HANDBOOK OF RESEARCH METHODS AND APPLICATIONS IN EMPIRICAL MACROECONOMICS

HANDBOOKS OF RESEARCH METHODS AND APPLICATIONS

Series Editor: Mark Casson, *University of Reading, UK*

The objective of this series is to provide definitive overviews of research methods in important fields of social science, including economics, business, finance and policy studies. The aim is to produce prestigious high quality works of lasting significance. Each *Handbook* consists of original contributions by leading authorities, selected by an editor who is a recognized leader in the field. The emphasis is on the practical application of research methods to both quantitative and qualitative evidence. The *Handbooks* will assist practising researchers in generating robust research findings that policy-makers can use with confidence.

While the *Handbooks* will engage with general issues of research methodology, their primary focus will be on the practical issues concerned with identifying and using suitable sources of data or evidence, and interpreting source material using best-practice techniques. They will review the main theories that have been used in applied research, or could be used for such research. While reference may be made to conceptual issues and to abstract theories in the course of such reviews, the emphasis will be firmly on real-world applications.

Titles in the series include:

Handbook of Research Methods and Applications in Urban Economies
Edited by Peter Karl Kresl and Jaime Sobrino

Handbook of Research Methods and Applications in Empirical Finance
Edited by Adrian R. Bell, Chris Brooks and Marcel Prokopczuk

Handbook of Research Methods and Applications in Empirical Macroeconomics
Edited by Nigar Hashimzade and Michael A. Thornton

Handbook of Research Methods and Applications in Empirical Macroeconomics

Edited by

Nigar Hashimzade

Durham University, UK

Michael A. Thornton

University of York, UK

HANDBOOKS OF RESEARCH METHODS AND APPLICATIONS

Edward Elgar
Cheltenham, UK • Northampton, MA, USA

Published by
Edward Elgar Publishing Limited
The Lypiatts
15 Lansdown Road
Cheltenham
Glos GL50 2JA
UK

Edward Elgar Publishing, Inc.
William Pratt House
9 Dewey Court
Northampton
Massachusetts 01060
USA

A catalogue record for this book
is available from the British Library

Library of Congress Control Number: 2012952654

This book is available electronically in the ElgarOnline.com
Economics Subject Collection, E-ISBN 978 0 85793 102 3

MIX
Paper from responsible sources
FSC® C013056
www.fsc.org

ISBN 978 0 85793 101 6 (cased)

Typeset by Servis Filmsetting Ltd, Stockport, Cheshire
Printed and bound in Great Britain by T.J. International Ltd, Padstow

Contents

Contributors

Badi H. Baltagi is Distinguished Professor of Economics and Senior Research Associate at the Center for Policy Research, Syracuse University. He received his PhD in Economics at the University of Pennsylvania in 1979. He is also part-time Chair in Economics, University of Leicester, and was a visiting Professor at the University of Arizona and the University of California, San Diego. He is the author of several books including *Econometric Analysis of Panel Data* (Wiley) and *Econometrics* (Springer), and an editor of *A Companion to Theoretical Econometrics* (Blackwell), *Recent Developments in the Econometrics of Panel Data*, Volumes I and II (Edward Elgar), and *Nonstationary Panels, Panel Cointegration, and Dynamic Panels* (Elsevier). He is also an author or a co-author of over 140 publications, all in leading economics and statistics journals. Professor Baltagi is the editor of *Economics Letters*, the editor of *Empirical Economics*, and an associate editor of the *Journal of Econometrics* and *Econometric Reviews*. He is the replication editor of the *Journal of Applied Econometrics* and the series editor for the *Contributions to Economic Analysis*. He is a fellow of the *Journal of Econometrics* and a fellow of *Advances in Econometrics*. Badi Baltagi is a recipient of the Multa and Plura Scripsit Awards from *Econometric Theory* journal and a recipient of the Distinguished Authors Award from the *Journal of Applied Econometrics*.

Luc Bauwens is Professor of Economics at the Université catholique de Louvain, where he is the President of the Center for Operations Research and Econometrics. His research focuses on financial and Bayesian econometrics. He received the Leonard J. Savage Thesis Award in 1984. He belongs to the editorial board of the *Journal of Applied Econometrics* and is associate editor of the *Journal of Financial Econometrics*.

Otilia Boldea is Assistant Professor in Econometrics at Tilburg University and research fellow at CentER. Her research focuses on time series econometrics in the presence of structural change and endogeneity, as well as on empirical monetary and macroeconomics.

Jörg Breitung is Professor of Econometrics at the University of Bonn, Germany and advisor of the German Central Bank (Deutsche Bundesbank). His research focuses on time series and panel data analysis. From 1994 to 2002 he was Assistant Professor at the Humboldt University of Berlin and Professor of Statistics at the University of Göttingen (Germany).

Cristiano Cantore is a Lecturer in the School of Economics and member of the Centre for International Macroeconomic Studies (CIMS) at the University of Surrey. He earned a PhD in Economics from the University of Kent, where his research focused on financial frictions and capital–labour substitution in dynamic stochastic general equilibrium (DSGE) models. Cristiano has also worked at the OECD and at the ECB as a trainee and at the Bank of Spain as a visiting research fellow. His current research interests include macroeconomic theory, business cycles, monetary economics, and production theory.

Marcus J. Chambers is Professor of Economics at the University of Essex. His research is mainly in the area of time series econometrics. Since 2004 he has been an Associate Editor of the *Journal of Econometrics*.

In Choi is Professor at Sogang University in Seoul, Korea. His research focus has been on time series and panel data analysis, and he has published numerous papers in leading journals in econometrics. He is a Fellow of the *Journal of Econometrics* and a recipient of the Plura Scripsit Award from *Econometric Theory*, one of the leading journals in econometrics. He is currently an Associate Editor of the *Journal of Business and Economics Statistics*.

James Davidson is Professor of Econometrics at the University of Exeter, and has previously held positions at Cardiff University and the London School of Economics. He is the author of two well-known econometrics texts, *Stochastic Limit Theory* (1994) and *Econometric Theory* (2000). His published research has focused on problems of estimation and inference in non-stationary and long memory processes.

Vasco J. Gabriel is a Senior Lecturer in Economics at the University of Surrey. He is a founding member of the Centre for International Macroeconomic Studies (CIMS) at Surrey and a Visiting Fellow of the Economic Policies Research Unit (NIPE) at the University of Minho. His research focuses on econometrics and applied macroeconomics.

Raffaella Giacomini is Associate Professor of Economics at University College London, British Academy Mid-Career Fellow and research fellow at CEPR and at the Center for Microdata Methods and Practice (Cemmap). Her research focuses on time series econometrics, forecasting, and applied macroeconomics. Previous faculty positions include UCLA and Boston College.

Paul Gomme is Professor of Economics at Concordia University and a Research Fellow at Centre Interuniversitaire de Recherche en Economie Quantitative (CIREQ) in Montreal, Canada. His research focuses on macroeconomics, business cycle theory, and the determinants of unemployment. He has previously worked at Simon Fraser University, the Federal Reserve Bank of Cleveland, and the University of Iowa.

Jesús Gonzalo is Professor of Econometrics at University Carlos III of Madrid. His research focuses on time series econometrics: persistence and non-linearities. Prior to his current position, he was on the faculty of Boston University.

Pablo A. Guerrón-Quintana is an Economic Adviser and Economist in the Research Department of the Federal Reserve Bank of Philadelphia. His research interests cover time series and macroeconomics with an emphasis on monetary policy and international finance. Prior to his current post, he was an Assistant Professor of Economics at North Carolina State University. He has served as a consultant for the International Monetary Fund, the Inter-American Development Bank, and the Corporación Andina de Fomento.

Niels Haldrup is Professor of Economics, Aarhus University, Denmark, and director for CREATES, a centre of excellence in time series econometrics funded by the Danish National Research Foundation. His research interests are broadly in time series econometrics with particular focus on non-stationary time series analysis, long memory, and the modelling of persistence in economic and financial time series.

Alastair R. Hall is Professor of Econometrics at the University of Manchester. He is a member of the Advisory Board for the Info-metrics Institute at American University and also an associate editor of *Econometric Reviews*, *Journal of Financial Econometrics*, and *Journal of Econometric Methods*; he has previously served as co-editor of the *Journal of Business and Economic Statistics*. He is the author of *Generalized Method of Moments* published by Oxford University Press in 2005. His current research focuses on statistical inference techniques for econometric models estimated from the information in moment conditions.

Nigar Hashimzade is Professor of Economics at Durham University. She undertakes research in economic theory and econometric theory. Prior to her current position she worked at the University of Exeter and the University of Reading. She holds a PhD in Economics from Cornell University. Her previous research career was in theoretical physics.

Menelaos Karanasos is Professor of Financial Economics at Brunel University, London. His research focuses on empirical finance and applied macroeconomics. Prior to his current position, he was on the faculty of the University of York.

Lutz Kilian is Professor of Economics at the University of Michigan and research fellow at CEPR. His research focuses on time series econometrics, empirical macroeconomics, and energy economics. He has also worked for the research department of the Inter-American Development Bank in Washington, DC, and has served as a research adviser to the European Central Bank in Frankfurt.a.M.

Soyoung Kim is Professor of Economics at Seoul National University. He received the Arnould O. Beckman Research Award, the Tae Sung Kim Research Award, the Chung Ram Research Award and the NEAR Research Award. Prior to his current position, he was on the faculty of the University of Illinois at Urbana-Champaign and Korea University. He was also involved with various institutions like IMF, ADB, ADB Institute, Bank of Spain, and HKIMR, Bank of Korea, KIEP, KIF, AIRI, Ministry of Strategy and Finance in Korea under various designations.

Dimitris Korobilis is Lecturer in Economics at the University of Glasgow, research fellow of the RCEA, and visiting researcher at the Deutsche Bundesbank. His research focuses on Bayesian time series analysis in empirical macroeconomics. His work has been published in the *International Economic Review* and the *Journal of Applied Econometrics*.

Robinson Kruse is Assistant Professor of Financial Statistics at the Leibniz University Hannover in Germany, and an international research fellow at CREATES, Aarhus University, Denmark. His research areas comprise time series econometrics in general, and inference in non-linear and fractionally integrated models in particular. He graduated from the University of Bonn, Germany, obtained his PhD from Leibniz University Hannover, and was a post-doctoral researcher at CREATES.

Paul Levine received a first-class BSc and a PhD, both in Mathematics, from the University of Manchester and an MSc in economics (distinction) at Queen Mary

University of London. In 1984 he became a senior research officer at the Centre for Economic Forecasting, London Business School, and was appointed Professor of Economics at the University of Leicester in 1989. In 1994 he moved to the University of Surrey where he now leads the Centre for International Macroeconomic Studies (CIMS). His main research activity is in constructing empirically-based DSGE models for the purpose of macroeconomic policy analysis for which he has acted as a consultant and/or visiting researcher at the IMF and the ECB.

Damba Lkhagvasuren is Assistant Professor at Concordia University, Montreal, Canada and Research Fellow at Centre Interuniversitaire de Recherche en Economie Quantitative (CIREQ). His research areas include macroeconomics, labour market dynamics and computational methods. Prior to his current position, he worked at the Kellogg School of Management of Northwestern University and Reinsurance Bureau of the Mongolian Ministry of Finance.

Alessandra Luati is Associate Professor of Statistics at the University of Bologna, Italy. Her research focuses on time series econometrics, likelihood based methods and spectral analysis. She completed a doctoral degree in Statistics at the University of Bologna and the University of Aarhus.

Helmut Lütkepohl is Bundesbank-Professor of Methods of Empirical Economics at the Free University Berlin and Dean of the Graduate Center of the DIW Berlin. His research interests are in the area of time series econometrics. He is an Associate Editor of *Econometric Theory*, *Macroeconomic Dynamics*, *Empirical Economics*, and other journals. He has published extensively in leading academic journals, and he is author, co-author and editor of a number of books in econometrics and time series analysis. Prior to his current position he was on the faculty of the European University Institute in Florence, at the Humboldt University in Berlin, and at the Christian-Albrechts-University Kiel.

João Madeira is a Lecturer in Economics at the University of Exeter. He obtained his PhD in Economics from Boston University in January 2009 under the supervision of François Gourio, Simon Gilchrist and Robert King. His research focuses on business cycle fluctuations and labour market rigidities.

Terence C. Mills is Professor of Applied Statistics and Econometrics at Loughborough University, having previously held professorial appointments at City University Business School and Hull University. His research focuses primarily on time series analysis and econometrics; he is the co-editor of the *Palgrave Handbooks of Econometrics* and has recently published *The Foundations of Time Series Analysis* and *A Very British Affair: Six Britons and the Development of Time Series Analysis* (Macmillan Palgrave).

James M. Nason is a Vice President and Economist in the Research Department at the Federal Reserve Bank of Philadelphia and a research associate at CAMA. His research covers the areas of macroeconomics, international finance, open economy macroeconomics, and time series econometrics.

Kerry Patterson is Professor of Econometrics at the University of Reading. His research interests include the econometrics of non-stationary time series and the development of semi-parametric methods for forecasting. He is co-editor of *Palgrave Texts in Econometrics* and *Palgrave Advanced Texts in Econometrics* and has recently published two books on testing for unit roots in economics.

Joseph Pearlman is Professor of Macroeconomics at City University, London. His research focuses on monetary policy, expectational learning, and growth. Prior to his current position he was Professor of Monetary Economics at Loughborough University.

Jean-Yves Pitarakis is a Professor of Economics at the University of Southampton. His research interests are in the area of theoretical and applied econometrics with an emphasis on time series econometrics. Prior to his current appointment he held positions at the University of Reading, the Centre for Operations Research and Econometrics, McGill University, and Boston University.

D.S.G. Pollock is Professor of Econometrics and Computational Statistics at the University of Leicester. His research focuses on time series analysis and statistical signal processing. He is the author of *The Algebra of Econometrics* (1979) and *A Handbook of Times-Series Analysis, Signal Processing and Dynamics* (1999). He is an associate editor of *Computational Statistics and Data Analysis* and *Interdisciplinary Science Reviews*, to which he has contributed articles on agronomy, palaeoanthropology and the history of medicine.

Tommaso Proietti is Associate Professor of Business Statistics at the University of Sydney, Australia, and Professor of Economic Statistics at the University of Rome Tor Vergata, Italy. His research interests are centred in the analysis of economic time series, forecasting, and signal extraction in economics.

Barbara Rossi is ICREA Professor at the University of Pompeu Fabra, BGSE and CREI, and research fellow at CEPR and EABCN. Her research focuses on time series econometrics, forecasting, and empirical macroeconometrics. She is an associate editor for the *Journal of Business and Economic Statistics*, *Journal of Economic Dynamics and Control* and *Journal of Applied Econometrics*. Prior to her current position, she was an associate professor (with tenure) at Duke University and held visiting researcher positions at St Louis Fed, UC Berkeley, Philadelphia Fed, University of Montreal, Atlanta Fed, UCSD, and Concordia University.

Francisco J. Ruge-Murcia is Professor of Economics at the University of Montreal. His research focuses on issues in monetary economics, collective decision making, and the econometrics of dynamic equilibrium models. He has previously held visiting positions at the University of California at San Diego, the University of Cambridge, Tel Aviv University, the International Monetary Fund, and various central banks.

Timo Teräsvirta is Professor of Economics, Aarhus University, Denmark, and member of CREATES, a centre of excellence for research in time series econometrics at the same university. He has published (with co-authors) two books on non-linear time series econometrics and a number of articles in international journals. His research and teaching interests include non-linear time series econometrics and volatility modelling.

Michael A. Thornton is a Lecturer in Economics at the University of York. His research focuses on time series econometrics, particularly on problems involving aggregation, both across time and across a population, and on filtering. Prior to his current position he was on the faculty of the University of Reading.

Rasmus T. Varneskov is a PhD Candidate in Economics at Aarhus University, Denmark and is also affiliated with CREATES. His research interests are time series econometrics, empirical finance and empirical macroeconomics with particular emphasis on modelling persistent time series, and the econometrics of high-frequency data.

Bo Yang is a Lecturer at Xi'an Jiaotong-Liverpool University (XJTLU), Suzhou, China and a part-time Lecturer in the School of Economics at the University of Surrey, UK. Following the completion of his PhD at the University of Surrey on the topic of DSGE modelling in 2008, Bo was appointed, by Surrey and London Metropolitan University, as a Research Fellow to support the research activities of the EU-funded project MONFISPOL. His Research Fellow include macroeconometrics, monetary economics, and Bayesian econometrics, focusing on the applications and quantitative analysis of DSGE models. He has published in the *Review of International Economics*, the *Oxford Handbook of the Indian Economy*, *Economics Letters*, and the *Economic Journal.*

Ning Zeng is a Lecturer at Jinan University, China. Her research focus is on applied macroeconomics. She holds a PhD in Economics from Brunel University, London.

1 Introduction

Nigar Hashimzade and Michael A. Thornton

This volume is part of the new series of Handbooks of Research Methods and Applications in the Social Sciences, compiled under the editorship of Mark Casson. While these *Handbooks* engage with general issues of research methodology, their primary focus is on the practical issues surrounding best-practice techniques and real world applications.

This *Handbook* provides a systematic account of a range of research methods in empirical macroeconomics. It is intended as a reference for graduate students and researchers interested in exploring new methodologies, but could also be deployed as a graduate text. The *Handbook* concentrates on the most important issues, models and techniques for research in macroeconomics. Each chapter highlights the key methodologies and their empirical application in an accessible way. The chapters are largely self-contained, and some background and key statistical concepts and methods are reviewed in the opening chapter. Given the breadth and the significance of the topics covered in the *Handbook*, no single chapter could claim to be comprehensive, but the chapters include the key references for each topic and provide a sound guide for further reading.

Distinctive features of the *Handbook* are:

- coverage of a wide range of methodologies from the well-established to relatively recent advances;
- a particular focus on examples illustrating the application of these methodologies to macroeconomic problems and datasets;
- the availability of resources and computer programs through a supporting website.

The opening chapter of the *Handbook* introduces the reader to the basic theoretical concepts of stochastic processes and stationarity. The chapter also presents a number of univariate and multivariate models that are useful for the analysis of macroeconomic data, and describes three most commonly used estimation methods: method of moments, generalized method of moments, and maximum likelihood. These models and estimation methods are further developed in greater detail with examples of application in later chapters. The first three sections of the volume set out a general theoretical framework, while also covering some important examples from macroeconomic research, whereas the remaining three sections focus on practical applications, providing further theoretical background where needed. Part I of the Handbook (Chapters 3, 4 and 5) describes the specific properties of macroeconomic data that require modelling and analysis differing from that typically applied in other fields of economics and the social sciences. The decomposition of a time series into trends and cycles, and the identification of unit roots, structural breaks and various non-linearities are presented in Chapters 3 and 4, whereas Chapter 5 introduces the theory of filtering, or isolating the components of data that are of particular interest (the signal), whilst removing the unwanted components (the noise).

Part II (Chapters 6 to 13) presents a number of fundamental models for macroeconomic data analysis. A detailed treatment of the vector autoregressive (VAR) modelling technique, from model specification and estimation to the structural analysis and forecasting, is given in Chapter 6. Chapter 7 introduces the concept of cointegration and describes the error correction approach to the modelling of non-stationary data. A set of threshold type regime switching models are described in Chapter 8; this approach is relevant when it can be assumed that the model parameters change once an economy experiences a change in regime, for example, following a policy intervention, while remaining constant within each regime. Econometric tests for instability in parameters and in the functional form of a model are presented in Chapter 9. Dynamic panel data models, introduced in Chapter 10, provide the advantage of accounting for heterogeneity across, say, countries, as well as for the dynamic nature of the relationships between economic variables. An overview of the dynamic factor analysis of large macroeconomic panel datasets is given in Chapter 11. Modelling data that exhibit conditional heteroskedasticity is commonly associated with the financial data analysis; Chapter 12 shows how this framework can be usefully applied to study the links between uncertainties in macroeconomic variables. Chapter 13 concludes this section by addressing a fundamental issue of temporal aggregation in time series and discussing, in particular, the implications of temporal aggregation in macroeconomic data for testing popular macroeconomic theories.

Part III (Chapters 14 to 17) presents the theoretical frameworks for estimation and evaluation of macroeconometric models. Chapter 14 describes in detail the generalized method of moments (GMM), arguably the most convenient and general way of estimation of an economic model that can be equally applied in a variety of frameworks. Maximum likelihood (ML) estimation and inference is presented in Chapter 15, as part of a detailed treatment of state space models in macroeconomics. Chapter 16 introduces Bayesian methods, as an alternative to the GMM and the ML estimation that has been gaining popularity in applied macroeconomic research with the development of powerful computers. Often researchers in empirical macroeconomics are interested in selecting, among competing models, the one that generates the most accurate forecast of the future values of economic variables. A review of traditional and modern methods of evaluation of the accuracy of forecasts, which are robust to instabilities, is provided in Chapter 17, along with the macroeconomic applications.

Part IV (Chapters 18 to 21) gives a detailed exposition of one important application of the theoretical and empirical methods developed in the previous sections, the dynamic stochastic general equilibrium (DSGE) framework. Currently, this framework is, perhaps, the most widely employed by academics and practitioners in the field of macroeconomics. Chapter 18 presents the building blocks of the New Keynesian (NK) DSGE model and describes how the Bayesian estimation methodology is applied in this framework. Chapter 19 provides a discussion of model comparison and validation, as well as the application of this framework for policy analysis. The application of two estimation methodologies for the DSGE models, Bayesian estimation and the GMM estimation, with an extension to the simulated method of moments (SMM), are developed in greater detail in Chapters 20 and 21, using an alternative version of the NK DSGE model.

Part V (Chapters 22 and 23) presents the application of the VAR as an alternative methodology for the macroeconomic modelling and policy analysis. Chapter 22 develops the structural VAR approach, presenting various methods for identification and discussing the relationship between the structural VAR and the DSGE framework. A number of examples of macroeconomic policy analysis in the VAR framework are developed in Chapter 23.

Part VI (Chapters 24 and 25), the final section of the volume, is dedicated to the calibration, simulation and estimation of macroeconomic models. Chapter 24 gives a detailed and careful description of the procedure for calibration and simulation using the neoclassical growth model as an example. Chapter 25 introduces Dynare, software (http://www.dynare.org) widely used for the simulation and estimation of macroeconomic models of the DSGE type, with detailed instruction from installation to writing a code for Bayesian estimation for a simple real business cycle model using macroeconomic data for the US.

Each chapter in this volume is an original contribution by a leading authority in the field.

2 A review of econometric concepts and methods for empirical macroeconomics

Kerry Patterson and Michael A. Thornton

1 INTRODUCTION

The aim of this chapter is to review some econometric terms and methods that are particularly useful for empirical macroeconomics. The technical level of the chapter assumes completion of an intermediate or good introductory course such as covered by, for example, Dougherty (2011) or Wooldridge (2011). Ideally, some knowledge of the linear regression model in matrix-vector notation would also be helpful, such as provided in Greene (2011).

This chapter proceeds as follows. The starting point for the analysis of macroeconomic time series is univariate modelling, a classic case being Nelson and Plosser's (1982) analysis of a number of macroeconomic time series to assess whether they were generated by unit root processes, a finding that would have implications not only for econometric analysis but, from a macroeconomic perspective, also for the persistence of shocks and the generation of the business cycle. There are two basic concepts that enable a better understanding of the framework of unit root tests, the first being that of a stochastic process and the second that of stationarity and non-stationarity, and these are outlined in section 2. Stationarity is a property related to the process generating the observable data of macroeconomic analysis, although one often finds a shorthand reference to the stationarity or non-stationarity of the data or of a particular time series.

The basic univariate modelling framework is outlined in section 3. Central to this framework and analysis is the autoregressive model of order p, $AR(p)$, which can be extended to include a moving average error process of order q, $MA(q)$; together they result in the ARMA(p, q) model. The unit root question then usually relates to the properties of the AR polynomial, although the possibility and implications of a unit root in the MA polynomial should not be overlooked; see, for example, Tanaka (1990), and for a textbook exposition of the ARMA modelling framework more generally see Brockwell and Davis (2006).

A test for a unit root is also often adopted as a pre-test that informs subsequent modelling, such as establishing balance (in the mean) in potentially cointegrated relationships. Chapter 4 by Niels Haldrup, Robinson Kruse, Timo Teräsvirta and Rasmus T. Varneskov takes up the issue of unit root testing in greater detail, including caveats and extensions such as the importance of non-linearities. Note, in particular, that the ARMA model is a linear framework whereas there is now a gathering body of evidence that non-linearities may characterize a number of macroeconomic variables; see for example Peel et al. (2001) on modelling the exchange rate, Taylor et al. (2003) on modelling money balances and Teräsvirta (2006) for a comparative forecasting assessment of linear and non-linear models.

A natural extension of the ARMA framework allows several variables to be modelled jointly and an outline of some key multivariate models is provided in section 4. The natural extension of the univariate AR and ARMA models is to the vector autoregressive, VAR, model and vector ARMA, VARMA models, although the focus in practice is largely on the former. Non-stationarity now refers to a property of the process generating the multivariate model and leads to the key concept of cointegration. This multivariate framework is followed up extensively in later chapters, see especially Chapters 6, 7, 22 and 23.

Estimation methods in empirical macroeconomics are largely based on parametric models and these are represented in this *Handbook* by variants of least squares, the generalized method of moments and maximum likelihood; section 5 outlines some of the preparatory background. Extensive reference to econometric and quantitative techniques that are useful in macroeconomics is provided in Bårsden (2005) and Canova (2007); and a good reference for non-parametric methods, which are becoming increasingly important, with applications in macroeconomics, is Li and Raccine (2006).

2 TWO BASIC CONCEPTS

The concepts of a stochastic process, which in essence is a sequence of random variables, or vector of random variables, ordered in time, and the stationarity or non-stationarity of that process, are central to time series analysis and especially to the analysis of macroeconomic time series. By considering a suitably defined vector stochastic process and fixing the time dimension of the process one obtains a cross section, whereas a sequence of vector stochastic processes can be interpreted as generating a panel of data.

2.1 Stochastic Processes

From the viewpoint of time series analysis, typically we are not interested in the outcome of a random variable at a single point in time, but in a sample path or realization of a sequence of random variables over an interval of time. The realizations are what we observe and collect for macroeconomic analysis, but it is important to realize that just as in tossing a coin, because we observe one particular outcome, for example the coin lands 'heads', this does not mean that was the only possible outcome. Moreover, to continue the analogy in the context of time series analysis, what we are interested in is a sequence of 'coin tosses', where that sequence is arranged in time; then a sample is a path or trajectory of length T, which comprises the realizations of T random variables. In a macroeconomic context, our 'coin tosses' are, for example, outcomes of the random processes generating GDP, exchange rates, unemployment and so on.

To establish some notation, let the sample space for the T random variables be denoted Ω_T, then the generic element of Ω_T, ω, refers to a T-dimensional *ordered* sequence. If the random variables underlying the sample space are independent, then Ω_T is the (Cartesian) product space of the sample spaces for each of the T random variables. Referring to the coin tossing example, the coin tosses are usually taken to be independent, in which case the sample space Ω_T is the product space, $\Omega_T = \Omega_1 \times \Omega_1 \times \ldots \times \Omega_1 = \Omega_1^T$, where Ω_1

is the sample space of a single random variable and the $\times$ symbol here indicates the Cartesian product.

A stochastic process conceptualizes how such sample paths or 'trajectories' arise; it is a collection of random variables, denoted Y, on a probability space (see, for example, Billingsley, 1995); usually it is indexed by $t \in T$ to emphasize time, although this aspect is not essential as a stochastic process is an example of a random vector for which one could equally use the index $j = 1, \ldots, n$. However, as the dominant application in this *Handbook* involves the dimension of time, the former notation will be used.

For brevity we will focus on the discrete time case, where the components of the stochastic process are denoted $y_t(\omega)$ and $t \in T$, where, typically T comprises the integers $N = (0, \pm 1, \pm 2, \ldots)$ or the non-negative integers $N^+ = (0, 1, 2, \ldots)$. A discrete-time stochastic process with $T \subseteq N^+$ is then summarized as the following collection of random variables:

$$Y = (y_t(\omega): t \in T \subseteq N^+, \omega \in \Omega_T).$$

For given $t \in T$, $y_t(\omega)$ is a single random variable as a function of $\omega \in \Omega_T$, with a distribution of outcomes at that point, one of which will be realized. For given $\omega \in \Omega_T$, $y_t(\omega)$ is a function of time, $t \in T$. In this case an 'outcome' is a complete sample path, that is a function of $t \in T$, rather than a single number. A description of the sample path would require a functional relationship rather than a single number. By varying ω we now get a different sample path; that is (potentially) different realizations for all $t \in T$.

We will often think of the index set T as comprising an infinite number of elements even in the case of discrete-time processes, where N is (countably) infinite; in the case of a continuous-time stochastic process even if T is a finite interval of time, such as [0, 1], the interval is infinitely divisible. In either case, the collection of random variables in Y is infinite. This is important in the context of taking the limit of partial sums, which appear in several contexts in the econometrics of macroeconomic analysis.

Often the reference to $\omega \in \Omega_T$ is suppressed and a single random variable in the stochastic process is written y_t, but the underlying dependence on the sample space should be noted. What is special about a stochastic process, other than that it is a sequence of random variables? In the case of a stochastic process, the sample space is the space of a sequence of length T in the case of a random variable with an inherent time dimension. By fixing ω we fix a whole path, not just a single element at a particular time; thus as ω is varied, the whole sample path is varied, at least potentially. This is why the appropriate space for a stochastic process is a function space: each sample path is a function, not a single outcome.

Replication of a stochastic process through simulation generates a distribution of sample paths associated with different realizations over the *complete* sample path. To illustrate this idea, Figure 2.1 shows four simulated trajectories for a Gaussian random walk defined by $y_t = y_{t-1} + \varepsilon_t$, where ε_t is niid (0, 1), that is ε_t is normally, independently and identically distributed with expected value of zero and variance of unity; the starting value is $y_0 = 0$ and $T = 1000$. The sample space is, therefore, the product space $\Omega_1^{T=1000}$; and in effect the random walk is a partial sum process (psp) defined on ε_t as $y_t = \sum_{i=1}^{t} \varepsilon_i$.

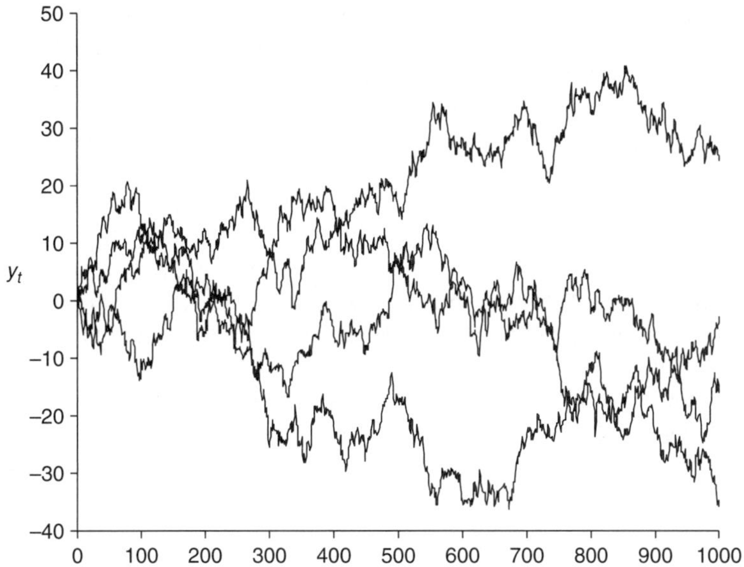

Figure 2.1 *Random walk trajectories*

The figure illustrates not only the nature of a random walk, but also the fundamental idea that a stochastic process relates to T-dimensional realizations of a sample path. It is this conceptual basis that underpins the analysis of macroeconomic time series.

2.2 Stationary Stochastic Processes

An important distinction in the analysis of macroeconomic series is whether the stochastic process generating the component random variables is stationary or non-stationary. The reader is likely to be aware of the Dickey–Fuller test for a unit root, which is a frequently used test for a particular form of non-stationarity; and throughout this volume, there is reference to the stationary/non-stationary distinction.

As a non-stationary process is one that is not stationary, we can focus on the definition of a stationary process. In an intuitive sense a stationary process is one that does not undergo any change, so that we can be assured that if we focus on one particular period then the process generating the data (the 'trajectories') is invariant if we then focus on another period or perhaps split one overall period into two sub-periods. This intuitive idea relates to the concept of strong or strict stationarity, which we now define. To simplify the definitions below, the focus is on discrete time, noting that the extension to continuous time is straightforward; further, the notation y_t refers to a single random variable, that is the univariate case, whereas the multivariate case is considered in section 4.1.

Strict stationarity: let $\tau \neq s$ and T be arbitrary, if Y is a strictly stationary, discrete time process for a discrete random variable, y_t, then:

$$P(y_{\tau+1}, y_{\tau+2}, \ldots, y_{\tau+T}) = P(y_{s+1}, y_{s+2}, \ldots, y_{s+T}), \tag{2.1}$$

where $P(.)$ is the joint probability mass function for the sequence of length T, which starting at time $\tau + 1$, is the same for any shift in the time index from τ to s and for any choice of T. These results imply that moments of y_t, including joint moments, such as the covariances, are invariant to arbitrary time shifts.

If the random variables are continuous, a strictly stationary random process satisfies the following condition:

$$F(y_{\tau+1}, y_{\tau+2}, \ldots, y_{\tau+T}) = F(y_{s+1}, y_{s+2}, \ldots, y_{s+T}), \tag{2.2}$$

where $F(.)$ is the joint distribution function of the random variables indicated in parentheses. If the probability density functions, $f(.)$, exist, then an analogous condition holds, replacing $F(.)$ by $f(.)$.

Strict stationarity is generally too strong a requirement for macroeconomic (and econometric) analysis and it is replaced with weak stationarity, WS (also referred to as covariance or second order stationarity), defined by satisfaction of the following three conditions, for arbitrary τ, s and k:

Weak stationarity

$$E(y_\tau) = E(y_s) = \mu$$

$$\text{Var}(y_\tau) = \text{Var}(y_s) = \sigma^2$$

$$\text{Cov}(y_\tau, y_{\tau+k}) = \text{Cov}(y_s, y_{s+k}),$$

where Var(.) and Cov(.) indicate the variance and covariance, respectively. The first condition states that the mean is constant, the second that the variance is constant and the third that the kth order autocovariance is invariant to an arbitrary shift in the time origin.

To illustrate the use of the defining conditions of weak stationarity, consider the simple random walk $y_t = y_{t-1} + \varepsilon_t$, then:

$$E(y_t) = \sum\nolimits_{i=1}^{t} E(\varepsilon_i) = 0; \text{Var}(y_t) = \text{Var}\left(\sum\nolimits_{i=1}^{t} \varepsilon_i\right) = t\sigma_\varepsilon^2;$$

$$\text{Cov}(y_t, y_{t+k}) = \text{Cov}\left(\sum\nolimits_{i=1}^{t} \varepsilon_i, \left(\sum\nolimits_{i=1}^{t} \varepsilon_i + \sum\nolimits_{i=t+1}^{k} \varepsilon_i\right)\right) = \text{Var}(y_t) = t\sigma_\varepsilon^2.$$

The last two results use $E(\varepsilon_t \varepsilon_s) = 0$ for $t \neq s$. (This assumption is not essential to the non-stationarity of the process generating y_t, but it simplifies this illustrative example.)

The extension of the definition of stationarity to the multivariate case, where y_t is a $K \times 1$ vector of random variables at time t, is considered in section 4.1. This is necessary to cover models such as variants of the vector autoregressive (VAR) models of Chapters 6, 7, 22 and 23, and the dynamic stochastic general equilibrium models of Chapters 18 to 21.

3 UNIVARIATE MODELS

Even if the object of macroeconomic analysis is multivariate analysis, for example the determination of output and unemployment, as in Blanchard and Quah (1989) or the variables of the IS–LM model of Gali (1992), this is often preceded by a univariate analysis of each component variable. Moreover, there are some influential studies, such as Nelson and Plosser (1982) and Perron (1989), whose primary concern is with macroeconomic variables considered individually. The most frequent parametric framework for such analysis is the autoregressive moving average, ARMA, model. An ARMA model is also an example of a linear time-invariant filter, which is considered more extensively, along with related concepts, by Stephen Pollock in Chapter 5 on filtering macroeconomic data.

3.1 ARMA(p, q) Models

The ARMA model of order p in the AR component and q in the MA component for the univariate process generating y_t, is written as follows:

$$(1 - \phi_1 L - \phi_2 L^2 - \ldots - \phi_p L^p) y_t = (1 + \theta_1 L + \theta_2 L^2 + \ldots + \theta_q L^q)\varepsilon_t, \quad (2.3)$$

where L is the lag operator defined as $L^j y_t \equiv y_{t-j}$ (sometimes referred as the backshift operator with equivalent notation $B^j y_t \equiv y_{t-j}$). The sequence $\{\varepsilon_t\}_{t=1}^{T}$ comprises the random variables ε_t, assumed to be independently and identically distributed for all t, with zero mean and constant variance, σ_ε^2, denoted $\varepsilon_t \sim \text{iid}(0, \sigma_\varepsilon^2)$, $\sigma_\varepsilon^2 < \infty$.

The ARMA model can be written more concisely by defining the AR and MA polynomials, respectively, as:

$$\phi(L) = (1 - \phi_1 L - \phi_2 L^2 - \ldots - \phi_p L^p) \text{ AR}(p) \text{ polynomial} \quad (2.4a)$$

$$\theta(L) = (1 + \theta_1 L + \theta_2 L^2 + \ldots + \theta_q L^q) \text{ MA}(q) \text{ polynomial.} \quad (2.4b)$$

The ARMA model is then written as:

$$\phi(L) y_t = \theta(L)\varepsilon_t. \quad (2.5)$$

Pure AR and pure MA models are clearly just the special cases corresponding to $q = 0$ and $p = 0$, respectively.

3.2 Deterministic Terms

For simplicity, the specification in (2.3) assumes $E(y_t) = 0$. If this is not the case, say $E(y_t) = \mu_t \neq 0$, then y_t is replaced by $y_t - \mu_t$, and the ARMA model is:

$$\phi(L)(y_t - \mu_t) = \theta(L)\varepsilon_t. \quad (2.6)$$

The term μ_t has the interpretation of a trend function, the simplest and most frequently occurring cases being where y_t has a constant mean, so that $\mu_t = \mu$, and y_t has a linear trend, so that $\mu_t = \beta_0 + \beta_1 t$. (There are other more complex models of the trend, and for an elaboration of the issues see Terence Mills in Chapter 3.) The ARMA model can then be written in deviations form by first defining $\tilde{y}_t \equiv y_t - \mu_t$, with the interpretation that $\tilde{y}_t$ is the detrended (or demeaned) data, so that (2.6) becomes:

$$\phi(L)\tilde{y}_t = \theta(L)\varepsilon_t. \tag{2.7}$$

In practice, μ_t is unknown and a consistent estimator, say $\hat{\mu}_t$, replaces μ_t, so that the estimated detrended data is $\hat{\tilde{y}}_t = y_t - \hat{\mu}_t$.

3.3 The Long Run and Persistence

An ARMA(p, q) model is described as being causal if there exists an absolutely summable sequence of constants $\{\omega_j\}_0^\infty$, such that:

$$\begin{aligned} y_t &= \sum\nolimits_{j=0}^{\infty} \omega_j L^j \varepsilon_t \\ &= \omega(L)\varepsilon_t. \end{aligned} \tag{2.8}$$

The condition of absolute summability is $\sum_{j=0}^{\infty}|\omega_j| < \infty$. The lag polynomial $\omega(L)$ is the causal linear filter governing the response of $\{y_t\}$ to $\{\varepsilon_t\}$. The representation in (2.8) is the MA form of the original model, which will be MA(∞) if $\phi(L)$ is not redundant. The causal ARMA(p, q) model is linear in the sense of (2.8), but it is not the only model that generates a linear form.

The MA polynomial is $\omega(L) = \sum_{j=0}^{\infty}\omega_j L^j = \phi(L)^{-1}\theta(L)$, with $\omega_0 = 1$; for this representation to exist, the roots of $\phi(z)$ must lie outside the unit circle so that $\phi(L)^{-1}$ is defined. The MA form (2.8) provides the basis of a number of tools of interpretation of the original model. In particular, the concepts of the impulse response function, the long-run solution, persistence and the long-run variance are all based on (2.8) and extend quite naturally to the multivariate case, as in VAR modelling; see section 4.1.

The impulse response function maps out the response of y_t to a one-unit (one-off) shock in ε_t; contemporaneously the effect is $\omega_0 = 1$, one period after the shock it is ω_1, two periods after the shock ω_2, and so on. The partial cumulative effect of the shock after s periods is $\sum_{j=0}^{s}\omega_j$ and in the limit as $s \to \infty$ this is $\omega(1)$, that is $\omega(L)$ evaluated at $L = 1$. The geometric pattern associated with an AR(1) model is probably the most familiar example, so that $\omega(L) = (1 - \phi_1 L)^{-1} = 1 + \sum_{j=1}^{\infty}\phi_1^j$, which converges to $(1 - \phi_1)^{-1}$ iff $|\phi_1| < 1$. A measure of long-run persistence is, therefore, provided by $\omega(1) = \sum_{j=0}^{\infty}\omega_j$. As to the long-run solution, assuming that the roots of $\phi(L)$ lie outside the unit circle, the eventual response of y_t to a one-unit, one-off shock in ε_t is to return to its initial equilibrium, which is $y_t = 0$ on setting all ε_t to their expected values of zero, or $\tilde{y}_t = 0$ if there is a trend function so that the long-run is $y_t = \mu_t$. The long-run variance of y_t is the variance of $\omega(1)\varepsilon_t$ which, given that μ_t, if it is present, is assumed to be a deterministic function, is also the long-run variance of y_t, denoted ω^2, where $\omega^2 = \omega(1)^2\sigma_\varepsilon^2$.

No constraints are needed on the polynomial $\theta(L)$ to ensure stationarity other than that its order, q, is finite. Our ARMA(p, q) is said to be invertible when the roots of $\theta(z)$

lie outside the unit circle. This has clear parallels with stationarity and ensures that it is possible to invert $\theta(L)$ and represent y_t as an AR(∞) process.

3.4 A Unit Root

Consider the pth order polynomial $\phi(z) = 1 - \sum_{i=1}^{p} \phi_i z^i$, then the solution to $\phi(z) = 0$ implies $\prod_{i=1}^{p}(z - \delta_i) = 0$, where δ_i are the p roots or solutions of $\phi(z) = 0$. The general condition for stability is that the modulus of the roots of $\phi(z)$ must lie outside the unit circle. In the AR(1) lag polynomial, there is one root $\delta_1 = \phi_1^{-1}$ and $|\delta_1| > 1$ for $|\phi_1| < 1$; hence the stability condition is satisfied. (If the stability condition is stated in the apparently opposite form as the roots must lie *inside* the unit circle, this refers to the reciprocals of δ_i.)

A special but important case arises when one of the roots of the polynomial $\phi(L)$ is equal to one and the others have modulus greater than one. If there is a single unit root, then the original pth order polynomial can be rewritten as the product of a first order polynomial, given by the first difference operator $(1 - L)$, and a polynomial of order $p - 1$. Multiplied together these polynomials are of the same order, p, as the original polynomial. This is as follows:

$$\begin{aligned} \phi(L) &= (1 - \phi_1 L - \phi_2 L^2 - \ldots - \phi_p L^p) \\ &= (1 - L)(1 - \phi_1^* L - \ldots - \phi_{p-1}^* L^{p-1}) \\ &= (1 - L)\phi^*(L), \end{aligned} \tag{2.9}$$

where $\phi^*(L)$ is of one order lower than $\phi(L)$, and the model in terms of Δy_t is $\phi^*(L)\Delta y_t = \varepsilon_t$ and thus by construction there are no further unit roots. It is for this reason that such a generating process is referred to as difference stationary.

This approach suggests a slightly different and informative way of (re)writing the ARMA(p, q) model that is more popular in the unit root literature, the idea being to isolate the potential unit root from the other stable roots. First, introduce $(1 - \rho L)$, a first order polynomial, so that the unit root null hypothesis is H_0: $\rho = 1$. That is:

$$(1 - \rho L)y_t = u_t \tag{2.10}$$

$$\varphi(L)u_t = \theta(L)\varepsilon_t, \quad \varphi(L) = (1 - \varphi_1 L - \ldots - \varphi_{p-1}L^{p-1}) \tag{2.11}$$

$\Rightarrow$

$$u_t = \varphi(L)^{-1}\theta(L)\varepsilon_t. \tag{2.12}$$

The components of the sequence $\{u_t\}$ are now referred to as errors rather than innovations, which are by assumption weakly dependent, in the sense that their autocovariances are summable, and this specification is, therefore, sometimes referred to as the error dynamics form of the ARMA model. In the context of the unit root hypothesis, the problem is to find a unit root test that is robust to weakly dependent errors or a modified test statistic that takes such structure into account, as in Phillips and Perron (1988). Note that $(1 - \rho L)\varphi(L) = \phi(L)$ and if $\rho = 1$, then $\varphi(L) = \phi^*(L)$. The principle can be applied to two unit roots first defining $(1 - \rho_1 L)(1 - \rho_2 L)$ and then redefining $\varphi(L)$ accordingly; the null hypothesis becomes H_0: $\rho_1 = \rho_2 = 1$; see for example, Hasza and Fuller (1979), Dickey and Pantula (1987) and Haldrup and Lildholt (2002, 2005). The number of unit roots leads to the *I*(*d*) notation.

3.5 The *I*(*d*) Notation

Engle and Granger (1987) defined an *I*(*d*) series as follows: 'A series with no deterministic component which has a stationary, invertible, ARMA representation after differencing *d* times, is said to be integrated of order *d*, denoted $y_t \sim I(d)$.' (Note x_t was used in the original definition.)

The *I*(*d*) property is readily apparent from the pure random walk $y_t = y_{t-1} + \varepsilon_t$, so that $\Delta y_t = \varepsilon_t$, hence $y_t \sim I(1)$. Some points arising from this definition follow. First note that *d* is the minimum number of times that y_t has to be differenced to achieve stationarity since, for example, the second difference of the random walk y_t is also stationary, but the $(d - 1)$th difference is not. If there is a deterministic component, for example the trend function μ_t, then the definition applies to $\tilde{y}_t \equiv y_t - \mu_t$. Whilst Engle and Granger (1987) had in mind that *d* is an integer, the definition may, with a suitable reinterpretation, be taken to apply to fractional *d*; see Patterson (2012, Chapter 3).

The qualification in the *I*(*d*) definition to a particular form of model after differencing (that is ARMA) is overly restrictive. As an alternative definition of an *I*(0) process, Davidson (2009) notes that one can instead look to the desired properties of a suitably scaled version of the partial sum of y_t, $S_T = \sum_{t=1}^{T} y_t$ (for convenience assume that $E(y_t) = 0$, otherwise subtract $E(y_t)$ from y_t). First note that this partial sum can be defined on the unit interval by introducing $0 \leq r \leq 1$ and defining $S_T(r) = \sum_{t=1}^{[Tr]} y_t$, where $[Tr]$ is the integer part of T times r. Let $\omega_T^2 = \text{Var}(S_T) = E(S_T^2)$ and $\omega^2 = \lim_{T\to\infty}(T^{-1}E(S_T^2)) = \lim_{T\to\infty}(T^{-1}\omega_T^2)$, where ω^2 is the long-run variance (of y_t).

Definition of an *I*(0) process (Davidson, 2009): A time series $\{y_t\}_{t=1}^{\infty}$ is *I*(0) if the partial sum process defined on the unit interval by $Y_T(r)$ converges in distribution to standard Brownian motion, that is:

$$Y_T(r) \equiv \frac{S_T(r)}{\omega_T} \Rightarrow_D B(r), \quad 0 \leq r \leq 1, \tag{2.13}$$

where $B(r)$ is standard Brownian motion ($\Rightarrow_D$ refers to weak convergence or convergence in distribution).

Whilst theoretically satisfactory, basing a test on such (2.13) is not possible because this condition is asymptotic. In part, the nature of the definition of an *I*(0) process depends on the problem being addressed. One possibility is that the distribution of an estimator based on y_t in finite samples is better guided by assuming that (2.13) holds than otherwise; another interest, as in Nelson and Plosser's (1982) original study, is what properties, especially as they relate to the persistence of shocks, better characterize such macroeconomic time series as GNP, unemployment and industrial production. The practical conclusion from the majority of the literature is that the Engle–Granger *I*(*d*) definition is useful partly because the parametric testing framework has largely focused on a maintained regression of AR form for which the definition, suitably qualified, is appropriate.

3.6 Basic Testing Framework

The basic testing framework is familiar from the Dickey–Fuller approach; see Fuller (1976, 1996) and Dickey and Fuller (1979, 1981). Suppose that the data are generated by $(1 - L)y_t = u_t$, so that there is a (single) unit root, $\rho = 1$, and also that the errors are in fact innovations, so that $u_t = \varepsilon_t$. Then the maintained regression is the test regression that enables a distinction to be drawn between the null and alternative hypotheses, where the latter depends upon the specification of the trend function, μ_t. For example suppose under H_A: $\mu_t = \mu$ and $|\rho| < 1$, then the maintained regression is $\hat{\tilde{y}}_t = \rho\hat{\tilde{y}}_{t-1} + \xi_t$, where $\hat{\tilde{y}}_t \equiv y_t - \hat{\mu}$, typically $\hat{\mu} = \bar{y}$, that is the 'global' sample mean, $T^{-1}\sum_{t=1}^{T} y_t$, although other estimators, such as the recursive mean, are possible (see Shin and So, 2002), and $\xi_t = \varepsilon_t + (1 - \rho)(\mu - \hat{\mu})$. Subtracting $\hat{\tilde{y}}_{t-1}$ and rearranging leads to the basic DF regression:

$$\Delta\hat{\tilde{y}}_t = \gamma\hat{\tilde{y}}_{t-1} + \xi_t, \qquad (2.14)$$

where $\gamma = (\rho - 1)$ and a unit root, therefore, corresponds to $\gamma = 0$. Note that imposing the null gives $\Delta y_t = \varepsilon_t$, whereas under the alternative $\hat{\tilde{y}}_t = \rho\hat{\tilde{y}}_{t-1} + \xi_t$, with $|\rho| < 1$; moreover the latter implies the estimated long-run solution $y_t = \hat{\mu}$, with stationary deviations about this long run, whereas the former does not have a well-defined long run.

The family of DF test statistics includes a joint F-type test on μ and ρ (see Dickey and Fuller, 1979, 1981) and the more familiar t-type test on γ, known as a $\hat{\tau}$-type test (see Fuller, 1976, 1996). There are many extensions of these tests, especially the latter. Of particular interest in this context is how to deal with weakly dependent errors. For the moment assume that the errors are generated by an AR(p – 1) model, so that the MA component is redundant, then a simple rearrangement results in what is known as the augmented Dickey–Fuller (ADF) regression:

$$\Delta\hat{\tilde{y}}_t = \gamma\hat{\tilde{y}}_{t-1} + \sum_{j=1}^{p-1}\alpha_j\Delta\hat{\tilde{y}}_{t-j} + \xi_t, \qquad (2.15)$$

where $\gamma = \phi(1) - 1$ and $\phi(1) = (1 - \rho)\varphi(1)$; thus, $\rho = 1$ corresponds to $\gamma = 0$, so that the $\hat{\tau}$ test is the t statistic corresponding to $\hat{\gamma}$, with the distribution of the test statistic depending on the specification of the trend function. In the case that $\hat{\tilde{y}}_t \equiv y_t - \hat{\mu}$, then current and lagged values of $\Delta\hat{\tilde{y}}_t$ can be replaced by the corresponding values of Δy_t.

In practice, the correct lag order is not known and a criterion, such as a fixed rule or data dependent method, has to be used to select p; see, for example, Schwert (1987, 1989) and Ng and Perron (1995). A rule with good empirical properties is the modified AIC, MAIC, due to Ng and Perron (2001). The ADF regression can also be subject to standard diagnostic tests, for example to ensure that the test regression is not subject to remaining residual serial correlation. As an informal guide, it is often helpful to compute the test statistic for each of the lags up to a maximum order and only select a particular pair of the lag order and test value if the test outcome is practically invariant to changes in the lag order past the selected lag.

The presence of an MA component complicates the choice since now there is not a single correct value of p, but a value of p that leads to a 'sufficiently good' approximation of the MA lag polynomial. Provided that the AR lag expands at an appropriate rate (see Said and Dickey, 1984 and Ng and Perron 1995), then the limiting distribution of $\hat{\tau}$ remains as in the simple DF case.

An alternative to the DF approach is direct maximum likelihood (ML) estimation of the error dynamics model in ARMA form, as suggested in Shin and Fuller (1998); the 'exact' taking into account the generation of the starting observation and leading to a difference in the estimator and the distribution of the test statistic compared to the case where estimation (by OLS, GLS or ML) is conditioned on the first observation (or first p observations in the more general case).

Other important developments include local detrending, a form of quasi-differencing familiar from the Cochrane–Orcut approach to AR(1) errors in the standard regression model, due to Elliott, Rothenberg and Stock (1996) and Elliott (1999); the former is usually referred to the ERS test and the latter differs only in how the initial value is treated. The importance of the initial value should not be overlooked as substantially different results can be obtained depending on how this is treated; see for example, Harvey and Leybourne (2005, 2006). Also, selecting the appropriate deterministic function for μ_t can be critical as superfluous deterministic terms can greatly reduce the power of unit root tests: for a discussion of the problem and possible solutions see the special issue of *Econometric Theory* (2009); and for an elaboration of different unit root tests and their properties see Patterson (2011, 2012).

The importance of a unit root has economic and econometric aspects. Many researchers since Nelson and Plosser's (1982) article have been interested in the importance of the random walk component in macroeconomic series (see for example Campbell and Mankiw, 1987a, 1987b), and its implications for the persistence of shocks. The econometric implications centre on avoiding spurious regressions (Granger and Newbold, 1974), that is for example in the simplest bivariate case where a regression of two unrelated random walks appears to be significant by conventional criteria such as R^2.

3.7 The Spectral Density Function

There are a number of semi-parametric methods for the estimation of the long memory parameter d based on the spectrum of the long memory process (see for example Shimotsu and Phillips, 2006). More generally frequency domain methods have an important role in econometrics and in the analysis of macroeconomic data; they are, for example, used in seasonal adjustment and more generally in filtering out or identifying particular frequency-based components of a time series. Stephen Pollock in Chapter 5 deals extensively with filters that have been applied to macroeconomic time series, for example the Hodrick–Prescott (HP) filter and the Butterworth filter.

This section introduces the power spectrum, which is an essential concept in the analysis and filtering of time series with frequency domain methods. Consider a stationary stochastic process, then the power spectrum is the Fourier transform of the autocovariance function, that is:

$$f(\lambda_j) = \frac{1}{2\pi}\left\{\gamma_0 + 2\sum\nolimits_{k=1}^{\infty}\gamma_k \cos(\lambda_j k)\right\}, \qquad \lambda_j \in [0, \pi], \tag{2.16}$$

$$= \frac{1}{2\pi}\left\{\gamma_0 + 2\sum\nolimits_{k=1}^{\infty}\gamma_k e^{-i\lambda_j k}\right\},$$

where γ_0 is the (unconditional) variance of y_t and γ_k is the kth order autocovariance of y_t. Considered as a function of the (angular) frequency λ_j, (2.16) is the spectral density function often referred as the sdf (for simplicity the subscript on λ_j is sometimes omitted from the definition). The range of λ_j assumes a real-valued time series. Anderson (1971, Chapter 7) contains an extensive discussion of these functions and the reader may also like to consult Hamilton (1994, Chapter 6). The power spectrum can be plotted as $f(\lambda_j)$ against $\lambda_j \in [0, \pi]$; alternatively $f(\lambda_j)$ may be plotted against F_j using $F_j = \lambda_j/2\pi$, so that the horizontal axis extends from 0 to 0.5. (The definition in (2.16) follows Anderson (1971, section 7.3). Some authors alternatively take the spectral density function to refer to the (scaled) Fourier transform of the autocorrelation function, that is $F(\lambda_j) = 2\pi\gamma(0)^{-1}f(\lambda_j)$.

As the frequency λ_j is a key input in the sdf, we consider its meaning in more detail. Consider a simple case with the sine and cosine functions $y_{t,\sin} = A\sin(\lambda t)$ and $y_{t,\cos} = B\cos(\lambda t)$, where λ is the angular frequency, measured in radians from 0 through to 2π. These are periodic functions in the sense that $y_{t,\sin} = y_{t+nP,\sin}$ and $y_{t,\cos} = y_{t+nP,\cos}$, for n an integer and a period of length $P = 2\pi/\lambda$. Initially, consider the case with $\lambda = \pi$, then each of these functions has a period of $P = 2\pi$, so that one complete cycle of the process is completed as the index t moves from 0 through to 2π; as t extends past 2π, or before 0, in integer multiples of 2π, a complete cycle is repeated. The amplitudes of these functions are A and B, respectively; for example, if $A = 3$, then the limits of $y_{t,\sin}$ are ± 3. The amplitude controls the importance of the contribution of each frequency to the whole when periodic signals are combined.

Different periods are obtained by varying the frequency λ; for example, if $\lambda = \pi/6 = 2\pi/12$, then the period is $P = 2\pi/(2\pi/12) = 12$ time units. Notice that by writing the frequency in this form, with 2π as the numerator, the period can be read off as the denominator, so that $\lambda = 2\pi/P$. The period P is sometimes referred to as the 'fundamental' period, since for $n = 1$ it is the smallest integer for which the periodicity condition $y_t = y_{t+nP}$ is satisfied; and the corresponding λ is then referred to as the 'fundamental' frequency. It is possible for a signal to have several different frequency components, and the different frequencies can then be distinguished by a subscript as in our notation; thus, λ_j is associated with the period $P_j = 2\pi/\lambda_j$.

A time series may have more than one period suggesting a modification of the definition of periodicity, so that $y_t = y_{t+nPj}$ indicates a repeating cycle with a period P_j. The period P_j is also the length, or span, of the cycle at the frequency λ_j. For example, if the time unit is a quarter and $\lambda_j = 2\pi/4$, then $P_j = 2\pi/\lambda_j = 4$ quarters (¼ cycle per quarter), so that a complete cycle takes four quarters = one year to complete; if $\lambda_j = 2\pi/2$, then $P_j = 2\pi/\lambda_j = 2$ quarters (½ cycle per quarter), so that a complete cycle takes two quarters to complete and there are two cycles in a year. In the case of quarterly data, the two frequencies corresponding to one cycle a year and two cycles a year are the seasonal frequencies. The inverse of the period, that is $F_j = 1/P_j = \lambda_j/2\pi$, is also referred to as a frequency, but in this case it has units of measurement that are the reciprocal of the time unit (not radians as in the case of λ_j). For example, if the time unit is a quarter and $\lambda_j = 2\pi/4$, then $F_j = \lambda_j/2\pi = $ ¼, with the interpretation that a ¼ of the cycle associated with this frequency is completed in the time unit (a calendar quarter); and, as noted above, $\lambda_j = 2\pi/2$ implies $F_j = ½$ cycle per calendar quarter. Note that P_j cannot be less than 2, implying that F_j cannot exceed ½; this follows from the observation that at least two time units are required to identify or resolve a cycle. This frequency is known as the Nyquist frequency which, in angular units, is simply $\lambda_j = 2\pi/2 = \pi$.

Returning to the interpretation of the (theoretical) sdf, a seasonal time series has peaks in the spectrum at the seasonal frequencies, $\lambda_j = 2\pi j/S$, j = 1, . . ., $S/2$ for S even and int[$S/2$] for S odd (where int[.] indicates the integer part of the expression); for example if $S = 4$, then the seasonal periodicities are $j = 1$, $\lambda_1 = \pi/2$, $P_1 = 4$, with one cycle per year; and $j = 2$, $\lambda_2 = \pi$, $P_2 = 2$, with two cycles per year. In practice, as Granger (1966) observed, many economic time series after the removal of any trend in the mean or seasonal components have a peak in the spectrum as $\lambda_j \rightarrow 0^+$; this is now easy to interpret as it corresponds to $f_j \rightarrow 0^+$ and $P_j \rightarrow \infty$; that is, the spectrum indicates that there is a very long (possibly) infinite cycle in the time series.

To estimate the sdf, γ_0 and γ_k are replaced by their sample counterparts, $\hat{\gamma}_0$ and $\hat{\gamma}_k$, and the sample spectral density function $\hat{f}(\lambda_j)$ is:

$$\hat{f}(\lambda_j) = \frac{1}{2\pi}\left\{\hat{\gamma}_0 + 2\sum_{k=1}^{T-1}\hat{\gamma}_k \cos(\lambda_j k)\right\}. \tag{2.17}$$

A range of frequencies for evaluating $\hat{f}(\lambda_j)$ is the set comprising $\lambda_j = 2\pi j/T, j = 0, \ldots,$ int[$T/2$].

There are a number of excellent texts to follow up spectral analysis. Two classics are Granger and Hatanka (1964) and Priestley (1981), the former being oriented to economic applications; and at an introductory level see Stoica and Moses (1997) and Warner (1998).

3.8 Conditional Heteroskedasticity

An important development in the econometric modelling of macroeconomic and financial time series is to allow for conditional heteroskedasticity, which is a particular form of stochastic volatility (see Baillie, 2006). The most popular framework is the ARCH/GARCH model due to Engle (1982) and Bollerslev (1986), which we outline briefly here as a precursor to the more extensive coverage in Chapter 12 by Menelaos Karanasos and Ning Zeng.

Consider the AR(1) model given by $y_t = \rho y_{t-1} + \varepsilon_t$ where $\varepsilon_t \sim \text{iid}(0, \sigma_\varepsilon^2)$. Solving the recursion we obtain $y_t = \rho^t y_0 + \sum_{i=1}^{t}\rho^{t-i}\varepsilon_i$ and for simplicity assume that $y_0 = 0$, hence $E(y_t) = \sum_{i=1}^{t}\rho^{t-i}E(\varepsilon_i) = 0$. Now consider forecasting y_t at time $t - 1$: should one use the unconditional mean $E(y_t) = 0$ or the conditional mean $E(y_t | y_{t-1}) = \rho y_{t-1}$? Using the latter rather than former is second nature, but it embodies a simple but important lesson, which is to allow the forecast to reflect past information on y_t, that is y_{t-1} in the context of an AR(1) model. However, forecasting focuses not only on a levels forecast, but also on forecast intervals; however, the variance that is paired with the use of the conditional mean is the conditional variance, that is $\text{Var}(y_t | y_{t-1})$, but this is assumed constant, it is just σ_ε^2; thus whilst the mean forecast takes the past into account, the conditional variance is assumed constant, that is it is assumed to be conditionally homoscedastic. Although the forecasts vary with y_{t-1}, the intervals around them do not. Engle, therefore, considered how to allow past information to affect the conditional variance, $\mathrm{Var}(y_t|y_{t-1})$, and so allow the forecast intervals to vary depending on the heteroskedasticity in the conditional variance.

The scheme of conditional heteroskedasticity suggested by Engle (1982) took the following form, known as autoregressive conditional heteroskedasticity, ARCH(s):

$$\varepsilon_t = u_t \sigma_t \tag{2.18}$$

$$\sigma_t^2 = \alpha_0 + \alpha_1 \varepsilon_{t-1}^2 + \ldots + \alpha_s \varepsilon_{t-s}^2, \tag{2.19}$$

where $u_t \sim \mathrm{iid}(0, 1)$, $\alpha_0 > 0$ and $\alpha_i \geq 0$ for $i = 1, \ldots, s$. The variable σ_t can be viewed as rescaling the innovation sequence $\{u_t\}$ in a way that is time dependent. The conditional variance is constant if $\alpha_i = 0$ for $i \geq 1$, otherwise it will depend on the s lags of ε_t^2. In practice, $\hat{\varepsilon}_t$ replaces ε_t, where $\hat{\varepsilon}_t = y_t - \hat{\rho} y_{t-1}$, or more generally $\hat{\varepsilon}_t = y_t - x_t'\hat{\beta}$ where $x_t = (x_{t1}, x_{t2}, \ldots, x_{tK})'$, $\beta = (\beta_1, \beta_2, \ldots, \beta_k)'$ and $\hat{\beta}$ is a consistent estimator of β. Given $\hat{\varepsilon}_t$, this will enable estimates of the α_j coefficients and the process can then be iterated. Engle (1982) suggested a maximum likelihood approach with the iterations based on a scoring algorithm. A test for an ARCH effect can be based on the joint significance of the α_j.

An important development of the ARCH model was due to Bollerslev (1986) who introduced the generalized ARCH model, known as GARCH(r, s), which nests the ARCH(r) model:

$$\varepsilon_t = u_t \sigma_t$$

$$\sigma_t^2 = \alpha_0 + \alpha(L)\varepsilon_t^2 + \gamma(L)\sigma_t^2,$$

where $\alpha(L) = \sum_{i=1}^{s} \alpha_i L^i$ and $\gamma(L) = \sum_{j=1}^{r} \gamma_j L^j$. Engle's original ARCH($s$) specification results when $\gamma(L) = 0$. Sufficient conditions for $\sigma_t^2 > 0$ are $\alpha_0 > 0$, $\alpha_i \geq 0$ and $\gamma_j \geq 0$, and a necessary and sufficient condition for stationarity is $\alpha(1) + \gamma(1) < 1$ (Bollerslev, 1986); this condition together with the assumption that all of the roots of the polynomials $1 - \alpha(L) - \gamma(L)$ and $1 - \gamma(L)$ lie outside the unit circle is sufficient for strict stationarity and ergodicity of $\{\varepsilon_t\}$, with finite variance (see Bougerol and Picard, 1992; Ling and McAleer, 2002; Wang, 2006; and Wang and Mao, 2008). The unconditional variance of ε_t is $\sigma^2 = \alpha_0(1 - \alpha(1) - \gamma(1))^{-1}$, hence for σ^2 to be positive given $\alpha_0 > 0$, requires $1 - \alpha(1) - \gamma(1) > 0$. Weak stationarity of the GARCH (r, s) process requires $0 < \alpha(1) + \gamma(1) < 1$; however, applications often find that $\alpha(1) + \gamma(1)$ is very close to 1, particularly in the popular GARCH(1, 1) model.

There have been many developments of GARCH models and good references are Engle (1995) and Baillie (2006), and for references to multivariate ARCH/GARCH models see Brooks (2006). Developments include introducing explanatory variables into the GARCH function (for example Lamoureux and Lastrapes, 1990), introducing a function of volatility into the regression model (Engle et al., 1987) and deriving the minimum mean squared error predictor explicitly accounting for the GARCH process (Baillie and Bollerslev, 2002). Variants of the basic GARCH model include the integrated GARCH, IGARCH, when $\alpha(1) + \gamma(1) \approx 1$, the extension to fractional integration in the FIGARCH model and asymmetric versions of GARCH including the exponential GARCH and the asymmetric GARCH. Bollerslev (2010) and Hamilton (2010) provide synoptic summaries of the many ARCH/GARCH variants. Although the dominant area of applications of these forms of stochastic volatility model is in finance, they also find applications in empirical macroeconomics; an example involving inflation and output is given in Chapter 12 and Hamilton (2010) gives two examples based on interest rates.

4 MULTIVARIATE MODELS

Univariate analysis is often undertaken as a precursor to multivariate modelling, which is the subject of this section. There is, however, no single dominant approach to multivariate model building, with a number of albeit related approaches existing side by side. Had a snapshot been taken in the mid-1970s, the dominant framework would have been that of the simultaneous equations model (SEM), which grew out of the pathbreaking work of Tinbergen (for example Tinbergen, 1939; and see also Klein, 1950), and the development of econometric methods associated with the Cowles Commission approach. For an outline of the latter approach see Bennion (1952), which in turn led to the development of large-scale macroeconometric models, such as the Wharton and Brookings models (Evans and Klein, 1967; Duesenberry, 1965), which came to dominate the 1970s and early 1980s. However, as with univariate analysis, the early 1980s marked a period of change. There were three central developments that have had (so far) permanent effects: Sims' (1980) critique of SEMs, especially of the reality of the identifying restrictions that were needed, was influential, and led to structural vector autoregressive, SVAR, models; cointegrated VARs, CVARs, with a seminal article by Engle and Granger (1987), explicitly recognized the importance of the distinction between non-stationary and stationary variables, and was more in the tradition of SEM model building with the interpretation of cointegrating vectors often depending upon exclusion type identifying restrictions; and dynamic stochastic general equilibrium, DSGE, models brought the ideas of microeconomic type optimizing models to the construction of models operating at a macroeconomic level (a section of this *Handbook* comprising Chapters 18–21 is devoted to the DSGE approach). One element that is, however, a common theme, is that of the VAR in its different forms.

4.1 Vector Autoregressions, VARs

A VAR is the natural extension of an AR model to more than one variable. Typically the notation used is either y_t or x_t to denote a vector of K random variables. The notation adopted here follows Lutz Kilian in Chapter 22, with $y_t = (y_{1t}, y_{2t}, \ldots, y_{Kt})'$.

The VAR of order p, VAR(p), is written:

$$\begin{aligned} y_t &= \eta + \sum\nolimits_{j=1}^{p} A_j y_{t-j} + \varepsilon_t \\ &= \eta + \sum\nolimits_{j=1}^{p} A_j L^j y_t + \varepsilon_t. \end{aligned} \qquad (2.20)$$

⇒

$$A(L)y_t = \eta + \varepsilon_t \tag{2.21}$$

where $A(L) = I_K - \sum_{j=1}^{p} A_j L^j$ and $\eta = (\eta_1, \eta_2, \ldots, \eta_K)'$ is a vector of intercepts. A_j is a $K \times K$ matrix of lag coefficients, $\varepsilon_t = (\varepsilon_{1t}, \varepsilon_{2t}, \ldots, \varepsilon_{Kt})'$ is a vector of shocks with $K \times K$ autocovariance matrices given by $E(\varepsilon_t \varepsilon_s') = \Sigma_\varepsilon(s)$, with typical element $E(\varepsilon_{it}\varepsilon_{js})$, so that the contemporaneous, time t, $K \times K$ (co)variance matrix is $E(\varepsilon_t \varepsilon_t') = \Sigma_\varepsilon(0)$, and the lag s autocovariance matrix is $\Sigma_\varepsilon(s)$; where there is no ambiguity $\Sigma_\varepsilon(0)$ is often written more simply as Σ_ε. We assume that $\Sigma_\varepsilon(s) = 0$ for $t \neq s$, so that ε_t is the multivariate extension of an innovations process. There are no subscripts on $\Sigma_\varepsilon(s)$, indicating that the covariance structure is the same for any translation of the t and s indices.

A VAR is a form of vector stochastic process in y_t, which is said to be weakly (or second order) stationary if the following three conditions are satisfied (see section 1.2 for the univariate case):

Mean:	$E(y_t) = \mu$, which is finite, for all t;
Variance:	$E(y_t - \mu)(y_t - \mu)' = \Sigma_y(0)$ for all t;
Autocovariance:	$E(y_t - \mu)(y_{t-s} - \mu)' = \Sigma_y(s) = \Sigma_y(-s)'$ for all t and $s \geq 1$.

The first condition states that the mean of each variable in the VAR is constant over time (bear in mind that μ is now a vector, interpreted as the vector of long-run means, which will be defined below); the second condition states that the contemporaneous variance–covariance matrix of y_t is invariant to t; the third condition requires that the autocovariance matrix just depends on the lag s. The second condition is the special case of the third with $s = 0$. (For the link between the covariance process for y_t and that for ε_t, see Lütkepohl, 2005.)

A VAR with two variables and two lags is:

$$y_{1t} = \eta_1 + a_{11,1}y_{1t-1} + a_{12,1}y_{2t-1} + a_{11,2}y_{1t\ \ 2} + a_{21,2}y_{2t\ \ 2} + \varepsilon_{1t}$$

$$y_{2t} = \eta_2 + a_{21,1}y_{1t-1} + a_{22,1}y_{2t-1} + a_{21,2}y_{1t-2} + a_{22,2}y_{2t-2} + \varepsilon_{2t}.$$

Each of these equations is like a univariate, autoregressive model but, in addition, includes lagged values of the other variable(s). The next step is to write the equations together using a matrix-vector notation:

$$y_t = \eta + A_1 L y_t + A_2 L^2 y_t + \varepsilon_t$$

⇒

$$(I_2 - A_1 L - A_2 L^2) y_t = \eta + \varepsilon_t$$

$$A_1 L = \begin{bmatrix} a_{11,1}L & a_{12,1}L \\ a_{21,1}L & a_{22,1}L \end{bmatrix}; \; A_2 L^2 = \begin{bmatrix} a_{11,2}L^2 & a_{12,2}L^2 \\ a_{21,2}L^2 & a_{22,2}L^2 \end{bmatrix}.$$

Just as in the univariate case, the sum of the lag weights is obtained by setting $L = 1$ in the lag polynomial $A(L)$, the shorthand for which is $A(1)$. Some other properties of the stationary VAR also follow by analogy with an AR model. The corresponding inverse matrix has the property that $A(L)^{-1}A(L) = I_K$ and, for future reference, adopting the notation of Lütkepohl (2005), define $\Phi(L) \equiv A(L)^{-1}$. Note that $A(z)^{-1} = \text{adj}[A(z)]/\det[A(z)]$, where adj indicates the adjoint matrix, that is the transpose of the matrix of cofactors, and invertibility requires that the determinant of $A(z)$, $\det[A(z)] \neq 0$ for $|z| < 1$. Note that $\det[A(z)] = 0$ for a non-stationary VAR, which leads to the concept of cointegration, considered below in section 4.3.

The VAR can also be expressed in deviations form, in this case as deviations from the vector of means (or trends), that is $y_t - \mu$ (respectively $y_t - \mu_t$). On letting $\mu = A(1)^{-1}\alpha = \Phi(1)\alpha$, then:

$$A(L)(y_t - \mu) = \varepsilon_t, \tag{2.22}$$

where μ has the interpretation of the long-run vector of means, an interpretation that can be maintained provided that the VAR is stable, so that $A(L)$ is invertible. (Note that in Chapter 6, Helmut Lütkepohl uses a slightly different notational convention; in the constant mean case, the model is set up as $y_t = \mu + x_t$ so that the VAR may be defined in terms of x_t; since $x_t = y_t - \mu$, one can equivalently write $A(L)x_t = \varepsilon_t$; the VAR of (2.20) in y_t is then known as the levels form of the VAR. In this chapter the notation x_t is reserved for an exogenous variable or vector of such variables.)

Stability can be expressed in one of two equivalent ways. However, before stating the condition note that the VAR(p) can always be written as a first order system by putting it in companion form, as follows:

$$Y_t = \Pi_0 + \Pi_1 Y_{t-1} + E_t$$

$\Rightarrow$

$$\Pi(L)Y_t = E_t,$$

where $\Pi(L) = I_{Kp} - \Pi_1 L$ and I_{Kp} is the identity matrix of order $Kp \times Kp$; $Y_t = (y_t, y_{t-1}, \ldots, y_{t-p+1})'$, $E_t = (\varepsilon_t, 0, \ldots, 0)'$ and remember that, for example, y_t is itself a K $\times$ 1 vector, so that Y_t is Kp $\times$ 1. Explicitly, the companion form of the VAR(p) is:

$$\begin{pmatrix} y_t \\ y_{t-1} \\ \vdots \\ y_{t-p+1} \end{pmatrix} = \begin{pmatrix} \eta \\ 0_K \\ \vdots \\ 0_K \end{pmatrix} + \begin{bmatrix} A_1 & A_2 & \cdots & A_{p-1} & A_p \\ I_K & \bar{0}_K & \cdots & \bar{0}_K & \bar{0}_K \\ \bar{0}_K & I_K & \cdots & \bar{0}_K & \bar{0}_K \\ \vdots & \vdots & \ddots & \vdots & \vdots \\ \bar{0}_K & \bar{0}_K & \cdots & I_K & \bar{0}_K \end{bmatrix} \begin{pmatrix} y_{t-1} \\ y_{t-2} \\ \vdots \\ y_{t-p} \end{pmatrix} + \begin{pmatrix} \varepsilon_t \\ 0_K \\ \vdots \\ 0_K \end{pmatrix}, \tag{2.23}$$

where 0_K is a K $\times$ 1 vector of 0*s* and $\bar{0}_K$ is a $K \times K$ matrix of 0*s*. Stability requires that the eigenvalues of Π_1 have modulus less than 1, where the eigenvalues are the roots of the characteristic polynomial $\det[\Pi_1 - \lambda I_{Kp}] = 0$. Equivalently, in terms of the reverse characteristic polynomial, the roots of $\Pi(\rho) = I_{Kp} - \Pi_1\rho$ have modulus greater than 1, where the roots of $\Pi(\rho)$ are obtained as the solutions of $\det[I_{Kp} - \rho\Pi_1] = 0$, which is identical to:

$$\det[I_K - \rho A_1 - \rho^2 A_2 - \ldots - \rho^p A_p] = 0.$$

We may also note (see Lütkepohl, 2005, Proposition 2.1), that stability implies stationarity of the VAR(p) process (but not vice versa).

The stationary VAR(p) has a vector MA (VMA) representation as follows:

$$y_t = \mu + \Phi(L)\varepsilon_t \tag{2.24}$$

$$= \mu + \sum\nolimits_{i=0}^{\infty} \Phi_i \varepsilon_{t-i}$$

As in the univariate case, the VMA provides the basis of a number of tools of analysis, such as the impulse response function and measures of persistence.

The VAR given by (2.20) is a closed VAR in the sense that there are the same number of equations as variables; an open VAR has more variables than equations, which implies that the variables are now treated asymmetrically, with some variables considered to be exogenous (or predetermined) to the system.

To illustrate, the VAR(2) amended to include two exogenous variables $x_t = (x_{1t}, x_{2t})'$, with a first order lag, is given by:

$$y_t = \eta + A_1 y_{t-1} + A_2 y_{t-2} + C_1 x_{t-1} + \varepsilon_t. \tag{2.25}$$

Just as in the single equation case, the long-run value of y_t can be obtained conditional on constant values for the exogenous variables. First write (2.25) collecting terms:

$$A(L)y_t = \eta + C(L)x_t + \varepsilon_t, \tag{2.26}$$

$$A(L) - (I - A_1 L - A_2 L^{?}) \text{ and } C(L) = C_1 L.$$

Multiplying through by $A(L)^{-1}$ gives:

$$y_t = A(1)^{-1}\eta + A(L)^{-1}C(L)x_t + A(L)^{-1}\varepsilon_t \tag{2.27}$$

$$= \Phi(1)\eta + \Phi(L)C(L)x_t + \Phi(L)\varepsilon_t$$

$$= \mu + D(L)x_t + \upsilon_t,$$

where $\mu = \Phi(1)\eta$, $D(L) = \Phi(L)C(L)$ and $\upsilon_t = \Phi(L)\varepsilon_t$. Equation (2.27) is sometimes referred to as the final form of the open VAR, with the matrix $D(L)$ referred to as the transfer function, which summarizes the effect of a unit change in the exogenous variables on the endogenous variables. $D(L)$ is the analogue of the rational lag function $w(L)$ in the single equation case and $D(1)$ is the matrix of long-run multipliers.

The VAR is a powerful way of analysing the evolution of data from one point in time to another. Most estimation techniques are based around the assumption that the evolution of the economic variables and the collection of the data occur simultaneously. In some circumstances, however, it may be preferable to allow the possibility that the process generating the data is operating more frequently than the resulting data is collected, for example, if households make decisions on the level of their consumption each month but data is only collected every quarter. Estimating the parameters of an equation like (2.20) when the available data suffer from such time aggregation is the subject of Chapter 13 by Michael Thornton and Marcus Chambers, which also extends the VAR framework to continuous time, where the analogue of (2.20) is written as a stochastic differential equation.

4.2 Structural VARs

The structural VAR, SVAR, is widely used in macroeconomics, and Chapter 22 by Lutz Kilian contains many examples that illustrate the macroeconomic context of SVARs. Given that extensive treatment, here we just draw out the distinction between the (reduced form) VAR of (2.20) and the corresponding SVAR and some implications for identification. For simplicity, in this section deterministic terms are assumed to be absent (otherwise y_t is replaced by $y_t - \mu_t$).

The VAR of (2.20) is a reduced form in the sense that no current dated values of the K variables in y_t appear in any of the equations: the right-hand side variables are predetermined. The genesis of the reduced form VAR could be as the solution of a dynamic structural form and in this sense structural refers to the representation of behavioural equations, such as aggregate demand and aggregate supply functions or demand for money functions and term structure equations. (However, see Sims, 2002, for a discussion of the distinction between structural and behavioural equations.)

The structural VAR is given by:

$$B_0 y_t = \sum_{j=1}^{p} B_j y_{t-j} + u_t \tag{2.28}$$

$\Rightarrow$

$$B(L)y_t = u_t,$$

where $B(L) = (B_0 - B_1 L - \ldots - B_p L^p)$, and $B(L)^{-1}$ is assumed to exist. $B_0 \neq I$ is a non-singular $K \times K$ matrix that summarizes the contemporaneous (or 'instantaneous') links between components of y_t; if $B_0 = I$, then (2.28) is a reduced form rather than a structural VAR as there are no such links. The instantaneous variance matrix of the structural shocks, u_t, is $E(u_t u_t') = \Sigma_u$.

Multiplying (2.28) through by B_0^{-1} gives the reduced form, which was previously referred to as *the* VAR:

$$y_t = \sum_{j=1}^{p} B_0^{-1} B_j y_{t-j} + B_0^{-1} u_t \tag{2.29}$$

$$= \sum_{j=1}^{p} A_j y_{t-j} + \varepsilon_t.$$

On comparison with the reduced form VAR of (2.20), the coefficient matrices are related as follows:

$$A_j = B_0^{-1}B_j, \text{ for } j = 1, \ldots, p, \tag{2.30}$$

$$\varepsilon_t = B_0^{-1}u_t \Rightarrow u_t = B_0\varepsilon_t. \tag{2.31}$$

The relationship between the covariance matrices of u_t and ε_t is $\Sigma_u = B_0\Sigma_\varepsilon B_0'$, which will be of interest later in identifying B_0; and, as B_0^{-1} is assumed to exist, $\Sigma_\varepsilon = B_0^{-1}\Sigma_u B_0'^{-1}$. A usual distinction in terminology is that the u_t and ε_t are referred to as structural shocks and (reduced form) innovations, respectively (note that Blanchard and Quah, 1989, refer to the u_t as disturbances and the innovations may be referred to as errors).

The VMA for the (reduced form) VAR is (see 2.24):

$$\begin{aligned} y_t &= \Phi(L)\varepsilon_t \\ &= \sum\nolimits_{i=0}^{\infty}\Phi_i\varepsilon_{t-i}. \end{aligned} \tag{2.32}$$

Whereas the corresponding VMA for the SVAR is:

$$\begin{aligned} y_t &= \Theta(L)u_t \\ &= \sum\nolimits_{i=0}^{\infty}\Theta_i u_{t-i} \\ \Theta(L) &= B(L)^{-1} \\ &= \Phi(L)B_0^{-1}. \end{aligned} \tag{2.33}$$

Suppose interest centres on the response of y_t to shocks (as in obtaining the impulse response functions), then one has to be precise about which shocks are being referred to and which are appropriate for the case at hand. From an economic point of view it is of interest to identify shocks as, for example, supply side shocks or demand side shocks but, for example, looking at the response of y_t to a one-unit shock to a component of ε_t is unlikely to have any economic meaning as $\varepsilon_t = B_0^{-1}u_t$, so that the reduced form innovations/errors are a non-linear function of the structural shocks and it is these latter that are likely to have more economic interest.

The VMA for the SVAR is the more meaningful representation for the analysis of shocks (although the reduced form VMA is more attractive from a forecasting perspective); however, the SVAR representation requires B_0, which was not required for the reduced form VAR. Why not, therefore, work with the structural form VAR and seek estimates of the B_j coefficients? The problem that has to be overcome in that approach, familiar from introductory econometrics texts, is that it requires that the structural form (or instantaneous) coefficients B_0 are identified. Identification in this sense means that there is a unique mapping from the reduced form coefficients back to the underlying structural form coefficients.

In the dynamic simultaneous equations model (SEM), identification is usually achieved by first imposing a set of normalization restrictions, namely that the diagonal elements of B_0 are unity, and then imposing a sufficient number of zero (exclusion) restrictions on the individual equations of (2.28), which correspond to the effect that not all equations contain all variables. In the case of the demand and supply of an agricultural good, a favoured example in textbooks, the normalization first implies that one equation is the demand equation and that the other is the supply equation; and, in respect of the exclusion restrictions, that income is a variable in the demand function but not in the supply function, and a weather indicator is a variable in the supply function but not in the demand function.

This SEM approach is distinguished from the SVAR approach in that it does not typically make any assumptions about a particular structure for Σ_u, whereas that is the leading case for SVARs using the relationship $\Sigma_u = B_0\Sigma_\varepsilon B_0'$. Identification in an SEM first focuses on normalizing B_0, whereas in an SVAR the focus is first on normalizing Σ_u, that is the variance–covariance matrix of the structural shocks. The shocks are assumed to be orthogonal so that Σ_u is a diagonal matrix, thus the shocks are uncorrelated or, further, independent if Gaussian. Next, once the initial focus switches to the role of the shocks, Σ_u, then by scaling each of the equations the individual variances can be set to unity so that $\Sigma_u = I$ and, hence, a perturbation to a shock is in units of the shock's standard deviation. This normalization will have implications for B_0, which will not now be normalized as unit elements on the diagonal as in the SEM approach. With these normalizations $B_0\Sigma_\varepsilon B_0' = I$, that is $\Sigma_\varepsilon = B_0^{-1}B_0'^{-1}$.

A consistent estimator of Σ_ε, say $\tilde{\Sigma}_\varepsilon$, can be obtained from LS estimation of (2.29), since that is in effect a system of seemingly unrelated equations (SURE). With $\tilde{\Sigma}_\varepsilon$ replacing Σ_ε, the equations to be solved are $\tilde{\Sigma}_\varepsilon = \tilde{B}_0^{-1}\tilde{B}_0'^{-1}$, where $\tilde{B}_0$ is the resulting estimator of B_0; identification, and hence whether this set of equations satisfies the necessary condition for $\tilde{B}_0$ to be obtained, then depends on the relationship between the number of equations and the number of unknowns in B_0. As in the standard SEM, this gives rise to an order (or necessary) condition comparing the number of unrestricted elements in Σ_ε and the number of unknowns. The former is the number of elements in Σ_ε excluding the diagonal elements, that is $K(K+1)/2$. If B_0 is unrestricted it has K^2 elements, therefore the minimum number of restrictions that it is necessary to impose on B_0 is $K^2 - K(K + 1)/2 = K(K - 1)/2$, imposing more restrictions results in B_0 being overidentified by the order condition. The nature of restrictions that are imposed in practice look like, for example, the zero and proportionality restrictions that are often applied in SEMs, but the focus in an SVAR is on the relationship between the shocks.

Setting $\Sigma_u = I$ or the diagonal elements of B_0 to unity are not the only normalization options (see Kilian in Chapter 22 and Lütkepohl in Chapter 6), and for some applications that illustrate the selection of restrictions in an economic context (see, for example, Blanchard and Quah, 1989; Blanchard and Perotti, 2002; and Sims and Zha, 2005, 2006). A popular choice is to seek a recursively identified structure so that B_0^{-1} is lower triangular $K \times K$ matrix, with a positive main diagonal; this imposes just enough restrictions to meet the order condition as there are $K(K - 1)/2$ zero elements on the upper triangle. Kilian (Chapter 22) gives macroeconomic examples of this kind of identification scheme and of several others that have been used in the macroeconomics literature.

It has so far been assumed that the VAR is a stationary process and indeed the typical practice in macroeconomic applications is to transform the variables so that the y_t vector comprises only $I(0)$ variables. For example, Blanchard and Quah (1989) use a two-variable VAR where y_{1t} is the first difference of the logarithm of GNP and y_{2t} is the unemployment rate, and each variable is assumed to be $I(0)$ resulting in a stationary VAR. However, some aspects of VAR modelling are still valid in the presence of $I(1)$ variables (see Toda and Phillips, 1993 and Toda and Yamamoto, 1995), and Lütkepohl provides more details and references in Chapter 6. If the multivariate system includes $I(d)$ variables, $d \geq 1$, the more usual macroeconomic modelling framework is that of the cointegrating VAR, CVAR.

4.3 Cointegration

As noted, one possible response to a unit root is to formulate the VAR in the first differences of the variables. However, such a formulation provides no information on the relationship between the levels of the variables in the VAR, and it is this aspect on which economic theory is usually most informative. This option is not, therefore, generally satisfactory even though a VAR in terms of Δy_t models is stationary.

A satisfactory alternative arises when the variables in y_t are cointegrated. Suppose that each of the variables in y_t is non-stationary, but on differencing once they become stationary, that is they are $I(1)$ and so modelling them jointly using a VAR in levels would reveal a unit root in the autoregressive polynomial. A linear combination of $I(1)$ variables can be $I(0)$, a situation summarized with the shorthand $CI(1,1)$ to indicate that $I(1)$ variables are reduced by one order of integration in a linear combination. In this case the candidate $I(0)$ variables are, therefore, not just the first differences but also the cointegrating combination(s) formed from the $I(1)$ variables. Note the use of the plural here: when $K>2$ there may be more than one linear combination of the K $I(1)$ variables which is stationary, each of which is a candidate regressor. Hence, a more promising way forward is to formulate models that capture short-run responses and the long-run relationships as represented in the cointegrating combinations. This is the topic of Chapter 7 by James Davidson, with some preliminary concepts reviewed here.

A result due to Engle and Granger (1987), which is part of what is known as the Granger Representation Theorem (implication 4), is of relevance; it states that if the $K \times 1$ vector of variables y_t is $CI(1, 1)$ then there exists an error correction representation of the general form:

$$\Delta y_t = A(1)^{-1}\eta + \alpha z_{t-1} + \sum_{j=1}^{p-1} \Gamma_j L^j \Delta y_t + \theta(L)\varepsilon_t \tag{2.34a}$$

$$= \mu + \Pi y_{t-1} + \sum_{j=1}^{p-1} \Gamma_j \Delta y_{t-j} + \theta(L)\varepsilon_t, \tag{2.34b}$$

where $\mu = A(1)^{-1}\eta$, $z_{t-1} = \beta' y_{t-1}$ are r linear, cointegrating combinations amongst the K variables, β' is the $r \times K$ matrix of r cointegrating vectors, α is the $K \times r$ matrix of adjustment or error correction coefficients and $\Pi = \alpha\beta'$. The coefficient vectors are related to those in the VAR as $\Pi = \Sigma_{j=1}^{p} A_j - I$ and $\Gamma_j = -\Sigma_{i=j+1}^{p} A_i$. There may be a moving average 'disturbance', $\theta(L)\varepsilon_t$, with $\theta(L)$ a lag polynomial but often, for practical purposes, $\theta(L)$ is degenerate, that is the identity matrix, which is an assumption we will adopt for this chapter.

The interpretation of the error correction representation is appealing: the long-run or equilibrium relationships amongst the levels of the variables are captured by the cointegrating combinations $z_{t-1} = \beta' y_{t-1}$; non-zero values of z_{t-1} indicate (lagged) disequilibria that are eradicated through the adjustment coefficients in α, with each column of α associated with one of the r stationary cointegrating combinations; short-run dynamic adjustments are captured by non-zero values for the elements in Γ_j. The error correction representation thus models entirely in $I(0)$ space: $\beta' y_{t-1}$ is $I(0)$ through cointegration and Δy_{t-j} is $I(0)$ by differencing; hence, the VAR is balanced in mean and, given cointegration, it may be referred to as a CVAR, a vector error correction model, VECM, or a vector equilibrium correction model, VEqCM.

Note that the cointegration 'space' can be isolated but not *the* cointegrating vector(s). The component matrices of Π, that is α and β, are not unique and so to refer to the former as the adjustment coefficients and the latter as the cointegrating coefficients is subject to a qualification. For example, if β' is scaled by a full rank $r \times r$ matrix Λ, such that $\overleftrightarrow{\beta}' = \Lambda\beta'$, with corresponding adjustment coefficients $\overleftrightarrow{\alpha}$, then we can write Π as $\Pi = \overleftrightarrow{\alpha}\overleftrightarrow{\beta}' = \alpha\Lambda^{-1}\Lambda\beta' = \alpha\beta'$. Hence, both $\overleftrightarrow{\beta}$ and β are matrices of cointegrating vectors and a normalization refers to a choice of the Λ matrix. A normalization is usually chosen that corresponds to an interpretation of α and β' in an economic context; for example, typical normalizations seek to interpret individual equations by way of a normalization such that a different coefficient in each of the r vectors in β' is set to unity (as in a traditional SEM normalization). For more on the role of normalization in a CVAR context see Phillips (1991), Boswijk (1996) and Luukkonen et al. (1999), and for examples see Juselius (2006).

Will it always be the case that a cointegrating vector or vectors exist? Intuition suggests that this cannot be the case. For example, in a bivariate VAR suppose that y_{1t} is unrelated to y_{2t}, or y_{1t} and y_{2t} are part of a larger system, then we should not be able to find a cointegrating vector for y_{1t} and y_{2t} or y_{1t} and y_{2t} alone. This prompts the question: what particular features of a VAR indicate the existence of cointegrating vectors? Π is an example of a matrix which does not have independent rows or columns and, therefore, is a matrix with less than full rank; it is said to have *reduced* or deficient rank. Whilst a matrix of reduced rank will have a determinant of zero, this does not tell us the order of the deficiency in rank. Another more fruitful possibility is to obtain the eigenvalues of Π, for which it is necessary to solve the characteristic equation given by:

$$\det[\Pi - \lambda I] = 0. \tag{2.35}$$

where λ is a scalar. A zero value for one of the eigenvalues alerts us to the deficient rank of Π and, in general, the number of non-zero eigenvalues of Π is its rank, which in turn is the number of cointegrating vectors. (Note that an eigenvalue of zero for Π corresponds to an eigenvalue of unity in the corresponding VAR.) The implications of the rank of Π are summarized in Table 2.1.

Table 2.1 Implication of the rank of Π

Rank	Implications
$r = K$ (maximum)	VAR is stationary in levels
$1 \leq r \leq K - 1$	Cointegration with r cointegrating vectors
$r = 0$	VAR can be reformulated entirely in first differences

Consider the following first order VECM in two variables:

$$\begin{pmatrix}\Delta y_{1t}\\ \Delta y_{2t}\end{pmatrix} = \begin{bmatrix}-1/2 & 1/16\\ 1/2 & -1/16\end{bmatrix}\begin{pmatrix}y_{1t-1}\\ y_{2t-1}\end{pmatrix} + \begin{pmatrix}\varepsilon_{1t}\\ \varepsilon_{2t}\end{pmatrix}$$

$$= \begin{pmatrix}-1/2\\ 1/2\end{pmatrix}(1 \quad -1/8)\begin{pmatrix}y_{1t-1}\\ y_{2t-1}\end{pmatrix} + \begin{pmatrix}\varepsilon_{1t}\\ \varepsilon_{2t}\end{pmatrix}.$$

The single cointegrating vector is $y_{1t} - 1/8y_{2t}$, with adjustment coefficients of $-½$ for the first equation and ½ for the second equation. The eigenvalues of Π are obtained as follows:

$$\begin{bmatrix}-1/2 & 1/16\\ 1/2 & -1/16\end{bmatrix} - \begin{bmatrix}\lambda & 0\\ 0 & \lambda\end{bmatrix} = \begin{bmatrix}-(1/2+\lambda) & 1/16\\ 1/2 & -(1/16+\lambda)\end{bmatrix},$$

so that $|\Pi - \lambda I|$ is:

$$\begin{Vmatrix}-(1/2+\lambda) & 1/16\\ 1/2 & -(1/16+\lambda)\end{Vmatrix} = (1/2+\lambda)(1/16+\lambda) - (1/2)(1/16)$$

$$= \lambda^2 + (9/16)\lambda = \lambda[\lambda + (9/16)].$$

Hence, setting this expression to zero gives the eigenvalues $\lambda_1 = 0$ and $\lambda_2 = -9/16$; as one of these is zero, the rank of Π is deficient, indeed the rank of Π is one and there is one cointegrating vector.

Johansen's procedure for testing for the cointegrating rank is based on the number of eigenvalues that are statistically different from zero using a likelihood ratio-based principle (see Johansen, 1988, 1995; Johansen and Juselius, 1990; and Juselius, 2006). There are two versions of the test known as the trace test and the λ_{max} (or maximal eigenvalue) test, although the former is more often used than the latter. The details of these and some other tests are given in Chapter 7.

4.4 Dynamic Panel Data

The recent growth in the quantity and coverage of macroeconomic data has made it possible to estimate a range of models where the vector of dependent variables, Y_t, and the matrix of exogenous variables, X_t, contain equivalent economic variables observed for a group of n countries. As n becomes large, however, the number of parameters to be estimated in a standard VAR rapidly becomes prohibitive. For example, the open VAR(2) given in equation (2.26) with one exogenous variable per country contains $n + 3n^2 + n(n+1)/2$ coefficients, which for a modest sample of 10 countries equates to 365 coefficients. To overcome this problem of dimensionality, panel data techniques from microeconomics have been adapted to the particularities of macroeconomic data, for example modelling with lagged endogenous variables and, quite often, longer time spans. This is discussed further in Chapter 10, by Badi Baltagi, which begins with a model that can be thought of as an open VAR(1) with restrictions on the parameters so that the heterogeneity between countries is captured in the vector η.

The availability of some very large macroeconomic datasets, such as the Penn World Table, has led to the development of methods that allow for a sophisticated treatment of the error term to capture unexplained correlations between the dependent variables. Chapter 11, by Jörg Breitung and In Choi, discusses models where the error has a factor structure; that is the error for each country contains a part that is idiosyncratic and the effects of a number of common factors which depend on the so-called factor loadings for that country.

5 ESTIMATION METHODS

As far as estimation is concerned, introductory texts in econometrics focus on the method of ordinary least squares, OLS, perhaps also including an outline of classical maximum likelihood, ML, estimation. The reader will note from the contents of this *Handbook* that the key estimation methods are the generalized method of moments, GMM, ML and Bayesian estimation, and these methods are briefly introduced in this chapter. Alastair Hall deals more extensively with GMM in Chapter 14 and Francisco Ruge-Murcia considers GMM estimation of DSGE models in Chapter 20; Tommaso Proietti and Alessandra Luati consider ML estimation and the Kalman Filter in Chapter 15; while Bayesian methods are the subject of Chapter 16 by Luc Bauwens and Dimitris Korobilis and their application to macroeconomic modelling is considered in Chapters 18, 21 and 24.

5.1 The Method of Moments

The method of moments (MM) first identifies a set of population moments that are equal to zero; the parameter estimates are then obtained by mimicking the chosen population moments by the corresponding sample moments. This is a unifying principle of estimation, which includes ordinary least squares, instrumental variables (IV), two-stage least squares (2SLS), and other methods for simultaneous equations, and maximum likelihood; it can be applied equally to data comprising time series observations, cross-section observations or a combination of both; it can be applied to situations where there is heteroskedasticity and/or serial correlation and to inherently non-linear models. When there are more moment conditions than parameters to be estimated, analogous to the case of over-identification in a standard simultaneous equations framework, it is not generally possible to simultaneously satisfy all of the sample moment conditions, and the development of MM for this case is referred to as the generalized method of moments (GMM).

MM and GMM not only include standard methods of estimation, they offer a general method of estimation that has found particular applications in macroeconomics and finance. (For a very readable introduction to GMM see Wooldridge, 2001, and a book length exposition with many examples is provided by Hall, 2005.) The moment conditions are essentially orthogonality conditions, which are familiar from standard models, such as the errors are orthogonal to the regressors or the errors are orthogonal to a set of instrumental variables (which may include some of the regressors). In an economic context the key is to obtain orthogonality conditions that derive from the underlying theory (for illustrations see, for example, Hansen and West, 2002). For example, a leading case is that the errors from a rational forecast based on an information set at time t, say Ω_t, are orthogonal to Ω_t. Orthogonality conditions also arise, and are exploited in a GMM framework, in dynamic stochastic general equilibrium (DSGE) models, and a section of this *Handbook* is devoted to that topic; see Chapters 18–21. Given the coverage of those chapters, this section provides a more basic underlying motivation for MM and GMM. Alastair Hall in Chapter 14 gives examples that show the flexibility of GMM applications in a macroeconomic context.

The notation used here emphasizes the standard linear regression model as a means of introducing the key unifying principles of estimation by MM and GMM, which are then extended later in the *Handbook*. The notation is, therefore, framed in terms of the parameter vector β. Considering the problem more generally, as in Chapter 17, the usual notational convention is to seek an estimator of the parameter vector generically denoted θ.

To continue let $E[g_t(\beta)]$denote the population moment function for index t, where $g_t(\beta)$ is a chosen function of the variables and parameter vector β. The simplest case for motivation is where $E(y_t) = \beta$, and β is a constant, with y_t a stationary, ergodic random variable; let $g_t(\beta) = y_t - \beta$, then the (population) moment condition is $E[g_t(\beta)] = E[y_t - \beta] = 0$. The sample analogue of this condition is then formed and solved to provide an estimator $\tilde{\beta}$ of β, that is:

$$T^{-1}\sum\nolimits_{t=1}^{T} g_t(\tilde{\beta}) = T^{-1}\sum\nolimits_{t=1}^{T} y_t - \tilde{\beta} = 0 \Rightarrow \tilde{\beta} = T^{-1}\sum\nolimits_{t=1}^{T} y_t.$$

The MM estimator $\tilde{\beta}$ uses the ensemble average $T^{-1}\Sigma_{t=1}^{T} y_t$ as an estimator of $E(y_t)$, hence the need for ergodic stationarity of y_t.

Two cases relevant to econometrics will serve to illustrate the principle of MM estimation. The first case is the standard linear regression model where the regressors are random variables:

$$y_t = x_t'\beta + \varepsilon_t \qquad t - 1, \ldots, T, \tag{2.36}$$

where $x_t - (x_{t1}, x_{t2}, \ldots, x_{tK})'$ and $\beta = (\beta_1, \beta_2, \ldots, \beta_k)'$. In familiar matrix vector notation, this is:

$$y = X\beta + \varepsilon, \tag{2.37}$$

where $y = (y_1, y_2, \ldots, y_T)'$, $\varepsilon = (\varepsilon_1, \varepsilon_2, \ldots, \varepsilon_T)'$ and x_t' is the tth row of X; further $E(x_t x_t') = \Sigma_{xx}$ and $E(x_t y_t) = \Sigma_{xy}$ are $K \times K$ and $K \times 1$ population moment matrices invariant to t. (In general the random variables in this and subsequent models are assumed to be jointly stationary and ergodic; see for example Hayashi, 2000.) For simplicity initially assume that $E(\varepsilon\varepsilon') = \sigma_\varepsilon^2 I$. (When the identity matrix is not subscripted it is of order T.) Note that in general a subscripted Σ indicates a population moment whereas the corresponding sample moment is indicated by $\hat{\Sigma}$; for example, the sample moment analogues of Σ_{xx} and Σ_{xy} are $\hat{\Sigma}_{xx} = T^{-1}\Sigma_{t=1}^{T} x_t x_t'$ and $\hat{\Sigma}_{xy} = T^{-1}\Sigma_{t=1}^{T} x_t y_t$.

In this set-up x_{tk} is a random variable, in contrast to the 'fixed in repeated samples' assumption of elementary texts, with the property that for all $t = 1, \ldots, T$, it is orthogonal to the error at time t, ε_t; hence (2.37) is described as a regression model. The moment conditions of interest relate to $g_t(\beta) = x_t\varepsilon_t$ and collecting these (orthogonality) conditions they can be expressed as:

$$E[g_t(\beta)] = E(x_t\varepsilon_t) = 0_K \qquad \text{for all } t, \tag{2.38}$$

where 0_K is a K $\times$ 1 vector of zeros as indicated by the K subscript.

As Wooldridge (2001) notes, these moment conditions are the weakest sense in which the x_{tk} can be regarded as 'exogenous' in (2.36). Note that (2.38) implies $E(x_{tk}\varepsilon_t) = 0$ for all t and $k = 1, \ldots, K$. If $x_{t1} = 1$, then this includes the condition that $E(\varepsilon_t) = 0$ for all t, the other conditions being interpreted as that each of the regressors is uncorrelated with the error term for all t. If the set (2.38) is satisfied, then the regressors are referred to as 'predetermined', whereas 'strict exogeneity' is a strengthening of (2.38) to $E(x_s\varepsilon_t) = 0$ for all s and t, so that the ε_t are orthogonal not only to x_t, but also to past regressors, $s < t$, and future regressors, $s > t$.

The sample analogue of (2.38) is:

$$\hat{\Sigma}_{x\hat{\varepsilon}} = T^{-1}\sum\nolimits_{t=1}^{T} x_t\hat{\varepsilon}_t = 0_K. \tag{2.39}$$

That is apart from T^{-1}, the $K \times 1$ vector in (2.39) is given by:

$$\begin{pmatrix} x_{11} \\ x_{12} \\ \vdots \\ x_{1K} \end{pmatrix} \hat{\varepsilon}_1 + \begin{pmatrix} x_{21} \\ x_{22} \\ \vdots \\ x_{2K} \end{pmatrix} \hat{\varepsilon}_2 + \ldots \begin{pmatrix} x_{T1} \\ x_{T2} \\ \vdots \\ x_{TK} \end{pmatrix} \hat{\varepsilon}_T = \begin{pmatrix} \sum_{t=1}^{T} x_{t1}\hat{\varepsilon}_t \\ \sum_{t=1}^{T} x_{t2}\hat{\varepsilon}_t \\ \vdots \\ \sum_{t=1}^{T} x_{tK}\hat{\varepsilon}_t \end{pmatrix} = \begin{pmatrix} 0 \\ 0 \\ \vdots \\ 0 \end{pmatrix}. \tag{2.40}$$

This is written more familiarly as $X'\hat{\varepsilon} = 0$, which follows from the normal equations derived from minimizing the residual sum of squares. If $x_{t1} = 1$, then the first column element is $\sum_{t=1}^{T} \hat{\varepsilon}_t = 0$. Substituting for $\hat{\varepsilon}_t = y_t - x_t'\hat{\beta}$, where $\hat{\beta}$ is the estimator of β that solves (2.39), results in the usual OLS estimator:

$$\begin{aligned} \hat{\beta}_{OLS} &= \left[\sum\nolimits_{t=1}^{T} x_t x_t'\right]^{-1} \sum\nolimits_{t=1}^{T} x_t y_t \\ &= \hat{\Sigma}_{xx}^{-1}\hat{\Sigma}_{xy} \\ &= (X'X)^{-1}X'y. \end{aligned} \tag{2.41}$$

An interesting way of deriving the OLS estimator, which enables its interpretation as a method of moments estimator, is to premultiply (2.37) by X' to obtain:

$$X'y = X'X\beta + X'\varepsilon. \tag{2.42}$$

The population moment conditions set $E(X'\varepsilon) = 0$, whereas the sample counterparts set $T^{-1}X'\tilde{\varepsilon} = 0$ for the choice of $\tilde{\varepsilon} = y - X\tilde{\beta}$, where $\tilde{\beta} = \hat{\beta}_{OLS} = (X'X)^{-1}X'y$. In this case the limiting distribution of $\hat{\beta}_{OLS}$ is summarized as $\sqrt{T}(\hat{\beta}_{OLS} - \beta) \Rightarrow_D N(0, \sigma_\varepsilon^2 \Sigma_{xx}^{-1})$, bearing in mind that $p\lim(T^{-1}\Sigma_{t=1}^{T} x_t x_t') = \Sigma_{xx}$. The asymptotic distribution (denoted $\Rightarrow_A$) of $\hat{\beta}_{OLS}$ is then $\hat{\beta}_{OLS} \Rightarrow_A N(\beta, \sigma_\varepsilon^2 T^{-1}\Sigma_{xx}^{-1})$; estimating Σ_{xx} by $\hat{\Sigma}_{xx}$ and σ_ε^2 by $\hat{\sigma}_\varepsilon^2 = \Sigma\hat{\varepsilon}_t^2/(T-k)$, where $\hat{\sigma}_\varepsilon^2 = y_t - x_t'\beta_{OLS}$, the estimated asymptotic variance (EAVAR) of $\hat{\beta}_{OLS}$ is $EAVAR(\hat{\beta}_{OLS}) = \hat{\sigma}_\varepsilon^2(X'X)^{-1}$.

The second case to consider is where some or all of the required orthogonality conditions do not hold, which in least squares terms leads to the instrumental variables (IV) estimator. Suppose that the orthogonality conditions of (2.38) hold for a set of random variables $z_t = (z_{t1}, z_{t2}, \ldots, z_{tL})'$, which are not necessarily the regressors in (2.36), so that:

$$E(z_t\varepsilon_t) = 0_L. \tag{2.43}$$

We can return to (2.38) by assuming that $z_t = x_t$ and, therefore, $K = L$; however, the new set-up allows some or all of the original orthogonality conditions to fail, as in simultaneous equation systems or in an errors in variables framework. For example, suppose the first K_1 conditions are valid, but the remaining K_2 fail and, initially, assume that $K = L$; then $z_t = (x_{t1}, \ldots, x_{tK_1}, z_{tK_1+1}, \ldots, z_{tK})'$, so that z_t' is the tth row of the matrix Z.

The method of moments approach proceeds as in the OLS case by using the sample analogue of the population moment conditions:

$$g(\tilde{\beta}) = T^{-1}\sum_{t=1}^{T} z_t\tilde{\varepsilon}_t = T^{-1}Z'\tilde{\varepsilon} = 0_K. \tag{2.44}$$

Resulting in:

$$\tilde{\beta}_{MM} = \left[T^{-1}\sum_{t=1}^{T} z_t x_t'\right]^{-1} T^{-1}\sum_{t=1}^{T} z_t y_t \tag{2.45}$$

$$= \hat{\Sigma}_{zx}^{-1}\hat{\Sigma}_{zy}$$

$$= (Z'X)^{-1}Z'y,$$

$$\text{EAVar}(\tilde{\beta}_{MM}) = \tilde{\sigma}_\varepsilon^2(Z'X)^{-1}Z'Z(X'Z)^{-1} \tag{2.46}$$

$$= \tilde{\sigma}_\varepsilon^2 T^{-1}\hat{\Sigma}_{zx}^{-1}\hat{\Sigma}_{zz}\hat{\Sigma}_{xz}^{-1}$$

$$\tilde{\sigma}_\varepsilon^2 = T^{-1}\sum_{t=1}^{T} \tilde{\varepsilon}_t^2$$

$$\tilde{\varepsilon}_t = y_t - x_t'\tilde{\beta}_{MM}.$$

$\tilde{\beta}_{MM}$ is also the instrumental variables estimator, $\tilde{\beta}_{IV}$, where $x_{tj}, j = 1, \ldots, K_1$ are their own instruments and $(z_{tK_1+1} \ldots, z_{tK})$ is a set of instruments for $(x_{tK_1+1}, \ldots, x_{tK})$. Given $L = K$, the dimension of β, the solution is unique requiring that $(Z'X)^{-1}$ exists, equivalently $(Z'X)$ is of full rank.

If $L > K$, and there are no linear dependencies amongst the Z variables, then in a sense there are 'too' many orthogonality conditions, a situation that leads to the generalized method of moments considered in the next section. In a simultaneous equations context this is referred as over-identification, which leads to non-uniqueness in the parameter estimates (in the sense that $L - K$ of the orthogonality conditions can be discarded to obtain a solution). The IV (also two-stage least squares, 2SLS) solution to this problem is to regress the columns of X on Z and use the predicted values of X. Consider:

$$X = Z\gamma + \upsilon. \tag{2.47}$$

The OLS estimator of the $L \times K$ vector γ is $\hat{\gamma} = (Z'Z)^{-1}Z'X$, with fitted values $\hat{X} = Z\hat{\gamma}$. The corresponding IV estimator uses the linear combinations given by $\hat{X}$ in place of Z, that is:

$$\hat{\beta}_{IV} = \hat{\Sigma}_{\hat{x}x}^{-1}\hat{\Sigma}_{\hat{x}y}$$

$$= [(X'Z)(Z'Z)^{-1}(Z'X)]^{-1}(X'Z)(Z'Z)^{-1}Z'Xy \tag{2.48}$$

$$\text{EAVar}(\hat{\beta}_{IV}) = \hat{\sigma}_{\varepsilon}^{2}[(X'Z)(Z'Z)^{-1}(Z'X)]^{-1} \tag{2.49}$$

$$\hat{\sigma}_{\varepsilon}^{2} = T^{-1}\sum_{t=1}^{T}\hat{\varepsilon}_t^2$$

$$\hat{\varepsilon}_t = y_t - x_t'\hat{\beta}_{IV}.$$

When a column (or columns) of X is (are) in Z, then it (they) will be reproduced in $\hat{X}$.

5.2 The Generalized Method of Moments

Continuing with the case $L > K$, the problem from this perspective is that there are more moment equations than there are parameters, hence it will not in general be possible to simultaneously satisfy all of the sample moment conditions by a choice, say, $\tilde{\beta}$ of β of dimension $K \times 1$. Instead, GMM proceeds by choosing a $\tilde{\beta}$ that results in $g(\tilde{\beta})$ as 'close' to 0_L as possible in a well defined sense. At this stage to show the generality of the approach, let $E(\varepsilon\varepsilon') = \Phi$, thus heteroskedasticity and serial correlation may be present.

Given that not all of the sample moment conditions can be satisfied, the 'close' to 0_L criterion refers to converting the L-dimensions of the sample moment conditions to a scalar using a particular metric. To this end let $\hat{W}$ and W be $L \times L$ symmetric positive definite matrices, referred to as weighting matrices, such that $\hat{W} \rightarrow_p W$ as $T \rightarrow \infty$. (In some notations, $\hat{W}$ is indexed or subscripted by T to emphasize its sample dependence; also $\hat{W}$ can be relaxed to be positive semi-definite, see Chapter 14, Definition 2.) Then the solution to the following minimization problem is the GMM estimator (indexed by $\hat{W}$):

$$\min_{\tilde{\beta}} \, [g(\tilde{\beta})']\hat{W}[g(\tilde{\beta})]. \tag{2.50}$$

The function to be minimized is a weighted quadratic form in the sample moment conditions where $g(\tilde{\beta}) = T^{-1}\Sigma_{t=1}^{T}z_t\tilde{\varepsilon}(\tilde{\beta}) = T^{-1}Z'\tilde{\varepsilon}(\tilde{\beta})$ and $\tilde{\varepsilon}(\tilde{\beta}) = y - X\tilde{\beta}$. Making the substitutions, $\tilde{\beta}_{GMM}$ solves:

$$\min_{\tilde{\beta}} \, T^{-2}\tilde{\varepsilon}'Z\hat{W}Z'\tilde{\varepsilon}. \tag{2.51}$$

This can then be viewed as minimizing the weighted sum of squares $\tilde{\varepsilon}'V\tilde{\varepsilon}$, where $V = Z\hat{W}Z'$. The explicit solution to this minimization problem is:

$$\tilde{\beta}_{GMM} = (X'Z\hat{W}Z'X)^{-1}X'Z\hat{W}Z'y. \quad (2.52)$$

The GMM residuals are then defined using $\tilde{\beta}_{GMM}$. The GMM estimator can be expressed in terms of the sample moments and $\hat{W}$ as:

$$\tilde{\beta}_{GMM} = (\hat{\Sigma}'_{zx}\hat{W}\hat{\Sigma}_{zx})^{-1}\hat{\Sigma}'_{zx}\hat{W}\hat{\Sigma}_{zy}. \quad (2.53)$$

There is not a unique GMM estimator (although $\tilde{\beta}_{GMM}$ is unique for a particular choice of $\hat{W}$), but rather a class of GMM estimators indexed by a choice of $\hat{W}$. Comparison of $\tilde{\beta}_{GMM}$ of (2.53) with $\hat{\beta}_{IV}$ of (2.48) shows that $\hat{\beta}_{GMM} = \hat{\beta}_{IV}$ for the choice $\hat{W} = (Z'Z)^{-1}$.

As in the case of the OLS estimator, the GMM estimator can be viewed as first pre-multiplying (2.37) by Z' to obtain:

$$Z'y = Z'X\beta + Z'\varepsilon. \quad (2.54)$$

In this context, the population moment conditions set $E(Z'\varepsilon) = 0$; in seeking an estimator by setting $Z'\tilde{\varepsilon} = 0$ for some choice of $\tilde{\varepsilon}$, note that $E[Z'\varepsilon(Z'\varepsilon)'] = E(Z'\varepsilon\varepsilon'Z) = Z'\Phi Z \equiv \Omega$. The estimator taking into account Ω (as in a GLS approach) sets $\hat{W} = \Omega^{-1} = (Z'\Phi Z)^{-1}$, thus:

$$\begin{aligned}\tilde{\beta}_{GMM} &= [(X'Z)\Omega^{-1}(Z'X)]^{-1}(X'Z)\Omega^{-1}Z'Xy \\ &= [(X'Z)(Z'\Phi Z)^{-1}(Z'X)]^{-1}(X'Z)(Z'\Phi Z)^{-1}Z'Xy. \quad (2.55)\end{aligned}$$

If Φ is unknown, as is generally the case, then $\tilde{\beta}_{GMM}$ is infeasible. The particular case $\Phi = \sigma^2_\varepsilon I$ has already been considered (that is the IV/2SLS case), and then $\tilde{\beta}_{GMM}$ reduces to:

$$\tilde{\beta}_{GMM} = [(X'Z)(Z'Z)^{-1}(Z'X)]^{-1}(X'Z)(Z'Z)^{-1}Z'Xy. \quad (2.56)$$

This is the 2SLS/IV estimator of (2.48); moreover, when $\Phi \neq \sigma^2_\varepsilon I$, $\tilde{\beta}_{GMM}$ in (2.55) can be viewed as the generalized IV estimator, GIVE (that is IV for the case when $E(\varepsilon\varepsilon') = \Phi$).

The next question to consider is whether there is an optimal choice of $\hat{W}$ in the sense of minimizing the asymptotic variance matrix of $\tilde{\beta}_{GMM}$. The answer is yes, and it corresponds to the lower bound for $\tilde{\beta}_{GMM}$ given by using $\hat{W}$ such that $\hat{W} \to_p \Omega^{-1}$; with this choice the GMM estimator is said to be efficient, for example see Chamberlain (1987).

Estimation is usually undertaken in two steps (and can be iterated). The first step uses a consistent but inefficient estimator of β, such as $\tilde{\beta}_{GMM}$ of (2.56), to obtain residuals that are used in the second stage to define $\hat{W} = \hat{\Omega}^{-1}$, and then $g(\tilde{\beta})'\hat{W}g(\tilde{\beta})$ is minimized to obtain the feasible (efficient) version of $\tilde{\beta}_{GMM}$. This procedure includes several familiar estimators. For example, if $E(Z'\varepsilon) = 0$, and the errors are heteroscedastic, then one possibility is to use $\hat{W} = I$ in the first stage, which obtains the IV/2SLS residuals $\hat{\varepsilon}_t$, and then in the second stage form $\hat{\Omega} = T^{-1}\sum^T_{t=1}\hat{\varepsilon}^2_t z_t z'_t$, which is a consistent estimator of $\Omega = T^{-1}\sum^T_{t=1}\sigma^2_t z_t z'_t$. Using $\hat{\Omega}^{-1}$ in place of Ω^{-1} in (2.55) gives the two-step feasible GMM estimator.

Whilst this section has shown that GMM includes estimators such as OLS, IV and 2SLS as special cases, GMM does more than unifying other estimators, it offers an estimation method that is valuable in an empirical macroeconomics context where the moment conditions arise from an underlying non-linear economic model; examples of this kind are included in Chapter 14.

5.3 Maximum Likelihood

The reader is likely to be familiar with the application of ML to the simple regression model, hence we use this as a simple way to link into the rather more complex cases as preparation for later chapters in this *Handbook*. Consider the simple linear model of (2.36) restated here for convenience:

$$y_t = x_t'\beta + \varepsilon_t \qquad t = 1, \ldots, T, \tag{2.57}$$

where $x_t = (x_{t1}, x_{t2}, \ldots, x_{tK})'$ is a vector of K random variables (the first of these may in practice be set equal to unity, that is $x_{t1} = 1$ for all t, to allow a constant in the regression, but the argument is easily modified in that case). Rather than simply add the assumption that ε_t is normally distributed and form the likelihood function based on $\varepsilon_t = y_t - x_t'\beta$, it is more satisfactory conceptually to first consider $f(y_t, x_t)$, the joint (probability) density function for y_t and x_t.

The joint density may then be factored as the product of a conditional density and a marginal density:

$$f(y_t, x_t; \psi) = f(y_t | x_t; \psi_1) f(x_t; \psi_2). \tag{2.58}$$

(Recall the simple rule in discrete probability calculus that $p(A \cap B) = p(A|B)p(B)$ where A and B are two random events.) The parameter vector $\psi = (\psi_1', \psi_2')'$ recognizes that, in principle, both the conditional and marginal densities will involve parameters. In the linear regression model the vector $\psi_1 = (\beta', \sigma_\varepsilon^2)'$ contains the parameters of interest, which combined with the standard assumption that there is no relationship between ψ_1 and ψ_2, implies that the ML estimator may then be obtained by maximizing the conditional likelihood function, where the conditioning is on x_t.

The likelihood function takes the data as given and views the density functions as a function of a parameter vector $\tilde{\psi}_1$, so that the true value ψ_1 is one element of $\tilde{\psi}_1$. To distinguish the pdf from the conditional likelihood function, the latter is written as $L(\tilde{\psi}_1 | y_t; x_t)$ and the ML estimator of ψ_1 is the one that maximizes this function. To proceed with this estimator it is necessary to make an assumption about the form of the pdfs; again this is done in two steps, first that y_t and x_t have a bivariate normal distribution, second it follows as an implication that the conditional pdfs, $f(y_t| x_t; \psi_1)$ and $f(x_t| y_t; \psi_1)$, are each univariate normal. This may now be put in context with the linear regression model, where the conditional pdf for the tth random variable is:

$$f(y_t | x_t, \psi_1) = \frac{1}{(2\pi\sigma_{y|x}^2)^{1/2}} \exp\left\{-\frac{(y_t - x_t'\beta)^2}{2\sigma_{y|x}^2}\right\} \qquad t = 1, \ldots, T,$$

$$= \frac{1}{(2\pi\sigma_\varepsilon^2)^{1/2}} \exp\left\{-\frac{\varepsilon_t^2}{2\sigma_\varepsilon^2}\right\} \qquad t = 1, \ldots, T, \tag{2.59}$$

where $\varepsilon_t = y_t - x_t'\beta$. Note that the variance of y_t conditional on x_t, $\sigma_{y|x}^2 = \sigma_\varepsilon^2$, is assumed to be invariant to t (that is homoscedastic conditional variances). To consider T such random variables requires an assumption about $E(\varepsilon_t\varepsilon_s)$ for $t \neq s$, the usual 'starting' assumption being that $E(\varepsilon_t\varepsilon_s) = 0$, so that the conditional pdf for all T random variables is the product of the T individual pdfs:

$$f(Y \mid X, \psi_1) = \prod\nolimits_{t=1}^{T} \frac{1}{(2\pi\sigma_\varepsilon^2)^{1/2}} \exp\left\{-\frac{(y_t - x_t'\beta)^2}{2\sigma_\varepsilon^2}\right\}, \qquad t = 1, \ldots, T. \tag{2.60}$$

Next, taking logarithms and considering this as a function to be maximized over $\tilde{\psi}_1 = (\tilde{\beta}', \tilde{\sigma}_\varepsilon^2)'$ gives the (conditional) log-likelihood (LL) function:

$$LL(\tilde{\psi}_1 \mid Y, X) = -\frac{T}{2}\ln(2\pi) - \frac{T}{2}\ln(\tilde{\sigma}_\varepsilon^2) - \frac{1}{2\tilde{\sigma}_\varepsilon^2}\sum\nolimits_{t=1}^{T}(y_t - x_t'\tilde{\beta})^2 \tag{2.61}$$

$$= -\frac{T}{2}\ln(2\pi) - \frac{T}{2}\ln(\tilde{\sigma}_\varepsilon^2) - \frac{1}{2\tilde{\sigma}_\varepsilon^2}(y - X\tilde{\beta})'(y - X\tilde{\beta}).$$

Maximizing $LL(\tilde{\psi}_1 \mid Y, X)$ with respect to $\tilde{\beta}$, taking $\tilde{\sigma}_\varepsilon^2$ as given, results in the ML estimator of β, which coincides with the (O)LS estimator; then setting $\tilde{\beta}$ to the ML estimator in the log-likelihood function, known as concentrating the function, and minimizing that function results in the ML estimator of σ_ε^2.

In practice many macroeconomic applications involve dynamic models so that lagged values of y_t are in the x_t vector. The simplest case will illustrate the distinction between the unconditional and the conditional likelihood function and the implications for the corresponding ML estimators. Suppose data are generated as $y_t = \rho y_{t-1} + \varepsilon_t$, $\varepsilon_t \sim N(0, \sigma_\varepsilon^2)$, $t = 2, \ldots, T$, then the likelihood function depends on how the initial observation y_1 is dealt with. To consider the difference, note that the joint density function for all T observations, $\{y_t\}_{t=1}^{T}$, is:

$$f(\{y_t\}_{t=1}^{T}) \equiv f(y_T, y_{T-1}, \ldots, y_2, y_1) \tag{2.62}$$

$$= f(y_T \mid \Psi_{T-1}) f(y_{T-1} \mid \Psi_{T-2}) \ldots f(y_2 \mid \Psi_1) f(y_1),$$

where $\Psi_t = (y_t, \ldots, y_1)$. Apart from $f(y_1)$, the log conditional densities are of the following form (for $t = 2, \ldots, T$):

$$\ln[f(y_t \mid \Psi_{t-1})] = -\frac{1}{2}\ln(2\pi) - \frac{1}{2}\ln(\sigma_\varepsilon^2) - \frac{1}{2\sigma_\varepsilon^2}(y_t - \rho y_{t-1})^2. \tag{2.63}$$

The complete joint density function also depends on how y_1 is generated; perhaps the leading case is to assume that it has been generated from the unconditional distribution for y_t, thus $y_1 \sim N(0, \sigma_y^2)$ where $\sigma_y^2 = (1 - \rho^2)^{-1}\sigma_\varepsilon^2$ (see Pantula et al., 1994); this is referred to as the stationarity assumption, as it implies that the process generating y_t does not differ comparing $t = 1$ and $t = 2, \ldots, T$. In this case the log of $f(y_1)$ is:

$$\ln[f(y_1)] = -\frac{1}{2}\ln(2\pi) - \frac{1}{2}\ln(\sigma_\varepsilon^2) - \frac{1}{2\sigma_\varepsilon^2}y_1^2. \tag{2.64}$$

Taking the sum of the $(T-1)$ identical terms and the one due to the generation of y_1, the log of the joint density function is:

$$\sum_{t=2}^{T}\ln[f(y_t\,|\,\Omega_{t-1})] + \ln[f(y_1)] =$$

$$-\frac{(T-1)}{2}\ln(2\pi) - \frac{(T-1)}{2}\ln(\sigma_\varepsilon^2) - \frac{1}{2\sigma_\varepsilon^2}\sum_{t=2}^{T}(y_t - \rho y_{t-1})^2 - \frac{1}{2}\ln(2\pi) - \frac{1}{2}\ln\frac{\sigma_\varepsilon^2}{(1-\rho^2)} - \frac{1}{2\sigma_\varepsilon^2}y_1^2$$

$$= -\frac{T}{2}\ln(2\pi) - \frac{T}{2}\ln(\sigma_\varepsilon^2) - \frac{1}{2\sigma_\varepsilon^2}\sum_{t=2}^{T}(y_t - \rho y_{t-1})^2 + \frac{1}{2}\ln(1-\rho^2) - \frac{1}{2\sigma_\varepsilon^2}y_1^2.$$

Treating this as a function of the parameters rather than the data gives the likelihood function, and maximizing accordingly over $\tilde{\rho}$ gives the unconditional (or exact) ML estimator. It is referred to as the unconditional ML estimator because it includes the terms relating to the generation of y_1, whereas the conditional likelihood function does not include these terms. Notice that the contribution of y_1 does involve the parameter of interest ρ, so that maximizing the conditional likelihood function is not the same as maximizing the unconditional likelihood function. Indeed the latter is a non-linear estimator that involves the solution of a cubic equation if the mean of the process is assumed known (here for simplicity it was set equal to zero) and a fifth order equation otherwise. For a unit root test based on the exact ML estimator, see Shin and Fuller (1998), and note that whilst maximizing the conditional likelihood function leads to a unit root test statistic with the same asymptotic distribution as its least squares counterpart, that is not the case for the same test statistic derived from exact ML estimation.

Whilst the AR(1) model is a simple illustration of the difference between the exact and conditional ML estimator, the implications carry across to VAR models including variants such as reduced form VARs, SVARs and cointegrating VARs; the exact ML will differ from the conditional ML estimator as it includes the terms in the likelihood that account for the generation of the initial vector $y_1 = (y_{11}, y_{12}, \ldots, y_{1K})'$.

A second consideration arises from macroeconomic applications in which maximizing the conditional log-likelihood function does not result in maximization of the joint likelihood function. Consider the following simple example:

$$\begin{bmatrix} 1 & -\gamma_{12} \\ -\gamma_{21} & 1 \end{bmatrix}\begin{pmatrix} y_{1t} \\ y_{2t} \end{pmatrix} = \begin{bmatrix} b_{11} & b_{12} \\ b_{21} & b_{22} \end{bmatrix}\begin{pmatrix} x_{1t} \\ x_{2t} \end{pmatrix} + \begin{pmatrix} u_{1t} \\ u_{2t} \end{pmatrix}. \tag{2.65}$$

This is an example of the following general (SEM) specification:

$$\Gamma y_t = Bx_t + u_t. \tag{2.66}$$

The parameters of interest are $\psi = (\gamma_{12}, \gamma_{21}, b_{11}, b_{12}, b_{21}, b_{22}, \Sigma_u)$. This is a 'traditional' SEM in the sense that y_t is a vector of endogenous variables assumed to be jointly normally distributed conditional on x_t, where x_t is a vector of exogenous variables; restrictions will have to be imposed if the structural coefficients are to be identified, typically these will be in the nature of exclusion restrictions such as $b_{12} = b_{21} = 0$.

To obtain the ML estimators, we might think of starting by factorizing the joint density as:

$$f(y_{1t}, y_{2t}, x_{1t}, x_{2t}) = f(y_{1t} \mid y_{2t}, x_{1t}, x_{2t}) f(y_{2t} \mid x_{1t}, x_{2t}) f(x_{1t}, x_{2t}). \tag{2.67}$$

However, basing ML estimation on $f(y_{1t} \mid y_{2t}, x_{1t}, x_{2t})$, which conditions y_{1t} on y_{2t}, x_{1t}, x_{2t}, is incorrect as, assuming that $\gamma_{12} \neq 0$, there is a functional relationship between y_{1t} and y_{2t}. Maximizing a LL function based on this conditioning will not result in maximization of the LL based on the joint density. The correct factorization is:

$$f(y_{1t}, y_{2t}, x_{1t}, x_{2t}) = f(y_{1t}\ y_{2t} \mid x_{1t}, x_{2t}) f(x_{1t}, x_{2t}). \tag{2.68}$$

In the general case, with M endogenous variables, the log likelihood function based on all T observations is:

$$\mathrm{LL}(\psi, \Sigma_u \mid Y, X) =$$

$$-\frac{MT}{2}\ln(2\pi) + T\ln[\det(\Gamma)] - \frac{T}{2}\ln[\det(\Sigma_u)] - \frac{1}{2}\sum\nolimits_{t=1}^{T}(\Gamma y_t - Bx_t)'\Sigma_u^{-1}(\Gamma y_t - Bx_t). \tag{2.69}$$

Estimation is based on maximizing this likelihood function and the resulting estimator is referred to as the full information ML (FIML) estimator; for excellent expositions of the FIML procedure see Greene (2011) and Hayashi (2000). A frequently used estimation method for cointegrating systems is based on the FIML method, and the log-likelihood on which that approach is based can be obtained as a specialization of (2.69) (see Johansen, 1995).

The maximum likelihood approach is attractive when one can be reasonably sure that the form of the density function is known and when a FIML approach is taken that the complete model is well specified. The method of GMM works with a much weaker assumption than that the form of the density function is known, focusing instead on conditions that specify that certain population moments are zero; GMM is also likely to be the estimation method of choice when moment conditions are available from an underlying economic model.

5.4 Bayesian Econometrics

Underlying the method of maximum likelihood the generalized method of moments estimation and the classical approach to statistics in general is the assumption that there is a 'true model' or data generating process and the job of the econometrician is to estimate the predetermined parameters, ψ, of that data generating process. Bayesian methods, on the other hand, acknowledge the uncertainty around ψ and attempt instead to describe this uncertainty in the form of a probability distribution. In contrast to the classical view, the process of estimation is not the discovery of an objective true value, but the ongoing refinement of the analyst's subjective views on the values that ψ might take. This distinction reflects two rival views on the nature of probability itself: the Bayesian view that probability is a subjective measure of the analyst's degree of belief that an event will happen; and, the 'frequentist' view that probability is an objective measure of how frequently an event will happen.

In Bayesian estimation, the analyst begins with some prior beliefs about the parameter vector captured by a density function $f(\psi)$. The requirement to provide such a prior, which could be the result of economic theory or of previous analyses, is the first and most obvious distinction between Bayesian and classical statistics. The prior is then updated in the light of the data, Y, to produce a posterior density, $f(\psi|Y)$, using Bayes theorem:

$$f(\psi|Y) = \frac{f(Y|\psi)f(\psi)}{f(Y)}, \tag{2.70}$$

where $f(Y|\psi)$ is the familiar likelihood function and $f(Y)$ is the marginal distribution of Y, which can be calculated as:

$$f(Y) = \int f(\psi)f(Y|\psi)\,d\psi.$$

Equation (2.70) can be read as: the posterior density is proportional to the likelihood function times the prior density. The posterior density provides a richer picture of ψ than is available through classical methods. In order to derive a single point estimate of ψ from this density, a loss function, $C(\hat{\psi},\psi)$ which specifies the cost of using $\hat{\psi}$ when the parameter is ψ, for example the quadratic loss function $C(\hat{\psi},\psi) = (\hat{\psi} - \psi)^2$, is deployed. The chosen point estimate, ψ^*, minimizes the expected value of the loss function, where the expectation is relative to the posterior density,

$$\psi = \operatorname{argmin}_{\hat{\psi}} \int C(\hat{\psi},\psi)f(\psi|Y)\,d\psi.$$

The estimation of an interval analogous to a $100(1-\alpha)$ per cent confidence interval can then be made by choosing the smallest region within the support of ψ that contains $100(1-\alpha)$ per cent of the posterior density, known as the highest posterior density.

Unfortunately, in many applications of interest to the macroeconomist, the updating in equation (2.70) cannot be performed analytically. Instead posterior densities are often elicited using Monte Carlo simulations, an approach that has increased greatly in popularity as computing power has risen. This approach has proven particularly popular in estimating DSGE models, which is the topic of Chapter 18 by Christiano Cantore, Vasco Gabriel, Paul Levine, Joseph Pearlman and Bo Yang and Chapter 21 by Pablo Guerrón-Quintana and James Nason. The use of the Dynare computer package for estimation is the subject of Chapter 25 by João Madeira.

6 CONCLUDING REMARKS

Many of the key developments in econometrics, especially over the last thirty years, have been focused on or motivated by applications in macroeconomics. For a historical perspective prior to 1991, see Bodkin et al. (1991). Some key developments include the following: (i) The seminal article by Nelson and Plosser (1982) drew attention to the difference between deterministic and stochastic trends in the context of 14 macroeconomic and financial time series. (ii) Hansen's (1982) generalized method of moments (GMM) estimation method has found many applications in macroeconomics, for example consumption and investment (Hansen and Singleton, 1982), and in estimating DGSE models (see for example, Long and Plosser, 1983 and Christiano and Eichenbaum, 1992 on modelling the real business cycle). (iii) Cointegration (Engle and Granger, 1987), and especially Johansen's (1988, 1995) methods for estimation and hypothesis testing, led to a fundamental rethinking of the way that macroeconometric models were specified and estimated. (iv) Sims (1980) called into question the validity of the traditional method of modelling simultaneous equations in the Cowles Commission approach, leading to SVARs that seek identification conditions through restrictions on the covariance matrix of the shocks rather than (primarily) through exclusion restrictions, an approach that has led to many macroeconomic applications. There is little doubt that the future developments in empirical macroeconomics will go hand in hand with developments in econometrics.

REFERENCES

Anderson, T.W.A (1971), *The Statistical Analysis of Time Series*, New York: John Wiley & Sons.
Baillie, R. (2006), 'Modeling volatility', Chapter 20 in T.C. Mills and K.D. Patterson, *Palgrave Handbook of Econometrics: Volume 1: Econometric Theory*, Basingstoke: Palgrave Macmillan.
Baillie, R.T. and T. Bollerslev (2002), 'Prediction in dynamic models with time dependent conditional variances', *Journal of Econometrics*, **74**, 3–30.
Bårsden, G., Ø. Eitrheim, E.S. Jansen and R. Nyomen (2005), *Econometrics of Macroeconomic Modelling*, Oxford: Oxford University Press.
Bennion, E.G. (1952), 'The Cowles Commission's "Simultaneous-equation approach": a simplified explanation', *The Review of Economics and Statistics*, **34**, 49–56.
Billingsley, P. (1995), *Probability and Measure*, 3rd edn, New York: John Wiley & Sons.
Blanchard, O.J. and R. Perotti (2002), 'An empirical characterization of the dynamic effects of changes in government spending and taxes on output', *Quarterly Journal of Economics*, **117**, 1329–68.
Blanchard, O.J. and D. Quah (1989), 'The dynamic effects of aggregate demand and supply disturbances', *American Economic Review*, **79**, 655–73.
Bodkin, R.G., L.R. Klein and K. Marwah (1991), *A History of Macroeconomic Model-Building*, Aldershot, UK and Brookfield, VT, USA: Edward Elgar Publishing.
Bollerslev, T. (1986), 'Generalized autoregressive conditional heteroskedasticity', *Journal of Econometrics*, **31**, 307–27.
Bollerslev, T. (2010), 'Glossary to ARCH (GARCH)', in T. Bollerslev, J.R. Russell and M. Watson, *Volatility and Time Series Econometrics, Essays in Honor of Robert Engle*, Oxford: Oxford University Press.
Boswijk, H.P. (1996), 'Testing identifiability of cointegrating vectors', *Journal of Business and Economic Statistics*, **14**, 153–60.
Bougerol, P. and N. Picard (1992), 'Stationarity of GARCH processes and of some nonnegative time series', *Journal of Econometrics*, **52**, 115–27.
Brockwell, P.J. and R.A. Davis (2006), *Time Series: Theory and Methods*, 2nd edn, New York: Springer.
Brooks, C. (2006), 'Multivariate volatility models', Chapter 21 in T.C. Mills and K.D. Patterson, *Palgrave Handbook of Econometrics: Volume 1: Econometric Theory*, Basingstoke: Palgrave Macmillan.

Campbell, J.Y. and N.G. Mankiw (1987a), 'Are output fluctuations transitory?', *Quarterly Journal of Economics*, **102**, 857–80.
Campbell, J.Y. and N.G. Mankiw (1987b), 'Permanent and transitory components in macroeconomic fluctuations', *American Economic Review*, **77**, 111–17.
Canova, F. (2007), *Methods for Applied Macroeconomic Research*, Princeton, NJ: Princeton University Press.
Chamberlain, G. (1987), 'Asymptotic efficiency in estimation with conditional moment restrictions', *Journal of Econometrics*, **34**, 305–34.
Christiano, L. and M. Eichenbaum (1992), 'Current real-business cycle theories and aggregate labor-market fluctuations', *American Economic Review*, **82**, 430–50.
Davidson, J. (2009), 'When is a time series I(0)?', in J. Castle and N. Shephard (eds), *The Methodology and Practice of Econometrics*, Oxford: Oxford University Press.
Dickey, D.A. and W.A. Fuller (1979), 'Distribution of the estimators for autoregressive time series with a unit root', *Journal of the American Statistical Association*, **74**, 427–31.
Dickey, D.A. and W.A. Fuller (1981), 'Likelihood ratio statistics for autoregressive time series with a unit root', *Econometrica*, **49**, 1057–72.
Dickey, D.A. and S.G. Pantula (1987), 'Determining the order of differencing in autoregressive processes', *Journal of Business & Economics Statistics*, **5**, 455–61.
Dougherty, C. (2011), *Introduction to Econometrics*, 4th edn, Oxford: Oxford University Press.
Duesenberry, J.S. (1965), *The Brookings Quarterly Econometric Model of the United States*, New York: Rand MacNally.
Elliott, G. (1999), 'Efficient tests for a unit root when the initial observation is drawn from its unconditional distribution', *International Economic Review*, **40**, 767–83.
Elliott, G., T.J. Rothenberg and J.H. Stock (1996), 'Efficient tests for an autoregressive root', *Econometrica*, **64**, 813–36.
Engle, R.F. (1982), 'Autoregressive conditional heteroskedasticity with estimates of the variance of United Kingdom inflation', *Econometrica*, **50**, 987–1007.
Engle, R.F. (1995), *ARCH Selected Readings*, Oxford: Oxford University Press.
Engle, R.F. and C.W.J. Granger (1987), 'Co-integration and error-correction: representation, estimation and testing', *Econometrica*, **55**, 251–76.
Engle, R.F., D.M. Lilien and R.P. Robins (1987), 'Estimating time varying risk premia in the term structure: the ARCH-M model', *Econometrica*, **55**, 391–407.
Evans, M.K. and L. Klein (1967), 'The Wharton econometric forecasting model', Philadelphia, PA: Wharton School of Finance and Commerce.
Fuller, W. (1976), *An Introduction to Statistical Time Series*, 1st edn, New York: John Wiley.
Fuller, W. (1996), *An Introduction to Statistical Time Series*, 2nd edn, New York: John Wiley.
Gali, J. (1992), 'How well does the IS-LM model fit postwar US data?', *Quarterly Journal*, **107**, 709–38.
Granger, C.W.J. (1966), 'The typical spectral shape of an economic variable', *Econometrica*, **34**, 150–61.
Granger, C.W.J. and M. Hatanka (1964), *Spectral Analysis of Economic Time Series*, Princeton, NJ: Princeton University Press.
Granger, C.W.J. and P. Newbold (1974), 'Spurious regressions in econometrics', *Journal of Econometrics*, **2**, 111–20.
Greene, W.H. (2011), *Econometric Analysis*, 7th edn, New York: Prentice Hall.
Haldrup, N. and P.M. Lildholt (2002), 'On the robustness of unit root tests in the presence of double unit roots', *Journal of Time Series Analysis*, **23**, 155–71.
Haldrup, N. and P.M. Lildholt (2005), 'Local power functions of tests for double unit roots', *Statistica Neerlandica*, **59**, 151–79.
Hall, A. (2005), *Generalised Method of Moments*, Oxford: Oxford University Press.
Hamilton, J.D. (1994), *Time Series Analysis*, Princeton, NJ: Princeton University Press.
Hamilton, J.D. (2010), 'Macroeconomics and ARCH', in T. Bollerslev, J.R. Russell and M. Watson, *Volatility and Time Series Econometrics: Essays in Honor of Robert Engle*, Oxford: Oxford University Press.
Hansen, B.E. and K.D. West (2002), 'Generalized method of moments and macroeconomics', *Journal of Business & Economic Statistics*, **20**, 460–69.
Hansen, L.P. (1982), 'Large sample properties of Generalized Method of Moments estimators', *Econometrica*, **50**, 1029–54.
Hansen, L.P. and K.J. Singleton (1982), 'Generalized instrumental variables estimation of nonlinear rational expectations models', *Econometrica*, **50**, 1269–86.
Harvey, D.I. and S.J. Leybourne (2005), 'On testing for unit roots and the initial observation', *Econometrics Journal*, **8**, 97–111.
Harvey, D.I, and S.J. Leybourne (2006), 'Power of a unit-root test and the initial condition', *Journal of Time Series Analysis*, **27**, 739–52.

Hasza, D.P. and W.A. Fuller (1979), 'Estimation for autoregressive processes with unit roots', *Annals of Statistics*, **7**, 1106–20.
Hayashi, F. (2000), *Econometrics*, Princeton, NJ: Princeton University Press.
Johansen, S. (1988), 'Statistical analysis of cointegration vectors', *Journal of Economic Dynamics and Control*, **12**, 231–54.
Johansen, S. (1995), *Likelihood-based Inference in Cointegrated Vector Autoregressive Models*, Oxford: Oxford University Press.
Johansen, S. and K. Juselius (1990), 'Maximum likelihood estimation and inference on cointegration with applications to the demand for money', *Oxford Bulletin of Economics and Statistics*, **52**, 169–210.
Juselius, K. (2006), *The Cointegrated VAR Model*, Oxford: Oxford University Press.
Klein, L.R. (1950), *Economic Fluctuations in the United States 1921–1941*: *Cowles Commission Monograph*: *Vol. 11*, New York: John Wiley & Sons.
Lamoureux, C.G. and W.D. Lastrapes (1990), 'Heteroskedasticity in stock return data: volume versus GARCH effects', *Journal of Finance*, **45**, 221–9.
Li, Q. and J.S. Raccine (2006), *Nonparametric Econometrics: Theory and Practice*, Princeton, NJ: Princeton University Press.
Ling, S., W.K. Li and M. McAleer (2002), 'Recent theoretical results for time series models with GARCH errors', *Journal of Economic Surveys*, **16**, 245–69.
Long, J.B. and C. Plosser (1983), 'Real business cycles', *Journal of Political Economy*, **91**, 39–69.
Lütkepohl, H. (2005), *New Introduction to Multiple Time Series Analysis*, Berlin: Springer Verlag.
Luukkonen, R., A. Ripatti and P. Saikkonen (1999), 'Testing for a valid normalization of cointegrating vectors in vector autoregressive processes', *Journal of Business and Economic Statistics*, **17**, 195–204.
Nelson, C. and C.I. Plosser (1982), 'Trends and random walks in macroeconomic time series', *Journal of Monetary Economics*, **10**, 139–62.
Ng, S. and P. Perron (1995), 'Unit root tests in ARMA models with data dependent methods for the selection of the truncation lag', *Journal of the American Statistical Association*, **90**, 268–81.
Ng, S. and P. Perron (2001), 'Lag length selection and the construction of unit root tests with good size and power', *Econometrica*, **69**, 1519–54.
Pantula, S.G., G. Gonzalez-Farias and W.A. Fuller (1994), 'A comparison of unit root test criteria', *Journal of Business and Economic Statistics*, **12**, 449–59.
Patterson, K.D. (2011), *Unit Root Tests in Time Series, Volume 1: Key Concepts and Problems*, London: Palgrave Macmillan.
Patterson, K.D. (2012), *Unit Root Tests in Time Series, Volume 2: Extensions and Developments*, London: Palgrave Macmillan.
Peel, D., L. Sarno and M.P. Taylor (2001), 'Nonlinear mean-reversion in real exchange rates: toward a solution to the purchasing power parity puzzles', *International Economic Review*, **42**, 1015–42.
Perron, P. (1989), 'The Great Crash, the oil price shock and the unit root hypothesis', *Econometrica*, **57**, 1361–401.
Phillips, P.C.B. (1991), 'Optimal inference in cointegrated systems', *Econometrica*, **59**, 283–306.
Phillips, P.C.B. and P. Perron (1988), 'Testing for a unit root in time series regression', *Biometrika*, **75**, 335–46.
Priestley, M.B. (1981), *Spectral Analysis and Time Series*, London: Academic Press.
Said, S.E. and D.A. Dickey (1984), 'Testing for unit roots in autoregressive-moving average models of unknown order', *Biometrika*, **71**, 599–607.
Schwert, G.W. (1987), 'Effects of model specification on tests for unit roots in macroeconomic data', *Journal of Momentry Economics*, **20**, 73–103.
Schwert, G.W. (1989), 'Tests for unit roots: a Monte Carlo investigation', *Journal of Business and Economic Statistics*, **7**, 147–59.
Shimotsu, K. and P.C.B. Phillips (2006), 'Local Whittle estimation of fractional integration and some of its variants', *Journal of Econometrics*, **103**, 209–33.
Shin, D.W. and B.A. So (2002), 'Recursive mean adjustment and tests for nonstationarities', *Economics Letters*, **75**, 203–8.
Shin, D.W. and W.A. Fuller (1998), 'Unit root tests based on unconditional maximum likelihood estimation for the autoregressive moving average', *Journal of Time Series Analysis*, **19**, 591–9.
Sims, C.A (1980), 'Macroeconomics and reality', *Econometrica*, **48**, 1–48.
Sims, C.A. (2002), 'Structural VARs', available at: http://sims.princeton.edu/yftp/Times02/StructuralVAR.pdf.
Sims, C.A. and T. Zha (2005), 'Does monetary policy generate recessions?', *Macroeconomic Dynamics*, **10**, 231–72.
Sims, C.A. and T. Zha (2006), 'Were there regime switches in US monetary policy?', *American Economic Review*, **96**, 54–81.
Stoica, P. and R. Moses (1997), *Introduction to Spectral Analysis*, Upper Saddle River, NJ: Prentice Hall.

Tanaka, K. (1990), 'Testing for a moving average unit root', *Econometric Theory*, **6**, 433–44.
Taylor, M.P., D. Peel and L. Sarno (2003), 'Nonlinear equilibrium correction in US real money balances, 1869–1997', *Journal of Money, Credit and Banking*, **35**, 787–99.
Teräsvirta, T. (2006), 'Forecasting economic variables with nonlinear models', in G. Elliott, C.W. Granger and A. Timmermann (eds), *Handbook of Economic Forecasting: Volume 1*, Amsterdam: Elsevier.
Tinbergen, J. (1939), *Business Cycles in the United States of America, 1919–1932*, Geneva: League of Nations Economic Intelligence Service.
Toda, H.Y. and P.C.B. Phillips (1993), 'Vector autoregressions and causality', *Econometrica*, **61**, 1367–93.
Toda, H.Y. and T. Yamamoto (1995), 'Statistical inference in vector autoregressions with possibly integrated processes', *Journal of Econometrics*, **66**, 225–50.
Wang, G. (2006), 'A note on unit root tests with heavy-tailed GARCH errors', *Statistics and Probability Letters*, **76**, 1075–9.
Wang, G. and W-L. Mao (2008), 'Unit root testing in the presence of heavy-tailed GARCH errors', *Australian Journal of Statistics*, **50**, 273–92.
Warner, R.M. (1998), *Spectral Analysis of Time Series Data*, New York: Guilford.
Wooldridge, J.M. (2001), 'Applications of generalised method of moments estimation', *Journal of Economic Perspectives*, **15**, 87–100.
Wooldridge, J.M. (2011), *Introductory Econometrics: A Modern Approach*, 5th edn, Mason, OH: Southwestern Cengage Learning.

PART I

PROPERTIES OF MACROECONOMIC DATA

3 Trends, cycles and structural breaks

Terence C. Mills

EARLY MODELLING OF TRENDS AND CYCLES

The analysis of cycles in macroeconomic time series began in earnest in the 1870s with the sunspot and Venus theories of William Stanley Jevons and Henry Ludwell Moore and the rather more conventional credit cycle theory of Clément Jugler (see Morgan, 1990, Chapter 1). Secular, or trend, movements were first studied somewhat later, with the term 'trend' only being coined in 1901 by Reginald Hooker when analysing British import and export data (Hooker, 1901). The early attempts to take into account trend movements, typically by detrending using simple moving averages or graphical interpolation, are analysed by Klein (1997), while the next generation of weighted moving averages, often based on actuarial graduation formulae using local polynomials, are surveyed in Mills (2011, Chapter 10).

The first half of the twentieth century saw much progress, both descriptive and theoretical, on the modelling of trends and cycles, as briefly recounted in Mills (2009a), but it took a further decade for techniques to be developed that would, in due course, lead to a revolution in the way trends and cycles were modelled and extracted. The seeds of this revolution were sown in 1961 – a year termed by Mills (2009a) as the 'annus mirabilis' of trend and cycle modelling – when four very different papers, by Klein and Kosobud (1961), Cox (1961), Leser (1961) and Kalman and Bucy (1961), were published. The influence of Klein and Kosobud for modelling trends in macroeconomic time series – the 'great ratios' of macroeconomics – is discussed in detail in Mills (2009b), and that of Cox in Mills (2009a). It is the last two papers that are of prime interest here. As is discussed in the next section, Leser's paper, in which he considered trend extraction from an observed series using a weighted moving average with the weights derived using the principle of penalized least squares, paved the way for one of the most popular trend extraction methods in use today, the Hodrick–Prescott filter. Kalman and Bucy (1961), along with its companion paper, Kalman (1960), set out the details of the Kalman filter algorithm, an essential computational component of many trend and cycle extraction techniques (see Young, 2011, for both historical perspective and a modern synthesis of the algorithm with recursive estimation techniques).

FILTERS FOR EXTRACTING TRENDS AND CYCLES

Leser (1961) implicitly considered the additive unobserved component (UC) decomposition of an observed series x_t into a trend, μ_t, and a cycle, ψ_t, that is, $x_t = \mu_t + \psi_t$. He invoked the penalized least squares principle, which minimizes, with respect to μ_t, $t = 1,2,\ldots,T$, the criterion:

$$\sum_{t=1}^{T}(x_t - \mu_t)^2 + \lambda\sum_{t=3}^{T}(\Delta^2\mu_t)^2 \tag{3.1}$$

The first term measures the goodness of fit of the trend, the second penalizes the departure from zero of the variance of the second differences of the trend, so that it is a measure of smoothness: λ is thus referred to as the smoothness parameter. Successive partial differentiation of (3.1) with respect to the sequence μ_t leads to the first order conditions:

$$\Delta^2\mu_{t+2} - 2\Delta^2\mu_{t+1} + \Delta^2\mu_t = (\lambda - 1)(x_t - \mu_t) \tag{3.2}$$

given T and λ, μ_t will then be a moving average of x_t with time-varying weights. Leser developed a method of deriving these weights and provided a number of examples in which the solutions were obtained in, it has to be said, laborious and excruciating detail, which must certainly have lessened the impact of the paper at the time!

Some two decades later, Hodrick and Prescott (1997) approached the solution of (3.1) rather differently. By recasting (3.1) in matrix form as $(\mathbf{x} - \mu)'(\mathbf{x} - \mu) + \lambda\mu'\mathbf{D}^{2\prime}\mathbf{D}^2\mu$, where $\mathbf{x} = (x_1, \ldots, x_T)'$, $\mu = (\mu_1, \ldots, \mu_T)'$ and $\mathbf{D}$ is the $T \times T$ 'first difference' matrix with elements $d_{t,t} = 1$, $d_{t-1,t} = -1$ and zero elsewhere, so that $\mathbf{D}\mu = (\mu_1, \mu_2 - \mu_1, \ldots, \mu_T - \mu_{T-1})'$, then differentiating with respect to μ allows the first-order conditions to be written as:

$$\mu = (\mathbf{I} + \lambda\mathbf{D}^{2\prime}\mathbf{D}^2)^{-1}\mathbf{x} \tag{3.3}$$

with the rows of the inverse matrix containing the filter weights for estimating the trend μ_t at each t. Hodrick and Prescott suggested setting $\lambda = 1600$ when extracting a trend from a quarterly macroeconomic series and other choices are discussed in, for example, Ravn and Uhlig (2002) and Maravall and del Rio (2007).[1]

In filtering terminology the H–P filter (3.3) is a *low-pass filter*. To understand this terminology, some basic concepts in filtering theory are useful. Define a *linear filter* of the observed series x_t to be the two-sided weighted moving average:

$$y_t = \sum_{j=-n}^{n} a_j x_{t-j} = (a_{-n}B^{-n} + a_{-n+1}B^{-n+1} + \ldots + a_0 + \ldots + a_n B^n)x_t = a(B)x_t$$

where use is made of the lag operator B, defined such that $B^j x_t \equiv x_{t-j}$. Two conditions are typically imposed upon the filter $a(B)$: (i) that the filter weights either (a) sum to zero, $a(1) = 0$, or (b) sum to unity, $a(1) = 1$; and (ii) that these weights are symmetric, $a_j = a_{-j}$. If condition (i)(a) holds, then $a(B)$ is a 'trend-elimination' filter, whereas if (i) (b) holds, it will be a 'trend-extraction' filter. If the former holds, then $b(B) = 1 - a(B)$ will be the corresponding trend-extraction filter, having the same, but oppositely signed, weights as the trend-elimination filter $a(B)$ except for the central value, $b_0 = 1 - a_0$, thus ensuring that $b(1) = 1$.

The *frequency response function* of the filter is defined as $a(\omega) = \sum_j a_j e^{-i\omega j}$ for a frequency $0 \leq \omega \leq 2\pi$. The *power transfer function* is then defined as:

$$|a(\omega)|^2 = \left(\sum_j a_j \cos \omega j\right)^2 + \left(\sum_j a_j \sin \omega j\right)^2$$

and the *gain* is defined as $|a(\omega)|$, measuring the extent to which the amplitude of the ω – frequency component of x_t is altered through the filtering operation. In general, $a(\omega) = |a(\omega)|e^{-i\theta(\omega)}$, where

$$\theta(\omega) = \tan^{-1}\frac{\sum_j a_j \sin \omega j}{\sum_j a_j \cos \omega j}$$

is the *phase shift*, indicating the extent to which the ω – frequency component of x_t is displaced in time. If the filter is indeed symmetric then $a(\omega) = a(-\omega)$, so that $a(\omega) = |a(\omega)|$ and $\theta(\omega) = 0$, known as phase neutrality.

With these concepts, an 'ideal' low-pass filter has the frequency response function:

$$a_L(\omega) = \begin{cases} 1 & \text{if } \omega < \omega_c \\ 0 & \text{if } \omega > \omega_c \end{cases} \tag{3.4}$$

Thus $a_L(\omega)$ passes only frequencies lower than the cut-off frequency ω_c, so that just slow-moving, low-frequency components of x_t are retained. Low-pass filters should also be phase-neutral, so that temporal shifts are not induced by filtering. The ideal low-pass filter will take the form:

$$a_L(B) = \frac{\omega_c}{\pi} + \sum_{j=1}^{\infty} \frac{\sin \omega_c j}{\pi j}(B^j + B^{-j})$$

In practice, low-pass filters will not have the perfect 'jump' in $a_L(\omega)$ as is implied by (3.4). The H–P trend extraction filter, that is, the one that provides an estimate of the trend component $\hat{\mu}_t = a_{H-P}(B)x_t$, where the weights are given by (3.3), has the frequency response function

$$a_{H-P}(\omega) = \frac{1}{1 + 4\lambda(1 - \cos\omega)^2} \tag{3.5}$$

while the H–P trend-elimination filter, which provides the cycle estimate $\hat{\psi}_t = b_{H-P}(B)x_t = (1 - a_{H-P}(B))x_t$, has the frequency response function:

$$b_{H-P}(\omega) = 1 - a_{H-P}(\omega) = \frac{4\lambda(1 - \cos\omega)^2}{1 + 4\lambda(1 - \cos\omega)^2}$$

The H–P frequency response function for $\lambda = 1600$ is compared to the ideal low-pass filter with cut-off at $\omega_c = 1/16$ in Figure 3.1. Rather than setting the smoothing parameter at an a priori value such as $\lambda = 1600$ for quarterly data or, as is often suggested, 100 for annual data, it could also be set at the value that equates the gain to 0.5, that is, at the value that separates frequencies between those mostly associated with the trend and those mostly associated with the cycle. Since the H–P weights are indeed symmetric, the gain

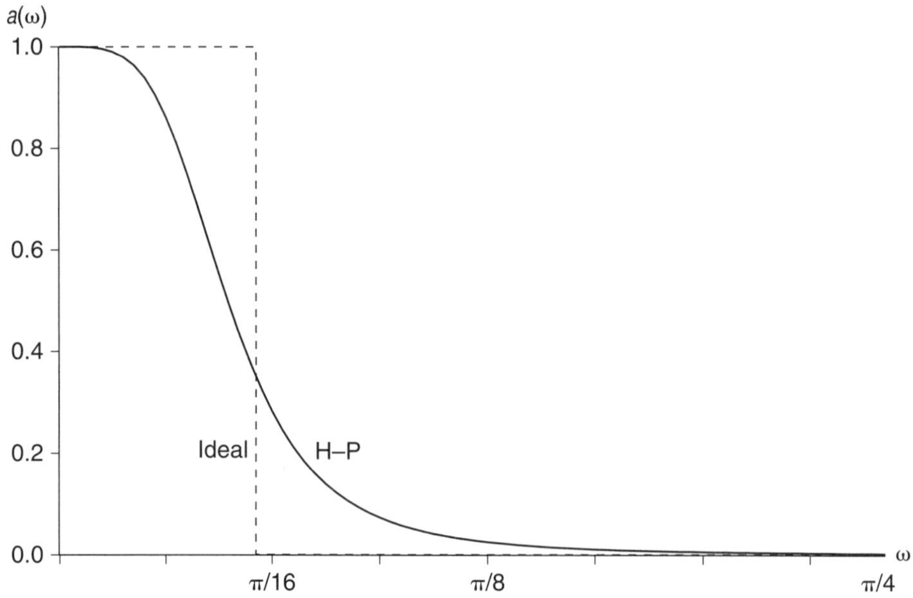

Figure 3.1 Frequency response functions for the ideal low-pass filter with $\omega_c = \pi/16$ *and H–P filter with* $\lambda = 1600$

is given by (3.5), so equating this to 0.5 yields $\lambda = 1/4(1 - \cos\omega_{0.5})^2$, where $\omega_{0.5}$ is the frequency at which the gain is 0.5 (for more on this idea, see Kaiser and Maravall, 2005).

The ideal low-pass filter removes high-frequency components while retaining low-frequency components. A high-pass filter does the reverse, so that the complementary high-pass filter to (3.4) has $a_H(\omega) = 0$ if $\omega < \omega_c$ and $a_H(\omega) = 1$ if $\omega \geq \omega_c$. The ideal band-pass filter passes only frequencies in the range $\omega_{c,1} \leq \omega \leq \omega_{c,2}$, so that it can be constructed as the difference between two low-pass filters with cut-off frequencies $\omega_{c,1}$ and $\omega_{c,2}$ and it will have the frequency response function $a_B(\omega) = a_{c,2}(\omega) - a_{c,1}(\omega)$, where $a_{c,2}(\omega)$ and $a_{c,1}(\omega)$ are the frequency response functions of the two low-pass filters, since this will give a frequency response of unity in the band $\omega_{c,1} \leq \omega \leq \omega_{c,2}$ and zero elsewhere. The weights of the band-pass filter will thus be given by $a_{c,2,j} - a_{c,1,j}$, where $a_{c,2,j}$ and $a_{c,1,j}$ are the weights of the two low-pass filters, so that:

$$a_B(B) = \frac{\omega_{c,2} - \omega_{c,1}}{\pi} + \sum_{j=1}^{\infty} \frac{\sin\omega_{c,2}j - \sin\omega_{c,1}j}{\pi j}(B^j + B^{-j}) \tag{3.6}$$

A conventional definition of the business cycle emphasizes fluctuations of between one and a half and eight years (see Baxter and King, 1999), which leads to $\omega_{c,1} = 2\pi/8s$ and $\omega_{c,2} = 2\pi/1.5s$, where s is the number of observations in a year. Assuming that x_t is observed quarterly, then a band-pass filter that passes only frequencies corresponding to these periods, that is, $\omega_{c,1} = \pi/16$ and $\omega_{c,2} = \pi/3$, is defined as $y_t = a_{B,n}(B)x_t$ with weights

$$a_{B,0} = a_{c,2,0} - a_{c,1,0} = \tfrac{1}{3} - \tfrac{1}{16} - (\zeta_{c,2,n} - \zeta_{c,1,n})$$

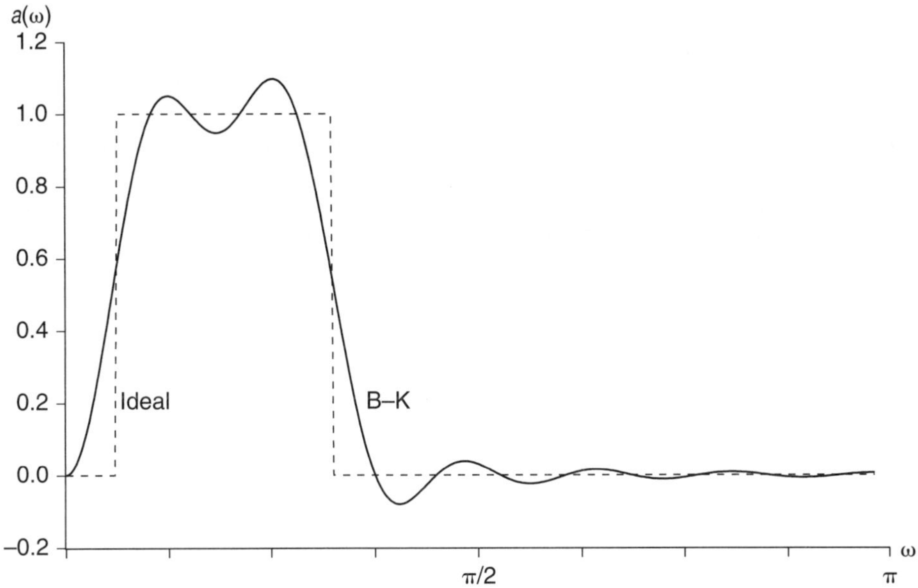

Figure 3.2 *Frequency response functions for the ideal band-pass filter with* $\omega_{c,1} = \pi/16$ *and* $\omega_{c,2} = \pi/3$ *and the B–K filter for* s = 4 *and* n = 12

$$a_{B,j} = a_{c,2,j} - a_{c,1,j} = \frac{1}{\pi j}\left(\sin\frac{\pi j}{3} - \sin\frac{\pi j}{16}\right) - (\zeta_{c,2,n} - \zeta_{c,1,n}) \quad j = 1,\ldots,n \tag{3.7}$$

where

$$\zeta_{c,i,n} = -\frac{\sum_{j=-n}^{n} a_{c,i,n}}{2n+1} \qquad i = 1,2$$

The infinite length filter in (3.6) has been truncated to have only n leads and lags and the appearance of the $\zeta_{c,i,n}$ terms ensures that the filter weights sum to zero, so that $a_{B,n}(B)$ is a trend-elimination (i.e., cycle) filter. The filter in (3.7) is known as the Baxter–King (B–K) filter, with further extensions being provided by Christiano and Fitzgerald (2003). The frequency response functions of the B–K and ideal band-pass filters for $\omega_{c,1} = \pi/16$ and $\omega_{c,2} = \pi/3$ (i.e., for quarterly data ($s = 4$)) and filter truncation $n = 12$ are shown in Figure 3.2: the 'ripples' in the former are a consequence of the truncation of the latter, an effect known as the Gibbs phenomenon.

FILTERS AND STRUCTURAL MODELS

Several filters in common use can be shown to be optimal for the following class of *structural* UC models:

$$x_t = \mu_t + \psi_t$$

$$\Delta^m \mu_t = (1 + B)^r \xi_t \qquad \xi_t \sim WN(0, \sigma_\xi^2)$$

$$\psi_t \sim WN(0, \lambda\sigma_\xi^2) \qquad E(\xi_t \psi_{t-j}) = 0 \text{ for all } j$$

Here the notation $y_t \sim WN(0, \sigma_y^2)$ is to be read as stating that the variable y_t is white noise (i.e., identically and independently distributed) with zero mean and variance σ_y^2. For (doubly) infinite samples, the minimum mean square error (MMSE) estimates of the components are $\hat{\mu}_t = a_\mu(B)x_t$ and $\hat{\psi}_t = x_t - \hat{\mu}_t = (1 - a_\mu(B))x_t = a_\psi(B)x_t$, where

$$a_\mu(B) = \frac{(1 + B)^r}{(1 + B)^r + (1 - B)^m}$$

and

$$|a_\mu(B)| = \frac{|1 + B|^{2r}}{|1 + B|^{2r} + \lambda|1 - B|^{2m}} \tag{3.8}$$

and the notation $|\alpha(B)| = \alpha(B)\alpha(B^{-1})$ is used. This result uses Weiner–Kolmogorov filtering theory and its derivation may be found in, for example, Proietti (2009a). This filter is therefore defined by the order of integration of the trend, m, which regulates its flexibility, by the parameter r (which technically is the number of unit poles at the Nyquist frequency and which thus regulates the smoothness of $\Delta^m\mu_t$) and by λ, which measures the relative variance of the noise component.

The H–P filter is obtained for $m = 2$ and $r = 0$, so that $\Delta^2\mu_t = \xi_t$. If $m = 1$ and $r = 0$, $\Delta\mu_t = \xi_t$ and the filter corresponds to a two-sided exponentially weighted moving average with smoothing parameter $((1 + 2\lambda) + \sqrt{1 + 4\lambda})/2\lambda$. If $r = 0$ then any setting of m defines a *Butterworth filter*, as does setting $m = r$, which is known as the Butterworth *square-wave* filter (see Gómez, 2001). Setting $m = r = 1$ and $\lambda = 1$ produces the multi-resolution Haar scaling and wavelet filters (see Percival and Walden, 1999).

Using (3.8) and the idea that the cut-off frequency can be chosen to be that at which the gain is 0.5 (as above) enables the smoothing parameter to be determined as:

$$\lambda = 2^{r-m} \frac{(1 + \cos\omega_{0.5})^r}{(1 - \cos\omega_{0.5})^m}$$

Detailed development of the models and techniques discussed in this and the preceding section may be found in Pollock (2009) and Proietti (2009a).

MODEL-BASED FILTERS

The set-up of the previous section is very assumption laden and implies, amongst other things, that the observed series is generated as

$$\Delta^m x_t = (1 + B)^r \zeta_t + (1 - B)^m \psi_t = \theta_q(B) a_t$$

that is, as a heavily restricted ARIMA$(0,m,q)$ process, where $\theta_q(B) = 1 - \theta_1 B - \ldots - \theta_q B^q$ with $q = \max(r,m)$ (the subscript q denoting the order of the polynomial will be dropped when appropriate to simplify notation). A less restrictive approach is to begin by assuming that the observed series has an ARIMA(p,d,q) representation:

$$\phi_p(B)(\Delta^d x_t - c) = \theta_q(B) a_t \qquad a_t \sim WN(0,\sigma_a^2)$$

where $\phi_p(B)$ has p stationary roots and $\theta_q(B)$ is invertible, and to derive filters with the desired properties from this representation. This is done by exploiting the idea that a_t can be decomposed into two orthogonal stationary processes (see, for example, Proietti, 2009a, 2009b, for technical details):

$$a_t = \frac{(1 + B)^r \zeta_t + (1 - B)^m \kappa_t}{\varphi_{q^*}(B)} \tag{3.9}$$

where $q^* = \max(r,m)$, $\zeta_t \sim WN(0,\sigma_a^2)$, $\kappa_t \sim WN(0,\lambda\sigma_a^2)$ and

$$|\varphi_{q^*}(B)|^2 = |1 + B|^{2r} + \lambda|1 - B|^{2m} \tag{3.10}$$

Given (3.9) and (3.10), the following orthogonal trend-cycle decomposition $x_t = \mu_t + \psi_t$ can be defined:

$$\phi(B)\varphi(B)(\Delta^d \mu_t - c) = (1 + B)^r \theta(B) \zeta_t \tag{3.11}$$

$$\phi(B)\varphi(B)\psi_t = \Delta^{m-d}\theta(B)\kappa_t$$

The trend, or low-pass component, has the same order of integration as x_t, regardless of m, whereas the cycle, or high-pass component, is stationary provided that $m \geq d$. The MMSE estimators of the trend and cycle are again given by (3.8) and its 'complement'.

Band-pass filters may be constructed by decomposing the low-pass component in (3.11). For fixed values of m and r and two cut-off frequencies $\omega_{c,1}$ and $\omega_{c,2} > \omega_{c,1}$, corresponding to smoothness parameters λ_1 and $\lambda_2 < \lambda_1$, Proietti (2009a) shows that x_t may be decomposed into low-pass (trend), band-pass (cycle) and high-pass (noise) components as:

$$x_t = \mu_t + \psi_t + \varepsilon_t$$

$$\Delta^d \mu_t = c + \frac{(1 + B)^r}{\varphi_1(B)} \frac{\theta(B)}{\phi(B)} \zeta_t \qquad \zeta_t \sim WN(0,\sigma_a^2)$$

$$\psi_t = \frac{(1+B)^r(1-B)^m}{\varphi_1(B)\varphi_2(B)} \frac{\theta(B)}{\Delta^d\phi(B)}\kappa_{1t} \qquad \kappa_{1t} \sim WN(0,(\lambda_1 - \lambda_2)\sigma_a^2)$$

$$\varepsilon_t = \frac{(1-B)^m}{\varphi_2(B)} \frac{\theta(B)}{\Delta^d\phi(B)}\kappa_{2t} \qquad \kappa_{2t} \sim WN(0,\lambda_2\sigma_a^2)$$

$$E(\zeta_j\kappa_{1t}) = E(\zeta_j\kappa_{2t}) = 0 \qquad E(\kappa_{1j}\kappa_{2t}) \quad \text{for all } j, t$$

$$|\varphi_i(B)|^2 = |1+B|^{2r} + \lambda_i|1+B|^{2m} \qquad i = 1, 2$$

The H–P and B–K filters are often referred to as being ad hoc, in the sense that they are invariant to the process actually generating x_t. This has the potential danger that such filters could produce a cyclical component, say, that might display cyclical features that are absent from the observed series, something that is known as the Slutsky–Yule effect. For example, it has been well documented that when the H–P filter is applied to a random walk, which obviously cannot contain any cyclical patterns, the detrended series can nevertheless display spurious cyclical behaviour. The (ARIMA) model-based filters are designed to overcome these limitations.

STRUCTURAL TRENDS AND CYCLES

An alternative approach to modelling trends and cycles is to take the UC decomposition $x_t = \mu_t + \psi_t + \varepsilon_t$ and to *assume* particular models for the components. The most general approach is that set out by Harvey and Trimbur (2003), Trimbur (2006) and Harvey et al. (2007), who consider the UC decomposition

$$x_t = \mu_{m,t} + \psi_{n,t} + \varepsilon_t \qquad \varepsilon_t \sim WN(0,\sigma_\varepsilon^2)$$

where the components are assumed to be mutually uncorrelated. The trend component is defined as the mth order stochastic trend

$$\mu_{1,t} = \mu_{1,t-1} + \zeta_t \qquad \zeta_t \sim WN(0,\sigma_\zeta^2)$$

$$\mu_{i,t} = \mu_{i,t-1} + \mu_{i-1,t} \qquad i = 2,\ldots,m$$

Note that repeated substitution yields $\Delta^m\mu_{m,t} = \zeta_t$. The random walk trend is thus obtained for $m = 1$ and the integrated random walk, or 'smooth trend', with slope $\mu_{1,t}$ for $m = 2$.

The component $\psi_{n,t}$ is an nth order stochastic cycle, for $n > 0$, if

$$\begin{bmatrix}\psi_{1,t}\\ \psi_{1,t}^*\end{bmatrix} = \rho\begin{bmatrix}\cos\varpi & \sin\varpi\\ -\sin\varpi & \cos\varpi\end{bmatrix}\begin{bmatrix}\psi_{1,t-1}\\ \psi_{1,t-1}^*\end{bmatrix} + \begin{bmatrix}\kappa_t\\ 0\end{bmatrix} \qquad \kappa_t \sim WN(0,\sigma_\kappa^2) \tag{3.12}$$

$$\begin{bmatrix} \psi_{i,t} \\ \psi^*_{i,t} \end{bmatrix} = \rho \begin{bmatrix} \cos \varpi & \sin \varpi \\ -\sin \varpi & \cos \varpi \end{bmatrix} \begin{bmatrix} \psi_{i,t-1} \\ \psi^*_{i,t-1} \end{bmatrix} + \begin{bmatrix} \psi_{i-1,t} \\ 0 \end{bmatrix} \qquad i = 2,\ldots,n$$

Here $0 \leq \varpi \leq \pi$ is the frequency of the cycle and $0 < \rho \leq 1$ is the damping factor. The reduced form representation of the cycle is

$$(1 - 2\rho \cos \varpi B + \rho^2 B^2)^n \psi_{n,t} = (1 - \rho \cos \varpi B)^n \kappa_t$$

and Harvey and Trimbur (2003) show that, as m and n increase, the optimal estimates of the trend and cycle approach the ideal low-pass and band-pass filters, respectively. Defining the 'signal to noise' variance ratios $q_\zeta = \sigma^2_\zeta/\sigma^2_\varepsilon$ and $q_\kappa = \sigma^2_\kappa/\sigma^2_\varepsilon$, the low-pass filter (of order m, n) is:

$$\hat{\mu}_t(m,n) = \frac{q_\zeta/|1 - B|^{2m}}{q_\zeta/|1 - B|^{2m} + q_k|c(B)|^n + 1}$$

where $c(B) = (1 - \rho \cos \varpi B)/(1 - 2\rho \cos \varpi B + \rho^2 B^2)$. The corresponding band-pass filter is

$$\hat{\psi}_t(m,n) = \frac{q_k|c(B)|^n}{q_\zeta/|1 - B|^{2m} + q_k|c(B)|^n + 1}$$

Harvey and Trimbur (2003) discuss many of the properties of this general model. They note that applying a band-pass filter of order n to a series that has been detrended by a low-pass filter of order m will not give the same result as applying a generalized filter of order (m, n), as a jointly specified model enables trends and cycles to be extracted by filters that are mutually consistent. Using higher order trends with a fixed order band-pass filter has the effect of removing lower frequencies from the cycle. However, setting m greater than 2 will produce trends that are more responsive to short term movements than is perhaps desirable.

Replacing the zero component in the right-hand side of (3.12) by a white noise uncorrelated with κ_t produces a *balanced cycle*, the statistical properties of which are derived in Trimbur (2006). For example, for $n = 2$ the variance of the cycle is given by

$$\sigma^2_\psi = \frac{1 + \rho^2}{(1 - \rho^2)^3}\sigma^2_\kappa$$

as opposed to $\sigma^2_\kappa/(1 - \rho^2)$ for the first-order case, while its autocorrelation function is

$$\rho_2(\tau) = \rho^\tau \cos \varpi\tau\left(1 + \frac{1 - \rho^2}{1 + \rho^2}\tau\right), \qquad \tau = 0, 1, 2,\ldots$$

compared to $\rho_1(\tau) = \rho^\tau \cos \varpi\tau$. Harvey and Trimbur prefer the balanced form as it seems to give better fits in empirical applications and offers computational advantages over (3.12).

MODELS WITH CORRELATED COMPONENTS

A feature of all the models introduced so far has been the identifying assumption that all component innovations are mutually uncorrelated, so that the components are orthogonal. Such an assumption can be relaxed: for example, Morley et al. (2003) consider the UC model $x_t = \mu_t + \psi_t$ with contemporaneously correlated innovations:

$$\begin{aligned} \mu_t &= \mu_{t-1} + c + \zeta_t & \zeta_t &\sim WN(0,\sigma_\zeta^2) \\ \psi_t &= \phi_1\psi_{t-1} + \phi_2\psi_{t-2} + \kappa_t & \kappa_t &\sim WN(0,\sigma_\kappa^2) \end{aligned} \tag{3.13}$$

with $\sigma_{\zeta\kappa} = E(\zeta_t\kappa_t) = r\sigma_\zeta\sigma_\kappa$, so that r is the contemporary correlation between the innovations. The reduced form of (3.13) is the ARIMA(2,1,2) process

$$(1 - \phi_1 B - \phi_2 B^2)(\Delta x_t - c) = (1 - \theta_1 B - \theta_2 B^2)a_t$$

Morley et al. (2003) show that the structural form is exactly identified, so that the correlation between the innovations can be estimated and the orthogonality assumption $\sigma_{\zeta\kappa} = 0$ tested.

A related model decomposes an ARIMA$(p,1,q)$ process $\phi(B)(\Delta x_t - c) = \theta(B)a_t$ into a random walk trend

$$\mu_t = \mu_{t-1} + c + \frac{\theta(1)}{\phi(1)}a_t = \frac{\theta(1)}{\phi(1)}\frac{\phi(B)}{\theta(B)}x_t$$

and a cyclical (or transitory) component

$$\psi_t = \frac{\phi(1)\theta(B) - \theta(1)\phi(B)}{\phi(1)\phi(B)\Delta}a_t = \frac{\phi(1)\theta(B) - \theta(1)\phi(B)}{\phi(1)\phi(B)}x_t$$

which has a stationary ARMA$(p,\max(p,q) - 1)$ representation. Thus for the ARIMA (2,1,2) process, the random walk trend will be:

$$\mu_t = \mu_{t-1} + c + \left(\frac{1 - \theta_1 - \theta_2}{1 - \phi_1 - \phi_2}\right)a_t$$

while the ARMA(2,1) cycle will be:

$$(1 - \phi_1 B - \phi_2 B^2)\psi_t = (1 + \vartheta B)\left(\frac{\theta_1 + \theta_2 - (\phi_1 + \phi_2)}{1 - \phi_1 - \phi_2}\right)a_t$$

$$\vartheta = \frac{\phi_2(1 - \theta_1 - \theta_2) + \theta_2(1 - \phi_1 - \phi_2)}{\theta_1 + \theta_2 - (\phi_1 + \phi_2)}$$

The two components are seen to be driven by the *same* innovation, a_t, and hence are perfectly correlated. Whether this correlation is +1 or −1 depends upon the *persistence* $\theta(1)/\phi(1)$: if this is less (greater) than 1, the correlation is +1 (−1). This decomposition is familiarly known as the Beveridge–Nelson decomposition (Beveridge and Nelson, 1981).

MULTIVARIATE EXTENSIONS OF STRUCTURAL MODELS

Since co-movement between macroeconomic series is a key aspect of business cycles, many of the filters and structural models have recently been extended to multivariate set-ups (see, for example, Kozicki, 1999). Multivariate structural models have been introduced by Carvalho and Harvey (2005) and Carvalho et al. (2007). Suppose there are N time series gathered together in the vector $\mathbf{x}_t = (x_{1t}, \ldots, x_{Nt})'$, which may be decomposed into trend, μ_t, cycle, ψ_t, and irregular, ε_t, vectors such that

$$\mathbf{x}_t = \mu_t + \psi_t + \varepsilon_t \qquad \varepsilon_t \sim MWN(\mathbf{0}, \Sigma_\varepsilon)$$

where $MWN(\mathbf{0}, \Sigma_\varepsilon)$ denotes zero mean multivariate white noise with $N \times N$ positive semi-definite covariance matrix Σ_ε. The trend is defined as:

$$\begin{aligned} \mu_t &= \mu_{t-1} + \beta_{t-1} + \eta_t \qquad & \eta_t &\sim MWN(\mathbf{0}, \Sigma_\eta) \\ \beta_t &= \beta_{t-1} + \zeta_t \qquad & \zeta_t &\sim MWN(\mathbf{0}, \Sigma_\zeta) \end{aligned} \tag{3.14}$$

With $\Sigma_\zeta = \mathbf{0}$ and Σ_η positive definite, each trend is a random walk with drift. If, on the other hand, $\Sigma_\eta = \mathbf{0}$ and Σ_ζ is positive definite, the trends are integrated random walks and will typically be much smoother than drifting random walks.

The *similar cycle* model is

$$\begin{bmatrix} \psi_t \\ \psi_t^* \end{bmatrix} = \left[\rho \begin{pmatrix} \cos \varpi & \sin \varpi \\ -\sin \varpi & \cos \varpi \end{pmatrix} \otimes \mathbf{I}_N \right] \begin{bmatrix} \psi_{t-1} \\ \psi_{t-1}^* \end{bmatrix} + \begin{bmatrix} \kappa_t \\ \kappa_t^* \end{bmatrix}$$

where ψ_t and ψ_t^* are N-vectors and κ_t and κ_t^* are N-vectors of mutually uncorrelated zero mean vector multivariate white noise with the same covariance matrix Σ_κ. As the damping factor ρ and cyclical frequency ϖ are the same for all series, the individual cycles have similar properties, being centred around the same period as well as being contemporaneously correlated, on noting that the covariance matrix of ψ_t is

$$\Sigma_\psi = (1 - \rho^2)^{-1}\Sigma_\kappa$$

Suppose $\Sigma_\zeta = \mathbf{0}$ in (3.14). The model will have common trends if Σ_η is less than full rank. If the rank of Σ_η is 1, then there will be a single common trend and

$$\mathbf{x}_t = \theta\mu_t + \alpha + \psi_t + \varepsilon_t \tag{3.15}$$

where the common trend is

$$\mu_t = \mu_{t-1} + \beta + \eta_t \qquad \mu_0 = 0 \qquad \eta_t \sim WN(0, \sigma_\eta^2)$$

and θ and α are N-vectors of constants. If $\Sigma_\eta = \mathbf{0}$, the existence of common trends depends on the rank of Σ_ζ. When this rank is less than N some linear combinations of the series will be stationary. A rank of 1 again leads to the model (3.15) but with

$$\mu_t = \mu_{t-1} + \beta_{t-1} \qquad \beta_t = \beta_{t-1} + \zeta_t \qquad \zeta_t \sim WN(0, \sigma_\zeta^2)$$

When $\theta = \mathbf{i}$, where $\mathbf{i}$ is an N-vector of ones, there is *balanced growth* and the difference between any pair of series in $\mathbf{x}_t$ is stationary.

A mechanism for capturing convergence to a common growth path can be incorporated by specifying the decomposition

$$\mathbf{x}_t = \alpha + \mu_t + \psi_t + \varepsilon_t$$

with

$$\mu_t = \Phi\mu_{t-1} + \beta_{t-1} \qquad \beta_t = \Phi\beta_{t-1} + \zeta_t$$

where $\Phi = \phi\mathbf{I} + (1 - \phi)\mathbf{i}\bar{\phi}$ and $\bar{\phi}$ is a vector of weights. With this set-up, a convergence mechanism can be defined to operate on both the gap between an individual series and the common trend and on the gap in the growth rates of the individual series and the common trend. When ϕ is less than but close to unity, the convergence components tend to be quite smooth and there is a clear separation of long-run movements and cycles. The forecasts for each series converge to a common growth path, although they may exhibit temporary divergences. If $\phi = 1$ there will be no convergence.

Extensions to incorporate multivariate mth order trends and nth order cycles may also be contemplated, as indeed may multivariate low-pass and band-pass filters (see Trimbur, 2010, for some analysis).

ESTIMATION OF STRUCTURAL MODELS

All the structural models introduced here may be estimated by recasting them in state space form, whence they can be estimated using the Kalman filter algorithm. This will produce a MMSE estimator of the state vector, along with its mean square error matrix, conditional on past information. This is then used to build the one-step-ahead predictor of $\mathbf{x}_t$ and its mean square error matrix. The likelihood of the model can be evaluated via the prediction error decomposition and both filtered (real time) and smoothed (full sample) estimates of the components may then be obtained using a set of recursive equations. Harvey and De Rossi (2006) and Proietti (2009a) are convenient references for technical details, while comprehensive software for the estimation and analysis of structural models is provided by the STAMP package (see Koopman et al., 2009).

STRUCTURAL BREAKS

A noticeable feature of many macroeconomic time series is the presence of 'structural breaks', typically characterized by shifts in the coefficients of the deterministic variables, perhaps a constant or a low-order polynomial trend, used to parameterize the trending non-stationarity of the series. Such breaks often play a decisive role in economic policy making and forecasting, where they are regularly a major source of forecast failure (see, for example, Hendry, 2000).

The literature on breaks in individual time series, and in particular on the impact such breaks have on unit root tests, has grown rapidly since the publication of Perron (1989), who showed that the presence of breaks has a major impact on unit root testing, requiring a new set of models and tests to determine the appropriate form of non-stationarity generating the data. A recent authoritative survey of the literature is Perron (2006), while Harris et al. (2009) contains the latest developments in testing for a unit root in the presence of a possible break of trend. A framework for modelling multiple structural breaks in multivariate regression is provided by Qu and Perron (2007) and forecasting time series that are subject to possible multiple structural breaks occurring in the future is discussed in Pesaran et al. (2006).

Rather than discuss such a widely disseminated literature, the focus here will be on the more recently developed modelling of breaks across a set of time series, known as *co-breaking*, as synthesized by Hendry and Massmann (2007). Their basic definition of co-breaking again focuses on the vector $\mathbf{x}_t = (x_{1t}, \ldots, x_{Nt})'$, which is now assumed to have an unconditional expectation around an initial parameterization of $E(\mathbf{x}_0) = \beta_0$, where β_0 depends only on deterministic variables whose parameters do not change: for example, $\beta_0 = \beta_{c,0} + \beta_{t,0}t$. A *location shift* in $\mathbf{x}_t$ is then said to occur if, for any t, $E(\mathbf{x}_t - \beta_0) = \beta_t$ and $\beta_t \neq \beta_{t-1}$, that is, if the expected value of $\mathbf{x}_t$ around its initial parameterization in one time period deviates from that in the previous time period. (Contemporaneous mean) co-breaking is then defined as the cancellation of location shifts across linear combinations of variables and may be characterized by there being an $n \times r$ matrix Ω, of rank $r < n$, such that $\Omega'\beta_t = \mathbf{0}$. It then follows that $\Omega' E(\mathbf{x}_t - \beta_0) - \Omega'\beta_t = \mathbf{0}$, so that the parameterization of the r co-breaking relationships $\Omega'\mathbf{x}_t$ is independent of the location shifts.

Various extensions of contemporaneous mean co-breaking may be considered, such as variance co-breaking and intertemporal mean co-breaking, defined as the cancellation of deterministic shifts across both variables and time periods. Co-breaking may also be related to cointegration: the 'common trends' incorporated in a VECM can be shown to be equilibrium-mean co-breaking while the cointegrating vector itself is drift co-breaking.

To formalize the co-breaking regression approach, consider the following regression model for $\mathbf{x}_t$:

$$\mathbf{x}_t = \pi_0 + \kappa\mathbf{d}_t + \delta\mathbf{w}_t + \varepsilon_t \tag{3.16}$$

where $\mathbf{w}_t$ is a vector of exogenous variables and $\mathbf{d}_t$ is a set of $k > n$ deterministic shift variables. Assuming that the rank of κ is $n - 1$ allows it to be decomposed as $\kappa = \xi\eta'$, where ξ is $n \times (n - 1)$, η is $k \times (n - 1)$ and both ξ and η are of full rank $n - 1$. There will then exist an $n \times 1$ vector $\xi_\perp$ such that $\xi'_\perp \xi = \mathbf{0}$, which then implies that the linear combination $\xi'_\perp \mathbf{x}_t = \xi'_\perp \pi_0 + \xi' \delta \mathbf{w}_t + \xi' \varepsilon_t$ will not contain the shift variables $\mathbf{d}_t$. Partitioning $\mathbf{x}_t$ as $(y_t \vdots \mathbf{z}_t)$ and partitioning and normalizing $\xi_\perp$ as $(1 \vdots -\xi'_{\perp,1})$ defines the structural break-free co-breaking regression:

$$y_t = \xi'_{\perp,1}\mathbf{z}_t + \tilde{\pi}_0 + \tilde{\delta}\mathbf{w}_t + \tilde{\varepsilon}_t \tag{3.17}$$

where $\tilde{\pi}_0 = \xi'_\perp \pi_0$, and so on. This co-breaking regression procedure may be implemented in two steps. First, test whether the k shifts $\mathbf{d}_t$ are actually present in each of the n components of $\mathbf{x}_t$ by estimating (3.16) and testing for the significance of κ: second, augment (3.17) by $\mathbf{d}_t$ and test whether the shifts are now insignificant, with the co-breaking vector either estimated or imposed. Various extensions of this basic approach are discussed by Hendry and Massmann (2007), who also relax the assumption that the number of co-breaking relationships is known (assumed to be 1 above), so that the rank of κ is $n - r$, where r is to be estimated. Although such procedures are still in their infancy, they represent an important advance in the co-breaking framework, in which linear combinations of the form $\Omega'\mathbf{x}_t$ depend on fewer breaks in their deterministic components than does $\mathbf{x}_t$ on its own.

WHAT ACTUALLY CONSTITUTES A TREND?

While cycles have been shown to be relatively straightforward to define in macroeconomics, there is much less consensus on what actually constitutes a trend, and trying to pin this down has attracted some attention recently for, as Phillips (2005) has memorably remarked, 'no one understands trends, but everyone sees them in the data', and that to 'capture the random forces of change that drive a trending process, we need sound theory, appropriate methods, and relevant data. In practice, we have to manage under shortcomings in all of them'.

White and Granger (2011) have set out 'working definitions' of various kinds of trends and this taxonomy may prove to be useful in developing further models of trending processes, in which they place great emphasis on 'attempting to relate apparent trends to appropriate underlying phenomena, whether economic, demographic, political, legal, technological or physical'. This would surely require taking account of possible co-breaking phenomena of the type discussed in the previous section as well, thereby producing a richer class of multivariate models for trending and breaking macroeconomic processes.

NOTE

1. Hodrick and Prescott (1997) was originally published as a discussion paper in 1980, but the widespread use of the H–P filter (3) eventually led to the paper's publication in the *Journal of Money, Credit and Banking* almost two decades later. That the penalized least squares approach, in various forms, anteceded the H–P filter by several decades was well known by Leser and Hodrick and Prescott, although the latter appear to be unaware of the former's paper. Pedregal and Young (2001) provide both historical and multidisciplinary perspective.

REFERENCES

Baxter, M. and R.G. King (1999), 'Measuring business cycles: approximate band-pass filters for economic time series', *Review of Economics and Statistics*, **81**(4), 575–93.

Beveridge, S. and C.R. Nelson (1981), 'A new approach to decomposition of economic time series into permanent and transitory components with particular attention to measurement of the "business cycle"', *Journal of Monetary Economics*, **7**(2), 151–74.

Carvalho, V. and A.C. Harvey (2005), 'Growth, cycles and convergence in US regional time series', *International Journal of Forecasting*, **21**(4), 667–86.

Carvalho, V., A.C. Harvey and T. Trimbur (2007), 'A note on common cycles, common trends and convergence', *Journal of Business and Economic Statistics*, **25**(1), 12–20.

Christiano, L. and T. Fitzgerald (2003), 'The band pass filter', *International Economic Review*, **44**(2), 435–65.

Cox, D.R. (1961), 'Prediction by exponentially weighted moving averages and related methods', *Journal of the Royal Statistical Society, Series B*, **23**(2), 414–22.

Gómez, V. (2001), 'The use of Butterworth filters for trend and cycle estimation in economic time series', *Journal of Business and Economic Statistics*, **19**(3), 365–73.

Harris, D., D.I. Harvey, S.J. Leybourne and A.M.R. Taylor (2009), 'Testing for a unit root in the presence of a possible break in trend', *Econometric Theory*, **25**(6), 1545–88.

Harvey, A.C. and P. De Rossi (2006), 'Signal extraction', in T.C. Mills and K. Patterson (eds), *Palgrave Handbook of Econometrics: Volume 1, Econometric Theory*, Basingstoke, UK: Palgrave Macmillan, pp. 970–1000.

Harvey, A.C. and T.M. Trimbur (2003), 'General model-based filters for extracting cycles and trends in economic time series', *Review of Economics and Statistics*, **85**(2), 244–55.

Harvey, A.C., T.M. Trimbur and H.K. van Dijk (2007), 'Trends and cycles in economic time series: a Bayesian approach', *Journal of Econometrics*, **140**(2), 618–49.

Hendry, D.F. and M. Massmann (2007), 'Co-breaking: recent advances and a synopsis of the literature', *Journal of Business and Economic Statistics*, **25**(1), 33–51.

Hodrick, R.J. and E.C. Prescott (1997), 'Postwar US business cycles: an empirical investigation', *Journal of Money, Credit and Banking*, **29**(1), 1–16.

Hooker, R.H. (1901), 'Correlation of the marriage rate with trade', *Journal of the Royal Statistical Society*, **64**(3), 485–92.

Kaiser, R. and A. Maravall (2005), 'Combining filter design with model-based filtering (with an application to business cycle estimation)', *International Journal of Forecasting*, **21**(4), 691–710.

Kalman, R.E. (1960), 'A new approach to linear filtering and prediction theory', *Journal of Basic Engineering, Transactions of the ASME, Series D*, **82**(1), 35–45.

Kalman, R.E. and R.E. Bucy (1961), 'New results in linear filtering and prediction theory', *Journal of Basic Engineering, Transactions of the ASME, Series D*, **83**(1), 95–108.

Klein, J.L. (1997), *Statistical Visions in Time. A History of Time Series Analysis, 1662–1938*, Cambridge, UK: Cambridge University Press.

Klein, L.R. and R.F. Kosobud (1961), 'Some econometrics of growth: great ratios in economics', *Quarterly Journal of Economics*, **75**(2), 173–98.

Koopman, S.J., A.C. Harvey, J.A. Doornik and N. Shephard (2009), *STAMP™ 8: Structural Time Series Analysis and Predictor*, London, UK: Timberlake Consultants.

Kozicki, S. (1999), 'Multivariate detrending under common trend restrictions: implications for business cycle research', *Journal of Economic Dynamics and Control*, **23**(4), 997–1028.

Leser, C.E.V. (1961), 'A simple method of trend construction', *Journal of the Royal Statistical Society, Series B*, **23**(1), 91–107.

Maravall, A. and A. del Rio (2007), 'Temporal aggregation, systematic sampling, and the Hodrick–Prescott filter', *Computational Statistics and Data Analysis*, **52**(2), 975–98.

Mills, T.C. (2009a), 'Modelling trends and cycles in economic time series: historical perspective and future developments', *Cliometrica*, **3**(3), 221–44.

Mills, T.C. (2009b), 'Klein and Kosobud's great ratios revisited', *Quantitative and Qualitative Analysis in Social Science*, **3**(3), 12–42.

Mills, T.C. (2011), *The Foundations of Modern Time Series Analysis*, Basingstoke, UK: Palgrave Macmillan.

Morgan, M.S. (1990), *The History of Econometric Ideas*, Cambridge, UK: Cambridge University Press.

Morley, J.C., C.R. Nelson and E. Zivot (2003), 'Why are Beveridge–Nelson and unobserved-component decompositions of GDP so different?', *Review of Economics and Statistics*, **85**(2), 235–43.

Pedregal, D.J. and P.C. Young (2001), 'Some comments on the use and abuse of the Hodrick–Prescott filter', *Review on Economic Cycles*, **2**.

Percival, D.B. and A.T. Walden (1999), *Wavelet Methods for Time Series Analysis*, Cambridge, UK: Cambridge University Press.
Perron, P. (1989), 'The great crash, the oil price shock, and the unit root hypothesis', *Econometrica*, **57**(6), 1361–401.
Perron, P. (2006), 'Dealing with structural breaks', in T.C. Mills and K. Patterson (eds), *Palgrave Handbook of Econometrics: Volume 1, Econometric Theory*, Basingstoke, UK: Palgrave Macmillan, pp. 278–352.
Pesaran, M.H., D. Pettenuzzo and A. Timmermann (2006), 'Forecasting time series subject to multiple structural breaks', *Review of Economic Studies*, **74**(4), 1057–84.
Phillips, P.C.B. (2005), 'Challenges of trending time series econometrics', *Mathematics and Computers in Simulation*, **68**(5–6), 401–16.
Pollock, D.S.G. (2009), 'Investigating economic trends and cycles', in T.C. Mills and K. Patterson (eds), *Palgrave Handbook of Econometrics: Volume 2, Applied Econometrics*, Basingstoke, UK: Palgrave Macmillan, pp. 243–307.
Proietti, T. (2009a), 'Structural time series models for business cycle analysis', in T.C. Mills and K. Patterson (eds), *Palgrave Handbook of Econometrics: Volume 2, Applied Econometrics*, Basingstoke, UK: Palgrave Macmillan, pp. 385–433.
Proietti, T. (2009b), 'On the model based interpretation of filters and the reliability of trend-cycle filters', *Econometric Reviews*, **28**(1–3), 186–208.
Qu, Z. and P. Perron (2007), 'Estimating and testing structural changes in multivariate regressions', *Econometrica*, **75**(2), 459–502.
Ravn, M.O. and H. Uhlig (2002), 'On adjusting the Hodrick–Prescott filter for the frequency of observation', *Review of Economics and Statistics*, **84**(2), 371–6.
Trimbur, T.M. (2006), 'Properties of higher order stochastic cycles', *Journal of Time Series Analysis*, **27**(1), 1–17.
Trimbur, T.M. (2010), 'The cyclical component of economic time series', Federal Reserve Board, July.
White, H. and C.W.J. Granger (2011), 'Consideration of trends in time series', *Journal of Time Series Econometrics*, **3**(1), Article 2.
Young, P.C. (2011), 'Gauss, Kalman and advances in recursive parameter estimation', *Journal of Forecasting*, **30**(1), 104–46.

4 Unit roots, non-linearities and structural breaks*

Niels Haldrup, Robinson Kruse, Timo Teräsvirta and Rasmus T. Varneskov

1 INTRODUCTION

It is widely accepted that many time series in economics and finance exhibit trending behaviour in the level (or mean) of the series. Typical examples include asset prices, exchange rates, real GDP, real wage series and so forth. In a recent paper White and Granger (2011) reflect on the nature of trends and make a variety of observations that seem to characterize these. Interestingly, as also noted by Phillips (2005), even though no one understands trends everybody still sees them in the data. In economics and other disciplines, almost all observed trends involve stochastic behaviour and purely deterministic trends are rare. However, a combination of stochastic and deterministic elements including structural changes seems to be a model class which is likely to describe the data well. Potentially the series may contain non-linear features and even the apparent deterministic parts like level and trend may be driven by an underlying stochastic process that determines the timing and the size of breaks.

In recent years there has been a focus on stochastic trend models caused by the presence of unit roots. A stochastic trend is driven by a cumulation of historical shocks to the process and hence each shock will have a persistent effect. This feature does not necessarily characterize other types of trends where the source of the trend can be different and some or all shocks may only have a temporary effect. Time series with structural changes and unit roots share similar features, which makes it difficult to discriminate between the two fundamentally different classes of processes. In principle, a unit root (or difference stationary) process can be considered as a process where each point in time has a level shift. On the other hand, if a time series process is stationary but is characterized by infrequent level shifts, certain (typically large) shocks tend to be persistent whereas other shocks have only a temporary influence. Many stationary non-linear processes contain features similar to level shifts and unit root processes. Some types of regime switching models belong to this class of processes.

It is not surprising that discriminating between different types of trend processes is difficult. Still, there is an overwhelming body of literature which has focused on unit root processes and how to distinguish these from other trending processes, and there are several reasons for this. One reason is the special feature of unit root processes regarding the persistence of shocks which may have important implications for the formulation of economic models and the measurement of impulse responses associated with economic policy shocks. Another reason concerns the fact that the presence of unit roots can result in spurious inference and hence should be appropriately accounted for in order to make valid inference when analysing multivariate time series. The development of the notion of cointegration by Granger (1981, 1983) and Engle and Granger (1987) shows how time series with stochastic trends can be represented and modelled to avoid spurious relations. This field has grown tremendously since the initial contributions. For the statistical theory and overview, see Johansen (1995) and Davidson in Chapter 7 of this volume.

The purpose of the present chapter is to review recent advances and the current status in the field of unit root testing when accounting for deterministic trends, structural breaks and non-linearities. We shall also consider some of the difficulties that arise due to other special features that complicate inference. There is a vast amount of literature on these topics. Review articles include Haldrup and Jansson (2006) who focus on the size and power of unit root tests, and Perron (2006) who deals with structural breaks in stationary and non-stationary time series models. See also Mills in Chapter 3 of this volume. Other general overviews of unit root testing can be found in Stock (1994), Maddala and Kim (1998), and Phillips and Xiao (1998). The present review updates the present state of the art and includes a number of recent contributions in the field.

In section 2 we introduce a general class of basic processes where the focus is on unit root processes that can be mixed with the presence of deterministic components that potentially may exhibit breaks. In section 3 we review existing unit root tests that are commonly used in practice, that is the augmented Dickey–Fuller, Phillips and Perron, and the trinity of M class of tests suggested by Perron and Ng (1996). We also briefly touch upon the literature on the design of optimal tests for the unit root hypothesis. The following two sections extend the analysis to the situation where the time series have a linear trend or drift and the initial condition is likely to affect inference. In particular, we address testing when there is general uncertainty about the presence of trends and the size of the initial condition. Section 6 extends the analysis to unit root testing in the presence of structural break processes for the cases where the break date is either known or unknown. Section 7 is concerned with unit root testing in non-linear models followed by a section on unit root testing when the data exhibit particular features such as being bounded by their definition or exhibiting trends in both the levels and growth rates of the series. The chapter finishes with an empirical illustration.

There are numerous relevant research topics which for space reasons we cannot discuss in this presentation. These include the literature on the design of optimal tests for the unit root hypothesis but also the highly relevant area of using the bootstrap in non-standard situations where existing procedures are likely to fail due to particular features of the data.

2 TRENDS IN TIME SERIES

We begin by reviewing some of the basic properties of unit root and trend-stationary processes including the possible structural breaks in such processes. Consider $T + 1$ observations from the time series process generated by

$$y_t = f(t) + u_t, \quad t = 0,1,2,\ldots,T \tag{4.1}$$

where

$$(1 - \alpha L)u_t = C(L)\varepsilon_t,$$

u_t is a linear process with $\varepsilon_t \overset{i.i.d.}{\sim} N(0,\sigma_\varepsilon^2)$ and $C(L) = \Sigma_{j=0}^{\infty} c_j L^j$, $\Sigma_{j=1}^{\infty} j|c_j| < \infty$, and $c_0 = 1$. L is the lag operator, $Lx_t = x_{t-1}$; $f(t)$ is a deterministic component to be defined later. When $\alpha = 1$ the series contains a unit root, and a useful decomposition due to Beveridge and Nelson (1981) reads

$$\Delta u_t = C(1)\varepsilon_t + \Delta C^*(L)\varepsilon_t,$$

where $C(1) \neq 0$ and $C^*(L)$ satisfies requirements similar to those of $C(L)$. With this representation

$$y_t = y_0 + f(t) + C(1)\sum_{j=1}^{t}\varepsilon_j + \sum_{j=1}^{t-1} c_j^* \varepsilon_{t-j} \tag{4.2}$$

where $\tau_t = C(1)\Sigma_{j=1}^{t}\varepsilon_j$ is a stochastic trend component and $C^*(L)\varepsilon_t$ is a stationary component.

When u_t has no unit root, $|\alpha| < 1$, and setting $v_t = C(L)\varepsilon_t$, the process reads

$$y_t = f(t) + (1 - \alpha L)^{-1} v_t$$

$$= \alpha^t y_0 + f(t) + \sum_{j=0}^{t-1} \alpha^j v_{t-j}. \tag{4.3}$$

Equations (4.2) and (4.3) encompass many different features of unit root and trend stationary processes. As seen from (4.2), the presence of a unit root means that shocks will have a permanent effect and the level of the series is determined by a stochastic trend component in addition to the trend component $f(t)$. In principle, each period is characterized by a level shift through the term $\Sigma_{j=0}^{t-1} v_{t-j}$. In the trend stationary case $|\alpha| < 1$ shocks will only have a temporary effect, but each period also has a level shift through the deterministic component $f(t)$.

The models point to many of the statistical difficulties concerned with unit root testing in practice and the complications with discriminating between the different types of processes. For instance, in (4.2) and (4.3) we have not made any assumptions regarding the initial condition. This could be assumed fixed, or it could be stochastic in a certain way. However, the assumptions made are not innocuous with respect to the properties of unit root tests, as we shall discuss later. The presence of deterministic components may also cause problems since deterministic terms can take many different forms. For instance the trend function can be prime linear in the parameters: $f(t) = d_t'\mu$ where d_t is a k-vector, for instance an intercept, a linear trend, and possibly a quadratic trend where $d_t' = (1,t,t^2)$, and μ is an associated parameter vector. Moreover, these different terms could have parameters that change over time within the sample. For example, the trend function may include changes in the level, the slope, or both, and these structural breaks may be at known dates (in which case the trend is still linear in parameters) or the break time may be generated according to a stochastic process, for example a Markov switching process.

Other difficulties concern the assumptions about the nature of the innovations governing the process. Generally, the short-run dynamics of the process are unknown, the innovation variance may be heteroscedastic, and ε_t need not be Gaussian. We are going to address many of these complications and how to deal with these in practice. First, we want to consider a range of specifications of the trend function $f(t)$ that are essential for practical unit root testing.

2.1 Assumptions about the Deterministic Component $f(t)$

Linear trend

Following the empirical analysis of Nelson and Plosser (1982) it has been commonplace to consider the unit root model against one containing a linear trend. Fundamentally, the question asked is whether the trending feature of the data can be best described as a trend that never changes versus a trend that changes in every period. Assume that $f(t) = \mu + \beta t$ is a linear-in-parameters trend, in which case (4.3) becomes

$$y_t = \mu + \beta t + (1 - \alpha L)^{-1} C(L)\varepsilon_t \tag{4.4}$$

and

$$\Delta y_t = (\alpha - 1)y_{t-1} + \mu(1 - \alpha) + \alpha\beta + (1 - \alpha)\beta t + C(L)\varepsilon_t. \tag{4.5}$$

By comparing (4.4) and (4.5) it is seen that the role of deterministic components is different in the levels and the first differences representations. When a unit root is present, $\alpha = 1$, the constant term $\mu(1 - \alpha) + \alpha\beta = \beta$ in (4.5) represents the drift, whereas the slope $(1 - \alpha)\beta = 0$. This shows the importance of carefully interpreting the meaning of the deterministic terms under the null and the alternative hypothesis. Note that when $\beta \neq 0$, the linear trend will dominate the series even in the presence of a stochastic trend component.

Structural breaks

As emphasized by Perron (2006), discriminating between trends that either change every period or never change can be a rather rigid distinction. In many situations a more appropriate question could be whether a trend changes at every period or whether it only changes occasionally. This line of thinking initiated research by Rappoport and Reichlin (1989) and Perron (1989, 1990) who considered the possibility of certain events having a particularly strong impact on trends. Examples could include the Great Depression, World War II, the oil crises in the 1970s and early 1980s, the German reunification in 1990, the recent financial crisis initiated in 2007 and so forth. In modelling, such events may be ascribed stochastic shocks but possibly of a different nature than shocks occurring each period. The former are thus likely to be drawn from a different statistical distribution than the latter.

Perron (1989, 1990) suggested a general treatment of the structural break hypothesis where four different situations were considered that allowed a single break in the sample: (a) a change in the level, (b) a change in the level in the presence of a linear trend, (c) a change in the slope and (d) a change in both the level and slope. In implementing these models, two different transition mechanisms were considered following the terminology of Box and Tiao (1975); one is labelled the *additive outlier (AO) model* where the transition is instantaneous and the trend break function is linear in parameters, and one is labelled the *innovation outlier (IO) model* where changes occur via the innovation process and hence a gradual adjustment of a 'big' shock takes place in accordance with the general dynamics of the underlying series. We will consider hypothesis testing later on and just note that distinguishing between these classes of break processes is important in the design of appropriate testing procedures.

Additive outlier models with level shift and trend break

Define the dummy variables DU_t and DT_t such that $DU_t = 1$ and $DT_t = t - T_1$ for $t > T_1$ and zero otherwise. The dummy variables allow various breaks to occur at time T_1. Using the classifications of Perron (2006) the following four AO models are considered:

$$\begin{aligned}
AO^a &: \quad y_t = \mu_1 + (\mu_2 - \mu_1)DU_t + (1 - \alpha L)^{-1}C(L)\varepsilon_t \\
AO^b &: \quad y_t = \mu_1 + \beta t + (\mu_2 - \mu_1)DU_t + (1 - \alpha L)^{-1}C(L)\varepsilon_t \\
AO^c &: \quad y_t = \mu_1 + \beta_1 t + (\beta_2 - \beta_1)DT_t + (1 - \alpha L)^{-1}C(L)\varepsilon_t \\
AO^d &: \quad y_t = \mu_1 + \beta_1 t + (\mu_2 - \mu_1)DU_t + (\beta_2 - \beta_1)DT_t + (1 - \alpha L)^{-1}C(L)\varepsilon_t.
\end{aligned}$$

We assume that $\beta_1 \neq \beta_2$ and $\mu_1 \neq \mu_2$. Notice that under the null of a unit root, the differenced series reads $\Delta y_t = \Delta f(t) + C(L)\varepsilon_t$ where $\Delta f(t)$ takes the form of an impulse at time T_1 for the AO^a and AO^b models, whereas the AO^c model will have a level shift and the AO^d model will have a level shift plus an impulse blip at the break date.

Innovation change level shift and trend break models

The nature of these models depends on whether a unit root is present or absent. Assume initially that $|\alpha| < 1$. Then the IO models read

$$\begin{aligned}
IO^a &: \quad y_t = \mu + (1 - \alpha L)^{-1}C(L)(\varepsilon_t + \theta DU_t) \\
IO^b &: \quad y_t = \mu + \beta t + (1 - \alpha L)^{-1}C(L)(\varepsilon_t + \theta DU_t) \\
IO^d &: \quad y_t = \mu + \beta t + (1 - \alpha L)^{-1}C(L)(\varepsilon_t + \theta DU_t + \gamma DT_t).
\end{aligned}$$

Hence, the impulse impact of a change in the intercept at time T_1 is given by θ and the long-run impact by $\theta(1 - \alpha)^{-1}C(1)$. Similarly, the immediate impact of a change in slope is given by γ with long-run impact $\gamma(1 - \alpha)^{-1}C(1)$. Note that these models have similar characteristics to those of the AO models apart from the temporal dynamic adjustments of the IO models. Note that model c is not considered in the IO case because linear estimation methods cannot be used and will cause difficulties for practical applications.

Under the null hypothesis of a unit root, $\alpha = 1$, the meaning of the breaks in the IO models will cumulate unintentionally to higher order deterministic processes. It will therefore be necessary to redefine the dummies in this case whereby the models read

$$\begin{aligned}
IO^{a_0} &: \quad y_t = y_{t-1} + C(L)(\varepsilon_t + \delta(1 - L)DU_t) \\
IO^{b_0} &: \quad y_t = y_{t-1} + \beta + C(L)(\varepsilon_t + \delta(1 - L)DU_t) \\
IO^{d_0} &: \quad y_t = y_{t-1} + \beta + C(L)(\varepsilon_t + \delta(1 - L)DU_t + \eta DU_t).
\end{aligned}$$

where $(1 - L)DU_t$ is an impulse dummy and $(1 - L)DT_t = DU_t$. The impulse impact on the level of the series is given by δ and the long-run impact is by $\delta C(1)$, whereas for the IO^{d_0} model the impulse impact on the trend slope is given by η with long-run slope equal to $\eta C(1)$. Qualitatively, the implications of the various break processes are thus similar to each other under the null and the alternative hypothesis.

2.2 Some Other Examples of Trends

It is obvious from the examples above that in practice it can be difficult to discriminate between unit root (or difference stationary) processes and processes that are trend stationary with a possibly changing trend or level shifts. A stochastic trend has (many) innovations that tend to persist. A break process implies the existence of 'big' structural breaks that tend to have a persistent effect. It goes without saying that distinguishing between these fundamentally different processes is even harder when one extends the above illustrations to cases with multiple breaks which potentially are generated by a stochastic process like a Bernoulli or Markov regime switching process.

As an example of this latter class of models, consider the so-called 'mean-plus-noise' model in state space form, see for example Diebold and Inoue (2001):

$$y_t = \mu_t + \varepsilon_t$$
$$\mu_t = \mu_{t-1} + v_t$$
$$v_t = \begin{cases} 0 & \text{with probability } (1 - p) \\ w_t & \text{with probability } p \end{cases}$$

where $w_t \overset{i.i.d.}{\sim} N(0,\sigma_w^2)$ and $\varepsilon_t \overset{i.i.d.}{\sim} N(0,\sigma_\varepsilon^2)$. Such a process consists of a mixture of shocks that have either permanent or transitory effect. If p is relatively small, then y_t will exhibit infrequent level shifts. Asymptotically, such a process which is really a generalization of the additive outlier level shift model AO^a, will behave like an $I(1)$ process. Granger and Hyung (2004) consider a related process in which the switches caused by a latent Markov chain have been replaced by deterministic breaks. A similar feature characterizes the STOPBREAK model of Engle and Smith (1999). A special case of the Markov-switching process of Hamilton (1989) behaves asymptotically as an $I(0)$ process: it has the same stationarity condition as a linear autoregressive model, but due to a Markov-switching intercept, it can generate a very high persistence in finite samples and can be difficult to discriminate from unit root processes, see for example Timmermann (2000) and Diebold and Inoue (2001). The intercept-switching threshold autoregressive process of Lanne and Saikkonen (2005) has the same property. It is a weakly stationary process but generates persistent realizations. Yet another model of the same type is the non-linear sign model by Granger and Teräsvirta (1999) that is stationary but has 'misleading linear properties'. This means that autocorrelations estimated from realizations of this process show high persistence, which may lead the practitioner to think that the data have been generated by a non-stationary (long-memory), that is, linear, model.

It is also possible to assume a deterministic intercept and generate realizations that have 'unit root properties'. The Switching-Mean Autoregressive model by González and Teräsvirta (2008) may serve as an example. In that model the intercept is characterized by a linear combination of logistic functions of time, which make both the intercept and with it the model quite flexible.

3 UNIT ROOT TESTING WITHOUT DETERMINISTIC COMPONENTS

In this section we will present unit root tests that are parametric or semiparametric extensions of the Dickey–Fuller test, see Dickey and Fuller (1979). We will state the underlying assumptions and consider generalizations in various directions.

3.1 The Dickey–Fuller Test

Historically, the Dickey–Fuller test initiated the vast literature on unit root testing. Let us consider the case when (4.1) takes the simplified form of an AR(1) process

$$y_t = \alpha y_{t-1} + \varepsilon_t \tag{4.6}$$

where we assume that the initial observation is fixed at zero and $\varepsilon_t \sim i.i.d\ (0,\sigma_\varepsilon^2)$. The hypothesis to be tested is $H_0 : \alpha = 1$, and is tested against the one-side alternative $H_1 : \alpha < 1$. The least squares estimator of α reads

$$\hat{\alpha} = \frac{\sum_{t=1}^{T} y_{t-1} y_t}{\sum_{t=1}^{T} y_{t-1}^2}.$$

The associated t-statistic of the null hypothesis is

$$t_\alpha = \frac{\hat{\alpha} - 1}{s/\sqrt{\sum_{t=1}^{T} y_{t-1}^2}}$$

where $s^2 = \frac{1}{T}\sum_{t=1}^{T}(y_t - \hat{\alpha} y_{t-1})^2$ is the estimate of the residual variance. Under the null hypothesis it is well known that these quantities have non-standard asymptotic distributions. In particular,

$$T(\hat{\alpha} - 1) \xrightarrow{d} \frac{\int_0^1 W(r)\,dW(r)}{\int_0^1 W^2(r)\,dr} \tag{4.7}$$

and

$$t_\alpha \xrightarrow{d} \frac{\int_0^1 W(r)\,dW(r)}{\sqrt{\int_0^1 W^2(r)\,dr}} \tag{4.8}$$

where $W(r)$ is a Wiener process (or standard Brownian motion) defined on the unit interval and $\xrightarrow{d}$ indicates convergence in distribution. These distributions are often referred to as the Dickey–Fuller distributions even though they can be traced back to White (1958).

3.2 The Augmented Dickey–Fuller Test

Because rather strict assumptions have been made regarding model (4.6) the limiting distributions (4.7) and (4.8) do not depend upon nuisance parameters under the null, that is the distributions are asymptotically pivotal. In particular, the assumption that innovations are *i.i.d.* is restrictive and a violation will mean that the relevant distributions are not as indicated above. To see this, assume that

$$y_t = \alpha y_{t-1} + u_t \tag{4.9}$$

where $u_t = C(L)\varepsilon_t$ with $C(L)$ satisfying the properties given in (4.1). We also assume that $y_0 = 0$.

This model allows more general assumptions regarding the serial correlation pattern of $y_t - \alpha y_{t-1}$ compared to the AR(1) model (4.6). Phillips (1987) shows that under these assumptions, the distributions (4.7) and (4.8) are modified as follows:

$$T(\hat{\alpha} - 1) \xrightarrow{d} \frac{\int_0^1 W(r)dW(r) + \lambda}{\int_0^1 W^2(r)dr} \tag{4.10}$$

and

$$t_\alpha \xrightarrow{d} \frac{\omega}{\sigma} \frac{\int_0^1 W(r)dW(r) + \lambda}{\sqrt{\int_0^1 W^2(r)dr}} \tag{4.11}$$

where $\lambda = (\omega^2 - \sigma^2)/(2\omega^2)$, $\sigma^2 = E[u_t^2] = \sigma_\varepsilon^2(\sum_{j=0}^{\infty} c_j^2)$ is the variance of u_t, and $\omega^2 = \lim_{T\to\infty} T^{-1}E[(\sum_{t=1}^{T} u_t)^2] = \sigma_\varepsilon^2(\sum_{j=0}^{\infty} c_j)^2$ is the 'long-run variance' of u_t. In fact, $\omega^2 = 2\pi f_u(0)$ where $f_u(0)$ is the spectral density of u_t evaluated at the origin. When the innovations are *i.i.d.*, $\omega^2 = \sigma^2$, the nuisance parameters vanish and the limiting distributions coincide with those given in (4.7) and (4.8).

Various approaches have been suggested in the literature to account for the presence of nuisance parameters in the limiting distributions of $T(\hat{\alpha} - 1)$ and t_α in (4.10) and (4.11). It was shown by Dickey and Fuller (1979) that when u_t is a finite order AR process of order k, then $T(\hat{\alpha} - 1)$ and t_α (known as the augmented Dickey–Fuller tests) based on the regression

$$y_t = \alpha y_{t-1} + \sum_{j=1}^{k-1} \gamma_j \Delta y_{t-j} + v_{tk} \qquad (t = k+1,\ldots,T) \tag{4.12}$$

have the asymptotic distributions (4.7) and (4.8). However, this result does not apply to more general processes when u_t is an ARMA(p,q) process (with $q \geq 1$). In this case a fixed truncation of the augmented Dickey–Fuller regression (4.12) with $k = \infty$ provides an inadequate solution to the nuisance parameter problem. Following results of Said and Dickey (1984) it has been shown by Chang and Park (2002), however, that when u_t follows an ARMA(p,q) process, then the limiting null distributions of $T(\hat{\alpha} - 1)$ and t_α coincide with the nuisance parameter free Dickey–Fuller distributions, provided that ε_t

has a finite fourth moment and k increases with the sample such that $k = o(T^{1/2-\delta})$ for some $\delta > 0$.

It has been documented in numerous studies, see for example Schwert (1989) and Agiakloglou and Newbold (1992), that the augmented Dickey–Fuller tests suffer from size distortion in finite samples in the presence of serial correlation, especially when the dependence is of (negative) moving average type. Ng and Perron (1995, 2001) have further scrutinized rules for truncating long autoregressions when performing unit root tests based on (4.12). Consider the information criterion

$$IC(k) = \log\tilde{\sigma}_k^2 + kC_T/T, \qquad \tilde{\sigma}_k^2 = (T-k)^{-1}\sum_{t=k+1}^{T}\tilde{v}_{tk}^2. \tag{4.13}$$

Here $\{C_T\}$ is a positive sequence satisfying $C_T = o(T)$. The Akaike Information Criterion (AIC) uses $C_T = 2$, whereas the Schwarz or Bayesian Information Criterion (BIC) sets $C_T = \log T$. Ng and Perron (1995) find that generally these criteria select too low a value of k, which is a source for size distortion. They also show that by using a sequential data dependent procedure, where the significance of coefficients of additional lags is sequentially tested, one obtains a test with improved size. This procedure, however, often leads to overparametrization and power losses. An information criterion designed for integrated time series which alleviates these problems has been suggested by Ng and Perron (2001). Their idea is to select some lag order k in the interval between 0 and a preselected value k_{max}, where the upper bound k_{max} satisfies $k_{max} = o(T)$. As a practical rule, Ng and Perron (2001) suggest that $k_{max} = \text{int}(12(T/100)^{1/4})$. Their modified form of the AIC is given by

$$MAIC(k) = \log\check{\sigma}_k^2 + 2(\tau_T(k) + k)/(T - k_{max}), \tag{4.14}$$

where $\check{\sigma}_k^2 = (T-k_{max})^{-1}\sum_{t=k_{max}+1}^{T}\tilde{v}_{tk}^2$ and $\tau_T(k) = \check{\sigma}_k^{-2}(\tilde{\rho}-1)^2\sum_{t=k_{max}+1}^{T}y_{t-1}^2$. Note that the penalty function is data dependent which captures the property that the bias in the sum of the autoregressive coefficients (i.e., $\hat{\alpha} - 1$) is highly dependent upon the selected truncation k. Ng and Perron have documented that the modified information criterion is superior to conventional information criteria in truncating long autoregressions with integrated variables when (negative) moving average errors are present.

3.3 Semi-parametric Z Tests

Instead of solving the nuisance parameter problem parametrically as in the augmented Dickey–Fuller test, Phillips (1987) and Phillips and Perron (1988) suggest to transform the statistics $T(\hat{\alpha} - 1)$ and $t_{\hat{\alpha}}$ based on estimating the model (4.6) in such a way that the influence of nuisance parameters is eliminated asymptotically. This can be done after consistent estimates of the nuisance parameters ω^2 and σ^2 have been found. More specifically, they suggest the statistics

$$Z_\alpha = T(\hat{\alpha} - 1) - \frac{\hat{\omega}^2 - \hat{\sigma}^2}{2T^{-2}\sum_{t=1}^{T}y_{t-1}^2} \tag{4.15}$$

and

$$Z_{t_\alpha} = \frac{\hat{\sigma}}{\hat{\omega}} t_{\hat{\alpha}} - \frac{\hat{\omega}^2 - \hat{\sigma}^2}{2\sqrt{\hat{\omega}^2 T^{-2} \sum_{t=1}^{T} y_{t-1}^2}}. \tag{4.16}$$

The limiting null distributions of Phillips' and Perron's Z statistics correspond to the pivotal distributions (4.7) and (4.8).

A consistent estimate of σ^2 is

$$\hat{\sigma}^2 = T^{-1} \sum_{t=1}^{T} \hat{u}_t^2, \quad \hat{u}_t = y_t - \hat{\alpha} y_{t-1},$$

whereas for the estimate of the long-run variance ω^2 a range of kernel estimators can been considered. These are typically estimators used in spectral density estimation and are of the form

$$\hat{\omega}_{KER}^2 = T^{-1} \sum_{t=1}^{T} \hat{u}_t^2 + 2 \sum_{j=1}^{T-1} w(j/M_T) \left(T^{-1} \sum_{t=j+1}^{T} \hat{u}_t \hat{u}_{t-j} \right), \tag{4.17}$$

where $w(\cdot)$ is a kernel (weight) function and M_T is a bandwidth parameter, see for example Newey and West (1987) and Andrews (1991).

Even though kernel estimators of the long-run variance ω^2 such as (4.17) are commonly used to remove the influence of nuisance parameters in the asymptotic distributions it has been shown by Perron and Ng (1996) that spectral density estimators cannot generally eliminate size distortions. In fact, kernel-based estimators tend to aggravate the size distortions, which is also documented in many Monte Carlo studies, for example Schwert (1989), Agiakloglou and Newbold (1992) and Kim and Schmidt (1990). The size distortions arise because the estimation of α and ω^2 are coupled in the sense that the least squares estimator $\hat{\alpha}$ is used in constructing $\hat{u}_t$ and hence affects $\hat{\omega}_{KER}^2$. The finite (and even large) sample bias of $\hat{\alpha}$ is well known when u_t exhibits strong serial dependence, and hence the nuisance parameter estimator $\hat{\omega}_{KER}^2$ is expected to be very imprecise.

Following work by Berk (1974) and Stock (1999), Perron and Ng (1996) have suggested a consistent autoregressive spectral density estimator which is less affected by the dependence on $\hat{\alpha}$. The estimator is based on estimation of the long autoregression (4.12):

$$\hat{\omega}_{AR}^2 = \frac{\tilde{\sigma}_k^2}{(1 - \sum_{j=1}^{k-1} \tilde{\gamma}_j)^2}, \tag{4.18}$$

where k is chosen according to the information criterion (4.14). The filtered estimator (4.18) decouples estimation of ω^2 from the estimation of α and is therefore unaffected by any bias that $\hat{\alpha}$ may otherwise have due the presence of serial correlation.

3.4 The *M* Class of Unit Root Tests

When comparing the size properties of the Phillips–Perron tests using the estimator $\hat{\omega}_{AR}^2$ and the tests applying the commonly used Bartlett kernel estimator of ω^2 with linearly decaying weights, Perron and Ng (1996) found significant size improvements in the most critical parameter space. Notwithstanding, size distortions can still be severe and remain so even if $\hat{\omega}^2_{AR}$ is replaced by the (unknown) true value ω^2. This suggests that the bias of $\hat{\alpha}$ is itself an important source of the size distortions. With this motivation Perron and Ng (1996) and Ng and Perron (2001) suggest further improvements of existing tests with much better size behaviour compared to other tests. Moreover, the tests can be designed in such a way that they satisfy desirable optimality criteria.

The trinity of M tests belongs to a class of tests which was originally suggested by Stock (1999). They build on the Z class of semiparametric tests but are modified in a particular way to deal with the bias of $\hat{\alpha}$ and exploit the fact that a series converges at different rates under the null and the alternative hypothesis. The first statistic can be formulated as

$$MZ_{\alpha} = Z_{\alpha} + \frac{T}{2}(\hat{\alpha} - 1)^2. \tag{4.19}$$

Since the least squares estimator $\hat{\alpha}$ is super-consistent under the null, that is $\hat{\alpha} - 1 = O_p(T^{-1})$, it follows that Z_{α} and MZ_{α} have the same asymptotic distribution. In particular, this implies that the limiting null distribution of MZ_{α} is the one given in (4.7). The next M statistic reads

$$MSB = \sqrt{\hat{\omega}_{AR}^{-2} T^{-2} \sum_{t=2}^{T} y_{t-1}^2}, \tag{4.20}$$

which is stochastically bounded under the null and $O_p(T^{-1})$ under the alternative; see also Sargan and Bhargava (1983) and Stock (1999). Note that $Z_{t_{\alpha}} = MSB \cdot Z_{\alpha}$, and hence a modified Phillips–Perron t-test can be constructed as

$$MZ_{t_{\alpha}} = Z_{t_{\alpha}} + \frac{1}{2}\left(\sqrt{\hat{\omega}_{AR}^{-2} \sum_{t=2}^{T} y_{t-1}^2}\right)(\hat{\alpha} - 1)^2. \tag{4.21}$$

The correction factors of MZ_{α} and $MZ_{t_{\alpha}}$ can be significant despite the super-consistency of $\hat{\alpha}$. Perron and Ng show that the M tests have lower size distortion relative to competing unit root tests. The success of the test is mainly due to the use of the sieve autoregressive spectral density estimator $\hat{\omega}^2_{AR}$ in (4.18) as an estimator of ω^2. Interestingly, the M tests also happen to be robust to, for example, measurement errors and additive outliers in the observed series; see Vogelsang (1999).

4 UNIT ROOT TESTING WITH DETERMINISTIC COMPONENTS BUT NO BREAKS

Since many macroeconomic time series are likely to have some kind of deterministic component, it is commonplace to apply unit root tests that yield inference which is invariant to the presence of a particular deterministic component. In practice, a constant term is always included in the model so the concern in most cases is that of whether to include or not to include a linear trend in the model. In many cases auxiliary information may be useful in ruling out a linear trend, for instance for interest rate data, real exchange rates, or inflation rates. However, for many other time series a linear trend is certainly a possibility such as GDP per capita, industrial production, and consumer prices (in logs).

In the previous section we excluded deterministic components from the analysis. Now we consider the model (4.1) in the special case where

$$f(t) = d_t'\mu. \tag{4.22}$$

In (4.22) d_t is a k-vector of deterministic terms, $(k \geq 1)$, and μ is a parameter vector of matching dimension. Hence the trend considered is linear-in-parameters. In particular, we will consider in this section the cases where $d_t = 1$ or $d_t = (1, t)'$ since these are the most relevant situations in applications. In principle, however, the analysis can even be extended to higher-order polynomial trends. Consequently we assume the possibility of a level effect or a level plus trend effect (without breaks) in the model. In fact, the linear-in-parameters specification also includes structural breaks of the additive outlier form discussed in section 2.1 when the break date is known. We return to this case later.

4.1 Linear-in-parameters Trends without Breaks

When allowing for deterministic components the augmented Dickey–Fuller (or Said–Dickey) regressions should take the alternative form

$$y_t = d_t'\mu + \alpha y_{t-1} + \sum_{j=1}^{k-1} \gamma_j \Delta y_{t-j} + v_{tk}. \tag{4.23}$$

In a similar fashion the Phillips–Perron Z tests allow inclusion of deterministic components in the auxiliary regressions, but alternatively one can also detrend the series prior to testing for a unit root. In all cases where the models are augmented by deterministic components the relevant distributions change accordingly; Brownian motion processes should be replaced with demeaned and detrended Brownian motions of the form

$$W^d(r) = W(r) - D(r)'\left(\int_0^1 D(s)D(s)'ds\right)^{-1}\left(\int_0^1 D(s)\,W(s)\,ds\right), \tag{4.24}$$

where $D(r) = 1$ when $d_t = 1$ and $D(r) = (1, r)'$ when $d_t = (1, t)'$. The relevant distributions of the ADF and Phillips–Perron tests are reported in Fuller (1996).

Concerning the M tests discussed in section 3.4, Ng and Perron (2001) suggest an alternative way to treat deterministic terms. They recommend to adopt the local *GLS* detrending/demeaning procedure initially developed by Elliott et al. (1996). This has the further advantage that tests are 'nearly' efficient in the sense that they nearly achieve the asymptotic power envelopes for unit root tests. For a time series $\{x_t\}_{t=1}^{T}$ of length T and any constant $\bar{c}$, define the vector $x^{\bar{c}} = (x_1, \Delta x_2 - \bar{c}T^{-1}x_1, \ldots, \Delta x_T - \bar{c}T^{-1}x_{T-1})'$. The so-called *GLS* detrended series $\{\tilde{y}_t\}$ reads

$$\tilde{y}_t = y_t - d_t'\tilde{\beta}, \quad \tilde{\beta} = \arg\min_{\beta}\,(y^{\bar{c}} - d^{\bar{c}\prime}\beta)'(y^{\bar{c}} - d^{\bar{c}\prime}\beta). \tag{4.25}$$

Elliott et al. (1996) suggested $\bar{c} = -7$ and $\bar{c} = -13.5$ for $d_t = 1$ and $d_t = (1, t)'$, respectively. These values of $\bar{c}$ correspond to the local alternatives against which the local asymptotic power envelope for 5 per cent tests equals 50 per cent. When the M tests are constructed by using GLS detrended data and the long-run variance estimator is $\hat{\omega}^2_{AR}$ defined in (4.18) together with the modified information criterion (4.14), the tests are denoted MZ^{GLS}_{α}, MSB^{GLS}, and MZ^{GLS}_{t}, respectively. Ng and Perron (2001) show that these tests have both excellent size and power when a moving average component is present in the error process.

The efficient tests suggested by Elliott et al. (1996) have become a benchmark reference in the literature. A class of these tests which we will later refer to is the GLS detrended or demeaned ADF tests, ADF^{GLS}_{t}. Basically these tests are constructed from the Dickey–Fuller t-statistic based on an augmented Dickey–Fuller regression without deterministic terms, like (4.12), where $\tilde{y}_t$ in (4.25) is used in place of y_t. The lag truncation again needs to be chosen via a consistent model selection procedure like the $MAIC$ criterion in (4.14). These tests can be shown to be near asymptotically efficient. The GLS detrended or demeaned ADF and M tests can thus be considered parametric and semi-nonparametric tests designed to be nearly efficient. Regarding the t-statistic-based tests ADF^{GLS}_{t} and MZ^{GLS}_{t}, the distribution for $d_t = 1$ is the Dickey–Fuller distribution for the case without deterministics (4.8) for which the critical values are reported in Fuller (1996). When $d_t = (1, t)'$ the relevant distribution can be found in Elliott et al. (1996) and Ng and Perron (2001) where the critical values for $\bar{c} = -13.5$ are also reported.

As a final note, Perron and Qu (2007) have shown that the selection of k using MAIC with GLS demeaned or detrended data may lead to power reversal problems, meaning that the power against non-local alternatives may be small. However, they propose a simple solution to this problem: first select k using the MAIC with OLS demeaned or detrended data and then use this optimal autoregressive order for the GLS detrended test.

4.2 Uncertainty about the Trend

The correct specification of deterministic components is of utmost importance to conduct consistent and efficient inference of the unit root hypothesis. Regarding the Dickey–Fuller class of tests one would always allow for a non-zero mean at least. However, it is not always obvious whether one should also allow for a linear trend. A general (conservative) advice is that if it is desirable to gain power against the trend-stationary alternative, then a trend should be included in the auxiliary regression (4.23), that is, $d_t = (1, t)'$. Note that under the null hypothesis the expression (4.5) shows that the coefficient of the trend regressor is zero in the model (4.23). However, if one does not include a linear time trend in (4.23) it will be impossible to have power against the trend-stationary alternative, that is asymptotic power will be trivial, leading to the conclusion that a unit root is present when the alternative is in fact true. In other words, the distribution of the unit root test statistic allowing for an intercept but no trend is not invariant to the actual value of the trend.

Although the use of a test statistic which is invariant to trends seems favourable in this light, it turns out that the costs in terms of power loss can be rather significant when there is no trend; see Harvey et al. (2009). In fact, this is a general finding for unit root tests where the decision of demeaning or detrending is an integral part of the testing procedure. Therefore, it would be of great value if some prior knowledge were available regarding the presence of a linear trend, but generally such information does not exist.

A possible strategy is to make pre-testing for a linear trend in the data an integral part of the unit root testing problem, that is the unit root test should be made contingent on the outcome of the trend pre-testing. However, this is complicated by the fact that we do not know whether the time series is I(1) or I(0) (this is what is being tested), and in the former case spurious evidence of trends may easily occur. A rather large body of literature exists on trend testing where test statistics are robust to the integration order of the data; a non-exhaustive list of references includes Phillips and Durlauf (1988), Vogelsang (1998), Bunzel and Vogelsang (2005), and Harvey et al. (2007). It turns out that testing for a trend prior to unit root testing generally is statistically inferior to alternative approaches.

Harvey et al. (2009) discuss a number of different approaches to dealing with the uncertainty about the trend. In particular, they consider a strategy which entails *pre-testing* of the trend specification, a strategy based on a *weighting scheme* of the Elliott et al. (1996) GLS demeaned or detrended ADF unit root tests, and finally a strategy based on a *union of rejections* of the GLS demeaned and detrended ADF tests. They find that the last procedure is better than the first two. It is also straightforward to apply since it does not require an explicit form of trend detection via an auxiliary statistic. Moreover, the strategy has practical relevance since it embodies what applied researchers already do, though in an implicit manner. Even though it is beyond the study of Harvey et al. (2009), our conjecture is that the strategy can be equally applied to the GLS filtered MZ_t^{GLS} tests.

The idea behind the union of rejections strategy is a simple decision rule stating that one should reject the $I(1)$ null if either $ADF_t^{GLS,1}$ (demeaning case) or $ADF_t^{GLS,(1,t)}$ (detrending case) rejects. The union of rejection test is defined as

$$UR = ADF_t^{GLS,1}\mathbf{I}(ADF_t^{GLS,1} < -1.94) + ADF_t^{GLS,(1,t)}\mathbf{I}(ADF_t^{GLS,1} \geq -1.94).$$

Here $\mathbf{I}(.)$ is the indicator function. If $UR = ADF_t^{GLS,1}$ the test rejects when $UR < -1.94$ and otherwise, if $UR = ADF_t^{GLS,(1,t)}$ a rejection is recorded when $UR < -2.85$. Alternatively, the $MZ_t^{GLS,1}$ and $MZ_t^{GLS,(1,t)}$ tests can be used in place of the ADF_t^{GLS} tests; the asymptotic distributions will be the same. Based on the asymptotic performance and finite sample analysis, Harvey et al. (2009) conclude that despite its simplicity the UR test offers very robust overall performance compared to competing strategies and is thus useful for practical applications.

5 THE INITIAL CONDITION

So far we have assumed that the initial condition $y_0 = 0$. This may seem to be a rather innocuous requirement since it can be shown that as long as $y_0 = o_p(T^{1/2})$ the impact of the initial observations is asymptotically negligible. For instance, this is the case when the initial condition is modelled as a constant nuisance parameter or as a random variable with a known distribution. However, problems occur under the alternative hypothesis and hence have implications for the power of unit root tests.

To clarify the argument, assume that y_t follows a stationary Gaussian AR(1) process with no deterministic components and let the autoregressive parameter be α. In this situation $y_0 \sim N(0,1/(1-\alpha^2))$. If we assume a local discrepancy from the unit root model, that is by defining $\alpha = 1 + c/T$ to be a parameter local to unity where $c < 0$, then it follows that $T^{-1/2}y_0 \sim N(0,-1/(2c))$. For the initial value to be asymptotically negligible we thus require this to be of a smaller order in probability than the remaining data points, which seems to be an odd property. Since stationarity is the reasonable alternative when testing for a unit root, this example shows that even for a rather simple model the impact of the initial observation is worth examining.

In practical situations it is hard to rule out small or large initial values a priori. As noted by Elliott and Müller (2006) there may be situations where one would not expect the initial condition to be exceptionally large or small relative to other observations. Müller and Elliott (2003) show that the influence of the initial condition can be rather severe in terms of power of unit root tests and the fact that what we observe is the initial observation, not the initial condition, see Elliott and Müller (2006). In practice this means that different conclusions can be reached with samples of the same data which only differ by the date at which the time series begins. Müller and Elliott (2003) derive a family of efficient tests which allow attaching different weighting schemes to the initial condition. They explore the extent to which existing unit root tests belong to this class of optimal tests. In particular they show that certain versions of the Dickey–Fuller class of tests are well approximated by members of efficient tests even though a complete removal of the initial observation influence cannot be obtained.

Harvey et al. (2009) undertake a very detailed study of strategies for dealing with uncertainty about the initial condition. The study embeds the set-up in the papers by Elliott and Müller as special cases. Interestingly, Harvey et al. find that when the initial condition is not negligible asymptotically, the ADF_t^{GLS} class of tests of Elliott et al. (1996) can perform extremely poorly in terms of asymptotic power which tends to zero as the magnitude of the initial value increases. This contrasts with the performance of the ADF_t^{GLS} tests when the initial condition is 'small'. However, the usual *ADF* tests using demeaned or detrended data from OLS regressions have power that increases with the initial observation, and hence are preferable when the initial value is 'large'. This finding made Harvey et al. suggest a union of rejections-based test similar to the approach adopted when there is uncertainty about the presence of a trend in the data. Their rule is to reject the unit root null if either the detrended (demeaned) ADF_t^{GLS} and the OLS detrended (demeaned) *ADF* test rejects. Their study shows that in terms of both asymptotic and finite sample behaviour the suggested procedure has properties similar to the optimal tests suggested by Elliott and Müller (2006). This means that despite its simplicity the procedure is extremely useful as a practical device for unit root testing.

In practical situations there will typically be uncertainty about both the initial condition and the deterministic components when testing for a unit root. In a recent paper Harvey et al. (2012) provide a joint treatment of these two major problems based on the approach suggested in their previous works.

6 UNIT ROOTS AND STRUCTURAL BREAKS

In section 2.1 it was argued that when structural breaks are present in the time series, they share features similar to unit root processes. This is most apparent when analysing the statistical properties of unit root tests in the presence of breaks. It follows from the work of Perron (1989, 1990) that in such circumstances inference can be strongly misleading. For instance, a deterministic level shift will cause $\hat{\alpha}$ from the augmented Dickey–Fuller regression to be biased towards 1 and a change in the trend slope makes the estimator tend to 1 in probability as the sample size increases. Thus, the DF test will indicate the presence of a unit root even when the time series is stationary around the deterministic break component. In fact, these problems concern most unit root tests including the tests belonging to the Phillips–Perron class of tests; see Montañés and Reyes (1998, 1999). A practical concern therefore is how to construct appropriate testing procedures for a unit root when breaks occur and power against the break alternative is wanted. In practice, what is important is to identify any major breaks in the data since these would otherwise give rise to the largest power loss of unit root tests. Minor breaks are more difficult to detect in finite samples than large ones, but then they only lead to minor power reductions. Hence the importance of focusing on 'large' breaks.

6.1 Unit Root Testing Accounting for a Break at Known Date

Additive outlier breaks

The way unit root tests should be formulated under the break hypothesis depends on the type of break considered. Also, it is crucial for the construction of tests that both the null and alternative is permitted in the model specification with the autoregressive root allowed to vary freely. Here we present variants of the Dickey–Fuller tests where the breaks allowed for are those of Perron (1989, 1990) with a known single break date. This corresponds to the models discussed in section 2.1.

First we consider breaks belonging to the additive outlier class. In this situation the testing procedure relies on two steps. In the first step the series y_t is detrended, and in the second step an appropriately formulated augmented Dickey–Fuller test with additional dummy regressors included is applied to the detrended series. For the additive outlier models $AO^a - AO^d$ the detrended series are obtained by regressing y_t on all the relevant deterministic terms that characterize the model. That is, the detrended series in the additive outlier model with breaks in both the level and the trend, (model AO^d), is constructed as

$$y_t = \tilde{\mu}_1 + \tilde{\beta}t + \tilde{\mu}^*{}_1 DU_t + \tilde{\beta}^* DT_t + \tilde{y}_t \tag{4.26}$$

where the parameters are estimated by the least squares method and $\tilde{y}_t$ is the detrended series. The detrended series for the other AO models are nested within the above detrending regression by appropriate exclusion of irrelevant regressors for the particular model considered. The unit root null is tested via a Dickey–Fuller t-test of $\tilde{y}_t$. For the additive outlier model (AO^c) (with DU_t absent from (4.26)) the Dickey–Fuller regression is like (4.12) applied to $\tilde{y}_t$. For the remaining AO models which all include DU_t as a deterministic component, the auxiliary regression takes the form

$$\tilde{y}_t = \hat{\alpha}\tilde{y}_{t-1} + \sum_{j=1}^{k-1} \hat{d}_j(1 - L)DU_{t-j} + \sum_{j=1}^{k-1} \hat{c}_j \Delta\tilde{y}_{t-j} + e_t \quad (t = k + 1,\ldots,T) \tag{4.27}$$

where k can be selected according to the criteria previously discussed. Note, however, that the selection of k using the *MAIC* criterion can be affected by the presence of breaks and hence other information criteria may by considered as well; see Ng and Perron (2001, Theorem 3). Observe that the inclusion of consecutive impulse dummy variables $(1 - L)DU_{t-j}$ is a temporary level shift patch that is caused by the general dynamics of the model. From this it can also be seen why this component is absent in the AO^c model. It can be shown that the null distribution of the Dickey–Fuller t-test from this regression will depend upon the actual timing of the break date T_1. If λ_1 determines the in-sample fraction of the full sample where the break occurs, that is $\lambda_1 = T_1/T$, then the distribution reads

$$t_{\alpha}(\lambda_1) \xrightarrow{d} \frac{\int_0^1 W^d(r,\lambda_1)\,dW(r)}{\sqrt{\int_0^1 W^d(r,\lambda_1)^2 dr}} \tag{4.28}$$

where $W^d(r,\lambda_1)$ is a process which is the residual function from a projection of $W(r)$ on the relevant continous time equivalent of the deterministic components used to detrend y_t, that is $1, I(r > r_1), r, I(r > \lambda_1)(r - \lambda_1)$ depending on the model. The relevant distributions (4.28) are tabulated in Perron (1989, 1990). Critical values for the AO^c case are reported in Perron and Vogelsang (1993).

Innovation outlier breaks

The innovation outlier models under both the null and alternative hypotheses can all be encompassed in the model

$$y_t = \mu + \theta DU_t + \beta t + \gamma DT_t + \delta(1 - L)DU_t + \alpha y_{t-1} + \sum_{j=1}^{k-1} c_i \Delta y_{t-j} + e_t. \tag{4.29}$$

The regressors t and DT_t are absent from the IO^a model. The IO^b model does not contain DT_t. Under the null hypothesis $\alpha = 1$ and for a components representation this would generally imply that many of the coefficients of the deterministic components would equal zero, even though these restrictions are typically not imposed when formulating tests. Note, however, that when there is in fact a level shift under the null, then $\delta \neq 0$, whereas under the alternative $\delta = 0$ and the remaining coefficients will typically be non-zero. By construction, the Dickey–Fuller t-statistic from this regression is invariant to the mean and trend as well as a possible break in them, provided the break date is correct. The distribution of $t_{\hat{\alpha}}(\lambda_1)$ is in this case identical to that given in (4.28).

The tests of Perron with known break dates have been generalized and extended in a number of directions. Saikkonen and Lütkepohl (2002) consider a class of the AO type of models that allow for a level shift whereas Lütkepohl et al. (2001) consider level shift models of the IO type. They propose a GLS-type detrending procedure and a unit root test statistic which has a limiting null distribution that does not depend upon the break date. Invariance with respect to the break date is a result of GLS detrending and in fact the relevant distribution is that of Elliott et al. (1996) for the case with a constant term included as a regressor in their model. This approach has been shown (see Lanne and Lütkepohl, 2002), to have better size and power than the test proposed by Perron (1990).

It is important to stress, however, that there are many ways of misspecifying break dates, and choosing an incorrect break model will affect inference negatively. The dates of possible breaks are usually unknown unless they refer to particular historical or economic events. Hence procedures for unit root testing when the break date is unknown are necessary. Such procedures will be discussed next.

6.2 Unit Root Testing Accounting for Break at Unknown Date

For the tests of Perron (1989, 1990) to be valid, the break date should be chosen independently of the given data, and it has been argued by Christiano (1992), for instance, that treating the break date as fixed in many cases is inappropriate. In practical situations the search and identification of breaks implies pretesting that will distort tests that use critical values for known break date unit root tests. Of course this criticism is only valid if in fact a search has been conducted to find the breaks. On the other hand, such a procedure, despite having a correct size, may result in power loss if the break date is given without pretesting. When the break date is unknown Banerjee et al. (1992) suggested to consider a sequence of rolling or recursive tests and then to use the minimal value of the unit root test and reject the null if the test value is sufficiently small. However, because such procedures will be based on sub-sampling, it is expected (and proven in simulations) that finite sample power loss will result.

Zivot and Andrews (1992) suggested a procedure which in some respects is closely linked to the methodology of Perron (1989) whereas in other respects it is somewhat different. Their model is of the IO type. For the IO^d model they consider the auxiliary regression model

$$y_t = \mu + \theta DU_t + \beta t + \gamma DT_t + \alpha y_{t-1} + \sum_{j=1}^{k-1} c_i \Delta y_{t-j} + e_t \tag{4.30}$$

which essentially is (4.29) leaving out $(1 - L)DU_t$ as a regressor. The test that $\alpha = 1$ is based on the minimal value of the associated t-ratio, $t_\alpha(\lambda_1)$, over all possible break dates in some range of the break fraction that is pre-specified, that is $[\varepsilon, 1 - \varepsilon]$. Typically one sets $\varepsilon = 0.15$ even though Perron (1997) has shown that trimming the break dates is unnecessary. The resulting test statistic has the distribution

$$t^*_\alpha = \inf_{\lambda_1 \in [\varepsilon, 1-\varepsilon]} t_\alpha(\lambda_1) \xrightarrow{d} \inf_{\lambda_1 \in [\varepsilon, 1-\varepsilon]} \frac{\int_0^1 W^d(r, \lambda_1)\, dW(r)}{\sqrt{\int_0^1 W^d(r, \lambda_1)^2 dr}} \tag{4.31}$$

with $W^d(r, \lambda_1)$ defined in section 6.1.

The analysis of Zivot and Andrews (1992) has been extended by Perron and Vogelsang (1992a) and Perron (1997) for the non-trending and trending cases, respectively. They consider both the IO and AO models based on the appropriately defined minimal value t-statistic of the null hypothesis. They also consider using the test statistics $t_\alpha(\lambda_1)$ for the case of known break date where the break date T_1 is determined by maximizing the numerically largest value of the t-statistic associated with the coefficient of the shift dummy DU_t (in case of a level shift) and DT_t (in case of slope change). Regarding the IO model they also consider using the regression (4.29) rather than (4.30) since this would be the right regression with a known break date.

A problem with the tests that build upon the procedure of Zivot and Andrews (1992) is that a break is not allowed under the null hypothesis of a unit root but only under the alternative. Hence the deterministic components are given an asymmetric treatment under the null and alternative hypotheses. This is a very undesirable feature, and Vogelsang and Perron (1998) showed that if a unit root exists and a break occurs in the trend function the Zivot and Andrews test will either diverge or will not be invariant to the break parameters. This caveat has motivated Kim and Perron (2009) to suggest a test procedure which allows a break in the trend function at unknown date under both the null and alternative hypotheses. The procedure has the advantage that when a break is present, the limiting distribution of the test is the same as when the break date is known, which increases the power whilst maintaining the correct size.

Basically, Kim and Perron (2009) consider the class of models initially suggested by Perron (1989) with the modification that a possible break date T_1 is assumed to be unknown. The models they address are the additive outlier models that allow for a non-zero trend slope AO^b, AO^c and AO^d, and the innovation outlier models associated with IO^b and IO^d, that is, the models implying a level shift, changing growth, or a combination of the two. The IO^c models are not considered since it is necessary to assume that no break occurs under the null hypothesis which contradicts the purpose of the analysis. When T_1 is an unknown parameter it is difficult in practice to estimate the models because the form of the regressors to be included is unknown. Notwithstanding, an estimate of the break date may be considered. The idea is to consider conditions under which the distribution of $t_\alpha(\hat{\lambda}_1)$ for the additive outlier case, for instance, is the same as the distribution of $t_\alpha(\lambda_1)$ given in (4.28); in other words, the limiting distribution of the Perron test is unaffected by whether the break is known in advance or has been estimated and hence the critical values for the known break date can be used. It turns out that such a result will depend upon the consistency rate of the estimate of the break fraction and also whether or not there is a non-zero break occurring in the trend slope of the model. Suppose that we have a consistent estimate $\hat{\lambda}_1 = \hat{T}_1/T$ of the break fraction such that

$$\hat{\lambda}_1 - \lambda_1 = O_p(T^{-a}) \tag{4.32}$$

for some $a \geq 0$. For the models AO^c, AO^d, and IO^d with a non-zero break the distribution of the unit root hypothesis for the estimated break date case is the same as the case of known break date when $\hat{\lambda}_1 - \lambda_1 = o_p(T^{-1/2})$. A consistent estimate of the break date is therefore not needed, but the break fraction needs to be consistently estimated at a rate larger than $\sqrt{T}$.

Kim and Perron (2009) consider a range of different estimators that can be used to estimate the break fraction with different rates of consistency. They also suggest an estimator using trimmed data whereby the rate of convergence can be increased. The reader is referred to Kim and Perron's (2009) paper for details.

So far we have assumed that a break in trend occurs under both the null and alternative hypotheses. When there is no such break the asymptotic results will no longer hold because the estimate of the break fraction will have a non-generate distribution on [0,1] under the null. Hence a pre-testing procedure is needed to check for a break, see for example Kim and Perron (2009), Perron and Yabu (2009a), Perron and Zhu (2005), and Harris et al. (2009). When the outcome of such a test indicates that there is no trend break, the usual Dickey–Fuller class of tests can be used.

In the models with a level shift, that is models AO^b and IO^b, Kim and Perron (2009) show that known break date asymptotics will apply as long as the break fraction is consistently estimated. On the other hand, if the break happens to be large in the sense that the magnitude of the break increases with the sample size, then a consistent estimate of the break fraction is not enough and a consistent estimate of the break date itself is needed.

Our review of unit root tests with unknown break dates is necessarily selective. Contributions not discussed here include Perron and Rodríguez (2003), Perron and Zhu (2005), and Harris et al. (2009) among others. Harris et al. (2009) suggest a procedure that is adequate when there is uncertainty about what breaks occur in the data. In so doing they generalize the approaches discussed in sections 4.2 and 5 where there is uncertainty about the trend or the initial condition.

There is also a large body of literature dealing with the possibility of *multiple* breaks in time series that are either known or unknown. We will not discuss these contributions but simply note that even though accounting for multiple breaks may give testing procedures with a controllable size, the cost will typically be a power loss that can often be rather significant; see Perron (2006) for a review.

7 UNIT ROOT TESTING AGAINST NON-LINEAR MODELS

This section is dedicated to recent developments in the field of unit root tests against stationary non-linear models. Amongst the non-linear models we consider (i) smooth transition autoregressive (STAR) models and (ii) threshold autoregressive (TAR) models. The model under validity of the null hypothesis is linear, which is in line with the majority of the literature. A notable exception is Yildirim et al. (2009) who suggest to consider non-linear models under both H_0 and H_1.

When smooth transition models are considered as an alternative to linear non-stationary models one often finds the Exponential STAR (ESTAR) model to be the most popular one; see, however, Eklund (2003) who considers the logistic version of the STAR model under the alternative. In particular, a three-regime ESTAR specification is used in most cases. The middle regime is non-stationary, while the two outer regimes are symmetric and mean-reverting. A prototypical model specification is given by

$$\Delta y_t = \rho y_{t-1}(1 - \exp(-\gamma y_{t-1}^2)) + \varepsilon_t, \gamma > 0, \rho < 0,$$

see Haggan and Ozaki (1981). Kapetanios et al. (2003) prove geometric ergodicity of such a model. A problem which is common to all linearity tests against smooth transition models (including TAR and Markov Switching (MS) models) is the Davies (1987) problem. Usually, at least one parameter is not identified under the null hypothesis; see Teräsvirta (1994). As unit root tests also take linearity as part of the null hypothesis, this problem becomes relevant here as well. The shape parameter γ is unidentified under

$H_0 : \rho = 0$. As shown by Luukkonen et al. (1988), this problem can be circumvented by using a Taylor approximation of the non-linear transition function $(1 - \exp(-\gamma y_{t-1}^2))$ around $\gamma = 0$. The resulting auxiliary test regression is very similar to a standard Dickey–Fuller test regression; see Kapetanios et al. (2003):

$$\Delta y_t = \delta y_{t-1}^3 + u_t.$$

The limiting distribution of the t-statistic for the null hypothesis of $\delta = 0$ is non-standard and depends on functionals of Brownian motions. The popularity of the test by Kapetanios et al. (2003) may stem from its ease of application. Regarding serially correlated errors, Kapetanios et al. (2003) suggest augmenting the test regression by lagged differences, while Rothe and Sibbertsen (2006) consider a Phillips–Perron-type adjustment. Another issue is tackled in Kruse (2011) who proposes a modification of the test by allowing for non-zero location parameter in the transition function. Park and Shintani (2005) and Kilic (2011) suggest dealing with the Davies problem in a different way. Rather than applying a Taylor approximation to the transition function, these authors consider an approach which is commonly used in the framework of TAR models, that is a grid search over the unidentified parameters; see also below.

Adjustment of deterministic terms can be handled in a similar way to the case of linear alternatives. Kapetanios and Shin (2008) suggest GLS adjustment, while Demetrescu and Kruse (2013) compare also recursive adjustment and the MAX procedure by Leybourne (1995) in a local-to-unity framework. The findings suggest that GLS adjustment performs best in the absence of a non-zero initial condition. Similar to the case of linear models, OLS adjustment proves to work best, when the initial condition is more pronounced. Another finding of Demetrescu and Kruse (2013) is that a combination of unit root tests against linear and non-linear alternatives would be a successful (union-of-rejections) strategy.

The ESTAR model specification discussed above can be viewed as restrictive in the sense that there is only a single point at which the process actually behaves like a random walk, namely at $y_{t-1} = 0$. In situations where it is more reasonable to assume that the middle regime contains multiple points, one may use a double logistic STAR model which is given by

$$\Delta y_t = \rho y_{t-1}(1 + \exp(-\gamma(y_{t-1} - c_1)(y_{t-1} - c_2))^{-1} + \varepsilon_t, \gamma > 0, \rho < 0,$$

see Jansen and Teräsvirta (1996). Kruse (2011) finds that unit root tests against ESTAR have substantial power against the double logistic STAR alternative although the power is somewhat lower than against ESTAR models. Such a result is due to similar Taylor approximations and suggests that a rejection of the null hypothesis does not necessarily contain information about the specific type of non-linear adjustment. This issue is further discussed in Kruse et al. (2012).

Another class of persistent non-linear models which permits a region of non-stationarity is the one of Self-Exciting Threshold Autoregressive (SETAR) models. Regarding unit root tests against three-regime SETAR models, important references are Bec et al. (2004), Park and Shintani (2005), Kapetanios and Shin (2006) and Bec et al. (2008). Similar to the case of smooth transition models, the middle regime often exhibits a unit root. Importantly, the transition variable is the lagged dependent variable y_{t-1} which is non-stationary under the null hypothesis. In Caner and Hansen (2001), stationary transition variables such as the first difference of the dependent variable are suggested. The TAR model with a unit root in the middle regime is given by (we abstract from intercepts here for simplicity)

$$\Delta y_t = \rho_1 y_{t-1} 1(y_{t-1} \leq -\lambda) + \rho_3 y_{t-1} 1(y_{t-1} \geq \lambda) + \varepsilon_t.$$

The non-stationary middle regime is defined by $\Delta y_t = \varepsilon_t$ for $|y_{t-1}| < \lambda$. Stationarity and mixing properties of a more general specification of the TAR model are provided in Bec et al. (2004). Similar to the STAR model, the parameter λ is not identified under the null hypothesis of a linear unit root process. In order to tackle this problem, sup-type Wald statistics can be considered:

$$\sup W \equiv \sup_{\lambda \in [\underline{\lambda}_T, \overline{\lambda}_T]} W_T(\lambda)$$

A nuisance parameter-free limiting distribution of the $\sup LM$ statistic can be achieved by choosing the interval $[\underline{\lambda}_T, \overline{\lambda}_T]$ appropriately. The treatment of the parameter space for λ distinguishes most of the articles. Seo (2008) for example suggests a test based on a compact parameter space similar to Kapetanios and Shin (2006). The test allows for a general dependence structure in the errors and uses the residual-block bootstrap procedure (see Paparoditis and Politis 2003) to calculate asymptotic p-values. Comparative studies are, amongst others, Maki (2009) and Choi and Moh (2007).

8 UNIT ROOTS AND OTHER SPECIAL FEATURES OF THE DATA

We have considered unit root testing for a range of different situations that may characterize economic time series processes. Here we will briefly describe some other features of the data that are often important for unit root testing. This non-exhaustible review will include issues related to higher order integrated processes, the choice of an appropriate functional form, the presence of heteroscedasticity, and unit root testing when economic variables by their construction are bounded upwards, downwards, or both.

8.1 I(2) Processes

So far we have addressed the unit root hypothesis implying that the time series of interest is I(1) under the null hypothesis. There has been some focus in the literature on time series processes with double unit roots, so-called I(2) processes. As seen from equation (4.2), an I(1) process is driven by a stochastic trend component of the form $\sum_{j=1}^{t} \varepsilon_j$. If, on the other hand, u_t in (4.1) is I(2), then $(1 - L)^2 u_t = C(L)\varepsilon_t$, and the series can be shown to include a stochastic trend component of the form

$$\sum_{k=1}^{t} \sum_{j=1}^{k} \varepsilon_j = t\varepsilon_1 + (t-1)\varepsilon_2 + \ldots + 3\varepsilon_{t-2} + 2\varepsilon_{t-1} + \varepsilon_t. \tag{4.33}$$

As seen, a shock to the process will have an impact that tends to increase over time. This may seem to be an odd feature but it is implied by the fact that (if the series is log transformed) then shocks to the growth rates are I(1), and hence will persist, and this will further amplify the effect on the level of the series when cumulated. In practice, testing for I(2) is often conducted by testing for whether the first differences of the series have a unit root under the null hypothesis. This can be tested using the range of tests available for the I(1) case. See for instance Haldrup (1998) for a review on the statistical analysis of I(2) processes.

8.2 Functional Form

From practical experience researchers have learned that unit root testing is often sensitive to non-linear transformations of the data. For instance, variables expressed in logarithms are sometimes found to be stationary, whereas the same variables in levels are found to be non-stationary. Granger and Hallman (1991) addressed the issue of appropriate non-linear transformations of the data and developed a test for unit roots that is invariant to monotone transformations of the data such as $y_t^2, y_t^3, |y_t|, sgn(y_t), \sin(y_t)$, and $\exp(y_t)$. Franses and McAleer (1998) developed a test of non-linear transformation to assess the adequacy of unit root tests of the augmented Dickey–Fuller type. They considered the following generalized augmented Dickey–Fuller regression (ignoring deterministic components) of a possibly unknown transformation of y_t

$$y_t(\delta) = \alpha y_{t-1}(\delta) + \sum_{j=1}^{k-1} \gamma_j \Delta y_{t-j}(\delta) + v_{tk} \qquad (t = k+1, \ldots, T) \tag{4.34}$$

where $y_t(\delta)$ denotes the transformation of Box and Cox (1964) given by

$$\begin{aligned} y_t(\delta) &= (y_t^\delta - 1)/\delta \qquad & \delta \neq 0, y_t \geq 0 \\ &= \log y_t(\delta) & \delta = 0, y_t > 0. \end{aligned} \tag{4.35}$$

For this model Franses and McAleer (1998) considered the null hypothesis of a unit root for some assumed value of the Box–Cox parameter δ, but without estimating the parameter directly. Based on a variable addition test they showed how the adequacy of the transformation could be tested. Fukuda (2006) suggested a procedure based on information criteria to jointly decide on the unit root hypothesis and the transformation parameter.

8.3 Bounded Time Series

Many time series in economics and finance are bounded by construction or are subject to policy control. For instance the unemployment rate and budget shares are variables bounded between zero and 1, and some variables, exchange rates for instance, may be subject to market intervention within a target zone. Conventional unit root tests will be seriously affected in this situation. Cavaliere (2005) showed that the limiting distributions in this case will depend upon nuisance parameters that reflect the position of the bounds. The tighter the bounds, the more will the distribution be shifted towards the left and thus bias the standard tests towards stationarity. Only when the bounds are sufficiently far away will conventional unit root tests behave according to standard asymptotic theory. Cavaliere and Xu (2013) have recently suggested a testing procedure for augmented Dickey–Fuller tests and the autocorrelation-robust M tests of Perron and Ng (1996) and Ng and Perron (2001), even though in principle the procedure can be used for any commonly used test.

The processes considered by Cavaliere and Xu (2013) behave like random walks but are bounded above, below or both; see also Granger (2010). The time series x_t is assumed to have (fixed) bounds at $\underline{b}, \overline{b}, (\underline{b} < \overline{b})$, and is a stochastic process $x_t \in [\underline{b}, \overline{b}]$ almost surely for all t. This means that the increments Δx_t necessarily have to lie in the interval $[\underline{b} - x_{t-1}, \overline{b} - x_{t-1}]$. Rewrite the process in the following form

$$x_t = \mu + y_t$$

$$y_t = \alpha y_{t-1} + u_t, \alpha = 1 \tag{4.36}$$

where u_t is further decomposed as

$$u_t = \varepsilon_t + \underline{\xi}_t - \overline{\xi}_t. \tag{4.37}$$

Furthermore, ε_t is a weakly dependent zero-mean unbounded process and $\underline{\xi}_t, \overline{\xi}_t$ are non-negative processes satisfying

$$\begin{aligned} \underline{\xi}_t > 0 \quad & \text{for } y_{t-1} + \varepsilon_t < \underline{b} - \theta \\ \overline{\xi}_t > 0 \quad & \text{for } y_{t-1} + \varepsilon_t > \overline{b} - \theta. \end{aligned} \tag{4.38}$$

A bounded I(1) process x_t will revert because of the bounds. When it is away from the bounds it behaves like a unit root process. When being close to the bounds the presence of the terms $\underline{\xi}_t$ and $\overline{\xi}_t$ will force x_t to lie between $\underline{b}$ and $\overline{b}$. In the stochastic control literature, see Harrison (1985), the stochastic terms $\underline{\xi}_t$ and $\overline{\xi}_t$ are referred to as 'regulators'.

To derive the appropriate asymptotic distributions of the augmented Dickey–Fuller test and the M tests defined in sections 3.2 and 3.4, Cavaliere and Xu (2013) relate the position of the bounds $\underline{b}$ and $\overline{b}$ (relative to the location parameter θ) to the sample size T as $(\underline{b} - \theta)/(\lambda T^{1/2}) = \underline{c} + o(1)$ and $(\overline{b} - \theta)/(\lambda T^{1/2}) = \overline{c} + o(1)$ where $\underline{c} \leq 0 \leq \overline{c}, \underline{c} \neq \overline{c}$. It occurs that the parameters c and $\overline{c}$ will appear as nuisance parameters in the relevant asymptotic distributions expressed in terms of a regulated Brownian motion $W(r; \underline{c}, \overline{c})$; see Nicolau (2002). When the bounds are one-sided $\underline{c} = -\infty$ or $\overline{c} = \infty$ and when there are no bounds $W(r; \underline{c}, \overline{c}) \rightarrow W(r)$ for $\underline{c} \rightarrow -\infty$ and $\overline{c} \rightarrow \infty$. Hence the usual bounds-free unit root distributions will apply as a special case.

The lesson to be learned from the analysis is that standard unit root inference is affected in the presence of bounds. If the null hypothesis is rejected on the basis of standard critical values, it is not possible to assess whether this is caused by the absence of a unit root or by the presence of the bounds. On the other hand, the non-rejection of the unit root hypothesis is very strong evidence for the null hypothesis under these circumstances. To provide valid statistical inference, Cavaliere and Xu (2013) suggest a testing procedure based on first estimating the nuisance parameters $\underline{c}$ and $\overline{c}$. Based on these estimates, they suggest simulating the correct asymptotic null distribution from which the asymptotic p-value of the unit root test can be inferred. In estimating the nuisance parameters $\underline{c}$ and $\overline{c}$ they define the consistent estimators

$$\hat{\underline{c}} = \frac{\underline{b} - x_0}{\hat{\omega}_{AR}^2 T^{1/2}}, \hat{\overline{c}} = \frac{\overline{b} - x_0}{\hat{\omega}_{AR}^2 T^{1/2}} \tag{4.39}$$

where $\underline{b}$ and $\overline{b}$ are assumed known in advance and $\hat{\omega}_{AR}^2$ is defined in (4.18). We will refer to Cavaliere and Xu (2013) for details about the algorithm that can be used to simulate the Monte Carlo p-values of the tests. In their paper they also suggest how heteroscedastic shocks can be accounted for. When the bounds $\underline{b}$ and $\overline{b}$ are unknown there are various ways to proceed. For instance the bounds can sometimes be inferred from historical observations or one can conduct a more formal (conservative) testing procedure by taking the minimum of the simulation-based p-values over a grid of admissible bound locations. In a different context, Lundbergh and Teräsvirta (2006) suggest a procedure for estimating implicit bounds, such as in unofficial exchange rate target zones inside announced ones, should they exist.

8.4 Non-constant Volatility

It is generally believed that (mild) heteroscedasticity is a minor issue in unit root testing because the tests allow for heterogenous mixing errors, see for example Kim and Schmidt (1993). This applies for the range of tests based on the Phillips–Perron type of unit root tests including the M class of tests, mainly because they are derived in a non-parameteric setting. But actually the parametric counterparts like the augmented (Said) Dickey–Fuller tests *are* robust to some form of heteroscedasticity. Notwithstanding, when volatility is non-stationary the standard unit root results no longer apply. Non-stationary volatility may occur for instance when there is a single or multiple permanent breaks in the volatility process, a property that seems to characterize a wide range of financial time series in particular. Cavaliere (2004) provides a general framework for investigating the effects of permanent changes in volatility on unit root tests.

Some attempts have been made in the literature to alleviate the problems with non-stationary volatility. Boswijk (2001) for instance has proposed a unit root test for the case where volatility is following a nearly integrated GARCH(1,1) process. Kim et al. (2002) consider the specific case of a single abrupt change in variance and suggest a procedure where the breakpoint together with the pre- and post-break variances are first estimated. These are then employed in modified versions of the Phillips–Perron unit root tests. The assumption of a single abrupt change in volatility is not, however, consistent with much empirical evidence, which seems to indicate that volatility changes smoothly and that multiple changes in volatility are common when the time series are sufficiently long; see for example van Dijk et al. (2002) and Amado and Teräsvirta (2012).

Cavaliere and Taylor (2007) propose a methodology that accommodates a fairly general class of volatility change processes. Rather than assuming a specific parametric model for the volatility dynamics they only require that the variance is bounded and implies a countable number of jumps and hence allow both smooth volatility changes and multiple volatility shifts. Based on a consistent estimate of the so-called variance profile they propose a numerical solution to the inference problem by Monte Carlo simulation to obtain the approximate quantiles from the asymptotic distribution of the *M* class of unit root tests under the null. Their approach can be applied to any of the commonly used unit root tests. We refer to the paper by Cavaliere and Taylor (2007) for details about the numerical procedure. Finally, bootstrap tests for a unit root under non-stationary volatility have been suggested by Chang and Park (2003), Park (2003), Cavaliere and Taylor (2007, 2008, 2009), among others.

9 EMPIRICAL ILLUSTRATION

To illustrate different approaches and methodologies discussed in this survey we conduct a small empirical analysis using four macroeconomic time series and a selected number of the tests presented. The time series are the monthly secondary market rate of the 3-month US Treasury bill (T-bill, henceforth) from 1938:1 to 2011:11 (935 observations), the monthly US civilian unemployment rate from 1948:1 to 2011:11 (767 observations), the monthly US CPI inflation from 1947:2 to 2012:1 (780 observations) and the quarterly log transformed US real GDP from 1947:1 to 2011:7 (259 observations). The series are depicted in Figure 4.1.

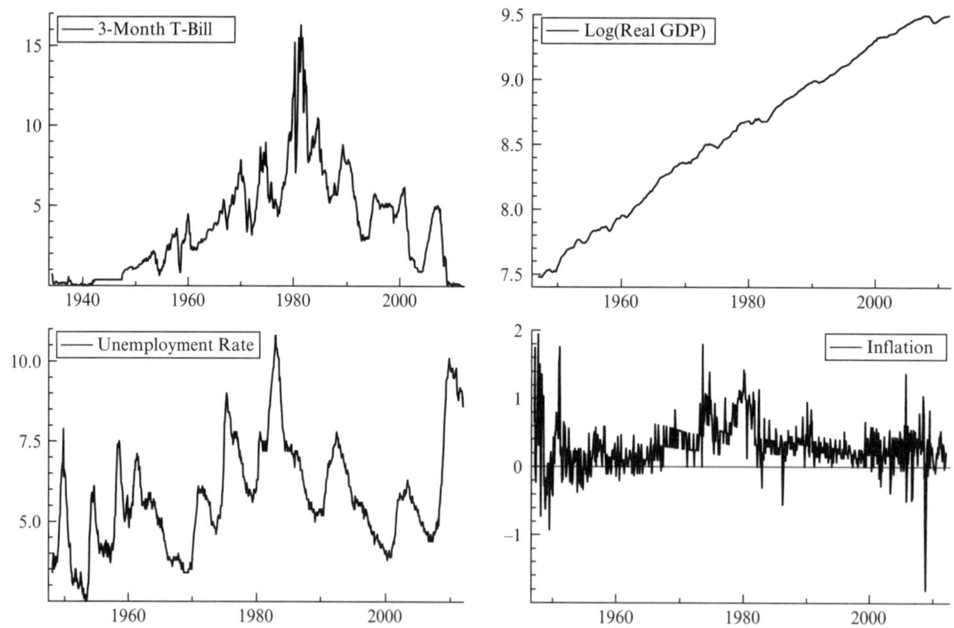

Note: The 3-month US T-bill rate (upper left), the log-transformed US real GDP (upper right), the US unemployment rate (lower left) and the US inflation (lower right).

Source: Federal Reserve Economic Data, Federal Reserve Bank of St Louis, http://research.stlouisfed.org/fred2/.

Figure 4.1 Four macroeconomic time series

Table 4.1 Full sample unit root testing

	3-Month T-bill			Log Real GDP		
	$d_t = 1$	$d_t = (1, t)'$	*UR*	$d_t = 1$	$d_t = (1, t)'$	*UR*
ADF	−2.06	−1.77	−1.77	−1.93	−1.45	−1.45
ADF^{GLS}	−1.43	−1.86	−1.86	3.52	−1.05	−1.05
Z_{t_α}	−2.02	−2.01	−2.01	−0.17	−1.71	−1.71
$Z_{t_\alpha}^{GLS}$	−1.73*	−2.10	−1.73*	−0.19	−1.59	−1.59
MZ_{t_α}	−2.01	−2.01	−2.01	−0.17	−1.71	−1.71
$MZ_{t_\alpha}^{GLS}$	−1.73*	−2.09	−1.73*	−0.19	−1.59	−1.59
	Unemployment Rate			Inflation		
	$d_t = 1$	$d_t = (1, t)'$	*UR*	$d_t = 1$	$d_t = (1, t)'$	*UR*
ADF	−2.33	−2.56	−2.33	−11.4***	−11.4***	−11.4***
ADF^{GLS}	−1.06	−2.43	−2.43	−2.61***	−12.5***	−2.61***
Z_{t_α}	−2.55	−2.97	−2.97	−16.31***	−16.24***	−16.31***
$Z_{t_\alpha}^{GLS}$	−1.55	−2.86*	−2.86*	−9.06***	−23.75***	−9.06***
MZ_{t_α}	−2.55	−2.97	−2.97	−13.72***	−13.64***	−13.72***
$MZ_{t_\alpha}^{GLS}$	−1.55	−2.86*	−2.86*	−4.45***	−22.68***	−4.45***

Notes: Unit root testing of four macroeconomic time series. (*), (**) and (***) denotes significance at a 10%, 5% and 1% level, respectively, based on the critical values from Fuller (1996) for the standard case and from Ng and Perron (2001) for the GLS detrended case.

The individual characteristics of the series look fundamentally different. The log real GDP series has a practically linear deterministic trend, the unemployment rate is a bounded variable, and the inflation rate series contains sharp fluctuations. Estimation of ARMA models (not reported) show that the model for the inflation rate series in particular has a strong negative moving average component, thus suggesting that standard ADF and Z tests may suffer from severe size distortions when applied to this series; see for example Perron and Ng (1996).

We implement six different tests using both $d_t = 1$ and $d_t = (1,t)'$ as deterministic components. These are the trinity of GLS demeaned/detrended tests ADF_t^{GLS}, $Z_{t_\alpha}^{GLS}$, and $MZ_{t_\alpha}^{GLS}$ defined in section 3 where the lag length k is selected using the MAIC with OLS demeaned/detrended data to avoid power reversal problems; see Perron and Qu (2007). The standard ADF_t, Z_{t_α} and MZ_{t_α} tests are based on the long autoregression in (4.23) using the same k. While Harvey et al. (2009) only consider a union of rejection (UR) strategies for ADF_t^{GLS},our conjecture is that similar procedures may be defined for the five remaining tests and results from these are reported as well. The results of full sample unit root tests are presented in Table 4.1

Several interesting observations can be made from results in Table 4.1. First, $\alpha = 1$ is clearly rejected for inflation, but the relative (negative) magnitude of the test statistics show the distortions due to a negative moving average component on standard ADF and Z tests. Second, it seems that the correction factor used in the construction of the MZ tests is often negligible, which may well be the result of large sample sizes and strongly consistent estimates of the unit root in the test regressions: often $\hat{\alpha} \approx 0.99$. Finally, we are likely to see an increase in the asymptotic power of the GLS demeaning/detrending procedure applied to the 3-month T-bill and unemployment series since only $Z_{t_\alpha}^{GLS}$ and $MZ_{t_\alpha}^{GLS}$ reject $\alpha = 1$ at the 10 per cent level. Before dismissing a unit root for unemployment it should be noted, however, that the critical values must be altered to reflect the bounds of $\underline{b} = 0$ and $\overline{b} = 100$. Because critical values are becoming numerically larger in this case, a consequence of this is that the unit root hypothesis cannot be rejected at 1 per cent and 5 per cent levels of significance.

9.1 Unit Root Testing in the Recent Financial Crisis

Figure 4.1 shows that we may have to be concerned with several structural breaks in each series. Nevertheless, for ease of exposition, we shall only treat the sample starting from 1990:1, and we assume that there is a known break in the series caused by the most recent financial crisis. We do not analyse inflation, since $\alpha = 1$ is clearly rejected even in the presence of structural breaks. For both the 3-month T-bill and unemployment series, we let T_1 correspond to 2008:9, such that $\lambda_1 \approx 0.85$. Similarly, for the real GDP T_1 corresponds to 2009:1, implying $\lambda_1 \approx 0.89$, since the decline in output seems to occur later corresponding to one quarter.

To emphasize the importance of correcting for a structural break in mean, we consider standard ADF, Z and MZ tests based on the AO^a and AO^b models. The ADF_t test is based on the auxiliary regression (4.27), whereas the Z_t and MZ_t tests, following Perron (1990) and Perron and Vogelsang (1992b), are based on the estimate $\hat{\alpha}$ from

$$\tilde{y}_t = \hat{\alpha}\tilde{y}_{t-1} + \hat{d}(1 - L)DU_t + \varepsilon_t,$$

Where (4.27) is used to estimate the long-run variance $\hat{\omega}_{AR}^2$. We use AIC to select k, since, as argued in section 6.1, it is unclear what the implications of structural breaks are on the MAIC criterion in finite samples. Table 4.2 shows the three unit root tests both with and without accounting for a structural break.

It follows from Table 4.2 that without accounting for a structural break caused by the financial crisis, we accept $\alpha = 1$ for all series. However, by allowing for the structural break, we are able to reject $\alpha = 1$ for the 3-month T-bill series, while the values of the test statistics for both the real GDP and unemployment are fairly close to the critical values at a 10 per cent level. While this small analysis is conducted under the simplifying and strong assumption of a single known break, it illustrates the importance of accounting for structural breaks when statistical properties of persistent and trending time series are considered.

10 CONCLUSION

This chapter has provided a selective review of the literature on testing for a unit root. As seen, the field has grown in numerous different directions. New tests have been developed over time to improve power and size properties of previous tests, and testing methodologies and procedures have been extended and modified to allow for an increasing complexity of models with breaks and non-linearities.

Table 4.2 Subsample unit root testing both with and without structural breaks

No Breaks	3-Month T-bill			Log Real GDP			Unemployment Rate		
	$d_t = 1$	$d_t = (1, t)'$	*UR*	$d_t = 1$	$d_t = (1, t)'$	*UR*	$d_t = 1$	$d_t = (1, t)'$	*UR*
ADF	−1.44	−1.79	−1.79	–	−0.453	−0.453	−0.783	−0.955	−0.955
Z_{t_α}	−0.969	−1.88	−1.88	–	−1.43	−1.43	−1.26	−1.47	−1.47
MZ_{t_α}	−0.969	−1.87	−1.87	–	−1.42	−1.42	−1.26	−1.46	−1.46
Breaks	**3-Month T-bill**			**Log Real GDP**			**Unemployment Rate**		
	$d_t = 1$	$d_t = (1, t)'$	*UR*	$d_t = 1$	$d_t = (1, t)'$	*UR*	$d_t = 1$	$d_t = (1, t)'$	*UR*
ADF	−2.96*	−3.21	−2.96*	–	−3.20	−3.20	−1.40	−3.25	−3.25
Z_{t_α}	−3.05*	−4.13**	−4.13**	–	−3.22	−3.22	−2.24	−3.16	−3.16
MZ_{t_α}	−3.04*	−4.13**	−4.13**	–	−3.15	−3.15	−2.22	−3.16	−3.16

Notes: Unit root testing of three macroeconomic time series both with and without structural breaks. (*), (**) and (***) denote significance at a 10%, 5% and 1% level, respectively, based on the critical values from Fuller (1996, Appendix 10.A) for the standard case and from Perron (1989, 1990) for the cases with breaks.

Unfortunately, there are many topics that we had to exclude from the exposition even though these areas deserve equal mention. For instance, the use of bootstrap methods for unit root testing in situations where standard assumptions are likely to fail has become a rapidly developing research area during the past decade or so and there still seems to be a potential for new results in this area; see for example Cavaliere and Taylor (2007, 2008, 2009), Chang and Park (2003), Paparoditis and Politis (2003), and Park (2003) among others.

Another topic concerns testing when the hypothesis being tested is reversed, that is the null of stationarity is tested against the alternative of a unit root; see for example Kwiatkowski et al. (1992).

In the review of tests for a unit root in the presence of structural breaks it has either been assumed that the break date was known or could be estimated consistently at a sufficiently fast rate. However, this is not always the case and testing for (possibly multiple) breaks in a time series is a separate research area which has attracted a lot of attention. See for instance Perron (2006) for a review, and Kejriwal and Perron (2010) and Perron and Yabu (2009a, 2009b) for recent contributions.

Finally, we would like to mention the fractional unit root literature where the order of differencing is fractional rather than being integer valued. Fractionally integrated processes have autocorrelations that die out at a slow hyperbolic rate and hence are often referred to as being long memory. Baillie (1996) provided an early review of this literature, but since then the field has grown tremendously. Velasco (2006) provides a recent review of semiparametric estimators of long memory models. More recently there has been an increased focus on how fractional integration and long memory interfere with persistent components caused by structural breaks or non-linearities; see for example Diebold and Inoue (2001), Perron and Qu (2010) and Varneskov and Perron (2011). Hence the known problems of discriminating a unit root from structural break models equally apply to fractional long memory models.

NOTE

* The authors acknowledge support from the Center for Research in Econometric Analysis of Time Series, CREATES, funded by the Danish National Research Foundation.

REFERENCES

Agiakloglou, C. and P. Newbold (1992), 'Empirical evidence on Dickey–Fuller type tests', *Journal of Time Series Analysis*, **13**, 471–83.

Amado, C. and T. Teräsvirta (2012), 'Modelling changes in the unconditional variance of long stock return series', Aarhus University, CREATES Research Paper 2012-07.

Andrews, D.W.K. (1991), 'Heteroscedasticity and autocorrelation consistent covariance matrix estimation', *Econometrica*, **59**, 817–58.

Baillie, R.T. (1996), 'Long memory processes and fractional integration in econometrics', *Journal of Econometrics*, **59**, 5–59.

Banerjee, A., R.L. Lumsdaine and J.H. Stock (1992), 'Recursive and sequential tests of the unit root and trend-break hypotheses: theory and international evidence', *Journal of Business and Economic Statistics*, **10**, 271–87.

Bec, F., M. Ben Salem and M. Carrasco (2004), 'Tests for unit root versus threshold specification with an application to the purchasing power parity relationship', *Journal of Business and Economic Statistics*, **22**, 382–95.

Bec, F., A. Guay and E. Guerre (2008), 'Adaptive consistent unit root tests based on autoregressive threshold model', *Journal of Econometrics*, **142**, 94–133.

Berk, K.N. (1974), 'Consistent autoregressive spectral estimates', *Annals of Statistics*, **2**, 489–502.

Beveridge, S. and C.R. Nelson (1981), 'A new approach to decomposition of economic time series into permanent and transitory components with particular attention to measurement of the "Business Cycle"', *Journal of Monetary Economics*, **7**, 151–74.

Boswijk, H.P. (2001), 'Testing for a unit root with near-integrated volatility', Tinbergen Institute Discussion Paper 01-077/4.

Box, G.E.P. and D.R. Cox (1964), 'An analysis of transformations', *Journal of the Royal Statistical Society*, series B, **26**, 211–52.

Box, G.E.P. and G.C. Tiao (1975), 'Intervention analysis with applications to economic and environmental problems', *Journal of American Statistical Association*, **70**, 70–9.

Bunzel, H. and T.J. Vogelsang (2005), 'Powerful trend function tests that are robust to strong serial correlation with an application to the Prebisch–Singer hypothesis', *Journal of Business and Economic Statistics*, **23**, 381–94.

Caner, M. and B. Hansen (2001), 'Threshold autoregression with a unit root', *Econometrica*, **69**, 1555–96.

Cavaliere, G. (2004), 'Unit root tests under time-varying variances', *Econometric Reviews*, **23**, 259–92.

Cavaliere, G. (2005), 'Limited time series with a unit root', *Econometric Theory*, **21**, 907–45.

Cavaliere, G. and A.M.R. Taylor (2007), 'Testing for unit roots in time series models with non-stationary volatility', *Journal of Econometrics*, **140**, 919–47.

Cavaliere, G. and A.M.R. Taylor (2008), 'Bootstrap unit root tests for time series models with non-stationary volatility', *Econometric Theory*, **24**, 43–71.

Cavaliere, G. and A.M.R. Taylor (2009), 'Bootstrap M unit root tests', *Econometric Reviews*, **28**, 393–421.

Cavaliere, G. and F. Xu (2013), 'Testing for unit roots in bounded time series', *Journal of Econometrics*, forthcoming.

Chang, Y. and J. Park (2002), 'On the asymptotics of ADF tests for unit roots', *Econometric Reviews*, **21**, 431–48.

Chang, Y. and J. Park (2003), 'A sieve bootstrap for the test of a unit root', *Journal of Time Series Analysis*, **24,** 379–400.

Choi, C.Y. and Y.K. Moh (2007), 'How useful are tests for unit root in distinguishing unit root processes from stationary but non-linear processes?', *Econometrics Journal*, **10**, 82–112.

Christiano, L.J. (1992), 'Searching for breaks in GNP', *Journal of Business and Economic Statistics*, **10**, 237–50.

Davies, R.B. (1987), 'Hypothesis testing when a nuisance parameter is present under the alternative', *Biometrika*, **74**, 33–43.

Demetrescu, M. and R. Kruse (2013), 'The power of unit root tests against nonlinear local alternatives', *Journal of Time Series Analysis*, **34**, 40–61.

Dickey, D.A. and W.A. Fuller (1979), 'Distribution of the estimators for autoregressive time series with a unit root', *Journal of American Statistical Association*, **74**, 427–31.
Diebold, F. and A. Inoue (2001), 'Long memory and regime switching', *Journal of Econometrics*, **105,** 131–59.
Eklund, B. (2003), 'Testing the unit root hypothesis against the logistic smooth transition autoregressive model', Stockholm School of Economics, SSE/EFI Working Paper Series in Economics and Finance, No. 546.
Elliott, G. and U. Müller (2006), 'Minimizing the impact of the initial condition on testing for unit roots', *Journal of Econometrics*, **135**, 285–310.
Elliott, G., T.J. Rothenberg and J.H. Stock (1996), 'Efficient tests for an autoregressive unit root', *Econometrica*, **64**, 813–36.
Engle, R.F. and C.W.J. Granger (1987), 'Co-integration and error correction: representation, estimation, and testing', *Econometrica*, **55**, 251–76.
Engle, R.F. and A.D. Smith (1999), 'Stochastic permanent breaks', *Review of Economics and Statistics*, **81,** 553–74.
Franses, P.H. and M. McAleer (1998), 'Testing for unit roots and non-linear transformations', *Journal of Time Series Analysis*, **19**, 147–64.
Fukuda, K. (2006), 'Time series forecast jointly allowing the unit-root detection and the Box–Cox transformation', *Communications in Statistics, Simulation and Computation*, **35**, 419–27.
Fuller, W.A. (1996), *Introduction to Statistical Time Series*, 2nd edn, New York: Wiley.
González, A. and T. Teräsvirta (2008), 'Modelling autoregressive processes with a shifting mean', *Studies in Nonlinear Dynamics and Econometrics*, **12**, Article 1.
Granger, C.W.J. (1981), 'Some properties of time series data and their use in econometric model specification', *Journal of Econometrics*, **16**, 121–30.
Granger, C.W.J. (1983), 'Co-integrated variables and error correcting models', UCSD Discussion Paper 1983-13.
Granger, C.W.J. (2010), 'Some thoughts on the development of cointegration', *Journal of Econometrics*, **158**, 3–6.
Granger, C.W.J. and J. Hallman (1991), 'Nonlinear transformations of integrated time series', *Journal of Time Series Analysis*, **12**, 207–24.
Granger, C.W.J. and N. Hyung (2004), 'Occasional structural breaks and long memory with an application to S&P 500 absolute stock returns ', *Journal of Empirical Finance*, **11**, 399–421.
Granger, C.W.J. and T. Teräsvirta (1999), 'A simple nonlinear time series model with misleading linear properties', *Economics Letters*, **62**, 161–5.
Haggan, V. and T. Ozaki (1981), 'Modelling nonlinear random vibrations using an amplitude-dependent autoregressive time series model', *Biometrika*, **68**, 189–96.
Haldrup, N. (1998), 'An econometric analysis of I(2) variables', *Journal of Economic Surveys*, **12(5)**, 595–650.
Haldrup, N. and M. Jansson (2006), 'Improving power and size in unit root testing', Chapter 7 in T.C. Mills and K. Patterson (eds), *Palgrave Handbooks of Econometrics: Vol. 1 Econometric Theory*, Basingstoke: Palgrave Macmillan.
Hamilton, J. (1989), 'A new approach to the economic analysis of nonstationary time series and the business cycle', *Econometrica*, **57**, 357–84.
Harris, D., D.I. Harvey, S.J. Leybourne and A.M.R. Taylor (2009), 'Testing for a unit root in the presence of a possible break in trend', *Econometric Theory*, **25**, 1545–88.
Harrison, J.M. (1985), *Brownian Motion and Stochastic Flow Systems*, New York: Wiley.
Harvey, D.I., S.J. Leybourne and A.M.R. Taylor (2007), 'A simple, robust and powerful test of the trend hypothesis', *Journal of Econometrics*, **141**, 1302–30.
Harvey, D.I., S.J. Leybourne and A.M.R. Taylor (2009), 'Unit root testing in practice: dealing with uncertainty over trend and initial condition (with commentaries and rejoinder)', *Econometric Theory*, **25**, 587–667.
Harvey, D.I., S.J. Leybourne and A.M.R. Taylor (2012), 'Testing for unit roots in the presence of uncertainty over both the trend and initial condition', *Journal of Econometrics*, **169**, 188–95.
Jansen, E.S. and T. Teräsvirta (1996), 'Testing parameter constancy and super exogeneity in econometric equations', *Oxford Bulletin of Economics and Statistics*, **58**, 735–63.
Johansen, S. (1995), *Likelihood-based Inference in Cointegrated Vector Autoregressive Models*, Oxford: Oxford University Press.
Kapetanios, G. and Y. Shin (2006), 'Unit root tests in three-regime SETAR models', *Econometrics Journal*, **9**, 252–78.
Kapetanios, G. and Y. Shin (2008), 'GLS detrending-based unit root tests in nonlinear STAR and SETAR models', *Economics Letters*, **100**, 377–80.
Kapetanios, G., Y. Shin and A. Snell (2003), 'Testing for a unit root in the nonlinear STAR framework', *Journal of Econometrics*, **112**, 359–79.

Kejriwal, M. and P. Perron (2010), 'A sequential procedure to determine the number of breaks in trend with an integrated or stationary noise component', *Journal of Time Series Analysis*, **31**, 305–28.
Kilic, R. (2011), 'Testing for a unit root in a stationary ESTAR process', *Econometric Reviews*, **30**, 274–302.
Kim, D. and P. Perron (2009), 'Unit root tests allowing for a break in the trend function at an unknown time under both the null and alternative hypothesis', *Journal of Econometrics*, **148**, 1–13.
Kim, K. and P. Schmidt (1990), 'Some evidence on the accuracy of Phillips–Perron tests using alternative estimates of nuisance parameters', *Economics Letters*, **34**, 345–50.
Kim, K. and P. Schmidt (1993), 'Unit root tests with conditional heteroskedasticity', *Journal of Econometrics*, **59**, 287–300.
Kim, T.H., S.J. Leybourne and P. Newbold (2002), 'Unit root tests with a break in innovation variance', *Journal of Econometrics*, **109**, 365–87.
Kruse, R. (2011), 'A new unit root test against ESTAR based on a class of modified statistics', *Statistical Papers*, **52**, 71–85.
Kruse, R., M. Frömmel, L. Menkhoff and P. Sibbertsen (2012), 'What do we know about real exchange rate nonlinearity?', *Empirical Economics*, **43**, 457–74.
Kwiatkowski, D., P.C.B. Phillips, P. Schmidt and Y. Shin (1992), 'Testing the null hypothesis of stationarity against the alternative of a unit root', *Journal of Econometrics*, **54**, 159–78.
Lanne, M. and H. Lütkepohl (2002), 'Unit root tests for time series with level shifts: a comparison of different proposals', *Economics Letters*, **75**, 109–14.
Lanne, M. and P. Saikkonen (2005), 'Nonlinear GARCH models with highly persistent volatility', *Econometrics Journal*, **8**, 251–76.
Leybourne, S.J. (1995), 'Testing for unit roots using forward and reverse Dickey–Fuller regressions', *Oxford Bulletin of Economics and Statistics*, **57**, 559–71.
Lundbergh, S. and T. Teräsvirta (2006), 'A time series model for an exchange rate in a target zone with applications', *Journal of Econometrics*, **131**, 579–609.
Lütkepohl, H., C. Müller and P. Saikkonen (2001), 'Unit root tests for time series with a structural break when the break point is known', in C. Hsiao, K. Morimune and J. Powell (eds), *Nonlinear Statistical Modelling: Essays in Honor of Takeshi Amemiya*, Cambridge: Cambridge University Press, pp. 327–48.
Luukkonen, R., P. Saikkonen and T. Teräsvirta (1988), 'Testing linearity against smooth transition autoregressive models', *Biometrika*, **75**, 491–99.
Maddala, G. and I.M. Kim (1998), *Unit Roots, Cointegration and Structural Change*, Cambridge: Cambridge University Press.
Maki, D. (2009), 'Tests for a unit root using three-regime TAR models: power comparison and some applications', *Econometric Reviews*, **28**, 335–63.
Montañés, A. and M. Reyes (1998), 'Effect of a shift in the trend function on Dickey–Fuller unit root tests', *Econometric Theory*, **14**, 355–63.
Montañés, A. and M. Reyes (1999), 'The asymptotic behavior of the Dickey–Fuller tests under the crash hypothesis', *Statistics and Probability Letters*, **42**, 81–9.
Müller, U. and G. Elliott (2003), 'Tests for unit roots and the initial condition', *Econometrica*, **71**, 1269–86.
Nelson, C.R. and C.I. Plosser (1982), 'Trends and random walks in macroeconomic time series: some evidence and implications', *Journal of Monetary Economics*, **10**, 139–62.
Newey, W.K. and K.D. West (1987), 'A simple, positive semi-definite, heteroscedasticity and autocorrelation consistent covariance matrix', *Econometrica*, **55**, 703–8.
Ng, S. and P. Perron (1995), 'Unit root tests in ARMA models with data-dependent methods for the selection of the truncation lag', *Journal of the American Statistical Association*, **90**, 268–81.
Ng, S. and P. Perron (2001), 'Lag length selection and the construction of unit root tests with good size and power', *Econometrica*, **69**, 1519–54.
Nicolau, J. (2002), 'Stationary processes that look like random walks – the bounded random walk process in discrete and continuous time', *Econometric Theory*, **18**, 99–118.
Paparoditis, E. and D.N. Politis (2003), 'Residual-based block bootstrap for unit root testing', *Econometrica*, **71**, 813–55.
Park, J.Y. (2003), 'Bootstrap unit root tests', *Econometrica*, **71**, 1845–95.
Park, J.Y. and M. Shintani (2005), 'Testing for a unit root against transitional autoregressive models', Working Paper.
Perron, P. (1989), 'The great crash, the oil price shock and the unit root hypothesis', *Econometrica*, **57**, 1361–401.
Perron, P. (1990), 'Testing for a unit root in a time series with a changing mean', *Journal of Business and Economic Statistics*, **8**, 153–62.
Perron, P. (1997), 'Further evidence on breaking trend functions in macroeconomic variables', *Journal of Econometrics*, **80**, 355–85.

Perron, P. (2006), 'Dealing with structural breaks', Chapter 8 in T.C. Mills and K. Patterson (eds), *Palgrave Handbooks of Econometrics: Vol. 1 Econometric Theory*, Basingstoke: Palgrave Macmillan.
Perron, P. and S. Ng (1996), 'Useful modifications to unit root tests with dependent errors and their local asymptotic properties', *Review of Economics Studies*, **63**, 435–65.
Perron, P. and Z. Qu (2007), 'A simple modification to improve the finite sample properties of Ng and Perron's unit root tests', *Economics Letters*, **94**, 12–19.
Perron, P. and Z. Qu (2010), 'Long memory and level shifts in the volatility of stock market indices', *Journal of Business and Economic Statistics*, **28**, 275–90.
Perron, P. and G.H. Rodríguez (2003), 'GLS detrending, efficient unit root tests and structural change', *Journal of Econometrics*, **115**, 1–27.
Perron, P. and T.J. Vogelsang (1992a), 'Nonstationarity and level shifts with an application to purchasing power parity', *Journal of Business and Economic Statistics*, **10**, 301–20.
Perron, P. and T. J. Vogelsang (1992b), 'Testing for a unit root in a time series with a changing mean: corrections and extensions', *Journal of Business and Economic Statistics*, **10**, 467–70.
Perron, P. and T.J. Vogelsang (1993), 'The great crash, the oil price shock and the unit root hypothesis, erratum', *Econometrica*, **61**, 248–9.
Perron, P. and T. Yabu (2009a), 'Testing for shifts in trend with an integrated or stationary noise component', *Journal of Business and Economic Statistics*, **27**, 369–96.
Perron, P. and T. Yabu (2009b), 'Estimating deterministic trends with an integrated or stationary noise components', *Journal of Econometrics*, **151**, 56–69.
Perron, P. and X. Zhu (2005), 'Testing for shifts in trend with integrated and stochastic trends', *Journal of Econometrics*, **129**, 65–119.
Phillips, P.C.B. (1987), 'Time series regression with unit root', *Econometrica*, **55**, 277–302.
Phillips, P.C.B. (2005), 'Challenges of trending time series econometrics', *Mathematics and Computers in Simulation*, **68**, 401–16.
Phillips, P.C.B. and S. Durlauf (1988), 'Trends versus random walks in time series analysis', *Econometrica*, **56**, 1333–54.
Phillips, P.C.B. and P. Perron (1988), 'Testing for a unit root in time series regression', *Biometrika*, **75**, 335–46.
Phillips, P.C.B. and Z. Xiao (1998), 'A primer on unit root testing', *Journal of Economic Surveys*, **12**, 423–69.
Rappoport, P. and L. Reichlin (1989), 'Segmented trends and non-stationary time series', *Economic Journal*, **99**, 168–77.
Rothe, C. and P. Sibbertsen (2006), 'Phillips–Perron-type unit root tests in the nonlinear ESTAR framework', *Allgemeines Statistisches Archiv*, **90**, 439–56.
Said, S.E. and D.A. Dickey (1984), 'Testing for unit roots in autoregressive moving average models of unknown order', *Biometrika*, **71**, 599–607.
Saikkonen, P. and H. Lütkepohl (2002), 'Testing for a unit root in a time series with a level shift at unknown time', *Econometric Theory*, **18**, 313–48.
Sargan, J. and A. Bhargava (1983), 'Testing for residuals from least squares regression being generated by Gaussian random walk', *Econometrica*, **51**, 153–74.
Schwert, G.W. (1989), 'Test for unit roots: a Monte Carlo investigation', *Journal of Business and Economic Statistics*, **7**, 147–60.
Seo, M.H. (2008), 'Unit root test in a threshold autoregression: asymptotic theory and residual-based block bootstrap', *Econometric Theory*, **24**, 1699–716.
Stock, J.H. (1994), 'Unit roots, structural breaks, and trends', in R.F. Engle and D.L. McFadden (eds), *Handbook of Econometrics*, Volume IV, New York: North Holland, pp. 2739–841.
Stock, J.H. (1999), 'A class of tests for integration and cointegration', in *Cointegration, Causality, and Forecasting: A Festschrift in Honour of Clive W.J. Granger*, Oxford: Oxford University Press, pp. 136–67.
Teräsvirta, T. (1994), 'Specification, estimation, and evaluation of smooth transition autoregressive models', *Journal of the American Statistical Association*, **89**, 208–18.
Timmermann, A. (2000), 'Moments of Markov switching models', *Journal of Econometrics*, **96**, 75–111.
van Dijk, D., D.R. Osborn and M. Sensier (2002), 'Changes in variability of the business cycle in the G7 countries', Econometric Institute Report EI 2002-28, Erasmus University Rotterdam.
Varneskov, R.T. and P. Perron (2011), 'Combining long memory and level shifts in modelling and forecasting the volatility of asset returns', CREATES Research Paper 2011-26, Aarhus University.
Velasco, C. (2006), 'Semi-parametric estimation of long memory models', Chapter 9 in T.C. Mills and K. Patterson (eds), *Palgrave Handbooks of Econometrics: Vol. 1 Econometric Theory*, Basingstoke: Palgrave Macmillan
Vogelsang, T.J. (1998), 'Trend function hypothesis testing in the presence of serial correlation', *Econometrica*, **66**, 123–48.
Vogelsang, T.J. and P. Perron (1998), 'Additional tests for a unit root allowing the possibility of breaks in the trend function', *International Economic Review*, **39**, 1073–100.

White, H. and C.W.J. Granger (2011), 'Consideration of trends in time series', *Journal of Time Series Econometrics*, **3**, 1–38.
White, J.S. (1958), 'The limiting distribution of the serial correlation coefficient in the explosive case', *Annals of Mathematical Statistics*, **29**, 1188–97.
Yildirim, D., R. Becker and D. Osborn (2009), 'Bootstrap unit root tests for nonlinear threshold models', University of Manchester, Economics Discussion Paper Series EDP-0915.
Zivot, E. and D.W.K. Andrews (1992), 'Further evidence on the great crash, the oil price shock and the unit root hypothesis', *Journal of Business and Economic Statistics*, **10**, 251–70.

5 Filtering macroeconomic data

D.S.G. Pollock

INTRODUCTION

The purpose of a filter is to remove unwanted components from a stream of data so as to enhance the clarity of the components of interest. In many engineering applications and in some econometric applications, there is a single component of interest, described as the signal, to which a component has been added that can be described as the noise.

A complete separation of the signal and the noise is possible only if they reside in separate frequency bands. If they reside in overlapping frequency bands, then their separation is bound to be tentative. The signal typically comprises elements of low frequency and the noise comprises elements of higher frequencies. Filters are, therefore, designed by engineers with reference to their frequency-selective properties.

In econometric applications, some additional components must be taken into account. The foremost of these is the trend, which may be defined as an underlying trajectory of the data that cannot be synthesized from trigonometrical functions alone. It is difficult to give a more specific definition, which may account for the wide variety of procedures that have been proposed for extracting trends from the economic data. A business cycle component might also be extracted from the data; but this is often found in combination with the trend.

Another component that is commonly present, if it has not been removed already by the providers of the economic data, is a pattern of seasonal fluctuations. In this case, given that the fluctuations reside in limited frequency bands, it is easier to provide a specific definition of the seasonal component, albeit that there is still scope for alternative definitions.

Notwithstanding the ill-defined nature of these components, econometricians have tended to adopt particular models for the trend and for the seasonal fluctuations. The trend is commonly modelled by a first-order random walk with drift, which is an accumulation of a white-noise sequence of independently and identically distributed random variables. The drift occurs when the variables have a nonzero mean – a positive mean giving rise to an upward drift. Second-order processes involving a double accumulation of white noise are also used to model the trend.

Econometricians commonly model the seasonal fluctuations by autoregressive moving-average processes in which the autoregressive operator contains complex roots with moduli of unity and with arguments that correspond to the fundamental seasonal frequency and to the harmonically related frequencies. The moving-average operator is usually instrumental in confining the effects of these roots to the vicinities of the seasonal frequencies.

Given a complete statistical specification of the processes generating the data, it is possible to derive the filters that provide the minimum mean-squared error estimates of the various components. This approach has been followed in the TRAMO–SEATS program of Caporello and Maravall (2004) for decomposing an econometric data sequence into its components. (See also Gómez and Maravall, 2001.) An account of their methods will be given in the penultimate section of this chapter.

The structural time series methodology that has been incorporated in the STAMP computer package of Koopmans et al. (2000) follows a similar approach. The STAMP program employs the Kalman filter, which is discussed elsewhere in this *Handbook* in the chapter by Tommaso Proietti. This powerful and all-encompassing method is capable of dealing with non-stationary data processes, provided that there are models to describe them.

Whereas the model-based approach to filtering has led to some refined computer programs that can often be used automatically to process the data, there are circumstances in which a significant mismatch occurs between the data and the models. Then, some alternative methods must be pursued which can be adapted more readily to the reflect the properties of the data. An aim of this chapter is to describe some methods that meet this requirement.

In this chapter, we shall also employ some statistical models of the processes underlying the data. However, these will be heuristic models rather than models that propose to be realistic. Their purpose is to enable us to derive filters that are endowed with whatever are the appropriate frequency-selective capabilities. Thus, the specifications of the resulting filters are to be determined flexibly in the light of the properties of the data.

In deriving these filters, we use an extension of the time-honoured Wiener–Kolmogorov principle, which is intended to provide minimum mean-squared error estimates of the components whenever these are truly described by the models. The original of Wiener–Kolmogorov theory was based on the assumption that the data are generated by stationary stochastic processes. Therefore, we have to adapt the theory to cater to non-stationary processes.

An alternative methodology will also be described that approaches the matter of frequency selection in a direct manner that does not depend on any models of the data. The resulting procedures, which employ what may be described as frequency-domain filters, perform the essential operations upon the trigonometrical functions that are the elements of the Fourier decomposition of the detrended data.

An advantage of these filters is that they enable one to separate elements that are at adjacent frequencies. Such sharp divisions of the frequency contents of the data cannot be achieved by the time-domain filters, which operate directly on the data, without incurring severe problems of numerical instability.

Some mathematical results must be provided in order to support the analysis of filtering. Some of these results will be presented at the outset in the sections that follow this introduction. Other results will be dispersed throughout the text. We shall begin with some basic definitions.

LINEAR TIME INVARIANT FILTERS

Whenever we form a linear combination of successive elements of a discrete-time signal $x(t) = \{x_t; t = 0, \pm 1, \pm 2, \ldots\}$, we are performing an operation that is described as linear filtering. In the case of a linear time-invariant filter, such an operation can be represented by the equation

$$y(t) = \sum_j \psi_j x(t - j). \tag{5.1}$$

To assist in the algebraic manipulation of such equations, we may convert the data sequences $x(t)$ and $y(t)$ and the sequence of filter coefficients $\{\psi_j\}$ into power series or polynomials. By associating z^t to each element y_t and by summing the sequence, we get

$$\sum_t y_t z^t = \sum_t \left\{ \sum_j \psi_j x_{t-j} \right\} z^t \quad \text{or} \quad y(z) = \psi(z)x(z), \tag{5.2}$$

where

$$x(z) = \sum_t x_t z^t, \; y(z) = \sum_t y_t z^t \; \text{ and } \; \psi(z) = \sum_j \psi_j z^j. \tag{5.3}$$

The convolution operation of equation (5.1) becomes an operation of polynomial multiplication in equation (5.2). We are liable to describe the z-transform $\psi(z)$ of the filter coefficients as the transfer function of the filter.

For a treatise on the z-transform, see Jury (1964).

THE IMPULSE RESPONSE

The sequence $\{\psi_j\}$ of the filter's coefficients constitutes its response, on the output side, to an input in the form of a unit impulse. If the sequence is finite, then $\psi(z)$ is described as a moving-average filter or as a finite impulse-response (FIR) filter. When the filter produces an impulse response of an indefinite duration, it is called an infinite impulse-response (IIR) filter. The filter is said to be causal or backward-looking if none of its coefficients is associated with a negative power of z. In that case, the filter is available for real-time signal processing.

CAUSAL FILTERS

A practical filter, which is constructed from a limited number of components of hardware or software, must be capable of being expressed in terms of a finite number of parameters. Therefore, linear IIR filters which are causal will invariably entail recursive equations of the form

$$\sum_{j=0}^{p} \phi_j y_{t-j} = \sum_{j=0}^{q} \theta_j x_{t-j}, \quad \text{with} \quad \phi_0 = 1, \tag{5.4}$$

of which the z-transform is

$$\phi(z)y(z) = \theta(z)x(z), \tag{5.5}$$

wherein $\phi(z) = \phi_0 + \phi_1 z + \cdots + \phi_p z^p$ and $\theta(z) = \theta_0 + \theta z + \cdots + \theta_q z^q$ are finite-degree polynomials. The leading coefficient of $\phi(z)$ may be set to unity without loss of generality; and thus the output sequence $y(t)$ in equation (5.4) becomes a function not only of past and present inputs but also of past outputs, which are described as feedback.

The recursive equation may be assimilated to the equation under (5.2) by writing it in rational form:

$$y(z) = \frac{\theta(z)}{\phi(z)}x(z) = \psi(z)x(z). \tag{5.6}$$

On the condition that the filter is stable, the expression $\psi(z)$ stands for the series expansion of the ratio of the polynomials.

The stability of a rational transfer function $\theta(z)/\phi(z)$ can be investigated via its partial-fraction decomposition, which gives rise to a sum of simpler transfer functions that can be analysed readily. If the degree of the numerator of $\theta(z)$ exceeds that of the denominator $\phi(z)$, then long division can be used to obtain a quotient polynomial and a remainder that is a proper rational function. The quotient polynomial will correspond to a stable transfer function, and the remainder will be the subject of the decomposition.

Assume that $\theta(z)/\phi(z)$ is a proper rational function in which the denominator is factorized as

$$\phi(z) = \prod_{j=1}^{r}(1 - z/\lambda_j)^{n_j}, \tag{5.7}$$

where n_j is the multiplicity of the root λ_j, and where $\sum_j n_j = p$ is the degree of the polynomial. Then, the so-called Heaviside partial-fraction decomposition is

$$\frac{\theta(z)}{\phi(z)} = \sum_{j=1}^{r}\sum_{k=1}^{n_j}\frac{c_{jk}}{(1 - z/\lambda_j)^k}; \tag{5.8}$$

and the task is to find the series expansions of the partial fractions. The stability of the transfer function depends upon the convergence of these expansions. For this, the necessary and sufficient condition is that $|\lambda_j| > 1$ for all j, which is to to say that all of the roots of the denominator polynomial must lie outside the unit circle in the complex plane.

The expansions of a pair of partial fractions with conjugate complex roots will combine to produce a sinusoidal sequence. The expansion of a partial fraction containing a root of multiplicity n will be equivalent to the n-fold auto-convolution of the expansion of a simple fraction containing the root.

It is helpful to represent the roots of the denominator polynomial, which are described as the poles of the transfer function, together with the roots of the numerator polynomial, which are described as the zeros, by showing their locations graphically within the complex plane.

It is more convenient to represent the poles and zeros of $\theta(z^{-1})/\phi(z^{-1})$, which are the reciprocals of those of $\theta(z)/\phi(z)$. For a stable and invertible transfer function, these must lie within the unit circle. This recourse has been adopted for Figure 5.2, which shows the pole–zero diagram for the transfer function that gives rise to Figure 5.1.

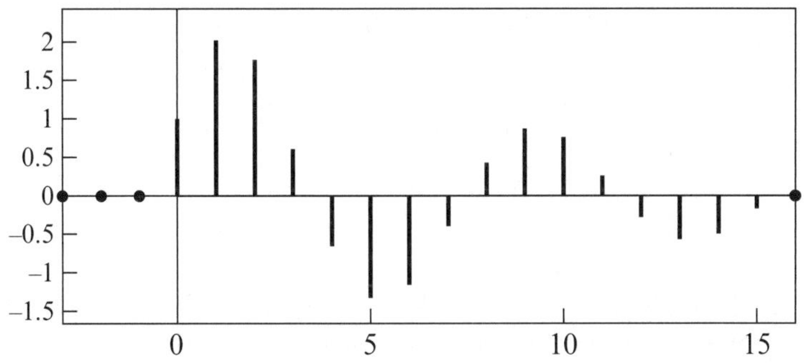

Figure 5.1 *The impulse response of the transfer function* $\theta(z)/\phi(z)$ *with* $\phi(z) = 1.0 - 1.2728z + 0.81z^2$ *and* $\theta(z) = 1.0 + 0.75z$

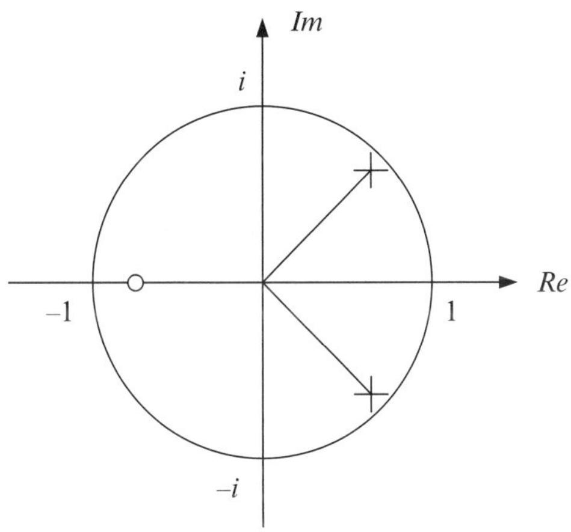

Figure 5.2 *The pole–zero diagram corresponding to the transfer function of Figure 5.1. The poles are conjugate complex numbers with arguments of* $\pm\pi/4$ *and with a modulus of* 0.9. *The single real-valued zero has the value of* -0.75

THE SERIES EXPANSION OF A RATIONAL TRANSFER FUNCTION

The method of finding the coefficients of the series expansion can be illustrated by the second-order case:

$$\frac{\theta_0 + \theta_1 z}{\phi_0 + \phi_1 z + \phi_2 z^2} = \{\psi_0 + \psi_1 z + \psi_2 z^2 + \cdots\}. \tag{5.9}$$

We rewrite this equation as

$$\theta_0 + \theta_1 z = \{\phi_0 + \phi_1 z + \phi_2 z^2\}\{\psi_0 + \psi_1 z + \psi_2 z^2 + \cdots\}. \tag{5.10}$$

The following table assists us in multiplying together the two polynomials:

	ψ_0	$\psi_1 z$	$\psi_2 z^2$	$\cdots$
ϕ_0	$\phi_0\psi_0$	$\phi_0\psi_1 z$	$\phi_0\psi_2 z^2$	$\cdots$
$\phi_1 z$	$\phi_1\psi_0 z$	$\phi_1\psi_1 z^2$	$\phi_1\psi_2 z^3$	$\cdots$
$\phi_2 z^2$	$\phi_2\psi_0 z^2$	$\phi_1\psi_2 z^3$	$\phi_2\psi_2 z^4$	$\cdots$

(5.11)

By performing the multiplication on the RHS of equation (5.10), and by equating the coefficients of the same powers of z on the two sides, we find that

$$\begin{aligned}
\theta_0 &= \phi_0\psi_0, & \psi_0 &= \theta_0/\phi_0,\\
\theta_1 &= \phi_0\psi_1 + \phi_1\psi_0, & \psi_1 &= (\theta_1 - \phi_1\psi_0)/\phi_0,\\
0 &= \phi_0\psi_2 + \phi_1\psi_1 + \phi_2\psi_0, & \psi_2 &= -(\phi_1\psi_1 + \phi_2\psi_0)/\phi_0,\\
&\vdots & &\vdots\\
0 &= \phi_0\psi_n + \phi_1\psi_{n-1} + \phi_2\psi_{n-2}, & \psi_n &= -(\phi_1\psi_{n-1} + \phi_2\psi_{n-2})/\phi_0.
\end{aligned} \tag{5.12}$$

BI-DIRECTIONAL (NON-CAUSAL) FILTERS

A two-sided symmetric filter in the form of

$$\psi(z) = \theta(z^{-1})\theta(z) = \psi_0 + \psi_1(z^{-1} + z) + \cdots + \psi_m(z^{-m} + z^m) \tag{5.13}$$

is often employed in smoothing the data or in eliminating its seasonal components. The advantage of such a filter is the absence of a phase effect. That is to say, no delay is imposed on any of the components of the signal.

The so-called Cramér–Wold factorization, which sets $\psi(z) = \theta(z^{-1})\theta(z)$, and which is available for any properly designed symmetric FIR filter, provides a straightforward way of explaining the absence of a phase effect. The factorization gives rise to two equations: (i) $q(z) = \theta(z)y(z)$ and (ii) $x(z) = \theta(z^{-1})q(z)$. Thus, the transformation of (5.1) is broken down into two operations:

$$\text{(i)}\ \ q_t = \sum_j \theta_j y_{t-j} \quad \text{and} \quad \text{(ii)}\ \ x_t = \sum_j \theta_j q_{t+j}. \tag{5.14}$$

The first operation, which runs in real time, imposes a time delay on every component of $x(t)$. The second operation, which works in reversed time, imposes an equivalent reverse-time delay on each component. The reverse-time delays, which are advances in other words, serve to eliminate the corresponding real-time delays.

If $\psi(z)$ corresponds to an FIR filter, then the processed sequence $x(t)$ may be generated via a single application of the two-sided filter $\psi(z)$ to the signal $y(t)$, or it may be generated in two operations via the successive applications of $\theta(z)$ to $y(z)$ and $\theta(z^{-1})$ to

$q(z) = \theta(z)y(z)$. The question of which of these techniques has been used to generate $y(t)$ in a particular instance should be a matter of indifference.

The final species of linear filter that may be used in the processing of economic time series is a symmetric two-sided rational filter of the form

$$\psi(z) = \frac{\theta(z^{-1})\theta(z)}{\phi(z^{-1})\phi(z)}. \tag{5.15}$$

Such a filter must, of necessity, be applied in two separate passes running forwards and backwards in time and described, respectively, by the equations

$$\text{(i)}\ \ \phi(z)q(z) = \theta(z)y(z) \quad \text{and} \quad \text{(ii)}\ \ \phi(z^{-1})x(z) = \theta(z^{-1})q(z). \tag{5.16}$$

Such filters represent a most effective way of processing economic data in pursuance of a wide range of objectives.

THE RESPONSE TO A SINUSOIDAL INPUT

One must also consider the response of the transfer function to a simple sinusoidal signal. Any finite data sequence can be expressed as a sum of discretely sampled sine and cosine functions with frequencies that are integer multiples of a fundamental frequency that produces one cycle in the period spanned by the sequence. The finite sequence may be regarded as a single cycle within a infinite sequence, which is the periodic extension of the data.

Consider, therefore, the consequences of mapping the perpetual signal sequence $\{x_t = \cos(\omega t)\}$ through the transfer function with the coefficients $\{\psi_0, \psi_1, \ldots\}$. The output is

$$y(t) = \sum_j \psi_j \cos(\omega[t - j]). \tag{5.17}$$

By virtue of the trigonometrical identity $\cos(A - B) = \cos A \cos B + \sin A \sin B$, this becomes

$$\begin{aligned} y(t) &= \Big\{\sum_j \psi_j \cos(\omega j)\Big\} \cos(\omega t) + \Big\{\sum_j \psi_j \sin(\omega j)\Big\} \sin(\omega t) \\ &= \alpha \cos(\omega t) + \beta \sin(\omega t) = \rho \cos(\omega t - \theta), \end{aligned} \tag{5.18}$$

Observe that using the trigonometrical identity to expand the final expression of (5.18) gives $\alpha = \rho\cos(\theta)$ and $\beta = \rho\sin(\theta)$. Therefore,

$$\rho^2 = \alpha^2 + \beta^2 \quad \text{and} \quad \theta = \tan^{-1}\left(\frac{\beta}{\alpha}\right). \tag{5.19}$$

Also, if $\lambda = \alpha + i\beta$ and $\lambda^* = \alpha - i\beta$ are conjugate complex numbers, then ρ would be their modulus. This is illustrated in Figure 5.3.

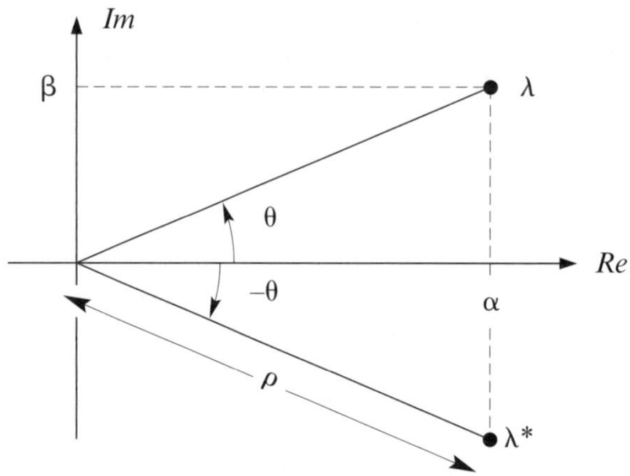

Figure 5.3 *The Argand Diagram showing a complex number* $\lambda = \alpha + i\beta$ *and its conjugate* $\lambda^* = \alpha - i\beta$

It can be seen, from (5.18), that the transfer function has a twofold effect upon the signal. First, there is a *gain effect*, whereby the amplitude of the sinusoid is increased or diminished by the factor ρ. Then, there is a *phase effect*, whereby the peak of the sinusoid is displaced by a time delay of θ/ω periods. The frequency of the output is the same as the frequency of the input, which is a fundamental feature of all linear dynamic systems.

Observe that the response of the transfer function to a sinusoid of a particular frequency is akin to the response of a bell to a tuning fork. It gives very limited information regarding the characteristics of the system. To obtain full information, it is necessary to excite the system over a full range of frequencies.

ALIASING AND THE SHANNON–NYQUIST SAMPLING THEOREM

In a discrete-time system, there is a problem of aliasing whereby signal frequencies (i.e. angular velocities) in excess of π radians per sampling interval are confounded with frequencies within the interval $[0, \pi]$. To understand this, consider a cosine wave of unit amplitude and zero phase with a frequency ω in the interval $\pi < \omega < 2\pi$ that is sampled at unit intervals. Let $\omega^* = 2\pi - \omega$. Then,

$$\begin{aligned}\cos(\omega t) &= \cos\{(2\pi - \omega^*)t\}\\ &= \cos(2\pi)\cos(\omega^* t) + \sin(2\pi)\sin(\omega^* t)\\ &= \cos(\omega^* t);\end{aligned} \tag{5.20}$$

which indicates that ω and ω^* are observationally indistinguishable. Here, $\omega^* \in [0, \pi]$ is described as the alias of $\omega > \pi$.

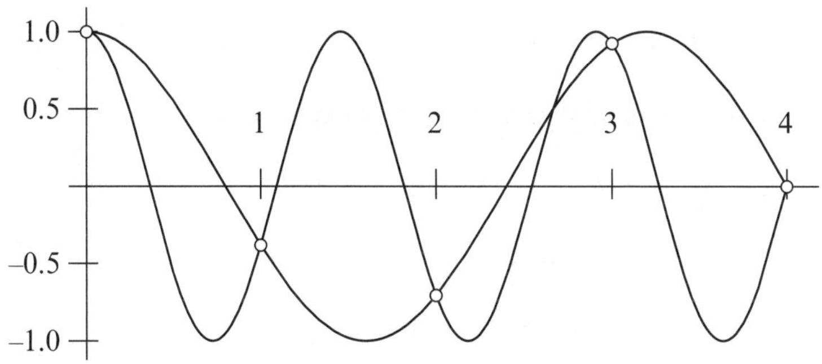

Figure 5.4 *The values of the function* $\cos\{(11/8)\pi t\}$ *coincide with those of its alias* $\cos\{(5/8)\pi t\}$ *at the integer points* $\{t = 0, \pm 1, \pm 2, \ldots\}$

The maximum frequency in discrete data is π radians per sampling interval and, as the Shannon–Nyquist sampling theorem indicates, aliasing is avoided only if there are at least two observations in the time that it takes the signal element of highest frequency to complete a cycle. In that case, the discrete representation will contain all of the available information on the system.

The consequences of sampling at an insufficient rate are illustrated in Figure 5.4. Here, a rapidly alternating cosine function is mistaken for one of less than half the true frequency.

The sampling theorem is attributable to several people, but it is most commonly attributed to Shannon (1949a, 1949b), albeit that Nyquist (1928) discovered the essential results at an earlier date.

THE FREQUENCY RESPONSE OF A LINEAR FILTER

The frequency response of a linear filter $\psi(z)$ is its response to the set of sinusoidal inputs of all frequencies ω that fall within the Nyquist interval $[0, \pi]$. This entails the squared gain of the filter, defined by

$$\rho^2(\omega) = \psi_\alpha^2(\omega) + \psi_\beta^2(\omega), \tag{5.21}$$

where

$$\psi_\alpha(\omega) = \sum_j \psi_j \cos(\omega j) \quad \text{and} \quad \psi_\beta(\omega) = \sum_j \psi_j \sin(\omega j), \tag{5.22}$$

and the phase displacement, defined by

$$\theta(\omega) = \text{Arg}\{\psi(\omega)\} = \tan^{-1}\{\psi_\beta(\omega)/\psi_\alpha(\omega)\}. \tag{5.23}$$

It is convenient to replace the trigonometrical functions of (5.22) by the complex exponential functions

$$e^{i\omega j} = \frac{1}{2}\{\cos(\omega j) + \sin(\omega j)\} \text{ and } e^{-i\omega j} = \frac{1}{2}\{\cos(\omega j) - \sin(\omega j)\}, \tag{5.24}$$

which enable the trigonometrical functions to be expressed as

$$\cos(\omega t) = \frac{1}{2}\{e^{i\omega j} + e^{-i\omega j}\} \text{ and } \sin(\omega j) = \frac{i}{2}\{e^{-i\omega j} - e^{i\omega j}\}. \tag{5.25}$$

Setting $z = \exp\{-i\omega j\}$ in $\psi(z)$ gives

$$\psi(e^{-i\omega j}) = \psi_\alpha(\omega) - i\psi_\beta(\omega), \tag{5.26}$$

which we shall write hereafter as $\psi(\omega) = \psi(e^{-i\omega j})$.

The squared gain of the filter, previously denoted by $\rho^2(\omega)$, is the square of the complex modulus:

$$|\psi(\omega)|^2 = \psi_\alpha^2(\omega) + \psi_\beta^2(\omega), \tag{5.27}$$

which is obtained by setting $z = \exp\{-i\omega j\}$ in $\psi(z^{-1})\psi(z)$.

THE SPECTRUM OF A STATIONARY STOCHASTIC PROCESS

Consider a stationary stochastic process $y(t) = \{y_t; t = 0, \pm 1, \pm 2, \ldots\}$ defined on a doubly-infinite index set. The generic element of the process can be expressed as $y_t = \Sigma_j \psi_j \varepsilon_{t-j}$, where ε_t is an element of a sequence $\varepsilon(t)$ of independently and identically distributed random variables with $E(\varepsilon_t) = 0$ and $V(\varepsilon_t) = \sigma^2$ for all t.

The autocovariance generating function of the process is

$$\sigma^2\psi(z^{-1})\psi(z) = \gamma(z) = \{\gamma_0 + \gamma_1(z^{-1} + z) + \gamma_2(z^{-2} + z^2) + \cdots\}. \tag{5.28}$$

The following table assists us in forming the product $\gamma(z) = \sigma^2\psi(z^{-1})\psi(z)$:

$$\begin{array}{c|cccc} & \psi_0 & \psi_1 z & \psi_2 z^2 & \cdots \\ \hline \psi_0 & \psi_0^2 & \psi_0\psi_1 z & \psi_0\psi_2 z^2 & \cdots \\ \psi_1 z^{-1} & \psi_1\psi_0 z^{-1} & \psi_1^2 & \psi_1\psi_2 z & \cdots \\ \psi_2 z^{-2} & \psi_2\psi_0 z^{-2} & \psi_2\psi_1 z^{-1} & \psi_2^2 & \cdots \\ \vdots & \vdots & \vdots & \vdots & \end{array} \tag{5.29}$$

The autocovariances are obtained by summing along the NW–SE diagonals:

$$\begin{aligned} \gamma_0 &= \sigma^2\{\psi_0^2 + \psi_1^2 + \psi_2^2 + \psi_3^2 + \cdots\}, \\ \gamma_1 &= \sigma^2\{\psi_0\psi_1 + \psi_1\psi_2 + \psi_2\psi_3 + \cdots\}, \\ \gamma_2 &= \sigma^2\{\psi_0\psi_2 + \psi_1\psi_3 + \psi_2\psi_4 + \cdots\}, \\ &\vdots \end{aligned} \tag{5.30}$$

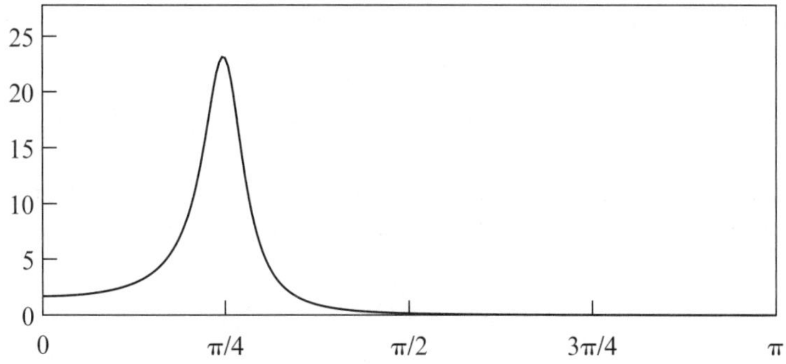

Figure 5.5 *The spectral density function of the ARMA (2, 1) process* $y(t) = 1.2728y(t-1) - 0.81y(t-2) + \varepsilon(t) + 0.75\varepsilon(t-1)$ *with* $V\{\varepsilon(t)\}=1$

By setting $z = \exp\{-i\omega j\}$ in $\gamma(z)$ and dividing by 2π, we get the spectral density function, or spectrum, of the process:

$$f(\omega) = \frac{1}{2\pi}\left\{\gamma_0 + 2\sum_{\tau=1}^{\infty}\gamma_\tau \cos(\omega\tau)\right\}. \tag{5.31}$$

This entails the cosine Fourier transform of the sequence of autocovariances.

The spectral density functions of an ARMA (2, 1) process, which incorporates the transfer function of Figures 5.1–5.3, is shown in Figure 5.5.

WIENER–KOLMOGOROV FILTERING OF STATIONARY SEQUENCES

The classical theory of linear filtering was formulated independently by Norbert Wiener (1941) and Andrei Nikolaevich Kolmogorov (1941) during the Second World War. They were both considering the problem of how to target radar-assisted anti aircraft guns on incoming enemy aircraft.

The purpose of a Wiener–Kolmogorov (W–K) filter is to extract an estimate of a signal sequence $\xi(t)$ from an observable data sequence

$$y(t) = \xi(t) + \eta(t), \tag{5.32}$$

which is afflicted by the noise $\eta(t)$. According to the classical assumptions, which we shall later amend in order to accommodate short non-stationary sequences, the signal and the noise are generated by zero-mean stationary stochastic processes that are mutually independent. Also, the assumption is made that the data constitute a doubly-infinite sequence. It follows that the autocovariance generating function of the data is the sum of the autocovariance generating functions of its two components. Thus,

$$\gamma^{yy}(z) = \gamma^{\xi\xi}(z) + \gamma^{\eta\eta}(z) \quad \text{and} \quad \gamma^{\xi\xi}(z) = \gamma^{y\xi}(z). \tag{5.33}$$

These functions are amenable to the so-called Cramér–Wold factorization, and they may be written as

$$\gamma^{yy}(z) = \phi(z^{-1})\phi(z), \quad \gamma^{\xi\xi}(z) = \theta(z^{-1})\theta(z), \quad \gamma^{\eta\eta}(z) = \theta_\eta(z^{-1})\theta_\eta(z). \tag{5.34}$$

The estimate x_t of the signal element ξ_t, generated by a linear time-invariant filter, is a linear combination of the elements of the data sequence:

$$x_t = \sum_j \psi_j y_{t-j}. \tag{5.35}$$

The principle of minimum mean-squared error estimation indicates that the estimation errors must be statistically uncorrelated with the elements of the information set. Thus, the following condition applies for all k:

$$\begin{aligned} 0 &= E\{y_{t-k}(\xi_t - x_t)\} \\ &= E(y_{t-k}\xi_t) - \sum_j \psi_j E(y_{t-k}y_{t-j}) \\ &= \gamma_k^{y\xi} - \sum_j \psi_j \gamma_{k-j}^{yy}. \end{aligned} \tag{5.36}$$

The equation may be expressed, in terms of the z-transforms, as

$$\gamma^{y\xi}(z) = \psi(z)\gamma^{yy}(z). \tag{5.37}$$

It follows that

$$\begin{aligned} \psi(z) &= \frac{\gamma^{y\xi}(z)}{\gamma^{yy}(z)} \\ &= \frac{\gamma^{\xi\xi}(z)}{\gamma^{\xi\xi}(z) + \gamma^{\eta\eta}(z)} = \frac{\theta(z^{-1})\theta(z)}{\phi(z^{-1})\phi(z)}. \end{aligned} \tag{5.38}$$

Now, by setting $z = \exp\{-i\omega\}$, one can derive the frequency-response function of the filter that is used in estimating the signal $\xi(t)$. The effect of the filter is to multiply each of the frequency elements of $y(t)$ by the fraction of its variance that is attributable to the signal. The same principle applies to the estimation of the residual or noise component. This is obtained using the complementary filter

$$\psi^c(z) = 1 - \psi(z) = \frac{\gamma^{\eta\eta}(z)}{\gamma^{\xi\xi}(z) + \gamma^{\eta\eta}(z)}. \tag{5.39}$$

The estimated signal component may be obtained by filtering the data in two passes according to the following equations:

$$\phi(z)q(z) = \theta(z)y(z), \quad \phi(z^{-1})x(z) = \theta(z^{-1})q(z). \tag{5.40}$$

The first equation relates to a process that runs forwards in time to generate the elements of an intermediate sequence, represented by the coefficients of $q(z)$. The second equation represents a process that runs backwards to deliver the estimates of the signal, represented by the coefficients of $x(z)$.

THE HODRICK–PRESCOTT (LESER) FILTER AND THE BUTTERWORTH FILTER

The Wiener–Kolmogorov methodology can be applied to non-stationary data with minor adaptations. A model of the processes underlying the data can be adopted that has the form of

$$\begin{aligned}\nabla^d(z)y(z) &= \nabla^d(z)\{\xi(z) + \eta(z)\} = \delta(z) + \kappa(z)\\ &= (1+z)^n\zeta(z) + (1-z)^m\varepsilon(z),\end{aligned} \tag{5.41}$$

where $\zeta(z)$ and $\varepsilon(z)$ are the z-transforms of two independent white-noise sequences $\zeta(t)$ and $\varepsilon(t)$ and where $\nabla(z) = 1 - z$ is the z-transform of the difference operator.

The model of $y(t) = \xi(t) + \eta(t)$ entails a pair of statistically independent stochastic processes, which are defined over the doubly-infinite sequence of integers and of which the z-transforms are

$$\xi(z) = \frac{(1+z)^n}{\nabla^d(z)}\zeta(z) \quad \text{and} \quad \eta(z) = \frac{(1-z)^m}{\nabla^d(z)}\varepsilon(z). \tag{5.42}$$

The condition $m \geq d$ is necessary to ensure the stationarity of $\eta(t)$, which is obtained from $\varepsilon(t)$ by differencing $m - d$ times.

It must be conceded that a non-stationary process such as $\xi(t)$ is a mathematical construct of doubtful reality, since its values will be unbounded, almost certainly. Nevertheless, to deal in these terms is to avoid the complexities of the finite-sample approach, which will be the subject of the next section.

The filter that is applied to $y(t)$ to estimate $\xi(t)$, which is the d-fold integral of $\delta(t)$, takes the form of

$$\psi(z) = \frac{\sigma_\zeta^2(1+z^{-1})^n(1+z)^n}{\sigma_\zeta^2(1+z^{-1})^n(1+z)^n + \sigma_\varepsilon^2(1-z^{-1})^m(1-z)^m}, \tag{5.43}$$

regardless of the degree d of differencing that would be necessary to reduce $y(t)$ to stationarity.

Two special cases are of interest. By setting $d = m = 2$ and $n = 0$ in (5.41), a model is obtained of a second-order random walk $\xi(t)$ affected by white-noise errors of observation $\eta(t) = \varepsilon(t)$. The resulting lowpass W–K filter, in the form of

$$\psi(z) = \frac{1}{1 + \lambda(1-z^{-1})^2(1-z)^2} \quad \text{with} \quad \lambda = \frac{\sigma_\varepsilon^2}{\sigma_\zeta^2}, \tag{5.44}$$

is the Hodrick–Prescott (H–P) filter. The complementary highpass filter, which generates the residue, is

$$\psi^c(z) = \frac{(1 - z^{-1})^2(1 - z)^2}{\lambda^{-1} + (1 - z^{-1})^2(1 - z)^2}. \tag{5.45}$$

Here, λ, which is described as the smoothing parameter, is the single adjustable parameter of the filter.

By setting $m = n$, a filter for estimating $\xi(t)$ is obtained that takes the form of

$$\begin{aligned}\psi(z) &= \frac{\sigma_\varsigma^2(1 + z^{-1})^n(1 + z)^n}{\sigma_\varsigma^2(1 + z^{-1})^n(1 + z)^n + \sigma_\varepsilon^2(1 - z^{-1})^n(1 - z)^n} \\ &= \frac{1}{1 + \lambda\left(i\dfrac{1 - z}{1 + z}\right)^{2n}} \quad \text{with} \quad \lambda = \frac{\sigma_\varepsilon^2}{\sigma_\varsigma^2}.\end{aligned} \tag{5.46}$$

This is the formula for the Butterworth lowpass digital filter. The filter has two adjustable parameters, and, therefore, it is a more flexible device than the H–P filter. First, there is the parameter λ. This can be expressed as

$$\lambda = \{1/\tan(\omega_d)\}^{2n}, \tag{5.47}$$

where ω_d is the nominal cut-off point of the filter, which is the mid-point in the transition of the filter's frequency response from its pass band to its stop band. The second of the adjustable parameters is n, which denotes the order of the filter. As n increases, the transition between the pass band and the stop band becomes more abrupt.

These filters can be applied to the non-stationary data sequence $y(t)$ in the bidirectional manner indicated by equation (5.40), provided that the appropriate initial conditions are supplied with which to start the recursions. However, by concentrating on the estimation of the residual sequence $\eta(t)$, which corresponds to a stationary process, it is possible to avoid the need for non-zero initial conditions. Then, the estimate of $\eta(t)$ can be subtracted from $y(t)$ to obtain the estimate of $\xi(t)$.

The H–P filter has been used as a lowpass smoothing filter in numerous macroeconomic investigations, where it has been customary to set the smoothing parameter to certain conventional values. Thus, for example, the econometric computer package *Eviews 4.0* (2000) imposes the following default values:

$$\lambda = \begin{cases} 100 & \text{for annual data,} \\ 1{,}600 & \text{for quarterly data,} \\ 14{,}400 & \text{for monthly data.} \end{cases}$$

Figure 5.6 shows the square gain of the filter corresponding to these values. The innermost curve corresponds to $\lambda = 14{,}400$ and the outermost curve to $\lambda = 100$.

Whereas they have become conventional, these values are arbitrary. The filter should

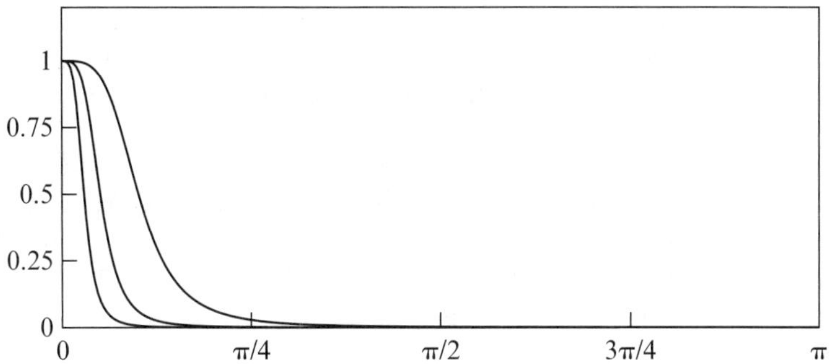

Figure 5.6 *The gain of the Hodrick–Prescott lowpass filter with a smoothing parameter set to* 100, 1,600 *and* 14,400

be adapted to the purpose of isolating the component of interest; and the appropriate filter parameters need to be determined in the light of the spectral structure of the component, such as has been revealed in Figure 5.10, in the case of the UK consumption data.

It will be observed that an H–P filter with $\lambda = 1{,}600$, which defines the middle curve in Figure 5.6, will not be effective in isolating the low-frequency component of the quarterly consumption data of Figure 5.9, which lies in the interval $[0, \pi/8]$. The curve will cut through the low-frequency spectral structure that is represented in Figure 5.10; and the effect will be greatly to attenuate some of the elements of the component that should be preserved intact.

Lowering the value of λ in order to admit a wider range of frequencies will have the effect of creating a frequency response with a gradual transition from the pass band to the stop band. This will be equally inappropriate to the purpose of isolating a component within a well-defined frequency band. For that purpose, a different filter is required.

A filter that may be appropriate to the purpose of isolating the low-frequency fluctuations in consumption is the Butterworth filter. The gain of the latter is illustrated in Figure 5.7. In this case, there is a well-defined nominal cut-off frequency, which is

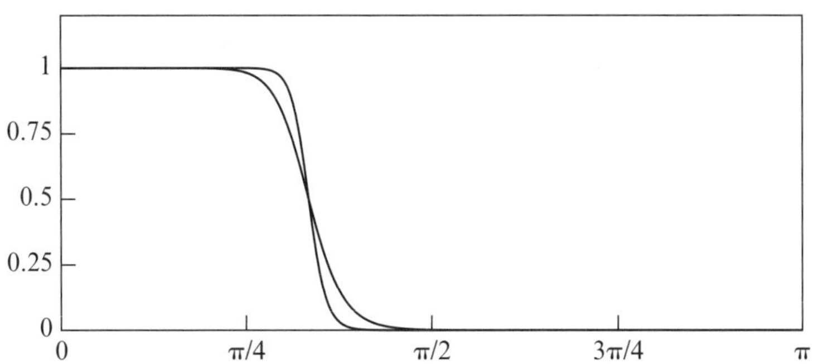

Figure 5.7 *The gain of the lowpass Butterworth filters of orders* $n = 6$ *and* $n = 12$ *with a nominal cut-off point of* $2\pi/3$ *radians*

at the mid point of the transition from the pass band to the stop band. The transition becomes more rapid as the filter order n increases. If a perfectly sharp transition is required, then the frequency-domain filter that will be presented later should be employed.

The Hodrick–Prescott filter has many antecedents. Its invention cannot reasonably be attributed to Hodrick and Prescott (1980, 1997), who cited Whittaker (1923) as one of their sources. Leser (1961) also provided a complete derivation of the filter at an earlier date. The analogue Butterworth filter is a commonplace of electrical engineering. The digital version has been described by Pollock (2000).

WIENER–KOLMOGOROV FILTERS FOR FINITE SEQUENCES

The classical Wiener–Kolmogorov theory can be adapted to finite data sequences generated by stationary stochastic processes.

Consider a data vector $y = [y_0, y_1, \ldots, y_{T-1},]'$ that has a signal component ξ and a noise component η:

$$y = \xi + \eta. \tag{5.48}$$

The two components are assumed to be independently normally distributed with zero means and with positive-definite dispersion matrices. Then,

$$\begin{aligned} E(\xi) &= 0, \quad D(\xi) = \Omega_\xi, \\ E(\eta) &= 0, \quad D(\eta) = \Omega_\eta, \\ \text{and} \quad & C(\xi,\eta) = 0. \end{aligned} \tag{5.49}$$

The dispersion matrices Ω_ξ and Ω_η may be obtained from the autocovariance generating functions $\gamma_\xi(z)$ and $\gamma_\eta(z)$, respectively, by replacing z by the matrix argument $L_T = [e_1, e_2, \ldots, e_{T-1}, 0]$, which is the finite sample-version of the lag operator. This is obtained from the identity matrix $I_T = [e_0, e_1, e_2, \ldots, e_{T-1}]$ by deleting the leading column and by appending a zero vector to the end of the array. Negative powers of z are replaced by powers of the forwards shift operator $F_T = L'_T$. A consequence of the independence of ξ and η is that $D(y) = \Omega_\xi + \Omega_\eta$.

We may begin by considering the determination of the vector of the T filter coefficients $\psi_{t.} = [\psi_{t,0}, \psi_{t,1}, \ldots, \psi_{t,T-1}]$ that determine x_t, which is the tth element of the filtered vector $x = [x_0, x_1, \ldots, x_{T-1}]'$ and which is the estimate of ξ_t. This is derived from the data in $y = [y_0, y_1, \ldots, y_{T-1}]'$ via the equation

$$x_t = \sum_{j=-t}^{T-1-t} \psi_{t,t+j} y_{t-j}. \tag{5.50}$$

The principle of minimum mean-squared error estimation continues to indicate that the estimation errors must be statistically uncorrelated with the elements of the information set. Thus

$$
\begin{aligned}
0 &= E\{y_{t-k}(\xi_t - x_t)\} \\
&= E(y_{t-k}\xi_t) - \sum_{j=-t}^{T-1-t} \psi_{t,t+j} E(y_{t-k} y_{t-j}) \\
&= \gamma^{\xi\xi}_{-k} - \sum_{j=-t}^{T-1+t} \psi_{t,t+j} \gamma^{yy}_{j-k}.
\end{aligned}
\tag{5.51}
$$

Here, $E(y_{t-k}\xi_t) = \gamma^{y\xi}_{-k} = \gamma^{\xi\xi}_{-k}$ in accordance with (5.33). Equation (5.51) can be rendered also in a matrix format. By running from $k = -t$ to $k = T-1-t$, and observing that $\gamma^{\xi\xi}_{-k} = \gamma^{\xi\xi}_{k}$, we get the following system:

$$
\begin{bmatrix} \gamma^{\xi\xi}_t \\ \gamma^{\xi\xi}_{t-1} \\ \vdots \\ \gamma^{\xi\xi}_{T-1-t} \end{bmatrix} = \begin{bmatrix} \gamma^{yy}_0 & \gamma^{yy}_1 & \cdots & \gamma^{yy}_{T-1} \\ \gamma^{yy}_1 & \gamma^{yy}_0 & \cdots & \gamma^{yy}_{T-2} \\ \vdots & \vdots & \ddots & \vdots \\ \gamma^{yy}_{T-1} & \gamma^{yy}_{T-2} & \cdots & \gamma^{yy}_0 \end{bmatrix} \begin{bmatrix} \psi_{t,0} \\ \psi_{t,1} \\ \vdots \\ \psi_{t,T-1} \end{bmatrix}. \tag{5.52}
$$

This equation above can be written in summary notation as $\Omega_\xi e_t = \Omega_y \psi'_{t.}$, where e_t is a vector of order T containing a single unit preceded by t zeros and followed by $T - 1 - t$ zeros. The coefficient vector $\psi_{t.}$ is given by

$$
\psi_{t.} = e'_t \Omega_\xi \Omega_y^{-1} = e'_t \Omega_\xi (\Omega_\xi + \Omega_\eta)^{-1}, \tag{5.53}
$$

and the estimate of ξ_t is $x_t = \psi_{t.} y$. The estimate of the complete vector $\xi = [\xi_0, \xi_1, \ldots, \xi_{T-1}]'$ of the signal elements is

$$
x = \Omega_\xi \Omega_y^{-1} y = \Omega_\xi (\Omega_\xi + \Omega_\eta)^{-1} y. \tag{5.54}
$$

THE ESTIMATES AS CONDITIONAL EXPECTATIONS

The linear estimates of (5.54) have the status of conditional expectations, when the vectors ξ and y are normally distributed. As such, they are, unequivocally, the optimal minimum mean-squared error predictors of the signal and the noise components:

$$
\begin{aligned}
E(\xi|y) &= E(\xi) + C(\xi, y) D^{-1}(y)\{y - E(y)\} \\
&= \Omega_\xi (\Omega_\xi + \Omega_\eta)^{-1} y = x,
\end{aligned}
\tag{5.55}
$$

$$
\begin{aligned}
E(\eta|y) &= E(\eta) + C(\eta, y) D^{-1}(y)\{y - E(y)\} \\
&= \Omega_\eta (\Omega_\xi + \Omega_\eta)^{-1} y = h.
\end{aligned}
\tag{5.56}
$$

The corresponding error dispersion matrices, from which confidence intervals for the estimated components may be derived, are

$$
\begin{aligned}
D(\xi|y) &= D(\xi) + C(\xi, y) D^{-1}(y) C(y,\xi) \\
&= \Omega_\xi - \Omega_\xi (\Omega_\xi + \Omega_\eta)^{-1} \Omega_\xi,
\end{aligned}
\tag{5.57}
$$

$$D(\eta|y) = D(\eta) - C(\eta, y)D^{-1}(y)C(y,\eta),$$
$$= \Omega_\eta - \Omega_\eta(\Omega_\xi + \Omega_\eta)^{-1}\Omega_\eta. \tag{5.58}$$

The equality $D(\xi|y) = D(\eta|y) = (\Omega_\xi^{-1} + \Omega_\eta^{-1})^{-1}$, which is in consequence of the constraint that $\xi + \eta = y$, can be demonstrated via the matrix inversion lemma.

THE LEAST-SQUARES DERIVATION OF THE ESTIMATES

The estimates of ξ and η, which have been denoted by x and h respectively, can also be derived according to the following criterion:

$$\text{Minimize } S(\xi,\eta) = \xi'\Omega_\xi^{-1}\xi + \eta'\Omega_\eta^{-1}\eta \text{ subject to } \xi + \eta = y. \tag{5.59}$$

Since $S(\xi,\eta)$ is the exponent of the normal joint density function $N(\xi,\eta)$, the resulting estimates may be described, alternatively, as the minimum chi-square estimates or as the maximum-likelihood estimates.

Substituting for $\eta = y - \xi$ gives the concentrated criterion function $S(\xi) = \xi'\Omega_\xi^{-1}\xi + (y-\xi)'\Omega_\eta^{-1}(y-\xi)$. Differentiating this function in respect of ξ and setting the result to zero gives the following condition of minimization: $0 = \Omega_\xi^{-1}x - \Omega_\eta^{-1}(y-x)$. From this, it follows that $y - x = \Omega_\eta\Omega_\xi^{-1}x$ and that $y = x + \Omega_\eta\Omega_\xi^{-1}x = (\Omega_\xi + \Omega_\eta)\Omega_\xi^{-1}x$. Therefore, the solution for x is

$$x = \Omega_\xi(\Omega_\xi + \Omega_\eta)^{-1}y. \tag{5.60}$$

Moreover, since the roles of ξ and η are interchangeable in this exercise, and since $h + x = y$, there are also

$$h = \Omega_\eta(\Omega_\xi + \Omega_\eta)^{-1}y \quad \text{and} \quad x = y - \Omega_\eta(\Omega_\xi + \Omega_\eta)^{-1}y. \tag{5.61}$$

The filter matrices $\Psi_\xi = \Omega_\xi(\Omega_\xi + \Omega_\eta)^{-1}$ and $\Psi_\eta = \Omega_\eta(\Omega_\xi + \Omega_\eta)^{-1}$ of (5.60) and (5.61) are the matrix analogues of the z-transforms displayed in equations (5.38) and (5.39).

A simple procedure for calculating the estimates x and h begins by solving the equation

$$(\Omega_\xi + \Omega_\eta)b = y \tag{5.62}$$

for the value of b. Thereafter, one can generate

$$x = \Omega_\xi b \quad \text{and} \quad h = \Omega_\eta b. \tag{5.63}$$

If Ω_ξ and Ω_η correspond to the narrow-band dispersion matrices of moving-average processes, then the solution to equation (5.62) may be found via a Cholesky factorization that sets $\Omega_\xi + \Omega_\eta = GG'$, where G is a lower-triangular matrix with a limited number of non-zero bands. The system $GG'b = y$ may be cast in the form of $Gp = y$ and solved for p. Then, $G'b = p$ can be solved for b.

THE DIFFERENCE AND SUMMATION OPERATORS

A simple expedient for eliminating the trend from the data sequence $y(t) = \{y_t; t = 0, \pm 1, \pm 2, \ldots\}$ is to replace the sequence by its differenced version $y(t) - y(t-1)$ or by its twice differenced version $y(t) - 2y(t-1) + y(t-2)$. Differences of higher orders are rare. The z-transform of the difference is $(1 - z)y(z) = y(z) - zy(z)$. On defining the operator $\nabla(z) = 1 - z$, the second differences can be expressed as $\nabla^2(z)y(t) = (1 - 2z + z^2)y(z)$.

The inverse of the difference operator is the summation operator

$$\Sigma(z) = (1 - z)^{-1} = \{1 + z + z^2 + \cdots\}. \tag{5.64}$$

The z-transform of the d-fold summation operator is as follows:

$$\Sigma^d(z) = \frac{1}{(1 - z)^d} = 1 + dz + \frac{d(d+1)}{2!}z^2 + \frac{d(d+1)(d+2)}{3!}z^3 + \cdots. \tag{5.65}$$

The difference operator has a powerful effect upon the data. It nullifies the trend and it severely attenuates the elements of the data that are adjacent in frequency to the zero frequency of the trend. It also amplifies the high frequency elements of the data. The effect is apparent in Figure 5.8, which shows the squared gain of the difference operator. The figure also shows the squared gain of the summation operator, which gives unbounded power to the elements that have frequencies in the vicinity of zero.

In dealing with a finite sequence, it is appropriate to consider a matrix version of the difference operator. In the case of a sample of T elements comprised by the vector $y = [y_0, y_1, \ldots, y_{T-1}]'$, it is appropriate to use the matrix difference operator $\nabla(L_T) = I_T - L_T$, which is obtained by replacing z within $\nabla(z) = 1 - z$ by the matrix argument $L_T = [e_1, e_2, \ldots, e_{T-1}, 0]$, which is obtained from the identity matrix $I_T = [e_0, e_1, e_2, \ldots, e_{T-1}]$ by deleting the leading column and by appending a zero vector to the end of the array.

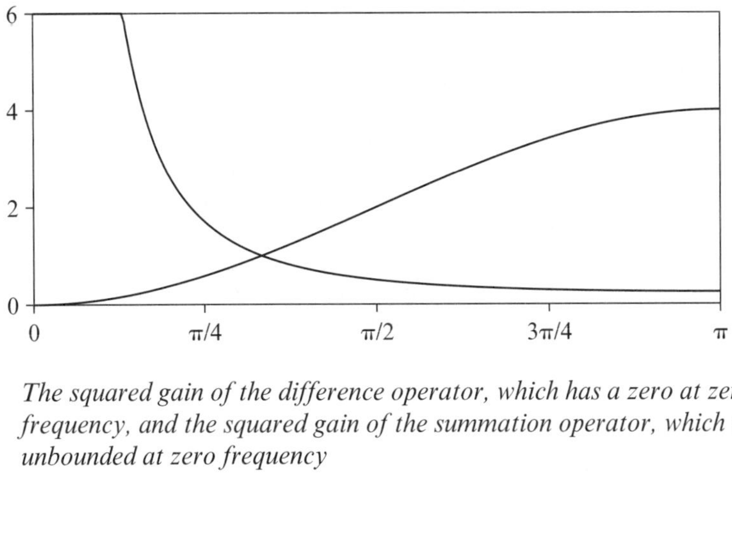

Figure 5.8 The squared gain of the difference operator, which has a zero at zero frequency, and the squared gain of the summation operator, which is unbounded at zero frequency

Examples of the first-order and second-order matrix difference operators are as follows:

$$\nabla_4 = \begin{bmatrix} 1 & 0 & 0 & 0 \\ -1 & 1 & 0 & 0 \\ 0 & -1 & 1 & 0 \\ 0 & 0 & -1 & 1 \end{bmatrix}, \quad \nabla_4^2 = \begin{bmatrix} 1 & 0 & 0 & 0 \\ -2 & 1 & 0 & 0 \\ 1 & -2 & 1 & 0 \\ 0 & 1 & -2 & 1 \end{bmatrix}. \tag{5.66}$$

The corresponding inverse matrices are

$$\Sigma_4 = \begin{bmatrix} 1 & 0 & 0 & 0 \\ 1 & 1 & 0 & 0 \\ 1 & 1 & 1 & 0 \\ 1 & 1 & 1 & 1 \end{bmatrix}, \quad \Sigma_4^2 = \begin{bmatrix} 1 & 0 & 0 & 0 \\ 2 & 1 & 0 & 0 \\ 3 & 2 & 1 & 0 \\ 4 & 3 & 2 & 1 \end{bmatrix}. \tag{5.67}$$

It will be seen that the elements of the leading vectors of these matrices are the coefficients associated with the expansion of $\Sigma^d(z)$ of (5.65) for the cases of $d = 1$ and $d = 2$. The same will be true for higher orders of d.

POLYNOMIAL INTERPOLATION

The first p columns of the matrix Σ_T^p provide a basis of the set of polynomials of degree $p - 1$ defined on the set of integers $t = 0, 1, 2, \ldots, T - 1$. An example is provided by the first three columns of the matrix Σ_4^3, which may be transformed as follows:

$$\begin{bmatrix} 1 & 0 & 0 \\ 3 & 1 & 0 \\ 6 & 3 & 1 \\ 10 & 6 & 3 \end{bmatrix} \begin{bmatrix} 1 & 1 & 1 \\ -2 & -1 & 1 \\ 1 & 0 & 0 \end{bmatrix} = \begin{bmatrix} 1 & 1 & 1 \\ 1 & 2 & 4 \\ 1 & 3 & 9 \\ 1 & 4 & 16 \end{bmatrix}. \tag{5.68}$$

The first column of the matrix on the LHS contains the ordinates of the quadratic function $(t^2 + t)/2$. The columns of the transformed matrix are recognizably the ordinates of the powers, t^0, t^1 and t^2 corresponding to the integers $t = 1, 2, 3, 4$. The natural extension of the matrix to T rows provides a basis for the quadratic functions $q(t) = at^2 + bt + c$ defined on T consecutive integers.

The matrix of the powers of the integers is notoriously ill-conditioned. In calculating polynomial regressions of any degree in excess of the cubic, it is advisable to employ a basis of orthogonal polynomials, for which purpose some specialized numerical procedures are available (see Pollock 1999). In the present context, which concerns econometric data sequences, the degrees of differencing and summation rarely exceed two. Nevertheless, it is appropriate to consider the algebra of the general case.

Consider, therefore, the matrix that takes the pth difference of a vector of order T, which is

$$\nabla_T^p = (I - L_T)^p. \tag{5.69}$$

This matrix can be partitioned so that $\nabla_T^p = [Q_*, Q]'$, where Q_*' has p rows. If y is a vector of T elements, then

$$\nabla_T^p y = \begin{bmatrix} Q_*' \\ Q' \end{bmatrix} y = \begin{bmatrix} g_* \\ g \end{bmatrix}; \tag{5.70}$$

and g_* is liable to be discarded, whereas g will be regarded as the vector of the pth differences of the data.

The inverse matrix may be partitioned conformably to give $\nabla_T^{-p} = [S_*, S]$. It follows that

$$[S_* \quad S] \begin{bmatrix} Q_*' \\ Q' \end{bmatrix} = S_* Q_*' + SQ' = I_T, \tag{5.71}$$

and that

$$\begin{bmatrix} Q_*' \\ Q' \end{bmatrix} [S_* \quad S] = \begin{bmatrix} Q_*' S_* & Q_*' S \\ Q' S_* & Q' S \end{bmatrix} = \begin{bmatrix} I_p & 0 \\ 0 & I_{T-p} \end{bmatrix}. \tag{5.72}$$

If g_* is available, then y can be recovered from g via

$$y = S_* g_* + Sg. \tag{5.73}$$

Since the submatrix S_* provides a basis for all polynomials of degree $p - 1$ that are defined on the integer points $t = 0, 1, \ldots, T - 1$, it follows that $S_* g_* = S_* Q_*' y$ contains the ordinates of a polynomial of degree $p - 1$, which is interpolated through the first p elements of y, indexed by $t = 0, 1, \ldots, p - 1$, and which is extrapolated over the remaining integers $t = p, p + 1, \ldots, T - 1$.

A polynomial that is designed to fit the data should take account of all of the observations in y. Imagine, therefore, that $y = \phi + \eta$, where ϕ contains the ordinates of a polynomial of degree $p - 1$ and η is a disturbance term with $E(\eta) = 0$ and $D(\eta) = \sigma_\eta^2 I_T$. Then, in forming an estimate $x = S_* r_*$ of ϕ, we should minimize the sum of squares $\eta'\eta$. Since the polynomial is fully determined by the elements of a starting-value vector r_*, this is a matter of minimizing

$$(y - x)'(y - x) = (y - S_* r_*)'(y - S_* r_*) \tag{5.74}$$

with respect to r_*. The resulting values are

$$r_* = (S_*' S_*)^{-1} S_*' y \quad \text{and} \quad x = S_* (S_*' S_*)^{-1} S_*' y. \tag{5.75}$$

An alternative representation of the estimated polynomial is available. This is provided by the identity

$$S_* (S_*' S_*)^{-1} S_*' = I - Q(Q'Q)^{-1} Q'. \tag{5.76}$$

To prove this identity, consider the fact that $Z = [Q, S_*]$ is square matrix of full rank and that Q and S_* are mutually orthogonal such that $Q' S_* = 0$. Then

$$Z(Z'Z)^{-1}Z' = [Q \quad S_*]\begin{bmatrix} (Q'Q)^{-1} & 0 \\ 0 & (S_*'S_*)^{-1} \end{bmatrix}\begin{bmatrix} Q' \\ S_*' \end{bmatrix}$$
$$= Q(Q'Q)^{-1}Q' + S_*(S_*'S_*)^{-1}S_*'. \tag{5.77}$$

The result of (5.76) follows from the fact that $Z(Z'Z)^{-1}Z' = Z(Z^{-1}Z'^{-1})Z' = I$. It follows from (5.76) that the vector of the ordinates of the polynomial regression is also given by

$$x = y - Q(Q'Q)^{-1}Q'y. \tag{5.78}$$

POLYNOMIAL REGRESSION AND TREND EXTRACTION

The use of polynomial regression in a preliminary detrending of the data is an essential part of a strategy for determining an appropriate representation of the underlying trajectory of an econometric data sequence. Once the trend has been eliminated from the data, one can proceed to assess their spectral structure by examining the periodogram of the residual sequence.

Often the periodogram will reveal the existence of a cut-off frequency that bounds a low-frequency trend/cycle component and separates it from the remaining elements of the spectrum.

An example is given in Figures 5.9 and 5.10. Figure 5.9 represents the logarithms of the quarterly data on aggregate consumption in the United Kingdom for the years 1955 to 1994. Through these data, a linear trend has been interpolated by least-squares regression. This line establishes a benchmark of constant exponential growth, against which the fluctuations of consumption can be measured. The periodogram of the residual sequence is plotted in Figure 5.10. This shows that the low-frequency structure is bounded by a frequency value of $\pi/8$. This value can used in specifying the appropriate filter for extracting the low-frequency trajectory of the data.

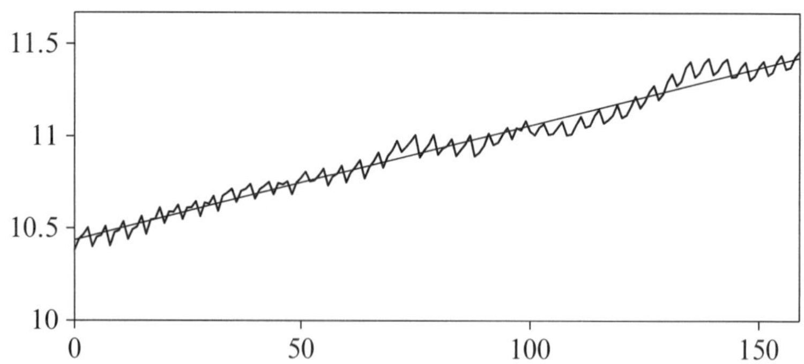

Figure 5.9 The quarterly series of the logarithms of consumption in the UK for the years 1955 to 1994, together with a linear trend interpolated by least-squares regression

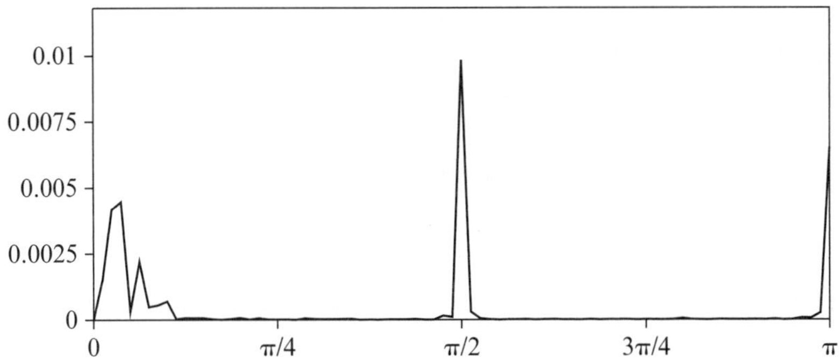

Figure 5.10 *The periodogram of the residual sequence obtained from the linear detrending of the logarithmic consumption data*

FILTERS FOR SHORT TRENDED SEQUENCES

One way of eliminating the trend is to take differences of the data. Usually, twofold differencing is appropriate. The matrix analogue of the second-order backwards difference operator in the case of $T = 5$ is given by

$$\nabla_5^2 = \begin{bmatrix} Q'_* \\ Q' \end{bmatrix} = \left[\begin{array}{ccccc} 1 & 0 & 0 & 0 & 0 \\ -2 & 1 & 0 & 0 & 0 \\ \hline 1 & -2 & 1 & 0 & 0 \\ 0 & 1 & -2 & 1 & 0 \\ 0 & 0 & 1 & -2 & 1 \end{array}\right]. \tag{5.79}$$

The first two rows, which do not produce true differences, are liable to be discarded. In general, the p-fold differences of a data vector of T elements will be obtained by pre-multiplying it by a matrix Q' of order $(T - p) \times T$. Applying Q' to the equation $y = \xi + \eta$, representing the trended data, gives

$$\begin{aligned} Q'y &= Q'\xi + Q'\eta \\ &= \delta + \kappa = g. \end{aligned} \tag{5.80}$$

The vectors of the expectations and the dispersion matrices of the differenced vectors are

$$\begin{aligned} E(\delta) &= 0, \quad D(\delta) = \Omega_\delta = Q'D(\xi)Q, \\ E(\kappa) &= 0, \quad D(\kappa) = \Omega_k = Q'D(\eta)Q. \end{aligned} \tag{5.81}$$

The difficulty of estimating the trended vector $\xi = y - \eta$ directly is that some starting values or initial conditions are required in order to define the value at time $t = 0$. However, since η is from a stationary mean-zero process, it requires only zero-valued initial conditions. Therefore, the starting-value problem can be circumvented by concentrating on the estimation of η. The conditional expectation of η, given the differenced data $g = Q'y$, is provided by the formula

$$\begin{aligned} h = E(\eta|g) &= E(\eta) + C(\eta, g)D^{-1}(g)\{g - E(g)\} \\ &= C(\eta, g)D^{-1}(g)g, \end{aligned} \tag{5.82}$$

where the second equality follows in view of the zero-valued expectations. Within this expression, there are

$$D(g) = \Omega_\delta + Q'\Omega_\eta Q \quad \text{and} \quad C(\eta, g) = \Omega_\eta Q. \tag{5.83}$$

Putting these details into (5.82) gives the following estimate of η:

$$h = \Omega_\eta Q(\Omega_\delta + Q'\Omega_\eta Q)^{-1}Q'y. \tag{5.84}$$

Putting this into the equation

$$x = E(\xi|g) = y - E(\eta|g) = y - h \tag{5.85}$$

gives

$$x = y - \Omega_\eta Q(\Omega_\delta + Q'\Omega_\eta Q)^{-1}Q'y. \tag{5.86}$$

THE LEAST-SQUARES DERIVATION OF THE FILTER

As in the case of the extraction of a signal from a stationary process, the estimate of the trended vector ξ can also be derived according to a least-squares criterion. The criterion is

$$\text{Minimize} \quad (y - \xi)'\Omega_\eta^{-1}(y - \xi) + \xi'Q\Omega_\delta^{-1}Q'\xi. \tag{5.87}$$

The first term in this expression penalizes the departures of the resulting curve from the data, whereas the second term imposes a penalty for a lack of smoothness. Differentiating the function with respect to ξ and setting the result to zero gives

$$\Omega_\eta^{-1}(y - x) = -Q\Omega_\delta^{-1}Q'x = Q\Omega_\delta^{-1}d, \tag{5.88}$$

where x stands for the estimated value of ξ and where $d = Q'x$. Pre-multiplying by $Q'\Omega_\eta$ gives

$$Q'(y - x) = Q'y - d = Q'\Omega_\eta Q\Omega_\delta^{-1}d, \tag{5.89}$$

whence

$$\begin{aligned} Q'y &= d + Q'\Omega_\eta Q\Omega_\delta^{-1}d \\ &= (\Omega_\delta + Q'\Omega_\eta Q)\Omega_\delta^{-1}d, \end{aligned} \tag{5.90}$$

which gives

$$\Omega_\delta^{-1}d = (\Omega_\delta + Q'\Omega_\eta Q)^{-1}Q'y. \tag{5.91}$$

Putting this into

$$x = y - \Omega_\eta Q\Omega_\delta^{-1}d, \tag{5.92}$$

which comes from pre-multiplying (5.88) by Ω_η, gives

$$x = y - \Omega_\eta Q(\Omega_\delta + Q'\Omega_\eta Q)^{-1}Q'y, \tag{5.93}$$

which is equation (5.86) again.

One should observe that

$$\begin{aligned} h &= \Omega_\eta Q(\Omega_\delta + Q'\Omega_\eta Q)^{-1}Q'y \\ &= \Omega_\eta Q(\Omega_\delta + Q'\Omega_\eta Q)^{-1}Q'e, \end{aligned} \tag{5.94}$$

where $e = Q(Q'Q)^{-1}Q'y$ is the vector of residuals obtained by interpolating a straight line through the data by a least-squares regression. That is to say, it makes no difference to the estimate h of the component that is complementary to the trend whether the filter is applied to the data vector y or the residual vector e. If the trend-estimation filter is applied to e instead of to y, then the resulting vector can be added to the ordinates of the interpolated line to create the estimate of the trend.

THE LESER (H–P) FILTER AND THE BUTTERWORTH FILTER

The specific cases that have been considered in the context of the classical form of the Wiener–Kolmogorov filter can now be adapted to the circumstances of short trended sequences. First, there is the Leser or H–P filter. This is derived by setting

$$D(\eta) = \Omega_\eta = \sigma_\eta^2 I, \quad D(\delta) = \Omega_\delta = \sigma_\delta^2 I \quad \text{and} \quad \lambda = \frac{\sigma_\eta^2}{\sigma_\delta^2} \tag{5.95}$$

within (5.93) to give

$$x = y - Q(\lambda^{-1}I + Q'Q)^{-1}Q'y. \tag{5.96}$$

Here, λ is the so-called smoothing parameter. It will be observed that, as $\lambda \to \infty$, the vector x tends to that of a linear function interpolated into the data by least-squares regression, which is represented by equation (5.78). The matrix expression $\Psi = I - Q(\lambda^{-1}I + Q'Q)^{-1}Q'$ for the filter can be compared to the polynomial expression

$\psi^c(z) = 1 - \psi(z)$ of the classical formulation, which entails the z-transform from (5.45).

The Butterworth filter that is appropriate to short trended sequences can be represented by the equation

$$x = y - \lambda\Sigma Q(M + \lambda Q'\Sigma Q)^{-1}Q'y. \tag{5.97}$$

Here, the matrices

$$\Sigma = \{2I_T - (L_T + L_T')\}^{n-2} \text{ and } M = \{2I_T + (L_T + L_T')\}^{n} \tag{5.98}$$

are obtained from the RHS of the equations $\{(1-z)(1-z^{-1})\}^{n-2} = \{2-(z+z^{-1})\}^{n-2}$ and $\{(1+z)(1+z^{-1})\}^{n} = \{2+(z+z^{-1})\}^{n}$, respectively, by replacing z by L_T and z^{-1} by L_T'. Observe that the equalities no longer hold after the replacements. However, it can be verified that

$$Q'\Sigma Q = \{2I_T - (L_T + L_T')\}^{n}. \tag{5.99}$$

FILTERING IN THE FREQUENCY DOMAIN

The method of Wiener–Kolmogorov filtering can also be implemented using the circulant dispersion matrices that are given by

$$\begin{aligned} &\Omega_\xi^\circ = \bar{U}\gamma_\xi(D)U, \quad \Omega_\eta^\circ = \bar{U}\gamma\eta(D)U \quad \text{and} \\ &\Omega^\circ = \Omega_\xi^\circ + \Omega_\eta^\circ = \bar{U}\{\gamma_\xi(D) + \gamma_\eta(D)\}U, \end{aligned} \tag{5.100}$$

wherein the diagonal matrices $\gamma_\xi(D)$ and $\gamma_\eta(D)$ contain the ordinates of the spectral density functions of the component processes. Accounts of the algebra of circulant matrices have been provided by Pollock (1999 and 2002). See, also, Gray (2002).

Here, $U = T^{-1/2}[W^{jt}]$, wherein $t,j = 0, \ldots, T-1$, is the matrix of the Fourier transform, of which the generic element in the jth row and tth column is $W^{jt} = \exp(-i2\pi tj/T)$, and $\bar{U} = T^{1/2}[W^{-jt}]$ is its conjugate transpose. Also, $D = \text{diag}\{1, W, W^2, \ldots, W^{T-1}\}$, which replaces z within each of the autocovariance generating functions, is a diagonal matrix whose elements are the T roots of unity, which are found on the circumference of the unit circle in the complex plane.

By replacing the dispersion matrices within (5.55) and (5.56) by their circulant counterparts, we derive the following formulae:

$$x = \bar{U}\gamma_\xi(D)\{\gamma_\xi(D) + \gamma_\eta(D)\}^{-1}Uy = P_\xi y, \tag{5.101}$$

$$h = \bar{U}\gamma_\eta(D)\{\gamma_\xi(D) + \gamma_\eta(D)\}^{-1}Uy = P_\eta y. \tag{5.102}$$

Similar replacements within the formulae (5.57) and (5.58) provide the expressions for the error dispersion matrices that are appropriate to the circular filters.

The filtering formulae may be implemented in the following way. First, a Fourier

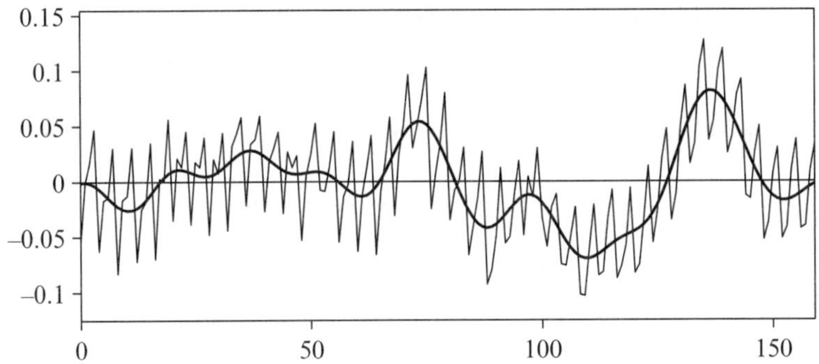

Figure 5.11 *The residual sequence from fitting a linear trend to the logarithmic consumption data with an interpolated line representing the business cycle, obtained by the frequency-domain method*

transform is applied to the data vector y to give Uy, which resides in the frequency domain. Then, the elements of the transformed vector are multiplied by those of the diagonal weighting matrices $J_\xi = \gamma_\xi(D)\{\gamma_\xi(D) + \gamma_\eta(D)\}^{-1}$ and $J_\eta = \gamma_\eta(D)\{\gamma_\xi(D) + \gamma_\eta(D)\}^{-1}$. Finally, the products are carried back into the time domain by the inverse Fourier transform, which is represented by the matrix $\bar{U}$.

An example of the method of frequency filtering is provided by Figure 5.11, which shows the effect applying a filter with a sharp cut-off at the frequency value of $\pi/8$ radians per period to the residual sequence obtained from a linear detrending of the quarterly logarithmic consumption data of the UK.

This cut-off frequency has been chosen in reference to the periodogram of the residual sequence, which is in Figure 5.10. This shows that the low-frequency structure of the data falls in the interval $[0, \pi/8]$. Apart from the prominent spike at the season frequency of $\pi/2$ and the smaller seasonal spike at the frequency of π, the remainder of the periodogram is characterized by wide spectral deadspaces.

The filters described above are appropriate only to stationary processes. However, they can be adapted in several alternative ways to cater to non stationary processes. One way is to reduce the data to stationarity by twofold differencing before filtering it. After filtering, the data may be reinflated by a process of summation.

As before, let the original data be denoted by $y = \xi + \eta$ and let the differenced data be $g = Q'y = \delta + \kappa$. If the estimates of $\delta = Q'\xi$ and $\kappa = Q'\eta$ are denoted by d and k respectively, then the estimates of ξ and η will be

$$x = S_*d_* + Sd \quad \text{where} \quad d_* = (S_*'S_*)^{-1}S_*'(y - Sd) \tag{5.103}$$

and

$$h = S_*k_* + Sk \quad \text{where} \quad k_* = -(S_*'S_*)^{-1}S_*'Sk. \tag{5.104}$$

Here, d_* an k_* are the initial conditions that are obtained via the minimization of the function

$$\begin{aligned}(y-x)'(y-x) &= (y-S_*d_*-Sd)'(y-S_*d_*-Sd)\\ &= (S_*k_*+Sk)'(S_*k_*+Sk) = h'h. \end{aligned} \tag{5.105}$$

The minimization ensures that the estimated trend x adheres as closely as possible to the data y.

In the case where the data are differenced twice, there is

$$S_*' = \begin{bmatrix} 1 & 2 & \dots & T-1 & T \\ 0 & 1 & \dots & T-2 & T-1 \end{bmatrix}. \tag{5.106}$$

The elements of the matrix $S_*'S_*$ can be found via the formulae

$$\begin{aligned}\sum_{t=1}^{T} t^2 &= \frac{1}{6}T(T+1)(2T+1) \quad \text{and}\\ \sum_{t=1}^{T} t(t-1) &= \frac{1}{6}T(T+1)(2T+1) - \frac{1}{2}T(T+1). \end{aligned} \tag{5.107}$$

A compendium of such results has been provided by Jolly (1961), and proofs of the present results were given by Hall and Knight (1899).

A fuller account of the implementation of the frequency filter has been provided by Pollock (2009).

Example Before applying a frequency-domain filter, it is necessary to ensure that the data are free of trend. If a trend is detected, then it may be removed from the data by subtracting an interpolated polynomial trend function. A test for the presence of a trend is required that differs from the tests that are used to detect the presence of unit roots in the processes generating the data. This is provided by the significance test associated with the ordinary-least squares estimate of a linear trend.

There is a simple means of calculating the adjusted sum of squares of the temporal index $t = 0, 1, \dots, T-1$, which is entailed in the calculation of the slope coefficient

$$b = \frac{\sum y_t^2 - \left(\sum y_t\right)^2 / T}{\sum t^2 - \left(\sum t\right)^2 / T}. \tag{5.108}$$

The formulae

$$\sum_{t=0}^{T-1} t^2 = \frac{1}{6}(T-1)T(2T-1) \quad \text{and} \quad \sum_{t=0}^{T-1} t = \frac{T(T-1)}{2} \tag{5.109}$$

are combined to provide a convenient means of calculating the denominator of the formula of (5.108):

$$\sum_{t=0}^{T-1} t^2 - \frac{\left(\sum_{t=0}^{T-1} t\right)^2}{T} = \frac{(T-1)T(T+1)}{12}. \tag{5.110}$$

Another means of calculating the low-frequency trajectory of the data via the frequency domain mimics the method of equation (5.93) by concentrating of the estimation the high-frequency component. This can be subtracted from the data to create an estimate of the complementary low-frequency trend component. However, whereas in the case of equation (5.93) the differencing of the data and the re-inflation of the estimated high-frequency component are deemed to take place in the time domain, now the re-inflation occurs in the frequency domain before the resulting vector of Fourier coefficients is transformed to the time domain.

The reduction of a trended data sequence to stationarity continues to be effected by the matrix Q but, in this case, the matrix can be seen in the context of a centralized difference operator. This is

$$\begin{aligned} N(z) &= z^{-1} - 2 + z = z^{-1}(1 - z)^2 \\ &= z^{-1}\nabla^2(z). \end{aligned} \tag{5.111}$$

The matrix version of the operator is obtained by setting $z = L_T$ and $z^{-1} = L'_T$, which gives

$$N(L_T) = N_T = L_T - 2I_T + L'_T. \tag{5.112}$$

The first and the final rows of this matrix do not deliver true differences. Therefore, they are liable to be deleted, with the effect that the two end points are lost from the twice-differenced data. Deleting the rows e'_0N_T and $e'_{T-1}N_T$ from N_T gives the matrix Q', which can also be obtained from $\nabla^2_T = (I_T - L_T)^2$ by deleting the matrix Q'_*, which comprises the first two rows $e'_0\nabla^2_T$ and $e'_1\nabla^2_T$. In the case of $T = 5$ there is

$$N_5 = \begin{bmatrix} Q'_{-1} \\ Q' \\ Q_{+1} \end{bmatrix} = \left[\begin{array}{ccccc} -2 & 1 & 0 & 0 & 0 \\ \hline 1 & -2 & 1 & 0 & 0 \\ 0 & 1 & -2 & 1 & 0 \\ 0 & 0 & 1 & -2 & 1 \\ \hline 0 & 0 & 0 & 1 & -2 \end{array}\right]. \tag{5.113}$$

On deleting the first and last elements of the vector N_Ty, which are $Q'_{-1}y = e'_1\nabla^2_T y$ and $Q_{+1}y$, respectively, we get $Q'y = [q_1, \ldots, q_{T-2}]'$.

The loss of the two elements from either end of the (centrally) twice-differenced data can be overcome by supplementing the original data vector y with two extrapolated end points y_{-1} and y_T. Alternatively, the differenced data may be supplemented by attributing appropriate values to q_0 and q_{T-1}. These could be zeros or some combination of the adjacent values. In either case, we will obtain a vector of order T denoted by $q = [q_0, q_1, \ldots, q_{T-1}]'$.

In describing the method for implementing a highpass filter, let Λ be the matrix that selects the appropriate ordinates of the Fourier transform $\gamma = Uq$ of the twice differenced data. These ordinates must be reinflated to compensate for the differencing operation, which has the frequency response

$$f(\omega) = 2 - 2\cos(\omega). \tag{5.114}$$

The response of the anti-differencing operation is $1/f(\omega)$; and γ is reinflated by pre-multiplying by the diagonal matrix

$$V = \text{diag}\{v_0, v_1, \ldots, v_{T-1}\}, \tag{5.115}$$

comprising the values $v_j = 1/f(\omega_j); j = 0, \ldots, T-1$, where $\omega_j = 2\pi j/T$.

Let $H = V\Lambda$ be the matrix that is applied to $\gamma = Uq$ to generate the Fourier ordinates of the filtered vector. The resulting vector is transformed to the time domain to give

$$h = \bar{U}H\gamma = \bar{U}HUq. \tag{5.116}$$

It will be seen that $f(\omega)$ is zero-valued when $\omega = 0$ and that $1/f(\omega)$ is unbounded in the neighbourhood of $\omega = 0$. Therefore, a frequency-domain reinflation is available only when there are no non-zero Fourier ordinates in this neighbourhood. That is to say, it can work only in conjunction with highpass or bandpass filtering. However, it is straightforward to construct a lowpass filter that complements the highpass filter. The low-frequency trend component that is complementary to h is

$$x = y - h = y - \bar{U}HUq. \tag{5.117}$$

BUSINESS CYCLES AND SPURIOUS CYCLES

Econometricians continue to debate the question of how macroeconomic data sequences should be decomposed into their constituent components. These components are usually described as the trend, the cyclical component or the business cycle, the seasonal component and the irregular component.

For the original data, the decomposition is usually a multiplicative one and, for the logarithmic data, the corresponding decomposition is an additive one. The filters are usually applied to the logarithmic data, in which case, the sum of the estimated components should equal the logarithmic data.

In the case of the Wiener–Kolmogorov filters, and of the frequency-domain filters as well, the filter gain never exceeds unity. Therefore, every lowpass filter $\psi(z)$ is accompanied by a complementary highpass filter $\psi^c(z) = 1 - \psi(z)$. The two sequences resulting from these filters can be recombined to create the data sequence from which they have originated.

Such filters can be applied sequentially to create an additive decomposition of the data. First, the tend is extracted. Then, the cyclical component is extracted from the detrended data, Finally, the residue can be decomposed into the seasonal and the irregular components.

Within this context, the manner in which any component is defined and how it is extracted are liable to affect the definitions of all of the other components. In particular, variations in the definition of the trend will have substantial effects upon the representation of the business cycle.

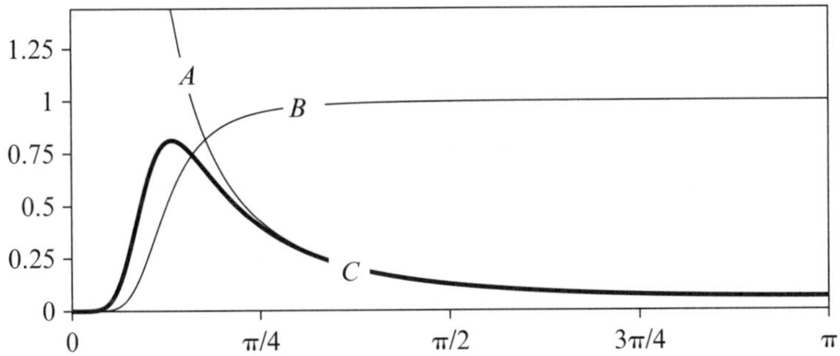

Figure 5.12 *The pseudo-spectrum of a random walk, labelled* A*, together with the squared gain of the highpass Hodrick–Prescott filter with a smoothing parameter of* $\lambda = 100$*, labelled* B*. The curve labelled* C *represents the spectrum of the filtered process*

It has been the contention of several authors, including Harvey and Jaeger (1993) and Cogley and Nason (1995), that the effect of using the Hodrick–Prescott filter to extract a trend from the data is to create or induce spurious cycles in the complementary component, which includes the cyclical component.

Others have declared that such an outcome is impossible. They point to the fact that, since their gains never exceeds unity, the filters cannot introduce anything into the data, nor can they amplify anything that is already present. On this basis, it can be fairly asserted that, at least, the verbs *to create* and *to induce* have been mis-applied, and that the use of the adjective *spurious* is doubtful.

The analyses of Harvey and Jaeger and of Cogley and Nason have both depicted the effects of applying the Hodrick–Prescott filter to a theoretical random walk that is supported on a doubly-infinite set of integers. They show that the spectral density function of the filtered process possesses a peak in the low-frequency region that is based on a broad range of frequencies. This seems to suggest that there is cyclicality in the processed data, whereas the original random walk has no central tendency.

This analysis is illustrated in Figure 5.12. The curve labelled A is the pseudo spectrum of a first-order random walk. The curve labelled B is the squared modulus of the frequency response of the highpass, detrending, filter with a smoothing parameter of 100. The curve labelled C is the spectral density function of a detrended sequence which, in theory, would be derived by applying the filter to the random walk.

The fault of the Hodrick–Prescott filter may be that it allows elements of the data at certain frequencies to be transmitted when, ideally, they should be blocked. However, it seems that an analysis based on a doubly-infinite random walk is of doubtful validity.

The effects that are depicted in Figure 5.12 are due largely to the unbounded nature of the pseudo spectrum labelled A, and, as we have already declared, there is a zero probability that, at any given time, the value generated by the random walk will fall within a finite distance of the horizontal axis.

An alternative analysis of the filter can be achieved by examining the effects of its finite-sample version upon a finite and bounded sequence that has been detrended by

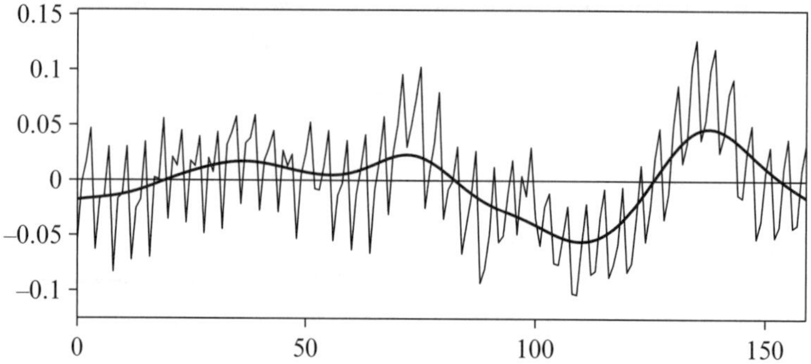

Figure 5.13 *The residual sequence obtained by extracting a linear trend from the logarithmic consumption data, together with a low-frequency trajectory that has been obtained via the lowpass Hodrick–Prescott filter*

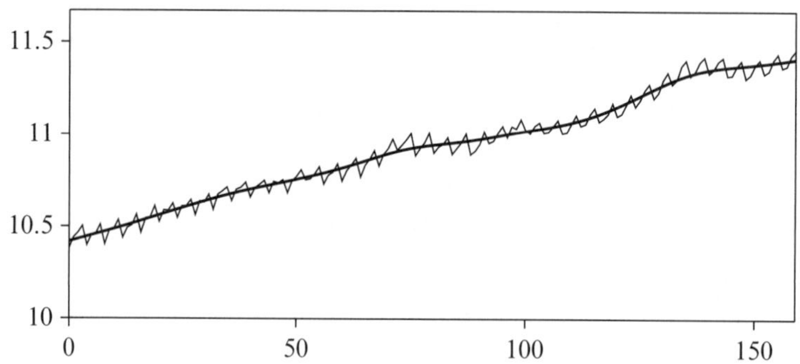

Figure 5.14 *The quarterly logarithmic consumption data together with a trend interpolated by the lowpass Hodrick–Prescott filter with the smoothing parameter set to $\lambda = 1{,}600$*

the interpolation of a linear regression function, according to the ordinary least-squares criterion.

If y is the vector of the data and if $P_Q = Q(Q'Q)^{-1}Q'$, where Q is the second-order difference operator, then the vector of the ordinates of the linear regression is $(I - P_Q)y$, and the detrended vector is the residual vector $e = P_Qy$. The highpass Hodrick–Prescott filter $\Psi_H = Q(\lambda^{-1}I + Q'Q)^{-1}Q'$ will generate the same output from the linearly detrended data as from the original data. Thus, it follows from (5.94) that $\Psi_Hy = \Psi_He$.

In characterizing the effects of the filter, it is reasonable to compare the linearly detrended data $e = P_Qy$ with the output Ψ_Hy of the filter. In the case of the logarithmic consumption data, these sequences are represented by the jagged lines that are, respectively, the backdrops to Figures 5.13 and 5.15.

Superimposed upon the residual sequence $e = P_Qy$ of Figure 5.13 is the low-frequency trajectory $(I - \Psi_H)P_Qy = (I - \Psi_H)e$ that has been obtained by subjecting e to the lowpass Hodrick–Prescott Filter with a smoothing parameter of 1,600.

Figure 5.14 shows the quarterly logarithmic consumption data together with a trend

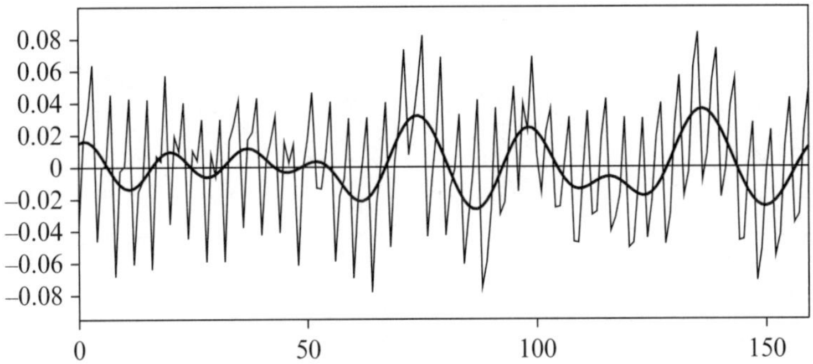

Figure 5.15 *The residual sequence obtained by using the Hodrick–Prescott filter to extract the trend, together with a fluctuating component obtained by subjecting the sequence to a lowpass frequency-domain filter with a cut-off point at π/8 radians*

$x = (I - \Psi_H)y$ interpolated by the lowpass Hodrick–Prescott filter. This trend can be obtained by adding the smooth trajectory of $(I - \Psi_H)e$ of Figure 5.13 to the linear trend $(I - P_Q)y$. That is to say,

$$\begin{aligned}(I - \Psi_H)y &= (I - \Psi_H)\{P_Q y + (I - P_Q)y\}\\ &= (I - \Psi_H)e + (I - P_Q)y, \qquad (5.118)\end{aligned}$$

which follows since $(I - \Psi_H)(I - P_Q) = (I - P_Q)$. (An implication of this identity is that a linear trend will be preserved by the lowpass H–P filter.)

Superimposed upon the jagged sequence $\Psi_H e$ of Figure 5.15 is the smoothed sequence $\Psi_\xi^\circ \Psi_H e$, where Ψ_ξ° is the lowpass frequency-domain filter with a cut-off at $\pi/8$ radians, which is the value that has been determined from the inspection of the periodogram of Figure 5.10.

Now, a comparison can be made of the smooth trajectory $\Psi_\xi^\circ e - \Psi_\xi^\circ P_Q y$ of Figure 5.11, which has been determined via linear detrending, and which has been regarded as an appropriate representation of the business cycle, with the trajectory $x^\circ = \Psi_\xi^\circ \Psi_H y$ of Figure 5.15, which has been determined using the Hodrick–Prescott filter to detrend the data.

Whereas the same essential fluctuations are present in both trajectories, it is apparent that the more flexible detrending of the Hodrick–Prescott filter has served to reduce and to regularize their amplitudes. Thus, some proportion of the fluctuations, which ought to be present in the trajectory of the business cycle, has been transferred into the trend.

Thus, although it cannot be be said that the Hodrick–Prescott filter induces spurious fluctuations in the filtered sequence, it is true that it enhances the regularity of fluctuations that are present in the data. However, the same can be said, without exception, of any frequency-selective filter.

To prevent it from absorbing the fluctuations, the trend should be maximally stiff, unless it is required to accommodate a structural break. The trend is to be regarded as a benchmark with which to measure the cyclical fluctuations. In times of normal economic

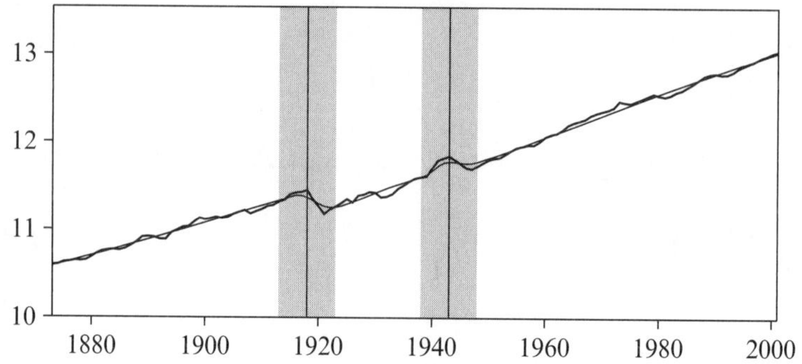

Figure 5.16 The logarithms of annual UK real GDP from 1873 to 2001 with an interpolated trend: the trend is estimated via a filter with a variable smoothing parameter

activity, a log linear trend, which represents a trajectory of constant exponential growth, may be appropriate. At other times the trend should be allowed to adapt to reflect untoward events.

A device that achieves this is available in the form of a version of the H–P filter that has a smoothing parameter that is variable over the sample. When the trajectory of the trend is required to accommodate a structural break, the smoothing parameter λ can be set to a value close to zero within the appropriate locality. Elsewhere, it can be given a high value to ensure that a stiff curve is created. Such a filter is available in the IDEOLOG computer program, of which the web address will be given at the end of the chapter.

Figure 5.16 shown an example of the use of this filter. There were brief disruptions to the steady upwards progress of GDP in the UK after the two world wars. These breaks have been absorbed into the trend by reducing the value of the smoothing parameter in their localities, which are highlighted in the figure. By contrast, the break that is evident in the data following the year 1929 has not been accommodated in the trend.

SEASONAL ADJUSTMENT IN THE TIME DOMAIN

The seasonal adjustment of economic data is performed preponderantly by central statistical agencies. The prevalent methods continue to be those that were developed by the US Bureau of Census and which are encapsulated in the X-11 computer program and its derivatives X-11-ARIMA and X-12. The X-11 program was the culmination of the pioneering work of Julius Shiskin in the 1960s (see Shiskin et al., 1967).

The X-11 program, which is difficult to describe concisely, depends on the successive application of the time-honoured Henderson moving-average filters that have proved to be very effective in practice but which lack a firm foundation in the modern theory of filtering. An extensive description of the program has been provided by Ladiry and Quenneville (2001).

Recently, some alternative methods of seasonal adjustment have been making headway amongst central statistical agencies. Foremost amongst these is the ARIMA-model-based method of the TRAMO–SEATS package. Within this program, the TRAMO (Time Series Regression with ARIMA Noise, Missing Observations and Outliers) module estimates a model of the composite process. Thereafter, the estimated parameters are taken to be the true parameters of the process, and they are passed to the SEATS (Signal Extraction in ARIMA Time Series) module, which extracts the components of the data.

The program employs the airline passenger model of Box and Jenkins (1976) as its default model. This is represented by the equation

$$y(z) = \frac{N(z)}{P(z)}\varepsilon(z) = \left\{\frac{(1-\rho z)(1-\theta z^s)}{(1-z)(1-z^s)}\right\}\varepsilon(z), \qquad (5.119)$$

where $N(z)$ and $P(z)$ are polynomial operators and $y(z)$ and $\varepsilon(z)$ are, respectively, the z-transforms of the output sequence $y(t)=\{y_t; t=0,\pm1,\pm2,\ldots\}$ and of the input sequence $\varepsilon(t)=\{\varepsilon_t; t=0,\pm1,\pm2,\ldots\}$ of unobservable white-noise disturbances. The integer s stands for the number of periods in the year, which are $s=4$ for quarterly data and $s=12$ for monthly data. Without loss of generality as far as the derivation of the filters is concerned, the variance of the input sequence can be set to unity.

Given the identity $1-z^s=(1-z)\Sigma(z)$, where $\Sigma(z)=1+z+\cdots+z^{s-1}$ is the seasonal summation operator, it follows that

$$P(z) = (1-z)(1-z^s) = \nabla^2(z)\Sigma(z), \qquad (5.120)$$

where $\nabla(z) = 1 - z$ is the backward difference operator. The polynomial $\Sigma(z)$ has zeros at the points $\exp\{i(2\pi/s)j\}; j=1,2,\ldots,s-1$, which are located on the circumference of the unit circle in the complex plane at angles from the horizontal that correspond to the fundamental seasonal frequency $\omega_s = 2\pi/s$ and its harmonics.

The TRAMO–SEATS program effects a decomposition of the data into a seasonal component and a non-seasonal component that are described by statistically independent processes driven by separate white-noise forcing functions. It espouses the principle of canonical decompositions that has been expounded by Hillmer and Tiao (1982).

The first step in this decomposition entails the following partial-fraction decomposition of the generating function of the autocovariances of $y(t)$:

$$\frac{N(z^{-1})N(z)}{P(z^{-1})P(z)} = \frac{U^*(z^{-1})U^*(z)}{\nabla^2(z^{-1})\nabla^2(z)} + \frac{V^*(z^{-1})V^*(z)}{\Sigma(z^{-1})\Sigma(z)} + \rho\theta. \qquad (5.121)$$

Here, $\rho\theta$ is the quotient of the division of $N(z^{-1})N(z)$ by $P(z^{-1})P(z)$, which must occur before the remainder, which will be a proper fraction, can be decomposed.

In the preliminary decomposition of (5.121), the first term on the RHS corresponds to the trend component, the second term corresponds to the seasonal component and the third term corresponds to the irregular component. Hillmer and Tiao have provided expressions for the numerators of the RHS, which are somewhat complicated, albeit that the numerators can also be found by numerical means.

When $z = e^{i\omega}$, equation (5.121) provides the spectral ordinates of the process and of its components at the frequency value of ω. The corresponding spectral density functions are obtained by letting ω run from 0 to π. The quotient $\rho\theta$ corresponds to the spectrum of a white-noise process, which is constant over the frequency range.

The principle of canonical decomposition proposes that the estimates of the trend and of the seasonal component should be devoid of any elements of white noise. Therefore, their spectra must be zero-valued at some point in the interval $[0, \pi]$. Let q_T and q_S be the minima of the spectral density functions associated with the trend and the seasonal components respectively. By subtracting these values from their respective components, a revised decomposition is obtained that fulfils the canonical principle. This is

$$\frac{N(z^{-1})N(z)}{P(z^{-1})P(z)} = \frac{U(z^{-1})U(z)}{\nabla^2(z^{-1})\nabla^2(z)} + \frac{V(z^{-1})V(z)}{\Sigma(z^{-1})\Sigma(z)} + q, \tag{5.122}$$

where $q = \rho\theta + q_T + q_S$.

The Wiener–Kolmogorov principle of signal extraction indicates that the filter that serves to extract the trend from the data sequence $y(t)$ should take the form of

$$\begin{aligned}\beta_T(z) &= \frac{U(z^{-1})U(z)}{\nabla^2(z^{-1})\nabla^2(z)} \times \frac{P(z^{-1})P(z)}{N(z^{-1})N(z)} \\ &= \frac{U(z^{-1})U(z)}{N(z^{-1})N(z)} \times \Sigma(z^{-1})\Sigma(z).\end{aligned} \tag{5.123}$$

This is the ratio of the autocovariance generating function of the trend component to that of the process as a whole. This filter nullifies the seasonal component in the process of extracting a trend that is relatively free of high-frequency elements. The nullification of the seasonal component is due to the factor $\Sigma(z)$.

The gain of the filter that serves to extract the trend from the quarterly logarithmic consumption data of Figure 5.9 is shown in Figure 5.17. This filter is derived from a model of the data based on equation (5.120), where $s = 4$ and where $\rho = 0.1698$ and $\theta = 0.6248$ are estimated parameters that determine the polynomial $N(z)$. The estimated trend is shown in Figure 5.18.

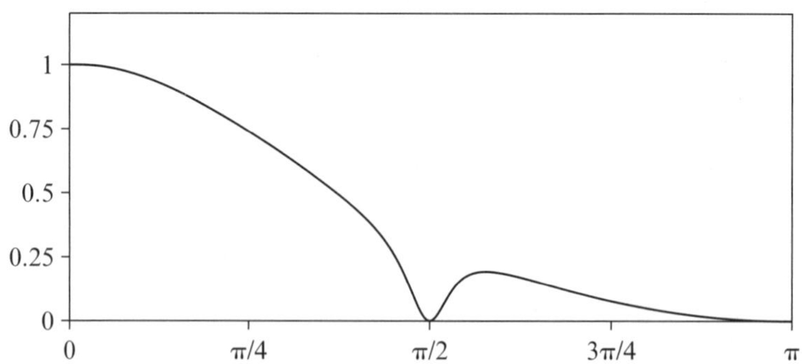

Figure 5.17 The gain of the filter for extracting the trend from the logarithmic consumption data

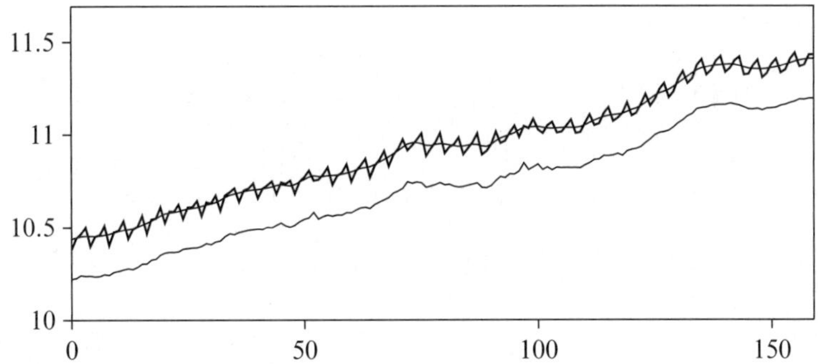

Figure 5.18 *The logarithmic consumption data overlaid by the estimated trend-cycle component. The plot of the seasonally-adjusted data, which should adhere closely to the trend-cycle trajectory, has been displaced downwards*

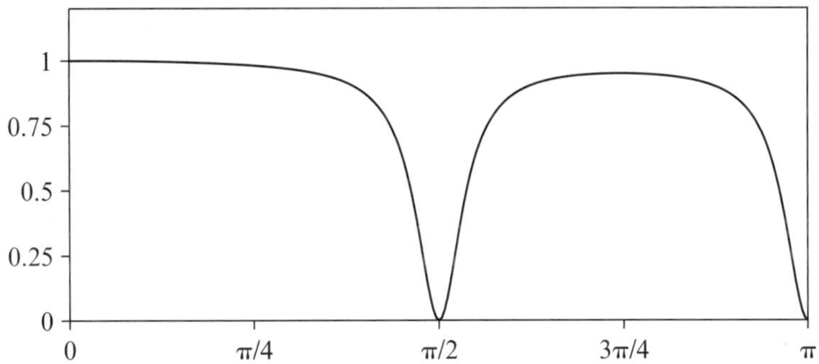

Figure 5.19 *The gain of the seasonal adjustment filter derived from a model of the logarithmic consumption data*

The filter that serves to extract the seasonal component from the data is constructed on the same principle as the trend extraction filter. It takes the form of

$$\beta_S(z) = \frac{V(z^{-1})V(z)}{N(z^{-1})N(z)} \times \nabla^2(z^{-1})\nabla^2(z). \tag{5.124}$$

The filter that serves the purposes of seasonal adjustment, and which nullifies the seasonal component without further attenuating the high-frequency elements of the data, is

$$\beta_A(z) = 1 - \beta_S(z). \tag{5.125}$$

The gain of the seasonal adjustment filter that is derived from the model of the logarithmic consumption data is in shown in Figure 5.19 and the seasonal component that is extracted from the data is shown in Figure 5.20.

Various procedures are available for effecting the canonical decomposition of the data. The method that is followed by the SEATS program is one that was expounded in a

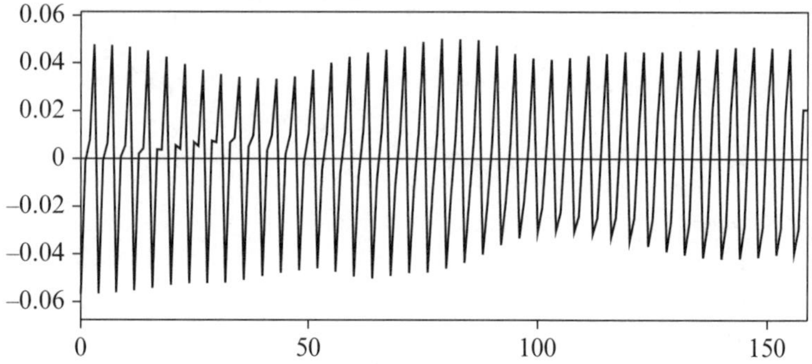

Figure 5.20 The component that is removed by the seasonal adjustment filter

paper of Burman (1980), which depends on a partial-fraction decomposition of the filter itself. The decomposition of the generic filter takes the form of

$$\beta(z) = \frac{C(z)}{N(z)N(z^{-1})} = \frac{D(z)}{N(z)} + \frac{D(z^{-1})}{N(z^{-1})}. \tag{5.126}$$

Compared with the previous approaches associated with the time-domain filters, this is a matter of implementing the filter via components that are joined in parallel rather than in series.

The estimate of the seasonal component obtained by Burman's method is therefore

$$x(z) = f(z) + b(z) = \frac{D(z)}{N(z)}y(z) + \frac{D(z^{-1})}{N(z^{-1})}y(z). \tag{5.127}$$

Thus, a component $f(t)$ is obtained by running forwards through the data, and a component $b(t)$ is obtained by running backwards through the data.

In order to compute either of these components, one needs some initial conditions. Consider the recursion running backwards through the data, which is associated with the equation

$$N(z^{-1})b(z) = D(z^{-1})y(z). \tag{5.128}$$

This requires some starting values for both $b(t)$ and $y(t)$. The SEATS program obtains these values by stepping outside the sample.

The post-sample values of $y(t)$ are generated in the usual way using a recursion based upon the equation of the ARIMA model, which is

$$\psi(L)y(t) = N(L)\varepsilon(t). \tag{5.129}$$

Here, the requisite post-sample elements of $\varepsilon(t)$ are represented by their zero-valued expectations. The post-sample values of $b(t)$ are calculated by a clever algorithm which was proposed to Burman by Granville Tunnicliffe-Wilson. (Tunnicliffe-Wilson was responsible for writing the programs that accompanied the original edition of the book of Box and Jenkins (1976) and he has played a major role in the development of the computational algorithms of modern time-series analysis.) The Burman–Wilson algorithm is expounded in the appendix to Burman's paper.

To initiate the recursion which generates the sequence $f(t)$, some pre-sample values are found by a method analogous to the one that finds the post-sample values.

SEASONAL ADJUSTMENT IN THE FREQUENCY DOMAIN

The TRAMO–SEATS program generates an abundance of diagrams relating to the spectra or pseudo-spectra of the component models and to the frequency responses of the associated filters. These diagrams are amongst the end products of the analysis. However, there is no frequency analysis of the data to guide the specification of the filters. Instead, they are determined by the component models that are derived from the aggregate ARIMA model that describes the data.

In this section, we shall pursue a method of seasonal adjustment that begins by looking at the periodogram of the detrended data. The detrending is by means of a polynomial regression. The residual sequence from the linear detrending of the logarithmic consumption data is shown in Figure 5.11 and the corresponding periodogram is shown in Figures 5.10 and 5.22.

Figure 5.22 shows that the significant elements of the data fall within three highlighted bands. The first band, which covers the frequency interval $[0, \pi/8]$, comprises the elements that constitute the low-frequency business cycle that is represented by the heavy line in Figure 5.11. When the cycle is added to the linear trend that is represented in Figure 5.9, the result is the trend-cycle component that is shown in Figure 5.21.

The second highlighted band, which covers the interval $[\pi/2 - 4\pi/T, \pi/2 + 4\pi/T]$, comprises five elements, which include two on either side of the seasonal frequency of $\pi/2$. The third band, which covers the interval $[\pi - 6\pi/T, \pi]$, contains the harmonic of the seasonal frequency and three elements at adjacent frequencies. The seasonal component, which is synthesized from the elements in the second and third bands, is represented in Figure 5.23.

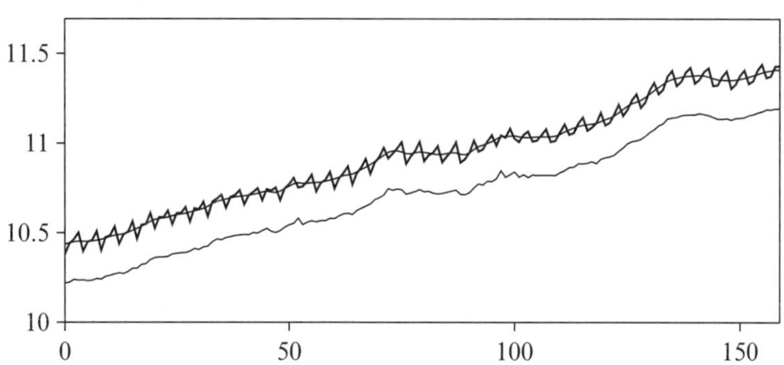

Figure 5.21 The trend-cycle component derived by adding the interpolated polynomial to the low-frequency components of the residual sequence

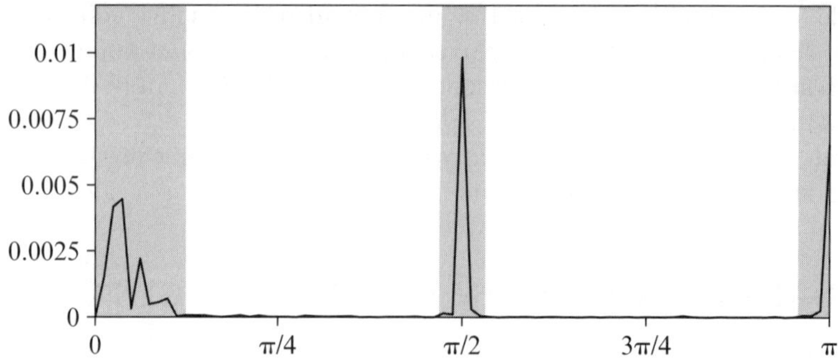

Figure 5.22 *The periodogram of the residual sequence obtained from the linear detrending of the logarithmic consumption data. The shaded bands in the vicinities of π/2 and π contain the elements of the seasonal component*

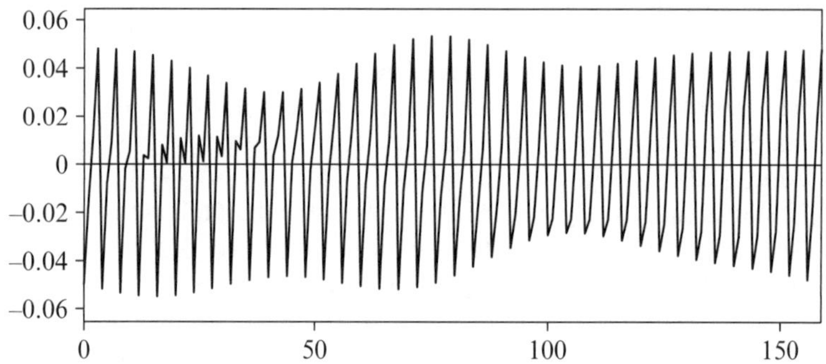

Figure 5.23 *The seasonal component, synthesized from Fourier ordinates in the vicinities of the seasonal frequency and its harmonic*

In addition to showing the logarithmic data sequence and the interpolated trend-cycle component, Figure 5.21 also shows a version of the seasonally-adjusted data. This is represented by the line that has been displaced downwards. It has been derived by subtracting the seasonal component from the data.

A comparison of Figure 5.17–5.20, which relate to the ARIMA-model-based filters, with Figures 5.21–5.23, which relate to the frequency-domain filters, shows that, notwithstanding the marked differences in the alternative methodologies of filtering, the results are virtually indistinguishable. This is a fortuitous circumstance that is largely attributable to the frequency composition of the data, which is revealed by the periodogram.

On the strength of what is revealed by Figure 5.22, it can be asserted that an ARIMA model misrepresents the data. The components of the detrended data are confined to bands that are separated by wide dead spaces in which there are no elements of any significant amplitudes. In contrast, the data generated by an ARIMA process is bound to extend, without breaks, over the entire frequency interval $[0, \pi]$, and there will be no dead spaces.

The nature of an ARIMA process is reflected in the gain of the trend-extraction filter of the TRAMO–SEATS program, which is represented by Figure 5.17. The filter allows the estimated trend to contain elements at all frequencies, albeit that those at the highest frequencies are strongly attenuated. This accords with the model of the trend, which is random walk.

Disregarding the seasonal component, there are no high-frequency elements in the data, nor any beyond the frequency limit of $\pi/8$. Therefore, there is no consequence in allowing such elements to pass through the filter, and its effects are virtually the same as those of the corresponding frequency-domain filter. If there were anything in the data beyond the limit that had not been removed by the seasonal adjustment, then the effect of the filter would be to produce a trend-cycle component with a profile roughened by the inclusion of high-frequency noise. It would resemble a slightly smoother version of the seasonally-adjusted data sequence.

THE PROGRAMS

The programs that have been described in this chapter are freely available from various sources. The H–P (Leser) filter and the Butterworth filter have been implemented in the program IDEOLOG, as have the frequency-domain filters. The program is available at the address: http://www.le.ac.uk/users/dsgp1/.

The H–P and Butterworth filters are also available in the gretl (Gnu Regression, Econometrics and Time-series Library) program, which can be downloaded from the address: http://gretl.sourceforge.net/.

The TRAMO–SEATS program which implements the ARIMA-model-based filters is available from the Bank of Spain at the address: http://www.bde.es/webbde/en/secciones/servicio/software/programas.html. The program, which is free-standing, can also be hosted by gretl.

REFERENCES

Box, G.E.P. and G.M. Jenkins (1976), *Time Series Analysis: Forecasting and Control, Revised Edition*, San Francisco: Holden Day.

Burman, J.P. (1980), 'Seasonal adjustment by signal extraction', *Journal of the Royal Statistical Society, Series A*, **143**, 321–37.

Caporello, G. and A. Maravall (2004), *Program TSW, Revised Reference Manual*, Servicio de Estudios, Banco de España.

Cogley, T. and J.M. Nason (1995), 'Effects of the Hodrick–Prescott filter on trend and difference stationary time series: implications for business cycle research', *Journal of Economic Dynamics and Control*, **19**, 253–78.

Gómez, V. and A. Maravall (2001), 'Seasonal adjustment and signal extraction in economic time series', in D. Peña, G. Tiao and R. Tsay (eds), *A Course in Time Series Analysis*, New York: John Wiley and Sons, Chapter 8.

Gray, R.M. (2002), *Toeplitz and Circulant Matrices: A Review*, Information Systems Laboratory, Department of Electrical Engineering, Stanford University, California, available at http://ee.stanford.edu/gray/~toeplitz.pdf.

Hall, H.S. and S.R. Knight (1899), *Higher Algebra*, London: Macmillan and Co.

Harvey, A.C. and A. Jaeger (1993), 'Detrending, stylised facts and the business cycle', *Journal of Applied Econometrics*, **8**, 231–47.

Hillmer, S.C. and G.C. Tiao (1982), 'An ARIMA-model-based approach to seasonal adjustment', *Journal of the American Statistical Association*, **77**, 63–70.
Hodrick, R.J. and E.C. Prescott (1980), *Postwar U.S. Business Cycles: An Empirical Investigation*, Working Paper, Carnegie–Mellon University, Pittsburgh, Pennsylvania.
Hodrick R.J. and E.C. Prescott (1997), 'Postwar U.S. business cycles: an empirical investigation', *Journal of Money, Credit and Banking*, **29**, 1–16.
Jolly, L.B.W. (1961), *Summation of Series*, 2nd revised edn, New York: Dover Publications.
Jury, E.I. (1964), *Theory and Applications of the z-Transform Method*, New York: John Wiley and Sons.
Kolmogorov, A.N. (1941), 'Interpolation and extrapolation', *Bulletin de l'Academie des Sciences de USSR*, Ser. Math., **5**, 3–14.
Koopman, S.J., A.C. Harvey, J.A. Doornik and N. Shephard (2000), *STAMP: Structural Time Series Analyser Modeller and Predictor*, London: Timberlake Consultants.
Ladiray, D. and B. Quenneville (2001), *Seasonal Adjustment with the X-11 Method*, Springer Lecture Notes in Statistics 158, Berlin: Springer Verlag.
Leser, C.E.V. (1961), 'A simple method of trend construction', *Journal of the Royal Statistical Society, Series B*, **23**, 91–107.
Nyquist, H. (1928), 'Certain topics in telegraph transmission theory', *AIEE Transactions, Series B*, 617–44.
Pollock, D.S.G. (1999), *A Handbook of Time-Series Analysis, Signal Processing and Dynamics*, London: Academic Press.
Pollock, D.S.G. (2000), 'Trend estimation and detrending via rational square wave filters', *Journal of Econometrics*, **99**, 317–34.
Pollock, D.S.G. (2002), 'Circulant matrices and time-series analysis', *The International Journal of Mathematical Education in Science and Technology*, **33**, 213–30.
Pollock, D.S.G. (2009), 'Realisations of finite-sample frequency-selective filters', *Journal of Statistical Planning and Inference*, **139**, 1541–58.
Shannon, C.E. (1949a), 'Communication in the presence of noise', *Proceedings of the Institute of Radio Engineers*, **37**, 10–21, reprinted in 1998, *Proceedings of the IEEE*, **86**, 447–57.
Shannon, C.E. (1949b) (reprinted 1998), *The Mathematical Theory of Communication*, Urbana, IL: University of Illinois Press.
Shiskin, J., A.H. Young and J.C. Musgrave (1967), 'The X-11 variant of the Census Method II Seasonal Adjustment Program', Technical Paper No. 15, Bureau of the Census, US Department of Commerce.
Whittaker, E.T. (1923), 'On a new method of graduations', *Proceedings of the Edinburgh Mathematical Society*, **41**, 63–75.
Wiener, N. (1941), *Extrapolation, Interpolation and Smoothing of Stationary Time Series*, report on the Services Research Project DIC-6037, published in book form in 1949 by MIT Technology Press and John Wiley and Sons, New York.

PART II

MODELS FOR MACROECONOMIC DATA ANALYSIS

6 Vector autoregressive models*

Helmut Lütkepohl

1 INTRODUCTION

Multivariate simultaneous equations models were used extensively for macroeconometric analysis when Sims (1980) advocated vector autoregressive (VAR) models as alternatives. At that time longer and more frequently observed macroeconomic time series called for models which described the dynamic structure of the variables. VAR models lend themselves to this purpose. They typically treat all variables as a priori endogenous. Thereby they account for Sims' critique that the exogeneity assumptions for some of the variables in simultaneous equations models are ad hoc and often not backed by fully developed theories. Restrictions, including exogeneity of some of the variables, may be imposed on VAR models based on statistical procedures.

VAR models are natural tools for forecasting. Their set-up is such that current values of a set of variables are partly explained by past values of the variables involved. They can also be used for economic analysis, however, because they describe the joint generation mechanism of the variables involved. Structural VAR analysis attempts to investigate structural economic hypotheses with the help of VAR models. Impulse response analysis, forecast error variance decompositions, historical decompositions and the analysis of forecast scenarios are the tools which have been proposed for disentangling the relations between the variables in a VAR model.

Traditionally VAR models are designed for stationary variables without time trends. Trending behaviour can be captured by including deterministic polynomial terms. In the 1980s the discovery of the importance of stochastic trends in economic variables and the development of the concept of cointegration by Granger (1981), Engle and Granger (1987), Johansen (1995) and others have shown that stochastic trends can also be captured by VAR models. If there are trends in some of the variables it may be desirable to separate the long-run relations from the short-run dynamics of the generation process of a set of variables. Vector error correction models offer a convenient framework for separating long-run and short-run components of the data generation process (DGP). In the present chapter levels VAR models are considered where cointegration relations are not modelled explicitly although they may be present. Specific issues related to trending variables will be mentioned occasionally throughout the chapter. The advantage of levels VAR models over vector error correction models is that they can also be used when the cointegration structure is unknown. Cointegration analysis and error correction models are discussed specifically in Chapter 7 in this *Handbook*.

1.1 Structure of the Chapter

Typically a VAR analysis proceeds by first specifying and estimating a reduced form model for the DGP and then checking its adequacy. Model deficiencies detected at the

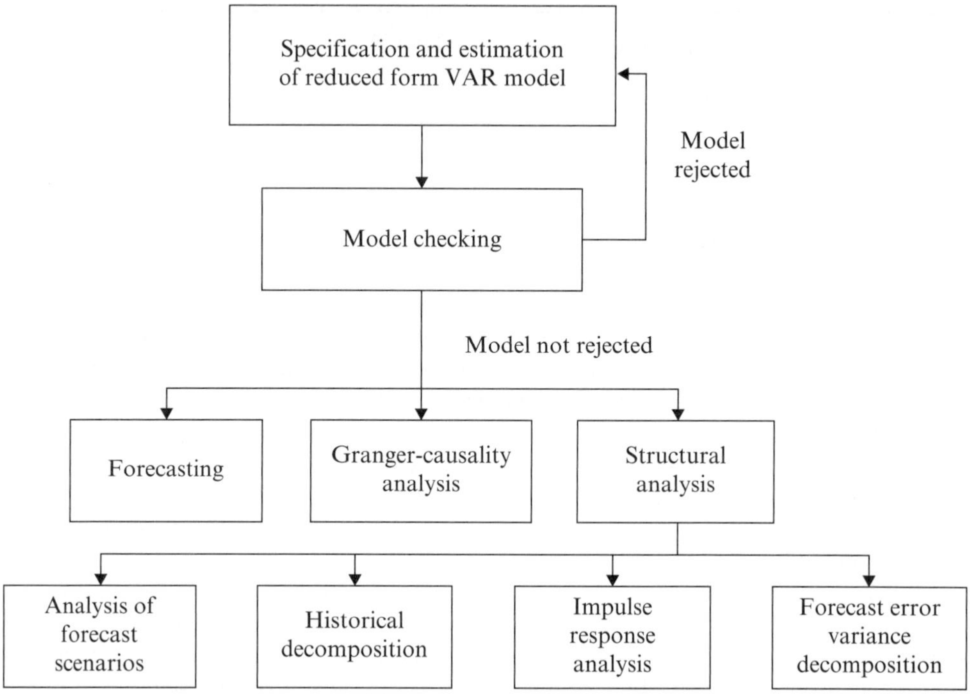

Figure 6.1 VAR analysis

latter stage are resolved by modifying the model. If the reduced form model passes the checking stage, it may be used for forecasting, Granger-causality or structural analysis. The main steps of this modelling approach are depicted in Figure 6.1. The basic VAR model will be introduced in section 2. Estimation and model specification issues are discussed in sections 3 and 4, respectively, and model checking is considered in section 5. Sections 6, 7 and 8 address forecasting, Granger-causality analysis and structural modelling including impulse response analysis, forecast error variance decomposition, historical decomposition of time series and analysis of forecast scenarios. Section 9 concludes and discusses extensions.

A number of textbooks and review articles deal with VAR models. Examples of books are Hamilton (1994), Johansen (1995), Hatanaka (1996), Lütkepohl and Krätzig (2004) and in particular Lütkepohl (2005). More formal and more detailed treatments of some of the issues discussed in the present chapter can be found in these references. The present chapter draws heavily on Lütkepohl and Krätzig (2004), Lütkepohl (2005) and earlier survey articles by Lütkepohl (2006b, 2009).

1.2 Terminology, Notation and General Assumptions

Given the importance of stochastic trends it is useful to have a special terminology in dealing with them. A time series variable y_t is called *integrated of order* $d(I(d))$ if stochastic trends can be removed by differencing the variable d times and a stochastic trend still remains after differencing only $d - 1$ times. Defining the differencing operator Δ such that $\Delta y_t = y_t - y_{t-1}$, the variable y_t is $I(d)$ if $\Delta^d y_t$ is stationary while $\Delta^{d-1} y_t$ still has a stochastic trend. A more formal definition of an integrated variable or process can be found in Johansen (1995). In this chapter all variables are assumed to be either $I(0)$ (that is, they do not have a stochastic trend) or $I(1)$ (if there are stochastic trends) if not explicitly stated otherwise. A K-dimensional vector of time series variables $y_t = (y_{1t}, \ldots, y_{Kt})'$ is called $I(d)$, in short, $y_t \sim I(d)$, if at least one of its components is $I(d)$. Using this terminology, it is possible that some components of y_t may be $I(0)$ individually if $y_t \sim I(1)$. A set of $I(d)$ variables is called *cointegrated* if a linear combination exists which is of lower integration order. In that case the variables have a common trend component.

The $I(d)$ terminology refers only to the stochastic properties of the variables. There can also be deterministic terms. For simplicity I assume that deterministic components will usually be at most linear trends of the form $E(y_t) = \mu_t = \mu_0 + \mu_1 t$. If $\mu_1 = 0$ there is just a constant or intercept term in the process. To further simplify matters it is occasionally assumed that there is no deterministic term so that $\mu_t = 0$. Other deterministic terms which are important in practice are seasonal dummies and other dummy variables. Including them in VAR models is a straightforward extension which is not considered explicitly in this chapter.

The following matrix notation is used. The transpose, inverse, trace, determinant and rank of the matrix A are denoted by A', A^{-1}, $\text{tr}(A)$, $\det(A)$ and $\text{rk}(A)$, respectively. For matrices A $(n \times m)$ and B $(n \times k)$, $[A : B]$ or (A, B) denotes the $(n \times (m + k))$ matrix which has A as its first m columns and B as the last k columns. For an $(n \times m)$ matrix A of full column rank $(n > m)$, an orthogonal complement is denoted by $A_\perp$, that is, $A_\perp' A = 0$ and $[A : A_\perp]$ is a non-singular square matrix. The zero matrix is the orthogonal complement of a non-singular square matrix and an identity matrix of suitable dimension is the orthogonal complement of a zero matrix. The symbol vec denotes the column vectorization operator, $\otimes$ signifies the Kronecker product and I_n is an $(n \times n)$ identity matrix.

The sets of all integers, positive integers and complex numbers are denoted by $\mathbb{Z}$, $\mathbb{N}$ and $\mathbb{C}$, respectively. The lag operator L shifts the time index backward by one period, that is, for a time series variable or vector y_t, $Ly_t = y_{t-1}$. Using this notation, the previously defined differencing operator may be written as $\Delta = 1 - L$. For a number x, $|x|$ denotes the absolute value or modulus. A sum is defined to be zero if the lower bound of the summation index exceeds the upper bound.

The following conventions are used with respect to distributions and stochastic processes. The symbol '$\sim (\mu, \Sigma)$' abbreviates 'has a distribution with mean (vector) μ and (co)variance (matrix) Σ' and $\mathcal{N}(\mu, \Sigma)$ denotes a (multivariate) normal distribution with mean (vector) μ and (co)variance (matrix) Σ. Convergence in distribution is denoted as $\xrightarrow{d}$ and plim stands for the probability limit. Independently, identically distributed is abbreviated as iid. A stochastic process u_t with $t \in \mathbb{Z}$ or $t \in \mathbb{N}$ is called *white noise* if the u_ts are iid with mean zero, $E(u_t) = 0$, and positive definite covariance matrix $\Sigma_u = E(u_t u_t')$.

The following abbreviations are used: DGP, VAR, SVAR and MA for data generation process, vector autoregression, structural vector autoregression and moving average, respectively; ML, OLS, GLS, LM, LR and MSE for maximum likelihood, ordinary least squares, generalized least squares, Lagrange multiplier, likelihood ratio and mean squared error, respectively. The natural logarithm is abbreviated as log.

2 VAR PROCESSES

2.1 The Reduced Form

Suppose the investigator is interested in a set of K related time series variables collected in $y_t = (y_{1t}, \ldots, y_{Kt})'$. Given the importance of distinguishing between stochastic and deterministic components of the DGPs of economic variables, it is convenient to separate the two components by assuming that

$$y_t = \mu_t + x_t, \tag{6.1}$$

where μ_t is the deterministic part and x_t is a purely stochastic process with zero mean. The deterministic term μ_t is at most a linear trend ($\mu_t = \mu_0 + \mu_1 t$) and may also be zero ($\mu_t = 0$) or just a constant ($\mu_t = \mu_0$) for simplicity. Deterministic trend terms have implausible implications in the context of forecasting. Hence, they are not recommendable in applied VAR analysis. The issue will be further discussed in section 6.1. The purely stochastic part, x_t, may be $I(1)$ and, hence, may include stochastic trends and cointegration relations. It has mean zero and a VAR representation. The properties of the observable process y_t are determined by those of μ_t and x_t. In particular, the order of integration and the cointegration relations are determined by x_t.

Suppose the stochastic part x_t is a VAR process of order p (VAR(p)) of the form

$$x_t = A_1 x_{t-1} + \cdots + A_p x_{t-p} + u_t, \tag{6.2}$$

where the A_i $(i = 1, \ldots, p)$ are $(K \times K)$ parameter matrices and the error process $u_t = (u_{1t}, \ldots, u_{Kt})'$ is a K-dimensional zero mean white noise process with covariance matrix $E(u_t u_t') = \Sigma_u$, that is, $u_t \sim (0, \Sigma_u)$. Using the lag operator and defining the matrix polynomial in the lag operator $A(L)$ as $A(L) = I_K - A_1 L - \cdots - A_p L^p$, the process (6.2) can be equivalently written as

$$A(L)x_t = u_t. \tag{6.3}$$

The VAR process (6.2)/(6.3) is *stable* if

$$\det A(z) = \det(I_K - A_1 z - \cdots - A_p z^p) \neq 0 \text{ for } z \in \mathbb{C}, |z| \leq 1. \tag{6.4}$$

In other words, x_t is stable if all roots of the determinantal polynomial are outside the complex unit circle. In that case x_t is $I(0)$. Under usual assumptions a stable process x_t has time invariant means, variances and covariance structure and is, hence, stationary. If, however, $\det A(z) = 0$ for $z = 1$ (that is, the process has a *unit root*) and all other roots of the determinantal polynomial are outside the complex unit circle, then some or all of the variables are integrated, the process is, hence, non-stationary and the variables may be cointegrated. Recall that all variables are either $I(0)$ or $I(1)$ by default.

Also, recall that x_t is the (typically unobserved) stochastic part whereas y_t is the vector of observed variables. Pre-multiplying (6.1) by $A(L)$, that is, considering $A(L)y_t = A(L)\mu_t + u_t$, shows that y_t inherits the VAR(p) representation from x_t. In other words, if $\mu_t = \mu_0 + \mu_1 t$, $A(L)y_t = \nu_0 + \nu_1 t + u_t$ or

$$y_t = \nu_0 + \nu_1 t + A_1 y_{t-1} + \cdots + A_p y_{t-p} + u_t, \tag{6.5}$$

where $\nu_0 = (I_K - \sum_{j=1}^{p} A_j)\mu_0 + (\sum_{j=1}^{p} jA_j)\mu_1$ and $\nu_1 = (I_K - \sum_{j=1}^{p} A_j)\mu_1$. Since all variables appear in levels, this form is known as the *levels form of the VAR process*. Alternatively, some or all variables may appear in first differences if the variables are $I(1)$ and not cointegrated.

If the parameters ν_i, $i = 0,1$, are unrestricted in (6.5), the variables may have quadratic trends if $y_t \sim I(1)$. Thus, the additive model set-up (6.1) imposes restrictions on the deterministic parameters in (6.5). Generally the additive set-up makes it necessary to think about the deterministic terms at the beginning of the analysis and allow for the appropriate polynomial order. Sometimes trend-adjustments are performed prior to a VAR analysis. The reason is that the stochastic part of the variables is often of main interest in econometric analysis because it is viewed as describing the behavioural relations. In that case there may be no deterministic term in the levels VAR form (6.5).

Using terminology from the simultaneous equations literature, the model (6.5) is in *reduced form* because all right-hand side variables are lagged or predetermined. The instantaneous relations between the variables are summarized in the residual covariance matrix. In economic analysis it is often desirable to model the contemporaneous relations between the variables directly. This may be done by setting up a structural form which is discussed next.

2.2 Structural Forms

In *structural form models* contemporaneous variables may appear as explanatory variables in some equations. For example,

$$\mathsf{A}y_t = \nu_0^* + \nu_1^* t + A_1^* y_{t-1} + \cdots + A_p^* y_{t-p} + v_t, \tag{6.6}$$

is a structural form. Here the $(K \times K)$ matrix A reflects the instantaneous relations, $\nu_i^* = \mathsf{A}\nu_i$ $(i = 0,1)$ and $A_j^* = \mathsf{A}A_j$ $(j = 1,\ldots,p)$. The structural form error term $v_t = \mathsf{A}u_t$ is iid white noise with covariance matrix $\Sigma_v = \mathsf{A}\Sigma_u\mathsf{A}'$. The matrix A usually has ones on its main diagonal so that the set of equations in (6.6) can be written such that each of the variables appears on the left-hand side of one of the equations and may depend on contemporaneous values of some or all of the other variables. Moreover, A is typically chosen such that Σ_v is a diagonal matrix. Structural VAR models are discussed in more detail by Lutz Kilian in Chapter 22 of this volume. Therefore they are only sketched briefly here. Other expository treatments are Amisano and Giannini (1997), Watson (1994), Breitung et al. (2004) and Lütkepohl (2005).

Multiplying (6.6) by any non-singular matrix results in a representation of the form (6.6). This shows that the parameters of the structural form (6.6) are not identified without further restrictions. Imposing restrictions on A and Σ_v to identify the structural form is a main focus of structural VAR (SVAR) analysis (see Chapter 22, this volume). Often zero restrictions are placed on A directly. In other words, some variables are not allowed to have an instantaneous impact on some other variables. For example, A may be lower-triangular if there is a recursive relation between the variables.

Alternatively, in SVAR analyses researchers sometimes think of specific shocks hitting the system. A suitable structural model set-up for that case is obtained by premultiplying (6.6) by $\mathsf{B} = \mathsf{A}^{-1}$ and considering

$$y_t = \nu_0 + \nu_1 t + A_1 y_{t-1} + \cdots + A_p y_{t-p} + \mathsf{B} v_t. \tag{6.7}$$

This set-up makes it easy to specify that a certain structural shock v_{it} does not have an instantaneous effect on one of the observed variables by restricting the corresponding element of $\mathsf{B} = \mathsf{A}^{-1}$ to be zero. In other words, zero restrictions are placed on $\mathsf{B} = \mathsf{A}^{-1}$.

Other popular identifying restrictions are placed on the accumulated long-run effects of shocks. For example, if some variables represent rates of change of some underlying quantity, one may postulate that a shock has no long-run effect on the level of a variable by enforcing that the accumulated changes in the variable induced by the shock add to zero. For instance, in a seminal article Blanchard and Quah (1989) consider a bivariate model consisting of output growth rates (y_{1t}) and an unemployment rate (y_{2t}). They assume that demand shocks have no long-run effects on output. In other words, the accumulated effects of a demand shock on the output growth rates are assumed to be zero. Such restrictions are effectively restrictions for A or/and B.

The SVAR models (6.6) and (6.7) are sometimes referred to as A- and B-models, respectively (see Lütkepohl, 2005). They can also be combined to an AB-model of the form

$$\mathsf{A} y_t = \nu_0^* + \nu_1^* t + A_1^* y_{t-1} + \cdots + A_p^* y_{t-p} + \mathsf{B} v_t, \tag{6.8}$$

which makes it easy to impose restrictions on the instantaneous effects of changes in observed variables and unobserved shocks. On the other hand, it involves many more parameters in A and B and, hence, requires more identifying restrictions. In the B- and AB-models, the residuals are usually assumed to be standardized to have identity covariance matrix, that is, $\Sigma_v = I_K$. In that case the reduced form covariance matrix is $\Sigma_u = \mathsf{BB}'$ for the B-model and $\Sigma_u = \mathsf{A}^{-1}\mathsf{BB}'\mathsf{A}^{-1\prime}$ for the AB-model.

As mentioned earlier, identifying the structural relations between the variables or identifying the structural shocks is a main concern of SVAR analysis. Other types of information and restrictions for identification than those mentioned previously have also been proposed. For instance, sign restrictions, using information from higher-frequency data or heteroscedasticity may be considered (see Chapter 22, this volume, for details).

Prior to a structural analysis, a reduced form model as a valid description of the DGP is usually constructed. The stages of reduced form VAR model construction are discussed in the following. Before model specification is considered, estimation of VAR models will be discussed because estimation is typically needed at the specification stage.

3 ESTIMATION OF VAR MODELS

Reduced form VAR models can be estimated with standard methods. Classical least squares and maximum likelihood (ML) methods are discussed in section 3.1 and Bayesian estimation is considered in section 3.2. Estimation of structural models is treated in section 3.3.

3.1 Classical Estimation of Reduced Form VARs

Consider the levels VAR(p) model (6.5) written in the more compact form

$$y_t = [\nu_0, \nu_1, A_1, \ldots, A_p]Z_{t-1} + u_t, \tag{6.9}$$

where $Z_{t-1} = (1, t, y'_{t-1}, \ldots, y'_{t-p})'$. The deterministic terms may be adjusted accordingly if there is just a constant in the model or no deterministic component at all. Given a sample of size T, $y_1, \ldots, y_T$, and p pre-sample vectors, $y_{-p+1}, \ldots, y_0$, the parameters can be estimated efficiently by ordinary least squares (OLS) for each equation separately. The estimator is easily seen to be

$$[\hat{\nu}_0, \hat{\nu}_1, \hat{A}_1, \ldots, \hat{A}_p] = \left(\sum_{t=1}^{T} y_t Z'_{t-1}\right)\left(\sum_{t=1}^{T} Z_{t-1}Z'_{t-1}\right)^{-1}. \tag{6.10}$$

This estimator is identical to the generalized least squares (GLS) estimator, if no restrictions are imposed on the parameters. For a normally distributed (Gaussian) process y_t, where $u_t \sim \mathcal{N}(0, \Sigma_u)$, this estimator is also identical to the ML estimator, conditional on the initial pre-sample values. Thus, the estimator has the usual desirable asymptotic properties of standard estimators. It is asymptotically normally distributed with smallest possible asymptotic covariance matrix and the usual inference procedures are available if the process is stable. In other words, in this case t-statistics can be used for testing individual coefficients and for setting up confidence intervals. Moreover, F-tests can be used for testing statistical hypotheses for sets of parameters. Of course, in the present framework these procedures are only valid asymptotically and not in small samples.

If there are integrated variables so that $y_t \sim I(1)$, the process is not stable and the variables may be cointegrated. In that case the OLS/ML estimator can still be used and it is still asymptotically normal under general conditions (see Park and Phillips, 1988, 1989; Sims et al., 1990; Lütkepohl, 2005, Chapter 7). However, in that case the covariance matrix of the asymptotic distribution is singular because some estimated parameters or linear combinations of them converge with a faster rate than the usual $\sqrt{T}$ rate when the sample size goes to infinity. This result implies that t-, χ^2- and F-tests for inference regarding the VAR parameters may be invalid asymptotically (Toda and Phillips, 1993). Although these properties require caution in doing inference for integrated processes, there are many situations where standard inference still holds (see Toda and Yamamoto, 1995; Dolado and Lütkepohl, 1996; Inoue and Kilian, 2002a). In particular, asymptotic inference on impulse responses as discussed in section 8.1 remains valid if the order of the VAR process is greater than 1.

If restrictions are imposed on the parameters, OLS estimation may be inefficient. In that case GLS estimation may be beneficial. Let $\boldsymbol{\alpha} = \text{vec}[\nu_1, \nu_2, A_1, \ldots, A_p]$ and suppose that there are linear restrictions for the parameters such as zero restrictions which exclude some of the lagged variables from some of the equations. Linear restrictions can often be written in the form

$$\boldsymbol{\alpha} = R\gamma, \tag{6.11}$$

where R is a suitable, known $((K^2p + 2K) \times M)$ restriction matrix with rank M which typically consists of zeros and ones and γ is the $(M \times 1)$ vector of unrestricted parameters. The GLS estimator for γ is then

$$\hat{\gamma} = \left[R'\left(\sum_{t=1}^{T} Z_{t-1}Z_{t-1}' \otimes \Sigma_u^{-1}\right)R\right]^{-1} R'\text{vec}\left(\Sigma_u^{-1}\sum_{t=1}^{T} y_t Z_{t-1}'\right). \tag{6.12}$$

The estimator $\hat{\gamma}$ has standard asymptotic properties if $y_t \sim I(0)$, that is, the GLS estimator is consistent and asymptotically normally distributed and usual methods for inference are valid asymptotically.

In practice, the white noise covariance matrix is usually unknown and has to be replaced by an estimator based on an unrestricted estimation of the model. The resulting feasible GLS estimator, say $\hat{\hat{\gamma}}$, has the same asymptotic properties as the GLS estimator under general conditions. The corresponding feasible GLS estimator of $\boldsymbol{\alpha}$, $\hat{\hat{\boldsymbol{\alpha}}} = R\hat{\hat{\gamma}}$, is also consistent and asymptotically normal and allows for standard asymptotic inference. For Gaussian white noise u_t, ML estimation may be used alternatively. Its asymptotic properties are the same as those of the GLS estimator under standard assumptions.

For $I(1)$ processes a specific analysis of the integration and cointegration properties of the left-hand and right-hand side variables of the individual equations is necessary to determine the asymptotic properties of the estimators and the associated inference procedures.

3.2 Bayesian Estimation of Reduced Form VARs

Standard Bayesian methods for estimating linear regression models can be applied for estimating the parameters of reduced form VAR models. They are not discussed here in detail because they are considered elsewhere in this volume. In the VAR literature specific priors have been used, however, which may be worth noting at this point. Assuming a normal distribution for the residuals and, hence, for the observed y_t together with a normal-Wishart prior distribution for the VAR coefficients results in a normal-Wishart posterior distribution. Such a set-up is rather common in the SVAR literature (see Uhlig, 2005, Appendix B). The so-called Minnesota prior is a specific example of a prior which has been used quite often in practice (see Doan et al., 1984; Litterman, 1986). It shrinks the VAR towards a random walk for each of the variables. Extensions and alternatives were proposed by Kadiyala and Karlsson (1997), Villani (2005), Sims et al. (2008), Giannone et al. (2010) and others. Other, recent proposals include shrinking towards some dynamic stochastic general equilibrium model (for example, Ingram and Whiteman, 1994 and Del Negro and Schorfheide, 2004). A more detailed exposition of Bayesian methods in VAR analysis may be found in Canova (2007, Chapters 9–11).

3.3 Estimation of Structural VARs

Properly identified structural form VAR models are also usually estimated by least squares, ML or Bayesian methods. The specific estimation algorithm depends to some extent on the type of restrictions used for identification. For example, if a just-identified A-model is used with ones on the main diagonal and diagonal residual covariance matrix Σ_v, equationwise OLS can be used for estimation. For the B-model (6.7) without restrictions on $\nu_0, \nu_1, A_1, \ldots, A_p$, the latter parameters can be concentrated out of the likelihood function by replacing them with their OLS estimators, using $\Sigma_u = \mathsf{B}\mathsf{B}'$ and estimating B by maximizing the concentrated Gaussian log-likelihood

$$l(\mathsf{B}) = \text{constant} - \frac{T}{2}\log\det(\mathsf{B})^2 - \frac{T}{2}\operatorname{tr}(\mathsf{B}'^{-1}\mathsf{B}^{-1}\hat{\Sigma}_u), \tag{6.13}$$

where $\hat{\Sigma}_u = T^{-1}\sum_{t=1}^{T}\hat{u}_t\hat{u}_t'$ is the estimator of Σ_u based on the OLS residuals (cf. Breitung et al., 2004). If the actual distribution of y_t (and, hence, of u_t) is not normal, the resulting estimators are quasi- or pseudo-ML estimators. They still allow for standard asymptotic inference under general conditions.

In the AB-model the concentrated log-likelihood function in terms of A and B is

$$l(\mathsf{A}, \mathsf{B}) = \text{constant} + \frac{T}{2}\log\det(\mathsf{A})^2 - \frac{T}{2}\log\det(\mathsf{B})^2 - \frac{T}{2}\operatorname{tr}(\mathsf{A}'\mathsf{B}'^{-1}\mathsf{B}^{-1}\mathsf{A}\hat{\Sigma}_u). \tag{6.14}$$

Numerical methods can be used for optimizing the functions in (6.13) and (6.14) with respect to the free parameters in B or A and B. The resulting estimators have the usual asymptotic properties of ML estimators (see, for example, Lütkepohl, 2005, Chapter 9 for details). Hence, asymptotic inference proceeds in the usual way. Alternatively, one may use Bayesian estimation methods (see, for example, Sims et al., 2008). The estimates will be of importance in the structural VAR analysis discussed in section 8 and Chapter 22 (this volume).

4 MODEL SPECIFICATION

Model specification in the present context involves selecting the VAR order and possibly imposing restrictions on the VAR parameters. Notably zero restrictions on the parameter matrices may be desirable because the number of parameters in a VAR model increases with the square of the VAR order. Lag order specification is considered next and some comments on setting zero restrictions on the parameters are provided at the end of this section.

The VAR order is typically chosen by sequential testing procedures or model selection criteria. Sequential testing proceeds by specifying a maximum reasonable lag order, say $p_{\max}$, and then testing the following sequence of null hypotheses: $H_0 : A_{p_{\max}} = 0$, $H_0 : A_{p_{\max}-1} = 0$, and so on. The procedure stops when the null hypothesis is rejected for the first time. The order is then chosen accordingly. For stationary processes the usual Wald or LR χ^2 tests for parameter restrictions can be used in this procedure. If there are $I(1)$ variables these tests are also asymptotically valid as long as the null hypothesis $H_0 : A_1 = 0$ is not tested. Unfortunately, the small sample distributions of the tests may be quite different from their asymptotic counterparts, in particular for systems with more than a couple of variables (for example, Lütkepohl, 2005, Section 4.3.4). Therefore it may be useful to consider small sample adjustments, possibly based on bootstrap methods (for example, Li and Maddala, 1996; Berkowitz and Kilian, 2000).

Alternatively, model selection criteria can be used. Some of them have the general form

$$C(m) = \log\det(\hat{\Sigma}_m) + c_T\varphi(m), \tag{6.15}$$

where $\hat{\Sigma}_m = T^{-1}\sum_{t=1}^{T}\hat{u}_t\hat{u}_t'$ is the OLS residual covariance matrix estimator for a reduced form VAR model of order m, $\varphi(m)$ is a function of the order m which penalizes large VAR orders and c_T is a sequence which may depend on the sample size and identifies the specific criterion. Popular examples are Akaike's information criterion (Akaike, 1973, 1974),

$$\text{AIC}(m) = \log\det(\hat{\Sigma}_m) + \frac{2}{T}mK^2,$$

where $c_T = 2/T$, the Hannan–Quinn criterion (Hannan and Quinn, 1979; Quinn, 1980),

$$\text{HQ}(m) = \log\det(\hat{\Sigma}_m) + \frac{2\log\log T}{T}mK^2,$$

with $c_T = 2\log\log T/T$, and the Schwarz (or Rissanen) criterion (Schwarz, 1978; Rissanen 1978),

$$\text{SC}(m) = \log\det(\hat{\Sigma}_m) + \frac{\log T}{T}mK^2,$$

with $c_T = \log T/T$. In all these criteria $\varphi(m) = mK^2$ is the number of VAR parameters in a model with order m. The VAR order is chosen such that the respective criterion is minimized over the possible orders $m = 0,\ldots,p_{\max}$. Among these three criteria, AIC always suggests the largest order, SC chooses the smallest order and HQ is in between (Lütkepohl, 2005, Chapters 4 and 8). Of course, the criteria may all suggest the same lag order. The HQ and SC criteria are both consistent, that is, under general conditions the order estimated with these criteria converges in probability or almost surely to the true VAR order p if $p_{\max}$ is at least as large as the true lag order. AIC tends to overestimate the order asymptotically with a small probability. These results hold for both $I(0)$ and $I(1)$ processes (Paulsen, 1984).

The lag order obtained with sequential testing or model selection criteria depends to some extent on the choice of $p_{\max}$. Choosing a small $p_{\max}$, an appropriate model may not be in the set of possibilities and choosing a large $p_{\max}$ may result in a large value which is spurious. At an early stage of the analysis, using a moderate value for $p_{\max}$ appears to be a sensible strategy. An inadequate choice should be detected at the model checking stage (see section 5).

Once the model order is determined, zero restrictions may be imposed on the VAR coefficient matrices to reduce the number of parameters. Standard testing procedures can be used for that purpose. The number of possible restrictions may be very large, however, and searching over all possibilities may result in excessive computations. Therefore a number of shortcuts have been proposed in the related literature under the name of subset model selection procedures (see Lütkepohl, 2005, Section 5.2.8).

If a model is selected by some testing or model selection procedure, that model is typically treated as representing the true DGP in the subsequent statistical analysis. Recent research is devoted to the problems and possible errors associated with such an approach (for example, Leeb and Pötscher, 2005). This literature points out that the actual distribution which does not condition on the model selected by some statistical procedure may be quite different from the conditional one. Suppose, for example, that the VAR order is selected by the AIC, say, the order chosen by this criterion is $\hat{p}$. Then a typical approach in practice is to treat a VAR($\hat{p}$) model as the true DGP and perform all subsequent analysis under this assumption. Such a conditional analysis can be misleading even if the true order coincides with $\hat{p}$ because the properties of the estimators for the VAR coefficients are affected by the post-model selection step. Conditioning on $\hat{p}$ ignores that this quantity is also a random variable based on the same data as the estimators of the VAR parameters. Since no general procedures exist for correcting the error resulting from this simplification, there is little to recommend for improving applied work in this respect.

5 MODEL CHECKING

Procedures for checking whether the VAR model represents the DGP of the variables adequately range from formal tests of the underlying assumptions to informal procedures such as inspecting plots of residuals and autocorrelations. Since a reduced form is underlying every structural form, model checking usually focuses on reduced form models. If a specific reduced form model is not an adequate representation of the DGP, any structural form based on it cannot represent the DGP well. Formal tests for residual autocorrelation, non-normality and conditional heteroscedasticity for reduced form VARs are briefly summarized in the following. For other procedures see, for example, Lütkepohl (2004).

5.1 Tests for Residual Autocorrelation

Portmanteau and Breusch–Godfrey–LM tests are standard tools for checking residual autocorrelation in VAR models. The null hypothesis of the portmanteau test is that all residual autocovariances are zero, that is, $H_0 : E(u_t u'_{t-i}) = 0$ $(i = 1, 2, \ldots)$. The alternative is that at least one autocovariance and, hence, one autocorrelation is non-zero. The test statistic is based on the residual autocovariances, $\hat{C}_j = T^{-1}\sum_{t=j+1}^{T} \hat{u}_t \hat{u}'_{t-j}$, where the $\hat{u}_t$s are the mean-adjusted estimated residuals. The portmanteau statistic is given by

$$Q_h = T\sum_{j=1}^{h} \text{tr}(\hat{C}_j'\hat{C}_0^{-1}\hat{C}_j\hat{C}_0^{-1}), \tag{6.16}$$

or the modified version

$$Q_h^* = T^2\sum_{j=1}^{h} \frac{1}{T-j}\text{tr}(\hat{C}_j'\hat{C}_0^{-1}\hat{C}_j\hat{C}_0^{-1})$$

may be used. The two statistics have the same asymptotic properties. For an unrestricted stationary VAR(p) process their null distributions can be approximated by a $\chi^2(K^2(h-p))$ distribution if T and h approach infinity such that $h/T \to 0$. For VAR models with parameter restrictions, the degrees of freedom of the approximate χ^2 distribution are obtained as the difference between the number of (non-instantaneous) autocovariances included in the statistic (K^2h) and the number of estimated VAR parameters (for example, Ahn, 1988; Hosking, 1980, 1981a, 1981b; Li and McLeod, 1981; or Lütkepohl, 2005, Section 4.4). Brüggemann et al. (2006) show that this approximation is unsatisfactory for integrated and cointegrated processes. For such processes the degrees of freedom also depend on the cointegrating rank. Thus, portmanteau tests are not recommended for levels VAR processes with unknown cointegrating rank.

The choice of h is crucial for the small sample properties of the test. If h is chosen too small the χ^2 approximation to the null distribution may be very poor while a large h reduces the power of the test. Using a number of different h values is not uncommon in practice.

The portmanteau test should be applied primarily to test for autocorrelation of high order. For low order autocorrelation the Breusch–Godfrey LM test is more suitable. It may be viewed as a test for zero coefficient matrices in a VAR model for the residuals,

$$u_t = B_1u_{t-1} + \cdots + B_hu_{t-h} + e_t.$$

The quantity e_t denotes a white noise error term. Thus, a test of

$$H_0: B_1 = \cdots = B_h = 0 \quad \text{versus} \quad H_1: B_i \neq 0 \text{ for at least one } i \in \{1, \ldots, h\}$$

may be used for checking that u_t is white noise. The precise form of the statistic can be found, for example, in Lütkepohl (2005, Section 4.4.4). It has an asymptotic $\chi^2(hK^2)$-distribution under the null hypothesis for both $I(0)$ and $I(1)$ systems (Brüggemann et al., 2006). As a consequence, the LM test is applicable for levels VAR processes with unknown cointegrating rank.

5.2 Other Popular Tests for Model Adequacy

Non-normality tests are often used for model checking, although normality is not a necessary condition for the validity of many of the statistical procedures related to VAR models. However, non-normality of the residuals may indicate other model deficiencies such as non-linearities or structural change. Multivariate normality tests are often applied to the residual vector of the VAR model and univariate versions are used to check normality of the errors of the individual equations. The standard tests check whether the third and fourth moments of the residuals are in line with a normal distribution, as proposed by Lomnicki (1961) and Jarque and Bera (1987) for univariate models. For details see Lütkepohl (2005, Section 4.5) and for small sample corrections see Kilian and Demiroglu (2000).

Conditional heteroscedasticity is often a concern for models based on data with monthly or higher frequency. Therefore suitable univariate and multivariate tests are available to check for such features in the residuals of VAR models. Again much of the analysis can be done even if there is conditional heteroscedasticity. Notice that the VAR model represents the conditional mean of the variables which is often of primary interest. Still, it may be useful to check for conditional heteroscedasticity to better understand the properties of the underlying data and to improve inference. Also, heteroscedastic residuals can indicate structural changes. If conditional heteroscedasticity is found in the residuals, modelling them by multivariate GARCH models or using heteroscedasticity robust inference procedures may be useful to avoid distortions in the estimators of the conditional mean parameters. For a proposal to robustify inference against conditional heteroscedasticity see Goncalves and Kilian (2004).

There are a number of tests for structural stability which check whether there are changes in the VAR parameters or the residual covariances throughout the sample period. Prominent examples are so-called Chow tests. They consider the null hypothesis of time invariant parameters throughout the sample period against the possibility of a change in the parameter values in some period T_B, say. One possible test version compares the likelihood maximum of the constant parameter model to the one with different parameter values before and after period T_B. If the model is time invariant, the resulting LR statistic has an asymptotic χ^2-distribution under standard assumptions. See Lütkepohl (2005, Section 4.6) for details and other tests for structural stability of VARs.

Stability tests are sometimes performed for a range of potential break points T_B. Using the maximum of the test statistics, that is, rejecting stability if one of the test statistics exceeds some critical value, the test is no longer asymptotically χ^2 but has a different asymptotic distribution (see Andrews, 1993; Andrews and Ploberger, 1994; and Hansen, 1997).

If a reduced form VAR model has passed the adequacy tests, it can be used for forecasting and structural analysis, which are treated next.

6 FORECASTING

Since reduced form VAR models represent the conditional mean of a stochastic process, they lend themselves for forecasting. For simplicity forecasting with known VAR processes will be discussed first and then extensions for estimated processes will be considered.

6.1 Forecasting Known VAR Processes

If y_t is generated by a VAR(p) process (6.5), the conditional expectation of y_{T+h} given y_t, $t \leq T$, is

$$y_{T+h|T} = E(y_{T+h}|y_T, y_{T-1}, \ldots) = \nu_0 + \nu_1(T+h) + A_1 y_{T+h-1|T} + \cdots + A_p y_{T+h-p|T}, \quad (6.17)$$

where $y_{T+j|T} = y_{T+j}$ for $j \leq 0$. If the white noise process u_t is iid, $y_{T+h|T}$ is the optimal, minimum mean squared error (MSE) h-step ahead forecast in period T. The forecasts can easily be computed recursively for $h = 1, 2, \ldots$. The forecast error associated with an h-step forecast is

$$y_{T+h} - y_{T+h|T} = u_{T+h} + \Phi_1 u_{T+h-1} + \cdots + \Phi_{h-1} u_{T+1}, \quad (6.18)$$

where the Φ_i matrices may be obtained recursively as

$$\Phi_i = \sum_{j=1}^{i} \Phi_{i-j} A_j, \quad i = 1, 2, \ldots, \quad (6.19)$$

with $\Phi_0 = I_K$ and $A_j = 0$ for $j > p$ (for example, Lütkepohl, 2005, Chapter 2). In other words, the Φ_i are the coefficient matrices of the infinite order polynomial in the lag operator $A(L)^{-1} = \sum_{j=0}^{\infty} \Phi_j L^j$. Obviously, the reduced form VAR residual u_t is the forecast error for a 1-step forecast in period $t - 1$. The forecasts are unbiased; that is, the errors have mean zero and the forecast error covariance or MSE matrix is

$$\Sigma_y(h) = E[(y_{T+h} - y_{T+h|T})(y_{T+h} - y_{T+h|T})'] = \sum_{j=0}^{h-1} \Phi_j \Sigma_u \Phi_j', \quad (6.20)$$

that is, $y_{T+h} - y_{T+h|T} \sim (0, \Sigma_y(h))$.

In fact, the conditional expectation in (6.17) is obtained whenever the conditional expectation of u_{T+h} is zero or in other words, if u_t is a martingale difference sequence. Even if the u_ts are just uncorrelated and do not have conditional mean zero, the forecasts obtained recursively from (6.17) are still best *linear* forecasts but may not be minimum MSE forecasts in a larger class which includes non-linear forecasts.

These results are valid even if the VAR process has $I(1)$ components. However, if y_t is $I(0)$ (stationary) the forecast MSEs are bounded as the horizon h goes to infinity. In contrast, for $I(1)$ processes the forecast MSE matrices are unbounded and, hence, forecast uncertainty increases without bounds for increasing forecast horizon.

Notice the major difference between considering deterministic and stochastic trends in a VAR model. The deterministic time trend in (6.17) does not add to the inaccuracy of the forecasts in this framework, where no estimation uncertainty is present, while stochastic trends have a substantial impact on the forecast uncertainty. Many researchers find it implausible that trending behaviour is not reflected in the uncertainty of long-term forecasts. Therefore deterministic trend components should be used with caution. In particular, higher order polynomial trends or even linear trends should be avoided unless there are very good reasons for them. Using them just to improve the fit of a VAR model can be counterproductive from a forecasting point of view.

For Gaussian VAR processes y_t with $u_t \sim$ iid $\mathcal{N}(0, \Sigma_u)$, the forecast errors are also multivariate normal, $y_{T+h} - y_{T+h|T} \sim \mathcal{N}(0, \Sigma_y(h))$, and forecast intervals can be set up in the usual way. For non-Gaussian processes y_t with unknown distribution, other methods for setting up forecast intervals are called for, for instance, bootstrap methods may be considered (see, for example, Findley, 1986; Masarotto, 1990; Grigoletto, 1998; Kabaila, 1993; Kim, 1999; and Pascual et al., 2004).

6.2 Forecasting Estimated VAR Processes

If the DGP is unknown and, hence, the VAR model only approximates the true DGP, the previously discussed forecasts will not be available. Let $\hat{y}_{T+h|T}$ denote a forecast based on a VAR model which is specified and estimated based on the available data. Then the forecast error is

$$y_{T+h} - \hat{y}_{T+h|T} = (y_{T+h} - y_{T+h|T}) + (y_{T+h|T} - \hat{y}_{T+h|T}). \qquad (6.21)$$

If the true DGP is a VAR process, the first term on the right-hand side is $\sum_{j=0}^{h-1}\Phi_j u_{T+h-j}$. It includes residuals u_t with $t > T$ only, whereas the second term involves just $y_T, y_{T-1}, \ldots,$ if only variables up to time T have been used for model specification and estimation. Consequently, the two terms are independent or at least uncorrelated, so that the MSE matrix has the form

$$\begin{aligned}\Sigma_{\hat{y}}(h) &= E[(y_{T+h} - \hat{y}_{T+h|T})(y_{T+h} - \hat{y}_{T+h|T})'] \\ &= \Sigma_y(h) + \text{MSE}(y_{T+h|T} - \hat{y}_{T+h|T}). \qquad (6.22)\end{aligned}$$

If the VAR model specified for y_t properly represents the DGP, the last term on the right-hand side approaches zero as the sample size gets large because the difference $y_{T+h|T} - \hat{y}_{T+h|T}$ vanishes asymptotically in probability under standard assumptions. Thus, if the theoretical model fully captures the DGP, specification and estimation uncertainty is not important asymptotically. On the other hand, in finite samples the precision of the forecasts depends on the precision of the estimators. Suitable correction factors for MSEs and forecast intervals for stationary processes are given by Baillie (1979), Reinsel (1980), Samaranayake and Hasza (1988) and Lütkepohl (2005, Chapter 3). A discussion of extensions with a number of further references may be found in Lütkepohl (2009).

7 GRANGER-CAUSALITY ANALYSIS

Because VAR models describe the joint generation process of a number of variables, they can be used for investigating relations between the variables. A specific type of relation was pointed out by Granger (1969) and is known as *Granger-causality*. Granger called a variable y_{2t} causal for a variable y_{1t} if the information in past and present values of y_{2t} is helpful for improving the forecasts of y_{1t}. This concept is especially easy to implement in a VAR framework. Suppose that y_{1t} and y_{2t} are generated by a bivariate VAR(p) process,

$$\begin{pmatrix} y_{1t} \\ y_{2t} \end{pmatrix} = \sum_{i=1}^{p} \begin{bmatrix} \alpha_{11,i} & \alpha_{12,i} \\ \alpha_{21,i} & \alpha_{22,i} \end{bmatrix} \begin{pmatrix} y_{1,t-i} \\ y_{2,t-i} \end{pmatrix} + u_t.$$

Then y_{2t} is not Granger-causal for y_{1t} if and only if $\alpha_{12,i} = 0$, $i = 1,2,\ldots,p$. In other words, y_{2t} is not Granger-causal for y_{1t} if the former variable does not appear in the y_{1t} equation of the model. This result holds for both stationary and integrated processes.

Because Granger-non-causality is characterized by zero restrictions on the levels VAR representation of the DGP, testing for it becomes straightforward. Standard Wald χ^2- or F-tests can be applied. If y_t contains integrated and possibly cointegrated variables, these tests may not have standard asymptotic properties, however (Toda and Phillips, 1993). For the presently considered case, there is a simple way to fix the problem. In this case the problem of getting a non-standard asymptotic distribution for Wald tests for zero restrictions can be resolved by adding an extra redundant lag to the VAR in estimating the parameters of the process and testing the relevant null hypothesis on the matrices $A_1,\ldots,A_p$ only (see Toda and Yamamoto, 1995 and Dolado and Lütkepohl, 1996). Since a VAR($p + 1$) is an appropriate model with $A_{p+1} = 0$ if the true VAR order is p, the procedure is sound. It will not be fully efficient, however, due to the redundant VAR lag.

If there are more than two variables the conditions for non-causality or causality become more complicated even if the DGP is a VAR process (see, for example, Lütkepohl, 1993 and Dufour and Renault, 1998). In practice, Granger-causality is therefore often investigated for bivariate processes. It should be clear, however, that Granger-causality depends on the information set considered. In other words, even if a variable is Granger-causal in a bivariate model, it may not be Granger-causal in a larger model involving more variables. For instance, there may be a variable driving both variables of a bivariate process. When that variable is added to the model, a bivariate causal structure may disappear. In turn it is also possible that a variable is non-causal for another one in a bivariate model and becomes causal if the information set is extended to include other variables as well. There are also a number of other limitations of the concept of Granger-causality which have stimulated an extensive discussion of the concept and have prompted alternative definitions. For further discussion and references see Lütkepohl (2005, Section 2.3.1) and for extensions to testing for Granger-causality in infinite order VAR processes see Lütkepohl and Poskitt (1996) and Saikkonen and Lütkepohl (1996).

8 STRUCTURAL ANALYSIS

Traditionally the interaction between economic variables is studied by considering the effects of changes in one variable on the other variables of interest. In VAR models changes in the variables are induced by non-zero residuals, that is, by shocks which may have a structural interpretation if identifying structural restrictions have been placed accordingly. Hence, to study the relations between the variables, the effects of non-zero residuals or shocks are traced through the system. This kind of analysis is known as impulse response analysis. It will be discussed in section 8.1. Related tools are forecast error variance decompositions and historical decompositions of time series of interest in terms of the contributions attributable to the different structural shocks. Moreover, forecasts conditional on a specific path of a variable or set of variables may be considered. These tools are discussed in sections 8.2, 8.3 and 8.4, respectively.

8.1 Impulse Response Analysis

In the reduced form VAR model (6.5) impulses, innovations or shocks enter through the residual vector $u_t = (u_{1t}, \ldots, u_{Kt})'$. A non-zero component of u_t corresponds to an equivalent change in the associated left-hand side variable which in turn will induce further changes in the other variables of the system in the next periods. The marginal effect of a single non-zero element in u_t can be studied conveniently by inverting the VAR representation and considering the corresponding moving average (MA) representation. Ignoring deterministic terms because they are not important for impulse response analysis gives

$$y_t = A(L)^{-1}u_t = \Phi(L)u_t = \sum_{j=0}^{\infty}\Phi_j u_{t-j}, \tag{6.23}$$

where $\Phi(L) = \sum_{j=0}^{\infty}\Phi_j L^j = A(L)^{-1}$. The $(K \times K)$ coefficient matrices Φ_j are precisely those given in (6.19). The marginal response of $y_{n,t+j}$ to a unit impulse u_{mt} is given by the (n, m)th elements of the matrices Φ_j, viewed as a function of j. Hence, the elements of Φ_j represent responses to u_t innovations. Because the u_t are just the 1-step forecast errors, these impulse responses are sometimes called *forecast error impulse responses* (Lütkepohl, 2005, Section 2.3.2) and the corresponding MA representation is called Wold MA representation.

The existence of the representation (6.23) is ensured if the VAR process is stable and, hence, y_t consists of stationary ($I(0)$) variables. In that case $\Phi_j \to 0$ as $j \to \infty$ and the effect of an impulse is *transitory*. If y_t has $I(1)$ components, the Wold MA representation (6.23) does not exist. However, for any finite j, Φ_j can be computed as in the stationary case, using the formula (6.19). Thus, impulse responses can also be computed for $I(1)$ processes. For such processes the marginal effects of a single shock may lead to *permanent* changes in some or all of the variables.

Because the residual covariance matrix Σ_u is generally not diagonal, the components of u_t may be contemporaneously correlated. Consequently, the u_{jt} shocks are not likely to occur in isolation in practice. Therefore tracing such shocks may not reflect what actually happens in the system if a shock hits. In other words, forecast error shocks may not be the right ones to consider if one is interested in understanding the interactions within the system under consideration. Therefore researchers typically try to determine structural shocks and trace their effects. A main task in structural VAR analysis is in fact the specification of the shocks of interest.

If an identified structural form such as (6.8) is available, the corresponding residuals are the structural shocks. For a stationary process their corresponding impulse responses can again be obtained by inverting the VAR representation,

$$y_t = (\mathsf{A} - A_1^* L - \cdots - A_p^* L^p)^{-1}\mathsf{B}v_t = \sum_{j=0}^{\infty}\Phi_j \mathsf{A}^{-1}\mathsf{B}v_{t-j} = \sum_{j=0}^{\infty}\Psi_j v_{t-j}, \tag{6.24}$$

where the $\Psi_j = \Phi_j \mathsf{A}^{-1}\mathsf{B}$ contain the structural impulse responses. The latter formulae can also be used for computing structural impulse responses for $I(1)$ processes even if the representation (6.24) does not exist.

Estimation of impulse responses is straightforward by substituting estimated reduced form or structural form parameters in the formulae for computing them. Suppose the structural form VAR parameters are collected in the vector $\boldsymbol{\alpha}$ and denote its estimator by $\hat{\boldsymbol{\alpha}}$. Moreover, let ψ be the vector of impulse response coefficients of interest. This vector is a (non-linear) function of $\boldsymbol{\alpha}$, $\psi = \psi(\boldsymbol{\alpha})$, which can be estimated as $\hat{\psi} = \psi(\hat{\boldsymbol{\alpha}})$. Using the delta method, it is easy to see that $\hat{\psi} = \psi(\hat{\boldsymbol{\alpha}})$ is asymptotically normal if $\hat{\boldsymbol{\alpha}}$ has this property. More precisely,

$$\sqrt{T}(\hat{\boldsymbol{\alpha}} - \boldsymbol{\alpha}) \xrightarrow{d} \mathcal{N}(0, \Sigma_{\hat{\alpha}})$$

implies

$$\sqrt{T}(\hat{\psi} - \psi) \xrightarrow{d} \mathcal{N}(0, \Sigma_{\hat{\psi}}), \tag{6.25}$$

where

$$\Sigma_{\hat{\psi}} = \frac{\partial \psi}{\partial \boldsymbol{\alpha}'} \Sigma_{\hat{\alpha}} \frac{\partial \psi'}{\partial \boldsymbol{\alpha}},$$

provided the matrix of partial derivatives $\partial\psi/\partial\boldsymbol{\alpha}'$ is such that none of the variances is zero and, in particular, $\partial\psi/\partial\boldsymbol{\alpha}' \neq 0$. If $\partial\psi/\partial\boldsymbol{\alpha}'$ does not have full row rank, the asymptotic covariance matrix $\Sigma_{\hat{\psi}}$ is singular. This problem will arise at specific points in the parameter space in the present situation because the function $\psi(\boldsymbol{\alpha})$ consists of sums of products of elements of $\boldsymbol{\alpha}$. Also, $\Sigma_{\hat{\alpha}}$ is generally singular if y_t is $I(1)$, which in turn may imply singularity of $\Sigma_{\hat{\psi}}$ even if $\partial\psi/\partial\boldsymbol{\alpha}'$ has full row rank. In the present case, both problems may occur jointly. A singular asymptotic covariance matrix may give rise to misleading inference for impulse responses. For further discussion see Benkwitz et al. (2000).

Even in those parts of the parameter space where standard asymptotic theory works, it is known that the actual small sample distributions of impulse responses may be quite different from their asymptotic counterparts. In particular, the accuracy of the confidence intervals tends to be low for large-dimensional VARs at longer horizons if the data are highly persistent, that is, if the process has roots close to the unit circle (see Kilian and Chang, 2000). Therefore attempts have been made to use local-to-unity asymptotics for improving inference in this situation. Earlier attempts in this context are Stock (1991), Wright (2000) and Gospodinov (2004), and more recent articles using that approach are Pesavento and Rossi (2006) and Mikusheva (2012).

In practice, bootstrap methods are often used in applied work to construct impulse response confidence intervals (for example, Kilian, 1998; Benkwitz et al., 2001). Although they have the advantage that complicated analytical expressions of the asymptotic variances are not needed, it is not clear that they lead to substantially improved inference. In particular, they are also justified by asymptotic theory. In general the bootstrap does not overcome the problems due to a singularity in the asymptotic distribution. Consequently bootstrap confidence intervals may have a coverage which does not correspond to the nominal level and may, hence, be unreliable (see Benkwitz et al., 2000). Using subset VAR techniques to impose as many zero restrictions on the parameters as possible and estimating only the remaining non-zero parameters offers a possible solution to this problem.

Bayesian methods provide another possible solution (for example Sims and Zha, 1999). If an a posteriori distribution is available for $\hat{\boldsymbol{\alpha}}$, it can be used to simulate the distribution of $\hat{\psi} = \psi(\hat{\boldsymbol{\alpha}})$ using standard Bayesian simulation techniques. That distribution can then be used for setting up confidence intervals or for inference on ψ. As Bayesian inference does not rely on asymptotic arguments, the singularity problem is not relevant. This does not mean that Bayesian estimation is necessarily more reliable. It requires extensive computations and is based on distributional assumptions which may be questionable.

8.2 Forecast Error Variance Decompositions

As mentioned earlier, forecast error variance decompositions are another tool for investigating the impacts of shocks in VAR models. In terms of the structural residuals the h-step forecast error (6.18) can be represented as

$$y_{T+h} - y_{T+h|T} = \Psi_0 v_{T+h} + \Psi_1 v_{T+h-1} + \cdots + \Psi_{h-1} v_{T+1}.$$

Using $\Sigma_v = I_K$, the forecast error variance of the kth component of y_{T+h} can be shown to be

$$\sigma_k^2(h) = \sum_{j=0}^{h-1} (\psi_{k1,j}^2 + \cdots + \psi_{kK,j}^2) = \sum_{j=1}^{K} (\psi_{kj,0}^2 + \cdots + \psi_{kj,h-1}^2),$$

where $\psi_{nm,j}$ denotes the (n,m)th element of Ψ_j. The quantity $(\psi_{kj,0}^2 + \cdots + \psi_{kj,h-1}^2)$ represents the contribution of the jth shock to the h-step forecast error variance of variable k. In practice, the relative contributions $(\psi_{kj,0}^2 + \cdots + \psi_{kj,h-1}^2)/\sigma_k^2(h)$ are often reported and interpreted for various variables and forecast horizons. A meaningful interpretation of these quantities requires that the shocks considered in the decomposition are economically meaningful.

The quantities of interest here can again be estimated easily by replacing unknown parameters by their estimators. Inference is complicated by the fact, however, that the relative variance shares may be zero or 1 and, hence, may assume boundary values. In such cases both classical asymptotic as well as bootstrap methods have problems.

8.3 Historical Decomposition of Time Series

Another way of looking at the contributions of the structural shocks to the observed series is opened up by decomposing the series as proposed by Burbidge and Harrison (1985). Neglecting deterministic terms and considering the structural MA representation (6.24), the jth variable can be represented as

$$y_{jt} = \sum_{i=0}^{\infty} (\psi_{j1,i} v_{1,t-i} + \cdots + \psi_{jK,i} v_{K,t-i}),$$

where $\psi_{jk,i}$ is the (j, k)th element of the structural MA matrix Ψ_i, as before. Thus,

$$y_{jt}^{(k)} = \sum_{i=0}^{\infty} \psi_{jk,i} v_{k,t-i}$$

is the contribution of the kth structural shock to the jth variable y_{jt}. Ideally one would like to plot the $y_{jt}^{(k)}$ for $k = 1,\ldots, K$, throughout the sample period, that is, for $t = 1,\ldots, T$, and interpret the relative contributions of the different structural shocks to the jth variable.

In practice, such a *historical decomposition* is, of course, not feasible because the structural shocks are not available. However, we can estimate the shocks associated with the sample period and use an estimated historical decomposition by noting that by successive substitution, the VAR process (6.5) can be written as

$$\begin{aligned} y_t &= \sum_{i=0}^{t-1} \Phi_i u_{t-i} + A_1^{(t)} y_0 + \cdots + A_p^{(t)} y_{-p+1} \\ &= \sum_{i=0}^{t-1} \Psi_i v_{t-i} + A_1^{(t)} y_0 + \cdots + A_p^{(t)} y_{-p+1}, \end{aligned} \tag{6.26}$$

where the Φ_i and Ψ_i are the MA coefficient matrices defined earlier and the $A_i^{(t)}$ are such that $[A_1^{(t)},\ldots, A_p^{(t)}]$ consists of the first K rows of the $(pK \times pK)$ matrix $\mathbf{A}^t$, where

$$\mathbf{A} = \begin{bmatrix} A_1 & \ldots & A_{p-1} & A_p \\ I_K & & 0 & 0 \\ & \ddots & & \vdots \\ 0 & & I_K & 0 \end{bmatrix}$$

(see Lütkepohl, 2005, Section 2.1). Hence, the $A_i^{(t)}$ go to zero for stationary VARs when t becomes large so that the contribution of the initial state becomes negligible for stationary processes as $t \to \infty$. On the other hand, for $I(1)$ processes the contribution of the initial values $y_0,\ldots, y_{-p+1}$ will remain important. In any case, y_{jt} may be decomposed as

$$y_{jt}^{(k)} = \sum_{i=0}^{t-1} \psi_{jk,i} v_{k,t-i} + \alpha_{j1}^{(t)} y_0 + \cdots + \alpha_{jp}^{(t)} y_{-p+1},$$

where $\psi_{jk,i}$ is the (j, k)th element of Ψ_i and $\alpha_{ji}^{(t)}$ is the jth row of $A_i^{(t)}$. The series $y_{jt}^{(k)}$ represents the contribution of the kth structural shock to the jth component series of y_t, given $y_0,\ldots, y_{-p+1}$. In practice all unknown parameters have to be replaced by estimators. The corresponding series $\hat{y}_{jt}^{(k)}$, $k = 1,\ldots, K$, represent a *historical decomposition* of y_{jt}. They are typically plotted to assess the contributions of the structural shocks to the jth series. Obviously, one may start the decomposition at any point in the sample and not necessarily at $t = 0$. In fact, for t close to the starting point of the decomposition the initial values may have a substantial impact even for stationary processes. So one may only want to consider the decomposition for periods some distance away from the starting point.

8.4 Analysis of Forecast Scenarios

SVAR models have also been used for analysing different forecast scenarios or conditional forecasts given restrictions for the future values of some of the variables. For example, in monetary policy analysis one may be interested in knowing the future development of the system under consideration for a given path of the interest rate or if the interest rate remains within a given range. Clearly, in a model where all variables are endogenous, fixing the future values of one or more variables may be problematic and one has to evaluate carefully how far the model can be stretched without being invalidated. In other words, SVAR models cannot be expected to reflect the changes induced in the future paths of the variables for arbitrary forecast scenarios (for applications see, for example, Waggoner and Zha, 1999; Baumeister and Kilian, 2012).

For describing the approach, a SVAR representation similar to (6.26) is particularly suitable,

$$y_{T+h} = \sum_{i=0}^{h-1} \Psi_i v_{T+h-i} + A_1^{(h)} y_T + \cdots + A_p^{(h)} y_{T-p+1}, \quad h = 1,2,\ldots, \tag{6.27}$$

where deterministic terms are again ignored for simplicity and all symbols are defined as in (6.26). The standard reduced form forecast $y_{T+h|T}$ discussed in section 6.1 is obtained from this expression by replacing all structural residuals in the first term on the right-hand side by zero. A forecast scenario different from this baseline forecast may be obtained by assigning other values to the structural shocks. For instance, a scenario where the jth variable has future values $y_{j,T+h}^*$ for $h = 1,\ldots,H$, amounts to choosing structural shocks v_{T+h}^*, $h = 1,\ldots,H$, such that

$$\sum_{i=0}^{h-1} \sum_{k=1}^{K} \psi_{jk,i} v_{k,T+h-i}^* = y_{j,T+h}^* - \alpha_{j1}^{(h)} y_T - \cdots - \alpha_{jp}^{(h)} y_{T-p+1} \quad h = 1,\ldots,H, \tag{6.28}$$

for periods $T + 1,\ldots,T + H$ or, more generally in matrix notation,

$$R_H \mathbf{v}_{T,T+H}^* = r_H, \tag{6.29}$$

where $\mathbf{v}_{T,T+H} = (v_{T+1}',\ldots,v_{T+H}')'$ is a $(KH \times 1)$ vector of stacked future structural shocks, R_H is a suitable $(Q \times KH)$ dimensional restriction matrix representing the left-hand side relations in (6.28) with $Q \leq KH$ and r_H is a $(Q \times 1)$ vector containing the right-hand side of (6.28). The forecasts conditional on the v_{T+h}^* shocks are then computed as

$$y_{T+h|T}^{cond} = \sum_{i=0}^{h-1} \Psi_i v_{T+h-i}^* + A_1^{(h)} y_T + \cdots + A_p^{(h)} y_{T-p+1}, \quad h = 1,\ldots,H. \tag{6.30}$$

For concreteness consider, for instance, the case of a B-model with lower-triangular initial effects matrix $\mathsf{B} = \Psi_0$. In that case, if the path of the first variable is pre-specified as $y_{1,T+h}^*$, $h = 1,\ldots,H$, this amounts to choosing the first residual as $v_{1,T+h}^* = y_{1,T+h}^* - \alpha_{11}^{(1)} y_{T+h-1|T}^{cond} - \cdots - \alpha_{1p}^{(1)} y_{T+h-p|T}^{cond}$, $h = 1,\ldots,H$. In general, the values for the v^*_{T+h}s will not be uniquely determined by the restrictions. In that case Doan et al. (1984) suggest using

$$\mathbf{v}^*_{T,T+h} = R'_H(R_H R'_H)^{-1} r_H$$

which is the least squares solution obtained by minimizing $\sum_{h=1}^{H} v'_{T+h} v_{T+h} = \mathbf{v}'_{T,T+h}\mathbf{v}_{T,T+h}$ subject to the restrictions (6.29).

Obviously, the conditional forecast $y^{cond}_{T+h|T}$ differs from the unconditional forecast $y_{T+h|T}$ of section 6.1 by the first term on the right-hand side of equation (6.30). Of course, other forecast scenarios may be of interest. For example, one may not want to condition on a particular path of a variable but on its values being in a given range. Such a scenario can be investigated by using the above formulae for computing forecast ranges accordingly.

For practical purposes the unknown parameters have to be replaced by estimates, as usual. Waggoner and Zha (1999) present a Bayesian method for taking into account the related estimation uncertainty in that case.

A critical question in the context of evaluating forecast scenarios in the context of SVAR models is whether such models are suitable for that purpose or whether they are stretched too much by restricting the future developments of some variables. The problem here is that all variables are regarded as endogenous and, hence, their values should be generated endogenously by the model and not be forced upon them exogenously. Of course, there could be cases where one or more of the variables are really exogenous and not affected by feedback relations within the system under consideration. In such cases a conditional analysis as described in the foregoing is plausible. In other cases the users should be cautious in interpreting the results and carefully evaluate whether the model can be expected to be informative about the questions of interest.

9 CONCLUSIONS AND EXTENSIONS

This chapter reviews VAR analysis. Specification, estimation, forecasting, causality and structural analysis are discussed. Finite order VAR models are popular for economic analysis because they are easy to use. There are several software products which can be used in performing a VAR analysis (see, for example, *PcGive* (Doornik and Hendry, 1997), *EViews* (EViews, 2000) and *JMulTi* (Krätzig, 2004)).

In many situations of practical interest the VAR models discussed in this chapter are too limited, however. For example, the assumption that the VAR order is finite is rather restrictive because theoretically omitted variables or linear transformations of the variables may lead to infinite order VAR processes. Hence, it may be appealing to extend the model class to infinite order VAR processes. Such an extension may be achieved by considering VAR models with MA error terms or by studying the implications of fitting approximate finite order VAR models to series which are generated by infinite order processes. This issue is dealt with in Lewis and Reinsel (1985), Lütkepohl and Saikkonen (1997), Inoue and Kilian (2002b) and Lütkepohl (2005, Part IV). An authoritative discussion of the theory of VARMA models is also available in Hannan and Deistler (1988) and a recent survey of the related literature is given by Lütkepohl (2006a).

As already mentioned in the introduction, if some variables are integrated and perhaps cointegrated, vector error correction models are suitable tools for modelling the cointegration relations in detail. Such models are presented in Chapter 7, 'Cointegration and error correction'. A possible advantage of the levels VAR models considered in the present chapter is that they are robust to cointegration of unknown form. They can be used even if the number of cointegration relations is unknown, not to speak of the precise cointegration relations. Of course, statistical tools are available for analysing the number and type of cointegration relations. However, such pretesting procedures have their limitations as well, in particular if some roots are only near unity, as pointed out, for instance, by Elliott (1998).

Other possible extensions are the inclusion of non-linear components (for example, Granger, 2001; Teräsvirta et al., 2010) or allowing the VAR coefficients to be time-varying (for example, Primiceri, 2005). Moreover, seasonal macroeconomic data are now available for many countries. Hence, accounting specifically for seasonal fluctuations may be necessary (for example, Ghysels and Osborn, 2001). Furthermore, heteroscedasticity or conditional heteroscedasticity in the residuals of VAR models may be of importance in practice, in particular, when higher frequency data are considered (see Lütkepohl, 2005, Chapter 16 for a textbook treatment and Bauwens et al., 2006 or Silvennoinen and Teräsvirta, 2009 for recent surveys). For some economic variables restricting the order of integration to zero or 1 may be unrealistic. Extensions to higher order integration have been considered by Boswijk (2000), Johansen (1997, 2006), and others.

NOTE

* Helpful comments by Lutz Kilian are gratefully acknowledged.

REFERENCES

Ahn, S.K. (1988), 'Distribution for residual autocovariances in multivariate autoregressive models with structured parameterization', *Biometrika*, **75**, 590–93.

Akaike, H. (1973), 'Information theory and an extension of the maximum likelihood principle', in B. Petrov and F. Csáki (eds), *2nd International Symposium on Information Theory*, Académiai Kiadó, Budapest, pp. 267–81.

Akaike, H. (1974), 'A new look at the statistical model identification', *IEEE Transactions on Automatic Control*, **AC-19**, 716–23.

Amisano, G. and C. Giannini (1997), *Topics in Structural VAR Econometrics*, 2nd edn, Berlin: Springer.

Andrews, D.W.K. (1993), 'Tests for parameter instability and structural change with unknown change point', *Econometrica*, **61**, 821–56.

Andrews, D.W.K. and W. Ploberger (1994), 'Optimal tests when a nuisance parameter is present only under the alternative', *Econometrica*, **62**, 1383–414.

Baillie, R.T. (1979), 'Asymptotic prediction mean squared error for vector autoregressive models', *Biometrika*, **66**, 675–8.

Baumeister, C. and L. Kilian (2012), 'Real-time forecasts of the real price of oil', *Journal of Business and Economic Statistics*, **30**, 326–36.

Bauwens, L., S. Laurent and J.V.K. Rombouts (2006), 'Multivariate GARCH models: a survey', *Journal of Applied Econometrics*, **21**, 79–109.

Benkwitz, A., H. Lütkepohl and M. Neumann (2000), 'Problems related to bootstrapping impulse responses of autoregressive processes', *Econometric Reviews*, **19**, 69–103.

Benkwitz, A., H. Lütkepohl and J. Wolters (2001), 'Comparison of bootstrap confidence intervals for impulse responses of German monetary systems', *Macroeconomic Dynamics*, **5**, 81–100.
Berkowitz, J. and L. Kilian (2000), 'Recent developments in bootstrapping time series', *Econometric Reviews*, **19**, 1–48.
Blanchard, O. and D. Quah (1989), 'The dynamic effects of aggregate demand and supply disturbances', *American Economic Review*, **79**, 655–73.
Boswijk, H.P. (2000), 'Mixed normality and ancillarity in I(2) systems', *Econometric Theory*, **16**, 878–904.
Breitung, J., R. Brüggemann and H. Lütkepohl (2004), 'Structural vector autogressive modeling and impulse responses', in H. Lütkepohl and M. Krätzig (eds), *Applied Time Series Econometrics*, Cambridge: Cambridge University Press, pp. 159–96.
Brüggemann, R., H. Lütkepohl and P. Saikkonen (2006), 'Residual autocorrelation testing for vector error correction models', *Journal of Econometrics*, **134**, 579–604.
Burbidge, J. and A. Harrison (1985), 'A historical decomposition of the great depression to determine the role of money', *Journal of Monetary Economics*, **16**, 45–54.
Canova, F. (2007), *Methods for Applied Macroeconomic Research*, Princeton, NJ: Princeton University Press.
Del Negro, M. and F. Schorfheide (2004), 'Priors from general equilibrium models for VARs', *International Economic Review*, **45**, 643–73.
Doan, T., R.B. Litterman and C.A. Sims (1984), 'Forecasting and conditional projection using realistic prior distributions', *Econometric Reviews*, **3**, 1–144.
Dolado, J.J. and H. Lütkepohl (1996), 'Making Wald tests work for cointegrated VAR systems', *Econometric Reviews*, **15**, 369–86.
Doornik, J.A. and D.F. Hendry (1997), *Modelling Dynamic Systems Using PcFiml 9.0 for Windows*, London: International Thomson Business Press.
Dufour, J-M. and E. Renault (1998), 'Short run and long run causality in time series: theory', *Econometrica*, **66**, 1099–125.
Elliott, G. (1998), 'On the robustness of cointegration methods when regressors almost have unit roots', *Econometrica*, **66**, 149–58.
Engle, R.F. and C.W.J. Granger (1987), 'Cointegration and error correction: representation, estimation and testing', *Econometrica*, **55**, 251–76.
EViews (2000), *EViews 4.0 User's Guide*, Irvine, CA: Quantitative Micro Software.
Findley, D.F. (1986), 'On bootstrap estimates of forecast mean square errors for autoregressive processes', in D.M. Allen (ed.), *Computer Science and Statistics: The Interface*, Amsterdam: North-Holland, pp. 11–17.
Ghysels, E. and D.R. Osborn (2001), *The Econometric Analysis of Seasonal Time Series*, Cambridge: Cambridge University Press.
Giannone, D., M. Lenza and G. Primiceri (2010), 'Prior selection for vector autoregressions', mimeo, Department of Economics, Free University of Brussels.
Goncalves, S. and L. Kilian (2004), 'Bootstrapping autoregressions with conditional heteroskedasticity of unknown form', *Journal of Econometrics*, **123**, 89–120.
Gospodinov, N. (2004), 'Asymptotic confidence intervals for impulse responses of near-integrated processes', *Econometrics Journal*, **7**, 505–27.
Granger, C.W.J. (1969), 'Investigating causal relations by econometric models and cross-spectral methods', *Econometrica*, **37**, 424–38.
Granger, C.W.J. (1981), 'Some properties of time series data and their use in econometric model specification', *Journal of Econometrics*, **16**, 121–30.
Granger, C.W.J. (2001), 'Overview of nonlinear macroeconometric empirical models', *Macroeconomic Dynamics*, **5**, 466–81.
Grigoletto, M. (1998), 'Bootstrap prediction intervals for autoregressions: some alternatives', *International Journal of Forecasting*, **14**, 447–56.
Hamilton, J.D. (1994), *Time Series Analysis*, Princeton, NJ: Princeton University Press.
Hannan, E.J. and M. Deistler (1988), *The Statistical Theory of Linear Systems*, New York: Wiley.
Hannan, E.J. and B.G. Quinn (1979), 'The determination of the order of an autoregression', *Journal of the Royal Statistical Society*, **B41**, 190–95.
Hansen, B.E (1997), 'Approximate asymptotic *p* values for structural-change tests', *Journal of Business & Economic Statistics*, **15**, 60–67.
Hatanaka, M. (1996), *Time-Series-Based Econometrics: Unit Roots and Co-Integration*, Oxford: Oxford University Press.
Hosking, J.R.M. (1980), 'The multivariate portmanteau statistic', *Journal of the American Statistical Association*, **75**, 602–608.
Hosking, J.R.M. (1981a), 'Equivalent forms of the multivariate portmanteau statistic', *Journal of the Royal Statistical Society*, **B43**, 261–2.

Hosking, J.R.M. (1981b), 'Lagrange-multiplier tests of multivariate time series models', *Journal of the Royal Statistical Society*, **B43**, 219–30.
Ingram, B.F. and C.H. Whiteman (1994), 'Supplanting the "Minnesota" prior: forecasting macroeconomic time series using real business cycle model priors', *Journal of Monetary Economics*, **34**, 497–510.
Inoue, A. and L. Kilian (2002a), 'Bootstrapping autoregressive processes with possible unit roots', *Econometrica*, **70**, 377–91.
Inoue, A. and L. Kilian (2002b), 'Bootstrapping smooth functions of slope parameters and innovation variances in VAR(∞) models', *International Economic Review*, **43**, 309–32.
Jarque, C.M. and A.K. Bera (1987), 'A test for normality of observations and regression residuals', *International Statistical Review*, **55**, 163–72.
Johansen, S. (1995), *Likelihood-based Inference in Cointegrated Vector Autoregressive Models*, Oxford: Oxford University Press.
Johansen, S. (1997), 'Likelihood analysis of the I(2) model', *Scandinavian Journal of Statistics*, **24**, 433–62.
Johansen, S. (2006), 'Statistical analysis of hypotheses on the cointegrating relations in the I(2) model', *Journal of Econometrics*, **132**, 81–115.
Kabaila, P. (1993), 'On bootstrap predictive inference for autoregressive processes', *Journal of Time Series Analysis*, **14**, 473–84.
Kadiyala, K.R. and S. Karlsson (1997), 'Numerical methods for estimation and inference in Bayesian VAR-models', *Journal of Applied Econometrics*, **12**, 99–132.
Kilian, L. (1998), 'Small-sample confidence intervals for impulse response functions', *Review of Economics and Statistics*, **80**, 218–30.
Kilian, L. and P.-L. Chang (2000), 'How accurate are confidence intervals for impulse responses in large VAR models?', *Economics Letters*, **69**, 299–307.
Kilian, L. and U. Demiroglu (2000), 'Residual-based tests for normality in autogressions: asymptotic theory and simulation evidence', *Journal of Business & Economic Statistics*, **18**, 40–50.
Kim, J.H. (1999), 'Asymptotic and bootstrap prediction regions for vector autoregression', *International Journal of Forecasting*, **15**, 393–403.
Krätzig, M. (2004), 'The software JMulTi', in H. Lütkepohl and M. Krätzig (eds), *Applied Time Series Econometrics*, Cambridge: Cambridge University Press, pp. 289–99.
Leeb, H. and B.M. Pötscher (2005), 'Model selection and inference: facts and fiction', *Econometric Theory*, **21**, 21–59.
Lewis, R. and G.C. Reinsel (1985), 'Prediction of multivariate time series by autoregressive model fitting', *Journal of Multivariate Analysis*, **16**, 393–411.
Li, H. and G.S. Maddala (1996), 'Bootstrapping time series models', *Econometric Reviews*, **15**, 115–58.
Li, W.K. and A.I. McLeod (1981), 'Distribution of the residual autocorrelations in multivariate ARMA time series models', *Journal of the Royal Statistical Society*, **B43**, 231–9.
Litterman, R.B. (1986), 'Forecasting with Bayesian vector autoregressions – five years of experience', *Journal of Business & Economic Statistics*, **4**, 25–38.
Lomnicki, Z.A. (1961), 'Tests for departure from normality in the case of linear stochastic processes', *Metrika*, **4**, 37–62.
Lütkepohl, H. (1993), 'Testing for causation between two variables in higher dimensional VAR models', in H. Schneeweiss and K.F. Zimmermann (eds), *Studies in Applied Econometrics*, Heidelberg: Physica-Verlag, pp. 75–91.
Lütkepohl, H. (2004), 'Vector autoregressive and vector error correction models', in H. Lütkepohl and M. Krätzig (eds), *Applied Time Series Econometrics*, Cambridge: Cambridge University Press, pp. 86–158.
Lütkepohl, H. (2005), *New Introduction to Multiple Time Series Analysis*, Berlin: Springer-Verlag.
Lütkepohl, H. (2006a), 'Forecasting with VARMA models', in G. Elliot, C.W.J. Granger and A. Timmermann (eds), *Handbook of Economic Forecasting, Volume 1*, Amsterdam: Elsevier, pp. 287–325.
Lütkepohl, H. (2006b), 'Vector autoregressive models', in T.C. Mills and K. Patterson (eds), *Palgrave Handbook of Econometrics, Volume 1, Econometric Theory*, Basingstoke: Palgrave Macmillan, pp. 477–510.
Lütkepohl, H. (2009), 'Econometric analysis with vector autoregressive models', in D.A. Belsley and E.J. Kontoghiorghes (eds), *Handbook of Computational Econometrics*, Chichester: Wiley, pp. 281–319.
Lütkepohl, H. and M. Krätzig (2004), *Applied Time Series Econometrics*, Cambridge: Cambridge University Press.
Lütkepohl, H. and D.S. Poskitt (1996), 'Testing for causation using infinite order vector autoregressive processes', *Econometric Theory*, **12**, 61–87.
Lütkepohl, H. and P. Saikkonen (1997), 'Impulse response analysis in infinite order cointegrated vector autoregressive processes', *Journal of Econometrics*, **81**, 127–57.
Masarotto, G. (1990), 'Bootstrap prediction intervals for autoregressions', *International Journal of Forecasting*, **6**, 229–39.

Mikusheva, A. (2012), 'One-dimensional inference in autoregressive models with the potential presence of a unit root', *Econometrica*, **80**, 173–212.
Park, J.Y. and P.C.B. Phillips (1988), 'Statistical inference in regressions with integrated processes: Part 1', *Econometric Theory*, **4**, 468–97.
Park, J.Y. and P.C.B. Phillips (1989), 'Statistical inference in regressions with integrated processes: Part 2', *Econometric Theory*, **5**, 95–131.
Pascual, L., J. Romo and E. Ruiz (2004), 'Bootstrap predictive inference for ARIMA processes', *Journal of Time Series Analysis*, **25**, 449–65.
Paulsen, J. (1984), 'Order determination of multivariate autoregressive time series with unit roots', *Journal of Time Series Analysis*, **5**, 115–27.
Pesavento, E. and B. Rossi (2006), 'Small-sample confidence intervals for multivariate impulse response functions at long horizons', *Journal of Applied Econometrics*, **21**, 1135–55.
Primiceri, G.E. (2005), 'Time varying structural vector autoregressions and monetary policy', *Review of Economic Studies*, **72**, 821–52.
Quinn, B.G. (1980), 'Order determination for a multivariate autoregression', *Journal of the Royal Statistical Society,* **B42**, 182–5.
Reinsel, G. (1980), 'Asymptotic properties of prediction errors for the multivariate autoregressive model using estimated parameters', *Journal of the Royal Statistical Society*, **B42**, 328–33.
Rissanen, J. (1978), 'Modeling by shortest data description', *Automatica*, **14**, 465–71.
Saikkonen, P. and H. Lütkepohl (1996), 'Infinite order cointegrated vector autoregressive processes: estimation and inference', *Econometric Theory*, **12**, 814–44.
Samaranayake, V.A. and D.P. Hasza (1988), 'Properties of predictors for multivariate autoregressive models with estimated parameters', *Journal of Time Series Analysis*, **9**, 361–83.
Schwarz, G. (1978), 'Estimating the dimension of a model', *Annals of Statistics*, **6**, 461–4.
Silvennoinen, A. and T. Teräsvirta (2009), 'Multivariate GARCH models', in T.G. Anderson, R.A. Davis, J.-P. Kreis and T. Mikosch (eds), *Handbook of Financial Time Series*, New York: Springer, pp. 201–28.
Sims, C.A. (1980), 'Macroeconomics and reality', *Econometrica*, **48**, 1–48.
Sims, C.A. and T. Zha (1999), 'Error bands for impulse responses', *Econometrica*, **67**, 1113–55.
Sims, C.A., J.H. Stock and M.W. Watson (1990), 'Inference in linear time series models with some unit roots', *Econometrica*, **58**, 113–44.
Sims, C.A., D.F. Waggoner and T. Zha (2008), 'Methods for inference in large multiple-equation Markov-switching models', *Journal of Econometrics*, **146**, 255–74.
Stock, J.H. (1991), 'Confidence intervals for the largest autoregressive root in US economic time series', *Journal of Monetary Economics*, **28**, 435–60.
Teräsvirta, T., D. Tjøstheim and C.W.J. Granger (2010), *Modelling Nonlinear Economic Time Series*, Oxford: Oxford University Press.
Toda, H.Y. and P.C.B. Phillips (1993), 'Vector autoregressions and causality', *Econometrica*, **61**, 1367–93.
Toda, H.Y. and T. Yamamoto (1995), 'Statistical inference in vector autoregressions with possibly integrated processes', *Journal of Econometrics*, **66**, 225–50.
Uhlig, H. (2005), 'What are the effects of monetary policy on output? Results from an agnostic identification procedure', *Journal of Monetary Economics*, **52**, 381–419.
Villani, M. (2005), 'Bayesian reference analysis of cointegration', *Econometric Theory*, **21**, 326–57.
Waggoner, D.F. and T. Zha (1999), 'Conditional forecasts in dynamic multivariate models', *Review of Economics and Statistics*, **81**, 639–51.
Watson, M.W. (1994), 'Vector autoregressions and cointegration', in R.F. Engle and D.L. McFadden (eds), *Handbook of Econometrics, Vol. IV*, New York: Elsevier.
Wright, J.H. (2000), 'Confidence intervals for univariate impulse responses with a near unit root', *Journal of Business & Economic Statistics*, **18**, 368–73.

7 Cointegration and error correction

James Davidson

1 THE BACKGROUND

Elementary courses in statistics introduce at an early stage the key assumption of 'random sampling'. In more technical language, the data set is assumed to be identically and independently distributed (i.i.d.). In this framework a range of simple and elegant results can be derived, for example, that the variance of the mean of n observations is $1/n$ times the variance of the observations themselves. Given a random sample of n pairs (x,y) with sample correlation coefficient r_{xy}, if at least one of the pair has a Gaussian (normal) distribution the existence of a relationship between them is tested by comparing the 't-statistic' $r_{xy}/\sqrt{(1 - r_{xy}^2)/(n - 2)}$ with the Student t-distribution with $n - 2$ degrees of freedom. All the inference procedures in classical regression analysis follow the same basic approach. The Gaussianity assumption may be dropped by appeal to a large sample and the central limit theorem, but independent sampling is strictly needed to validate these procedures.

The received theory notwithstanding, often the first data sets that students meet in econometrics class are time series for GDP, aggregate consumption, money stock and the like – samples that are neither independently nor identically distributed. Such disjunctions between theory and practice often sow confusion in the understanding of statistical relationships in economics.

One of the first authors to study the problem of inference in time series was G. Udny Yule (1926), who reflected in his presidential address to the Royal Statistical Society on the high correlation (0.9512) between standardized mortality and the proportion of marriages solemnized by the Church of England, recorded in the years 1866 to 1911. It is interesting with the benefit of hindsight to read of the difficulties that professional statisticians would have – both then and much more recently – with the interpretation of such facts. The two series of Yule's example share a pronounced downward drift over the 46 years of the observations. 'Large goes with large and small with small', which is the classic indicator of a positive correlation. In what sense is this correlation to be regarded as spurious? It is true that both variables are subject to systematic variation with the passage of time. However, to be driven by a common factor is a perfectly legitimate way of understanding the phenomenon of correlation between variables. This fact alone does not explain why we regard this particular correlation as spurious.

The true explanation requires us to distinguish between correlation as a description of data, and correlation as a theoretical construct; an expected association as a feature of a fixed joint distribution of random variables. Our problem arises when this fixed joint distribution does not exist. The examples Yule analyses in his paper include integrated processes, formed by a cumulation of independent random shocks. As is well known, such processes – often called *random walks* – can 'wander anywhere', having no central tendency. Short realizations often give the appearance of deterministic-seeming time trends. Averages of repeated drawings from such processes do not converge to fixed limits as the sample size increases; in other words, they do not obey the law of large numbers. The sample variances of such processes, and likewise covariances, diverge to infinity. While correlation coefficients are normalized to lie between -1 and $+1$, the correlations of pairs of mutually independent random walk processes do not converge to zero, but remain random variables even asymptotically. As famously demonstrated in a set of computer simulations by Granger and Newbold (1974), independent random walks exhibit 'significant' correlations, such that the t-statistic defined above diverges to infinity as n increases. Additional data do not serve to resolve a spurious correlation but, rather, to reinforce the false conclusion. It follows that the conventional equating of sample and theoretical correlations in an estimation exercise has no validity.

These phenomena presented a dilemma for econometricians in the middle years of the twentieth century, as they attempted to model macroeconomic and financial data sets that are well described as the integrals (cumulations) of stationary series. One approach was to model the relationships between the differences (the changes from period to period) but clearly a great deal of information about relationships between series is lost in such transformations. It is easy to construct examples where the correlation between the differences of time series have signs opposite to that between the levels. A second approach is to treat trends as deterministic, and remove them by regression on dummy (straight-line) trend variables. Although the relations between fitted trend components can be discounted as spurious (one straight line always 'explains' another) the deviations of economic series from linear trend often exhibit random walk characteristics in practice, so the problem is not resolved.

It was in the context of this unsatisfactory hiatus in the progress of time series econometrics, in the course of the 1970s, that Clive Granger initiated his researches into the modelling of economic trends. The culmination of this research was the key idea that relationships between integrated time series must be understood as a sharing of common trends; not correlation, but cointegration. The story of these discoveries, well told in an article by David Hendry (2004) celebrating Granger's 2003 Nobel Prize, provides a fascinating mix of debates and disagreements, false trails, penetrating intuitions and the insightful re-interpretation of applied studies. Hendry's (1980) inaugural lecture at LSE is often cited as an accessible exposition of the issues, although the term 'cointegration' had yet to be coined at that date.

The complete story of the cointegration concept has to acknowledge the indispensable contributions of two other researchers, Peter C.B. Phillips at Yale, who developed the essential links with mathematical stochastic process theory that were needed for a theory of inference in non-stationary data, and Søren Johansen in Copenhagen, who developed a rigorous theory of vector autoregressions in non-stationary data. The net result of these endeavours is that econometrics can deal effectively with time series data, whether or not the 'identically and independently distributed' sampling paradigm has any practical relevance.

2 A LINEAR MODEL OF NON-STATIONARY DATA

To fix ideas, consider first the simplest multiple time series model, the first-order VAR. Let $\boldsymbol{x}_t$ $(m \times 1)$ denote a vector of variables evolving according to the equation

$$\boldsymbol{x}_t = \boldsymbol{a}_0 + \boldsymbol{A}\boldsymbol{x}_{t-1} + \varepsilon_t \tag{7.1}$$

where $\boldsymbol{A}$ is an $m \times m$ matrix of coefficients and ε_t $(m \times 1)$ is i.i.d. with mean vector $\boldsymbol{0}$ and variance matrix $\boldsymbol{\Sigma}$. Suppose that this process has been running for a large number of periods that we can treat as effectively infinite. Then the equation has the solution

$$\boldsymbol{x}_t = \sum_{j=0}^{\infty} \boldsymbol{A}^j(\boldsymbol{a}_0 + \varepsilon_{t-j})$$

where $\boldsymbol{A}^j = \boldsymbol{AA}...\boldsymbol{A}$ (the j-fold product) and $\boldsymbol{A}^0 = \boldsymbol{I}_m$, the identity matrix of order m.

Write the Jordan canonical form of the matrix as $\boldsymbol{A} = \boldsymbol{PMP}^{-1}$, where if the eigenvalues are all distinct, $\boldsymbol{M}$ is a diagonal matrix with the eigenvalues of $\boldsymbol{A}$ (either real or complex valued) on the diagonal.[1] Provided the eigenvalues all have modulus strictly less than unity, it is easy to see that $\boldsymbol{A}^j = \boldsymbol{PM}^j\boldsymbol{P}^{-1} \to \boldsymbol{0}$ and $\sum_{j=0}^{\infty}\boldsymbol{A}^j = (\boldsymbol{I}_m - \boldsymbol{A})^{-1} < \infty$. In this case, we note that $\boldsymbol{x}_t$ has a distribution independent of t, with mean $(\boldsymbol{I}_m - \boldsymbol{A})^{-1}\boldsymbol{a}_0$ and variance matrix $\boldsymbol{\Sigma}_x = \sum_{j=0}^{\infty}\boldsymbol{A}^j\boldsymbol{\Sigma}(\boldsymbol{A}^j)'$.[2] We say that the process is stationary.

If $\boldsymbol{A}$ has one or more eigenvalues equal to 1, on the other hand, $\boldsymbol{A}^j$ does not converge to zero and $\boldsymbol{I}_m - \boldsymbol{A}$ is singular, by construction. In this case, the assumption that it has been running for an infinite number of periods is not compatible with a well-defined distribution for $\boldsymbol{x}_t$; such a process has infinite magnitude with probability 1. We must instead postulate a finite initial condition $\boldsymbol{x}_0$ and consider the cases $t = 1, 2, 3,...$ to see what happens. Clearly, this process is non-stationary, and its variance is increasing with time. A particularly simple case is $\boldsymbol{A} = \boldsymbol{I}_m$, where all m eigenvalues are equal to 1, and

$$\boldsymbol{x}_t = \boldsymbol{x}_0 + t\boldsymbol{a}_0 + \sum_{j=0}^{t-1}\varepsilon_{t-j}. \tag{7.2}$$

This is a vector of so-called random walks, with drifts $\boldsymbol{a}_0$. Note how the equation intercepts no longer measure a unique location, or central tendency of the distribution, but the rate of divergence of the central tendency with time. The variance matrix of the process, treating $\boldsymbol{x}_0$ as fixed, is $t\Sigma$. Even with $\boldsymbol{a}_0 = \boldsymbol{0}$ the average distance from the starting point, as measured by the standard deviation of the coordinates, increases like $\sqrt{t}$.

More generally, we may have some of the eigenvalues of the system equal to unity, and others in the stable range. It is convenient in this case to recast the model in the form in which the singular matrix appears explicitly. Write $\boldsymbol{\Pi} = \boldsymbol{A} - \boldsymbol{I}_m$ and then (7.1) can be written

$$\Delta\boldsymbol{x}_t = \boldsymbol{a}_0 + \boldsymbol{\Pi}\boldsymbol{x}_{t-1} + \varepsilon_t \tag{7.3}$$

where $\Delta\boldsymbol{x}_t = \boldsymbol{x}_t - \boldsymbol{x}_{t-1}$.[3] Note that the eigenvalues of $\boldsymbol{\Pi}$ are the diagonal elements of $\boldsymbol{M} - \boldsymbol{I}_m$ and, hence, unit eigenvalues of $\boldsymbol{A}$ are zero eigenvalues of $\boldsymbol{\Pi}$. With one or more zero eigenvalues, $\boldsymbol{\Pi}$ is singular, say with rank $s < m$, and note that the case $s = 0$ implies $\boldsymbol{\Pi} = \boldsymbol{0}$ and hence corresponds to the random walk model (7.2).[4]

An $m \times m$ matrix with rank s always has a representation $\mathbf{\Pi} = \alpha\beta'$ where α and β are $m \times s$ matrices with full rank s. This decomposition is not of course unique, since we can also write $\mathbf{\Pi} = \alpha^*\beta^{*\prime}$ where $\alpha^* = \alpha \boldsymbol{D}^{-1}$ and $\beta^* = \beta\boldsymbol{D}'$ for any $s \times s$ non-singular matrix $\boldsymbol{D}$. However. the columns of β must always span the same space.[5] It is also possible that known restrictions on the model could allow α and β to be identified uniquely, an issue that we discuss further in section 6.

Consider the relationship between the processes $\boldsymbol{x}_t$ and $\Delta\boldsymbol{x}_t$ appearing in (7.3). Differencing is the inverse of the operation of integrating (that is, cumulating) a series. If $\boldsymbol{x}_0 = \boldsymbol{0}$ and $\boldsymbol{x}_t = \boldsymbol{y}_1 + \boldsymbol{y}_2 + \cdots + \boldsymbol{y}_t$, then $\Delta\boldsymbol{x}_t = \boldsymbol{y}_t$ for $t \geq 1$. We define the notion of the 'order of integration' of a series, denoted d, such that if $\boldsymbol{x}_t$ has order of integration d, then $\Delta\boldsymbol{x}_t$ has order of integration $d - 1$. A convenient shorthand for this is to write $\boldsymbol{x}_t \sim \mathrm{I}(d)$. If we (arbitrarily) assign $d = 0$ to the case where the process is stationary with finite variance, then a random walk of the type shown in (7.2) must be assigned $d = 1$. Differencing an I(0) process yields the case I(−1), again a stationary process but this one is also stationary after integrating; hence this case, sometimes called an *over-differenced* process, is distinct from I(0).

The interesting feature of (7.3) is that processes with different orders of integration feature on the two sides of the equation. It is not too difficult to deduce from the definitions that $\mathrm{I}(d) + \mathrm{I}(d-p) \sim \mathrm{I}(d)$ for any $p > 0$, and also that $\varepsilon_t \sim \mathrm{I}(0)$. Writing (7.3) in the form

$$\Delta\boldsymbol{x}_t = \boldsymbol{a}_0 + \alpha\beta'\boldsymbol{x}_{t-1} + \varepsilon_t \tag{7.4}$$

we see, given that α is a full-rank matrix, that $\beta'\boldsymbol{x}_t$ must be $\mathrm{I}(d-1)$ when $\boldsymbol{x}_t \sim \mathrm{I}(d)$. Taking a certain linear combination of the variables in the model results in a process of lower integration order than that of the variables themselves. While we have not shown by this argument that $d = 1$ in the 'reduced rank VAR' (7.4), this is intuitively clear from considering the limiting cases $s = m$ and $s = 0$, the stationary and random walk models respectively.

With no loss of generality the intercept may be decomposed as $\boldsymbol{a}_0 = \delta - \alpha\mu$ where μ is $s \times 1$. Then the model can be further rearranged as

$$\Delta\boldsymbol{x}_t = \delta + \alpha\boldsymbol{z}_{t-1} + \varepsilon_t \tag{7.5}$$

where $\boldsymbol{z}_t$ is the s-vector of *cointegrating residuals*, defined as

$$\boldsymbol{z}_t = \beta'\boldsymbol{x}_t - \mu \ (s \times 1). \tag{7.6}$$

The elements of α are often referred to as the 'loadings coefficients' or 'error correction coefficients'. Pre-multiplying (7.5) by β' and rearranging yields the VAR(1) representation of the residuals,

$$\boldsymbol{z}_t = \beta'\delta + (\boldsymbol{I}_s + \beta'\alpha)\boldsymbol{z}_{t-1} + \beta'\varepsilon_t. \tag{7.7}$$

This relation defines a modified form of stability condition. If the matrix $\boldsymbol{I}_s + \beta'\alpha$ has all its eigenvalues in the stable region, then the series possess s stationary linear combinations. If $\boldsymbol{\delta} \neq \mathbf{0}$ the system contains a drift, the variables of the system having a persistent tendency to either rise or fall depending on the signs of the elements, although if $\boldsymbol{\beta}'\boldsymbol{\delta} = \mathbf{0}$ the cointegrating relations cancel the drift and $E(z_t) = \mathbf{0}$. On the other hand, if $\boldsymbol{\delta} = \mathbf{0}$ the processes are drift-neutral, their variances increasing with time but as likely to fall as to rise in any period. Such a process is said to exhibit a pure stochastic trend. Take care to note that $\boldsymbol{\mu}$ does not contribute to the drift so that $\boldsymbol{a}_0 = \mathbf{0}$ is not necessary for drift-neutrality.

We have now derived a simple form of the celebrated Granger representation theorem, which says, in essentials, the following. A vector autoregression containing unit roots generates non-stationary processes, but if the number of these roots is smaller than the dimension of the system there must at the same time exist a set of $s < m$ stationary linear combinations of the variables, forming the so-called *cointegrating relations*: s is called the *cointegrating rank* of the system. A necessary feature of the system is that the cointegrating residuals Granger-cause[6] future changes of the process, so that the model can always be cast in the so-called *error-correction* form. The variables of the model are said to exhibit *m* − *s common trends*. The variables evolve along non-stationary paths, but these paths are tied together by the cointegrating relations. The error correction form has a very natural interpretation, that to maintain the common trends through time requires that changes in the variables must respond to deviations from the cointegrating relations measured by z_t. For this to happen requires the elements of $\boldsymbol{\alpha}$ to have appropriate signs and magnitudes to ensure stable adjustment, according to (7.7). This feature is of course implicit in the requirement that the non-unit eigenvalues of $\boldsymbol{A}$ fall in the stable region.

3 THE GENERAL LINEAR CASE

We next consider the standard generalization of the foregoing simple case. An *m*-dimensional *linear process* is defined as a process whose non-deterministic component (after subtracting intercepts, trends, and so on) has the representation

$$\boldsymbol{y}_t = \boldsymbol{C}(L)\boldsymbol{\varepsilon}_t \tag{7.8}$$

where[7] $\boldsymbol{C}(z) = \sum_{j=0}^{\infty} \boldsymbol{C}_j z^j$ $(m \times m)$ and $\{\boldsymbol{\varepsilon}_t, -\infty < t < \infty\}$ is an i.i.d. sequence of random *m*-vectors with mean $\mathbf{0}$ and variance $\boldsymbol{\Sigma}$. This is sometimes called the Wold representation of the process (Wold, 1938) although remember that Wold's representation exists for any stationary process if the innovation process is white noise (that is, stationary and uncorrelated). The definition of a linear process specifies independence of the innovations, a stronger condition than white noise. We assume $\boldsymbol{C}_0 = \boldsymbol{I}_m$, although this entails no loss of generality if $\boldsymbol{\Sigma}$ is arbitrary, and could be replaced by the requirement $\boldsymbol{\Sigma} = \boldsymbol{I}_m$.

If (a) $\sum_{j=0}^{\infty} \|\boldsymbol{C}_j\| < \infty$[8] and (b) $\sum_{j=0}^{\infty} \boldsymbol{C}_j \neq \mathbf{0}$, we call the process I(0). Note that (a) is a stronger condition than is required for stationarity. Define

$$\boldsymbol{\Gamma}_k = E(\boldsymbol{y}_t \boldsymbol{y}'_{t+k}) = \sum_{j=0}^{\infty} \boldsymbol{C}_j \boldsymbol{\Sigma} \boldsymbol{C}'_{j+k}$$

for $k > 0$, where $\boldsymbol{\Gamma}_{-k} = \boldsymbol{\Gamma}'_k$. Then, writing $\boldsymbol{C}$ as shorthand for $\boldsymbol{C}(1) = \sum_{j=0}^{\infty} \boldsymbol{C}_j$, note that (a) is sufficient for $\boldsymbol{\Omega} < \infty$ where

$$\mathbf{\Omega} = \sum_{k=-\infty}^{\infty} \mathbf{\Gamma}_k = \mathbf{C\Sigma C}'. \tag{7.9}$$

This matrix is called the 'long-run variance' of the process,[9] and observe that

$$\mathbf{\Omega} = \lim_{T\to\infty} \frac{1}{T} E\left(\sum_{t=1}^{T} \mathbf{y}_t \sum_{t=1}^{T} \mathbf{y}_t'\right).$$

Thus, the I(0) property embodies the 'square root rule', which says that the average variability of the partial sums grows like the square root of the sample size. Condition (b) rules out the case of an over-differenced process. It is easy to verify that if $\mathbf{y}_t$ is given by (7.8), then $\Delta\mathbf{y}_t$ is a linear process with coefficients $\mathbf{C}_0$, $\mathbf{C}_1 - \mathbf{C}_0$, $\mathbf{C}_2 - \mathbf{C}_1$,. . ., and condition (b) is violated in this case if condition (a) holds.

The significance of these properties is that they suffice to validate the standard asymptotic distribution results, such as the central limit theorem for re-scaled sums of the $\mathbf{y}_t$. Simple stationarity is not sufficient for this by itself, and over-differencing presents an obvious counter-example, featuring $\mathbf{\Omega} = \mathbf{0}$. We shall appeal to some stronger assumptions on the sequence of coefficients for our present development, in particular (c) $\sum_{j=0}^{\infty} j\|\mathbf{C}_j\| < \infty$, which we call 1-summability (the '1' referring to the power of j).[10] Note that 1-summability is equivalent to the condition $\sum_{j=0}^{\infty}\sum_{k=j+1}^{\infty}\|\mathbf{C}_k\| < \infty$. Many operational models in econometrics, in particular stable finite-order vector ARMAmodels, satisfy the still stronger condition $\|\mathbf{C}(z)\| < \infty$ for $|z| \leq 1 + \delta$, for some $\delta > 0$, implying that the coefficients converge to zero at an exponential rate. However, this is not required for present purposes.

The particular case we consider here is the I(1) linear process $\mathbf{x}_t$, such that the Wold representation of the differences is

$$\Delta\mathbf{x}_t = \mathbf{C}(L)\varepsilon_t \tag{7.10}$$

where conditions (a), (b) and (c) are satisfied in the right-hand side. The key relation in this analysis is commonly known as the *Beveridge–Nelson* (BN) *decomposition* (Beveridge and Nelson, 1981). This is nothing but an easily verified identity for polynomials,

$$\mathbf{C}(z) = \mathbf{C}(1) + (1 - z)\mathbf{C}^*(z)$$

where $\mathbf{C}^*(z) = \sum_{j=0}^{\infty}\mathbf{C}_j^* z^j$ and $\mathbf{C}_j^* = -\sum_{k=j+1}^{\infty}\mathbf{C}_k$. Thus, we can write,

$$\Delta\mathbf{x}_t = \mathbf{C}\varepsilon_t + \zeta_t - \zeta_{t-1}.$$

where $\zeta_t = \mathbf{C}^*(L)\varepsilon_t$ is a I(0) process, by 1-summability. Integrating[11] this sequence from an initial value $\mathbf{x}_0$,[12] which we must assume finite, yields

$$\mathbf{x}_t - \mathbf{x}_0 = \mathbf{C}\mathbf{w}_t + \zeta_t \tag{7.11}$$

where $\mathbf{w}_t = \sum_{s=1}^{t}\varepsilon_s$ is a random walk process. Thus, we are able to decompose a linear process rather straightforwardly into stationary and non-stationary components. Since the first right-hand side term is $O_p(t^{1/2})$ and the second one is $O_p(1)$,[13] equation (7.11) can be used to verify directly the result that was previously determined by substitution in (7.9), that is,

$$\lim_{T\to\infty}\frac{1}{T}E(\boldsymbol{x}_T - \boldsymbol{x}_0)(\boldsymbol{x}_T - \boldsymbol{x}_0)' = \boldsymbol{C}\Sigma\boldsymbol{C}' = \boldsymbol{\Omega}. \tag{7.12}$$

Now, consider the case where $\boldsymbol{C}$, and hence $\boldsymbol{\Omega}$, is singular with rank $m - s$. There must exist in this case a matrix β $(m \times s)$ of rank s such that $\beta'\boldsymbol{C} = \boldsymbol{0}$, and it follows immediately that

$$z_t = \beta'(\boldsymbol{x}_t - \boldsymbol{x}_0) = \beta'\zeta_t$$

is an I(0) process. In other words, deficient rank of the matrix **C** implies the existence of cointegration in the non-stationary series $\boldsymbol{x}_t$. In the extreme case, $\boldsymbol{C} = \boldsymbol{0}$ implies that $\boldsymbol{x}_t$ is stationary, since the factor Δ cancels in (7.10).

Next, consider an autoregressive representation of the process. Suppose

$$\boldsymbol{A}(L)(\boldsymbol{x}_t - \boldsymbol{x}_0) = \varepsilon_t.$$

Writing $\boldsymbol{A}(z) = \boldsymbol{A}^+(z)(1 - z)$ shows that the Wold polynomial $\boldsymbol{C}(z)$ must have the representation $\boldsymbol{A}^+(z)^{-1}$.[14] Substituting the BN decomposition $\boldsymbol{A}(z) = (1 - z)\boldsymbol{A}^*(z) + \boldsymbol{A}$ where $\boldsymbol{A} = \boldsymbol{A}(1)$ yields

$$\varepsilon_t = \boldsymbol{A}^*(L)\Delta\boldsymbol{x}_t + \boldsymbol{A}(\boldsymbol{x}_t - \boldsymbol{x}_0). \tag{7.13}$$

For this equation to balance requires $\boldsymbol{A}(\boldsymbol{x}_t - \boldsymbol{x}_0) \sim \mathrm{I}(0)$, so there must exist a decomposition of the form $\boldsymbol{A} = -\alpha\beta'$ for some α $(m \times s)$ of rank s. Therefore, note from (7.13) and (7.10) that

$$\begin{aligned}(1 - z)\boldsymbol{I}_m &= \boldsymbol{C}(z)\boldsymbol{A}(z)\\ &= \boldsymbol{C}(z)\boldsymbol{A}^*(z)(1 - z) - \boldsymbol{C}(z)\alpha\beta'\\ &= \boldsymbol{C}(z)\boldsymbol{B}(z)(1 - z) - z\boldsymbol{C}(z)\alpha\beta'\end{aligned} \tag{7.14}$$

where $\boldsymbol{B}(z) = \boldsymbol{A}^*(z) - \alpha\beta'$. Evaluating (7.14) at the point $z = 1$ yields $\boldsymbol{C}\alpha = \boldsymbol{0}$, since β has full rank, and hence $\boldsymbol{C}\boldsymbol{A} = \boldsymbol{0}$ and also note that $\boldsymbol{A}\boldsymbol{C} = -\alpha\beta'\boldsymbol{C} = \boldsymbol{0}$. The matrices $\boldsymbol{A}$ and $\boldsymbol{C}$ span orthogonal spaces, respectively the cointegrating space of dimension s and the space of dimension $m - s$ containing the common trends, through (7.11).

Evaluating (7.14) at the point $z = 0$, noting $\boldsymbol{C}_0 = \boldsymbol{I}_m$, also yields $\boldsymbol{B}_0 = \boldsymbol{I}_m$. Accordingly, defining $\boldsymbol{\Gamma}(z)$ by $\boldsymbol{B}(z) = \boldsymbol{I}_m - z\boldsymbol{\Gamma}(z)$, the error correction form of the system is obtained from (7.13), after some rearrangement, as

$$\Delta\boldsymbol{x}_t = \boldsymbol{\Gamma}(L)\Delta\boldsymbol{x}_{t-1} + \alpha z_{t-1} + \varepsilon_t \tag{7.15}$$

where $z_t = \beta'\boldsymbol{x}_t - \mu$ and $\mu = \beta'\boldsymbol{x}_0$. This is the generalization of (7.5), although it is also a simplification since the possibility of drift terms has been excluded here. (To re-introduce these would be a useful exercise for the reader.) Note that an intercept appears in the cointegrating relation, in general, unless the data are explicitly initialized at zero.

This system has the feature that $\Delta \boldsymbol{x}_t$ is explained only by lagged variables, whereas the macroeconometrics literature generally allows for the existence of contemporaneous interactions between variables, which might either be truly simultaneous relations, or involve some kind of causal ordering within the period of observation. The extension to cover this case is a simple matter of treating (7.15) as a solved form. Writing

$$\boldsymbol{B}_0 \Delta \boldsymbol{x}_t = \boldsymbol{B}_1(L)\Delta \boldsymbol{x}_{t-1} + \rho \boldsymbol{z}_{t-1} + \boldsymbol{u}_t, \tag{7.16}$$

where $\boldsymbol{B}_0$ is a square non-singular matrix, we then recover (7.15) with the substitutions $\boldsymbol{\Gamma}(L) = \boldsymbol{B}_0^{-1}\boldsymbol{B}_1(L)$, $\alpha = \boldsymbol{B}_0^{-1}\rho$ and $\varepsilon_t = \boldsymbol{B}_0^{-1}\boldsymbol{u}_t$, so that $E(\boldsymbol{u}_t\boldsymbol{u}_t') = \boldsymbol{B}_0\Sigma\boldsymbol{B}_0'$. We call (7.16) a structural form, where $\boldsymbol{B}_0 = \boldsymbol{I}_m$ is a permissible case but not a requisite.

While (7.15) is perhaps the commonest representation of a cointegrated system in the applied literature, the Park–Phillips triangular form (see Park and Phillips, 1988, 1989; Phillips and Loretan, 1991; Phillips, 1991 *inter alia*) has considerable virtues of simplicity and ease of manipulation. Partitioning the vector of variables as $\boldsymbol{x}_t = (\boldsymbol{x}_{1t}', \boldsymbol{x}_{2t}')'$ where $\boldsymbol{x}_{1t}$ is $s \times 1$ and $\boldsymbol{x}_{2t}$ $(m-s) \times 1$, write[15]

$$\boldsymbol{x}_{1t} = \boldsymbol{B}\boldsymbol{x}_{2t} + \boldsymbol{v}_{1t} \tag{7.17a}$$

$$\Delta \boldsymbol{x}_{2t} = \boldsymbol{v}_{2t} \tag{7.18b}$$

where $\boldsymbol{v}_{1t}$ and $\boldsymbol{v}_{2t}$ are constrained solely to be I(0) stochastic processes. If we form the partition

$$\beta = \begin{bmatrix} \beta_1 \\ \beta_2 \end{bmatrix} \begin{matrix} s \times s \\ (m-s) \times s \end{matrix}$$

after re-ordering variables as necessary to ensure β_1 has full rank, the first equation shows the cointegrating relations expressed as a reduced form with $\boldsymbol{B} = -\beta_1^{-1}\beta_2$. This matrix is accordingly unique, given this partition of the variables.

The second block of equations is merely the relevant block from the Wold representation (7.10). Writing the system as $\boldsymbol{A}(L)\boldsymbol{x}_t = \boldsymbol{v}_t$ where

$$\boldsymbol{A}(L) = \begin{bmatrix} \boldsymbol{I}_s & -\boldsymbol{B} \\ \boldsymbol{0} & \Delta \boldsymbol{I}_{m-s} \end{bmatrix},$$

the Wold form is obtained as $\Delta \boldsymbol{x}_t = \Delta \boldsymbol{A}(L)^{-1}\boldsymbol{v}_t$ or, in partitioned form,

$$\begin{bmatrix} \Delta \boldsymbol{x}_{1t} \\ \Delta \boldsymbol{x}_{2t} \end{bmatrix} = \Delta \begin{bmatrix} \boldsymbol{I}_s & \Delta^{-1}\boldsymbol{B} \\ \boldsymbol{0} & \Delta^{-1}\boldsymbol{I}_{m-s} \end{bmatrix} \begin{bmatrix} \boldsymbol{v}_{1t} \\ \boldsymbol{v}_{2t} \end{bmatrix} = \begin{bmatrix} \Delta \boldsymbol{v}_{1t} + \boldsymbol{B}\boldsymbol{v}_{2t} \\ \boldsymbol{v}_{2t} \end{bmatrix}.$$

This simple case gives a little insight into the mechanism of cointegration. The $m - s$ common trends are supplied as the integrals of $\boldsymbol{v}_{2t}$, whereas $\boldsymbol{v}_{1t}$ contributes only the noise component in the cointegrating relations. We discuss below how the triangular form can be the basis for a useful approach to estimation and inference.

Let's summarize the conclusions of this section. We have shown that an arbitrary linear model, that need not have a finite-order VAR representation but has 1-summable coefficients in its Wold representation, satisfies the Granger representation theorem. In other words, if the matrix $\boldsymbol{C}$ has reduced rank $m - s$ in the representation $\Delta \boldsymbol{x}_t = \boldsymbol{C}(L)\varepsilon_t$, then the variables are cointegrated with rank s and the system admits an error-correction representation. Note that the choice of a first-order lag in (7.15) is completely arbitrary. It can be set to any finite value, p, by a suitable redefinition of the polynomial $\boldsymbol{\Gamma}(L)$. It is customary in the literature to let p match the order of the VAR when this is finite, such that $\boldsymbol{\Gamma}(L)$ is a polynomial of order $p - 1$.

4 INTERPRETING COINTEGRATION

In his earliest contributions on the topic of cointegration, Granger (1981) was keen to emphasize his debt to the macroeconometric research of the time, in particular Sargan (1964) on wages and prices and Davidson et al. (1978) on consumption and income. These authors had explicitly built dynamic equations for non-stationary series that correlated logarithmic changes with the logarithms of 'long-run' ratios, which were now to be recognized as cointegrating relations. In both the cited cases the relations happily involved no unknown parameters so the resulting regressions were easily fitted by ordinary least squares. The technical challenges involved for estimation when z_t in (7.15) involves unknown parameters (of which more later) did not have to be faced.

However, these models were somewhat casual in their approach to the dynamics of economic behaviour. It was assumed, first, that there existed identifiable economic relations that described behaviour in a 'steady state', abstracting from business cycle fluctuations but possibly allowing for a secular drift; and second, that these relations are not expected to hold period-to-period (nor of course are they observed to) due to unspecified dynamic effects about which economic theory is taken to be mute. There was a simple presumption that in a dynamic setting agents would formulate plans (say, for the consumption/savings balance as income changes) that combined 'rule of thumb' responses to changes in driving variables represented by the $\boldsymbol{\Gamma}(L)$ coefficients in (7.15) with compensating adjustments, represented by the α coefficients, to achieve a proportion of the required adjustment towards the long-run (steady state) relation in each period. The actual behavioural mechanisms were treated as beyond the reach of economics to explain, and hence this modelling approach is often spoken of as ad hoc, with a mildly pejorative tone.

We should not overlook that the error correction form is only nominally dynamic, and subsumes instantaneous adjustment. The static equation $y_t = \beta x_t + \varepsilon_t$, where ε_t is an independent disturbance, can of course be written equivalently as

$$\Delta y_t = \beta \Delta x_t + \alpha(y_{t-1} - \beta x_{t-1}) + \varepsilon_t$$

with $\alpha = -1$. However, empirical work with such equations invariably shows α closer to zero than to -1, and also no match between the 'dynamic' and 'long run' coefficients. These observed adjustment dynamics called for some explanation, and a number of authors have attempted to lay more rigorous economic foundations for the ECM scheme, notably Salmon (1982), Nickell (1985) and Campbell and Shiller (1988). Natural precursors are the partial adjustment model of Lovell (1961) and the habit persistence model of Brown (1952). Assuming that agents face costs associated with speedy adjustment (physical building costs in the case of inventory investment, psychological costs of changing behaviour in the case of decisions by consumers) it is straightforward to formulate a quadratic loss function for a decision variable y_t involving both the costs of change $y_t - y_{t-1}$, and the costs of deviation from equilibrium $y_t - y_t^*$, where y_t^* is the function of forcing variables defining equilibrium. Optimizing with respect to the choice of y_t leads directly to a plan to set y_t to a value intermediate between y_t^* and y_{t-1},

$$y_t = \lambda y_{t-1} + (1 - \lambda)y_t^*, \quad 0 \leq \lambda \leq 1$$

which, after a simple rearrangement, and the addition of a shock representing random deviations from the plan, can be cast in the ECM form

$$\Delta y_t = (1 - \lambda)\Delta y_t^* + (1 - \lambda)(y_{t-1}^* - y_{t-1}) + \varepsilon_t$$

replacing y^* in practice by a linear combination of forcing variables.

The constraints across these dynamic adjustment coefficients are a consequence of the extreme simplicity (or maybe we should say *naïveté*) of this particular set-up. However, the framework is easily elaborated to allow for forward-looking behaviour and multi-step dynamic optimization. See Nickell (1985) also Davidson (2000, Section 5.5.4) for illustrations. What these examples show is that the solved form of the dynamic adjustment depends not only on the agent's optimization rule but also on the form of the processes generating the forcing variables.

Campbell and Shiller (1988) argue that error-correction behaviour can be observed even without the existence of adjustment costs, and illustrate their case with the class of present value models. Theory has the spread between long and short rates depending mechanically on the difference between the former and rational forecasts of the latter; but if these forecasts use information not available to the modeller, the spread involves a random component that, moreover, must Granger-cause the future changes in the short rate. This gives rise to an error correction structure with the spread representing the cointegrating residual, but note that this structure does not arise through agents reacting to resolve perceived disequilibria, as the classic ECM framework suggests.

Cointegration has been derived in the preceding sections as the attribute of a system of dynamic equations. However, many of the models that appear in the applied literature, the prototypical examples of Sargan (1964), Davidson et al. (1978), Hendry (1979) and many others, are cast as single equations and estimated by least squares. The driving variables are assumed to be *weakly exogenous* within the time frame of observation. Weak exogeneity is a technical concept, defined formally in Engle et al. (1982), but it can be loosely interpreted to describe a variable that is regarded as given and conditionally fixed by agents within the decision period, even though it could be endogenous in the wider sense of depending on past values of the variables it drives. A key implication of weak exogeneity is that the variable is uncorrelated with the shocks in the regression model, and hence ordinary least squares is a consistent estimator for the dynamic equation.

Without loss of generality, assume that the equation of interest is the first equation in the system, and so partition the variables as $\boldsymbol{x}_t = (x_{1t}, \boldsymbol{x}'_{2t})'$. Further assume, in concert with the cited references, that the cointegrating rank is 1. The structural system (7.16) is then partitioned as

$$\begin{bmatrix} 1 & \boldsymbol{b}'_{0,12} \\ \boldsymbol{b}_{0,21} & \boldsymbol{B}_{0,22} \end{bmatrix} \begin{bmatrix} \Delta x_{1t} \\ \Delta \boldsymbol{x}_{2t} \end{bmatrix}$$

$$= \begin{bmatrix} b_{1,11}(L) & \boldsymbol{b}'_{1,12}(L) \\ \boldsymbol{b}_{1,21}(L) & \boldsymbol{B}_{1,22}(L) \end{bmatrix} \begin{bmatrix} \Delta x_{1,t-1} \\ \Delta \boldsymbol{x}_{2,t-1} \end{bmatrix} + \begin{bmatrix} \rho_1 \\ \boldsymbol{\rho}_2 \end{bmatrix} z_{t-1} + \begin{bmatrix} u_{1t} \\ \boldsymbol{u}_{2t} \end{bmatrix} \tag{7.18}$$

where $z_t = \beta'\boldsymbol{x}_t - \mu$. The noteworthy feature of this set-up is the potential dependence of all the variables on z_{t-1}. If β is known then z_t can be treated as a datum and there is no obstacle to estimating the first equation by least squares, subject to the usual weak exogeneity restrictions on the distribution of $\boldsymbol{x}_{2t}$, specifically that $\boldsymbol{b}_{0,21} = \boldsymbol{0}$ and $E(u_{1t}\boldsymbol{u}_{2t}) = \boldsymbol{0}$. On the other hand, if β is unknown, then it is potentially involved in all the equations of the system. Weak exogeneity of $\boldsymbol{x}_{2t}$ in the first equation requires the extra condition $\boldsymbol{\rho}_2 = \boldsymbol{0}$, so that the error correction effect is wholly focused on the evolution of x_{1t}. Under these circumstances, the first equation can be studied in isolation, conditional on $\boldsymbol{x}_{2t}$. Note that β could be estimated by non-linear least squares applied to this equation. We say more about this estimation question below.

5 ESTIMATING COINTEGRATING RELATIONS

We start the discussion of estimation with the focus of attention on the matrix β of cointegrating coefficients. Immediately, we run into the difficulty that this matrix is not in general unique. It is defined merely to span a space of m-vectors having the property that any element of the space cointegrates the variables of the model. One approach to estimation is to impose normalization restrictions, such as having the columns orthogonal and with unit length. The structural modelling approach, on the other hand, supposes that cointegration is to be explained by the existence of some long-run economic relations, and the cointegrating space is relevant because these structural vectors span it, in particular. When the cointegrating rank s is greater than 1, however, any linear combination of the hypothesized structural vectors is also a cointegrating vector. We therefore face a problem of identifying the parameters of interest.

Before approaching that more difficult case, assume initially that $s = 1$. Then β ($m \times 1$) is unique up to a choice of normalization and, normalizing on x_{1t} in the partition $\boldsymbol{x}_t = (x_{1t}, \boldsymbol{x}'_{2t})'$, with *almost* no loss of generality,[16] we can write the cointegrating relation as a regression model,

$$x_{1t} = \gamma'\boldsymbol{x}_{2t} + \mu + z_t \tag{7.19}$$

where $\beta = (1, -\gamma')'$, and it is natural to consider the possibility of OLS estimation. If

$$S(\boldsymbol{g}, m) = \sum_{t=1}^{T} (x_{1t} - \boldsymbol{g}'\boldsymbol{x}_{2t} - m)^2$$

it can be shown that $S(\gamma, m) = O_p(T)$ for any m, whereas $S(\boldsymbol{g}, m) = O_p(T^2)$ at points where $\boldsymbol{g} \neq \gamma$. The proof of consistency of least squares is therefore very direct, and (letting hats denote the least squares estimators) $\hat{\gamma} - \gamma = O_p(T^{-1})$ by comparison with the usual convergence rate of $O_p(T^{-1/2})$ in stationary data. This property is known as *superconsistency*.[17] The other features of this regression include $R^2 \to 1$ as $T \to \infty$.

However, notwithstanding these desirable properties, the large-sample distribution of $T(\hat{\gamma} - \gamma)$ is non-standard, and depends critically on the structure of the model. Consider the OLS formula in the standard notation $\hat{\gamma} = (\boldsymbol{X}'\boldsymbol{X})^{-1}\boldsymbol{X}'\mathbf{y}$, the rows of $\boldsymbol{X}$ having the form $(\boldsymbol{x}_{2t} - \bar{\boldsymbol{x}}_2)'$ for $t = 1,\ldots,T$ where $\bar{\boldsymbol{x}}_2$ is the vector of sample means, and $\boldsymbol{y} = (x_{11},\ldots,x_{1T})'$. The problem with cointegrating regression is that the regressors do not obey the law of large numbers. It can be shown that

$$\begin{aligned} T(\hat{\gamma} - \gamma) &= \left(\frac{\boldsymbol{X}'\boldsymbol{X}}{T^2}\right)^{-1}\frac{\boldsymbol{X}'\boldsymbol{u}}{T} \\ &\xrightarrow{d} \boldsymbol{P}^{-1}\boldsymbol{q} \end{aligned} \tag{7.20}$$

where $\xrightarrow{d}$ denotes convergence in distribution, and $\boldsymbol{u} = (z_1,\ldots,z_T)'$. $\boldsymbol{P}$ and $\boldsymbol{q}$, the limits in distribution of the normalized sums of squares and products matrices, are in general random variables and correlated with each other. Since $\boldsymbol{q}$ typically has a mean different from zero, there can be substantial finite sample biases. Similarly, the usual regression standard errors do not converge to constants, as in the stationary data analysis, but to random elements proportional to the square roots of the diagonal elements of $\boldsymbol{P}^{-1}$. The asymptotic distributions of the regression t-ratios are therefore not merely non-standard, but depend on nuisance parameters and cannot be tabulated. All these facts are bad news for making inferences on cointegrating vectors.

However, there is a favourable special case. Suppose that $\boldsymbol{x}_{2t}$ is strictly exogenous in equation (7.19), which means that $E(\Delta\boldsymbol{x}_{2t-j}z_t) = \mathbf{0}$ for $-\infty < j < \infty$. For this condition to be satisfied, note that in (7.18) the parameters $\boldsymbol{b}_{0,21}$, $\boldsymbol{b}_{1,21}(L)$ and ρ_2 will all need to be zero, and in addition, $E(u_{1t}\boldsymbol{u}_{2t}') = \mathbf{0}$. In this case, the distribution of $T(\hat{\gamma} - \gamma)$ is *asymptotically mixed normal*. Under strict exogeneity, $\boldsymbol{X}$ in (7.20) can be treated as conditionally fixed when considering the distribution of $\boldsymbol{u}$. It can be shown that $T(\hat{\gamma} - \gamma)$ is asymptotically normally distributed under the *conditional* distribution, holding $\boldsymbol{X}$ fixed, although its variance matrix is a random drawing under the unconditional distribution, hence 'mixed normal'. Further, we can compute t-ratios that (on the null hypothesis) are *conditionally* N(0,1) in the limit. However, since this distribution is the same for any set of conditioning variables, the same limit result holds *un*conditionally. This means that standard inference procedures, using tabulations of the standard normal and chi-squared distributions, are asymptotically valid. The only modification of the usual least squares inference procedure that may be necessary, since the residuals are typically autocorrelated, is to use a heteroscedasticity and autocorrelation consistent (HAC) estimator for the residual variance, such as that derived by Newey and West (1987).[18]

Unfortunately, strict exogeneity is a very strong assumption in macroeconomic data, and this favourable case is the exception to the rule. An alternative approach, while maintaining the single-equation framework, is to estimate the dynamic error correction model itself by non-linear least squares. This method is analysed by Stock (1987). The first equation of (7.18) may be written

$$\Delta x_{1t} = a_0 - \boldsymbol{b}'_{0,12}\Delta \boldsymbol{x}_{2t} + \boldsymbol{b}_{1,1}(L)'\Delta \boldsymbol{x}_{t-1} + \rho_1(x_{1,t-1} - \gamma' \boldsymbol{x}_{2,t-1}) + u_{1t} \tag{7.21}$$

This equation can be estimated unrestrictedly by least squares, and $\hat{\gamma}$ recovered by dividing the coefficients of $\boldsymbol{x}_{2,t-1}$ by minus the coefficient of $x_{1,t-1}$. Alternatively, a non-linear optimization algorithm may be used. This estimator can be shown to be superconsistent, and it is also asymptotically mixed normal (meaning that standard inference applies, as above) subject to the weak exogeneity condition detailed following (7.18). In particular, in addition to the usual requirements of no simultaneity, the condition $\boldsymbol{\rho}_2 = \boldsymbol{0}$ is needed to ensure that all the sample information about the cointegrating relation is contained in (7.21). Without these conditions, there is once again a failure of mixed normality, and a dependence of the limit distributions on nuisance parameters. However, note that these conditions are less severe than those required to obtain the equivalent result for the OLS estimator of the cointegrating relation itself.

To achieve standard asymptotic inference in arbitrary cases of (7.18), a number of proposals have been made to modify the least squares estimator. Saikkonen (1991) and Stock and Watson (1993) independently proposed similar procedures. Consider the triangular representation in (7.17), assuming $s = 1$ for present purposes. Saikkonen shows that the $\boldsymbol{x}_{2t}$ variables can be treated as conditionally fixed in the regression of the first block if $E(v_{1t}\boldsymbol{v}'_{2,t-j}) = \boldsymbol{0}$ for $-\infty < j < \infty$ where, in this context, $\boldsymbol{v}_{2t} = \Delta \boldsymbol{x}_{2t}$. However, by augmenting the first equation in (7.17) with these observed variables, the same condition can be engineered. Substituting from the second block, the ideal set of additional regressors are $\Delta \boldsymbol{x}_{2,t-j}$ for $-\infty < j < \infty$. Whereas this is not a feasible choice, the same asymptotic distribution is obtained by running the finite-order regression

$$x_{1t} = \gamma' \boldsymbol{x}_{2t} + \sum\nolimits_{j=-K_T}^{K_T} \pi_j \Delta \boldsymbol{x}_{2,t-j} + \mu + e_t \tag{7.22}$$

where K_T increases with T, although at a slower rate. Saikkonen proposes $K_T = o(T^{1/3})$.[19] In this regression, the regressors are 'as if' strictly exogenous. The coefficients π_j are merely projection parameters and their values are generally not of direct interest. The unusual (from an econometric modelling point of view) step of including leads as well as lags in the regression has to be understood as allowing for the possibility that x_{1t} Granger-causes $\boldsymbol{x}_{2t}$ through endogenous feedbacks, hence the disturbance term must be purged of both past and future dependence on $\boldsymbol{x}_{2t}$. Thus, (7.22) must *not* be confused with a conventional structural equation describing agents' behaviour. Implicitly, we need the full multi-equation system to do this correctly.

The augmented least squares estimator is asymptotically mixed normal when correctly specified. Note that the regression in (7.22) does not make allowance for autocorrelation in the residual disturbance e_t, which can clearly exist even following the projection onto the $\Delta \boldsymbol{x}_{2,t-j}$ variables. This fact does not invalidate the asymptotic distribution results, provided that the covariance matrix is computed in the correct manner. As already noted for the strictly exogenous case, it is typically necessary to use a HAC estimator for the residual variance. Conventional t- and F-test statistics then have standard distributions asymptotically and the usual normal and chi-squared tables can be used to get approximate critical values. Saikkonen also shows that the augmented estimator is optimal, in the sense of achieving the maximum concentration of the asymptotic distribution about the true values.

An alternative approach to this type of correction is the fully modified least squares (FMLS) estimator of Phillips and Hansen (1990). The essential idea here is to derive the limiting distribution of $\boldsymbol{P}^{-1}\boldsymbol{q}$ in (7.20), identify the components of this formula that produce the deviation from the centred mixed normal distribution, and estimate these components using the sample. The ingredients of these modifications include the covariance matrix of the data increments and disturbances, estimated by an HAC formula using the consistent OLS estimator of the parameters computed in a preliminary step. The resulting formulae are somewhat technical, and will not be reproduced here. The main thing to be aware of is that the asymptotic distribution of this estimator matches that of the Saikkonen–Stock–Watson augmented least squares estimator. Both of these methods are suitable for dealing with arbitrary forms of the distribution of the cointegrating VAR, and hence are inherently more robust than the single-equation ECM method of (7.21).

We have discussed the estimation of the vector γ, but naturally we shall also be interested in inference on the dynamic parameters of an equation such as (7.21). In particular, we may be interested in knowing how rapidly the error-correction mechanism moves the variables towards their cointegrating relations. However, given an efficient estimator of γ, we can now exploit the super-consistency property. Construct $\hat{z}_t = x_{1t} - \hat{\gamma}'\boldsymbol{x}_{2t}$, and insert this constructed sequence into (7.21) with coefficient ρ_1. These residuals can be treated effectively as data from the standpoint of the asymptotic distribution, and are (by hypothesis) I(0), so the usual asymptotics for stationary data can be used to make inferences about ρ_1 and the other parameters of the equation.

6 MULTIPLE COINTEGRATING VECTORS

Consider the case when there are two or more linearly independent vectors spanning the cointegrating space. Here is a simple example with $m = 3$. Suppose that $\boldsymbol{x}_t = (x_{1t}, x_{2t}, x_{3t})' \sim \mathrm{I}(1)$ and

$$p_t = x_{1t} - \mu x_{2t} \sim \mathrm{I}(0) \tag{7.23a}$$

$$q_t = x_{2t} - \nu x_{3t} \sim \mathrm{I}(0). \tag{7.23b}$$

Then, for any λ,

$$p_t + \lambda q_t = x_{1t} - (\mu - \lambda)x_{2t} - \lambda\nu x_{3t} \sim \mathrm{I}(0).$$

The vectors $\beta_\lambda = (1, -(\mu - \lambda), -\lambda\nu)'$ are cointegrating for all choices of λ. If an attempt is made to estimate this vector, say by OLS regression of x_{1t} onto x_{2t} and x_{3t}, then the estimated coefficients will merely correspond to the case of λ that minimizes the sum of squares, which in turn depends on the relative sample variances of the variables p_t and q_t. It cannot tell us anything about the values of μ or ν, as such. While setting $\lambda = 0$ returns us relation (7.23a), there is in fact no value of λ that can return (7.23b) because of the choice of normalization.

Nonetheless, there is a simple way to estimate μ and ν, given that we know the structure. This is to run two regressions,[20] the first one excluding x_{3t} and the second one excluding x_{1t} and normalized on x_{2t}. In fact the regression of x_{1t} onto x_{3t} will estimate a third cointegrating vector of the system, $\beta_\mu = (1, 0, -\mu\nu)'$.

On the other hand, suppose that (7.23a) holds, but not (7.23b), and instead there exists a cointegrating relation of the form

$$x_{1t} - \delta_1 x_{2t} - \delta_2 x_{3t} \sim \mathrm{I}(0) \tag{7.24}$$

It is easy to see that while the same restricted regression procedure will consistently estimate μ, there is no way to estimate the coefficients of (7.24). Running the regression with all three variables inevitably gives us an arbitrary linear combination of (7.23a) and (7.24). We say in this situation that the coefficients δ_1 and δ_2 are *unidentified.*

Generalizing from this example we see that the problem has a strong affinity with the analysis of static simultaneous equations that we now associate with the research agenda of the Cowles Commission at the University of Chicago in the 1940s (see Koopmans, 1949, and also any number of econometrics texts, such as Johnston and DiNardo, 1997). If β ($m \times s$) is a matrix spanning the cointegrating space, any vector of the form $\beta\boldsymbol{r}$ is a cointegrating vector where $\boldsymbol{r}$ ($s \times 1$) is arbitrary. The only way that one of these vectors can be distinguished from another is by the existence of known restrictions on the coefficients. Assume for the sake of argument that the columns of β are 'structural' in the sense that the elements have a specific interpretation in terms of economic behaviour. In particular, some of these elements are known to be zero, since structural economic relations do not in general involve all the variables in a system. Such a relation (say, the first column of β with no loss of generality) is said to be identified if the only choice of $\boldsymbol{r}$ that preserves the known restrictions is $\boldsymbol{r} = \boldsymbol{e}_1 = (1, 0, \ldots, 0)'$. Assume, without loss of generality, that the variables are ordered so that the first g_1 of the elements of column 1 of β are non-zero, with the first element set to 1 as normalization, and the last $m - g_1$ elements are zeros. Accordingly, partition β by rows as $\beta = \begin{bmatrix}\beta_1\\ \beta_2\end{bmatrix}$ where β_2 ($m - g_1 \times s$) has first column equal to zero by construction, so that its rank cannot exceed $s - 1$. The following well-known proposition is the *rank condition for identification*:

- Equation 1 is identified if and only if β_2 has rank $s - 1$

Clearly, β_2 having maximum rank means that it is not possible to construct a zero linear combination of its columns except for the specific cases of $a\boldsymbol{e}_1$ for scalar a, where the normalization rules out all of these cases except $a = 1$. An important by-product of this result is the *order condition for identification* (necessary but not sufficient) that requires $g_1 \leq m - s + 1$.

We now have the following result: a structural cointegrating relation that is identified by zero restrictions is consistently estimated by a least squares regression (or efficient counterpart) imposing these zero restrictions.[21] In text-book accounts of the simultaneous equations model, recall that it is necessary to separate the variables of the model into endogenous and exogenous categories, and implement estimation by (for example) two-stage least squares, where the order condition for identification determines whether sufficient instruments are available to estimate the unrestricted coefficients. Here, there is no such separation. All the variables are on the same footing and least squares is consistent, with identification achieved by excluding variables to match the known restrictions. Every identified structural cointegrating relation can be consistently and efficiently estimated by running either the Saikkonen–Stock–Watson or Phillips–Hansen procedures on equations containing only the non-excluded variables. For example, following Saikkonen's notation, equation (7.22) would become

$$x_{1t} = \gamma' \boldsymbol{x}_{2t} + \sum\nolimits_{j=-K_T}^{K_T} \pi_j \Delta \boldsymbol{x}_{c,t-j} + \mu + e_t \tag{7.25}$$

where $\boldsymbol{x}_{ct} = (\boldsymbol{x}'_{2t}, \boldsymbol{x}'_{3t})'$, and the subscript 3 denotes the excluded variables. Each identified relation is estimated with a different partition of the variables into inclusions and exclusions, not overlooking the fact that the identity of the normalizing variable x_{1t} needs to be changed if it is itself to be excluded from the relation.

A further point of interest about identified structural relations is that they are *irreducible*. In other words, no variable can be dropped without the relation ceasing to be cointegrating. The examples in (7.23) are a good case in point, and this is how in practice we can detect the fact that a relation such as (7.24) cannot be both structural and identified. To appreciate the role of irreducibility, consider the triangular form (7.17) once again. We had assumed $s = 1$. Suppose however that, contrary to the implicit assumption, the variables $\boldsymbol{x}_{2t}$ in fact featured a cointegrating relation amongst themselves. Clearly, in this case, the first relation is not irreducible, although to discover this it may be necessary to change the normalization. Likewise if there are two or more cointegrating vectors containing x_{1t}, so that the estimated γ is a composite relation, there will necessarily exist a linear combination of these vectors that excludes one of the variables, and is cointegrating. So, again, it cannot be irreducible. Ideally, the irreducibility property should be checked (see section 8 on cointegration testing) on each postulated structural relation. However, it's important to note that irreducibility is not an exclusive property of identified structures. In the three-variable example, it is of course shared by the solved relation involving x_{1t} and x_{3t}. There is no way except by prior knowledge of the structure that we can be sure of distinguishing structural from irreducible solved forms.

7 ESTIMATING COINTEGRATED SYSTEMS

In a series of papers focusing chiefly on the triangular parameterization (7.17), Peter Phillips and co-authors (Phillips, 1988; Park and Phillips, 1988, 1989; Phillips and Hansen, 1990; Phillips, 1991; Phillips and Loretan, 1991) have provided a careful analysis of the issue of valid inference in cointegrated systems. One feature of their approach is that the cointegrated relations are always parameterized in reduced form. In other words, if

$$\beta = \begin{bmatrix} \beta_1 \\ \beta_2 \end{bmatrix} \begin{matrix} s \times s \\ (m - s) \times s \end{matrix}$$

then, in (7.17), $\boldsymbol{B} = -\beta_1^{-1}\beta_2$. While the normalization on $\boldsymbol{x}_{1t}$ is basically arbitrary – any partition of the variables that delivers a β_1 of full rank will do – there is no reason in principle why the matrix $[\boldsymbol{I}: -\boldsymbol{B}]'$ should not be replaced with a matrix β of structural vectors, subject to identifying restrictions. Such an approach is less easy to implement in practice, however.

The primary lesson of this research is that the number of cointegrating vectors in the system is the crucial piece of information for efficient, mixed normal estimation. It's convenient as a pedagogical device to consider the case where $\boldsymbol{v}_t = (\boldsymbol{v}_{1t}', \boldsymbol{v}_{2t}')'$ in (7.17) is an i.i.d. vector. Then the efficient, asymptotically mixed normal estimator of the system is simply computed by applying least squares to the s augmented equations.

$$\boldsymbol{x}_{1t} = \boldsymbol{B}\boldsymbol{x}_{2t} + \boldsymbol{\Gamma}_{12}\Delta\boldsymbol{x}_{2t} + \boldsymbol{e}_t$$

where we define $\boldsymbol{\Gamma}_{12} = \boldsymbol{\Omega}_{22}^{-1}\boldsymbol{\Omega}_{21}$ with $\boldsymbol{\Omega}_{22} = E(v_{2t}v_{2t}')$, $\boldsymbol{\Omega}_{21} = E(v_{2t}v_{1t}')$, and, with Gaussian disturbances,

$$\boldsymbol{e}_t = \boldsymbol{v}_{1t} - \boldsymbol{\Gamma}_{12}\Delta\boldsymbol{x}_{2t} = \boldsymbol{v}_{1t} - E(\boldsymbol{v}_{1t}|\boldsymbol{v}_{2t}).$$

In the event that $\boldsymbol{v}_t$ is autocorrelated, the further augmentation by leads and lags of $\Delta\boldsymbol{x}_{2t}$ will provide efficiency, as detailed in section 5 above. Contrast this with the case of the triangular model

$$\boldsymbol{x}_{1t} = \boldsymbol{B}\boldsymbol{x}_{2t} + \boldsymbol{v}_{1t} \tag{7.26}$$

$$\boldsymbol{x}_{2t} = \boldsymbol{\Pi}\boldsymbol{x}_{2t-1} + \boldsymbol{v}_{2t}$$

where $\boldsymbol{\Pi}$ is unrestricted. The roots of the autoregressive system could be either unity or stable and the identity $\boldsymbol{v}_{2t} = \Delta\boldsymbol{x}_{2t}$ no longer obtains. Phillips (1991) shows that the maximum likelihood estimator of $\boldsymbol{B}$ in this system has an asymptotic distribution contaminated by nuisance parameters such that conventional inference is not possible. The knowledge that $\Pi = \boldsymbol{I}_{m-s}$ is the key to mixed-normal asymptotics.

Thanks largely to the influential contributions of Søren Johansen (1988a, 1988b, 1991, 1995), the most popular approach to system estimation is the *reduced rank regression* estimator. This works with the representation in (7.15), although specialized by assuming a finite-order vector autoregressive specification. To describe how this method works with the maximum clarity we develop the case of the first-order VECM

$$\Delta\boldsymbol{x}_t = \boldsymbol{a}_0 + \alpha\beta'\boldsymbol{x}_{t-1} + \varepsilon_t \tag{7.27}$$

as in (7.4). As before, the key piece of prior information is the cointegrating rank of the system.

The natural estimator for a system of reduced form equations is *least generalized variance* (LGV), which is also the maximum likelihood estimator when the disturbances are Gaussian. This minimizes the determinant of the system covariance matrix,

$$\Lambda_s(\alpha,\beta) = |\textstyle\sum_{t=2}^{T}\varepsilon_t\varepsilon_t'| = |\boldsymbol{S}_{00} - \alpha\beta'\boldsymbol{S}_{10} - \boldsymbol{S}_{01}\beta\alpha' + \alpha\beta'\boldsymbol{S}_{11}\beta\alpha'| \tag{7.28}$$

where

$$S_{00} = \sum_{t=2}^{T}(\Delta x_t - \overline{\Delta x})(\Delta x_t - \overline{\Delta x})'$$

$$S_{01} = \sum_{t=2}^{T}(\Delta x_t - \overline{\Delta x})(x_{t-1} - \overline{x}_{-1})'$$

$$S_{11} = \sum_{t=2}^{T}(x_{t-1} - \overline{x}_{-1})(x_{t-1} - \overline{x}_{-1})'$$

and $S_{10} = S'_{01}$. Note that the value of s is built into this function through the dimensions of the unknown matrices α and β, and so is indicated in the subscript in (7.28). If additional non-I(1) variables are to be included in (7.27), such as dummy variables and lagged values of Δx_t, these are removed by regressing Δx_t and x_{t-1} onto them and taking the residuals. The mean-deviations shown here are just the simplest possible case of this 'partialling out' operation. It's conventional to replace x_{t-1} by x_{t-p} where p is the maximum lag order, but this is optional. Either choice of lag will yield the same asymptotic properties.

To minimize Λ_s, first fix β temporarily and regress Δx_t onto $\beta' x_{t-1}$ to get a conditional estimate of α; that is,

$$\hat{\alpha} = (\beta' S_{11}\beta)^{-1}\beta' S_{10}. \tag{7.29}$$

Substitution of (7.29) into (7.28) yields the concentrated criterion function

$$\Lambda_s^*(\beta) = |S_{00} - S_{01}\beta(\beta' S_{11}\beta)^{-1}\beta' S_{10}|. \tag{7.30}$$

Now, the rule for determinants of partitioned matrices gives the twin identities

$$\begin{vmatrix} S_{00} & S_{01}\beta \\ \beta' S_{10} & \beta' S_{11}\beta \end{vmatrix} = |\beta' S_{11}\beta||S_{00} - S_{01}\beta(\beta' S_{11}\beta)^{-1}\beta' S_{10}|$$

$$= |S_{00}||\beta' S_{11}\beta - \beta' S_{10} S_{00}^{-1} S_{01}\beta|$$

from which we obtain the alternative form of (7.30),

$$\Lambda_s^*(\beta) = |S_{00}|\frac{|\beta'(S_{11} - S_{10}S_{00}^{-1}S_{01})\beta|}{|\beta' S_{11}\beta|} \tag{7.31}$$

where $|S_{00}|$ does not depend on β and so can be omitted from the function. The next step is to appeal to a well-known result from multivariate analysis. The minimum with respect to β of the ratio of determinants in (7.31) is obtained by solving the generalized eigenvalue problem

$$|\lambda S_{11} - S_{10}S_{00}^{-1}S_{01}| = 0. \tag{7.32}$$

Specifically, $\Lambda_s^*(\beta)$ is minimized uniquely when the columns of β are the solutions $q_1, \ldots, q_s$ of the s homogeneous equations

$$(\lambda_j \boldsymbol{S}_{11} - \boldsymbol{S}_{10}\boldsymbol{S}_{00}^{-1}\boldsymbol{S}_{01})\boldsymbol{q}_j = \boldsymbol{0} \tag{7.33}$$

where $\lambda_1, \ldots, \lambda_s$ are the *s largest* solutions to (7.32), subject to the normalization

$$\boldsymbol{q}_i'\boldsymbol{S}_{11}\boldsymbol{q}_j = \begin{cases} 1, & i = j \\ 0, & \text{otherwise.} \end{cases} \tag{7.34}$$

The eigenvalues must fall in the interval $[0, 1]$. Noting that $\boldsymbol{S}_{11} = O(T^2)$ whereas $\boldsymbol{S}_{10}\boldsymbol{S}_{00}^{-1}\boldsymbol{S}_{01} = O(T)$, observe how necessarily $\lambda_j = O_p(T^{-1})$ unless the solution to (7.33) is a cointegrating vector. The normalization in (7.34) is not convenient, but letting $\boldsymbol{L}$ $(m \times m)$ be defined by $\boldsymbol{S}_{11}^{-1} = \boldsymbol{L}\boldsymbol{L}'$, so that $\boldsymbol{L}'\boldsymbol{S}_{11}\boldsymbol{L} = \boldsymbol{I}_m$, the $\lambda_1,\ldots,\lambda_m$ are also the simple eigenvalues of the matrix $\boldsymbol{L}'\boldsymbol{S}_{10}\boldsymbol{S}_{00}^{-1}\boldsymbol{S}_{01}\boldsymbol{L}$, whereas the eigenvectors are $\hat{\beta}_j = \boldsymbol{L}\boldsymbol{q}_j$, which are orthonormal (orthogonal with unit length).

Care is needed in interpreting this result. The orthonormal matrix $\hat{\beta} = (\hat{\beta}_1,\ldots,\hat{\beta}_s)$ asymptotically spans the cointegrating space, but it is not a reduced form nor, of course, a structural form. Given the arbitrary nature of the normalization, it is difficult to give an interpretation to these vectors, but for the fact that any structural cointegrating vector can be found asymptotically as a linear combination of the columns.

While inference on the elements of $\hat{\beta}$ itself is neither possible nor indeed useful, it is possible to impose and test linear restrictions on the cointegrating space. Following Johansen and Juselius (1992), one can write for example

$$\beta = \boldsymbol{H}\phi$$

where $\boldsymbol{H}$ is an $m \times (m - r)$ matrix of known constants (0 and 1 typically) and $\phi(m - r \times s)$ is an unrestricted matrix of parameters. This parameterization allows the cointegrating space to satisfy a certain type of linear restriction, and permits a likelihood ratio test of these restrictions.

Davidson (1998a) shows how to test a set of p restrictions expressed in the form

- There exists a vector $\boldsymbol{a}$ $(s \times 1)$ such that $\boldsymbol{H}\beta\boldsymbol{a} = \boldsymbol{0}$

where here, $\boldsymbol{H}$ is a $p \times m$ matrix of known constants. This approach allows testing of hypotheses such as 'a vector subject to p specified zero restrictions lies in the cointegrating space'. Given asymptotic mixed normality of the estimators $\hat{\beta}$, which can be demonstrated subject to regularity conditions, these tests can be performed making use of the standard chi-squared tables in large samples.

8 TESTING COINTEGRATION

We have shown that the cointegrating rank of a collection of I(1) processes is the key piece of information, without which inference on the system cannot realistically proceed. It is in this context in particular that Søren Johansen's contributions have proved essential. The discussion of the last section has already provided the clue. Consider the m

solutions to (7.32), ordered as $\lambda_1 \geq \lambda_2 \geq \cdots \geq \lambda_m$. These are functions of the data set but their computation does not depend on a choice of s. The $m - s$ smallest converge to zero as $T \to \infty$, because the corresponding eigenvectors $\boldsymbol{q}_j$ are not cointegrating vectors, and the terms $\boldsymbol{S}_{11}\boldsymbol{q}_j$ and $\boldsymbol{S}_{10}\boldsymbol{S}_{00}^{-1}\boldsymbol{S}_{01}\boldsymbol{q}_j$ in (7.33) are therefore diverging at different rates, respectively $O_p(T^2)$ and $O_p(T)$. Balancing the equation imposes $\lambda_j = O_p(T^{-1})$ for $s < j \leq m$, while $\lambda_j = O_p(1)$ for $1 \leq j \leq s$.

This provides the basis for a test based on the statistics $T\lambda_j$, which are computed as a by-product of the reduced rank regression. If $j \leq s$ then $T\lambda_j = O_p(T)$, otherwise $T\lambda_j = O_p(1)$. Suppose that the distributions of the $T\lambda_j$ in the second case can be tabulated. We can then proceed to compare the statistic with this distribution for the cases $j = 1,2,\ldots,m$, in decreasing order of magnitude, until the chosen critical value is not exceeded. Then, s can be estimated as the last case of j before this non-rejection occurs. For any choice of s, the tests can be formally cast in the form H_0: *cointegrating rank* $= s$ against the alternative H_1: *cointegrating rank* $\geq s + 1$.

It is shown by an ingenious argument that, under the null hypothesis, the non-divergent $T\lambda_j$ (the cases $j = s + 1\ldots,m$) are tending as $T \to \infty$ to the eigenvalues of a certain random matrix of dimension $(m - s) \times (m - s)$ whose distribution is free of nuisance parameters. This limiting distribution is shared with matrices that can be generated on the computer using pseudo-random numbers, so the distribution of its eigenvalues can be tabulated in a Monte Carlo simulation exercise.

There are two ways in which this idea might be implemented as a test. One is to look at $T\lambda_{s+1}$, the largest of the set of the $m - s$ smallest rescaled eigenvalues. This is called the *maximum eigenvalue test*. The second implementation is to look at $\sum_{j=s+1}^{m} T\lambda_j$. This latter statistic converges to the trace of the limit matrix, and so this is known as the *trace test*. Each of these distributions has been tabulated for a range of values of $m - s$, although not depending on m, note, since the cases (m, s) and $(m + 1, s + 1)$ are equivalent.

It can also be shown that the minimized value of the generalized variance is

$$\Lambda_s^*(\hat{\beta}) = \prod_{j=1}^{s}(1 - \lambda_j)$$

(the product of the s terms) and hence, using the fact that $\log(1 + x) \approx x$ when x is small,

$$T\log\Lambda_s^*(\hat{\beta}) - T\log\Lambda_{s+1}^*(\hat{\beta}) = -T\log(1 - \lambda_{s+1}) \sim T\lambda_{s+1}$$

and

$$T\log\Lambda_s^*(\hat{\beta}) - T\log\Lambda_m^*(\hat{\beta}) = -T\sum_{j=s+1}^{m}\log(1 - \lambda_j) \sim \sum_{j=s+1}^{m} T\lambda_j$$

where '$\sim$' denotes that the ratio of the two sides converges to 1. Hence, asymptotically equivalent tests can be based on the estimation minimands. If the disturbances are Gaussian, the maximized likelihood takes the form $-\frac{1}{2}T\log\Lambda_s^*(\hat{\beta})$ and then these forms have the natural interpretation of likelihood ratio tests. However, be careful to note that these limiting distributions are not chi-squared. It is a general rule of I(1) asymptotics that restrictions affecting the orders of integration of variables – in other words that concern unit roots – give rise to non-standard distributions. Be careful to note that the standard asymptotic tests that we have described in this chapter all share the feature that the cointegrating rank is given and not part of the tested hypothesis.

An interesting special case is the test based on the statistic $T\lambda_m$, for the null hypothesis of a single common trend (cointegrating rank $s = m - 1$) against the alternative that the data are stationary. In this case the trace and maximal eigenvalue statistics coincide and, interestingly enough, the null limiting distribution is none other than the square of the Dickey–Fuller distribution associated with the standard test for a unit root.

An alternative approach to testing cointegration is to estimate a single equation and test whether the resulting residual is I(0). In these tests, non-cointegration is the null hypothesis. This is basically comparable to testing the hypothesis H_0: $s = 0$ in the cointegrating VECM framework, but avoids modelling the complete system. A well-known paper by Phillips and Ouliaris (1990) compares a range of alternative implementations of this idea. The best known is based on the augmented Dickey–Fuller (ADF) test for a unit root (Dickey and Fuller, 1979, 1981; Said and Dickey, 1984) applied to the residuals from an ordinary least squares regression. The test statistic takes the form of the t-ratio for the parameter estimate $\hat{\phi}$ in the regression

$$\Delta\hat{u}_t = \phi\hat{u}_{t-1} + \sum\nolimits_{j=1}^{K_T}\pi_j\Delta\hat{u}_{t-j} + e_t \tag{7.35}$$

where $\hat{u}_t = x_{1t} - \hat{\mu} - \hat{\gamma}'\boldsymbol{x}_{2t}$ and $K_T = o(T^{1/3})$.

Although this test closely resembles the augmented Dickey–Fuller test for a unit root, there are a number of important issues to be aware of. When the null hypothesis is true, there is no cointegration and $\hat{\gamma}$ does not converge in probability and is a random vector even in the limit as $T \to \infty$. A linear combination of random walks with random coefficients, where these coefficients are computed specifically to minimize the variance of the combination, is not itself a random walk, in the sense that the regular Dickey–Fuller distribution should be expected to apply. In fact, the asymptotic distribution of this test depends only on the number of elements in $\boldsymbol{x}_{2t}$, and tabulation of the distributions is therefore feasible (see Engle and Yoo, 1987). However, while it might be assumed that an efficient single-equation estimator would be a better choice than OLS for the estimator of γ, in fact the limit distributions have been derived on the assumption of OLS estimation and depend on this for their validity. The requirement that $K_T \to \infty$ is important because, under H_0, $\Delta\hat{u}_t$ is a random combination of stationary processes. Even if these have finite-order autoregressive structures individually, there is no reason to assume this of the combination. The idea of approximating a finite-order ARMA process by an AR(∞), approximated in finite samples by the AR(K_T), is due to Said and Dickey (1984). In practice it should give an adequate account of the autocorrelation structure of most I(0) processes.

Leading alternatives to the ADF statistic are the statistics denoted $\hat{Z}_\alpha$ and $\hat{Z}_t$ in Phillips (1987), where the coefficient $\hat{\phi}$ is subjected to specifically tailored corrections that play an equivalent role to the lag-difference terms in (7.35). These corrections are similar in principle to those in the Phillips–Hansen (1990) fully modified least squares estimator of γ, and make use of HAC estimates of the data long-run covariance matrix.

9 CONCLUSION

This chapter has aimed to survey the main issues in the specification and estimation of cointegrating relationships in non-stationary data. This is now a very large body of literature, and inevitably there are many aspects which there has been no space to deal with here. In particular, while a number of conclusions about the large-sample distributions of estimators have been asserted, no attempt has been made to describe the asymptotic analysis on which these conclusions rest. This theory makes a clever use of the calculus of Brownian motion, following from the fundamental idea that non-stationary economic time series, when viewed in the large, move much like pollen grains suspended in water as first observed microscopically by the botanist Robert Brown. The same mathematics can be used to analyse either phenomenon. The key result in this theory is the functional central limit theorem, generalizing the ordinary central limit theorem to show the limiting Gaussianity of every increment of the path of a normalized partial sum process. Interested readers can find many of the details omitted here in Part IV of the present author's text *Econometric Theory* (Davidson, 2000).

NOTES

1. With repeated eigenvalues $\boldsymbol{M}$ is generally not diagonal. When $\mu_k = \mu_{k+1}$, a '1' appears in position $\{k, k+1\}$. However, note that $\boldsymbol{A}$ and $\boldsymbol{M}$ have the same rank and $\boldsymbol{M}$ is either diagonal or upper triangular. While only in symmetric matrices is the rank always equal to the number of non-zero eigenvalues, a singular matrix always has one or more zero eigenvalues.
2. This matrix can be written in closed form only with the use of Vec notation, but it's easy to see that it must satisfy the identity $\boldsymbol{\Sigma}_x - \boldsymbol{A}\boldsymbol{\Sigma}_x\boldsymbol{A}' = \boldsymbol{\Sigma}$.
3. The difference operator is $\Delta = 1 - L$ where L is the lag operator.
4. s cannot be less than the number of non-zero eigenvalues, but could be greater.
5. The space spanned by β is the collection of vectors $\beta\boldsymbol{r}$ for all s-vectors $\boldsymbol{r} \neq \boldsymbol{0}$. Clearly, this is identical with the collection $\beta\boldsymbol{D}'\boldsymbol{r}$, for any $s \times s$ non-singular $\boldsymbol{D}$.
6. A variable x is said to Granger-cause another variable y if knowledge of x_t improves the forecasts of y_{t+j} for $j > 0$. This concept is defined in Granger (1969), Clive Granger's first notable contribution to time series econometrics.
7. It is convenient to give the properties of a lag polynomial in the context of a dummy numerical argument z, in general complex-valued.
8. $\|\boldsymbol{A}\| = \sqrt{\mathrm{tr}(\boldsymbol{A}'\boldsymbol{A})}$ is one of several alternative definitions of the matrix norm. This is a simple way to specify absolute summability, ruling out the possibility of offsetting signs allowing elements to be summable while their squares, for example, are not summable.
9. In the VAR(1) case (1), $\Omega = (\boldsymbol{I} - \boldsymbol{A})^{-1}\boldsymbol{\Sigma}(\boldsymbol{I} - \boldsymbol{A}')^{-1}$. Be careful to distinguish between this formula and $\boldsymbol{\Sigma}_x$.
10. Some of the results in this theory can be proved under the weaker condition (c') $\sum_{j=0}^{\infty} j^{1/2}\|\boldsymbol{C}_j\| < \infty$, see for example Phillips and Solo (1992). The conditions stated here are sufficient for the properties we discuss, and are hopefully the most intuitive ones.
11. Note the conventions governing the use of the difference operator Δ and its inverse, the integration operator $\Delta^{-1} = 1 + L + \cdots + L^t$. Consider a sequence $y_1, \ldots, y_T$. Since $\Delta^{-1}y_1 = y_1$, the operator Δ must be accordingly defined by $\Delta y_1 = y_1$ and $\Delta y_t = y_t - y_{t-1}$ for $t > 1$.
12. Some care is needed in the treatment of initial conditions. Expressing the observed process as the deviation from an initial value $\boldsymbol{x}_0$ allows assumptions about how $\boldsymbol{x}_0$ is generated to be sidelined. To avoid infinities, this clearly has to be by a different mechanism from that generating $\boldsymbol{x}_t$ for $t > 0$.
13. We write $X_T = O_p(T^k)$ to denote that for every $\varepsilon > 0$, there exists $B_\varepsilon < \infty$ such that $P(|X_T|/T^k > B_\varepsilon) < \varepsilon$. In particular, a stationary process is $O_p(1)$.
14. Be careful to note that $\boldsymbol{A}^+(z)$ is an invertible autoregressive polynomial, of finite or infinite order, driving the stationary differences, whereas $\boldsymbol{A}(z)$ involves the finite-order integration operator Δ^{-1}. Cumulation

must be initiated at some finitely remote date. However, considering the sequence $\boldsymbol{x}_t - \boldsymbol{x}_0$ allows us to set this date as $t = 1$ without loss of generality.

15. We follow the cited papers by Phillips and co-authors in using $\boldsymbol{B}$ for the reduced form cointegrating coefficients. Don't confuse this usage with the lag polynomial $\boldsymbol{B}(z)$ appearing earlier.
16. Where the choice of normalization has unintended consequences as in the case where the first element of β is actually zero, so that x_{1t} is not in the cointegrating set. This is a valid special case of the model and obviously needs to be ruled out by assumption. To pre-empt this possibility it's desirable to compare alternative normalizations.
17. Note, however, that $\hat{\mu} - \mu = O_p(T^{1/2})$ in the usual way.
18. Think of this as a method for estimating (an element of) Ω in (7.9), rather than the corresponding (element of) $\boldsymbol{\Sigma}$.
19. The $o()$ notation is a shorthand for the condition $|K_T|/T^{1/3} \to 0$ as $T \to \infty$.
20. Here we use the term 'regression' generically, to denote any of the consistent methods described in section 5.
21. Further discussion of this and related results can be found in Davidson (1994, 1998b).

REFERENCES

Beveridge, S. and C.R. Nelson (1981), 'A new approach to decomposition of economic time series into permanent and transitory components with particular attention to the measurement of the business cycle', *Journal of Monetary Economics*, **7**, 151–74.

Brown, T.M. (1952), 'Habit persistence and lags in consumer behaviour', *Econometrica*, **20**, 355–71.

Campbell, J.Y. and R.J. Shiller (1988), 'Interpreting cointegrated models', *Journal of Economic Dynamics and Control*, **12**, 505–22.

Davidson, J., D.F. Hendry, F. Srba and S. Yeo (1978), 'Econometric modelling of the aggregate time-series relationship between consumers' expenditure and income in the United Kingdom', *Economic Journal*, **88**, 661–92.

Davidson, J. (1994), 'Identifying cointegrating regressions by the rank condition', *Oxford Bulletin of Economics and Statistics*, **56**, 103–8.

Davidson, J. (1998a), 'A Wald test of restrictions on the cointegrating space based on Johansen's estimator', *Economics Letters*, **59**, 183–7.

Davidson, J. (1998b), 'Structural relations, cointegration and identification: some simple results and their application', *Journal of Econometrics*, **87**, 87–113.

Davidson, J. (2000), *Econometric Theory*, Oxford: Blackwell Publishers.

Dickey, David A. and W.A. Fuller (1979), 'Distribution of estimates for autoregressive time series with unit root', *Journal of the American Statistical Association*, **74**, 427–31.

Dickey, D.A. and W.A. Fuller (1981), 'Likelihood ratio statistics for autoregressive time series with a unit root', *Econometrica*, **49**, 1057–72.

Engle, R.F., D.F. Hendry and J-F. Richard (1983), 'Exogeneity', *Econometrica*, **51**, 277–304.

Engle, R.F. and B.S. Yoo (1987), 'Forecasting and testing in cointegrated systems', *Journal of Econometrics*, **35**, 143–59.

Granger, C.W.J. (1969), 'Investigating causal relations by econometric models and cross-spectral methods', *Econometrica*, **37**, 424–38.

Granger, C.W.J. (1981), 'Some properties of time series data and their use in econometric model specification', *Journal of Econometrics*, **16**, 121–30.

Granger, C.W.J. and P. Newbold (1974), 'Spurious regressions in econometrics', *Journal of Econometrics*, **2**, 111–20.

Hendry, D.F. (1979), 'Predictive failure and econometric modelling in macroeconomics: the transactions demand for money', Chapter 9 in P. Ormerod (ed.), *Economic Modelling*, London: Heinemann (reprinted in *Econometrics: Alchemy or Science* by D.F. Hendry, Blackwell Publishers 1993).

Hendry, D.F. (1980), 'Econometrics: Alchemy or science?', *Economica*, **47**, 387–406.

Hendry, D.F. (2004), 'The Nobel Memorial Prize for Clive W.J. Granger', *Scandinavian Journal of Economics*, **106**(2), 187–213.

Johansen, S. (1988a), 'The mathematical structure of error correction models', *Contemporary Mathematics*, **80**, 359–86.

Johansen, S. (1988b), 'Statistical analysis of cointegration vectors', *Journal of Economic Dynamics and Control*, **12**, 231–54.

Johansen, S. (1991), 'Estimation and hypothesis testing of cointegration vectors in Gaussian vector autoregressive models', *Econometrica*, **59**, 1551–80.

Johansen, S. (1995), *Likelihood-Based Inference in Cointegrated Vector Autoregressive Models*, Oxford: Oxford University Press.
Johansen, S. and K. Juselius (1992), 'Testing structural hypotheses in a multivariate cointegration analysis of the PPP and the UIP for UK', *Journal of Econometrics*, **53**, 211–44.
Johnston, J. and J. DiNardo (1997), *Econometric Methods*, 4th edn, New York: McGraw-Hill.
Koopmans, T.C.C (1949), 'Identification problems in economic model construction', *Econometrica*, **17**, 125–44.
Lovell, M.C. (1961), 'Manufacturers' inventories, sales expectations and the acceleration principle', *Econometrica*, **29**, 293–314.
Newey, W.K. and K.D. West (1987), 'A simple, positive semi-definite, heteroscedasticity and autocorrelation consistent covariance matrix', *Econometrica*, **55**, 703–8.
Nickell, S.J. (1985), 'Error correction, partial adjustment and all that: an expository note', *Oxford Bulletin of Economics and Statistics*, **47**, 119–30.
Park, J.Y. and P.C.B. Phillips (1988), 'Statistical inference in regressions with integrated processes: Part 1', *Econometric Theory*, **4**, 468–97.
Park, J.Y. and P.C.B. Phillips (1989), 'Statistical inference in regressions with integrated processes: Part 2', *Econometric Theory*, **5**, 95–131.
Phillips, P.C.B. (1987), 'Time series regression with a unit root', *Econometrica*, **55**, 277–301.
Phillips, P.C.B. (1988), 'Reflections on econometric methodology', *Economic Record*, **64**, 544–59.
Phillips, P.C.B. (1991), 'Optimal inference in cointegrated systems', *Econometrica*, **59**, 283–306.
Phillips, P.C.B. and B.E. Hansen (1990), 'Statistical inference in instrumental variables regression with I(1) processes', *Review of Economic Studies*, **57**, 99–125.
Phillips, P.C.B. and M. Loretan (1991), 'Estimating long-run economic equilibria', *Review of Economic Studies*, **58**, 407–37.
Phillips, P.C.B. and S. Ouliaris (1990), 'Asymptotic properties of residual based tests for cointegration', *Econometrica*, **58**, 165–93.
Phillips, P.C.B. and V. Solo (1992), 'Asymptotics for linear processes', *Annals of Statistics*, **2**, 971–1001.
Said, S.E. and D.A. Dickey (1984), 'Testing for unit roots in autoregressive moving average models of unknown order', *Biometrika*, **71**, 599–607.
Saikkonen, P. (1991), 'Asymptotically efficient estimation of cointegration regressions', *Econometric Theory*, **7**, 1–21.
Salmon, M. (1982), 'Error correction mechanisms', *The Economic Journal*, **92**, 615–29.
Sargan, J.D. (1964), 'Wages and prices in the United Kingdom: a study in econometric methodology', in P.E. Hart, G. Mills and J.K. Whitaker (eds), *Econometric Analysis for National Economic Planning*, London: Butterworth, pp. 25–54, reprinted in D.F. Hendry and K.F.Wallis (eds) (1984), *Econometrics and Quantitative Economics*, Oxford: Basil Blackwell.
Stock, J.H. (1987), 'Asymptotic properties of least squares estimators of cointegrating vectors', *Econometrica*, **55**, 1035–56.
Stock, J.H. and M.W. Watson (1993), 'A simple estimator of cointegrating vectors in higher order integrated systems', *Econometrica*, **61**, 783–820.
Wold, H. (1938), *A Study in the Analysis of Stationary Time Series*, Uppsala: Almqvist and Wiksell.
Yule, G.U. (1926), 'Why do we sometimes get nonsense correlations between time series?', *Journal of the Royal Statistical Society*, **89**, 1–64.

8 Estimation and inference in threshold type regime switching models*

Jesús Gonzalo and Jean-Yves Pitarakis

1 INTRODUCTION

The recognition that linear time series models may be too restrictive to capture economically interesting asymmetries and empirically observed non-linear dynamics has over the past twenty years generated a vast research agenda on designing models which could capture such features while remaining parsimonious and analytically tractable. Models that are capable of capturing non-linear dynamics have also been the subject of a much earlier and extensive research led by statisticians as well as practitioners in fields as broad as biology, physics and engineering with a very wide range of proposed specifications designed to capture, model and forecast field specific phenomena (for example bilinear models, random coefficient models, state dependent models and so on). The amount of research that has been devoted to describing the non-linear dynamics of sunspot numbers and Canadian lynx data is an obvious manifestation of this quest (see Tong, 1990; Granger and Terasvirta, 1993; Hansen, 1999; Terasvirta et al., 2010, and references therein).

A particular behaviour of interest to economists has been that of regime change or regime switching whereby the parameters of a model are made to change depending on the occurrence of a particular event, episode or policy (for example recessions or expansions, periods of low/high stock market valuations, low/high interest rates) but are otherwise constant within regimes. Popular models that can be categorized within this group are the well known Markov switching models popularized by Hamilton's early work (see Hamilton, 1989) which model parameter change via the use of an unobservable discrete time Markov process. This class of models in which parameter changes are triggered by an unobservable binary variable has been used extensively as an intuitive way of capturing policy shifts in macroeconomic models as well as numerous other contexts such as forecasting economic growth and dating business cycles. In Leeper and Zha (2003), Farmer et al. (2009), Davig and Leeper (2007) and Benhabib (2010), for instance, the authors use such models to introduce the concept of monetary policy switches and regime-specific Taylor rules. Other particularly fruitful areas of application of such regime switching specifications have involved the dating of business cycles and the modelling of time variation in expected returns, among numerous others (see Hamilton, 2011; Perez-Quiros and Timmermann, 2000).

An alternative, parsimonious and dynamically very rich way of modelling regime switching behaviour in economic data is to take an explicit stand on what might be triggering such switches and adopt a piecewise linear setting in which regime switches are triggered by an *observed* variable crossing an unknown threshold. Such models have been proposed by Howell Tong in the mid-1970s and have gone through an important revival following their adoption by economists and econometricians during the 1980s and 1990s following the methodological work of Bruce Hansen (see also Hansen, 2011 and references therein for a historical overview), Ruey Tsay (Tsay, 1989, 1991), Koop et al. (1996), Koop and Potter (1999) and others. When each regime is described by an autoregressive process and the threshold variable causing the regime change is also a lagged value of the variable being modelled we have the well known Self Exciting Threshold AutoRegressive class of models (SETAR) extensively studied in the early work of Tong and others (see Tong and Lim, 1980; Tong, 1983, 1990; Chan, 1990, 1993). In general, however, the threshold principle may apply to a wider range of linear univariate or multivariate models and need not be solely confined to autoregressive functional forms. Similarly the threshold variable triggering regime switches may or may not be one of the variables included in the linear part of the model. Despite their simplicity, such models have been shown to be able to capture a very diverse set of dynamics and asymmetries particularly relevant to economic data. Important examples include the modelling of phenomena such as costly arbitrage whereby arbitrage occurs solely after the spread in prices exceeds a threshold due, for instance, to transport costs (see Lo and Zivot, 2001; Obstfeld and Taylor, 1997; O'Connell and Wei, 1997; Balke and Fomby, 1997). Other areas of application include the study of asymmetries in the business cycles explored in Beaudry and Koop (1993), Potter (1995), Koop and Potter (1999), Altissimo and Violante (1999), the modelling of asymmetries in gasoline and crude oil prices (Borenstein et al., 1997) and other markets (Balke, 2000; Gospodinov, 2005; Griffin et al., 2007 among others).

Threshold models are particularly simple to estimate and conduct inferences on, and despite the lack of guidance offered by economic theory for a particular non-linear functional form such piecewise linear structures can be viewed as approximations to a wider range of functional forms as discussed in Petruccelli (1992) and Tong (1990, pp. 98–100). Two key econometric problems that need to be addressed when contemplating the use of such models for one's own data involve tests for detecting the presence of threshold effects and if supported by the data the subsequent estimation of the underlying model parameters.

The purpose of this chapter is to offer a pedagogical overview of the most commonly used inference and estimation techniques developed in the recent literature on threshold models. In so doing, we also aim to highlight the key strengths, weaknesses and limitations of each procedure and perhaps more importantly discuss potential areas requiring further research and interesting extensions. The plan of the chapter is as follows. Section 2 concentrates on tests for detecting the presence of threshold non-linearities against linear specifications. Section 3 explores methods of estimating the model parameters and their properties. Section 4 discusses important extensions and interesting areas for future work. Section 5 concludes.

2 DETECTING THRESHOLD EFFECTS

In what follows we will be interested in methods for assessing whether the dynamics of a univariate time series y_t and a p-dimensional regressor vector x_t may be plausibly described by a threshold specification given by

$$y_t = \begin{cases} x_t'\beta_1 + u_t & q_t \leq \gamma \\ x_t'\beta_2 + u_t & q_t > \gamma \end{cases} \tag{8.1}$$

with q_t denoting the threshold variable triggering the regime switches and u_t the random disturbance term. At this stage it is important to note that our parameterization in (8.1) is general enough to also be viewed as encompassing threshold autoregressions by requiring x_t to contain lagged values of y_t. Similarly, the threshold variable q_t may be one of the components of x_t or some external variable. The threshold parameter γ is assumed unknown throughout but following common practice we require $\gamma \in \Gamma$ with $\Gamma = [\underline{\gamma}, \overline{\gamma}]$ denoting a compact subset of the threshold variable sample space. Given our specification in (8.1) the first concern of an empirical investigation is to test the null hypothesis of linearity $H_0 : \beta_1 = \beta_2$ against $H_1 : \beta_1 \neq \beta_2$.

Before proceeding with the various testing procedures it is useful to document alternative and occasionally more convenient formulations of the threshold model by introducing relevant indicator functions. Letting $I(q_t \leq \gamma)$ be such that $I(q_t \leq \gamma) = 1$ when $q_t \leq \gamma$ and $I(q_t \leq \gamma) = 0$ otherwise we define $x_{1t}(\gamma) = x_t{*}I(q_t \leq \gamma)$ and $x_{2t}(\gamma) = x_t{*}I(q_t > \gamma)$ so that (8.1) can also be written as

$$y_t = x_{1t}(\gamma)'\beta_1 + x_{2t}(\gamma)'\beta_2 + u_t \tag{8.2}$$

or in matrix notation as

$$y = X_1(\gamma)\beta_1 + X_2(\gamma)\beta_2 + u \tag{8.3}$$

with $X_i(\gamma)$ stacking the elements of $x_{it}(\gamma)$ for $i = 1,2$ and which is such that $X_1(\gamma)'X_2(\gamma) = 0$. Our notation in (8.2) and (8.3) also makes it clear that for a known γ, say $\gamma = 0$, the above models are linear in their parameters and we are in fact in a basic textbook linear regression setting. This latter observation also highlights the importance of recognizing the role played by the unknown threshold parameter when it comes to conducting inferences in threshold models. The price to pay for our desire to remain agnostic about the possible magnitude of γ and whether it exists at all is that we will need to develop tests that are suitable for any $\gamma \in \Gamma$. Naturally, we will also need to develop methods of obtaining a good estimator of γ once we are confident that the existence of such a quantity is supported by the data.

Within the general context of threshold models such as (8.1) the main difficulty for testing hypotheses such as $H_0 : \beta_1 = \beta_2$ arises from the fact that the threshold parameter γ is unidentified under this null hypothesis of linearity. This can be observed very clearly from our formulation in (8.3) since setting $\beta_1 = \beta_2$ leads to a linear model via $X_1(\gamma) + X_2(\gamma) \equiv X$ and in which γ plays no role. This problem is occasionally referred to as the Davies problem (see Davies, 1977, 1987 and Hansen 1996) and is typically addressed by viewing the traditional Wald, LM or LR type test statistics as functionals of γ and subsequently focusing inferences on quantities such as the supremum or average of the test statistics across all possible values of γ.

Letting $X = X_1(\gamma) + X_2(\gamma)$ denote the p-dimensional regressor matrix in the linear model we can write its corresponding residual sum of squares as $S_T = y'y - y'X(X'X)^{-1}X'y$ while that corresponding to the threshold model is given by

$$S_T(\gamma) = y'y - \sum_{i=1}^{2} y'X_i(\gamma)\,(X_i(\gamma)'X_i(\gamma))^{-1}X_i(\gamma)'y \tag{8.4}$$

for any $\gamma \in \Gamma$. This then allows us to write a Wald type test statistic for testing $H_0 : \beta_1 = \beta_2$ as

$$W_T(\gamma) = \frac{T(S_T - S_T(\gamma))}{S_T(\gamma)}. \tag{8.5}$$

Naturally we could also formulate alternative test statistics such as the likelihood ratio or LM in a similar manner, for example $LR_T(\gamma) = T \ln S_T/S_T(\gamma)$ and $LM_T(\gamma) = T(S_T - S_T(\gamma))/S_T$. Due to the unidentified nuisance parameter problem, inferences are typically based on quantities such as $\sup_{\gamma \in \Gamma} W_T(\gamma)$ or their variants (see Hansen, 1996).

For practical purposes the maximum Wald statistic is constructed as follows.

- Step 1: Let qs denote the $T \times 1$ dimensional sorted version of q_t. Since we operate under the assumption that $\gamma \in \Gamma$ a compact subset of {qs[1],. . .,qs[T]} we trim a given fraction π from the top and bottom components of the $T \times 1$ vector qs so as to obtain a new vector of threshold variable observations $\text{qss} = \text{qs}[T\pi : T(1-\pi)]$. If $T = 1000$ for instance and $\pi = 10$ per cent the new sorted and trimmed version of the threshold variable is given by qss = qs[100 : 900]. Let T_s denote the number of observations included in qss.
- Step 2: For each $i = 1,. . .,T_s$ construct the top and bottom regime regressor matrices given by $X_1[i] = x[1:T]*I(q_t \leq qss[i])$ and $X_2[i] = x[1:T]*I(q_t > qss[i])$. Note that for each possible value of i, $X_1[i]$ and $X_2[i]$ are $T \times p$ regressor matrices with * denoting the element by element multiplication operator and x[1 : T] refers to the $T \times p$ original regressor matrix X.
- Step 3: Using $X_1[i]$, $X_2[i]$ and X construct, $S_T[i] = y'y - y'X_1[i](X_1[i]'X_1[i])^{-1}X_1[i]'y - y'X_2[i](X_2[i]'X_2[i])^{-1}X_2[i]'y$, $S_T = y'y - y'X(X'X)^{-1}X'y$ and obtain a magnitude of the Wald statistics as defined above for each i, say $W_T[i]$ with $i = 1,. . .,T_s$.
- Step 4: Use $\max_{1 \leq i \leq T_s} W_T[i]$ as the supremum Wald statistic and proceed similarly for $\max_{1 \leq i \leq T_s} LR_T[i]$ or $\max_{1 \leq i \leq T_s} LM_T[i]$ as required. Alternative test statistics may involve the use of averages such as $\sum_{i=1}^{T_s} W_T[i]/T_s$.

Upon completion of the loop, the decision regarding $H_0 : \beta_1 = \beta_2$ involves rejecting the null hypothesis for *large* values of the test statistics. Cut-offs and implied p-values are obviously dictated by the limiting distribution of objects such as $\max_i W_T[i]$ which may or may not be tractable, an issue we concentrate on below.

The early research on tests of the null hypothesis of linearity focused on SETAR versions of (8.1) and among the first generation of tests we note the CUSUM type of tests developed in Petruccelli and Davies (1986) and Tsay (1989). Chan (1990, 1991) subsequently extended this testing toolkit by obtaining the limiting distribution of a maximum LR type test statistic whose construction we described above. Chan (1990, 1991) established that under the null hypothesis $H_0 : \beta_1 = \beta_2$, suitable assumptions requiring stationarity, ergodicity and the iid-ness of the $u_t's$, the limiting distribution of the supremum

LR is such that $\sup_\gamma LR_T(\gamma) \Rightarrow \sup_\gamma \zeta(\gamma)'\Omega(\gamma)\zeta(\gamma) \equiv \sup_\gamma G_\infty(\gamma)$ with $\zeta(\gamma)$ denoting a zero mean Gaussian process and $\Omega(\gamma)$ its corresponding covariance kernel. Naturally the same result would hold for the Sup Wald or Sup LM statistics.

These results were obtained within a SETAR setting with the covariance kernel of $\zeta(\gamma)$ depending on model-specific population moments in a complicated manner (for example unknown population quantities such as $E[x_t^2 I(q_t \leq \gamma)]$ and so on). This latter aspect is important to emphasize since it highlights the unavailability of universal tabulations for $\sup_\gamma G_\infty(\gamma)$. Differently put the limiting distribution given by $G_\infty(\gamma)$ depends on model-specific nuisance parameters and can therefore not be tabulated for practical inference purposes. There are, however, some very restrictive instances under which $G_\infty(\gamma)$ may simplify into a random variable with a familiar distribution that is free of any nuisance parameters. This can happen for instance if the threshold variable is taken as external, say independent of x_t and u_t. In this instance $G_\infty(\gamma)$ can be shown to be equivalent to a normalized squared Brownian Bridge process identical to the limiting distribution of the Wald, LR or LM statistic for testing the null of linearity against a single structural break tabulated in Andrews (1993). More specifically, the limiting distribution is given by $[W(\lambda) - \lambda W(1)]^2/\lambda(1 - \lambda)$ with $W(\lambda)$ denoting a standard Brownian Motion associated with u_t. Tong (1990, pp. 240–44) documents some additional special cases in which the limiting random variable takes the simple Brownian Bridge type formulation. See also Wong and Li (1997) for an application of the same test to a SETAR model with conditional heteroscedasticity. Note also that inferences would be considerably simplified if we were to proceed for a given value of γ, say $\gamma = 0$. This scenario could arise if one were interested in testing for the presence of threshold effects at a specific *location* such as q_t crossing the zero line. In this instance it can be shown that since $\zeta(\gamma = 0)$ is a multivariate normally distributed random variable with covariance $\Omega(\gamma = 0)$, the resulting Wald statistic evaluated at $\gamma = 0$, say $W_T(0)$, will have a χ^2 limit.

The lack of universal tabulations for test statistics such as $\max_i W_T[i]$ perhaps explains the limited take-up of threshold-based specifications by economists prior to the 1990s. In an important paper, Hansen (1996) proposed a broadly applicable simulation-based method for obtaining asymptotic p-values associated with $\max_i W_T[i]$ and related test statistics. Hansen's method is general enough to apply to both SETAR or any other threshold model setting, and bypasses the constraint of having to deal with unknown nuisance parameters in the limiting distribution. Hansen's simulation-based method proposes to replace the population moments of the limiting random variable with their sample counterparts and simulates the score under the null using NID(0,1) draws. This simulation-based method is justified by the multiplier CLT (see Van der Vaart and Wellner, 1996) and can in a way be viewed as an *external bootstrap*. It should not be confused, however, with the idea of obtaining critical values from a bootstrap distribution.

A useful exposition of Hansen's simulation-based approach which we repeat below can be found in Hansen (1999). For practical purposes Hansen's (1996) method involves writing the sample counterpart of $G_\infty(\gamma)$, say $G_T(\gamma)$ obtained by replacing the population moments with their sample counterparts (the scores are simulated using NID(0,1) random variables). One can then obtain a large sample of draws, say N=10000, from $\max_{1 \leq i \leq T_s} G_T[i]$ so as to construct an approximation to the limiting distribution given by $\sup_\gamma G_\infty(\gamma)$. The computed test statistic $\max_{1 \leq i \leq T_s} W_T[i]$ can then be compared with either the quantiles of the simulated distribution (for example 9750th sorted value) or alternatively p-values can be computed.

It is important to note that this approach is applicable to general threshold specifications and is not restricted to the SETAR family. Gauss, Matlab and R codes applicable to a general threshold specification as in (8.1) can be found as a companion code to Hansen (1997). The general format of the procedure involves the arguments y, x and q (i.e. the data) together with the desired level of trimming π and the number of replications N. The output then consists of $\max_{1 \leq i \leq T_s} W_T[i]$ together with its p-value, say

$$\text{TEST}(y,x,q,\pi,N) \rightarrow (\max_{1 \leq i \leq T_s} W_T[i], \text{pval}). \tag{8.6}$$

The above approach allows one to test the null hypothesis $H_0 : \beta_1 = \beta_2$ under quite general conditions and is commonly used in applied work.

An alternative and equally general model selection-based approach that does not require any simulations has been proposed more recently by Gonzalo and Pitarakis (2002). Here, the problem of detecting the presence of threshold effects is viewed as a model selection problem among two competing models given by the linear specification $y_t = x_t'\beta + u_t$, say M_0, and M_1 its threshold counterpart (8.2). The decision rule is based on an information theoretic criterion of the type

$$IC_T(\gamma) = \ln S_T(\gamma) + 2p\frac{c_T}{T}. \tag{8.7}$$

Here $2p$ refers to the number of estimated parameters in the threshold model (i.e. p slopes in each regime) and c_T is a deterministic penalty term. Naturally, under the linear model M_0, we can write the criterion as

$$IC_T = \ln S_T + p\frac{c_T}{T}. \tag{8.8}$$

Intuitively, as we move from the linear to the less parsimonious threshold specification, the residual sum of squares declines and this decline is balanced by a greater penalty term (i.e. $2p\ c_T$ versus $p\ c_T$). The optimal model is then selected as the model that leads to the smallest value of the IC criterion. More formally, we choose the linear specification if

$$IC_T < \min_{\gamma \in \Gamma} IC_T(\gamma) \tag{8.9}$$

and opt for the threshold model otherwise. It is interesting to note that this decision rule is very much similar to using a maximum LR type test statistic since $IC_T - \min_\gamma IC_T(\gamma) = \max_\gamma[IC_T - IC_T(\gamma)] = \max_\gamma[\ln(S_T/S_T(\gamma)) - p\,c_T/T]$. Equivalently, the model selection-based approach points to the threshold model when $\max_\gamma LR_T(\gamma) > p\,c_T$. Thus, rather than basing inferences on the quantiles of the limiting distribution of $\max_\gamma LR_T(\gamma)$ we instead reach our decision by comparing the magnitude of $\max_\gamma LR_T(\gamma)$ with the deterministic quantity $p\,c_T$. This also makes it clear that the practical implementation of this model selection approach follows trivially once Steps 3 and 4 above have been completed. More specifically noting that the model selection-based approach points to the threshold specification when

Table 8.1 Size properties of $\max_i W_T[i]$ *and model selection-based correct decision frequencies under a linear DGP*

	0.010	0.025	0.050	*MSEL*
$T = 100$	0.009	0.019	0.041	0.862
$T = 200$	0.013	0.029	0.055	0.902
$T = 400$	0.011	0.023	0.052	0.964

$$\max_{\gamma} \frac{T(S_T - S_T(\gamma))}{S_T(\gamma)} > T(e^{\frac{pc_T}{T}} - 1). \tag{8.10}$$

it is easy to see that the decision rule can be based on comparing $\max_{1 \leq i \leq T_s} W_T[i]$ with the deterministic term $T(e^{\frac{pc_T}{T}} - 1)$.

Gonzalo and Pitarakis (2002) further established that this model selection-based approach leads to the *correct* choice of models (i.e. $\lim_{T\to\infty} P(M_1|M_0) = \lim_{T\to\infty} P(M_0|M_1) = 0$) provided that the chosen penalty term is such that $c_T \to \infty$ and $c_T/T \to 0$. Through extensive simulations Gonzalo and Pitarakis (2002) further argued that a choice of $c_T = \ln T$ leads to excellent finite sample results.

In Table 8.1 we present a small simulation experiment in which we contrast the size properties of the test-based approach with the ability of the model selection approach to point to the linear specification when the latter is true (that is, correct decision frequencies). Our Data Generating Process (DGP) is given by $y_t = 1 + 0.5x_{t-1} + u_t$ with x_t generated from an AR(1) process given by $x_t = 0.5x_{t-1} + v_t$. The random disturbances $w_t = (u_t, v_t)$ are modelled as an $NID(0, \Omega_2)$ random variable with $\Omega = \{(1.0.5), (0.5, 1)\}$. The empirical size estimates presented in Table 8.1 are obtained as the number of times across the N replications that the empirical p-value exceeds 1 per cent, 2.5 per cent and 5 per cent respectively. The empirical p-values associated with the computed Wald type $\max W_T[i]$ test statistic are obtained using Bruce Hansen's publicly available *thrtest* routine. The correct decision frequencies associated with the model selection procedure MSEL correspond to the number of times across the N replications that $\max_\gamma T(S_T - S_T(\gamma))/S_T(\gamma) < T(e^{p \ln T/T} - 1)$.

The above figures suggest that the test based on $\sup_\gamma W_T(\gamma)$ has good size properties even under small sample sizes. We also note that the ability of the model selection procedure to point to the true model converges to 1 as we increase the sample size. This is expected from the underlying theory since the choice of a BIC type of penalty $c_T = \ln T$ satisfies the two conditions ensuring vanishing probabilities of over- and under-fitting.

In summary, we have reviewed two popular approaches for conducting inferences about the presence or absence of threshold effects within multiple regression models that may or may not include lagged variables. Important operating assumptions include stationarity and ergodicity, absence of serial correlation in the error sequence u_t, absence of endogeneity, and a series of finiteness of moments assumptions ensuring that laws of large numbers and CLTs can be applied. Typically, existing results are valid under a martingale difference assumption on u_t (see for instance Hansen, 1999) so that some forms of heterogeneity (for example conditional heteroscedasticity) would not be invalidating inferences. In fact all of the test statistics considered in Hansen (1996) are heteroscedasticity robust versions of Wald, LR and LM. It is important to note, however, that regime-dependent heteroscedasticity is typically ruled out. A unified theory that may allow inferences in a setting with threshold effects in both the conditional mean and variance (with possibly different threshold parameters) is not readily available although numerous authors have explored the impact of allowing for GARCH type effects in threshold models (see Wong and Li, 1997; Gospodinov, 2005, 2008). It will also be interesting to assess the possibility of handling serial correlation in models such as (8.1). Finally, some recent research has also explored the possibility of including persistent variables (for example near unit root processes) in threshold models. This literature was triggered by the work of Caner and Hansen (2001) who extended tests for threshold effects to models with unit root processes, but much more remains to be done in this area (see Pitarakis (2008), Gonzalo and Pitarakis (2012a, 2012b)).

3 ESTIMATION OF THRESHOLD MODELS AND FURTHER TESTS

The natural objective of an empirical investigation following the rejection of the null hypothesis of linearity is the estimation of the unknown true threshold parameter, say γ_0, together with the unknown slope coefficients β_{10} and β_{20}.

3.1 Threshold and Slope Parameter Estimation

The true model is now understood to be given by $y_t = x_{1t}(\gamma_0)'\beta_{10} + x_{2t}(\gamma_0)'\beta_{20} + u_t$ and our initial goal is the construction of a suitable estimator for γ_0. A natural choice is given by the least squares principle, which we write as

$$\hat{\gamma} = \arg\min_{\gamma \in \Gamma} S_T(\gamma) \tag{8.11}$$

with $S_T(\gamma)$ denoting the concentrated sum of squared errors function. In words, the least squares estimator of γ is the value of γ that minimizes $S_T(\gamma)$. It is also important to note that this argmin estimator is numerically equivalent to the value of γ that maximizes the *homoscedastic* Wald statistic for testing $H_0 : \beta_1 = \beta_2$, that is $\hat{\gamma} = \arg\max_\gamma W_T(\gamma)$ with $W_T(\gamma) = T(S_T - S_T(\gamma))/S_T(\gamma)$. From a practical viewpoint therefore $\hat{\gamma}$ is a natural by-product of the test procedure described earlier (see Appendix for a simple Gauss code for estimating $\hat{\gamma}$). We have

- Step 1: Record the index i = 1,. . .,T_s that maximizes W_T[i], say $\hat{i}$
- Step 2: $\hat{\gamma}$ is obtained as qss[$\hat{i}$].

The asymptotic properties of $\hat{\gamma}$ that have been explored in the literature have concentrated on its superconsistency properties together with its limiting distribution. Early work on these properties was completed in Chan (1993) in the context of SETAR-type threshold models (see also Koul and Qian, 2002). Chan (1993) established the important result of the T-consistency of $\hat{\gamma}$ in the sense that $T(\hat{\gamma} - \gamma_0) = O_p(1)$. This result was also obtained by Gonzalo and Pitarakis (2002) who concentrated on general threshold models with multiple regimes instead. Proving the consistency of the argmin estimator $\hat{\gamma}$ is typically done following a standard two-step approach. In a first instance it is important to show that the objective function, say $S_T(\gamma)/T$, satisfies

$$\sup_{\gamma \in \Gamma} \left| \frac{S_T(\gamma)}{T} - S_\infty(\gamma) \right| \xrightarrow{p} 0 \tag{8.12}$$

with $S_\infty(\gamma)$ denoting a non-stochastic limit with a unique minimum. The consistency of $\hat{\gamma}$ then follows by showing that $S_\infty(\gamma)$ is uniquely minimized at $\gamma = \gamma_0$, that is $S_\infty(\gamma) > S_\infty(\gamma_0)$ for $\gamma < \gamma_0$ and $S_\infty(\gamma) > S_\infty(\gamma_0)$ for $\gamma > \gamma_0$.

In Chan (1993) the author also obtained the limiting distribution of $T(\hat{\gamma} - \gamma_0)$, with the latter shown to be a function of a compound Poisson process. This limit did not lend itself to any practical inferences, however, since it was dependent on a large number of nuisance parameters besides being particularly difficult to simulate due to the presence of continuous time jump processes.

As a way out of these difficulties and for the purpose of developing a toolkit that can be used by practitioners, Hansen (2000) adopted an alternative parameterization of the threshold model that was then shown to lead to a convenient nuisance parameter-free limiting distribution for $\hat{\gamma}$. The price to pay for this more favourable limiting theory was a rate of convergence for $\hat{\gamma}$ that was slightly lower than T. The main idea behind Hansen's approach was to reparameterize the threshold model in (8.1) in such a way that the threshold effect vanishes with T in the sense that $\delta_T = \beta_2 - \beta_1 \to 0$ as $T \to \infty$. Assuming Gaussian errors and using this vanishing threshold framework, Hansen (2000) was able to obtain a convenient distribution theory for $\hat{\gamma}$ that is usable for conducting inferences and confidence interval construction. In particular, Hansen (2000) derived the limiting distribution of a likelihood ratio test for testing the null hypothesis $H_0 : \gamma = \gamma_0$ and showed it to be free of nuisance parameters provided that $\delta_T \to 0$ at a suitable rate. As mentioned earlier, the price to pay for this asymptotically vanishing threshold parameterization is the slightly slower convergence rate of $\hat{\gamma}$. More specifically $T^{1-2\alpha}(\hat{\gamma} - \gamma_0) = O_p(1)$ for $0 < \alpha < \frac{1}{2}$ which can be contrasted with the T-consistency documented under non-vanishing threshold effects. Note that here α is directly linked to the rate of decay of $\delta_T = \beta_2 - \beta_1 = c/T^\alpha$ so that the faster the threshold is allowed to vanish, the slower the ensuing convergence of $\hat{\gamma}$.

Hansen (2000) subsequently showed that a likelihood ratio-type test for testing the null hypothesis $H_0 : \gamma = \gamma_0$ takes a convenient and well known limiting expression that is free of nuisance parameters provided that u_t is assumed to be homoscedastic in the sense that $E[u_t^2|q_t] = \sigma_u^2$. More specifically, Hansen (2000) established that

$$LR_T(\gamma_0) \xrightarrow{d} \zeta \tag{8.13}$$

with $P(\zeta \leq x) = (1 - e^{-x/2})^2$. The practical implementation of the test is now trivial and can be performed in two simple steps. Suppose for instance that one wishes to test $H_0 : \gamma = 0$. This can be achieved as follows:

- Step 1: Construct $LR_T = T(S_T(\gamma = 0) - S_T(\hat{\gamma}))/S_T(\hat{\gamma})$ with $\hat{\gamma} = \text{argmin}_{\gamma \in \Gamma} S_T(\gamma)$.
- Step 2: The p-value corresponding to the test statistic is $p = 1 - (1 - e^{-LR_T/2})^2$.

Following the work of Hansen (2000) numerous authors explored the possibility of developing inferences about γ (for example confidence intervals) without the need to operate within a vanishing threshold framework with Gaussian errors and/or assuming error variances that cannot shift across regimes. In Gonzalo and Wolf (2005) the authors developed a flexible subsampling approach in the context of SETAR models, while more recently Li and Ling (2012) revisited the early work of Chan (1993) and explored the possibility of using simulation methods to make the compound Poisson type of limit usable for inferences. The above discussions have highlighted the important complications that are caused by the presence of the discontinuity induced by the threshold variable. This prompted Seo and Linton (2007) to propose an alternative approach for estimating the parameters of a threshold model that relies on replacing the indicator functions that appear in (8.2) with a smoothed function *à la* smoothed maximum score of Horowitz (1992).

Finally, following the availability of an estimator for γ, the remaining slope parameter estimators can be constructed in a straightforward manner as

$$\hat{\beta}_i(\hat{\gamma}) = (X_i(\hat{\gamma})'X_i(\hat{\gamma}))^{-1}X_i(\hat{\gamma})'y \tag{8.14}$$

for $i = 1,2$. An important result that follows from the consistency of $\hat{\gamma}$ and that makes inferences about the slopes simple to implement is the fact that $\hat{\beta}_i(\hat{\gamma})$ and $\hat{\beta}_i(\gamma_0)$ are asymptotically equivalent. More formally, we have $\sqrt{T}(\hat{\beta}_i(\hat{\gamma}) - \hat{\beta}_i(\gamma_0)) \xrightarrow{p} 0$ so that inferences about the slopes can proceed as if γ were known. Under conditional homoscedasticity, for instance, t-ratios can be constructed in the usual manner via the use of covariances given by $\hat{\sigma}^2_u(\hat{\gamma})\,(X_i(\hat{\gamma})'X_i(\hat{\gamma}))^{-1}$ with $\hat{\sigma}^2_u(\hat{\gamma}) = S_T(\hat{\gamma})/T$.

3.2 Finite Sample Properties

At this stage it is also useful to gain some insights on the behaviour of estimators such as $\hat{\gamma}$ and $\hat{\beta}_i(\hat{\gamma})$ in finite samples commonly encountered in economics. The bias and variability of $\hat{\gamma}$ is of particular importance since the asymptotics of $\hat{\beta}_i(\hat{\gamma})$ rely on the fact that we may proceed as if γ_0 were known. As noted in Hansen (2000) it is unlikely that we will ever encounter a scenario whereby $\hat{\gamma} = \gamma_0$, and taking this uncertainty into account in subsquent confidence intervals about the $\beta_i's$ becomes particulary important.

In order to evaluate the finite sample behaviour of the threshold and slope parameter estimators we consider a simple specification given by

$$y_t = \begin{cases} \beta_{10} + \beta_{11}x_{t-1} + u_t & q_{t-1} \leq \gamma_0 \\ \beta_{20} + \beta_{21}x_{t-1} + u_t & q_{t-1} > \gamma_0 \end{cases} \tag{8.15}$$

with $x_t = \phi_x x_{t-1} + v_t$ and $q_t = \phi_q q_{t-1} + e_t$. Letting $w_t = (u_t, v_t, e_t)$ we take $w_t \equiv NID(0, \Omega)$ and set $\Omega = \{(1, 0.5, -0.3), (0.3, 1.0.4), (-0.5, 0.4, 1)\}$ so as to allow for some dependence across the random shocks while satisfying the assumptions of the underlying distributional theory. Regarding the choice of parameters we use $\{\phi_q, \phi_x\} = \{0.5, 0.5\}$ throughout and set the threshold parameter $\gamma_0 = 0.25$.

Our initial goal is to assess the finite sample bias and variability of $\hat{\gamma} = \arg\min S_T(\gamma)$. For this purpose we distinguish between two scenarios of strong and weak threshold

Table 8.2 Finite sample properties of $\hat{\gamma}$ and $\hat{\beta}_i(\hat{\gamma})$

	$E(\hat{\gamma})$	$\sigma(\hat{\gamma})$	$E(\hat{\beta}_{10})$	$\sigma(\hat{\beta}_{10})$	$E(\hat{\beta}_{20})$	$\sigma(\hat{\beta}_{20})$	$E(\hat{\beta}_{11})$	$\sigma(\hat{\beta}_{11})$	$E(\hat{\beta}_{21})$	$\sigma(\hat{\beta}_{21})$
	Case 1 (*strong*): $\beta_{10} = 1, \beta_{20} = 2, \beta_{11} = 0.5, \beta_{12} = 1, \gamma_0 = 0.25$									
$T = 100$	0.227	0.183	0.991	0.142	2.012	0.199	0.515	0.138	1.009	0.163
$T = 200$	0.243	0.080	0.996	0.099	2.004	0.128	0.507	0.087	1.014	0.104
$T = 400$	0.246	0.034	0.999	0.069	2.000	0.087	0.502	0.059	1.004	0.073
	Case 2 (*weak*): $\beta_{10} = 1, \beta_{20} = 1, \beta_{11} = 0.5, \beta_{12} = 1, \gamma_0 = 0.25$									
$T = 100$	0.156	0.621	1.016	0.239	0.962	0.276	0.494	0.201	1.052	0.212
$T = 200$	0.219	0.396	0.994	0.126	0.981	0.156	0.489	0.109	1.041	0.131
$T = 400$	0.248	0.215	1.000	0.074	0.987	0.098	0.495	0.064	1.021	0.082

effects. Results for this experiment are presented in Table 8.2 which displays averages and standard deviations across N = 1000 replications.

The figures in Table 8.2 suggest that both the threshold and slope parameter estimators have good small sample properties as judged by their bias and variability. We note that $\hat{\gamma}$ has negligible finite sample bias even under small sample sizes such as T = 200. However, an interesting distinguishing feature of $\hat{\gamma}$ is its substantial variability relative to that characterizing the slope parameter estimators. Under the weak threshold scenario for instance and the moderately large sample size of T = 400, we note that $\sigma(\hat{\gamma}) \approx E(\hat{\gamma})$, whereas the standard deviations of the $\hat{\beta}_i(\hat{\gamma})'s$ are substantially smaller. It will be interesting in future work to explore alternative estimators that may have lower variability.

The above data generating process can also be used to assess the properties of the LR-based test for testing hypotheses about γ. Using the same parameterization as in Table 8.2 we next consider the finite sample size properties of the likelihood ratio test for testing $H_0 : \gamma = 0.25$. Results for this experiment are presented in Table 8.3, which contrasts nominal and empirical sizes. Empirical sizes have been estimated as the number of times (across N replications) that the estimated p-value is smaller than 1 per cent, 2.5 per cent and 5 per cent respectively. The scenario under consideration corresponds to Case 2 under a weak threshold parameterization.

Table 8.3 suggests an excellent match of theoretical and empirical sizes across a wide range of small to moderately large sample sizes. Note also that this happens under a rather weak threshold effect forcing solely the slope parameters to switch once q_{t-1} cross the value 0.25. It is also important to recall that the above inferences based on a nuisance

Table 8.3 Size Properties of the LR test for H_0: $\gamma = 0.25$

	0.010	0.025	0.050
$T = 100$	0.010	0.025	0.065
$T = 200$	0.017	0.030	0.065
$T = 400$	0.015	0.032	0.054
$T = 800$	0.010	0.024	0.055

parameter-free limiting distribution are valid solely under a homoscedasticity restriction forcing $E[u_t^2|q_t]$ to be constant.

4 GOING BEYOND THE STANDARD ASSUMPTIONS AND SUGGESTIONS FOR FURTHER WORK

The various methods for detecting the presence of threshold effects and subsequently estimating the model parameters that we reviewed above crucially depend on the stationarity and ergodicity of the series being modelled. It is indeed interesting to note that, despite the enormous growth of the unit root literature, the vast majority of the research agenda on exploring non-linearities in economic data has operated under the assumption of stationarity, highlighting the fact that non-stationarity and non-linearities have been mainly treated in isolation. In fact one could also argue that they have often been viewed as mutually exclusive phenomena with an important strand of the literature arguing that neglected non-linearities may be the underlying cause of the observed persistence in numerous series.

One area through which threshold specifications entered the world of unit roots is through the concept of cointegration, a statistical counterpart to the notion of a long-run equilibrium linking two or more variables. This naturally avoided the technical problems one may face when interacting non-linearities with non-stationarities, since cointegrated relationships are by definition stationary processes and their residuals can be interpreted as mean-reverting equilibrium errors whose dynamics may describe the adjustment process to the long-run equilibrium. Consider for instance two I(1) variables y_t and x_t and assume that they are cointegrated in the sense that the equilibrium error z_t is such that $|\rho| < 1$ in

$$y_t = \beta x_t + z_t$$

$$z_t = \rho z_{t-1} + u_t. \tag{8.16}$$

Researchers such as Balke and Fomby (1997) proposed to use threshold type specifications for error correction terms for capturing the idea that adjustments to long-run equilibria may be characterized by discontinuities or that there may be periods during which the speed of adjustment to equilibrium (summarized by ρ) may be slower or faster depending on how far we are from the equilibrium, or alternatively depending on some external variable summarizing the state of the economy. More formally the equilibrium error or error correction term can be formulated as

$$\Delta \hat{z}_t = \begin{cases} \rho_1 \hat{z}_{t-1} + v_t & q_{t-1} \leq \gamma \\ \rho_2 \hat{z}_{t-1} + v_t & q_{t-1} > \gamma \end{cases} \tag{8.17}$$

with $\hat{z}_t = y_t - \hat{\beta} x_t$ typically taken as the threshold variable q_t. Naturally one could also incorporate more complicated dynamics to the right-hand side of (8.17) in a manner similar to an Augmented Dickey–Fuller regression. The natural hypothesis to test in this context is again that of linear adjustment versus threshold adjustment via $H_0 : \rho_1 = \rho_2$.

This simple example highlights a series of important issues that triggered a rich body of literature on testing for the presence of non-linear dynamics in error correction models. First, the above framework assumes that y_t and x_t are *known* to be cointegrated so that z_t is stationary under both the null and alternative hypotheses being tested. In principle therefore the theory developed in Hansen (1996) should hold and standard tests discussed earlier should be usable (see also Enders and Siklos, 2001). Another difficulty with the specification of a SETAR type of model for $\hat{z}_t$ is that its stationarity properties are still not very well understood beyond some simple cases (see Chan and Tong, 1985 and Caner and Hansen, 2001, pp. 1567–8).[1]

One complication with alternative tests such as $H_0 : \rho_1 = \rho_2 = 0$ is that under this null the threshold variable (when $q_t \equiv \hat{z}_t$) is no longer stationary. It is our understanding that some of these issues are still in need of a rigorous methodological research agenda. Note for instance that fitting a threshold model to $\hat{z}_t$ in (8.17) involves using a generated variable via $y_t - \hat{\beta} x_t$ unless one is willing to assume that the cointegrating vector is known.

Perhaps a more intuitive and rigorous framework for handling all of the above issues is to operate within a multivariate vector error correction setting *à la* Johansen. Early research in this area has been developed in Hansen and Seo (2002) who proposed a test of the null hypothesis of linear versus threshold adjustment in the context of a vector error correction model (VECM). Assuming a VECM with a single cointegrating relationship and a known cointegrating vector, Hansen and Seo (2002) showed that the limiting theory developed in Hansen (1996) continues to apply in this setting. However, and as recognized by the authors, the validity of the distributional theory under an estimated cointegrating vector is unclear. These two points are directly relevant to our earlier claim about testing $H_0 : \rho_1 = \rho_2$ in (8.17). If we are willing to operate under a known β then the theory of Hansen (1996) applies, and inferences can be implemented using a $\sup_\gamma W_T(\gamma)$ or similar test statistic.

In Seo (2006) the author concentrates on the null hypothesis of no linear cointegration which would correspond to testing the joint null hypothesis $H_0 : \rho_1 = \rho_2 = 0$ within our earlier ECM specification. Seo's work clearly highlights the impact that a non-stationary threshold variable has since under this null hypothesis the error correction term used as the threshold variable is also I(1), and Hansen's (1996) distributional framework is no longer valid. It is also worth emphasizing that Seo's distributional results operate under the assumption of a known cointegrating vector. In a more recent paper Seo (2011) explores in greater depth the issue of an unknown cointegrating vector and derives a series of large sample results about $\hat{\beta}$ and $\hat{\gamma}$ via a smoothed indicator function approach along the same lines as Seo and Linton (2007).

Overall there is much that remains to be done. We can note for instance that all of the above research operated under the assumption that threshold effects were relevant solely in the adjustment process to the long-run equilibrium with the latter systematically assumed to be given by a single linear cointegrating regression. An economically interesting feature that could greatly enhance the scope of the VECMs is the possibility of allowing the cointegrating vectors also to be characterized by threshold effects. This would be particularly interesting for the statistical modelling of *switching equilibria*. Preliminary work in this context can be found in Gonzalo and Pitarakis (2006a, 2006b).

5 CONCLUSIONS

The purpose of this chapter was to provide a comprehensive methodological overview of the econometrics of threshold models as used by economists in applied work. We started our review with the most commonly used methods for detecting threshold effects and subsequently moved towards the techniques for estimating the unknown model parameters. Finally we also briefly surveyed how the originally developed stationary threshold specifications have evolved to also include unit root variables for the purpose of capturing economically interesting phenomena such as asymmetric adjustment to equilibrium. Despite the enormous methodological developments over the past ten to twenty years this line of research is still in its infancy. Important new developments should include the full development of an estimation and testing methodology for threshold VARs similar to Johansen's linear VAR analysis, together with a full representation theory that could allow for switches in both the cointegrating vectors and their associated adjustment process. As discussed in Gonzalo and Pitarakis (2006a, 2006b) such developments are further complicated by the fact that it is difficult to associate a formal definition of threshold cointegration with the rank properties of VAR-based long-run impact matrices, as is the case in linearly cointegrated VARs.

NOTES

* Financial support from the ESRC is gratefully acknowledged.

1. Caner and Hansen (2001) was in fact one of the first papers that sought to combine the presence of unit root type of non-stationarities and threshold type non-linear dynamics. Their main contribution was the development of a new asymptotic theory for detecting the presence of threshold effects in a series which was restricted to be a unit root process under the null of linearity (for example testing $H_0 : \beta_1 = \beta_2$ in $\Delta y_t = \beta_1 y_{t-1} I(q_{t-1} \leq \gamma) + \beta_2 y_{t-1} I(q_{t-1} > \gamma) + u_t$ with $q_t \equiv \Delta y_{t-k}$ for some $k \geq 1$ when under the null of linearity we have $\Delta y_t = u_t$ so that y_t is a pure unit root process). Pitarakis (2008) has shown that when the fitted threshold model contains solely deterministic regressors such as a constant and deterministic trend together with the unit root regressor y_{t-1} the limiting distribution of $\max_i \mathrm{W}_T[\mathrm{i}]$ takes a familiar form given by a normalized quadratic form in Brownian Bridges and readily tabulated in Hansen (1997). Caner and Hansen (2001) also explore further tests such as $H_0 : \beta_1 = \beta_2 = 0$ which are directly relevant for testing $H_0 : \rho_1 = \rho_2 = 0$ in the above error correction model (ECM).

REFERENCES

Altissimo, F. and G.L. Violante (1999), 'The nonlinear dynamics of output and unemployment in the US', *Journal of Applied Econometrics*, **16**, 461–86.

Andrews, D.K.W. (1993), 'Tests for parameter instability and structural change with unknown change point', *Econometrica*, **61**, 821–56.

Balke, N. (2000), 'Credit and economics activity: credit regimes and nonlinear propagation of shocks', *Review of Economics and Statistics*, **82**, 344–9.

Balke, N. and T. Fomby (1997), 'Threshold cointegration', *International Economic Review*, **38**, 627–45.

Beaudry, P. and G. Koop (1993), 'Do recessions permanently change output?', *Journal of Monetary Economics*, **31**, 149–64.

Benhabib, J. (2010), 'Regime switching, monetary policy and multiple equilibria', unpublished manuscript, Department of Economics, New York University.

Borenstein, S., A.C. Cameron and R. Gilbert (1997), 'Do gasoline prices respond asymmetrically to crude oil price changes?', *Quarterly Journal of Economics*, **112**, 305–39.

Caner, M. and B.E. Hansen (2001), 'Threshold autoregression with a unit root', *Econometrica*, **69**, 1555–96.

Chan, K.S. (1990), 'Testing for threshold autoregression', *Annals of Statistics*, **18**, 1886–94.
Chan, K.S. (1991), 'Percentage points of likelihood ratio tests for threshold autoregression', *Journal of the Royal Statistical Society, Series B*, **53**, 691–6.
Chan, K.S. (1993), 'Consistency and limiting distribution of the least squares estimator of a threshold autoregressive model', *Annals of Statistics*, **21**, 520–33.
Chan, K.S. and H. Tong (1985), 'On the use of the deterministic Lyapunov function for the ergodicity of stochastic difference equations', *Advances in Applied Probability*, **17**, 666–78.
Davies, R.B. (1977), 'Hypothesis testing when a nuisance parameter is present only under the alternative', *Biometrika*, **64**, 247–54.
Davies, R.B. (1987), 'Hypothesis testing when a nuisance parameter is present only under the alternative', *Biometrika*, **74**, 33–43.
Davig, T. and E.M. Leeper (2007), 'Generalizing the Taylor principle', *American Economic Review*, **97**, 607–35.
Enders, W. and P.L. Siklos (2001), 'Cointegration and threshold adjustment', *Journal of Business and Economic Statistics*, **19**, 166–76.
Farmer, R.E.A, D.F. Waggoner and T. Zha (2009), 'Indeterminacy in a forward-looking regime switching model', *International Journal of Economic Theory*, **5**, 69–84.
Gonzalo, J. and J. Pitarakis (2002), 'Estimation and model selection based inference in single and multiple threshold models', *Journal of Econometrics*, **110**, 319–52.
Gonzalo, J. and J. Pitarakis (2006a), 'Threshold effects in cointegrating relationships', *Oxford Bulletin of Economics and Statistics*, **68**, 813–33.
Gonzalo, J. and J. Pitarakis (2006b), 'Threshold effects in multivariate error correction models', Chapter 18 in T.C. Mills and K. Patterson (eds), *Palgrave Handbook of Econometrics: Econometric Theory*, Volume 1, Basingstoke: Palgrave Macmillan.
Gonzalo, J. and J. Pitarakis (2012a), 'Detecting episodic predictability induced by a persistent variable', unpublished manuscript, Economics Division, University of Southampton.
Gonzalo, J. and J. Pitarakis (2012b), 'Regime specific predictability in predictive regressions', *Journal of Business and Economic Statistics*, **30**, 229–41.
Gonzalo, J. and M. Wolf (2005), 'Subsampling inference in threshold autoregressive models', *Journal of Econometrics*, **127**, 201–24.
Gospodinov, N. (2005), 'Testing for threshold nonlinearity in short-term interest rates', *Journal of Financial Econometrics*, **3**, 344–71.
Gospodinov, N. (2008), 'Asymptotic and bootstrap tests for linearity in a TAR-GARCH(1,1) model with a unit root', *Journal of Econometrics*, **146**, 146–61.
Granger, C.W.J. and T. Terasvirta (1993), *Modelling Nonlinear Economic Relationships*, Oxford: Oxford University Press.
Griffin, J.M., F. Nardari and R.M. Stultz (2007), 'Do investors trade more when stocks have performed well? evidence from 46 countries', *Review of Financial Studies*, **20**, 905–51.
Hamilton, J.D. (1989), 'A new approach to the economic analysis of nonstationary time series and the business cycle', *Econometrica*, **57**, 357–84.
Hamilton, J.D. (2011), 'Calling recessions in real time', *International Journal of Forecasting*, **27**, 1006–26.
Hansen, B.E. (1996), 'Inference when a nuisance parameter is not identified under the null hypothesis', *Econometrica*, **64**, 413–30.
Hansen, B.E. (1997), 'Inference in TAR models', *Studies in Nonlinear Dynamics and Econometrics*, **2**, 1–14.
Hansen, B.E. (1999), 'Testing for linearity', *Journal of Economic Surveys*, **13**, 551–76.
Hansen, B.E. (2000), 'Sample splitting and threshold estimation', *Econometrica*, **68**, 575–603.
Hansen, B.E. (2011), 'Threshold autoregressions in economics', *Statistics and Its Interface*, **4**, 123–7.
Hansen, B.E. and B. Seo (2002), 'Testing for two-regime threshold cointegration in vector error correction models', *Journal of Econometrics*, **110**, 293–318.
Horowitz, J.L. (1992), 'A smoothed maximum score estimator for the binary response model', *Econometrica*, **60**, 505–31.
Koop, G. and S.M. Potter (1999), 'Dynamic asymmetries in US unemployment', *Journal of Business and Economic Statistics*, **17**, 298–312.
Koop, G., H.M. Pesaran and S.M. Potter (1996), 'Impulse response analysis in nonlinear multivariate models', *Journal of Econometrics*, **74**, 119–47.
Koul, L.H. and L.F. Qian (2002), 'Asymptotics of maximum likelihood estimator in a two-phase linear regression model', *Journal of Statistical Planning and Inference*, **108**, 99–119.
Leeper, E.M. and T. Zha (2003), 'Modest policy interventions', *Journal of Monetary Economics*, **50**, 1673–700.
Li, D. and S. Ling (2012), 'On the least squares estimation of multiple-regime threshold autoregressive models', *Journal of Econometrics*, **167**, 240–53.
Lo, M.C. and E. Zivot (2001), 'Threshold cointegration and nonlinear adjustment to the law of one price', *Macroeconomic Dynamics*, **5**, 533–76.

Obstfeld, M. and A. Taylor (1997), 'Nonlinear aspects of goods market arbitrage and adjustment', *Journal of Japanese and International Economics*, **11**, 441–79.
O'Connell, P.G.J. and S. Wei (1997), 'The bigger they are the harder they fall: how price differences across US cities are arbitraged', *NBER Working Paper No. W6089.*
Perez-Quiros, G. and A. Timmermann (2000), 'Firm size and cyclical variations in stock returns', *Journal of Finance*, **55**, 1229–62.
Petruccelli, J.D. (1992), 'On the approximation of time series by threshold autoregressive models', *Sankhya, Series B*, **54**, 54–61.
Petruccelli, J.D. and N. Davies (1986), 'A portmanteau test for self-exciting threshold autoregressive-type nonlinearity in time series', *Biometrika*, **73**, 687–94.
Pitarakis, J. (2008), 'Comment on: Threshold autoregressions with a unit root', *Econometrica*, **76**, 1207–17.
Potter, S.M. (1995), 'A nonlinear approach to US GNP', *Journal of Applied Econometrics*, **2**, 109–25.
Seo, M.H. (2006), 'Bootstrap testing for the null of no cointegration in a threshold vector error correction model', *Journal of Econometrics*, **134**, 129–50.
Seo, M.H. (2011), 'Estimation of nonlinear error correction models', *Econometric Theory*, **27**, 201–34.
Seo, M.H. and O. Linton (2007), 'A smoothed least squares estimator for threshold regression models', *Journal of Econometrics*, **141**, 704–35.
Terasvirta, T., D. Tjostheim and C.W.J. Granger (2010), *Modelling Nonlinear Economic Time Series*, New York: Oxford University Press.
Tong, H. (1983), *Threshold Models in Non-Linear Time Series Analysis: Lecture Notes in Statistics*, **21**, Berlin: Springer-Verlag.
Tong, H. (1990), *Non-Linear Time Series: A Dynamical System Approach,* Oxford: Oxford University Press.
Tong, H. and K.S. Lim (1980), 'Threshold autoregression, limit cycles and cyclical data', *Journal of The Royal Statistical Society, Series B*, **4**, 245–92.
Tsay, R.S. (1989), 'Testing and modeling threshold autoregressive processes', *Journal of the American Statistical Association*, **84**, 231–40.
Tsay, R.S. (1991), 'Detecting and modeling nonlinearity in univariate time series analysis', *Statistica Sinica*, **1**, 431–51.
Tsay, R.S. (1998), 'Testing and modeling multivariate threshold models', *Journal of the American Statistical Association*, **93**, 1188–202.
Van der Vaart, A.W. and J.A. Wellner (1996), *Weak Convergence and Empirical Processes*, New York: Springer-Verlag.
Wong, C.S. and W.K. Li (1997), 'Testing of threshold autoregression with conditional heteroscedasticity', *Biometrika*, **84**, 407–18.

APPENDIX

The code below estimates the threshold parameter $\hat{\gamma} = \arg\min_{\gamma} S_T(\gamma)$ using the specification in (8.15). It takes as inputs the variables $y \equiv y_t$, $x \equiv x_{t-1}$ and $q_t \equiv q_{t-1}$ and outputs $\hat{\gamma}$. The user also needs to input the desired percentage of data trimming used in the determination of Γ (for example trimper=0.10).

```
proc gamhatLS(y,x,q,trimper);
local   t,qs,top,bot,qss,sigsq1,r,xmat1,xmat2,thetahat,zmat,
  res1,idx;
t=rows(y); /* sample size */
qs=sortc(q[1:t-1],1); /* threshold variable */
top=t*trimper;
bot=t*(1-trimper);
qss=qs[top+1:bot]; /* Sorted and Trimmed Threshold Variable
  */
sigsq1=zeros(rows(qss),1); /* Initialisation: Defining some
  vector of length (bot-top) */
r=1; /* Looping over all possible values of qss */
do while r<=rows(qss);
xmat1=ones(t-1,1).*(q[1:t-1].<=qss[r])~x[1:t-1].*(q[1:t-1].
  <=qss[r]);
xmat2=ones(t-1,1).*(q[1:t-1].>qss[r])~x[1:t-1].*(q[1:t-1].
  >qss[r]);
zmat=xmat1~xmat2;
thetahat=invpd(zmat'zmat)*zmat'y[2:t];
res1=y[2:t]-zmat*thetahat;
sigsq1[r]=res1'res1;  /* Residual Sum of Squares for each
  possible value of qss */
r=r+1;
endo;
idx=minindc(sigsq1); /* Fetch the index where the smallest
  value of sigsq1 is located */
retp(qss[idx]); /* Returns the threshold parameter estimator
  */
endp;
```

9 Testing structural stability in macroeconometric models*

Otilia Boldea and Alastair R. Hall

1 INTRODUCTION

Since the earliest days of macroeconometric analysis, researchers have been concerned about the appropriateness of the assumption that model parameters remain constant over long periods of time; for example see Tinbergen (1939).[1] This concern is also central to the so-called Lucas (1976) critique which has played a central role in shaping macroeconometric analysis in the last thirty years. Lucas (1976) emphasizes the fact that the decision models of economic agents are hard to describe in terms of stable parameterizations, simply because changes in policy may change these decision models and their respective parameterization. These arguments underscore the importance of using structural stability tests as diagnostic checks for macroeconometric models.

A large body of empirical macroeconomic studies provides evidence for parameter instability in a variety of macroeconomic models. For example, considerable evidence exists that the New Keynesian Phillips curve has become flat and/or less persistent in recent years; see for example Alogoskoufis and Smith (1991), Cogley and Sargent (2001), Zhang et al. (2008), Kang et al. (2009). Similarly, there is evidence that the interest rate reaction function is asymmetric over the business cycle; see for example Boivin and Giannoni (2006), Surico (2007), Benati and Surico (2008), Liu et al. (2009). Examples of parameter instability are not confined to monetary policy, but also extend to: growth models (Ben-David et al., 2003); output models (Perron, 1997, Hansen, 1992); exchange rate models (Rossi, 2006); unemployment rate models (Weber, 1995, Papell et al., 2000, Hansen, 1997b), and many more. If such instabilities are ignored in the estimation procedure, they lead to incorrect policy recommendations and flawed macroeconomic forecasts.

Thus, it is essential – and it has become common practice – to test for instability in macroeconomic models. Instabilities can be of many types. In this chapter, we describe econometric tests for three main types of instability: *parameter breaks*, *other parameter instabilities* and *model instabilities*.

The first category, *parameter breaks*, focuses on sudden parameter changes. It may be desired to test for change that occurs at a particular time. In this case, the time of change, called *break-point* in econometrics and *change-point* in statistics, is said to be known. It can also be that it is desired to test for change at some unspecified point in the sample. In this case, the break-point is said to be unknown. We discuss tests for both a known and an unknown break. We also present methods for detecting multiple break-points, and their practical implementation.

For the second category, *other parameter instabilities*, we give a brief but thorough account of the state-of-the-art tests for threshold models, smooth transition models and Markov-switching models.

In practice, there is no reason to assume that only parameters change, while the underlying functional form stays the same. Therefore, the third category of tests we describe is for *model instabilities*, when the functional form of the model is allowed to change after a known or unknown break.

In macroeconomics, the tests we present are often viewed as tests for Lucas critique. Lucas critique, at the time it was written, was directed against the use of backward-looking expectations, which did not take into account that agents will change their decision making when policy changes occur, leading to parameter or model instability. However, as Estrella and Fuhrer (2003) point out, using forward-looking expectations that incorporate certain policy changes does not make a model immune either to Lucas critique or to parameter or model instability. To see this, note that even if a structural model of the economy exists – with forward-looking behaviour, based on solid microeconomic foundations, with important policy functions specified – it is unclear whether one can derive the complete model, or estimate it in practice. Any simplification, parameter calibration, omission or misspecification of relevant policy functions and other agent decisions can lead to parameter or model instability. Thus, even though it is often stated that Lucas critique implies that only reduced-form models suffer from instability (see for instance Lubik and Surico, 2010), in practice all models are prone to this problem and need to be tested for instability.[2]

In this chapter, we discuss Wald-type tests for breaks that are based on least-squares (LS) type methods, suitable for reduced-form models, and also on two-stage least-squares (2SLS) and generalized method of moments (GMM) estimation, more suitable for structural models. The chapter is organized as follows. In section 2, we present structural stability tests for a single break based on GMM estimation. In section 3, we discuss testing strategies for multiple break-points. Section 4 provides a brief but thorough account of tests for other types of parameter instability, with comments on the most recent developments in this literature. Section 5 focuses on testing for model instabilities rather than parameter instabilities. Section 6 concludes.

2 TESTING FOR DISCRETE PARAMETER CHANGE AT A SINGLE POINT

In this section, we summarize the literature on testing for discrete parameter change in macroeconometric models based on GMM. GMM provides a method for estimation of the parameters of a macroeconomic model based on the information in a population moment condition. GMM is described elsewhere in this Handbook, see Chapter 14 by Alastair Hall, and so here we assume knowledge of the basic GMM framework. For ease of reference, we adopt the same generic notation as in Chapter 14: thus, the population moment condition is written as $E[f(v_t, \theta_0)] = 0$ in which θ_0 denotes the true value of the $p \times 1$ parameter, v_t is a random vector, and $f(\cdot)$ is a $q \times 1$ vector of continuous differentiable functions.[3] The sample is assumed to consist of observations on $\{v_t, t = 1, 2, \ldots T\}$.

As befits the GMM framework, the null and alternative hypotheses are expressed in terms of the population moment condition. The null hypothesis is that the population moment condition holds at the same parameter value throughout the sample. The alternative of interest here is that the population moment condition holds at one value of the parameters up until a particular point in the sample, called break-point, after which the population moment condition holds at a different parameter value. To formally present the hypotheses of interest here, we need a notation for the break-point. Following the convention in the literature, we let λ be a constant defined on $(0, 1)$ and let $[T\lambda]$ denote the potential break-point at which some aspect of the model changes.[4] For our purposes here, it is convenient to divide the original sample into two subsamples. Subsample 1 consists of the observations before the break-point, namely $\mathcal{T}_1(\lambda) = \{1, 2, \ldots, [\lambda T]\}$, and subsample 2 consists of the observations after the break-point, $\mathcal{T}_2(\lambda) = \{[\lambda T] + 1, \ldots T\}$.

As mentioned in the introduction, this break-point may be treated as *known* or *unknown* in the construction of the tests. If it is known, then the break-point is specified a priori by the researcher and it is only desired to test for instability at this point alone. For example, Clarida et al. (2000) investigate whether the monetary policy reaction function of the Federal Reserve Board is different during the tenure of different chairmen. Of particular interest in their study is whether or not the reaction function is different pre- and post-1979, the year Paul Volcker was appointed as Chairman. Since their analysis uses quarterly data, this involves exploring whether or not there is parameter change at the fixed break date with $[T\lambda] = 1979.2$. If the break-point is unknown, the alternative is the broader hypothesis that there is parameter change at some point in the sample. We begin our discussion with the simpler case in which the break-point is known, and then consider the extension to the unknown break-point case.

For a fixed break-point indexed by λ, the null hypothesis of interest can be expressed mathematically as

$$H_0: E[f(v_t, \theta_0)] = 0, \qquad \text{for } t = 1, 2, \ldots, T, \tag{9.1}$$

and the alternative hypothesis as

$$H_1(\lambda): \begin{array}{ll} E[f(v_t, \theta_1)] = 0, & \text{for } t \in \mathcal{T}_1(\lambda) \\ E[f(v_t, \theta_2)] = 0, & \text{for } t \in \mathcal{T}_2(\lambda), \end{array}$$

where $\theta_1 \neq \theta_2$.

This statement of the alternative allows all elements of the parameter vector to change; this scenario is referred to in the literature as 'pure structural change'. It is also possible to restrict attention to an alternative in which only certain elements of the parameter vector are allowed to change with the remainder taking the same value before and after the break-point; this scenario is referred to as 'partial structural change'. Given space limitations, we focus on the case of pure structural change, which is arguably of most practical interest. We note parenthetically that all the methods discussed can be adapted to test for partial structural change in a relatively straightforward fashion, and that the qualitative discussion of the properties of the tests below also extends to those for partial structural change.

Andrews and Fair (1988) propose Wald, Lagrange Multiplier (LM) and Difference

(D) statistics to test H_0 versus $H_1(\lambda)$. These statistics are actually derived by applying the test principles concerned to a different but equivalent specification of the null and alternative hypothesis in terms of a set of linear restrictions on an augmented parameter vector that indexes an augmented population moment condition. Since all three statistics have the same limiting properties under null and local alternatives, we focus exclusively on the Wald statistic and use it to discuss issues common to all three tests. As emerges below, the Wald statistic has an appealing intuitive structure that can be motivated without appealing to Andrews and Fair's (1988) framework involving augmented parameter vectors and moments; we therefore do not describe their approach, leaving the interested reader to refer to their paper or to Hall (2005, Chapter 5.4).

The form of the Wald statistic can be motivated as follows. The null hypothesis is that the parameters take the same value before and after the break-point, and the alternative hypothesis is that the parameters take a different value before and after the break-point. Given this structure, a natural way to assess which is true is to estimate the parameters based on the observations in $\mathcal{T}_1(\lambda)$ and $\mathcal{T}_2(\lambda)$ separately and then compare these estimators. If the null is true there should be no difference between them – allowing for sampling variation – while if the alternative is true, there should be a difference. This is the essence of the Wald statistic.

To present the formula for the statistic, we require certain notation. For $i = 1, 2$, let $g_{i,T}(\theta;\lambda) = T^{-1}\Sigma_{t\in\mathcal{T}_i(\lambda)} f(v_t, \theta)$, where $\Sigma_{t\in\mathcal{T}_i(\lambda)}$ denotes summation over t for all values in $\mathcal{T}_i(\lambda)$, $G_{i,T}(\theta;\lambda) = \partial g_{i,T}(\theta;\lambda)/\partial\theta'$, $S_i(\lambda) = \lim_{T\to\infty} Var[T^{1/2} g_{i,T}(\theta;\lambda)]$ and $S_{i,T}(\lambda)$ be a consistent estimator for $S_i(\lambda)$. The subsample parameter estimators referred to in the previous paragraph are calculated in the following way.

Definition 1 For $i = 1, 2$, $\hat{\theta}_{i,T}(\lambda)$ is defined to be the GMM estimator of θ_i based on the population moment condition $E[f(v_t, \theta_i)] = 0$ calculated from observations in $\mathcal{T}_i(\lambda)$ and using weighting matrix $W_{i,T} = \{S_{i,T}(\lambda)\}^{-1}$.

In the literature, $\hat{\theta}_{i,T}(\lambda)$, $i = 1, 2$, are often referred to as 'partial-sum' GMM estimators because they are based on the part of the sample, either up to or after the break-point. Notice that the specified choice of weighting matrix is optimal, and that in practice the estimators would be obtained using a two-step or iterated estimation; see Chapter 14 in this volume for further details.

The Wald test statistic is as follows:

$$\mathcal{W}_T(\lambda) = T[\hat{\theta}_{1,T}(\lambda) - \hat{\theta}_{2,T}(\lambda)]'\hat{V}_W(\lambda)^{-1}[\hat{\theta}_{1,T}(\lambda) - \hat{\theta}_{2,T}(\lambda)], \tag{9.2}$$

where, using $\hat{\theta}_i = \hat{\theta}_{i,T}(\lambda)$ for ease of notation,

$$\hat{V}_W(\lambda) = [G_{1,T}(\hat{\theta}_1;\lambda)' W_{1,T}(\lambda) G_{1,T}(\hat{\theta}_1;\lambda)]^{-1}$$

$$+ [G_{2,T}(\hat{\theta}_2;\lambda)' W_{2,T}(\lambda) G_{2,T}(\hat{\theta}_2;\lambda)]^{-1}. \tag{9.3}$$

The limiting distribution of the Wald statistic under the null hypothesis is given in the following proposition:

Proposition 1 If certain regularity conditions hold then under H_0, $\mathcal{W}_T(\lambda) \xrightarrow{d} \chi^2_p$.

The regularity conditions referred to in Proposition 1 are the same as those needed for the standard first order asymptotic theory of GMM estimators (see Andrews and Fair, 1988 or Hall, 2005, Chapter 5.4). They include the crucial assumptions that v_t is non-trending, the function $f(v_t, \cdot)$ is smooth in θ, and that the parameters are identified.[5]

As anticipated in our motivation of the test above, the test statistic behaves very differently under $H_1(\lambda)$. For in this case, we have

$$\hat{\theta}_{1,T}(\lambda) - \hat{\theta}_{2,T}(\lambda) \xrightarrow{p} \theta_1 - \theta_2 = \mu(\lambda),$$

say, with $\mu(\lambda) \neq 0$ because $\theta_1 \neq \theta_2$. As a result, it can be shown that $\mathcal{W}_T(\lambda)$ diverges as $T \to \infty$, in consequence of which $\mathcal{W}_T(\lambda)$ is said to be a *consistent* test of $H_0(\lambda)$ versus $H_1(\lambda)$.[6]

While the statistic is designed to test for parameter change at a particular point in the sample and is consistent against that alternative, caution needs to be exercised in interpreting the outcome of the test. To see why, we now consider the behaviour of $\mathcal{W}_T(\lambda)$ if the parameters do not change at $[T\lambda]$ but *do* change at some other point in the sample. Let this true break-point be indexed by λ^* and, for sake of argument, assume $\lambda^* > \lambda$, that is, $\mathcal{W}_T(\lambda)$ is designed to test for parameter change at a point in the sample before it actually occurs. Further assume the population moment condition is satisfied at θ_1^* for observations $t \leq [T\lambda^*]$, and is satisfied at θ_2^* for observations $t > [T\lambda^*]$. In this case, $\mathcal{T}_1(\lambda)$ contains observations for which $E[f(v_t, \theta_1^*)] = 0$, and so $\hat{\theta}_{1,T}(\lambda) \xrightarrow{p} \theta_1^*$; but $\mathcal{T}_2(\lambda)$ contains some observations for which $E[f(v_t, \theta_1^*)] = 0$ and some for which $E[f(v_t, \theta_2^*)] = 0$, and, as a result, it can be shown that $\hat{\theta}_{2,T}(\lambda) \xrightarrow{p} h(\theta_1^*, \theta_2^*)$ for some function $h(\cdot, \cdot)$. Therefore, under this scenario, we have

$$\hat{\theta}_{1,T}(\lambda) - \hat{\theta}_{2,T}(\lambda) \xrightarrow{p} \theta_1^* - h(\theta_1^*, \theta_2^*) = \mu^*(\lambda, \lambda^*), \text{ say.}$$

In general, $\mu^*(\lambda, \lambda^*) \neq 0$, and so by similar arguments to the above the test diverges in this case as well.[7] Thus in the limit, the test rejects with probability 1 when T is large even if the wrong break-point has been specified under the alternative. In finite samples, the impact is less clear because – loosely speaking – $h(\theta_1^*, \theta_2^*)$ is a weighted average of θ_1^* and θ_2^*: if $h(\theta_1^*, \theta_2^*)$ is close to θ_2^* then the test is more likely to reject than if $h(\theta_1^*, \theta_2^*)$ is close to θ_1^* *ceteris paribus*. Either way, the possibility of parameter change at other points in the sample complicates the interpretation of the outcome of the fixed break-point test, and motivates the use of the unknown break-point tests to which we now turn.

If the break-point is unknown, then it is necessary to test whether there is evidence of instability at any point in the sample. However, in practice, it is necessary to limit attention to potential breaks indexed by λ values within a closed subset of the unit interval that is, $\lambda \in \Lambda = [\lambda_l, \lambda_u] \subset [0, 1]$. The choice of Λ is critical and typically governed by two main considerations: on the one hand, given the alternative of interest, it is desirable for Λ to be as wide as possible; on the other hand, it must not be so wide that asymptotic theory is a poor approximation in the subsamples. In applications to models of economic time series, it has become customary to use Λ equal to $[0.15, 0.85]$ or (less often) $[0.20, 0.80]$. The null hypothesis is again H_0 in (9.1). The alternative is

$$H_1(\Lambda) = H_1(\lambda) \quad \text{holds for some } \lambda \in \Lambda.$$

The construction of statistics for testing H_0 versus $H_1(\Lambda)$ is a natural extension of the fixed break-point methods. In this setting, $\mathcal{W}_T(\lambda)$ is calculated for each possible λ to produce a sequence of statistics indexed by λ, and inference is based on some function of this sequence.[8] Three functions of this sequence have become popular in the literature and these lead to the so-called 'Sup-, 'Av-' and 'Exp-' statistics which are respectively given by,[9]

$$Sup\mathcal{W}_T = \sup_{\lambda \in \Lambda} \{\mathcal{W}_T(\lambda)\},$$

$$Av\mathcal{W}_T = \int_\Lambda \mathcal{W}_T(\lambda) dJ(\lambda),$$

$$Exp\mathcal{W}_T = \log\left\{\int_\Lambda \exp[0.5\mathcal{W}_T(\lambda)] dJ(\lambda)\right\},$$

where $J(\lambda) = (\lambda_u - \lambda_l)^{-1} d\lambda$. As they stand, these statistics are not operational because we have treated λ as continuous, whereas in practice it is discrete. For a given sample size, the set of possible break-points are $\mathcal{T}_b = \{i/T;\ i = [\lambda_l T], [\lambda_l T] + 1, \ldots, [\lambda_u T]\}$. So in practice, inference is based on the discrete analogs to $Sup\mathcal{W}_T$, $Av\mathcal{W}_T$ and $Exp\mathcal{W}_T$:

$$Sup\mathcal{W}_T = \sup_{i \in \mathcal{T}_b} \{\mathcal{W}_T(i/T)\}$$

$$Av\mathcal{W}_T = d_b^{-1} \sum_{i=[\lambda_l T]}^{[\lambda_u T]} \mathcal{W}_T(i/T)$$

$$Exp\mathcal{W}_T = \log\left\{d_b^{-1} \sum_{i=[\lambda_l T]}^{[\lambda_u T]} \exp[0.5\mathcal{W}_T(i/T)]\right\}$$

where $d_b = [\lambda_u T] - [\lambda_l T] + 1$. Various statistical arguments can be made to justify one statistic over another, but it has become common practice to report all three in the empirical literature.

The limiting distribution of the three statistics is given in the following proposition.[10]

Proposition 2 If certain regularity conditions hold then under H_0, we have: $Sup\mathcal{W}_T \Rightarrow Sup_{\lambda \in \Lambda}\mathcal{W}(\lambda)$, $Av\mathcal{W}_T \Rightarrow \int_\Lambda \mathcal{W}(\lambda)dJ(\lambda)$, and $Exp\mathcal{W}_T \Rightarrow log[\int_\Lambda exp\{0.5\mathcal{W}(\lambda)\} dJ(\lambda)]$ where $\mathcal{W}(\lambda) = \{\lambda(1-\lambda)\}^{-1} BB_p(\lambda)' BB_p(\lambda)$ and $BB_p(\lambda)$ denotes a $p \times 1$ Brownian Bridge on $[0, 1]$.

The limiting distributions in Proposition 2 are non-standard but depend only on p, the dimension of the parameter vector. Percentiles are reported in Andrews (2003)

(Sup-) and Andrews and Ploberger (1994) (Av- and Exp-). These percentiles enable the researcher to ascertain whether the statistic is significant at a prescribed level. Hansen (1997a) reports response surfaces which can be used to calculate approximate p-values for all three versions of these tests.

The use of unknown break-point tests removes the concern about the interpretation of fixed break-point tests, but the tests are still only designed against an alternative in which there is one break-point. This is a limitation because in many cases of interest there are likely to be multiple events in the sample which may have caused the parameters to change. In the next section, we describe various tests that can be used to test for parameter change at multiple unknown break-points.

3 TESTING DISCRETE PARAMETER CHANGE AT MULTIPLE POINTS

Tests for multiple break-points have been proposed predominantly in the context of models that can be estimated via LS-type criteria, such as ordinary least-squares (OLS), two-stage least-squares (2SLS) and non-linear least-squares (NLS). The most widely used testing strategy for multiple breaks in linear models estimated via ordinary least-squares is the one proposed by Bai and Perron (1998). This strategy involves three types of tests: (i) testing no breaks versus a known number of breaks; (ii) testing no breaks against an unknown number of breaks up to a fixed upper bound, and (iii) testing ℓ versus $\ell + 1$ breaks.

These tests are useful as their by-products are consistent estimates for the break locations (see Bai and Perron, 1998). The strategy for determining the number of break-points in a sample involves, as a first step, testing zero versus a known or unknown number of breaks, via tests in (i)–(ii), described below. It is common to test for a maximum of five breaks. If the null of zero breaks is not rejected, we conclude that there are no breaks. If the null is rejected, it implies we have at least one break, and so we employ the tests in (iii), described below, for one versus two breaks. If we do not reject, then we conclude we have one break; if we reject, then we have at least two breaks and test via the tests in (iii) for two versus three breaks. If we do not reject, then we conclude we have two breaks. If we reject, then we continue testing for an additional break until we cannot reject the null or a maximum number of breaks has been reached. This is a simple sequential strategy for estimating the number of breaks, and provided the significance level of each test is shrunk in each step towards zero,[11] we will obtain the true number of breaks with probability 1 for large T.

To describe these tests, consider the following univariate linear model, estimable via OLS:

$$y_t = x_t'\theta_i + u_t \quad (t = T_{i-1}^0 + 1, \ldots, T_i^0) \quad (i = 1, \ldots, m + 1) \tag{9.4}$$

where y_t is a scalar dependent variable, x_t is a $p \times 1$ vector of exogenous regressors, uncorrelated with u_t, possibly including lags of y_t. Also, the number of breaks m is fixed, $T_i^0 = [\lambda_i^0 T]$ are the true break-points, λ_i^0 are the true break-fractions, for $i = 0, \ldots, m + 1$, and $\lambda_0^0 = 0$, $\lambda_{m+1}^0 = 1$ by convention. Here, we treat λ_i^0 as unknown quantities; the tests for unknown break-points simplify as in the previous section when the λ_i^0s are known.

(i) Tests for a Fixed Number of Breaks

Under the notation above, the tests for a fixed number of breaks are for the following null and alternative hypotheses:

$$H_0: m = 0 \quad H_1: m = k, \quad \text{for a fixed } k. \tag{9.5}$$

Since the LM and LR tests are asymptotically equivalent to the Wald test, we restrict our attention to the latter. To derive Wald tests from their principles, rewrite the null hypothesis in terms of restricting the parameters to be the same across subsamples:

$$H_0 : \theta_1 = \theta_2 = \ldots = \theta_{k+1} \tag{9.6}$$

$$H_1 : \theta_i \neq \theta_j \text{ for all } i \neq j, \quad (i,j = 1,\ldots,k+1). \tag{9.7}$$

To define the Wald test, let $\widetilde{R}_k$ be the $k \times (k+1)$ matrix with the (j,j)th element equal to 1, the $(j,j+1)$th element equal to -1, and the rest equal to zero, for $j = 1,2,\ldots,k$. Also let $R_k = \widetilde{R}_k \otimes I_p$, where $\otimes$ denotes the Kronecker product. Then H_0 above can be written as $R_k\theta^c = 0$, where θ^c is a $(k+1)p$ vector that vertically stacks $\theta_1,\ldots,\theta_{k+1}$. Let $\lambda^c = (0,\lambda_1,\lambda_2,\ldots,\lambda_k,1)'$ the break-fractions associated with any candidate partition of the sample $T^c = (0,T_1,T_2,\ldots,T_k,T)'$, where $T_i = [\lambda_i T]$ for $i = 1,2,\ldots,k$. Also, let the corresponding subsamples be denoted by $\mathcal{T}_i(\lambda^c) = \{[\lambda_{i-1}T]+1,[\lambda_{i-1}T]+2,\ldots,[\lambda_i T]\}$ for $i = 1,2,\ldots,k+1$. Since the Wald tests are constructed using estimates under the alternative, we have to estimate $\theta_1,\ldots,\theta_{k+1}$.

Definition 2 For $i = 1,2,\ldots,k+1$, $\hat{\theta}_{i,T}(\lambda^c)$ is defined to be the OLS estimator of θ_i, based on minimizing the sum of squared residuals calculated from observations in $\mathcal{T}_i(\lambda^c)$. Also, $\hat{\theta}^c_{i,T}(\lambda^c)$ is the $(k+1)p$ vector that vertically stacks $\hat{\theta}_{i,T}(\lambda^c)$, for $i = 1,\ldots,m+1$.

Let also $V_i(\lambda^c) = \lim_{T\to\infty} Var(T^{1/2}[\theta_{i,T}(\lambda^c) - \theta_i])$, $V_{i,T}(\lambda^c)$ be a consistent estimator of $V_i(\lambda^c)$ and $V_T(\lambda^c)$ the $(k+1) \times (k+1)$ block-diagonal matrix with the (i,i)th diagonal block equal to $V_{i,T}(\lambda^c)$. Then the Wald test for a particular sample partition λ^c is defined as follows:

$$\mathcal{W}_T(\lambda^c) = T[R_k\,\hat{\theta}^c_{i,T}(\lambda^c)]'\,[R_k\,V_T(\lambda^c)\,R_k']^{-1}[R_k\,\hat{\theta}^c_{i,T}(\lambda^c)] \tag{9.8}$$

For $k = 1$, this test is the OLS equivalent of its GMM counterpart in equation (9.2). As in the previous section, it depends on the particular partition of the sample used, so for unknown break-points, we use its $Sup\mathcal{W}_T$ version, defined as:

$$Sup\mathcal{W}_T(k) = \sup_{\lambda^c \in \Lambda^c_\varepsilon} \{\mathcal{W}_T(\lambda^c)\}, \tag{9.9}$$

where $\Lambda_e^c = \{(0, \lambda_1, \ldots, \lambda_k, 1) : |\lambda_i - \lambda_{i-1}| \geq \varepsilon, (i = 1, \ldots, k), \lambda_1 \geq \varepsilon, 1 - \lambda_k \geq \varepsilon$ for some positive ε. In practice, ε is usually chosen to be 0.15; this implies not only that the breaks cannot be too close to the beginning or end of the sample, but also that there are enough observations in each subsample so that OLS estimation can be performed. The asymptotic distribution of this test is given below.

Proposition 3 Under certain regularity conditions and H_0 in (9.6), $SupW_T(k) \Rightarrow \sup_{\lambda^c \in \Lambda_\varepsilon^c} \mathcal{W}(\lambda^c)$, where

$$\mathcal{W}(\lambda^c) = B'_{p(k+1)} \{[C_k^{-1} \widetilde{R}'_k (\widetilde{R}_k C_k^{-1} \widetilde{R}'_k)^{-1} \widetilde{R}_k C_k^{-1}] \otimes I_p\} B_{p(k+1)},$$

with $B_{p(k+1)} = [B'_p(\lambda_1), B'_p(\lambda_2) - B'_p(\lambda_1), \ldots, B'_p(\lambda_{k+1}) - B'_p(\lambda_k)]'$, a $p(k+1) \times 1$ vector of pairwise independent vector of Brownian motion increments of dimensions p, C_k is a $k \times k$ diagonal matrix with elements $\lambda_1, \lambda_2 - \lambda_1, \ldots, \lambda_{k+1} - \lambda_k$ on the diagonal, and $\lambda_{k+1} = 1$ by convention.

The most important regularity conditions in Proposition 3 are that the regressors are not trending, they are orthogonal to the errors, that there is no unit root, and that there are no changes in the marginal distribution of x_t.[12] Unlike for LR-type tests, these regularity conditions allow for heteroscedasticity and autocorrelation. In particular, they allow for the variance of u_t to change at the same time as the parameters. As pointed out by Lubik and Surico (2010), this is an important feature of the $SupW_T(k)$ test that allows practitioners to test more accurately for monetary policy breaks during the Great Moderation.

The $SupW_T(k)$ test is consistent against H_1. For $k = 1$, its distribution reduces to the one in Proposition 1, and its optimality properties are the same as for GMM settings,[13] but they are not known for $k > 1$. However, for most practical purposes, it suffices to know that in the OLS setting, the $SupW_T(k)$ delivers consistent estimators of the true k break-fractions indexing the break-points.

(ii) Tests for an Unknown Number of Breaks

The test in (9.9) also rejects with probability 1 when T is large, if the true number of breaks under the alternative is $k^* \neq k$. However, if the true alternative is $H_1 : m = k^*$, in small samples it might not have good power properties because it is not designed for this alternative. To address this issue, Bai and Perron (1998) propose a second set of tests, presented below, against the alternative of an unknown number of breaks up to a maximum:

$$H_0 : m = 0 \quad H_1 : 1 \leq m \leq M, \text{ for a fixed } M. \tag{9.10}$$

These tests are known as *double-maximum* or *Dmax*-type tests. The idea behind these tests is to construct for each $m \in \{1, \ldots, M\}$ a $SupW_T(m)$-test (thus a maximum for each m), and then to maximize over weighted versions of these statistics to obtain a unique test statistic for the null and alternative hypotheses in (9.10). This test is defined below:

$$DmaxW_T = \max_{1 \le m \le M} \frac{a_m}{p} SupW_T(m), \tag{9.11}$$

for some fixed, strictly positive weights a_m. The distribution of this test generalizes in a straightforward fashion from Proposition 3:

Proposition 4 Under certain regularity conditions and H_0,

$$DmaxW_T \Rightarrow \max_{1 \le m \le M} \frac{a_m}{p} \sup_{\lambda^c \in \Lambda_\varepsilon^c} \sum_{i=1}^{m+1} W_i(\lambda^c)$$

The regularity conditions are the same as for $SupW_T(m)$ test, for each m. The weights for the $DmaxW_T$ test should be set larger for a certain m if one believes that m is more likely to be the correct number of breaks. If there is no clear a priori belief about the true number of breaks, one can use equal weights $a_m = 1/M$, in which case the test is known as a *UDmax* test. However, note that the scaling p is used because in its absence and with equal weights a_m, this test will be equivalent to testing zero against M breaks, since the critical values increase in m for a fixed p. Since, despite the scaling, the critical values still tend to increase with m, let $c(m,p,\alpha)$ be the asymptotic critical value of the test $SupW_T(m)/p$ at significance level $100\alpha\%$.[14] Then the problem of increasing critical values is alleviated by setting $a_1 = 1$ and $a_m = c(1,p,\alpha)/c(m,p,\alpha)$, and the corresponding test is called a *WDmax* test.

(iii) Tests for an Additional Break

The third category of tests for multiple breaks (iii) are called *sequential Wald tests*, since they are Wald tests for an additional break. The null and alternative hypotheses are, for any given ℓ:

$$H_0: m = \ell \qquad H_1: m = \ell + 1. \tag{9.12}$$

An LR-type test is proposed in Bai and Perron (1998). However, asymptotically equivalent Wald-type tests can be derived as a special case of the sequential Wald tests in Boldea and Hall (2013) and Hall et al. (2012). For the Wald test, one ideally uses the estimates only under the alternative hypothesis.[15] However, for computational ease, it has become routine among practitioners to use Bai and Perron's (1998) approach of pre-estimating the model with ℓ breaks. This implies that estimates of the ℓ breaks are obtained as a by-product of calculating the Wald statistic $SupW_T(\ell)$, imposed as if they were the true ones, and for the alternative hypothesis in (9.12), evidence is maximized for exactly one additional break, occurring in only one of the $\ell + 1$ subsamples obtained by partitioning the sample with the pre-estimated ℓ breaks. To define the test, let μ denote each candidate additional break-fraction in the pre-estimated $\ell + 1$ subsamples $\Lambda_q (q = 1, 2, \ldots, \ell + 1)$, with

$$\Lambda_q = \{\mu : \hat{T}_{q-1} + (\hat{T}_q - \hat{T}_{q-1})\eta \le [\mu T] \le \hat{T}_q - (\hat{T}_q - \hat{T}_{q-1})\eta\}.$$

In these subsamples, the OLS parameter estimates before and after each candidate additional break are denoted by $\vartheta_q(\mu) = [\hat{\theta}_1(\mu,q)',\hat{\theta}_2(\mu,q)']'$, where $q = 1,2,\ldots,\ell + 1$, and the restriction that they are equal is defined through the restriction matrix $R^* = [I_p; -I_p]$. Then the sequential Wald test is:

$$\mathcal{W}_T(\ell + 1|\ell) = \max_{1\leq q\leq \ell+1} \sup_{\mu\in\Lambda_q} \mathcal{W}_{T,\ell}(\mu,q) \tag{9.13}$$

where

$$\mathcal{W}_{T,\ell}(\mu,q) = T[R^*\hat{\vartheta}_q(\mu)]'[R^* V_T^*(\mu,q) R^{*\prime}]^{-1} R^*\hat{\vartheta}_q(\mu)$$

and $V_T^*(\mu,q)$ is the $2p \times 2p$ block-diagonal matrix with diagonal blocks $V_{1,T}(\mu,q)$ and $V_{2,T}(\mu,q)$. The latter two are defined as consistent estimators of their asymptotic equivalents $V_1(\mu,q) = \lim_{T\to\infty} Var\, T^{1/2}[\hat{\theta}_1(\mathcal{M},q) - \mathcal{Q}_q]$, respectively $V_2(\mu,q) = \lim_{T\to\infty} Var\, T^{1/2}[\hat{\theta}_{\mu,q} - \theta_{q+1}]$, for $q = 1,2,\ldots,\ell$.

The asymptotic distribution of the test is described below:

Proposition 5 Under certain regularity conditions and H_0 in (9.3), $\lim P(\mathcal{W}_T(\ell + 1|\ell) \leq x) = G_{p,\eta}^{\ell+1}$, where $G_{p,\eta}$ is the cumulative distribution function of $\sup_{\eta\leq\mu\leq 1-\eta} \frac{\| B_p(\mu) - \mu B_p(1)\|^2}{\mu(1-\mu)}$.

The regularity conditions follow directly from Hall et al. (2012), by treating all endogenous variables as exogenous. They allow for breaks in the error variance occurring at the same time as the parameters under H_1 in (9.12). Critical values for the tests (i)–(iii) can be found in Bai and Perron (1998), and p-values based on approximate response surfaces can be found in Hall and Sakkas (2013).

As mentioned above, these tests are useful for models that can be estimated by OLS, thus with exogenous regresssors. When some regressors are endogenous, Hall et al. (2012) show that a similar sequential procedure for finding the number of breaks in models with endogenous regressors can be developed, based on tests constructed with 2SLS estimates.

However, unlike for OLS, with 2SLS, one needs first to assess whether there are any breaks in the first-stage regression. To see why this is important, assume that the researcher has in mind an economic model, from which the first and second stages of 2SLS estimation arise naturally. For example, consider the following structural model:

$$y_t = \theta x_t + u_t \tag{9.14}$$

$$x_t = \gamma_1 y_t + \gamma_2 h_t + \gamma_3 z_{1,t} + v_{1,t} \tag{9.15}$$

$$h_t = \delta_1 x_t + \delta_2 z_{2,t} + v_{2,t} \tag{9.16}$$

where y_t, x_t, h_t are scalar dependent variables, $z_t = (z_{1,t}, z_{2,t})'$ are scalar exogenous regressors, u_t, $v_{1,t}$, $v_{2,t}$ are errors and $\theta, \gamma_1, \gamma_2, \gamma_3, \delta_1, \delta_2$ are scalar unknown parameters that may break at unknown locations in the sample.

If one is interested in estimating θ, the equation of interest is (9.14), and will be the second stage in a 2SLS regression, with the first stage instrumenting for the endogeneity of x_t via instruments z_t. In this example, the first stage arises naturally, since the reduced form for x_t can be found by substituting (9.16) and (9.14) into (9.15):

$$x_t = z_t'\Delta + v_t$$

$$\Delta = \left(\frac{\gamma_3}{1 - \theta\gamma_1 - \delta_1\gamma_2}, \frac{\gamma_2\delta_2}{1 - \theta\gamma_1 - \delta_1\gamma_2}\right)'$$

$$v_t = \frac{\gamma_1 u_t + v_{1,t} + \gamma_2 v_{2,t}}{1 - \theta\gamma_1 - \delta_1\gamma_2}. \tag{9.17}$$

In this context, we can see that all breaks in θ, thus in (9.14), will also be in (9.17) by default, unless $\gamma_1 = 0$. When $\gamma_1 = 0$, if no other parameters change besides θ, (9.17) will have no breaks. If any of the parameters $\gamma_j (j = 1,2,3), \delta_1, \delta_2$ change, then these changes are only reflected in (9.17). Thus the first stage can have no breaks, or breaks that are common to the second stage, or breaks that are idiosyncratic to the first stage.

In practice, one does not necessarily know which scenario occurs, so it is important to consider both the case where the first stage is stable and where it is unstable. For simplicity, consider a data generating process with m and m^* breaks in the second and first stage regressions respectively:

$$y_t = x_t\theta_i + u_t \quad (t = T^0_{i-1} + 1, \ldots, T^0_i) \quad (i = 1, \ldots, m + 1) \tag{9.18}$$

where x_t is a scalar endogenous regressor, that is, correlated with u_t, and thus needs to be predicted via the first stage OLS regression with $s \times 1$ strong instruments z_t:

$$x_t = z_t'\Delta_j + v_t \quad (t = T^*_{j-1} + 1, \ldots, T^*_j) \quad (j = 1, \ldots, m^* + 1) \tag{9.19}$$

with u_t correlated with v_t, $T_0 = T^*_0 = 1$, $T^0_i = [\lambda^0_i T]$, $T^*_j = [\lambda^*_j T]$, $T_{m+1} = T_{m^*+1} = T$, and some breaks may be common to both equations.

If there are no breaks in the first stage, that is, $m^* = 0$, the 2SLS structural stability tests are computed exactly as their OLS conterparts in (i)–(iii), but for the second stage equation (9.18), and with x_t replaced by $\hat{x}_t$, its predicted counterpart from an OLS regression in (9.19). For clarity, the 2SLS estimators are defined below.

Definition 3 For $i = 1, 2, \ldots, k + 1$, $\hat{\theta}_{i,T}(\lambda^c)$ is defined to be the 2SLS estimator of θ_i, based on minimizing the OLS sum of squared residuals calculated for the second stage (9.18), from observations in $\mathcal{T}_i(\lambda^c)$ – defined as before – using as regressors $\hat{x}_t$ instead of x_t, where $\hat{x}_t$ is the full-sample OLS estimator from the first stage equation (9.19). Also, $\hat{\theta}^c_T(\lambda^c)$ is the $(k + 1)p$ vector that vertically stacks $\hat{\theta}_{i,T}(\lambda^c)$, for $i = 1, \ldots, m + 1$.

(iv) Sequential Testing Strategy for Stable First Stage Regression

For sequential testing, the tests in (i)–(iii), $SupW_T$, $DmaxW_T$ and $W_T(\ell + 1|\ell)$, are defined in the same way as before, except that the 2SLS estimators replace their OLS counterparts in the definition of the tests. As Hall et al. (2012) show, the asymptotic distributions of these tests are also the same as in Propositions 3–5. Thus, a 2SLS sequential strategy for estimating the number and location of breaks can be constructed in the same way from these tests as before, when the first stage equation (9.19) is stable.

However, in general (9.19) may also have breaks, that is, $m^* \neq 0$. One can test this equation for breaks, and find their locations, via the OLS sequential testing strategy in (i)–(iii). As discussed above, these tests also provide consistent estimators of the number of break-points, m^*, and their locations, T_j^*, $(j = 1, 2, \ldots, m^*)$.

It remains to find the number of breaks in the second stage, for which $\hat{x}_t$, a prediction of x_t based on estimating the first stage equation (9.19), needs to be computed. If one ignores the breaks found in (9.19) in computing $\hat{x}_t$, the 2SLS tests in the second stage will pick up these breaks and reject with probability 1 for large T even if there are no breaks in the second stage. If one computes $\hat{x}_t$ by OLS in each subsample constructed via the estimates of T_j^*, and then proceeds with testing for breaks in the full sample of the second stage (9.18) via the tests in (i)–(iii), but with x_t replaced by $\hat{x}_t$, then the asymptotic distributions in Propositions 3–5 are no longer valid.[16]

Fortunately, there is a simple way to side-step these issues and sequentially test for breaks in (9.18). A strategy for finding these breaks is described below.

(v) Sequential Testing Strategy for Unstable First Stage Regression

(v-i) Tests for Breaks that are Idiosyncratic to the Second Stage

If breaks are found in the first stage, a strategy for finding the breaks that only occur in the second stage is described below.

- Obtain estimates $\hat{m}^*$ for the number of breaks m^* and $\hat{T}_j^*(j = 1, \ldots, \hat{m}^*)$ for the associated break-points $T_j^*(j = 1, \ldots, m^*)$, either as a by-product of the OLS sequential strategy in (9.19), or by global estimation via the methods in Bai and Perron (1998). If the sequential strategy is used, reduce the critical value in each step to make sure that $\hat{m}^* = m^*$ with probability 1 as T grows larger. This ensures that we can treat $\hat{m}^*$ as if it were m^* in the next steps.
- Split the sample into subsamples $\hat{\mathcal{T}}_j^* = \{\hat{T}_{j-1}^* + 1, \hat{T}_{j-1}^* + 2, \ldots, \hat{T}_j^*\}$ for $(j = 1, \ldots, \hat{m}^*)$. In each subsample $\hat{\mathcal{T}}_j^*$, compute $\hat{x}_t$ via OLS, and run the sequential testing strategy in (iv) for each of these subsamples of the second stage model (9.18).
- As a by-product of the testing strategy, or the re-estimation of the breaks in sub-samples $\hat{\mathcal{T}}_j^*$ (see Boldea et al., 2012), one obtains consistent estimates of the non-common break fractions in (9.18). Denote their break-point counterparts by $\hat{T}_n, (n = 1, 2, \ldots, N)$, with $N \leq m$. These are the breaks that are idiosyncratic to the second stage.
- Let $\hat{T}_0 = 0$ and $\hat{T}_{N+1} = T$, to include sample ends. Obtain the union of sample end-points and the breaks in the first stage and second stage, ordered, as $\mathcal{B} = \{\hat{T}_0, \ldots, \hat{T}_{N+1}\} \cup \{\hat{T}_1^*, \ldots, \hat{T}_{\hat{m}^*}^*\}$. Thus, $\mathcal{B}$ contains all the breaks in the first and second stage equation in (9.18) and (9.19).

Thus, via this strategy, the researcher knows the idiosyncratic breaks to the second stage, and all the breaks in the first stage. However, for practical purposes, one needs to know which breaks are common to the two stages. This is not only important for correct estimation of the subsamples in the second stage, it is also of interest to practitioners. For example, in the estimation of a hybrid New Keynesian Phillips Curve (NKPC), with measured expectations, Boldea et al. (2012) show that a break at the end of 1980 occurred in the modelled inflation expectations, but that break did not further occur in the NKPC itself once the change in expectations was taken into account. The test they use to detect common breaks is a usual Wald test for a known break-point, and is defined below.

(v-ii) Tests for breaks that are common to both stages

To describe these tests, let the ordered breaks in $\mathcal{B}$ be $\tilde{T}_1, \tilde{T}_2, \ldots, \tilde{T}_H$, with $H = \hat{m}^* + N$. Then for any $s = 1, 2, \ldots, H$ such that $\hat{T}_j^* = \tilde{T}_s$, take the smallest subsample encompassing it, $\{\tilde{T}_{s-1} + 1, \ldots, \tilde{T}_{s+1}\}$, and calculate the 2SLS estimators $\hat{\theta}_s$ and $\hat{\theta}_{s+1}$, based on subsamples $\mathcal{B}_s = \{\tilde{T}_{s-1} + 1, \ldots, \tilde{T}_s\}$, respectively $\mathcal{B}_{s+1} = \{\tilde{T}_s + 1, \ldots, \tilde{T}_{s+1}\}$. Treat the end-points $\tilde{T}_{s-1}$ and $\tilde{T}_{s+1}$, and $\hat{T}_j^*$ as known. Then the Wald test for a common break $\tilde{T}_s$, to both equations (9.18) and (9.19), is:

$$\mathcal{W}_T = T(\hat{\theta}_s - \hat{\theta}_{s+1})'[V_{s,T} + V_{s+1,T}]^{-1}(\hat{\theta}_s - \hat{\theta}_{s+1}), \qquad (9.20)$$

where $V_{i,T}$ are consistent estimates of the asymptotic variances $V_i = \lim_{T\to\infty} Var[T^{1/2}(\hat{\theta}_i - \theta_i)]$, for $i = s, s + 1$. Because we test in the second stage for a break pre-estimated from another equation, the first stage, the distribution is the same as if the break-point $\hat{T}_s$ were known.

Proposition 6 Under certain regularity conditions,[17] under the null hypothesis of no common break in the subsample tested,

$$\mathcal{W}_T \xrightarrow{d} \chi_1^2 \qquad (9.21)$$

Thus, all the breaks in the equation of interest (9.18) can be retrieved via the sequential strategy in (v), or (iv) if no breaks are found in the first stage regression.

This procedure was defined for one endogenous regressor, but can be generalized to p multiple endogenous regressors X_t in which case the degrees of freedom become p. Intuitively, one just needs to consistently predict the endogenous regressors from the first stage, so the OLS sequential strategy in (i)–(iii) can be applied to the first stage equation pertaining to each endogenous regressor separately.[18] If the second stage equation also has exogenous regressors a_t, then the tests in (iv)–(v) remain valid, with $\hat{x}_t$ replaced by $(\hat{x}_t', a_t')'$. The optimality of these procedures is, as for OLS methods, unclear, but all the tests reject with probability 1 for large T, regardless of whether the breaks are small or large.

In non-linear models, a similar sequential procedure as in (i)–(iii) is available for models that can be estimated via non-linear least squares (see Boldea and Hall, 2013).

Given a known parametric regression function with multiple parameter changes, the tests in (i)–(iii) remain valid, and so do their distributions, as long as the OLS estimators in (i)–(iii) are replaced by their NLS counterparts.

Even though a procedure for testing for multiple breaks in linear models estimated via GMM is not known, its 2SLS counterpart can be used, and as a by-product, one obtains consistent break-points as well as parameter estimates. Thanks to the dynamic programming algorithm introduced in Bai and Perron, the computational burden for a sample size of T is less than $T(T + 1)/2$ operations, independent of the number of breaks. MATLAB code for testing for multiple breaks can be found at https://sites.google.com/site/otiliaboldea/home.

The testing procedures above are all designed for multiple breaks, when the parameter changes infrequently and permanently from one value to another at a few locations in the sample. Other types of parameter instability are summarized in the next section.

4 TESTING FOR OTHER TYPES OF PARAMETER CHANGE

Break-points are by default exogenous to the model, since time is an exogenous quantity. When parameter changes are believed to be driven by some observed variables that indicate the state of the business cycle or some other important economic indicators, researchers resort to other types of parameter change models, called threshold and smooth transition models.

Threshold and smooth transition models have been used to model GDP growth, unemployment, interest rates, prices, stock returns and exchange rates (for a review of the empirical and theoretical econometrics literature, see Van Dijk et al., 2002 and Hansen, 2011).

The threshold model, introduced by Howell Tong,[19] in many ways resembles the break-point model. To see the connection, for simplicity we revert to an exposition with one break. Thus, consider the model (9.4) but $m = 1$, rewritten in the following way:

$$y_t = x_t'\theta_t + u_t \text{ with } \theta_t = \theta_1 + (\theta_2 - \theta_1)\mathbf{1}\{t \geq T_1\} \tag{9.22}$$

where $\mathbf{1}$ is the indicator function. If instead, θ_t is defined as:

$$y_t = x_t'\theta_t + u_t \text{ with } \theta_t = \theta_1 + (\theta_2 - \theta_1)\mathbf{1}\{q_t \geq c\}, \tag{9.23}$$

where y_t is a scalar dependent variable, c is an unknown parameter, to be estimated, and x_t and q_t are exogenous observed regressors, uncorrelated with u_t, one obtains the *threshold model.* If x_t contains lags of y_t, this model is known as the *threshold autoregressive (TAR) model.*

In this model, the parameter change is driven by the observed variable q_t, called a state variable, and c denotes the threshold above which the parameters of the model change from θ_1 to θ_2. If one orders the data (y_t, x_t) on the values of q_t, say in ascending order, one obtains two subsamples, one for which the true parameter is θ_1, and another for which the true parameter is θ_2. These two subsamples resemble the break-point subsamples; the break-point here is the point in the newly ordered sample where q_t changes from a value below c to a value above c. Hansen (1997b) shows that by re-ordering of the data as described above, a $SupW_T$ of the type described in the previous section can be constructed, and its asymptotic distribution for one threshold is the same as in Proposition 3 for $k = 1$. This procedure is extended to estimating multiple thresholds in Gonzalo and Pitarakis (2002).

When some of the regressors in x_t are endogenous, but q_t is exogenous, for one threshold model, Caner and Hansen propose the *Sup*-type Wald test constructed with a 2SLS estimator of the threshold c and GMM estimators of the other parameters. Its asymptotic distribution is computed by simulation in Caner and Hansen (2004). For endogenous q_t, no tests are known so far, although estimation of models with one endogenous threshold can be done via 2SLS estimation with bias correction (see Kourtellos et al., 2008).

An equally influential model in empirical macroeconomics is the *smooth transition autoregressive (STAR) model*, introduced by Teräsvirta (1994). This model is mostly suitable for policy functions such as the interest rate functions, where the parameter is not changing in a sudden fashion from θ_1 to θ_2, but in a smooth way. The smoothness is imputed by replacing the indicator function with a smooth function, with values in the interval $(0, 1)$, meaning that true parameters at each point in time no longer take two values, θ_1 and θ_2, but are most of the time in between these values. We present here the simplest STAR model, called the logistic STAR, where the indicator function is replaced by the smooth logistic function $f(\cdot,\cdot,\cdot)$, defined below:

$$y_t = x_t'\theta_t + u_t \text{ with } \theta_t = \theta_1 + (\theta_2 - \theta_1)f(q_t, \gamma, c) \tag{9.24}$$

$$f(q_t, \gamma, c) = \frac{exp\{\gamma(q_t - c)\}}{1 + exp\{\gamma(q_t - c)\}} \tag{9.25}$$

Here q_t and x_t are observed and uncorrelated with the errors u_t, and may contain lags of y_t, γ is an unknown smoothness parameter and c is the unknown 'threshold' parameter. The latter two need to be estimated. When γ is large, the transition is faster as the transition function moves faster from 0 to 1 when q_t is above c; when γ is small, the transition is slower.

This model is different from the threshold or break model in the sense that it can be written as a smooth non-linear regression. Unfortunately, the usual non-linear regression Wald tests do not directly apply. The reason is because, under the null hypothesis of $\theta_1 = \theta_2$, or no non-linearity, the parameters γ, c are not identified, since any value of these parameters will render the same linear regression function. This implies that we may have a similar problem to the break-point or threshold model, of unidentified parameters under the null hypothesis. However, because the regression function in (9.24) is smooth under the alternative, one can write a third-order Taylor expansion of $f(q_t, \cdot, c)$ around $\gamma = 0$. This yields a model that has the parameters γ, c also identified under the null hypothesis, and Eitrheim and Teräsvirta (1996) show that the resulting model can be tested for no non-linearity via a usual *LM* test. If one doesn't use this expansion, the optimality properties of a *Sup*-type LR test over all possible values of γ, c, are studied in Andrews et al. (2011), who show that this test may not have the right size.

STAR models have recently been shown to be estimable via GMM in the presence of endogenous regressors using the usual GMM asymptotic theory (see Areosa et al., 2011). Thus, we conjecture that the tests discussed here for STAR models can be used in their equivalent GMM form with no further complications.

So far, we have discussed models for parameter change driven by an observed variable. However, one may think that the behaviour of macroeconomic variables changes with an unobserved variable such as the state of the business cycle. Such models are called regime-switching models (or Markov-switching under certain regularity conditions) and were introduced in econometrics by Hamilton (1989). To write down a Markov-switching model, let s_t be an unobserved state variable, with values zero or one (that is, for recession or expansion). Then:

$$y_t = x_t'\theta_t + u_t \text{ with } \theta_t = \theta_1 + (\theta_2 - \theta_1)s_t \tag{9.26}$$

$$P(s_t = 1|s_{t-1} = 1, \mathcal{I}_t) = p_1; P(s_t = 0|s_{t-1} = 0, \mathcal{I}_t) = p_2 \tag{9.27}$$

Here, x_t usually includes some lags of y_t, and is uncorrelated with u_t. Also, $s_t \in \{0, 1\}$, and the probabilities of being in a certain state are entirely determined by the previous state and the information set at time t, $\mathcal{I}_t$, which includes x_t and all its previous values.

Suppose one wants to test whether the parameter change $\theta_2 - \theta_1$ is zero or not. In this case, p_1 and q_2 are the parameters that are not identified under the null hypothesis, but there are other complications related to the cases of p_1 or q_2 being close to zero or 1. This presence implies that we cannot use Taylor expansions as in the STAR example to test for parameter change. Hansen (1992) proposes an upper bound for a *Sup*-type LR test, but this bound depends on the data and is often burdensome to compute. Garcia (1998) proposes to restrict testing to cases where p_1, q_2 are bounded away from 0, 1, and use the *Sup*-LR test, where the supremum is taken over (p_1, q_2), and gives the asymptotic distribution of the test. However, because the framework he uses to justify his test, taken from Andrews and Ploberger (1994), does not apply to Markov-switching models, this test may not have optimal power. To that end, we recommend the test by Carrasco et al. (2009), an information-matrix type LM test that is shown to have certain desired optimality properties.

When x_t is endogenous, Kim (2004) and Kim (2009) show that either a bias-corrected maximum-likelihood estimation or a two-step maximum likelihood ignoring the bias can be used to estimate the Markov-switching model with two regimes. Similarly, when s_t is endogenous but x_t is exogenous, Kim et al. (2008) propose a bias-corrected filter to estimate the model. As for STAR, we conjecture that tests can be constructed based on these inference procedures, adapted from the Markov switching tests for exogenous regressors.

There are many other types of parameter change, but the main types are summarized here and they all have their merits for the applied researcher.

5 TESTING FOR OTHER TYPES OF STRUCTURAL INSTABILITY

So far, the focus of this chapter has been on testing for parameter change; however, this is not the only scenario that can lead to structural instability. In this section, we explore tests for other forms of structural instability that have been developed within the GMM framework. To this end, we return to the framework in section 2.

A natural alternative to H_0 in (9.1) that captures the notion of structural instability at a fixed break-point $T_1 = [T\lambda]$ is

$$H_1'(\lambda): \begin{array}{ll} E[f(v_t, \theta_0)] = 0 & \text{for } t = 1, 2, \ldots, T_1, \\ E[f(v_t, \theta_0)] \neq 0 & \text{for } t = T_1 + 1, \ldots, T. \end{array}$$

Under $H_1'(\lambda)$, the population moment holds at θ_0 before the break-point, but fails to hold after. Before proceeding further, we note that all that follows applies equally if the population moment condition holds at θ_0 after but not before the break-point.

If $q = p$ – and so there are the same number of moment conditions as parameters – then it can be shown that $H_1(\lambda)$ and $H_1'(\lambda)$ are equivalent.[20] However, if $q > p$ – and so there are more moment conditions than parameters – then this equivalence does not hold. Exploiting the decomposition of the population moment condition inherent in GMM estimation,[21] Hall and Sen (1999) show that $H_1'(\lambda)$ can be decomposed into two parts: structural instability in the identifying restrictions at $[T\lambda]$ and structural instability in the overidentifying restrictions at $[T\lambda]$. Instability of the identifying restrictions is equivalent to $H_1(\lambda)$, that is, to parameter change at $[T\lambda]$. Instability of the overidentifying restrictions means that some aspect of the model beyond the parameters alone has changed at $[T\lambda]$. Rather than specifying this alternative mathematically, we present an intuitive explanation. To this end, consider Hansen and Singleton's (1982) consumption-based asset pricing in which a representative agent makes consumption and investment decisions to maximize discounted expected lifetime utility based on a utility function,

$$U_t(c_t) = \frac{c_t^{\gamma} - 1}{\gamma}.$$

The parameters of this model are γ, with $1 - \gamma$ being the coefficient of relative risk aversion, and β, the discount factor; so, in our notation, $\theta = (\gamma, \beta)'$. It is customary to estimate θ_0 via GMM based on $E[u_t(\theta_0)z_t] = 0$ where $u_t(\theta_0)$ is the so-called Euler residual derived from the underlying economic model, and z_t is a vector of variables contained in the representative agent's information set. Within this setting, $H_1(\lambda)$ implies that the parameters have changed but the functional form of $u_t(\theta)$ has stayed the same: this state of the world occurs if the functional form of the agent's utility function is the same before and after the break-point but either his/her coefficient of relative risk aversion or his/her discount factor changes. Instability of the overidentifying restrictions implies that the structural change involves more than the parameters: this state of the world would occur if the functional form of the agent's utility function changes at the break-point.

Since instability of the identifying and overidentifying restrictions have different implications for the underlying model, Hall and Sen (1999) argue that it is advantageous to test $H_0(\lambda)$ against each separately. To test against instability of the identifying restrictions, we can use the statistics for testing against $H_1(\lambda)$ described in section 2. To test against instability of the overidentifying restrictions, Hall and Sen (1999) propose the use of the following statistic,

$$\mathcal{O}_T(\lambda) = \mathcal{O}_{1,T}(\lambda) + \mathcal{O}_{2,T}(\lambda)$$

where $\mathcal{O}_{i,T}(\lambda)$ is the overidentifying restrictions tests based on the subsample $\mathcal{T}_i$ for $i = 1, 2$.[22] The following proposition gives the limiting distribution of $\mathcal{O}_T(\lambda)$:

Proposition 7 If certain regularity conditions hold then under H_0, we have: $\mathcal{O}_T(\lambda) \xrightarrow{d} \chi_{2(q-p)}$.

Hall and Sen (1999) show that under H_0, $\mathcal{O}_T(\lambda)$ is asymptotically independent of the statistics, such as $\mathcal{W}_T(\lambda)$, used to test parameter change. They further show that under local alternatives each of $\mathcal{W}_T(\lambda)$ and $\mathcal{O}_T(\lambda)$ has power against its own specific alternative but none against the alternative of the other test. These properties underscore the notion that the two statistics are testing different aspects of instability and this provides some guidance on the interpretation of significant statistics, although the local nature of the results needs to be kept in mind.[23]

Hall and Sen (1999) also propose the following statistics for testing for instability of the overidentifying restrictions at an unknown break-point,[24]

$$SupO_T = \sup_{i \in T_b} \{\mathcal{O}_T(i/T)\}$$

$$AvO_T = d_b^{-1} \sum_{i=[\lambda_l T]}^{[\lambda_u T]} \mathcal{O}_T(i/T)$$

$$ExpO_T = \log\left\{ d_b^{-1} \sum_{i=[\lambda_l T]}^{[\lambda_u T]} \exp[0.5\mathcal{O}_T(i/T)] \right\}$$

The limiting distribution of these statistics is as follows:

Proposition 8 If certain regularity conditions hold then under H_0, we have: $SupO_T \Rightarrow Sup_{\lambda \in \Lambda} \mathcal{O}(\lambda)$, $AvO_T \Rightarrow \int_\Lambda \mathcal{O}(\lambda) dJ(\lambda)$, and $ExpO_T \Rightarrow log[\int_\Lambda exp\{0.5\mathcal{O}(\lambda)\} dJ(\lambda)]$ where $\mathcal{O}(\lambda) = \frac{1}{\lambda} B'_{q-p}(\lambda) B_{q-p}(\lambda) + \frac{1}{1-\lambda}[B_{q-p}(1) - B_{q-p}(\lambda)]'[B_{q-p}(1) - B_{q-p}(\lambda)]$ and $B_{q-p}(\lambda)$ denotes a $(q - p) \times 1$ Brownian motion on $[0, 1]$.

The limiting distributions in Proposition 8 are non-standard but depend only on $q - p$, the number of overidentifying restrictions. The percentiles of these limiting distributions are reported in Hall and Sen (1999). Sen and Hall (1999) report response surfaces which can be used to calculate approximate p-values for all three versions of these tests.

6 CONCLUSIONS

In this chapter we describe various structural stability tests that are best suited for empirical analysis in macroeconomics. We discuss tests for parameter breaks, other types or parameter changes and also model instability. Most of our discussion is focused around

Wald-type tests, which are robust to heteroscedasticity and autocorrelation. The tests we described do not cover all possible scenarios, such as the presence of unit roots, long memory, cointegrating relationships. Instead, we strive to provide practitioners with a broad set of tools that cover most cases of interest – excluding the above – in empirical macroeconometrics. We emphasize structural stability tests for models with exogenous and endogenous regressors and the differences between the two.

The tools we summarize here can be readily applied to a wide range of macroeconomic and monetary policy models, contributing to important macroeconomic debates such as whether the New Keynesian Phillips curve has become less predictable, or whether the Great Moderation is due to good monetary policy or good luck (see Lubik and Surico, 2010).

NOTES

* Boldea acknowledges the support of NWO VENI grant 415-11-001 and Hall acknowledges the support of the ESRC grant RES-062-23-1351. We thank Denise Osborn for useful conversations in the preparation of this manuscript.

1. See Morgan (1990) for a review of Tinbergen's contributions.
2. The name 'structural instability' refers to the economic structure being unstable, encompassing instability in both structural and reduced-form models.
3. We adopt the convention of using '0' to denote either a scalar, vector or matrix of zero(s) with the dimension determined by the term on the other side of the equation.
4. Here, $[\cdot]$ stands for the integer part.
5. In instrumental variables estimation, identification is commonly referred to as the case of 'strong instruments'. For break-point tests in the presence of weak instruments, see Caner (2011).
6. See Andrews and Fair (1998) for a local power analysis of the test.
7. See Hall and Sen (1999, Theorem 3.2) and Sen (1997) for a similar analysis using local alternatives.
8. Inference can also be based on the D or LM statistics mentioned above and the discussion below equally applies to these statistics as well.
9. This function is chosen to maximize power against a local alternative in which a weighting distribution is used to indicate the relative importance of departures from parameter constancy in different directions (*i.e.* $\theta_1 - \theta_2$) at different break-points and also the relative importance of different break-points; see Andrews and Ploberger (1994) and Sowell (1996). The distribution over break-points is commonly taken to be uniform on Λ which is imposed in the presented formulae (via the specified $J(\pi)$) for the Av- and Exp- statistics in the text.
10. For regularity conditions and proofs see: Sup-test, Andrews (1993); Av-, Exp- tests, Andrews and Ploberger (1994) (in context of maximum likelihood) and Sowell (1996) (in context of GMM). In this context '$\Rightarrow$' denotes weak convergence in distribution.
11. For details, see Bai and Perron (1998).
12. For tests that allow for changes in the marginal distribution of regressors, see Hansen (2000).
13. Corresponding $AveW_T$ and $ExpW_T$ and their optimality properties for one break in an OLS setting are discussed in Kim and Perron (2009).
14. These critical values can be found in Bai and Perron (1998).
15. For an equivalent LR test that estimates the model in 4 with ℓ, respectively $\ell + 1$ breaks, see Bai (1999).
16. These distributions are much more complicated and depend on the relative positioning of the breaks in the first and second stage. To obtain critical values, bootstrap-based methods are proposed (see Boldea et al., 2011).
17. See Hall et al. (2012).
18. For estimating the breaks by considering a multivariate first stage for all endogenous regressors jointly, a comprehensive procedure can be found in Qu and Perron (2007).
19. For an early review of the threshold literature in statistics, see Tong (1983).
20. This result presumes that certain (relatively weak) regularity conditions hold and can be established via a similar argument to Hall and Inoue (2003, Proposition 1).
21. For example, see Chapter 14 in this volume.

22. See Chapter 14 in this volume for a description of the overidentifying restrictions test.
23. To elaborate, $\mathcal{W}_T(\lambda)$ significant but $\mathcal{O}_T(\lambda)$ insignificant is consistent with instability confined to the parameters alone; $\mathcal{O}_T(\lambda)$ significant is consistent with more general forms of instability. However, important caveats are the local nature of these results and concerns about the interpretation of fixed break-point tests discussed in section 2.
24. Although the functionals are the same as the parameter change tests, it has proved impossible to date to deduce any optimality properties for the versions based on $\mathcal{O}_T(\lambda)$ due to the nature of the alternative in this case; see Hall (2005, p. 182) for further discussion.

REFERENCES

Alogoskoufis, G. and R. Smith (1991), 'The Phillips curve, the persistence of inflation, and the Lucas critique: evidence from exchange-rate regimes', *American Economic Review*, **81**, 1254–75.

Andrews, D., X. Cheng and P. Guggenberger (2011), 'Generic results for establishing the asymptotic size of confidence sets and tests', Cowles Foundation Discussion Paper No. 1813.

Andrews, D.W.K. (1993), 'Tests for parameter instability and structural change with unknown change point', *Econometrica*, **61**, 821–56.

Andrews, D.W.K. (2003), 'Tests for parameter instability and structural change with unknown change point: a corrigendum', *Econometrica*, **71**, 395–8.

Andrews, D.W.K. and R. Fair (1988), 'Inference in econometric models with structural change', *Review of Economic Studies*, **55**, 615–40.

Andrews, D.W.K. and W. Ploberger (1994), 'Optimal tests when a nuisance parameter is present only under the alternative', *Econometrica*, **62**, 1383–414.

Areosa, W., M. McAleer and M. Medeiros (2011), 'Moment-based estimation of smooth transition regression models with endogenous variables', *Journal of Econometrics*, **165**, 100–111.

Bai, J. (1999), 'Likelihood ratio tests for multiple structural changes', *Journal of Econometrics*, **91**, 299–323.

Bai, J. and P. Perron (1998), 'Estimating and testing linear models with multiple structural changes', *Econometrica*, **66**, 47–78.

Bai, J. and P. Perron (2003), 'Computation and analysis of multiple structural change models', *Journal of Applied Econometrics*, **18**, 1–23.

Ben-David, D., R. Lumsdaine and D. Papell (2003), 'Unit roots, postwar slowdowns and long-run growth: evidence from two structural breaks', *Empirical Economics*, **28**, 303–19.

Benati, L. and P. Surico (2008), 'Evolving US monetary policy and the decline of inflation predictability', *Journal of the European Economic Association*, **6**, 634–46.

Boivin, J. and M. Giannoni (2006), 'Has monetary policy become more effective?', *The Review of Economics and Statistics*, **88**, 445–62.

Boldea, O. and A.R. Hall (2013), 'Estimation and inference in unstable non-linear least squares models', *Journal of Econometrics*, **172**, 158–67.

Boldea, O., A. Cornea and A. Hall (2011), 'Bootstrapping multiple structural change tests in models estimated via 2SLS', Working Paper.

Boldea, O., A.R. Hall and S. Han (2012), 'Asymptotic distribution theory for break point estimators in models estimated via 2SLS', *Econometric Reviews*, **33**, 1–33.

Caner, M. (2011), 'Pivotal structural change tests in linear simultaneous equations with weak identification', *Econometric Theory*, **27**, 413–26.

Caner, M. and B. Hansen (2004), 'Instrumental variable estimation of a threshold model', *Econometric Theory*, **20**, 813–43.

Carrasco, M., L. Hu and W. Ploberger (2009), 'Optimal test for Markov switching parameters', Working Paper, University of Montreal, Canada.

Clarida, R., J. Gali and M. Gertler (2000), 'Monetary policy rules and macroeconomic stability: evidence and some theory', *Quarterly Journal of Economics*, **115**, 147–80.

Cogley, T. and T. Sargent (2001), 'Evolving post-world war II US inflation dynamics', in B. Bernanke and K. Rogoff (eds), *NBER Macroeconomics Annual* vol. 16, Cambridge, MA: MIT Press.

Eitrheim, Ø. and T. Teräsvirta (1996), 'Testing the adequacy of the smooth transition autoregressive models', *Journal of Econometrics*, **74**, 59–75.

Estrella, A. and C. Fuhrer (2003), 'Monetary policy shifts and the stability of monetary policy models', *The Review of Economics and Statistics*, **85**, 94–104.

Garcia, R. (1998), 'Asymptotic null distribution of the likelihood ratio test in Markov Switching models', *International Economic Review*, **39**, 763–88.

Gonzalo, J. and J-Y. Pitarakis (2002), 'Estimation and model selection based inference in single and multiple threshold models', *Journal of Econometrics*, **110**, 319–52.
Hall, A.R. (2005), *Generalized Method of Moments*, Oxford: Oxford University Press.
Hall, A.R. and A. Inoue (2003), 'The large sample behaviour of the Generalized Method of Moments estimator in misspecified models', *Journal of Econometrics*, **114**, 361–94.
Hall, A.R. and N. Sakkas (2013), 'Approximate p-values of certain tests involving hypotheses about multiple breaks', *Journal of Econometric Methods*, forthcoming.
Hall, A.R. and A. Sen (1999), 'Structural stability testing in models estimated by Generalized Method of Moments', *Journal of Business and Economic Statistics*, **17**, 335–48.
Hall, A.R., S. Han and O. Boldea (2012), 'Inference regarding multiple structural changes in linear models with endogenous regressors', *Journal of Econometrics*, **170**, 281–302.
Hamilton, J. (1989), 'A new approach to the economic analysis of nonstationary time series and the business cycle', *Econometrica*, **57**, 357–84.
Hansen, B.E. (1992), 'The likelihood ratio test under nonstandard conditions: testing the Markov switching model of GNP', *Journal of Applied Econometrics*, **7**, S61–S82.
Hansen, B.E. (1997a), 'Approximate asymptotic p-values for structural change tests', *Journal of Business and Economic Statistics*, **15**, 60–67.
Hansen, B.E. (1997b), 'Inference in TAR models', *Studies in Nonlinear Dynamics and Econometrics*, **2**.
Hansen, B.E. (2000), 'Testing for structural change in conditional models', *Journal of Econometrics*, **97**, 93–115.
Hansen, B.E. (2011), 'Threshold autoregression in economics', *Statistics and its Interface*, **4**, 123–7.
Hansen, L.P. and K.J. Singleton (1982), 'Generalized instrumental variables estimation of nonlinear rational expectations models', *Econometrica*, **50**, 1269–86.
Kang, K., C. Kim and J. Morley (2009), 'Changes in US inflation persistence', *Studies in Nonlinear Dynamics & Econometrics*, **13**.
Kim, C-J. (2004), 'Markov-switching models with endogenous explanatory variables', *Journal of Econometrics*, **122**, 127–36.
Kim, C.-J. (2009), 'Markov-switching models with endogenous explanatory variables II: a two-step MLE procedure', *Journal of Econometrics*, **148**, 46–55.
Kim, C-J., J. Piger and R. Startz (2008), 'Estimation of Markov regime-switching regression models with endogenous switching', *Journal of Econometrics*, **143**, 263–73.
Kim, D. and P. Perron (2009), 'Assessing the relative power of structural break tests using a framework based on the approximate Bahadur slope', *Journal of Econometrics*, **149**, 26–51.
Kourtellos, A., T. Stengos and C. Tan (2008), 'THRET: Threshold Regression with Endogenous Threshold Variables', University of Cyprus Discussion Paper No. 3.
Liu, Z., D. Waggoner and T. Zha (2009), 'Asymmetric expectation effects of regime shifts in monetary policy', *Review of Economic Dynamics*, **12**, 284–303.
Lubik, T. and P. Surico (2010), 'The Lucas critique and the stability of empirical models', *Journal of Applied Econometrics*, **25**, 177–94.
Lucas, R. (1976), 'Econometric policy evaluation: a critique', in K. Brunner and A. Melzer (eds), *The Phillips Curve and Labor Markets*, vol. 1 of Carnegie-Rochester Conference Series on Public Policy, New York: Elsevier, pp. 19–46.
Morgan, M. (1990), *The History of Econometric Ideas*, New York: Cambridge University Press.
Papell, D., C. Murray and H. Ghiblawi (2000), 'The structure of unemployment', *Review of Economics and Statistics*, **82**, 309–15.
Perron, P. (1997), 'Further evidence on breaking trend functions in macroeconomic variables', *Journal of Econometrics*, **80**, 355–85.
Qu, Z. and P. Perron (2007), 'Estimating and testing structural changes in multivariate regressions', *Econometrica*, **75**, 459–502.
Rossi, B. (2006), 'Are exchange rates really random walks? Some evidence robust to parameter instability', *Macroeconomic Dynamics*, **10**, 20–38.
Sen, A. (1997), 'New tests of structural stability and applications to consumption based asset pricing models', Ph.D. thesis, Department of Economics, North Carolina State University, Raleigh, NC.
Sen, A. and A.R. Hall (1999), 'Two further aspects of some new tests for structural stability', *Structural Change and Economic Dynamics*, **10**, 431–43.
Sowell, F. (1996), 'Optimal tests of parameter variation in the Generalized Method of Moments framework', *Econometrica*, **64**, 1085–108.
Surico, P. (2007), 'The Fed's monetary policy rule and US inflation: the case of asymmetric preferences', *Journal of Economic Dynamics and Control*, **31**, 305–24.
Teräsvirta, T. (1994), 'Specification, estimation, and evaluation of smooth transition autoregressive models', *Journal of the American Statistical Association*, **89**, 208–18.

Tinbergen, J. (1939), *Statistical Testing of Business-cycle Theories, Volumes I & II*, Geneva: League of Nations.
Tong, H. (1983), *Threshold Models in Non-linear Time Series Analysis*, vol. 21 of *Lecture Notes in Statistics*, Berlin: Springer.
van Dijk, D., T. Teräsvirta and P. Franses (2002), 'Smooth transition autoregressive models: a survey of recent developments', *Econometric Reviews*, **21**, 1–47.
Weber, C. (1995), 'Cyclical output, cyclical unemployment, and Okun's coefficient: a new approach', *Journal of Applied Econometrics*, **10**, 433–45.
Zhang, C., D. Osborn and D. Kim (2008), 'The new Keynesian Phillips curve: from sticky inflation to sticky prices', *Journal of Money, Credit and Banking*, **40**, 667–99.

10 Dynamic panel data models

Badi H. Baltagi

1 INTRODUCTION

Many macroeconomic relationships are dynamic in nature in that they include at least one lagged dependent variable among the regressors:

$$y_{it} = \delta y_{i,t-1} + x'_{it}\beta + u_{it} \quad i = 1,\ldots,N \quad t = 1,\ldots,T \tag{10.1}$$

where δ is a scalar, x'_{it} is $1 \times K$ and β is $K \times 1$. The index i denotes countries, regions, firms, banks, and so on, while the index t denotes time.[1] Some early examples include Islam (1995) on empirical growth models, Attanasio et al. (2000) on the relationship between saving, growth and investment, to mention a few. A simple and popular method for tackling *heterogeneity* among the countries is to allow the disturbances to follow a one-way error component model (see Hsiao, 2003)

$$u_{it} = \mu_i + \nu_{it} \tag{10.2}$$

where μ_i could be a *fixed* or a *random* country-specific effect and $\nu_{it} \sim \text{IID}\,(0, \sigma^2_\nu)$. Note that μ_i is time-invariant and it accounts for any country-specific effect that is not included in the regression. This could be the fact that this country is an island, French speaking, was colonized by the French, predominantly Catholic, and so on. Let us start with some of the basic problems introduced by the inclusion of a lagged dependent variable. In a static model with no lagged dependent variable, if the $\mu'_i s$ are correlated with the regressors, the standard *fixed effects* (FE) estimator wipes out the $\mu'_i s$, by performing the *within transformation* $(y_{i,t} - \bar{y}_{i.})$ where $\bar{y}_{i.} = \sum_{t=1}^{T} y_{i,t}/T$ is the average over time. This yields a consistent estimator of β because the resulting disturbances $(\nu_{it} - \bar{\nu}_{i.})$ are not correlated with $(x_{it} - x_{i.})$. Wiping out the $\mu'_i s$ could have been also achieved by *first-differencing* (FD) the model and regressing $(y_{it} - y_{i,t-1})$ on $(x_{it} - x_{i,t-1})$. The latter transformation loses the initial N observations due to lagging. The FE estimator is in general more efficient than the FD estimator when the remainder disturbance $\nu_{it} \sim \text{IID}\,(0, \sigma^2_\nu)$. The FD estimator is more efficient than the FE estimator when the remainder disturbance ν_{it} is a random walk. The presence of $y_{i,t-1}$ complicates matters because it renders the FE estimator inconsistent for small T; see Nickell (1981), who showed that the FE estimator is biased of $O(1/T)$. In fact, $(y_{i,t-1} - \bar{y}_{i.-1})$ will be correlated with $(\nu_{it} - \bar{\nu}_{i.})$. To see this, note that $y_{i,t-1}$ is correlated with $\bar{\nu}_{i.}$ by construction. The latter average contains $\nu_{i,t-1}$, which is obviously correlated with $y_{i,t-1}$. Also, ν_{it} is correlated with $\bar{y}_{i.-1} = \sum_{t=1}^{T} y_{i,t-1}/T$ because the latter average contains y_{it}. These are two leading terms causing the correlation and they are both of order T. This bias does not vanish as N increases. However, as T gets large, the FE estimator becomes consistent. Several suggestions to correct for the bias of the popular FE estimator have been proposed. Most notable of these is Kiviet

(1995), who proposes a bias corrected FE estimator that subtracts a consistent estimator of this bias from the original FE estimator. However, in order to make this estimator feasible, an initial estimator for δ is needed.[2] For large T, large N, as in macro-panel studies, such that $\lim(N/T) = c$ is finite, Hahn and Kuersteiner (2002) derive a bias corrected FE estimator which reduces to

$$\hat{\delta}_c = \left(\frac{T+1}{T}\right)\tilde{\delta}_{FE} + \frac{1}{T}$$

with $\sqrt{NT}(\hat{\delta}_c - \delta) \rightarrow N(0, 1 - \delta^2)$. Under the assumption of normality of the disturbances, $\hat{\delta}_c$ is asymptotically efficient as $N, T \rightarrow \infty$ at the same rate. Hahn and Moon (2006) showed that this result can be extended to dynamic linear panel data models with both individual and time effects. Hence, the same higher order bias correction approach as in Hahn and Kuersteiner (2002) can be adopted even when time effects are present. They stress that such robustness is limited only to linear models.

In summary, for typical *micro-panels* where N is *large* and T is *short* and fixed, the FE estimator is *biased* and inconsistent, and it is worth emphasizing that only if $T \rightarrow \infty$ will the FE estimator of δ and β be consistent for the dynamic error component model. For *macro-panels*, T is not very small relative to N, hence, some researchers may still favor the FE estimator, arguing that its bias may not be large. Judson and Owen (1999) performed some Monte Carlo experiments for $N = 20$ or 100 and $T = 5, 10, 20$ and 30 and found that the bias in the FE estimator can be as much as 20 per cent of the true value of the coefficient of interest, even when $T = 30$. This bias increases with δ, the coefficient of the lagged dependent variable, and decreases with T. For an empirical example, Attanasio et al. (2000) studied the relationship between saving, growth and investment using a panel of $N = 123$ countries over the period 1961–94. However, not all variables were available for every country and for every year. Hence, they used three different data sets in their empirical investigation. One data set included $N = 50$ countries for which all variables are available every year in the interval 1965–93 ($T = 29$). Another data set included $N = 38$ countries whose variables are available every year from 1961 to 1994 ($T = 34$). The last data set has comparable N and T and it is not clear that we have N asymptotics as in the micro-panel case. For large N and T asymptotics, see Phillips and Moon (1999).

For the first difference (FD) estimator, the right-hand differenced regressor $(y_{i,t-1} - y_{i,t-2})$ is correlated with the differenced error $(\nu_{i,t} - \nu_{i,t-1})$, but this correlation is easier to handle than FE. In fact, Anderson and Hsiao (1981) suggested using $\Delta y_{i,t-2} = (y_{i,t-2} - y_{i,t-3})$ or simply $y_{i,t-2}$ as an instrument for $\Delta y_{i,t-1} = (y_{i,t-1} - y_{i,t-2})$. These instruments will not be correlated with $\Delta\nu_{it} = \nu_{i,t} - \nu_{i,t-1}$, as long as the ν_{it} themselves are not serially correlated. This instrumental variable (IV) estimation method leads to consistent but not necessarily efficient estimates of the parameters in the model because it does not make use of all the available moment conditions (see Ahn and Schmidt, 1995), and it does not take into account the differenced structure on the residual disturbances $(\Delta\nu_{it})$. Arellano (1989) finds that for simple dynamic error components models, the estimator that uses *differences* $\Delta y_{i,t-2}$ rather than *levels* $y_{i,t-2}$ for instruments in a *first-differenced* equation, will yield a singularity point and very large variances over a significant range of parameter values. In contrast, the estimator that uses instruments in *levels*, that is, $y_{i,t-2}$, for the *first-differenced* equation, has no singularities and much smaller variances and is therefore recommended.

Dessi and Robertson (2003) estimate dynamic panel regressions relating debt and Tobin's Q using a panel of $N = 557$ UK firms observed over the period 1967–89 ($T = 23$). They find that firm fixed effects are highly significant, concluding that unobserved firm characteristics are important determinants of both capital structure and expected performance (as measured by Tobin's Q). Applying the Anderson and Hsiao (1981) estimator, they find highly significant dynamic effects in the determination of debt and Tobin's Q, hence emphasizing the importance of capturing firm *heterogeneity* and *dynamics*, two of the main advantages of applying panel data methods.

2 THE ARELLANO AND BOND ESTIMATOR

Arellano and Bond (1991) proposed a Generalized Method of Moments (GMM) procedure that is more efficient than the Anderson and Hsiao (1981) estimator. This can be demonstrated using the simple autoregressive model with no regressors:

$$y_{it} = \delta y_{i,t-1} + u_{it} \quad i = 1,\ldots,N \quad t = 1,\ldots,T \tag{10.3}$$

Differencing this equation to eliminate the individual effects, one gets

$$y_{it} - y_{i,t-1} = \delta(y_{i,t-1} - y_{i,t-2}) + (\nu_{it} - \nu_{i,t-1}) \tag{10.4}$$

and note that $(\nu_{it} - \nu_{i,t-1})$ is $MA(1)$ with unit root. If we only observe this panel for three periods, that is, $t = 3$, then this is a cross-section regression

$$y_{i3} - y_{i2} = \delta(y_{i2} - y_{i1}) + (\nu_{i3} - \nu_{i2}) \quad i = 1,\ldots,N$$

with y_{i1} being a valid instrument, since it is highly correlated with $(y_{i2} - y_{i1})$ and not correlated with $(\nu_{i3} - \nu_{i2})$ as long as the ν_{it} are not serially correlated. But note what happens when we observe the panel for four periods, that is, $t = 4$:

$$y_{i4} - y_{i3} = \delta(y_{i3} - y_{i2}) + (\nu_{i4} - \nu_{i3}) \quad i = 1,\ldots,N$$

In this case, y_{i2} as well as y_{i1} are valid instruments for $(y_{i3} - y_{i2})$, since both y_{i2} and y_{i1} are not correlated with $(\nu_{i4} - \nu_{i3})$. One can continue in this fashion, adding an extra valid instrument with each additional period of observation, so that for period T, the set of valid instruments becomes $(y_{i1}, y_{i2},\ldots,y_{i,T-2})$.

Define the matrix of instruments

$$W_i = \begin{bmatrix} [y_{i1}] & & & 0 \\ & [y_{i1}, y_{i2}] & & \\ & & \ddots & \\ 0 & & & [y_{i1},\ldots,y_{i,T-2}] \end{bmatrix} \quad i = 1,\ldots,N \tag{10.5}$$

based on the moment conditions given by $E(W_i'\Delta v_i) = 0$. It is important to emphasize that the number of instruments increases with T and this estimation method relies on N being very large (N asymptotics) and T being very small (N much larger than T). For the whole panel, stacked such that the country index is slow and the time index is fast, the matrix of instruments becomes $W = [W_1', \ldots, W_N']'$. Pre-multiplying the differenced equation in vector form by W', one gets

$$W'\Delta y = W'(\Delta y_{-1})\delta + W'\Delta v \tag{10.6}$$

The differenced $MA(1)$ error term Δv_i has mean zero and variance

$$E(\Delta v_i \Delta v_i') = \sigma_v^2 G \tag{10.7}$$

where $\Delta v_i' = (v_{i3} - v_{i2}, \ldots, v_{iT} - v_{i,T-1})$ and

$$G = \begin{pmatrix} 2 & -1 & 0 & \cdots & 0 & 0 & 0 \\ -1 & 2 & -1 & \cdots & 0 & 0 & 0 \\ 0 & -1 & 2 & \cdots & 0 & 0 & 0 \\ \vdots & \vdots & \vdots & \ddots & \vdots & \vdots & \vdots \\ 0 & 0 & 0 & \cdots & 2 & -1 & 0 \\ 0 & 0 & 0 & \cdots & -1 & 2 & -1 \\ 0 & 0 & 0 & \cdots & 0 & -1 & 2 \end{pmatrix}.$$

The Arellano and Bond (1991) *one-step* GMM estimator performs GLS using this G matrix:

$$\hat{\delta}_1 = [(\Delta y_{-1})' W (W'(I_N \otimes G) W)^{-1} W'(\Delta y_{-1})]^{-1} \times [(\Delta y_{-1})' W (W'(I_N \otimes G) W)^{-1} W'(\Delta y)] \tag{10.8}$$

The optimal generalized method of moments (GMM) estimator replaces

$$W'(I_N \otimes G) W = \sum_{i=1}^{N} W_i' G W_i$$

by

$$V_N = \sum_{i=1}^{N} W_i'(\Delta v_i)(\Delta v_i)' W_i$$

where Δv is replaced by differenced residuals obtained from the one step estimator $\hat{\delta}_1$. The resulting estimator is the *two-step* Arellano and Bond (1991) GMM estimator:

$$\hat{\delta}_2 = [(\Delta y_{-1})' W \hat{V}_N^{-1} W'(\Delta y_{-1})]^{-1} [(\Delta y_{-1})' W \hat{V}_N^{-1} W'(\Delta y)] \tag{10.9}$$

The *one-step* Arellano and Bond estimator $\hat{\delta}_1$ is the *default* option in Stata's command *xtabond*. Adding the option *two-step* gives the estimator $\hat{\delta}_2$. Of course, this is also available in other software such as EViews.

If there are additional *strictly exogenous* regressors x_{it} satisfying $E(x_{it}\nu_{is}) = 0$ for all $t, s = 1, 2, \ldots, T$, but where all the x_{it} are correlated with μ_i, then all the x_{it} are valid instruments for the first differenced equation. In this case, $[x'_{i1}, x'_{i2}, \ldots, x'_{iT}]$ should be added to each diagonal element of W_i.

If x_{it} are *predetermined* rather than *strictly exogenous* with $E(x_{it}\nu_{is}) \neq 0$ for $s < t$, and zero otherwise, then only $[x'_{i1}, x'_{i2}, \ldots, x'_{i(s-1)}]$ are valid instruments for the differenced equation at period s. In this case, the matrix of instruments becomes:

$$W_i = \begin{bmatrix} [y_{i1}, x'_{i1}, x'_{i2}] & & & 0 \\ & [y_{i1}, y_{i2}, x'_{i1}, x'_{i2}, x'_{i3}] & & \\ & & \ddots & \\ 0 & & & [y_{i1}, \ldots, y_{i,T-2}, x'_{i1}, \ldots, x'_{i,T-1}] \end{bmatrix}. \quad (10.10)$$

2.1 Diagnostics for the Arellano and Bond Estimator

Arellano and Bond (1991) propose a test for the hypothesis that there is *no second-order serial correlation* for the disturbances of the first-differenced equation. This test is important because the consistency of the GMM estimator relies upon the fact that ν_{it} is not serially correlated. A test for *first order* and *second order* serial correlation of $\Delta\nu_{it}$ can be obtained with Stata 11 using the command *estat abond*. One should reject the absence of first order serial correlation of $\Delta\nu_{it}$, but not reject the absence of second order serial correlation of $\Delta\nu_{it}$.

Additionally, Arellano and Bond (1991) suggest *Sargan's test* of *over-identifying restrictions* given by

$$m = \Delta\hat{\nu}' W \left[\sum_{i=1}^{N} W_i'(\Delta\hat{\nu}_i)(\Delta\hat{\nu}_i)' W_i \right]^{-1} W'(\Delta\hat{\nu}) \sim \chi^2_{p-K-1}$$

where p refers to the number of columns of W and $\Delta\hat{\nu}$ denote the residuals from the two-step estimator. Using Monte Carlo experiments, this test performs well for large N and very small T. However, Bowsher (2002) finds that the use of too many moment conditions (large T) causes the Sargan test for overidentifying restrictions to be *undersized* and have extremely *low power*. The Sargan test never rejects when T is too large for a given N. The test had *zero size and power* for the following (N, T) pairs $(125, 16)$, $(85, 13)$, and $(40, 10)$. This is attributed to poor estimates of the weighting matrix in GMM.

To summarize, dynamic panel data estimation with fixed effects suffers from the Nickell (1981) bias for small T. Hence FE in a dynamic panel model is only recommended for very large T. The recommended estimator for large N and small T is the GMM estimator suggested by Arellano and Bond (1991). However, the Arellano and Bond two-step estimator suffers from two weaknesses. The first one is poor estimation of the weight matrix, which leads to biased asymptotic standard errors and weak inference. In fact, Arellano and Bond warned that the estimated standard error of their two-step

GMM estimator is *downward biased*. Windmeijer (2005) suggests a correction term based on a Taylor-series expansion that accounts for the estimation of this *weight matrix*. He shows that this correction term provides a more accurate approximation in finite samples when all the moment conditions are linear. These corrected standard errors are available using Stata 11 with the option *vce (robust)*.

The second weakness of the Arellano and Bond GMM estimator is that it relies on too many moment conditions which were shown to suffer from the weak instruments problems (see Blundell and Bond, 1998). One solution suggested by Ziliak (1997) is not to use *all* the moment conditions but a *sub-optimal number* of instruments. Using Monte Carlo experiments, Ziliak showed that there is a bias/efficiency trade-off as one uses more moment conditions. Even though it is desirable from an asymptotic efficiency point of view to include as many moment conditions as possible, it may be infeasible or impractical to do so in many cases. The practical problem of not being able to use more moment conditions as well as the statistical problem of the trade-off between small sample bias and efficiency prompted Ahn and Schmidt (1999) to pose the following questions: 'Under what conditions can we use a smaller set of moment conditions without incurring any loss of asymptotic efficiency? In other words, under what conditions are some moment conditions redundant in the sense that utilizing them does not improve efficiency?' These questions were first dealt with by Im et al. (1999) who considered panel data models with strictly exogenous explanatory variables. They argued that, for example, with ten strictly exogenous time-varying variables and six time periods, the moment conditions available for the random effects (RE) model is 360 and this reduces to 300 moment conditions for the FE model. GMM utilizing all these moment conditions leads to an efficient estimator. However, these moment conditions exceed what the simple RE and FE estimators use. Im et al. (1999) provide the assumptions under which this efficient GMM estimator reduces to the simpler FE or RE estimator. In other words, Im et al. (1999) show the redundancy of the moment conditions that these simple estimators do not use. Ahn and Schmidt (1999) provide a more systematic method by which redundant instruments can be found, and generalize this result to models with time-varying individual effects.

Blundell et al. (1992) apply the Arellano and Bond estimator to a panel of $N = 532$ UK manufacturing companies over the period 1975–86 ($T = 12$). They study the importance of Tobin's Q in the determination of investment decisions. Tobin's Q is allowed to be endogenous and possibly correlated with the firm-specific effects. Utilizing past variables as instruments, Tobin's Q effect is found to be small but significant. These results are sensitive to the choice of dynamic specification, exogeneity assumptions and measurement error in Q.

Becker et al. (1994) estimate a rational addiction model for cigarettes using a panel of 50 states (and the District of Columbia) over the period 1955–85 ($T = 31$). They apply fixed effects 2SLS to estimate a second-order difference equation in consumption of cigarettes, finding support for forward-looking consumers and rejecting myopic behavior. Their long-run price elasticity estimate is -0.78 as compared to -0.44 for the short run. Baltagi and Griffin (2001) apply the FD-2SLS, FE-2SLS and Arellano and Bond GMM dynamic panel estimation methods to the Becker, Grossman and Murphy rational addiction model for cigarettes. Although the results are in general supportive of rational addiction, the estimates of the implied discount rate are not precise.

Bond et al. (2003) estimate dynamic investment equations using company panel data for manufacturing firms in Belgium, France, Germany and the United Kingdom, covering the period 1978–89. Using GMM first difference estimation methods, they find that cash flow and profits appear to be both statistically and quantitatively more significant in the United Kingdom than in the three continental European countries. This is consistent with the suggestion that financial constraints on investment may be relatively severe in the more market-oriented UK financial system.

More recently, Baltagi et al. (2009) use panel data of $N = 42$ developing countries over the period 1980–2003 ($T = 24$) to address the empirical question of whether trade and financial openness can help explain the recent pace in financial development, as well as its variation across countries in recent years. Using Arellano and Bond (1991) GMM dynamic panel estimation, they show that both types of openness are statistically significant determinants of banking sector development. They also show that the marginal effects of trade (financial) openness are negatively related to the degree of financial (trade) openness, indicating that relatively closed economies stand to benefit most from opening up their trade and/or capital accounts. Although these economies may be able to accomplish more by taking steps to open both their trade and capital accounts, opening up one without the other could still generate gains in terms of banking sector development.

3 SYSTEM ESTIMATION

Ahn and Schmidt (1995) show that under the standard assumptions used in a dynamic panel data model, there are additional *non-linear* moment conditions that are ignored by the Arellano and Bond (1991) estimator. The standard assumptions for the dynamic panel model are that:

(A.1) For all i, ν_{it} is uncorrelated with y_{i0} for all t.
(A.2) For all i, ν_{it} is uncorrelated with μ_i for all t.
(A.3) For all i, the ν_{it} are mutually uncorrelated.

Under these assumptions, one obtains the following $T(T-1)/2$ moment conditions:

$$E(y_{is}\Delta u_{it}) = 0 \quad t = 2, \ldots, T \quad s = 0, \ldots, t-2 \tag{10.11}$$

These are the same moment restrictions exploited by Arellano and Bond (1991). However, Ahn and Schmidt (1995) find $T-2$ *additional* moment conditions given by

$$E(u_{iT}\Delta u_{it}) = 0 \quad t = 2, \ldots, T-1 \tag{10.12}$$

These $T(T-1)/2 + (T-2)$ moment conditions represent *all* of the moment conditions implied by the assumptions that the v_{it} are mutually uncorrelated among themselves and with μ_i and y_{i0}.

Wansbeek and Bekker (1996) considered a simple dynamic panel data model with no exogenous regressors considered in (10.3). They derived an expression for the optimal instrumental variable estimator, that is, one with minimal asymptotic variance. A striking result is the difference in efficiency between the IV and ML estimators under the normality assumption. They find that for regions of the autoregressive parameter δ which are likely in practice, ML is superior. The gap between IV (or GMM) and ML can be narrowed down by adding moment restrictions of the type considered by Ahn and Schmidt (1995). Hence, Wansbeek and Bekker (1996) find support for adding these non-linear moment restrictions and warn against the loss in efficiency as compared with MLE by ignoring them.

Blundell and Bond (1998) revisit the importance of exploiting the initial condition in generating efficient estimators of the dynamic panel data model when T is small. Blundell and Bond (1998) focus on the case where $T = 3$ with only one orthogonality condition given by $E(y_{i1}\Delta v_{i3}) = 0$, so that δ is just-identified. In this case, the first stage IV regression is obtained by running Δy_{i2} on y_{i1}. Note that this regression can be obtained from (10.3) evaluated at $t = 2$ by subtracting y_{i1} from both sides of this equation, that is,

$$\Delta y_{i2} = (\delta - 1)y_{i,1} + \mu_i + v_{i2} \tag{10.13}$$

Since we expect $E(y_{i1}\mu_i) > 0$, $(\delta - 1)$ will be biased upwards with

$$\text{plim}\,(\hat{\delta} - 1) = (\delta - 1)\frac{c}{c + (\sigma_\mu^2/\sigma_u^2)} \tag{10.14}$$

where $c = (1 - \delta)/(1 + \delta)$. The bias term effectively scales the estimated coefficient on the instrumental variable y_{i1} towards zero. They also find that the F-statistic of the first stage IV regression converges to χ_1^2 with non-centrality parameter

$$\tau = \frac{(\sigma_u^2 c)^2}{\sigma_\mu^2 + \sigma_u^2 c} \to 0 \text{ as } \delta \to 1 \tag{10.15}$$

As $\tau \to 0$, the instrumental variable estimator performs poorly. Hence, Blundell and Bond attribute the bias and the poor precision of the first difference Arellano and Bond GMM estimator to the problem of *weak instruments* and characterize this by its concentration parameter τ.

Next, Blundell and Bond (1998) show that an additional *mild stationarity restriction* on the initial conditions process allows the use of an extended system GMM estimator that uses *lagged differences* of y_{it} as instruments for equations in *levels*, in addition to *lagged levels* of y_{it} as instruments for equations in *first differences*. More specifically, this stationarity condition on y_{i1} requires $E[(y_{i1} - \frac{\mu_i}{1-\delta})\mu_i] = 0$, so that y_{it} converges towards its mean $\frac{\mu_i}{1-\delta}$ for each individual from period $t = 2$ onwards. This in turn yields the condition $E[\Delta y_{i,t-1}\mu_i] = 0$ for $i = 1,2,..,N$. Using the usual mild assumption that $E[\Delta v_{it}\mu_i] = 0$ for $i = 1,2,..,N$ and $t = 3,4,\ldots,T$, we get the additional $T - 2$ non-redundant linear moment conditions $E[\Delta y_{i,t-1}(\mu_i + v_{it})] = 0$ for $t = 3,4,\ldots,T$, obtained by Ahn and Schmidt (1995). Together with the Arellano and Bond (1991) conditions on the first differenced equation, these moment conditions on equations in levels yield the system GMM estimator.[3] Blundell and Bond (1998) show that this system GMM estimator produces *dramatic efficiency gains* over the basic first difference GMM as $\delta \to 1$ and $(\sigma_\mu^2/\sigma_u^2)$ increases. In fact, for $T = 4$ and $(\sigma_\mu^2/\sigma_u^2) = 1$, the asymptotic variance ratio of the first difference Arellano and Bond GMM estimator to this system GMM estimator is 1.75 for $\delta = 0$ and increases to 3.26 for $\delta = 0.5$ and 55.4 for $\delta = 0.9$. This clearly demonstrates that the *levels restrictions* remain informative in cases where first differenced instruments become weak. Things improve for first difference GMM as T increases. However, with short T and persistent series, the Blundell and Bond findings support the use of the extra moment conditions.

Blundell and Bond (2000) estimate a Cobb–Douglas production function using data on $N = 509$ R&D performing US manufacturing companies observed over $T = 8$ years (1982–89). The Arellano and Bond (1991) GMM estimator that uses moment conditions on the first differenced model finds a low estimate of the capital coefficient and low precision for all coefficients estimated. However, the system Blundell and Bond (2000) GMM estimator gives reasonable and more precise estimates of the capital coefficient, and constant returns to scale is not rejected. Blundell and Bond (2000) conclude that 'a careful examination of the original series and consideration of the system GMM estimator can usefully overcome many of the disappointing features of the standard GMM estimator for dynamic panel models'.

Acemoglu et al. (2005) use a dynamic panel data specification to revisit the relationship between education and democracy across countries. They show that the positive and significant cross-sectional relationship between schooling and democracy across countries disappears when panel data fixed effects are included in the regression. Democracy is measured using the Freedom House Political Rights Index (from 1 to 7): these are transformed to lie between 0 and 1, with 1 corresponding to the most democratic set of institutions. Education is measured by the average years of schooling in the total population of age 25 and above. Since the specification is dynamic, and the FE estimator is known to be biased, a two-step robust Arellano and Bond (1991) GMM estimator is applied, which also results in a negative and insignificant coefficient estimate for lagged education. Bobba and Coviello (2007) apply Blundell and Bond (1998) system GMM to the same equation and find that the lagged education coefficient estimate is now positive and significant.

4 LIMITED INFORMATION MAXIMUM LIKELIHOOD

The dynamic panel model generates many overidentifying restrictions even for moderate values of T. Also, the number of instruments increases with T, but the quality of these instruments is often *poor* because they tend to be only weakly correlated with first differenced endogenous variables that appear in the equation. From the classic literature on simultaneous equations, it is well known that Limited Information Maximum Likelihood (LIML) is strongly preferred to 2SLS if the number of instruments gets large as the sample size tends to infinity. In fact, Alonso-Borrego and Arellano (1999) and Alvarez and Arellano (2003) advocate the use of LIML in dynamic panel models. The latter paper derives the asymptotic properties of the FE, GMM and LIML estimators of a dynamic model with random effects. When both T and $N \to \infty$, GMM and LIML are *consistent* and asymptotically equivalent to the FE estimator. When ($T/N \to 0$), the fixed T results for GMM and LIML remain valid, but FE, although consistent, still exhibits an asymptotic bias term in its asymptotic distribution. When $T/N \to c$, where $0 < c \leq 2$, all three estimators are consistent. The basic intuition behind this result is that, contrary to the simultaneous equation setting where too many instruments produce over-fitting and undesirable closeness to OLS, with dynamic panels, a larger number of instruments is associated with larger values of T and closeness to FE is desirable since the endogeneity bias $\to 0$ as $T \to \infty$. Nevertheless, FE, GMM and LIML exhibit a bias term in their asymptotic distributions; the biases are of order $1/T$, $1/N$ and $1/(2N - T)$, respectively. Provided $T < N$, the asymptotic bias of GMM is always *smaller* than the FE bias, and the LIML bias is *smaller* than the other two. When $T = N$, the asymptotic bias is the same for all three estimators.

Alvarez and Arellano (2003) find that as $T \to \infty$, regardless of whether N is fixed or tends to ∞, provided $N/T^3 \to 0$,

$$\sqrt{NT}\left[\tilde{\delta}_{FE} - \left(\delta - \frac{1}{T}(1 + \delta)\right)\right] \to N(0, 1 - \delta^2). \tag{10.16}$$

Also, as $N, T \to \infty$ such that $(logT^2)/N \to 0$, $\hat{\delta}_{GMM} \to \delta$. Moreover, provided $T/N \to c$, $0 < c < \infty$,

$$\sqrt{NT}\left[\hat{\delta}_{GMM} - \left(\delta - \frac{1}{N}(1 + \delta)\right)\right] \to N(0, 1 - \delta^2). \tag{10.17}$$

When $T \to \infty$, the number of GMM orthogonality conditions $T(T - 1)/2 \to \infty$. In spite of this fact, $\hat{\delta}_{GMM} \to \delta$. Also, as $N, T \to \infty$ provided $T/N \to c$, $0 \le c \le 2, \hat{\delta}_{LIML} \to \delta$. Moreover,

$$\sqrt{NT}\left[\hat{\delta}_{LIML} - \left(\delta - \frac{1}{2N - T}(1 + \delta)\right)\right] \to N(0, 1 - \delta^2). \tag{10.18}$$

LIML, like GMM, is consistent for δ despite $T \to \infty$ and $T/N \to c$.

Provided $T < N$, the bias of LIML $<$ bias of GMM $<$ bias of FE.

Wansbeek and Knaap (1999) consider a simple dynamic panel data model with *heterogeneous* coefficients on the lagged dependent variable and the time trend, i.e.,

$$y_{it} = \delta_i y_{i,t-1} + \xi_i t + \mu_i + u_{it} \tag{10.19}$$

This model results from Islam's (1995) version of Solow's model on growth convergence among countries. Wansbeek and Knaap (1999) show that double differencing gets rid of the individual country effects (μ_i) on the first round of differencing and the heterogeneous coefficient on the time trend (ξ_i) on the second round of differencing. Modified OLS, IV and GMM methods are adapted to this model and LIML is suggested as a viable alternative to GMM to guard against the small sample bias of GMM. Simulations show that LIML is the superior estimator for $T \ge 10$ and $N \ge 50$. Macroeconomic data are subject to measurement error and Wansbeek and Knaap (1999) show how these estimators can be modified to account for measurement error that is white noise. For example,

GMM is modified so that it discards the orthogonality conditions that rely on the absence of measurement error.

Bun and Kiviet (2006) analyze the finite sample behavior of the FE, GLS and a range of GMM estimators in dynamic panel data models with individual effects and an additional regressor. The additional regressor may be correlated with the individual effects and is predetermined. Asymptotic expansions indicate how the order of magnitude of bias of these estimators depends on N and T. For example, they show that FE and GLS are biased of $O(1/T)$ irrespective of the value of N, while the GMM estimators are biased of the order $O(1/N)$, assuming T fixed. They also reveal how the bias of the GMM estimators tends to increase with the number of moment conditions exploited. They study both GMM based on the levels equation and those based on the forward orthogonalization procedure. They provide analytic evidence on how the bias of the various estimators depends on the feedbacks and on other model characteristics such as prominence of individual effects and correlation between observed and unobserved heterogeneity. Simulation results show that none of the techniques examined dominates regarding bias and mean squared error over all parametrization examined. For N and T of moderate size, all estimators show substantial bias and poor RMSE performance leading the authors to conclude that 'standard first-order asymptotic theory is of little use indeed to establish and rank the qualities of the estimators'.

Andrews and Lu (2001) develop consistent model and moment *selection criteria* and downward testing procedures for GMM estimation that are able to select the correct model and moments with probability that goes to 1 as the sample size goes to infinity. This is applied to dynamic panel data models with unobserved individual effects. The selection criteria can be used to select the lag length for the lagged dependent variables, to determine the exogeneity of the regressors, and/or to determine the existence of correlation between some regressors and the individual effects. Monte Carlo experiments are performed to study the small sample performance of the selection criteria and the testing procedures and their impact on parameter estimation.

Hahn et al. (2007) consider the simple autoregressive panel data model in (10.3) with the following strong assumptions: (i) $\nu_{it} \sim IIN(0, \sigma_\nu^2)$ over i and t, (ii) stationarity conditions $(y_{i0}/\mu_i) \sim N(\frac{\mu_i}{1-\delta}, \frac{\sigma_\nu^2}{1-\delta^2})$ and $\mu_i \sim N(0, \sigma_\mu^2)$. They show that the Arellano and Bover (1995) GMM estimator, based on the forward demeaning transformation, can be represented as a linear combination of 2SLS estimators and therefore may be subject to a substantial finite sample bias. Using Monte Carlo experiments, they show that this is indeed the case. For example, for $T = 5$, $N = 100$ and $\delta = 0.1$, the %bias of the GMM estimator is -16%. For $\delta = 0.8$, the %bias is -28%, and for $\delta = 0.9$, the %bias is -51%. Hahn et al. suggest two different approaches to eliminate this bias. The first is a second order Taylor series type approximation and the second is a long-difference estimator. The Monte Carlo results show that the second order Taylor series type approximation does a reasonably good job except when δ is close to 1 and N is small. For $T = 5, N = 100$ and $\delta = 0.1, 0.8, 0.9$ the %bias for this bias corrected estimator is 0.25%, -11% and -42%, respectively.

The second order asymptotics fails to be a good approximation around $\delta = 1$. This is due to the *weak instrument* problem discussed in Blundell and Bond (1998). Hahn et al. turn to the *long difference* estimator to deal with weak IV around the unit circle avoiding the stationarity assumption:

$$y_{it} - y_{i1} = \delta(y_{it} - y_{i0}) + \nu_{it} - \nu_{i1} \tag{10.20}$$

Here y_{i0} is a valid instrument. The residuals $(y_{i,T-1} - \delta y_{i,T-2}),.., (y_{i,2} - \delta y_{i,1})$ are also valid instruments. To make it operational, they suggest using the Arellano and Bover estimator for the first step and iterating using the long difference estimator. Hahn et al. analyze the class of GMM estimators that exploit the Ahn and Schmidt (1995) complete set of moment conditions and show that a strict subset of the full set of moment restrictions should be used in estimation in order to minimize bias. They show that the long difference estimator is a good approximation to the bias minimal procedure. They report the numerical values of the biases of the Arellano and Bond, Arellano and Bover and Ahn and Schmidt estimators under near unit root asymptotics and compare them with biases for the long difference estimator as well as the bias minimal estimator. Despite the fact that the long difference estimator does not achieve small bias reduction as the fully optimal estimator, it has significantly less bias than the more commonly used implementations of the GMM estimator.

5 THE KEANE AND RUNKLE ESTIMATOR

Keane and Runkle (1992) suggest an alternative estimation method to dynamic panel models with small T and large N. This method of estimation eliminates the general serial correlation pattern in the data, while preserving the use of predetermined instruments in obtaining consistent parameter estimates. This is based on the forward filtering idea from the time-series literature. More specifically, they allow for a general variance–covariance structure Σ of dimension $T \times T$ for the disturbances across time. This Σ is invariant across $i = 1,\ldots,N$, so that

$$\Omega = E(uu') = I_N \otimes \Sigma.$$

Keane and Runkle assume the existence of a set of predetermined instruments W such that $E(u_{it}/W_{is}) = 0$ for $s \leq t$, but $E(u_{it}/W_{is}) \neq 0$ for $s > t$. In other words, W may contain lagged values of y_{it}. For this model, the 2SLS estimator will provide a consistent estimator of the residuals. Using the consistent 2SLS residuals, say $\hat{u}_i$ for the ith individual, where $\hat{u}_i$ is of dimension $(T \times 1)$, one can get a consistent estimate of Σ as follows:

$$\hat{\Sigma} = \hat{U}'\hat{U}/N = \sum_{i=1}^{N} \hat{u}_i\hat{u}_i'/N$$

where $\hat{U}' = [\hat{u}_1, \hat{u}_2, \ldots, \hat{u}_N]$ is of dimension $(T \times N)$. Obtain $\hat{\Sigma}^{-1}$ and its corresponding Cholesky's decomposition $\hat{P}$.[4] Next, one pre-multiplies the model by $\hat{Q} = (I_N \otimes \hat{P})$ and estimates the model by 2SLS using the original set of predetermined instruments.

Keane and Runkle suggest first differencing if one is worried about the presence of individual specific effects. To find out whether one should difference or not, they perform a Hausman (1978) type test based on the difference between FD-2SLS and 2SLS. If the null is not rejected, there is no need to first difference. If the null is rejected, they perform their estimation procedure on the first-differenced (FD) model. They also suggest testing the null hypothesis of the strong exogeneity of the instruments based on the contrast between FE-2SLS and FD-2SLS. Keane and Runkle apply their testing and estimation procedures to a simple version of the rational expectations life-cycle consumption model, based on a sample of 627 households surveyed between 1972 and 1982 by the Michigan Panel Study on Income Dynamics (PSID). They reject the strong exogeneity of the instruments, but fail to reject the null hypothesis of no correlation between the individual effects and the instruments. This means that there is no need to first-difference to get rid of the individual effects. Based on the KR-2SLS estimates, the authors cannot reject the simple life-cycle model. However, they show that if one uses the Within estimates, one would get misleading evidence against the life-cycle model.

6 HETEROGENEOUS PANELS

Robertson and Symons (1992) and Pesaran and Smith (1995) questioned the poolability of the data across *heterogeneous* countries. In fact, Robertson and Symons (1992) consider the case of, say, two countries ($N = 2$), where the asymptotics depend on $T \rightarrow \infty$. Their true model is a simple *heterogeneous static* regression model with one regressor

$$y_{it} = \beta_i x_{it} + \nu_{it} \quad i = 1, 2 \quad t = 1, \ldots, T$$

where ν_{it} is independent for $i = 1, 2$, and β_i varies across $i = 1, 2$. However, their estimated model is *dynamic and homogeneous* with $\beta_1 = \beta_2 = \beta$ and assumes an identity covariance matrix for the disturbances:

$$y_{it} = \delta y_{i,t-1} + \beta x_{it} + w_{it} \quad i = 1, 2$$

The regressors are assumed to follow a stationary process $x_{it} = \rho x_{i,t-1} + \varepsilon_{it}$ with $|\rho| < 1$ but different variances σ_i^2 for $i = 1, 2$. Robertson and Symons (1992) obtain the probability limits of the resulting $\hat{\delta}$ and $\hat{\beta}$ as $T \rightarrow \infty$. They find that the coefficient δ of $y_{i,t-1}$ is overstated, while the mean effect of the regressors (the x_{it}) is underestimated. In case the regressors are random walks ($\rho = 1$), then plim $\hat{\delta} = 1$ and plim $\hat{\beta} = 0$. Therefore, false imposition of parameter *homogeneity*, and *dynamic* estimation of a static model when the regressors follow a random walk lead to perverse results. Using Monte Carlo experiments they show that the dynamics become misleading even for T as small as 40, which corresponds to the annual post-war data period. Even though these results are derived for $N = 2$, one regressor and no lagged dependent variable in the true model, Robertson and Symons (1992) show that the same phenomenon occurs for an empirical example of a real wage equation for a panel of 13 OECD countries observed over the period 1958–86. Parameter homogeneity across countries is rejected and the true relationship appears dynamic. Imposing false equality restriction biases the coefficient of the lagged wage upwards and the coefficient of the capital–labor ratio downwards.

Pesaran and Smith (1995) estimate a *heterogeneous dynamic* panel data model given by

$$y_{it} = \lambda_i y_{i,t-1} + \beta_i x_{it} + u_{it} \quad i = 1, \ldots, N \quad t = 1, \ldots, T$$

where λ_i is IID $(\lambda, \sigma^2_\lambda)$ and β_i is IID (β, σ^2_β). Further λ_i and β_i are independent of y_{is}, x_{is} and u_{is} for all s. The objective in this case is to obtain consistent estimates of the *mean* values of λ_i and β_i. Pesaran and Smith (1995) present four different estimation procedures:

1. aggregate time-series regressions of group averages;
2. cross-section regressions of averages over time;
3. pooled regressions allowing for fixed or random intercepts, or
4. separate regressions for each group, where coefficients estimates are averaged over these groups.

They show that when T is small (even if N is large), all the procedures yield *inconsistent* estimators. When both N and T are large, Pesaran and Smith (1995) show that the cross-section regression procedure will yield consistent estimates of the mean values of λ and β. Intuitively, when T is large, the individual parameters λ_i and β_i can be consistently estimated using T observations of each country i, say $\hat{\lambda}_i$ and $\hat{\beta}_i$, then averaging these individual estimators, $\sum_{i=1}^{N}\hat{\lambda}_i/N$ and $\sum_{i=1}^{N}\hat{\beta}_i/N$, will lead to consistent estimators of the mean values of λ and β.

Maddala et al. (1997) on the other hand argued that the heterogeneous time series estimates yield inaccurate estimates and even wrong signs for the coefficients, while the panel data estimates are not valid when one rejects the hypothesis of homogeneity of the coefficients. They argued that shrinkage estimators are superior to either heterogeneous or homogeneous parameter estimates especially for prediction purposes. In fact, Maddala et al. (1997) considered the problem of estimating short-run and long-run elasticities of residential demand for electricity and natural gas for each of 49 states over the period 1970–90. They conclude that individual heterogeneous state estimates were hard to interpret and had the wrong signs. Pooled data regressions were not valid because the hypothesis of homogeneity of the coefficients was rejected. They recommend shrinkage estimators if one is interested in obtaining elasticity estimates for each state since these give more reliable results.

In the context of dynamic demand for gasoline across $N = 18$ OECD countries over the period 1960–90 ($T = 31$), Baltagi and Griffin (1997) argued for pooling the data as the best approach for obtaining reliable price and income elasticities. They also pointed out that pure cross-section studies cannot control for unobservable country effects, whereas pure time-series studies cannot control for unobservable oil shocks or behavioral changes occurring over time. Baltagi and Griffin (1997) compared the homogeneous and heterogeneous estimates in the context of gasoline demand based on the plausibility of the price and income elasticities as well as the speed of adjustment path to the long-run equilibrium. They found considerable variability in the parameter estimates among the heterogeneous estimators, some giving implausible estimates, while the homogeneous estimators gave similar plausible short-run estimates that differed only in estimating the long-run effects. Baltagi and Griffin (1997) also compared the forecast performance of these homogeneous and heterogeneous estimators over a one-, five- and ten-year horizon. Their findings show that the homogeneous estimators outperformed their heterogeneous counterparts based on mean squared forecast error.

Attanasio et al. (2000) estimated both *homogeneous* as well as *heterogeneous* dynamic panel relationships between saving, growth and investment using a panel of $N = 123$ countries over the period 1961–94. Even though they find evidence of parameter heterogeneity across countries, they conclude that, appropriately taking it into account, by applying the Pesaran and Smith (1995) pooled mean group estimator, does not modify the general picture obtained using estimators that erroneously impose homogeneity.

In another application, Driver et al. (2004) utilize the Confederation of British Industry's (CBI) survey data to measure the impact of uncertainty on UK investment authorizations. The panel consists of $N = 48$ industries observed over $T = 85$ quarters 1978(Q1) to 1999(Q1). The uncertainty measure is based on the dispersion of beliefs across survey respondents about the general business situation in their industry. The heterogeneous estimators considered are OLS and 2SLS at the industry level, as well as the unrestricted SUR estimation method. Fixed effects, random effects, pooled 2SLS and restricted SUR are the homogeneous estimators considered. The panel estimates find that uncertainty has a negative, non-negligible effect on investment, while the heterogeneous estimates vary considerably across industries. Forecast performance for 12 out of sample quarters 1996(Q2) to 1999(Q1) are compared. The pooled homogeneous estimators outperform their heterogeneous counterparts in terms of RMSE.

Hsiao and Tahmiscioglu (1997) use a panel of $N = 561$ US firms over the period 1971–92 ($T = 12$) to study the influence of financial constraints on company investment. They find substantial differences across firms in terms of their investment behavior. When a homogeneous pooled model is assumed, the impact of liquidity on firm investment is seriously underestimated. The authors recommend a mixed fixed and random coefficients framework based on the recursive predictive density criteria.

Pesaran et al. (1996) investigated the small sample properties of various estimators of the long-run coefficients for a dynamic heterogeneous panel data model using Monte Carlo experiments. Their findings indicate that the mean group estimator performs reasonably well for large T. However, when T is small, the mean group estimator could be seriously biased, particularly when N is large relative to T. Pesaran and Zhao (1999) examine the effectiveness of alternative bias-correction procedures in reducing the small sample bias of these estimators using Monte Carlo experiments. An interesting finding is that when the coefficient of the lagged dependent variable is greater than or equal to 0.8, none of the bias correction procedures seem to work. Hsiao et al. (1999) suggest a Bayesian approach for estimating the mean parameters of a dynamic heterogeneous panel data model. The coefficients are assumed to be normally distributed across cross-sectional units and the Bayes estimator is implemented using Markov Chain Monte Carlo methods. Hsiao et al. (1999) argue that Bayesian methods can be a viable alternative in the estimation of mean coefficients in dynamic panel data models even when the initial observations are treated as fixed constants. They establish the asymptotic equivalence of this Bayes estimator and the mean group estimator proposed by Pesaran and Smith (1995). The asymptotics are carried out for both N and $T \to \infty$ with $\sqrt{N}/T \to 0$. Monte Carlo experiments show that this Bayes estimator has better sampling properties than other estimators for both small and moderate size T. Hsiao et al. also caution against the use of the mean group estimator unless T is sufficiently large relative to N. The bias in the mean coefficient of the lagged dependent variable appears to be serious when T is small and the true value of this coefficient is larger than 0.6. Hsiao et al. apply their methods to estimate the q-investment model using a panel of $N = 273$ US firms over the period 1972–93 ($T = 22$).

Holtz-Eakin et al. (1989) formulate a coherent set of procedures for estimating and testing vector autoregressions (VAR) with panel data. Tests for parameter stationarity, minimum lag length and causality are performed. They emphasize the importance of testing for the appropriate lag length before testing for causality, especially in short panels. Otherwise, misleading results on causality can be obtained. They suggest a simple method of estimating VAR equations with panel data that has a straightforward GLS interpretation. This is based on applying instrumental variables to the quasi-differenced autoregressive equations. They demonstrate how inappropriate methods that deal with individual effects in a VAR context can yield misleading results. They apply these methods to estimating the dynamic relationships between local government revenues and expenditures. The data are based on $N = 171$ municipal governments over the period 1972–80 and are drawn from the Annual Survey of Governments between 1973 and 1980 and the Census of Governments conducted in 1972 and 1977. The main findings include the following:

1. Lags of one or two years are sufficient to summarize the dynamic interrelationships in local public finance.
2. There are important intertemporal linkages among expenditures, taxes and grants.
3. Results of the stationarity test cast doubt over the stability of parameters over time.
4. Contrary to previous studies, this study finds that past revenues help predict current expenditures, but past expenditures do not alter the future path of revenues.

Rapach and Wohar (2004) show that the monetary model of exchange rate determination performs poorly on a country-by-country basis for US dollar exchange rates over the post-Bretton Woods period for $N = 18$ industrialized countries for quarterly data over the period 1973:1–1997:1. However, they find considerable support for the monetary model using panel procedures. They reject tests for the homogeneity assumptions inherent in panel procedures. Hence, they are torn between obtaining panel cointegrating coefficient estimates that are much more plausible in economic terms than country-by-country estimates. Yet these estimates might be spurious since they are rejected by formal statistical test for pooling. Rapach and Wohar (2004) perform an out-of-sample forecasting exercise using the panel and country-by-country estimates employing the RMSE criteria for a 1, 4, 8, 12 and 16 step ahead quarters. For the 1-step and 4-step ahead, the RMSEs of the homogeneous and heterogeneous estimates are similar. At the 8-step ahead horizon, homogeneous estimates generate better forecasts in comparison to five of the six heterogeneous estimates. At the 16-step horizon, the homogeneous estimates have RMSE that is smaller than each of the heterogeneous estimates. In most cases the RMSE is reduced by 20 per cent. They conclude that while there are good reasons to favor the panel estimates over the country-by country estimates of the monetary model, there are also good reasons to be suspicious of these panel estimates since the homogeneity assumption is rejected. Despite this fact, they argue that panel data estimates should not be dismissed based on tests for homogeneity alone, because they may eliminate certain biases that plague country-by-country estimates. In fact, panel estimates of the monetary model were more reliable and generated superior forecasts to those of country-by-country estimates. Rapach and Wohar's (2004) suspicion of panel data estimates comes from Monte Carlo evidence that shows that 'it is not improbable to find evidence in support of the monetary model by relying on panel estimates, even when the true data generating process is characterized by a heterogeneous structure that is not consistent with the monetary model'. Other papers in this vein are Mark and Sul (2003) and Groen (2005). The latter paper utilizes a panel of vector error-correction models based on a common long-run relationship to test whether the euro exchange rates of Canada, Japan and the United States have a long-run link with monetary fundamentals. Out-of-sample forecasts show that this common long-run exchange model is superior to both the naive random walk-based forecasts and the standard cointegrated VAR model-based forecasts, especially for horizons of 2 to 4 years.

Gavin and Theodorou (2005) use forecasting criteria to examine the macrodynamic behavior of $N = 15$ OECD countries observed quarterly over the period 1980 to 1996. They utilize a small set of familiar, widely used core economic variables (output, price level, interest rates and exchange rates), omitting country-specific shocks. They find that this small set of variables and a simple VAR common model strongly support the hypothesis that many industrialized nations have similar macroeconomic dynamics. In sample, they often reject the hypothesis that coefficient vectors estimated separately for each country are the same. They argue that these rejections may be of little importance if due to idiosyncratic events since macro time series are typically too short for standard methods to eliminate the effects of idiosyncratic factors. Panel data can be used to exploit the heterogeneous information in cross-country data, hence increasing the data and eliminating the idiosyncratic effects. They compare the forecast accuracy of the individual country models with the common models in a simulated out-of-sample experiment. They calculate four forecasts with increasing horizons at each point in time, one quarter ahead and four quarters ahead. For the four equations, at every horizon, the panel forecasts are significantly more accurate more often than are the individual country model forecasts. The biggest differences are for the exchange rate and the interest rate. They conclude that the superior out-of-sample forecasting performance of the common model supports their hypothesis that market economies tend to have a common macrodynamic pattern related to a small number of variables.

7 FURTHER READING

For classic influential papers on dynamic panels, see Baltagi (2002). Recent surveys on dynamic panel data models include Harris et al. (2008) and Hsiao (2011). The latter has an extensive treatment of the maximum likelihood approach to dynamic panels, the importance of initial value assumptions, and multiplicative individual and time-specific effects. Space limitations prevent the inclusion of semi-parametric, non-parametric and Bayesian methods using dynamic panel data, also, of non-stationary panels (see the recent survey by Breitung and Pesaran, 2008). More extensive treatment of dynamic panel data models are given in textbooks on the subject by Arellano (2003), Hsiao (2003), and Baltagi (2008).

NOTES

1. This can easily be extended to the case of additional lags of the dependent variable without loss of generality.
2. See also Bun and Kiviet (2003) and Everaert and Pozzi (2007), to mention two.
3. Another system estimator is suggested by Arellano and Bover (1995) who stack the forward orthogonalization demeaned equation on top of the levels time averaged equation.
4. Note that there are $T(T + 1)/2$ distinct elements of Σ and this has to be much smaller than N. This is usually the case for large consumer or labor panels where N is very large and T is very small, but not necessarily true for macro-panels. It is also worth emphasizing that if $T > N$, this procedure will fail since $\hat{\Sigma}$ will be singular with rank N. Also, the estimation of an unrestricted P matrix will be difficult with unbalanced panels due to missing data.

REFERENCES

Acemoglu, D., S. Johnson, J.A. Robinson and P. Yared (2005), 'From education to democracy?', *American Economic Review*, **95**, 44–9.

Ahn, S.C. and P. Schmidt (1995), 'Efficient estimation of models for dynamic panel data', *Journal of Econometrics*, **68**, 5–27.

Ahn, S.C. and P. Schmidt (1999), 'Modified generalized instrumental variables estimation of panel data models with strictly exogenous instrumental variables', Chapter 7 in C. Hsiao, K. Lahiri, L.F. Lee and M.H. Pesaran (eds), *Analysis of Panels and Limited Dependent Variable Models*, Cambridge: Cambridge University Press pp. 171–98.

Alonso-Borrego, C. and M. Arellano (1999), 'Symmetrically normalized instrumental variable estimation using panel data', *Journal of Business and Economic Statistics*, **17**, 36–49.

Alvarez, J. and M. Arellano (2003), 'The time series and cross-section asymptotics of dynamic panel data estimators', *Econometrica*, **71**, 1121–59.

Anderson, T.W. and C. Hsiao (1981), 'Estimation of dynamic models with error components', *Journal of the American Statistical Association*, **76**, 598–606.

Andrews, D.W.K. and B. Lu (2001), 'Consistent model and moment selection procedures for GMM estimation with application to dynamic panel data models', *Journal of Econometrics*, **101**, 123–64.

Arellano, M. (1989), 'A note on the Anderson–Hsiao estimator for panel data', *Economics Letters*, **31**, 337–41.

Arellano, M. (2003), *Panel Data Econometrics*, Oxford: Oxford University Press.

Arellano, M. and S. Bond (1991), 'Some tests of specification for panel data: Monte Carlo evidence and an application to employment equations', *Review of Economic Studies*, **58**, 277–97.

Arellano, M. and O. Bover (1995), 'Another look at the instrumental variables estimation of error-component models', *Journal of Econometrics*, **68**, 29–51.

Attanasio, O.P., L. Picci and A.E. Scorcu (2000), 'Saving, growth, and investment: a macroeconomic analysis using a panel of countries', *The Review of Economics and Statistics*, **82**, 182–211.

Baltagi, B.H. (2002), *Recent Developments in the Econometrics of Panel Data*, Volumes I and II, Cheltenham, UK and Northampton, MA, USA: Edward Elgar Publishing.

Baltagi, B.H. (2008), *Econometric Analysis of Panel Data*, Chichester: John Wiley.

Baltagi, B.H. and J.M. Griffin (1997), 'Pooled estimators vs. their heterogeneous counterparts in the context of dynamic demand for gasoline', *Journal of Econometrics*, **77**, 303–27.

Baltagi, B.H. and J.M. Griffin (2001), 'The econometrics of rational addiction: the case of cigarettes', *Journal of Business and Economic Statistics*, **19**, 449–54.

Baltagi, B.H., P.O. Demetriades and S.H. Law (2009), 'Financial development and openness: evidence from panel data', *Journal of Development Economics*, **89**, 285–96.

Becker, G.S., M. Grossman and K.M. Murphy (1994), 'An empirical analysis of cigarette addiction', *American Economic Review*, **84**, 396–418.

Blundell, R. and S. Bond (1998), 'Initial conditions and moment restrictions in dynamic panel data models', *Journal of Econometrics*, **87**, 115–43.

Blundell, R. and S. Bond (2000), 'GMM estimation with persistent panel data: an application to production functions', *Econometric Reviews*, **19**, 321–40.

Blundell, R., S. Bond, M. Devereux and F. Schiantarelli (1992), 'Investment and Tobin's q: evidence from company panel data', *Journal of Econometrics*, **51**, 233–57.

Bobba, M. and D. Coviello (2007), 'Weak instruments and weak identification in estimating the effects of education on democracy', *Economics Letters*, **96**, 301–6.

Bond, S., J.A. Elston, J. Mairesse and B. Mulkay (2003), 'Financial factors and investment in Belgium, France, Germany, and the United Kingdom: a comparison using company panel data', *The Review of Economics and Statistics*, **85**, 153–65.

Bowsher, C.G. (2002), 'On testing overidentifying restrictions in dynamic panel data models', *Economics Letters*, **77**, 211–20.

Breitung, J. and M.H. Pesaran (2008), 'Unit roots and cointegration in panels', Chapter 9 in L. Matyas and P. Sevestre (eds), *The Econometrics of Panel Data: Fundamentals and Recent Developments in Theory and Practice*, Berlin: Springer, pp. 279–322.

Bun, M.J.G. and J.F. Kiviet (2003), 'On the diminishing returns of higher-order terms in asymptotic expansions of bias', *Economics Letters*, **79**, 145–52.

Bun, M.J.G. and J.F. Kiviet (2006), 'The effects of dynamic feedbacks on LS and MM estimator accuracy in panel data models', *Journal of Econometrics*, **132**, 409–44.

Dessi, R. and D. Robertson (2003), 'Debt, incentives and performance: evidence from UK panel data', *The Economic Journal*, **113**, 903–19.

Driver, C., K. Imai, P. Temple and A. Urga (2004), 'The effect of uncertainty on UK investment authorisation: homogeneous vs. heterogeneous estimators', *Empirical Economics*, **29**, 115–28.

Everaert, G. and L. Pozzi (2007), 'Bootstrap-based bias correction for dynamic panels', *Journal of Economic Dynamics and Control*, **31**, 1160–84.

Gavin, W.T. and A.T. Theodorou (2005), 'A common model approach to macroeconomics: using panel data to reduce sampling error', *Journal of Forecasting*, **24**, 203–19.

Groen, J.J.J. (2005), 'Exchange rate predictability and monetary fundamentals in a small multi-country panel', *Journal of Money, Credit, and Banking*, **37**, 495–516.

Hahn, J. and G. Kuersteiner (2002), 'Asymptotically unbiased inference for a dynamic panel model with fixed effects when both n and T are large', *Econometrica*, **70**, 1639–57.

Hahn, J. and H.R. Moon (2006), 'Reducing bias of MLE in a dynamic panel model', *Econometric Theory*, **22**, 499–512.

Hahn, J., J. Hausman and G. Kuersteiner (2007), 'Long difference instrumental variables estimation for dynamic panel models with fixed effects', *Journal of Econometrics*, **140**, 574–617.

Harris, M.N., L. Matyas and P. Sevestre (2008), 'Dynamic models for short panels', Chapter 8 in L. Matyas and P. Sevestre (eds), *The Econometrics of Panel Data: Fundamentals and Recent Developments in Theory and Practice*, Berlin: Springer, pp. 249–78.

Hausman, J.A. (1978), 'Specification tests in econometrics', *Econometrica*, **46**, 1251–71.

Holtz-Eakin, D., W. Newey and H.S. Rosen (1989), 'The revenues–expenditures nexus: Evidence from local government data', *International Economic Review*, **30**, 415–29.

Hsiao, C. (2003), *Analysis of Panel Data*, Cambridge: Cambridge University Press.

Hsiao, C. (2011), 'Dynamic panel data models', Chapter 13 in A. Ullah and D.E.A. Giles (eds), *Handbook of Empirical Economics and Finance*, Boca Raton, FL: Chapman & Hall, pp. 373–96.

Hsiao, C. and A.K. Tahmiscioglu (1997), 'A panel analysis of liquidity constraints and firm investment', *Journal of the American Statistical Association*, **92**, 455–65.

Hsiao, C., M.H. Pesaran and A.K. Tahmiscioglu (1999), 'Bayes estimation of short run coefficients in dynamic panel data models', Chapter 11 in C. Hsiao, K. Lahiri, L.F. Lee and M.H. Pesaran (eds), *Analysis of Panels and Limited Dependent Variable Models*, Cambridge: Cambridge University Press, pp. 268–96.

Im, K.S., S.C. Ahn, P. Schmidt and J.M. Wooldridge (1999), 'Efficient estimation of panel data models with strictly exogenous explanatory variables', *Journal of Econometrics*, **93**, 177–201.

Islam, N. (1995), 'Growth empirics: a panel data approach', *Quarterly Journal of Economics*, **110**, 1127–70.

Judson, R.A. and A.L. Owen (1999), 'Estimating dynamic panel data models: a guide for macroeconomists', *Economics Letters*, **65**, 9–15.

Keane, M.P. and D.E. Runkle (1992), 'On the estimation of panel-data models with serial correlation when instruments are not strictly exogenous', *Journal of Business and Economic Statistics*, **10**, 1–9.

Kiviet, J.F. (1995), 'On bias, inconsistency and efficiency of various estimators in dynamic panel data models', *Journal of Econometrics*, **68**, 53–78.

Maddala, G.S., R.P. Trost, H. Li and F. Joutz (1997), 'Estimation of short-run and long-run elasticities of energy demand from panel data using shrinkage estimators', *Journal of Business and Economic Statistics*, **15**, 90–100.

Mark, N.C. and D. Sul (2003), 'Cointegration vector estimation by panel dynamic OLS and long-run money demand', *Oxford Bulletin of Economics and Statistics*, **65**, 655–80.

Nickell, S. (1981), 'Biases in dynamic models with fixed effects', *Econometrica*, **49**, 1417–26.

Pesaran, M.H. and R. Smith (1995), 'Estimating long-run relationships from dynamic heterogenous panels', *Journal of Econometrics*, **68**, 79–113.

Pesaran, M.H. and Z. Zhao (1999), 'Bias reduction in estimating long-run relationships from dynamic heterogeneous panels', Chapter 12 in C. Hsiao, K. Lahiri, L.F. Lee and M.H. Pesaran (eds), *Analysis of Panels and Limited Dependent Variable Models*, Cambridge: Cambridge University Press, pp. 297–322.
Pesaran, M.H., Y. Shin and R. Smith (1999), 'Pooled mean group estimation of dynamic heterogeneous panels', *Journal of the American Statistical Association*, **94**, 621–34.
Pesaran, M.H., R. Smith and K.S. Im (1996), 'Dynamic linear models for heterogeneous panels', Chapter 8 in L. Mátyás and P. Sevestre (eds), *The Econometrics of Panel Data: A Handbook of the Theory with Applications*, Dordrecht: Kluwer Academic Publishers, pp. 145–95.
Phillips, P.C.B. and H. Moon (1999), 'Linear regression limit theory for nonstationary panel data', *Econometrica*, **67**, 1057–111.
Rapach, D.E. and M.E. Wohar (2004), 'Testing the monetary model of exchange rate determination: a closer look at panels', *Journal of International Money and Finance*, **23**, 867–95.
Robertson, D. and J. Symons (1992), 'Some strange properties of panel data estimators', *Journal of Applied Econometrics*, **7**, 175–89.
Wansbeek, T.J. and P. Bekker (1996), 'On IV, GMM and ML in a dynamic panel data model', *Economics Letters*, **51**, 145–52.
Wansbeek, T.J. and T. Knaap (1999), 'Estimating a dynamic panel data model with heterogeneous trends', *Annales D'Economie et de Statistique*, **55–56**, 331–49.
Windmeijer, F. (2005), 'A finite sample correction for the variance of linear efficient two-step GMM estimators', *Journal of Econometrics*, **126**, 25–51.
Ziliak, J.P. (1997), 'Efficient estimation with panel data when instruments are predetermined: an empirical comparison of moment-condition estimators', *Journal of Business and Economic Statistics*, **15**, 419–31.

11 Factor models

Jörg Breitung and In Choi

1 INTRODUCTION

Factor models are becoming increasingly popular in economics because they can utilize large data sets in an effective manner. Factor models have been used for various purposes. First, they have been used to construct economic indicators. Monthly coincident business cycle indicators such as the Chicago Fed National Activity index (CFNAI) for the US and EuroCOIN for the Euro area (cf. Altissimo et al., 2001) are related examples. Second, factor models have widely been used in order to forecast real and nominal economic variables. They often provide more accurate forecasts than autoregressive and vector autoregressive models (see Eickmeier and Ziegler, 2008 and the literature cited therein). Third, factor models have been used for monetary policy analysis in combination with a vector autoregressive (VAR) system as in Bernanke et al. (2005). In many cases only five to ten factors are sufficient to capture more than a half of the total variation within a data set of more than three hundred macroeconomic variables. Therefore, adding a few common factors to a macroeconomic VAR system is supposed to control for a variety of omitted variables within a typical low-dimensional VAR analysis. Fourth, factor models are used for instrumental variables estimation. Bai and Ng (2010) assume that endogenous regressors are driven by a small number of unobserved, exogenous factors and suggest using the estimated factors as instruments. Fifth, factor models have been used in panel regressions as a way of modelling cross-sectional correlation. See Bai and Ng (2004), Bai (2009), Moon and Perron (2004), Pesaran (2006) and Phillips and Sul (2003).

In this chapter we review classical and more recent results from the (dynamic) factor analysis of large macroeconomic panels. As the literature is evolving rapidly, it is not possible to give a full account of all current research activities within this field. More comprehensive reviews emphasizing different aspects of recent work are provided by Breitung and Eickmeier (2006), Deistler and Zinner (2007), Bai and Ng (2008), and Stock and Watson (2011).

2 MODEL ASSUMPTIONS

2.1 The Strict Factor Model

Assume that each of the N variables $y_{1t},\ldots,y_{Nt}$ with t being a time index can be represented by the factor model

$$\begin{aligned} y_{it} &= \lambda_{i1}f_{1t} + \cdots + \lambda_{ir}f_{rt} + u_{it}, \quad (i = 1,\ldots,N;\ \ t = 1,\ldots,T) \qquad (11.1) \\ &= \lambda_i' f_t + u_{it}, \end{aligned}$$

where $f_t = (f_{1t}, \ldots, f_{rt})'$ denotes the vector of r factors and $\lambda_i = (\lambda_{i1}, \ldots, \lambda_{ir})'$ is the associated $r \times 1$ vector of factor loadings. Furthermore, $u_{it} \overset{iid}{\sim} \mathcal{N}(0, \sigma_u^2)$, $f_t \overset{iid}{\sim} \mathcal{N}(0, \Sigma_f)$, and $E(f_t u_{it}) = 0$ for all i and t.[1] The component $\chi_{it} = \lambda_i' f_t$ is called the *common component* and u_{it} is the *idiosyncratic error*. The covariance between the variables is given by

$$E(y_{it} y_{jt}) = \lambda_i' \Sigma_f \lambda_j, \quad \text{for } i \neq j,$$

that is, any cross-section dependence among the variables is due to the presence of common factors. Note that the $N(N-1)/2$ covariances are determined by the $r \cdot N + r(r+1)/2$ parameters stemming from $\lambda_1, \ldots, \lambda_N$ and Σ_f. Thus, the factor model implies a substantial number of restrictions if $N >> r$.

In matrix notation, the model is written as

$$y_t = \Lambda f_t + u_t \tag{11.2}$$

$$Y = F\Lambda' + U, \tag{11.3}$$

where $\Lambda = (\lambda_1, \ldots, \lambda_N)'$, $Y = (y_1, \ldots, y_T)'$, $y_t = (y_{1t}, \ldots, y_{Nt})'$, $F = (f_1, \ldots, f_T)'$ and $U = (u_1, \ldots, u_T)'$ with $u_t = (u_{1t}, \ldots, u_{Nt})'$.

It is important to note that Λ and Σ_f are not separately identified. An observationally equivalent model is obtained by

$$\begin{aligned} y_t &= \Lambda Q^{-1} Q f_t + u_t \\ &= \Lambda^* f_t^* + u_t, \end{aligned}$$

where Q is any non-singular $r \times r$ matrix. Therefore, r^2 restrictions on Λ and Σ_f are required to identify the model. In explanatory factor analysis these restrictions are not derived from a formal structural identification guided by economic theory but are selected just for computational convenience. In particular, it is often assumed that $\Sigma_f = I_r$ (implying $r(r+1)/2$ restrictions) and that $\Lambda'\Lambda$ is a diagonal matrix (yielding the remaining $r(r-1)/2$ restrictions). Although there are good reasons to normalize the variance of the factors to unity and assume that the factors are orthogonal, the restrictions on the factor loading matrix are less appealing intuitively. Indeed it is possible to introduce some 'rotation matrix' Q with $Q'Q = I_r$ such that the rotated factors $f_t^* = Q' f_t$ remain orthonormal. This raises the question of how to choose the rotation matrix. The 'varimax approach' (Kaiser, 1958) determines the rotation of the factor space with maximal variance of the factor loadings. The notion behind this method is to find a clear pattern of the factor loadings such that a subset of variables are explained well by some particular factors, whereas the factors do not explain some other variables. This sometimes helps to find some interpretation of the associated factors.

2.2 Approximate Factor Models

The 'strict' factor model considered so far is overly restrictive in most economic applications. It sometimes seems unrealistic to assume that both components f_t and u_{it} are i.i.d. First, since f_{jt} and u_{it} are time series it is natural to assume that the components are generated by dynamic processes that give rise to some forms of serial correlation. Second, the idiosyncratic component of unit i may be correlated with the idiosyncratic components of some other unit $j(j \neq i)$. Third, the variances of the common and idiosyncratic components may vary across i and t. The approximate factor model allow for some 'mild' form of cross-sectional and temporal dependence as well as heteroscedasticity.

It is important to note that allowing for cross-sectional correlation raises severe identification problems. The covariance matrix of the data $\Omega_y = E(y_t y_t')$ entails only $N(N + 1)/2$ parameters, whereas the factor model with $\Sigma_f = I_r$ and unrestricted covariance matrix $\Sigma_u = E(u_t u_t')$ involves $N(N + 1)/2 + rN$ parameters. Accordingly, different specifications of the factor model may result in an identical covariance matrix Ω_y and, thus, in observationally equivalent structures. However, under certain conditions it is possible to consistently estimate the factor space even if the covariance parameters of the idiosyncratic components are left unidentified. To see this, assume that there exist some $N \times r$ matrix Γ such that as $N \to \infty$, $N^{-1}\Gamma'\Gamma \to \Psi_\Gamma$ and $N^{-1}\Gamma'\Lambda \to Q$ with $rank(\Gamma) = rank(Q) = r$. Pre-multiplying the factor model (11.2) by Γ' yields

$$N^{-1}\Gamma' y_t = N^{-1}\Gamma'\Lambda f_t + v_t,$$

where $v_t = N^{-1}\Gamma' u_t$ is $O_p(N^{-1/2})$. As $N \to \infty$ we obtain $N^{-1}\Gamma' y_t \xrightarrow{p} Qf_t$, and therefore $N^{-1}\Gamma' y_t$ is a consistent estimator of the factor space irrespective of the covariance parameters of u_t (which are in fact not identified). Thus, imposing assumptions that ensure that some linear combination of u_t tends to zero in probability is sufficient for a consistent estimator of the factor space. For example, a sufficient condition is $\|N^{-1}\Gamma'\Sigma_u\Gamma\| < \infty$ for all N. Chamberlain and Rothschild (1983) assume that all eigenvalues of Σ_u are bounded, whereas Stock and Watson (2002) and Bai and Ng (2002) assume

$$\frac{1}{N}\sum_{i=1}^{N}\sum_{j=1}^{N}\tau_{ij} \leq M < \infty \quad \text{for all } N,$$

with $\tau_{ij} = \sup_t\{|E(u_{it}u_{jt})|\}$. Note that this condition involves the sum over N^2 upper bounds of the covariance parameters which is divided only by the factor N. Hence, this condition rules out that all covariances are different from zero. However, we may still allow for some 'spots of local correlation' (for example some spatial correlation) among a finite group of neighbours (cf. Chudik et al., 2011).

2.3 Dynamic Factor Models

A dynamic version of the factor model is given by

$$y_{it} = \lambda_i^*(L)' f_t^* + u_t, \tag{11.4}$$

where $\lambda_i^*(L) = \lambda_{0,i} + \lambda_{1,i}L + \cdots + \lambda_{q_i,i}L^{q_i}$ is an $r \times 1$ lag polynomial (for example Geweke, 1977 and Stock and Watson, 2002). This model can be reformulated as a static factor model by using $\tilde{f}_t = (f_t^{*\prime}, f_{t-1}^{*\prime}, \ldots, f_{t-\tilde{q}}^{*\prime})'$ and $\tilde{\lambda}_i = (\lambda_{0,i}', \ldots, \lambda_{\tilde{q},i}')'$ such that

$$y_{it} = \tilde{\lambda}_i' \tilde{f}_t + u_{it},$$

where $\tilde{q} = \max_i(q_i)$. Although this 'static representation' is convenient as it allows one to cope with a dynamic factor model by using the usual (static) framework, this representation has a number of drawbacks. First, the static representation may severely inflate the number of factors leading to a substantial loss of efficiency when estimating the factor space. Second, since the estimated factors are linear combinations of the original factors (also called the dynamic or primitive factors) and their lags, the estimated factors are difficult to interpret. Third, if some lags enter only for a subset of the variables (example: a few variables have a lag-order $q_i = 2$ whereas all other variables have lag order $q_i = 0$), then the associated factors are difficult to distinguish from the idiosyncratic components. Finally, no static factor model exists if $\lambda_i^*(L)$ is an infinite order lag polynomial. Consider, for instance, the following dynamic factor model:

$$y_{it} = \alpha_i y_{i,t-1} + \lambda_i' f_t + \varepsilon_{it}.$$

This model may be rewritten in a form like (11.4) with $\lambda_i^*(L) = (1 - \alpha_i L)^{-1}\lambda_i$ and $u_{it} = (1 - \alpha_i L)^{-1}\varepsilon_{it}$. Obviously, this model implies an infinite number of static factors and, therefore, the static factor representation does not make sense in this case (see Hallin and Liska, 2011 in relation to this).

3 ESTIMATION AND INFERENCE

3.1 Estimators Based on Principal Components

The most popular estimation method is obtained from applying a principal component (PC) analysis. This estimator results from applying the least-squares principle. Define the (unweighted) sum of squared residuals as

$$\mathrm{SSR}(\Lambda, F) = \sum_{i=1}^{N}\sum_{t=1}^{T} u_{it}^2 = \sum_{t=1}^{T}(y_t - \Lambda f_t)'(y_t - \Lambda f_t)$$

$$= tr[(Y - F\Lambda')'(Y - F\Lambda')].$$

The PC estimator is obtained by minimizing SSR with respect to Λ and F subject to the constraint $\Lambda'\Lambda = I_r$. Using the OLS estimator $\hat{F} = (\Lambda'\Lambda)^{-1}\Lambda' Y = \Lambda' Y$, we can concentrate out the parameter Λ yielding

$$\mathrm{SSR}_c(\Lambda, F) = tr(Y'Y) - tr(\Lambda' Y' Y\Lambda).$$

Accordingly, minimizing SSR is equivalent to maximizing $tr(\Lambda' Y' Y\Lambda)$.

For a single-factor model with $r = 1$, the PC estimator of the $N \times 1$ vector Λ is obtained from maximizing

$$\Lambda'\hat{\Omega}_y\Lambda - \mu(\Lambda'\Lambda - 1),$$

where $\hat{\Omega}_y = T^{-1}Y'Y$ and μ is the Lagrange multiplier. Since the first order condition is

$$(\mu I_N - \hat{\Omega}_y)\hat{\Lambda} = 0,$$

the desired PC estimator of $\Lambda, \hat{\Lambda}$, is the eigenvector corresponding to the largest eigenvalue of $\hat{\Omega}_y$. Similarly, the PC estimator of Λ for an r -factor model is the $N \times r$ matrix of r eigenvectors associated with the r largest eigenvalues of $\hat{\Omega}_y$. The PC estimator of the factor matrix is obtained as

$$\hat{F} = Y\hat{\Lambda}(\hat{\Lambda}'\hat{\Lambda})^{-1} = Y\hat{\Lambda},$$

which can be seen to be the (system) OLS estimator of F, where Λ is replaced by $\hat{\Lambda}$ in (11.3). Since $T^{-1}\hat{F}'\hat{F} = \hat{\Lambda}'\hat{\Omega}_y\hat{\Lambda}$ is a diagonal matrix with the eigenvalues of $\hat{\Omega}_y$ on the diagonal, it follows that the estimated factors are orthogonal with variances identical to the respective eigenvalues of $\hat{\Omega}_y$.

Alternatively, we may put the eigenvectors associated with the r largest eigenvalues of the $T \times T$ matrix YY' in the matrix $\tilde{V}_r$ and define the PC estimator of the factor space as $\tilde{F} = \sqrt{T}\tilde{V}_r$. The PC estimator satisfies the normalization $T^{-1}\tilde{F}'\tilde{F} = I_r$. The corresponding loading matrix is obtained as $\tilde{\Lambda} = T^{-1}Y'\tilde{F}$.

If u_{it} is assumed to be heteroscedastic, efficiency gains for the estimation of the factor loading space may be expected from minimizing the GLS criterion function

$$\tilde{S}(\Lambda, F, \Sigma_u) = \sum_{i=1}^{N}\sum_{t=1}^{N}\frac{1}{\sigma_i^2}(y_{it} - \lambda_i' f_t)^2, \tag{11.5}$$

where it is assumed that $\Sigma_u = \text{diag}(\sigma_1^2, \ldots, \sigma_N^2)$. However, since the system of regression equations forms an SUR system with identical regressors, the GLS estimator of Λ is equivalent to the OLS (i.e. PC) estimator (cf. Breitung and Tenhofen, 2011).

Minimizing the GLS criterion function (11.5) improves the efficiency in estimating f_t. The PC estimator is equivalent to the OLS estimator of f_t in the regression

$$y_{it} = \hat{\lambda}_i' f_t + v_{it}, \quad (i = 1, \ldots, N),$$

where $\hat{\lambda}_i$ is the PC estimator of λ_i. Since the errors of this regression are heteroscedastic, a more efficient estimator results from applying the (feasible) GLS principle based on the estimated weights $1/\hat{\sigma}_i$, where $\hat{\sigma}_i^2$ is the PC-based estimator of the variance of the ith variable's idiosyncratic component. The resulting estimator yields the two-step PC–GLS estimator of Breitung and Tenhofen (2011). A related estimator is introduced by Choi (2012b) who suggests applying the PC estimator to the transformed data $\tilde{Y} = Y\hat{\Sigma}_u^{-1/2}$, where $\hat{\Sigma}_u^{-1/2} = \text{diag}(\hat{\sigma}_1, \ldots, \hat{\sigma}_N)$. The resulting estimator can also obtained from the eigenvectors of the generalized eigenvalue problem

$$|\gamma\hat{\Sigma}_u - \hat{\Omega}_y| = 0.$$

Note that the normalizations of Breitung and Tenhofen's and Choi's estimators are different. While Breitung and Tenhofen's PC–GLS estimator is normalized such that $T^{-1}\tilde{F}_{2S}'\tilde{F}_{2S} \xrightarrow{p} I_r$, Choi's generalized PC estimator obeys $T^{-1}\tilde{F}_{gls}'\hat{\Sigma}_u^{-1}\tilde{F}_{gls} = I_r$. These estimators can be shown to be asymptotically equivalent to the local maximizer of the Gaussian likelihood function that treats $f_1, \ldots, f_N$ as fixed parameters (cf. Breitung and Tenhofen, 2011).

Further efficiency gains can be achieved if possible (weak) cross-sectional correlation represented by some non-zero off-diagonal elements of Σ_u is exploited as shown in Choi (2012). Such covariance matrix may arise in the spatial model where off-diagonal entries of the covariance matrix represent the correlations among regional neighbours.

Efficiency gains are also possible for the estimation of the factor loadings. Assume that the errors are generated by the autoregressive process $\rho_i(L)u_t = \varepsilon_{it}$, where $\rho_i(L)$ is a polynomial in the lag operator L. A GLS transformation of the model yields

$$\rho_i(L)y_{it} = [\rho_i(L)f_t]'\lambda_i + \varepsilon_{it}.$$

The (two-step) PC–GLS estimator of Breitung and Tenhofen (2011) is obtained from replacing $\rho_i(L)$ and f_t by the estimated autoregressive polynomial that uses the PC residuals $\hat{u}_{it} = y_{it} - \hat{\lambda}_i'\hat{f}_t$ and the PC estimator $\hat{f}_t$, respectively. Monte Carlo simulations indicate substantial efficiency improvements whenever the dynamic process of u_{it} is highly persistent.

3.2 ML-type Estimators

Two different set-ups may be employed to obtain an ML estimator for the strict factor model. First, assume that f_t is a vector of random variables with $f_t \sim \mathcal{N}(0, I)$ and $\Lambda'\Sigma_u\Lambda$ is a diagonal matrix (for example Anderson, 1984, p. 557). Under this set-up, Lawley and Maxwell (1963) propose a scoring algorithm based on the first and second derivatives of the log-likelihood function

$$\log L(\Lambda, F, \Sigma_u) = \text{const} - \frac{T}{2}\log|\Lambda\Lambda' + \Sigma_u| - \frac{T}{2}\text{tr}\{(\Lambda\Lambda' + \Sigma_u)^{-1}\hat{\Omega}_y\},$$

where $\hat{\Omega}_y$ is the $N \times N$ sample covariance matrix of y_t. Another possibility is to assume that the factors are fixed unknown constants. In this case it is important to note that if $\Sigma_u = \text{diag}(\sigma_1^2, \ldots, \sigma_N^2)$, the likelihood function is unbounded. For example, we may choose $\lambda_i = 1$ and $f_t = y_{it}$ resulting in $\hat{\sigma}_i^2 = T^{-1}\Sigma_{t=1}^T(y_{it} - \lambda_i f_t)^2 = 0$ and an infinite likelihood function. Breitung and Tenhofen (2011) argue that there is a local maximum in the neighbourhood of the true parameter values that can be found by initializing the maximization algorithm by some consistent estimators (such as the PC estimators).

These ML estimators are based on fairly restrictive assumptions which rule out realistic scenarios such as (weakly) serially and cross-sectionally correlated idiosyncratic errors, time dependent heteroscedasticity and serially correlated factors. A dynamic version of the factor model is typically formulated within a state space framework (for example Kapetanios and Marcellino, 2009). In this framework, the factor model (11.2) constitutes the *signal equation*, whereas (if the factors are assumed to follow a VAR(1) process) the transition equation is given by

$$f_t = \Phi f_{t-1} + \upsilon_t.$$

An obvious computational challenge is to deal with the typically high dimension of the signal equation. To reduce the computational burden, Kapetanios and Marcellino (2009) suggest a subspace algorithm, whereas Doz et al. (2011) use conventional algorithms based on the Kalman filter, arguing that 'the estimator is feasible when N is large and easily implementable using the Kalman smoother and the EM algorithm as in traditional factor analysis'. Jungbacker and Koopman (2008) combine traditional techniques based on the Kalman filter and Bayesian methods (MCMC techniques).

3.3 Frequency-domain Estimators

Forni et al. (2000, 2004) and Forni and Lippi (2001) consider the generalized factor model

$$\begin{aligned} y_{it} &= b_i(L)'\varepsilon_t + u_{it}, \\ &= \chi_{it} + u_{it} \end{aligned} \tag{11.6}$$

or in vector notation

$$y_t = \chi_t + u_t, \tag{11.7}$$

where $b_i(L) = (b_{i1}(L),\ldots,b_{ir}(L))'$, $\varepsilon_t = (\varepsilon_{1t},\ldots,\varepsilon_{rt})'$ is a vector white noise process, u_{it} is a stationary process representing idiosyncratic errors, $y_t = (y_{1t},\ldots,y_{Nt})'$ and χ_t and u_t are defined analogously. The vector ε_t comprises the common shocks of model (11.6), and $\chi_t = (\chi_{1t},\ldots,\chi_{Nt})'$ denotes the $N \times 1$ vector of the common components. As before, we assume that r is known.

Under the model assumptions, $\{y_t\}$ is a stationary N-dimensional process. Let $\Sigma^y(\theta)$, $\Sigma^\chi(\theta)$ and $\Sigma^u(\theta)$ be the spectral density matrices of y_t, χ_t and u_t, respectively. The jth eigenvalues of the matrices $\Sigma^y(\theta), \Sigma^\chi(\theta)$ and $\Sigma^u(\theta)$ (in descending order) are denoted as $\mu_j^y(\theta)$, $\mu_j^\chi(\theta)$ and $\mu_j^u(\theta)$. Note that all these spectral density matrices and eigenvalues depend on the index N, though we suppress it to simplify the notation. In order to identify the common components, Forni et al. (2000, 2004) and Forni and Lippi (2001) assume that r eigenvalues of the spectral density matrix $\Sigma^y(\theta)$ are $O(N)$ for all $\theta \in [-\pi,\pi]$, whereas the remaining $N - r$ eigenvalues are bounded for all N.

Since it is assumed that the common and idiosyncratic components are independent, we have

$$\Sigma^y(\theta) = \Sigma^\chi(\theta) + \Sigma^u(\theta) \quad \text{for any } \theta \in [-\pi,\pi].$$

Consider the (complex) eigenvector of the matrix $\Sigma^y(\theta)$ corresponding to the eigenvalue $\mu_j^y(\theta)$, denoted as $p_j(\theta)$ with

(i) $p_j^*(\theta)p_j(\theta) = 1$;

(ii) $p_h^*(\theta)p_j(\theta) = 0$ for any $j \neq h$ and any $\theta \in [-\pi, \pi]$,

where p^* denote the conjugate transpose of p.

The inverse Fourier transform of $p_j(\theta)$ is written as

$$p_j(\theta) = \frac{1}{2\pi}\sum_{k=-\infty}^{\infty}\Gamma_{jk}e^{-ik\theta},$$

where Γ_{jk} is the Fourier transform of $p_j(\theta)$, that is, $\Gamma_{jk} = \int_{-\pi}^{\pi} p_j(\theta)e^{ik\theta}d\theta$. Using $\{\Gamma_{jk}\}$ we can construct a scalar time series $\{z_{jt}\}$ such that

$$z_{jt} = \frac{1}{2\pi}\sum_{k=-\infty}^{\infty}\Gamma_{jk}y_{t-k}$$

with spectral density:

$$p_j(\theta)\Sigma^y(\theta)p_j^*(\theta) = \mu_j^y(\theta).$$

Thus, $\{z_{1t}\}, \ldots, \{z_{rt}\}$ have $\mu_1^y(\theta), \ldots, \mu_r^y(\theta)$ as spectral densities and, therefore, these components represent the dynamic principal components. Note that if y_t is white noise, then $\Sigma^y(\theta)$ is proportional to Ω_y and, therefore, the eigenvector $p_j(\theta) = v_j$ is real and does not depend on the frequency θ. In this case $z_{jt} = v_j'y_t$ is the ordinary principal component.

Forni et al. (2000) suggest an estimator of χ_{it} as

$$\hat{\chi}_{it} = \sum_{j=1}^{r} p_{ji}^*(L)z_{jt},$$

where $p_j(L) = \frac{1}{2\pi}\sum_{k=-\infty}^{\infty}\Gamma_{jk}L^k$ and $p_{ji}^*(L)$ is the ith element of $p_j^*(L)$. This estimator is a linear combination of all the past, present and future values of $\{z_{1t}, \ldots, z_{rt}\}$ with weights coming from the ith element of $\{\Gamma_{jk}\}$. The estimator $\hat{\chi}_{it}$ is not feasible in practice because it assumes that the true spectral density matrix $\Sigma^y(\theta)$ is known and it requires time series data with an index running from $-\infty$ to ∞. A feasible version of $\hat{\chi}_{it}$ is based on a consistent estimator of the spectral density matrix $\Sigma^y(\theta)$ and a suitable truncation of the infinite sums. Due to the leads and lags only $\{\chi_{it}\}$ with t belonging to a certain interval can be estimated consistently. The feasible version of $\hat{\chi}_{it}$ is shown to be consistent when both N and T go to infinity.

The two-sided nature of the filter used to construct $\hat{\chi}_{it}$ prevents this estimator from being useful for forecasting. To overcome this difficulty, Forni et al. (2005) propose a one-sided estimator of the common component.

4 DETERMINING THE NUMBER OF FACTORS

So far we have supposed that the number of factors r is known. In empirical practice, however, the number of factors is unknown and has to be determined from data. The characteristic feature of the factor structure (11.1) is that r eigenvalues of the variance-covariance matrix of $(y_{1t},\ldots,y_{Nt})'$ are 'large' relative to the remaining $N - r$ eigenvalues. Therefore, it is natural to select the number of factors by assessing the magnitude of the eigenvalues. A somewhat arbitrary but nevertheless popular criterion (sometimes called the Kaiser–Guttman criterion) is to determine the number of factors as the number of eigenvalues of the sample correlation matrix that exceed unity (which is the average size of the eigenvalue of the correlation matrix). Since the largest r eigenvalues are $O_p(N)$, these eigenvalues eventually exceed the threshold as $N \rightarrow \infty$.

Another simple and very popular selection criterion is the 'scree plot'. Cattell (1966) suggests selecting the number of factors from the plot of the ordered eigenvalues, where the smooth decrease of eigenvalues appears to level off to the right of the plot (the 'elbow' of the scree plot). Since the rth eigenvalue is $O(N)$ whereas the $(r + 1)$th eigenvalue is $O(1)$, it is expected that the eigenvalues show a sharp drop from r to $r + 1$. Using this observation, Onatski (2009) suggests selecting the number of common factors according to the slope of the eigenvalue function. Let $\hat{\mu}_i$ denote the ith ordered eigenvalue of the sample covariance matrix $\hat{\Omega}_y$. A measure of the slope of the scree plot is

$$\hat{\delta}_i = \frac{\hat{\mu}_i - \hat{\mu}_{i+1}}{\hat{\mu}_{i+1} - \hat{\mu}_{i+2}}.$$

It is not difficult to see that $\hat{\delta}_i$ is $O_p(N)$ for $i = r$ but $O_p(1)$ if $i > r$. To test the null hypothesis $H_0 : r = r_0$ against $H_1 : r_0 < r < r_{\max}$, Onatski (2009) introduces the test statistic $R = \max(\hat{\delta}_{r_0+1},\ldots,\hat{\delta}_{r_{\max}})$ and derives its (rather complex) limiting distribution. The number of factors can be determined by testing the sequence of hypotheses $r_0 = r_{\max}, r_{\max} - 1,\ldots$. The procedure suggests selecting the number of factors where the test rejects the null hypothesis for the first time.

Bai and Ng (2002) propose consistent information criteria for the number of factors in approximate factor models. Although the criteria are originally formulated in terms of the total sum of squared residuals, it can also be written as a function of the eigenvalues $\hat{\mu}_i$ of the sample covariance matrix $\hat{\Omega}_y$ by noting that

$$V_{NT}(r^*) = \frac{1}{NT}\sum_{i=1}^{N}\sum_{t=1}^{T}(y_{it} - \hat{\lambda}_i'\hat{F}_t)^2 = \frac{1}{N}\sum_{i=r^*+1}^{N}\hat{\mu}_i,$$

where $r^* = \dim(\hat{f}_t)$ and $\{\hat{f}_t, \hat{\lambda}_i\}$ denote the PC estimators (cf. Ahn and Horenstein, 2013). Bai and Ng (2002) propose two different classes of information criteria:

$$\mathrm{PCP}(r^*) = V_{NT}(r^*) + \bar{\sigma}^2 r^* g(N,T)$$

$$\mathrm{IC}(r^*) = \log[V_{NT}(r^*)] + r^* g(N,T),$$

where $\overline{\sigma}^2 = V_{NT}(r_{\max})$. The estimated number of common factors is obtained from minimizing the information criteria $PCP(r^*)$ or $IC(r^*)$ with respect to r^*. The penalty function $g(N, T)$ obeys $g(N, T) \to 0$ and $\min(N, T) \cdot g(N, T) \to \infty$ as N and T tend to infinity.

To study the properties of the information criteria, it is instructive to consider the difference

$$PCP(r^* - 1) - PCP(r^*) = \frac{\hat{\mu}_{r^*}}{N} - \overline{\sigma}^2 g(N, T). \tag{11.8}$$

We prefer r^* to $r^* - 1$ if this difference is positive, that is, if the r^*th eigenvalue is larger than $N\overline{\sigma}^2 g(N, T)$. If the number of factors is equal to (or larger than) r^*, then the corresponding eigenvalue is $O(N)$ and, therefore, the eigenvalue eventually exceeds the threshold if N is sufficiently large. On the other hand, if the true number of factors is smaller than r^*, the r^*th eigenvalue is bounded and, since the threshold is increasing in N, the information criterion tends to select the smaller number of factors. A similar reasoning applies to the criterion $IC(r^*)$ by invoking the approximation $\log(1 + \Delta) \approx \Delta$ for small Δ.

Bai and Ng (2008) recommend the penalty function

$$g(N, T) = \frac{N + T}{NT} \log[\min(N, T)].$$

In empirical applications these information criteria perform well if N is sufficiently large (for example $N > 100$). For small sample sizes the information criteria overestimate the number of factors and tend to select the upper limit $r_{\max}$. This is not surprising since N needs to be large enough to push the largest eigenvalue above the threshold implied by (11.8). Another drawback of this approach is that the eigenvalues depend on nuisance parameters stemming from the cross-sectional and serial correlations of the idiosyncratic errors, which makes it sensitive to the particular features of the data generating process. Therefore, Greenaway-McGrevy et al. (2012a) suggest filtering the data before applying the Bai–Ng method.

Ahn and Horenstein (2013) suggest a simple and appealing alternative approach to selecting the number of factors. They consider maximizing the eigenvalue ratio

$$ER(r^*) = \frac{\hat{\mu}_{r^*}}{\hat{\mu}_{r^*+1}} \tag{11.9}$$

or the growth ratio

$$GR(r^*) = \frac{\log(1 + \hat{\mu}_{r^*})}{\log(1 + \hat{\mu}_{r^*+1})}. \tag{11.10}$$

The notion behind this approach is that for the true number of factors $r^* = r$ these ratios are $O_p(N)$, whereas for all other values of r^* the ratios are $O_p(1)$. Thus, it follows that maximizing the ratios with respect to r^* yields a consistent estimator of r as $N \to \infty$. An attractive feature of this approach is that it does not involve any (more or less arbitrary) threshold for the eigenvalues. Monte Carlo simulations of the authors suggest that these criteria perform well relative to the alternative approaches proposed by Bai and Ng (2002) and Onatski (2010).

All the methods considered so far were developed for the static factor model. In the dynamic factor model where the factors enter in the form of distributed lags, these criteria estimate the number of factors in the static representation (see section 2.3). For the purpose of illustration, consider the dynamic factor model with a single factor:

$$y_{it} = \lambda_{1i} f_t^* + \lambda_{2i} f_{t-1}^* + u_{it}. \tag{11.11}$$

The selection criteria considered so far treat the lagged factor as an additional factor and, therefore, tend to indicate the existence of two factors. Bai and Ng (2007), Amengual and Watson (2007), Hallin and Liska (2007) and Breitung and Pigorsch (2013) propose selection procedures for the number of the dynamic (or 'primitive') factors. In model (11.11), there is only one dynamic factor that can be written as a linear combination of the two static factors. To estimate the number of dynamic factors, Amengual and Watson (2007) suggest a sequential approach. In the first step, a PC analysis is applied to obtain consistent estimators of the vector of static factors $\hat{f}_t$. In the second step, the lagged factors are removed by regressing all variables y_{it} on the lags $\hat{f}_{t-1}, \ldots, \hat{f}_{t-p}$. Finally, the number of dynamic factors are estimated by applying some consistent selection criterion to the residuals of the second step regression. The approaches of Bai and Ng (2007) and Breitung and Pigorsch (2009) are based on a VAR of the estimated factors. Since the rank of the residual covariance matrix of the VAR is identical to the number of dynamic factors, their selection procedure is based on the number of significant eigenvalues. Hallin and Liska (2007) develop information criteria for the generalized PC estimator considered in section 3.3. Since in a dynamic PC analysis the common shocks are associated with unbounded eigenvalues, this approach directly estimates the number of the original dynamic factors.

5 ASYMPTOTIC THEORY

As has been argued in section 2.1, the vectors of common factors and factor loadings are not separably identified as the transformed vectors $f_t^* = Qf_t$ and $\lambda_i^* = Q'^{-1}\lambda_i$ provide observationally equivalent representations. Thus, instead of estimating the true factors f_t, the estimators merely render some particular basis of the factor space. Specifically, the PC estimator imposes the normalization $T^{-1}\Sigma_{t=1}^{T}\hat{f}_t\hat{f}_t' = I_r$ and, therefore, the statement that $\hat{f}_t$ converges in probability to f_t^* makes sense only if we choose $Q = H$ such that $T^{-1}\Sigma_{t=1}^{T} Hf_t f_t' H' \xrightarrow{p} I_r$. As shown by Bai and Ng (2002) the matrix

$$H = T\Lambda'\Lambda F'\hat{F}(\hat{F}'YY'\hat{F})^{-1}.$$

has the desired property.

Let $\hat{f}_t$ denote the PC estimator of the vector of factors f_t. The estimator of the vector of factor loadings λ_i is equivalent to the least-squares estimator of the time series regression

$$y_{it} = \lambda_i' \hat{f}_t + v_{it}, \quad (t = 1, \ldots, T),$$

where $v_{it} = \lambda_i'(f_t - \hat{f}_t) + u_{it}$. Similarly, the (transformed) factors can be estimated from the cross-section regression

$$y_{it} = f_t'\hat{\lambda}_i + \nu_{it}, \quad (i = 1,\ldots,N),$$

with $\nu_{it} = f_t'(\lambda_i - \hat{\lambda}_i) + u_{it}$. Under some fairly weak conditions it was shown by Stock and Watson (2002) and Bai (2003) that the estimation errors $\lambda_i'(Hf_t - \hat{f}_t)$ and $f_t'(H'^{-1}\lambda_i - \hat{\lambda}_i)$ in these regressions are asymptotically negligible in the sense that the PC estimators are asymptotically equivalent to the corresponding regression using the (appropriately normalized) true factors and factor loadings. Accordingly, the limiting distributions are given by

$$\sqrt{T}(\hat{\lambda}_i - H'^{-1}\lambda_i) \xrightarrow{d} \mathcal{N}(0, V_i^{\lambda});$$

$$\sqrt{N}(\hat{f}_t - Hf_t) \xrightarrow{d} \mathcal{N}(0, V_t^{f}).$$

For example, if it is assumed that $u_{it} \overset{iid}{\sim} \mathcal{N}(0,\sigma^2)$ it follows that

$$V_i^{\lambda} = \lim_{T\to\infty} \sigma^2\left(\frac{1}{T}\sum_{t=1}^{T} \hat{f}_t\hat{f}_t'\right)^{-1} = \sigma^2 I_r$$

$$V_t^{f} = \lim_{N\to\infty} \sigma^2\left(\frac{1}{N}\sum_{i=1}^{N} \hat{\lambda}_i\hat{\lambda}_i'\right)^{-1} = \sigma^2 \operatorname{diag}\left(\frac{1}{\mu_1^*},\ldots,\frac{1}{\mu_r^*}\right),$$

where $\mu_j^* = \lim_{N\to\infty} N^{-1}\mu_j$ for $j = 1,\ldots,r$ and μ_j denotes the jth eigenvalue of $\Omega_y = E(y_t y_t')$. If the errors are heteroscedastic and correlated, the asymptotic variance–covariance matrices have to be estimated by using a Newey–West type HAC estimator (cf. Newey and West, 1987). The full set of assumptions required to derive these limiting results are provided in Bai (2003). Here we just mention the most important assumptions for empirical applications:[2]

1. The idiosyncratic errors are weakly cross-sectionally correlated in the sense that the largest eigenvalue of the error covariance matrix is bounded:

$$\mu_1^u \leq \frac{1}{N}\sum_{i=1}^{N}\sum_{j=1}^{N}|\sigma_{ij}| \leq M < \infty$$

   for all N, where μ_1^u is the largest eigenvalue of Σ_u and σ_{ij} denotes the (i,j)-element of Σ_u.
2. The errors are weakly serially correlated in the sense that

$$\frac{1}{T}\sum_{t=1}^{T}\sum_{s=1}^{T}|E(u_{it}u_{is})| \leq M < \infty$$

   for all i, j and T.
3. The errors obey the following central limit theorems:

$$\frac{1}{\sqrt{N}}\sum_{i=1}^{N}\lambda_i u_{it} \xrightarrow{d} \mathcal{N}(0, V_{\lambda u,t})$$

$$\frac{1}{\sqrt{T}}\sum_{t=1}^{T}F_t u_{it} \xrightarrow{d} \mathcal{N}(0, V_{Fu,i})$$

with some positive definite covariance matrices $V_{\lambda u,t}$ and $V_{Fu,i}$.

Assumption (1) implies that the idiosyncratic errors are weakly cross-sectionally dependent in the sense of Chudik et al. (2011). Furthermore, assumptions (2) and (3) rule out that the errors are integrated processes (see section 6 for related discussions).

It is easy to see that if the errors are heteroscedastic and/or autocorrelated the PC estimator fails to be asymptotically efficient. For example, if $E(u_{it}^2) = \sigma_i^2$, then a more efficient estimator of the factors is obtained by a GLS estimation of the form

$$\frac{1}{\sigma_i}y_{it} = f_t'\left(\frac{1}{\sigma_i}\hat{\lambda}_i\right) + \frac{1}{\sigma_i}v_i, \tag{11.12}$$

whereas no gain in efficiency can be achieved when estimating λ_i. Breitung and Tenhofen (2011) propose a feasible GLS estimator that employs the variance estimator $\hat{\sigma}_i^2 = T^{-1}\sum_{t=1}^{T}\hat{u}_{it}^2$, where $\hat{u}_{it}$ denotes the PC estimator of the idiosyncratic component. Alternatively, the factors may be estimated by applying a PC analysis to the transformed data $y_{it}^* = y_{it}/\hat{\sigma}_{it}$ (cf. Choi, 2011).

In many econometric applications, the model includes observed variables and unobserved factors. For example, factors may be employed as predictors to improve the forecast of some economic variables as in the predictive regression model (for example Stock and Watson, 2002):

$$y_{t+h} = \alpha_0 y_t + \cdots + \alpha_p y_{t-p} + \beta_0' f_t + \cdots + \beta_q' f_{t-q} + \varepsilon_t.$$

Another related example is the factor-augmented VAR regression (for example Stock and Watson, 2005 and Bernanke et al., 2005):

$$y_t = A_1 y_{t-1} + \cdots + A_p y_{t-p} + B_1 f_{t-1} + \cdots + B_q f_{t-q} + \varepsilon_t.$$

In the panel data model with interactive effects (cf. Pesaran, 2006 and Bai, 2009), the cross-sectional correlation among the errors is represented by the factor augmented panel regression

$$y_{it} = \beta' x_{it} + \lambda_i' f_t + u_{it}$$

where x_{it} is a vector of observed regressors.

In those variants of factor-augmented regressions it is natural to replace the unobserved factor by consistent estimators and apply OLS to the resulting regression equation. The previous asymptotic properties suggest that replacing the unobserved factors by PC estimators (or some more efficient PC–GLS estimators) does not affect the asymptotic properties of the second-stage OLS estimators whenever $\sqrt{T/N} \rightarrow 0$, that is, if N is large relative to T. Indeed, this finding was established by Bai and Ng (2006) for a wide class of factor-augmented regressions. In some cases, however, these findings also hold under some less restrictive assumptions such as $T/N \rightarrow 0$ (cf. Bai, 2009 and Greenaway-McGrevy et al., 2012b).

6 NON-STATIONARY FACTOR MODELS

Bai (2004) studies the non-stationary factor model for which the factors are generated by a (multivariate) unit-root process

$$f_t = f_{t-1} + \eta_t,$$

where $\{\eta_t\}$ is an r-dimensional stationary process. For the idiosyncratic components two cases are considered: (i) u_{it} is stationary and (ii) u_{it} is $I(1)$, that is, Δu_{it} has a stationary and invertible MA representation. The implications of these assumptions for the factor model can easily be analysed by assuming that the factors are known. It is well known from the literature on non-stationary time series analysis that if u_{it} is stationary the OLS estimator of λ_i in the regression model

$$y_{it} = \lambda_i' f_t + u_{it} \quad t = 1, \ldots, T \tag{11.13}$$

is T-consistent with a non-standard limiting distribution. On the other hand, if u_{it} is $I(1)$, model (11.13) gives rise to a 'spurious regression' and the OLS estimator of λ_i does not converge to the true values.

Bai and Ng (2004) propose a robust estimator that is consistent whether the errors are stationary or not. Taking first differences of (11.13) yields

$$\Delta y_{it} = \lambda_i' \Delta f_t + \Delta u_{it}. \tag{11.14}$$

Since the error Δu_{it} is stationary, the PC estimator of Δf_t is consistent even if the errors are 'over-differenced'. Bai and Ng suggest estimating the original factors by using $\Delta f_2 + \cdots + \Delta f_t = f_t - f_1$. Although this approach elegantly sidesteps the problems due to possible non-stationary idiosyncratic errors, it may imply a severe loss of efficiency if the errors are over-differenced. In empirical practice it is standard to apply unit root test to the components of y_{it} in order to find out whether the variables need to be differenced or not.

Choi (2011) studies the same model as in Bai (2004), but adopts the assumption that $E(u_t u_t') = \Sigma_u$ for all t. With the standardization $T^{-2}F'F = I_r$, his estimator of the factor space, denoted as $\hat{F}_g$, is T times the matrix consisting of the eigenvectors corresponding to the r largest eigenvalues of the matrix $Y\Sigma_u^{-1}Y'$. The matrix of factor loadings Λ is estimated by $\hat{\Lambda} = \frac{1}{T^2}Y'\hat{F}_g$. It is shown that the resulting estimator of F_t is more efficient than the PC estimator since the generalized PC estimator corresponds to the GLS estimator in the linear regression while the PC estimator corresponds to the OLS estimator. Regarding the estimation of λ_i, Choi shows that the GLS version of the principal components estimator is asymptotically equivalent to the original PC estimator. A set of conditions that makes the generalized principal components estimator of F_t and its feasible version equivalent in the limit are stated. Choi (2011) also extends his theory to the models with an intercept and with an intercept and a linear time.

7 CONCLUSION

In recent years dynamic factor models have become popular for analysing and forecasting large macroeconomic data sets. In this chapter we focused on recent developments in the modelling and estimation of (dynamic) factor models. The premise of these models is that a few latent factors are able to capture the pervasive co-movement among a large set of economic variables. Employing dynamic factor models in empirical practice raises a number of important problems: how many factors are required to summarize the cross-correlation among the variables? How can we efficiently estimate the latent factors? Is it possible to provide the extracted factors with a meaningful economic interpretation? How can we perform statistical inference based on estimated factors? In the past decade, econometric work provided a variety of statistical methods to address these issues. There is no doubt that future research will further complement the econometric toolbox for analysing macroeconomic co-movement based on factor models.

NOTES

1. For notational convenience we assume that $E(y_t) = 0$. In practice, the variable specific means $\bar{y}_i = T^{-1}\Sigma_{t=1}^{T} y_{it}$ are subtracted and in many applications the variables are further divided by their sample standard deviations.
2. To simplify the exposition we assume that the errors are stationary with $\Sigma_u = E(u_t u_t')$.

REFERENCES

Ahn, S.C. and A.R. Horenstein (2013), 'Eigenvalue ratio test for the number of factors', *Econometrica*, forthcoming.

Altissimo, F., A. Bassanetti, R. Cristadoro, M. Forni, M. Hallin, M. Lippi and L. Reichlin (2001), 'EuroCOIN: a real time coincident indicator of the euro area business cycle', CEPR Working Paper no. 3108.

Amengual, D. and M.W. Watson (2007), 'Consistent estimation of the number of dynamic factors in a large N and T panel', *Journal of Business & Economic Statistics*, **25**, 91–6.

Anderson, T.W. (1984), *Introduction to Multivariate Statistical Analysis*, 2nd edn, New York: John Wiley.

Bai, J. (2003), 'Inferential theory for factor models of large dimensions', *Econometrica*, **71**, 135–72.

Bai, J. (2004), 'Estimating cross-section common stochastic trends in nonstationary panel data', *Journal of Econometrics*, **122**, 137–83.

Bai, J. (2009), 'Panel data models with interactive fixed effects', *Econometrica*, **77**, 1229–79.

Bai, J. and S. Ng (2002), 'Determining the number of factors in approximate factor models', *Econometrica*, **70**, 191–221.

Bai, J. and S. Ng (2004), 'A PANIC attack on unit roots and cointegration', *Econometrica*, **72**, 1127–77.

Bai, J. and S. Ng (2006), 'Evaluating latent and observed factors in macroeconomics and finance', *Journal of Econometrics*, **113**, 507–37.

Bai, J. and S. Ng (2007), 'Determining the number of primitive shocks in factor models', *Journal of Business and Economic Statistics*, **25**, 52–60.

Bai, J. and S. Ng (2008), 'Large dimensional factor models', *Foundations and Trends in Econometrics*, **3**, 89–163.

Bai, J. and S. Ng (2010), 'Instrumental variable estimation in data rich environment', *Econometric Theory*, **26**, 1577–606.

Bernanke, B., J. Boivin and P. Eliasz (2005), 'Measuring the effects of monetary policy: a factor-augmented vector autoregressive (FAVAR) approach', *Quarterly Journal of Economics*, **120**, 387–422.

Breitung, J. and S. Eickmeier (2006), 'Dynamic factor models', Chapter 3 in O. Hübler and J. Frohn (eds), *Modern Econometric Analysis*, Heidelberg: Springer.

Breitung, J. and U. Pigorsch (2013), 'A canonical correlation approach for selecting the number of dynamic factors', *Oxford Bulletin of Economics and Statistics*, **75**, 23–36.

Breitung, J. and J. Tenhofen (2011), 'GLS estimation of dynamic factor models', *Journal of the American Statistical Association*, **106**, 1150–66.

Cattell, R.B. (1966), 'The scree test for the number of factors', *Multivariate Behavioral Research*, **1**, 245–76.

Chamberlain, G. and M. Rothschild (1983), 'Arbitrage, factor structure, and mean-variance analysis on large asset markets', *Econometrica*, **51**, 1281–304.

Choi, I. (2011), 'Efficient estimators of nonstationary factor models', mimeo.

Choi, I. (2012), 'Efficient estimators of factor models', *Econometric Theory*, **28**, 274–308.

Chudik, A., M.H. Pesaran and E. Tosetti (2011), 'Weak and strong cross section dependence and estimation of large panels', *Econometrics Journal*, **14**, C45–C90.

Deistler, M. and C. Zinner (2007), 'Modelling high dimensional time series by generalized linear factor models: an introductory survey, festschrift for Tyrone Duncan', *Communications in Information and Systems*, **7**, 153–66.

Doz, C., D. Giannone and L. Reichlin (2011), 'A quasi maximum likelihood approach for large approximate dynamic factor models', *The Review of Economics and Statistics*, **94**, 1014–24.

Eickmeier, S. and C. Ziegler (2008), 'How successful are dynamic factor models at forecasting output and inflation? A meta-analytic approach', *Journal of Forecasting*, **27**, 237–65.

Forni, M. and F. Lippi (2001), 'The generalized dynamic factor model: representation theory', *Econometric Theory*, **17**, 1113–41.

Forni, M., M. Hallin, F. Lippi and L. Reichlin (2000), 'The generalized dynamic factor model: identification and estimation', *The Review of Economics and Statistics*, **82**, 540–54.

Forni, M., M. Hallin, M. Lippi and L. Reichlin (2004), 'The generalized factor model: consistency and rates', *Journal of Econometrics*, **119**, 231–55.

Forni, M., M. Hallin, M. Lippi and L. Reichlin (2005), 'The generalized dynamic factor model: one-sided estimation and forecasting', *Journal of the American Statistical Association*, **100**, 830–40.

Geweke, J. (1977), 'The dynamic factor analysis of economic time series', in D.J. Aigner and A. Goldberger (eds), *Latent Variables in Socio-economic Models*, Amsterdam: North Holland.

Greenaway-McGrevy, R., C. Han and D. Sul (2012a), 'Estimating the number of common factors in serially dependent approximate factor models', *Economics Letters*, **116**, 531–4.

Greenaway-McGrevy, R., C. Han and D. Sul (2012b), 'Asymptotic distribution of factor augmented estimators for panel regression', *Journal of Econometrics*, **169**, 48–53.

Hallin, M. and R. Liska (2007), 'Determining the number of dynamic factors in the general dynamic factor model', *Journal of the American Statistical Association*, **102**, 603–17.

Hallin, M. and R. Liska (2011), 'Dynamic factors in the presence of blocks', *Journal of Econometrics*, **163**, 29–41.

Jungbacker, B. and S.J. Koopman (2008), 'Likelihood-based analysis for dynamic factor models', mimeo, Free University of Amsterdam.

Kaiser, H.F. (1958), 'The varimax criterion for analytic rotation in factor analysis', *Psychometrika*, **23**, 187–200.

Kapetanios, G. and M. Marcellino (2009), 'A parametric estimation method for dynamic factor models of large dimensions', *Journal of Time Series Analysis*, **30**, 208–38.

Lawley, D.N. and A.E. Maxwell (1963), *Factor Analysis as a Statistical Method*, London: Butterworths.

Moon, H.R. and B. Perron (2004), 'Testing for a unit root in panels with dynamic factors', *Journal of Econometrics*, **122**, 81–126.

Newey, W.K. and K.D. West (1987), 'A simple, positive semi-definite, heteroskedasticity and autocorrelation consistent covariance matrix', *Econometrica*, **55**, 703–8.

Onatski, A. (2009), 'Testing hypotheses about the number of factors in large factor models', *Econometrica*, **77**, 1447–79.

Onatski, A. (2010), 'Determining the number of factors from empirical distribution of Eigenvalues', *Review of Economics and Statistics*, **92**, 1004–16.

Pesaran, M.H. (2006), 'Estimation and inference in large heterogeneous panels with multifactor error structure', *Econometrica*, **74**, 967–1012.

Phillips, P.C.B and D. Sul (2003), 'Dynamic panel estimation and homogeneity testing under cross-section dependence', *Econometrics Journal*, **6**, 217–59.

Stock, J.H. and M.W. Watson (2002), 'Forecasting using principal components from a large number of predictors', *Journal of the American Statistical Association*, **97**, 1167–79.
Stock, J.H. and M.W. Watson (2005), 'Implications of dynamic factor models for VAR analysis', NBER Working Paper no. 11467.
Stock, J.H. and M.W. Watson (2011), 'Dynamic factor models', Chapter 2 in M.P. Clements and D.F. Hendry (eds), *Oxford Handbook of Economic Forecasting*, New York: Oxford University Press.

12 Conditional heteroskedasticity in macroeconomics data: UK inflation, output growth and their uncertainties*

Menelaos Karanasos and Ning Zeng

1 INTRODUCTION

The conditional heteroskedasticity models are widely used in the financial economics and less frequently so in other fields, including macroeconomics. However, certain applications lend themselves naturally to the investigation of possible links between macroeconomic variables and their volatilities, and here the conditional heteroskedasticity approach proved to be a powerful tool. The basics of the univariate models with conditional heteroskedasticity have been introduced in Chapter 2 in this volume. In this chapter, we extend this to a bivariate model and illustrate how this approach can be used to investigate the link between UK inflation, growth and their respective uncertainties, using a particular bivariate model with conditional heteroskedasticity.[1] For recent surveys on multivariate GARCH specifications and their importance in various areas such as asset pricing, portfolio selection, and risk management see, for example, Bauwens et al. (2006) and Silvennoinen and Teräsvirta (2007).

The ARCH and GARCH models were introduced by Engle (1982) and Bollerslev (1986), respectively, and quickly gained currency in the finance literature.[2] Consider the process y_t augmented by a risk premium defined in terms of volatility (h_t):

$$y_t = \mathbb{E}(y_t|\Omega_{t-1}) + kh_t + \varepsilon_t, \tag{12.1}$$

with

$$\varepsilon_t = e_t h_t^{\frac{1}{2}},$$

where Ω_{t-1} is the information set. In addition, $\{e_t\}$ are independently and identically distributed (i.i.d) random variables with $\mathbb{E}(e_t) = \mathbb{E}(e_t^2 - 1) = 0$, while h_t denotes the conditional variance of y_t. In particular, h_t is specified as a GARCH(1,1) process:

$$h_t = \omega + \alpha\varepsilon_{t-1}^2 + \beta h_{t-1}, \tag{12.2}$$

where α and β are the ARCH and GARCH coefficients respectively. h_t is positive with probability 1 if and only if $\omega, \alpha > 0$, and $\beta \geq 0$. It can also be seen that, if $\alpha + \beta < 1$, the unconditional variance of the errors is given by

$$\mathbb{E}(h_t) = \mathbb{E}(\varepsilon_t^2) = \frac{\omega}{1 - (\alpha + \beta)}$$

(see Francq and Zakoian, 2010).

A general bivariate VAR(p) (GARCH-in-mean) model can be written as

$$\left(\mathbf{I} - \sum_{i=1}^{p} \mathbf{\Phi}_i L^i\right)(\mathbf{x}_t - \mathbf{\Delta h}_{t-n}) = \mathbf{\Phi}_0 + \boldsymbol{\varepsilon}_t, \quad t \in \mathbb{N}, \tag{12.3}$$

with

$$\mathbf{\Phi}_i = \begin{bmatrix} \phi_{\pi\pi}^{(i)} & \phi_{\pi y}^{(i)} \\ \phi_{y\pi}^{(i)} & \phi_{yy}^{(i)} \end{bmatrix}, \quad \mathbf{\Delta} = \begin{bmatrix} \delta_{\pi\pi} & \delta_{\pi y} \\ \delta_{y\pi} & \delta_{yy} \end{bmatrix}, \quad \mathbf{\Phi}_0 = \begin{bmatrix} \phi_{\pi 0} \\ \phi_{y0} \end{bmatrix},$$

where $\mathbf{I}$ is a 2×2 identity matrix, $\mathbf{x}_t$ and $\mathbf{h}_t$ are 2×1 column vectors given by $\mathbf{x}_t = (\pi_t\, y_t)'$ and $\mathbf{h}_t = (h_{\pi t}\, h_{yt})'$ respectively, and $n = 0, \ldots, 4$.

We use a bivariate model to simultaneously estimate the conditional means, variances, and covariances of inflation and output growth. Let π_t and y_t denote the inflation rate and real output growth respectively, and define the residual vector $\boldsymbol{\varepsilon}_t$ as $\boldsymbol{\varepsilon}_t = (\varepsilon_{\pi t}\ \varepsilon_{yt})'$.[3] Regarding $\boldsymbol{\varepsilon}_t$ we assume that it is conditionally normal with mean vector $\mathbf{0}$ and covariance matrix $\mathbf{H}_t$ where vech $(\mathbf{H}_t) = (h_{\pi t}\ h_{\pi y,t}\ h_{yt})'$.[4] That is $(\boldsymbol{\varepsilon}_t|\Omega_{t-1}) \sim N(\mathbf{0}, \mathbf{H}_t)$, where Ω_{t-1} is the information set up to time $t-1$. Following Conrad and Karanasos (2010, 2012) we impose the extended constant conditional correlation (eccc) GARCH (1,1)-level structure on the conditional covariance matrix $\mathbf{H}_t$:

$$\mathbf{h}_t = \boldsymbol{\omega} + \mathbf{A}\boldsymbol{\varepsilon}_{t-1}^2 + \mathbf{B}\mathbf{h}_{t-1} + \mathbf{\Gamma}\mathbf{x}_{t-1}, \tag{12.4}$$

with

$$\boldsymbol{\omega} = \begin{bmatrix} \omega_\pi \\ \omega_y \end{bmatrix}, \quad \mathbf{A} = \begin{bmatrix} a_{\pi\pi} & a_{\pi y} \\ a_{y\pi} & a_{yy} \end{bmatrix}, \quad \mathbf{B} = \begin{bmatrix} \beta_{\pi\pi} & \beta_{\pi y} \\ \beta_{y\pi} & \beta_{yy} \end{bmatrix}, \quad \mathbf{\Gamma} = \begin{bmatrix} \gamma_{\pi\pi} & \gamma_{\pi y} \\ \gamma_{y\pi} & \gamma_{yy} \end{bmatrix}.$$

Moreover, $h_{\pi y,t} = \rho\sqrt{h_{\pi t}}\sqrt{h_{yt}}$, $(-1 \leq \rho \leq 1)$. We will use the acronym BVAR(p)-GARCH$(1,1)$-ML$(n,1)$ to refer to this model.

There are many controversies in the theoretical literature on the relationship between the four variables. The debate about the inflation–growth interaction is linked to another ongoing dispute, that of the existence or absence of a variance relationship. As Fuhrer (1997) puts it,

> It is difficult to imagine a policy that embraces targets for the level of inflation or output growth without caring about their variability around their target levels. The more concerned the monetary policy is about maintaining the level of an objective as its target, the more it will care about the variability of that objective around its target.

Thus, Fuhrer focuses his attention on the trade-off between the volatility of inflation and that of output. The extent to which there is an interaction between them is an issue that cannot be resolved on merely theoretical grounds. To paraphrase the words of Temple (2000):

> When one lists ideas about the influence of macroeconomic performance on uncertainty, it is striking that theoretical models are less common than hypotheses or conjectures.[5] Not only that, the models regarding the opposite link (the impact of uncertainty on performance) that do exist are often ambiguous in their predictions. These considerations reinforce a widespread awareness of the need for more empirical evidence, but also make clear that a good empirical framework is lacking.

The last ten years have seen an outpouring of empirical work intended to explain the links among the four variables. Many researchers who have worked on this field over the last decade or so have endorsed the GARCH model (see, for example, Grier et al., 2004, Shields et al., 2005, Fountas et al., 2006, Fountas and Karanasos, 2007 and Conrad et al., 2010). Indeed, this model has been the driving force behind the quest to examine the interactions between macroeconomic performance and its uncertainty.[6] Despite numerous empirical studies, there still exists controversy over the robustness of these relationships. The GARCH studies by Karanasos et al. (2004), Karanasos and Kim (2005a) and Karanasos and Schurer (2005) focus almost exclusively on the empirical linkages between any of the following three: (i) inflation and its volatility; (ii) nominal and real uncertainty; and (iii) growth and its variability. It makes good sense to treat these issues together as answers to one relationship are usually relevant to the other two.

In this chapter we use a bivariate GARCH model to investigate the interactions between the four variables. Our work has many distinguishing features. We examine in a single empirical framework all the possible causal relationships among inflation, output growth, and their respective variabilities that are predicted by economic theory. If well estimated, this model can help identify the relative contributions of different influences more precisely than previous studies. Rather than selecting one specification as pre-eminent, we compare various formulations and investigate the similarities and differences between them.

One potentially controversial aspect of nearly all bivariate GARCH processes is the way in which the conditional variance–covariance matrix is formulated. The two most commonly used models are the constant conditional correlation (ccc) specification and the BEKK representation.[7] At the one extreme, the former assumes that there is no link between the two uncertainties, whereas, near the other extreme, the latter only allows for a positive variance relationship. At this point one alternative model suggests itself. That is, we construct a formulation of the ccc GARCH-in-mean model which allows for a bidirectional feedback between the two volatilities, which can be of either sign, positive or negative, and so no restriction is imposed. This has the advantage of allowing us to derive sufficient conditions for the non-negativity of the two conditional variances.[8]

The studies by Grier and Perry (2000) and Grier et al. (2004) focus on the impact of uncertainty on performance (the so-called in-mean effects). These studies simultaneously estimate a system of equations that allows only the current values of the two conditional variances to affect inflation and growth (see also Elder, 2004). However, any relationship where macroeconomic performance is influenced by its variability takes time to show up and cannot be fairly tested in a model that restricts the effect to be contemporaneous. In this chapter we estimate a system of equations that allows various lags of the two variances to affect the conditional means.

Perhaps a more promising approach is to construct a model allowing for effects in the opposite direction as well. There exists relatively little empirical work documenting the influence of performance on uncertainty (the so-called level effects). Dotsey and Sarte (2000) point out that countries which have managed to live with relatively high levels of inflation should exhibit greater variability in their real growth rate. Inflation breeds uncertainty in many forms. The fact that higher inflation has implications for the volatility of growth has thus far been overlooked in empirical studies. One could also imagine that when economic growth decreases, there is some uncertainty generated about the future path of monetary policy, and consequently, inflation variability increases (Brunner, 1993). Although Dotsey and Sarte's and Brunner's hypotheses are merely suggestive, their conjectures suggest the importance of devoting greater explicit attention to the effects of inflation and growth on nominal and real uncertainty. This study employs a ueccc model with lagged inflation and growth included in the variance specifications. Various lags of the two variables are considered, with the best model chosen on the basis of the minimum value of the information criteria. In other words, we examine the bidirectional causality between the four variables in contrast with the existing literature that focuses almost exclusively on the effect of uncertainty on performance.

The above considerations, along with the just mentioned complexity, have led to a protracted chicken-or-egg debate about the causal relations between inflation, growth and their respective uncertainties. This chapter examines simultaneously all the interactions among the four variables. In doing so we are able to highlight some key behavioral features that are present across various bivariate formulations. The following observations, among other things, are noted about the interlinkages. Of significant importance is that in all cases, growth tends to increase inflation, whereas inflation is detrimental to growth. This finding is robust to the choice of the model. Another useful piece of evidence is that increased nominal uncertainty leads to higher real variability as predicted by Logue and Sweeney (1981).

We also draw attention to one particularly dramatic finding. Some in-mean effects are found to be quite robust to the various specifications that were considered. In particular, inflation is independent of changes in its volatility whereas real uncertainty affects inflation positively, as predicted by Cukierman and Gerlach (2003). Some others are found to be 'fragile' in the sense that either their statistical significance disappears or their sign changes when a different formulation is used. Slight variations in the specification of the regressions appear to yield substantially different results for the influence of the two volatilities on output growth. It is also worth pointing out that robustness is not a necessary condition for useful information. We would like to make clear that lack of robustness should often spur further investigation into causality and interrelationships. Finding that some results are fragile could in itself be valuable information (Temple, 1999).

Moreover, inflation has a positive impact on macroeconomic uncertainty. Whereas the link between inflation and its volatility is well documented, not much attention has been paid to the effect of inflation on real variability. Theoretically speaking this impact is based on the interaction of two effects: a higher inflation will raise its variance and, therefore, real uncertainty. The evidence for both these effects confirms the positive impact of inflation on output volatility. That is, direct and indirect effects point to the same conclusion. Finally, we find some evidence for a positive causal effect from growth to the variability of inflation. The indirect impact works through the channel of inflation.

This effect has also been overlooked in the literature. There has been surprisingly little work of this kind. When we examine simultaneously the direct and indirect impact of growth on the variance of inflation, the former disappears. In doing so, we show that accounting for the indirect effect reduces the strength of the direct one.

The remainder of this chapter is organized as follows. Section 2 discusses the economic theory concerning the link between macroeconomic performance and uncertainty. In section 3 we describe the time series model for the inflation and growth. The empirical results are reported in section 4. In section 5 we interpret these results and relate them to the predictions of economic theory. Section 6 contains summary remarks and conclusions.

2 ECONOMIC THEORIES, HYPOTHESES AND CONJECTURES

To motivate the application of the bivariate GARCH approach in the macroeconomic context, in this section we provide a discussion of the economic theory concerning the relationship between macroeconomic uncertainty and performance.

2.1 The Link Between Inflation (Uncertainty) and Growth (Uncertainty)

Mean inflation and output growth are interrelated. Temple (2000) presents a critical review of the emerging literature which tends to discuss how inflation affects growth. Gillman and Kejak (2005) bring together for comparison several main approaches to modeling the inflation–growth effect by nesting them within a general monetary endogenous growth model with both human and physical capital. Their summary of the findings across the different formulations clearly establishes a robust significant negative effect. Other researchers also find evidence that inflation negatively Granger causes real growth (see Gillman and Kejak, 2005, and the references therein).

Briault (1995) argues that there is a positive relationship between growth and inflation, at least over the short run, with the direction of causation running from higher growth (at least in relation to productive potential) to higher inflation. For simplicity, in what follows we will refer to this positive influence as the Briault conjecture. A study by Fountas et al. (2006), involving the G7, finds that growth has a significant positive impact on inflation.

The inflation–output variability relationship

There are some reasons to suspect a relationship between nominal uncertainty and the volatility of real growth. For example, models with a stable inflation–unemployment trade-off imply a positive relationship between the two variabilities (see Logue and Sweeney, 1981, for details). Moreover, the discretionary equilibrium of Devereux's (1989) model predicts a close relationship between the mean rate of inflation, its volatility and the variance of output. Although in his model there is no direct causal link whatever from real to nominal uncertainty, for simplicity, in what follows we will refer to this positive effect as the 'Devereux' hypothesis.

In contrast to the positive relationship, Fuhrer (1997) explores the nature of the long-run variance trade-off. The short-run trade-off between inflation and output that exists in the models he explores implies a long-run trade-off in the volatilities. Karanasos and Kim (2005a, 2005b) discuss a number of arguments, advanced over the last 30 years, that predict a positive association between the two variables.

2.2 The Impact of Macroeconomic Uncertainty on Performance

Macroeconomists have placed considerable emphasis on the impact of economic uncertainty on the state of the macroeconomy. The profession seems to agree that the objectives of monetary policy are inflation and output stabilization around some target levels.

Variability about future inflation affects the average rate of inflation. However, the direction of the effect is ambiguous from a theoretical point of view. One possible reason for greater nominal variability to precede lower inflation is that an increase in uncertainty is viewed by policymakers as costly, inducing them to reduce inflation in the future (Holland, 1995). We will refer to this negative effect as the Holland conjecture. Cukierman and Meltzer's (1986) model, on the other hand, explains the positive association between the two variables. In the words of Holland (1995):

> The policy maker chooses monetary control procedures that are less precise, so that uncertainty about inflation is higher. The reason is that greater ambiguity about the conduct of monetary policy makes it easier for the government to create the monetary surprises that increase output. This causes the rate of inflation to be higher on average.

The impact of nominal uncertainty on output growth has received considerable attention in the literature. However, there is no consensus among macroeconomists on the direction of this effect. Theoretically speaking, the influence is ambiguous. In his Nobel address, Friedman (1977) explains a possible positive correlation between inflation and unemployment by arguing that high inflation produces more uncertainty about future inflation. This uncertainty then lowers economic efficiency and temporarily reduces output and increases unemployment. In sharp contrast, Dotsey and Sarte (2000) employ a model where money is introduced via a cash-in-advance constraint and find that variability increases average growth through a precautionary savings motive.

Next, real variability may affect the rate of inflation. Cukierman and Gerlach (2003), using an expectations-augmented Phillips curve, demonstrate that in the presence of a precautionary demand for expansions and uncertainty about the state of the economy there is an inflation bias even if policymakers target the potential level of output. Their bias-producing mechanism implies that countries with more volatile shocks to output should have, on average, higher rates of inflation. Their approach implies a positive relationship between inflation and the variance of growth where causality runs from the latter to the former.

Finally, of particular interest has been the relationship between growth and its variance with different analyses reaching different conclusions depending on what type of model is employed, what values for parameters are assumed and what types of disturbance are considered (see Blackburn and Pelloni, 2005, and the references therein). Pindyck (1991), among others, proposes a theory for which the negative impact of volatility on growth relies on uncertainty through the link of investment (see Martin and

Rogers, 2000, and the references therein). In another class of models the relationship between short-term variance and long-term growth is positive (see Blackburn, 1999, and the references therein). Blackburn (1999) presents a model of imperfect competition with nominal rigidities and 'learning-by-doing' technology. He argues that it is possible that the additional learning during expansions more than compensates for the loss of learning during recessions so that, on average, the rate of technological progress increases when there is an increase in volatility. Under such circumstances, there is a positive relationship between growth and uncertainty. A positive correlation between the two variables does not imply a causal link. However, in our analysis a positive effect from real variability to growth implies a positive correlation between the two variables. Thus, in what follows we will refer to a positive influence as the 'Blackburn' theory.

2.3 The Influence of Macroeconomic Performance on Uncertainty

The positive relationship between inflation and its uncertainty has often been noted. According to Holland (1993) if regime changes cause unpredictable changes in the persistence of inflation, then lagged inflation squared is positively related to volatility. In addition, Ungar and Zilberfarb (1993) provide a theoretical framework in order to specify the necessary conditions for the existence of a positive or negative impact.

A number of theories have been put forward to examine the impact of inflation on real uncertainty. In a nutshell, the sign of such an effect is ambiguous. Dotsey and Sarte (2000) present a model which suggests that as average money growth rises, nominal variability increases and real growth rates become more volatile. The models developed by Ball et al. (1988) assume menu costs and imply that the slope of the short-run Phillips curve should be steeper when average inflation is higher. In their New Keynesian model, nominal shocks have real effects because nominal prices change infrequently. Higher average inflation reduces the real effects of nominal disturbances and hence also lowers the variance of output.

The sign of the impact of output growth on macroeconomic volatility is also ambiguous. Consider first the influence on nominal uncertainty. As Brunner (1993) puts it: 'While Friedman's hypothesis is plausible, one could also imagine that when economic activity falls off, there is some uncertainty generated about the future path of monetary policy, and consequently, about the future path of inflation.' We will use the term 'Brunner conjecture' as a shorthand for this negative effect. In sharp contrast, a higher growth rate will raise inflation according to the Briault conjecture, and therefore this raises/lowers its variability, as predicted by the Ungar–Zilberfarb theory. We will term this positive/negative impact the Karanasos conjecture (I).

Finally, consider now the effect of growth on its variability. An increase in growth, given that the Briault conjecture and Dotsey–Sarte conjecture hold, pushes its variance upward. However, if the impact of inflation on real uncertainty is negative (the Ball–Mankiw–Romer theory), the opposite conclusion applies. We will refer to this causal effect as the Karanasos conjecture (II).

The causal relationships and the associated theories presented in section 2 are summarized in Table 12.1.

Table 12.1 Theories-hypotheses-conjectures

Macroeconomic performance
Inflation Granger causes growth
Gillman–Kejak theory: −
Growth Granger causes inflation
Briault conjecture: +
Macroeconomic uncertainty
Inflation uncertainty Granger causes growth uncertainty
Logue–Sweeney theory: +; Fuhrer theory: −
Growth uncertainty Granger causes inflation uncertainty
'Devereux' hypothesis: +; Fuhrer theory: −
In-Mean effects
Inflation uncertainty Granger causes inflation
Cukierman–Meltzer theory: +; Holland conjecture: −
Inflation uncertainty Granger causes growth
Dotsey–Sarte theory: +; Friedman hypothesis: −
Growth uncertainty Granger causes inflation
Cukierman–Gerlach theory: +
Growth uncertainty Granger causes growth
Pindyck (Blackburn) theory: − (+)
Level effects
Inflation Granger causes inflation uncertainty
Ungar–Zilberfarb theory: ±
Inflation Granger causes growth uncertainty
Dotsey–Sarte conjecture: +; Ball–Mankiw–Romer theory: −
Growth Granger causes inflation uncertainty
Karanasos conjecture (I): ±; Brunner conjecture: −
Growth Granger causes growth uncertainty
Karanasos conjecture (II): ±

3 EMPIRICAL STRATEGY

Regarding the model, we follow Zellner's (1998) 'KISS' approach. That is, we 'keep it sophisticatedly simple'. It is important to notice that, despite the fact that it is simple and convenient, the model remains very general in its scope.[9] It is worth reiterating in just a few sentences what we see to be the main benefits of our model. Its greatest advantage is that it does not require us to make the dubious assumption that there is a positive link between the two uncertainties. That is, the coefficients that capture the variance-relationship ($\beta_{\pi y}$, $\beta_{y\pi}$) are allowed to be negative.[10] It has the convenience of allowing us to derive sufficient conditions for the non-negativity of the two conditional variances. These conditions can be seen as analogous to those derived by Nelson and Cao (1992) and Tsai and Chan (2008) for the univariate GARCH model (see Conrad and Karanasos 2010, 2012).

Another advantage is that several lags of the conditional variances are added as regressors in the mean equation. Further, distinguishing empirically between the in-mean and level effects found in theoretical models is extremely difficult in practice so it makes sense

Table 12.2 Causality effects

Twelve Links	Coefficients
Macroeconomic performance	*Matrix* $\mathbf{\Phi}$
Inflation Granger causes output growth	$\phi_{y\pi} \neq 0$
Output growth Granger causes inflation	$\phi_{\pi y} \neq 0$
Macroeconomic uncertainty	*Matrix* $\mathbf{B}$
Inflation uncertainty Granger causes output growth uncertainty	$\beta_{y\pi} \neq 0$
Output growth uncertainty Granger causes inflation uncertainty	$\beta_{\pi y} \neq 0$
In-Mean effects	*Matrix* $\mathbf{\Delta}$
Inflation uncertainty Granger causes inflation	$\delta_{\pi\pi} \neq 0$
Inflation uncertainty Granger causes output growth	$\delta_{y\pi} \neq 0$
Output growth uncertainty Granger causes inflation	$\delta_{\pi y} \neq 0$
Output growth uncertainty Granger causes output growth	$\delta_{yy} \neq 0$
Level effects	*Matrix* $\mathbf{\Gamma}$
Inflation Granger causes inflation uncertainty	$\gamma_{\pi\pi} \neq 0$
Inflation Granger causes output growth uncertainty	$\gamma_{y\pi} \neq 0$
Output growth Granger causes inflation uncertainty	$\gamma_{\pi y} \neq 0$
Output growth Granger causes output growth uncertainty	$\gamma_{yy} \neq 0$

to emphasize that both are relevant. Our approach is promising because we construct a model allowing for effects in both directions. However, there are great difficulties in drawing conclusions for the interlinkages, because the relationships between the four variables are not well understood, and theoretical models can only be used to illustrate a range of possibilities. Our methodology is interesting because it tests the various theories in a variety of ways and it emphasizes that the empirical evidence is not clear cut. The causality links and the relevant coefficients are summarized in Table 12.2.

3.1 Notation

In order to make our analysis easier to understand we will introduce the following matrix notation. The subscripts d and f will denote diagonal and full matrices respectively, whereas the subscripts c and u (l) will denote cross-diagonal and upper (lower) triangular matrices respectively. For example, $\mathbf{\Phi}_{id}$ is a diagonal matrix: diag$\{\phi_{\pi\pi}^{(i)}, \phi_{yy}^{(i)}\}$, whereas $\mathbf{B}_d$ and $\mathbf{\Gamma}_d$ are diagonal matrices with $\beta_{\pi y}, \beta_{y\pi} = 0$ and $\gamma_{\pi y}, \gamma_{y\pi} = 0$ respectively. In addition, $\mathbf{\Phi}_{if}$, $\mathbf{B}_f$, and $\mathbf{\Gamma}_f$ are full matrices (see Table 12.3).

To distinguish between four alternative models, we will refer to the specifications with $\mathbf{\Delta}, \mathbf{\Gamma} = \mathbf{0}$ and $\mathbf{\Delta}, \mathbf{\Gamma} \neq \mathbf{0}$ as the simple and the in-mean-level models respectively. Similarly, we will refer to the formulations with $\mathbf{\Delta} \neq \mathbf{0}, \mathbf{\Gamma} = \mathbf{0}$ and $\mathbf{\Delta} = \mathbf{0}, \mathbf{\Gamma} \neq \mathbf{0}$ as the in-mean and level models respectively. For typographical convenience we will use the letters S, M, L and ML for reference to the simple, in-mean, level and in-mean-level models respectively (see Table 12.4).

In order to simplify the description of the various models we will introduce the following notation as shorthand. S($\mathbf{\Phi}_d$, $\mathbf{B}_f$) denotes the simple model with the $\mathbf{\Phi}$ matrix diagonal and the $\mathbf{B}$ matrix full. Further, $\underset{n=0}{\text{M}}(\mathbf{\Phi}_d, \mathbf{B}_d)$ describes the in-mean model with the $\mathbf{\Phi}$ and the $\mathbf{B}$ matrices diagonal and the current value of the macroeconomic uncertainty

Table 12.3 Matrix notation

Matrices	Diagonal	Cross-Diagonal	Upper Triangular	Lower Triangular	Full
$\mathbf{\Phi}$	$\mathbf{\Phi}_{id}$ $(\phi^{(i)}_{\pi y}, \phi^{(i)}_{y\pi} = 0)$	–	$\mathbf{\Phi}_{iu}$ $(\phi^{(i)}_{y\pi} = 0)$	–	$\mathbf{\Phi}_{if}$ $(\phi^{(i)}_{\pi y}, \phi^{(i)}_{y\pi} \neq 0)$
$\mathbf{B}$	$\mathbf{B}_d$ $(\beta_{\pi y}, \beta_{y\pi} = 0)$	–	–	$\mathbf{B}_l$ $(\beta_{\pi y} = 0)$	$\mathbf{B}_f$ $(\beta_{\pi y}, \beta_{y\pi} \neq 0)$
$\mathbf{\Gamma}$	$\mathbf{\Gamma}_d$ $(\gamma_{\pi y}, \gamma_{y\pi} = 0)$	$\mathbf{\Gamma}_c$ $(\gamma_{\pi\pi}, \gamma_{yy} = 0)$	–	–	$\mathbf{\Gamma}_f$ $(\gamma_{\pi y}, \gamma_{y\pi} \neq 0)$

Notes:
$\mathbf{\Phi}_{id}$, $\mathbf{B}_d$, and $\mathbf{\Gamma}_d$ denote diagonal matrices. $\mathbf{\Phi}_{if}$, $\mathbf{B}_f$, and $\mathbf{\Gamma}_f$ denote full matrices.
$\mathbf{\Phi}_{iu}$ ($\mathbf{B}_l$), and $\mathbf{\Gamma}_c$ denote upper, lower triangular and cross-diagonal matrices respectively.

Table 12.4 Models notation

Models	Simple	In-Mean	Level	In-Mean-Level
Matrices	$\mathbf{\Delta} = \mathbf{0}, \mathbf{\Gamma} = \mathbf{0}$	$\mathbf{\Delta} \neq \mathbf{0}, \mathbf{\Gamma} = \mathbf{0},$	$\mathbf{\Delta} = \mathbf{0}, \mathbf{\Gamma} \neq \mathbf{0}$	$\mathbf{\Delta} \neq \mathbf{0}, \mathbf{\Gamma} \neq \mathbf{0}$
Notation $\xi(\kappa) = d, u(l), f; \zeta = d, f$	$\mathrm{S}(\mathbf{\Phi}_\xi, \mathbf{B}_\kappa)$	$\underset{n=0}{\mathrm{M}}(\mathbf{\Phi}_\xi, \mathbf{B}_\kappa)$	$\mathrm{L}(\mathbf{\Phi}_\xi, \mathbf{B}_\kappa, \mathbf{\Gamma}_\zeta)$	$\underset{n=0}{\mathrm{ML}}(\mathbf{\Phi}_\xi, \mathbf{B}_\kappa, \mathbf{\Gamma}_\zeta)$

Notes:
S and ML refer to the simple and the in-mean-level models respectively.
M and L refer to the in-mean and level models respectively.
The *d*, *u* (*l*) and *f* subscripts denote diagonal, upper (lower) triangular and full matrices respectively. *n* is the lag order of the in-mean effect.

to affect performance. Moreover, $\mathrm{L}(\mathbf{\Phi}_f, \mathbf{B}_d, \mathbf{\Gamma}_d)$ stands for the level process with the $\mathbf{\Phi}$ matrix full and the $\mathbf{B}$ and $\mathbf{\Gamma}$ matrices diagonal (see Table 12.4).

Before analysing our results, in order to make our analysis more concise, we will discuss some specific models. For example, in the $\mathrm{S}(\mathbf{\Phi}_f, \mathbf{B}_f)$ model four out of the twelve effects are present. In particular,there is a bidirectional feedback between inflation (uncertainty) and growth (uncertainty). Moreover, in the $\underset{n=0}{\mathrm{M}}(\mathbf{\Phi}_f, \mathbf{B}_f, \mathbf{\Delta}_f)$ model eight influences are present. Specifically, in addition to the four impacts above, the four in-mean effects are also present. Further, in the $\mathrm{L}(\mathbf{\Phi}_f, \mathbf{B}_d, \mathbf{\Gamma}_f)$ model six effects are present. Namely, the four level effects are present and there is also a bidirectional feedback between inflation and growth.

4 DATA AND EMPIRICAL SPECIFICATIONS

4.1 Data and Estimation Results

Monthly data, obtained from the OECD Statistical Compendium, are used to provide a reasonable number of observations. The inflation and output growth series are calculated as the monthly difference in the natural logarithm of the Consumer Price

Index and Industrial Production Index respectively. The data range from 1962:01 to 2004:01. Allowing for differencing this implies 504 usable observations.[11]

Within the BVAR–GARCH–ML framework we will analyze the dynamic adjustments of both the conditional means and the conditional variances of UK inflation and output growth, as well as the implications of these dynamics for the direction of causality between the two variables and their respective uncertainties. The estimates of the various formulations were obtained by maximum likelihood estimation (MLE) as implemented by James Davidson (2006) in time series modeling (TSM) software. To check for the robustness of our estimates we used a range of starting values and hence ensured that the estimation procedure converged to a global maximum. The best model is chosen on the basis of Likelihood Ratio (LR) tests and three alternative information criteria. For the conditional means [variances] of inflation and growth, we choose AR(14) [GARCH(1, 1)] and AR(2) [ARCH(1)] models respectively.[12]

To select our best S model we estimate specifications with the $\mathbf{\Phi}(\mathbf{B})$ matrix either diagonal or upper (lower) triangular or full. To test for the presence of an inflation–growth link we examine the LR statistic for the linear constraints $\phi_{\pi y} = \phi_{y\pi} = 0$. To test for the existence of a variance relationship we employ the LR test for the constraints $\beta_{\pi y} = \beta_{y\pi} = 0$. The LR tests (not reported) clearly reject the $S(\mathbf{\Phi}_f, \mathbf{B}_d)$ and $S(\mathbf{\Phi}_d, \mathbf{B}_f)$ null hypotheses against the $S(\mathbf{\Phi}_f, \mathbf{B}_f)$ model. In accordance with this result, the Akaike and Hannan–Quinn Information Criteria (AIC and HQIC respectively) choose the $S(\mathbf{\Phi}_f, \mathbf{B}_f)$ specification,[13] that is the formulation with the simultaneous feedback between inflation (uncertainty) and growth (uncertainty).

Further, for the L, M and ML models the estimation routine did not converge when the $\mathbf{B}_f$ matrix was used. In accordance with the results for the S models, the three criteria (not reported) favor the $L(\mathbf{\Phi}_f, \mathbf{B}_d, \mathbf{\Gamma}_f)$ specification while the $L(\mathbf{\Phi}_f, \mathbf{B}_l, \mathbf{\Gamma}_f)$ process is ranked second. When the $\mathbf{\Phi}_f$ and either the $\mathbf{B}_d$ or the $\mathbf{B}_l$ matrices are used, all criteria favor the level model over the simple one. According to the three information criteria the optimal ML formulation is the $\underset{n=0}{ML}(\mathbf{\Phi}_f, \mathbf{B}_d, \mathbf{\Gamma}_f)$ while the second ranked model is the $\underset{n=0}{ML}(\mathbf{\Phi}_f, \mathbf{B}_l, \mathbf{\Gamma}_f)$. Finally, it is worth noting that for the specification with the $\mathbf{\Phi}_f$, and either the $\mathbf{B}_d$ or the $\mathbf{B}_l$ matrices the criteria favor the ML model over both the M and S ones. Thus, purely from the perspective of searching for a model that best describes the link between macroeconomic performance and uncertainty, the ML model appears to be the most satisfactory representation.

4.2 Interconnections Among the Four Variables

In this section we analyze the results from the various specifications and examine the sign and the significance of the estimated coefficients to provide some statistical evidence on the nature of the relationship between the four variables.

4.2.1 Inflation–growth link

There is strong evidence supporting the Gillman–Kejak theory and the Briault conjecture. That is, there is strong bidirectional feedback between inflation and output growth. In particular, inflation affects growth negatively, whereas growth has a positive effect on inflation (see Table 12.5). This causal relationship is not qualitatively altered by changes in the specification of the model (results not reported).

Table 12.5 Inflation–growth link

	The effect of growth on inflation				The impact of inflation on growth			
Models	$\phi_{\pi y,5}$		$\phi_{\pi y,7}$		$\phi_{y\pi,7}$		$\phi_{y\pi,11}$	
$\underset{n=0}{\mathrm{ML}}(\boldsymbol{\Phi}_f, \mathbf{B}_l \mid \mathbf{B}_d, \boldsymbol{\Gamma}_f)$*	**0.04** [0.01]	**0.04*** [0.01]	**0.03** [0.01]	**0.03** [0.01]	**−0.20** [0.02]	**−0.20** [0.02]	**0.13** [0.10]	**0.13** [0.09]

Notes:
* The two numbers refer to the models with the $\mathbf{B}_l$ and $\mathbf{B}_d$ matrices respectively.
The numbers in bold indicate significant effects. The numbers in brackets are p-values.

Table 12.6 Variance relationship

Models	$\beta_{\pi y}$			$\beta_{y\pi}$		
$S(\boldsymbol{\Phi}_f \mid \boldsymbol{\Phi}_u \mid \boldsymbol{\Phi}_d, \mathbf{B}_f)$*	0.01 [0.26]	0.00 [0.85]	0.01* [0.35]	**2.96** [0.00]	**2.96** [0.00]	**2.95** [0.00]

Notes:
* The three numbers refer to the models with the $\boldsymbol{\Phi}_f$, $\boldsymbol{\Phi}_u$ and $\boldsymbol{\Phi}_d$ matrices respectively. The numbers in bold indicate significant effects.
The numbers in brackets are p-values. For the L, M and ML models the estimation routine did not converge when the $\mathbf{B}_f$ matrix was used.

4.2.2 Variance relationship

There is evidence that nominal uncertainty has a positive impact on real volatility as predicted by Logue and Sweeney (1981). The influence is invariant to the formulation of the $\boldsymbol{\Phi}$ matrix. In particular, in all three $S(\boldsymbol{\Phi}_\xi, \mathbf{B}_f)$, $\xi = d, u, f$ models the effect is significant at the 1 per cent level (see Table 12.6). When we tried to estimate M, L and ML models, with the **B** matrix full, the estimation routine did not converge. In all specifications with the **B** matrix lower triangular (not reported) the influence disappears.

4.2.3 In-mean effects

Our objective in the following analysis is to consider several changes in the specification of the model and to discuss how these changes affect the in-mean effects. In some cases we find that by making very small changes in the formulation of the model the estimated effects vary considerably.

First, when the current values ($n = 0$) of the conditional variances are included in the mean equations we find some very weak evidence for the Friedman hypothesis. This result is invariant to changes in the **B** matrix. For example, in the $\underset{n=0}{\mathrm{M}}(\boldsymbol{\Phi}_d, \mathbf{B}_d)$ and $\underset{n=0}{\mathrm{M}}(\boldsymbol{\Phi}_d, \mathbf{B}_l)$ models the effect is significant at the 18 per cent and 20 per cent levels respectively (see Table 12.7). However, when we control for the impact of inflation on growth, that is when the $\boldsymbol{\Phi}_f$ matrix is used, the effect disappears (result not reported). On the other hand, the negative influence of nominal uncertainty on growth becomes stronger when we account for level effects. More specifically, in the $\underset{n=0}{\mathrm{ML}}(\boldsymbol{\Phi}_d, \mathbf{B}_d, \boldsymbol{\Gamma}_d)$ and $\underset{n=0}{\mathrm{ML}}(\boldsymbol{\Phi}_u, \mathbf{B}_d, \boldsymbol{\Gamma}_d)$ models the in-mean coefficient becomes more significant, at the 13 per cent and 10 per cent levels respectively (see Table 12.7).

In sharp contrast, Dotsey and Sarte (2000) argue that as inflation rises, the growth

Table 12.7 Friedman hypothesis: estimated $\delta_{y\pi}$ coefficients

$\boldsymbol{\Phi}_d$, $n = 0$			$\boldsymbol{\Phi}_u$, $n = 0$		
M ($\mathbf{B}_d$)	ML ($\mathbf{B}_d,\boldsymbol{\Gamma}_d$)	M ($\mathbf{B}_l$)	M ($\mathbf{B}_d$)	ML ($\mathbf{B}_d,\boldsymbol{\Gamma}_d$)	M ($\mathbf{B}_l$)
−0.67 [0.18]	**−0.78** [0.13]	−0.62 [0.20]	−0.68 [0.19]	**−0.77** [0.10]	−0.59 [0.20]

Notes: p-values are reported in brackets. For the $\underset{n=0}{\mathrm{ML}}(\underset{\varsigma=d,u}{\boldsymbol{\Phi}_\varsigma}, \mathbf{B}_d, \boldsymbol{\Gamma}_f)$ and $\underset{n=0}{\mathrm{ML}}(\underset{\varsigma=d,u}{\boldsymbol{\Phi}_\varsigma}, \mathbf{B}_l, \underset{\zeta=d,f}{\boldsymbol{\Gamma}_\zeta})$ the estimation routine did not converge.

Table 12.8 Cukierman–Gerlach theory: estimated $\delta_{\pi y}$ coefficients

$\boldsymbol{\Phi}_f$, $n = 0$						$\boldsymbol{\Phi}_f$, $n = 4$					
M ($\mathbf{B}_d$)	ML ($\mathbf{B}_d,\boldsymbol{\Gamma}_d$)	ML ($\mathbf{B}_d,\boldsymbol{\Gamma}_f$)	M ($\mathbf{B}_l$)	ML ($\mathbf{B}_l,\boldsymbol{\Gamma}_d$)	ML ($\mathbf{B}_l,\boldsymbol{\Gamma}_f$)	M ($\mathbf{B}_d$)	ML ($\mathbf{B}_d,\boldsymbol{\Gamma}_d$)	ML ($\mathbf{B}_d,\boldsymbol{\Gamma}_f$)	M ($\mathbf{B}_l$)	ML ($\mathbf{B}_l,\boldsymbol{\Gamma}_d$)	ML ($\mathbf{B}_l,\boldsymbol{\Gamma}_f$)
0.02 [0.08]	**0.02** [0.08]	**0.02** [0.09]	**0.02** [0.07]	**0.02** [0.04]	**0.02** [0.09]	**0.02** [0.08]	**0.01** [0.15]	**0.02** [0.12]	**0.02** [0.08]	**0.01** [0.15]	**0.02** [0.12]

Notes: p-values are reported in brackets. The estimation routine did not converge when the $\mathbf{B}_f$ matrix was used.

begins to fall. However, as inflation continues to rise, the positive effects of higher nominal uncertainty begin to dominate and growth starts to increase. The mitigating effect of inflation variability may help partially to explain why inflation might seem unrelated to growth. However, in our work weak (significant at the 14 per cent level) evidence (not reported) for the Dotsey–Sarte theory appears in the model with the third lags of the in-mean effects and a bidirectional feedback between inflation and growth ($\underset{n=3}{\mathrm{M}}(\boldsymbol{\Phi}_f, \mathbf{B}_d)$).

Second, we find evidence supporting the Cukierman–Gerlach theory when either the current values ($n = 0$) or the fourth lags ($n = 4$) of the conditional variances are allowed to affect inflation and growth. When the current values are used the impact of real uncertainty on inflation is stronger (see Table 12.8) and is not qualitatively altered by using different versions (diagonal or upper triangular) of the $\boldsymbol{\Phi}$ matrix (results not reported). However, at lag 4 the effect disappears when the $\boldsymbol{\Phi}_d$ matrix is used. Moreover, when the current values are used the impact is robust to the inclusion or exclusion of level effects and to whether the $\mathbf{B}$ matrix is diagonal or lower triangular and the $\boldsymbol{\Gamma}$ matrix is diagonal or full. For example, when the $\underset{n=0}{\mathrm{ML}}(\boldsymbol{\Phi}_f, \mathbf{B}_l, \boldsymbol{\Gamma}_d)$ and $\underset{n=0}{\mathrm{M}}(\boldsymbol{\Phi}_f, \mathbf{B}_l)$ models are estimated the effect is significant at the 4 per cent and 7 per cent levels respectively. However, at lag 4, the impact becomes weaker in the presence of level effects (see Table 12.8).

Third, there is weak evidence (significant at the 16 per cent level) for the 'Blackburn' theory when the $\boldsymbol{\Phi}$ matrix is full and the first lags of the two uncertainties are allowed to affect their means. This result is invariant to the formulation of the $\mathbf{B}$ matrix. When adding level effects, the impact becomes stronger. In particular, in the model with the $\mathbf{B}_l$ matrix, when the $\boldsymbol{\Gamma}_d$ matrix is used it is significant at the 11 per cent level while when the full $\boldsymbol{\Gamma}$ matrix is employed it is significant at the 9 per cent level (see Table 12.9).

Table 12.9 'Blackburn'/Pindyck theories: estimated δ_{yy} coefficients

'Blackburn' theory; $\mathbf{\Phi}_f$, $n = 1$						Pindyck theory; $\mathbf{\Phi}_f$, $n = 3$			
M ($\mathbf{B}_d$)	ML ($\mathbf{B}_d, \mathbf{\Gamma}_d$)	ML ($\mathbf{B}_d, \mathbf{\Gamma}_f$)	M ($\mathbf{B}_l$)	ML ($\mathbf{B}_l, \mathbf{\Gamma}_d$)	ML ($\mathbf{B}_l, \mathbf{\Gamma}_f$)	M ($\mathbf{B}_d$)	ML ($\mathbf{B}_d, \mathbf{\Gamma}_f$)	M ($\mathbf{B}_l$)	ML ($\mathbf{B}_l, \mathbf{\Gamma}_f$)
0.04	**0.04**	**0.04**	**0.04**	**0.04**	**0.04**	0.03	**−0.04**	**−0.03**	**−0.04**
[0.16]	[0.10]	[0.09]	[0.14]	[0.11]	[0.09]	[0.58]	[0.14]	[0.12]	[0.15]

Notes: p-values are reported in brackets. For the $\underset{n=3}{\mathrm{ML}}(\mathbf{\Phi}_f, \underset{k=d,l}{\mathbf{B}_k}, \mathbf{\Gamma}_d)$ the estimation routine did not converge.

On the other hand, there is evidence for the Pindyck theory when we allow the third lags of the macroeconomic uncertainty to affect performance. However, the significance of the effect varies substantially with changes in the specification of the model. For example, in the $\underset{n=3}{\mathrm{M}}(\mathbf{\Phi}_d, \mathbf{B}_l)$ (not reported) and $\underset{n=3}{\mathrm{M}}(\mathbf{\Phi}_f, \mathbf{B}_l)$ models the effect is significant at the 19 per cent and 12 per cent levels respectively, whereas in the $\underset{n=3}{\mathrm{M}}(\mathbf{\Phi}_f, \mathbf{B}_d)$ it disappears. That is, when we account for the bi(uni)-directional feedback between inflation (uncertainty) and growth (uncertainty) the impact is stronger. When we include all four level effects the impact becomes weaker. In particular, for the $\underset{n=3}{\mathrm{ML}}(\mathbf{\Phi}_f, \mathbf{B}_l, \mathbf{\Gamma}_f)$ model the effect is significant at the 15 per cent level (see Table 12.9).

4.2.4 Level effects

There is strong evidence in favor of the Ungar–Zilberfarb theory and the Dotsey–Sarte conjecture that higher inflation has a positive impact on nominal and real uncertainty respectively (see Table 12.10, columns 2 and 3). We also demonstrate the invariance of these findings to changes in the specification of the model (results not reported). Moreover, some evidence (see the last row of Table 12.10) for the Karanasos conjecture (I) regarding the positive effect of growth on inflation variability appears in the ML model with the first lags of the two conditional variances in the mean equations, the $\mathbf{\Phi}$ and the $\mathbf{B}$ matrices diagonal, and the $\mathbf{\Gamma}$ matrix cross-diagonal ($\underset{n=1}{\mathrm{ML}}(\mathbf{\Phi}_d, \mathbf{B}_d, \mathbf{\Gamma}_c)$). Finally, there is a lack (negative and insignificant) of a direct link from growth to its volatility.

Table 12.10 Level effects

<table>
<tr><td>ML Models</td><td colspan="2">$\gamma_{\pi\pi}$</td><td colspan="2">$\gamma_{y\pi}$</td><td colspan="2">$\gamma_{\pi y}$</td><td colspan="2">γ_{yy}</td></tr>
<tr><td>$\underset{n=0}{\mathrm{ML}}(\mathbf{\Phi}_f, \mathbf{B}_l | \mathbf{B}_d, \mathbf{\Gamma}_f)$*</td><td>0.07
[0.02]</td><td>0.07*
[0.02]</td><td>0.53
[0.00]</td><td>0.53
[0.00]</td><td>0.00
[0.84]</td><td>0.00
[0.83]</td><td>−0.10
[0.57]</td><td>−0.10
[0.57]</td></tr>
<tr><td>$\underset{n=1}{\mathrm{ML}}(\mathbf{\Phi}_d, \mathbf{B}_d, \mathbf{\Gamma}_c)$</td><td colspan="2">–</td><td colspan="2">0.48
[0.00]</td><td colspan="2">0.01
[0.03]</td><td colspan="2">–</td></tr>
</table>

Notes: * The two numbers refer to the models with the $\mathbf{B}_l$ and $\mathbf{B}_d$ matrices respectively. The numbers in bold indicate significant effects. The numbers in brackets are p-values. For the ML models the estimation routine did not converge when the $\mathbf{B}_f$ matrix was used.

Table 12.11 Relatively robust effects

$\pi \xrightarrow{-} y$	$y \xrightarrow{+} \pi$	$h_\pi \xrightarrow{+} h_y$	$h_y \nrightarrow h_\pi$	$h_\pi \nrightarrow \pi$	$\pi \xrightarrow{+} h_\pi$	$\pi \xrightarrow{+} h_y$	$y \nrightarrow h_y$

Notes: ($\nrightarrow$) $\rightarrow$ (does not) Granger causes. A + (−) indicates that the effect is positive (negative).

Table 12.12 In-mean effects sensitive to the choice of the lag

Lags:	0	1	2	3	4		0	1	2	3	4		0	1	2	3	4
$h_\pi \rightarrow y$	–	0	0	+	0	$h_y \rightarrow \pi$	+	0	0	0	+	$h_y \rightarrow y$	0	+	0	–	0

Notes: $\rightarrow$: Granger causes. A + (−) indicates that the effect is positive (negative).

5 DISCUSSION

5.1 Summary

In general, there are three bidirectional feedbacks. There is a positive one, between inflation and real uncertainty, and two mixed ones. That is, growth has a positive direct impact on inflation and an indirect one on nominal uncertainty, whereas it is affected negatively by the two variables (see Tables 12.11 and 12.12). Moreover, there are two positive unidirectional feedbacks. That is, causality runs only from nominal to real uncertainty, and from inflation to its variability. Finally, there is a third unidirectional feedback. Causality runs only from real uncertainty to growth. However, the sign of the influence is altered by changes in the choice of the lag of the in-mean effect. More specifically, at lag 1 the effect is positive whereas at lag 3 it switches to negative. In sharp contrast, when the current values or the second lags or the fourth lags of the conditional variances are included as regressors in the mean equations, growth and its uncertainty are independent of each other.

5.2 Sensitivity of the In-mean Effects

Choice of the lag

When the current values of the in-mean effects are used there is evidence supporting the Friedman hypothesis and the Cukierman–Gerlach theory, whereas at lag 1 there is evidence that real uncertainty affects growth positively as predicted by Blackburn (1999). Moreover, when the third lags of the conditional variances are allowed to affect their means there is evidence in support of the Dotsey–Sarte and Pindyck theories, whereas at lag 4 there is evidence that the variability of growth has a positive impact on inflation, which squares with the Cukierman–Gerlach theory (see Table 12.12).

Level effects

We examined how changes in the specification of the model affect the in-mean effects. First, we checked their sensitivity to the inclusion or exclusion of level effects. When we account for level effects, the evidence for the Cukierman–Gerlach theory, at lag 4, becomes weaker whereas, at lag 0, it remains the same (see Table 12.8). Moreover, the evidence in support of the Friedman hypothesis and the 'Blackburn' theory becomes stronger in the presence of level effects (see Tables 12.7 and 12.9). Further, if we assume that the two variances are independent of each other, then when we exclude the level effects the negative impact of real uncertainty on growth disappears. In sharp contrast, if we assume that the volatility of inflation affects real variability, then the evidence for the Pindyck theory becomes weaker when we include the level effects (see Table 12.9).

Inflation–growth link

We also investigate the invariance of the results to the inflation–growth link. The (lack of) evidence for the (Holland conjecture) Cukierman–Gerlach theory is not qualitatively altered by the presence or absence of an inflation–growth link. However, when we assume that either there is no inflation–growth link or that growth is independent of changes in inflation, the evidence for the Blackburn/Pindyck theory disappears/becomes weaker (results not reported).

An empirically important issue is that it is difficult to separate the nominal uncertainty from inflation as the source of the possible negative impact of the latter on growth. As a policy matter this distinction is important. As Judson and Orphanides (1999) point out:

> If inflation volatility is the sole culprit, a high but predictably stable level of inflation achieved through indexation may be preferable to a lower, but more volatile, inflation resulting from an activist disinflation strategy. If on the other hand, the level of inflation per se negatively affects growth, an activist disinflation strategy may be the only sensible choice.

In our analysis, we find that when we control for the impact of inflation on growth, that is when the $\mathbf{\Phi}_f$ matrix is used, the effect of uncertainty on growth disappears (result not reported).

Variance relationship

The Friedman hypothesis and the Cukierman–Gerlach and 'Blackburn' theories are invariant to the choice of the matrix **B** (see Tables 12.7, 12.8 and 12.9). Moreover, in the absence of level effects, when there is unidirectional feedback between nominal and real uncertainty there is mild evidence for the Pindyck theory, whereas when there is no variance relationship the evidence disappears (see Table 12.9). That is, the evidence for the Pindyck theory is qualitatively altered by the inclusion or exclusion of a variance relationship.

5.3 Direct and Indirect Events

In-mean effects

For our purposes it helped to distinguish between direct and indirect impacts. Our analysis has highlighted reciprocal interactions in which two or more variables influence each other, either directly or indirectly. As we have already seen, these kinds of interactions can be very important. Panel A of Figure 12.1 presents the direct and indirect impacts for the in-mean effects. It is noteworthy that the indirect effect of nominal uncertainty

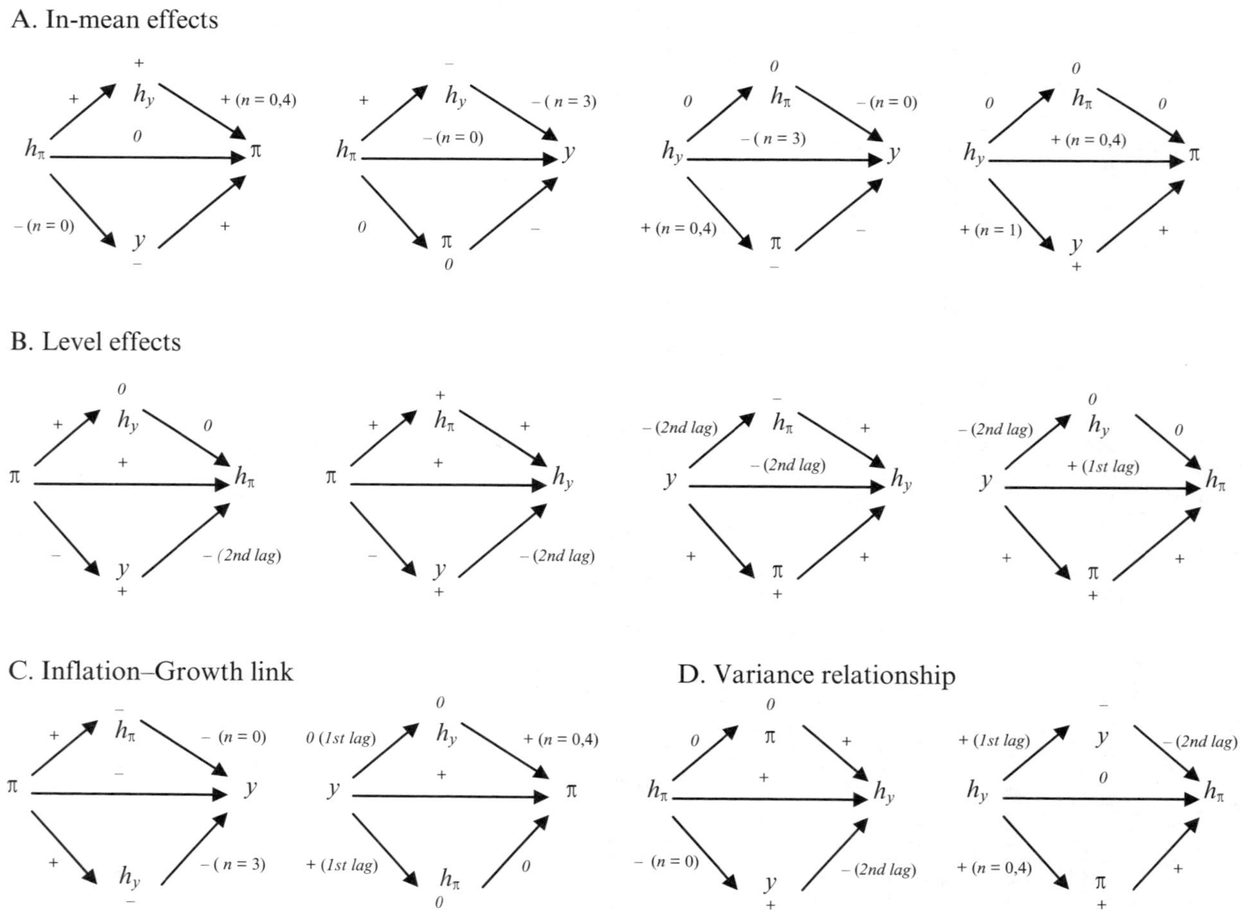

Figure 12.1 Direct and indirect effects between macroeconomic performance and uncertainty

on inflation that works via the growth is opposite to the one that works through growth variability. In particular, the former impact is negative whereas the latter influence is positive. One possible implication of this finding is that inflation is independent of changes in its uncertainty. In essence, the offsetting indirect effects provide a partial rationale for the lack of evidence for either the Cukierman–Meltzer theory or the Holland conjecture.

Regarding the other three in-mean effects, direct and indirect influences point to the same conclusion. First, the indirect negative influence of inflation variability on growth through its impact on the uncertainty about growth tells essentially the same story, with the direct evidence supporting the Friedman hypothesis. Second, the indirect evidence (via the inflation channel) regarding the negative impact of real uncertainty on growth agrees well with the direct evidence supporting the Pindyck theory. Finally, both types of evidence point unequivocally to a positive effect of real uncertainty on inflation. That is, the evidence supporting the Cukierman–Gerlach theory is in line with the evidence for the 'Blackburn' theory and the Briault conjecture.

Level effects

Panel B of Figure 12.1 presents the direct and indirect impacts for the level effects. Both types of evidence point unequivocally to a positive effect of inflation on its uncertainty. That is, the evidence supporting the Friedman hypothesis is in line with the evidence for the Gillman–Kejak theory and Brunner conjecture (when we include the second lag of growth as a regressor in the two variances; see the next section). In addition, the indirect effect (via the channel of nominal uncertainty) regarding the positive impact of inflation on the variability of growth agrees well with the direct evidence supporting the Dotsey–Sarte conjecture.

Moreover, the indirect positive influence of growth on its uncertainty through its (first lag) impact on the inflation variability (see the last row of Table 12.10) tells essentially the same story, with the indirect evidence supporting the Briault and Dotsey–Sarte conjectures. In sharp contrast, there is a lack of a direct effect. On the other hand, when we include the second lag of growth as a regressor in the two variances, direct and indirect (via the channel of nominal uncertainty) evidence points to a negative impact (see the next section and Panel B of Figure 12.1).

Finally, we hypothesize that the effects of growth on inflation variability could work through changes in inflation. Theoretically speaking the impact is based on the interaction of two effects. A higher growth will raise inflation and, therefore, nominal uncertainty. The evidence for both these influences confirms the positive direct effect. The four variables are connected by a rich network of relationships, which may be causal (direct effects), or reflect shared causal pathways (indirect effects). Direct and indirect effects often occur together. Co-occurrence depends on the strength and number of these relationships. However, in order to understand the mechanisms that are responsible for these effects sometimes it is necessary to consider them in isolation. For example, as we have just mentioned, the indirect impact of growth on volatility works via the channel of inflation. It is worth noting that the direct relationship is qualitatively altered by the presence of the indirect effects. That is, when we include in the model the influence of growth on inflation and of inflation on its uncertainty, the direct impact disappears (see Table 12.10).

Table 12.13 Level effects

L Models	$\gamma_{\pi\pi}$	$\gamma_{y\pi}$	$\gamma_{\pi y}$	γ_{yy}
Panel A. Models with $\tilde{x}_{t-1} = [(\pi_{t-1} - \bar{\pi}_{t-1})^2 \ (y_{t-1} - \bar{y}_{t-1})^2]'$				
$\tilde{\text{L}}(\mathbf{\Phi}_f, \mathbf{B}_l \vert \mathbf{B}_d, \mathbf{\Gamma}_f)$*	0.06 | 0.06* [0.22] | [0.22]	**0.36** | **0.16** [0.00] | [0.05]	0.00 | 0.00 [0.87] | [0.87]	−0.16 | −0.19 [0.69] | [0.64]
Panel B. Models with $x_{t-1,2} = (\pi_{t-1} \ y_{t-2})'$				
$\text{L}_2(\mathbf{\Phi}_u, \mathbf{B}_l \vert \mathbf{B}_d, \mathbf{\Gamma}_f)$	**0.08** | **0.08** [0.03] | [0.03]	**0.55** | **0.49** [0.00] | [0.00]	**−0.01** | **−0.01** [0.01] | [0.01]	**−0.11** | **−0.11** [0.11] | [0.11]

Notes:
* The two numbers refer to the models with the $\mathbf{B}_l$ and $\mathbf{B}_d$ matrices respectively.
The numbers in bold indicate significant effects.

5.4 Level Effects: Second Lags and Squared Terms

In this section we check the sensitivity of our results (regarding the level effects) to the linear form and the choice of the lag. We consider the ccc GARCH(1, 1)-level structure eq. (12.4) with the $\mathbf{x}_{t-1}$ replaced by (i) $\tilde{\mathbf{x}}_{t-1}$, and (ii) $\mathbf{x}_{t-1,2}$ where $\tilde{\mathbf{x}}_{t-1}$ and $\mathbf{x}_{t-1,2}$ are 2×1 column vectors given by $\tilde{\mathbf{x}}_{t-1} = [(\pi_{t-1} - \bar{\pi})^2 \ (y_{t-1} - \bar{y})^2]'$ (with $\bar{\pi}$, $\bar{y}$ the two sample means) and $\mathbf{x}_{t-1,2} = (\pi_{t-1} \ y_{t-2})'$ respectively. The estimated level parameters are reported in Table 12.13.

According to Holland (1993) if regime changes cause unpredictable changes in the persistence of inflation, then lagged inflation squared is positively related to inflation uncertainty. Uncertainty about inflation regimes is a source of inflation uncertainty. As seen from Panel A of Table 12.13, inflation variability is independent from changes in $(\pi_{t-1} - \bar{\pi}_{t-1})^2$. In other words, over against the Holland conjecture there is a lack of a causal impact from squared inflation to the variance of inflation. Regarding the other three level effects, the results from the linear causality tests and those obtained by the non-linear procedure are basically identical.

When we include the second lag of growth as a regressor in the two variances the results change dramatically. That is, the impact of growth on nominal uncertainty is negative as predicted by Brunner (1993). This result is invariant to the formulation of the **B** matrix (see the fourth column of Panel B) and the $\mathbf{\Phi}$ matrix (results not reported). Recall, however, that the effect disappears with the first lag (see Table 12.10). Moreover, in the L model with the second lag of growth and the $\mathbf{\Phi}$ matrix, upper triangular growth affects its volatility negatively, thus supporting the Karanasos (II) conjecture (see the last column of panel B). Recall that, theoretically speaking, the negative indirect impact is based on the interaction of the Brunner conjecture and the Logue–Sweeney theory. The evidence for these two effects confirms the direct negative influence of growth on its uncertainty, that is, direct and indirect effects point to the same conclusion. However, when we control for the impact of inflation on growth, that is when the $\mathbf{\Phi}_f$ matrix is used, the negative influence of growth on its variance disappears (result not reported).

6 CONCLUSIONS

In this chapter we showed how a bivariate version of the conditional heteroskedasticity model can be applied to macroeconomic data. Specifically, we have investigated the link between UK inflation, growth and their respective uncertainties. The variables under consideration are inextricably linked. Informal stories are common and there are few theoretical models that come to grips with the main relationships. Partly as a result of this, and partly as a result of many econometric difficulties, much of the empirical evidence is dubious. We know from the previous literature how hard it is to arrive at definitive conclusions on this topic. One of the objectives of our analysis was to consider several changes in the specification of the bivariate model and discuss how these changes would affect the twelve interlinkages among the four variables.

Most of the empirical studies which have been carried out in this area concentrate on the impact of uncertainty on performance and do not examine the effects in the opposite direction. The 'one-sidedness' of these methodologies is an important caveat and any such attempts to analyze the link between the four variables are doomed to imperfection. In our analysis, we have shown that not only does volatility affect performance but the latter influences the former as well. Another advantage of our approach was that several lags of the conditional variances were used as regressors in the mean equations. Finally, our methodology allowed for either a positive or a negative bidirectional feedback between the two volatilities, and so no restriction was imposed in the variance relationship.

The core findings that are quite robust to changes in the specification of the model are: (i) growth tends to increase inflation, whereas inflation is detrimental to growth, which are in line with the Briault conjecture and the Gillman–Kejak theory respectively; (ii) inflation, under linearity, has a positive impact on macroeconomic uncertainty thus supporting the Ungar–Zilberfarb theory and the Dotsey–Sarte conjecture; and (iii) nominal variability, when we allow for both cross-effects, affects real volatility positively as argued by Logue and Sweeney (1981). In addition, of significant importance is that in all specifications inflation is independent of changes in its variance, and real uncertainty does not affect inflation variability and is unaffected by the first lag of growth.

The significance and even the sign of the in-mean effects vary with the choice of the lag. Thus our analysis suggests that the behavior of macroeconomic performance depends upon its uncertainty, but also that the nature of this dependence varies with time. In particular, at lag 1, the impact of real variability on growth is positive, as predicted by Blackburn (1999), but at lag 3, it turns negative. At lags 1 to 3 there is no causal effect from real volatility to inflation, whereas at lags 0 and 4 a positive impact appears, offering support for the Cukierman–Gerlach theory. We also show that accounting for the level effects reduces the strength of the impact of real uncertainty on inflation. In sharp contrast, the evidence in support of the Friedman hypothesis and the 'Blackburn' theory becomes stronger in the presence of level effects.

In contrast, note that the lack of an effect from nominal uncertainty to inflation exhibits much less sensitivity. That is, we have been unable to verify, for the UK, the more conventional view that greater volatility in the inflation either lowers or increases inflation. This astonishing result cries out for explanation. It is worth noting that the indirect effect that works via the real variability is opposite to the one that works via output growth. That is, on the one hand, nominal uncertainty has a positive impact on real volatility, which in turn affects inflation positively. On the other hand, it has a negative effect on growth, which in turn affects inflation positively. In essence, the offsetting indirect effects of nominal uncertainty on inflation might provide a rationale for the lack of a direct impact. The account we have just given has been fairly speculative – it is more an agenda for further research than a polished theory. In addition, when we control for the impact of inflation on growth, the evidence for the Friedman hypothesis disappears. The interlinkage between levels of the two variables may, therefore, be an important element masking the negative effects of nominal volatility on growth.

The possibly causal effect of growth, on uncertainty has hardly been investigated, perhaps because most researchers have decided to reject this possibility from the outset. Nonetheless, we found some evidence that growth predicts future nominal variability. We hypothesize that the effects of growth on macroeconomic volatility could work through changes in inflation. In particular, when the positive impacts of growth on inflation and of the latter on uncertainty are combined, the net effect is to create a positive influence of growth on either nominal or real volatility.

The attendant danger is that one might see technical sophistication as an end in itself, and lose sight of the reasons for interest in the various relationships. Be that as it may, one of the contributions of our work was to clarify the kinds of mechanisms that may be at play. Some of the conclusions we have reached in this chapter are fairly speculative. In these circumstances we focus on the general principles that we are attempting to explain rather than the details, which may have to be amended as more evidence becomes available. However, our ideas about the mechanism linking performance to uncertainty at least offer plenty of opportunities for further research. It seems likely that many more of these kinds of relationships between the four variables will be uncovered by researchers.

NOTES

* We are grateful to J. Davidson, C. Conrad and M. Karanassou for their valuable suggestions.

1. We will use the terms variance, variability, uncertainty and volatility interchangeably in the remainder of the text.
2. For example, Campos et al. (2012) use this process to model output growth and financial development in Argentina.
3. Throughout the chapter we will adhere to the following convention: in order to distinguish matrices (vectors) from scalars, the former are denoted by upper(lower)-case boldface symbols.
4. vech is the operator that stacks the lower triangle of an $N \times N$ matrix as an $N(N + 1)/2 \times 1$ vector.
5. We tend to use the term macroeconomic performance (uncertainty) as a shorthand for inflation (uncertainty) and output growth (uncertainty).
6. Of course, the GARCH process is not the only possible model of the performance–uncertainty link.
7. The ccc and BEKK GARCH models were introduced by Bollerslev (1990) and Engle and Kroner (1995) respectively.
8. In a recent paper Conrad and Karanasos (2010) consider a formulation of the extended ccc (eccc) GARCH model that allows for volatility feedback of either positive or negative sign. This model was termed unrestricted eccc (ueccc) GARCH. They show that the positive definiteness of the conditional covariance matrix can be guaranteed even if some of the parameters are negative. Thus, they extended the results of Nelson and Cao (1992) and Tsai and Chan (2008) to a multivariate setting. Conrad and Karanasos (2012) employed an augmented version of the ueccc GARCH specification which allows for lagged in-mean effects, level effects (see below) as well as asymmetries in the conditional variances. They applied this model to US inflation and output.

9. And it is well known that Einstein advised in connection with theorizing in the natural sciences, 'Make it as simple as possible but no simpler' (Zellner, 1998).
10. Of course the conditional correlation ($h_{\pi y,t}/\sqrt{h_{\pi t}}\sqrt{h_{yt}}$,) is constant (ρ). This is the price that we have to pay for allowing for a negative relationship between nominal and real uncertainty. The model that we have estimated has some more limitations. However, it is easy to see how the model might be modified to overcome some of its limitations, and we will leave this task for future research (see also the 'robustness' section below).
11. For our inflation series, based on the Phillips–Perron (PP) unit root test (not reported), we are able to reject the unit root hypothesis. The results from the two Elliot–Rothenberg–Stock (ERS) unit root tests (the point optimal test and the ERS version of the Dickey–Fuller test) concur with the PP results.
12. The GARCH coefficient is significant only in the conditional variance of inflation. For our bivariate process the estimation shows a significant improvement in the likelihood value of the ARCH growth specification over the GARCH model. Due to space limitations, we have not reported the estimated equations for the conditional means and variances. They are available upon request from the authors.
13. In particular, the seventh and eleventh lags of inflation have a joint significant negative impact on growth while the fifth and seventh lags of growth affect inflation positively (see Table 12.5).

REFERENCES

Ball, L., N. Mankiw and D. Romer (1988), 'The new Keynesian economics and the output–inflation trade-off', *Brookings Papers on Economic Activity*, **1**, 1–65.

Bauwens, L., S. Laurent and J.V.K. Rombouts (2006), 'Multivariate GARCH models: a survey', *Journal of Applied Econometrics*, **21**, 79–109.

Blackburn, K. (1999), 'Can stabilisation policy reduce long-run growth?', *Economic Journal*, **109**, 67–77.

Blackburn, K. and A. Pelloni (2005), 'Growth, cycles and stabilisation policy', *Oxford Economic Papers*, **57**, 262–82.

Bollerslev, T. (1986), 'Generalized autoregressive conditional heteroskedasticity', *Journal of Econometrics*, **31**, 307–27.

Bollerslev, T. (1990), 'Modelling the coherence in short-run nominal exchange rates: a multivariate generalized ARCH approach', *Review of Economics and Statistics*, **72**, 498–505.

Briault, C. (1995), 'The costs of inflation', *Bank of England Quarterly Bulletin*, February, pp. 33–45.

Brunner, A. (1993), 'Comment on inflation regimes and the sources of inflation uncertainty', *Journal of Money, Credit, and Banking*, **25**, 512–14.

Campos, N., M. Karanasos and B. Tan (2012), 'Two to tangle: financial development, political instability and growth in Argentina', *Journal of Banking and Finance*, **36**, 290–304.

Conrad, C. and M. Karanasos (2010), 'Negative volatility spillovers in the unrestricted ECCC-GARCH model', *Econometric Theory*, **26**, 838–62.

Conrad, C. and M. Karanasos (2012), 'Modeling the link between US inflation and output: the importance of the uncertainty channel', unpublished paper.

Conrad, C., M. Karanasos and N. Zeng (2010), 'The link between macroeconomic performance and variability in the UK', *Economics Letters*, **106**, 154–7.

Cukierman, A. and S. Gerlach (2003), 'The inflation bias revisited: theory and some international evidence', *The Manchester School*, **71**, 541–65.

Cukierman, A. and A. Meltzer (1986), 'A theory of ambiguity, credibility, and inflation under discretion and asymmetric information', *Econometrica*, **54**, 1099–128.

Davidson, J. (2006), 'Time Series Modelling 4.20', available at: http://www.timeseriesmodelling.com.

Devereux, M. (1989), 'A positive theory of inflation and inflation variance', *Economic Inquiry*, **27**, 105–16.

Dotsey, M. and P. Sarte (2000), 'Inflation uncertainty and growth in a cash-in-advance economy', *Journal of Monetary Economics*, **45**, 631–55.

Elder, J. (2004), 'Another perspective on the effects of inflation uncertainty', *Journal of Money, Credit and Banking*, **5**, 911–28.

Engle, R.F. (1982), 'Autoregressive conditional heteroskedasticity with estimates of the variance of UK inflation', *Econometrica*, **50**, 987–1008.

Engle, R. and K. Kroner (1995), 'Multivariate simultaneous generalized ARCH', *Econometric Theory*, **11**, 122–50.

Fountas, S. and M. Karanasos (2007), 'Inflation, output growth, and nominal and real uncertainty: empirical evidence for the G7', *Journal of International Money and Finance*, **26**, 229–50.

Fountas, S., M. Karanasos and J. Kim (2006), 'Inflation uncertainty, output growth uncertainty and macroeconomic performance', *Oxford Bulletin of Economics and Statistics*, **3**, 319–43.
Francq, C. and J. Zakoian (2010), GARCH Models: Structure, Statistical Inference and Financial Applications, Chichester: Wiley.
Friedman, M. (1977), 'Nobel lecture: inflation and unemployment', *Journal of Political Economy*, **85**, 451–72.
Fuhrer, J. (1997), 'Inflation/output variance trade-offs and optimal monetary policy', *Journal of Money, Credit, and Banking*, **29**, 214–34.
Gillman, M. and M. Kejak (2005), 'Contrasting models of the effect of inflation on growth', *Journal of Economic Surveys*, **1**, 113–36.
Grier, K. and M. Perry (2000), 'The effects of real and nominal uncertainty on inflation and output growth: some GARCH-M evidence', *Journal of Applied Econometrics*, **15**, 45–58.
Grier, K., O. Henry, N. Olekalns and K. Shields (2004), 'The asymmetric effects of uncertainty on inflation and output growth', *Journal of Applied Econometrics*, **5**, 551–65.
Holland, S. (1993), 'Comment on inflation regimes and the sources of inflation uncertainty', *Journal of Money, Credit, and Banking*, **25**, 514–20.
Holland, S. (1995), 'Inflation and uncertainty: tests for temporal ordering', *Journal of Money, Credit, and Banking*, **27**, 827–37.
Judson, R. and O. Orphanides (1999), 'Inflation, volatility and growth', *International Finance*, **2**, 117–38.
Karanasos, M. and J. Kim (2005a), 'The inflation–output variability relationship in the G3: a bivariate GARCH (BEKK) approach', *Risk Letters*, **2**, 17–22.
Karanasos, M. and J. Kim (2005b), 'On the existence or absence of a variance relationship: a study of macroeconomic uncertainty', *WSEAS Transactions on Computers*, **4**, 1475–82.
Karanasos, M. and S. Schurer (2005), 'Is the reduction in output growth related to the increase in its uncertainty? The case of Italy', *WSEAS Transactions on Business and Economics*, **3**, 116–22.
Karanasos, M., M. Karanassou and S. Fountas (2004), 'Analyzing US inflation by a GARCH model with simultaneous feedback', *WSEAS Transactions on Information Science and Applications*, **1**, 767–72.
Logue, D. and R. Sweeney (1981), 'Inflation and real growth: some empirical results', *Journal of Money, Credit, and Banking*, **13**, 497–501.
Martin, P. and C. Rogers (2000), 'Long-term growth and short-term economic instability', *European Economic Review*, **44**, 359–81.
Nelson, D. and C. Cao (1992), 'Inequality constraints in the univariate GARCH model', *Journal of Business and Economic Statistics*, **10**, 229–35.
Pindyck, R. (1991), 'Irreversibility, uncertainty, and investment', *Journal of Economic Literature*, **29**, 1110–48.
Shields, K., N. Olekalns, O. Henry and C. Brooks (2005), 'Measuring the response of macroeconomic uncertainty to shocks', *Review of Economics and Statistics*, **2**, 362–70.
Silvennoinen, A. and T. Teräsvirta (2007), 'Multivariate GARCH models', in T.G. Andersen, R.A. Davis, J.P. Kreiss and T. Mikosh (eds), *Handbook of Financial Time Series*, Heidelberg: Springer.
Temple, J. (1999), 'The new growth evidence', *Journal of Economic Literature*, **1**, 112–56.
Temple, J. (2000), 'Inflation and growth: stories short and tall', *Journal of Economic Surveys*, **4**, 395–426.
Tsai, H. and K.S. Chan (2008), 'A note on inequality constraints in the GARCH model', *Econometric Theory*, **24**, 823–8.
Ungar, M. and B. Zilberfarb (1993), 'Inflation and its unpredictability: theory and empirical evidence', *Journal of Money, Credit, and Banking*, **25**, 709–20.
Zellner, A. (1998), 'Keep it sophisticatedly simple', unpublished paper, University of Chicago.

13 Temporal aggregation in macroeconomics

Michael A. Thornton and Marcus J. Chambers

1 INTRODUCTION

1.1 Variables and Observations of Variables

When trying to draw inferences about economic behaviour from a set of data it is important to disentangle the process driving the economic variables of interest from extraneous effects generated by the process of data collection itself. Such considerations are familiar to microeconometricians, who must contend with the effects of sampling, measurement error, mis-reporting, truncation and other causes of bias, but they have not received the same level of attention in macroeconomics. This chapter examines one such feature that has, however, received considerable attention: the frequency of data collection. Very often the data of interest to the macroeconomist are based on observations taken quarterly, possibly monthly or annually, but in a modern economy the activity to which they relate is ongoing. These macroeconomic data stand in stark contrast to some financial data, which are available in real time. For example, one can find the market price of an asset for any given moment when the market is open, but there is no measure of inflation or gross domestic product for that moment, only one relating to the month or quarter in which the moment falls. Having such gaps between observations is a limitation in the data, especially when underlying events are fast moving and the economic relationships are dynamic.

One can credibly imagine the economy as a system in which information flows round to agents, leading them to re-evaluate their behaviour, more frequently than information about the state of the economy becomes available to researchers. The effects of temporal aggregation have been considered in relation to a wide range of macroeconomic topics; see, for example, Rossanna and Seater (1995), who examine a range of macroeconomic variables including real GDP, investment, real wages and money stock, or Marcellino (1999) for an overview. Here we pick out two strands: consumption, and large-scale macroeconomic modelling, these two examples being used to emphasize key concepts throughout the chapter:

Example 1 (the permanent income hypothesis) Since Hall's (1978) ground-breaking paper, there has been considerable interest in whether and at what level consumption is a martingale, that is to say whether current information can be used to predict future changes in consumption. A number of empirical studies, following Flavin (1981), have provided evidence that aggregate consumption is not martingale: shocks to aggregate consumption appear to persist beyond one period.

The consumer's problem is to choose a path for consumption, $\{c_t\}_{t=0}^{\infty}$, adjusted for deterministic tastes, to maximize the present expected value of the sum of time separable felicity functions, $U(.)$, discounted at rate δ,

$$E_0 \sum_{t=0}^{\infty} \frac{U(c_t)}{(1+\delta)^t},$$

subject to a resource constraint. This problem has the familiar solution that future changes to consumption must be orthogonal to previous income shocks – the well-known martingale hypothesis. In Hall's corollary 3, which features quadratic utility, after setting the discount rate equal to the interest rate the path for consumption follows a random walk without drift,

$$C_t - C_{t-1} = e_t, \tag{13.1}$$

where e_t is a white noise process. □

Example 2 (models of complete economies) There is a long tradition of modelling macroeconomies in continuous time, starting with Bergstrom and Wymer's (1976) model of the UK; see section 1.5 of Bergstrom and Nowman (2007) for an overview of, and references for, work on other countries. The most recent work, Bergstrom and Nowman's (2007) model of the UK economy, involves 15 endogenous variables (a mixture of stocks and flows), 12 exogenous variables and three unobservable stochastic trends. The model consists of mixed first and second order stochastic differential equations, examples of which shall be provided later at appropriate points. □

So how should the economist proceed in the face of such data limitations? One approach is simply to ignore them, which would be the natural and correct thing to do if the economy lurched from one state to another every three months, with no activity in between. This is patently not the case, but all modelling uses acceptable approximations to draw out important relationships from complicated systems, and turning a blind eye to some features of data collection is often only one of many well-intended sins. The consequences of ignoring temporal aggregation for estimation and inference will be discussed throughout this chapter. In reality, an economy evolves and mutates more subtly and almost constantly. The main focus of this chapter is how to build models that incorporate this feature explicitly: that is to say how to take a model that operates on a finer time scale than can be observed through the available data. We begin with some key concepts and a little terminology.

1.2 Time and Data: Continuous and Discrete; Stocks and Flows

Let $\{y_t\}$, $t = 0, 1, 2, 3, \ldots, T$, denote our observed variable or vector of variables, which is only available at discrete points in time, denoted t. We accept that the process generating the y_t values operates more frequently than we obtain the observations. Since we are interested in the workings of the economy, rather than the workings of the data, our aim is to model that underlying process. We start by being explicit about how time operates on this underlying process. We could imagine that the underlying process operates at discrete points in time, which are more frequent. We denote this underlying process as $y_{[\tau]}$ (with brackets around the time subscript), where $\tau = 0, 1, \ldots, m, m+1, \ldots, 2m, \ldots, mT$, where $m > 1$. If this process is observed every m period then time for our observations is

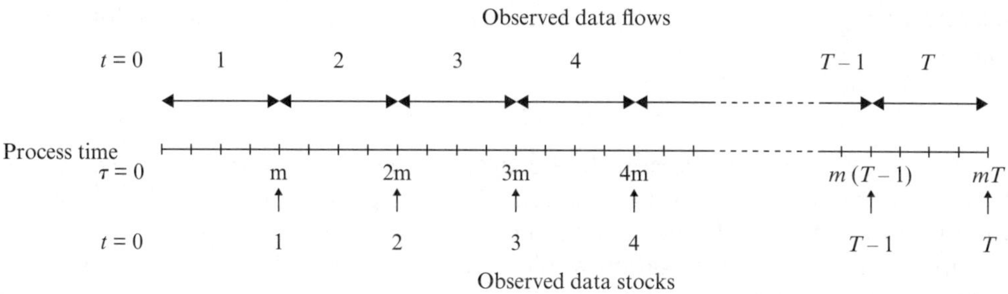

Figure 13.1 Temporal aggregation of discrete time processes

$t = \tau/m$. This is illustrated in Figure 13.1, where the central line denotes the time scale, τ, in which the underlying process operates. As m gets larger, that is the number of process-time units per observation interval increases, this discrete time model approaches a continuous time model, in which our time parameter takes real values. We denote a process that operates continuously through time as $y(t)$, $0 \leq t \leq T$, putting the time parameter in parentheses.

Then consider what our observed value y_t is telling us. For something like a price index, an exchange rate or an interest rate, it might be telling us the value of the variable at that moment in time, so $y_t = y_{[mt]}$ in discrete time or $y_t = y(t)$ in continuous time, shown as vertical arrows in Figure 13.1. This type of variable is known as a stock and the limitation in the data is often referred to as 'systematic sampling', because we do observe the underlying variable, but miss some of its values. For example, the published data on consumer prices is typically available monthly, but it seems likely that prices continue to change during each month.

For variables like gross domestic product, industrial production and investment, on the other hand, what we observe is the aggregate of the underlying variable since the previous observation, y_{t-1}, ended. In discrete time $y_t = \sum_{\tau=m(t-1)+1}^{mt} y_{[\tau]}$ is the sum of m realizations of the underlying y variable, shown as horizontal arrows in Figure 13.1. In continuous time $y_t = \int_{s=t-1}^{t} y(s)ds$ becomes an integral of the underlying process. This type of variable is known as a flow and the limitation in the data is often referred to as 'time aggregation', because we never observe the underlying variable directly, only an aggregate over time. In this chapter we use the term 'temporal aggregation' as a catch-all, making clear in each case whether the data are composed of stocks or flows or both. Systematic sampling and time aggregation have different impacts on the observed series. To get a better idea of the impact we present a simple example.

1.3 Temporal Aggregation of a Unit Root Process

The unit root process is widely used in modelling macroeconomic variables following the work of Nelson and Plosser (1982), who found evidence of unit roots across a range of US data including employment, GNP and prices. The following example, based on an influential article by Working (1960), illustrates the effect that temporal aggregation has on a flow variable, such as GDP or consumption, with a unit root. To keep things simple, we postpone consideration of short-run dynamics to the next section and imagine that the underlying process $y_{[\tau]}$, $\tau = 0,1,2,3,\ldots,mT$, is a discrete time scalar random walk, that is

$$y_{[\tau]} - y_{[\tau-1]} = e_{[\tau]},$$

where $e_{[\tau]}$ is a white noise process with zero mean and constant variance σ_e^2. Suppose also that the observed series, y_t, is time aggregated over m periods, so that $y_t = \sum_{j=0}^{m-1} y_{[\tau-j]}$. In terms of observational time, $\tau = mt$ and so we can also write $y_t = \sum_{j=0}^{m-1} y_{[mt-j]}$. An example of this type of aggregation would be using quarterly data for household consumption when the process operates monthly.

How does this aggregation impact on the properties of the observed series, y_t? The most notable impact is that y_t is no longer a random walk. To see why, note that now

$$y_t - y_{t-1} = \sum_{j=0}^{m-1} (y_{[mt-j]} - y_{[m(t-1)-j]}).$$

But for each j the m-period differences in the above summation can be written in terms of the sum of the intra-period differences as follows:

$$\begin{aligned} y_{[mt-j]} - y_{[m(t-1)-j]} &= y_{[mt-j]} - y_{[mt-j-1]} + y_{[mt-j-1]} - y_{[mt-j-2]} \\ &\quad + \ldots + y_{[m(t-1)-j+1]} - y_{[m(t-1)-j]} \\ &= \sum_{k=0}^{m-1} (y_{[mt-j-k]} - y_{[mt-j-k-1]}) \\ &= \sum_{k=0}^{m-1} e_{[mt-j-k]}. \end{aligned}$$

Hence we find that the first difference of the observed series satisfies

$$y_t - y_{t-1} = \sum_{j=0}^{m-1} \sum_{k=0}^{m-1} e_{[mt-j-k]} \equiv u_t,$$

in which the driving process, u_t, features lags of $e_{[\tau]}$ going back $2m - 2$ periods. That means for $m > 2$ it aggregates realizations $e_{[\tau-m]},\ldots,e_{[\tau-2m+2]}$ that also contribute to u_{t-1}. It follows that $E\{u_t u_{t-1}\} \neq 0$ and, hence, the time aggregation means that the observed y_t is no longer a pure random walk, even though the underlying series $y_{[\tau]}$ is. In fact, it is possible to show that

$$E\{u_t^2\} = \sigma_e^2 \left\{ \frac{m(2m^2+1)}{3} \right\}, E\{u_t u_{t-1}\} = \sigma_e^2 \left\{ \frac{m(m^2-1)}{6} \right\};$$

see Working (1960) (although note that Working normalizes y_t by $1/m$). It follows that the correlation between u_t and u_{t-1} is then

$$\text{Corr}\{u_t u_{t-1}\} = \frac{m^2-1}{2(2m^2+1)},$$

which approaches 0.25 as $m \to \infty$.

This simple example offers some specific insights for the applied researcher working with flow variables. First, when testing for a unit root the researcher needs to take the correlation present in u_t into account or the test will be biased. Secondly, that temporal aggregation destroys the martingale property that future changes in the data cannot be predicted from past changes. This is of interest as the martingale hypothesis has a close association with rational expectations and the efficient operation of markets. This effect, commonly known as time aggregation bias, would push the researcher to reject the martingale hypothesis when it is actually true.

Example 1 (continued) Suppose the above version of the martingale hypothesis holds for consumption, so that equation (13.1) is the correct model for disaggregated data. Given that household consumption is a flow variable, measured over a month, quarter or year, suppose that observations are of the form $C_t = \Sigma_{j=0}^{m-1} C_{[mt-j]}$. Then the above analysis suggests that $C_t - C_{t-1}$ will not be white noise but an MA(1) process, meaning that the observed series is not martingale. A test based on the ability of information available at time $t - 1$ to predict observed consumption at time t would incorrectly reject the martingale hypothesis. □

There has been a great deal of interest in whether the features outlined in the above analysis could cause one of the well known implications of the permanent income hypothesis to be rejected incorrectly. Ermini (1989) notes that the first order correlation between the differenced consumption series is negative for monthly data but positive for quarterly data and that this is consistent with the permanent income hypothesis if decisions are taken at intervals somewhere between monthly and quarterly. Ermini (1993), working in a discrete time framework, shows that US monthly consumption data are consistent with the permanent income hypothesis when transitory consumption and temporal aggregation effects are both incorporated into the modelling.

Christiano et al. (1991) investigate a variety of reasons why lagged consumption and output help predict the change in measured aggregate quarterly US consumption. Using an atheoretical econometric model, which is estimated by the generalized method of moments (see Chapter 14), they find much less evidence that the martingale hypothesis fails to hold in (unobservable) continuous time. They then build a continuous time dynamic stochastic general equilibrium model (see Chapter 18), which is estimated by frequency domain likelihood techniques, nesting the continuous time martingale hypothesis as a special case. They fail to find overwhelming evidence against this special case.

Although we have not yet considered estimation of the underlying model, the above example hints at a general point: that, in most cases, the effect of using data observed at a lower frequency than the underlying process is to induce autocorrelation in the error term. If ignored this is a source of bias; but handled correctly it is a source of information.

1.4 Advantages of Modelling Temporal Aggregation

The advantages of modelling a series in a way that takes account of temporal aggregation are elegantly set out in the introduction to Bergstrom (1990) and Bergstrom and Nowman (2007). Perhaps the major advantage is that, as we discuss in the following two sections, doing so is the most efficient, in terms of making the best use of information, way of estimating the underlying model. Another advantage is that a priori restrictions or hypotheses from economic theory can be imposed easily and accurately on the parameters of the underlying model. Where these restrictions are correct they will improve the efficiency of our estimates and where, as is likely, they restrict some parameters to take on zero values they also improve the efficiency of computation. A further advantage is that it becomes possible to 'forecast' the underlying economic variable, rather than the data series. One could use such a model to interpolate a measure of gross domestic product over any range consistent with the underlying model; or one could decompose a forecast for the next observation into the underlying component forecasts. The method also ensures that stock and flow data receive appropriately different treatments.

Given these clear advantages, many econometricians working in the field wonder why temporal aggregation is not taken into account in every macroeconomic model. There are two main reasons for this. One is that conceding that the data employed are aggregated over time makes the use of common non-linear transforms slightly dubious. For example, suppose we have in mind a model that uses the natural logarithm of $y_{[\tau]}$. Can this be estimated on an observed flow variable, $y_t = \sum_{\tau=m(t-1)+1}^{mt} y_{[\tau]}$? Only if we can observe $\sum_{\tau=m(t-1)+1}^{mt} \ln(y_{[\tau]})$, which we cannot when $m \geq 2$. We must work instead with $\ln(\sum_{\tau=m(t-1)+1}^{mt} y_{[\tau]})$, in effect using an arithmetic mean in place of a geometric mean. This is a general feature of all aggregation problems, cross-section as well as time, and its effects are known as Theil's entropy.

The second reason is the technical sophistication involved in the efficient estimation of such models, which is the main subject of this chapter. As will be discussed in more detail later, the estimation of a simple reduced form vector autoregression is transformed from an application of least squares to a sophisticated non-linear optimization problem. While ongoing developments in computing power make such considerations far less relevant than once they were, the econometrician is usually dependent on statistical software that is either directly programmable, such as GAUSS or Matlab, or capable of implementing a bespoke Kalman iteration. Even before computation can begin, there is often the extra intellectual effort needed to translate the underlying model into a model consistent with the observable data.

Aggregation in discrete time and continuous time have evolved as largely separate strands within the empirical macroeconomics literature and here they are separated into sections 2 and 3 respectively. The two are almost never seen side by side as rivals to be applied to the same data. This chapter, nevertheless, covers both because many of the key estimation techniques, covered in section 4, are equally applicable. Moreover, it is hoped that appreciation of one will help with understanding of the other. We begin with the (possibly) more intuitive modelling of temporal aggregation in discrete time.

2 TEMPORAL AGGREGATION IN DISCRETE TIME

2.1 A First Order Model

Consider the $n \times 1$ vector $y_{[\tau]} = [y_{[1,\tau]}, y_{[2,\tau]}, \ldots, y_{[n,\tau]}]'$, which follows a first order autoregressive process

$$y_{[\tau]} = Ay_{[\tau-1]} + e_{[\tau]}, \tag{13.2}$$

where A is an $n \times n$ matrix of parameters. The error process $e_{[\tau]}$ is an $n \times 1$ vector that, for now, we specify to be vector white noise with covariance matrix $\mathrm{E}\{e_{[\tau]}e'_{[\tau]}\} = \Sigma$. Now suppose we observe $y_{[\tau]}$ as a vector of stock variables every m periods. How are the dynamics of the observed process y_t governed? Lagging equation (13.2) and substituting in m times produces

$$y_t = A^m y_{t-1} + u_t, \tag{13.3}$$

where, in this case,

$$u_t = \sum_{j=0}^{m-1} A^j e_{t-j}.$$

If the error $e_{[\tau]}$ driving the underlying process is white noise then u_t, which drives the observed process, is as well. Ordinary least squares would provide a consistent estimator of A^m, from which an estimator of A can be derived, subject to the effects of aliasing, discussed below.

The use of summation notation rapidly becomes cumbersome for sophisticated models. Equation (13.2) can be written equivalently as

$$(I - AL)y_{[\tau]} = e_{[\tau]},$$

where L is the lag operator defined as $Lx_{[\tau]} = x_{[\tau-1]}$ and I is an $n \times n$ identity matrix. The observable equation (13.3) is then the underlying equation (13.2) multiplied by $[1 - A^mL^m][1 - AL]^{-1} = \sum_{k=0}^{m-1} A^k L^k$.

Suppose instead that the observed variables are flows,[1] that is

$$y_t = \sum_{j=0}^{m-1} y_{[\tau-j]} = \sum_{j=0}^{m-1} L^j y_{[\tau]} = (1 - L^m)(1 - L)^{-1} y_{[\tau]}.$$

This change does not affect the autoregressive structure; the equivalent procedures of repeated lagging and substitution and of multiplying by the polynomial $[I - A^mL^m][I - AL]^{-1}$ apply as they do for a stock. The nature of the error process, u_t, has, however, changed dramatically and can provide useful insights into the issues involved in temporal aggregation; we now have

$$\begin{aligned}
u_t &= [I - A^mL^m][I - AL]^{-1}[I - IL^m][I - IL]^{-1}e_{[\tau]} \\
&= \sum_{i=0}^{m-1}\sum_{j=0}^{m-1} A^j e_{[\tau-i-j]} \\
&= Ie_{[\tau]} + [I + A]e_{[\tau-1]} + [I + A + A^2]e_{[\tau-2]} + \ldots + [I + A + \ldots + A^{m-1}]e_{[\tau-m+1]} \\
&\quad + [A + \ldots + A^{m-1}]e_{[\tau-m]} + [A^2 + \ldots + A^{m-1}]e_{[\tau-m-1]} + \ldots + A^m e_{[\tau-2m+2]},
\end{aligned}$$

recognizing the coefficients on the e_{t-k} terms as geometric progressions. Purely for ease of algebra we now assume that the $n \times n$ matrix $[I - A]$ is full rank so that the above expression can be simplified to

$$u_t = [I - A]^{-1}\left\{\sum_{k=0}^{m-1}[I - A^{k+1}]e_{[\tau-k]} + [A^{k+1} - A^m]\sum_{k=0}^{m-1}e_{[\tau-m-k]}\right\}.$$

The first summation in the final expression contains shocks which occur between period t and $t - 1$, while the second summation contains shocks occurring at or before period $t - 1$, that is to say shocks which will also have featured in u_{t-1}. Note that the coefficient on $e_{[\tau-2m+1]}$ is zero, making the two expressions above for u_t equivalent. Two main insights may be gleaned from these expressions. The first is that, in this case, u_t has a first order moving average structure and so least squares estimation of equation (13.3) based on the observed series y_t will not produce consistent estimates of A^m. The second is that the covariance structure of u_t is itself a function of the matrix of parameters A. It follows that

$$\begin{aligned}
\mathrm{E}\{u_t u_t'\} &= [I-A]^{-1}\left\{\sum_{k=0}^{m-1}[I-A^{k+1}]\Sigma[I-A^{k+1}]'\right\}[I-A']^{-1}\\
&\quad+[I-A]^{-1}\left\{\sum_{k=0}^{m-1}[A^{k+1}-A^m]\Sigma[A^{k+1}-A^m]'\right\}[I-A']^{-1},\\
\mathrm{E}\{u_t u_{t-1}'\} &= [I-A]^{-1}\left\{\sum_{k=0}^{m-1}[I-A^{k+1}]\Sigma[A^{k+1}-A^m]'\right\}[I-A']^{-1},\\
\mathrm{E}\{u_t u_{t-s}'\} &= 0,\ \forall|s|>1. \qquad (13.4)
\end{aligned}$$

The first order moving average error is then more than the usual nuisance to be overcome in estimation. It is itself a source of information that an efficient estimator of the parameter matrix A will exploit.

2.2 Aliasing

The phenomenon of aliasing arises because it is impossible to discern cycles in a series that operate at higher frequencies than one observes, as discussed in Chapter 4 of Priestley (1981). In macroeconomics, this basic lack of information manifests itself in the problem of identifying the matrix A uniquely given the matrix A^m. Using the spectral decomposition theorem, it is possible to show that the eigenvalues of A^m are the eigenvalues of A raised to the mth power, while their (normalized) eigenvectors are the same. For any given scalar, x, it is a property of the exponential function that $x^m = [x\exp(2\pi ij/m)]^m$, where $i = \sqrt{-1}$, for any real integer j. In general, any eigenvalue of A^m could be the mth power of a range of values, each varying by a multiple of $\exp(2\pi i/m)$, so A^m could be the exponent of a range of matrices.

2.3 More General Models

We have seen that when our underlying model was an AR(1), the observed model for stock variables was also an AR(1) while for flow variables it became an ARMA(1,1).

We now consider the effects of including a moving average error in the underlying model. It is straightforward to show that making $e_{[\tau]}$ into an MA(q) process, $e_{[\tau]} = \varepsilon_{[\tau]} + \theta_1\varepsilon_{[\tau-1]} + \ldots + \theta_q\varepsilon_{[\tau-q]}$, means that when u_t is decomposed into terms in $\varepsilon_{[\tau]}$ there are q additional lags. In discrete time aggregation, this may or may not have an impact on the orders of the observed models. For example, in the flow case, having $e_{[\tau]}$ follow an MA(1) adds a term corresponding to $2m - 1$ lags of $\varepsilon_{[\tau]}$ to u_t, meaning that u_t remains an MA(1) process; whereas in the stock case the added term is of m lags, meaning that u_t becomes an MA(1) process. Results for the orders of processes are summarized in Table 1 of Brewer (1973). In order to provide a quick guide, note following the above example that each autoregressive root in the underlying model, including unit roots, translates to one autoregressive root in the observed model and it also adds $m - 1$ (unobservable) lags to the error term, as does observing a flow. By this reasoning if the underlying model is an ARMA(p,q), then the autoregressive order in the observed series is p, while the moving average order is $Int\{[p(m-1)+q]/m\}$ in the stock case and $Int\{[(p+1)(m-1)+q]/m\}$ in the flow case, where $Int\{x\}$ denotes the integer part of a non-negative number x. For example, if the variables are stocks then the observed series is an ARMA$(p,p-1)$ when $q + m > p > q$ and an ARMA(p,p) when $m + p > q \geq p$; if they are flows then the observed series is an ARMA(p,p) if $q + m > p + 1 > q$ and an ARMA$(p,p+1)$ when $m + p + 1 > q \geq p + 1$. It is an important feature of these models that the orders of the moving average error in the observable process are largely determined by the orders of the autoregressive elements in the underlying process.

Understanding the orders of the processes is not itself enough to achieve efficient estimation. For that we need to know how the parameters of the underlying model relate to the parameters fitting the observed data. While it is possible to repeat the procedure outlined above for each root of the autoregressive process when the observed data are scalars, this quickly becomes tedious and it cannot usually be generalized to vector processes. Results for scalar processes are set out in Weiss (1984). Marcellino (1999) proposed an elegant general method to generate parameter matrices recursively as part of a system where the coefficients on time periods between the observable periods are set to zero. It is of course entirely possible to treat the order of temporal aggregation, m, as a parameter to be estimated itself.

2.4 Unit Roots and Cointegration

We saw in the previous section that an autoregressive unit root is preserved after time aggregation. In general, since the eigenvalues of the matrix of autoregressive parameters for the observed series, A^m, are simply those of the underlying series raised to the power m, the stationarity of the observed variables is the same as the underlying variables. If, for example, the underlying process is non-stationary because one or more of the eigenvalues, λ_i, of the matrix A lie on the unit circle, then the corresponding eigenvalues of A^m, λ_i^m, also lie on the unit circle and the observed process is also non-stationary. If all of the eigenvalues of A lie inside the unit circle, then so do all of the eigenvalues of A^m.

Cointegration between certain elements of $y_{[\tau]}$ occurs if those elements individually are non-stationary (unit root) but certain linear combinations of them are stationary. Suppose, for example, that all of the elements of $y_{[\tau]}$ are unit root processes and that there are r such linearly independent relationships so that there exists an $n \times r$ matrix, β, with $1 \leq r < n$, such that $\beta' y_{[\tau]}$ is stationary. It is shown in Granger (1990) that these linear combinations remain stationary after temporal aggregation. For further discussion of the impact on the loadings of the error correction terms see Marcellino (1999).

3 TEMPORAL AGGREGATION IN CONTINUOUS TIME

As in the previous section, we first consider a simple first order model, using it to discuss the appropriateness of standard estimation techniques and the treatment of exogenous variables and the phenomenon of aliasing, which are also relevant in discrete time models.

3.1 A First Order Model

For the researcher accustomed to economic models in discrete time, continuous time models have some novel features. The most obvious is that continuous time models are expressed as stochastic differential equations rather than stochastic difference equations. Consider the $n \times 1$ vector $y(t) = [y_1(t), y_2(t), \ldots, y_n(t)]'$. A first order system of stochastic differential equations takes the form

$$dy(t) = [Ay(t) + a]dt + \zeta(dt), \tag{13.5}$$

where A is an $n \times n$ matrix, a is an $n \times 1$ vector of constants and $\zeta(dt)$ is a random disturbance. As with a fully deterministic system, the solution of equation (13.5) involves integration. Perhaps the greatest technical difference is the difficulty in defining, with any rigour, a continuous time white noise process that can be integrated, as opposed to a discrete time one that can be summed. Heuristically, while it is possible to imagine a series of completely unrelated dots at discrete intervals it is not possible to draw a continuous line that is sufficiently smooth to be integrable but where the position of each point is unrelated to the points in its near vicinity. This issue is discussed in more detail in Bergstrom (1984). Bergstrom's solution, which has been widely adopted, is to define the process $\zeta(dt)$ as an $n \times 1$ vector of random measures. These are stochastic processes defined over subsets of (rather than points on) the real line; see the technical appendix accompanying this chapter for details. Denoting an arbitrary subset (or interval) by Δ, such processes maintain a finite variance, $E[\zeta(\Delta)\zeta(\Delta)'] = \Sigma|\Delta|$, where Σ is a symmetric, positive definite matrix of order n and $|\Delta|$ denotes the length of the interval, and are integrable over the intervals between observations, while remaining uncorrelated over disjoint intervals.

A further complication is that a process, $y(t)$, satisfying (13.5) is not mean square differentiable (see the technical appendix for a definition of mean square differentiability). The process $y(t)$ is then interpreted as satisfying (for $t_1 < t$)

$$y(t) - y(t_1) = A\int_{t_1}^{t} y(r)dr + \int_{t_1}^{t} a\,dr + \int_{t_1}^{t} \zeta(dr), \tag{13.6}$$

where $\int_{t_1}^{t}\zeta(dr)=\zeta((t_1,t])$, $\int_{t_1}^{t} adr = a(t - t_1)$ and $\int_{t_1}^{t} y(r)dr$ is a wide sense integral (see the technical appendix for a definition).

Estimation of the system involves finding values for the matrices A and the covariance matrix of the error term, Σ, as well as the vector a. In line with the solution to deterministic systems, the solution to equation (13.5), given initial conditions $y(0)$, is

$$y(t) = \int_0^t e^{A(t-r)}\zeta(dr) + \int_0^t e^{A(t-r)}adr + e^{At}y(0), (\mathrm{t} > 0), \qquad (13.7)$$

where e^{As} is the matrix exponential defined by

$$e^{As} = I + As + \frac{1}{2!}(As)^2 + \frac{1}{3!}(As)^3 + \ldots = \sum_{j=0}^{\infty}\frac{1}{j!}(As)^j.$$

Note that the matrix exponential is not formed simply by taking the scalar exponential of each element.

The compensation for mastering these features is that the resulting models are usually more straightforward to solve than discrete time temporally aggregated models. The solution in equation (13.7) contains the integral of a function of the parameters through time with respect to a random measure, which is defined more carefully in the technical appendix. The time series properties of the observed data y_t depend on whether the individual series $[y_{1,t}, y_{2,t}, \ldots, y_{n,t}]'$ are stocks or flows. If y_t is composed entirely of stock variables, that is $y_t = y(t)$, then it satisfies

$$y_t = \Phi y_{t-1} + \alpha + \eta_t, (t = 1, \ldots, T),$$

where $\Phi = e^A$, $\eta_t = \int_{t-1}^{t} e^{A(t-s)}\zeta(ds)$ and the vector α can be written[2]

$$\alpha = \int_{t-1}^{t} e^{A(t-s)}ads = \sum_{j=0}^{\infty}\frac{1}{(j+1)!}A^j a.$$

For y_t to be stationarity, the eigenvalues of the matrix Φ must lie inside the unit circle, which happens if and only if the eigenvalues of the matrix A have negative real parts.

In this case the discrete process η_t is vector white noise since it is drawn as an integral only over $(t-1, t]$, so that $E\{\eta_t\eta'_{t-s}\}=0$, $\forall s = \pm 1, \pm 2, \ldots$ and y_t is therefore a first order vector autoregressive (VAR) process.

If, on the other hand, y_t contains flow variables, the process $y_t = \int_{t-1}^{t} y(s)ds$ satisfies

$$y_t = \Phi y_{t-1} + \alpha + u_t, (t = 1, \ldots, T).$$

where the disturbance $u_t = \int_{t-1}^{t}\int_{s-1}^{s} e^{A(s-r)}\zeta(dr)ds$ is a vector MA(1) process. To see this, it is possible, as, for example, in McCrorie and Chambers (2006), to express the double integral as the sum of two single non-overlapping integrals of the form

$$u_t = \int_{t-1}^{t}\int_{r}^{t} e^{A(s-r)}ds\zeta(dr) + \int_{t-2}^{t-1}\int_{t-1}^{r+1} e^{A(s-r)}ds\zeta(dr)$$

$$= A^{-1}\int_{t-1}^{t}[1 - e^{A(t-r)}]\zeta(dr) + A^{-1}\int_{t-2}^{t-1}[e^{A} - e^{A(t-1-r)}]\zeta(dr).$$

The autocovariance structure of u_t, analogously to equation (13.4), is

$$\begin{aligned}
E\{u_t u_t'\} &= \int_0^1 \{A^{-1}[1 - e^{As}]\Sigma[1 - e^{As}]' A'^{-1} \\
&\quad + A^{-1}[e^{A} - e^{As}]\Sigma[e^{A} - e^{As}]' A'^{-1}\} ds \\
E\{u_t u_{t-1}'\} &= \int_0^1 A^{-1}[1 - e^{As}]\Sigma[e^{A} - e^{As}]' A'^{-1} ds \\
E\{u_t u_{t-s}'\} &= 0, \forall s = \pm 2, \ldots
\end{aligned}$$

In this case the observed process y_t does not follow a simple VAR(1), even though the underlying process does, but a vector autoregressive moving average – VARMA(1, 1) – process. A standard VAR would not provide consistent estimates of Φ. Note also that the covariance structure is a function of the autoregressive matrix A and is, as in the discrete case, not merely a nuisance, but a source of information that can be used to improve the efficiency of estimates.

Very often a macroeconomic model will contain both stock and flow variables. We partition the vector $y(t) = [y^s(t)', y^f(t)']'$, where $y^s(t)$ is an $n^s \times 1$ vector of stock variables and $y^f(t)$ is an $n^f \times 1$ vector of flow variables with $n^s + n^f = n$. In this case the observed vector is of the form

$$y_t = \begin{bmatrix} y_t^s \\ y_t^f \end{bmatrix} = \begin{bmatrix} y^s(t) - y^s(t-1) \\ \int_{t-1}^{t} y^f(r)\,dr \end{bmatrix}, \quad t = 1, \ldots, T;$$

(see Bergstrom, 1986). Similar arguments can be used to show that y_t is a vector ARMA(1,1) process.

Example 2 (continued) The Bergstrom and Nowman (2007) macroeconomic model contains both first and second order stochastic differential equations. An example of the former is the equation for real private consumption, C, given by

$$D\log C = \lambda_1 + \lambda_2 + \gamma_1 \log\left[\frac{\beta_1 e^{-\{\beta_2(r - D\log p) + \beta_3 D\log p\}}(Q + P)}{T_1 C}\right],$$

where λ_1 and λ_2 are the growth rates of productivity and labour supply trends, respectively, r denotes the interest rate, p denotes the price level, Q and P are real net output and real profits, interest and dividends from abroad, respectively, T_1 is a taxation policy variable, and γ_1 is the speed of adjustment of the logarithm of consumption to its partial equilibrium level. As it stands, the equation is neither stochastic nor linear, but all the equations in the model are linearized around the steady state solution before a white noise random measure is introduced, prior to estimation. □

In the main, this chapter concentrates on the dynamics of the underlying model and the observed data, but we pause to consider the treatment of exogenous variables and the phenomenon of aliasing.

3.2 Exogenous Variables

The above example is a closed system, one containing all relevant variables. Although this is an elegant approach to any system, there may be times where an open model, containing exogenous variables, is needed. Open systems allow models to take account of the movement of additional variables without having to incorporate them into the y vector, saving the additional computation that a larger dimension A matrix implies. Suppose a further q exogenous variables, contained in the vector $z(t)$ are added to the right-hand side of equation (13.5) in the form $Bz(t)$, with B an $n \times q$ matrix of parameters. The solution to the model would then contain $\int_{t-1}^{t} e^{A(t-s)} Bz(s)ds$. The problem is that we are unlikely to be able to observe $z(s)$ continuously through time and are forced to make assumptions interpolating its path between discrete observations. This is discussed further in Bergstrom (1986) and McCrorie (2001).

3.3 Aliasing

As in discrete time models, continuous time models are subject to the phenomenon of aliasing, which manifests itself in the problem of identifying the matrix A uniquely given the matrix Φ. Again using the spectral decomposition theorem, it is possible to show that the eigenvalues of Φ are the exponents of the eigenvalues of A, while their (normalized) eigenvectors are the same. For any given scalar, x, it is a property of the exponential function that $\exp(x) = \exp(x + 2\pi ij)$, where $i = \sqrt{-1}$, for any real integer j. It follows that any eigenvalue of Φ could be the exponent of a range of values, each varying by a multiple of $2\pi i$ and so Φ could be the exponent of a range of matrices.

3.4 Higher Order and ARMA Models

In many applications, a first order model fails to deliver sufficiently rich dynamics to fit the data. Fortunately, higher order models can be translated into state-space form and then treated as first order processes, such as in Bergstrom (1983), and it is also possible to include MA disturbances in the system. The continuous time ARMA(p, q) model for the $n \times 1$ vector $y(t)$ is given by

$$D^p y(t) = a_0 + A_{p-1} D^{p-1} y(t) + \ldots + A_0 y(t) + u(t) + \Theta_1 Du(t) + \ldots + \Theta_q D^q u(t), t > 0, \tag{13.8}$$

where D denotes the mean square differential operator (see the technical appendix for details), $A_0, \ldots, A_{p-1}$ and $\Theta_1, \ldots, \Theta_q$ are $n \times n$ matrices of unknown coefficients, a_0 is an $n \times 1$ vector of unknown constants, and $u(t)$ is an $n \times 1$ continuous time white noise vector with variance matrix Σ. The condition that $q < p$ must be imposed so that $y(t)$ itself has finite variance. This type of process is considered by Zadrozny (1988), Brockwell (2004) and Chambers and Thornton (2012), the latter authors demonstrating that the presence of MA disturbances in a continuous time model can have empirical content by capturing additional serial correlation that pure AR processes are unable to capture.

Example 2 (continued) Second order differential equations appear in the Bergstrom and Nowman (2007) macroeconomic model, an example being the equation for employment, L, which is given by

$$D^2\log L = \gamma_2(\lambda_2 - D\log L) + \gamma_3\log\left[\frac{\beta_4 e^{-\mu_1}\{Q^{-\beta_6} - \beta_5 K^{-\beta_6}\}^{-1/\beta_6}}{L}\right],$$

where γ_2 and γ_3 are speed of adjustment parameters, μ_1 is the productivity trend variable, K is private non-residential fixed capital, and Q and λ_2 were defined earlier. As with the equation for consumption, defined earlier, this equation is first linearized around the model's steady state solution before a random disturbance is appended prior to estimation. □

3.5 Zero Roots and Cointegration

Zero roots in a stochastic differential equation manifest themselves as unit roots in the discrete time difference equation. That this is so is most easily seen by considering the equation $dy(t) = \alpha y(t)dt + \zeta(dt)$, where $y(t)$ is a scalar random process. The characteristic equation is $(z - \alpha) = 0$ and the root is clearly equal to α; negative values of α are required for stationarity. Clearly, if $\alpha = 0$ there will exist a unit root in the continuous time model. In this case, $dy(t) = \zeta(dt)$ and it follows that (by integrating once) $y(t) - y(t-1) = \int_{t-1}^{t}\zeta(dr)$, thereby yielding a unit root in the first-differenced discrete time process.

Cointegration between a set of non-stationary (zero root) processes occurs when one or more linear combinations of them is stationary. For example, if $y_1(t),\ldots,y_n(t)$ have zero roots in continuous time then if the linear combinations represented by $\beta' y(t)dt$ are stationary, where β is $n \times r$ with $1 \leq r < n$, there will exist r cointegrating relations between these variables. It is possible to define a continuous time error correction model in the form

$$dy(t) = \alpha\beta' y(t)dt + \zeta(dt),$$

where α is an $n \times r$ matrix of adjustment coefficients. For further details of cointegrated continuous time processes see, for example, Phillips (1991) and Chambers (2009).

4 ESTIMATION TECHNIQUES

We describe two popular time domain methods for the estimation of temporally aggregated models based on a Gaussian likelihood function: one is based on the exact discrete model while the other employs Kalman Filtering of the state space form. A third set of techniques is based in the frequency domain; details of Fourier estimation methods as well as frequency domain-based likelihood methods can be found in Robinson (1976, 1993).

4.1 Estimation Based on Exact Discrete Models

Gaussian estimation based on the exact discrete model was proposed by Bergstrom (1983) and developed further by him in a sequence of subsequent papers. It is a quasi-likelihood method in which the parameters of the underlying model are translated into the coefficients of a VARMA process that describes the observed data, known as the exact discrete model. This is then used to evaluate a likelihood function under the assumption that the process generating the errors is Gaussian. The exact discrete representation of a continuous time model was proposed by Bergstrom (1983) following work by Phillips (1972) which showed that an exact model could be used to obtain estimates that were not only consistent and asymptotically efficient but also, Monte Carlo evidence suggested, performed better in finite samples than the approximate methods then in use. The technique has since been extended to cope with higher order models, stochastic trends and exogenous regressors; see for example Bergstrom (1983, 1986, 1997) and Chambers (1999, 2009). Given the similarities between the effects of temporal aggregation in discrete and continuous time, it is natural to extend the approach beyond continuous time modelling. The essential algorithm involves the computationally efficient evaluation of the likelihood function for an observed sample of n variables over T periods, which is defined as

$$\log L = -\frac{nT}{2}\log(2\pi) - \frac{1}{2}\log|\Omega| - \frac{1}{2}u'\Omega^{-1}u, \qquad (13.9)$$

where $u = [u_1', u_2', \ldots, u_T']'$ and u_t is the n by 1 vector of residuals from each observation. Note that, in general, the $nT \times nT$ covariance matrix $\Omega \equiv \mathrm{E}\{uu'\}$ will not be block diagonal because temporal aggregation induces MA correlation in the error terms. However, the finite order MA structure ensures that Ω has a block Toeplitz form, the $n \times n$ non-zero blocks being known functions of the parameters of interest. This can be exploited to ease computation. Since Ω is positive definite and symmetric we can find a lower triangular matrix, M with i,jth element $m_{i,j}$, such that $MM' = \Omega$. A straightforward recursive procedure then produces a vector μ such that $M\mu = u$. Finally, equation (13.9) can be evaluated as

$$\log L = -\frac{nT}{2}\log(2\pi) - \frac{1}{2}\sum_{i=1}^{nT}(\mu_i^2 + 2\log(m_{i,i})). \qquad (13.10)$$

Bergstrom (1990) uses this transformed vector of errors, μ, which should be uncorrelated standard normal variables if the model is correctly specified, in a portmanteau-type statistic looking for correlation over the first l lags; it is defined by

$$S_l = \frac{1}{T-l}\sum_{r=1}^{l}\left(\sum_{t=l+1}^{T}\mu_t\mu_{t-r}\right)^2. \qquad (13.11)$$

Under the null hypothesis that the model is correctly specified the statistic S_l will have an approximate chi-square distribution with l degrees of freedom for sufficiently large l and $T - l$.

Example 2 (continued) Bergstrom and Nowman (2007) use the Gaussian estimation algorithm to estimate their macroeconomic model which includes deeply embedded stochastic trends. This approach treats the stochastic trends as random forcing functions that help to generate the solution to the model, whereas the earlier approach of Harvey and Stock (1988), which exploits Kalman filtering techniques (see below), adds the stochastic trends after the model has been solved. □

4.2 Kalman Filtering

A different approach to evaluating the likelihood function is based around the Kalman–Bucy filter discussed in Chapter 15; see Harvey and Stock (1985, 1988, 1989) and Zadrozny (1988) for applications to continuous time models. It has the advantages of coping with irregular observations, missing observations and measurement error through the observation equation, but comes with some computational cost. As an example of this approach consider the system in equation (13.8) without moving average error and no intercept vector, that is with $a_0 = 0$ and $\Theta_1 = \Theta_2 = \ldots = \Theta_q = 0$. Such a system has a representation in the form of the following continuous time state equation:

$$\frac{d}{dt}x(t) = \tilde{A}x(t) + \zeta(t), \tag{13.12}$$

where $x(t)$ is an $np \times 1$ vector containing $y(t)$ and its first $(p - 1)$ derivatives, $\tilde{A}$ is an $np \times np$ transition matrix containing the parameter matrices $A_0, \ldots, A_p$, and $\zeta(t)$ is an $np \times 1$ vector containing the $n \times 1$ disturbance vector $u(t)$. Assuming that $y(t)$ contains stock variables, the solution to (13.12) yields the discrete time state equation

$$x(t) = e^{\tilde{A}}x(t - 1) + \zeta_t,$$

where the transition matrix is now $e^{\tilde{A}}$. The set-up is completed with the observation equation

$$y_t = Zx(t), \tag{13.13}$$

where the $n \times np$ selection matrix Z picks out $y_t = y(t)$ from $x(t)$ and could be allowed to vary over time if there are missing observations; an observation error vector could also be added to (13.13). In the absence of missing observations, the rows of Z are made up of the rows of an $n \times n$ identity matrix and an $n \times np$ null matrix, so as to select the observable elements of y_t (see Harvey and Stock, 1985). It is possible to incorporate a moving average error into the model either through the observation equation, as in Brockwell (2004), or by adopting a slightly different form of state equation, as in Zadrozny (1988). Extensions to handle flow variables, and mixtures of stocks and flows, can also be incorporated in this approach.

5 CONCLUDING COMMENTS

This chapter has considered the treatment of temporal aggregation in empirical macroeconomics. We have discussed the implications of using standard techniques to test some well known macroeconomic theories on aggregated data and shown how the explicit treatment of temporal aggregation makes efficient use of the available information. The chapter has featured models where the aggregation is over discrete time periods and over real time. Although the languages of the two systems are quite different, they share many common features and are largely amenable to the same estimation techniques. Although the computations underlying those techniques are often more intensive than standard methods, advances in computing power make this a diminishing concern.

It is inevitable that any overview chapter must leave many areas uncovered. Temporal aggregation has implications for many analyses presented in the *Handbook*, of which we have highlighted relatively few. Theoretical research into the implications for testing non-stationary and other areas is ongoing. At the same time, the use of techniques covered in this chapter in modelling macroeconomic and financial data, as highlighted in Bergstrom and Nowman (2007), continues to expand.

NOTES

1. Similar results to this can be derived when the vector contains a mixture of stocks and flows.
2. For algebraic simplicity the form $A^{-1}[e^A - I]a$ is sometimes used if A is non-singular.

REFERENCES

Bergstrom, A.R. (1983), 'Gaussian estimation of structural parameters in higher order continuous time dynamic models', *Econometrica*, **51**, 117–52.

Bergstrom, A.R. (1984), 'Continuous time stochastic models and issues of aggregation over time', in Z. Griliches and M.D. Intriligator (eds), *Handbook of Econometrics, Vol. 2*, Amsterdam: North-Holland, pp. 1145–212.

Bergstrom, A.R. (1986), 'The estimation of open higher-order continuous time dynamic models with mixed stock and flow data', *Econometric Theory*, **2**, 350–73.

Bergstrom, A.R. (1990), *Continuous Time Econometric Modelling*, Oxford: Oxford University Press.

Bergstrom, A.R. (1997), 'Gaussian estimation of mixed-order continuous-time dynamic models with unobservable stochastic trends from mixed stock and flow data', *Econometric Theory*, **13**, 467–505.

Bergstrom, A.R. and K.B. Nowman (2007), *A Continuous Time Econometric Model of the United Kingdom with Stochastic Trends*, New York: Cambridge University Press.

Berstrom, A.R. and C.R. Wymer (1976), 'A model of disequilibrium neoclassical growth and its application to the United Kingdom', in A.R. Bergstrom (ed.), *Statistical Inference in Continuous Time Economic Models*, Amsterdam: North Holland.

Brewer, K.R.W. (1973), 'Some consequences of temporal aggregation and systematic sampling for ARMA and ARMAX models', *Journal of Econometrics*, **1**, 133–54.

Brockwell, P.A. (2004), 'Representations of continuous-time ARMA processes', *Journal of Applied Probability*, **41A**, 375–82.

Chambers, M.J. (1999), 'Discrete time representation of stationary and nonstationary continuous time systems', *Journal of Economic Dynamics and Control*, **23**, 619–39.

Chambers, M.J. (2009), 'Discrete time representation of cointegrated continuous time models with mixed sample data', *Econometric Theory*, **25**, 1030–49.

Chambers, M.J. and M.A. Thornton (2012), 'Discrete time representation of continuous time ARMA processes', *Econometric Theory*, **28**, 219–38.

Christiano, L.J., M. Eichenbaum and D.A. Marshall (1991), 'The permanent income hypothesis revisited', *Econometrica*, **59**, 397–423.
Ermini, L. (1989), 'Some new evidence on the timing of consumption decision and on their generating process', *The Review of Economics and Statistics*, **71**, 643–50.
Ermini, L. (1993), 'Effects of transitory consumption and temporal aggregation on the permanent income hypothesis', *The Review of Economics and Statistics*, **75**, 736–40.
Flavin, M. (1981), 'The adjustment of consumption to changing expectations about future income', *Journal of Political Economy*, **89**, 974–1009.
Granger, C.W.J. (1990), 'Aggregation of time series variables: a survey', in T. Barker and M.H. Peseran (eds), *Disaggregation in Econometric Modelling*, London: Routledge, pp. 17–34.
Hall, R.E. (1978), 'Stochastic implications of the life cycle – permanent income hypothesis: theory and evidence', *Journal of Political Economy*, **86**, 971–87.
Harvey, A.C. and J.H. Stock (1985), 'The estimation of higher-order continuous time autoregressive models', *Econometric Theory*, **1**, 97–117.
Harvey, A.C. and J.H. Stock (1988), 'Continuous time autoregressive models with common stochastic trends', *Journal of Economic Dynamics and Control*, **42**, 319–36.
Harvey, A.C. and J.H. Stock (1989), 'Estimating integrated higher-order continuous time autoregressions with an application to money–income causality', *Journal of Econometrics*, **12**, 365–84.
Marcellino, M. (1999), 'Some consequences of temporal aggregation in empirical analysis', *Journal of Business & Economic Statistics*, **17**, 129–36.
McCrorie, J.R. (2001), 'Interpolating exogenous variables in continuous time dynamic models', *Journal of Economic Dynamics & Control*, **25**, 1399–427.
McCrorie, J.R. and M.J. Chambers (2006), 'Granger causality and the sampling of economic processes', *Journal of Econometrics*, **132**, 311–36.
Nelson, C.R. and C.R. Plosser (1982), 'Trends and random walks in macroeconomic time series: some evidence and implications', *Journal of Monetary Economics*, **10**, 139–62.
Phillips, P.C.B. (1972), 'The structural estimation of a stochastic differential equation system', *Econometrica*, **40**, 1021–41.
Phillips, P.C.B. (1991), 'Error correction and long-run equilibrium in continuous time', *Econometrica*, **59**, 967–80.
Priestley, M.B (1981), *Spectral Analysis and Time Series*, London: Academic Press.
Robinson, P.M. (1976), 'Fourier estimation of continuous time model', in A.R. Bergstrom (ed.), *Statistical Inference in Continuous Time Economic Models*, Amsterdam: North-Holland, pp. 215–66.
Robinson, P.M. (1993), 'Continuous-time models in econometrics: closed and open systems, stock and flows', in P.C.B. Phillips (ed.), *Models, Methods, and Applications of Econometrics: Essays in Honor of A.R. Bergstrom*, Oxford: Blackwell, pp. 71–90.
Rossana, R.J. and J.J. Seater (1995), 'Temporal aggregation and economic time series', *Journal of Business & Economic Statistics*, **13**, 441–51.
Weiss, A.A. (1984), 'Systematic sampling and temporal aggregation in time series models', *Journal of Econometrics*, **26**, 271–81.
Working, H. (1960), 'Note on the correlation of first difference of averages in a random chain', *Econometrica*, **28**, 916–18.
Zadrozny, P. (1988), 'Gaussian likelihood of continuous-time ARMAX models when data are stocks and flows at different frequencies', *Econometric Theory*, **4**, 108–24.

TECHNICAL APPENDIX ON STOCHASTIC CALCULUS AND RANDOM MEASURE

The following material is a more formal account of the processes and operations underpinning continuous time econometrics. It is intended to supplement the intuitive explanations given in the chapter.

A1 Mean Square Differentiation

The mean square differential operator D is defined as operating on a stochastic process, $x(t)$ such that $Dx(t) = \xi(t)$ implies the process $\xi(t)$ has the property that

$$\lim_{h\to 0} E\left\{\frac{x(t+h) - x(t)}{h} - \xi(t)\right\}^2 = 0.$$

A2 Random Measure

Let ζ be a random set function which associates with any set Δ on the real line a random variable $\zeta(\Delta)$ with the properties:

1. $E[\zeta(\Delta)] = 0$;
2. $E[\zeta(\Delta)^2] = F(\Delta)$;
3. if Δ_1 and Δ_2 are disjoint the $E[\zeta(\Delta_1)\zeta(\Delta_2)] = 0$;
4. if Δ_1 and Δ_2 are disjoint the $\zeta(\Delta_1 \cup \Delta_2) = \zeta(\Delta_1) + \zeta(\Delta_2)$.

Properties 1 to 3 define a random measure, while properties 1 to 4 define a σ-additive random measure.

A3 Integration with Respect to a Random Measure

To define integration with respect to a random measure, some further concepts are required. A function $f(t)$ is said to be *simple* on the interval $[c, d]$ if it assumes a finite or countable set of values $f_k (k = 1, 2, \ldots)$ on disjoint sets Δ_k whose union is $[c, d]$. A simple function $f(t)$ is *integrable* with respect to ζ on $[c, d]$ if the series $\sum_k f_k \zeta(\Delta_k)$ converges in mean square. The *integral* of $f(t)$ with respect to ζ over $[c, d]$ is then the limit in mean square (l.i.m.) to which this sum converges. That is

$$\int_c^d f(x)\zeta(dx) = \text{l.i.m.} \sum_{k=1}^{n} f_k \zeta(\Delta_k) \text{ as } n \to \infty,$$

which is to say

$$\lim_{n\to\infty} E\left[\sum_{k=1}^{n} f_k \zeta(\Delta_k) - \int_c^d f(x)\zeta(dx)\right]^2 = 0,$$

where the function $f(t)$ has been assumed to be simple.

An arbitrary (measurable) function $f(x)$ is *integrable* with respect to ζ on $[c, d]$ if there exists a sequence $f_n(x)$ $(n = 1, 2, \ldots)$ of simple integrable functions that converges in mean square to $f(x)$ on $[c, d]$, that is

$$\lim_{n \to \infty} \int_c^d [f(x) - f_n(x)]^2 F(dx) = 0.$$

In this case the integral of $f(x)$ with respect to ζ on $[c, d]$ is

$$\int_c^d f(x)\zeta(dx) = \text{l.i.m.} \int_c^d f_n(x)\zeta(dx) \text{ as } n \to \infty. \tag{13.14}$$

A necessary and sufficient condition for the integral in (13.14) to exist is

$$\int_c^d |f(x)|^2 F(dx) < \infty. \tag{13.15}$$

This, in turn, implies that

$$E\left|\int_c^d f(x)\zeta(dx)\right|^2 = \int_c^d |f(x)|^2 F(dx).$$

Furthermore, if $f(x)$ and $g(x)$ both satisfy the property defined by (13.15), then

$$E\left[\int_c^d f(x)\zeta(dx) \int_c^d g(x)\zeta(dx)\right] = \int_c^d f(x)g(x)F(dx). \tag{13.16}$$

Another important property that is an implication of property 3 of random measures is that, if $a < b \leq c < d$, then

$$E\left[\int_a^b f(x)\zeta(dx) \int_c^d f(x)\zeta(dx)\right] = 0. \tag{13.17}$$

These properties of stochastic integrals are useful when the random measure is used to characterize the disturbance term in a stochastic differential equation.

A4 Integration of Arbitrary Random Processes

A random process $x(t)$ is *simple* on $[c,d]$ if there exists a finite or countable family of sets Δ_k $(k = 1, 2, \ldots)$ whose union is $[c, d]$, and corresponding random variables x_k $(k = 1, 2, \ldots)$, such that $x(t) = x_k$ $(t \in \Delta_k)$. If $|\Delta_k|$ denotes the Lebesgue measure of Δ_k (that is the length of the interval), then $x(t)$ is *integrable in the wide sense* on $[c, d]$ if the series $\sum_k x_k |\Delta_k|$ converges in mean square. The *wide sense integral* of $x(t)$ is then

$$\int_c^d x(r)\,dr = \text{l.i.m.} \sum_{k=1}^{n} x_k |\Delta_k| \text{ as } n \to \infty.$$

An arbitrary random process $x(t)$ is *integrable in the wide sense* if there exists a sequence $x_n(t)$ of simple integrable processes which converges uniformly on $[c, d]$ to $x(t)$, that is if

$$E[x(t) - x_n(t)]^2 \rightarrow 0,$$

as $n \rightarrow \infty$ uniformly in t. Then the wide sense integral of $x(t)$ over $[c, d]$ is

$$\int_c^d x(r)\,dr = \text{l.i.m.}\int_c^d x_n(r)\,dr \text{ as } n \rightarrow \infty.$$

PART III

ESTIMATION AND EVALUATION FRAMEWORKS IN MACROECONOMICS

14 Generalized Method of Moments*

Alastair R. Hall

1 INTRODUCTION

Generalized Method of Moments (GMM) estimation provides a computationally convenient way of estimating parameters of economic models. It can be applied equally in linear or non-linear models, in single equations or systems of equations, and to models involving cross-section, panel or time series data. This convenience and generality has led to the application of GMM in many areas of empirical economics, and the method is used frequently in macroeconomics. In fact, the emergence of GMM can be argued to be one of the most important developments in the econometric analysis of macroeconomic models over the last 35 years.[1]

The method was first introduced in a seminal paper by Lars Hansen published in *Econometrica* in 1982. While GMM had its origins in work on financial economics,[2] it was also soon recognized that the method offered a relatively simple method for estimating the parameters of rational expectations models in macroeconomics. Early applications involved models for: business cycles (Singleton, 1988), consumption (Miron, 1986), interest rates (Dunn and Singleton, 1986), inventory holding (Miron and Zeldes, 1988) and labour demand (Pindyck and Rotemberg, 1983).[3]

Whatever the application, the cornerstone of GMM estimation is a quantity known as the population moment condition:

Definition 1 Population Moment Condition Let θ_0 be a $p \times 1$ vector of unknown parameters which are to be estimated, v_t be a vector of random variables and $f(.)$ a $q \times 1$ vector of functions, then a population moment condition takes the form

$$E[f(v_t, \theta_0)] = 0 \tag{14.1}$$

for all t.

In other words, a population moment is a statement that some function of the data and parameters has expectation equal to zero when evaluated at the true parameter value.

Estimation based on population moment conditions has a long tradition in statistics going back at least to the Method of Moments (MM) principle introduced by Pearson in the late nineteenth century.[4] The MM principle can be applied in cases where $q = p$ and involves estimating θ by $\hat{\theta}_T$, the value that solves the analogous sample moment condition, $g_T(\hat{\theta}_T) = 0$, where $g_T(\theta) = T^{-1}\sum_{t=1}^{T} f(v_t, \theta)$ and T is the sample size. However, in by far the majority of cases in macroeconomics, the underlying model implies more moment conditions than there are parameters to be estimated, that is, $q > p$. In such cases, as we show below, the MM principle does not work, but *Generalized* Method of Moments does.

The popularity of GMM can be understood by comparing the requirements for the method to those for Maximum Likelihood (ML). While ML is the best available estimator within the Classical statistics paradigm, its optimality stems from its basis on the joint probability distribution of the data. However, in many scenarios of interest in macroeconomics, this dependence on the probability distribution can become a weakness. The reason is that the underlying theoretical model places restrictions on the distribution of the data but does not completely specify its form, with the result that ML is infeasible unless the researcher imposes an arbitrary assumption about the distribution. The latter is an unattractive strategy because if the assumed distribution is incorrect then the optimality of ML is lost, and the resulting estimator may even be inconsistent, for example in non-linear Euler equation models (see Hansen and Singleton, 1982). It turns out that in many cases where the macroeconomic model does not specify the complete distribution, it does specify population moment conditions. Therefore, in these settings, GMM can be preferred to ML because it offers a way to estimate the parameters based solely on the information deduced from the underlying macroeconomic model.

In this chapter, we provide an introduction to GMM estimation in macroeconomic models, focusing on the main aspects of its associated inference framework and various practical matters that arise in its implementation. Since most applications in macroeconomics involve time series, we concentrate on this case. An outline of the chapter is as follows. In section 2 we provide an illustration of how population moment conditions arise in macroeconomic models. Section 3 defines the GMM estimator and discusses certain issues relating to its calculation. In section 4 we summarize the large sample properties of the GMM estimator and discuss the construction of the so-called two-step (or iterated) GMM estimator. This section also presents various methods for inference about the parameter. Section 5 contains a discussion of methods for assessing whether the underlying model is correctly specified. In section 6 we comment briefly on the finite sample behaviour of the GMM estimator and examine reasons why it may not be well approximated by the large sample theory in certain cases. The latter leads to a discussion of a variant of GMM known as the Continuous Updating GMM estimator. Section 7 discusses the behaviour of the GMM estimator in the case of so-called weak identification, and section 8 concludes with a discussion of some recent developments involving estimation based on moment inequalities.

In keeping with the tone of this volume, the discussion is aimed at practitioners. Readers interested in the statistical arguments are referred to the articles cited below or to Hall (2005) for a formal statement of the underlying regularity conditions and proofs of the main statistical results.

2 EXAMPLE: NEW KEYNESIAN MODEL

To ilustrate the use of GMM in macroeconomics, we consider the problem of estimating the parameters of a New Keynesian (NK) macroeconomic model. At the heart of this model are an aggregate supply equation (or Phillips curve), an aggregate demand equation (or IS curve), and a monetary policy rule (or Taylor rule). There are a number of variants of this model and our discussion focuses on the version presented in Bekaert, Cho and Moreno (2010) (BCM hereafter).

In presenting the model, we adopt the following conventions and notations: p_t denotes inflation at time t, y_t denotes detrended log output at time t, i_t denotes the short-term (nominal) interest rate at time t, y_t^n is the natural rate of detrended log output that would arise with perfectly flexible prices, $e_{..,t}$ denotes an error term in which '..' is replaced by an acronym to denote the equation in which it occurs, $\mathcal{I}_t$ denotes the information set at time t, $E_t[\cdot]$ denotes expectations conditional on $\mathcal{I}_t$, and Greek letters denote unknown parameters of the model that need to be estimated.

The aggregate supply equation relates inflation today to expected future inflation, past inflation and the output gap, $y_t - y_t^n$, as follows:[5]

$$\dot{p}_t = \delta_0 E_t[\dot{p}_{t+1}] + (1 - \delta_0)\dot{p}_{t-1} + \kappa_0(y_t - y_t^n) + e_{AS,t}. \tag{14.2}$$

The aggregate demand equation relates output to expected future output, past output and the real interest rate, $i_t - E_t[\dot{p}_{t+1}]$ that is:

$$y_t = \mu_0 E_t[y_{t+1}] + (1 - \mu_0)y_{t-1} - \phi_0(i_t - E_t[\dot{p}_{t+1}]) + e_{AD,t}. \tag{14.3}$$

The monetary policy rule relates the interest rate to its past values, the expected deviation of future inflation from its desired level, $\dot{p}_t^*$, and the output gap via

$$i_t = \rho_0 i_{t-1} + (1 - \rho_0)\{\beta_0(E_t[\dot{p}_{t+1}] - \dot{p}_t^*) + \gamma_0(y_t - y_t^n)\} + e_{MP,t}. \tag{14.4}$$

Estimation of the parameters of this model raises a number of issues that can be resolved in a variety of ways. Given that our purpose here is to illustrate the use of GMM, we focus on the construction of the types of population moment conditions that have been used as a basis for GMM estimation of part or all of this model. We consider two specific studies: Zhang et al. (2008), who estimate the parameters of the aggregate supply equation, and BCM, who estimate the parameters of all three equations simultaneously. Taken together, these two examples illustrate the wide applicability of GMM as they cover both linear and non-linear models and parameters from both single equations and systems of equations.

Estimation of the Aggregate Supply Equation

An immediate problem is that the right-hand side of (14.2) involves the unobservable variables $E_t[\dot{p}_{t+1}]$ and y_t^n. To implement their GMM estimation, Zhang et al. (2008) replace these variables by proxy variables: for $E_t[\dot{p}_{t+1}]$, they use actual forecasts of inflation based on survey data, denoted here by $\dot{p}_{t+1,t}^f$; for y_t^n, they use estimates of real potential GDP, denoted y_t^p.[6] To present the population moment condition used in their GMM estimation,[7] it is convenient to define

$$e_{AS,t}(\phi) = \dot{p}_t - \delta\dot{p}_{t+1,t}^f - \eta\dot{p}_{t-1} - \kappa(y_t - y_t^p), \tag{14.5}$$

where $\phi = (\delta, \eta, \kappa)'$. Note that to begin we treat the coefficient on $\dot{p}_{t-1}$ as unrestricted and ignore restriction in (14.2) that $\eta = 1 - \delta$. The theory underlying the NK model implies that $E_{t-1}[e_{AS,t}(\phi_0)] = 0$ and this conditional moment restriction can be translated into a set of population moment conditions because we have, for any $w_{t-1} \in \mathcal{I}_{t-1}$,[8]

$$E[e_{AS,t}(\phi_0)w_{t-1}] = E[E_{t-1}[e_{AS,t}(\phi_0)w_{t-1}]] = E[E_{t-1}[e_{AS,t}(\phi_0)]w_{t-1}] = 0.$$

This population moment condition fits within our generic structure by writing $f(v_t,\theta) = e_{AS,t}(\phi)w_{t-1}$ with $v_t' = (\dot{p}_t,\dot{p}^f_{t+1,t},\dot{p}_{t-1},y_t - y^p_t,w'_{t-1})$ and $\theta = \phi$. It can be recognized that $E[e_{AS,t}(\phi_0)w_{t-1}] = 0$ is the statement that the error of the aggregate supply equation is uncorrelated with the variables in w_{t-1}. Since $e_{AS,t}(\phi)$ is linear in both the data variables and parameters, it follows that GMM estimation based on $E[e_{AS,t}(\phi_0)w_{t-1}] = 0$ exploits the same information as IV estimation of the supply equation using w_{t-1} as instruments.[9]

In line with the original specification, it may be desired to impose the restriction $\eta = (1 - \delta)$ in which case, we can use similar arguments as above to deduce the population moment condition $E[\tilde{e}_{AS,t}(\psi_0)w_{t-1}] = 0$ where the parameter vector, ψ, now only consists of two elements, $\psi = (\delta,\kappa)$, and $\tilde{e}_{AS,t}(\psi)$ is defined as $e_{AS,t}(\phi)$ in (14.5) except that η is replaced by $1 - \delta$. In this case, the GMM estimation exploits the same information as restricted IV estimation of (14.2) subject to the (linear) restriction $\eta = (1 - \delta)$ using w_{t-1} as instruments.

The population moment conditions discussed in this example both involve the statement that the expectation of some function of the data and unknown parameters times a vector of variables is zero. This generic structure occurs in many macroeconomic models, and moment conditions of this form are referred to as *orthogonality conditions.* ◇

Estimation of All Model Parameters Simultaneously

BCM estimate all the parameters of the model simultaneously using GMM. To do so, they adopt a model-based solution to the presence of unobservable variables on the right-hand side. They specify equations for y^n_t and $\dot{p}^*_t$ that combined with (14.2)–(14.4) yield a macroeconomic model of the generic form

$$Bx_t = \alpha + AE_t[x_{t+1}] + Cx_{t-1} + De_t \tag{14.6}$$

where $x_t = (\dot{p}_t,y_t,i_t,y^n_t,\dot{p}^*_t)'$, e_t is a vector of errors, and A, B, C and D are matrices whose elements are functions of the parameters of the model. Equation (14.6) implies that the rational expectations equilibrium solution path for x_t follows a VAR(1), the parameters of which are functions of the parameters of the underlying model. While the latter representation is a relatively simple structure, it is not convenient for estimation as x_t includes two unobservables.[10] However, BCM demonstrate that by including an equation for the term structure of interest rates it is possible to obtain the following

$$z_t = \alpha(\theta_0) + \Omega(\theta_0)z_{t-1} + \Gamma(\theta_0)u_t \tag{14.7}$$

where $z_t = (\dot{p}_t,y_t,i_t,s_{n_1,t},s_{n_2,t})$, $s_{n_j,t}$ is the spread between the n_j-period bond yield and i_t; θ_0 is the true value of θ, the vector of the parameters of the model, and $\alpha(\theta)$, $\Omega(\theta)$ and $\Gamma(\theta)$ vectors/matrices whose elements are functions of θ; and u_t is an innovation process. The key advantage of (14.7) is that all the elements of z_t are observable. If we put $u_t(\theta) = \Gamma(\theta)^{-1}(z_t - \alpha(\theta) - \Omega(\theta)z_{t-1})$ then BCM show that the innovation process satisfies $E_{t-1}[u_t(\theta_0)] = 0$ and $E[u_t(\theta_0)u_t(\theta_0)'] = I_5$, the identity matrix of dimension 5. The first of these conditions implies the innovations have zero mean given $\mathcal{I}_{t-1}$; the second set implies that the innovations all have unit variance and are contemporaneously uncorrelated. It therefore follows that within this model we have

$$E[f(v_t, \theta_0)] = 0 \tag{14.8}$$

where

$$f(v_t, \theta) = \begin{bmatrix} u_t(\theta) \otimes z_{t-1} \\ vech\{u_t(\theta)u_t(\theta)' - I_5\} \end{bmatrix},$$

$v_t = (z_t', z_{t-1}')'$ and $vech(\cdot)$ denotes the operator that stacks the lower diagonal elements of a matrix into a vector. Notice that some elements of $f(v_t, \theta)$ are non-linear functions of θ; also that the model leads naturally to a case in which the number of population moment conditions ($q = 40$, here) exceeds the number of parameters ($p = 15$) ◇

3 THE GMM ESTIMATOR AND THE FIRST ORDER CONDITIONS

In this section, we present the GMM estimator and discuss certain issues pertaining to its computation. It is noted in the introduction that the strength of GMM comes from its flexibility in that it works for a wide variety of choices of $f(.)$. While this is true, the $f(.)$ must satisfy certain restrictions and it is useful to discuss these briefly before defining the estimator itself.

The population moment condition states that $E[f(v_t, \theta)]$ equals zero when evaluated at θ_0. For the GMM estimation to be successful in a sense defined below, this must be a unique property of θ_0, that is $E[f(v_t, \theta)]$ is not equal to zero when evaluated at any other value of θ. If that holds, then θ_0 is said to be *identified* by $E[f(v_t, \theta_0)] = 0$. A first order condition for identification (often referred to as a 'local condition') is that $rank\{G(\theta_0)\} = p$, where $G(\theta) = E[\partial f(v_t, \theta)/\partial\theta']$, and this condition plays a crucial role in standard asymptotic distribution theory for GMM. By definition the moment condition involves q pieces of information about p unknowns, therefore identification can only hold if $q \geq p$. For reasons that emerge below it is convenient to split this scenario into two parts: $q = p$, in which case θ_0 is said to be *just-identified*, and $q > p$, in which case θ_0 is said to be *over-identified.*

Recalling that $g_T(\theta)$ denotes the analogous sample moment to $E[f(v_t, \theta)]$, the GMM estimator is then as follows.

Definition 2 Generalized Method of Moments Estimator The Generalized Method of Moments estimator based on (14.1) is $\hat{\theta}_T$, the value of θ which minimizes:

$$Q_T(\theta) = g_T(\theta)' W_T g_T(\theta) \tag{14.9}$$

where W_T is known as the *weighting matrix* and is restricted to be a positive semi-definite matrix that converges in probability to W, some positive definite matrix of constants.

To understand the intuition behind GMM, it is useful to first consider what happens in the just-identified case. If $q = p$ then there is in general a value of θ that sets the sample moment equal to zero. By definition, this value also sets $Q_T(\theta)$ to zero and so will be the GMM estimator. Thus in the just-identified case, the GMM estimator is the value of θ that satisfies the analogous sample moment condition, namely, $g_T(\hat{\theta}_T) = 0$. Now if θ_0 is over-identified then there is typically no solution for θ to the sample moment condition, $g_T(\theta) = 0$, and $Q_T(\theta)$ is a measure of how far $g_T(\theta)$ is from zero. Since the GMM estimator minimizes $Q_T(\theta)$, it is the value of θ that sets $g_T(\theta)$ as close as possible to zero or – put another way – the GMM estimator is the value of θ that is closest to solving the sample moment condition. The restrictions on W_T are required to ensure that $Q_T(\theta)$ is a meaningful measure of the distance the sample moment is from zero at different values of θ. Clearly $Q_T(\theta) = 0$ for $g_T(\theta) = 0$, and the positive semi-definiteness of W_T ensures $Q_T(\theta) \geq 0$. However, *semi*-definiteness leaves open the possibility that $Q_T(\theta) = 0$ without $g_T(\theta) = 0$. Positive definiteness ensures $Q_T(\theta) = 0$ if and only if $g_T(\theta) = 0$, but, since all our statistical analysis is based on asymptotic theory, positive definiteness is only required in the limit. The choice of weighting matrix is discussed further below.

In some cases, it is possible to solve analytically for the GMM estimator; an example is the case of estimation of the parameters of the aggregate supply equation based on $E[e_{AS,t}(\phi_0)w_{t-1}] = 0$.[11] However, in most cases, it is not possible to obtain a closed form solution for $\hat{\theta}_T$, and so the estimator must be found via numerical optimization. These routines involve an algorithm that performs an 'informed' iterative search over the parameter space to find the value that minimizes $Q_T(\theta)$. Many computer packages now contain specific commands for the implementation of GMM that produce both the estimates and associated statistics of interest such as standard errors and model diagnostics. Examples are the GMM option in *Eviews* and proc model in *SAS*.[12] However, in both these cases, the moment conditions must take the form of orthogonality conditions.[13] Kostas Kyriakoulis has provided a user-friendly MATLAB toolbox for GMM estimation that provides a wide variety of GMM statistics irrespective of the form of the moment condition.[14]

Various numerical optimization routines lie behind these procedures. While we do not review the generic structure of such algorithms here, it is worth highlighting two features common to most: the *starting values* and *convergence criterion*, both of which can impact on the estimates. In many programs, the user must specify starting values for the parameters which represent the point in the parameter space at which the search for the minimum begins. It is good practice to initiate the numerical optimization multiple times with different starting values on each. This offers protection against the twin possibilities that either the algorithm converges to a local but not global minimum or it has stalled in an area of the parameter space in which $Q_T(\theta)$ is relatively flat as a function of θ. In most cases, the user also has control of the convergence criterion which is the rule by which the numerical optimization routine decides if the minimum has been found. An example of such a rule is as follows: letting $\hat{\theta}(k)$ denote the value of θ after k iterations of the routine, the routine is judged to have converged if $\|\hat{\theta}(k) - \hat{\theta}(k-1)\| < \varepsilon$, where ε is some small positive number. In other words, if the numerical optimization routine returns essentially the same value for θ from two consecutive iterations then the minimum is judged to have been found. This decision is clearly sensitive to the chosen value of ε, and the choice of ε can have more impact than might be imagined; see Hall (2005, Chapter 3.2) for an example. Convergence can also be assessed by evaluation of the derivatives of $Q_T(\theta)$ at $\hat{\theta}(k)$, and this may yield different conclusions about whether the minimum has been reached. It is therefore good practice to assess convergence using multiple criteria.[15]

In many cases of interest, the GMM estimator can be characterized equivalently as the solution to the first order conditions for this minimization, that is,

$$G_T(\hat{\theta}_T)'W_T g_T(\hat{\theta}_T) = 0, \tag{14.10}$$

where $G_T(\theta) = T^{-1}\Sigma_{t=1}^{T}\partial f(v_t,\theta)/\partial\theta'$, a matrix often referred to as the 'Jacobian' in our context here. The structure of these conditions reveals some interesting insights into GMM estimation. Since $G_T(\theta)$ is $q \times p$, it follows that (14.10) involves calculating $\hat{\theta}_T$ as the value of θ that sets the p linear combinations of $g_T(.)$ to zero. Therefore, if $p = q$, and $G_T(\hat{\theta}_T)'W_T$ is non-singular, then $\hat{\theta}_T$ satisfies the analogous sample moment condition to (14.1), $g_T(\hat{\theta}_T) = 0$, and is, thus, the Method of Moments estimator based on the original moment condition. However, if $q > p$ then the first order conditions are not equivalent to solving the sample moment condition. Instead, $\hat{\theta}_T$ is equivalent to the Method of Moments estimator based on

$$G(\theta_0)'WE[f(v_t,\theta_0)] = 0, \tag{14.11}$$

where $G(\theta) = E[G_T(\theta)]$. Although (14.1) implies (14.11), the reverse does not hold because $q > p$; therefore, in this case, the estimation is actually based on only part of the original information. As a result, if $q > p$ then GMM can be viewed as decomposing the original moment condition into two parts, the *identifying restrictions*, which contain the information actually used in the estimation, and the *overidentifying restrictions*, which represent a remainder. Furthermore, GMM estimation produces two fundamental statistics and each is associated with a particular component: the estimator $\hat{\theta}_T$ is a function of the information in the identifying restrictions, and the estimated sample moment, $g_T(\hat{\theta}_T)$, is a function of the information in the overidentifying restrictions. While unused in estimation, the overidentifying restrictions play a crucial role in inference about the validity of the model as is discussed below.

In some circumstances, it may be desired to impose restrictions on the parameter vector as part of the estimation. Suppose the restrictions take the form: $r(\theta_0) = 0$, where $r(\theta)$ is an $s \times 1$ vector of continuous, differentiable functions. These restrictions must form a coherent set of equations, and so satisfy $rank\{R(\theta_0)\} = s$ where $R(\theta) = \partial r(\theta)/\partial\theta'$. This can be handled straightforwardly by using the so-called restricted GMM estimation.

Definition 3 The Restricted GMM Estimator Suppose the underlying economic model implies both the population moment condition in (14.1) and also the (non)linear restrictions on θ_0, $r(\theta_0) = 0$, then the restricted GMM estimator is defined to be $\tilde{\theta}_T$, the value of θ that minimizes $Q_T(\theta)$ subject to $r(\theta) = 0$, where $Q_T(\theta)$ is defined in Definition 2. $\hat{\theta}_{r,T}$ is referred to as the restricted GMM estimator.

In practice, the restricted GMM estimator is calculated on the computer by using a constrained optimization routine that directly imposes the restrictions specified by the user.

4 LARGE SAMPLE PROPERTIES, THE CHOICE OF W_T AND INFERENCE ABOUT θ_0

In this section we summarize the (so-called) first order asymptotic theory for $\hat{\theta}_T$ that forms the basis for the standard inference framework associated with GMM. Implementation of this framework raises a number of practical issues that are also addressed. Chief among them are the issue of covariance matrix estimation and the choice of weighting matrix, the latter of which leads to the so-called two-step or iterated GMM estimators. Since our focus here is on practical issues, our discussion only highlights certain key assumptions and we present neither a complete accounting of the necessary regularity conditions underlying the statistical results nor any proofs; the interested reader is referred to Hall (2005, Chapter 3.4).

This first order asymptotic theory is obtained using statistical theorems, such as the Law of Large Numbers and Central Limit Theorem, that involve statements about the behaviour of sample moments as $T \to \infty$. Such theory is therefore only strictly valid for infinite samples and is used as an approximation to *finite* sample behaviour. In section 6, we briefly discuss the evidence on the accuracy of this approximation in practical circumstances.

We begin with an important assumption about the data.

Assumption 1 Time series properties of v_t The $(r \times 1)$ random vectors $\{v_t; -\infty < t < \infty\}$ form a strictly stationary ergodic process with sample space $\mathbf{V} \subseteq \Re^r$.

The stationarity assumption implies that the moment of functions of v_t are independent of time. Ergodicity places restriction on the memory of time v_t. Taken together, stationarity and ergodicity essentially place sufficient restrictions on v_t to permit the development of the limit theorems that underlie the large sample theory discussed here. While this assumption applies to many of the time series that occur in macroeconomic models, it does exclude some important cases such as processes with deterministic trends or unit root processes. However, in cases where the population moment condition derives from a conditional moment restriction, it is sometimes possible to find a transformation that delivers a population moment condition that involves stationary ergodic variables even if the original conditional moment in question did not. To illustrate, suppose the model implies the conditional moment restriction $E_{t-1}[u_t(\theta_0)] = 0$ where $u_t(\theta)$ depends on unit root processes; then it may be possible to find $h_{t-1}(\theta_0) \in \mathcal{I}_{t-1}$ such that $k_t(\theta_0) = h_{t-1}(\theta_0)u_t(\theta_0)$ is a function of stationary ergodic variables. Notice that, given the properties of $u_t(\theta_0)$ and $h_{t-1}(\theta_0)$, $E_{t-1}[k_t(\theta_0)] = 0$ and this conditional moment restriction can form the basis of population moment conditions in the way discussed in section 2. This type of transformation is often used (implicitly) in Euler equation models in which the first order condition for the representative agent's optimization involves levels of macroeconomic variables but it is manipulated to create an equation involving growth rates of the same variables.[16]

To emphasize their importance in the theory, we also state the population moment and identification conditions as an assumption. Note that for what follows, it is important that the first order identification condition holds.[17]

Assumption 2 Population moment condition and identification condition

(i) $E[f(v_t, \theta_0)] = 0$; (ii) $E[f(v_t, \bar{\theta})] \neq 0$ for all $\bar{\theta} \in \Theta$ such that $\bar{\theta} \neq \theta_0$; (iii) $rank\{G(\theta_0)\} = p$.

The large sample properties of the GMM estimator are summarized in the following proposition.[18]

Proposition 1 Large sample behaviour of $\hat{\theta}_T$ Let Assumptions 1, 2, and certain other regularity conditions hold then: (i) $\hat{\theta}_T \xrightarrow{p} \theta_0$; (ii) $T^{1/2}(\hat{\theta}_T - \theta_0) \xrightarrow{d} N(0, V)$ where

$$V = [G(\theta_0)' WG(\theta_0)]^{-1} G(\theta_0)' WS(\theta_0) WG(\theta_0) [G(\theta_0)' WG(\theta_0)]^{-1}$$

and $S(\theta) = \lim_{T\to\infty} Var[T^{1/2} g_T(\theta)]$.

Proposition 1 states that the GMM is both consistent and $T^{1/2}(\hat{\theta}_T - \theta_0)$ converges to a normal distribution. The latter result forms the basis of inference procedures about θ_0, but before discussing these, we consider the implications of Proposition 1 for the choice of weighting matrix.

In the discussion of the first order conditions above, it is noted that if $p = q$ then the GMM estimator can be found by solving $g_T(\hat{\theta}_T)$. As a result, the estimator does not depend on W_T. The asymptotic properties must also be invariant to W_T and it can be shown that V reduces to $\{G(\theta_0)' S(\theta_0)^{-1} G(\theta_0)\}^{-1}$ in this case. However, if $q > p$ then the first order conditions depend on W_T and therefore so does $\hat{\theta}_T$ in general. This dependence is unattractive because it raises the possibility that subsequent inferences can be affected by the choice of weighting matrix. However, in terms of asymptotic properties, Proposition 1 reveals that the choice of weighting matrix only manifests itself in V, the asymptotic variance of the estimator. Since this is the case, it is natural to choose W_T such that V is minimized in a matrix sense. Hansen (1982) shows that this can be achieved by setting $W_T = \hat{S}_T^{-1}$ where $\hat{S}_T$ is a consistent estimator of $S(\theta_0)$. The resulting asymptotic variance is $V = V^0 = \{G(\theta_0)' S(\theta_0)^{-1} G(\theta_0)\}^{-1}$; Chamberlain (1987) shows V^0 represents the asymptotic efficiency bound – that is, the smallest asymptotic variance possible – for an estimator of θ_0 based on (14.1).

In practical terms, two issues arise in the implementation of GMM with this choice of weighting matrix: (i) how to construct $\hat{S}_T$ so that it is a consistent estimator of $S(\theta_0)$; (ii) how to handle the dependence of $\hat{S}_T$ on $\hat{\theta}_T$. We treat each in turn.

Estimation of $S(\theta_0)$

Under stationarity and ergodicity and certain other technical restrictions, it can be shown that $S(\theta_0) = \Gamma_0(\theta_0) + \sum_{i=1}^{\infty}\{\Gamma_i(\theta_0) + \Gamma_i(\theta_0)'\}$ where $\Gamma_i(\theta_0) = Cov[f(v_t, \theta_0), f(v_{t-i}, \theta_0)]$ is known as the i-lag autocovariance matrix of $f(v_t, \theta_0)$; see Andrews (1991). In some cases, the structure of the model implies $\Gamma_i(\theta_0) = 0$ for all $i > k$ for some k, and this simplifies the estimation problem; see Hall (2005, Chapter 3.5). In the absence of such a restriction on the autocovariance matrices, the long-run variance can be estimated by a member of the class of *heteroscedasticity autocorrelation covariance (HAC)* estimators defined as

$$\hat{S}_{HAC} = \hat{\Gamma}_0 + \sum_{i=1}^{T-1} \omega(i;b_T)(\hat{\Gamma}_i + \hat{\Gamma}_i'), \qquad (14.12)$$

where $\hat{\Gamma}_j = T^{-1}\Sigma_{t=j+1}^{T} \hat{f}_t \hat{f}_{t-j}'$, $\hat{f}_t = f(v_t, \hat{\theta}_T)$, $\omega(.)$ is known as the *kernel*, and b_T is known as the *bandwidth*. The kernel and bandwidth must satisfy certain restrictions to ensure $\hat{S}_{HAC}$ is both consistent and positive semi-definite. As an illustration, Newey and West (1987b) propose the use of the kernel $\omega(i, b_T) = \{1 - i/(b_T + 1)\}\mathcal{I}\{i \leq b_T\}$ where $\mathcal{I}\{i \leq b_T\}$ is an indicator variable that takes the value of 1 if $i \leq b_T$ and zero otherwise. This choice is an example of a truncated kernel estimator because the number of included autocovariances is determined by b_T. For consistency, we require $b_T \to \infty$ with $T \to \infty$ but at a slower rate than $T^{1/2}$. Various choices of kernel have been proposed and their properties analysed: while theoretical rankings are possible, the evidence suggests that the choice of b_T is a far more important determinant of finite sample performance. Andrews (1991) and Newey and West (1994) propose data-based methods for the selection of b_T. Simulation evidence suggests that the properties of HAC estimators are sensitive to the time series properties of $f(v_t, \theta_0)$ and are adversely affected if $f(v_t, \theta_0)$ contains a strong autoregressive component. Since this feature is common to many macroeconomic series, Andrews and Monahan (1992) propose the use of the so-called *prewhitening and recolouring* method for covariance matrix estimation in which the autoregressive component is filtered out of $f(v_t, \hat{\theta}_T)$ – the 'prewhitening' – and then an HAC matrix is used to estimate the long-run variance of the filtered series; the estimator $S(\theta_0)$ is then constructed from the properties of the filter and the HAC of the filtered series – the 'recolouring'. To illustrate, suppose the filter is a Vector Autoregressive (VAR) model of order 1, in this case $\hat{S}_T$ is calculated in three steps: Step 1, regress $f(v_t, \hat{\theta}_T)$ on $f(v_{t-1}, \hat{\theta}_T)$ to obtain estimated coefficient matrix $\hat{A}$ and residuals $d_t = f(v_t, \hat{\theta}_T) - \hat{A}f(v_{t-1}, \hat{\theta}_T)$; Step 2, construct $\hat{D}$, an HAC estimator of the long-run variance of d_t; Step 3, $\hat{S}_T = (I - \hat{A})^{-1}\hat{D}\{(I - \hat{A})^{-1}\}'$. Newey and West (1994) argue that the use of a VAR(1) filter suffices to substantially improve the properties of the long-run covariance matrix estimator in most cases encountered in macroeconomics.[19] ◇

Dependence of $\hat{S}_T$ on $\hat{\theta}_T$

As is apparent from the above discussion, the calculation of a consistent estimator for $S(\theta_0)$ requires knowledge of a (consistent) estimator of θ_0. Therefore, in order to calculate a GMM estimator that attains the efficiency bound, a multi-step procedure is used. On the first step, GMM is performed with an arbitrary weighting matrix; this preliminary estimator is then used in the calculation of $\hat{S}_T$. On the second step, GMM estimation is performed with $W_T = \hat{S}_T^{-1}$. For obvious reasons, the resulting estimator is commonly referred to as the *two-step GMM estimator*. Instead of stopping after just two steps, the procedure can be continued so that on the ith step the GMM estimation is performed using $W_T = \hat{S}_T^{-1}$, where $\hat{S}_T$ is based on the estimator from the $(i - 1)$th step. This yields the so-called *iterated GMM estimator*. While two steps are sufficient to attain the efficiency bound, simulation evidence suggests that there are often considerable gains to iteration in the sense of improvements in the quality of asymptotic theory as an approximation to finite sample behaviour; see Hall (2005, Chapter 6). ◇

The distributional result in Proposition 1 can be used as a basis for inference procedures about θ_0. Two types of inference are commonly of interest: confidence intervals for elements of θ_0, and statistics for testing the hypothesis that the parameters satisfy a set of (non)linear restrictions. We consider each in turn; since such inferences are typically performed using the two-step or iterated estimator, we confine attention to this case.

Confidence Interval for a Parameter

Proposition 1(ii) implies that an approximate $100(1 - \alpha)$ per cent confidence interval for $\theta_{0,i}$, the ith element of θ_0, is given by

$$\hat{\theta}_{T,i} \pm z_{\alpha/2}\sqrt{\hat{V}_{T,ii}/T}, \tag{14.13}$$

where $\hat{V}_{T,ii}$ is the $i - i$th element of $\hat{V}_T = [G_T(\hat{\theta}_T)'\hat{S}_T^{-1}G_T(\hat{\theta}_T)]^{-1}$, $\hat{S}_T$ is a consistent estimator of $S(\theta_0)$ and $z_{\alpha/2}$ is the $100(1 - \alpha/2)$th percentile of the standard normal distribution. ◇

Testing Hypotheses about the Parameters

Newey and West (1987a) propose Wald, Lagrange Multiplier (LM) and Difference (D) statistics for testing the null hypothesis that θ_0 satisfies a set of s non-linear restrictions $r(\theta_0) = 0$, where $r(\theta)$ satisfies the conditions imposed in section 3. For brevity, we consider only the Wald test statistic,

$$\mathcal{W}_T = Tr(\hat{\theta}_T)'[R(\hat{\theta}_T)\hat{V}_T R(\hat{\theta}_T)']^{-1}r(\hat{\theta}_T). \tag{14.14}$$

and, as a reminder, $R(\bar{\theta}) = \partial r(\theta)/\partial\theta'|_{\theta=\bar{\theta}}$. Newey and West (1987a) establish that the large sample distribution of $\mathcal{W}_T$ is as follows.

Proposition 2 Large sample behaviour of $\mathcal{W}_T$ Let Assumptions 1, 2, and certain other regularity conditions hold. If $r(\theta_0) = 0$ then $\mathcal{W}_T \xrightarrow{d} \chi^2_s$. where χ^2_s denotes the χ^2 distribution with s degrees of freedom.

Thus, an approximate 100α per cent significance level test of $H_0 : r(\theta_0) = 0$ versus $H_1 : r(\theta_0) \neq 0$ can be performed using the decision rule: reject H_0 if $\mathcal{W}_T > c_s(\alpha)$, where $c_s(\alpha)$ is the $100(1 - \alpha)$th percentile of the χ^2_s distribution.

To illustrate, suppose the aggregate supply equation is estimated based on $E[e_{AS,t}(\phi_0)w_{t-1}]$ – in other words ignoring the restriction on the coefficients implied by (2) – and it is then desired to test if this restriction, $\eta = 1 - \delta$, holds. For consistency with our discussion here, we set this model in our generic notation so that $f(v_t,\theta) = e_{AS,t}(\phi_0)w_{t-1}$ and $\theta = \phi$, implying that $p = 3$ and the individual elements of θ are $\theta_1 = \delta$, $\theta_2 = \eta$ and $\theta_3 = \kappa$. Using this generic notation, the restriction of interest can be written as $r(\theta) = 0$ where $r(\theta) = 1 - \theta_1 - \theta_2$. It follows that $R(\theta)$ is the 1×3 vector $(-1, -1, 0)$. ◇

We conclude this section by summarizing the properties of the restricted GMM estimator defined in Definition 2.[20]

Proposition 3 Large sample behaviour of $\tilde{\theta}_T$ Let Assumptions 1, 2, and certain other regularity conditions hold. (i) If $r(\theta_0) = 0$ then $\tilde{\theta}_T \xrightarrow{p} \theta_0$, but if $r(\theta_0) \neq 0$ then $\tilde{\theta}_T \not\xrightarrow{p} \theta_0$; (ii) If $r(\theta_0) = 0$ then $T^{1/2}(\hat{\theta}_T - \theta_0) \xrightarrow{d} N(0, V_R)$ where $V - V_R$ is a positive semi-definite matrix, and V is defined in Proposition 1.

Proposition 3(i) states that the restricted GMM estimator is only consistent for θ_0 if the restrictions imposed are valid information about θ_0. Proposition 3(ii) states that if we impose valid restrictions, then $T^{1/2}(\tilde{\theta}_T - \theta_0)$ converges to a normal distribution, the variance of which is either smaller than or equal to the variance $T^{1/2}(\hat{\theta}_T - \theta_0)$. The latter implies the restricted estimator is at least as efficient in large samples as its unrestricted counterpart. Taken together, the results in Proposition 3 indicate we are never worse off in large samples from imposing restrictions on the parameters – *provided* they are correct.

5 TESTING THE MODEL SPECIFICATION

The large sample theory in the previous section is predicated on the assumption that the model is correctly specified in the sense that $E[f(v_t, \theta_0)] = 0$. If this assumption is false then the arguments behind Proposition 1 break down, and it is no longer possible to establish the consistency of the estimator. Since the validity of the population moment condition is central to GMM, it is desirable to assess whether the data appear consistent with the restriction implied by the population moment condition. As noted above, if $p = q$ then the first order conditions force $g_T(\hat{\theta}_T) = 0$ irrespective of whether or not (14.1) holds and so the latter cannot be tested directly using the estimated sample moment, $g_T(\hat{\theta}_T)$. However, if $q > p$ then $g_T(\hat{\theta}_T) \neq 0$ because GMM estimation only imposes the identifying restrictions and ignores the overidentifying restrictions. The latter represent $q - p$ restrictions which are true if (14.1) is itself true and can be used as a basis for a test of the model specification. To motivate the most commonly applied test statistic, it is useful to recall two aspects of our discussion above: (a) the GMM minimand measures the distance of $g_T(\theta)$ from zero; (b) the estimated sample moment contains information about overidentifying restrictions. Combining (a) and (b), it can be shown that GMM minimand evaluated at $\hat{\theta}_T$ is a measure of how far the sample is from satisfying the overidentifying restrictions. This leads to *overidentifying restrictions test* statistic,

$$J_T = Tg_T(\hat{\theta}_T)'\hat{S}_T^{-1}g_T(\hat{\theta}_T),$$

where $\hat{\theta}_T$ is the two-step (or iterated) GMM estimator and, once again, $\hat{S}_T$ denotes a consistent estimator of $S(\theta_0)$. The choice of notation reflects a tendency in some articles to refer to this quantity as the 'J-statistic'. Hansen (1982) establishes that the large sample behaviour of J_T is as follows.

Proposition 4 Let Assumptions 1, 2, and certain other regularity conditions hold then $J_T \xrightarrow{d} \chi^2_{q-p}$.

Thus, an approximate 100α per cent significance level test of $H_0: E[f(v_t,\theta_0)] = 0$ versus $H_1: E[f(v_t,\theta_0)] \neq 0$ can be performed using the decision rule: reject H_0 if $J_T > c_{q-p}(\alpha)$; where $c_a(b)$ is defined following Proposition 2.

Notice that J_T is conveniently calculated as the sample size times the two-step (or iterated) GMM minimand evaluated at the associated estimator. The overidentifying restrictions test is the standard model diagnostic within the GMM framework and is routinely reported in applications. Nevertheless, J_T is not able to detect all possible misspecifications of the model. In particular, Ghysels and Hall (1990) show that J_T can be insensitive to misspecification due to neglected parameter variation. This 'blind spot' may be a particular concern in macroeconomic models with time series data as parameter variation is a natural source of potential misspecification, and so it is prudent to complement the overidentifying restrictions test with tests of structural stability; see Chapter 9 in this volume for further discussion of this issue and structural stability testing in macroeconometric models.

6 FINITE SAMPLE PERFORMANCE AND THE CONTINUOUS UPDATING GMM ESTIMATOR

The foregoing discussion has rested upon asymptotic theory. In finite samples, such theory can only provide an approximation. It is therefore important to assess the quality of this approximation in the types of model and sample sizes that are encountered in economics. Intuition suggests that the quality is going to vary from case to case depending on the form of the non-linearity and the dynamic structure. A number of simulation studies have examined this question; see *inter alia* Tauchen (1986), Kocherlakota (1990) and the seven papers included in the July 1996 issue of *Journal of Business and Statistics*. It is beyond the scope of this chapter to provide a comprehensive review of these studies.[21] However, it should be noted that in certain circumstances of interest the quality of the approximation is poor.

There are two possible explanations for the failure of this first order asymptotic theory to provide a good approximation to the behaviour of the estimator in a particular model with a particular data set. First, the key assumptions behind the distribution theory may be valid but the sample may simply not be large enough for the first order asymptotic theory to be a good guide. Second, the key assumptions behind the distribution theory may be inappropriate for the case in hand. Both can occur in macroeconomic models. In the remainder of this section, we focus on an aspect of the structure of estimation that may retard convergence in models where the key assumptions behind GMM are valid. This discussion leads us to a modified version of the estimator known as the *Continuous Updating* GMM (CUGMM) estimator. In the next section, we discuss a scenario in which the poor approximation may be due to the near failure of the key assumptions behind GMM.

So for the rest of this section, we suppose that the population moment condition is valid and θ_0 is first order identified (*that is* Assumption 2 holds). We also focus on the two-step estimator and so set $W_T = \hat{S}_T^{-1}$ and $W = S^{-1}$. To understand why the first asymptotic theory in Proposition 1 may not provide a good approximation in some settings, it is instructive to re-examine the structure of the first order conditions of GMM estimation. Recall from our earlier discussion that GMM can be considered an MM estimator based on the information in (14.11) that is, the information that a certain linear combination of the population moment condition is zero. As seen above, the weights of this linear combination, $G_0'W$, involve unknown matrices that are replaced by their sample analogs in GMM estimation.

However, for the purposes of our discussion here, suppose those weights were actually known and thus that one could obtain an estimator of θ_0 by solving the equations

$$G_0' W g_T(\hat{\theta}_T^*) = 0$$

for $\hat{\theta}_T^*$. Newey and Smith (2004) show that $\hat{\theta}_T^*$ has the same first order asymptotic distribution as $\hat{\theta}_T$ but has better finite sample bias properties; for the purposes of exposition, it is useful to have a name for $\hat{\theta}_T^*$ and we refer to this as the 'ideal' GMM estimator. Further Newey and Smith (2004) trace the source of this comparative advantage to the equations solved for $\hat{\theta}_T^*$ and $\hat{\theta}_T$ as we now describe.

From Assumption 2(i) and $G_0'W$ constant (by definition), it follows that $\hat{\theta}_T^*$ is obtained by solving a set of equations that has the property that

$$E[G(\theta_0)' W g_T(\theta_0)] = 0 \text{ for any } T.$$

Thus, the 'ideal' GMM estimator can be seen to be based on valid information about θ_0 in the sense that $\hat{\theta}_T^*$ solves a set of equations that when evaluated at θ_0 are satisfied in expectation *for any T*.

In contrast, GMM estimation is based on solving the equations $h_T(\theta) = 0$ where $h_T(\theta) = G_T(\theta)' W_T g_T(\theta)$. Since $G_T(\theta_0)' W_T$ are functions of the data, it no longer follows automatically from Assumption 2(i) that $E[h_T(\theta_0)] = 0$: in fact, if $G_T(\theta_0)' W_T$ is correlated with $g_T(\theta_0)$ then $E[h_T(\theta_0)] \neq 0$. In such cases, GMM is based on a set of equations that represent invalid information about θ_0 for finite T and it thus may be anticipated that the GMM estimator is more biased than its 'ideal' counterpart. However, since both the Jacobian and sample moment involve averages, they are converging to constants as $T \to \infty$ and this combined with our assumptions about the limit of W_T ensure that

$$E[G_T(\theta_0)' W_T g_T(\theta_0)] \to 0 \text{ as } T \to \infty$$

In other words, GMM *is* based on a set of equations that represent valid information about θ_0 in the limit as $T \to \infty$.

It should be noted that there are cases in which $E[h_T(\theta_0)] = 0$ and so GMM estimation is based on information that is valid for any T: a leading example is estimation of linear models via instrumental variables with conditionally homoscedastic and symmetrically distributed errors.[22] But such a scenario is the exception rather than the rule. Thus in general, GMM can be viewed as being based on information that is only valid in large samples, and as a result the first order asymptotic theory can be anticipated only to provide a good approximation in large samples.

This aspect of GMM estimation has stimulated research into alternative estimators based on information in the population moment condition. We focus on just one here, the Continuous Updating GMM (CUGMM) estimator proposed by Hansen et al.

(1996), because it is both the most closely related to GMM and also relatively straightforward to apply to time series data. To motivate the form of the CUGMM estimator, we recall that the optimal weighting matrix has been shown to be $S(\theta_0)^{-1}$. It was remarked earlier that this optimal choice is in most cases dependent on θ_0 and that one way to resolve this dependence is to use a multi-step procedure in which $W_T = \hat{S}_T^{-1}$ with $\hat{S}_T$ based on the estimator of θ_0 from the previous step. An alternative way to handle this dependence is estimate θ_0 by minimizing

$$Q_T^{cu}(\theta) = g_T(\theta)' S_T(\theta)^{-1} g_T(\theta),$$

where $S_T(\theta)$ is a (matrix) function of θ such that $S_T(\theta_0) \xrightarrow{p} S(\theta_0)$. Hansen et al. (1996) refer to the resulting estimator as CUGMM and show it has the same limiting distribution as the iterated GMM estimator. However, Newey and Smith (2004) and Anatolyev (2005) demonstrate analytically that the continuous-updating estimator can be expected to exhibit lower finite sample bias than its two-step counterpart. Interestingly, this comparative advantage can be linked back to the first order equations of CUGMM. Donald and Newey (2000) show that the first order conditions of CUGMM take the form

$$\tilde{G}_T(\theta)' S_T(\theta)^{-1} g_T(\theta) = 0,$$

where $\tilde{G}_T(\theta)' S_T(\theta)^{-1}$ can be thought of as estimating the weights $G(\theta_0)' W$. The first order conditions of CUGMM and GMM thus have the same generic form: the crucial difference is that $\tilde{G}_T(\theta)$ is uncorrelated with $g_T(\theta)$ by construction. Recalling that it is the correlation between $G_T(\theta_0)' W_T$ and $g_T(\theta_0)$ that is argued to be the source of the finite sample biases of GMM, it can be anticipated that the CUGMM estimator leads to an estimator whose finite sample behaviour is better approximated by its first order asymptotic distribution.

While it may dominate in terms of statistical properties, it should be noted that CUGMM involves a much more complex minimand than GMM, and thus finding its minimum can be challenging; see Hall (2005, Chapter 3.7) for further discussion and a numerical illustration.

We conclude this section by briefly mentioning two other approaches to improving inference based on GMM in settings where the key assumptions behind the first order asymptotic theory apply. The first such approach is the use of the bootstrap, and this has been explored in the context of GMM by Hall and Horowitz (1996). The second is the use of formal data-based moment selection techniques that are designed to uncover which moments lead to estimators whose finite sample behaviour is best approximated by standard first order asymptotic theory. Since neither approach has been widely employed in macroeconomic applications to our knowledge, we do not explore them in detail here but refer the interested reader to reviews in Hall (2005, Chapters 7.3 and 8.1).

7 WEAK IDENTIFICATION

The first order asymptotic theory in Proposition 1 is predicated on the assumption that θ_0 is first order identified by the population moment condition. In a very influential paper, Nelson and Startz (1990) pointed out that this proviso may not be so trivial in situations which arise in practice and provided the first evidence of the problems it causes for the inference framework we have described above. Their paper has prompted considerable interest and has led to a vast amount of literature on what has become known as *weak identification*. The problem of weak identification can arise in macroeconomic models: for example, Mavroeidis (2005) demonstrates conditions in which it arises in GMM estimation of versions of the aggregate supply curve, equation (14.2) above, in which $E_t[\dot{p}_{t+1}]$ is replaced by $\dot{p}_{t+1}$.[23] In this section, we briefly review the problems caused by weak identification and some potential solutions.

The statistical analysis of GMM under weak identification involves some quite subtle and sophisticated arguments, and so we do not attempt to reproduce them here. Instead, we focus on the essence of the concept. We first consider the consequences of failure of the first order identification condition. Consider the population analog to the first order conditions for GMM estimation. Recall that if θ_0 is first order identified then (14.11) can be thought of as the information on which GMM estimation is based. Now if $rank\{G(\theta_0)\} = \ell < p$ then this set of equations represents only ℓ pieces of unique information about the p elements of θ_0 and is thus insufficient information to tie down their value. As a consequence the first order asymptotic theory in Proposition 1(ii) no longer holds. Consistency may also be lost but this depends on the behaviour of the minimand and the Jacobian.[24] Following Stock and Wright (2000), weak identification is the term used to denote the case in which $E[G_T(\theta_0)] \rightarrow 0$ at a rate of $T^{-1/2}$. In this case, Stock and Wright (2000) show the GMM estimator is not consistent and conventional inference procedures based on first order asymptotic theory are no longer valid.

Kleibergen (2005) proposes inference procedures that can be used irrespective of whether or not the parameter vector is identified. Suppose it is desired to test $H_0: \theta_0 = \bar{\theta}$. The so-called K-statistic for testing this hypothesis is

$$K_T(\bar{\theta}) = Tk_T(\bar{\theta})'\{\tilde{G}_T(\bar{\theta})'\{S_T(\bar{\theta})\}^{-1}\tilde{G}_T(\bar{\theta})\}^{-1}k_T(\bar{\theta})$$

where $k_T(\bar{\theta}) = \tilde{G}_T(\bar{\theta})'\{S_T(\bar{\theta})\}^{-1}g_T(\bar{\theta})$, $S_T(\theta_0)$ is a consistent estimator of $S(\theta_0)$ and $\tilde{G}_T(\bar{\theta})$ is the estimator of the Jacobian employed in CUGMM (discussed in the previous section). Kleibergen (2005) establishes the following.

Proposition 5 If Assumption 1, 2(i) and certain other regularity conditions hold then under $H_0: \theta_0 = \bar{\theta}$, $K_T(\theta^d) \rightarrow \chi^2_p$.

Crucially, the conditions for Proposition 5 do not include any statements about the identification of θ_0. Two aspects of $K_T(\bar{\theta})$ explain this invariance to identification: first, the test is based on the Lagrange Multiplier principle and thus requires an 'estimation' under the null hypothesis and, with this H_0, there is no estimation as the value of θ_0 is completely specified; second, as noted in the previous section, $\tilde{G}_T(\bar{\theta})$ is orthogonal to $g_T(\theta)$ by construction, and this means the behaviour of the sample moment is independent of the behaviour of the Jacobian.[25]

The null hypothesis above involves all elements of θ. Kleibergen (2005) also presents a modified version of the tests that allows the null hypothesis to involve only a subset of the parameters. So suppose $\theta = (\beta', \gamma')'$, where β is $p_\beta \times 1$, and the hypothesis of interest is $H_0 : \beta_0 = \bar{\beta}$. In this case, β_0 may be unidentified but γ_0 must be first order identified *given* β_0; let $\hat{\gamma}^*_T(\bar{\beta})$ denote the two-step GMM estimator of γ_0 based on $E[f(v_t, \theta_0)] = 0$ with $\beta_0 = \bar{\beta}$. Kleibergen's (2005) statistic for $H_0 : \beta_0 = \bar{\beta}$ is of similar structure to $K_T(\theta)$ but is evaluated at $\theta = (\bar{\beta}', \hat{\gamma}(\bar{\beta})')'$, and is shown to converge to a $\chi^2_{p_\beta}$ under this null.[26]

$K_T(\theta)$ can also be inverted to construct a confidence set for θ_0 as follows: the $100(1-\alpha)$ per cent confidence set for θ_0 contains all values of θ for which $K_T(\theta) < c_p(\alpha)$. Notice that unlike the intervals in (14.13), the result is a set of values for the entire parameter vector. A further important difference is that the intervals in (14.13) are of finite length by construction whereas the sets based on $K_T(\theta)$ may be infinite, reflecting cases where the population moment condition is completely uninformative about θ_0, being consistent with all possible values of θ.[27] While such confidence sets have the attractive feature of being robust to failures of identification, the computational burden associated with their calculation increases with p and makes this approach infeasible for large p.

A potential weakness of using the K-statistic is that it may fail to reject $H_0 : \theta_0 = \bar{\theta}$ in circumstances when $E[f(v_t, \bar{\theta})] \neq 0$ and so the parameter value $\bar{\theta}$ is incompatible with the population moment condition, and thus the underlying economic model. To protect against this eventuality, Kleibergen (2005) proposes testing $E[f(v_t, \bar{\theta})] = 0$ using a statistic, $\tilde{J}_T(\bar{\theta})$, that is variant of the overidentifying restrictions. Notice that like the K-statistic, $\tilde{J}_T(\bar{\theta})$ does not involve an estimated value of θ and thus avoids problems that face conventional GMM statistics caused by lack of identification. Kleibergen (2005) shows that under $E[f(v_t, \bar{\theta})] = 0$ the $\tilde{J}_T(\bar{\theta})$ converges to a χ^2_{q-p} distribution. Exploiting the independence of $\tilde{J}_T(\bar{\theta})$ and $K_T(\bar{\theta})$ in large samples, Kleibergen (2005) recommends examining both statistics to assess whether $\bar{\theta}$ is compatable with the model.[28]

8 INFERENCE BASED ON MOMENT INEQUALITIES

So far, we have considered the situation in which the information about the parameter vector consists entirely of a population moment condition. This is by far the leading case in applications to date. However, in recent years, there has been interest in settings where the information consists either partially or exclusively of moment inequalities. For example, moment inequalities naturally arise in models for the behaviour of central banks; for example see Moon and Schorfheide (2009) and Coroneo et al. (2011). In this section, we briefly discuss the *Generalized Moment Selection* method that has been proposed by Andrews and Soares (2010) for performing inference about the parameters in these kinds of models.

Suppose the underlying macroeconomic model implies

$$E[f(v_t, \theta_0)] \begin{cases} = 0 & \text{for } i = 1, 2 \ldots q_1, \\ \geq 0 & \text{for } i = q_1 + 1, \ldots q. \end{cases} \qquad (14.15)$$

Thus, the information about the parameters consists of q_1 population moment conditions – or moment equalities – and $q_2 = q - q_1$ moment inequalities.[29] In what follows, no presumption is made about whether or not this information identifies θ_0.

Andrews and Soares (2010) introduce a framework for constructing confidence sets for θ_0 in this setting based on the inversion of a member of a suitably defined class of test statistics.[30] To summarize the basic ideas behind their approach, we focus on one particular member of this class,

$$A_T(\theta) = \sum_{i=1}^{q_1}\left\{\frac{g_{T,i}(\theta)}{\hat{s}_T^{(i)}(\theta)}\right\}^2 + \sum_{i=q_1+1}^{q}\left\{\frac{[g_{T,i}(\theta)]_-}{\hat{s}_T^{(i)}(\theta)}\right\}^2 \qquad (14.16)$$

where $g_{T,i}(\theta)$ is the ith element of $g_T(\theta)$, $\{\hat{s}_T^{(i)}(\theta)\}^2$ is the (i,i)th element of $S_T(\theta)$ (defined in section 6), $[x]\_=x\mathcal{I}(x<0)$ and $\mathcal{I}(a)$ is an indicator variable that takes the value 1 if the event a occurs and is zero otherwise.

It can be recognized that $A_T(\theta)$ is the sum of two terms, one reflecting the sample moments associated with the moment equalities and one reflecting the the sample moments associated with the moment inequalities. Notice that in both these terms, a sample moment only affects the value of $A_T(\theta)$ if it does not satisfy the restriction in (14.15). So, for example, the first element of $f(\cdot)$ appears in an equality in (14.15) and $g_{T,1}(\theta)$ only impacts on $A_T(\theta)$ if $g_{T,1}(\theta) \neq 0$; and the $(q_1 + 1)$th element of $f(\cdot)$ appears in an inequality in (14.15), and $g_{T,q_1+1}(\theta)$ only impacts on $A_T(\theta)$ if $g_{T,q_1+1}(\theta) < 0$.

The confidence set for θ_0 is then constructed as $\{\bar{\theta}: A_T(\bar{\theta}) < c_T(\alpha)\}$ where $c_T(\alpha)$ is the $100(1 - \alpha)$th percentile of the distribution of $A_T(\bar{\theta})$ under the assumption that (14.15) holds at $\theta_0 = \bar{\theta}$. It turns out that the (limiting) distribution of A_T does not have a convenient form, such as χ^2, because it depends on the degree of *slackness* of each of the inequality constraints, that is, it depends on whether or not each of the moment inequalities is close or far from being an equality. Andrews and Soares (2010) consider a number of ways of calculating $c_T(\alpha)$ and recommend the use of bootstrap methods. Given the construction of $A_T(\theta)$ its value is unaffected by any moment inequality that is far from being an equality. It is therefore desirable not to allow such moments to affect the simulated sampling distribution of the statistic. To achieve this goal, Andrews and Soares (2010) propose a data-based method for determining which moment inequalities are close and which far from being equalities. It is this feature that gives the method the name of 'Generalized Moment Selection'.

NOTES

* I am grateful to Ralf Becker, Mardi Dungey and Kostas Kyriakoulis for useful conversations during the preparation of this chapter, to Laura Coroneo and Denise Osborn for valuable comments on an earlier draft. The support of ESRC grant RES-062-23-1351 is gratefully acknowledged.

1. For example, see Hansen and West (2002).
2. See Ghysels and Hall (2002).
3. For a list of other applications of GMM in macroeconomics and other areas, see Hall (2005, Table 1.1, pp. 3–4).
4. See Pearson (1893, 1894, 1895) and Hall (2005, Chapter 1.2) for summary of this and other statistical antecedents of GMM.
5. For brevity, we omit the constant term from the aggregate supply and monetary policy equations as these terms do not play a role in the subsequent discussion.
6. Zhang et al. (2008) estimate the model using US data. They consider different inflation forecasts obtained from the Survey of Professional Forecasts, the Greenbook published by the Federal Reserve Board and the Michigan survey. The estimates of real GDP are published by the Congressional Budget Office.

7. It should be noted that Zhang et al. (2008) include additional variable on the right-hand side for reasons discussed in their paper. For our purposes here, it suffices to focus on the simpler specification in (14.2).
8. This argument appeals to the Law of Iterated Expectations (e.g. see White, 1984, p. 54) and the fact that if $w_{t-1} \in \mathcal{I}_{t-1}$ then w_{t-1} can be treated as a constant when taking expectations conditional on $\mathcal{I}_{t-1}$.
9. See Hall (2005, Chapter 2).
10. BCM show that this VAR(1) model implies that the observables $(\dot{p}_t, y_t, i_t)$ follow a VARMA(3,2) process; the presence of a VMA component create computational problems that render this representation unattractive as a vehicle for estimating the parameters of the model.
11. See Hall (2005, Chapter 2) for further discussion of this case.
12. See, respectively, '*Eviews 6 User's Guide II*' (http://www.eviews.com) and '*SAS/ETS(R) 9.2 User's Guide*' (http://www.sas.com).
13. It should be noted that *SAS* also offers numerical optimization routines that can be used to obtain GMM estimators but do not provide related statistics of interest: see proc optmodel and proc nlp in '*SAS/OR(R) 9.2 User's Guide: Mathematical Programming*'.
14. See http://www.kostaskyriakoulis.com/. This toolbox is linked to the presentation in Hall (2005).
15. See Hall (2005, Chapter 3.2) for further discussion.
16. For example see Hall (2005, pp. 100–101).
17. Contrary to the claim on Hall (2005, p. 53) this first order condition is not necessary for identification. It is necessary, however, for the first order asymptotic theory of the GMM estimator presented below; see Dovonon and Renault (2011).
18. '$\xrightarrow{p}$' signifies convergence in probability; '$\xrightarrow{d}$' signifies convergence in distribution.
19. See Hall (2005, Chapter 3.5) for discussion of other choices of kernel and other approaches to long-run variance matrix estimation.
20. For brevity we do not present the formula for V_R and refer the interested reader to Hall (2005, Chapter 5.3).
21. The interested reader is referred to Hall (2005, Chapter 6).
22. See Newey and Smith (2004, p. 228).
23. See Kleibergen and Mavroeidis (2009) for an application of the methods described in this section to the aggregate supply curve.
24. The characterization of the GMM estimator via the first order conditions is crucial for the derivation of asymptotic normality result in Proposition 1(ii). However, this characterization is not needed to establish consistency; for example see Hansen (1982).
25. In contrast, if this hypothesis is tested using the conventional Wald, D or LM statistics based for GMM (Newey and West, 1987a and discussed in Section 4 above) then these statistics only have a limiting χ^2_p under the null if θ_0 is identified; see Kleibergen (2005).
26. See Kleibergen (2005) for further details.
27. If θ_0 is not first order identified then the intervals in (14.13) are invalid; see Dufour (1997) for further discussion.
28. See Kleibergen (2005) for further details of the construction of these statistics and some other approaches to inference in this setting.
29. Note that the sign of the inequality does not matter. If the underlying model implies $E[f(v_t, \theta_0)] \leq 0$ then this can be fit within the framework here by rewriting this condition as $E[\tilde{f}(v_t, \theta_0)] \geq 0$ with $\tilde{f}(\cdot) = -f(\cdot)$.
30. Also see Chernozhukov et al. (2007).

REFERENCES

Anatolyev, S. (2005), 'GMM, GEL, Serial correlation, and asymptotic bias', *Econometrica*, **73**, 983–1002.

Andrews, D.W.K. (1991), 'Heteroscedasticity and autocorrelation consistent covariance matrix estimation', *Econometrica*, **59**, 817–58.

Andrews D.W.K. and J.C. Monahan (1992), 'An improved heteroscedasticity and autocorrelation consistent covariance matrix', *Econometrica*, **60**, 953–66.

Andrews, D.W.K. and G. Soares (2010), 'Inference for parameters defined by moment inequalities using Generalized Moment Selection', *Econometrica*, **78**, 119–58.

Bekaert, G., S. Cho and A. Moreno (2010), 'New Keynesian macroeconomics and the term structure', *Journal of Money, Credit and Banking*, **42**, 33–62.

Chamberlain, G. (1987), 'Asymptotic efficiency in estimation with conditional moment restrictions', *Journal of Econometrics*, **34**, 305–34.

Chernozhukov, V., H. Hong and E. Tamer (2007), 'Estimation and confidence regions for parameter sets in econometric models', *Econometrica*, **75**, 1243–84.
Coroneo, L., V. Corradi and P.S. Monteiro (2011), 'Testing for degree of commitment via set-identification', Discussion paper, Economics, School of Social Sciences, University of Manchester, UK.
Donald, S.G. and W.K. Newey (2000), 'A jackknife interpretation of the continuous updating estimator', *Economics Letters*, **67**, 239–43.
Dovonon, P. and E. Renault (2011), 'Testing for common GARCH factors', Discussion paper, Department of Economics, Concordia University, Montreal, Canada.
Dufour, J-M. (1997), 'Some impossibility theorems in econometrics with applications to structural and dynamic models', *Econometrica*, **65**, 1365–87.
Dunn, K. and K.J. Singleton (1986), 'Modelling the term structure of interest rates under nonseparable utility and durable goods', *Journal of Financial Economics*, **17**, 27–55.
Ghysels, E. and A.R. Hall (1990), 'Are consumption-based intertemporal asset pricing models structural?', *Journal of Econometrics*, **45**, 121–39.
Ghysels, E. and A.R. Hall (2002), 'Interview with Lars Peter Hansen', *Journal of Business and Economic Statistics*, **20**, 442–7.
Hall, A.R. (2005), *Generalized Method of Moments*, Oxford: Oxford University Press.
Hall, P. and J.L. Horowitz (1996), 'Bootstrap critical values for tests based on generalized Method of Moments', *Econometrica*, **64**, 891–917.
Hansen, B.E. and K.D. West (2002), 'Generalized Method of Moments and macroeconomics', *Journal of Business and Economic Statistics*, **20**, 460–69.
Hansen, L.P. (1982), 'Large sample properties of Generalized Method of Moments estimators', *Econometrica*, **50**, 1029–54.
Hansen, L.P. and K.S. Singleton (1982), 'Generalized instrumental variables estimation of nonlinear rational expectations models', *Econometrica*, **50**, 1269–86.
Hansen, L.P., J. Heaton and A. Yaron (1996), 'Finite sample properties of some alternative GMM estimators obtained from financial market data', *Journal of Business and Economic Statistics*, **14**, 262–80.
Kleibergen, F. (2005), 'Testing parameters in GMM without assuming that they are identified', *Econometrica*, **73**, 1103–24.
Kleibergen, F. and S. Mavroeidis (2009), 'Weak instrument robust tests in GMM and the new Keynesian Phillips curve', *Journal of Business and Economic Statistics*, **27**, 293–310.
Kocherlakota, N.R. (1990), 'On tests of representative consumer asset pricing models', *Journal of Monetary Economics*, **26**, 285–304.
Mavroeidis, S. (2005), 'Identification issues in forward-looking models estimated by GMM, with an application to the Phillips curve', *Journal of Money, Credit and Banking*, **37**, 421–48.
Miron, J.A. (1986), 'Seasonal fluctuations and the life cycle-permanent income model of consumption', *Journal of Political Economy*, **94**, 1258–79.
Miron, J.A. and S.P. Zeldes (1988), 'Seasonality, cost shocks and the production smoothing model of inventories', *Econometrica*, **56**, 877–908.
Moon, H.R. and F. Schorfheide (2009), 'Estimation with overidentifying inequality moment conditions', *Journal of Econometrics*, **153**, 136–54.
Nelson, C.R. and R. Startz (1990), 'The distribution of the instrumental variables estimator and its *t* ratio when the instrument is a poor one', *Journal of Business*, **63**, S125–S140.
Newey, W.K. and R.J. Smith (2004), 'Higher order properties of GMM and generalized empirical likelihood estimators', *Econometrica*, **72**, 219–56.
Newey, W.K. and K.D. West (1987a), 'Hypothesis testing with efficient method of moments testing', *International Economic Review*, **28**, 777–87.
Newey, W.K. and K.D. West (1987b), 'A simple positive semi-definite heteroscedasticity and autocorrelation consistent covariance matrix', *Econometrica*, **55**, 703–708.
Newey, W.K. and K.D. West (1994), 'Automatic lag selection in covariance matrix estimation', *Review of Economic Studies*, **61**, 631–53.
Pearson, K.S. (1893), 'Asymmetrical frequency curves', *Nature*, **48**, 615–16.
Pearson, K.S. (1894), 'Contributions to the mathematical theory of evolution', *Philosophical Transactions of the Royal Society of London (A)*, **185**, 71–110.
Pearson, K.S. (1895), 'Contributions to the mathematical theory of evolution, II: skew variation', *Philosophical Transactions of the Royal Society of London (A)*, **186**, 343–414.
Pindyck, R. and J. Rotemberg (1983), 'Dynamics factor demands and the effects of energy price shocks', *American Economic Review*, **73**, 1066–79.
Singleton, K.J. (1988), 'Econometric issues in the analysis of equilibrium business cycle models', *Journal of Monetary Economics*, **21**, 361–86.
Stock, J. and J. Wright (2000), 'GMM with weak identification', *Econometrica*, **68**, 1055–96.

Tauchen, G. (1986), 'Statistical properties of Generalized Method of Moments estimators of structural parameters obtained from financial market data', *Journal of Business and Economic Statistics*, **4**, 397–416.
White, H. (1984), *Asymptotic Theory for Econometricians*, New York: Academic Press.
Zhang, C., D. Osborn and D. Kim (2008), 'The new Keynesian Phillips curve: from sticky inflation to sticky prices', *Journal of Money, Credit and Banking*, **40**, 667–99.

15 Maximum likelihood estimation of time series models: the Kalman filter and beyond

Tommaso Proietti and Alessandra Luati

1 INTRODUCTION

The purpose of this chapter is to provide a comprehensive treatment of likelihood inference for state space models. These are a class of time series models relating an observable time series to quantities called states, which are characterized by a simple temporal dependence structure, typically a first order Markov process.

The states sometimes have substantial interpretation. Key estimation problems in economics concern latent variables, such as the output gap, potential output, the non-accelerating inflation rate of unemployment, or NAIRU, core inflation, and so forth. Time-varying volatility, which is quintessential to finance, is also an important feature in macroeconomics. In the multivariate framework relevant features can be common to different series, meaning that the driving forces of a particular feature and/or the transmission mechanism are the same.

The main macroeconomic applications of state space models have dealt with the following topics.

- The extraction of signals such as trends and cycles in macroeconomic time series: see Watson (1986), Clark (1987), Harvey and Jäger (1993), Hodrick and Prescott (1997), Morley et al. (2003), Proietti (2006), Luati and Proietti (2010).
- Dynamic factor models: for the extraction of a single index of coincident indicators see Stock and Watson (1989) and Frale et al. (2011), and for large dimensional systems see Jungbacker et al. (2011).
- Stochastic volatility models: see Shephard (2005) and Stock and Watson (2007) for applications to US inflation.
- Time varying autoregressions with stochastic volatility: see Primiceri (2005); Cogley et al. (2010).
- Structural change in macroeconomics: see Kim and Nelson (1999); Giordani et al. (2007).
- The class of dynamic stochastic general equilibrium (DSGE) models: see Sargent (1989); Fernandez-Villaverde and Rubio-Ramirez (2005); Smets and Wouters (2003); Fernandez-Villaverde (2010).

Leading macroeconomics books, such as Ljungqvist and Sargent (2004) and Canova (2007), provide a comprehensive treatment of state space models and related methods. The above list of references and topics is all but exhaustive and the literature has been growing at a fast rate.

State space methods are tools for inference in state space models, since they allow one to estimate any unknown parameters along with the states, to assess the uncertainty of the estimates, to perform diagnostic checking, to forecast future states and observations, and so forth.

The Kalman filter (Kalman, 1960; Kalman and Bucy, 1961) is a fundamental algorithm for the statistical treatment of a state space model. Under the Gaussian assumption, it produces the minimum mean square estimator of the state vector along with its mean square error matrix, conditional on past information; this is used to build the one-step-ahead predictor of y_t and its mean square error matrix. Due to the independence of the one-step-ahead prediction errors, the likelihood can be evaluated via the prediction error decomposition.

The objective of this chapter is to review this algorithm and discuss maximum likelihood inference, starting from the linear Gaussian case and discussing the extensions to a non-linear and non-Gaussian framework. Due to space constraints we shall provide a self-contained treatment of the standard case and an overview of the possible modes of inference in the non-linear and non-Gaussian case. For more details we refer the reader to Jazwinski (1970); Anderson and Moore (1979); Hannan and Deistler (1988); Harvey (1989); West and Harrison (1997); Kitagawa and Gersch (1996); Kailath et al. (2000); Durbin and Koopman (2012); Harvey and Proietti (2005); Cappé et al. (2005) and Kitagawa (2010).

The chapter is structured as follows. Section 2 introduces state space models and provides the state space representation of some commonly applied linear processes, such as univariate and multivariate autoregressive moving average processes (ARMA) and dynamic factor models. Section 3 is concerned with the basic tool for inference in state space models, that is the Kalman filter. Maximum likelihood estimation is the topic of section 4, which discusses the profile and marginal likelihood, when non-stationary and regression effects are present; section 5 deals with estimation by the Expectation Maximization (EM) algorithm. Section 6 considers inference in non-linear and non-Gaussian models along with stochastic simulation methods and new directions of research. Section 7 concludes the chapter.

2 STATE SPACE MODELS

We begin our treatment with the linear Gaussian state space model. Let $\mathbf{y}_t$ denote an $N \times 1$ vector time series related to an $m \times 1$ vector of unobservable components, the states, α_t, by the so-called measurement equation,

$$\mathbf{y}_t = \mathbf{z}_t\alpha_t + \mathbf{G}_t\varepsilon_t, \quad t = 1,\ldots,n, \tag{15.1}$$

where $\mathbf{Z}_t$ is an $N \times m$ matrix, $\mathbf{G}_t$ is $N \times g$ and $\varepsilon_t \sim \text{NID}(0, \sigma^2\mathbf{I}_g)$.

The evolution of the states is governed by the transition equation:

$$\alpha_{t+1} = \mathbf{T}_t\alpha_t + \mathbf{H}_t\varepsilon_t, \quad t = 1,2,\ldots,n, \tag{15.2}$$

where the transition matrix $\mathbf{T}_t$ is $m \times m$ and $\mathbf{H}_t$ is $m \times g$.

The specification of the state space model is completed by the initial conditions concerning the distribution of α_1. In the sequel we shall assume that this distribution is independent of $\varepsilon_t, \forall t \geq 1$ When the system is time-invariant and α_t is stationary (the eigenvalues of the transition matrix, $\mathbf{T}$, are inside the unit circle), the initial conditions are provided by the unconditional mean and covariance matrix of the state vector, $\mathbf{E}(\alpha_1) = \mathbf{0}$ and $\text{Var}(\alpha_1) = \sigma^2\mathbf{P}_{1|0}$, satisfying the matrix equation $\mathbf{P}_{1|0} = \mathbf{TP}_{1|0}\mathbf{T}' + \mathbf{HH}'$. Initialization of the system turns out to be a relevant issue when non-stationary components are present.

Often the models are specified in a way that the measurement and transition equation disturbances are uncorrelated, that is $\mathbf{H}_t\mathbf{G}_t' = 0, \forall t$.

The system matrices, $\mathbf{Z}_t$, $\mathbf{G}_t$, $\mathbf{T}_t$, and $\mathbf{H}_t$, are non-stochastic, that is they are allowed to vary over time in a deterministic fashion, and are functionally related to a set of hyperparameters, $\theta \in \Theta \subseteq \mathbb{R}^k$, which are usually unknown. If the system matrices are constant, that is $\mathbf{Z}_t = \mathbf{Z}, \mathbf{G}_t = \mathbf{G}, \mathbf{T}_t = \mathbf{T}$ and $\mathbf{H}_t = \mathbf{H}$, the state space model is time invariant.

2.1 State Space Representation of ARMA Models

Let y_t be a scalar time series with ARMA(p, q) representation:

$$y_t = \phi_1 y_{t-1} + \cdots + \phi_p y_{t-p} + \xi_t + \theta_1\xi_{t-1} + \cdots + \theta_q\xi_{t-q}, \xi_t \sim \text{NID}(0,\sigma^2),$$

or $\phi(L)y_t = \theta(L)\xi_t$, where L is the lag operator, and $\phi(L) = 1 - \phi_1 L - \cdots - \phi_p L^p$, $\theta(L) = 1 + \theta_1 L + \cdots + \theta_q L^q$.

The state space representation proposed by Pearlman (1980) (see Burridge and Wallis, 1988 and de Jong and Penzer, 2004), is based on $m = \max(p,q)$ state elements and it is such that $\varepsilon_t = \xi_t$. The time invariant system matrices are

$$\mathbf{Z} = [1,\ \mathbf{0}'_{m-1}], \mathbf{G} = 1, \mathbf{T} = \begin{bmatrix} \phi_1 & 1 & 0 & \cdots & 0 \\ \phi_2 & 0 & 1 & \ddots & 0 \\ \vdots & \vdots & \ddots & \ddots & 0 \\ \vdots & \cdots & \cdots & 0 & 1 \\ \phi_m & 0 & \cdots & \cdots & 0 \end{bmatrix}, \mathbf{H} = \begin{bmatrix} \theta_1 + \phi_1 \\ \theta_2 + \phi_2 \\ \vdots \\ \vdots \\ \theta_m + \phi_m \end{bmatrix}.$$

If y_t is stationary, the eigenvalues of $\mathbf{T}$ are inside the unit circle (and vice versa). State space representations are not unique. The representation adopted by Harvey (1989) is based on $m = \max(p, q + 1)$ states and has $\mathbf{Z}, \mathbf{T}$ as above, but $\mathbf{G} = 0$ and $\mathbf{H}' = [1, \theta_1, \ldots, \theta_m]$. The canonical observable representation in Brockwell and Davis (1991) has minimal state dimension, $m = \max(p,q)$, and

$$\mathbf{Z} = [1,\ \mathbf{0}'_{m-1}], \mathbf{G} = 1, \mathbf{T} = \begin{bmatrix} 0 & 1 & 0 & \cdots & 0 \\ 0 & 0 & 1 & \ddots & 0 \\ \vdots & \vdots & \ddots & \ddots & 0 \\ \vdots & \cdots & \cdots & 0 & 1 \\ \phi_m & \phi_{m-1} & \cdots & \cdots & \phi_1 \end{bmatrix}, \mathbf{H} = \begin{bmatrix} \psi_1 \\ \psi_2 \\ \vdots \\ \vdots \\ \psi_m \end{bmatrix},$$

where ψ_j are the coefficients of the Wold polynomial $\psi(L) = \theta(L)/\phi(L)$. The virtue of this representation is that $\boldsymbol{\alpha}_t = [\tilde{y}_{t|t-1}, \tilde{y}_{t+1|t-1}, \ldots, \tilde{y}_{t+m-1|t-1}]'$ where $\tilde{y}_{t+j|t-1} = \mathrm{E}(y_{t+j}|Y_{t-1}), Y_t = \{y_t, y_{t-1}, \ldots\}$. In fact, the transition equation is based on the forecast updating recursions:

$$\tilde{y}_{t+j|t} = \tilde{y}_{t+j|t-1} + \psi_j \xi_t, j = 1, \ldots, m-1, \tilde{y}_{t+m|t} = \sum_{k=1}^{m} \phi_k \tilde{y}_{t+k-1|t-1} + \psi_m \xi_t.$$

2.2 AR and MA Approximations of Fractional Noise

The fractional noise process $(1-L)^d y_t = \xi_t, \xi_t \sim \mathrm{NID}(0, \sigma^2)$, is stationary if $d < 0.5$. Unfortunately such a process is not finite order Markovian and does not admit a state space representation with finite m. Chan and Palma (1998) obtained the finite m AR and MA approximations by truncating respectively the AR polynomial $\phi(L) = (1-L)^d = 1 - \sum_{j=1}^{\infty} \frac{\Gamma(j+d)}{\Gamma(d)\Gamma(j+1)} L^j$ and the MA polynomial $\theta(L) = (1-L)^{-d} = 1 + \sum_{j=1}^{\infty} \frac{\Gamma(j-d)}{\Gamma(-d)\Gamma(j+1)} L^j$. Here $\Gamma(\cdot)$ is the Gamma function. A better option is to obtain the first m AR coefficients applying the Durbin–Levinson algorithm to the Toeplitz variance covariance matrix of the process.

2.3 AR(1) Plus Noise Model

Consider an AR(1) process μ_t observed with error:

$$\begin{aligned} y_t &= \mu_t + \varepsilon_t, & \varepsilon_t &\sim \mathrm{NID}(0, \sigma_\varepsilon^2), \\ \mu_{t+1} &= \phi\mu_t + \eta_t, & \eta_t &\sim \mathrm{NID}(0, \sigma_\eta^2), \end{aligned}$$

where $|\phi| < 1$ to ensure stationarity and $\mathrm{E}(\eta_t \varepsilon_{t+s}) = 0, \forall s$. The initial condition is $\mu_1 \sim \mathrm{N}(\tilde{\mu}_{1|0}, P_{1|0})$.

Assuming that the process has started in the indefinitely remote past $\tilde{\mu}_{1|0} = 0, P_{1|0} = \frac{\sigma_\eta^2}{1-\phi^2}$. Alternatively, we may assume that the process started at time 1, so that $P_{1|0} = 0$ and μ_1 is a fixed (though possibly unknown) value.

If $\sigma_\varepsilon^2 = 0$ then $y_t \sim$ AR(1); on the other hand, if $\sigma_\eta^2 = 0$ then $y_t \sim \mathrm{NID}(0, \sigma_\varepsilon^2)$; finally, if $\phi = 0$ then the model is not identifiable.

When $\phi = 1$, the local level (random walk plus noise) model is obtained.

2.4 Time Varying AR Models

Consider the time varying vector autoregressive (VAR) model $\mathbf{y}_t = \sum_{k=1}^{p} \Phi_{kt}\mathbf{y}_{t-k} + \boldsymbol{\xi}_t$, $\boldsymbol{\xi}_t = \mathrm{N}(\mathbf{0}, \Sigma_t)$ with random walk evolution for the coefficients:

$$\mathrm{vec}(\boldsymbol{\Phi}_{k,t+1}) = \mathrm{vec}(\boldsymbol{\Phi}_{k,t}) + \eta_{kt}, \eta_{kt} \sim NID(0, \Sigma_\eta);$$

(see Primiceri, 2005). Often Σ_η is taken as a scalar or a diagonal matrix.

The model can be cast in state space form, setting $\alpha_t = [\mathrm{vec}(\Phi_1)', \ldots, \mathrm{vec}(\Phi p)']'$, $\mathbf{Z}_t = [(\mathbf{y}'_{t-1} \otimes \mathbf{I}), \ldots, (y'_{t-p} \otimes \mathbf{I})]$, $\mathbf{G} = \Sigma^{1/2}$, $\mathbf{T}_t = \mathbf{I}$, $\mathbf{H} = \Sigma_\eta^{1/2}$.

Time varying volatility is incorporated by writing $\mathbf{G}_t = \mathbf{C}_t\mathbf{D}_t$ where $\mathbf{C}_t$ is lower diagonal with unit diagonal elements and $c_{ij,t+1} = c_{ij,t} + \zeta_{ij,t}, j < i, \zeta_{ij,t} \sim \mathrm{NID}(0, \sigma_\zeta^2)$, and $\mathbf{D}_t = \mathrm{diag}(d_{it}, i = 1, \ldots, N)$, $\ln d_{i,t+1} = \ln d_{it} + \kappa_{it}$, $\kappa_{it} \sim \mathrm{NID}(0, \sigma_\kappa^2)$. Allowing for time varying volatility makes the model non-linear.

2.5 Dynamic Factor Models

A simple model is $\mathbf{y}_t = \boldsymbol{\Lambda}\mathbf{f}_t + \mathbf{u}_t$ where $\boldsymbol{\Lambda}$ is the matrix of factor loadings, $\mathbf{f}_t$ are q common factors admitting a VAR representation, $\mathbf{f}_{t+1} = \boldsymbol{\Phi}\mathbf{f}_t + \eta_t, \eta_t \sim \mathrm{N}(\mathbf{0}, \Sigma_\eta)$ (see Sargent and Sims, 1977; Stock and Watson, 1989). For identification we need to impose $q(q + 1)/2$ restrictions (see Geweke and Singleton, 1981). One possibility is to set $\Sigma_\eta = \mathbf{I}$; alternatively, we could set $\boldsymbol{\Lambda}$ equal to a lower triangular matrix with 1's on the main diagonal.

2.6 Contemporaneous and Future Representations

The transition equation (15.2) has been specified in the so-called future form; in some treatment, for example Harvey (1989) and West and Harrison (1989, 1997), the contemporaneous form of the model is adopted, with (15.2) replaced by $\boldsymbol{\alpha}_t^* = \mathbf{T}_t\boldsymbol{\alpha}_{t-1}^* + \mathbf{H}_t\varepsilon_t$, $t = 1, \ldots, n$, whereas the measurement equation retains the form $\mathbf{y}_t = \mathbf{Z}^*\boldsymbol{\alpha}_t^* + \mathbf{G}^*\varepsilon_t$. The initial conditions are usually specified in terms of $\boldsymbol{\alpha}_0^* \sim \mathrm{N}(\mathbf{0}, \sigma^2\mathbf{P}_0)$, which is assumed to be distributed independently of $\varepsilon_t, \forall t \geq 1$.

Simple algebra shows that we can reformulate the model in future form (15.1)–(15.2) with $\boldsymbol{\alpha}_t = \boldsymbol{\alpha}_{t-1}^*$, $\mathbf{Z} = \mathbf{Z}^*\mathbf{T}^*$, $\mathbf{G} = \mathbf{G}^* + \mathbf{Z}^*\mathbf{H}^*$.

For instance, consider the AR(1) plus noise model in contemporaneous form, specified as $y_t = \mu_t^* + \varepsilon_t^*$, $\mu_t^* = \phi\mu_{t-1}^* + \eta_t^*$, with ε_t^* and η_t^* mutually and serially independent. Substituting from the transition equation, $y_t = \mu_{t-1}^* + \eta_t^* + \varepsilon_t^*$, and setting $\mu_t = \mu_{t-1}^*$, we can rewrite the model in future form, but the disturbances $\varepsilon_t = \eta_t^* + \varepsilon_t^*$ and $\eta_t = \eta_t^*$ will be (positively) correlated.

2.7 Fixed Effects and Explanatory Variables

The linear state space model can be extended to introduce fixed and regression effects. There are essentially two ways for handling them.

If we let $\mathbf{X}_t$ and $\mathbf{W}_t$ denote fixed and known matrices of dimension $N \times k$ and $m \times k$, respectively, the state space form can be generalized as follows:

$$\mathbf{y}_t = \mathbf{Z}_t\boldsymbol{\alpha}_t + \mathbf{X}_t\boldsymbol{\beta} + \mathbf{G}_t\varepsilon_t, \quad \boldsymbol{\alpha}_{t+1} = \mathbf{T}_t\boldsymbol{\alpha}_t + \mathbf{W}_t\boldsymbol{\beta} + \mathbf{H}_t\varepsilon_t. \tag{15.3}$$

In the sequel we shall express the initial state vector in terms of the vector $\boldsymbol{\beta}$ as follows:

$$\boldsymbol{\alpha}_1 = \tilde{\boldsymbol{\alpha}}^*_{1|0} + \mathbf{W}_0\boldsymbol{\beta} + \mathbf{H}_0\varepsilon_0, \varepsilon_0 \sim \mathrm{N}(\mathbf{0}, \sigma^2\mathbf{I}), \tag{15.4}$$

where $\tilde{\boldsymbol{\alpha}}^*_{1|0}$, $\mathbf{W}_0$, $\mathbf{H}_0$, are known quantities.

Alternatively, $\boldsymbol{\beta}$ is included in the state vector and the state space model becomes:

$$\mathbf{y}_t = \mathbf{Z}^\dagger_t\boldsymbol{\alpha}^\dagger_t + \mathbf{G}_t\varepsilon_t, \quad \boldsymbol{\alpha}^\dagger_{t+1} = \mathbf{T}^\dagger_t\boldsymbol{\alpha}^\dagger_t + \mathbf{H}^\dagger_t\varepsilon_t$$

where

$$\boldsymbol{\alpha}^\dagger_t = \begin{bmatrix}\boldsymbol{\alpha}_t \\ \boldsymbol{\beta}_t\end{bmatrix}, \mathbf{Z}^\dagger_t = [\mathbf{Z}_t\ \mathbf{X}_t], \mathbf{T}^\dagger_t = \begin{bmatrix}\mathbf{T}_t & \mathbf{W}_t \\ \mathbf{0} & \mathbf{I}_k\end{bmatrix}, \mathbf{H}^\dagger_t = \begin{bmatrix}\mathbf{H}_t \\ \mathbf{0}\end{bmatrix}$$

This representation opens the way to the treatment of $\boldsymbol{\beta}$ as a time varying vector.

3 THE KALMAN FILTER

Consider a stationary state space model with no fixed effect (15.1)–(15.2) with initial condition $\boldsymbol{\alpha}_1 \sim \mathrm{N}(\mathbf{0}, \sigma^2\mathbf{P}_{1|0})$, independent of ε_t, $t \geq 1$, and define $\mathbf{Y}_t = \{\mathbf{y}_1, \mathbf{y}_2, \ldots, \mathbf{y}_t\}$, the information set up to and including time t, $\tilde{\boldsymbol{\alpha}}_{t|t-1} = \mathrm{E}(\boldsymbol{\alpha}_t|\mathbf{Y}_{t-1})$, and $\mathrm{Var}(\boldsymbol{\alpha}_t|\mathbf{Y}_{t-1}) = \sigma^2\mathbf{P}_{t|t-1}$.

The Kalman filter (KF) is the following recursive algorithm: for $t = 1, \ldots, n$,

$$\nu_t = \mathbf{y}_t - \mathbf{Z}_t\tilde{\boldsymbol{\alpha}}_{t|t-1}, \quad \mathbf{F}_t = \mathbf{Z}_t\mathbf{P}_{t|t-1}\mathbf{Z}'_t + \mathbf{G}_t\mathbf{G}'_t,$$

$$\mathbf{K}_t = (\mathbf{T}_t\mathbf{P}_{t|t-1}\mathbf{Z}'_t + \mathbf{H}_t\mathbf{G}'_t)\mathbf{F}_t^{-1},$$

$$\tilde{\boldsymbol{\alpha}}_{t+1|t} = \mathbf{T}_t\tilde{\boldsymbol{\alpha}}_{t|t-1} + \mathbf{K}_t\nu_{t1}, \quad \mathbf{P}_{t+1|t} - \mathbf{T}_t\mathbf{P}_{t|t-1}\mathbf{T}'_t + \mathbf{H}_t\mathbf{H}'_t - \mathbf{K}_t\mathbf{F}_t\mathbf{K}'_t \tag{15.5}$$

Hence, the KF computes recursively the optimal predictor of the states and thereby of $\mathbf{y}_t$ conditional on past information as well as the variance of their prediction error. The vector $\mathbf{v}_t = \mathbf{y}_t - \mathrm{E}(\mathbf{y}_t|\mathbf{Y}_{t-1})$ is the time t innovation, that is the new information in $\mathbf{y}_t$ that could not be predicted from knowledge of the past, also known as the one-step-ahead prediction error; $\sigma^2\mathbf{F}_t$ is the prediction error variance at time t, that is $\mathrm{Var}(\mathbf{y}_t|\mathbf{Y}_{t-1})$. The one-step-ahead predictive distribution is $\mathbf{y}_t|\mathbf{Y}_{t-1} \sim \mathrm{N}(\mathbf{Z}_t\tilde{\boldsymbol{\alpha}}_{t|t-1}, \sigma^2\mathbf{F}_t)$. The matrix $\mathbf{K}_t$ is sometimes referred to as the Kalman gain.

3.1 Proof of the Kalman Filter

Let us assume that $\tilde{\boldsymbol{\alpha}}_{t|t-1}$, $\mathbf{P}_{t|t-1}$ are given at the tth run of the KF. The available information set is $\mathbf{Y}_{t-1}$. Taking the conditional expectation of both sides of the measurement equations yields $\tilde{\mathbf{y}}_{t|t-1} = \mathrm{E}(\mathbf{y}_t|\mathbf{Y}_{t-1}) = \mathbf{Z}_t\tilde{\boldsymbol{\alpha}}_{t|t-1}$. The innovation at time t is $\mathbf{v}_t = \mathbf{y}_t - \mathbf{Z}_t\tilde{\boldsymbol{\alpha}}_{t|t\ 1} = \mathbf{Z}_t(\boldsymbol{\alpha}_t - \tilde{\boldsymbol{\alpha}}_{t|t\ 1}) + \mathbf{G}_t\varepsilon_t$. Moreover, $\mathrm{Var}(\mathbf{y}_t|\mathbf{Y}_{t\ 1}) = \sigma^2\mathbf{F}_t$, where $\mathbf{F}_t = \mathbf{Z}_t\mathbf{P}_{t|t-1}\mathbf{Z}_t' + \mathbf{G}_t\mathbf{G}_t'$. From the transition equation, $\mathrm{E}(\boldsymbol{\alpha}_{t+1}|\mathbf{Y}_{t-1}) = \mathbf{T}_t\tilde{\boldsymbol{\alpha}}_{t|t-1}$ $\mathrm{Var}(\boldsymbol{\alpha}_{t+1}|\mathbf{Y}_{t-1}) = \mathrm{Var}[\mathbf{T}_t(\boldsymbol{\alpha}_t - \tilde{\boldsymbol{\alpha}}_{t|t-1}) + \mathbf{H}_t\varepsilon_t] = \sigma^2(\mathbf{T}_t\mathbf{P}_{t|t-1}\mathbf{T}_t' + \mathbf{H}_t\mathbf{H}_t')$, and $\mathrm{Cov}(\boldsymbol{\alpha}_{t+1}, \mathbf{y}_t|\mathbf{Y}_{t-1}) = \sigma^2(\mathbf{T}_t\mathbf{P}_{t|t-1}\mathbf{Z}_t' + \mathbf{H}_t\mathbf{G}_t')$.

The joint conditional distribution of $(\boldsymbol{\alpha}_{t+1}, \mathbf{y}_t)$ is thus:

$$\begin{array}{c}\alpha_{t+1}\\ \mathbf{y}_t\end{array}\Bigg|\mathbf{Y}_{t-1} \sim \mathrm{N}\left[\begin{pmatrix}\mathbf{T}_t\tilde{\boldsymbol{\alpha}}_{t|t-1}\\ \mathbf{Z}_t\tilde{\boldsymbol{\alpha}}_{t|t-1}\end{pmatrix}, \sigma^2\begin{pmatrix}\mathbf{T}_t\mathbf{P}_{t|t-1}\mathbf{T}_t' + \mathbf{H}_t\mathbf{H}_t', & \mathbf{T}_t\mathbf{P}_{t|t-1}\mathbf{Z}_t' + \mathbf{H}_t\mathbf{G}_t'\\ \mathbf{Z}_t\mathbf{P}_{t|t-1}\mathbf{T}_t' + \mathbf{G}_t\mathbf{H}_t', & \mathbf{F}_t\end{pmatrix}\right],$$

which implies $\boldsymbol{\alpha}_{t+1}|\mathbf{Y}_{t-1}, \mathbf{y}_t \equiv \boldsymbol{\alpha}_{t+1}|\mathbf{Y}_t \sim \mathrm{N}(\tilde{\boldsymbol{\alpha}}_{t+1|t}, \sigma^2\mathbf{P}_{t+1|t})$, with $\tilde{\boldsymbol{\alpha}}_{t+1|t} = \mathbf{T}_t\tilde{\boldsymbol{\alpha}}_{t|t-1} + \mathbf{K}_t\boldsymbol{\nu}_t$, $\mathbf{K}_t = (\mathbf{T}_t\mathbf{P}_{t|t-1}\mathbf{Z}_t' + \mathbf{H}_t\mathbf{G}_t')\mathbf{F}_t^{-1}$, $\mathbf{P}_{t+1|t} = \mathbf{T}_t\mathbf{P}_{t|t-1}\mathbf{T}_t' + \mathbf{H}_t\mathbf{H}_t' + \mathbf{K}_t\mathbf{F}_t\mathbf{K}_t'$. Hence, $\mathbf{K}_t = \mathrm{Cov}(\boldsymbol{\alpha}_t, \mathbf{y}_t|\mathbf{Y}_{t-1})$ $[\mathrm{Var}(\mathbf{y}_t|\mathbf{Y}_{t-1})]^{-1}$ is the regression matrix of $\boldsymbol{\alpha}_t$ on the new information $\mathbf{y}_t$, given $\mathbf{Y}_{t-1}$.

3.2 Real Time Estimates and an Alternative Kalman Filter

The updated (real time) estimates of the state vector, $\tilde{\boldsymbol{\alpha}}_{t|t} = \mathrm{E}(\boldsymbol{\alpha}_t|\mathbf{Y}_t)$, and their covariance matrix $\mathrm{Var}(\boldsymbol{\alpha}_t|\mathbf{Y}_t) = \sigma^2\mathbf{P}_{t|t}$ are:

$$\tilde{a}_{t|t} = \tilde{a}_{t|t-1} + \mathbf{P}_{t|t-1}\mathbf{Z}_t'\mathbf{F}_t^{-1}\boldsymbol{\nu}_t, \quad \mathbf{P}_{t|t} = \mathbf{P}_{t|t-1} - \mathbf{P}_{t|t-1}\mathbf{Z}_t'\mathbf{F}_t^{-1}\mathbf{Z}_t\mathbf{P}_{t|t-1}. \tag{15.6}$$

The proof of (15.6) is straightforward. We start writing the joint distribution of the states and the last observation, given the past:

$$\begin{array}{c}\boldsymbol{\alpha}_t\\ \mathbf{y}_t\end{array}\Bigg|\mathbf{Y}_{t-1} \sim \mathrm{N}\left[\begin{pmatrix}\tilde{\boldsymbol{\alpha}}_{t|t-1}\\ \mathbf{Z}_t\tilde{\boldsymbol{\alpha}}_{t|t-1}\end{pmatrix}, \sigma^2\begin{pmatrix}\mathbf{P}_{t|t-1}, & \mathbf{P}_{t|t-1}\mathbf{Z}_t'\\ \mathbf{Z}_t\mathbf{P}_{t|t-1}, & \mathbf{F}_t\end{pmatrix}\right],$$

whence it follows $\boldsymbol{\alpha}_t|\mathbf{Y}_{t-1}, \mathbf{y}_t \equiv \boldsymbol{\alpha}_t|\mathbf{Y}_t \sim \mathrm{N}(\tilde{\boldsymbol{\alpha}}_{t|t}, \sigma^2\mathbf{P}_{t|t})$ with (15.6) providing, respectively,

$$\mathrm{E}(\boldsymbol{\alpha}_t|\mathbf{Y}_t) = \mathrm{E}(\boldsymbol{\alpha}_t|\mathbf{Y}_{t-1}) + \mathrm{Cov}(\boldsymbol{\alpha}_t, \mathbf{y}_t|\mathbf{Y}_{t-1})[\mathrm{Var}(\mathbf{y}_t|\mathbf{Y}_{t-1})]^{-1}[\mathbf{y}_t - \mathrm{E}(\mathbf{y}_t|\mathbf{Y}_{t-1})],$$

$$\mathrm{Var}(\boldsymbol{\alpha}_t|\mathbf{Y}_t) = \mathrm{Var}(\boldsymbol{\alpha}_t|\mathbf{Y}_{t-1}) - \mathrm{Cov}(\boldsymbol{\alpha}_t, \mathbf{y}_t|\mathbf{Y}_{t-1})[\mathrm{Var}(\mathbf{y}_t|\mathbf{Y}_{t-1})]^{-1}\mathrm{Cov}(\mathbf{y}_t, \boldsymbol{\alpha}_t|\mathbf{Y}_{t-1}).$$

The KF recursions for the states can be broken up into an updating step, followed by a prediction step: for $t = 1, \ldots, n$,

$$\begin{aligned}
\boldsymbol{\nu}_t &= \mathbf{y}_t - \mathbf{Z}_t\tilde{\boldsymbol{\alpha}}_{t|t-1}, & \mathbf{F}_t &= \mathbf{Z}_t\mathbf{P}_{t|t-1}\mathbf{Z}_t' + \mathbf{G}_t\mathbf{G}_t',\\
\tilde{\boldsymbol{\alpha}}_{t|t} &= \tilde{\boldsymbol{\alpha}}_{t|t-1} + \mathbf{P}_{t|t-1}\mathbf{Z}_t'\mathbf{F}_t^{-1}\boldsymbol{\nu}_t, & \mathbf{P}_{t|t} &= \mathbf{P}_{t|t-1} - \mathbf{P}_{t|t-1}\mathbf{Z}_t'\mathbf{F}_t^{-1}\mathbf{Z}_t\mathbf{P}_{t|t-1},\\
\tilde{\boldsymbol{\alpha}}_{t+1|t} &= \mathbf{T}_t\tilde{\boldsymbol{\alpha}}_{t|t} + \mathbf{H}_t\mathbf{G}_t'\mathbf{F}_t^{-1}\boldsymbol{\nu}_t, & \mathbf{P}_{t+1|t} &= \mathbf{T}_t\mathbf{P}_{t|t}\mathbf{T}_t' + \mathbf{H}_t\mathbf{H}_t' - \mathbf{H}_t\mathbf{G}_t'\mathbf{F}_t^{-1}\mathbf{G}_t\mathbf{H}_t'.
\end{aligned} \tag{15.7}$$

The last row follows from $\varepsilon_t|\mathbf{Y}_t \sim \mathrm{N}(\mathbf{G}_t'\mathbf{F}_t^{-1}\boldsymbol{\nu}_t, \sigma^2(\mathbf{I} - \mathbf{G}_t'\mathbf{F}_t^{-1}\mathbf{G}_t))$. Also, when $\mathbf{H}_t\mathbf{G}_t' = 0$ (uncorrelated measurement and transition disturbances), the prediction equations in (15.7) simplify considerably.

3.3 Illustration: The AR(1) Plus Noise Model

For the AR(1) plus noise process considered above, let $\sigma^2 = 1$ and $\mu_1 \sim N(\tilde{\mu}_{1|0}, P_{1|0}), \tilde{\mu}_{1|0} = 0, P_{1|0} = \sigma_\eta/(1 - \phi^2)$. Hence, $\tilde{y}_{1|0} = \mathrm{E}(y_1|Y_0) = \tilde{\mu}_{1|0} = 0$, so that at the first update of the KF,

$$\nu_1 = y_1 - \tilde{y}_{1|0} = y_1, \quad F_1 = \mathrm{Var}(y_1|Y_0) = \mathrm{Var}(\nu_1) = P_{1|0} + \sigma_\varepsilon^2 = \frac{\sigma_\eta^2}{1 - \phi^2} + \sigma_\varepsilon^2.$$

Note that F_1 is the unconditional variance of y_t. The updating equations will provide the mean and variance of the distribution of μ_1 given y_1:

$$\tilde{\mu}_{1|1} = \mathrm{E}(\mu_1|Y_1) = \tilde{\mu}_{1|0} + P_{1|0}F_1^{-1}\nu_1 = \frac{\sigma_\eta^2}{1 - \phi^2}\left[\frac{\sigma_\eta^2}{1 - \phi^2} + \sigma_\varepsilon^2\right]^{-1} y_1,$$

$$P_{1|1} = \mathrm{Var}(\mu_1|Y_1) = P_{1|0} - P_{1|0}F_1^{-1}P_{1|0} = \frac{\sigma_\eta^2}{1 - \phi^2}\left[1 - \frac{\sigma_\eta^2/(1 - \phi^2)}{\sigma_\eta^2/(1 - \phi^2) + \sigma_\varepsilon^2}\right].$$

It should be noticed that if $\sigma_\varepsilon^2 = 0$, $\tilde{\mu}_{1|1} = y_1$ and $P_{1|1} = 0$ as the AR(1) process is observed without error. Conversely, when $\sigma_\varepsilon^2 > 0$, y_1 will be shrunk towards zero by an amount depending on the relative contribution of the signal to the total variation.

The one-step-ahead prediction of the state and the state prediction error variance are:

$$\tilde{\mu}_{2|1} = \mathrm{E}(\mu_2|Y_1)\tilde{\mu}_{2|1} = \phi\mathrm{E}(\mu_1|Y_1) + \mathrm{E}(\eta_1|Y_1) = \phi\tilde{\mu}_{1|1},$$

$$P_{2|1} = \mathrm{Var}(\mu_2|Y_1) = \mathrm{E}(\mu_2 - \phi\tilde{\mu}_{1|0})^2 = \mathrm{E}[\phi(\mu_1 - \tilde{\mu}_{1|0}) + \eta_1]^2 = \phi^2 P_{1|1} + \sigma_\eta^2.$$

At time $t = 2$, $\tilde{y}_{2|1} = \mathrm{E}(y_2|Y_1) = \tilde{\mu}_{2|1} = \phi\tilde{\mu}_{1|1}$, so that $\nu_2 = y_2 - \tilde{y}_{2|1} = y_2 - \tilde{\mu}_{2|1}$ and $F_2 = \mathrm{Var}(y_2|Y_1) = \mathrm{Var}(\nu_2) = P_{2|1} + \sigma_\varepsilon^2$, and so forth.

The KF equations (15.5) give for $t = 1, \ldots, n$,

$$\begin{aligned} \nu_t &= y_t - \tilde{\mu}_{t|t-1}, & F_t &= P_{t|t-1} + \sigma_\varepsilon^2, \\ & & K_t &= \phi P_{t|t-1}F_t^{-1}, \\ \tilde{\mu}_{t+1|t} &= \phi\tilde{\mu}_{t|t-1} + K_t\nu_t, & P_{t+1|t} &= \phi^2 P_{t|t-1} + \sigma_\eta^2 - \phi^2 P_{t|t-1}^2 F_t^{-1}. \end{aligned}$$

Notice that $\sigma_\varepsilon^2 = 0 \Rightarrow F_t = P_{t|t-1} = \sigma_\eta^2$ and $\tilde{y}_{t+1|t} = \tilde{\mu}_{t+1|t} = \phi y_t$.

3.4 Non-stationarity and Regression Effects

Consider the local level model,

$$\begin{aligned} y_t &= \mu_t + \varepsilon_t, & \varepsilon_t &\sim \mathrm{NID}(0, \sigma_\varepsilon^2), \\ \mu_{t+1} &= \mu_t + \eta_t, & \eta_t &\sim \mathrm{NID}(0, \sigma_\eta^2), \end{aligned}$$

which is obtained as a limiting case of the above AR(1) plus noise model, letting $\phi = 1$. The signal is a non-stationary process. How do we handle initial conditions in this case? We may alternatively assume:

i Fixed initial conditions: the latent process has started at time $t = 0$ with μ_0 representing a fixed and unknown quantity.
ii Diffuse (random) initial conditions: the process has started in the remote past, so that at time $t = 1$, μ_1 has a degenerate distribution centred at zero, $\tilde{\mu}_{1|0} = 0$, but with variance tending to infinity: $P_{1|0} = \kappa, \kappa \to \infty$.

In the first case, the model is rewritten as $y_t = \mu_0 + \alpha_t + \varepsilon_t, \alpha_{t+1} = \alpha_t + \eta_t$, $\alpha_1 \sim N(\tilde{\alpha}_{1|0}, P_{1|0}), \tilde{\alpha}_{1|0} = 0, P_{1|0} = \sigma^2_\eta$, which is a particular case of the augmented state space model (15.3). The generalized least squares estimator of μ_0 is $\hat{\mu}_0 = (\mathbf{i}'\Sigma^{-1}\mathbf{i})^{-1}\mathbf{i}\Sigma^{-1}\mathbf{y}$, where $\mathbf{y}$ is the stack of the observations, $\mathbf{i}$ is a vector of 1's and $\Sigma = \sigma^2_\varepsilon \mathbf{I} + \sigma^2_\eta CC'$, where C is lower triangular with unit elements. We shall provide a more systematic treatment of the filtering problem for non-stationary processes in section (4.2). In particular, the GLS estimator can be computed efficiently by the augmented KF. For the time being we show that, under diffuse initial conditions, after processing one observation, the usual KF provides proper inferences. At time $t = 1$ the first update of the KF, with initial conditions $\tilde{\mu}_{1|0} = 0$ and $P_{1|0} = \kappa$, gives:

$$\begin{aligned} \nu_1 &= y_1, & F_1 &= \kappa + \sigma^2_\varepsilon, \\ & & K_1 &= \kappa/(\kappa + \sigma^2_\varepsilon), \\ \tilde{\mu}_{2|1} &= y_1\kappa/(\kappa + \sigma^2_\varepsilon) & P_{2|1} &= \sigma^2_\varepsilon\kappa/(\kappa + \sigma^2_\varepsilon) + \sigma^2_\eta. \end{aligned}$$

The distribution of ν_1 is not proper, as y_1 is non-stationary and $F_1 \to \infty$ if we let $\kappa \to \infty$. Also, by letting $\kappa \to \infty$, we obtain the limiting values $K_1 = 1$, $\tilde{\mu}_{2|1} = y_1 P_{2|1} = \sigma^2_\varepsilon + \sigma^2_\eta$. Notice that $P_{2|1}$ no longer depends upon κ and $\nu_2 = y_2 - y_1$ has a proper distribution, $\nu_2 \sim \mathrm{N}(0, F_2)$, with finite $F_2 = \sigma^2_\eta + 2\sigma^2_\varepsilon$. In general, the innovations ν_t, for $t > 1$, can be expressed as a linear combination of $\Delta y_t, \Delta y_{t-1}, \ldots$, and thus they possess a proper distribution.

4 MAXIMUM LIKELIHOOD ESTIMATION

Let $\boldsymbol{\theta} \in \boldsymbol{\Theta} \subseteq \mathbb{R}^k$ denote a vector containing the so-called hyperparameters, that is the vector of structural parameters other than the scale factor σ^2. The state space model depends on $\boldsymbol{\theta}$ via the system matrices $\mathbf{Z}_t = \mathbf{Z}_t(\boldsymbol{\theta}), \mathbf{G}_t = \mathbf{G}_t(\boldsymbol{\theta}), \mathbf{T}_t = \mathbf{T}_t(\boldsymbol{\theta}), \mathbf{H}_t = \mathbf{H}_t(\boldsymbol{\theta})$ and via the initial conditions $\tilde{\boldsymbol{\alpha}}_{1|0}, \mathbf{P}_{1|0}$.

Whenever possible, the constraints in the parameter space $\boldsymbol{\Theta}$ are handled by transformations. Also, one of the variance parameters is attributed the role of the scale parameter σ^2. For instance, for the local level model, we set: $\mathbf{Z} = \mathbf{T} = 1, \mathbf{G} = [1, 0], \sigma^2 = \sigma^2_\varepsilon$, $\varepsilon_t \sim \mathrm{NID}(0, \sigma^2_\varepsilon I_2), \mathbf{H} = [0, e^\theta], \theta = \frac{1}{2}\ln q$, where $q = \sigma^2_\eta/\sigma^2_\varepsilon$ is the signal to noise ratio.

As a second example, consider the Harvey–Jäger (1993) decomposition of US gross domestic product (GDP): $y_t = \mu_t + \psi_t$, where μ_t is a local linear trend and ψ_t is a stochastic cycle. The state space representation has $\boldsymbol{\alpha}_t = [\mu_t \beta_t \psi_t \psi_t^*]'$, $\mathbf{Z} = [1,0,1,0]$, $\mathbf{G} = [0,0,0,0]$, $\mathbf{T} = \text{diag}(\mathbf{T}_\mu, \mathbf{T}_\psi)$,

$$\mathbf{T}_\mu = \begin{bmatrix} 1 & 1 \\ 0 & 1 \end{bmatrix}, \ \mathbf{T}_\psi = \rho \begin{bmatrix} \cos\lambda & \sin\lambda \\ -\sin\lambda & \cos\lambda \end{bmatrix},$$

$$\mathbf{H} = \text{diag}\left(\frac{\sigma_\eta}{\sigma_\kappa}, \frac{\sigma_\zeta}{\sigma_\kappa}, 1, 1\right); \ \varepsilon_t = \begin{bmatrix} \eta_t \sigma_\kappa / \sigma_\eta \\ \zeta_t \sigma_\kappa / \sigma_\zeta \\ \kappa_t \\ \kappa_t^* \end{bmatrix} \sim \text{N}(0, \sigma_\kappa^2 I_4)$$

The parameter ρ is a damping factor, taking values in (0,1), and λ is the cycle frequency, restricted in the range $[0, \pi]$. Moreover, the parameters σ_η^2 and σ_ζ^2 take non-negative values. The parameter σ_κ^2 is the scale of the state space disturbance which will be concentrated out of the likelihood function.

We reparameterize the model in terms of the vector $\boldsymbol{\theta}$, which has four unrestricted elements, so that $\boldsymbol{\Theta} \subseteq \mathbb{R}^4$, related to the original hyperparameters by:

$$\frac{\sigma_\eta^2}{\sigma_\kappa^2} = \exp(2\theta_1), \quad \frac{\sigma_\zeta^2}{\sigma_\kappa^2} = \exp(2\theta_2),$$

$$\rho = \frac{|\theta_3|}{\sqrt{1 + \theta_3^2}}, \quad \lambda = \frac{2\pi}{2 + \exp\theta_4}.$$

Let $\ell(\boldsymbol{\theta}, \sigma^2)$ denote the log-likelihood function (LF), that is the logarithm of the joint density of the sample time series $\{y_1, \ldots, y_n\}$ as a function of the parameters $\boldsymbol{\theta}, \sigma^2$.

The log-likelihood can be evaluated by the prediction error decomposition:

$$\ell(\boldsymbol{\theta}, \sigma^2) = \ln g(\mathbf{y}_1, \ldots, \mathbf{y}_n; \boldsymbol{\theta}, \sigma^2) = \sum_{t=1}^{n} \ln g(\mathbf{y}_t | \mathbf{Y}_{t-1}; \boldsymbol{\theta}, \sigma^2).$$

Here $g(\cdot)$ denotes the Gaussian probability density function. The predictive density $g(\mathbf{y}_t|\mathbf{Y}_{t-1}; \boldsymbol{\theta}, \sigma^2)$ is evaluated with the support of the KF, as $\mathbf{y}_t|\mathbf{Y}_{t-1} \sim \text{NID}(\tilde{\mathbf{y}}_{t|t-1}, \sigma^2\mathbf{F}_t)$, so that

$$\ell(\boldsymbol{\theta}, \sigma^2) = -\frac{1}{2}\left(Nn \ln\sigma^2 + \sum_{t=1}^{n} \ln|\mathbf{F}_t| + \frac{1}{\sigma^2}\sum_{t=1}^{n} \mathbf{v}_t'\mathbf{F}_t^{-1}\mathbf{v}_t\right). \tag{15.8}$$

The scale parameter σ^2 can be concentrated out of the LF: maximizing $\ell(\boldsymbol{\theta}, \sigma^2)$ with respect to σ^2 yields

$$\hat{\sigma}^2 = \sum_t \mathbf{v}_t'\mathbf{F}_t^{-1}\mathbf{v}_t/(Nn).$$

The profile (or concentrated) likelihood is

$$\ell_{\sigma^2}(\boldsymbol{\theta}) = -\frac{1}{2}\left[Nn(\ln\hat{\sigma}^2 + 1) + \sum_{t=1}^{n}\ln|F_t|\right]. \quad (15.9)$$

This function can be maximized numerically by a quasi-Newton optimization routine, by iterating the following updating scheme:

$$\tilde{\boldsymbol{\theta}}_{k+1} = \tilde{\boldsymbol{\theta}}_k - \lambda_k[\nabla^2\ell_{\sigma^2}(\tilde{\boldsymbol{\theta}}_k)]^{-1}\nabla\ell_{\sigma^2}(\tilde{\boldsymbol{\theta}}_k),$$

where λ_k is a variable step-length, and $\nabla\ell_{\sigma^2}(\tilde{\boldsymbol{\theta}}_k)$ and $\nabla^2\ell_{\sigma^2}(\tilde{\boldsymbol{\theta}}_k)$ are respectively the gradient and hessian, evaluated at $\tilde{\boldsymbol{\theta}}_k$. The analytical gradient and hessian can be obtained in parallel to the Kalman filter recursions; see Harvey (1989) and Proietti (1999), for an application.

The innovations are a martingale difference sequence, $\mathbf{E}(\mathbf{v}_t|\mathbf{Y}_{t-1}) = 0$, which implies that they are uncorrelated with any function of their past: using the law of iterated expectations $\mathbf{E}(\mathbf{v}_t\mathbf{v}_{t-j}|\mathbf{Y}_{t-1}) = 0$. Under Gaussianity they will also be independent.

The KF performs a linear transformation of the observations with unit Jacobian: if $\mathbf{v}$ denotes the stack of the innovations and $\mathbf{y}$ that of the observations: then $\mathbf{v} = \mathbf{C}^{-1}\mathbf{y}$, where $\mathbf{C}^{-1}$ is a lower triangular matrix such that $\Sigma_y = \text{Cov}(\mathbf{y}) = \sigma^2\mathbf{CFC}'$,

$$\mathbf{C} = \begin{bmatrix} \mathbf{I} & \mathbf{0} & \mathbf{0} & \cdots & \mathbf{0} & \mathbf{0} \\ -\mathbf{Z}_2\mathbf{K}_1 & \mathbf{I} & \mathbf{0} & \cdots & \mathbf{0} & \mathbf{0} \\ -\mathbf{Z}_3\mathbf{L}_{3,2}\mathbf{K}_1 & -\mathbf{Z}_3\mathbf{K}_2 & \mathbf{I} & \ddots & \mathbf{0} & \mathbf{0} \\ \vdots & \vdots & \ddots & \ddots & \ddots & \vdots \\ -\mathbf{Z}_{n-1}\mathbf{L}_{n-1,2}\mathbf{K}_1, & -\mathbf{Z}_{n-1}\mathbf{L}_{n-1,3}\mathbf{K}_2, & \cdots & \ddots & \mathbf{I} & \mathbf{0} \\ -\mathbf{Z}_n\mathbf{L}_{n,2}\mathbf{K}_1, & -\mathbf{Z}_n\mathbf{L}_{n,3}\mathbf{K}_2, & -\mathbf{Z}_n\mathbf{L}_{n,4}\mathbf{K}_3, & \cdots & -\mathbf{Z}_n\mathbf{K}_{n-1}, & \mathbf{I} \end{bmatrix} \quad (15.10)$$

where $\mathbf{L}_t = \mathbf{T}_t - \mathbf{K}_t\mathbf{Z}_t'$, and $\mathbf{L}_{t,s} = \mathbf{L}_{t-1}\mathbf{L}_{t-2}\cdots\mathbf{L}_s$ for $t > s$, $\mathbf{L}_{t,t} = \mathbf{I}$ and $\mathbf{F} = \text{diag}(\mathbf{F}_1,\ldots,\mathbf{F}_t,\ldots,\mathbf{F}_n)$. Hence, $\mathbf{v}_t$ is a linear combination of the current and past observations and is orthogonal to the information set $\mathbf{Y}_{t-1}$. As a result $|\Sigma_y| = \sigma^{2n}|\mathbf{F}| = \sigma^{2n}\Pi_t|\mathbf{F}_t|$ and $\mathbf{y}'\Sigma_y^{-1}\mathbf{y} = \frac{1}{\sigma^2}\mathbf{v}'\mathbf{F}^{-1}\mathbf{v} = \frac{1}{\sigma^2}\Sigma_t\mathbf{v}_t\mathbf{F}_t^{-1}\mathbf{v}_t$.

4.1 Properties of Maximum Likelihood Estimators

Under regularity conditions, the maximum likelihood estimator of $\boldsymbol{\theta}$ is consistent and asymptotically normal, with covariance matrix equal to the inverse of the asymptotic Fisher information matrix (see Caines, 1988). Besides the technical conditions regarding the existence of derivatives and their continuity about the true parameter, regularity requires that the model is identifiable and the true parameter values do not lie on the boundary of the parameter space. For the AR(1) plus noise model introduced in section 2.3 these conditions are violated, for instance, when $\phi = 0$ and when $\phi = 1$ or $\sigma_\varepsilon^2 = 0$, respectively. While testing for the null hypothesis $\phi = 0$ against the alternative $\phi \neq 0$ is standard, based on the t-statistics of the coefficient y_{t-1} in the regression of y_t on y_{t-1} or on the first order autocorrelation, testing for unit roots or deterministic effects is much more involved, since likelihood ratio tests do not have the usual chi square distribution.

Testing for deterministic and non-stationary effects in unobserved component models is considered in Nyblom (1986) and Harvey (2001).

Pagan (1980) has derived sufficient conditions for asymptotic identifiability in stationary models and sufficient conditions for consistency and asymptotic normality of the maximum likelihood estimators in non-stationary but asymptotically identifiable models. Strong consistency of the maximum likelihood estimator in the general case of a non-compact parameter space is proved in Hannan and Deistler (1988). Recently, full asymptotic theory for maximum likelihood estimation of non-stationary state space models has been provided by Chang et al. (2009).

4.2 Profile and Marginal Likelihood for Non-stationary Models with Fixed and Regression Effects

Let us consider the state space model (15.3), with initial conditions stated in (15.4).

Let us start from the simple case when the vector $\boldsymbol{\beta}$ is fixed and known, so that $\boldsymbol{\alpha}_1 \sim \mathrm{N}(\tilde{\boldsymbol{\alpha}}_{1|0}, \sigma^2 \mathbf{P}_{1|0})$, where $\tilde{\boldsymbol{\alpha}}_{1|0} = \tilde{\boldsymbol{\alpha}}^*_{1|0} + \mathbf{W}_0\boldsymbol{\beta}$ and $\mathbf{P}_{1|0} = \mathbf{H}_0\mathbf{H}_0'$.

The KF for this model becomes, for $t = 1, \ldots, n$:

$$\mathbf{v}_t = \mathbf{y}_t - \mathbf{Z}_t\tilde{\boldsymbol{\alpha}}_{t|t-1} - \mathbf{X}_t\boldsymbol{\beta}_t, \qquad \mathbf{F}_t = \mathbf{Z}_t\mathbf{P}_{t|t-1}\mathbf{Z}_t' + \mathbf{G}_t\mathbf{G}_t',$$

$$\mathbf{K}_t = (\mathbf{T}_t\mathbf{P}_{t|t-1}\mathbf{Z}_t' + \mathbf{H}_t\mathbf{G}_t')\mathbf{F}_t^{-1}$$

$$\tilde{\boldsymbol{\alpha}}_{t+1|t} = \mathbf{T}_t\tilde{\boldsymbol{\alpha}}_{t|t-1} + \mathbf{W}_t\boldsymbol{\beta} + \mathbf{K}_t\mathbf{v}_t, \quad \mathbf{P}_{t+1|t} = \mathbf{T}_t\mathbf{P}_{t|t-1}\mathbf{T}_t' + \mathbf{H}_t\mathbf{H}_t' - \mathbf{K}_t\mathbf{F}_t\mathbf{K}_t' \quad (15.11)$$

We refer to this filter as KF($\boldsymbol{\beta}$). Apart from a constant term, the log likelihood is as given in (15.8), whereas (15.9) is the profile likelihood.

The KF and the definition of the likelihood need to be amended when we remove the assumption that $\boldsymbol{\beta}$ is a known vector and that the state vector has a stationary distribution. An instance is provided by the local level model, for which $\mathbf{Z}_t = 1, \mathbf{X}_t = 0, \boldsymbol{\alpha}_t = \mu_t$, $\mathbf{G}_t = [1, 0], \sigma^2 = \sigma^2_\varepsilon, \varepsilon_t = [\varepsilon_t, \sigma_\varepsilon\eta_t/\sigma_\eta]', \mathbf{H}_t = [0, \sigma_\eta/\sigma_\varepsilon], \mathbf{T}_t = 1, \mathbf{W}_t = 0$,

$$\tilde{\boldsymbol{\alpha}}^*_{1|0} - 0, \mathbf{W}_0 - 1, \boldsymbol{\beta} - \mu_0, \mathbf{H}_0 - [0, \sigma_\eta/\sigma_\varepsilon].$$

If a scalar explanatory variable is present in the measurement equation, x_t, with coefficient γ: $\mathbf{X}_t = [0, x_t], \boldsymbol{\beta} = [\mu_0, \gamma]', \mathbf{W}_0 = [1,0], \mathbf{W}_t = [0,0], t > 0$.

When $\boldsymbol{\beta}$ is fixed but unknown, Rosenberg (1973) showed that it can be concentrated out of the likelihood function and that its generalized least square estimate is obtained from the output of an augmented KF. In fact, $\boldsymbol{\alpha}_1$ has mean $\tilde{\boldsymbol{\alpha}}_{1|0} = \tilde{\boldsymbol{\alpha}}^*_{1|0} + \mathbf{W}_0\boldsymbol{\beta}$ and covariance matrix $\mathbf{P}^*_{1|0} = \sigma^2\mathbf{H}_0\mathbf{H}_0'$. Defining $\mathbf{A}_{1|0} = -\mathbf{W}_0$, rewriting $\tilde{\boldsymbol{\alpha}}_{1|0} = \tilde{\boldsymbol{\alpha}}^*_{1|0} - \mathbf{A}_{1|0}\boldsymbol{\beta}$, and running the KF recursions for a fixed $\boldsymbol{\beta}$, we obtain the set of innovations $\mathbf{v}_t = \mathbf{v}_t^* - \mathbf{V}_t\boldsymbol{\beta}$ and one-step-ahead state predictions $\tilde{\boldsymbol{\alpha}}_{t+1|t} = \tilde{\boldsymbol{\alpha}}^*_{t+1|t} - \mathbf{A}_{t+1|t}\boldsymbol{\beta}$, as a linear function of $\boldsymbol{\beta}$.

In the above expressions the starred quantities, $\mathbf{v}_t^*$ and $\tilde{\boldsymbol{\alpha}}^*_{t+1|t}$, are produced by the KF in (15.11), run with $\boldsymbol{\beta} = \mathbf{0}$, that is with initial conditions $\tilde{\boldsymbol{\alpha}}^*_{1|0}$ and $\mathbf{P}^*_{1|0} = \mathbf{H}_0\mathbf{H}_0'$, hereby denoted KF($\mathbf{0}$). The latter also computes the matrices $\mathbf{F}_t^*$, $\mathbf{K}_t^*$ and $\mathbf{P}^*_{t+1|t}$, $t = 1, \ldots, n$, that do not depend on $\boldsymbol{\beta}$.

The matrices $\mathbf{V}_t$ and $\mathbf{A}_{t+1|t}$ are generated by the following recursions, that are run in parallel to KF(**0**):

$$\mathbf{V}_t = \mathbf{X}_t - \mathbf{Z}_t\mathbf{A}_{t|t-1},\ \mathbf{A}_{t+1|t} = \mathbf{T}_t\mathbf{A}_{t|t-1} + \mathbf{W}_t + \mathbf{K}_t^*\mathbf{V}_t,\ t = 1,\ldots,T, \tag{15.12}$$

with initial value $\mathbf{A}_{1|0} = -\mathbf{W}_0$. Notice that this amounts to running the same filter, KF(**0**), on each of the columns of the matrix $\mathbf{X}_t$.

Then, replacing $\mathbf{v}_t = \mathbf{v}_t^* - \mathbf{V}_t\boldsymbol{\beta}$ into the expression for the log-likelihood (15.8), and defining $\mathbf{s}_n = \sum_1^n \mathbf{V}_t'\mathbf{F}_t^{*-1}\mathbf{v}_t^*$ and $\mathbf{S}_n = \sum_1^n \mathbf{V}_t'\mathbf{F}_t^{*-1}\mathbf{V}_t$, yields, apart from a constant term:

$$\ell(\boldsymbol{\theta},\sigma^2,\boldsymbol{\beta}) = -\frac{1}{2}\left(Nn\ln\sigma^2 + \sum_{t=1}^{n}\ln|\mathbf{F}_t^*| + \sigma^{-2}\left[\sum_{t=1}^{n}\mathbf{v}_t^{*\prime}\mathbf{F}_t^{*-1}\mathbf{v}_t^* - 2\boldsymbol{\beta}'\mathbf{s}_n + \boldsymbol{\beta}'\mathbf{S}_n\boldsymbol{\beta}\right]\right). \tag{15.13}$$

Hence, the maximum likelihood estimator of $\boldsymbol{\beta}$ is $\hat{\boldsymbol{\beta}} = \mathbf{S}_n^{-1}\mathbf{s}_n$. This is coincident with the generalized least square estimator. The profile likelihood (with respect to $\boldsymbol{\beta}$) is

$$\ell_\beta(\boldsymbol{\theta},\sigma^2) = -\frac{1}{2}\left(Nn\ln\sigma^2 + \sum_{t=1}^{n}\ln|\mathbf{F}_t^*| + \sigma^{-2}\left[\sum_{t=1}^{n}\mathbf{v}_t^{*\prime}\mathbf{F}_t^{*-1}\mathbf{v}_t^* - \mathbf{s}_n'\mathbf{S}_n^{-1}\mathbf{s}_n\right]\right) \tag{15.14}$$

The MLE of σ^2 is

$$\hat{\sigma}^2 = \frac{1}{Nn}\left[\sum_{t=1}^{n}\mathbf{v}_t^{*\prime}\mathbf{F}_t^{*-1}\mathbf{v}_t^* - \mathbf{s}_n'\mathbf{S}_n^{-1}\mathbf{s}_n\right]$$

and the profile likelihood (also with respect to σ^2) is

$$\ell_{\beta,\sigma^2}(\boldsymbol{\theta}) = -\frac{1}{2}\left[Nn(\ln\hat{\sigma}^2 + 1) + \sum_{t=1}^{n}\ln|\mathbf{F}_t^*|\right]. \tag{15.15}$$

The vector $\boldsymbol{\beta}$ is said to be diffuse if $\boldsymbol{\beta} \sim \mathrm{N}(0,\Sigma_\beta)$, where $\Sigma_\beta^{-1} \to \mathbf{0}$. Writing $\Sigma_\beta = \kappa\mathbf{I}_d$, where d is the number of elements of $\boldsymbol{\beta}$ and $\kappa > 0$, so that the prior log-density is, up to a constant, $\ell(\boldsymbol{\beta}) = \ln p(\boldsymbol{\beta}) = -0.5d\ln\kappa - 0.5\boldsymbol{\beta}'\boldsymbol{\beta}/\kappa$, the diffuse likelihood is defined as the limit of $\ell(\boldsymbol{\theta},\sigma^2,\boldsymbol{\beta}) + 0.5d\ln\kappa$ as $\kappa \to \infty$. Using $\ell(\mathbf{y}) = \ell(\boldsymbol{\beta}) + \ell(\mathbf{y}|\boldsymbol{\beta}) - \ell(\boldsymbol{\beta}|\mathbf{y})$, this yields

$$\ell_\infty(\boldsymbol{\theta},\sigma^2) = -\tfrac{1}{2}\{N(n-k)\ln\sigma^2 + \sum\ln|\mathbf{F}_t^*| + \ln|\mathbf{S}_n| + \sigma^{-2}[\sum \mathbf{v}_t^{*\prime}\mathbf{F}_t^{*-1}\mathbf{v}_t^* - \mathbf{s}_n'\mathbf{S}_n^{-1}\mathbf{s}_n],\}$$

where k is the number of elements of $\boldsymbol{\beta}$. The MLE of σ^2 is

$$\hat{\sigma}^2 = \frac{1}{N(n-k)}\left[\sum_{t=1}^{n}\mathbf{v}_t^{*\prime}\mathbf{F}_t^{*-1}\mathbf{v}_t^* - \mathbf{s}_n'\mathbf{S}_n^{-1}\mathbf{s}_n\right]$$

and the profile likelihood is

$$\ell_{\infty,\sigma^2}(\boldsymbol{\theta}) = -\frac{1}{2}\left[N(n-k)(\ln\hat{\sigma}^2 + 1) + \sum_{t=1}^{n}\ln|\mathbf{F}_t^*| + \ln|\mathbf{S}_n|\right]. \tag{15.16}$$

The notion of a diffuse likelihood is close to that of a marginal likelihood, being based on reduced rank linear transformation of the series that eliminates dependence on $\boldsymbol{\beta}$; see the next subsection and Francke et al. (2010).

De Jong (1991) has further shown that the limiting expressions for the innovations, the one-step-ahead prediction of the state vector and the corresponding covariance matrices are

$$\mathbf{v}_t = \mathbf{v}_t^* - \mathbf{V}_t\mathbf{S}_{t-1}^{-1}\mathbf{s}_{t-1}, \qquad \mathbf{F}_t = \mathbf{F}_t^* + \mathbf{V}_t\mathbf{S}_{t-1}^{-1}\mathbf{V}_t',$$

$$\tilde{\boldsymbol{\alpha}}_{t|t-1} = \tilde{\boldsymbol{\alpha}}_{t|t-1}^* - \mathbf{A}_{t|t-1}\mathbf{S}_{t-1}^{-1}\mathbf{s}_{t-1}, \quad \mathbf{P}_{t|t-1} = \mathbf{P}_{t|t-1}^* + \mathbf{A}_{t|t-1}\mathbf{S}_{t-1}^{-1}\mathbf{A}_{t|t-1}'. \qquad (15.17)$$

De Jong and Chu-Chun-Lin (1994) show that the additional recursions (15.12), referring to initial conditions, can be collapsed after a suitable number of updates (equal to the rank of $\mathbf{W}_0$).

4.3 Discussion

The augmented state space model (15.3) can be represented as a linear regression model $\mathbf{y} = \mathbf{X}\boldsymbol{\beta} + \mathbf{u}$ for a suitable choice of the matrix $\mathbf{X}$. Under the Gaussian assumption $\mathbf{y} \sim \mathrm{N}(\mathbf{X}\boldsymbol{\beta}, \Sigma_u)$, the MLE of $\boldsymbol{\beta}$ is the GLS estimator

$$\hat{\beta} = (\mathbf{X}'\boldsymbol{\Sigma}_u^{-1}\mathbf{X})^{-1}\mathbf{X}'\boldsymbol{\Sigma}_u^{-1}\mathbf{y}.$$

Consider the LDL decomposition (see, for instance, Golub and Van Loan, 1996) of the matrix $\boldsymbol{\Sigma}_u$, $\boldsymbol{\Sigma}_u = \mathbf{C}^*\mathbf{F}^*\mathbf{C}^{*\prime}$, where $\mathbf{C}^*$ has the same structure as (15.10). The KF($\mathbf{0}$) applied to $\mathbf{y}$ yields $\mathbf{v}^* = \mathbf{C}^{*-1}\mathbf{y}$. When applied to each of the deterministic regressors making up the columns of the $\mathbf{X}$ matrix, it gives $\mathbf{V} = \mathbf{C}^{*-1}\mathbf{X}$. The GLS estimate of $\boldsymbol{\beta}$ is thus obtained from the augmented KF as follows:

$$\begin{aligned}\hat{\boldsymbol{\beta}} &- (\mathbf{X}'\mathbf{C}^{*-1\prime}\mathbf{F}^{*-1}\mathbf{C}^{*-1}\mathbf{X})^{-1}\mathbf{X}'\mathbf{C}^{*-1\prime}\mathbf{F}^{*-1}\mathbf{C}^{*-1}\mathbf{y}\\ &= (\mathbf{V}'\mathbf{F}^{*-1}\mathbf{V})^{-1}\mathbf{V}'\mathbf{F}^{*-1}\mathbf{v}^*\\ &= (\boldsymbol{\Sigma}_t\mathbf{V}_t\mathbf{F}_t^{*-1}\mathbf{V}_t')^{-1}\boldsymbol{\Sigma}_t\mathbf{V}_t\mathbf{F}_t^{*-1}\mathbf{v}_t^*.\end{aligned}$$

The restricted or marginal log-likelihood estimator of $\boldsymbol{\theta}$ is the maximizer of the marginal likelihood defined by Patterson and Thompson (1971) and Harville (1977):

$$\ell_R(\boldsymbol{\theta}, \sigma^2) = \ell_\beta(\boldsymbol{\theta}, \sigma^2) - \tfrac{1}{2}[\ln|\mathbf{X}'\boldsymbol{\Sigma}_u^{-1}\mathbf{X}| - \ln|\mathbf{X}'\mathbf{X}|]$$

$$= -\tfrac{1}{2}\{\ln|\boldsymbol{\Sigma}_u| + \ln|\mathbf{X}'\boldsymbol{\Sigma}_u^{-1}\mathbf{X}| - \ln|\mathbf{X}'\mathbf{X}| + \mathbf{y}'\boldsymbol{\Sigma}_u^{-1}\mathbf{y} - \mathbf{y}'\boldsymbol{\Sigma}_u^{-1}\mathbf{X}(\mathbf{X}'\boldsymbol{\Sigma}_u^{-1}\mathbf{X})^{-1}\mathbf{X}'\boldsymbol{\Sigma}_u^{-1}\mathbf{y}\}.$$

Simple algebra shows that $\ell_R(\boldsymbol{\theta}, \sigma^2) = \ell_\infty(\boldsymbol{\theta}, \sigma^2) + 0.5\ln|\mathbf{X}'\mathbf{X}|$. Thus the marginal MLE is obtained from the assumption that the vector $\boldsymbol{\beta}$ is a diffuse random vector, that is it has an improper distribution with a mean of zero and an arbitrarily large variance matrix.

The restricted likelihood is the likelihood of a non-invertible linear transformation of the data, $(\mathbf{I}-\mathbf{Q}_X)\mathbf{y}$, $\mathbf{Q}_X = \mathbf{X}(\mathbf{X}'\boldsymbol{\Sigma}_y^{-1}\mathbf{X})^{-1}\mathbf{X}'\boldsymbol{\Sigma}_y^{-1}$, which eliminates the dependence on $\boldsymbol{\beta}$. The maximizer of $\ell_R(\boldsymbol{\theta},\sigma^2)$ is preferable to the profile likelihood estimator when n is small and the variance of the random signal is small compared to that of the noise.

4.4 Missing Values and Sequential Processing

In univariate models missing values are handled by skipping the KF updating operations: if y_i is missing at time i, ν_i and F_i cannot be computed and $\tilde{\boldsymbol{\alpha}}_{i+1|i-1} = \mathbf{T}_i\tilde{\boldsymbol{\alpha}}_{i|i-1}$, $\mathbf{P}_{i+1|i-1} = \mathbf{T}_i\mathbf{P}_{i|i-1}\mathbf{T}' + \mathbf{H}_i\mathbf{H}_i'$ are the moments of the two-step-ahead predictive distribution.

For multivariate models, when $\mathbf{y}_i$ is only partially missing, sequential processing must be used. This technique, illustrated by Anderson and Moore (1979) and further developed by Koopman and Durbin (2000) for non-stationary models, provides a very flexible and convenient device for filtering and smoothing and for handling missing values. Our treatment is prevalently based on Koopman and Durbin (2000). However, for the treatment of regression effects and initial conditions we adopt the augmentation approach by de Jong (1991).

Assume, for notation simplicity, a time invariant model with $\mathbf{HG}' = \mathbf{0}$ (uncorrelated measurement and transition disturbances) and $\mathbf{GG}' = \text{diag}\{g_i^2, i = 1,\ldots,N\}$, so that the measurements $y_{t,i}$ are conditionally independent, given $\boldsymbol{\alpha}_t$. The latter assumption can be relaxed: a possibility is to include $\mathbf{G}\varepsilon_t$ in the state vector, and set $g_i^2 = 0, \forall i$; alternatively, we can transform the measurement equation so as to achieve that the measurement disturbances are fully idiosyncratic.

The multivariate vectors $\mathbf{y}_t, t = 1,\ldots,n$, where some elements can be missing, are stacked one on top of the other to yield a univariate time series $\{y_{t,i}, i = 1,\ldots,N, t = 1,\ldots,n\}$, whose elements are processed sequentially. The state space model for the univariate time series $\{y_{t,i}\}$ is constructed as follows.

The new measurement equation for the ith element of the vector $\mathbf{y}_t$ is:

$$y_{t,i} = \mathbf{z}_i'\boldsymbol{\alpha}_{t,i} + \mathbf{x}_{t,i}'\boldsymbol{\beta} + g_i\varepsilon_{t,i}^*, \quad t = 1,\ldots,n, \quad i = 1,\ldots,N, \quad \varepsilon_{t,i}^* \sim \text{NID}(0,\sigma^2) \qquad (15.18)$$

where $\mathbf{z}_i'$ and $\mathbf{x}_{t,i}'$ denote the ith rows of $\mathbf{Z}$ and $\mathbf{X}_t$, respectively. Notice that (15.18) has two indices: the time index runs first and it is kept fixed as series index runs.

The transition equation varies with the two indices. For a fixed time index, the transition equation is the identity $\boldsymbol{\alpha}_{t,i} = \boldsymbol{\alpha}_{t,i-1}$, for $i = 2,\ldots,N$, whereas for $i = 1$,

$$\boldsymbol{\alpha}_{t,1} = \mathbf{T}\boldsymbol{\alpha}_{t-1,N} + \mathbf{W}\boldsymbol{\beta} + \mathbf{H}\varepsilon_{t,1}$$

The state space form is completed by the initial state vector which is $\boldsymbol{\alpha}_{1,1} = \mathbf{a}_{1,1} + \mathbf{W}_0\boldsymbol{\beta} + \mathbf{H}_0\varepsilon_{1,1}$, where $\text{Var}(\varepsilon_{1,1}) = \text{Var}(\varepsilon_{t,1}) = \sigma^2\mathbf{I}$.

The augmented Kalman filter, taking into account the presence of missing values, is given by the following definitions and recursive formulae.

- Set the initial values $\mathbf{a}_{1,1} = \mathbf{0}, \mathbf{A}_{1,1} = -\mathbf{W}_0, \mathbf{P}_{1,1} = \mathbf{H}_0\mathbf{H}_0', q_{1,1} = 0, \mathbf{s}_{1,1} = \mathbf{0}, \mathbf{S}_{1,1} = \mathbf{0}$, $d_{1,1} = 0$,

- for $t = 1,\ldots,n$, $i = 1,\ldots,N-1$,
  - if $y^{\dagger}_{t,i}$ is available:

$$\begin{array}{lllllll} v_{t,i} & = & y_{t,i} - \mathbf{z}_i'\mathbf{a}_{t,i}, & \mathbf{V}'_{t,i} & = & \mathbf{x}'_{t,i} - \mathbf{z}_i'\mathbf{A}_{t,i}, \\ f_{t,i} & = & \mathbf{z}_i'\mathbf{P}_{t,i}\mathbf{z}_i' + g_i^2, & \mathbf{K}_{t,i} & = & \mathbf{P}_t\mathbf{z}_i'/f_{t,i} \\ \mathbf{a}_{t,i+1} & = & \mathbf{a}_{t,i} + \mathbf{K}_{t,i}v_{t,i}, & \mathbf{A}_{t,i+1} & = & \mathbf{A}_{t,i} + \mathbf{K}_{t,i}\mathbf{V}'_{t,i}, \\ \mathbf{P}_{t,i+1} & = & \mathbf{P}_{t,i} - \mathbf{K}_{t,i}\mathbf{K}'_{t,i}f_t, & & & \\ q_{t,i+1} & = & q_{t,i} + v_{t,i}^2/f_{t,i}, & \mathbf{s}_{t,i+1} & = & \mathbf{s}_{t,i} + \mathbf{V}_{t,i}v_{t,i}/f_{t,i} \\ \mathbf{S}_{t,i+1} & = & \mathbf{S}_{t,i} + \mathbf{V}_{t,i}\mathbf{V}'_{t,i}/f_{t,i} & d_{t,i+1} & = & d_{t,i} + \ln f_{t,i} \\ cn & = & cn + 1 & & & \end{array} \tag{15.19}$$

  - Here, cn counts the number of observations.
  - Else, if $y_{t,i}$ is missing:

$$\begin{array}{lll} \mathbf{a}_{t,i+1} & = & \mathbf{a}_{t,i},\ \ \mathbf{A}_{t,i+1} = \mathbf{A}_{t,i}, \\ \mathbf{P}_{t,i+1} & = & \mathbf{P}_{t,i}, \\ q_{t,i+1} & = & q_{t,i},\ \ \mathbf{s}_{t,i+1} = \mathbf{s}_{t,i},\ \ \mathbf{S}_{t,i+1} = \mathbf{S}_{t,i},\ \ d_{t,i+1} = d_{t,i}. \end{array} \tag{15.20}$$

- For $i = N$, compute:

$$\begin{array}{llllll} \mathbf{a}_{t+1,1} & = & \mathbf{T}\mathbf{a}_{t,N}, & \mathbf{A}_{t+1,1} & = & \mathbf{W} + \mathbf{T}\mathbf{A}_{t,N}, \\ \mathbf{P}_{t+1,1} & = & \mathbf{T}\mathbf{P}_{t,N}\mathbf{T}' + \mathbf{H}\mathbf{H}', & & & \\ q_{t+1,1} & = & q_{t,N},\ \ \mathbf{s}_{t+1,1} = \mathbf{s}_{t,N}, & \mathbf{S}_{t+1,1} & = & \mathbf{S}_{t,N},\ \ d_{t+1,1} = d_{t,N}. \end{array} \quad 15.21)$$

Under the fixed effects model maximizing the likelihood with respect to $\boldsymbol{\beta}$ and σ^2 yields:

$$\hat{\boldsymbol{\beta}} = \mathbf{S}^{-1}_{n+1,1}\mathbf{s}_{n+1,1},\ \mathrm{Var}(\hat{\boldsymbol{\beta}}) = \mathbf{S}^{-1}_{n+1,1},\ \ \hat{\sigma}^2 = \frac{q_{n+1,1} - \mathbf{s}'_{n+1,1}\mathbf{S}^{-1}_{n+1,1}\mathbf{s}_{n+1,1}}{cn}. \tag{15.22}$$

The profile likelihood is $\ell_{\beta,\sigma^2} = -0.5[d_{n+1,1} + cn(\ln\hat{\sigma}^2 + \ln(2\pi) + 1)]$.

When $\boldsymbol{\beta}$ is diffuse, the maximum likelihood estimate of the scale parameter is

$$\hat{\sigma}^2 = \frac{q_{n+1,1} - \mathbf{s}'_{n+1,1}\mathbf{S}^{-1}_{n+1,1}\mathbf{s}_{n+1,1}}{cn - k},$$

and the diffuse profile likelihood is:

$$\ell_\infty = -0.5[d_{n+1,1} + (cn - k)(\ln\hat{\sigma}^2 + \ln(2\pi) + 1) + \ln|\mathbf{S}_{n+1,1}|]. \tag{15.23}$$

This treatment is useful for handling estimation with mixed frequency data. Also, temporal aggregation can be converted into a systematic sampling problem, see Harvey and Chung (2000), and handled by sequential processing; see Frale et al. (2011).

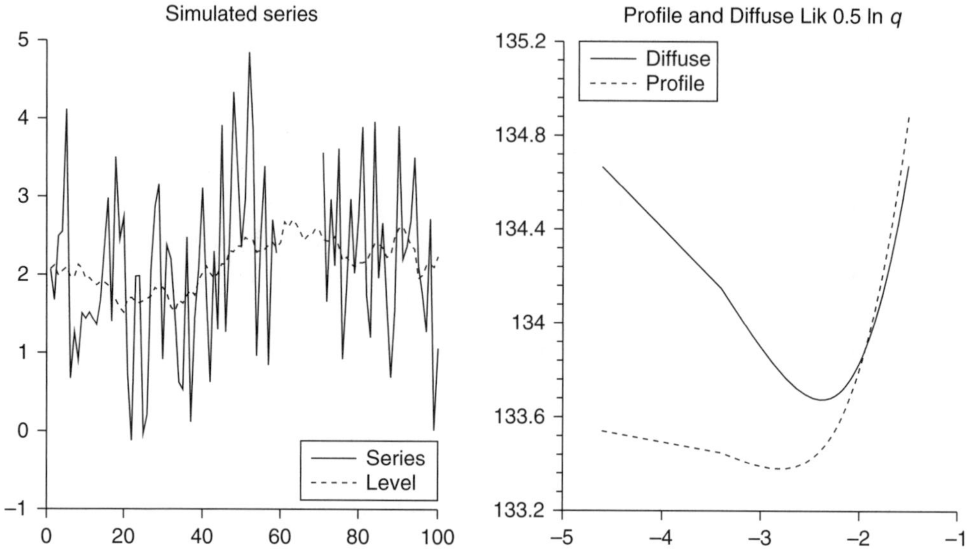

Figure 15.1 *Simulated series from a local level model with* q = *0.1 (0.5 ln* q = *−2.3) and underlying level (left): plot of the profile and diffuse likelihood of the parameter 0.5 ln* q

4.5 Linear Constraints

Suppose that the vector $\boldsymbol{\alpha}_t$ is subject to c linear binding constraints $\mathbf{C}_t\boldsymbol{\alpha}_t = \mathbf{c}_t$, with $\mathbf{C}_t$ and $\mathbf{c}_t$ fixed and known. An example is a Cobb–Douglas production function with time varying elasticities, but constant returns to scale in every time period. See Doran (1992) for further details.

These constraints are handled by augmenting the measurement equation with further c observations:

$$\begin{bmatrix} \mathbf{y}_t \\ \mathbf{c}_t \end{bmatrix} = \begin{bmatrix} \mathbf{Z}_t \\ \mathbf{C}_t \end{bmatrix} \boldsymbol{\alpha}_t + \begin{bmatrix} \mathbf{G}_t \\ \mathbf{0} \end{bmatrix} \varepsilon_t.$$

Non-binding constraints are easily accommodated.

4.6 A Simulated Example

We simulated $n = 100$ observations from a local level model with signal to noise ratio $q = 0.01$. Subsequently, 10 observations (for $t = 60$–69) were deleted, and the parameter $0.5 \ln q$ estimated by profile and diffuse MLE. Figure 15.1 displays the simulated series and true level (left), and the profile and diffuse likelihood (right).

The maximizer of the diffuse likelihood is higher and closer to the true value, which amounts to −2.3. This illustrates that the diffuse likelihood in small samples provides a more accurate estimate of the signal to noise ratio when the latter is close to the boundary of the parameter space.

5 THE EM ALGORITHM

Maximum likelihood estimation of the standard time invariant state space model can be carried out by the EM algorithm (see Shumway and Stoffer, 1982, and Cappé et al., 2005). In the sequel we will assume without loss of generality $\sigma^2 = 1$.

Let $\mathbf{y} = [\mathbf{y}_1', \ldots, \mathbf{y}_n']'$, $\boldsymbol{\alpha} = [\boldsymbol{\alpha}_1', \ldots, \boldsymbol{\alpha}_n']'$. The log-posterior of the states is $\ln g(\boldsymbol{\alpha}|\mathbf{y};\boldsymbol{\theta}) = \ln g(\mathbf{y}, \boldsymbol{\alpha}; \boldsymbol{\theta}) - \ln g(\mathbf{y};\boldsymbol{\theta})$, where the first term on the right-hand side is the joint probability density function of the observations and the states, also known as the complete data likelihood, and the subtrahend is the likelihood, $\ell(\boldsymbol{\theta}) = \ln g(\mathbf{y};\boldsymbol{\theta})$, of the observed data.

The complete data log-likelihood can be evaluated as follows: $\ln g(\mathbf{y}, \boldsymbol{\alpha}; \boldsymbol{\theta}) = \ln g(\mathbf{y}|\boldsymbol{\alpha};\boldsymbol{\theta}) + \ln g(\boldsymbol{\alpha};\boldsymbol{\theta})$, where $\ln g(\mathbf{y}|\boldsymbol{\alpha};\boldsymbol{\theta}) = \sum_{t=1}^n \ln g(\mathbf{y}_t|\boldsymbol{\alpha}_t)$, and $\ln g(\boldsymbol{\alpha};\boldsymbol{\theta}) = \sum_{t=1}^n \ln g(\boldsymbol{\alpha}_{t+1}|\boldsymbol{\alpha}_t;\boldsymbol{\theta}) + \ln g(\boldsymbol{\alpha}_1;\boldsymbol{\theta})$. Thus, from (15.1)–(15.2),

$$\begin{aligned}\ln g(\mathbf{y}, \boldsymbol{\alpha}; \boldsymbol{\theta}) = & -\tfrac{1}{2}[n \ln|\mathbf{GG}'| + \operatorname{tr}\{(\mathbf{GG}')^{-1}\textstyle\sum_{t=1}^n(\mathbf{y}_t - \mathbf{Z}\boldsymbol{\alpha}_t)(\mathbf{y}_t - \mathbf{Z}\boldsymbol{\alpha}_t)'\}] \\ & -\tfrac{1}{2}n\ln|\mathbf{HH}'| + \operatorname{tr}\{(\mathbf{HH}')^{-1}\textstyle\sum_{t=2}^n(\boldsymbol{\alpha}_{t+1} - \mathbf{T}\boldsymbol{\alpha}_t)(\boldsymbol{\alpha}_{t+1} - \mathbf{T}\boldsymbol{\alpha}_t)'\}] \\ & -\tfrac{1}{2}\{\ln|\mathbf{P}_{1|0}| + \operatorname{tr}\{\mathbf{P}_{1|0}^{-1}\boldsymbol{\alpha}_1\boldsymbol{\alpha}_1'\}]\end{aligned}$$

where $\mathbf{P}_0$ satisfies the matrix equation $\mathbf{P}_{1|0} = \mathbf{TP}_{1|0}\mathbf{T}' + \mathbf{HH}'$ and we take, with little loss in generality, $\tilde{\boldsymbol{\alpha}}_{1|0} = \mathbf{0}$.

Given an initial parameter value, $\boldsymbol{\theta}^*$, the EM algorithm iteratively maximizes, with respect to $\boldsymbol{\theta}$, the intermediate quantity (Dempster et al., 1977):

$$Q(\boldsymbol{\theta};\boldsymbol{\theta}^*) = E_{\boldsymbol{\theta}^*}[\ln g(\mathbf{y}, \boldsymbol{\alpha}; \boldsymbol{\theta})] = \int \ln g(\mathbf{y}, \boldsymbol{\alpha}; \boldsymbol{\theta}) g(\boldsymbol{\alpha}|\mathbf{y};\boldsymbol{\theta}^*)\, d\boldsymbol{\alpha},$$

which is interpreted as the expectation of the complete data log-likelihood with respect to $g(\boldsymbol{\alpha}|\mathbf{y};\boldsymbol{\theta}^*)$, which is the conditional probability density function of the unobservable states, given the observations, evaluated using $\boldsymbol{\theta}^*$. Now,

$$\begin{aligned}Q(\boldsymbol{\theta};\boldsymbol{\theta}^*) = & -\tfrac{1}{2}[n \ln|\mathbf{GG}'| + \operatorname{tr}\{(\mathbf{GG}')^{-1}\textstyle\sum_{t=1}^n[(\mathbf{y}_t - \mathbf{Z}\tilde{\boldsymbol{\alpha}}_{t|n})(\mathbf{y}_t - \mathbf{Z}\tilde{\boldsymbol{\alpha}}_{t|n})' + \mathbf{ZP}_{t|n}\mathbf{Z}']\}] \\ & -\tfrac{1}{2}[n\ln|\mathbf{HH}'| + \operatorname{tr}\{(\mathbf{HH}')^{-1}(\mathcal{S}_\alpha - \mathcal{S}_{\alpha,\alpha-1}\mathbf{T}' - \mathbf{T}\mathcal{S}_{\alpha,\alpha-1}' + \mathbf{T}\mathcal{S}_{\alpha-1}\mathbf{T}')\}] \\ & -\tfrac{1}{2}[\ln|\mathbf{P}_0| + \operatorname{tr}\{\mathbf{P}_0^{-1}(\tilde{\boldsymbol{\alpha}}_{0|n}\tilde{\boldsymbol{\alpha}}_{0|n}' + \mathbf{P}_{0|n})\}]\end{aligned}$$

where $\tilde{\boldsymbol{\alpha}}_{t|n} = \mathrm{E}(\boldsymbol{\alpha}_t|\mathbf{y};\boldsymbol{\theta}^{(j)}), \mathbf{P}_{t|n} = \mathrm{Var}(\boldsymbol{\alpha}_t|\mathbf{y};\boldsymbol{\theta}^{(j)})$, and

$$\mathcal{S}_\alpha = \left[\sum_{t=2}^n (\mathbf{P}_{t+1|n} + \tilde{\boldsymbol{\alpha}}_{t+1|n}\tilde{\boldsymbol{\alpha}}_{t+1|n}')\right],$$

$$\mathcal{S}_{\alpha-1} = \left[\sum_{t=2}^n \left(\mathbf{P}_{t|n} + \tilde{\boldsymbol{\alpha}}_{t|n}\tilde{\boldsymbol{\alpha}}_{t|n}'\right)\right], \mathcal{S}_{\alpha,\alpha-1} = \left[\sum_{t=2}^n (\mathbf{P}_{t+1,t|n} + \tilde{\boldsymbol{\alpha}}_{t+1|n}\tilde{\boldsymbol{\alpha}}_{t|n}')\right].$$

These quantities are evaluated with the support of the Kalman filter and smoother (KFS, see below), adapted to the state space model (15.1)–(15.2) with parameter values $\boldsymbol{\theta}^*$. Also, $\mathbf{P}_{t+1,t|n} = \text{Cov}(\boldsymbol{\alpha}_{t+1}, \boldsymbol{\alpha}_t|\mathbf{y};\boldsymbol{\theta}^*)$ is computed using the output of the KFS recursions, as will be detailed below.

Dempster et al. (1977) show that the parameter estimates maximizing the log-likelihood $\ell(\boldsymbol{\theta})$, can be obtained by a sequence of iterations, each consisting of an expectation step (E-step) and a maximization step (M-step), that aim at locating a stationary point of $Q(\boldsymbol{\theta};\boldsymbol{\theta}^*)$. At iteration j, given the estimate $\boldsymbol{\theta}^{(j)}$, the E-step deals with the evaluation of $Q(\boldsymbol{\theta};\boldsymbol{\theta}^{(j)})$; this is carried out with the support of the KFS applied to the state space representation (15.1)–(15.2) with hyperparameters $\boldsymbol{\theta}^{(j)}$.

The M-step amounts to choosing a new value $\boldsymbol{\theta}^{(j+1)}$, so as to maximize with respect to $\boldsymbol{\theta}$ the criterion $Q(\boldsymbol{\theta};\boldsymbol{\theta}^{(j)})$, that is, $Q(\boldsymbol{\theta}^{(j+1)};\boldsymbol{\theta}^{(j)}) \geq Q(\boldsymbol{\theta}^{(j)};\boldsymbol{\theta}^{(j)})$. The maximization is in closed form, if we assume that $\mathbf{P}_0$ is an independent unrestricted parameter. Actually, the latter depends on the matrices $\mathbf{T}$ and $\mathbf{HH}'$, but we will ignore this fact, as is usually done. For the measurement matrix the M-step consists of maximizing $Q(\boldsymbol{\theta};\boldsymbol{\theta}^{(j)})$ with respect to $\mathbf{Z}$, which gives

$$\hat{\mathbf{Z}}^{(j+1)} = \left(\sum_{t=1}^{n} \mathbf{y}_t \tilde{\boldsymbol{\alpha}}'_{t|n}\right) S_{\alpha}^{-1}.$$

The $(j + 1)$ update of the matrix $\mathbf{GG}'$ is given by

$$\widehat{\mathbf{GG}}'^{(j+1)} = \text{diag}\left\{\frac{1}{n}\sum_{t=1}^{n} [\mathbf{y}_t\mathbf{y}_t' - \hat{\mathbf{Z}}^{(j+1)}\tilde{\boldsymbol{\alpha}}_{t|n}\mathbf{y}_t']\right\}$$

Further, we have:

$$\hat{\mathbf{T}}^{(j+1)} = S_{\alpha,\alpha-1}S_{\alpha-1}^{-1}, \quad \widehat{\mathbf{HH}}'^{(j+1)} = \frac{1}{n}(S_f - \hat{\mathbf{T}}^{(j+1)}S'_{\alpha,\alpha-1}).$$

5.1 Smoothing Algorithm

The smoothed estimates $\tilde{\boldsymbol{\alpha}}_{t|n} = \text{E}(\boldsymbol{\alpha}_t|\mathbf{y};\boldsymbol{\theta})$, and their covariance matrix $\mathbf{P}_{t|n} = \text{E}[(\boldsymbol{\alpha}_t - \tilde{\boldsymbol{\alpha}}_{t|n})(\boldsymbol{\alpha}_t - \tilde{\boldsymbol{\alpha}}_{t|n})'|\mathbf{y};\boldsymbol{\theta}]$, are computed by the following backwards recursive formulae, given by Bryson and Ho (1969) and de Jong (1989), starting at $t = n$, with initial values $\mathbf{r}_n = 0$, $\mathbf{R}_n = \mathbf{0}$ and $\mathbf{N}_n = 0$: for $t = n - 1, \ldots, 1$,

$$\mathbf{r}_{t-1} = \mathbf{L}_t'\mathbf{r}_t + \mathbf{Z}_t'\mathbf{F}_t^{-1}\mathbf{v}_t, \quad \mathbf{M}_{t-1} = \mathbf{L}_t'\mathbf{M}_t\mathbf{L}_t + \mathbf{Z}_t'\mathbf{F}_t^{-1}\mathbf{Z}_t,$$

$$\tilde{\boldsymbol{\alpha}}_{t|n} = \tilde{\boldsymbol{\alpha}}_{t|t-1} + \mathbf{P}_{t|t-1}\mathbf{r}_{t-1}, \quad \mathbf{P}_{t|n} = \mathbf{P}_{t|t-1} - \mathbf{P}_{t|t-1}\mathbf{M}_{t-1}\mathbf{P}_{t|t-1}. \tag{15.24}$$

where $\mathbf{L}_t = \mathbf{T}_t - \mathbf{K}_t\mathbf{Z}'$.

Finally, it can be shown that $\mathbf{P}_{t,t-1|n} = \text{Cov}(\boldsymbol{\alpha}_t, \boldsymbol{\alpha}_{t-1}|\mathbf{y}) = \mathbf{T}_t\mathbf{P}_{t-1|n} - \mathbf{H}_t\mathbf{H}_t'\mathbf{M}_{t-1}\mathbf{L}_{t-1}\mathbf{P}_{t-1|t-2}$.

6 NON-LINEAR AND NON-GAUSSIAN MODELS

A general state space model is such that the density of the observations is conditionally independent, given the states, that is

$$p(\mathbf{y}_1,\ldots,\mathbf{y}_n|\boldsymbol{\alpha}_1,\ldots,\boldsymbol{\alpha}_n;\boldsymbol{\theta}) = \prod_{t=1}^{n} p(\mathbf{y}_t|\boldsymbol{\alpha}_t;\boldsymbol{\theta}), \tag{15.25}$$

and the transition density has the Markovian structure,

$$p(\boldsymbol{\alpha}_0,\boldsymbol{\alpha}_1,\ldots,\boldsymbol{\alpha}_n|\boldsymbol{\theta}) = p(\boldsymbol{\alpha}_0|\boldsymbol{\theta})\prod_{t=0}^{n-1} p(\boldsymbol{\alpha}_{t+1}|\boldsymbol{\alpha}_t;\boldsymbol{\theta}). \tag{15.26}$$

The measurement and the transition density belong to a given family. The linear Gaussian state space model (15.1)–(15.2) arises when $p(y_t|\boldsymbol{\alpha}_t;\boldsymbol{\theta}) \sim \mathrm{N}(\mathbf{Z}_t\boldsymbol{\alpha}_t, \sigma^2\mathbf{G}_t\mathbf{G}_t')$ and $p(\boldsymbol{\alpha}_{t+1}|\boldsymbol{\alpha}_t;\boldsymbol{\theta}) \sim \mathrm{N}(\mathbf{T}_t\boldsymbol{\alpha}_t, \sigma^2\mathbf{H}_t\mathbf{H}_t')$.

An important special case is the class of generalized linear state space models, which are such that the states are Gaussian and the transition model retains its linearity, whereas the observation density belongs to the exponential family. Models for time series observations originating from the exponential family, such as count data with Poisson, binomial, negative binomial and multinomial distributions, and continuous data with skewed distributions such as the exponential and gamma have been considered by West and Harrison (1997), Fahrmeir and Tutz (1994) and Durbin and Koopman (2012), among others. In particular, the latter perform MLE by importance sampling; see section 6.2.

Models for which some or all of the state have discrete support (multinomial) are often referred to as Markov switching models; usually, conditionally on those states, the model retains a Gaussian and linear structure. See Cappé et al. (2005) and Kim and Nelson (1999) for macroeconomic applications.

In a more general framework, the predictive densities required to form the likelihood via the prediction error decomposition need not be available in closed form and their evaluation calls for Monte Carlo or deterministic integration methods. Likelihood inference is straightforward only for a class of models with a single source of disturbance, known as observation driven models; see Ord et al. (1997) and section 6.5.

6.1 Extended Kalman Filter

A non-linear time series model is such that the observations are functionally related in a non-linear way to the states, and/or the states are subject to a non-linear transition function. Non-linear state space representations typically arise in the context of DSGE models. Assume that the state space model is formulated as

$$\mathbf{y}_t = \mathcal{Z}_t(\boldsymbol{\alpha}_t) + \mathcal{G}_t(\boldsymbol{\alpha}_t)\varepsilon_t$$

$$\boldsymbol{\alpha}_{t+1} = \mathcal{T}_t(\boldsymbol{\alpha}_t) + \mathcal{H}_t(\boldsymbol{\alpha}_t)\varepsilon_t, \quad \boldsymbol{\alpha}_1 \sim \mathrm{N}(\tilde{\boldsymbol{\alpha}}_{1|0}, \mathbf{P}_{1|0}), \tag{15.27}$$

where $\mathcal{Z}_t(\cdot)$ and $\mathcal{T}_t(\cdot)$ are known smooth and differentiable functions.

Let $\mathbf{a}_t$ denote a representative value of $\boldsymbol{\alpha}_t$. Then, by Taylor series expansion, the model can be linearized around the trajectory $\{\mathbf{a}_t, t = 1,\ldots,n\}$, giving,

$$\mathbf{y}_t = \widetilde{\mathbf{Z}}_t\boldsymbol{\alpha}_t + \mathbf{c}_t + \mathbf{G}_t\varepsilon_t,$$

$$\boldsymbol{\alpha}_{t+1} = \widetilde{\mathbf{T}}_t\boldsymbol{\alpha}_t + \mathbf{d}_t + \mathbf{H}_t\varepsilon_t,\ \ \boldsymbol{\alpha}_1 \sim \mathrm{N}(\tilde{\boldsymbol{\alpha}}_{1|0},\mathbf{P}_{1|0}), \qquad (15.28)$$

where

$$\widetilde{\mathbf{Z}}_t = \frac{\partial \mathcal{Z}_t(\boldsymbol{\alpha}_t)}{\partial \boldsymbol{\alpha}_t}\Big|_{\boldsymbol{\alpha}_t=\mathbf{a}_t},\ \mathbf{c}_t = \mathcal{Z}_t(\mathbf{a}_t) - \widetilde{\mathbf{Z}}_t\mathbf{a}_t, \mathbf{G}_t = \mathcal{G}_t(\mathbf{a}_t),$$

and

$$\widetilde{\mathbf{T}}_t = \frac{\partial \mathcal{T}_t(\boldsymbol{\alpha}_t)}{\partial \boldsymbol{\alpha}_t}\Big|_{\boldsymbol{\alpha}_t=\mathbf{a}_t},\ \mathbf{d}_t = \mathcal{T}_t(\mathbf{a}_t) - \widetilde{\mathbf{T}}_t\mathbf{a}_t, \mathbf{H}_t = \mathcal{H}_t(\mathbf{a}_t).$$

The extended Kalman filter results from applying the KF to the linearized model. The latter depends on $\mathbf{a}_t$ and we stress this dependence by writing KF($\mathbf{a}_t$). The likelihood of the linearized model is then evaluated by KF($\mathbf{a}_t$), and can be maximized with respect to the unknown parameters. See Jazwinski (1970) and Anderson and Moore (1979, Chapter 8).

The issue is the choice of the value $\mathbf{a}_t$ around which the linearization is taken. One possibility is to choose $\mathbf{a}_t = \boldsymbol{\alpha}_{t|t-1}$, where the latter is delivered recursively on line as the observations are processed in (15.5). A more accurate solution is to use $\mathbf{a}_t = \boldsymbol{\alpha}_{t|t-1}$ for the linearization of the measurement equation and $\mathbf{a}_t = \boldsymbol{\alpha}_{t|t}$ for that of the transition equation, using the prediction-updating variant of the filter of section 3.2.

Assuming, for simplicity $\mathcal{G}_t(\boldsymbol{\alpha}_t) = \mathbf{G}_t$, $\mathcal{H}_t(\boldsymbol{\alpha}) = \mathbf{H}_t$, and $\varepsilon_t \sim \mathrm{NID}(\mathbf{0}, \sigma^2\mathbf{I})$, the linearization can be performed using the *iterated extended KF* (Jazwinski, 1970, Chapter 8), which determines the trajectory $\{\mathbf{a}_t\}$ as the maximizer of the posterior kernel:

$$\sum_t (\mathbf{y}_t - \mathcal{Z}_t(\mathbf{a}_t))'(\mathbf{G}_t\mathbf{G}_t')^{-1}(\mathbf{y}_t - \mathcal{Z}_t(\mathbf{a}_t)) + \sum_t (\mathbf{a}_{t+1} - \mathcal{T}_t(\mathbf{a}_t))'(\mathbf{H}_t\mathbf{H}_t')^{-1}(\mathbf{a}_{t+1} - \mathcal{T}_t(\mathbf{a}_t))$$

with respect to $\{\mathbf{a}_t, t = 1,\ldots,n\}$. This is referred to as *posterior mode estimation*, as it locates the posterior mode of $\boldsymbol{\alpha}$ given $\mathbf{y}$, and is carried out iteratively by the following algorithm:

1. Start with trial trajectory $\{\mathbf{a}_t\}$;
2. Linearize the model around it;
3. Run the Kalman filter and smoothing algorithm (15.24) to obtain a new trajectory $\mathbf{a}_t = \boldsymbol{\alpha}_{t|n}$;
4. Iterate steps 2–3 until convergence.

Rather than approximating a non-linear function, the unscented KF (Julier and Uhlmann, 1996, 1997), is based on an approximation of the distribution of $\boldsymbol{\alpha}_t|\mathbf{Y}_t$ based on a deterministic sample of representative *sigma points*, characterized by the same mean and covariance as the true distribution of $\boldsymbol{\alpha}_t|\mathbf{Y}_t$. When these points are propagated using the true non-linear measurement and transition equations, the mean and covariance of the predictive distributions $\boldsymbol{\alpha}_{t+1}|\mathbf{Y}_t$ and $\mathbf{y}_{t+1}|\mathbf{Y}_t$ can be approximated accurately (up to the second order) by the weighted average of the transformation of the chosen sigma points.

6.2 Likelihood Evaluation via Importance Sampling

Let $p(\mathbf{y})$ denote the joint density of the n observations (as a function of $\boldsymbol{\theta}$, omitted from the notation), as implied by the original non-Gaussian and non-linear model. Let $g(\mathbf{y})$ be the likelihood of the associated linearized model. See Durbin and Koopman (2012) for the linearization of exponential family models, non-Gaussian observation densities such as Student's t, as well as non-Gaussian state disturbances; for functionally non-linear models see above.

The estimation of the likelihood via importance sampling is based on the following identity:

$$p(\mathbf{y}) = \int p(\mathbf{y}, \boldsymbol{\alpha}) d\boldsymbol{\alpha} = g(\mathbf{y}) \int \frac{p(\mathbf{y}, \boldsymbol{\alpha})}{g(\mathbf{y}, \boldsymbol{\alpha})} g(\boldsymbol{\alpha}|\mathbf{y}) d\boldsymbol{\alpha} = g(\mathbf{y}) \mathrm{E}_g\left[\frac{p(\mathbf{y}, \boldsymbol{\alpha})}{g(\mathbf{y}, \boldsymbol{\alpha})}\right]. \quad (15.29)$$

The expectation, taken with respect to the conditional Gaussian density $g(\boldsymbol{\alpha}|\mathbf{y})$, can be estimated by Monte Carlo simulation using importance sampling: in particular, after having linearized the model by posterior mode estimation, M samples $\boldsymbol{\alpha}^{(m)}, m = 1, \ldots, M$, are drawn from $g(\boldsymbol{\alpha}|\mathbf{y})$, the importance sampling weights

$$w_m = \frac{p(\mathbf{y}, \boldsymbol{\alpha}^{(m)})}{g(\mathbf{y}, \boldsymbol{\alpha}^{(m)})} = \frac{p(\mathbf{y}|\boldsymbol{\alpha}^{(m)}) p(\boldsymbol{\alpha}^{(m)})}{g(\mathbf{y}|\boldsymbol{\alpha}^{(m)}) g(\boldsymbol{\alpha}^{(m)})},$$

are computed and the above expectation is estimated by the average $\frac{1}{M}\sum_m w_m$. Sampling from $g(\boldsymbol{\alpha}|\mathbf{y})$ is carried out by the simulation smoother illustrated in the next subsection. The proposal distribution is multivariate normal with mean equal to the posterior mode $\tilde{\boldsymbol{\alpha}}_{t|n}$. The curvature around the mode can also be matched in special cases, in the derivation of the Gaussian linear auxiliary model. See Shephard and Pitt (1997), Durbin and Koopman (2012) and Richard and Zhang (2007) for further details.

6.3 The Simulation Smoother

The simulation smoother is an algorithm which draws samples from the conditional distribution of the states, or the disturbances, given the observations and the hyper-parameters. We focus on the simulation smoother proposed by Durbin and Koopman (2002).

Let $\boldsymbol{\eta}_t$ denote a random vector (for example a selection of states or disturbances) and let $\tilde{\boldsymbol{\eta}} = \mathrm{E}(\boldsymbol{\eta}|\mathbf{y})$, where $\boldsymbol{\eta}$ is the stack of the vectors $\boldsymbol{\eta}_t$; $\tilde{\boldsymbol{\eta}}$ is computed by the Kalman filter and smoother. We can write $\boldsymbol{\eta} = \tilde{\boldsymbol{\eta}} + \mathbf{e}$, where $\mathbf{e} = \boldsymbol{\eta} - \tilde{\boldsymbol{\eta}}$ is the smoothing error, with conditional distribution $\mathbf{e}|\mathbf{y} \sim \mathrm{N}(\mathbf{0}, \mathbf{V})$, such that the covariance matrix $\mathbf{V}$ does not depend on the observations, and thus does not vary across the simulations (the diagonal blocks are computed by the smoothing algorithm).

A sample $\boldsymbol{\eta}^*$ from $\boldsymbol{\eta}|\mathbf{y}$ is constructed as follows:

- Draw $(\boldsymbol{\eta}^+, \mathbf{y}^+) \sim g(\boldsymbol{\eta}, \mathbf{y})$.
  As $p(\boldsymbol{\eta}, \mathbf{y}) = g(\boldsymbol{\eta})g(\mathbf{y}|\boldsymbol{\eta})$, this is achieved by first drawing $\boldsymbol{\eta}^+ \sim g(\boldsymbol{\eta})$ from an unconditional Gaussian distribution, and constructing the pseudo observations $\mathbf{y}^+$ recursively from $\boldsymbol{\alpha}_{t+1}^+ = \mathbf{T}_t\boldsymbol{\alpha}_t^+ + \mathbf{H}_t\boldsymbol{\varepsilon}_t^+, \mathbf{y}_t^+ = \mathbf{Z}_t\boldsymbol{\alpha}_t^+ + \mathbf{G}_t\boldsymbol{\varepsilon}_t^+$, $t = 1,2,\ldots,n$, where the initial draw is $\boldsymbol{\alpha}_1^+ \sim \mathrm{N}(\tilde{\boldsymbol{\alpha}}_{1|0}, \mathbf{P}_{1|0})$, so that $\mathbf{y}^+ \sim g(\mathbf{y}|\boldsymbol{\eta})$.
- The Kalman filter and smoother computed on the simulated observations $\mathbf{y}_t^+$ will produce $\tilde{\boldsymbol{\eta}}^+$ and $\boldsymbol{\eta}^+ - \tilde{\boldsymbol{\eta}}^+$ will be the required draw from $\mathbf{e}|\mathbf{y}$.

Hence, $\tilde{\boldsymbol{\eta}} + \boldsymbol{\eta}^+ - \tilde{\boldsymbol{\eta}}^+$ is the required sample from $\boldsymbol{\eta}|\mathbf{y} \sim \mathrm{N}(\tilde{\boldsymbol{\eta}}, \mathbf{V})$.

6.4 Sequential Monte Carlo Methods

For a general state space model, the one-step-ahead predictive densities of the states and the observations, and the filtering density are respectively:

$$\begin{aligned} p(\boldsymbol{\alpha}_{t+1}|\mathbf{Y}_t) &= \int p(\boldsymbol{\alpha}_{t+1}|\boldsymbol{\alpha}_t)p(\boldsymbol{\alpha}_t|\mathbf{Y}_t)\,d\boldsymbol{\alpha}_t = \mathbf{E}_{\alpha_t|Y_t}[p(\boldsymbol{\alpha}_{t+1}|\boldsymbol{\alpha}_t)] \\ p(\mathbf{y}_{t+1}|\mathbf{Y}_t) &= \int p(\mathbf{y}_{t+1}|\boldsymbol{\alpha}_{t+1})p(\boldsymbol{\alpha}_{t+1}|\mathbf{Y}_t)\,d\boldsymbol{\alpha}_{t+1} = \mathbf{E}_{\alpha_{t+1}|Y_t}[p(\mathbf{y}_{t+1}|\boldsymbol{\alpha}_{t+1})] \\ p(\boldsymbol{\alpha}_{t+1}|\mathbf{Y}_{t+1}) &= p(\boldsymbol{\alpha}_{t+1}|\mathbf{Y}_t)p(\mathbf{y}_{t+1}|\boldsymbol{\alpha}_{t+1})/p(\mathbf{y}_{t+1}|\mathbf{Y}_t) \end{aligned} \tag{15.30}$$

Sequential Monte Carlo methods provide algorithms, known as *particle filters*, for recursive, or *on-line*, estimation of the predictive and filtering densities in (15.30). They deal with the estimation of the above expectations as averages over Monte Carlo samples from the reference density, exploiting the fact that $p(\boldsymbol{\alpha}_{t+1}|\boldsymbol{\alpha}_t)$ and $p(\mathbf{y}_{t+1}|\mathbf{Y}_t)$ are easy to evaluate, as they depend solely on the model prior specification.

Assume that at any time t an IID sample of size M from the filtering density $p(\boldsymbol{\alpha}_t|\mathbf{Y}_t)$ is available, with each draw representing a 'particle', $\boldsymbol{\alpha}_t^{(i)}$, $i = 1,\ldots, M$, so that the true density is approximated by the empirical density function:

$$\hat{p}(\boldsymbol{\alpha}_t \in A|\mathbf{Y}_t) = \frac{1}{M}\sum_{i=1}^{M} I(\boldsymbol{\alpha}_t^{(i)} \in A), \tag{15.31}$$

where $I(\cdot)$ is the indicator function.

The Monte Carlo approximation to the state and measurement predictive densities is obtained by generating $\boldsymbol{\alpha}_{t+1|t}^{(i)} \sim p(\boldsymbol{\alpha}_{t+1}|\boldsymbol{\alpha}_t^{(i)})$, $i = 1,\ldots, M$ and $\mathbf{y}_{t+1|t}^{(i)} \sim p(\mathbf{y}_{t+1}|\boldsymbol{\alpha}_{t+1}^{(i)})$, $i = 1,\ldots, M$.

The crucial issue is to obtain a new particle characterization of the filtering density $p(\boldsymbol{\alpha}_{t+1}|\mathbf{Y}_{t+1})$, avoiding particle degeneracy, that is a non-representative sample of particles. To iterate the process it is necessary to generate new particles from $p(\boldsymbol{\alpha}_{t+1}|\mathbf{Y}_{t+1})$ with probability mass equal to $1/M$, so that the approximation to the filtering density will have the same form as (15.31), and the sequential simulation process can progress. Direct application of the last row in (15.30) suggests weighted resampling (Rubin, 1987) of the particles $\boldsymbol{\alpha}_{t+1|t}^{(i)} \sim p(\boldsymbol{\alpha}_{t+1}|\boldsymbol{\alpha}_t^{(i)})$, with importance weights

$w_i = p(\mathbf{y}_{t+1}|\boldsymbol{\alpha}^{(i)}_{t+1|t}) / \sum_{j=1}^{M} p(\mathbf{y}_{t+1}|\boldsymbol{\alpha}^{(j)}_{t+1|t})$. The resampling step eliminates particles with low importance weights and propagates those with high w_i's. This basic particle filter is known as the bootstrap (or Sampling/Importance Resampling, SIR) filter; see Gordon et al. (1993) and Kitagawa (1996).

A serious limitation is that the particles, $\boldsymbol{\alpha}^{(i)}_{t+1|t}$, originate from the prior density and are 'blind' to the information carried by $\mathbf{y}_{t+1}$; this may deplete the representativeness of the particles when the prior is at conflict with the likelihood, $p(\mathbf{y}_{t+1}|\boldsymbol{\alpha}^{(i)}_{t+1|t})$, resulting in a highly uneven distribution of the weights w_i. A variety of sampling schemes have been proposed to overcome this conflict, such as the *auxiliary particle filter*; see Pitt and Shephard (1999) and Doucet et al. (2001).

More generally, in a sequential setting, we aim at simulating $\boldsymbol{\alpha}^{(i)}_{t+1}$ from the target distribution:

$$p(\boldsymbol{\alpha}_{t+1}|\boldsymbol{\alpha}_t, \mathbf{Y}_{t+1}) = \frac{p(\boldsymbol{\alpha}_{t+1}|\boldsymbol{\alpha}_t) p(\mathbf{y}_{t+1}|\boldsymbol{\alpha}_{t+1})}{p(\mathbf{y}_{t+1}|\boldsymbol{\alpha}_t)},$$

where, typically, only the numerator is available in closed form. Let $g(\boldsymbol{\alpha}_{t+1}|\boldsymbol{\alpha}_t, \mathbf{Y}_{t+1})$ be an importance density, available for sampling $\boldsymbol{\alpha}^{(i)}_{t+1} \sim g(\boldsymbol{\alpha}_{t+1}|\boldsymbol{\alpha}^{(i)}_t, \mathbf{Y}_{t+1})$ and let

$$w_i \propto \frac{p(\mathbf{y}_{t+1}|\boldsymbol{\alpha}^{(i)}_{t+1}) p(\boldsymbol{\alpha}^{(i)}_{t+1}|\boldsymbol{\alpha}^{(i)}_t)}{g(\boldsymbol{\alpha}_{t+1}|\boldsymbol{\alpha}^{(i)}_t, \mathbf{Y}_{t+1})};$$

M particles are resampled with probabilities proportional to w_i. Notice that SIR arises as a special case with proposals $g(\boldsymbol{\alpha}_{t+1}|\boldsymbol{\alpha}_t, \mathbf{Y}_{t+1}) = p(\boldsymbol{\alpha}_{t+1}|\boldsymbol{\alpha}_t)$ that ignore $\mathbf{y}_{t+1}$. Van der Merwe et al. (2000) used the unscented transformation of Julier and Uhlmann (1997) to generate a proposal density. Amisano and Tristani (2010) obtain the proposal density by a local linearization of the observation and transition density. Winschel and Krätzig (2010) proposed a particle filter that obtains the first two moments of the predictive distributions in (15.30) by Smolyak Gaussian quadrature, using a normal proposal $g(\boldsymbol{\alpha}_{t+1}|\boldsymbol{\alpha}_t, \mathbf{y}_{t+1})$, with mean and variance resulting from a standard updating Kalman filter step (see section 3.2).

Essential and comprehensive references for the literature on sequential MC are Doucet et al. (2001) and Cappé et al. (2005). For macroeconomic applications see Fernández-Villaverde and Rubio Ramírez (2007) and the recent survey by Creal (2012). Poyiadjis et al. (2011) propose sequential MC methods for approximating the score and the information matrix and use it for recursive and batch parameter estimation of non-linear state space models.

At each update of the particle filter, the contribution to the likelihood of each observation can be thus estimated. However, maximum likelihood estimation by quasi-Newton method is infeasible as the likelihood is not a continuous function of the parameters. Grid search approaches are only feasible when the size of the parameter space is small. A pragmatic solution consists of adding the parameters in the state vector and assigning a random walk evolution with fixed disturbance variance, as in Kitagawa (1998). In the iterated filtering approach proposed by Ionides et al. (2006), generalized in Ionides et al. (2011), the evolution variance is allowed to tend deterministically to zero.

6.5 Observation Driven Score Models

Observation driven models based on the score of the conditional likelihood are a class of models independently developed by Harvey (2013) and Creal et al. (2011a, 2011b).

The model specification starts with the conditional probability distribution of $\mathbf{y}_t$, for $t = 1,\ldots,n$,

$$p(\mathbf{y}_t|\boldsymbol{\lambda}_{t|t-1}, \mathbf{Y}_{t-1}; \boldsymbol{\theta}),$$

where $\boldsymbol{\lambda}_{t|t-1}$ is a set of time varying parameters that are fixed at time $t-1$, $\mathbf{Y}_{t-1}$ is the information set up to time $t-1$, and $\boldsymbol{\theta}$ is a vector of static parameters that enter in the specification of the probability distribution of $\mathbf{y}_t$ and in the updating mechanism for $\boldsymbol{\lambda}_t$. The defining feature of these models is that the dynamics that govern the evolution of the time varying parameters are driven by the score of the conditional distribution:

$$\boldsymbol{\lambda}_{t+1|t} = f(\boldsymbol{\lambda}_{t|t-1}, \boldsymbol{\lambda}_{t-1|t-2}, \ldots, \mathbf{s}_t, \mathbf{s}_{t-1}, \ldots, \boldsymbol{\theta})$$

where

$$\mathbf{s}_t \propto \frac{\partial \ell(\boldsymbol{\lambda}_{t|t-1})}{\partial \boldsymbol{\lambda}_{t|t-1}}$$

and $\ell(\boldsymbol{\lambda}_{t|t-1})$ is the log-likelihood function of $\boldsymbol{\lambda}_{t|t-1}$. Given that $\boldsymbol{\lambda}_t$ is updated through the function f, maximum likelihood estimation eventually concerns the parameter vector $\boldsymbol{\theta}$. The proportionality constant linking the score function to $\mathbf{s}_t$ is a matter of choice and may depend on $\boldsymbol{\theta}$ and other features of the distribution, as the following examples show.

The basic GAS(p, q) models (Creal et al., 2011a, 2011b) consists in the specification of the conditional observation density

$$p(\mathbf{y}_t|\boldsymbol{\lambda}_{t|t-1}, \mathbf{Y}_{t-1}, \boldsymbol{\theta})$$

along with the generalized autoregressive updating mechanism

$$\boldsymbol{\lambda}_{t+1|t} = \boldsymbol{\delta} + \sum_{i=1}^{p} \mathbf{A}_i(\boldsymbol{\theta})\mathbf{s}_{t-i+1} + \sum_{j=1}^{q} \mathbf{B}_i(\boldsymbol{\theta})\boldsymbol{\lambda}_{t-i+1}$$

where $\boldsymbol{\delta}$ is a vector of constants and $\mathbf{A}_i(\boldsymbol{\theta})$ and $\mathbf{B}_i(\boldsymbol{\theta})$ are coefficient matrices and where $\mathbf{s}_t$ is defined as the standardized score vector, that is the score pre-multiplied by the inverse Fisher information matrix $\mathcal{I}^{-1}_{t|t-1}$,

$$\mathbf{s}_t = \mathcal{I}^{-1}_{t|t-1} \frac{\partial \ell(\boldsymbol{\lambda}_{t|t-1})}{\partial \boldsymbol{\lambda}_{t|t-1}}.$$

The recursive equation for $\boldsymbol{\lambda}_{t+1|t}$ can be interpreted as a Gauss–Newton algorithm for estimating $\boldsymbol{\lambda}_{t+1|t}$ through time.

The first order Beta-t-EGARCH model (Harvey and Chakravarty, 2008) is specified as follows,

$$p(y_t|\lambda_{t|t-1}, Y_{t-1}, \boldsymbol{\theta}) \sim t_\nu(0, e^{\lambda_{t|t-1}})$$

$$\lambda_{t+1|t} = \delta + \phi\lambda_{t|t-1} + \kappa s_t$$

where

$$s_t = \frac{(\nu + 1)y_t^2}{\nu e^{\lambda_{t|t-1}} + y_t^2} - 1$$

is the score of the conditional density and $\boldsymbol{\theta} = (\delta, \phi, \kappa, \nu)$. It follows from the properties of the Student-t distribution that the random variable

$$b_t = \frac{s_t + 1}{\nu + 1} = \frac{(s_t + 1)/(\nu e^{\lambda_{t|t-1}})}{(\nu + 1)/(\nu e^{\lambda_{t|t-1}})}$$

is distributed like a Beta $(\frac{1}{2}, \frac{\nu}{2})$. Based on this property of the score, it is possible to develop full asymptotic theory for the maximum likelihood estimator of $\boldsymbol{\theta}$ (Harvey, 2013). In practice, having fixed an initial condition such as, for $|\phi| < 1$, $\lambda_{1|0} = \frac{\delta}{1 - \phi}$, likelihood optimization may be carried out with a Fisher scoring or Newton–Raphson algorithm.

7 CONCLUSIONS

The focus of this chapter was on likelihood inference for time series models that can be represented in state space. Although we have not touched upon the vast area of Bayesian inference, the state space methods presented in this chapter are a key ingredient in designing and implementing Markov chain Monte Carlo sampling schemes.

REFERENCES

Amisano, G. and O. Tristani (2010), 'Euro area inflation persistence in an estimated nonlinear DSGE model', *Journal of Economic Dynamics and Control*, **34**, 1837–58.

Anderson, B.D.O. and J.B. Moore (1979), *Optimal Filtering*, Englewood Cliffs, NJ: Prentice-Hall.

Brockwell, P.J. and R.A. Davis (1991), *Time Series: Theory and Methods*, New York: Springer.

Bryson, A.E. and Y.C. Ho (1969), *Applied Optimal Control: Optimization, Estimation, and Control*, Waltham, MA: Blaisdell Publishing.

Burridge, P. and K.F. Wallis (1988), 'Prediction theory for autoregressive-moving average processes', *Econometric Reviews*, **7**, 65–9.

Caines, P.E. (1988), *Linear Stochastic Systems*, New York: John Wiley & Sons.

Canova, F. (2007), *Methods for Applied Macroeconomic Research*, Princeton, NJ: Princeton University Press.

Cappé, O., E. Moulines and T. Rydén (2005), *Inference in Hidden Markov Models*, New York: Springer.

Chan, N.H. and W. Palma (1998), 'State space modeling of long-memory processes', *Annals of Statistics*, **26**, 719–40.

Chang, Y., J.I. Miller and J.Y. Park (2009), 'Extracting a common stochastic trend: theory with some applications', *Journal of Econometrics*, **15**, 231–47.

Clark, P.K. (1987), 'The cyclical component of US economic activity', *The Quarterly Journal of Economics*, **102**(4), 797–814.
Cogley, T., G.E. Primiceri and T.J. Sargent (2010), 'Inflation-gap persistence in the US', *American Economic Journal: Macroeconomics*, **2**(1), 43–69.
Creal, D. (2012), 'A survey of sequential Monte Carlo methods for economics and finance', *Econometric Reviews*, **31**(3), 245–96.
Creal, D., S.J. Koopman and A. Lucas (2011a), 'Generalized autoregressive score models with applications', *Journal of Applied Econometrics*, forthcoming.
Creal, D., S.J. Koopman and A. Lucas (2011b), 'A dynamic multivariate heavy-tailed model for time-varying volatilities and correlations', *Journal of Business and Economics Statistics*, **29**(4), 552–63.
De Jong, P. (1989), 'Smoothing and interpolation with the state space model', *Journal of the American Statistical Association*, **84**, 1085–88.
De Jong, P. (1991), 'The diffuse Kalman filter', *Annals of Statistics*, **19**, 1073–83.
De Jong, P. and S. Chu-Chun-Lin (1994), 'Fast likelihood evaluation and prediction for nonstationary state space models', *Biometrika*, **81**, 133–42.
De Jong, P. and J. Penzer (2004), 'The ARMA model in state space form', *Statistics and Probability Letters*, **70**, 119–25.
Dempster, A.P., N.M. Laird and D.B. Rubin (1977), 'Maximum likelihood estimation from incomplete data', *Journal of the Royal Statistical Society*, **14**(1), 1–38.
Doran, E. (1992), 'Constraining Kalman filter and smoothing estimates to satisfy time-varying restrictions', *Review of Economics and Statistics*, **74**, 568–72.
Doucet, A., J.F.G. de Freitas and N.J. Gordon (2001), *Sequential Monte Carlo Methods in Practice*, New York: Springer-Verlag.
Durbin, J. and S.J. Koopman (2002), 'A simple and efficient simulation smoother for state space time series analysis', *Biometrika*, **89**, 603–15.
Durbin, J. and S.J. Koopman (2012). *Time Series Analysis by State Space Methods*, 2nd edn, Oxford: Oxford University Press.
Farhmeir, L. and G. Tutz (1994), *Multivariate Statistical Modelling Based on Generalized Linear Models*, New York: Springer-Verlag.
Fernández-Villaverde, J. (2010), 'The econometrics of DSGE models', *Journal of the Spanish Economic Association*, **1**, 3–49.
Fernández-Villaverde, J. and J.F. Rubio-Ramírez (2005), 'Estimating dynamic equilibrium economies: linear versus non-linear likelihood', *Journal of Applied Econometrics*, **20**, 891–910.
Fernández-Villaverde, J. and J.F. Rubio-Ramírez (2007), 'Estimating macroeconomic models: a likelihood approach', *Review of Economic Studies*, **74**, 1059–87.
Frale, C., M. Marcellino, G. Mazzi and T. Proietti (2011), 'EUROMIND: a monthly indicator of the euro area economic conditions', *Journal of the Royal Statistical Society, Series A*, **174**(2), 439–70.
Francke, M.K., S.J. Koopman and A. de Vos (2010), 'Likelihood functions for state space models with diffuse initial conditions', *Journal of Time Series Analysis*, **31**, 407–14.
Geweke, J.F. and K.J. Singleton (1981), 'Maximum likelihood confirmatory factor analysis of economic time series', *International Economic Review*, **22**, 37–54.
Giordani, P., R. Kohn and D. van Dijk (2007), 'A unified approach to nonlinearity, structural change, and outliers', *Journal of Economics*, **137**, 112–33.
Golub, G.H. and C.F. van Loan (1996), *Matrix Computations*, 3rd edn, Baltimore, MD: The Johns Hopkins University Press.
Gordon, N.J., D.J. Salmond and A.F.M. Smith (1993), 'A novel approach to non-linear and non-Gaussian Bayesian state estimation', *IEE-Proceedings F 140*, 107–13.
Hannan, E.J. and M. Deistler (1988), *The Statistical Theory of Linear systems*, New York: John Wiley & Sons.
Harvey, A.C. (1989), *Forecasting, Structural Time series and the Kalman Filter*, Cambridge: Cambridge University Press.
Harvey, A.C. (2001), 'Testing in unobserved components models', *Journal of Forecasting*, **20**, 1–19.
Harvey, A.C. (2013), *Dynamic Models for Volatility and Heavy Tails: With Applications to Financial and Economic Time Series*, Economic Society Monograph, Cambridge University Press.
Harvey, A.C. and T. Chakravarty (2008), *Beta-t(E)GARCH*, Working Paper, CWPE 0840.
Harvey, A.C. and C.H. Chung (2000), 'Estimating the underlying change in unemployment in the UK', *Journal of the Royal Statistics Society, Series A*, Statistics in Society, **163**, Part 3, 303–39.
Harvey, A.C. and A. Jäger (1993), 'Detrending, stylized facts and the business cycle', *Journal of Applied Econometrics*, **8**, 231–47.
Harvey, A.C. and T. Proietti (2005), *Readings in Unobserved Components Models*, Oxford: Oxford University Press.

Harville, D.A. (1977), 'Maximum likelihood approaches to variance component estimation and to related problems', *Journal of the American Statistical Association*, **72**, 320–40.
Hodrick, R. and E.C. Prescott (1997), 'Postwar US business cycle: an empirical investigation', *Journal of Money, Credit and Banking*, **29**(1), 1–16.
Ionides, E.L., C. Breto and A.A. King (2006), 'Inference for nonlinear dynamical systems', *Proceedings of the National Academy of Sciences*, **103**, 18438–43.
Ionides, E.L., A. Bhadra, Y. Atchade and A.A. King (2011), 'Iterated filtering', *Annals of Statistics*, **39**, 1776–802.
Jazwinski, A.H. (1970), *Stochastic Processes and Filtering Theory*, New York: Academic Press.
Julier, S.J. and J.K. Uhlmann (1996), 'A general method for approximating nonlinear transformations of probability distributions', Robotics Research Group, Oxford University, **4**(7), 1–27.
Julier, S.J. and J.K. Uhlmann (1997), 'A new extension of the Kalman filter to nonlinear systems', *Proceedings of AeroSense: The 11th International Symposium on Aerospace/Defense Sensing, Simulation and Controls*, Orlando, FL.
Jungbacker, B., S.J. Koopman and M. van der Wel (2011), 'Maximum likelihood estimation for dynamic factor models with missing data', *Journal of Economic Dynamics and Control*, **35**(8), 1358–68.
Kailath, T., A.H. Sayed and B. Hassibi (2000), *Linear Estimation*, Upper Saddle River, NJ: Prentice Hall.
Kalman, R.E. (1960), 'A new approach to linear filtering and prediction problems', *Journal of Basic Engineering, Transactions ASME, Series D*, **82**, 35–45.
Kalman, R.E. and R.S. Bucy (1961), 'New results in linear filtering and prediction theory', *Journal of Basic Engineering, Transactions ASME, Series D*, **83**, 95–108.
Kim, C.J. and C. Nelson (1999), *State-Space Models with Regime-Switching*, Cambridge, MA: MIT Press.
Kitagawa, G. (1996), 'Monte Carlo filter and smoother for non-Gaussian nonlinear state-space models', *Journal of Computational and Graphical Statistics*, **5**, 125.
Kitagawa, G. (1998), 'A self-organising state-space model', *Journal of the American Statistical Association*, **93**, 1203–15.
Kitagawa, G. (2010), *Introduction to Time Series Models*, Boca Raton, FL: Chapman and Hall/CRC.
Kitagawa, G. and W. Gersch (1996), *Smoothness Priors Analysis of Time Series*, Berlin: Springer-Verlag.
Koopman, S.J. and J. Durbin (2000), 'Fast filtering and smoothing for multivariate state space models', *Journal of Time Series Analysis*, **21**, 281–96.
Ljungqvist, L. and T.J. Sargent (2004), *Recursive Macroeconomic Theory*, 2nd edn, Cambridge, MA: MIT Press.
Luati, A. and T. Proietti (2010), 'Hyper-spherical and elliptical stochastic cycles', *Journal of Time Series Analysis*, **31**, 169–81.
Morley, J.C., C.R. Nelson and E. Zivot (2003), 'Why are Beveridge–Nelson and unobserved-component decompositions of GDP so different?', *Review of Economics and Statistics*, **85**, 235–43.
Nyblom, J. (1986), 'Testing for deterministic linear trend in time series', *Journal of the American Statistical Association*, **81**, 545–9.
Ord, J.K., A.B. Koehler and R.D. Snyder (1997), 'Estimation and prediction for a class of dynamic nonlinear statistical models', *Journal of the American Statistical Association*, **92**, 1621–29.
Pagan, A. (1980), 'Some identification and estimation results for regression models with stochastically varying coefficients', *Journal of Econometrics*, **13**, 341–63.
Patterson, H.D. and R. Thompson (1971), 'Recovery of inter-block information when block sizes are unequal', *Biometrika*, **58**, 545–54.
Pearlman, J.G. (1980), 'An algorithm for the exact likelihood of a high-order autoregressive-moving average process', *Biometrika*, **67**, 232–3.
Pitt, M.K. and N. Shephard (1999), 'Filtering via simulation: auxiliary particle filters', *Journal of the American Statistical Association*, **94**, 590–99.
Poyiadjis, G., A. Doucet and S.S. Singh (2011), 'Particle approximations of the score and observed information matrix in state space models with application to parameter estimation', *Biometrika*, **98**, 65–80.
Primiceri, G.E. (2005), 'Time varying structural vector autoregressions and monetary policy', *The Review of Economic Studies*, **72**, 821–52.
Proietti, T. (1999), 'Characterising business cycle asymmetries by smooth transition structural time series models', *Studies in Nonlinear Dynamics and Econometrics*, **3**, 141–56.
Proietti, T. (2006), 'Trend-cycle decompositions with correlated components', *Econometric Reviews*, **25**, 61–84.
Richard, J.F. and W. Zhang (2007), 'Efficient high-dimensional importance sampling', *Journal of Econometrics*, **127,** 1385–411.
Rosenberg, B. (1973), 'Random coefficient models: the analysis of a cross-section of time series by stochastically convergent parameter regression', *Annals of Economic and Social Measurement*, **2**, 399–428.
Rubin, D.B. (1987), 'A noniterative sampling/importance resampling alternative to the data augmentation

algorithm for creating a few imputations when the fraction of missing information is modest: the SIR algorithm. Discussion of Tanner and Wong (1987)', *Journal of the American Statistical Association*, **82**, 543–6.
Sargent, T.J. (1989), 'Two models of measurements and the investment accelerator', *Journal of Political Economy*, **97**(2), 251–87.
Sargent, T.J. and C.A. Sims (1977), 'Business cycle modeling without pretending to have too much a-priori economic theory', in C. Sims *et al.* (eds), *New Methods in Business Cycle Research*, Minneapolis, MN: Federal Reserve Bank of Minneapolis.
Shephard, N. (2005), *Stochastic Volatility: Selected Readings*, Oxford: Oxford University Press.
Shephard, N. and M.K. Pitt (1997), 'Likelihood analysis of non-Gaussian measurement time series', *Biometrika*, **84**, 653–67.
Shumway, R.H. and D.S. Stoffer (1982), 'An approach to time series smoothing and forecasting using the EM algorithm', *Journal of Time Series Analysis*, **3**, 253–64.
Smets, F. and R. Wouters (2003), 'An estimated dynamic stochastic general equilibrium model of the euro area', *Journal of the European Economic Association*, **1**(5), 1123–75.
Stock, J.H. and M.W. Watson (1989), 'New indexes of coincident and leading economic indicators', *NBER Macroeconomics Annual 1989*, pp. 351–93.
Stock, J.H. and M.W. Watson (2007), 'Why has US inflation become harder to forecast?', *Journal of Money, Credit and Banking*, **39**(1), 3–33.
Van der Merwe, R., A. Doucet, N. De Freitas and E. Wan (2000), 'The unscented particle filter', *Advances in Neural Information Processing Systems*, **13**, 584–90.
Watson, M.W. (1986), 'Univariate detrending methods with stochastic trends', *Journal of Monetary Economics*, **18**, 49–75.
West, M. and P.J. Harrison (1989), *Bayesian Forecasting and Dynamic Models*, New York: Springer-Verlag.
West, M. and P.J. Harrison (1997), *Bayesian Forecasting and Dynamic Models*, 2nd edn, New York: Springer-Verlag.
Winschel, W. and M. Krätzig (2010), 'Solving, estimating, and selecting nonlinear dynamic models without the curse of dimensionality', *Econometrica*, **39**(1), 3–33.

16 Bayesian methods*

Luc Bauwens and Dimitris Korobilis

1 INTRODUCTION

The scope of this chapter is to introduce applied macroeconomists to the world of Bayesian estimation methods. Why would an empirical macroeconomist invest in learning Bayesian estimation after having invested hours learning estimation methods like maximum likelihood and generalized method of moments (see previous chapters)?

Nowadays, with the advancement of computing power and the establishment of new simulation techniques, it is probably much easier to answer this question compared to, say, thirty years ago. First, Bayesian methods offer a wide range of estimation tools for macroeconomic models, ranging from simple time series models to structural macroeconometric models. When optimizing the likelihood function becomes a daunting task (due to its high dimensionality or multimodality, or due to underidentification of specific model parameters), Bayesian methods can prove more robust since they do not rely on using complex optimization techniques that might get stuck in local optima. Second, Bayesian methods allow the researcher to incorporate prior beliefs in her model. We argue in this chapter that such beliefs are not so difficult to formalize as one may fear a priori, and that they may help to get reasonable estimates and forecasts, for example through soft shrinkage constraints.

The purpose of this chapter is to provide the reader with a soft introduction to the Bayesian world. Exhaustively presenting the advances of Bayesian methods in macroeconomics is beyond the scope of this chapter. The interested reader should consult Bauwens et al. (1999), Koop (2003), Lancaster (2004) and Geweke (2005), in order to delve deeper into Bayesian methods in econometrics. We start by introducing the basic principles of Bayesian inference and the numerical tools that are necessary for its implementation (section 2). We apply all this in section 3 to the dynamic linear regression model. The last section contains a short guide to the Bayesian literature for more sophisticated models.

2 BASICS OF BAYESIAN INFERENCE

2.1 Prior, Posterior and Likelihood

At the core of the Bayesian paradigm lies 'Bayes theorem'. This is our starting point for statistical inference. Assume two random events A and B, and a probability measure P such that $P(B) \neq 0$, then Bayes Theorem states that

$$P(A|B) = \frac{P(B|A)P(A)}{P(B)}.$$

It holds, by definition of conditional probability, that $P(A|B) = P(A \cap B)/P(B)$ and similarly $P(B|A) = P(A \cap B)/P(A)$, which gives $P(A|B)P(B) = P(A \cap B) = P(B|A)P(A)$, and by rearranging terms we end up with Bayes theorem. However, this exposition from probability theory may not be interesting to the applied econometrician who wants to estimate a parametric model which could potentially be connected to economic theory. Subsequently assume that the random event B is a stochastic process y from which our observed data (for instance US inflation) occur, and the random event A is our parameters θ which take values in a space Θ. An econometric model might have other assumptions apart from observed data and model parameters, but we can ignore them at this level of generality. The parameters θ might come from a regression model, a vector autoregressive (VAR) model, a dynamic stochastic general equilibrium (DSGE) model, or another type of model. We can write Bayes theorem in terms of y and θ in the following form:

$$p(\theta|y) = \frac{p(y|\theta)p(\theta)}{p(y)}. \tag{16.1}$$

where p denotes generically a probability density function. The density $p(\theta)$ is representing our prior beliefs about the values of our parameters. The conditional density of the data given the parameters, $p(y|\theta)$, is the familiar likelihood function $L(\theta; y)$ (once y is 'realized' into observations). The density $p(y)$ is the marginal 'likelihood' or prior predictive density of the data. It is the density $p(y|\theta)$ marginalized with respect to the parameters θ, that is

$$p(y) = \int_{\Theta} p(y|\theta)\, p(\theta)\, d\theta, \text{ when } \theta \text{ is continuous} \tag{16.2}$$

$$p(y) = \sum_{\Theta} p(y|\theta)\, p(\theta), \text{ when } \theta \text{ is discrete} \tag{16.3}$$

The resulting conditional density $p(\theta|y)$ in equation (16.1) is called the posterior of the parameters: it is the density of the parameters after observing the data (hence conditional on y). Note that $p(y)$ does not depend on θ since it is integrated out from this density. Subsequently the formula of the posterior can be written as

$$p(\theta|y) \propto p(y|\theta)p(\theta) \tag{16.4}$$

or

$$p(\theta|y) \propto L(\theta; y)p(\theta), \tag{16.5}$$

where the symbol $\propto$ means 'proportional to' and is used extensively to avoid writing uninteresting constants in many formulae. This formulation makes it clear that the posterior density of the parameters, $p(\theta|y)$, updates our prior beliefs (before seeing the data) with the data information embedded in the likelihood function that measures the probability that our data come from the specified model.

Consequently, the Bayesian econometrician tries to average the likelihood with the prior $p(\theta)$, whereas the frequentist tries to maximize the likelihood $L(\theta;y) \propto p(y|\theta)$. The equation above has several implications. One of those is that we assumed that we can assign a probability density not only to our data, but also to our parameters θ. That is, the parameters are considered as random variables, with a well defined probability density. Subsequently, for the Bayesian, a parameter θ is not only identified by the likelihood, but also by the prior distribution, something that has very important implications in possibly underidentified macroeconometric models, especially DSGE models.

Thus, what is common to Bayesian and frequentist econometricians is the need to define a model that is assumed to have generated the data, yielding a likelihood function. What differentiates them is that the Bayesian finds it convenient to treat the parameters as random variables, while the frequentist views the parameters as unknown fixed constants. Notice that these viewpoints are not necessarily contradictory, since the Bayesian is just adding that unknown true constants may be the object of (subjective or objective) probability judgements, precisely because they are unknown. The frequentist then maximizes the likelihood (or another) function and reports point estimates and typically asymptotic standard errors. The Bayesian computes the posterior by integral calculus and reports posterior means as point estimates and posterior standard deviations as measures of uncertainty about these estimates.

The presence of a prior distribution is thus one of the main elements that differentiate substantially frequentist from Bayesian analysis. At the same time, the prior is a useful tool for the modern macroeconomist in that it allows the incorporation of beliefs from economic theory, personal experience and opinions about the structure or the future of the economy coming from analysts in business, academia, or simply consumers' beliefs. Given that macroeconomic series at monthly or quarterly frequencies are short, thus making the likelihood not very informative (especially when trying to model the economy using many variables), the prior often plays a favourable role in producing reasonable results. Subsequently the prior should be seen as an ally for the applied macroeconomist, and not as one more trouble to solve during the process of statistical inference. In the next section, we discuss in detail the elaboration of priors for the parameters of regression models, and we give examples of informative priors that have been adopted by applied econometricians.

This explains why applied macroeconomics is one of the few fields in economics where the philosophical dispute about being subjective (as opposed to being objective) plays less of a significant role. Nevertheless, Bayesian analysis allows us to produce results that are comparable to maximizing the likelihood (objective analysis). For instance, it is customary in Bayesian econometrics to use a non-informative prior on a parameter θ when we have no prior information about this parameter. Suppose that this parameter is the mean of a normal density with possible values (support) on the space $(-\infty,+\infty)$ and that since we have no information to restrict this support a priori,[1] we use the uniform prior $p(\theta) \propto c$ (an arbitrary constant), so that all values of θ are a priori equally likely. This leads to the posterior being written as $p(\theta|y) \propto L(\theta;y) \times c \propto L(\theta;y)$, so that the posterior is proportional to the likelihood function (up to a normalizing constant that does not involve θ). Subsequently the mode of the posterior density is equal to the maximum likelihood estimate (MLE), and the posterior mean is close to the MLE if the likelihood is symmetric around its mode.

Finally we should note that another benefit of using Bayesian analysis is that the computation of the posterior (see next subsection) usually does not require optimization techniques that can fail in complex models, when the likelihood function is multimodal or highly dimensional. Additionally, basing predictions (that are often essential for applied macroeconomists) on the predictive density of future observations means that uncertainty about the values of the parameters is accounted for. Let y_f denote future observations to be predicted, that is y_f occurs after our sample y that serves to compute $p(\theta|y)$. Then the predictive density of y_f is obtained as

$$p(y_f|y) = \int p(y_f|y,\theta)p(\theta|y)\,d\theta. \tag{16.6}$$

The integrand in the previous formula shows that the density of future observations conditional on the past data and the parameters (that is the likelihood function of the potential future data) is weighted by the evidence obtained about the parameters from the past data. The integration means that this evidence is taken into account for all possible values of θ, and not only at the MLE as in a frequentist analysis. Indeed, a natural frequentist point predictor of y_f is $E(y_f|y,\hat{\theta})$, where $\hat{\theta}$ is the MLE, whereas a Bayesian point predictor is naturally taken to be $E(y_f|y)$ (or any other central measure like the median). Notice that $E(y_f|y) = E[E(y_f|y,\theta)]$, implying that $E(y_f|y,\hat{\theta})$ is just one of the averaged values in the Bayesian formula.

2.2 Methods to Compute the Posterior

In essence all Bayesian computation techniques try to estimate the formula in (16.5). In the Bayesian context, 'estimate' means finding the normalizing constant of the posterior (which is nothing else but $p(y)$), and, more importantly, whatever features of it are of interest. Such features typically include the expected value, the covariance matrix, univariate marginal densities of θ and their quantiles, and often also of functions of θ, denoted by $g(\theta)$. In general the quantities we wish to compute can be expressed as

$$E[g(\theta)|y] = \int g(\theta)p(\theta|y)\,d\theta, \tag{16.7}$$

where it is understood that $p(\theta|y)$ is a properly normalized density, that is $\int p(\theta|y)\,d\theta = 1$. To be concrete, if $g(\theta) = \theta$, we get the expected value of θ, if $g(\theta) = \theta\theta'$, we get the matrix of uncentred second moments, and from these two, we easily get the covariance matrix of θ. If we are interested in the posterior probability that the ith element of θ is in the interval (a, b), we define $g(\theta)$ as the indicator function that is equal to 1 if $\theta_i \in (a, b)$ and to zero otherwise. Moreover, if $g(\theta)$ is taken to be $p(y_f|y,\theta)$, we get $p(y_f|y)$, and if it is $E(y_f|y,\theta)$ (which may be available analytically), we get $E(y_f|y)$.

For a few (simple) econometric models (in particular the normal linear regression model), some choices of prior densities, and some simple functions g, there is no need to compute the integrals above by numerical methods, because they are known analytically. For example, if the posterior is a Normal density, we know all its moments, but if we are interested in a special function of θ, we may not know the result.[2] In this case, we need numerical methods to compute integrals as in (16.7). We also need these numerical integration techniques in most econometric models. This is due to the fact that their likelihood function is so complex that whatever the prior we choose and the functions g we are interested in, the integrals are not known analytically. In this kind of situation, the typical tool to compute integrals as in (16.7) is Monte Carlo simulation. The principle of this technique is to simulate on a computer a large sample of values of θ that are distributed according to the posterior density $p(\theta|y)$. Let us denote by $\{\theta^{(r)}\}_{r=1}^{R}$ a sample of size R of such values, called (random) draws or replicates (of the posterior). Then we can estimate consistently[3] $E[g(\theta)|y]$ (if it is finite) by the sample mean of the draws, that is

$$\frac{1}{N}\sum_{r=1}^{R} g(\theta^{(r)}) \xrightarrow{p} E[g(\theta)|y] \tag{16.8}$$

as R tends to infinity. We present next the most useful ways of generating draws of the posterior density of the parameters of econometric models.

2.2.1 Direct sampling

As mentioned above, in linear regression models under the normality assumption, it is possible to obtain the posterior analytically. Write the regression model for observation t as $y_t = \beta' x_t + \varepsilon_t$, where x_t and β are vectors of k elements, $\varepsilon_t \sim N(0,\sigma^2)$ and $t = 1,2,\ldots,T$. In matrix form, this is written as $y = X\beta + \varepsilon$ where X is the matrix of T observations on the k regressors, and we assume $T > k$. The likelihood function is then

$$L(\beta,\sigma^2;y,X) \propto (\sigma^2)^{-T/2}\exp\left[-\frac{(y - X\beta)'(y - X\beta)}{2\sigma^2}\right]. \tag{16.9}$$

We use the non-informative prior $p(\beta,\sigma^2|) \propto 1/\sigma^2$. This means that we consider each regression coefficient and the logarithm of σ^2 to be uniformly distributed on the real line.[4] For sure, such a prior is not a density, since it is not integrable ('improper'). However the posterior is integrable (proper) as we explain below. The reader who feels uneasy about using an improper prior may be reassured by the following argument: instead of saying that a regression coefficient is uniformly distributed on $(-\infty, +\infty)$, we could decide that it should be uniformly distributed on the bounded interval $(-B,+B)$. By choosing B to be very large but finite, the prior is proper and the posterior will be the same as if we used the improper uniform prior. A way to choose B that ensures this equivalence is to choose B as the smallest value such that when the likelihood function is evaluated at $\beta = \pm B$, the computer returns zero (an underflow). It would be a waste of time to search for this value, so that using an improper uniform prior is a convenient shortcut.

By multiplication of the likelihood and the prior, we get the posterior

$$p(\beta,\sigma^2|y,X) \propto (\sigma^2)^{-(T+2)/2}\exp\left[-\frac{(\beta - \hat{\beta})'X'X(\beta - \hat{\beta}) + s^2}{2\sigma^2}\right] \tag{16.10}$$

where $\hat{\beta} = (X'X)^{-1}X'y$ is the OLS estimator and $s^2 = (y - X\hat{\beta})'(y - X\hat{\beta})$ is the sum of squared OLS residuals. The equality of $(y - X\beta)'(y - X\beta)$ and $(\beta - \hat{\beta})'X'X(\beta - \hat{\beta}) + s^2$ can be checked by using the definitions of $\hat{\beta}$ and s^2 in the latter. To obtain the posterior density of β alone, we must integrate the above expression with respect to σ^2. This yields a proper density if $T > k$, given by

$$p(\beta|y, X) \propto [(\beta - \hat{\beta})'X'X(\beta - \hat{\beta}) + s^2]^{-\frac{\nu+k}{2}}, \tag{16.11}$$

where $\nu = T - k$ is the degrees of freedom parameter. The posterior density of β is a multivariate t, with parameters $\hat{\beta}$, $X'X$, s^2 and ν. To write it as a normalized density, we should multiply the expression in the above formula by some constants (see Bauwens et al., 1999, Appendix A, for a complete definition and properties). Using the properties of the t density, we can state that the posterior mean of β is $\hat{\beta}$, and its posterior covariance matrix is $s^2(X'X)^{-1}/(T - k - 2)$. Thus the posterior mean is the OLS estimator, and the posterior covariance differs only slightly from the covariance of the OLS estimator, which is equal to $s^2(X'X)^{-1}/(T - k)$. For the reader who is not familiar with the multivariate t density, but who is familiar with the Normal density, the difference disappears as ν tends to infinity. Thus if the sample size is large relative to the number of regressors, the posterior (16.11) is very well approximated by the $N(\hat{\beta}, s^2(X'X)^{-1}/(T - k))$ density.

This is an example of a model and prior which give numerical results that are quasi-identical from the frequentist and Bayesian perspectives. However, the interpretation of the results is different. The Bayesian says that given the observed unique sample that is available, the unknown parameter β has a posterior density centred on $\hat{\beta}$, while the frequentist says that the (sampling) distribution of $\hat{\beta}$ is centred on the (unknown) true value of β. Thus the frequentist refers to a hypothetically infinitely many times repeated experiment of sampling the data from the population model, whereas the Bayesian just refers to the single sample that has been observed.

Subsequently all we need to do to obtain features of the posterior density that are not known analytically is to generate independent draws of the t density with the parameters specified above. This can be done easily in any programming language using a random number generator from the t density (see Bauwens et al., 1999, Appendix B, for a generator). For example, if we are interested in generating the marginal posterior density of $(\beta_1 + \beta_2)/(1 - \beta_3)$, we proceed as follows:

1. Generate R draws $\{\beta^{(r)}\}_{r=1}^{R}$ of β from the t density with parameters $\hat{\beta}$, $X'X$, s^2 and ν.
2. Compute $(\beta_1^{(r)} + \beta_2^{(r)})/(1 - \beta_3^{(r)})$ for $r = 1, 2, \ldots, R$.
3. Use a kernel method to obtain an estimate of the posterior density.

We draw the reader's attention to the fact that the posterior mean of $(\beta_1 + \beta_2)/(1 - \beta_3)$ does not exist, so that a point estimator of that quantity could be the median of its posterior. The median is obtained by ordering the R draws of $(\beta_1^{(r)} + \beta_2^{(r)})/(1 - \beta_3^{(r)})$ by increasing value and selecting the value ranked in position $R/2$ (if R is an even number).

2.2.2 Methods to simulate posteriors that are not tractable

There are cases where multiplying the prior with the likelihood gives a mathematical expression of the posterior density that does not belong to any known family of densities or is not easy to simulate by direct sampling. If this happens, we are unable to simulate directly samples $\{\theta^{(r)}\}_{r=1}^{R}$ from the posterior of the parameters using known random number generators. In these cases we need to rely on other simulation methods. One useful class of methods to do this is called 'Markov chain Monte Carlo' (MCMC). Two MCMC sampling methods, very much used, are the Metropolis–Hastings (MH) algorithm and the Gibbs algorithm. The 'Markov chain' part of the name reveals that the samples generated by these methods have a 'Markov property', implying that the draws are not independent, contrary to the direct sampling method. To explain MCMC, we first define the Markov property.

A Markov chain is a stochastic process (that is a sequence of random variables) which has the Markov property, that is the probability of the next state of the stochastic process depends only the current state, and not on any other state in the distant past. Formally, consider a process $\{s_t\}$, $t = 1, 2, \ldots, T$. If the probability of moving from one state s_t to the next s_{t+1} satisfies $P(s_{t+1}|s_t, s_{t-1}, \ldots, s_1) = P(s_{t+1}|s_t)$, the process satisfies the Markov property. If the variable s_t is continuous, the above property holds using densities (that is P is replaced by p). All you need to remember in order to understand MCMC is that we have a variable s_t, with initial state (or initial condition) s_0, and *transition density* $p(s_{t+1}|s_t)$ which satisfies the Markov property.

Gibbs sampling In the rest of this section, we denote the posterior by $p(\theta)$ instead of $p(\theta|y)$. The Gibbs sampler requires us to partition the parameter vector θ (of k elements) into b sub-vectors ('blocks'), with $b \leq k$, denoted by $\theta_{[i]}$, that is $\theta = (\theta'_{[1]}\theta'_{[2]} \ldots \theta'_{[b]})'$, such that for each block, the 'full' conditional density $p(\theta_{[i]}|\theta_{-[i]})$, where $\theta_{-[i]}$ denotes θ without $\theta_{[i]}$, can be directly simulated. To generate a sample of size R of draws from $p(\theta)$ (after warming up the algorithm with R_0 draws), the algorithm proceeds as follows:

1. Choose an initial value $\theta^{(0)}_{-[1]}$ that belongs to the parameter space.
2. Set $r = 1$.
3. Draw successively

$$\theta^{(r)}_{[1]} \text{ from } p(\theta_{[1]}|\theta^{(r-1)}_{-[1]})$$

$$\theta^{(r)}_{[2]} \text{ from } p(\theta_{[2]}|\theta^{(r)}_{[1]}, \theta^{(r-1)}_{[3]}, \ldots, \theta^{(r-1)}_{[b]})$$

$$\vdots$$

$$\theta^{(r)}_{[i]} \text{ from } p(\theta_{[i]}|\theta^{(r)}_{[1]}, \ldots, \theta^{(r)}_{[i-1]}, \theta^{(r-1)}_{[i+1]}, \ldots, \theta^{(r-1)}_{[b]})$$

$$\vdots$$

$$\theta^{(r)}_{[b]} \text{ from } p(\theta_{[b]}|\theta^{(r)}_{-[b]}).$$

4. Set $r = r + 1$ and go to step 3 unless $r > R_0 + R$.
5. Discard the first R_0 values of $\theta^{(r)} = (\theta^{(r)\prime}_{[1]}\theta^{(r)\prime}_{[2]} \ldots \theta^{(r)\prime}_{[b]})'$. Compute what you are interested in (estimates of posterior means, variances . . .) from the last R generated values.

In step 3, we sample successively from the full conditional posterior densities of each block. Each full conditional density is updated by the values of the previously generated blocks in the current iteration (r), while the blocks that have not yet been generated are set at the values of the previous iteration ($r - 1$). This creates the dependence in the sample (through the Markov property). Note that if there is only one block, the method boils down to direct sampling, which should be used whenever possible. The number of blocks should be chosen as small as possible but this choice is constrained by our ability to find full conditional densities that can be directly simulated. It may happen that for some blocks, we are not able to perform the direct simulation of the full conditional. We then resort to an indirect method to sample from the full conditional (a 'Metropolis step'; see section 3.2.2 for an example) within the Gibbs sampler.

Note that we must warm up the algorithm with R_0 draws that are discarded. The purpose of this is to get rid of the impact of the initial value $\theta_{[1]}^{(0)}$ and to let the algorithm converge to the target distribution. Convergence means that the sampled values of θ are a valid sample from the target. The issue of convergence is important and too often overlooked by applied researchers. Though it is often easy to state theoretical conditions for convergence,[5] it is not possible to prove convergence practically (for a given run). There are convergence diagnostics that should always be used and reported (see for example Bauwens et al., 1999, Chapter 3, pp. 90–92 for details and references).

Metropolis–Hastings algorithm This is a useful algorithm when Gibbs sampling is not applicable, because there is no way to partition the parameter θ into blocks whose full conditional densities are easy to simulate. The MH algorithms require elaborating a density that approximates the target (posterior) and is easy to simulate (for example a Normal, a finite mixture of Normals . . .). Parameter values are drawn from the approximating density (called candidate density) and subject to an acceptance-rejection test to decide if the drawn value (called candidate) is a draw of the target, in which case it is kept as a valid draw $\theta^{(r)}$. If the candidate is rejected, the previously accepted draw is accepted once again (that is $\theta^{(r)} = \theta^{(r-1)}$). Thus there will be sequences of identical draws in the posterior sample, which directly indicates that the draws are dependent. If the approximating density is identical to the target, all draws are accepted and the method boils down to direct simulation of independent draws of the posterior. Thus, the approximating density should be designed to be as close as possible to the target, which is more easily said than done in a large dimension.

The candidate density may depend on the last accepted draw and is therefore denoted by $q(\theta|\theta^{(r-1)})$. The steps of the MH algorithm are:

1. Set $r = 1$. Choose an initial value $\theta^{(0)}$ that belongs to the parameter space.
2. Draw $\theta^{(cand)} \sim q(\theta|\theta^{(r-1)})$. Compute $p = \min\{\frac{p(\theta^{(cand)})}{p(\theta^{(r-1)})}\frac{q(\theta^{(r-1)}|\theta^{(cand)})}{q(\theta^{(cand)}|\theta^{(r-1)})}, 1\}$.
3. Set $\theta^{(r)} = \theta^{(cand)}$ with probability p, and set $\theta^{(r)} = \theta^{(r-1)}$ with probability $1 - p$.
4. Set $r = r + 1$ and go to step 2 unless $r > R_0 + R$.
5. Identical to step 5 of the Gibbs algorithm.

Step 3 is implemented by drawing a random number U from the Uniform $(0,1)$ density, and if $U < p$, setting $\theta^{(r)} = \theta^{(cand)}$, otherwise to $\theta^{(r-1)}$. The ratio in the min of Step 2 is called the MH ratio. It may be larger than 1, in which case the candidate is definitely accepted. Indeed it is the ratio of the posterior to candidate densities evaluated at the candidate draw, to the same ratio evaluated at the previous draw. If that ratio is larger than 1, the new candidate must be accepted. If it is smaller than 1, it is accepted only with probability $p < 1$.

Some choices of proposal density are of interest. If q does not depend on $\theta^{(r-1)}$, the algorithm is known as the independent MH algorithm. If q is symmetric in the sense that $q(\theta^{(r-1)}|\theta^{(cand)}) = q(\theta^{(cand)}|\theta^{(r-1)})$ the MH ratio is simplified. One way to let q depend on $\theta^{(r-1)}$ is the random walk MH algorithm. This generates $\theta^{(cand)}$ as $\theta^{(r-1)} + v$ where v is a draw from a distribution (for example Normal) centred on 0 and with a variance matrix to be selected not too small so as to allow the candidate draw to walk in the parameter space without staying too close to the previous draw.

3 LINEAR REGRESSION MODELS

Since choosing a prior is an important step in an application using Bayesian inference, and this step may look like a daunting task (which it is not), we provide in this section several useful approaches to do this in the context of the dynamic linear regression model. We also describe the corresponding algorithms to compute the posterior.

Consider a univariate time-series of interest y_t (GDP, price inflation . . .) observed over the period $t = 1, \ldots, T$. The empirical macroeconomist usually assumes that y_t depends on an intercept, some own lags, and current or past values of some predictor variables z_t. Then a popular model for y_t is the dynamic regression model of the form

$$y_t = \kappa + \sum_{i=1}^{p} \varphi_i y_{t-i} + \sum_{j=0}^{q} \lambda_j' z_{t-q} + \varepsilon_t \tag{16.12}$$

with the usual assumption that $\varepsilon_t \sim N(0, \sigma^2)$. This model can be cast in the standard regression form already introduced in section 2.2.1, $y_t = \beta' x_t + \varepsilon_t$, where $x_t = (1, y_{t-1}', \ldots, y_{t-p}', z_{t-1}', \ldots, z_{t-q}')'$ collects all the regressors, and $\beta' = (\kappa, \varphi_1, \ldots, \varphi_p, \lambda_1', \ldots, \lambda_q')$ the coefficients. The first thing the researcher needs to do is choose a 'sensible' prior for the parameters $\theta = (\beta')$. Here we will guide the reader step by step on what exactly Bayesians mean by choosing a sensible prior. We have already presented an easy-to-use and sensible prior in section 2.2.1. It is actually a particular case of what is called a conjugate prior.

3.1 Conjugate Priors

The uninformative prior presented in section 2.2.1 does not allow the researcher to add information: it just allows the likelihood to determine the final result about β. Presumably the researcher is free to use any other prior density of the form

$$p(\theta) = f(\theta|\underline{a}_1, \underline{a}_2, \ldots, \underline{a}_n) \tag{16.13}$$

where $f(\cdot)$ is a generic density function (Beta, Gamma, Dirichlet, Normal and so on) and $(\underline{a}_1, \underline{a}_2, \ldots, \underline{a}_n)$ are parameters of this distribution. In practice, there are three major considerations to keep in mind when deciding on the specific form of the prior:

1. The prior distribution must be congruent with the support of the parameters. As an example, an inverse-Gamma density[6] denoted by iG (ν, q) has support on $[0,\infty)$, so it is not an appropriate choice for a regression coefficient β that is expected to take

negative values, but it is appropriate for the variance parameter σ^2 of the regression model.

2. The prior must be of a form that allows sensible values of the prior parameters $(\underline{a}_1, \underline{a}_2, \ldots, \underline{a}_n)$ to be chosen easily. Subsequently Bayesians usually focus on standard distributions, such as the Normal, Bernoulli, Beta, Gamma, Exponential and so on which have one or two prior parameters to choose from.
3. The prior distribution must be such that the resulting posterior is either known analytically or easy to sample from using simulation methods such as those reviewed in section 2.2.

In that respect, for many models that are the focus of macroeconomists, default choices of prior densities exist. In practice, Bayesian macroeconomists usually focus on *conjugate priors* that have all three of the above properties. A prior distribution such as (16.13) is said to be conjugate to the likelihood function $L(\theta; y)$ if the resulting posterior $p(\theta|y)$ also belongs to the family $f(\theta|\bar{a}_1, \bar{a}_2, \ldots, \bar{a}_n)$, but obviously the posterior parameters (overlined) update the prior ones (underlined) with some functions of the data.

3.1.1 Conjugate prior for the regression model

The conjugate prior on β is the Normal density $N(\underline{\beta}, \sigma^2 \underline{V}_\beta)$ where the parameters $\underline{\beta}, \sigma^2 \underline{V}_\beta$ are the prior mean and prior covariance matrix. Notice that for conjugacy the inclusion of σ^2 is needed as a proportionality factor in the prior covariance. This is not very convenient since it forces us to interpret the variances and covariances in units of σ, an unknown parameter, though an idea of its value is given by the usual OLS estimator. We explain how to avoid this problem in section 3.2. Written explicitly, that normal prior is

$$p(\beta|\sigma^2) \propto (\sigma^2)^{-\frac{k}{2}} |\underline{V}_\beta|^{-\frac{1}{2}} \exp\left[-\frac{(\beta - \underline{\beta})' \underline{V}_\beta^{-1} (\beta - \underline{\beta})}{2\sigma^2}\right]. \tag{16.14}$$

Since the likelihood has the same functional form, that is, Normal – see (16.9) and (16.10) – the resulting posterior of β given σ^2 has the same form: $\beta|\sigma^2, y \sim N(\bar{\beta}, \sigma^2 \bar{V}_\beta)$,[7] where

$$\bar{V}_\beta = (\underline{V}_\beta^{-1} + X'X)^{-1}, \quad \bar{\beta} = \bar{V}_\beta(\underline{V}_\beta^{-1}\underline{\beta} + X'X\hat{\beta}). \tag{16.15}$$

We notice an interesting feature: the posterior mean $\bar{\beta}$ does not depend on σ^2 and it is therefore the unconditional mean of β, $E(\beta|y)$, as well as its conditional mean, $E(\beta|y, \sigma^2)$. That posterior mean is a matrix weighted average of the prior mean and of the OLS estimator. On the other hand, the posterior covariance matrix $Var(\beta|y, \sigma^2)$ is proportional to σ^2 and is thus not the unconditional covariance matrix that we need to make inferences. For example, to compute a highest posterior density (HPD) interval for a particular element of β, we need to know its marginal variance.[8]

Since the posterior we have obtained for β is conditioned on σ^2, we must still marginalize it to use it for inferences. For this we need the posterior of σ^2, since marginalization means computing $\int p(\beta|\sigma^2, y) p(\sigma^2|y) d\sigma^2$ to get $p(\beta|y)$. The conjugate prior for σ^2 is the iG$(\underline{\nu}, \underline{q})$ density. The resulting posterior density of σ^2 is iG $(\bar{\nu}, \bar{q})$, where

$$\overline{\nu} = \underline{\nu} + T,\ \overline{q} = \underline{q} + y'y + \underline{\beta}'\underline{V}_\beta^{-1}\underline{\beta} - \overline{\beta}'\overline{V}_\beta^{-1}\overline{\beta}.$$

Finally, the marginal density of $\beta|y$ is multivariate t with parameters $\overline{\beta}$ (the mean), $\overline{V}_\beta^{-1}$, $\overline{\nu}$ (degrees of freedom) and $\overline{q}$, such that the posterior covariance matrix is $\overline{q}\overline{V}_\beta/(\overline{\nu} - 2)$. The posterior mean of σ^2 is $\overline{q}/(\overline{\nu} - 2)$, so that we have obtained that the posterior marginal (or unconditional) covariance of β is equal to the posterior mean of σ^2 multiplied by the matrix $\overline{V}_\beta$.

The above results are fully analytical and useful if we are just interested in β and σ^2. However, if we are interested in functions of these parameters, we may need to simulate the posterior. Though we can do this by direct simulation (as explained at the end of section 2.2.1) we can also use the Gibbs sampler to sample from the posterior. The algorithm iterates between the conditional posterior of β given σ^2, which is none other than $N(\overline{\beta}, \sigma^2\overline{V}_\beta)$, and that of σ^2 given β, which can be easily shown to be $iG(\overline{\nu}^*, \overline{q}^*)$, where

$$\overline{\nu}^* = \underline{\nu} + T + k,\ \overline{q}^* = \underline{q} + (y - X\beta)'(y - X\beta) + (\beta - \underline{\beta})'\underline{V}_\beta^{-1}(\beta - \underline{\beta}).$$

Here is the Gibbs sampling algorithm to generate a sample of size R of draws from the posterior distribution of β and σ^2 (after warming up the algorithm with R_0 draws):

1. Choose an initial value $(\sigma^2)^{(0)}$ (e.g. the OLS sum of squared residuals divided by $T - k$).
2. Set $r = 1$.
3. Draw successively $\beta^{(r)}$ from $N(\overline{\beta}, (\sigma^2)^{(r-1)}\overline{V}_\beta)$ and $(\sigma^2)^{(r)}$ from $iG(\overline{\nu}^*, (\overline{q}^*)^{(r)})$, where $(\overline{q}^*)^{(r)}$ is $\overline{q}^*$ evaluated at $\beta = \beta^{(r)}$.
4. Set $r = r + 1$ and go to step 3 unless $r > R_0 + R$.
5. Discard the first R_0 values of $\beta^{(r)}$ and $(\sigma^2)^{(r)}$. Compute what you are interested in (estimates of posterior means, variances . . .) from the last R generated values.

3.1.2 Non-informative conjugate prior

It is worth mentioning at this point that even though conjugate priors are not by default non-informative, they can (almost) always become non-informative by taking their parameters to some limit. For instance, the bell-shaped Normal density becomes almost flat when its variance is large. Therefore, the conjugate prior $N(0, \sigma^2 10^6 I_k)$ implies that for each element of β, values in the range (–1000, 1000) are practically speaking 'equally likely' a priori. For the regression variance parameter, the inverse Gamma density becomes non-informative (variance close to infinity) when both $\underline{\nu}$ and $\underline{q}$ tend to zero. Then it is customary in practice to use the $iG(0.001, 0.001)$ in the absence of prior information. The fully non-informative prior $p(\beta, \sigma^2|) \propto 1/\sigma^2$ of section 2.2.1 is the conjugate prior for β, σ^2 given by $N(\underline{\beta}, \sigma^2\underline{V}_\beta) \times iG(\underline{\nu}, \underline{q})$ when $\underline{\beta} = 0$ (a vector), $\underline{V}_\beta^{-1} = 0$ (a matrix) and $\underline{\nu} = \underline{q} = 0$ (scalars).

3.1.3 Practical recommendations for fixing $\underline{\beta}$ and $\underline{V}_\beta$

It is recommended to choose a value for the inverse of $\underline{V}_\beta$ since it is the inverse that appears in the formulae (16.15) defining the posterior parameters. The researcher who wants to be very little informative on an element of β should choose a very small positive value for the corresponding diagonal element of $\underline{V}_\beta$, and zero values for the off-diagonal elements on the corresponding row and column of that matrix. For the prior mean, the element of β should be fixed to zero. For being informative on an element of β, the researcher should assign his or her belief of what could be the most likely value of this coefficient to the corresponding element of $\underline{\beta}$. Such a belief may be inspired by theory or by empirical results on similar (but different) data. For example, if a theory or past results suggest that the parameter should be between two values, the average of these is a sensible prior mean. The prior variance can then be fixed in such a way that with high prior probability the parameter lies in the interval in question. The corresponding diagonal element of $\underline{V}_\beta^{-1}$ is then just the inverse of this variance if one assumes, as is almost always the case, that $\underline{V}_\beta^{-1}$ is a diagonal matrix. More examples and ways to choose the prior parameters are discussed in Bauwens et al. (1999, Chapter 4).

A researcher might have a subjective opinion about a parameter of choice. For instance if in the dynamic regression model written in (16.12) the GDP growth rate is the dependent variable, one might want to incorporate the belief that the intercept should be in the bounds, say, –15 to 15 per cent since the researcher might not expect with certainty to observe a growth rate beyond these bounds in his or her economy of interest. This could be translated to the subjective conjugate prior for the intercept $\kappa/\sigma \sim N(0,9)$. This prior gives almost all the prior weight in the support $(-15,15)$. Additionally, due to the bell shape of the Normal distribution, more prior probability goes to values of the growth rate around zero and less probability is given to tail (extreme) values.

As another example, consider the AR(1) coefficient in a dynamic regression model for the case of price inflation. The AR(1) coefficient is not expected to be more than 1 (the process can be assumed to be stationary or near-stationary, but definitely not explosive); hence the prior $\varphi_1/\sigma \sim \mathrm{N}(0,1)$ seems more appropriate than the non-informative option $\mathrm{N}(0,10^6)$, since it will attract the likelihood towards a more realistic posterior mean value. In models with several lags, the researcher might choose for more distant lags to use the prior $\varphi_i/\sigma \sim \mathrm{N}(0,1/i)$, so that more distant lags are increasingly penalized.[9]

Other than these specific examples to elicit the prior parameters, macroeconomists (for instance working in central banks) have well defined economic theories to guide them empirically[10] as well as strong opinions about the state of the economy. In that respect, researchers have used estimates from national econometric models to form priors for regional models for which data are sparse or simply at yearly frequency (see Adkins et al., 2003). Other researchers have used priors informed from estimated DSGE models (see Ingram and Whiteman, 1994).

3.1.4 The *g*-prior

Zellner (1986) proposed to use a conjugate prior of the form

$$\beta|\sigma^2, X \sim N(0, g\sigma^2(X'X)^{-1})$$

that is, scale the prior variance by using the inverse of the information matrix. The resulting Bayes estimate also provides shrinkage over the least squares estimate, since the posterior mean in (16.15) is simplified into

$$\bar{\beta} = \frac{g}{1+g}\hat{\beta}.$$

For $g \rightarrow \infty$ we get the least squares estimate, while for $g \rightarrow 0$ we have shrinkage towards zero (the prior mean). Despite the shrinkage properties, this prior has mainly been used because it allows analytical calculation of the marginal likelihood. The latter is a prevalent model choice criterion among Bayesian econometricians. Between two models for the same data y, the model that has the highest marginal likelihood is preferred.

This prior has been used extensively in situations where (macroeconomic) theory fails to give directions for constructing the empirical model. This is the case of the famous 'growth regressions' where researchers try to identify factors affecting growth from a large pool of potential factors (see Fernandez et al., 2001). A major criticism of the g-prior in dynamic models is that X includes data from y (the vector of data of the dependent variable) through lags, so that prior depends on y and Bayes theorem is inapplicable. The ridge prior presented in the next subsection is a shrinkage prior that avoids this criticism.

3.2 Non-conjugate Priors

A reason for using a non-conjugate prior is convenience in choosing the parameters of the prior. We have seen that the normal (conjugate) prior for β depends on σ^2 through its covariance matrix that is proportional to σ^2. Thus if we choose for example the prior $\beta \sim N(0, \sigma^2 \underline{V}_\beta)$ (assume β is scalar here) and $\sigma^2 \sim IG(\underline{\nu}, \underline{q})$ with ν smaller than 2, the unconditional prior variance of β is 'infinite' (that is it does not exist). This implies that however small we fix the value of $\underline{V}_\beta$, a choice we would like to make if we have precise information on β, we will be actually non-informative on β. This happens because a value of $\underline{a}$ smaller than 2 implies that $E(\sigma^2)$ does not exist, and though $E(\beta|\sigma^2) = \sigma^2 \underline{V}_\beta$ exists for any finite value of σ^2, $E(\beta) = E(\sigma^2)\underline{V}_\beta$ does not exist if $E(\sigma^2)$ does not exist. In practice, it is very practical to be non-informative on σ^2 since this is a parameter about which we usually have no prior ideas. A convenient non-informative prior on σ^2 is proportional to $1/\sigma^2$, even if an iG(0.001, 0.001) is practically non-informative as well. To avoid the problem outlined above when we want to be informative about at least one element of β, we recommend therefore to use a prior on β that does not depend on σ^2.

3.2.1 Normal priors

There are many possible choices on non-conjugate priors for β, and we consider first the case where the prior is Normal, say $\beta \sim N(\underline{\beta}, \underline{V}_\beta)$, multiplied by the non-informative prior $1/\sigma^2$ for the variance parameter of the regression model. The price to pay for avoiding conjugacy is that the posterior results are not available analytically and must be computed numerically. However, a Gibbs sampling algorithm is easily constructed to simulate the posterior. It is the same as the algorithm described in section 3.1 except that the distributions to simulate in step 3 are given below. Indeed, calculations similar to those of section 2.2.1 provide the following conditional posteriors:[11]

$$\beta | y, X, \sigma^2 \sim N(\bar{\beta}^*, \bar{V}_\beta^*)$$

$$\sigma^2 | y, X, \beta \sim iG(T, (y - X\beta)'(y - X\beta))$$

where

$$\overline{V}^*_{\beta} = (\underline{V}_{\beta}^{-1} + \sigma^{-2}X'X)^{-1}, \quad \overline{\beta^*} = \overline{V}^*_{\beta}(\underline{V}_{\beta}^{-1}\underline{\beta} + \sigma^{-2}X'X\hat{\beta}). \tag{16.16}$$

Apart from subjective choices of $\underline{\beta}$ and $\underline{V}_{\beta}$, we briefly review other choices that have been proposed and are less demanding in terms of prior elicitation.

Ridge regression priors A Normal prior of the form

$$p(\beta) \sim \mathrm{N}(0, \tau I_k)$$

where τ is a prior parameter, is called a 'ridge regression' prior. It leads to a posterior mean similar to the estimate obtained from classical ridge regression. In this case, $\beta|\sigma^2$ has a Normal posterior with posterior mean

$$\overline{\beta}^* = \left(\sigma^{-2}X'X + \frac{1}{\tau}I_k\right)^{-1}\sigma^{-2}X'y.$$

As for the g-prior, the case where the prior variance is infinite ($\tau \to \infty$) leads to the OLS estimate as unconditional posterior mean. For $\tau \to 0$ the unconditional posterior mean of β also tends to zero, thus this prior can provide shrinkage over the OLS estimate. Apart from these two limit cases, the unconditional posterior mean must be computed by Gibbs sampling. Ridge regression priors impose prior independence between the coefficients β, since the prior covariance matrix is diagonal, and cannot incorporate prior beliefs of correlations between elements of β.

Empirical Bayes priors The Empirical Bayes technique relies on the information in the observations to estimate the parameters of the prior distribution. In that respect, they are subject to the major criticism that Bayes theorem is not applicable if the prior depends on the data y. Depending on the problem at hand, there are many options for defining an Empirical Bayes prior. For instance, Judge and Bock (1978) suggested the Empirical Bayes prior

$$\beta \sim \mathrm{N}(0, \tau(X'X)^{-1})$$

where $\tau = \frac{\hat{\sigma}^2}{\hat{\xi}^2}$, $\hat{\sigma}^2 = (y - X\hat{\beta})'(y - X\hat{\beta})/T$ and $\hat{\xi}^2 = \frac{\hat{\beta}'\hat{\beta}}{\mathrm{tr}(X'X)^{-1}} - \hat{\sigma}^2$. This empirical Bayes prior is Stein-like, also shrinking β towards zero, since the posterior mean of β given σ^2 writes

$$\overline{\beta}^* = \left(\frac{\tau}{\tau + \sigma^2}\right)\hat{\beta}.$$

Full-Bayes (hierarchical) priors Ridge and g-priors are based on the subjective choice of a 'tuning' prior parameter that provides shrinkage, and hence are difficult to justify among objective researchers. On the other hand, Empirical Bayes priors are less favoured by Bayesians because they do not respect Bayes Theorem, though from an empirical viewpoint, they often prove to be helpful. Since anyway the coefficients β are assumed to be random variables, why not also treat the prior parameters as random variables which admit a prior on their own and can be updated from information in the likelihood (using again Bayes Theorem)? Although this choice may seem abstract conceptually, by definining a *hyperprior* distribution on unknown prior parameters, we can accommodate a variety of shrinkage and model selection estimators.

To give an example, we consider hierarchical shrinkage priors. In the ridge regression prior $\beta \sim N(0, \tau I_k)$, all k coefficients in β share the same shrinkage factor τ. If we want the different coefficients in β to be shrunk to a different degree, we can use the prior

$$\beta_i | \tau_i \sim N(0, \tau_i) \tag{16.17}$$

for $i = 1, 2, \ldots, k$. Choosing all the different τ_i is very demanding. If instead we assume a common prior on all τ_is, we allow the data to determine their values. To see this, assume the conjugate prior for this variance parameter of the form

$$\tau_i \sim iG(q_1, q_2). \tag{16.18}$$

Then we can easily derive the conditional posterior densities for this model and use the Gibbs sampler to simulate all parameters:

1) Draw τ_i conditional on β_i from

$$iG(q_1 + 1, q_2 + \beta_i^2), \text{ for } i = 1, 2, \ldots, k. \tag{16.19}$$

2) Draw σ^2 conditional on β and the data from $iG(T, (y - X\beta)'(y - X\beta))$.
3) Draw β conditional on all τ_is, σ^2 and the data from

$$N((\sigma^{-2}X'X + (\underline{V})^{-1})^{-1}X'y, (\sigma^{-2}X'X + (\underline{V})^{-1})^{-1}) \tag{16.20}$$

where $\underline{V} = \text{diag}(\tau_1, \ldots, \tau_k)$ is the prior covariance matrix constructed from the τ_i.

Note that in step 1 the data do not revise τ_i directly but only through β_i, in step 2 the τ_is influence σ^2 only through β, and in step 3 they influence β directly. The data appear directly only in steps 2 and 3.

Numerous such examples exist in the literature. For instance, one can specify a Uniform (non-informative) prior on τ_i, while an Exponential prior on τ_i gives a posterior mean with shrinkage properties identical to the LASSO (least absolute shrinkage and selection operator) algorithm. Other authors have used hierarchical priors for model selection and model averaging. For instance, one can replace the prior in (16.17) by

$$p(\beta_i) \sim N(0, \gamma_i \tau_i) \tag{16.21}$$

where τ_i may, or may not, have a prior but the crucial assumption is that γ_i is a 0/1 variable. This prior is a mixture of Normal priors: when $\gamma_i = 0$, we have a $N(0,0)$ prior, that is a point mass at zero, which by definition will restrict the posterior of β_i to have point mass at zero; when $\gamma_i = 1$, we have a $N(0, \tau_i)$ prior, that is an unrestricted prior (for non-zero values of τ_i) and hence β_i is updated by the likelihood. The Bayesian can allow the information in the likelihood to determine which γ_i will be zero and which will be 1, by placing a prior on γ_i. The conjugate prior is of the form

$$\gamma_i \sim \text{Bernoulli}(\pi_i). \tag{16.22}$$

It leads to a Gibbs sampler algorithm which gives: (i) a posterior estimate of β_i, which is shrunk towards zero if and only if $\gamma_i = 0$; and (ii) a posterior estimate of γ_i indicating which coefficients (and hence which predictor variables) should be included in the model.

One can take this hierarchical analysis to a further step and combine algorithms and ideas. For instance, if in (16.21) we assume $\tau_i \rightarrow \infty$ we just let all coefficients with $\gamma_i = 1$ have a very flat and uninformative prior. However, we can use the prior (16.18) instead. In that case, if a coefficient is not restricted to be exactly 0 (that is if $\gamma_i = 1$), it can still be shrunk towards zero by allowing τ_i to vary according to information in the likelihood. Similarly, if we are unsure about choosing a precise value for the hyperparameter π_i in (16.22), we can easily introduce one more hierarchical layer and place a prior on this hyperparameter! In this case, the conjugate prior on π_i is in the family of Beta densities, so that the posterior of π_i is also a Beta density, and hence is easy to sample from.

3.2.2 Non-Normal priors

If a researcher wishes to use a non-Normal prior for β, denoted by $p(\beta)$, the conditional posterior of $\beta|y, X, \sigma^2$ is not Normal.[12] We can only say that

$$p(\beta|y, X, \sigma^2) \propto p(\beta) \exp[-(\beta - \hat{\beta})'X'X(\beta - \hat{\beta})/(2\sigma^2)], \tag{16.23}$$

and that it will not be possible to simulate it directly. In such a case, the simulation of $\beta|y, X, (\sigma^2)^{(r-1)}$ in step 3 of the Gibbs sampling algorithm of section 3.1 has to be done using a Metropolis step. To do this, at iteration r, we must approximate (16.23) (where σ^2 is set at the value $(\sigma^2)^{(r-1)}$ generated at step 3 of the previous iteration) by a density that we can simulate directly, denoted by $q(\beta|(\sigma^2)^{(r-1)})$. The sampling of β at step 3 of the algorithm of section 3.1 is done like this:

- Draw $\beta^{(cand)}$ from $q(\beta|(\sigma^2)^{(r-1)})$. Set $\beta^{(r)} = \beta^{(cand)}$ with probability α and $= \beta^{(r-1)}$ with probability $1 - \alpha$, where $\alpha = \min\{\frac{p(\beta^{(cand)}|y, X, (\sigma^2)^{(r-1)})}{p(\beta^{(r-1)}|y, X, (\sigma^2)^{(r-1)})} \frac{q(\beta^{(r-1)}|\beta^{(cand)}, (\sigma^2)^{(r-1)})}{q(\beta^{(cand)}|\beta^{(r-1)}, (\sigma^2)^{(r-1)})}, 1\}$ and $p(.|.)$ defined in (16.23).

If the prior $p(\beta)$ is not very informative, or if it is not highly non-normal, (16.23) can be easily approximated by replacing the non-normal prior by a normal prior approximating it. Then the candidate $q(\beta|\sigma^2)$ will be the normal posterior defined in section 3.2.1 above formula (16.16), and the Metropolis step is easy to implement. If the prior is highly non-normal and very sharp, one will have to think harder to design a good proposal, that is one that does not lead to frequent rejections of the candidate draws of β. Too many rejections would slow down (or prevent) the convergence of the algorithm to the targeted posterior distribution.

4 OTHER MODELS: A SHORT GUIDE TO THE LITERATURE

Several books cover Bayesian inference in econometrics in detail. The most comprehensive ones for applied macroeconomists are probably Bauwens et al. (1999) and Koop (2003). Geweke et al. (2011) has chapters on time series state space models, macroeconometrics and MCMC methods. Geweke (2005) and Lancaster (2004) each include one chapter on time series models.

Bayesian inference on DSGE models is covered in Chapters 18 and 21 of this *Handbook*.

Bayesian inference for VAR models is reviewed in Chapter 9 of Bauwens et al. (1999). A recent treatment of VAR models with shrinkage, time-varying parameters and stochastic volatility, as well as factor augmented VARs can be found in Koop and Korobilis (2010). The authors also provide MATLAB code to estimate the models using analytical or MCMC methods of the form introduced in section 2 of this chapter.

Markov switching and state-space models are covered extensively in the two excellent books by Frühwirth-Schnatter (2006) and Kim and Nelson (1999).

The list of resources related to Bayesian analysis in macroeconomics is by no means restricted to the books and monographs just presented. However, this referenced material is a good starting point for the inexperienced student or researcher who wishes to start conducting research using Bayesian methods.

NOTES

* Research supported by the contract 'Projet d'Actions de Recherche Concertées' 07/12-002 of the 'Communauté française de Belgique', granted by the 'Académie universitaire Louvain'. This chapter presents research results of the Belgian programme on Interuniversity Poles of Attraction initiated by the Belgian State, Prime Minister's Office, Science Policy Programming. The scientific responsibility is assumed by the authors.

1. As an alternative, if θ is the mean of GDP growth, a prior belief would be to restrict this parameter on the interval, say, −20 to 25 per cent, implying that we do not realistically expect to observe growth beyond these bounds. Letting the bounds become arbitrarily large may be viewed as a convenient simplification.
2. For example, if $\theta = (\theta_1 \theta_2)$, and we are interested in θ_1/θ_2, we do not know the density of this ratio.
3. Invoking the ergodic theorem, we do not even need the sample to be independent.
4. If $p(\log \sigma^2) \propto 1$, then $p(\sigma^2) \propto 1/\sigma^2$ due to the Jacobian $\partial \log \sigma^2/\partial\sigma^2$.
5. A sufficient condition is that the full conditional densities are always strictly positive in the parameter space.
6. The $iG(\nu, q)$ density with $\nu > 0$ degrees of freedom and scale parameter $q > 0$, for the random variable U, is given by $[1/\Gamma(\nu/2)](q/2)^{\nu/2}u^{-(\nu+2)/2}\exp-[q/(2u)]$. Its mean is $q/(\nu - 2)$ (if $\nu > 2$) and its variance is $2q^2/[(\nu - 2)(\nu - 4)]$ (if $\nu > 4$).
7. For a detailed proof, see Bauwens et al. (1999, Chapter 2, pp. 58–9).
8. An HPD interval of (probability) level α for a scalar parameter θ is the shortest interval of values (θ_i, θ_s) such that $P[\theta \in (\theta_i, \theta_s)] = \alpha$. If the density of θ is $N(m, s^2)$, it is given by $(m - z_{\alpha/2}, m + z_{\alpha/2}s)$, where $z_{\alpha/2}$ is the quantile of level $\alpha/2$ of the right tail of the standard Normal. For a Bayesian, an HPD interval is an interval estimator. An HPD interval resembles a frequentist confidence interval, but it has a quite different interpretation: for a Bayesian, θ is random, for a frequentist, the interval is random.
9. This is similar in spirit, but not identical to, the so-called Minnesota prior for VAR models; see Doan et al. (1984).
10. At least, one can argue that macroeconomic theory can guide the empirical researcher on what outcome to expect, as well as what empirical result makes sense. In that respect, empirical results like the price puzzle in VAR models (the fact that inflation responds with an increase after a contractionary monetary policy shock), have been solved by using prior restrictions about the expected signs of the responses of each variable; see Uhlig (2001).

11. The normality of $p(\beta|y, X, \sigma^2)$ comes from the fact that its functional form is the product of two functions that are like Normal densities: $\exp[-(\beta-\hat{\beta})'X'X(\beta-\hat{\beta})/(2\sigma^2)]$ (from the likelihood) and $\exp[-(\beta-\underline{\beta})'\underline{V}_{\beta}^{-1}(\beta-\underline{\beta})/2]$ (from the prior). Actually, the Normal prior used here is conjugate for the likelihood when σ^2 is fixed, though the joint prior of β and σ^2 is not conjugate to the likelihood for both parameters. Thus we have 'partial conjugacy'.
12. For example, we may wish to use an asymmetric prior if our prior belief is that a parameter is of the order of 0.95 (prior mean or mode), definitely smaller than 1, and with high probability in the interval (0.5, 1). A normal prior centred on 0.9 with a small standard deviation (such as 0.015) implies that the parameter has a negligible probability to be larger than 1, but it also implies that the parameter is in the interval (0.9,1) with probability (very close to) 1 rather than in the desired interval (0.5, 1). A Beta density for that parameter can be easily chosen to satisfy all the prior beliefs.

REFERENCES

Adkins, L.C., D.S. Rickman and A. Hameed (2003), 'Bayesian estimation of regional production for CGE modeling', *Journal of Regional Science*, **43**, 641–61.

Bauwens, L., M. Lubrano and J. Richard (1999), *Bayesian Inference in Dynamic Econometric Models*, Oxford: Oxford University Press.

Doan, T., R.B. Litterman and C. Sims (1984), 'Forecasting and conditional projection under realistic prior distributions', *Econometric Reviews*, **3**, 1–100.

Fernandez, C., E. Ley and M. Steel (2001), 'Model uncertainty in cross-country growth regressions', *Journal of Applied Econometrics*, **16**, 563–76.

Frühwirth-Schnatter, S. (2006), *Finite Mixture and Markov Switching Models*, New York: Springer.

Geweke, J. (2005), *Contemporary Bayesian Econometrics and Statistics*, Hoboken, NJ: Wiley.

Geweke, J., G. Koop and H. van Dijk (2011), *The Oxford Handbook of Bayesian Econometrics*, Oxford: Oxford University Press.

Ingram, B.F. and C.H. Whiteman (1994), 'Supplanting the Minnesota prior: forecasting macroeconomic time series using real business cycle model priors', *Journal of Monetary Economics*, **34**, 497–510.

Judge, G.G. and M. Bock (1978), *Statistical Implications of Pre-Test and Stein Rule Estimators in Econometrics*', Amsterdam: North-Holland.

Kim, C-J. and C.R. Nelson (1999), *State-Space Models with Regime Switching*, Cambridge, MA: MIT Press.

Koop, G. (2003), *Bayesian Econometrics*, Hoboken, NJ: Wiley.

Koop, G. and D. Korobilis (2010), 'Bayesian multivariate time series methods for empirical macroeconomics', *Foundations and Trends in Econometrics*, **3**, 267–358.

Lancaster, T. (2004), *Introduction to Modern Bayesian Econometrics*, Oxford: Blackwell.

Uhlig, H. (2001), 'Did the Fed surprise the markets in 2001? A case study for VARs with sign restrictions', Technical report, CESifo Working Paper Series.

Zellner, A. (1986), 'On assessing prior distributions and Bayesian regression analysis with g-prior distributions', in P. Goel and A. Zellner (eds), *Bayesian Inference and Decision Techniques*, Amsterdam: North-Holland.

17 Forecasting in macroeconomics

Raffaella Giacomini and Barbara Rossi

1 INTRODUCTION

This chapter offers a review of forecasting methodologies and empirical applications that are useful for macroeconomists. The chapter is divided in two parts. The first part overviews econometric methods available for forecast evaluation, including both traditional methods as well as new methodologies that are robust to instabilities. We discuss their usefulness, their assumptions as well as their implementation, to provide practical guidance to macroeconomists. The second part addresses special issues of interest to forecasters, including forecasting output growth and inflation as well as the use of real-time data and structural models for forecasting.

PART I ECONOMETRIC METHODOLOGIES FOR FORECASTING IN MACROECONOMICS

2 Methods for Forecast Evaluation

An important area of research over the past couple of decades has been the development of formal econometric techniques for evaluating the accuracy of forecasts. The problem can be viewed in a decision-theoretic context: if y_{t+1} is the variable of interest and f_t its forecast made at time t, the accuracy of f_t is judged by the expected loss $E[L(y_{t+1}, f_t)]$, for a choice of loss function $L(\cdot)$ that reflects the type of forecast (point-, interval- or density-) and the decision problem of the forecaster. The vast majority of empirical work has typically focused on the quadratic or absolute error loss, but there is some literature discussing different choices of loss function, for example, Diebold and Lopez (1996), Amisano and Giacomini (2007), Giacomini and Komunjer (2005), Leitch and Tanner (1991), West et al. (1993). See also Elliott et al. (2005) for a method for eliciting forecasters' loss functions from survey data. Most of the methods discussed in the remainder of this chapter will be applicable to a general loss function, and we will provide some concrete examples below.

The expected loss of a forecast is in practice estimated using sample data. This can be done in a relatively straightforward manner if the data consists of a sequence of forecasts and corresponding realizations, as is the case for applications analysing the accuracy of survey-based forecasts. The econometric methods for this case are standard, and we refer to, for example, Diebold's (2007) textbook for further discussion. In many empirically relevant situations, however, a forecaster is interested in assessing the accuracy of model-based forecasts using macroeconomic and financial time series data. In this case a sequence of forecasts is obtained by a so-called 'pseudo-out-of-sample' forecasting exercise, which we describe formally below. Informally, this involves pretending that one could go back in time to a given date R in the sample (of total size T) and mimic what an actual forecaster would have done as time went by: estimate the model using the data up to time R, produce a forecast for time $R + 1$, wait until $R + 1$, observe the realization of the variable and compare it to the forecast, re-estimate the model including the data at time $R + 1$, produce a forecast for $R + 2$, wait until $R + 2$ and compare it to the actual realization and so on. This procedure results in a sequence of $P = T - R$ forecasts $\{f_t(\hat{\theta}_t)\}_{t=R}^{T-1}$ and of corresponding out-of-sample losses $\{L(y_{t+1}, f_t(\hat{\theta}_t))\}_{t=R}^{T-1}$ which depend on the data and on parameters estimated over a sequence of overlapping samples. The accuracy of the forecast is then estimated by the average of the out-of-sample losses

$$E[\widehat{L(y_{t+1}, f_t)}] = \frac{1}{P}\sum_{t=R}^{T-1} L(y_{t+1}, f_t(\hat{\theta}_t)), \tag{17.1}$$

which, in the typical case of a quadratic loss, is the Mean Square Forecast Error (MSFE).

This estimate of the accuracy of the forecast is not in general directly interpretable, as it depends on the units of measurement of y_t. In practice therefore one typically relates the accuracy of a model to that of a benchmark model, or compares the accuracy of multiple competing models by comparing their out-of-sample average losses (17.1). In the remainder of this section we focus on testing the relative predictive ability of models, and separately consider the case of pairwise and multiple comparisons. Even though the technicalities are different, the basic idea of all the approaches that we discuss below is to develop statistical tests to assess whether the average out-of-sample losses of competing models are significantly different from each other in a way that takes into account their dependence on out-of-sample data, in-sample data and recursively estimated parameters.

A further econometric challenge that arises in the context of developing such tests is the fact that one needs to pay attention to whether the models compared are nested (in the sense that one model can be obtained from the other by imposing parameter restrictions) or non-nested. We will discuss this issue and the possible solutions below.

Finally, we will briefly consider the extension to conditional predictive ability testing, which goes beyond assessing the forecasting performance of models on average.

2.1 The econometric environment

In the following, we assume that the researcher is interested in forecasting the scalar variable y_t and that he or she has available a number of competing forecasting models. Out-of-sample testing involves dividing a sample of size T into an in-sample portion of size R and an out-of-sample portion of size P. The models are then first estimated using data from 1 to R and the parameters are used to produce $h-$ step ahead forecasts. We denote the first forecast from model i by $f_R^{(i)}(\hat{\theta}_R)$. Some of the approaches that we discuss below do not impose restrictions on the type of model (for example, linear or non-linear) or the estimation method used in-sample, whereas others are only applicable in special cases (for example, the linear model estimated by OLS). We will make these assumptions explicit in each subsection. The forecasts at time R are then compared to the realization y_{R+h} and the corresponding loss for model i is denoted by $L^{(i)}(y_{R+h}, f_R^{(i)}(\hat{\theta}_R))$. The second sets of $h-$ step ahead forecasts are obtained at time $R + 1$ by either: keeping the parameter estimates fixed at $\hat{\theta}_R$ (fixed scheme); re-estimating the models over data indexed $1, \ldots, R + 1$ (recursive scheme) or re-estimating the models over data indexed $2, \ldots, R + 1$ (rolling scheme). The loss for model i is then given by $L^{(i)}(y_{R+1+h}, f^{(i)}_{R+1}(\hat{\theta}_{R+1}))$, where the definition of $\hat{\theta}_{R+1}$ depends on the estimation scheme used. Iterating this procedure until all sample observations are exhausted yields a sequence of $P = T - h - R + 1$ out-of-sample losses $\{L^{(i)}(y_{t+h}, f^{(i)}_t(\hat{\theta}_t))\}_{t=R}^{T-h}$ for each model i.

It is important to note that most of the techniques described below can be applied regardless of whether the forecasts are point-, volatility-, interval-, probability- or density-forecasts. The only difference lies in selecting the appropriate loss function for each type of forecast. Examples of loss functions for point forecasts are: (i) (quadratic) $L(y_{t+h}, f_t) = (y_{t+h} - f_t)^2$; (ii) (absolute error) $L(y_{t+h}, f_t) = |y_{t+h} - f_t|$; (iii) (lin-lin) $L(y_{t+h}, f_t) = (\alpha - 1(y_{t+h} - f_t < 0))(y_{t+h} - f_t)$ for $\alpha \in (0,1)$; (iv) (linex) $L(y_{t+h}, f_t) = \exp(a(y_{t+h} - f_t)) - a(y_{t+h} - f_t) - 1$ for $a \in \mathbb{R}$; (v) (direction-of-change) $L(y_{t+h}, f_t) = 1\{sign(y_{t+h} - y_t) \neq sign(f_t - y_t)\}$. Loss functions for conditional variance forecasts are (i) $L(y_{t+h}, f_t) = (\log(y^2_{t+h}) - \log(f_t))^2$; (ii) $L(y_{t+h}, f_t) = (\frac{y^2_{t+h}}{f_t} - 1)^2$; (iii) $L(y_{t+h}, f_t) = \log(f_t) + \frac{y^2_{t+h}}{f_t}$. For probability forecasts, we have $L(y_{t+h}, f_t) = (f_t - I_t)^2$, where $I_t = 1$ if the event occurred and is 0 otherwise. For density forecasts one can consider $L(y_{t+h}, f_t) = \log f_t(y_{t+h})$.

2.2 Pairwise (unconditional) predictive ability testing

When there are only two models, one can compare their accuracy by computing the difference in, say, MSFEs, ask whether the difference is significantly different from zero and, if so, choose the model with the smallest MSFE. For a general loss function, a test of equal predictive ability can be implemented by first constructing the time series of P out-of-sample loss differences $\{\Delta L_{t+h}(\hat{\theta}_t)\}_{t=R}^{T-h}$ where[1] $\Delta L_{t+h} = L^{(1)}(y_{t+h}, f^{(1)}_t(\hat{\theta}_t)) - L^{(2)}(y_{t+h}, f^{(2)}_t(\hat{\theta}_t))$ and then conducting a t-test of the hypothesis $H_0 : \mu = 0$ in the regression

$$\Delta L_{t+h}(\hat{\theta}_t) = \mu + \varepsilon_{t+h}, \; t = R, \ldots, T - h. \tag{17.2}$$

The test has a standard normal asymptotic distribution, provided one uses the correct standard errors which take into account the time-series properties of ε_{t+h} and the dependence of ΔL_{t+h} in (17.2) on estimated in-sample parameters. The former challenge is relatively easy to deal with and has long been addressed in the literature, starting from Diebold and Mariano (1995), who suggested considering the test statistic

$$\left|\frac{\sqrt{P}\,\hat{\mu}}{\hat{\sigma}}\right| = \left|\frac{1}{\sqrt{P}} \sum_{t=R}^{T-h} \frac{\Delta L_{t+h}(\hat{\theta}_t)}{\hat{\sigma}}\right|, \tag{17.3}$$

where $\hat{\sigma}$ is a heteroscedasticity- and autocorrelation-consistent standard error, for example,

$$\hat{\sigma}^2 = \sum_{j=-q+1}^{q-1} (1 - |j/q|) P^{-1} \sum_{t=R}^{T-h} \Delta L_{t+h} \Delta L_{t+h-j}, \tag{17.4}$$

with truncation lag $q = h - 1$. The challenge of accounting for estimation uncertainty is trickier and has been the subject of a sizable body of literature. Broadly speaking, there are two strands of the literature, which correspond to two different asymptotic approximations in the derivation of a test of equal predictive ability. The two approaches are exemplified by West (1996) and Giacomini and White (2006).

2.2.1 West (1996) The key insight of West (1996) is to acknowledge the dependence of (17.2) on $\hat{\theta}_t$ and propose a test of equal predictive ability that is valid as both the in-sample size R and the out-of-sample size P grow to infinity. West (1996) considers a t-test of $H_0 : \mu = 0$ in a modification of the regression in (17.2) where the dependent variable is a function of the population parameter θ^* (interpretable as the probability limit of $\hat{\theta}_t$ as the size of the estimation sample grows to infinity):

$$\Delta L_{t+h}(\theta^*) = \mu + \varepsilon_{t+h}, t = R,\ldots,T - h. \tag{17.5}$$

The practical implication of this focus on population parameters is that one needs to take into account that the test statistic depends on in-sample parameter estimates, which may have an effect on the estimator of the asymptotic variance to be used in the test. Formally, West's (1996) test statistic is

$$\frac{1}{P}\sum_{t=R}^{T-h}\frac{\Delta L_{t+h}(\hat{\theta}_t)}{\hat{\sigma}},$$

where $\hat{\sigma}$ is an asymptotically valid standard error that reflects the possible contribution of in-sample parameter estimation uncertainty. The main technical contribution of West (1996) is to show how to construct $\hat{\sigma}$ for a fairly wide class of models and estimation procedures, as well as point out special cases in which estimation uncertainty is asymptotically irrelevant and $\hat{\sigma}$ is the same standard error (17.4) as in the Diebold and Mariano (1995) test statistic (for example, this occurs in the case of MSFE comparisons of models estimated by OLS).

West's (1996) test has two main 'disadvantages'. The first, which is merely an issue of convenience of implementation, is that $\hat{\sigma}$ is not as easily computed as the corresponding standard error in the Diebold and Mariano (1995) test, because in general it depends on the estimators used by the two models and on the estimation scheme. The second disadvantage is of a more fundamental nature, and has been discussed in a series of papers by Clark and McCracken (2001, 2005) and McCracken (2007). The key limitation of West's (1996) result is that it is only applicable to comparisons between non-nested models and thus rules out the empirically relevant comparison between a model and a nested benchmark such as an autoregression or a random walk. The technical reason for this is that West's (1996) result requires the probability limit of $\hat{\sigma}$ to be positive as both R and P grow to infinity, which may be violated in the case of nested models. Clark and McCracken (2001, 2005) and McCracken (2007) show that it is nonetheless possible to derive a valid test of equal predictive ability for nested models within a more restrictive class of models and estimation procedures (that is, linear models estimated by OLS and direct multi-step forecasting). The asymptotic distribution is however non-standard, so critical values for the t-test must be simulated in each specific case.

2.2.2 Giacomini and White (2006) Giacomini and White (2006) propose deriving predictive ability tests in a different asymptotic environment with growing out-of-sample size P and fixed in-sample size R. Importantly, this assumption rules out the use of the recursive scheme in the construction of the out-of-sample test, but allows for both fixed and rolling schemes. The basic idea is to propose a test of $H_0 : \mu = 0$ in the regression

$$\Delta L_{t+h}(\hat{\theta}_t) = \mu + \varepsilon_{t+h}, \; t = R, \ldots, T - h, \tag{17.6}$$

where the dependent variable $\Delta L_{t+h}(\hat{\theta}_t)$ is now a function of estimated – rather than population – parameters. This corresponds to taking a different 'philosophical' view on what the relevant object of interest of the forecasting exercise is.[2] In practice, the test statistic considered by Giacomini and White (2006) is the same as the Diebold and Mariano (1995) test statistic, and thus the key message is that Diebold and Mariano's (1995) test is valid regardless of whether the models are nested or non-nested, as long as the estimation window does not grow with the sample size. The reason for the test being valid regardless of whether the models are nested or non-nested is that, in a context with non-vanishing estimation uncertainty (due to the finite estimation window), the estimator $\hat{\theta}_t$ does not converge to its probability limit and thus the denominator $\hat{\sigma}$ of the Diebold and Mariano (1995) test cannot converge to zero.

The asymptotic framework with non-vanishing estimation uncertainty allows Giacomini and White (2006) to weaken many of the assumptions used by West (1996), Clark and McCracken (2001, 2005) and McCracken (2007), and as a result yields a test that is applicable to a wide class of models and estimation procedures, including any linear or non-linear model estimated by classical, Bayesian, semi-parametric or non-parametric procedures. The only restriction to keep in mind is that the forecasts cannot be obtained by using the recursive scheme (see Clark and McCracken, 2009 for an example of a test of the Giacomini and White (2006) null hypothesis that permits recursive estimation, applicable in the special case of linear models estimated by OLS).

2.3 Pairwise (conditional) predictive ability testing

The central idea of conditional predictive ability testing (also in Giacomini and White, 2006) is to ask whether one could use available information – above and beyond past average performance – to predict which of the two forecasts will be more accurate in the future. Another way to look at this is to argue that more could be learned about the forecasting performance of models by studying the time series properties of the sequence of loss differences in its entirety, rather than limiting oneself to asking whether it has mean zero. For example, one could extend the regression (17.6) to

$$\Delta L_{t+h}(\hat{\theta}_t) = \beta' X_t + \varepsilon_{t+h}, \; t = R, \ldots, T - h, \tag{17.7}$$

where X_t contains elements from the information set at time t, such as a constant, lags of ΔL_t and economic indicators that could help predict the relative performance of the models under analysis. One could then test $H_0 : \beta = 0$ by a Wald test:

$$W = P(\hat{\beta})' \, \hat{\Sigma}^{-1}(\hat{\beta}), \tag{17.8}$$

where, because of the finite-estimation window asymptotic framework, $\hat{\Sigma}$ is the standard HAC estimator computed by any regression software. The test is also applicable to both nested and non-nested models.

One useful feature of the extension to conditional predictive ability testing is that rejection of the null $H_0 : \beta = 0$ implies that the future relative performance of the models is predictable using current information, which suggests the following simple decision rule for choosing at time T a forecasting model for time $T + h$: choose the second model if $\hat{\beta}' X_T > 0$ and the first model otherwise, where $\hat{\beta}$ is estimated from (17.7).

2.4 Multiple predictive ability testing

It is often the case that a forecaster is interested in comparing the performance of several models to that of a benchmark model, which can be viewed as a problem of multiple hypothesis testing. Referring back to the notation in section 2.1, suppose there are N models and a benchmark denoted by 0, so that $\Delta L^{(i)}_{t+h} = L^{(0)}_{t+h} - L^{(i)}_{t+h}$ is the loss difference between the benchmark and model i. The null hypothesis of interest is that none of the N models outperforms the benchmark, and the key econometric challenge is to propose procedures that control the overall Type I error of the procedure, while taking into account the dependence of the forecast losses on each other and on the in-sample parameter estimates. White (2000) does so by proposing a 'reality check' test of

$$
\begin{aligned}
H_0\colon \max_{i=1,\ldots,N} E[\Delta L^{(i)}_{t+h}] \leq 0 \text{ against} \\
H_1\colon \max_{i=1,\ldots,N} E[\Delta L^{(i)}_{t+h}] > 0,
\end{aligned}
\tag{17.9}
$$

where the alternative states that there is at least one model outperforming the benchmark. White (2000) uses the asymptotic framework of West (1996) to derive the asymptotic distribution of the test statistic, which is the (out-of-) sample analogue of (17.9). The asymptotic distribution is the maximum of a Gaussian process and thus the p-values must be obtained by simulation. White (2000) suggests a bootstrap procedure for obtaining p-values that are valid under the assumption that at least one model is not nested in (and non-nesting) the benchmark and that estimation uncertainty is asymptotically irrelevant as in the special cases considered by West (2006) (for example, MSFE comparison in linear models estimated by OLS).

Hansen (2005) modifies White's (2000) procedure to obtain a test that is less sensitive to the inclusion of poor-performing models and thus has higher power than White's (2000) test. Romano and Wolf (2005) suggest a further possible power improvement by adopting a 'step-wise' multiple testing approach.

While the approaches described above are useful for identifying the best performing model relative to the benchmark, if there is one, they are silent about what to do in case the null hypothesis is not rejected (which could mean that the benchmark is more accurate than all the competing models or that it is as accurate as all or some of them). One may try to take a further step and ask whether it is possible to eliminate the worst-performing models and retain all the models that have equal performance, which is related to the notion of constructing a 'model confidence set' (MCS), as described by Hansen et al. (2011). The procedure consists of the following steps:

1. Let M be the set of all possible models. Test $H_0 : E[L^{(i)}_{t+h} - L^{(j)}_{t+h}] = 0$ for all $i,j \in M$ using the statistic

$$T = \max_{i,j \in M} t_{i,j}, \tag{17.10}$$

   where $t_{i,j}$ is the Diebold and Mariano (1995) test statistic in (17.3).
2. If fail to reject, all models in M are equally accurate. If reject, eliminate the worst model (that with the highest average loss) and repeat step 1 until no model is eliminated.

As in the case of the tests described above, the p-value for the test in step 1 is obtained by bootstrap methods as the test statistic (17.10) is not pivotal since it depends on the cross-sectional correlation of the $t_{i,j}$. The bootstrap p-values are computed by considering the bootstrap test statistic $T^{(b)} = max_{i,j \in M} \left| \frac{\sqrt{P}(\hat{\mu}^{*(b)} - \hat{\mu})}{\hat{\sigma}^*} \right|$ for $b = 1, \ldots, B$, where $\hat{\sigma}^* = \frac{P}{B} \sum_{b=1}^{B} (\hat{\mu}^{*(b)} - \hat{\mu})^2$ and computing $p^* = \frac{1}{B} \sum_{b=1}^{B} 1_{\{T^{(b)} > T\}}$.

2.5 Open issues in forecast evaluation

An important issue that has been largely ignored by the literature so far, at least from a theoretical standpoint, is how to choose the sample split and/or rolling window size for the out-of-sample evaluation exercise. The question is in part linked to which asymptotic approximation one considers. There is limited evidence based on Monte Carlo simulations that shows that Giacomini and White's (2006) approximation works best when the in-sample size is small relative to the out-of-sample size, as one would expect given the finite-estimation window assumption. Regarding West's (1996) approximation, instead, no clear guidelines seem to emerge from the simulations in the literature, except that it might not work very well when the in-sample size is small. Note that a direct comparison between the two approximations is not possible, as they test different null hypotheses. This issue has attracted a lot of attention and several new techniques have been proposed to help researchers reach empirical conclusions that are robust to the choice of the rolling window size and/or the split point, or where the latter are chosen optimally. Section 3.4 will review the recently proposed techniques that address this issue.

Another important issue is that the methodologies previously discussed are applicable only in stationary environments, which for example rules out unit roots or highly persistent variables. Analyses of the properties of forecast tests in the presence of high persistence are provided by Corradi et al. (2001) and Rossi (2005).

A more general question that has received no clear answer in the literature is if, why and when out-of-sample testing is preferable to in-sample testing, particularly when the null hypothesis is formulated in terms of (pseudo-) true parameters, as in (17.5). An argument against out-of-sample testing is for example made by Inoue and Kilian (2005), who show that out-of-sample tests may in fact have lower power than in-sample tests and they may not necessarily guard against data-mining, as is generally believed. An argument in favour is indirectly given by Clark and McCracken (2005), who show that out-of-sample tests may have an advantage over in-sample tests in that they are more 'robust' to changes in predictive ability due to un-modelled structural change. Rossi and Sekhposyan (2011a) propose a new methodology to explain the difference between in-sample fit and out-of-sample forecasting performance. They propose to decompose models' forecasting ability into asymptotically uncorrelated components that measure the contribution of instabilities, predictive content and over-fitting. We will discuss these contributions more in detail in section 3.5.

The last result suggests that the link between predictive ability testing and structural change is worth exploring in greater depth, which is the subject of the research summarized in the next section.

3 Methods for Forecast Evaluation in the Presence of Instabilities

Stock and Watson (2003) and Rossi (2011) have discussed two main stylized facts existing in the forecasting literature on macroeconomic variables. The first stylized fact is that the predictive ability is unstable over time. For example, instabilities have been found when forecasting GDP growth using the term spread for both the US (Giacomini and Rossi, 2006, and Bordo and Haubrich, 2008) as well as other major developed countries (Schrimpf and Wang, 2010, and Wheelock and Wohar, 2009). Instabilities have been found in a variety of predictors for forecasting inflation and output growth over time, as shown in Stock and Watson (2007) and Rossi and Sekhposyan (2010).

More in detail, Stock and Watson (2003) assess the lack of stability using parameter instability tests in Granger-causality type regressions. In-sample Granger-causality tests assess the significance of the proposed predictors in a regression of the dependent variable (say y_{t+h}) onto the lagged predictors (say, x_t), where h is the forecast horizon. That is, the Granger-causality test is a simple F-test on the parameter vector β_h, where:

$$y_{t+h} = \beta_h' x_t + \gamma_h' z_t + \varepsilon_{t,h}, \; t = 1, \ldots, T \tag{17.11}$$

and z_t are other control variables (for example, lags of y: $y_t, y_{t-1}, \ldots$) and the total sample size available to the researcher is $T + h$. Stock and Watson (2003) evaluate the stability of β_h in regression (17.11) by using Andrews' (1993) test for structural breaks, and reject stability for most of the regressors. In addition, they evaluate the forecasting ability of predictors in subsamples and find that the existence of predictability in a subsample does not necessarily imply existence of predictability in the other subsamples.

A second stylized fact existing in the literature is that the existence of in-sample predictive ability does not necessarily imply out-of-sample forecasting ability. That is, predictors that Granger-cause macroeconomic variables in the in-sample regression (17.11) do not necessarily perform well in an out-of-sample forecasting framework. A well-known example is the fact that, while exchange rate models fit well in-sample, their forecasting ability is poorer than that of a random walk (Meese and Rogoff, 1983). For other examples, see Swanson and White (1995) in forecasting interest rates, Swanson (1998) for forecasting monetary aggregates, Stock and Watson (2003) for forecasting output growth and inflation using a large dataset of predictors. That is, out-of-sample forecasting ability is harder to find than in-sample predictive ability, and therefore it is a tougher metric to be used in evaluating the performance of macroeconomic models.

How does one then assess predictive ability or estimate forecast models in the presence of instabilities? Does the widespread evidence of instabilities in macroeconomic forecasting models change our evaluation of whether it is possible to forecast macroeconomic variables? In what follows, we will review several methodologies that can be used to answer these questions; for a more detailed discussion of several test statistics as well as estimation strategies that have been proposed explicitly to address the presence of instabilities, see Rossi (2011).

In what follows, we will focus on a simplified situation where researchers are interested in predicting the h-steps ahead value of the dependent variable (say y_{t+h}) using lagged predictors (say, x_t), where h is the forecast horizon. That is,

$$y_{t+h} = \beta_h' x_t + \varepsilon_{t,h},\ t = 1, \ldots, T. \tag{17.12}$$

3.1 Granger-causality tests robust to instabilities

Traditional Granger-causality tests are invalid in the presence of instabilities. In fact, Rossi (2005) showed that traditional Granger-causality tests may have no power in the presence of instabilities. Rossi (2005) proposed a test that is robust to the presence of instabilities.

Rossi (2005) is interested in testing whether the variable x_t has no predictive content for y_t in the situation where the parameter β_t might be time-varying.[3] Her procedure is based on testing jointly the significance of the predictors and their stability over time. Among the various forms of instabilities that she considers, we focus on the case in which β_t may shift from β_1 to $\beta_2 \neq \beta_1$ at some unknown point in time, τ. That is, $\beta_t = \beta_1 \cdot 1(t < \tau) + \beta_2 \cdot 1(t \geq \tau)$.

The test is implemented as follows. Let $\hat{\beta}_{1\tau}$ and $\hat{\beta}_{2\tau}$ denote the OLS estimators before and after the break:

$$\hat{\beta}_{1\tau} = \left(\frac{1}{\tau}\sum_{t=1}^{\tau-1} x_t x_t'\right)^{-1}\left(\frac{1}{\tau}\sum_{t=1}^{\tau-1} x_t y_{t+h}\right),$$

$$\hat{\beta}_{2\tau} = \left(\frac{1}{T-\tau}\sum_{t=\tau}^{T} x_t x_t'\right)^{-1}\left(\frac{1}{T-\tau}\sum_{t=\tau}^{T} x_t y_{t+h}\right).$$

The test builds on two components: $\frac{\tau}{T}\hat{\beta}_{1\tau} + (1 - \frac{\tau}{T})\hat{\beta}_{2\tau}$ and $\hat{\beta}_{1\tau} - \hat{\beta}_{2\tau}$. The first is simply the full-sample estimate of the parameter, $\frac{\tau}{T}\hat{\beta}_{1\tau} + (1 - \frac{\tau}{T})\hat{\beta}_{2\tau} = (\frac{1}{T}\sum_{t=1}^{T} x_t x_t')^{-1}(\frac{1}{T}\sum_{t=1}^{T} x_t y_{t+h})^{-1}$; a test on whether this component is zero is able to detect situations in which the parameter β_t is constant and different from zero. However, if the regressor Granger-causes the dependent variable in such a way that the parameter changes but the average of the estimates equals zero (as in the example previously discussed), then the first component would not be able to detect such situations. The second component is introduced to perform this task. It is the difference between the parameters estimated in the two subsamples; a test on whether this component is zero is able to detect situations in which the parameter changes. Rossi (2005) proposes several test statistics, among which the following:

$$QLR_T^* = \sup_{\tau = [0.15T], \ldots, [0.85T]} \Phi_T^*$$

$$Exp - W_T^* = \frac{1}{T}\sum_{\tau=[0.15T]}^{[0.85T]} \frac{1}{0.7}\exp\left\{\left(\frac{1}{2}\right)\Phi_T^*\right\}$$

$$Mean - W_T^* = \frac{1}{T}\sum_{\tau=[0.15T]}^{[0.85T]}\frac{1}{0.7}\Phi_T^* \tag{17.13}$$

where $\Phi_T^* \equiv ((\hat{\beta}_{1\tau} - \hat{\beta}_{2\tau})' (\frac{\tau}{T}\hat{\beta}_{1\tau} + (1 - \frac{\tau}{T})\hat{\beta}_{2\tau})') \hat{V}^{-1}\begin{pmatrix} (\hat{\beta}_{1\tau} - \hat{\beta}_{2\tau}) \\ (\frac{\tau}{T}\hat{\beta}_{1\tau} + (1-\frac{\tau}{T})\hat{\beta}_{2\tau}) \end{pmatrix}$,

$$\hat{V} = \begin{pmatrix} \frac{\tau}{T} S'_{xx}\hat{S}_1^{-1}S_{xx} & 0 \\ 0 & \frac{T-\tau}{T} S'_{xx}\hat{S}_2^{-1}S_{xx} \end{pmatrix},$$

$$S_{xx} \equiv \frac{1}{T}\sum_{t=1}^{T} x_t x_t'$$

$$\hat{S}_1 = \left(\frac{1}{\tau}\sum_{t=1}^{\tau} x_t\hat{\varepsilon}_{t+h}\hat{\varepsilon}_{t+h}x_t'\right) + \sum_{j=1}^{\tau-1}\left(1 - \left|\frac{j}{\tau^{1/3}}\right|\right)\left(\frac{1}{\tau}\sum_{t=j+1}^{\tau} x_t\hat{\varepsilon}_{t+h}\hat{\varepsilon}_{t+h-j}x_{t-j}'\right), \tag{17.4}$$

$$\hat{S}_2 = \left(\frac{1}{T-\tau}\sum_{t=\tau+1}^{T-\tau} x_{t-1}\hat{\varepsilon}_{t+h}\hat{\varepsilon}_{t+h}x_t'\right)$$

$$+ \sum_{j=\tau+1}^{T-\tau}\left(1 - \left|\frac{j}{(T-\tau)^{1/3}}\right|\right)\left(\frac{1}{T-\tau}\sum_{t=j+1}^{T-\tau} x_t\hat{\varepsilon}_{t+h}\hat{\varepsilon}_{t+h-j}x_{t-j}'\right), \tag{17.5}$$

for $\hat{\varepsilon}_{t+h} \equiv y_{t+h} - x_t'\hat{\beta}$. If there is no serial correlation in the data, only the first component in (17.14) and (17.15) is relevant. Under the joint null hypothesis of no Granger-causality and no time-variation in the parameters ($\beta_t = \beta = 0$), QLR_T^*, $Mean - W_T^*$ and $Exp - W_T^*$ have asymptotic distributions whose critical values depend on the number of predictors, p, and are tabulated in Rossi's (2005) Table B1. For example, the 5 per cent critical values of the QLR_T^*, $Mean - W_T^*$ and $Exp - W_T^*$ tests are, respectively: (9.826, 3.134, 5.364) in the presence of one regressor, and (14.225, 5.015, 8.743) in the presence of two regressors.

3.2 Forecast comparisons tests robust to instabilities

If researchers are interested in establishing which model forecasts the best in the presence of instabilities, they could use Giacomini and Rossi's (2010) Fluctuation test. To simplify notation, let $\Delta L_{t+h}(\hat{\theta}_t)$, defined in (17.2), be denoted by ΔL_{t+h}. To test the null hypothesis of equal performance at each point in time:

$$H_0 : E(\Delta L_{t+h}) = 0 \text{ for all } t, \tag{17.16}$$

they propose computing the sequence of statistics

$$F_t = \hat{\sigma}^{-1}m^{-1/2}\sum_{j=t-m/2}^{t+m/2-1}\Delta L_j,\ t = R + h + m/2, \ldots, T - m/2 + 1, \tag{17.17}$$

where $m(< R)$ is a user-defined 'bandwidth', $\hat{\sigma}^2$ is an HAC estimator of the asymptotic variance of the forecast losses, for example,

$$\hat{\sigma}^2 = \sum_{j=-\tilde{q}+1}^{\tilde{q}-1} (1-|j/\tilde{q}|)P^{-1} \sum_{t=R+h}^{T} \Delta L_{t+h}\Delta L_{t+h-j}, \tag{17.18}$$

and $\tilde{q}$ is appropriately chosen (see for example, Andrews, 1991 and Newey and West, 1987). Giacomini and Rossi (2010) rely on an asymptotic approximation that assumes $\lim_{T\to\infty} \frac{m}{P} = \delta$. The null hypothesis is rejected at the 100α per cent significance level against the two-sided alternative $E(\Delta L_{t+h}) \neq 0$ for some t when $\max_t |F_t| > k_\alpha^{GR}$, where k_α^{GR} is the appropriate critical values, which depend on δ. The critical values depend on δ, and are reported in their Table 1. For example, for values of δ equal to (.1, .2, .3, .4, .5, .6, .7, .8 and .9), the critical values are 3.393, 3.179, 3.012, 2.890, 2.779, 2.634, 2.560, 2.433, 2.248 respectively.[4]

The test statistic F_t in (17.17) is equivalent to Diebold and Mariano's (1995) and Giacomini and White's (2006) (unconditional) test statistic, computed over rolling out-of-sample windows of size m. Giacomini and Rossi (2010) show that their approach can be generalized to allow for any other commonly used test for out-of-sample predictive ability comparisons discussed in section 2, as long as their asymptotic distribution is Normal. In particular, one could use the test statistics proposed by West (1996) or by Clark and West (2007), which are respectively applicable to non-nested and nested models.[5] The adoption of West's (1996) framework involves replacing $\hat{\sigma}$ in (17.18) with an estimator of the asymptotic variance that reflects the contribution of estimation uncertainty (see Theorem 4.1 of West, 1996). For the nested case, the use of the Clark and West (2007) test statistic in practice amounts to replacing ΔL_{t+h} in (17.17) with Clark and West's (2007) corrected version.

Also note that West's (1996) approach allows the parameters to be estimated using a recursive scheme, in addition to a rolling or fixed scheme. In that case, let $\{W_t^{OOS}\}$ denote a sequence of West's (1996) test statistics for h-steps ahead forecasts calculated over recursive windows (with an initial window of size R) for $t = R + h + m/2, \ldots, T - m/2 + 1$. Giacomini and Rossi (2010) show that the null hypothesis of equal predictive ability is rejected when $\max_t |W_t^{OOS}| > k_\alpha^{rec}\sqrt{\frac{T-R}{t}}(1 + 2\frac{t-R}{T-R})$, where (α, k_α^{rec}) are $(0.01, 1.143)$, $(0.05, 0.948)$ and $(0.10, 0.850)$.

Empirically, taking into account instabilities when assessing predictive ability is very important. For example, Rossi and Sekhposyan (2010) used the Fluctuation test to empirically investigate whether the relative performance of competing models for forecasting US industrial production growth and consumer price inflation has changed over time. Their predictors include interest rates, measures of real activity (such as unemployment and GDP growth), stock prices, exchange rates and monetary aggregates. Their benchmark model is the autoregressive model. Using both fully revised and real-time data, they find sharp reversals in the relative forecasting performance. They also estimate the time of the reversal in the relative performance, which allows them to relate the changes in the relative predictive ability to economic events that might have happened simultaneously. In particular, when forecasting output growth, interest rates and the spread were useful predictors in the mid-1970s, but their performance worsened at the beginning of the 1980s. Similar results hold for money growth (M2), the index of supplier deliveries, and the index of leading indicators. When forecasting inflation, the empirical evidence in favour of predictive ability is weaker than that of output growth, and the predictive ability of most variables breaks down around 1984, which dates the beginning of the Great Moderation. Such predictors include employment and unemployment measures, among others, thus implying that the predictive power of the Phillips curve disappeared around the time of the Great Moderation.

3.3 Forecast optimality tests robust to instabilities

Rossi and Sekhposyan's (2011b) proposed robust tests of forecast optimality that can be used in case researchers are interested in assessing whether forecasts are rational. In fact, traditional tests for forecast rationality are subject to the same issues as the other tests previously discussed: they are potentially invalid in the presence of instabilities.

Consider the forecast optimality regression:

$$v_{t+h} = g_t' \cdot \alpha + \eta_{t,h}, \text{ for } t = R, \ldots, T, \tag{17.19}$$

where α is a $(p \times 1)$ parameter vector. The null hypothesis of interest is $H_0 : \alpha = \alpha_0$, where typically $\alpha_0 = 0$. For example, in forecast rationality tests (Mincer and Zarnowitz, 1969), $v_{t+h} = y_{t+h}$, $g_t = [1, y_{t+h|t}]$, $\alpha = [\alpha_1, \alpha_2]'$, and typically a researcher is interested in testing whether α_1 and α_2 are jointly zero. For forecast unbiasedness, $g_t = 1$, for forecast encompassing g_t is the forecast of the encompassed model, and for serial uncorrelation $g_t = v_t$.

To test forecast optimality, one typically uses the re-scaled Wald test:

$$\mathcal{W}_T = \hat{\alpha}'\hat{V}_\alpha^{-1}\hat{\alpha}, \tag{17.20}$$

where $\hat{V}_\alpha$ is a consistent estimate of the long-run variance of the parameter vector obtained following West and McCracken (1998).[6]

Rossi and Sekhposyan (2011b) propose the following procedure, inspired by Giacomini and Rossi (2010). Let $\hat{\alpha}_t$ be the parameter estimate in regression (17.19) computed over centred rolling windows of size m (without loss of generality, we assume m to be an even number). That is, consider estimating regression (17.20) using data from $t - m/2$ up to $t + m/2 - 1$, for $t = m/2, \ldots, P - m/2 + 1$. Also, let the Wald test in the corresponding regressions be defined as:

$$\mathcal{W}_{t,m} = \hat{\alpha}_t'\hat{V}_{\theta,t}^{-1}\hat{\alpha}_t, \text{ for } t = m/2, \ldots, P - m/2 + 1, \tag{17.21}$$

where $\hat{V}_{\alpha,t}$ is a consistent estimator of the asymptotic variance of the parameter estimates in the rolling windows obtained following West and McCracken (1998). Rossi and Sekhposyan (2011b) refer to $\mathcal{W}_{t,m}$ as the Fluctuation optimality test. The test rejects the null hypothesis $H_0 : E(\hat{\alpha}_t) = 0$ for all $t = m/2, \ldots, P - m/2 + 1$ if $\max_t \mathcal{W}_{t,m} > k_{\alpha,k}^{RS}$, where $k_{\alpha,k}^{RS}$ are the critical values at the 100α per cent significance level. The critical values are reported in their Table 1 for various values of $\mu = [m/P]$ and the number of restrictions, p.[7]

3.4 The choice of the window size

In the presence of breaks, it might be useful to use a rolling window. But which size of the rolling window should be used? Similarly, recursive window forecasts require researchers to split the sample between an in-sample and an out-of-sample portion. Again, which split-point should be used? For simplicity, in this section we will focus on the choice of the window size, although we note that similar issues and solutions are applicable to the choice of split-point. The choice of the estimation window size has always been a concern for practitioners, and they raise several concerns. The first concern is that the use of different window sizes may lead to different empirical results in practice. In addition, arbitrary choices of window sizes have consequences about how the sample is split into in-sample and out-of-sample portions. Notwithstanding the choice of the window size is crucial, in the forecasting literature it is common to only report empirical results for one window size.

Pesaran and Timmermann (2007) study the problem of determining the optimal window size that guarantees the best forecasting performance, especially in the presence of breaks. They propose several methods in practice, among which several are available if the researcher possesses an estimate of the break, in which case, using either only the post-break window data to estimate the parameter or a combination of pre- and post-break data according to weights that trade-off bias against reduction in parameter estimation error, might improve forecasting performance. A difficulty in the latter methods is the fact that, in practice, it may be difficult to precisely estimate the time and magnitude of the break. Thus, rather than selecting a single window, they propose to combine forecasts based on several estimation windows. For example, they propose an average ('Ave') forecast:

$$y_{t+h|t}^{AVE,f} = (T - \underline{R} + 1)^{-1} \sum_{R=t-\underline{R}}^{t} y_{t+h|t}^{f}(R) \tag{17.22}$$

where R is the size of the rolling window, $\underline{R}$ is the researcher's minimum number of observations to be used for estimation, and the forecast for the target variable h-steps into the future made at time t based on data from the window size R (that is data from time $t - R + 1$ to t) is denoted by $y_{t+h|t}^{f}(R)$.

An alternative approach is suggested by Inoue and Rossi (2012). Inoue and Rossi (2012) are interested in assessing the robustness of conclusions of predictive ability tests to the choice of the estimation window size. They argue that the common practice of reporting empirical results for only one window size raises two types of concerns. First, it might be possible that satisfactory results (or lack thereof) were obtained simply by chance, and are not robust to other window sizes. Second, it might be possible that the data were used more than once for the purpose of selecting the best forecasting model and thus the empirical results were the result of data snooping over many different window sizes and the search process was not ultimately taken into account when reporting the empirical results. Inoue and Rossi (2012) propose new methodologies for comparing the out-of-sample forecasting performance of competing models that are robust to the choice of the estimation and evaluation window size by evaluating the models' relative forecasting performance for a variety of estimation window sizes, and then taking summary statistics. Their methodology can be applied to most of the tests of predictive ability that have been proposed in the literature, such as those discussed in section 2.

Inoue and Rossi's (2012) proposed methodology is as follows. Let $\Delta L_T(R)$ denote the test of equal predictive ability implemented using forecasts based either on a rolling window of size R or recursive/split estimation starting at observation R. For example, for the case of Diebold and Mariano's (1995) and West's (1996) test, $\Delta L_T(R)$ is defined as in (17.3). Similarly, let $\Delta L_T^{\varepsilon}(R)$ denote Clark and McCracken's (2001) ENCNEW test for nested models comparison based either on rolling window estimation with window size R or recursive/split window estimation starting at observation R. Finally, let $\mathcal{W}_T(R)$ denote tests for forecast optimality analysed by West and McCracken (1998), including tests of forecast encompassing (Clements and Hendry, 1993; Harvey et al., 1998), tests for forecast rationality (Mincer and Zarnowitz, 1969) and tests of forecast uncorrelatedness (Granger and Newbold, 1986; and Diebold and Lopez, 1996) based on forecast errors obtained either by estimation on a rolling window of size R or recursive/split estimation starting at observation R.

They suggest the following statistics:

$$\mathcal{R}_T = \sup_{R \in \{\underline{R},\ldots\overline{R}\}} |\Delta L_T(R)|, \text{ and } \mathcal{A}_T = \frac{1}{\overline{R} - \underline{R} + 1} \sum_{R=\underline{R}}^{\overline{R}} |\Delta L_T(R)|, \tag{17.23}$$

$$\mathcal{R}_T^{\varepsilon} = \sup_{R \in \{\underline{R},\ldots\overline{R}\}} \Delta L_T^{\varepsilon}(R) \text{ and } \mathcal{A}_T^{\varepsilon} = \frac{1}{\overline{R} - \underline{R} + 1} \sum_{R=\underline{R}}^{\overline{R}} \Delta L_T^{\varepsilon}(R), \tag{17.24}$$

$$\mathcal{R}_T^{W} = \sup_{R \in \{\underline{R},\ldots\overline{R}\}} W_T(R), \text{ and } A_T^{W} = \frac{1}{\overline{R} - \underline{R} + 1} \sum_{R=\underline{R}}^{\overline{R}} W_T(R), \tag{17.25}$$

where $\underline{R}$ is the smallest window size considered by the researcher, $\overline{R}$ is the largest window size, and $\hat{\Omega}_R$ is a consistent estimate of the long run variance matrix.[8] Inoue and Rossi (2012) obtain asymptotic approximations to (17.23), (17.24) and (17.25) by letting the size of the window R be asymptotically a fixed fraction of the total sample size: $\zeta = \lim_{T\to\infty}(R/T) \in (0,1)$. The null hypothesis of equal predictive ability or forecast optimality at each window size for the $\mathcal{R}_T$ test is rejected when the test statistics are larger than the critical values reported in the tables in Inoue and Rossi (2012). For example, at the 5 per cent significance level and for $\underline{R} = [0.15T]$ and $\overline{R} = [0.85T]$, the critical values for the $\mathcal{R}_T$ and $\mathcal{A}_T$ test are, respectively, 2.7231 and 1.7292. Inoue and Rossi (2012) also consider cases where the window size is fixed – we refer interested readers to their paper for more details. Hansen and Timmermann (2012) propose a similar approach; the difference is that they focus on nested models' comparisons based on recursive window estimation procedure. The advantage of their method is to provide analytic power calculations for the test statistic under very general assumptions. Unlike Inoue and Rossi (2012), however, they do not consider rolling window estimation, nor the effects of time-varying predictive ability on the power of the test.

3.5 Empirical evidence on forecasting in the presence of instabilities

In an empirical analysis focusing on the large dataset of macroeconomic predictors used in Stock and Watson (2003), Rossi (2011) finds that the Granger-causality test robust to instability proposed by Rossi (2005) is capable of overturning existing stylized facts about macroeconomic predictability and identifies more empirical evidence in favour of macroeconomic predictability, due to the fact that, in several cases, predictability only appears in subsamples of the data. She also finds similar results when evaluating the out-of-sample forecasting ability of macroeconomic predictors: using tests of predictive ability that are robust to instabilities (such as Giacomini and Rossi, 2010) is key to uncovering more predictive ability than previously found. On the other hand, tests of forecast rationality that are robust to instability (such as Rossi and Sekhposyan, 2011b) find instead more evidence that typical macroeconomic predictors of inflation and output growth lead to forecasts that are not optimal.

Finally, in the presence of instabilities, as discussed in Inoue and Rossi (2012), traditional tests may encounter two problems due to the fact that they are performed conditional on a given estimation window: they might either find spurious predictability (if the researcher had performed data-mining over several window sizes) or too little predictive ability (if the window chosen for estimation was not the optimal one given the instability in the data). Inoue and Rossi (2012) and Hansen and Timmermann (2012) propose methods to assess forecasting ability in a way that is robust to the choice of the estimation window size.

Rossi (2011) also notes that there are several estimation procedures that have been proposed to improve models' estimation in the presence of instabilities. One should note that, as shown in Elliott and Muller (2007), it is very difficult to estimate break dates in the data, which complicates estimation in the presence of instabilities; in addition, Pesaran and Timmermann (2002) have shown that, unlike what one might suspect, it is not necessarily optimal to use only observations after a break to forecast. Estimation methods that perform well in forecasting are therefore a bit more sophisticated than models in subsamples estimated according to possible break-dates. For example, Pesaran and Timmermann (2002, 2007) propose to adapt the estimation window to the latest break in a more sophisticated manner; Pesaran et al. (2006) and Koop and Potter (2007) propose time-varying parameter models where the size and duration of the process is modelled explicitly, and Clements and Hendry (1996) propose intercept corrections. Alternative methods include forecast combinations (Timmermann, 2006) and Bayesian model averaging (Wright, 2008, 2009). In her empirical analysis on the large dataset of macroeconomic predictors for inflation and output growth, Rossi (2011) finds that, among the estimation and forecasting methodologies robust to instabilities discussed above, forecast combinations with equal weights are the best.

Should one rely on in-sample measures of fit or out-of-sample measures of forecast performance when evaluating models? The short answer is that the two provide very different assessments of models' validity. Clark and McCracken (2005) show that out-of-sample forecasting procedures have more power in finding predictive ability than traditional in-sample Granger-causality tests in the presence of instabilities since they re-estimate the models' parameters over time. On the other hand, Inoue and Kilian (2005) argue that in-sample tests are based on a larger sample size than out-of-sample forecast tests, and thus may be better when designed appropriately. In fact, Clark and McCracken (2005) also show that the Granger-causality tests designed to be robust to instabilities (Rossi, 2005) perform even better. However, instabilities are only one of the sources of the difference between in-sample fit and out-of-sample forecasting performance. Giacomini and Rossi (2009) show that the difference depends on parameter instabilities, instabilities in other aspects of the forecasting model, as well as estimation uncertainty (including over-fitting). They also propose a 'Forecast Breakdown' test to determine whether, empirically, models' in-sample fit differs from out-of-sample forecasting ability. How does one determine empirically why in-sample fit differs from out-of-sample forecasting ability? Rossi and Sekhposyan (2011a) provide a methodology to decompose the models' forecasting ability into asymptotically uncorrelated components that measure the contribution of instabilities, predictive content and over-fit in explaining the differences between in-sample fit and out-of-sample forecasting performance. Using their method, one can uncover the source of the difference between the two. In an empirical analysis on a large dataset of macroeconomic predictors, Rossi (2011) finds that most predictors for output growth and inflation experienced a forecast breakdown based on Giacomini and Rossi's (2009) test. She investigates the reasons for the breakdown using Rossi and Sekhposyan's (2011a) decomposition, and finds that, when forecasting inflation, instabilities are a major determinant when using interest rates as predictors, whereas when using real measures of activity (such as unemployment) not only are there instabilities but the predictive content is misleading (that is, out-of-sample forecasting ability goes in the opposite direction relative to in-sample fit). When forecasting output growth, overfitting drives a wedge between in-sample and out-of-sample measures of performance even for predictors that have significant predictive content.

PART II SPECIAL EMPIRICAL ISSUES IN FORECASTING IN MACROECONOMICS

In the second part of the chapter we will focus on special issues that arise in practice when forecasting with macroeconomic data. Given the space constraints we will focus only on four issues that are especially important in practice, in particular: forecasting real activity with leading indicators, forecasting inflation, forecasting with real-time data, and including economic theory in forecasting.

4 Forecasting Real Economic Activity with Leading Indicators

An important goal of forecasting is to identify and evaluate leading indicators of real economic activity. Typically, the target variable for the leading indicator is either Gross Domestic Product (GDP) or industrial production or a composite index. For example, Burns and Mitchell (1946) define business cycles as co-movements, happening at the same time, in a large number of economic variables, which fluctuate from expansions and recessions and whose duration can last between 1 and 8 years (see Stock and Watson, 1999a). Since typically most measures of economic activity are highly correlated with GDP, one can use the latter as the measure of the business cycle, or an index (weighted average of several real economic variables) summarizing the joint co-movements among the real variables. An example of the latter is the Stock and Watson (1989) coincident index of economic activity based on industrial production, real disposable income, hours and sales.

The objective of the leading indicators literature is to predict the future values of such target variables, and successful leading indicators either: (i) successfully predict turning points while at the same time maintaining good predictive power across the various stages of the business cycle; for example, a good leading indicator should systematically anticipate the target variable with a stable lead time and be capable of predicting peaks and troughs with sufficient lead times; (ii) are economically and statistically significant predictors; for example, one would expect that good leading indicators have significant marginal predictive content and Granger-cause the target variable. In order for a leading indicator to have the aforementioned properties, it is often necessary to transform (or filter) the leading indicator to remove high frequency fluctuations and very long-run components that do not contain useful information on the business cycle. Typically, filtering the data is done by using Baxter and King's (1999) bandpass filter, which allows research to focus on the frequencies of interest (see Stock and Watson, 1999a); note that Hodrick–Prescott filters, while removing very long frequencies, do keep very high frequency movements and therefore are not ideal.

Widely used leading indicators include model-free composite indexes as well as model-based indexes. The former apply statistical methods such as detrending, seasonal adjustment and removal of outliers to the candidate leading indicator series. An example is the composite coincident index (CCI) by the Conference Board. A major problem of model-free composite indexes is that it is not possible to construct measures of uncertainty around them, since they are not estimated models. Model-based leading indicators instead rely on either dynamic factor models or Markov-switching models to estimate the index, and the estimation procedure does provide a measure of uncertainty around the point forecast. The difference between the two is that the underlying unobservable state of the economy is modelled as a continuous variable in the former and as a discrete variable in the latter. Examples of the former include the dynamic factor models of Geweke (1977), Sargent and Sims (1977), Stock and Watson (1991, 1993) and Forni et al. (2000); examples of the latter include Hamilton (1989), Diebold and Rudebusch (1989), Chauvet (1998) and Kim and Nelson (1998), among others. For a detailed technical description of these models, see Marcellino (2009). It is also possible to model directly the state of the business cycle (that is, the expansions/recessions) using probit or logit models, as in Stock and Watson (1991) or Estrella and Mishkin (1998), for example.

Marcellino (2009) provides an extensive empirical analysis of the success of leading indicators in practice as well as an excellent overview of the theoretical literature. He notes that most CCI indicators behave similarly for the US, and their peaks and troughs coincide with the recession dates identified by the NBER.

To evaluate the success of a leading indicator, it is common practice to compare its out-of-sample predictions with the realized values of the target variable, either the business cycle indicator (expansion/recession) or the state of the business cycle. In the latter case, the tests for forecast comparisons listed in section 2 can be used; in the former case, one often constructs probability scores. For example, Diebold and Rudebusch (1989) have proposed using the quadratic probability score:

$$QPS = \frac{2}{P} \sum_{t=R+1}^{P} (P_{t+h|t} - R_{t+h}),$$

where R_{t+h} is a binary indicator indicating whether the economy is in a recession or expansion at time $t + h$, and $P_{t+h|t}$ is the probability of recession/expansion at time $t + h$ based on the leading indicator using information up to time t. The lower the quadratic probability score, the better the forecast; a value close to zero indicates perfect forecasts.

Marcellino (2009) compares the success of several leading indicators at the one and six months ahead forecast horizon in an out-of-sample forecast exercise over the period 1989 to 2003, which includes two recessions.

Stock and Watson (1999a) examine co-movements across many series and real GDP, which they think of as a proxy for the overall business cycle. They find large correlations between several variables and real GDP growth at a variety of leads and lags. Variables that Granger-cause output can be thought of as leading indicators for the business cycle, although the predictive ability of several such indicators is unstable over time, according to parameter stability tests in the Granger-causality regressions. For example, housing starts and new orders lead output growth.

Rossi and Sekhposyan (2010) evaluate various economic models' relative performance in forecasting future US output growth. They show that the models' relative performance has, in fact, changed dramatically over time, both for revised and real-time data. In addition, they find that most predictors for output growth lost their predictive ability in the mid-1970s, and became essentially useless in the last two decades.

More recent developments focus on developing better methods to handle data irregularities and improve nowcasts of macroeconomic variables in real time. Nowcasts are the current period forecasts of unobserved macroeconomic variables which will be revealed or revised subsequently. Giannone et al. (2008) develop a formal methodology to evaluate the information content of intra-monthly data releases for nowcasts of GDP growth. They show that their method can handle large data sets with staggered data-release dates and successfully tracks the information in real time.

5 Forecasting Inflation

In a classic paper, Stock and Watson (1999b) investigated one-year ahead forecasts of US inflation. They focused on predicting inflation using the unemployment rate, according to the Phillips curve. In a sample of monthly data from 1959 to 1997, they found that the latter produces more accurate forecasts than other macroeconomic variables, including commodity prices and monetary aggregates. They also found statistical evidence of instabilities in the parameters of the Phillips curve. In addition, they showed that, by including index measures of real activity, it is possible to improve inflation forecasts beyond those based on unemployment.

Rossi and Sekhposyan (2010) evaluate various economic models' relative performance in forecasting inflation by taking into account the possibility that the models' relative performance can be varying over time. They show that fewer predictors are significant for forecasting inflation than forecasting output growth, and their predictive ability significantly worsened around the time of the Great Moderation.

Faust and Wright (2011) investigate subjective forecasts, which empirically appear to have an advantage over traditional model-based forecasts. They attempt to incorporate subjective forecast's information into model-based forecasts. They argue that, by exploiting boundary values provided by subjective forecasts (for example where inflation will be in the medium and long run), it might be possible to improve model-based forecasts. However, they find that, given good boundary values, models cannot improve much on trivial paths between the boundaries and, overall, perform equally well.

6 Forecasting with Real-time Data

When conducting a forecasting exercise, typically researchers utilize data that they have collected at the time of the analysis for the macroeconomic variables of interest from the beginning of the sample up to the most recent data available. Then, using these data, they mimic what a forecaster would have done in the past to obtain a series of pseudo out-of-sample forecasts over time. However, these data are not necessarily the same as the data that were available at the time forecasters were actually producing a forecast. In fact, data are constantly subject to data revisions, changes and updates, which not only change the contemporaneous value of the variables but also their past values. To avoid this problem, Croushore and Stark (2001, 2003) introduced a database (the 'Real-time data set for macroeconomists') that is available free at the Federal Reserve Bank of Philadelphia. The database consists of a series of datasets of macroeconomic variables collected at each point in time (vintage); at each time, the dataset contains data of macroeconomic variables as they existed at that point in time, starting from the first datapoint up to the time of collection. Each dataset is a snapshot of the data that a forecaster would have been able to observe and use at each point in time. Using real-time data effectively allows the actual forecasting ability of models or predictors to be evaluated.

Using real-time data is important in practice. Orphanides (2001) has shown that implications of macroeconomic models for studying the effects of monetary policy in-sample might change if one uses real-time as opposed to revised data. Similarly, the empirical results of forecasting exercises might differ depending on whether the researcher uses real-time as opposed to revised data. In fact, Orphanides and Van Norden (2005) show that, although ex-post measures of the output gap are useful for predicting inflation, in real time the predictive content disappears. Edge et al. (2007) also find the same result when forecasting long-run productivity growth. Similarly, Faust et al. (2003) show that exchange rates are much more difficult to forecast using real-time data. Swanson (1996) finds that Granger causality test results change depending on whether one uses the first release of the data or the latest available data. Finally, Amato and Swanson (2001) show that money supply has predictive content for output only when using fully revised data rather than real-time data.

There are three main reasons why forecasts may be affected by revisions (Croushore, 2006). First, the data are different: real time databases provide vintages of data; thus, the data to be forecasted are different. In contrast, typical forecasting exercises are implemented and evaluated using the last revised data available at the time the data are collected. Secondly, the estimated coefficients change. In fact, the forecasting exercise can be implemented by either using the data available in the latest vintage of data (that is, what the forecaster would have had available at that point in time) or by using for each time the data that were immediately released at that time. Again, this is different from estimating coefficients using data that are available at the time the data are collected (fully revised data). Koenig et al. (2003) find that it is best to use the first release of the data in forecasting rather than real-time data. Third, the model used for forecasting may be different as well (for example, the number of lags estimated using real-time data might differ from that estimated in fully revised data). See Croushore (2006) for more details.

Finally, the fact that data are revised might be exploited to improve forecasts as well.

For example, one might optimally take into account data revisions by using a Kalman filter or a state-space model. See Howrey (1978) for how to do so in practice.

7 Economic Theory and Forecasting

Can economic theory help us produce better forecasts? This is a fundamental question that has received little attention in the literature. In fact, a general picture that emerges from the recent literature on forecasting methodology is the almost exclusive focus on 'a-theoretical' econometric models. This may be partly due to the fact that some of these methods have proven to be quite successful, in particular those that provide a way to extract the information contained in large datasets while at the same time controlling the dimensionality of the problem, such as factor models (Stock and Watson, 2002; Forni et al., 2000), Bayesian VARs (BVARs, for example, Litterman, 1986; Giannone et al., 2010) and forecast combination methods such as Bayesian model averaging (Raftery et al., 1997; Aiolfi et al., 2010) and bagging (Inoue and Kilian, 2008). On the other hand, there has been some call in the literature (particularly from researchers at central banks and policy institutions) for forecasts that are based on models that can 'tell a story' (Edge et al., 2010). As a response, a small amount of literature has investigated the forecasting performance of the new generation of dynamic stochastic general equilibrium (DSGE) models that are large-scale theoretical models built on microfoundations with optimizing agents (for example, Smets and Wouters, 2003). See, for example, Adolfson et al. (2007), Wang (2009), Lees et al. (2011) and Edge et al. (2010). The evidence from this literature is, however, still limited and the conclusions should be taken with caution as they are typically based on short evaluation samples that moreover do not include the most recent periods of recession. A more thorough evaluation of the forecasting performance of DSGE models is clearly needed.

In particular, Gurkaynak and Edge (2010) empirically assess the forecasting performance of the Smets and Wouters DSGE model. They explore how this model would have forecasted, from 1 to 8 quarters ahead, movements in inflation, output growth and interest rates between 1997 and 2006 and evaluate how good forecasts based on DSGE models are using real-time data. They find that their forecasts are not worse than those based on several competing alternatives, including official forecasts such as the Greenbook and Blue Chip Consensus forecasts. Greenbook forecasts are judgemental forecasts produced by the Board of Governors of the Federal Reserve System; they are produced before each FOMC meeting, approximately eight times a year, and are made available to the public with a five-year delay. Importantly, Greenbook forecasts are produced conditional on expected paths for financial variables such as the policy interest rate. The Blue Chip Consensus forecasts are forecasts of several important macroeconomic variables (such as output growth, inflation and interest rates) made monthly by a sample of approximately 50 banks and consulting firms; the average forecast across the sample is called the Consensus forecast. However, their absolute performance is very poor, especially during the Great Moderation period, since there was basically nothing to be forecasted. Similarly, Edge et al. (2010) compared the forecasts from the Federal Reserve Board's DSGE model with alternative forecasts based on time series models as well as Greenbook forecasts.

A further branch of the literature has looked for a middle ground and proposed 'hybrid' approaches. One example in the context of model estimation is the use of theoretical models to construct priors for the parameters of econometric models (An and Schorfheide, 2007; Schorfheide, 2000), or the idea of constructing an optimal combination of the theoretical and econometric models (Del Negro and Schorfheide, 2004).

We will next discuss two different hybrid approaches applied to the specific case of out-of-sample forecasting.

7.1 Carriero and Giacomini (2011)

The idea of optimally combining the theoretical and the econometric model can be easily extended to the context of out-of-sample forecasting, as shown by Carriero and Giacomini (2011). The basic idea is to first acknowledge that the theoretical model can often be viewed as an econometric model with theory-based parameter restrictions. This is the case of the DSGE models considered in the literature mentioned above, since they are linearized DSGE models that can therefore be written as vector ARMA models subject to cross-equation restrictions implied by theory. The problem is therefore that of combining two forecasts in a non-standard framework in which there is only one model, but the forecaster has the option of either imposing the parameter restrictions implied by the theoretical model or of forecasting with the unrestricted model. The forecast combination problem is non-standard because the combination is between forecasts based on the same model but that use different estimators, which may yield perfectly correlated forecasts in large samples. This problem can be overcome by adopting the asymptotic framework of Giacomini and White (2006), where the estimation uncertainty is non-vanishing.

Carriero and Giacomini (2011) propose estimating the optimal combination weight out-of-sample and constructing an out-of-sample encompassing test. Let the forecast combination be $f_t^* = f_t^R + (1 - \lambda)(f_t^U - f_t^R)$, and define the optimal weight λ^* as the one that minimizes a general expected out-of-sample loss

$$\begin{aligned}\lambda^* &= \arg\min_{\lambda \in R} E\left[\frac{1}{P}\sum_{t=R}^{T-h} L(y_{t+h}, f_t^*)\right] \\ &= \arg\min_{\lambda \in R} E[Q_P(\lambda)], \end{aligned} \tag{17.26}$$

which can be estimated by

$$\begin{aligned}\hat{\lambda} &= \arg\min_{\lambda \in R} \frac{1}{P}\sum_{t=R}^{T-h} L(y_{t+h}, f_t^*) \\ &= \arg\min_{\lambda \in R} Q_P(\lambda). \end{aligned} \tag{17.27}$$

Under suitable assumptions, Carriero and Giacomini (2011) show that a test of the 'usefulness' of the parameter restrictions for out-of-sample forecasting can be obtained by first constructing

$$\begin{aligned} t^U &= \frac{\sqrt{n}(\hat{\lambda} - 1)}{\hat{\sigma}} \text{ and} \\ t^R &= \frac{\sqrt{n}\hat{\lambda}}{\hat{\sigma}}, \end{aligned} \tag{17.28}$$

where $\hat{\sigma}$ is given by

$$\hat{\sigma} = \sqrt{\hat{H}^{-1}\hat{\Omega}\hat{H}^{-1}};$$

$$\hat{H} = \nabla_{\lambda\lambda}Q_n(\hat{\lambda});$$

$$\hat{\Omega} = \sum_{j=-p+1}^{p-1}\left(1-\left|\frac{j}{p}\right|\right)n^{-1}\sum_{t=R+j}^{T-h} s_t(\hat{\lambda})s_{t-j}(\hat{\lambda});$$

$$s_t(\hat{\lambda}) = \nabla_{\lambda}L(y_{t+h}, f_t^R + (1-\hat{\lambda})(f_t^U - f_t^R)), \quad (17.29)$$

where p is a bandwidth that increases with the sample size (Newey and West, 1987). Then the hypotheses $H_0^U : \lambda^* = 1$ (the unrestricted forecast is useless) and $H_0^R : \lambda^* = 0$ (the restricted forecast is useless) are rejected at a significance level α respectively when $|t^U| > c_{\alpha/2}$ and $|t^R| > c_{\alpha/2}$, with $c_{\alpha/2}$ indicating the $1 - \alpha/2$ quantile of an $N(0,1)$ distribution. If both hypotheses are rejected, the estimated weight $\hat{\lambda}$ yields the forecast combination that optimally exploits the theoretical restrictions, given the user-defined loss function.

Note that the same test can be used to combine forecasts based on any two competing estimators, and it is not necessary that the forecast f_t^U be based on the unrestricted models (in other words, f_t^U could be a forecast based on any other estimator, for example, a-theoretical restrictions such as a BVAR or a random walk).

7.2 Giacomini and Ragusa (2011)

The approach discussed in the previous section requires one being able to construct forecasts based on the theoretical model. A model that fully specifies a likelihood for all the variables of interest (for example, in the multivariate case) is not, however, always available, and there might be a concern that a fully-fledged DSGE is misspecified. One may for example be interested in asking whether the restrictions embedded in, say, a Euler equation are useful for forecasting, which is a difficult question to answer as the Euler equation does not provide a conditional likelihood that can be used for forecasting.

Giacomini and Ragusa (2011) propose adopting a hybrid approach to forecasting that starts from a forecast based on the econometric model (for example, a BVAR or a factor model) and modifies it in a way that results in a forecast that satisfies theoretical restrictions written in the form of non-linear moment conditions, such as, for example, Euler equations or moment conditions implied by Taylor rules.

This is obtained by projection methods as follows. Suppose the theory-based moment restrictions for the vector y_{t+h} are

$$E_t[g(y_{t+h}, \theta_0)] = 0, \quad (17.30)$$

where the subscript t indicates conditioning on the information set at time t and θ_0 is assumed to be known, calibrated, or estimated on a different data set from the one used for forecasting (note that the moment conditions could possibly only involve a subset of y_{t+h}). One proceeds as follows:

1. Produce a sequence of h-step ahead density forecasts from an econometric model, $f_t(y_{t+h})$ for $t = R,\ldots,T-h$.
2. Project each $f_t(y_{t+h})$ onto the space of distributions that satisfy the moment condition $E_t[g(y_{t+h},\theta_0)] = 0$. This yields a new density $\tilde{f}_t(y_{t+h})$ given by:

$$\tilde{f}_t(y_{t+h}) = f_t(y_{t+h})\exp\{\eta_t + \lambda_t' g(y_{t+h},\theta_0)\}. \tag{17.31}$$

   The new density by construction satisfies the moment condition (17.30).
3. For each t, estimate η_t and λ_t by (numerically) solving:

$$\lambda_t = \min_{\lambda} \int f_t(x)\exp\{\lambda' g(x,\theta_0)\}\,dx$$

$$\eta_t = \log\left\{\int f_t(x)\exp\{\lambda_t' g(x,\theta_0)\}\,dx\right\}^{-1} \tag{17.32}$$

The new forecast $\tilde{f}_t(y_{t+h})$ can be interpreted as the density which, out of all the densities that satisfy the moment condition, is the closest to the initial density $f_t(y_{t+h})$ according to a Kullback–Leibler measure of divergence. The paper shows that the theory-coherent density forecast $f_t(y_{t+h})$ is weakly more accurate than the initial, a-theoretical forecast, when accuracy is measured by a logarithmic scoring rule, provided the moment restrictions are true at all time periods.

The method is an alternative to forecasting with fully-fledged DSGE models and can be used to investigate the role of theory in forecasting in a variety of empirical applications. Because of the possibility of accommodating non-linearity in the moment conditions (a task that may be difficult to accomplish in a likelihood-based context) the method can also be used to ask whether incorporating the non-linearity suggested by theory into forecasts can lead to improvements in accuracy in practice.

8 Conclusions

This chapter provides an overview of forecast methodologies and empirical results that are useful for macroeconomists and practitioners interested in forecasting using macroeconomic databases. A more detailed exposition of these techniques as well as other available techniques that we did not include due to space constraints is provided in Elliott et al. (2009) and Elliott and Timmermann (2011).

NOTES

1. For ease of notation we stack the parameters of the two models in $\hat{\theta}_t$.
2. From a technical point of view, the reason why things work is that the assumption of a finite estimation window means that $\Delta L_{t+h}(\hat{\theta}_t)$ can be viewed as a function of the finite history of the predictor and predictands, and as such it inherits their time series properties, which makes it easy to derive the test.
3. Rossi (2005) also considers the general case of testing possibly non-linear restrictions in models estimated with Generalized Method of Moments (GMM). She also considers the case of tests on subsets of parameters, that is, in the case of Granger-causality regressions, tests on whether x_t Granger-causes y_t in the model $y_{t+h} = x_t'\beta_t + z_t'\gamma + \varepsilon_{t,h}$.
4. They also derive critical values for one-sided tests.

5. The fundamental difference between these approaches and Giacomini and White (2006) is that they test two different null hypotheses: the null hypothesis in West (1996) and Clark and West (2006, 2007) concerns forecast losses that are evaluated at the population parameters, whereas in Giacomini and White (2006) the losses depend on estimated in-sample parameters. This reflects the different focus of the two approaches on comparing forecasting models (West, 1996, and Clark and West, 2006, 2007) versus comparing forecasting methods (Giacomini and White, 2006).
6. West and McCracken (1998) have shown that it is necessary to correct (17.20) for parameter estimation error in order to obtain test statistics that have good size properties in small samples, and proposed a general variance estimator as well as adjustment procedures that take into account estimation uncertainty.
7. Rossi and Sekhposyan (2011b) also note that a simple, two-sided t-ratio test on the *s*th parameter, $\alpha^{(s)}$, can be obtained as $\hat{\alpha}_t^{(s)} \hat{V}_{\alpha^{(s)},t}^{-1/2}$, where $\hat{V}_{\alpha^{(s)},t}$ is element in the *s*th row and *s*th column of $\hat{V}_{\alpha,t}$; then, reject the null hypothesis $H_0 : E(\hat{\alpha}_t^{(s)}) = \alpha_0^{(s)}$ for all $t = m/2, \ldots, P - m/2 + 1$ at the 100α per cent significance level if $\max_t |\hat{\alpha}_t^{(s)} \hat{V}_{\alpha^{(s)},t}^{-1/2}| > k_\alpha^{GR}$, where k_α^{GR} are the critical values provided by Giacomini and Rossi (2010).
8. See West (1996) for consistent variance estimates in (17.23), Clark and McCracken (2001) for (17.24) and West and McCracken (1998) for (17.25).

REFERENCES

Adolfson, M., J. Linde and M. Villani (2007), 'Forecasting performance of an open economy DSGE model', *Econometric Reviews*, **26**, 289–328.

Aiolfi, M., C. Capistrán and A. Timmermann (2010), 'Forecast combinations', CREATES Research Paper No. 2010-21.

Amato, J.D. and N.R. Swanson (2001), 'The real time predictive content of money for output', *Journal of Monetary Economics*, **48**, 3–24.

Amisano, G. and R. Giacomini (2007), 'Comparing density forecasts via weighted likelihood ratio tests', *Journal of Business and Economic Statistics*, **25**, 177–90.

An, S. and F. Schorfheide (2007), 'Bayesian analysis of DSGE models', *Econometric Reviews*, **26**, 113–72.

Andrews, D.W. (1993), 'Tests for parameter instability and structural change with unknown change point', *Econometrica*, **61**(4), 821–56.

Andrews, D.W.K. (1991), 'Heteroskedasticity and autocorrelation consistent covariance matrix estimation', *Econometrica*, **59**, 817–58.

Baxter, M. and R. King (1999), 'Measuring business cycles: approximate band-pass filters for economic time series', *Review of Economics and Statistics*, **81**(4), 575–93.

Bordo, M.D. and J.G. Haubrich (2008), 'The yield curve as a predictor of growth: long-run evidence, 1875–1997', *Review of Economics and Statistics*, **90**(1), 182–5.

Burns, A.F. and W.C. Mitchell (1946), *Measuring Business Cycles*, New York: NBER.

Carriero, A. and R. Giacomini (2011), 'How useful are no-arbitrage restrictions for forecasting the term structure of interest rates?', *Journal of Econometrics*, **164**, 21–34.

Chauvet, M. (1998), 'An econometric characterization of business cycle dynamics with factor structure and regime switching', *International Economic Review*, **39**(4), 969–96.

Clark, T. and M. McCracken (2001), 'Tests of equal forecast accuracy and encompassing for nested models', *Journal of Econometrics*, **105**(1), 85–110.

Clark, T. and M. McCracken (2009), 'Nested forecast model comparisons: a new approach to testing equal accuracy', *mimeo*.

Clark, T.E. and M.W. McCracken (2005), 'The power of tests of predictive ability in the presence of structural breaks', *Journal of Econometrics*, **124**, 1–31.

Clark, T.E. and K.D. West (2006), 'Using out-of-sample mean squared prediction errors to test the martingale difference hypothesis', *Journal of Econometrics*, **135**(1–2), 155–86.

Clark, T.E. and K.D. West (2007), 'Approximately normal tests for equal predictive accuracy in nested models', *Journal of Econometrics*, **138**, 291–311.

Clements, M.P. and D.F. Hendry (1993), 'On the limitations of comparing mean square forecast errors', *Journal of Forecasting*, **12**, 617–37.

Clements, M.P. and D.F. Hendry (1996), 'Intercept corrections and structural change', *Journal of Applied Econometrics*, **11**, 475–94.

Corradi, V., N. Swanson and C. Olivetti (2001), 'Predictive ability with cointegrated variables', *Journal of Econometrics*, **104**(2), 315–58.

Croushore, D. (2006), 'Forecasting with real-time macroeconomic data', in G. Elliott, C.W.J. Granger and A. Timmermann (eds), *Handbook of Economic Forecasting*, Amsterdam: Elsevier/North-Holland.

Croushore, D. and T. Stark (2001), 'A real-time data set for macroeconomists', *Journal of Econometrics*, **105**, 111–30.
Croushore, D. and T. Stark (2003), 'A real-time data set for macroeconomists: does the data vintage matter?', *Review of Economics and Statistics*, **85**, 605–17.
Del Negro, M. and F. Schorfheide (2004), 'Priors from general equilibrium models for VARs', *International Economic Review*, **45**(2), 643–73.
Diebold, F.X. (2007), *Elements of Forecasting*, 4th edn, Cincinnati, OH: South-Western College Publishing.
Diebold, F.X. and J. Lopez (1996), 'Forecast evaluation and combination', in G.S. Maddala and C.R. Rao (eds), *Handbook of Statistics*, Amsterdam: North-Holland, pp. 241–68.
Diebold, F.X. and R.S. Mariano (1995), 'Comparing predictive accuracy', *Journal of Business and Economic Statistics*, **13**, 253–63.
Diebold, F.X. and G.D. Rudebusch (1989), 'Scoring the leading indicators', *The Journal of Business*, **62**(3), 369–91.
Edge, R.M., M.T. Kiley and J.-P. Laforte (2010), 'A comparison of forecast performance between Federal Reserve staff forecasts, simple reduced-form models, and a DSGE model', *Journal of Applied Econometrics*, **25**, 720–54.
Edge, R.M., T. Laubach and J.C. Williams (2007), 'Learning and shifts in long-run productivity growth', *Journal of Monetary Economics*, **54**, 2421–38.
Elliott, G. and U. Muller (2007), 'Confidence sets for the date of a single break in linear time series regressions', *Journal of Econometrics*, **141**, 1196–218.
Elliott, G. and A. Timmermann (2011), *Handbook of Economic Forecasting*, Vol. 2, Amsterdam: Elsevier/North Holland.
Elliott, G., C. Granger and A. Timmermann (2009), *Handbook of Economic Forecasting*, Vol. 1, Amsterdam: Elsevier/North Holland.
Elliott, G., I. Komunjer and A. Timmermann (2005), 'Estimation and testing of forecast rationality under flexible loss', *Review of Economic Studies*, **72**, 1107–25.
Estrella, A. and F.S. Mishkin (1998), 'Predicting US recessions: financial variables as leading indicators', *The Review of Economics and Statistics*, **80**(1), 45–61.
Faust, J. and J. Wright (2011), 'Forecasting inflation', in G. Elliott and A. Timmermann (eds), *Handbook of Economic Forecasting*, Vol. 2, Amsterdam: Elsevier/North Holland.
Faust, J., J.H. Rogers and J.H. Wright (2003), 'Exchange rate forecasting: the errors we've really made', *Journal of International Economics*, **60**, 35–59.
Forni, M., M. Hallin, M. Lippi and L. Reichlin (2000), 'The generalized factor model: identification and estimation', *The Review of Economics and Statistics*, **82**(4), 540–54.
Geweke, J. (1977), 'The dynamic factor analysis of economic time series', Chapter 19 in D.J. Aigner and A.S. Goldberger (eds), *Latent Variables in Socio-Economic Models*, Amsterdam: Elsevier/North Holland.
Giacomini, R. and I. Komunjer (2005), 'Evaluation and combination of conditional quantile forecasts', *Journal of Business and Economic Statistics*, **23**, 416–31.
Giacomini, R. and G. Ragusa (2011), 'Incorporating theoretical restrictions into forecasting by projection methods', mimeo.
Giacomini, R. and B. Rossi (2006), 'How stable is the forecasting performance of the yield curve for output growth?', *Oxford Bulletin of Economics and Statistics*, **68**(s1), 783–95.
Giacomini, R. and B. Rossi (2009), 'Detecting and predicting forecast breakdowns', *Review of Economic Studies*, **76**(2), 669–705.
Giacomini, R. and B. Rossi (2010), 'Forecast comparisons in unstable environments', *Journal of Applied Econometrics*, **25**(4), 595–620.
Giacomini, R. and H. White (2006), 'Tests of conditional predictive ability', *Econometrica*, **74**, 1545–78.
Giannone, D., M. Lenza and G. Primiceri (2010), 'Prior selection for vector autoregressions', mimeo.
Giannone, D., L. Reichlin and D. Small (2008), 'Nowcasting: the real-time informational content of macroeconomic data', *Journal of Monetary Economics*, **55**(4), 665–76.
Granger, C.W.J. and P. Newbold (1986), *Forecasting Economic Time Series*, 2nd edn, New York: Academic Press.
Gurkaynak, R. and R. Edge (2010), 'How useful are estimated DSGE model forecasts for central bankers?', *Brookings Papers on Economic Activity*, **2**, 209–59.
Hamilton, J.D. (1989), 'A new approach to the economic analysis of nonstationary time series and the business cycle', *Econometrica*, **57**, 357–84.
Hansen, P.R. (2005), 'A test for superior predictive ability', *Journal of Business and Economic Statistics*, **23**, 365–80.
Hansen, P.R. and A. Timmermann (2011), 'Choice of sample split in out-of-sample forecast evaluation', mimeo.

Hansen, P.R., A. Lunde and J.M. Nason (2011), 'The model confidence set', *Econometrica*, **79**, 452–97.

Harvey, D.I., S.J. Leybourne and P. Newbold (1998), 'Tests for forecast encompassing', *Journal of Business and Economic Statistics*, **16**(2), 254–9.

Howrey, E.P. (1978), 'The use of the preliminary data in econometric forecasting', *Review of Economics and Statistics*, **60**, 193–200.

Inoue, A. and L. Kilian (2005), 'In-sample or out-of-sample tests of predictability: which one should we use?', *Econometric Reviews*, **23**(4), 371–402.

Inoue, A. and L. Kilian (2008), 'How useful is bagging in forecasting economic time series? A case study of US consumer price inflation', *Journal of the American Statistical Association*, **103**, 511–22.

Inoue, A. and B. Rossi (2012), 'Out of sample forecast tests robust to the window size choice', *Journal of Business and Economics Statistics*, **30**(3), 432–53.

Kim, C.J. and C.R. Nelson (1998), 'Business cycle turning points, a new coincident index, and tests of duration dependence based on a dynamic factor model with regime switching', *The Review of Economics and Statistics*, **80**, 188–201.

Koenig, E., S. Dolmas and J. Piger (2003), 'The use and abuse of "real-time" data in economic forecasting', *Review of Economics and Statistics*, **85**, 618–28.

Koop, G. and S.M. Potter (2007), 'Estimation and forecasting in models with multiple breaks', *Review of Economic Studies*, **74**, 763–89.

Lees, K., T. Matheson and C. Smith (2011), 'Open economy forecasting with a DSGE-VAR: head to head with the RBNZ published forecasts', *International Journal of Forecasting*, **27**, 512–28.

Leitch, G. and E.J. Tanner (1991), 'Economic forecast evaluation: profits versus the conventional error measures', *American Economic Review*, **81**(3), 580–90.

Litterman, R. (1986), 'A statistical approach to economic forecasting', *Journal of Business & Economic Statistics*, **4**, 1–4.

Marcellino, M. (2009), 'Leading indicators', in G. Elliott, C. Granger and A. Timmermann, *Handbook of Economic Forecasting*, Vol. 1, Amsterdam: Elsevier/North Holland.

McCracken, M. (2007), 'Asymptotics for out-of-sample tests of Granger causality', *Journal of Econometrics*, **140**, 719–52.

Meese, R. and K.S. Rogoff (1983), 'Exchange rate models of the seventies. Do they fit out of sample?', *Journal of International Economics*, **14**, 3–24.

Mincer, J. and V. Zarnowitz (1969), 'The evaluation of economic forecasts', in J. Mincer (ed.), *Economic Forecasts and Expectations*, New York: National Bureau of Economic Research, pp. 81–111.

Newey, W. and K. West (1987), 'A simple, positive semi-definite, heteroskedasticity and autocorrelation consistent covariance matrix', *Econometrica*, **55**, 703–708.

Orphanides, A. (2001), 'Monetary policy rules based on real-time data', *American Economic Review*, **91**, 964–85.

Orphanides, A. and S. van Norden (2005), 'The reliability of inflation forecasts based on output gaps in real time', *Journal of Money, Credit, and Banking*, **37**, 583–601.

Pesaran, M.H. and A. Timmermann (2002), 'Market timing and return prediction under model instability', *Journal of Empirical Finance*, **9**(5), 495–510.

Pesaran, M.H. and A. Timmermann (2007), 'Selection of estimation window in the presence of breaks', *Journal of Econometrics*, **137**(1), 134–61.

Pesaran, M.H., D. Pettenuzzo and A. Timmermann (2006), 'Forecasting time series subject to multiple structural breaks', *Review of Economic Studies*, **73**, 1057–84.

Raftery, A., D. Madigan and J. Hoeting (1997), 'Bayesian model averaging for linear regression models', *Journal of the American Statistical Association*, **92**, 179–91.

Romano, J.P. and M. Wolf (2005), 'Stepwise multiple testing as formalized data snooping', *Econometrica*, **73**, 1237–82.

Rossi, B. (2005), 'Optimal tests for nested model selections with underlying parameter instabilities', *Econometric Theory*, **21**(5), 962–90.

Rossi, B. (2011), 'Advances in forecasting under instabilities', in G. Elliott and A. Timmermann (eds), *Handbook of Economic Forecasting*, Vol. 2, Amsterdam: Elsevier/North Holland.

Rossi, B. and T. Sekhposyan (2010), 'Have models' forecasting performance changed over time, and when?', *International Journal of Forecasting*, **26**(4).

Rossi, B. and T. Sekhposyan (2011a), 'Understanding models' forecasting performance', *Journal of Econometrics*, **164**, 158–72.

Rossi, B. and T. Sekhposyan (2011b), 'Forecast optimality tests in the presence of instabilities', mimeo, Duke University.

Sargent, T.J. and C.A. Sims (1977), 'Business cycle modeling without pretending to have too much a priori economic theory', in C. Sims et al. (eds), *New Methods in Business Cycle Research*, Minneapolis, MN: Federal Reserve Bank of Minneapolis.

Schorfheide, F. (2000), 'Loss function-based evaluation of DSGE models', *Journal of Applied Econometrics*, **15**, 645–70.
Schrimpf, A. and Q.W. Wang (2010), 'A reappraisal of the leading indicator properties of the yield curve under structural instability', *International Journal of Forecasting*, **26**(4), 836–57.
Smets, F. and R. Wouters (2003), 'An estimated dynamic stochastic general equilibrium model of the euro area', *Journal of the European Economic Association*, **1**, 1123–75.
Stock, J.H. and M.W. Watson (1989), 'New indexes of coincident and leading economic indicators', in O.J. Blanchard and S. Fisher (eds), *NBER Macroeconomics Annual 1989*, Vol. 4, MIT Press, pp. 351–409.
Stock, J.H. and M.W. Watson (1991), 'A probability model of the coicident indicators', in K. Lahiri and G.H. Moore (eds), *Leading Economic Indicators: New Approaches and Forecasting Records*, Cambridge: Cambridge University Press.
Stock, J.H. and M.W. Watson (1993), 'A procedure for predicting recessions with leading indicators: econometric issues and recent experience', in J.H. Stock and M.W. Watson (eds), *Business Cycles, Indicators, and Forecasting*, Chicago, IL: The University of Chicago Press, pp. 95–153.
Stock, J.H. and M.W. Watson (1999a), 'Business cycle fluctuations in US macroeconomic time series', in J.B. Taylor and M. Woodford (eds), *Handbook of Macroeconomics*, Vol. 1A, Amsterdam: Elsevier Science/North-Holland.
Stock, J.H. and M.W. Watson (1999b), 'Forecasting inflation', *Journal of Monetary Economics*, **44**, 293–335.
Stock, J.H. and M.W. Watson (2002), 'Forecasting using principal components from a large number of predictors', *Journal of the American Statistical Association*, **97**, 1167–79.
Stock, J.H. and M.W. Watson (2003), 'Forecasting output and inflation: the role of asset prices', *Journal of Economic Literature*, **XLI**, 788–829.
Stock, J.H. and M.W. Watson (2007), 'Has inflation become harder to forecast?', *Journal of Money, Credit and Banking*, **39**(1), 3–34.
Swanson, N.R. (1996), 'Forecasting using first available versus fully revised economic time series data', *Studies in Nonlinear Dynamics and Econometrics*, **1**, 47–64.
Swanson, N.R. (1998), 'Money and output viewed through a rolling window', *Journal of Monetary Economics*, **41**, 455–73.
Swanson, N.R. and H. White (1995), 'A model selection approach to assessing the information in the term structure using linear models and artifical neural networks', *Journal of Business and Economic Statistics*, **13**, 265–75.
Timmermann, A. (2006), 'Forecast combinations', in G. Elliott, C. Granger and A. Timmermann, *Handbook of Economic Forecasting*, Vol. 1, Amsterdam: Elsevier/North Holland.
Wang, M.C. (2009), 'Comparing the DSGE model with the factor model: an out-of-sample forecasting experiment', *Journal of Forecasting*, **28**, 167–82.
West, K.D. (1996), 'Asymptotic inference about predictive ability', *Econometrica*, **64**, 1067–84.
West, K.D. and M.W. McCracken (1998), 'Regression-based tests of predictive ability', *International Economic Review*, **39**(4), 817–40.
West, K.D., H.J. Edison and D. Cho (1993), 'A utility-based comparison of some models of exchange rate volatility', *Journal of International Economics*, **35**, 23–45.
Wheelock, D.C. and M.E. Wohar (2009), 'Can the term spread predict output growth and recessions? A survey of the literature', *Federal Reserve Bank of St. Louis Review*, **91**(5), 419–40.
White, H. (2000), 'A reality check for data snooping', *Econometrica*, **68**, 1097–127.
Wright, J.H. (2008), 'Bayesian model averaging and exchange rate forecasts', *Journal of Econometrics*, **146**(2), 329–41.
Wright, J.H. (2009), 'Forecasting US inflation by Bayesian model averaging', *Journal of Forecasting*, **28**(2), 131–44.

PART IV

APPLICATIONS I: DYNAMIC STOCHASTIC GENERAL EQUILIBRIUM MODELS

18 The science and art of DSGE modelling: I – construction and Bayesian estimation*

Cristiano Cantore, Vasco J. Gabriel, Paul Levine, Joseph Pearlman and Bo Yang

1 INTRODUCTION

The past forty years or so have seen a remarkable transformation in macro-models used by central banks, policymakers and forecasting bodies. In this chapter and the next, we discuss how the different elements of modern macroeconomic models can be seamlessly integrated in a framework encompassing the different stages of model building, estimation and policy analysis. We describe the development of the building blocks of such models, showing that the main features of New Keynesian (NK) Dynamic Stochastic General Equilibrium (DSGE) models consist of a 'Real Business Cycle' (RBC) core, with an outer shell that includes nominal rigidities and other frictions. We then discuss how to take these models to the data, focusing on empirical implementations based on Bayesian system estimation methods.

The road of macroeconomic modelling is full of twists and turns, but the different directions taken seem to have converged to what is still, to a large extent, the consensual synthesis. Indeed, the models that are now the mainstay for policy analysis and forecasting depart significantly from previous approaches in that they strike a balance between internal consistency, empirical adherence and adequacy for policy analysis.

In contrast, in the 1960s–1970s econometric models were mostly based on equation-by-equation estimation of what were essentially Keynesian reduced form behavioural equations, without explicit expectations. Large models were then constructed using these behavioural relationships as building blocks, alongside identities defining aggregate demand, trade balances and the government budget constraint.

The introduction of first adaptive and then rational expectations led to what proved to be a fatal blow for this generation of models – the Lucas Critique (Lucas,1976, seconded by Sims, 1980 and Sargent, 1981). As Pesaran and Smith (1995) suggest, these models 'did not represent the data. . . did not represent the theory . . . [and] . . . were ineffective for practical purposes of forecasting and policy'. In the context of forward-looking agents with rational expectations, this critique showed that apparently stable empirical backward-looking relationship between, for example, consumption, post-tax income and real consumption, were not independent of the policy rule in place. The implication of this finding is that these (apparently structural) models were at best suitable for forecasting on the basis of a continuation of an existing policy and were, therefore, unfit for the purpose of examining the consequences of different policies.[1]

Early models certainly lacked coherence in that different behavioural relationships involving the same optimizing agent often led an independent existence. Within what is often termed the new classical macroeconomics approach, the seminal paper by Kydland

and Prescott (1982) produced the first small coherent dynamic general equilibrium macro model built from solid micro-foundations with expected utility optimizing forward-looking agents. This first RBC model was stochastic and therefore of DSGE form, with only one exogenous shock to technology. Despite this simple structure, the model was remarkably successful at reproducing the volatilities of some observed variables.

RBC models provided a fundamental methodological shift, but it soon became apparent that their contribution in terms of policy analysis in central banks and policy institutions was of limited impact and usefulness. Indeed, their very stylized, frictionless nature, implied that any change in the monetary policy instrument induced immediate changes in inflation and, in consequence, little or no impact on real variables, which runs counter to empirical evidence (see Bernanke and Mihov, 1998 and Christiano et al., 1999, for example).

Although there were many other dimensions along which the RBC framework failed on its own terms (notably in reproducing observed output persistence and the volatility of hours), subsequent developments did not abandon what is an otherwise intellectually sound approach. Indeed, the so-called New Keynesian (NK) macroeconomics attempted to address the shortcomings of RBC models, relying on rigorous micro-foundations. A crucial distinction of the Keynesian perspective, though, is the view that real economies are not perfectly flexible nor perfectly competitive, thus providing a powerful cause for (inefficient) business cycle fluctuations and the non-neutrality of money. This, consequently, implies that economic policy has a significant role in minimizing welfare distortions caused by these imperfections and rigidities.

Thus, much of the research from the mid-1980s onwards was devoted to developing mechanisms that provide a rationale for price stickiness. These include models of imperfect competition, imperfect information and nominal price rigidities, which eventually made their way into current NK DSGE models.[2] In fact, incorporating price stickiness in a rigorous way requires that firms are price setters, as opposed to price takers in a perfectly competitive world. This can be achieved in a tractable way by using the monopolistic competition approach of Dixit and Stiglitz (1977), in which firms produce (and set prices for) differentiated goods.

Nominal price inertia then requires some form of staggered pricing, so that only a proportion of firms adjust prices at a given time. While different formulations are possible, the Calvo (1983) formulation has become standard, as it greatly simplifies aggregation.[3] An extension with similar persistence mechanisms to wage setting was suggested by Erceg et al. (2000), which, while playing an important role in explaining output and inflation dynamics, has also important implications for optimal monetary policy, as now a welfare-maximizing central bank should be concerned with both price and wage stability.

In the quest for increased theoretical and empirical adequacy, additional frictions have been suggested in order to further capture the observed inertial behaviour of inflation and other aggregate variables. Carlstrom and Fuerst (1997) and Bernanke et al. (1999), for example, propose the introduction of financial frictions, while Christiano et al. (2005) stress the role played by habit persistence in consumption preferences, adjustment costs in investment and variable capital utilization.

The endeavours on the theoretical front have greatly benefited from major advances in the econometric techniques that are used to estimate and assess DSGE models.

Interestingly, a synthesis of apparently divergent approaches has also been gathering pace as the dominant paradigm in the empirical analysis of DSGE models. The initial response to the Lucas critique was radical in both directions. On one hand, the Vector Autoregression (VAR) approach of Sims (1980) circumvented the 'incredible' exogeneity identification assumptions of the 1970s by (initially, at least) abandoning them altogether, that is, a VAR model should provide an a-theoretical, non-structural empirical account of macroeconomic relationships.

On the other hand, Kydland and Prescott (1982) suggested an alternative methodology of evaluating dynamic macroeconomic models.[4] Given that empirical macro models were merely capturing reduced-form relationships, rather than deep parameters arising from agents' inter-temporal optimization, Kydland and Prescott (1982) propose dropping any attempts to estimate these models, focusing instead on quantitative exercises based on calibrated parameters. Thus, having selected a metric for model evaluation (usually involving comparisons of model moments and their data counterparts), the parametrization of the structural parameters is obtained by weighing information suggested by economic theory and previous evidence taken from microeconometric studies, so that the model replicates particular 'stylized facts' of the actual economy.

Some alternatives have sought to find a middle ground, between the a-theoretical VAR approach and the a-statistical calibration methodology. These include the use of the Generalized Method of Moments (see Christiano and Eichenbaum, 1992, for example, and Chapter 20 by Francisco Ruge-Murcia in this *Handbook*) or the Matching Moments method of Christiano et al. (2005), whereby parameters are estimated so that the difference between the impulse response functions (IRF) of a VAR and those of a DSGE model is minimized. However, these (mostly) limited-information methods have been superseded by full-information methods. Given a chosen probabilistic structure, a likelihood function can be constructed so that the DSGE model provides a full statistical characterization of the observed data. Different choices for parameters will lead to different values of the likelihood function (that is, the probability of observing the data given the model's parameters), so the practitioner is interested in finding the parametrization that maximizes the 'likelihood' of the model originating the data at hand.

Classical maximum likelihood estimation (MLE) treats parameters as unknown, but fixed, and these are chosen so that the likelihood function is maximized, given a realization of the observables. On the other hand, a Bayesian framework assumes that parameters are random variables, about which the researcher may have prior information (for example theoretical ranges for the parameters, previous studies, and so on). Combined with the likelihood function, this then forms the posterior density, from which one can draw inferences about the parameters. Notice that, on one hand, this approach constrains the parameter space, thus reducing the possibility of obtaining 'absurd' estimates that may occur when classical MLE is used (see An and Schorfheide, 2007). On the other hand, it provides a more sophisticated and flexible form of calibration, whereby several, rather than just one, potential values of the parameter are considered, weighted by the relevant prior density.

There is now a substantial body of literature devoted to understanding business cycle dynamics, in which empirical DSGE models have been found to provide good empirical fit and forecasting performance (see Smets and Wouters, 2003; Fernandez-Villaverde and Rubio-Ramirez, 2004; Smets and Wouters, 2007; Adolfson et al., 2007; Del Negro et al., 2007; Gabriel et al., 2010, to name a few). Given its advantages, the Bayesian approach has become particularly popular with policy institutions, as it encapsulates the idea that good policy making requires utilizing formal models alongside judgement. Indeed, as demonstrated in Levine et al. (2012), it is also very important to design policy rules that are 'robust' to model uncertainty.

In section 2 we describe the RBC core, while in section 3 we introduce the main NK features found in modern DSGE models. Their impulse response functions are addressed in section 4. The models are increasingly estimated by systems estimation using Bayesian-Maximum Likelihood Estimation, which is described in section 5. Section 6 summarizes this chapter.

2 RBC MODEL WITHOUT INVESTMENT COSTS

The construction of a DSGE model requires the specification of agents' preferences, the economy's technological constraints and the set of exogenous shocks to which the economy is subject. The agents' decision rules are derived from the first order conditions of the dynamic optimization problem for each agent. Aggregating over agents and assuming that markets clear allow us to derive a system of non-linear stochastic difference equations, involving the endogenous variables, the parameters and a set of shocks. The purpose is then to find a stable and unique solution to the model, which requires an additional set of procedures. The model should be written in stationary form, so that the variables are written as deviations from a balanced-growth steady-state. Often DSGE models are log-linearized and written in state-space form. Standard methods then result in a linear Rational Expectations solution of the model. We demonstrate this procedure for the NK model that follows, but using the software package Dynare[5] the modeller can simply set up the non-linear model and either compute the steady state or in the RBC model write down an analytical solution. Dynare then performs the linearization to produce a first-order solution. These different stages are detailed next.

First we consider a simple RBC model with a wholesale and monopolistic retail sector, but no costs of investment (see Lucas, 1987; Wickens, 2008; Lim and McNelis, 2008, chapter 6). This lies at the core of the NK model that follows later. We include a retail sector with monopolistic competition that is usually omitted in the standard RBC model that assumes perfect competition. However, it is convenient to include it at this stage in order to allow a seamless progression to the New Keynesian model with staggered price setting.

2.1 RBC Model without Investment Costs

First for the household we have

$$\text{Utility} : \Lambda_t = \Lambda(C_t, L_t) \tag{18.1}$$

$$\text{Euler Consumption} : \Lambda_{C,t} = \beta R_t E_t[\Lambda_{C,t+1}] \tag{18.2}$$

$$\text{Labour Supply}: \frac{\Lambda_{h,t}}{\Lambda_{C,t}} = -\frac{W_t}{P_t} \tag{18.3}$$

$$\text{Leisure and Hours}: L_t \equiv 1 - h_t \tag{18.4}$$

where C_t is real consumption, L_t is leisure, R_t is the gross real interest rate set in period t to pay out interest in period $t + 1$, h_t are hours worked and $\frac{W_t}{P_t}$ is the real wage. The Euler consumption equation, (18.2), where $E_t[\cdot]$ denotes rational expectations based on agents observing all current macroeconomic variables (that is, 'complete information'), describes the optimal consumption–savings decisions of the household and is derived in Appendix A. It equates the marginal utility from consuming one unit of income in period t with the discounted marginal utility from consuming the gross income acquired, R_t, by saving the income. For later use it is convenient to write the Euler consumption equation as

$$1 = R_t E_t[D_{t,t+1}] \tag{18.5}$$

where $D_{t,t+1} \equiv \beta\frac{\Lambda_{C,t+1}}{\Lambda_{C,t}}$ is the *real stochastic discount factor* over the interval $[t, t + 1]$. Equation (18.3) equates the real wage with the marginal rate of substitution between consumption and leisure.

Output and the firm's behaviour is summarized by:

$$\text{Wholesale Output}: Y_t^W = F(A_t, h_t, K_{t-1}) \tag{18.6}$$

$$\text{Retail Output}: Y_t = (1 - c)\, Y_t^W \tag{18.7}$$

$$\text{Labour Demand}: \frac{P_t^W}{P_t} F_{h,t} = \frac{W_t}{P_t} \tag{18.8}$$

$$\text{Capital Demand}: E_t\left[\frac{P_{t+1}^W}{P_{t+1}} F_{K,t}\right] = R_t - 1 + \delta \tag{18.9}$$

$$\text{Price Mark Up}: P_t = \frac{1}{1 - \frac{1}{\zeta}} P_t^W \tag{18.10}$$

Equation (18.6) is a production function for the wholesale sector that is converted into differentiated goods in (18.7) at a cost cY_t^W. Note here K_t is *end-of-period t* capital stock. Equation (18.8) equates the marginal product of labour with the real wage. Equation (18.9) equates the marginal product of capital with the cost of capital. P_t and P_t^W are the aggregate price indices in the retail and wholesale sectors respectively and the mark-up in (18.10) is simply the flexi-price case of the monopolistic competition set-up described in the NK model below. The model is completed with an output equilibrium, law of the motion for capital and a balanced budget constraint with lump-sum taxes.

$$Y_t = C_t + G_t + I_t$$

$$I_t = K_t - (1 - \delta) K_{t-1}$$

$$G_t = T_t$$

We now specify functional forms for production and utility and we assume AR(1) processes for exogenous variables A_t and G_t. For production we assume a Cobb–Douglas function. The utility function is non-separable and consistent with a balanced growth path when the inter-temporal elasticity of substitution, $1/\sigma_c$, is not unitary (see Barro and Sala-i-Martin, 2004, Chapter 9, section 9.4). These functional forms, the associated marginal utilities and marginal products, and exogenous processes are given by

$$F(A_t, h_t, K_{t-1}) = (A_t h_t)^{\alpha} K_{t-1}^{1-\alpha} \tag{18.11}$$

$$F_h(A_t, h_t, K_{t-1}) = \frac{\alpha Y_t^W}{h_t} \tag{18.12}$$

$$F_K(A_t, h_t, K_{t-1}) = \frac{(1-\alpha) Y_t^W}{K_{t-1}} \tag{18.13}$$

$$\log A_t - \log \overline{A}_t = \rho_A(\log A_{t-1} - \log \overline{A}_{t-1}) + \varepsilon_{A,t} \tag{18.14}$$

$$\log G_t - \log \overline{G}_t = \rho_G(G_{t-1} - \overline{G}_{t-1}) + \varepsilon_{G,t} \tag{18.15}$$

$$\Lambda_t = \frac{(C_t^{(1-\varrho)} L_t^{\varrho})^{1-\sigma_c} - 1}{1-\sigma_c} \tag{18.16}$$

$$\Lambda_{C,t} = (1-\varrho) C_t^{(1-\varrho)(1-\sigma_c)-1} (1-h_t)^{\varrho(1-\sigma_c)} \tag{18.17}$$

$$\Lambda_{h,t} = -\varrho C_t^{(1-\varrho)(1-\sigma_c)} (1-h_t)^{\varrho(1-\sigma_c)-1} \tag{18.18}$$

Equation (18.1)–(18.18) describe an equilibrium in Λ_t, C_t, $\frac{W_t}{P_t}$, Y_t, Y_t^W, L_t, h_i, $\frac{P_t^W}{P_t}$ K_t, I_t, R_t, T_t, given A_t and G_t where for the latter we assume AR1 processes about possibly trending steady states $\overline{A}_t, \overline{G}_t$ driven by zero mean iid shocks $\varepsilon_{A,t}$ and $\varepsilon_{G,t}$. Figure 18.1 illustrates the model.

2.2 Investment Costs

A common form of investment costs makes the convenient assumption that they disappear in the long run (see, for example, Smet and Wouters, 2007). With their form of investment costs the model becomes

$$K_t = (1-\delta)K_{t-1} + (1 - S(X_t))I_t;\ S', S'' \geq 0;\ S(1+g) = S'(1+g) = 0$$

$$X_t \equiv \frac{I_t}{I_{t-1}}$$

It is convenient to introduce capital-producing firms that at time t convert I_t of output into $(1 - S(X_t))I_t$ of new capital sold at a real price Q_t. They then maximize with respect to $\{I_t\}$ expected discounted profits

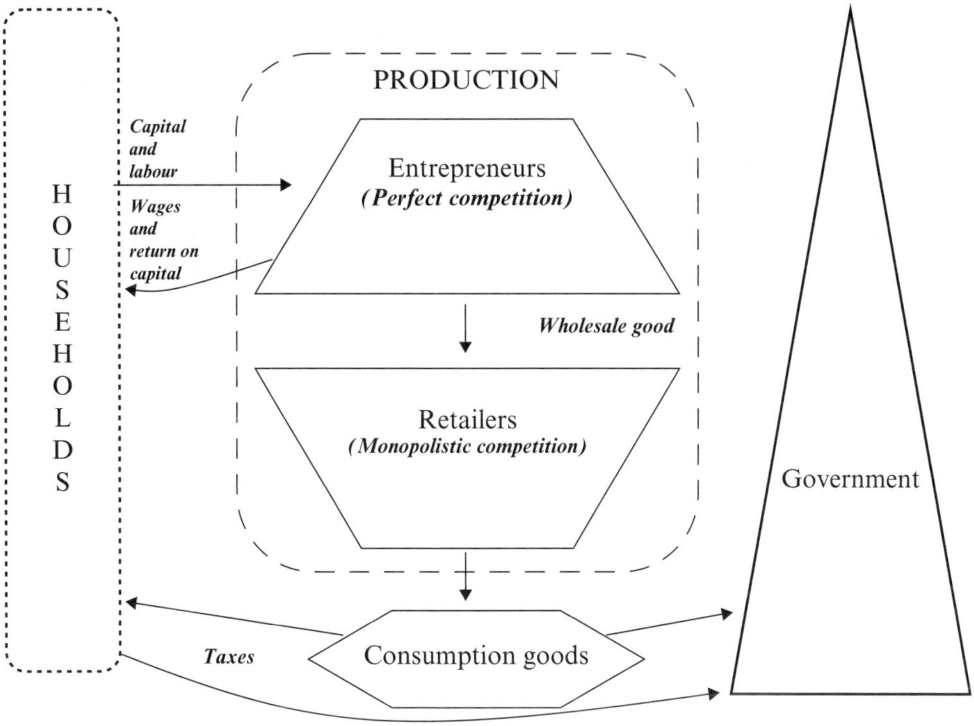

Figure 18.1 RBC model with retail sector

$$E_t \sum_{k=0}^{\infty} D_{t,t+k}[Q_{t+k}(1 - S(I_{t+k}/I_{t+k-1}))I_{t+k} - I_{t+k}]$$

where $D_{t,t+k} = \beta^k(\frac{\Lambda_{C,t+1}}{\Lambda_{C,t}})$ is the real stochastic discount rate over the interval $[t, t + k]$.

This results in the first-order condition (see Appendix B).

$$Q_t(1 - S(X_t) - X_t S'(X_t)) + E_t[D_{t,t+1} Q_{t+1} S'(X_{t+1}) X_{t+1}^2] = 1$$

Demand for capital by firms must satisfy

$$R_t = \frac{E_t[(1 - \alpha)\frac{P_{t+1}^W Y_{t+1}^W}{P_{t+1} K_t} + (1 - \delta) Q_{t+1}]}{Q_t} \tag{18.19}$$

In (18.19) the right-hand side is the gross return to holding a unit of capital from t to $t + 1$. The left-hand side is the gross return from holding bonds, the opportunity cost of capital. Note that without investment costs, $S = 0$, $Q_t = 1$ and (18.19) reduces to (18.9). We complete this set-up with the functional form

$$S(X) = \phi_X(X_t - (1 + g))^2$$

where g is the balanced growth rate. Note that along a balanced growth path $X_t = 1 + g$ and investment costs disappear. This is a convenient property because then the steady state to which we now turn is unchanged from introducing investment costs.

2.3 The Steady State

The balanced growth steady state path (bgp) driven by labour-augmenting technical change growing at a rate g of the model economy (with or without investment costs) is given by $Q = 1$ and

$$\frac{\bar{\Lambda}_{C,t+1}}{\bar{\Lambda}_{C,t}} \equiv 1 + g_{\Lambda_C} = \left[\frac{\bar{C}_{t+1}}{\bar{C}_t}\right]^{((1-\varrho)(1-\sigma_c)-1)} = (1 + g)^{((1-\varrho)(1-\sigma_c)-1)} \tag{18.20}$$

using (18.17). Thus from (18.12)

$$R = \frac{(1 + g)^{1+(\sigma_c - 1)(1-\varrho)}}{\beta} \tag{18.21}$$

To set up a bgp steady state we must stationarize the bgp by defining stationary variables such as $C \equiv \bar{C}_t/\bar{A}_t$, $Y \equiv \bar{Y}_t/\bar{A}_t$, $K \equiv \bar{K}_t/\bar{A}_t$, $\frac{W_t}{P_t}$ and so on. We must also stationarize $\Lambda_{C,t}$ by defining $\Lambda_C \equiv \Lambda_{C,t}/\bar{\Lambda}_{C,t}$. Then the bgp is given by

$$Y = (1 - c)h^{\alpha}K^{1-\alpha}$$

$$\frac{\varrho C}{(1 - \varrho)(1 - h)} = \frac{W}{P}$$

$$\frac{\alpha P^W Y^W}{Ph} = \frac{W}{P}$$

$$\frac{K}{Y^W} = \frac{1 - \alpha}{R - 1 + \delta}$$

$$I = (\delta + g)K$$

$$Y = C + I + G$$

$$G = T$$

$$1 = \frac{1}{1 - \frac{1}{\zeta}}\frac{P^W}{P}$$

where consumption, labour augmenting productivity, the real wage and tax rates, and government spending are growing at the common growth rate g. We can impose a free entry condition on retail firms in this steady state which drives monopolistic profits to zero. This implies that costs of converting wholesale to retail goods are given by

$$c = 1/\zeta$$

Given exogenous trends for $\bar{A}_t$ and $\bar{G}_t$, this gives us nine relationships in nine stationary variables $R, \frac{P^W}{P}, C, Y, W, h, I, K, T$ describing the exogenous balanced-growth steady-state equilibrium.

Our RBC and subsequent NK models are all special cases of the following general set-up recognized by Dynare in non-linear form

$$Z_t = J(Z_{t-1}, X_t, \varepsilon_{t+1})$$

$$E_t X_{t+1} = K(Z_t, X_t, \varepsilon_{t+1})$$

where Z_{t-1}, X_t are $(n - m) \times 1$ and $m \times 1$ vectors of backward and forward-looking variables, respectively, and ε_t is a $\ell \times 1$ shock variable of zero mean iid stochastic processes.

2.4 Calibration

We have carefully set out the steady state of the RBC (and NK) models because it is needed to calibrate a number of parameters. The idea is to assume an observed baseline steady state equilibrium. We then use this observed equilibrium to solve for model parameters consistent with this observation. In general terms, our baseline steady state can be described in terms of a vector $\underline{X} = f(\underline{\theta})$ of outcomes where $\underline{\theta}$ is a vector of parameters. The calibration strategy is to choose a subset $\underline{X}_1$ of n observed outcomes to calibrate a subset $\underline{\theta}_1$ of n parameters. Partition $\underline{X} = [\underline{X}_1, \underline{X}_2]$ and $\underline{\theta} = [\underline{\theta}_1, \underline{\theta}_2]$. Then $\underline{\theta}_1$ is found by solving

$$[\underline{X}_1, \underline{X}_2] = f([\underline{\theta}_1, \underline{\theta}_2]) \tag{18.22}$$

for $\underline{X}_2$ and $\underline{\theta}_1$, given $\underline{X}_1$ and $\underline{\theta}_2$. If such a solution exists for economically meaningful parameter values for $\underline{\theta}_1$ then a successful calibration has been achieved.

To illustrate this, suppose we have data for factor shares in the wholesale sector, the price mark-up, hours (h), growth (g), the real interest rate (R) and expenditure shares $c_y \equiv \frac{C}{Y}$, $i_y \equiv \frac{I}{Y}$ and $g_y \equiv \frac{G}{Y}$. First we calibrate ζ and c using data on the price mark-up in the retail sector. This mark-up is given by $\frac{1}{1-\frac{1}{\zeta}}$, so $\zeta = 1/c = 7$ corresponds to a mark-up of 17 per cent. Next, α is the wage share in the wholesale sector and is therefore determined. Then write the Cobb–Douglas production function as

$$Y^W = Ah(K/Y^W)^{\frac{1-\alpha}{\alpha}}$$

where K/Y^W is the capital–labour ratio in the wholesale sector. We can choose units of output and capital stock so that $A = 1$. Then using $K/Y^W = \frac{1-\alpha}{R-1+\delta}$ from the RBC steady state we can now write

$$i_y \equiv \frac{I}{Y} = \frac{(\delta + g)K}{(1 - c)Y^W} = \frac{(\delta + g)(1 - \alpha)}{(1 - c)(R - 1 + \delta)}$$

from which δ can be calibrated and both Y^W and K are now determined.

Table 18.1 Calibration with imposed $\sigma_c = 2$

Observed Equilibrium	Value
h^{obs}	45/100
wage share = α	0.6
c_y	0.70
i_y	0.15
g_y	0.15
R	1.01
g	0.025/4
mark-up = $\frac{1}{1-\frac{1}{\zeta}}$	0.17
ϕ_x	1.24
Calibrated Parameters	**Value**
ϱ	0.69
δ	0.025
β	0.998
ζ	7.0

From the steady state equation $\frac{\varrho C}{(1-\varrho)(1-h)} = \frac{W}{P}$ we have

$$\frac{\varrho}{(1-\varrho)(1-h)} = \frac{W}{C} = \frac{(Wh/Y)}{C/Yh} = \frac{\alpha}{c_y h}$$

from which ϱ is obtained. Having calibrated ϱ, from observations of R and g we can calibrate either σ_c or β from

$$R = \frac{(1+g)^{1+(\sigma_c-1)(1-\varrho)}}{\beta}$$

Since there is a sizeable body of literature on the microeconometric estimation of the latter risk aversion parameter, it is usual to use this and calibrate β. This completes the calibration – typical US observations and calibrated parameters are illustrated in Table 18.1.

3 NEW KEYNESIAN MODEL

The NK model with investment costs and monopolistic competition has the RBC model at its core. Monopolistic competition plays a minor role until we come to the feature that makes the model Keynesian, namely price stickiness in the form of staggered price setting in the retail sector. These are the aspects on which we now concentrate.

3.1 The Retail Sector and Price Stickiness

This uses a homogeneous wholesale good to produce a basket of differentiated goods for consumption

$$C_t = \left(\int_0^1 C_t(m)^{(\zeta - 1)/\zeta} dm \right)^{\zeta/(\zeta - 1)} \tag{18.23}$$

where ζ is the elasticity of substitution. For each m, the consumer chooses $C_t(m)$ at a price $P_t(m)$ to maximize (18.23) given total expenditure $\int_0^1 P_t(m) C_t(m) dm$. This results in a set of demand equations for each differentiated good m with price $P_t(m)$ of the form

$$C_t(m) = \left(\frac{P_t(m)}{P_t} \right)^{-\zeta} C_t \tag{18.24}$$

where $P_t = [\int_0^1 P_t(m)^{1-\zeta} dm]^{\frac{1}{1-\zeta}}$. P_t is the aggregate price index. C_t and P_t are Dixit–Stiglitz aggregates – see Dixit and Stiglitz (1977).

Now we assume that there is a probability of $1 - \xi$ at each period that the price of each retail good m is set optimally to $P_t^0(m)$. If the price is not re-optimized, then it is held fixed.[6] For each retail producer m, given its real marginal cost MC_t, the objective is at time t to choose $\{P_t^0(m)\}$ to maximize discounted profits

$$E_t \sum_{k=0}^{\infty} \xi^k D_{t,t+k} Y_{t+k}(m) [P_t^0(m) - P_{t+k} MC_{t+k}] \tag{18.25}$$

subject to (18.24), where $D_{t,t+k} \equiv \beta \frac{\Lambda_{C,t+k}/P_{t+k}}{\Lambda_{C,t}/P_t}$ is now the *nominal* stochastic discount factor over the interval $[t, t + k]$. The solution to this is

$$E_t \sum_{k=0}^{\infty} \xi^k D_{t,t+k} Y_{t+k}(m) \left[P_t^0(m) - \frac{1}{(1 - 1/\zeta)} P_{t+k} MC_{t+k} \right] = 0 \tag{18.26}$$

and by the law of large numbers the evolution of the price index is given by

$$P_{t+1}^{1-\zeta} = \xi P_t^{1-\zeta} + (1 - \xi)(P_{t+1}^0)^{1-\zeta} \tag{18.27}$$

In order to set up the model in non-linear form as a set of difference equations, required for software packages such as Dynare, we need to represent the price dynamics as difference equations. Both sides of the first-order condition for pricing, (18.26), are of the form considered in Appendix C. Using the Lemma inflation dynamics are given by

$$\frac{P_t^0}{P_t} = \frac{J_t}{H_t} \tag{18.28}$$

$$H_t - \xi\beta E_t[\Pi_{t+1}^{\zeta-1} H_{t+1}] = Y_t \Lambda_{C,t} \tag{18.29}$$

$$J_t - \xi\beta E_t[\Pi_{t+1}^{\zeta} J_{t+1}] = \left(\frac{1}{1 - \frac{1}{\zeta}} \right) Y_t \Lambda_{C,t} MC_t MS_t \tag{18.30}$$

$$\Pi_t: \quad 1 = \xi \Pi_t^{\zeta - 1} + (1 - \xi)\left(\frac{J_t}{H_t}\right)^{1-\zeta} \tag{18.31}$$

$$MC_t = \frac{P_t^W}{P_t} \tag{18.32}$$

where we have introduced a mark-up shock MS_t. Notice that the real marginal cost, MC_t, is no longer fixed as it was in the RBC model. With a nominal side of the model we need to distinguish between the *ex ante* nominal gross interest rate $R_{n,t}$ set at time t and the *ex post* real interest rate, R_t^{ex}. These are related by the Fischer equation

$$R_t^{ex} = \frac{R_{n,t-1}}{\Pi_t} \tag{18.33}$$

The nominal interest rate is a policy variable, typically given by a simple Taylor-type rule:

$$\log\left(\frac{R_{n,t}}{R_n}\right) = \rho \log\left(\frac{R_{n,t-1}}{R_n}\right) + \theta_\pi \log\left(\frac{\Pi_t}{\Pi}\right) + \theta_y \log\left(\frac{Y_t}{Y}\right) + \log \varepsilon_{e,t} \tag{18.34}$$

where $\varepsilon_{e,t}$ is a monetary policy shock.

The stochastic Euler equation must now take the form

$$\Lambda_{C,t} = E_t\left[\frac{R_{n,t}}{\Pi_{t+1}}\Lambda_{C,t+1}\right] = E_t[R_{t+1}^{ex}\Lambda_{C,t+1}] \tag{18.35}$$

Demand for capital is now given by

$$E_t[R_{t+1}^{ex}] = \frac{E_t[(1-\alpha)\frac{P_{t+1}^W}{P_{t+1}}\frac{Y_{t+1}^W}{K_{t+1}} + (1-\delta)Q_{t+1}]}{Q_t}$$

The final change is that price dispersion Δ_t reduces output which, as shown in Appendix D, is now given by

$$Y_t = (1 - c)\frac{(A_t h_t)^\alpha K_{t-1}^{1-\alpha}}{\Delta_t} \tag{18.36}$$

$$\Delta_t \equiv \frac{1}{n}\sum_{j=1}^{n}(P_t(j)/P_t)^{-\zeta} = \xi \Pi_t^{\zeta}\Delta_{t-1} + (1-\xi)\left(\frac{J_t}{H_t}\right)^{-\zeta} \tag{18.37}$$

However, Δ_t is of second order so for a first-order approximation we can put $\Delta = 1$, its steady state value.

To summarize, the NK model consists of the RBC model of real variables with a time-varying real marginal cost (18.32) and price dynamics given by (18.29)–(18.31). The expected *ex post* real interest rate $E_t[R_{t+1}^{ex}]$ over the interval $[t, t+1]$ replaces R_t in the RBC model and price dispersion given by (18.37) reduces output as in (18.36). By proceeding from the RBC to the NK model in this fashion we see how price stickiness

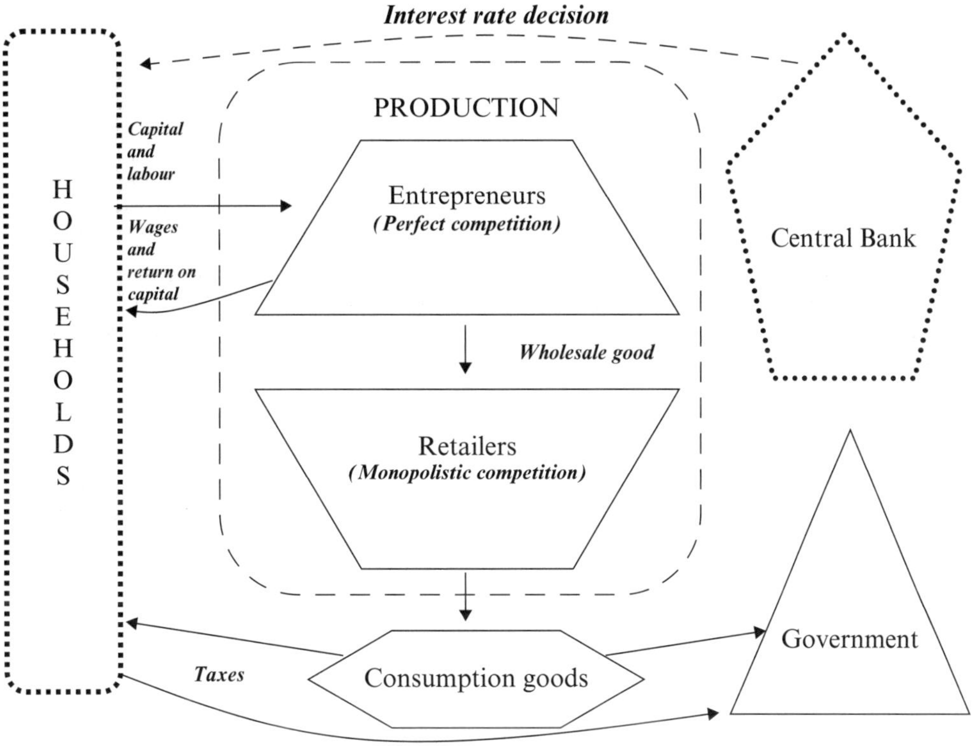

Figure 18.2 NK model

introduces an inefficiency through the price dispersion mechanism. Figure 18.2 illustrates the NK model.

3.2 Steady State

For a particular steady state inflation rate Π the NK features of the steady state are

$$\frac{J}{H} = \left(\frac{1 - \xi\Pi^{\zeta-1}}{1 - \xi}\right)^{\frac{1}{1-\zeta}}$$

$$MC = \left(1 - \frac{1}{\zeta}\right)\frac{J(1 - \beta\xi\Pi^{\zeta})}{H(1 - \beta\xi\Pi^{\zeta-1})}$$

$$\Delta = \frac{(1 - \xi)^{\frac{1}{1-\zeta}}(1 - \xi\Pi^{\zeta-1})^{\frac{\zeta}{1-\zeta}}}{1 - \xi\Pi^{\zeta}}$$

For a zero-inflation steady state $\Pi = 1$ we arrive at $\frac{J}{H} = \Delta = 1$ and $MC = (1 - \frac{1}{\zeta})$ but in general there is a long-run inflation–output trade-off in the choice of the steady-state inflation rate. We return to this issue later in this section and in Chapter 19 when we discuss optimal monetary policy. The implications of introducing a *non-zero* inflation steady state into the standard NK model are explored by Ascari and Ropele (2007).

3.3 Linearization

To solve the model it is usual to linearize about the steady state. In fact this is the easiest way to set up a model in Dynare for estimation, simulation and policy analysis. It is also useful as the linearized form can be used for some partial analysis providing insights into the workings of the model. That said, in Dynare it is not necessary to go through this step, which becomes more arduous as models become larger.

The technique of linearization uses a Taylor series expansion. Consider a general function of two variables $F(X_t, Y_t)$. Then up to first-order terms we have

$$F(X_t, Y_t) \approx F(X, Y) + \frac{\partial F}{\partial X_t}(X_t - X) + \frac{\partial F}{\partial Y_t}(Y_t - Y) \tag{18.38}$$

where partial derivatives are evaluated at the steady-state values X, Y. Now use the following notation

$$\frac{X_t - X}{X} = x \tag{18.39}$$

Then (18.38) becomes

$$f \approx \frac{X}{F}\frac{\partial F}{\partial X_t}x + \frac{Y}{F}\frac{\partial F}{\partial Y_t}y \tag{18.40}$$

Note that

$$\log\left[\frac{X_t}{X}\right] = \log\left[1 + \frac{X_t - X}{X}\right] \approx x \tag{18.41}$$

which is why this technique is referred to as 'log-linearization'.

Define lower case variables $x_t = \log\frac{X_t}{X_t} \approx x$ if X_t has a long-run trend or $x_t = \log\frac{X_t}{X}$ otherwise where X is the steady state value of a non-trended variable. For the variable h_t define $\hat{x}_t = \log\frac{X_t}{X}$. Then using this technique for the case of a zero-inflation steady state, $\Pi = 1$, the complete state space representation is given by

$$\begin{aligned}
a_t &= \rho_A a_{t-1} + \varepsilon_{a,t} \\
g_t &= \rho_G g_{t-1} + \varepsilon_{g,t} \\
ms_t &= \rho_{MS} ms_{t-1} + \varepsilon_{ms,t} \\
k_t &= \frac{1-\delta}{1+g}k_{t-1} + \frac{\delta+g}{1+g}i_t \\
E_t[\lambda_{C,t+1}] &= \lambda_{C,t} - E_t[r_{t+1}] \\
\beta E_t[\pi_{t+1}] &= \pi_t - \frac{(1-\xi)(1-\xi\beta)}{\xi}(mc_t + ms_t)
\end{aligned}$$

$$E_t[x_{t+1}] = E_t[r_{t+1}] + \rho_{rps} rps_t + q_t$$

$$\left(1 + \frac{1+g}{R}\right)i_t = \frac{1+g}{R}E_t i_{t+1} + i_{t-1} + \frac{1}{(1+g)^2 S''(1+g)}q_t$$

with outputs of interest defined by

$$r_t = r_{n,t-1} - \pi_t$$

$$\lambda_{C,t} = -(1 + (\sigma_c - 1)(1-\varrho))c_t + (\sigma_c - 1)\varrho\frac{h}{1-h}\hat{h}_t$$

$$\lambda_{L,t} = \lambda_{C,t} + c_t + \frac{h}{1-h}\hat{h}_t$$

$$w_t - p_t = \lambda_{L,t} - \lambda_{C,t}$$

$$y_t = \alpha(a_t + \hat{h}_t) + (1-\alpha)k_{t-1}$$

$$y_t = c_y c_t + i_y i_t + g_y g_t$$

$$g_t = t_t$$

$$Rx_t \equiv (R - 1 + \delta)(mc_t + y_t - k_{t-1}) + (1-\delta)q_t$$

$$mc_t = w_t - p_t - (y_t^w - \hat{h}_t)$$

$$y_t^w = y_t$$

$$r_{n,t} = \rho r_{n,t-1} + (1-\rho)(\theta_\pi \pi_t + \theta_y y_t) + \varepsilon_{e,t}$$

This provides the basis for some insightful partial analysis, but before proceeding with this we now add two more features, namely external habit and indexing, to arrive at what can be regarded as a 'workhorse NK model'.

3.4 Persistence Mechanisms: Habit and Indexation

Both habit and indexation are motivated by the need to introduce mechanisms to reproduce the persistence seen in the data for output and inflation. Whereas indexation is an ad hoc feature vulnerable to the Lucas critique, the existence of habit by contrast is a plausible formulation of utility that addresses issues examined in the recent 'happiness' literature.[7]

First, introducing external habit ('keeping up with the Joneses') for household j we replace, (18.16), (18.17) and (18.18) with

$$\Lambda_t^j = \frac{((C_t^j - \chi C_{t-1})^{(1-\varrho)} L_t^{\varrho})^{1-\sigma_c} - 1}{1-\sigma_c} \tag{18.42}$$

$$\Lambda_{C,t}^j = (1-\varrho)(C_t^j - \chi C_{t-1})^{(1-\varrho)(1-\sigma_c)-1}((1-h_t)^{\varrho(1-\sigma_c)})$$

$$\Lambda_{L,t}^j = \varrho(C_t^j - \chi C_{t-1})^{(1-\varrho)(1-\sigma_c)}(1-h_t)^{\varrho(1-\sigma_c)-1}$$

where aggregate per capita consumption C_{t-1} is taken as given. The external habit parameter $\chi \in [0,1]$. Then in an equilibrium of identical households, $C_t^j = C_t$.

With indexing by an amount $\gamma \in [0,1]$ and an exogenous mark-up shock MS_t as before, the optimal price-setting first-order condition for a firm j setting a new optimized price $P_t^0(j)$ is now given by

$$P_t^0(j) E_t\left[\sum_{k=0}^{\infty} \xi^k D_{t,t+k} Y_{t+k}(j) \left(\frac{P_{t+k-1}}{P_{t-1}}\right)^{\gamma}\right] = \frac{1}{(1-1/\zeta)} E_t\left[\sum_{k=0}^{\infty} \xi^k D_{t,t+k} P_{t+k} MC_{t+k} MS_{t+k} Y_{t+k}(j)\right]$$

Price dynamics are now given by

$$\begin{aligned} \frac{P_t^0}{P_t} &= \frac{J_t}{H_t} \\ H_t - \xi\beta E_t[\tilde{\Pi}_{t+1}^{\zeta-1} H_{t+1}] &= Y_t MU_t^C \\ J_t - \xi\beta E_t[\tilde{\Pi}_{t+1}^{\zeta} J_{t+1}] &= \frac{1}{1-\frac{1}{\zeta}} MC_t MS_t Y_t MU_t^C \\ \tilde{\Pi}_t &\equiv \frac{\Pi_t}{\Pi_{t-1}^{\gamma}} \end{aligned}$$

The linearized NK model about a zero inflation steady state with habit and indexing is as before with the following changes:

$$\lambda_{C,t} = -(1 + (\sigma_c - 1)(1 - \varrho))\frac{(c_t - \chi c_{t-1})}{1 - \chi} + (\sigma_c - 1)\varrho\frac{h}{1-h}\hat{h}_t$$

$$\lambda_{L,t} = \lambda_{C,t} + \frac{c_t - \chi c_{t-1}}{1 - \chi} + \frac{h}{1-h}\hat{h}_t$$

$$\pi_t = \frac{\beta}{1 + \beta\gamma} E_t\pi_{t+1} + \frac{\gamma}{1 + \beta\gamma}\pi_{t-1} + \frac{(1 - \beta\xi)(1 - \xi)}{(1 + \beta\gamma)\xi}(mc_t + ms_t)$$

For the special case of no capital ($\alpha = 1$) and government consumption fixed at the steady state ($g_t = 0$) then $c_t = g_t$. Substituting $mc_t = w_t - p_t - y_t + \hat{h}_t = \frac{1}{1-h}\hat{h}_t + \frac{\chi}{1-\chi}(y_t - y_{t-1})$ and putting $y_t = \hat{h}_t + a_t$ for this special case, we arrive at the Phillips curve

$$\begin{aligned} \pi_t = {} & \frac{\beta}{1 + \beta\gamma} E_t\pi_{t+1} + \frac{\gamma}{1 + \beta\gamma}\pi_{t-1} + \frac{(1 - \beta\xi)(1 - \xi)}{(1 + \beta\gamma)\xi}\left(\frac{1}{1-h}(y_t - a_t)\right. \\ & \left. + \frac{\chi}{1 - \chi}(y_t - y_{t-1}) + ms_t\right) \end{aligned}$$

Thus both habit ($\chi > 0$) and indexation ($\lambda > 0$) introduce persistence effects for inflation and output. In the space of (y_t,π_t) given expectations $E_t\pi_{t+1}$ and lagged variables π_{t-1} and y_{t-1}, the short-run Phillips curve is upward sloping and shifts to the right as

$E_t\pi_{t+1}$, π_{t-1} or ms_t increase, and to the left if y_{t-1} or a_t increase. In the long run with $y_t = y_{t-1} = y$ and $\pi_t = \pi_{t-1}$ and no shocks the Phillips curve is given by

$$\pi = \frac{(1-\beta\xi)(1-\xi)y}{(1-\beta)(1-\gamma)(1-h)\xi}$$

so we can see that there is a long-run output–inflation trade-off as long as $\beta, \gamma, h < 1$.

4 IMPULSE RESPONSES TO A TECHNOLOGY SHOCK

We are now in a position to compare the RBC and NK models. For the RBC model we adopt the calibration set out in Table 18.1. The additional parameters in the NK model are set as $\xi = 0.75$, $h = 0$ and $\gamma = 0$, $\rho = 0.75$, $\theta_{pi} = 1.5$ and $\theta_y = 0.15$ so we leave out habit and indexation for this comparison. $\xi = 0.75$ corresponds to an average price contract length of four quarters.

We compare the impulse response functions (IRFs), as percentage deviations about the steady state, for two AR(1) shocks with persistence parameters 0.7 (as with the policy rule). The first is a 1 per cent supply-side shock to total factor productivity, $\varepsilon_{A,t}$ and the second is a 1 per cent demand-side shock to government expenditure $\varepsilon_{G,t}$. Figures 18.3

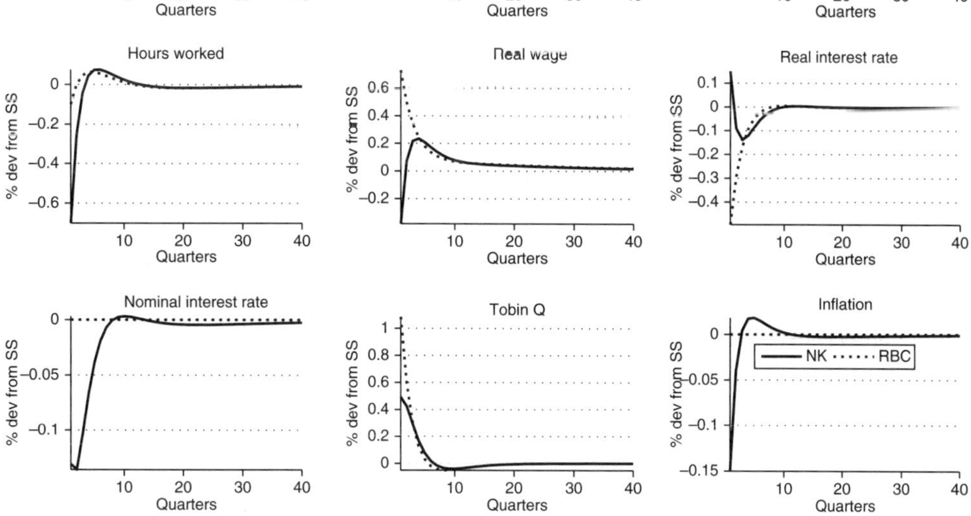

Figure 18.3 RBC model with investment costs and NK model: IRFs to $\varepsilon_{A,t}$ shock

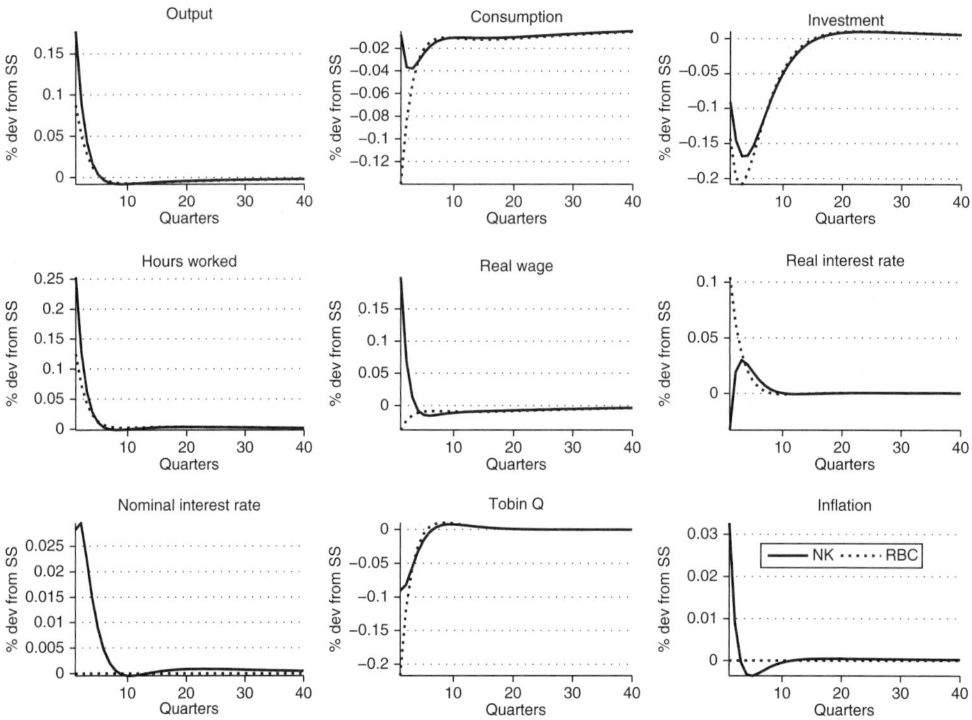

Figure 18.4 RBC model with investment costs and NK model: IRFs to $\varepsilon_{G,t}$ *shock*

and 18.4 show the IRFs as proportional deviations about the steady state for RBC variables: real output, consumption, investment, hours, the real wage, the real interest rate and the real price of capital and the same for the NK model with, in addition, inflation and the nominal interest rate (set to zero in the RBC model). In the NK model the *ex post* real interest rate replaces the *ex ante* rate of the RBC model.

Consider first a positive technology shock. For both RBC and NK models output, consumption and investment rise and then fall back to the steady state as the shock fades away. The increase in the supply of capital reduces its cost, the real interest rate. Thus the discounted sum of future profits rises, bringing about a rise in the price of capital. Real wage increases because labour supply increases less than proportionally with output, the substitution effect outweighs the income effect and hours worked increase. In the NK model inflation falls sharply at first then quickly returns and slightly overshoots the steady state. With our chosen Taylor rule this calls for a reduction in the nominal interest rate, a lower immediate increase in output and consumption and an initial decline in the real wage that is now affected by the increase in marginal costs and the reduction of labour supply. In the long run the real wage increases as soon as hours worked overshoot their steady state value. There are rather small differences between the IRFs of real variables except for hours worked and the real wage in the short run. Whereas in the short-run, hours and the real wage increase in the RBC model,[8] the opposite is the case in the NK model. For the latter case sticky prices result in an hours–technology debate which is probably one of the most controversial issues in business cycle theory and, as shown by our simulations, the major point of distinction between these two models. The reason is that the sign and response of hours to a productivity shock can have important consequences for policy analysis. For comprehensive reviews about the hours–technology debate see Gali and Rabanal (2005) and Whelan (2009).

Turning to the demand shock (in effect a fiscal stimulus), we now observe significant differences between the two models. The response of a shock to government spending is to crowd out consumption and investment in both RBC and NK worlds, the latter occurring through an increase in the real interest rate. The fall in consumption increases the marginal utility of consumption and induces the household to switch from consumption and leisure. Hours therefore increase and with capital only able to change gradually we see output increase in both the RBC and NK models. However, in the NK model with sticky prices firms respond to an increase in demand by raising output and there is an additional demand effect on aggregate output. In both cases there is an increase in hours supplied which, in the RBC model, leads to a reduction in the real wage. In the NK model demand for labour increases, offsetting the decrease in the real wage which in fact now increases.

So sticky prices in the NK model lead to important differences in the response to both supply but especially demand shocks. It is interesting to compare the impact on fiscal multipliers at $t = 0$ in the two models. The IRFs are elasticities which for output is $\frac{G\Delta Y}{Y\Delta G} = g_y\frac{\Delta Y}{\Delta G}$. With $g_y = 0.2$, the multiplier $\frac{\Delta Y}{\Delta G}$ as a percentage is therefore $5 \times 100 \times$ the values shown; so for the RBC model the fiscal multiplier is around 0.38 and rises to about twice that in the NK model.

5 BAYESIAN ESTIMATION OF DSGE MODELS

In the preceding sections, we showed how to construct a small-scale NK DSGE model. This section focuses on the empirical implementation of such models, through the use of Bayesian methods for direct estimation and comparison of structural DSGE models.[9] First, distributional assumptions for the shock processes are needed, so that the Kalman filter is used to compute the likelihood function. In addition, the researcher can specify prior assumptions about the model parameters (say θ) to be estimated, which then allows us to evaluate their posterior distribution conditional on the data. Using Bayes' theorem, the posterior density is obtained as:

$$p(\theta|y) = \frac{L(y|\theta)p(\theta)}{\int L(y|\theta)p(\theta)d\theta} \tag{18.43}$$

where $p(\theta)$ denotes the prior density of the parameter vector θ, $L(y|\theta)$ is the likelihood of the sample $y \in Y$ with T observations (evaluated with the Kalman filter) and $\int L(y|\theta)p(\theta)d\theta$ is the marginal likelihood. However, an additional technical difficulty arises in Bayesian inference, in that the objects of interest are integrals for which, in general, no closed-form analytical is available. This is overcome by the use of computationally intensive numerical integration methods, which entail generating draws of the set of parameters from the posterior density and then computing statistics of interest based on the simulations. One can then perform sensitivity analysis, model evaluation and model comparisons. The discussion below largely bypasses the technical details (we refer the interested reader to the relevant literature), focusing instead on the perspective of a potential user.

We favour using a Bayesian approach for several reasons. First, these procedures, unlike full information maximum likelihood, for example, allow us to use prior information to identify key structural parameters. In addition, the Bayesian methods employed here utilize all the cross-equation restrictions implied by the general equilibrium set-up, which makes estimation more efficient when compared to partial equilibrium approaches. Moreover, Bayesian estimation and model comparison are consistent even when the models are misspecified, as shown by Fernandez-Villaverde and Rubio-Ramirez (2004). Finally, this framework provides a straightforward method of evaluating the ability of the models to capture the cyclical features of the data, while allowing for a fully structural approach to analyse the sources of fluctuations.

5.1 Implementation

5.1.1 Prior selection

As noted above, (18.43) requires the specification of a prior density $p(\theta)$. In general, we can distinguish between non-informative priors (representing the *subjective* beliefs a researcher has in the occurrence of an event) and informative priors (which reflect an *objective* evaluation. The former, employed in the Bayesain approach, are invariant in location and scale, or invariant to parametrization (if one wants to minimize the influence of priors on the posterior). Objective priors are data-based, formulated using the predictive density of the data since, according to the Bayes theorem.

In defining appropriate priors for the parameters, the researcher should consider the theoretical domain of each parameter (whether or not the parameter is bounded, strictly positive, larger than a specific value, and so on) and the shape of the prior distribution. Usually, inverse gamma distributions are used for parameters constrained to be positive (such as variances, standard deviations and so on), the beta distribution for parameters constrained to be between 0 and 1 (probabilities, fractions, and so on), while the normal distribution is employed for non-bounded parameters.

5.1.2 Posterior computation and simulation

In general, the objective of Bayesian inference can be expressed as $E[g(\theta)|y]$ where $g(\theta)$ is a function of interest (for example, the posterior mean/mode, the marginal density and so on):

$$E[g(\theta)|y] = \int g(\theta)p(\theta|y)d\theta = \frac{\int g(\theta)p^*(\theta|y)d\theta}{\int p^*(\theta|y)d\theta} = \frac{\int g(\theta)L(y|\theta)p(\theta)d\theta}{\int L(y|\theta)p(\theta)d\theta} \quad (18.44)$$

where $p^*(\theta|y) \propto p(\theta|y) \propto L(y|\theta)p(\theta)$ is any posterior density kernel for θ. Given that these integrals do not normally allow a closed-form analytical solution, one resorts to simulation methods such as the Markov Chain Monte Carlo (MCMC) Metropolis–

Hastings (MH) Algorithm) in order to obtain random draws from the posterior density.

The general simulation strategy is: (1) choose a starting value θ_0; (2) run MCMC simulation; (3) check convergence; (4) summarize inference. The MCMC specifies a transition kernel for a Markov Chain such that, starting from some initial value and iterating a number of times, one produces a limiting distribution which is the target distribution from which one needs to sample (see Geweke, 1999 for details).

The (Random Walk) Metropolis–Hastings (RWMH), in turn, allows sampling from the region with highest probability, while visiting the whole parameter space as much as possible. The algorithm starts from an arbitrary candidate density $\alpha(\theta_i^*, \theta_{i-1})$, given that the latest value of θ is θ_{i-1}. A draw from $\alpha(\theta_i^*, \theta_{i-1})$ is accepted with a certain probability that depends on $\frac{p(\theta_i^*)L(y|\theta_i^*)\alpha(\theta_i^*,\theta_{i-1})}{p(\theta_{i-1}^*)L(y|\theta_{i-1}^*)\alpha(\theta_{i-1},\theta_i^*)}$, so that there is sufficient variability in the sampling. If a candidate is rejected, then $\theta_i = \theta_{i-1}$. By changing the acceptance rate, one can ensure that the chain moves in an appropriate direction, that is, it is more likely that a draw in a state of high probability is accepted.

5.2 Estimating the Linear NK Model

5.2.1 Preparing the data

We estimate the NK model with habit and indexation set out in section 3.4 around a zero steady state inflation using Bayesian methods. We use the same data set as in Smets and Wouters (2007) in first differences at quarterly frequency. The observable variables are the log difference of real GDP, the log difference of the GDP deflator and the federal funds rate. All series are seasonally adjusted. Since the variables in the model state space are measured as deviations from a trending steady state, we take the first difference of the real GDP in order to obtain stationary processes. The raw data consists of real variables and for GDP we take the log of the original data. Inflation and nominal interest rates are used directly as they are in percentage terms. The original data are taken from the FRED Database available through the Federal Reserve Bank of St. Louis. The sample period is 1984:1 to 2004:4. A full description of the data used can be found in Smets and Wouters (2007).[10]

The corresponding measurement equations for the three observables are:[11]

$$\begin{bmatrix} D(\log GDP_t) \\ \log(GDPDEF_t/GDPDEF_{t-1}) \\ FEDFUNDS_t/4 \end{bmatrix} = \begin{bmatrix} \log(\frac{Y_t}{\bar{Y}_t}) - \log(\frac{Y_{t-1}}{\bar{Y}_{t-1}}) + \text{trend growth} \\ \log(\frac{\Pi_t}{\Pi}) + \text{constant}_{\Pi} \\ \log(\frac{1 + R_{n,t}}{1 + R_n}) + \text{constant}_{R_n} \end{bmatrix} \quad (18.45)$$

where we introduce an observation trend (constant) to the real variable (real GDP) and a specific one to inflation and nominal interest rate instead of demeaning the series.

5.2.2 Estimation

This section presents an empirical example of Bayesian estimation using the linearized NK model in section 4.[12] A few structural parameters are kept fixed in the estimation procedure, in accordance with the usual practice in the literature (see

Table 18.2 Calibrated parameters

Calibrated parameter	Symbol	Value
Discount factor	β	0.987
Depreciation rate	δ	0.025
Growth rate	g	0
Substitution elasticity of goods	ζ	7
Fixed cost	c	$\frac{1}{\zeta} = 0.143$
Implied steady state relationship		
Government expenditure–output ratio	g_y	0.2
Consumption–output ratio	c_y	0.64
Investment–output ratio	i_y	$1-g_y-c_y$

Table 18.2). The choice of priors for the estimated parameters is usually determined by the theoretical implications of the model, stylized facts and evidence from other microeconometric studies. In general, inverse gamma distributions are used as priors when non-negativity constraints are necessary, and beta distributions for fractions or probabilities. Normal distributions are used when more informative priors seem to be necessary.

In order to avoid a stochastic singularity when evaluating the likelihood function, Dynare requires at least as many shocks (or measurement errors) in the models as observable variables (that is, it requires the covariance matrix of endogenous variables to be non-singular). In this estimation an additional structural shock is included to capture to some extent aggregation effects (for example monetary policy shock) and there are no measurement errors in the data set.

In the process of parameter estimation, the mode of the posterior is first estimated using Chris Sims' csminwel[13] after the models' log-prior densities and log-likelihood functions have been obtained by running the Kalman recursion and maximized. Then a sample from the posterior distribution is obtained with the Metropolis–Hastings (MH) algorithm using the inverse Hessian at the estimated posterior mode as the covariance matrix of the jumping distribution. The covariance matrix needs to be adjusted in order to obtain reasonable acceptance rates. Thus the scale used for the jumping distribution in the MH is set to 0.40, allowing good acceptance rates (around 20–30 per cent). Two parallel Markov chains of 100000 runs each are run from the posterior kernel for the MH.[14] The first 25 per cent of iterations (initial burn-in period) are discarded in order to remove any dependence of the chain from its starting values (use *mh_drop*: sets the percentage of discarded draws).

The estimation outputs report the Bayesian inference which summarizes the prior distribution – posterior mean and 95 per cent confident interval. The marginal data density of the model is computed using the Geweke (1999) modified harmonic-mean estimator. The outputs are displayed on the MATLAB Command Window:

```
ESTIMATION RESULTS
Log marginal likelihood is -68.263710.
parameters
```

	prior mean	post. mean	conf.	inter-val	prior	pstdev
rho_A	0.500	0.9306	0.8870	0.9768	beta	0.2000
rho_G	0.500	0.9622	0.9242	0.9982	beta	0.2000
phi_X	2.000	4.1235	2.4401	5.7525	norm	1.5000
sigma_c	1.500	1.5710	0.9533	2.1905	norm	0.3750
chi	0.700	0.8999	0.7413	0.9896	beta	0.1000
varrho	0.500	0.4128	0.0987	0.7284	beta	0.2000
xi	0.500	0.6797	0.5755	0.7913	beta	0.1000
gamma	0.500	0.2216	0.0681	0.3699	beta	0.1500
alp	0.700	0.7485	0.6731	0.8216	norm	0.0500
alpha_pi	1.500	1.7398	1.3671	2.1517	norm	0.2500
alpha_r	0.750	0.8204	0.7734	0.8689	beta	0.1000
alpha_y	0.125	0.1445	0.0716	0.2184	norm	0.0500
average pi	0.625	0.5827	0.5208	0.6444	gamm	0.1000
trend	0.400	0.4141	0.2905	0.5343	norm	0.1000
standard deviation of shocks						
	prior mean	post. mean	conf.	inter-val	prior	pstdev
eps_A	0.100	1.1543	0.5793	1.6989	invg	2.0000
eps_G	0.500	2.8338	2.3745	3.2691	invg	2.0000
eps_MS	0.100	0.1594	0.1361	0.1843	invg	2.0000

All the estimates are plausible. Noticeably habit is strong with an estimated parameter $\chi = 0.90$ whereas the indexation effect is rather small at $\gamma = 0.2$. The estimated sticky-price parameter $\xi = 0.68$ corresponds to a contract length $\frac{1}{1-\xi} = 3.12$ quarters, a value within the range of those found in surveys for the US. The posterior means are for the most part away from the priors, suggesting that the data is informative, but one exception is the parameter σ_c, which appears to be weakly identified. We discuss the identification issue and how to deal with it formally at the end of Chapter 19.

The output shows the log of the posterior marginal likelihoods which facilitates a formal comparison of different models through their posterior marginal likelihoods through likelihood race. But such an assessment of model fit is only relative to its other rivals with different restrictions. The outperforming model in the space of competing models may still be poor (potentially misspecified) in capturing the important dynamics in the data. To further evaluate the absolute performance of one particular model against data, it is necessary to compare the model's implied characteristics with those of the actual data and with a benchmark model, a DSGE-VAR that by construction must outperform both a structural VAR and the DSGE model. These issues are pursued in Chapter 19.

6 CONCLUSION

This chapter has taken the first steps in the construction and estimation of a DSGE model suitable for monetary policy experiments. We have shown how the New Keynesian model builds on the Real Business Cycle Model and how it can be calibrated to observed outcomes using the steady state. Impulse response functions to a supply and demand shock demonstrate the important differences between the two models. We have argued for and demonstrated a Bayesian approach to the estimation of the NK model. The next chapter will show how model comparisons can be made and how the model fit can be assessed by comparing second moments and by a comparison with a benchmark DSGE-VAR. We then proceed to using the estimated model for computing optimal monetary policy.

NOTES

* We acknowledge financial support for the preparation of this chapter from the Foreign & Commonwealth Office as a contribution to the project 'Building Capacity and Consensus for Monetary and Financial Reform' led by the National Institute of Public Finance and Policy, from the EU Framework Programme 7 in support of the project 'MONFISPOL' led by Michel Juillard, CEPREMAP and from the ESRC, project no. RES-000-23-1126.

1. A notable example is what has been labelled the 'case of missing money' in the 1970s, in which economic analysts were surprised by sudden surges in the velocity of money circulation and therefore conventional money demand functions over-predicted actual money growth.
2. See Mankiw and Romer (1991), which contains a collection of the most influential articles in the early New Keynesian tradition.
3. See Rotemberg (1982) for an alternative and equally convenient specification of price stickiness.
4. See also the special issues of the *Journal of Applied Econometrics* (1994, vol. 9, December), the *Economic Journal* (1995, vol. 105, November) and Cooley (1997).
5. Dynare is a software platform that carries out all the computational aspects of these two chapters. It handles a wide class of dynamic economic models and, in particular, those of a DSGE variety. See Adjemian et al. (2011) for full details.
6. Thus we can interpret $\frac{1}{1-\xi}$ as the average duration for which prices are left unchanged.
7. In particular the 'Easterlin paradox', Easterlin (2003). See also Layard (2006) and Choudhary et al. (2012) for the role of external habit in the explanation of the paradox.
8. The actual reduction in hours on impact for the RBC model showed in the simulations is due to the presence of investment adjustment costs. In this case it is costly to adjust capital so firms respond to a TFP shock by reducing hours worked in the first period. From the second quarter on the usual result that hours increase in RBC models still applies.
9. Bayesian methods have also been employed in the study of reduced-form VAR models, giving rise to the literature on Bayesian VAR (BVAR) models; see Canova (2007) for a review.
10. An alternative to this two-step procedure of first filtering the data and then estimating the model in deviation form is a hybrid framework (one-step method) where the cyclical fluctuations of the data are represented by the solution of the DSGE model and the non-cyclical fluctuations are captured by a flexible reduced form representation. We discuss this in Chapter 19.
11. $Y_t = GDP_t$, $\overline{Y}_t =$ trend and trend growth $= \log \overline{Y}_t - \log \overline{Y}_{t-1} =$ constant.
12. The terminology, commands and theory used in the Estimation/Validation sections of these notes closely follow the Dynare Reference Manual and Dynare User Guide, distributed with Dynare and also available from the official Dynare website.
13. See, for more details, Chris Sims' homepage: http://www.princeton.edu/sims/.
14. In this example, the univariate diagnostic statistics produced by Dynare indicate convergence by comparing between and within moments of multiple chains (Brooks and Gelman, 1998).

REFERENCES

Adjemian, S., H. Bastani, M. Juillard, F. Mihoubi, G. Perendia, M. Ratto and S. Villemot (2011), 'Dynare: reference manual, Version 4', Dynare Working Papers 1, CEPREMAP.

Adolfson, M., S. Laseen, J. Linde and M. Villani (2007), 'Bayesian estimation of an open economy DSGE model with incomplete pass-through', *Journal of International Economics*, **72**(2), 481–511.

An, S. and F. Schorfheide (2007), 'Bayesian analysis of DSGE models', *Econometric Reviews*, **26**, 113–72.

Ascari, G. and T. Ropele (2007), 'Optimal monetary policy under low trend inflation', *Journal of Monetary Economics*, **54**(8), 2568–83.

Barro, R. and X. Sala-i-Martin (2004), *Economic Growth*, 2nd edn, Boston, MA: McGraw-Hill.

Bernanke, B., M. Gertler and S. Gilchrist (1999), 'The financial accelerator in quantitative business cycles', in M. Woodford and J.B. Taylor (eds), *Handbook of Macroeconomics*, vol, 1C, Amsterdam: Elsevier Science.

Bernanke, B.S. and I. Mihov (1998), 'Measuring monetary policy', *Quarterly Journal of Economics*, **113**, 869–902.

Brooks, P. and A. Gelman (1998), 'General methods for monitoring convergence of iterative simulations', *Journal of Computational and Graphical Statistics*, **7**(4), 434–55.

Calvo, G.A. (1983), 'Staggered prices in a utility-maximising framework', *Journal of Monetary Economics*, **12**(3), 383–98.

Canova, F. (2007), *Methods for Applied Macroeconomic Research*, Princeton, NJ: Princeton University Press.

Carlstrom, C.T. and T.S. Fuerst (1997), 'Agency costs, net worth and business cycle fluctuations: a computable general equilibrium analysis', *American Economic Review*, **87**, 893–910.

Choudhary, A., P. Levine, P. McAdam and P. Welz (2012), 'The happiness puzzle: analytical aspects of the Easterlin paradox', *Oxford Economic Papers*, **64**(1), 27–42.

Christiano, L.L. and M. Eichenbaum (1992), 'Current real-business-cycle theories and aggregate labor-market fluctuations', *American Economic Review*, **82**(2), 430–50.

Christiano, L.J., M Eichenbaum and C.L. Evans (1999), 'Monetary policy shocks: what have we learned and to what end?', in J.B. Taylor and M. Woodford (eds), *Handbook of Macroeconomics*, vol. 1, Amsterdam: Elsevier Science, pp. 65–148.

Christiano, L.L., M. Eichenbaum and C.L. Evans (2005), 'Nominal rigidities and the dynamic effects of a shock to monetary policy', *Journal of Political Economy*, **113**(1), 1–45.

Cooley, T.F. (1997), 'Calibrated models', *Oxford Review of Economic Policy*, **13**, 55–69.

Del Negro, M., F. Schorfheide, F. Smets and R. Wouters (2007), 'On the fit of new Keynesian models', *Journal of Business and Economic Statistics*, **25**(2), 123–62.

Dixit, A.K. and J.E. Stiglitz (1977), 'Monopolistic competition and optimal product diversity', *American Economic Review*, **67**(3), 297–308.

Easterlin, R.A. (2003), 'Explaining happiness', *Proceeding of the National Academy of Sciences of the United States*, **100**(19), 11176–83.

Erceg, C.J., D. Henderson and A.T. Levin (2000), 'Optimal monetary policy with staggered wage and price contracts', *Journal of Monetary Economics*, **46**(2), 281–313.

Fernandez-Villaverde, J. and Rubio-Ramirez, J.F. (2004), 'Comparing dynamic equilibrium models to data: a Bayesian approach', *Journal of Econometrics*, **123**, 153–87.

Gabriel, V., P. Levine, J. Pearlman and B. Yang (2010), 'An estimated model of the Indian economy', University of Surrey Discussion Paper DP 12/10 and forthcoming in Chetan Ghate (ed.), *Handbook of the Indian Economy*, Oxford University Press.

Gali, J. and P. Rabanal (2005), 'Technology shocks and aggregate fluctuations: how well does the real business cycle model fit postwar US data?', in *NBER Macroeconomics Annual 2004, Volume 19*, NBER Chapters, National Bureau of Economic Research, pp. 225–318.

Geweke, J. (1999), Computational Experiments and Reality. University of Minnesota and Federal Reserve Bank of Minneapolis.

Kydland, F.F and E.C. Prescott (1982), 'Time to build and aggregate fluctuations', *Econometrica*, **50**, 1345–70.

Layard, R. (2006), 'Happiness and public policy: a challenge to the profession', *Economic Journal*, **116**(510), C24–C33.

Levin, P., P. McAdam and J. Pearlman (2012), 'Probability modal and robust policy rules', *European Economic Review*, **56**(2), 246–62.

Lim, G.C. and P.D. McNelis (2008), *Computational Macroeconomics for the Open Economy*, Cambridge, MA: MIT Press.

Lucas, R. (1976), 'Econometric policy evaluation: a critique', in K. Brunner and A. Meltzer (eds), *The Phillips Curve and Labor Markets, Carnegie-Rochester Conference Series on Public Policy*, New York: American Elsevier, p. 1946.

Lucas, R.E. (1987), *Modal of Business Cycle*, Oxford: Basil Blackwell.

Mankiw, N.G. and P. Romer (1991), *New Keynesian Economics*, Cambridge, MA: MIT Press.

Pesaran, H. and R.P. Smith (1995), 'The role of theory in econometrics', *Journal of Econometrics*, **67**, 61–79.

Rotemberg, J. (1982), 'Monopolistic price adjustment and aggregate output', *Review of Economic Studies*, **49**, 517–31.

Sargent, T. (1981), 'Interpreting economic time series', *Journal of Political Economy*, **99**, 213–48.

Sims, C.A. (1980), 'Macroeconomics and reality', *Econometrica*, **48**, 1–48.

Smets, F. and R. Wouters (2003), 'An estimated stochastic dynamic general equilibrium model of the euro area', *Journal of the European Economic Association*, **1**(5), 1123–75.
Smets, F. and R. Wouters (2007), 'Shocks and frictions in US business cycle: a Bayesian DSGE approach', *American Economic Review*, **97**(3), 586–606.
Whelan, K.T. (2009), 'Technology shocks and hours worked: checking for robust conclusions', *Journal of Macroeconomics*, **31**(2), 231–9.
Wickens, M. (2008), *Macroeconomics Theory*, Princeton, NJ: Princeton University Press.

APPENDIX

A The Euler Consumption Equation

Households choose between work and leisure and therefore how much labour they supply. Let L_t be the proportion of the total time available for work (say 16 hours per day) that consists of leisure time and h_t the proportion of this time spent at work. Then clearly $L_t + h_t = 1$. The single-period utility is

$$\Lambda = \Lambda(C_t, L_t) \qquad (18A.1)$$

and we assume that[1]

$$\Lambda_C > 0, \Lambda_L > 0\ \Lambda_{CC} \leq 0, \Lambda_{LL} \leq 0 \qquad (18A.2)$$

In a stochastic environment, the value function of the representative household at time t is given by

$$H_t = H_t(B_t) = E_t\left[\sum_{s=0}^{\infty}\beta^s\Lambda(C_{t+s}, L_{t+s})\right] \qquad (18A.3)$$

For the household's problem at time t is to choose paths for consumption $\{C_t\}$, leisure, $\{L_t\}$, labour supply $\{h_t = 1 - L_t\}$ and holdings of financial savings to maximize H_t given by (18A.3) given its budget constraint in period t

$$B_{t+1} = (1 + R_t)B_t + W_t h_t - C_t \qquad (18A.4)$$

where B_t is the given net stock of financial assets at the beginning of period t, W_t is the wage rate and R_t is the interest rate paid on assets held at the beginning of period t. All variables are expressed in real terms relative to the price of output.

There are two ways of solving this optimization problem, by dynamic programming or by Lagrangian methods. Here we present the former. The Bellman equation is given by

$$\begin{aligned} H_t B_t &= \max_{C_t, L_t, B_t}[\Lambda(C_t, L_t) + \beta E_t[H_{t+1}(B_{t+1})]] \\ &= \max_{C_t, L_t}[\Lambda(C_t, L_t) + \beta E_t[H_{t+1}((1 + R_t)B_t + W_t(1 - L_t) - C_t)]] \end{aligned} \qquad (18A.5)$$

We seek a solution of the form $C_t = C_t(B_t)$ and $L_t = L_t(B_t)$. The first-order conditions for consumption and leisure are

$$\Lambda_{C,t} - \beta E_t[H'_{t+1}(B_{t+1})] = 0 \qquad (18A.6)$$

$$\Lambda_{L,t} - \beta W_t E_t[H'_{t+1}(B_{t+1})] = 0 \qquad (18A.7)$$

Hence we arrive at the standard result that equates the MRS with the real wage:

$$\frac{\Lambda_{L,t}}{\Lambda_{C,t}} = W_t \qquad (18A.8)$$

To obtain the Euler consumption equation put $C_t = C_t(B_t)$ and $L_t = L_t(B_t)$ at the optimal holding of assets and differentiate (18A.5) with respect to B_t. By the envelope theorem we can drop all terms involving $C_t'(B_t)$ and $L_t'(B_t)$ to obtain[2]

$$H_t'(B_t) = \beta(1 + R_t)E_t[H_{t+1}'(B_{t+1})] \tag{18A.9}$$

Therefore using (18A.6) we have $H_t'(B_t) = (1 + R_t)\Lambda_{C,t}$. Substituting back into (18A.9) we arrive at the Euler consumption equation

$$\Lambda_{C,t} = \beta E_t[(1 + R_t)\Lambda_{C,t+1}] = \beta(1 + R_t)E_t[\Lambda_{C,t+1}] \tag{18A.10}$$

B Optimal Investment with Investment Costs

Firms maximize with respect to $\{I_t\}$ expected discounted profits

$$E_t\sum_{k=0}^{\infty} D_{t,t+k}[Q_{t+k}(1 - S(I_{t+k}/I_{t+k-1}))I_{t+k} - I_{t+k}] \tag{18A.11}$$

where $D_{t,t+k} = \beta^k(\frac{\Lambda_{C,t+1}}{\Lambda_{C,t}})$ is the real stochastic discount rate over the interval $[t, t + k]$.

Consider the first two terms of this summation in (18A.11)

$$E_t[D_{t,t}[Q_t(1 - S(I_t/I_{t-1}))I_t - I_t] + D_{t,t+1}[Q_{t+1}(1 - S(I_{t+1}/I_t))I_{t+1} - I_{t+1}]]$$

Noting that $D_{t,t} = 1$, the first order condition with respect to I_t is then

$$E_t\left[Q_t(1 - S(I_t/I_{t-1})) - 1 - Q_tS'(I_t/I_{t-1})\frac{I_t}{I_{t-1}} - D_{t,t+1}Q_{t+1}S'(I_t/I_{t-1}) \times \left(-\frac{I_{t+1}}{I_t^2}I_{t+1}\right)\right]$$

Putting $X_t \equiv \frac{I_t}{I_{t-1}}$ results in the first-order condition in the main text:

$$Q_t(1 - S(X_t) - X_tS'(X_t)) + E_t[D_{t,t+1}Q_{t+1}S'(X_{t+1})X_{t+1}^2] = 1$$

C Expressing Summations as Difference Equations

In the first order conditions for Calvo contracts and expressions for value functions we are confronted with expected discounted sums of the general form

$$\Omega_t = E_t\left[\sum_{k=0}^{\infty}\beta^k X_{t,t+k}Y_{t+k}\right] \tag{18A.12}$$

where $X_{t,t+k}$ has the property $X_{t,t+k} = X_{t,t+1}X_{t+1,t+k}$ (for example an inflation, interest or discount rate over the interval $[t, t + k]$).

Lemma

Ω_t can be expressed as

$$\Omega_t = X_{t,t}Y_t + \beta E_t[X_{t,t+1}\Omega_{t+1}] \tag{18A.13}$$

Proof

$$\begin{aligned}\Omega_t &= X_{t,t}Y_t + E_t\left[\sum_{k=1}^{\infty}\beta^k X_{t,t+k}Y_{t+k}\right] \\ &= X_{t,t}Y_t + E_t\left[\sum_{k'=0}^{\infty}\beta^{k'+1}X_{t,t+k'+1}Y_{t+k'+1}\right] \\ &= X_{t,t}Y_t + \beta E_t\left[\sum_{k'=0}^{\infty}\beta^{k'}X_{t,t+1}X_{t+1,t+k'+1}Y_{t+k'+1}\right] \\ &= X_{t,t}Y_t + \beta E_t[X_{t,t+1}\Omega_{t+1}] \qquad \square\end{aligned}$$

D Dynamics of Price Dispersion

Price dispersion lowers aggregate output as follows. As with consumption goods, the demand equations for each differentiated good m with price $P_t(m)$ forming aggregate investment and public services takes the form

$$I_t(m) = \left(\frac{P_t(m)}{P_t}\right)^{-\varsigma} I_t;\ G_t(m) = \left(\frac{P_t(m)}{P_t}\right)^{-\varsigma} G_t \tag{18A.14}$$

Hence equilibrium for good m gives

$$Y_t(m)^w = A_t h_t(m)\left(\frac{K_t(m)}{Y_t(m)}\right)^{\frac{1-\alpha}{\alpha}} = \frac{1}{1-c}(C_t + I_t + G_t)\left(\frac{P_t(m)}{P_t}\right)^{-\varsigma} \tag{18A.15}$$

where $Y_t(m)$, $h_t(m)$ and $K_t(m)$ are the quantities of output, hours and capital needed in the wholesale sector to produce good m in the retail sector. Since the capital–labour ratio is constant integrating over m, and using $h_t = \int_0^1 h_t(m)\,dm$ we obtain

$$Y_t = \frac{(1-c)\,Y_t^w}{\Delta_t} = \frac{(1-c)\,F(A_t,h_t,K_t)}{\Delta_t} \tag{18A.16}$$

as in (18.36)

Price dispersion is linked to inflation as follows. Assuming as before that the number of firms is large we obtain the following dynamic relationship:

$$\Delta_t = \xi\Pi_t^{\varsigma}\Delta_{t-1} + (1-\xi)\left(\frac{J_t}{H_t}\right)^{-\varsigma} \tag{18A.17}$$

Proof

In the next period, ξ of these firms will keep their old prices, and $(1-\xi)$ will change their prices to P_{t+1}^O. By the law of large numbers, we assume that the distribution of prices among those firms that do not change their prices is the same as the overall distribution in period t. It follows that we may write

$$\begin{aligned}
\Delta_{t+1} &= \xi \sum_{j_{no\ change}} \left(\frac{P_t(j)}{P_{t+1}}\right)^{-\varsigma} + (1-\xi)\left(\frac{J_{t+1}}{H_{t+1}}\right)^{-\varsigma} \\
&= \xi\left(\frac{P_t}{P_{t+1}}\right)^{-\varsigma} \sum_{j_{no\ change}} \left(\frac{P_t(j)}{P_t}\right)^{-\varsigma} + (1-\xi)\left(\frac{J_{t+1}}{H_{t+1}}\right)^{-\varsigma} \\
&= \xi\left(\frac{P_t}{P_{t+1}}\right)^{-\varsigma} \sum_{j} \left(\frac{P_t(j)}{P_t}\right)^{-\varsigma} + (1-\xi)\left(\frac{J_{t+1}}{H_{t+1}}\right)^{-\varsigma} \\
&= \xi \Pi_{t+1}^{\varsigma} \Delta_t + (1-\xi)\left(\frac{J_{t+1}}{H_{t+1}}\right)^{-\varsigma} \qquad \square
\end{aligned}$$

Notes

1. Our notation is $\Lambda_c \equiv \frac{\partial \Lambda}{\partial C}$, $\Lambda_{cc} \equiv \frac{\partial^2 \Lambda}{\partial C^2}$ etc
2. This can be verified by retaining such terms which then cancel out.

19 The science and art of DSGE modelling: II – model comparisons, model validation, policy analysis and general discussion*

Cristiano Cantore, Vasco J. Gabriel, Paul Levine, Joseph Pearlman and Bo Yang

1 INTRODUCTION

The previous chapter described the construction, calibration and the Bayesian estimation of DSGE models with a particular focus on the New Keynesian model. This chapter shows how model comparisons can be made and how the model's success in fitting data can be assessed by comparing second moments and by a comparison with a benchmark DSGE-VAR. We then demonstrate how the estimated model can be used for computing optimal monetary policy.

Our two chapters as a whole will then describe a seamless construction, estimation and policy analysis methodology for macroeconomics summarized by the following steps.

1. The construction of a DSGE model describing the first-order conditions for economic agents in the form of a set of non-linear difference equations;
2. the solution of the steady state to be used for both solution and calibration;
3. Bayesian estimation of the linearized model;
4. model comparisons between different models or variants of the same model;
5. model validation by comparison with second moments and a benchmark DSGE-VAR;
6. optimal policy analysis with
    a) optimal commitment (the 'Ramsey problem')
    b) optimal policy under discretion
    c) optimized simple commitment Taylor-type rules.

The previous chapter has covered steps 1 to 3. This chapter proceeds from step 4 through to step 6 in sections 2 to 4. The final two sections of this chapter switch from a practical to a more reflective mode. Although we have claimed that the DSGE approach to macroeconomic modelling enjoys a reasonable consensus at the moment, there is a growing debate that is either demanding new types of DSGE model or a totally different approach. The final two sections 5 and 6 join this debate.

2 MODEL COMPARISONS

One of the main advantages of adopting a Bayesian approach is that it facilitates a formal comparison of different models through their posterior marginal likelihoods, computed using the Geweke (1999) modified harmonic-mean estimator. For a given model $m_i \in M$ and common data set, the marginal likelihood is obtained by integrating out vector θ,

$$L(y|m_i) = \int_{\Theta} L(y|\theta, m_i)p(\theta|m_i)d\theta \tag{19.1}$$

where $p_i(\theta|m_i)$ is the prior density for model m_i, and $L(y|\theta, m_i)$ is the likelihood of the sample $y \in Y$ given the parameter vector θ and the model m_i. To compare models (say, m_i and m_j) we calculate the posterior odds ratio which is the ratio of their posterior model probabilities, or the Bayes Factor when the prior odds ratio, $\frac{p(m_i)}{p(m_j)}$, is set to unity:

$$PO_{i,j} = \frac{p(m_i|y)}{p(m_j|y)} = \frac{L(y|m_i)p(m_i)}{L(y|m_j)p(m_j)} \tag{19.2}$$

$$BF_{i,j} = \frac{L(y|m_i)}{L(y|m_j)} = \frac{\exp(LL(y|m_i))}{\exp(LL(y|m_j))} \tag{19.3}$$

in terms of the log-likelihoods. Components (19.2) and (19.3) provide a framework for comparing alternative and potentially misspecified models based on their marginal likelihood. Such comparisons are important in the assessment of rival models, as the model which attains the highest odds outperforms its rivals and is therefore favoured.

Given Bayes factors, we can easily compute the model probabilities $p_1, p_2, \ldots, p_n$ for n models. Since $\sum_{i=1}^{n} p_i = 1$ we have that $\frac{1}{p_1} = \sum_{i=2}^{n} BF_{i,1}$, from which p_1 is obtained. Then $p_i = p_1 BF(i,1)$ gives the remaining model probabilities.

We now use these results to compare three variants of our estimated NK model: 'Model GH' is the full model with both indexation ($\gamma > 0$) and habit ($\chi > 0$). In 'Model H' we shut down indexation by putting $\gamma = 0$. In 'Model Z' there are zero extra persistence mechanisms and $\gamma = \chi = 0$.

Table 19.1 provides a formal Bayesian comparison of models GH, H and Z. To interpret the marginal log-likelihood (LL) differences we appeal to Jeffries (1996) who judges that a BF of 3–10 is 'slight evidence' in favour of model i over j. This corresponds to a LL difference in the range [ln 3, ln 10] = [1.10,2.30]. A BF of 10–100 or a LL range of [2.30, 4.61] is 'strong to very strong evidence'; a BF over 100 (LL over 4.61) is 'decisive evidence'.[1] Thus according to this assessment, our model comparison analysis provides 'decisive evidence' against the inclusion of price indexation. The poor performance of indexation is in a sense encouraging as this feature of the NK is ad hoc and vulnerable to the Lucas critique. The existence of habit by contrast is a plausible formulation of utility that addresses issues examined in the recent literature.[2] However, there is no evidence

Table 19.1 Marginal log-likelihood values and posterior model odds across model variants

	Model GH	Model H	Model Z
LLs	−68.26	−62.75	−61.33
prob.	0.0008	0.1945	0.8047

that habit improves upon model Z with neither habit nor indexation. The most basic NK then comes out of this exercise well and it appears that the other persistence mechanisms in the model associated with investment costs and interest rate smoothing are sufficient to render indexation and habit irrelevant, at least for fitting the model to only output, inflation and the nominal interest rate.[3]

3 MODEL VALIDATION

A limitation of the likelihood race methodology is that the assessment of model fit is only relative to its other rivals with different restrictions. The outperforming model in the space of competing models may still be poor (potentially misspecified) in capturing the important dynamics in the data. Summary statistics consisting of second moments have been commonly used for model validation in the RBC literature. To further evaluate the absolute performance of one particular model against data, in a later section we compare the model's implied characteristics with those of the actual data and with a benchmark DSGE-VAR model. But first we carry out a traditional RBC second moments comparison.

3.1 Second Moments Comparisons with Data

For the simulation and computation of moments, Dynare assumes that the shocks follow a normal distribution. In a stochastic set-up, shocks are only allowed to be temporary. A permanent shock cannot be accommodated because of the need to stationarize the model. Also the expectations of future shocks in a stochastic model must be zero. Table 19.2 presents some selected second moments implied by the above estimations and

Table 19.2 Selected second moments of the model variants

Standard Deviation			
Model	Output	Inflation	Interest rate
Data	0.59	0.25	0.64
Model GH	0.58	0.31	0.38
Model H	0.57	0.28	0.37
Model Z	0.64	0.26	0.32
Cross-correlation with Output			
Data	1.00	−0.14	0.15
Model GH	1.00	−0.13	−0.26
Model H	1.00	−0.09	−0.24
Model Z	1.00	−0.003	−0.16
Autocorrelations (Order = 1)			
Data	0.31	0.53	0.96
Model GH	0.14	0.63	0.91
Model H	0.13	0.57	0.91
Model Z	0.01	0.52	0.89

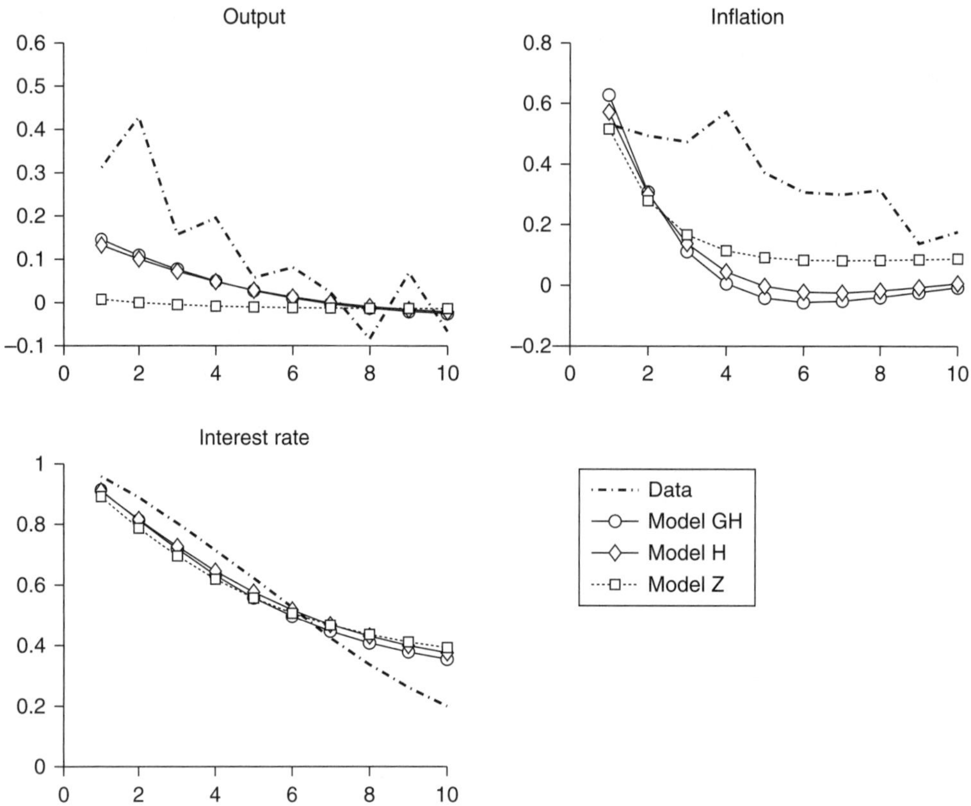

Figure 19.1 Autocorrelations of observables in the actual data and in the estimated models

compares with those in the actual data. In particular, we compute these model-implied statistics by solving the models at the posterior means obtained from estimation. The results of the model's second moments are compared with the second moments in the actual data to evaluate the models' empirical performance.

We can see that model Z performs best in some dimensions, such as capturing the standard deviation of inflation, but worse in others, such as the standard deviation of output. This applies also to models GH versus H and it is not obvious from Table 19.2 in terms of volatility and co-movement with output that GH is outperformed by H.

We have so far considered autocorrelation only up to order 1. To further illustrate how the estimated models capture the data statistics and persistence in particular, we now plot the autocorrelations up to order 10 of the actual data and those of the endogenous variables generated by the model variants in Figure 19.1. Here we can see that habit does improve the ability of the models to fit the persistence seen in output data, but not in inflation where model Z performs best. Again there is only a slight indication that model GH is outperformed by H as indicated by the LL comparison. Perhaps the main message to emerge from this RBC type of model validity exercise is that it can be misleading to assess model fit using a selective choice of second moment comparisons.

LL comparisons provide the most comprehensive form of assessment that will still leave trade-offs in terms of fitting some second moments well, at the expense of others.

3.2 The DSGE-VAR Benchmark

An alternative way of validating the model performance is to follow Del Negro and Schorfheide (2004) and Del Negro et al. (2007) and to compare it with a hybrid model that is a combination of an unrestricted VAR and the VAR implied by the estimated DSGE model. Levine et al. (2012b) show that under weak conditions the solution to the DSGE model can be approximated by a finite VAR approximation to

$$\Psi(L)Y_t = \eta_t = \tilde{D}\varepsilon_t;\ \ E_t[\varepsilon_t\varepsilon_t'] = I$$

where Y_t is a vector of observables and the shocks have been suitably normalized. The DSGE-VAR approach uses the DSGE model itself to construct a prior distribution for the VAR coefficients so that DSGE-VAR estimates are tilted toward DSGE model restriction, thus identifying the shocks for the IRFs. To see how this differs from standard identification, we first perform a Cholesky decomposition $\Sigma_\eta \equiv E_t[\eta_t\eta_t'] = \Sigma_{tr}\Sigma_{tr}'$, $\tilde{D} = \Sigma_{tr}\Omega$ where Σ_{tr} is lower triangular and Ω (the 'rotation matrix') is an orthonormal matrix. Then we can set priors for the VAR and identify shocks (that is, choose Ω) by putting

$$\tilde{D} = \Sigma_{tr}\Omega^{DSGE}(\theta)$$

where $\Omega^{DSGE}(\theta)$ is obtained from the DSGE model (see Del Negro and Schorfheide, 2004).[4]

This method constructs the DSGE prior by generating dummy observations from the DSGE model, and adding them to the actual data and leads to an estimation of the VAR based on a mixed sample of artificial and actual observations. The ratio of dummy over actual observations (called the hyper-parameter λ) controls the variance and therefore the weight of the DSGE prior relative to the sample. For extreme values of this parameter (0 or ∞) either an unrestricted VAR or the DSGE is estimated. If λ is small the prior is diffuse. When $\lambda = \infty$, we obtain a VAR approximation of the log-linearized DSGE model. As λ becomes small the cross-equation restrictions implied by the DSGE model are gradually relaxed. The empirical performance of a DSGE-VAR will depend on the tightness of the DSGE prior. Details on the algorithm used to implement this DSGE-VAR are to be found in Del Negro and Schorfheide (2004) and Del Negro et al. (2007).

We fit our VAR to the same data set used to estimate the DSGE model. We consider a VAR with 4 lags.[5] We use a data-driven procedure to determine the tightness of prior endogenously based on the marginal data density. Our choice of the optimal λ is 0.5 and this is found by comparing different VAR models using the estimates of the marginal data density (Figure 19.2). In particular, we iterate over a grid that contains the values of $\lambda = [0.2; 0.5; 1; 1.2; 1.5; 5; \infty]$, we find that $\lambda = 0.5$ has the highest posterior probability for both models. Note that 0.2 is the smallest λ value for which we have a proper prior. This implies that the mixed sample that is used to estimate the VAR has relatively lower weight on the DSGE model (artificial observations) than on the VAR (actual observations).

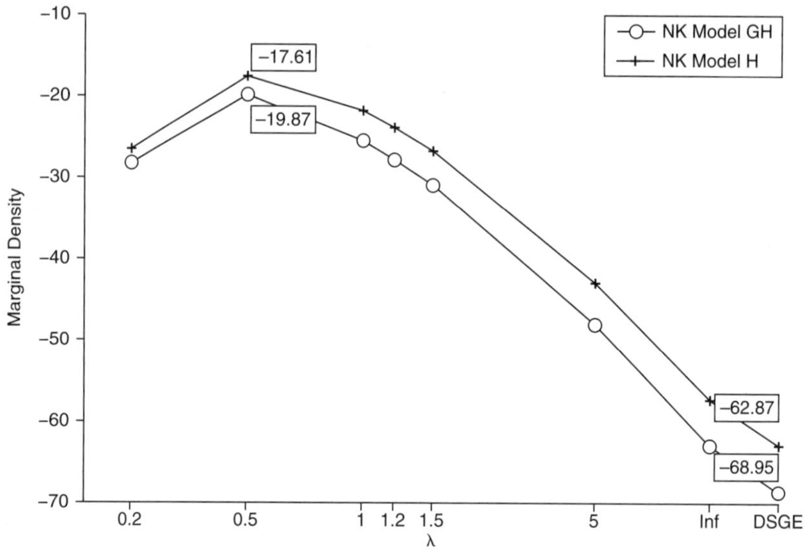

Figure 19.2 Marginal likelihood as a function of λ

The optimum $\hat{\lambda}$ represents how much the economic model (DSGE) is able to explain the real data. Figure 19.2 applies this procedure to models H and GH. We see that both models with the optimal λ clearly dominate VARs with very diffuse priors since the marginal likelihood values increase sharply as λ moves from 0.2 to the optimal values. This suggests that the cross-equation restrictions imposed by our DSGE models are important in fitting the data. More importantly, the results from comparing across different models H and GH show that Model H generally outperforms Model GH when the weight on the DSGE model becomes higher (when λ tends to ∞). Overall the LL plots then confirm the fact that model H is less misspecified.

4 OPTIMAL MONETARY POLICY IN THE NK MODEL

The welfare-optimal policy problem at time $t = 0$ is to choose policy instruments over time to maximize the household's inter-temporal utility function

$$\Omega_0 = E_0\left[(1 - \beta)\sum_{t=0}^{\infty}\beta^t U(C_t, L_t)\right]$$

subject to constraints described by the model. The latter consists of the models RBC with government spending G_t chosen as the fiscal policy instrument, rather than imposed as an exogenous process, and the NK model with, in addition, the nominal interest rate $R_{n,t}$ as the monetary instrument. For the latter, optimal policy then replaces the ad hoc Taylor rule we have used up to now.

We adopt a linear-quadratic (LQ) approximation approach to this non-linear dynamic optimization problem in macroeconomics for a number of reasons. First, for LQ problems the characterization of time-consistent and commitment equilibria for a single policymaker, and even more so for many interacting policymakers, are well understood. Second, the certainty equivalence property results in optimal rules that are robust in the sense that they are independent of the variance–covariance matrix of additive disturbances. Third, policy can be decomposed into deterministic and stochastic components. This is a very convenient property since it enables the stochastic stabilization component to be pursued using simple Taylor-type feedback rules rather than the exceedingly complex optimal counterpart. Fourth, in an imperfect information context the conditional welfare loss (in deviation form about the deterministic steady state) conveniently decomposes into a deterministic component and two stochastic components, one of which describes the effect of imperfect information. Finally for sufficiently simple models, LQ approximation allows analytical rather than numerical solution.

The solution to linear rational expectations models goes back to Blanchard and Kahn (1980) and has since been generalized in various dimensions by Pearlman et al. (1986), Klein (2000) and Sims (2003). The early literature on optimal policy with commitment developed LQ infinite time horizon control theory for engineering, non-forward-looking models into a rational expectations (RE) forward-looking context (Driffill, 1982; Calvo, 1978; Miller and Salmon, 1985; Levine and Currie, 1987).

In a stochastic environment the feedback representation of policy is crucial. For the standard infinite time horizon LQ engineering problem, optimal policy can be represented as a linear time-invariant feedback rule on the state variables; but this is no longer the case when rational expectations are introduced. Then as is shown in the literature the optimal policy can only be implemented as very complicated rules, even in the 'timeless' form advocated by Woodford (2003). The added complexity of such a rule adds force to the case for designing policy in the form of simple optimized, but sub-optimal rules. The *normative case* for such rules was first put forward by Vines et al. (1983), Levine and Currie (1985), Currie and Levine (1985) and (1993). This early literature considered both monetary and fiscal policy and, in the case of Vines et al. (1983), incomes and exchange rate targeting policies. The *positive case* for a particular form of monetary policy interest rate rule feeding back on current inflation and the output gap was advocated by Taylor (1999), so simple 'Maciejowski–Meade–Vines–Currie–Levine Rules' eventually became known as 'Taylor Rules'. More recently, in the context of DSGE models, we have seen a renewed interest in simple rules in general (referred to by Woodford, 2003 as 'explicit instrument rules') and interest rate rules in particular.

Following the pioneering contributions of Kydland and Prescott (1977) and Barro and Gordon (1983), the credibility problem associated with monetary policy has stimulated a huge academic literature that has been influential with policymakers. The central message underlying these contributions is the existence of significant macroeconomic gains, in some sense, from 'enhancing credibility' through formal commitment to a policy rule or through institutional arrangements for central banks such as independence, transparency, and forward-looking inflation targets, that achieve the same outcome. The technical reason for this result is that optimal policy formulated by Pontryagin's maximum principle is time-inconsistent – the simple passage of time, even in a deterministic environment, leads to an incentive to re-optimize and renege on the initial optimal plan. Appreciation of this problem has motivated the examination of policies that are optimal within the constraint of being time consistent (Levine and Currie, 1985; Miller and Salmon, 1985; Currie and Levine, 1987; Cohen and Michel, 1988; and Söderlind, 1999). Comparing optimal policy with and without commitment enables us then to quantify the stabilization gains from commitment.

A further important consideration when considering monetary policy is the existence of a nominal interest rate zero lower bound. A number of papers have studied optimal commitment policy with this constraint (for example, Coenen and Wieland, 2003; Eggertsson and Woodford, 2003; Woodford, 2003, Chapter 6). In an important contribution to the credibility literature, Adam and Billi (2007) show that ignoring the zero lower bound constraint for the setting of the nominal interest rate can result in considerably underestimating the stabilization gain from commitment. The reason for this is that under discretion the monetary authority cannot make credible promises about future policy. For a given setting of future interest rates the volatility of inflation is driven up by the expectations of the private sector that the monetary authority will re-optimize in the future. This means that to achieve a given low volatility of inflation the lower bound is reached more often under discretion than under commitment. All these authors study a simple New Keynesian model and are able to employ non-linear techniques. In a more developed model such as Smets and Wouters (2003), Levine et al. (2008b) adopt the more tractable linear-quadratic (LQ) framework adopted here.

4.1 State-space Set-up

Following the LQ approach to optimal policy we consider linearized forms of the models expressed in a general linear minimal[6] state-space form

$$\begin{bmatrix} \mathbf{z}_{t+1} \\ E_t\mathbf{x}_{t+1} \end{bmatrix} = A\begin{bmatrix} \mathbf{z}_t \\ \mathbf{x}_t \end{bmatrix} + Br_{n,t} + C\varepsilon_{t+1};\ \mathbf{o}_t = E\begin{bmatrix} \mathbf{z}_t \\ \mathbf{x}_t \end{bmatrix} \tag{19.4}$$

where $\mathbf{z}_t$ is an $(n - m) \times 1$ vector of predetermined variables at time t with $\mathbf{z}_0$ given, $\mathbf{x}_t$ is an $m \times 1$ vector of non-predetermined variables and $\mathbf{o}_t$ is a vector of outputs. All variables are expressed as absolute or proportional deviations about a steady state. A, B, C and E are fixed matrices and ε_t is a vector of random zero-mean shocks. Rational expectations are formed assuming an information set $\{z_s, x_s, \varepsilon_s\}$, $s \leq t$, the model and the monetary rule. For example the linearized NK model can be expressed in this form where $\mathbf{z}_t$ consists of exogenous shocks, lags in non-predetermined and output variables and capital stock; $\mathbf{x}_t$ consists of current inflation, investment, Tobin's Q, consumption and flexi-price outcomes for the latter two variables, and outputs o_t consist of marginal costs, the marginal rate of substitution between consumption and leisure, the cost of capital, labour supply, output, flexi-price outcomes, the output gap and other target variables for the monetary authority.

4.2 LQ Approximation of the Optimization Problem

In our models there are many sets of distortions that result in the steady state output being below the social optimum: these are from monopolistic competition, external habit and labour and credit market frictions. We cannot assume that these distortions are small in the steady state and use the 'small distortions' (Woodford, 2003), quadratic approximation to the household's single period utility which is accurate in the vicinity of the steady state.[7]

In Woodford (2003) and many other recent papers a *separable* household utility of the form

$$\Lambda_t^j = \left[\frac{(C_t^j - \chi C_{t-1})^{1-\sigma_c}}{1-\sigma_c} - \kappa\frac{(h_t^j)^{1+\phi}}{1+\phi}\right] \tag{19.5}$$

replaces the *non-separable* utility utilized up to now. This form of utility is actually inconsistent with a balanced growth path unless $\sigma_c = 1$. Nonetheless we proceed to consider the NK model with habit (but no indexing), with only one shock A_t. To make the analysis tractable we consider a special case of the NK model and no capital ($\alpha = 1$). Then following the procedure set out in the Appendix, the large distortions approximation to this welfare function is given by

$$\begin{aligned}\Lambda_t = -\frac{\kappa}{2\varpi}h^{1+\phi}\Bigg[&\frac{\sigma_c}{1-\chi}(y_t - \chi y_{t-1})^2 + \phi(\varpi + \lambda_5(1+\phi))y_t^2 \\ &- 2(1+\phi)(\varpi + \lambda_5(1+\phi))y_t a_t + 2\lambda_5\frac{\sigma_c}{1-\chi}(y_t - \chi y_{t-1})y_t \\ &- \lambda_5\frac{\sigma_c(\sigma_c+1)}{(1-\chi)^2}(y_t - \chi y_{t-1})^2 + \frac{\xi\zeta}{(1-\xi)(1-\beta\xi)}(\varpi + (1+\phi)\lambda_5)\pi_t^2\Bigg]\end{aligned} \tag{19.6}$$

where we define $\varpi = (1 - 1/\zeta)$ which is 1 for the efficient steady state case, $\zeta \rightarrow \infty$ and

$$\lambda_5 = \frac{1 - \beta\chi - \varpi}{\frac{\sigma_c(1-\chi\beta)}{1-\chi} + \phi} \tag{19.7}$$

The small distortion case assumes that the zero-inflation steady state about which we have linearized is approximately efficient. We are now in a position to examine the nature of the small distortions approximation by examining the correctly quadratified single-period utility (19.6). From (19.6) we can see that this means that λ_5 must be small and that the small distortion case, which would omit all terms involving λ_5, is valid only if $|\lambda_5(1+\phi)| << \varpi$ or, using the definition of λ_5, only if

$$(1+\phi)\frac{|1 - \beta\chi - \varpi|}{\frac{\sigma_c(1-\chi\beta)}{1-\chi} + \phi} << \varpi \tag{19.8}$$

Typical estimated parameter values are $\sigma_c = 2$, $\phi = 1.3$. With χ at the mid-point of the range of estimates at $\chi = 0.7$ this gives the left-hand side of (19.8) as 0.22 and the right-hand side as 0.69. Neglected terms are therefore of the order of one third of those retained.

Finally consider the case without habit ($\chi = 0$). After some further effort (and subtracting an appropriate term in a_t^2), (19.6) then reduces to

$$\frac{-\kappa h^{1+\phi}}{2\varpi}(\phi + \sigma_c\varpi + 1 - \varpi)\left[\left(y_t - \frac{1+\phi}{\sigma_c + \phi}a_t\right)^2 + \frac{\zeta\xi}{(1-\xi)(1-\beta\xi)(\sigma_c + \phi)}\pi_t^2\right] \quad (19.9)$$

This is a loss function with a stochastic output target $y_t^* = \frac{1+\phi}{\sigma_c+\phi}a_t$ and inflation target of zero (the steady state about which we have formed the LQ approximation). In fact y_t^* is the solution in the flexi-price case, so $y_t^* - y_t$ is the output gap and (19.9) now becomes the familiar 'welfare-based' loss function that appears in much of the literature using a NK model to evaluate optimal policy. *It should be stressed that this is only welfare based under the extreme restrictions that NK model has no capital, no habit, no indexing, has only one shock A_t and uses a separable utility function.* Generally then the numerical procedure set out in the Appendix must be used for welfare-based optimal policy.

4.3 Optimal Policy with Commitment

For both ad hoc and welfare-based loss function the inter-temporal loss function can be expressed in quadratic form:

$$\Omega_0 = E_0\left[(1-\beta)\sum_{t=0}^{\infty}\beta^t L_t\right]$$

where the single-period loss function is given by a quadratic form $L_t = \mathbf{y}_t^T Q \mathbf{y}_t$, where Q is a fixed matrix.

To derive the *ex ante* optimal policy with commitment (OP) following Currie and Levine (1993) we maximize the Lagrangian

$$\mathcal{L}_0 = E_0\left[(1-\beta)\sum_{t=0}^{\infty}\beta^t[\mathbf{y}_t^T Q\mathbf{y}_t + w_r r_{n,t}^2 + \mathbf{p}_{t+1}(A\mathbf{y}_t + Br_{n,t} - \mathbf{y}_{t+1})]\right]$$

with respect to $\{r_{n,t}\}$, $\{\mathbf{y}_t\}$ and the row vector of co-state variables, $\mathbf{p}_t$, given $\mathbf{z}_0$. From Currie and Levine (1993) where more details are provided, this leads to an optimal rule

$$r_{n,t} = D\begin{bmatrix}\mathbf{z}_t \\ \mathbf{p}_{2t}\end{bmatrix} \quad (19.10)$$

where

$$\begin{bmatrix}\mathbf{z}_{t+1} \\ \mathbf{p}_{2t+1}\end{bmatrix} = F\begin{bmatrix}\mathbf{z}_t \\ \mathbf{p}_{2t}\end{bmatrix}$$

and the optimality condition[8] at time $t = 0$ imposes $\mathbf{p}_{20} = 0$. In (19.10) $\mathbf{p}_t^T = [\mathbf{p}_{1t}^T\ \mathbf{p}_{2t}^T]$ is partitioned so that $\mathbf{p}_{1t}$, the co-state vector associated with the predetermined variables, is of dimension $(n - m) \times 1$ and $\mathbf{p}_{2t}$, the co-state vector associated with the non-predetermined variables, is of dimension $m \times 1$. The (conditional) loss function is then given by

$$\Omega_t^{OP} = -(1-\beta)\,\mathrm{tr}\left(N_{11}\left(Z_t + \frac{\beta}{1-\beta}\Sigma\right) + N_{22}\mathbf{p}_{2t}\mathbf{p}_{2t}^T\right)$$

where $Z_t = z_t z_t^T$, $\Sigma = \text{cov}(C\varepsilon_t)$,

$$N = \begin{bmatrix} S_{11} - S_{12}S_{22}^{-1}S_{21} & S_{12}S_{22}^{-1} \\ -S_{22}^{-1}S_{21} & S_{22}^{-1} \end{bmatrix} = \begin{bmatrix} N_{11} & N_{12} \\ N_{21} & N_{22} \end{bmatrix} \tag{19.11}$$

and $n \times n$ matrix S is the solution to the steady-state Ricatti equation. In (19.11) matrices S and N are partitioned conformably with $y_t = [z_t^T x_t^T]^T$ so that S_{11} for instance has dimensions $(n - m) \times (n - m)$.

Note that in order to achieve optimality, the policymaker sets $p_{20} = 0$ at time $t = 0$. At time $t > 0$ there then exists a gain from reneging by resetting $p_{2t} = 0$. It can be shown that matrices N_{11} and N_{22} are negative definite, so the loss in Ω is positive and an incentive to renege exists at all points along the trajectory of the optimal policy by resetting $p_{2t} = 0$. This essentially is the time-inconsistency problem facing stabilization policy in a model with structural dynamics.

4.4 Discretion

To evaluate the discretionary (time-consistent) policy we write the expected loss Ω_t at time t as

$$\Omega_t = E_t\left[(1 - \beta)\sum_{\tau=t}^{\infty}\beta^{\tau-t}L_\tau\right] = (1 - \beta)(y_t^T Q y_t + w_r r_{n,t}^2) + \beta\Omega_{t+1}$$

The dynamic programming solution then seeks a stationary solution of the form $r_{n,t} = -Fz_t$, $\Omega_t = z^T S z$ and $x = -Nz$ where matrices S and N are different matrices from those under commitment (unless there is no forward-looking behaviour), now of lower dimensions $(n - m) \times (n - m)$ and $m \times (n - m)$ respectively. The value function Ω_t is minimized at time t, subject to (19.4), in the knowledge that a similar procedure will be used to minimize Ω_{t+1} at time $t + 1$.[9] Both the instrument $r_{n,t}$ and the forward-looking variables x_t are now proportional to the predetermined component of the state-vector z_t and the equilibrium we seek is therefore *Markov Perfect*. In Currie and Levine (1993) an iterative process for F_t, N_t and S_t starting with some initial values is set out. If the process converges to stationary values independent of these initial values,[10] F, N and S say, then the time-consistent (TC) feedback rule is $r_{n,t} = -Fz_t$ with loss at time t given by

$$\Omega_t^{TC} = (1 - \beta)\,\text{tr}\left(S\left(Z_t + \frac{\beta}{1 - \beta}\Sigma\right)\right)$$

4.5 Optimized Simple Commitment Rules

We now address a problem with the optimal commitment rule (19.10): in all but very simple models it is extremely complex, with the interest rate feeding back at time t on the full state vector z_t and all past realizations of z_t back to the initiation of the rule at $t = 0$. We therefore seek to mimic the optimal commitment rule with simpler rules of the form

$$r_{n,t} = Dy_t = D\begin{bmatrix} z_t \\ x_t \end{bmatrix} \tag{19.12}$$

where D is constrained to be sparse in some specified way. In Currie and Levine (1993) we show that the loss at time t is given by

$$\Omega_t^{SIM} = (1 - \beta)\mathrm{tr}\left(V\left(Z_t + \frac{\beta}{1 - \beta}\Sigma\right)\right)$$

where $V = V(D)$ satisfies a Lyapunov equation. Ω_t^{SIM} can now be minimized with respect to D to give an *optimized simple rule* of the form (19.12) with $D = D^*$. A very important feature of optimized simple rules is that unlike their optimal commitment or optimal discretionary counterparts they are *not certainty equivalent*. In fact if the rule is designed at time $t = 0$ then $D^* = f^*(Z_0 + \frac{\beta}{1-\beta}\Sigma)$ and so depends on the displacement $\mathbf{z}_0$ at time $t = 0$ and on the covariance matrix of innovations $\Sigma = \mathrm{cov}(\varepsilon_t)$. From non-certainty equivalence it follows that if the simple rule were to be redesigned at any time $t > 0$, since the re-optimized D^* will then depend on Z_t the new rule will differ from that at $t = 0$. This feature is true in models with or without rational forward-looking behaviour and it implies that *simple rules are time-inconsistent even in non-RE models.*

4.6 Stability and Indeterminacy

Substituting (19.12) into (19.4), the condition for a stable and unique equilibrium depends on the magnitude of the eigenvalues of the matrix $A + BD$. If the number of eigenvalues outside the unit circle is equal to the number of non-predetermined variables, the system has a unique equilibrium which is also stable with saddle-path $x_t = -Nz_t$ where $N = N(D)$ (see Blanchard and Kahn, 1980; Currie and Levine, 1993). In our model NK under a Taylor rule with forward horizons $j = 0, 1$, there are 2 non-predetermined variables. Instability occurs when the number of eigenvalues of $A + BD$ outside the unit circle is larger than the number of non-predetermined variables. This implies that when the economy is pushed off its steady state following a shock, it cannot ever converge back to it, but rather finishes up with explosive inflation dynamics (hyper-inflation or hyper-deflation).

By contrast, indeterminacy occurs when the number of eigenvalues of $A + BD$ outside the unit circle is smaller than the number of non-predetermined variables. Put simply, this implies that when a shock displaces the economy from its steady state, there are many possible paths leading back to equilibrium, that is there are multiple well-behaved rational expectations solutions to the model economy. With forward-looking rules this can happen when policymakers respond to the private sector's inflation expectations and these in turn are driven by non-fundamental exogenous random shocks (that is they are not based on preferences or technology), usually being referred to as 'sunspots'. If policymakers set the coefficients of the rule so that this accommodates such expectations, the latter become self-fulfilling. Then the rule is unable to uniquely pin down the behaviour of one or more real and/or nominal variables, making many different paths compatible with equilibrium (see Chari et al., 1998; Clarida et al., 2000; Carlstrom and Fuerst, 1999; 2000; Benhabib et al., 2001 and Woodford, 2003). The fact that the rule itself may introduce indeterminacy and generate so-called 'sunspot equilibria' is of interest because sunspot fluctuations – that is, persistent movements in inflation and output

Table 19.3 Optimal policy and optimized rules

Rule	Loss	ρ	θ_π	θ_y
Ramsey = 0	0.0596	n.a.	n.a.	n.a.
Simple: $j = 0$	0.0679	0.955	1.017	0.015
Simple: $j = 1$	0.0677	0.970	8.198	0.0617
Simple: $j = 2$	0.0820	0.962	7.380	0.125
Simple: $j = 3$	0.2792	0.953	1.134	−0.119
Simple: $j = 4$	0.5760	1.000	1.107	0.088

that materialize even in the absence of shocks to preferences or technology – are typically welfare-reducing and can potentially be quite large.

4.7 Results for Optimal Monetary Policy

The optimal policy results for the linearized NK model using Dynare are set out in Table 19.3. The loss function is of the ad hoc form

$$\Omega_0 = (1 - \beta)E_0\left[\sum_{t=0}^{\infty}\beta^t(\pi_t^2 + \lambda_1 y_t^2 + \lambda_2 r_{n,t}^2)\right]$$

$$\simeq \text{var}(\pi_t) + \lambda_1\text{var}(y_t) + \lambda_2\text{var}(r_{n,t}) \text{ as } \beta \to 1$$

where the variances are conditional variances at the steady state. Dynare currently computes the Ramsey policy (optimal commitment) and optimized simple rules.[11] The following forward-looking simple rules are investigated:

$$r_{n,t} = \rho r_{n,t-1} + \theta_\pi E_t[\pi_{t+j}] + \theta_y E_t[y_{t+j}] \quad j = 0, 1, 2, 3, 4$$

Thus we see that two simple rules, $j = 0, 1$ can closely mimic the optimal policy. Otherwise rules that are very forward-looking give rise to substantial losses, a familiar result in the literature (see Batini et al., 2006).

5 CRITIQUE OF DSGE MODELS

There are a number of criticisms levelled at DSGE models. The first is fundamental and common to RBC and NK models alike – problems with rationality and Expected Utility Maximization (EUM). The second is that DSGE models examine fluctuations about an exogenous balanced growth path and there is no role for endogenous growth. The third consists of a number of empirical concerns. The fourth is the rudimentary nature of earlier models that lacked unemployment and a banking sector. We discuss this in the final section of this chapter. Finally there is another fundamental problem with any micro-founded macro-model – that of heterogeneity and aggregation. We consider these in turn.

5.1 Rationality

The assumption of rationality in general and that of rational expectations in particular has naturally generated a lively debate in economics and the social sciences. The assumption of perfect rationality has come under scrutiny since the 1950s when Herbert A. Simon claimed that agents are not realistically so rational so as to aspire to pay-off maximization. Instead he proposed 'bounded rationality' as a more realistic alternative to the assumption of rationality, incorporating players' inductive reasoning processes. This is the route that the Agent-based Computational Economics (ACE) models take (see, for example, LeBaron Tesfatsion, 2008). Certainly, experimental studies of decision-making show human behaviour to be regularly inconsistent and contradictory to the assumption of perfect rationality. That said, experiments using people and ACE models suggest agents can *learn* to be rational so that rationality may well be a reasonable empirical postulate to describe behaviour near a long-run steady state. This view is supported by *statistical learning* in theoretical macro-models which converges to rational expectations equilibria (see Evans and Honkapohja, 2001)

Models can only be beaten by alternative models. A model of irrationality has to pin down why one decision is preferred to another and here we observe that analytically tractable theories of the inconsistency and irrationality in human behaviour simply have not yet been developed. Hence our best analytical models are based on the rationality assumption as we unfortunately have nothing superior on offer. However, we can be more positive than that at least when it comes to competitive behaviour. Darwinian selection helps rational (that is, profit-maximizing) firms to succeed in competition.

Perhaps the most convincing argument for adopting the rationality assumption is provided by Myerson (1999. If we view the aim of social sciences to be not only to predict human behaviour in the abstract, but also, crucially, to analyse social institutions and assess proposals for their reform, it is useful to evaluate these institutions under the assumption of perfect rationality. In this way, we can solve for flaws as either defects in the institutional structure (and thereby institutional reform is the required solution) or as flaws in the rationality of the agents (which begs for improved education and/or provision of information for individuals). Accordingly this has become a logical and useful assumption for economists in order to see with more clarity when social problems must be solved by institutional reform. This argument can be refined to illustrate why this individual perfection assumption should be one of intelligent rational maximization, as in the models of non-cooperative game theory. Thus an argument for reform of social institutions (rather than for re-education of individuals) is most persuasive when it is based on a model which assumes that individuals intelligently understand their environment and rationally act to maximize their own welfare.[12]

Even if we accept utility maximization, there still is an issue of whether it should be *expected* utility maximization (EUM). An alternative supported by experiments is *Prospect Theory* which takes into account that people behave as if extremely improbable events are impossible and extremely probable events are certain (see Shiller, 1999). Prospect theory can explain phenomena such as the equity premium puzzle. However, it is extremely difficult to incorporate into general equilibrium modelling; in the words of Shiller, 'EUM can be a workhorse for some sensible research'.

5.2 Integrating Endogenous Growth and Business Cycles

Turning to our second limitation – the lack of a role for endogenous growth. As Lucas (1987) pointed out, the welfare gains from eliminating business cycle fluctuations in the standard RBC model are very small and are dwarfed by the gains from increased growth. It is true that adding New Keynesian frictions significantly increases the gains from stabilization policy, but they still remain small compared with those from increased growth.

Recently a number of papers have introduced long-run growth into DSGE models. Wang and Wen (2008) and Annicchiarico et al. (2010) do so within the simple AK approach. Examples of R&D-led endogenous growth are Comin and Gertler (2006), Comin et al. (2009a), (2009b) and Holden (2011). Comin et al. (2009b) introduce new layers of differentiated goods into wholesale output and capital goods sectors with expanding varieties that lead to endogenous growth. Crucial variables are the numbers of final and intermediate varieties in output and capital goods sectors pinned down by free entry. Efficiency of production then depends on exogenous productivity and numbers of adopted intermediate goods. New intermediate goods arrive exogenously in Comin et al. (2009b) but endogenously in Holden (2011) and Comin and Gertler (2006). For the latter two there are both innovators who develop new intermediate goods, and adopters in Comin et al. (or appropriators in Holden) who convert them into a usable input. Innovation depends on 'news shocks' about future growth prospects. These features result in new endogenous persistence mechanisms as well as an endogenous growth path. These models allow for both exogenous and endogenous movements in total factor productivity and the empirical strategy is to let the data determine the importance of each. The R&D-led EG model can encompass the basic NK model and a likelihood race can assess the empirical relevance of the endogenous growth element of the DSGE model.

5.3 Empirical Concerns

Our third limitation centres on the empirical dimension. Although Bayesian Maximum-Likelihood estimation is a giant step forward from the calibration methods of earlier RBC models there are concerns associated with identification, ability to match VARs, too many shocks required, too little attention to priors and the parametric assumptions surrounding technology and consumer preferences. Identification issues are a very active area of research (see Canova and Sala, 2006; Iskrev, 2008; Ratto, 2008), for example, research that is feeding into toolboxes available in Dynare.

Another critique of Bayesian estimation is the method of pre-filtering the data. As we showed in Chapter 18, models are currently estimated with a two-step approach: data are first filtered and then structural parameters are estimated. This means that the choice of the statistical filter might be arbitrary and can affect the structural estimation. To bridge the models and the raw data an alternative is to implement a hybrid framework where the cyclical fluctuations of the data are seized by the solution of the DSGE model and the non-cyclical fluctuations are captured by a flexible reduced form representation. This approach links the observables to the model counterparts via a flexible specification which does not require that the cyclical component be solely located at business cycle frequencies (see Canova, 2009), and allows the non-cyclical component to take various time series patterns (see Ferroni, 2011 and Cantore et al., 2011). The critique by Chari et al. (2008) is essentially empirical and focuses mainly on ill-conceived shocks in a standard NK model that are not structural or consistent with microeconometric evidence or have plausible estimated standard errors. Many of the other empirical issues are discussed in an excellent recent review, Fernandez-Villaverde (2009).

Not all these empirical concerns can be addressed by better econometrics. Although asset prices make an appearance in the standard DSGE model they still do a terrible job at matching them with data. Our models cannot account for a range of financial observations ranging from the equity premium (Mehra and Prescott, 1985) to the slope of the yield curve (Campbell, 2003). As Smith (2008) points out these are first-order conflicts between data and theory about levels and not the second-order considerations about covariances considered up to now. One response is to compromise theoretical rigour for statistical fit by combining DSGE and VAR (or rather global VAR or GVAR) structures as Pesaran and Smith (2006) and (2011). Another response is to improve the models by exploring different utility functions (or 'exotic preferences') as in Barro (2007).

5.4 Heterogeneous Agents and Aggregation

Finally we turn to what is perhaps the most important issue in micro-founded macroeconomics – that of heterogeneous agents and aggregation. The first generation of DSGE models, the RBC models, stayed within the representative agent paradigm. The current wave of New Keynesian models have made only the slightest deviation from this framework by assuming consumers have access to complete markets. Then although they may differ in their initial tastes, are subject to staggered wage contracts and to idiosyncratic shocks, they still face a common budget constraint and the economy in aggregate does not depend on the distribution of individual qualities. By contrast a recent body of literature is developing macroeconomics from the study of average consumption, output and inputs involving the interaction of these representative households and firms, to the study of the entire distribution of these variables. A recent insightful survey of these developments is provided by Heathcote et al. (2009).

Aggregation certainly matters! For example in a standard RBC model but with indivisible labour, An et al. (2008) show that a representative agent model can only explain the data if one assumes an implausible household utility function. However, progress in embracing heterogeneity has been confined to simple RBC models and still faces technical problems in solving for a rational expectations equilibrium. ACE models (again see LeBaron and Tesfatsion, 2008) certainly tackle aggregation head-on and dispense with the latter problem by ditching rational expectations. But should central banks go down this path for their models? To quote LeBaron and Tesfatsion they (ACE models) 'raise some practical complications for the applied econometrician . . . computational methods such as method of moments might be too computationally costly to undertake . . . Researchers at central banks might never decide to fit giant ACE macro models to data.' Aggregation remains a difficult problem in macroeconomics. Economics cannot copy the success of statistical physics in tackling this problem because, unlike atoms and molecules in physics, economic agents are conscious and calculating!

6 THE 'ROAD AHEAD'?

'All models are wrong, but some are useful.' (Box, 1979).

These notes provide an indication of the 'journey so far' for DSGE macroeconomic modelling. Where does that leave the 'road ahead'? To organize our conclusions it is useful to view a macro-model as being constructed in two stages: first a model of the aggregate economy given a particular model of how expectations are formed by economic agents; and second, the model of expectations formation. We consider these two stages in turn:

6.1 Better Models Given Expectations Formation

There are a number of areas where DSGE models need developing, especially for emerging economies. Our NK model is of a closed economy. A large body of literature now extends the models to open economies; see Galí (2008) and Lim and McNelis (2008). Examples of some work on DSGE models for emerging economies are Batini et al. (2007), (2009) and Gabriel et al. (2010).

Until recently, as with their RBC antecedents, the New Keynesian forms still omitted involuntary unemployment. We are now seeing labour market models with unemployment in both RBC and DSGE models (for the latter, see for example Blanchard and Galí, 2007; Thomas, 2008; and Cantore et al., 2013). Another major lacuna in the NK models has been the absence of a banking sector. The monetary transmission mechanism existed simply through one nominal interest on a riskless bond, 'set' by the central bank. The seminal work on financial frictions by Bernanke et al. (1999) introduced a risk premium paid by firms with an implicit intermediary financial institution. But it is only very recently that a comprehensive banking sector has appeared – see Gertler and Kiyotaki (2010) as a representative example of this development on which our banking model is based. In general, to move toward more heterogeneous models rather than attempting to model the full distribution of agents, it makes sense to first work on more disaggregated models by introducing multi sectors, credit-constrained non-Ricardian (poor) households alongside Ricardian (well-off) households, entrepreneurs, workers and so on.

6.2 Better Models of Expectations Formation

Staying broadly within the rational expectations paradigm a number of refinements are on offer that assume that agents are not able to perfectly observe states that define the economy. The 'rational inattention' literature (Sims, 2005; Luo and Young, 2009; Luo, 2006) fits into this agenda, as does the 'sticky information' approach of Reis (2009). The basic idea is that agents can process information subject to a constraint that places an upper bound on the information flow. Borrowing from information theory (which in turn borrows from statistical physics) the idea is formalized by an upper bound on the decrease in entropy that ensues as agents proceed from a prior to a posterior of a signal. Levine et al. (2007) and (2012b) propose a general framework for introducing information limitations at the point at which agents form expectations.[13]

A more drastic deviation from rational expectations is provided by the statistical rational learning literature already mentioned when discussing rationality. This introduces a specific form of bounded rationality in which utility-maximizing agents make forecasts in each period based on standard econometric techniques such as least squares. In many cases this converges to a rational expectations equilibrium. All these refinements contrast with the drastic alternative offered by the very recent 'Animal Spirits' approach (Akerlof and Shiller, 2009; DeGrauwe, 2009). The latter paper is particularly apposite as it proposes a radical alternative to a standard New Keynesian model with rational expectations. Some agents are optimists and some are pessimists and use ad hoc simple rules to forecast future output. There are shifts from optimism to pessimism that are driven by a form of adaptive expectations which drive *endogenous* cycles and inertia without inertial mechanisms such as habit and indexing. This framework provides an interesting challenge to the existing paradigm which needs to show that, with the refinements set out here, it can also explain the same stylized facts without recourse to these inertial mechanisms.

DSGE models estimated by Bayesian-Maximum-Likelihood methods can be considered as probability models in the sense described by Sims (2007) and be used for risk assessment and policy design. This is true for any one model, but with a range of models on offer it is possible also to design interest rate rules that are simple and robust across the rival models and across the distribution of parameter estimates for each of these rivals as in Levine et al. (2012a) and another forthcoming Dynare facility. After making models better in the sense described in the first part of this section, a possible road ahead is to consider rival models as being distinguished by the model of expectations. This would avoid becoming 'a prisoner of a single system' at least with respect to expectations formation where, as we have seen, there is relatively less consensus on the appropriate modelling strategy.

NOTES

* We acknowledge financial support for the preparation of this chapter from the Foreign & Commonwealth Office as a contribution to the project 'Building Capacity and Consensus for Monetary and Financial Reform' led by the National Institute of Public Finance and Policy, from the EU Framework Programme 7 in support of the project 'MONFISPOL' led by Michel Juillard, CEPREMAP and from the ESRC, project no. RES-000-23-1126.

1. These assertions belong to the art rather than science of DSGE modelling!
2. In particular the 'Easterlin paradox', Easterlin (2003). See also Layard (2006) and Choudhary et al. (2012) for the role of external habit in the explanation of the paradox.
3. For expositional reasons we have confined ourselves to a simple NK model without wage stickiness, capacity utilization and without shocks to preferences, investment and the wage mark-up as in Smets and Wouters (2007). The irrelevance of habit especially does not carry over to a richer model with these features and indeed other labour market and financial frictions.
4. By contrast the standard way of identification is to put $\Omega = I$ and order the variables to make some economic sense.
5. Since we estimated the VAR in levels there is a potential problem of non-stationarity; however, tests on the residuals indicated stationarity. The choice of the lag length maximizes the marginal data density associated with the DSGE-VAR($\hat{\lambda}$).
6. See Levine and Pearlman (2011).
7. In a forthcoming Dynare facility we employ a large distortions approximation to this welfare function as described in Levine et al. (2008a).
8. Optimality from a 'timeless perspective' imposes a different condition at time $t = 0$, but this has no bearing on the stochastic component of policy.

9. See Currie and Levine (1993) and Söderlind (1999).
10. Indeed we find this is usually the case.
11. The current version Dynare 4.2.3 computes a welfare-based Ramsey policy, but only optimized simple rules for ad hoc quadratic loss functions as in (19.13). To make comparisons between the two we therefore confine ourselves to an ad hoc loss function. Discretionary optimal policy is not yet available in Dynare, but will be in future versions, as will welfare-based optimized simple rules and the imposition of a ZLB on the nominal interest rate.
12. I am grateful to Mustapha Doukoure for this summary of the Myerson argument.
13. This is now a Dynare facility.

REFERENCES

Adam, K. and R.M. Billi (2007), 'Discretionary monetary policy and the zero lower bound on nominal interest rates', *Journal of Monetary Economics*, **54**(3), 728–52.

Akerlof, G.A. and R.J. Shiller (2009), *Animal Spirits*, Princeton, NJ: Princeton University Press.

An, S., Y. Chang and S-B. Kim (2008), 'Can a representative-agent model represent a heterogeneous-agent economy?', Working Paper No. 542, University of Rochester.

Annicchiarico, B., A. Pelloni and L. Rossi (2010), 'Endogenous growth, monetary shocks and nominal rigidities', mimeo.

Barro, R.J. (2007), 'Rare disasters, asset prices and welfare costs', NBER Working Paper No. 13690.

Barro, R.J. and D.B. Gordon (1983), 'Rules, discretion, and reputation in a model of monetary policy', *Journal of Monetary Economics*, **12**, 101–20.

Batini, N., P. Levine and J. Pearlman (2007), 'Monetary rules in emerging economics with financial market imperfections', Paper presented to the NBER Conference on International Dimensions of Monetary Policy, S'Agaro, Spain, 11–13 June, 2007 and in J. Gali and M. Gertler (eds), NBER Conference Volume, *International Dimensions of Monetary Policy*.

Batini, N., P. Levine and J. Pearlman (2009), 'Monetary rules and fiscal rules in an emerging small open economy', IMF Working Paper No. 9/22.

Batini, N., A. Justiniano, P. Levine and J. Pearlman (2006), 'Robust inflation-forecast-based rules to shield against indeterminacy', *Journal of Economic Dynamics and Control*, **30**, 1491–526.

Benhabib, J., S. Schmitt-Grohe and M. Uribe (2001), 'Monetary policy and multiple equilibria', *American Economic Review*, **91**(1), 167–86.

Bernanke, B., M. Gertler and S. Gilchrist (1999), 'The financial accelerator in quantitative business cycles', in M. Woodford and J.B. Taylor (eds), *Handbook of Macroeconomics*, vol. 1C, Amsterdam: Elsevier Science.

Blanchard, O. and J. Galí (2007), 'A New Keynesian model with unemployment', Centre for Financial Studies Working Paper No. 2007/08.

Blanchard, O.J. and C.M. Kahn (1980), 'The solution of linear difference models under rational expectations', *Econometrica*, **48**(5), 1305–11.

Box, G.E.P. (1979), 'Robustness in the strategy of scientific model building', in R.L. Launer and G.N. Wilkinson (eds), *Robustness in Statistics*, New York: Academic Press, pp. 210–36.

Calvo, G.A. (1978), 'On the time consistency of optimal policy in a monetary economy', *Econometrica*, **46**, 1411–28.

Campbell, J.Y. (2003), 'Consumption-based asset pricing', in G.M. Constantinides, M. Harris and R.M. Stulz (eds), *Handbook of the Economics of Finance 1*, Amsterdam: Elsevier/North Holland, pp. 803–87.

Canova, F. (2009), 'Bridging raw data to cyclical DSGE models', mimeo, Universitat Pompeu Fabra.

Canova, F. and L. Sala (2006), 'Back to square one: identification issues in DSGE models', ECB Working Paper Series No. 583.

Cantore, C., P. Levine and G. Melina (2013), 'A fiscal simulus and jobless recovery', *Scandinavian Journal of Economics*, forthcoming.

Cantore, C., F. Ferroni, P. Levine and B. Yang (2011), 'CES technology and business cycle fluctuations', Paper presented at the Conference 'Growth and Business Cycles', Durham Business School, 12–13 March, 2011 and the MONFISPOL Conference, 4–5 November, 2010 London Metropolitan University.

Carlstrom, C.T. and T.S. Fuerst (1999), 'Real indeterminacy in monetary models with nominal interest rate distortions', Federal Reserve Bank of Cleveland working paper.

Carlstrom, C.T. and T.S. Fuerst (2000), 'Forward-looking versus backward-looking Taylor rules', Federal Reserve Bank of Cleveland working paper.

Chari, V.V., L.J. Christiano and M. Eichenbaum (1988), 'Expectation traps and discretion', *Journal of Economic Theory*, **81**(2), 462–92.

Chari, V.V., E.R. McGrattan and P.J. Kehoe (2008), 'New Keynesian models: not yet useful for policy analysis', NBER Working Paper No. 14313.
Choudhary, A., P. Levine, P. McAdam and P. Welz (2012), 'The happiness puzzle: analytical aspects of the Easterlin paradox', *Oxford Economic Papers*, **64**(1), 27–42.
Clarida, R., J. Galí and M. Gertler (2000), 'Monetary policy rules and macroeconomic stability: evidence and some theory', *The Quarterly Journal of Economics*, **115**(1), 147–80.
Coenen, G. and V. Wieland (2003), 'The zero-interest rate bound and the role of the exchange rate for monetary policy in Japan', *Journal of Monetary Economics*, **50**, 1071–101.
Cohen, D. and P. Michel (1988), 'How should control theory be used to calculate a time consistent policy', *Review of Economic Studies*, **55**, 263–74.
Comin, D. and M. Gertler (2006), 'Medium-term business cycles', *American Economic Review*, **96**(3), 523–51.
Comin, D., M. Gertler and A.M. Santacreu (2009b), 'Technology innovation and diffusion as sources of output and asset price fluctuations', Harvard Business School Working Paper No. 09-134.
Comin, D., N. Loayza, F. Pasha and L. Serven (2009a), 'Medium term business cycles in developing countries', NBER Working Paper No. 15428.
Currie, D. and P. Levine (1985), 'Optimal feedback rules in an open economy macro-model with rational expectations', *European Economic Review*, **27**, 141–63.
Currie, D. and P. Levine (1987), 'Credibility and time inconsistency in a stochastic world', *Journal of Economics*, **47**(3), 225–52.
Currie, D. and P. Levine (1993), *Rules Reputation and Macroeconomic Policy Coordination*, Cambridge: Cambridge University Press.
DeGrauwe, P. (2009), 'Animal spirits and monetary policy', mimeo, University of Leuven.
Del Negro, M. and F. Schorfheide (2004), 'Priors from general equilibrium models for VARs', *International Economic Review*, **45**, 643–73.
Del Negro, M., F. Schorfheide, F. Smets and R. Wouters (2007), 'On the fit of New Keynesian models', *Journal of Business and Economic Statistics*, **25**(2), 123–62.
Driffill, J. (1982), 'Optimal money and exchange rate polices', *Greek Economic Review*, **4**, 161–83.
Easterlin, R.A. (2003), 'Explaining happiness', *Proceedings of the National Academy of Science of the United States*, **100**(19), 11176–83.
Eggertsson, G. and M. Woodford (2003), 'The zero interest-rate bound and optimal monetary policy', *Brooking Papers on Economic Activity*, **1**, 139–211.
Evans, G.W. and S. Honkapohja (2001), *Learning and Expectations in Macroeconomics*, Princeton, NJ: Princeton University Press.
Fernandez-Villaverde, J. (2009), 'The econometrics of DSGE models', CEPR Discussion Paper No. 7159.
Ferroni, F. (2011), 'Trend agnostic one-step estimation of DSGE models', *The B.E. Journal of Macroeconomics, Advance*, **11**(1).
Gabriel, V., P. Levine, J. Pearlman and B. Yang (2010), 'An estimated model of the Indian economy', University of Surrey Discussion Paper DP 12/10 and forthcoming in Chetan Ghate (ed.), *Handbook of the Indian Economy*, Oxford University Press.
Galí, J. (2008), *Monetary Policy, Inflation and the Business Cycle*, Princeton, NJ: Princeton University Press.
Gertler, M. and N. Kiyotaki (2010), 'Financial intermediation and credit policy in business cycle analysis', mimeo and forthcoming in *Handbook of Macroeconomics*, Elsevier.
Geweke, J. (1999), 'Computational experiments and reality', University of Minnesota and Federal Reserve Bank of Minneapolis.
Heathcote, J., K. Storesletten and G.L. Violante (2009), 'Quantitative macroeconomics with heterogeneous households', NBER Working Paper No. 1468.
Holden, T. (2011), 'Products, patents and productivity persistence', mimeo, University of Oxford.
Iskrev, N. (2008), 'How much do we learn from the estimation of DSGE models? A case study of identification issues in a New Keynesian business cycle model', mimeo, University of Michigan.
Jeffries, H. (1996), *Theory of Probability*, 3rd edn, Oxford: Clarendon Press.
Klein, P. (2000), 'Using the generalized Schur form to solve a multivariate linear rational expectations model', *Journal of Economic Dynamics and Control*, **24**, 405–23.
Kydland, F.E. and E.C. Prescott (1977), 'Rules rather than discretion: the inconsistency of optimal plans', *Journal of Political Economy*, **85**, 473–92.
Layard, R. (2006), 'Happiness and public policy: a challenge to the profession', *Economic Journal*, **116**(510), C24–C33.
LeBaron, B. and L. Tesfatsion (2008), 'Modeling macroeconomics as open-ended dynamic systems of interacting agents', *American Economic Review*, **98**(2), 246–50.
Levine, P. and D. Currie (1985), 'Simple macro-policy rules for the open economy', *Economic Journal*, **95**, 60–70.

Levine, P. and D. Currie (1987), 'The design of feedback rules in linear stochastic rational expectations models', *Journal of Economic Dynamics and Control*, **11**, 1–28.
Levine, P. and J. Pearlman (2011), 'Computation of LQ approximations to optimal policy problems in different information settings under zero lower bound constraints', Dynare Working Papers No. 10, CEPREMAP.
Levine, P., P. McAdam and J. Pearlman (2008b), 'Quantifying and sustaining welfare gains from monetary commitment', *Journal of Monetary Economics*, **55**(7), 1253–76.
Levine, P., J. Pearlman and G. Perendia (2007), 'Estimating DSGE models under partial information', Department of Economics Discussion Papers No. 1607, University of Surrey.
Levine, P., J. Pearlman and R. Pierse (2008a), 'Linear-quadratic approximation, efficiency and target-implementability', *Journal Economic Dynamics and Control*, **32**, 3315–49.
Levine, P., P. McAdam and J. Pearlman (2012a), 'Probability models and robust policy rules', *European Economic Review*, **56**(2), 246–62.
Levine, P., J. Pearlman, G. Perendia and B. Yang (2012b), 'Endogenous persistence in an estimated DSGE model under imperfect information', *Economic Journal*, **122**(565), 1287–1312.
Lim, G.C. and P.D. McNelis (2008), *Computational Macroeconomics for the Open Economy*, Cambridge, MA: MIT Press.
Lucas, R.E. (1987), *Models of Business Cycles*, Oxford: Basil Blackwell.
Luo, Y. (2006), 'Consumption dynamics under information processing', mimeo, University of Hong Kong.
Luo, Y. and E.R. Young (2009), 'Rational inattention and aggregate fluctuations', *The B.E. Journal of Macroeconomics*, **9**(1), Article 14.
Magill, M. (1977), 'A local analysis of capital accumulation under uncertainty', *Journal of Economic Theory*, **15**(2), 211–19.
Mehra, R. and E.C. Prescott (1985), 'The equity premium: a puzzle', *Journal of Monetary Economics*, **15**(2), 145–61.
Miller, M.H. and M. Salmon (1985), 'Dynamic games and the time inconsistency of optimal policy in open economics', *Economic Journal*, **85**, 124–37.
Myerson, R. (1999), 'Nash equilibrium and the history of economic theory', *Journal of Economic Literature*, **37**(3), 1067–82.
Pearlman, J.G., D. Currie and P. Levine (1986), 'Rational expectations models with private information', *Economic Modelling*, **3**(2), 90–105.
Pesaran, M.H. and R.P. Smith (2006), 'Macroeconomic modelling with a global perspective', *Manchester School*, **74**(s1), 24–49.
Pesaran, M.H. and R.P. Smith (2011), 'Beyond the DSGE straitjacket', *Manchester School*, IZA Discussion Paper No. 5661.
Ratto, M. (2008), 'Analyzing DSGE models with global sensitivity analysis', *Computational Economics*, **115**, 115–39.
Reis, R. (2009), 'A sticky information general equilibrium model for policy analysis', NBER Working Paper No. 14732.
Shiller, R.J. (1999), 'Human behavior and the efficiency of the financial system', in J.B Taylor and M. Woodford (eds), *Handbook of Macroeconomics, Volume 1C*, Amsterdam: Elsevier, pp. 1305–40.
Sims, C. (2003), 'Solving linear rational expectations models', *Computational Economics*, **20**(1), 1–20.
Sims, C. (2005), 'Rational inattention: a research agenda', Deutsche Bundesbank Working Paper No. 34/2005.
Sims, C.A. (2007), 'Monetary policy rules', CEPS Working Paper No. 155.
Smets, F. and R. Wouters (2003), 'An estimated stochastic dynamic general equilibrium model of the euro area', *Journal of the European Economic Association*, **1**(5), 1123–75.
Smets, F. and R. Wouters (2007), 'Shocks and frictions in US business cycles: a Bayesian DSGE approach', *American Economic Review*, **97**(3), 586–606.
Smith, R. (2008), 'Real-financial interactions in macro-finance models', mimeo, Birkbeck College, University of London.
Söderlind, P. (1999), 'Solution and estimation of RE macromodels with optimal policy', *European Economic Review*, **43**, 813–23.
Taylor, J.B. (1999), 'A historical analysis of monetary policy rules', in J.B. Taylor (ed.), *Monetary Policy Rules*, Chicago, IL: University of Chicago Press, pp. 319–41.
Thomas, C. (2008), 'Search and matching frictions and optimal policy', *Journal of Monetary Economics*, **55**(5), 936–56.
Vines, D., J. Maciejowski and J. Meade (1983), *Demand Management*, London: Allen and Unwin.
Wang, P. and Y. Wen (2008), 'Volatility, growth and welfare', Federal Reserve Bank of St Louis, Working Paper No. 2006–032C, revised.
Woodford, M. (2003), *Interest and Prices. Foundations of a Theory of Monetary Policy*, Princeton, NJ: Princeton University Press.

APPENDIX

A The Hamiltonian Quadratic Approximation of Welfare

Consider the following general deterministic optimization problem

$$\max \sum_{t=0}^{\infty} \beta^t U(X_{t-1}, W_t) \;\; s.t. \;\; X_t = f(X_{t-1}, W_t) \qquad (19A.1)$$

where X_{t-1} is a vector of state variables and W_{t-1} a vector of instruments.[1] There are given initial and the usual tranversality conditions. For our purposes, we consider this as including models with forward-looking expectations, so that the optimal solution to the latter set-up is the pre-commitment solution. Suppose the solution converges to a steady state X, W as $t \to \infty$ for the states X_t and the policies W_t. Define $x_t = X_t - X$ and $w_t = W_t - W$ as representing the first-order approximation to absolute deviations of states and policies from their steady states.[2]

The Lagrangian for the problem is defined as,

$$\sum_{t=0}^{\infty} \beta^t [U(X_{t-1}, W_t) - \lambda_t^T (X_t - f(X_{t-1}, W_t))] \qquad (19A.2)$$

so that a necessary condition for the solution to (19A.1) is that the Lagrangian is stationary at all $\{X_s\}$, $\{W_s\}$, that is

$$U_W + \lambda_t^T f_W = 0 \quad U_X - \frac{1}{\beta}\lambda_{t-1}^T + \lambda_t^T f_X = 0 \qquad (19A.3)$$

Assume a steady state λ for the Lagrange multipliers exists as well. Now define the Hamiltonian $H_t = U(X_{t-1}, W_t) + \lambda^T f(X_{t-1}, W_t)$. The following is the discrete time version of Magil (1977):

Theorem

If a steady state solution (X, W, λ) to the optimization problem (19A.1) exists, then any perturbation (x_t, w_t) about this steady state can be expressed as the solution to

$$\max \frac{1}{2} \sum_{t=0}^{\infty} \beta^t [x_{t-1} \;\; w_t] \begin{bmatrix} H_{XX} & H_{XW} \\ H_{WX} & H_{WW} \end{bmatrix} \begin{bmatrix} x_{t-1} \\ w_t \end{bmatrix} \;\; s.t. \;\; x_t = f_X x_{t-1} + f_W w_t \qquad (19A.4)$$

where H_{XX}, etc. denote second-order derivatives evaluated at (X, W). This can be directly extended to the case incorporating disturbances.

Thus our general procedure is as follows:

1. Set out the deterministic non-linear problem for the Ramsey problem, to maximize the representative agents' utility subject to non-linear dynamic constraints.
2. Write down the Lagrangian for the problem.
3. Calculate the first-order conditions. We do not require the initial conditions for an optimum since we ultimately only need the steady state of the Ramsey problem.

4. Calculate the steady state of the first-order conditions. The terminal condition implied by this procedure is such that the system converges to this steady state.
5. Calculate a second-order Taylor series approximation, about the steady state, of the Hamiltonian associated with the Lagrangian in (2).
6. Calculate a first-order Taylor series approximation, about the steady state, of the first-order conditions and the original constraints.
7. Use (4) to eliminate the steady-state Lagrangian multipliers in (5). By appropriate elimination both the Hamiltonian and the constraints can be expressed in minimal form as described in Levine and Pearlman (2011). This then gives us the accurate LQ approximation of the original non-linear optimization problem in the form of a minimal linear state-space representation of the constraints and a quadratic form of the utility expressed in terms of the states.

B Dynare-based Software Available for *Handbook* Chapters

Three Dynare model (.mod) files are available on the website: http://surrey.ac.uk/economics/research/groups/centreinternationalmacro/ for reproducing and building on the example in these chapters. They consist of:

- **RBC model** with investment costs
- **NK model** with habit and indexing
- **NK linear model** for estimation and DSGE-VAR

Notes

1. An alternative representation of the problem is $U(X_t, W_t)$ and $E_t[X_{t+1}] = f(X_t, W_t)$ where X_t includes forward-looking non-predetermined variables and $E_t[X_{t+1}] = X_{t+1}$ for the deterministic problem where perfect foresight applies. Whichever one uses, it is easy to switch from one to the other by a simple re-definition. As we demonstrate in Levine et al. (2008b), although the inclusion of forward-looking variables significantly alters the nature of the optimization problem, these changes only affect the boundary conditions and the second-order conditions, but not the steady state of the optimum which is all we require for LQ approximation.
2. Alternatively $x_t = (X_t - X)/X$ and $w_t = (W_t - W)/W$, depending on the nature of the economic variable. Then the theorem follows in a similar way with an appropriate adjustment to the Jacobian matrix.

20 Generalized Method of Moments estimation of DSGE models*

Francisco J. Ruge-Murcia

1 INTRODUCTION

This chapter examines the application of the Generalized Method of Moments (GMM) to the estimation of dynamic stochastic general equilibrium (DSGE) models. The goal is to present the use of GMM in a pedagogical manner and to provide evidence on its small sample properties. The version of GMM where the moment conditions are computed via simulation – that is, the Simulated Method of Moments (SMM) – is examined in this chapter as well.

The use of the method of moments for the estimation of DSGE models is attractive for several reasons. First, it delivers consistent and asymptotically normal parameter estimates under the hypothesis that the model is correctly specified. Of course, other estimators (for example, Maximum Likelihood (ML)) have these properties and, thus, the difference between them is statistical efficiency and computational ease. Second, GMM is relatively fast because the evaluation of the statistical objective function is cheap. Ruge-Murcia (2007) compares the computing time required by different methods used for the estimation of DSGE models and finds that GMM is the fastest, followed, in that order, by ML, SMM and indirect inference. Third, the method of moments is more robust than ML to the stochastic singularity of DSGE models. DSGE models are stochastically singular because they generate implications about a large number of observable variables using as input a relatively small number of structural shocks. Thus, the model predicts that certain linear combinations of observable variables should hold without noise. Needless to say, this prediction is not satisfied by actual economic data. For the purpose of estimation, stochastic singularity affects ML more severely than moment-based methods because the former requires linearly independent variables while the latter requires linearly independent moments. The latter is a weaker restriction because one can find independent moments that involve more variables than those which are linearly independent. Finally, more generally, the method of moments is more robust than ML to misspecification. See Ruge-Murcia (2007) for a detailed discussion of these issues and supporting Monte Carlo evidence.

The Generalized Method of Moments was first introduced in the literature by Lars Hansen (Hansen, 1982) and earlier applications (for example, Hansen and Singleton, 1982) involved the estimation and testing of Euler equations derived from utility maximization. Regarding the estimation of DSGE models by GMM, one approach consists in estimating parameters by applying GMM to a subset of the model equations (for example, the first-order conditions). For an example of this strategy, see Braun (1994). This limited-information approach does not involve the solution of the DSGE model and, consequently, it does not exploit its cross-equation restrictions.

The GMM approach studied here is closely related to the minimum distance estimator in Malinvaud (1970). The GMM estimator is the value that minimizes the weighted distance between the empirical moments of the data and theoretical moments predicted by the model. This approach requires solving the model in each iteration of the minimization routine, which may be computationally demanding but also leads to efficiency improvements because it exploits the cross-equation restrictions. Earlier applications of this approach include Christiano and Eichenbaum (1992) and Burnside et al. (1993). More recent contributions include, among many others, Gorodnichenko and Ng (2010), who examine the implications of different detrending methods for the GMM estimation of DSGE models; Ruge-Murcia (2010), who studies the estimation of non-linear DGSE models by the method of moments; and Christiano et al. (2011), who study the use of DSGE models of monetary policy analysis. A nice presentation of GMM, including historical antecedents, a large bibliography and a discussion of practical issues, can be found in Hall (2005).

This chapter is organized as follows. Section 2 presents the DSGE model that will be used through this chapter. Section 3 describes the application of GMM and SMM to the estimation of DSGE models. Section 4 studies the small-sample properties of these estimators using Monte Carlo analysis. The Monte Carlo experiments complement the ones in my earlier work (Ruge-Murcia, 2007), where the focus was on the role of moment conditions involving different combinations of observable variables. Instead, the experiments here study the role of different weighting matrices and sample sizes. Finally, section 5 concludes. Codes and replication material are made available separately on the *Handbook*'s web page.

2 A DSGE MODEL

In order to illustrate the application of the Generalized Method of Moments (GMM) to the estimation of DSGE models, it is convenient to focus on a specific model. I focus on the neoclassical growth model because it is simple, widely known, and constitutes the core of more sophisticated DSGE models used by researchers in the field.

Consider an economy populated by identical agents with instantaneous utility function

$$u(c_t, n_t) = \frac{(c_t)^{1-\gamma} - 1}{1 - \gamma} + b(1 - n_t), \tag{20.1}$$

where c_t is consumption, n_t is hours worked, γ and b are positive preference parameters, and the time endowment is normalized to 1. Under this specification, the disutility of labor is linear (see Hansen, 1985), and consumption preferences are isoelastic and characterized by constant relative risk aversion. The population size is constant and normalized to 1.

The only perishable good in this economy is produced using the technology

$$f(k_t, n_t, z_t) = z_t k_t^{\alpha} n_t^{1-\alpha}, \tag{20.2}$$

where $\alpha \in (0, 1)$ is a parameter, k_t is the capital stock, and z_t is an exogenous productivity shock. Technology is homogeneous of degree 1, and so it features constant returns to scale. The productivity shock follows the process

$$\ln(z_t) = (1 - \rho)\ln(z) + \rho\ln(z_{t-1}) + e_t, \tag{20.3}$$

where $\rho \in (-1, 1)$, $\ln(z)$ is the unconditional mean of $\ln(z_t)$, and e_t is an innovation assumed to be identically and independently distributed (*i.i.d.*) with mean zero and variance equal to σ^2. In what follows, I set $z = 1$ and, thus, $\ln(z) = 0$. Since z is just a scaling factor, this normalization entails no loss of generality.

Economic decisions are made by a central planner who maximizes the expected lifetime utility of agents,

$$E_s \sum_{t=s}^{\infty} \beta^{t-s} u(c_t, n_t), \tag{20.4}$$

where $\beta \in (0, 1)$ is the discount factor. The central planner takes as given the initial capital stock and is subject in every period to the resource constraint

$$c_t + k_{t+1} - (1 - \delta)k_t = z_t k_t^{\alpha} n_t^{1-\alpha}, \tag{20.5}$$

where $\delta \in (0, 1)$ is the depreciation rate. Notice that this specification implicitly assumes that there exists a technology to costlessly convert one unit of perishable consumption good into one unit of productive capital and vice versa.

In addition to the transversality condition, the first-order necessary conditions associated with the optimal choice of consumption and labor supply are

$$(c_t)^{-\gamma} = \beta E_t((c_{t+1})^{-\gamma}(1 + \alpha z_{t+1} k_{t+1}^{\alpha-1} n_{t+1}^{1-\alpha} - \delta)), \tag{20.6}$$

$$b/(c_t)^{-\gamma} = (1 - \alpha) z_t k_t^{\alpha} n_t^{-\alpha}. \tag{20.7}$$

Equation (20.6) is the Euler equation for consumption whereby the central planner is indifferent between allocating the marginal unit of good to current consumption or saving it in the form of capital. Equation (20.7) equates the marginal rate of substitution between leisure and consumption with the marginal productivity of labor.

2.1 A Special Case

It will be useful below to consider the version of the growth model due to Brock and Mirman (1972). This version is interesting because it has an exact, closed-form solution and, consequently, its exact unconditional moments can be derived analytically.

The Brock–Mirman model corresponds to the case where $b = 0$ (leisure is not an argument of the utility function), $\gamma = 1$ (consumption preferences are logarithmic), $\delta = 1$ (depreciation is complete), and the productive technology is

$$f(k_t, z_t) = z_t k_t^{\alpha}, \tag{20.8}$$

with all other notation as previously defined. The resource constraint is then

$$c_t + k_{t+1} = z_t k_t^{\alpha}, \tag{20.9}$$

and the Euler equation for consumption becomes

$$1/c_t = \beta E_t((1/c_{t+1})(\alpha z_{t+1} k_{t+1}^{\alpha-1})). \tag{20.10}$$

2.2 Solution

In the case of the Brock–Mirman model, it is easy to verify that the dynamic system of non-linear first-difference equations (20.9) and (20.10) is solved by the decision rules

$$c_t = c(k_t, z_t) = (1 - \alpha\beta) z_t k_t^{\alpha}, \tag{20.11}$$

$$k_{t+1} = k(k_t, z_t) = (\alpha\beta) z_t k_t^{\alpha}. \tag{20.12}$$

This solution is exact (that is, no approximation is involved) and holds regardless of the time-series properties of the productivity shock. Since $z_t k_t^{\alpha}$ is total output, this model implies that agents optimally consume a fixed proportion of their current income, just as in the celebrated Solow model (see Solow, 1956). These decision rules are non-linear in the level of the variables but by taking logs in both sides of (20.11) and (20.12), one obtains the linear relationships

$$\begin{bmatrix} \ln(c_t) \\ \ln(k_{t+1}) \end{bmatrix} = \begin{bmatrix} \ln(1 - \alpha\beta) \\ \ln(\alpha\beta) \end{bmatrix} + \begin{bmatrix} \alpha & 1 \\ \alpha & 1 \end{bmatrix} \begin{bmatrix} \ln(k_t) \\ \ln(z_t) \end{bmatrix}.$$

These log-linear decision rules will be used below to derive exact expressions for the second-order moments of consumption and investment in the Brock–Mirman economy.

More generally, however, the solution of DSGE models requires some degree of approximation. See Taylor and Uhlig (1990) and the papers therein for a survey of different approximate solution methods. In this chapter, I use a perturbation method that approximates the policy rules around the deterministic steady state with a first-order polynomial in the state variables and characterizes the local dynamics. For the neoclassical growth model, this strategy delivers the (approximate) solution

$$\begin{bmatrix} \ln(c_t) \\ \ln(n_t) \\ \ln(k_{t+1}) \end{bmatrix} = \begin{bmatrix} \ln(c) \\ \ln(n) \\ \ln(k) \end{bmatrix} + \begin{bmatrix} \phi_{ck} & \phi_{cz} \\ \phi_{nk} & \phi_{nz} \\ \phi_{kk} & \phi_{kz} \end{bmatrix} \begin{bmatrix} \ln(k_t) - \ln(k) \\ \ln(z_t) \end{bmatrix},$$

where c, n and k respectively denote the levels of consumption, hours worked and capital in the deterministic steady state, the ϕ coefficients are non-linear function of the structural parameters of the model, and I have used the normalization $\ln(z) = 0$. These log-linear decision rules will be used below to derive expressions for the second-order moments of the model variables in percentage deviation from their steady state values.

3 THE GENERALIZED METHOD OF MOMENTS

Consider a DSGE model with unknown parameters $\theta \in \Theta \subset \Re^q$, where θ is a $q \times 1$ vector and Θ is a compact set. For example, in the case of the growth model $\theta = \{\beta, \gamma, b, \alpha, \rho, \sigma, \delta\}$, while in the case of the Brock–Mirman model $\theta = \{\beta, \alpha, \rho, \sigma\}$. Denote by $\{x_t\}$ a sample of T observations of data available to estimate the model. The data series in $\{x_t\}$ are assumed to be stationary and ergodic with these properties possibly the result of a prior transformation of the raw data (for example, by means of a detrending procedure.)

The key input in the GMM estimation of DSGE models is the set of p moment conditions

$$\mathbf{M}(\theta) = \left((1/T) \sum_{t=1}^{T} \mathbf{m}(x_t) - E(\mathbf{m}(\theta)) \right), \tag{20.13}$$

which are collected here in a $p \times 1$ vector. The first term in the right-hand side of (20.13), $(1/T) \sum_{t=1}^{T} \mathbf{m}(x_t)$, is statistics computed using the time average of some function of the data, while the second term, $E(\mathbf{m}(\theta))$, is the theoretical counterpart of the same statistics predicted by the economic model. The GMM estimator is

$$\hat{\theta} = \underset{\theta \in \Theta}{\text{argmin}}\, \mathbf{M}(\theta)' \mathbf{W} \mathbf{M}(\theta), \tag{20.14}$$

with $\mathbf{W}$ a $p \times p$ positive-definite weighting matrix. In words, the GMM estimator is the value of θ that makes the (weighted) distance between the empirical moments of the data and theoretical moments predicted by the model as small as possible, and, hence, the moment conditions in (20.13) as close to zero as possible. This formulation of GMM is closely related to the minimum distance estimator in Malinvaud (1970).

A necessary, but not sufficient, condition for identification is $p \geq q$ (that is, at least as many moment conditions as the number of parameters). Sufficient conditions for global identification are difficult to verify in practice, but local identification requires that

$$rank \left\{ \frac{\partial E(\mathbf{m}(\theta))}{\partial \theta} \right\} = q, \tag{20.15}$$

where (with some abuse of the notation) θ is the point in the parameter space Θ where the rank condition is evaluated. For an extensive discussion of identification issues in DSGE models, see Canova and Sala (2009), Iskrev (2010), and Komunjer and Ng (2011).

Under the regularity conditions in Hansen (1982), the GMM estimator is consistent and asymptotically normal:

$$\sqrt{T}(\hat{\theta} - \theta_0) \to N(0, (\mathbf{D}'\mathbf{W}\mathbf{D})^{-1}\mathbf{D}'\mathbf{W}\mathbf{S}\mathbf{W}\mathbf{D}(\mathbf{D}'\mathbf{W}\mathbf{D})^{-1}), \tag{20.16}$$

where $\mathbf{D} = \partial E(\mathbf{m}(\theta))/\partial \theta$ is a $p \times q$ matrix of full column rank and

$$\mathbf{S} = \sum_{s=-\infty}^{\infty} (\mathbf{m}(x_t) - E(\mathbf{m}(x_t)))(\mathbf{m}(x_{t-s}) - E(\mathbf{m}(x_{t-s})))'. \tag{20.17}$$

In the special case where $\mathbf{W} = \mathbf{S}^{-1}$, the GMM estimator has the smallest possible variance among all possible positive-definite weighting matrices and the asymptotic distribution simplifies to

$$\sqrt{T}(\hat{\theta} - \theta_0) \rightarrow N(0, (\mathbf{D}'\mathbf{S}^{-1}\mathbf{D})^{-1}). \tag{20.18}$$

Moreover, when the model is overidentified (meaning that $p > q$), a general specification test of the model can be easily constructed using the chi-square statistic proposed by Hansen (1982):

$$T(\mathbf{M}(\hat{\theta})'\mathbf{W}\mathbf{M}(\hat{\theta})) \rightarrow \chi^2(p - q),$$

where $\mathbf{M}(\hat{\theta})'\mathbf{W}\mathbf{M}(\hat{\theta})$ is the value of the objective function at the optimum.

3.1 An Illustration

In order to help develop the reader's intuition, this section illustrates the general structure of GMM in the case of the Brock–Mirman model. Let us assume that the macroeconomist has at his or her disposal data series on log consumption and the log of the end-of-period capital stock (that is, $\ln(k_{t+1})$). Thus $x_t = \{\ln(c_t)\ \ln(k_{t+1})\}$. Define

$$\mathbf{m}(x_t) = [\ln(c_t)\ \ln(k_{t+1})\ (\ln(c_t))^2\ (\ln(k_{t+1}))^2\ \ln(c_t)\ln(c_{t-1})\ \ln(k_{t+1})\ln(k_t)]'$$

Then, the first part of $\mathbf{M}(\theta)$ in equation (20.13) is

$$(1/T)\sum_{t=1}^{T}\mathbf{m}(x_t) = (1/T)\sum_{t=1}^{T}[\ln(c_t)\ \ln(k_{t+1})\ (\ln(c_t))^2\ (\ln(k_{t+1}))^2\ \ln(c_t)\ln(c_{t-1})\ \ln(k_{t+1})\ln(k_t)]'.$$

It is clear that the elements of this vector are just the sample mean, the variance, and the autocovariance of both consumption and capital. Note that latter two moments (that is, the variances and autocovariances) are defined around zero, rather than around the mean. This involves no loss of generality and one could specify instead the moments around the mean. However, for the purpose of this chapter, the notation is a bit cleaner if one specifies the moments around zero. Finally, recall that these moments are computed using the actual data series.

The second part of $\mathbf{M}(\theta)$ contains the unconditional moments of consumption and capital predicted by the model. These moments depend on the structural parameters $\theta = \{\beta, \alpha, \rho, \sigma\}$ and are derived in the Appendix from the decision rules that (exactly) solve the model and using the time series process of the productivity shock.

Then, the moment conditions for this model are

$$\mathbf{M}(\theta) = (1/T)\sum_{t=1}^{T}\begin{bmatrix} \ln(c_t) \\ \ln(k_{t+1}) \\ (\ln(c_t))^2 \\ (\ln(k_{t+1}))^2 \\ \ln(c_t)\ln(c_{t-1}) \\ \ln(k_{t+1})\ln(k_t) \end{bmatrix} - \begin{bmatrix} \ln(1-\alpha\beta) + \alpha\ln(\alpha\beta)/(1-\alpha) \\ \ln(\alpha\beta)/(1-\alpha) \\ \sigma^2(1+\alpha\rho)/\lambda + (\ln(1-\alpha\beta) + \alpha\ln(\alpha\beta)/(1-\alpha))^2 \\ \sigma^2(1+\alpha\rho)/\lambda + (\ln(\alpha\beta)/(1-\alpha))^2 \\ \sigma^2(\alpha+\rho)/\lambda + (\ln(1-\alpha\beta) + \alpha\ln(\alpha\beta)/(1-\alpha))^2 \\ \sigma^2(\alpha+\rho)/\lambda + (\ln(\alpha\beta)/(1-\alpha))^2 \end{bmatrix},$$

where $\lambda = (1-\rho^2)(1-\alpha^2)(1-\alpha\rho)$ and the elements in the vector furthest to the right correspond to those in equations (20A.6), (20A.5), (20A.9), (20A.8), (20A.10) and (20A.11) in the Appendix. Estimates of $\theta = \{\beta, \alpha, \rho, \sigma\}$ may obtained by the numerical minimization of the objective function (20.14).

3.2 Using Simulations to Compute the Moments

In the case of linearized DSGE models, it is straightforward to compute the theoretical moments using the decision rules that solve the model. However, this computation requires matrix inversions that can be time consuming if the model has a large number of variables. In such situations, it may be more efficient to compute the theoretical moments via simulation. That is, instead of using $E(\mathbf{m}(\theta))$ in (20.13) and, thus, in the objective function (20.14), one would use the simulation-based estimate $(1/\tau T)\sum_{\iota=1}^{\tau T}\mathbf{m}(x_\iota(\theta))$ where $\tau \geq 1$ is an integer, τT is the length of the simulated sample, and $\mathbf{m}(x_\iota(\theta))$ is the $p \times 1$ vector of variables analogous to $\mathbf{m}(x_t)$ but based on data simulated from the model using parameter values θ. In what follows, I denote this artificial sample by $x_\iota(\theta)$.

Under the assumption that $\{x_\iota(\theta)\}$ is geometrically ergodic and by the Law of large numbers (see Duffie and Singleton, 1993, p. 939)

$$(1/\tau T)\sum_{\iota=1}^{\tau T}\mathbf{m}(x_\iota(\theta)) \rightarrow E(\mathbf{m}(x_\iota(\theta)) \text{ almost surely, as } \tau T \rightarrow \infty.$$

Moreover, under the assumption that the model is correctly specified $E(\mathbf{m}(x_\iota(\theta_0)) = E(\mathbf{m}(x_t))$. These assumptions and results underpin the substitution of $E(\mathbf{m}(\theta))$ by $(1/\tau T)\sum_{\iota=1}^{\tau T}\mathbf{m}(x_\iota(\theta))$ proposed above. Then, the moment conditions become

$$\mathbf{M}(\theta) = \left((1/T)\sum_{t=1}^{T}\mathbf{m}(x_t) - (1/\tau T)\sum_{\iota=1}^{\tau T}\mathbf{m}(x_\iota(\theta))\right),$$

and the simulated method moments (SMM) estimator is

$$\hat{\theta} = \underset{\theta\in\Theta}{\operatorname{argmin}}\, \mathbf{M}(\theta)'\mathbf{W}\mathbf{M}(\theta), \tag{20.19}$$

with $\mathbf{W}$ a positive-definite weighting matrix of dimension $p \times p$. Intuitively, the SMM estimator is the value of θ that minimizes the (weighted) distance between the moments implied by the model and those computed from the observed data, where the former are obtained using artificial data simulated from the model. The application of SMM to the estimation of time series models was first examined by Lee and Ingram (1991) and Duffie and Singleton (1993).

Under the regularity conditions spelled out in Duffie and Singleton (1993), $\hat{\theta}$ is consistent for θ_0 and has asymptotic distribution

$$\sqrt{T}(\hat{\theta} - \theta_0) \rightarrow N(0, (1 + 1/\tau)(\mathbf{J}'\mathbf{W}\mathbf{J})^{-1}\mathbf{J}'\mathbf{W}\mathbf{S}\mathbf{W}\mathbf{J}(\mathbf{J}'\mathbf{W}\mathbf{J})^{-1}), \qquad (20.20)$$

where $\mathbf{J} = E(\partial \mathbf{m}(x_t(\theta))/\partial\theta)$ is a finite matrix of full column rank and dimension $p \times q$. In the special case where $\mathbf{W} = \mathbf{S}^{-1}$, the asymptotic distribution simplifies to

$$\sqrt{T}(\hat{\theta} - \theta_0) \rightarrow N(0, (1 + 1/\tau)(\mathbf{J}'\mathbf{W}\mathbf{J})^{-1}). \qquad (20.21)$$

As before, when p is strictly larger than q – that is, when the model is over-identified – it is possible to construct a general specification test using the chi-square statistic proposed in Lee and Ingram (1991, p. 204) and based on Hansen (1982). The test statistic is easiest to compute in the case where $\mathbf{W} = \mathbf{S}^{-1}$. Then,

$$T(1 + 1/\tau)(\mathbf{M}(\hat{\theta})'\mathbf{W}\mathbf{M}(\hat{\theta})) \rightarrow \chi^2(p - q), \qquad (20.22)$$

where $\mathbf{M}(\hat{\theta})'\mathbf{W}\mathbf{M}(\hat{\theta})$ is the value of the objective function at the optimum.

It is interesting to compare the asymptotic distributions of the GMM and SMM estimators in (20.16) and (20.20), respectively. The distributions differ primarily by the term $(1 + 1/\tau)$ in the SMM distribution, which captures the effect of simulation uncertainty on our confidence regarding the parameter estimates. Since $(1 + 1/\tau) > 1$, SMM asymptotic standard errors are generally larger than those obtained under GMM, meaning that SMM is less statistically efficient than GMM. However, in practice, this difference in efficiency can be controlled by the researcher through the choice of τ. To see this, notice that $(1 + 1/\tau)$ decreases asymptotically towards 1 as τ increases so that, for example, when $\tau = 5$, 10 and 20, the asymptotic SMM standard errors are only 1.10, 1.05 and 1.025 times larger than those implied by GMM.

4 SMALL-SAMPLE PROPERTIES

The asymptotic distributions in the previous section hold, by definition, in the theoretical case where the sample size increases without bound. On the other hand, macroeconomists have at their disposal only relatively short time series to estimate DSGE models. It is, therefore, important to ask whether asymptotic distributions constitute a good approximation in the latter, more realistic, case. To that effect, I carry out a limited number of Monte Carlo experiments. These Monte Carlo experiments complement the ones reported in my earlier work (Ruge-Murcia, 2007), where the focus was on the role of moment conditions involving different combinations of observable variables. Instead, the experiments here study the role of different weighting matrices and sample sizes.

4.1 Monte Carlo Design

The neoclassical growth model has seven structural parameters. The parameters are the discount factor (β), the consumption curvature (γ), the weight of leisure in the utility function (b), the autoregressive coefficient of the productivity shock (ρ), the standard deviation of the productivity innovation (σ), the elasticity parameter in the production function (α), and the depreciation rate (δ). In order to reduce the computational burden in the Monte Carlo experiments, I focus on four parameters so that $\theta = \{\beta, \rho, \sigma, \gamma\}$ and fix α to 1/3, δ to 0.02, and b to a value such that the time spent working in steady state is one third of the time endowment. The value $\alpha = 1/3$ is consistent with data from the National Income and Product Accounts (NIPA), which implies that the share of capital in total income is approximately one third. The value for δ and the strategy for fixing b are standard in the literature.

The artificial data in all experiments is generated using $\beta = 0.96$ and I consider two possible values for each of the parameters ρ, σ, and γ. The two values are $\rho = 0.5$ and 0.9; $\sigma = 0.05$ and 0.1; and $\gamma = 1$ and 5. In all experiments, the moments used to estimate the model are the variances of consumption and hours, their covariance, and their first-order autocovariances. That is, I use five moments to estimate four parameters, and so the model is over-identified with degrees of freedom equal to 1.

I study the small-sample properties of GMM using two possible sample sizes, $T = 200$ and $T = 600$. Loosely speaking the former corresponds to, say, fifty years of quarterly observations, while the latter corresponds to fifty years of monthly observations. In order to study the role of the weighting matrix, I consider two possible weighting matrices. First, the optimal matrix $\mathbf{W} = \mathbf{S}^{-1}$, that is the inverse of the matrix with the long-run variance of the moments defined in (20.17). This weighting matrix is optimal in the sense that it delivers the smallest possible asymptotic variance among the class of positive-definite matrices. Second, the identity matrix $\mathbf{W} = \mathbf{I}$. By construction, the identity matrix gives equal weight to all moments in the objective function, which becomes simply (the square of) the Euclidean distance between the empirical and theoretical moments. One goal of this analysis is to examine the efficiency loss associated with using weighting matrices which are not asymptotically optimal but may have practical advantages in actual applications. For GMM, the combination of all possible parameter values, weighting matrices and sample sizes delivers a total of 32 configurations.

I also use this design to study the small-sample properties of SMM. In all SMM experiments I use the optimal matrix $\mathbf{W} = \mathbf{S}^{-1}$ and the value $\tau = 5$, meaning that the simulated sample is five times longer than the original sample. In preliminary work, I also performed experiments using $\tau = 10$ and 20 but conclusions are basically the same to those reported here. For SMM, the combination of all possible parameter values and sample sizes delivers a total of 16 configurations.

Finally, the matrix $\mathbf{S}$ is computed using the Newey–West estimator with a Bartlett kernel and bandwidth given by the integer of $4(T/100)^{2/9}$, where T is the sample size. Hence in the case where $T = 200$, the bandwidth is 4 while in the case where $T = 600$, the bandwidth is 5.

Results in each experiment are based on 500 replications. That is, for each configuration, I generate artificial series and estimate the parameters 500 times. Various statistics are then computed using these 500 estimates (for example, the mean, average asymptotic standard error, and so on). In all experiments the DGP is the linearized version of the neoclassical growth model.

4.2 Results

Results for GMM are reported in Tables 20.1 to 20.4. In all tables, Mean is the average of the estimated parameter values and A.S.E. is the average asymptotic standard error where averages are taken over the 500 replications in each experiment. Median and S.D. are the median and standard deviation of the empirical parameter distribution (that is, the distribution of the 500 observations of the parameters). Size is the proportion of times that the null hypothesis that the parameter takes its true value is rejected using a t-test with nominal size of 5 per cent. In other words, Size is the empirical size of this t-test. S.E. is the standard error of this empirical size and is computed as the standard deviation of a Bernoulli variable. Finally, O.I. is the empirical size of the chi-square test of the overidentification restrictions.

These tables support four conclusions. First, GMM estimates are numerically close to the true values used to generate the data: notice that in all tables, the mean and median of the estimated parameters are very close to the true values. This result is driven by the consistency of the GMM estimator, but it is useful to know that GMM yields accurate parameter estimates for the relatively small samples and regardless of the weighting matrix employed.

Second, asymptotic standard errors tend to overstate the actual variability of the parameter estimates: notice that in all tables, the A.S.E. is usually larger than the standard deviation of the estimates. This result suggests a discrepancy between the asymptotic and the small-sample distributions. Ruge-Murcia (2007, 2010) reports similar findings for other methods applied to both linear and non-linear DSGE models. Thus, this discrepancy is not specific to either the Generalized Method of Moments or to linear models. Figure 20.1 plots the empirical distribution of the parameters for experiments where $\beta = 0.96$, $\rho = 0.90$, $\sigma = 0.1$, and $\gamma = 5$ and using the optimal weighting matrix. (This configuration illustrates general results obtained in the Monte Carlo and so the same conclusions are drawn from plots based on other experiments.) The top and bottom rows respectively correspond to the sample sizes $T = 200$ and $T = 600$. These plots show an additional dimension in which the small-sample distributions differ from the asymptotic ones: while the latter are Normal and, hence, their skewness is zero, the former are skewed. Notice also that, as one would expect, the distributions are more tightly concentrated around the true value in the larger sample.

Third, the empirical size of the *t*-test of the null hypothesis that the parameter takes its true value is statistically different from the nominal size of 5 per cent: notice that in all tables, the size is quantitatively far from 0.05 and that the 95 per cent confidence interval around it seldom contains the nominal size. In particular, notice that since the empirical size is usually smaller than the nominal size, the *t*-test tends to under-reject the null hypothesis.

Finally, note in Tables 20.1 and 20.2 that the empirical size of the chi-square test of the over-identification restrictions is frequently below its nominal size of 5 per cent. The result that the chi-square test easily fails to detect a misspecified model is well known in the literature (see, for example, Newey, 1985) and has been previously reported by

Table 20.1 Small-sample properties: optimal weighting matrix T = *200*

Mean A.S.E. Size	Median S.D. S.E.	Mean A.S.E. Size	Median S.D. S.E.	Mean A.S.E. Size	Median S.D. S.E.	Mean A.S.E. Size	Median S.D. S.E.	O.I. S.E.
$\beta = 0.96$		$\rho = 0.50$		$\sigma = 0.10$		$\gamma = 1$		
0.9600	0.9600	0.4892	0.4933	0.0987	0.0986	1.0008	0.9993	
0.0054	0.0040	0.0546	0.0685	0.0047	0.0056	0.0971	0.0548	0.0320
0.0440	0.0092	0.1140	0.0142	0.1060	0.0138	0.0080	0.0040	0.0079
$\beta = 0.96$		$\rho = 0.90$		$\sigma = 0.10$		$\gamma = 1$		
0.9594	0.9600	0.8922	0.9000	0.0978	0.0974	0.9926	0.9949	
0.0127	0.0047	0.0222	0.0274	0.0089	0.0090	0.0593	0.0229	0.0320
0.0160	0.0056	0.1000	0.0134	0.0860	0.0125	0.0060	0.0035	0.0079
$\beta = 0.96$		$\rho = 0.50$		$\sigma = 0.05$		$\gamma = 1$		
0.9604	0.9600	0.4883	0.4884	0.0492	0.0493	1.0052	1.0006	
0.0054	0.0048	0.0543	0.0659	0.0023	0.0028	0.0972	0.0640	0.0220
0.0820	0.0123	0.1160	0.0143	0.1340	0.0152	0.0100	0.0044	0.0066
$\beta = 0.96$		$\rho = 0.90$		$\sigma = 0.05$		$\gamma = 1$		
0.9599	0.9600	0.8920	0.9000	0.0489	0.0489	0.9911	0.9935	
0.0128	0.0024	0.0226	0.0265	0.0045	0.0045	0.0596	0.0211	0.0340
0.0040	0.0028	0.0880	0.0127	0.0800	0.0121	0.0000	0.0000	0.0081
$\beta = 0.96$		$\rho = 0.50$		$\sigma = 0.10$		$\gamma = 5$		
0.9600	0.9600	0.4885	0.4909	0.0987	0.0991	5.0047	5.0051	
0.0051	0.0039	0.0574	0.0586	0.0045	0.0058	0.4851	0.2336	0.0400
0.0480	0.0096	0.0600	0.0106	0.1520	0.0161	0.0000	0.0000	0.0088
$\beta = 0.96$		$\rho = 0.90$		$\sigma = 0.10$		$\gamma = 5$		
0.9601	0.9602	0.8956	0.8958	0.0975	0.0979	4.9560	4.9719	
0.0230	0.0007	0.0440	0.0153	0.0155	0.0131	0.4506	0.1445	0.0180
0.0000	0.0000	0.0000	0.0000	0.0820	0.0123	0.0000	0.0000	0.0059
$\beta = 0.96$		$\rho = 0.50$		$\sigma = 0.05$		$\gamma = 5$		
0.9600	0.9600	0.4895	0.4933	0.0494	0.0495	5.0014	5.0030	
0.0051	0.0039	0.0571	0.0599	0.0023	0.0032	0.4856	0.2313	0.0500
0.0520	0.0099	0.0640	0.0109	0.1940	0.0177	0.0040	0.0028	0.0097
$\beta = 0.96$		$\rho = 0.90$		$\sigma = 0.05$		$\gamma = 5$		
0.9601	0.9601	0.8962	0.8965	0.0491	0.0494	4.9662	4.9805	
0.0232	0.0007	0.0442	0.0152	0.0078	0.0067	0.4521	0.1406	0.0220
0.0000	0.0000	0.0000	0.0000	0.0580	0.0105	0.0000	0.0000	0.0066

Notes: Mean is the average of the estimated parameter values; A.S.E. is the median asymptotic standard error; Median and S.D. are, respectively, the median and standard deviation of the empirical parameter distribution; Size is the empirical size of the *t*-test; O.I. is the empirical size of the chi-square test of the overidentification restrictions; and S.E. is the standard error of the empirical test size.

Table 20.2 Small-sample properties: optimal weighting matrix T = *600*

Mean A.S.E. Size	Median S.D. S.E.	Mean A.S.E. Size	Median S.D. S.E.	Mean A.S.E. Size	Median S.D. S.E.	Mean A.S.E. Size	Median S.D. S.E.	O.I. S.E.
$\beta = 0.96$		$\rho = 0.50$		$\sigma = 0.10$		$\gamma = 1$		
0.9601	0.9600	0.4933	0.4952	0.0995	0.0996	1.0015	1.0003	
0.0032	0.0012	0.0325	0.0356	0.0028	0.0032	0.0569	0.0175	0.0840
0.0240	0.0068	0.0680	0.0113	0.1120	0.0141	0.0080	0.0040	0.0124
$\beta = 0.96$		$\rho = 0.90$		$\sigma = 0.10$		$\gamma = 1$		
0.9599	0.9600	0.8978	0.9000	0.0996	0.0994	0.9994	0.9989	
0.0076	0.0013	0.0127	0.0144	0.0052	0.0055	0.0350	0.0104	0.0580
0.0020	0.0020	0.0800	0.0121	0.0640	0.0109	0.0000	0.0000	0.0105
$\beta = 0.96$		$\rho = 0.50$		$\sigma = 0.05$		$\gamma = 1$		
0.9601	0.9600	0.4960	0.4999	0.0498	0.0498	1.0008	1.0006	
0.0032	0.0013	0.0325	0.0369	0.0014	0.0016	0.0573	0.0182	0.0780
0.0220	0.0066	0.0800	0.0121	0.1180	0.0144	0.0120	0.0049	0.0120
$\beta = 0.96$		$\rho = 0.90$		$\sigma = 0.05$		$\gamma = 1$		
0.9600	0.9600	0.8967	0.9000	0.0495	0.0495	0.9980	0.9982	
0.0077	0.0005	0.0128	0.0143	0.0026	0.0026	0.0352	0.0105	0.0920
0.0000	0.0000	0.0980	0.0133	0.0700	0.0114	0.0000	0.0000	0.0129
$\beta = 0.96$		$\rho = 0.50$		$\sigma = 0.10$		$\gamma = 5$		
0.9600	0.9600	0.4956	0.4948	0.0995	0.0994	4.9996	5.0010	
0.0030	0.0009	0.0336	0.0297	0.0027	0.0035	0.2811	0.0749	0.0740
0.0160	0.0056	0.0280	0.0074	0.1240	0.0147	0.0000	0.0000	0.0117
$\beta = 0.96$		$\rho = 0.90$		$\sigma = 0.10$		$\gamma = 5$		
0.9600	0.9600	0.8983	0.8999	0.0989	0.0987	4.9859	4.9939	
0.0144	0.0004	0.0274	0.0088	0.0097	0.0078	0.2806	0.0793	0.0060
0.0000	0.0000	0.0000	0.0000	0.0440	0.0092	0.0000	0.0000	0.0035
$\beta = 0.96$		$\rho = 0.50$		$\sigma = 0.05$		$\gamma = 5$		
0.9600	0.9600	0.4955	0.4958	0.0497	0.0498	5.0013	5.0000	
0.0030	0.0010	0.0333	0.0301	0.0014	0.0018	0.2807	0.0800	0.0800
0.0180	0.0059	0.0360	0.0083	0.1300	0.0150	0.0000	0.0000	0.0121
$\beta = 0.96$		$\rho = 0.90$		$\sigma = 0.05$		$\gamma = 5$		
0.9600	0.9600	0.8993	0.9000	0.0498	0.0499	4.9909	4.9985	
0.0144	0.0004	0.0273	0.0089	0.0049	0.0039	0.2787	0.0745	0.0040
0.0000	0.0000	0.0000	0.0000	0.0340	0.0081	0.0000	0.0000	0.0028

Notes: Mean is the average of the estimated parameter values; A.S.E. is the median asymptotic standard error; Median and S.D. are, respectively, the median and standard deviation of the empirical parameter distribution; Size is the empirical size of the *t*-test; O.I. is the empirical size of the chi-square test of the overidentification restrictions; and S.E. is the standard error of the empirical test size.

Table 20.3 Small-sample properties: identity weighting matrix T = *200*

Mean A.S.E. Size	Median S.D. S.E.	Mean A.S.E. Size	Median S.D. S.E.	Mean A.S.E. Size	Median S.D. S.E.	Mean A.S.E. Size	Median S.D. S.E.
$\beta = 0.96$		$\rho = 0.50$		$\sigma = 0.10$		$\gamma = 1$	
0.9640	0.9600	0.4879	0.4897	0.0974	0.0971	0.9283	0.9860
0.0262	0.0177	0.0708	0.0641	0.0175	0.0122	0.5123	0.2038
0.0100	0.0044	0.0680	0.0113	0.0100	0.0044	0.0000	0.0000
$\beta = 0.96$		$\rho = 0.90$		$\sigma = 0.10$		$\gamma = 1$	
0.9616	0.9607	0.8785	0.8962	0.0945	0.0964	0.9267	0.9911
0.0138	0.0142	0.0259	0.0710	0.0126	0.0180	0.1147	0.2352
0.0640	0.0109	0.1920	0.0176	0.1000	0.0134	0.0640	0.0109
$\beta = 0.96$		$\rho = 0.50$		$\sigma = 0.05$		$\gamma = 1$	
0.9597	0.9600	0.4972	0.4980	0.0501	0.0502	1.0393	1.0356
0.0193	0.0039	0.0563	0.0622	0.0071	0.0041	0.3238	0.2069
0.0040	0.0028	0.0800	0.0121	0.0040	0.0028	0.0080	0.0040
$\beta = 0.96$		$\rho = 0.90$		$\sigma = 0.05$		$\gamma = 1$	
0.9605	0.9603	0.8763	0.8943	0.0482	0.0485	0.9358	0.9926
0.0142	0.0034	0.0340	0.0775	0.0068	0.0086	0.1358	0.2031
0.0080	0.0040	0.1460	0.0158	0.0980	0.0133	0.0360	0.0083
$\beta = 0.96$		$\rho = 0.50$		$\sigma = 0.10$		$\gamma = 5$	
0.9601	0.9600	0.4944	0.4980	0.0996	0.0991	6.0963	4.9990
0.0227	0.0046	0.0752	0.0592	0.0161	0.0072	21.2870	8.1660
0.0020	0.0020	0.0420	0.0090	0.0120	0.0049	0.0000	0.0000
$\beta = 0.96$		$\rho = 0.90$		$\sigma = 0.10$		$\gamma = 5$	
0.9602	0.9600	0.9005	0.9002	0.0961	0.0970	5.0734	5.0218
0.0538	0.0011	0.0915	0.0154	0.0915	0.0186	0.6003	0.3384
0.0000	0.0000	0.0000	0.0000	0.0000	0.0000	0.0000	0.0000
$\beta = 0.96$		$\rho = 0.50$		$\sigma = 0.05$		$\gamma = 5$	
0.9600	0.9600	0.4947	0.5000	0.0500	0.0498	5.0003	5.0000
0.0178	0.0000	0.0635	0.0580	0.0064	0.0032	0.8836	0.0099
0.0000	0.0000	0.0400	0.0088	0.0000	0.0000	0.0000	0.0000
$\beta = 0.96$		$\rho = 0.90$		$\sigma = 0.05$		$\gamma = 5$	
0.9599	0.9600	0.9011	0.9001	0.0483	0.0477	5.0246	5.0002
0.0518	0.0006	0.0915	0.0051	0.0198	0.0103	0.5777	0.1771
0.0000	0.0000	0.0000	0.0000	0.0000	0.0000	0.0000	0.0000

Notes: Mean is the average of the estimated parameter values; A.S.E. is the median asymptotic standard error; Median and S.D. are, respectively, the median and standard deviation of the empirical parameter distribution; Size is the empirical size of the *t*-test; O.I. is the empirical size of the chi-square test of the overidentification restrictions; and S.E. is the standard error of the empirical test size.

Table 20.4 Small-sample properties: identity weighting matrix T = *600*

Mean	Median	Mean	Median	Mean	Median	Mean	Median
A.S.E.	S.D.	A.S.E.	S.D.	A.S.E.	S.D.	A.S.E.	S.D.
Size	S.E.	Size	S.E.	Size	S.E.	Size	S.E.
$\beta = 0.96$		$\rho = 0.50$		$\sigma = 0.10$		$\gamma = 1$	
0.9607	0.9600	0.4949	0.4966	0.0993	0.0992	0.9824	0.9968
0.0117	0.0101	0.0335	0.0377	0.0085	0.0070	0.1976	0.1107
0.0180	0.0059	0.0900	0.0128	0.0100	0.0044	0.0000	0.0000
$\beta = 0.96$		$\rho = 0.90$		$\sigma = 0.10$		$\gamma = 1$	
0.9605	0.9602	0.8959	0.9000	0.0985	0.0989	0.9861	0.9972
0.0083	0.0082	0.0131	0.0350	0.0078	0.0087	0.0725	0.0877
0.0640	0.0109	0.1200	0.0145	0.0500	0.0097	0.0080	0.0040
$\beta = 0.96$		$\rho = 0.50$		$\sigma = 0.05$		$\gamma = 1$	
0.9600	0.9600	0.4967	0.4965	0.0499	0.0498	1.0068	1.0034
0.0114	0.0000	0.0329	0.0359	0.0042	0.0021	0.1876	0.1153
0.0000	0.0000	0.0820	0.0123	0.0000	0.0000	0.0020	0.0020
$\beta = 0.96$		$\rho = 0.90$		$\sigma = 0.05$		$\gamma = 1$	
0.9601	0.9601	0.8935	0.8972	0.0494	0.0495	0.9852	0.9953
0.0084	0.0011	0.0140	0.0299	0.0039	0.0043	0.0744	0.0742
0.0000	0.0000	0.1380	0.0154	0.0560	0.0103	0.0040	0.0028
$\beta = 0.96$		$\rho = 0.50$		$\sigma = 0.10$		$\gamma = 5$	
0.9600	0.9600	0.4959	0.4976	0.0996	0.0994	5.0075	4.9994
0.0106	0.0001	0.0366	0.0328	0.0078	0.0035	0.5235	0.1792
0.0000	0.0000	0.0360	0.0083	0.0000	0.0000	0.0060	0.0035
$\beta = 0.96$		$\rho = 0.90$		$\sigma = 0.10$		$\gamma = 5$	
0.9601	0.9600	0.8994	0.9001	0.0990	0.0987	4.9978	5.0000
0.0290	0.0005	0.0511	0.0093	0.0237	0.0098	0.3362	0.0829
0.0000	0.0000	0.0000	0.0000	0.0020	0.0020	0.0000	0.0000
$\beta = 0.96$		$\rho = 0.50$		$\sigma = 0.05$		$\gamma = 5$	
0.9600	0.9600	0.4971	0.5000	0.0500	0.0500	4.9998	5.0000
0.0106	0.0000	0.0363	0.0319	0.0039	0.0018	0.5220	0.0053
0.0000	0.0000	0.0300	0.0076	0.0000	0.0000	0.0000	0.0000
$\beta = 0.96$		$\rho = 0.90$		$\sigma = 0.05$		$\gamma = 5$	
0.9600	0.9600	0.9002	0.9000	0.0500	0.0499	4.9917	5.0000
0.0289	0.0001	0.0512	0.0015	0.0117	0.0064	0.3328	0.0603
0.0000	0.0000	0.0000	0.0000	0.0000	0.0000	0.0000	0.0000

Notes: Mean is the average of the estimated parameter values; A.S.E. is the median asymptotic standard error; Median and S.D. are, respectively, the median and standard deviation of the empirical parameter distribution; Size is the empirical size of the *t*-test; O.I. is the empirical size of the chi-square test of the overidentification restrictions; and S.E. is the standard error of the empirical test size.

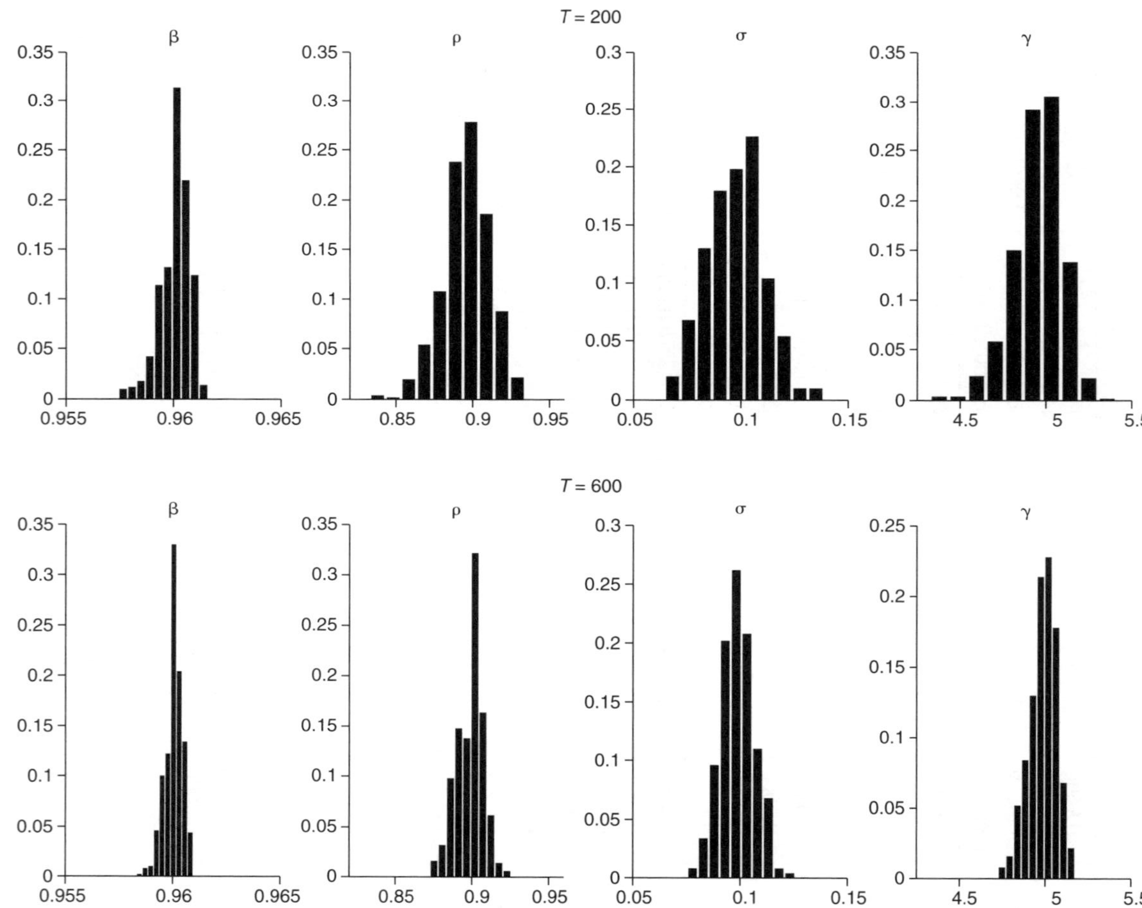

Figure 20.1 Empirical distributions

Ruge-Murcia (2007) for the case of DSGE models. The discrepancy between the asymptotic and the sample-distribution of the test statistics can be seen in Figure 20.2, which shows the empirical distribution of the *t*- and chi-square test statistics for the first experiment in Table 20.1.

A possible strategy to construct accurate small-sample critical values and confidence intervals is to use bootstrap methods. Hall and Horowitz (1996) present theoretical results and some Monte Carlo evidence for the application of the bootstrap to tests based on GMM estimators. One possible concern regarding the use of the bootstrap is the numerically-intensive nature of this method. However, among the estimation methods available to estimate DSGE models, GMM is the fastest (see Ruge-Murcia, 2007, p. 2633) and so it is probably the most promising avenue for both estimation and accurate small-sample inference. Alternatively, Racine and MacKinnon (2004) propose a bootstrap of the critical value of the *t*-test that is accurate even for a small number of simulations and, hence, it is very attractive in set-ups where simulation is expensive.

Finally, comparing asymptotic standard errors across different weighting matrices, notice that those obtained under $\mathbf{W} = \mathbf{I}$ are larger than those under $\mathbf{W} = \mathbf{S}^{-1}$. This result, of course, was expected because the latter weighting matrix is the optimal one. The point is, however, that the quantitative difference between standard errors is moderate. Thus, the efficiency loss of using weighting matrices other than the optimal may not be so large as to overcome other practical considerations. For example, Cochrane (2001, p. 215) argues that in certain circumstances a researcher may want to use a weighting matrix that pays more attention to economically, rather than statistically, important moments.

Results for SMM are reported in Tables 20.5 and 20.6. By comparing Table 20.5 and 20.1 (and Tables 20.6 and 20.2), it is easy to see that the results for SMM are very similar to those for GMM. The main is difference is that, as discussed in section 3.2, asymptotic standard errors tend to be larger for former case as result of simulation uncertainty. Since (1) the loss of statistical efficiency is relatively small for reasonable values of τ, and (2) computing the moments via simulation may be more computationally efficient in the case of models with a large number of variables, it follows that this 'simulated' version of GMM may be an attractive method for such cases.

5 CONCLUSIONS

This chapter examines the application of the methods of moments to the estimation of the DSGE models. In particular, this chapter explains GMM and SMM in a pedagogical manner, illustrates their use to estimate macro models, and examines their small-sample properties using a limited set of Monte Carlo experiments. Results show that GMM and SMM deliver accurate parameter estimates, even for the relatively small samples and regardless of the weighting matrix used. On the other hand, there are discrepancies between the small-sample and asymptotic distributions of the estimates which may be important for statistical inference. For example, the empirical size of the t-test of the null hypothesis that a parameter takes its true value is frequently different from the nominal size. However, it is important to point out that, as reported by Ruge-Murcia (2007),

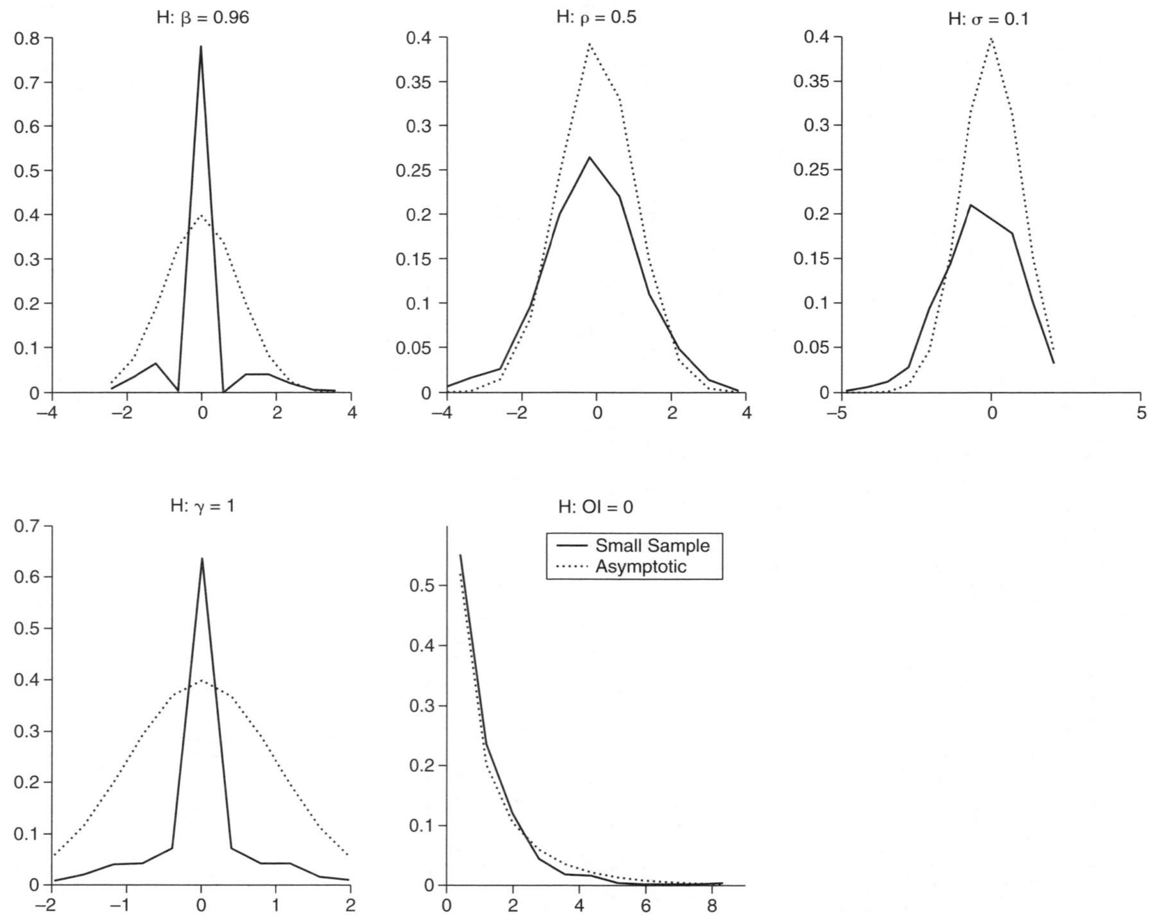

Figure 20.2 Distribution of test statistics

Table 20.5 Small-sample properties: computing the moments using simulation T = *200*

Mean A.S.E. Size	Median S.D. S.E.	Mean A.S.E. Size	Median S.D. S.E.	Mean A.S.E. Size	Median S.D. S.E.	Mean A.S.E. Size	Median S.D. S.E.	 O.I. S.E.
$\beta = 0.96$		$\rho = 0.50$		$\sigma = 0.10$		$\gamma = 1$		
0.9583	0.9600	0.4870	0.4923	0.1004	0.1003	0.9774	0.9867	
0.0054	0.0050	0.0602	0.0649	0.0052	0.0058	0.1091	0.0714	0.0240
0.0400	0.0088	0.0760	0.0119	0.0740	0.0117	0.0020	0.0020	0.0068
$\beta = 0.96$		$\rho = 0.90$		$\sigma = 0.10$		$\gamma = 1$		
0.9564	0.9595	0.8924	0.9000	0.1015	0.1008	0.9891	0.9943	
0.0149	0.0117	0.0259	0.0373	0.0100	0.0094	0.0688	0.0340	0.0100
0.0260	0.0071	0.1320	0.0151	0.0440	0.0092	0.0100	0.0044	0.0044
$\beta = 0.96$		$\rho = 0.50$		$\sigma = 0.05$		$\gamma = 1$		
0.9582	0.9600	0.4813	0.4833	0.0504	0.0502	0.9760	0.9817	
0.0054	0.0052	0.0604	0.0639	0.0026	0.0028	0.1087	0.0757	0.0200
0.0560	0.0103	0.0660	0.0111	0.0660	0.0111	0.0080	0.0040	0.0063
$\beta = 0.96$		$\rho = 0.90$		$\sigma = 0.05$		$\gamma = 1$		
0.9577	0.9597	0.8963	0.9000	0.0507	0.0506	0.9937	0.9969	
0.0147	0.0104	0.0254	0.0309	0.0049	0.0047	0.0691	0.0276	0.0000
0.0340	0.0081	0.0920	0.0129	0.0460	0.0094	0.0000	0.0000	0.0000
$\beta = 0.96$		$\rho = 0.50$		$\sigma = 0.10$		$\gamma = 5$		
0.9585	0.9599	0.4858	0.4881	0.1004	0.1003	4.9297	4.9444	
0.0052	0.0046	0.0628	0.0580	0.0050	0.0058	0.5450	0.2712	0.0600
0.0540	0.0101	0.0440	0.0092	0.0960	0.0132	0.0000	0.0000	0.0106
$\beta = 0.96$		$\rho = 0.90$		$\sigma = 0.10$		$\gamma = 5$		
0.9594	0.9598	0.9017	0.9031	0.1019	0.1008	5.0173	5.0278	
0.0257	0.0050	0.0469	0.0196	0.0159	0.0137	0.5129	0.1617	0.0140
0.0020	0.0020	0.0100	0.0044	0.0520	0.0099	0.0000	0.0000	0.0053
$\beta = 0.96$		$\rho = 0.50$		$\sigma = 0.05$		$\gamma = 5$		
0.9585	0.9599	0.4836	0.4833	0.0502	0.0503	4.9279	4.9485	
0.0051	0.0046	0.0631	0.0615	0.0025	0.0029	0.5445	0.2692	0.0420
0.0440	0.0092	0.0480	0.0096	0.1040	0.0137	0.0000	0.0000	0.0090
$\beta = 0.96$		$\rho = 0.90$		$\sigma = 0.05$		$\gamma = 5$		
0.9593	0.9598	0.9002	0.9024	0.0508	0.0504	4.9845	5.0166	
0.0254	0.0038	0.0469	0.0188	0.0079	0.0069	0.5005	0.1579	0.0180
0.0040	0.0028	0.0100	0.0044	0.0620	0.0108	0.0060	0.0035	0.0059

Notes: Mean is the average of the estimated parameter values; A.S.E. is the median asymptotic standard error; Median and S.D. are, respectively, the median and standard deviation of the empirical parameter distribution; Size is the empirical size of the *t*-test; O.I. is the empirical size of the chi-square test of the overidentification restrictions; and S.E. is the standard error of the empirical test size.

Table 20.6 Small-sample properties: computing the moments using simulation T= *600*

Mean	Median	Mean	Median	Mean	Median	Mean	Median	
A.S.E.	S.D.	A.S.E.	S.D.	A.S.E.	S.D.	A.S.E.	S.D.	O.I.
Size	S.E.	Size	S.E.	Size	S.E.	Size	S.E.	S.E.
$\beta = 0.96$		$\rho = 0.50$		$\sigma = 0.10$		$\gamma = 1$		
0.9609	0.9600	0.5045	0.5080	0.1003	0.1002	1.0125	1.0022	
0.0035	0.0031	0.0352	0.0351	0.0030	0.0031	0.0611	0.0412	0.0320
0.0440	0.0092	0.0540	0.0101	0.0620	0.0108	0.0140	0.0053	0.0079
$\beta = 0.96$		$\rho = 0.90$		$\sigma = 0.10$		$\gamma = 1$		
0.9609	0.9600	0.5045	0.5080	0.1003	0.1002	1.0125	1.0022	
0.0035	0.0031	0.0352	0.0351	0.0030	0.0031	0.0611	0.0412	0.0320
0.0440	0.0092	0.0540	0.0101	0.0620	0.0108	0.0140	0.0053	0.0079
$\beta = 0.96$		$\rho = 0.50$		$\sigma = 0.05$		$\gamma = 1$		
0.9606	0.9600	0.4999	0.5000	0.0502	0.0502	1.0086	1.0017	
0.0035	0.0029	0.0354	0.0346	0.0015	0.0016	0.0613	0.0386	0.0200
0.0260	0.0071	0.0480	0.0096	0.0840	0.0124	0.0040	0.0028	0.0063
$\beta = 0.96$		$\rho = 0.90$		$\sigma = 0.05$		$\gamma = 1$		
0.9587	0.9600	0.8963	0.9000	0.0502	0.0503	0.9964	0.9978	
0.0079	0.0053	0.0140	0.0167	0.0027	0.0026	0.0379	0.0113	0.0060
0.0320	0.0079	0.1000	0.0134	0.0480	0.0096	0.0000	0.0000	0.0035
$\beta = 0.96$		$\rho = 0.50$		$\sigma = 0.10$		$\gamma = 5$		
0.9607	0.9600	0.5023	0.5016	0.1003	0.1003	5.0375	5.0150	
0.0033	0.0027	0.0364	0.0317	0.0030	0.0035	0.3042	0.1506	0.0780
0.0220	0.0066	0.0280	0.0074	0.1000	0.0134	0.0000	0.0000	0.0120
$\beta = 0.96$		$\rho = 0.90$		$\sigma = 0.10$		$\gamma = 5$		
0.9600	0.9600	0.8992	0.8999	0.0999	0.0996	4.9937	5.0003	
0.0154	0.0004	0.0304	0.0091	0.0103	0.0078	0.3163	0.0783	0.0180
0.0000	0.0000	0.0000	0.0000	0.0220	0.0066	0.0000	0.0000	0.0059
$\beta = 0.96$		$\rho = 0.50$		$\sigma = 0.05$		$\gamma = 5$		
0.9605	0.9600	0.5027	0.5044	0.0503	0.0503	5.0319	5.0089	
0.0033	0.0026	0.0364	0.0324	0.0015	0.0018	0.3046	0.1451	0.0460
0.0220	0.0066	0.0280	0.0074	0.1020	0.0135	0.0000	0.0000	0.0094
$\beta = 0.96$		$\rho = 0.90$		$\sigma = 0.05$		$\gamma = 5$		
0.9600	0.9600	0.8994	0.8999	0.0498	0.0496	5.0036	5.0077	
0.0154	0.0004	0.0303	0.0086	0.0052	0.0039	0.3157	0.0807	0.0040
0.0000	0.0000	0.0000	0.0000	0.0100	0.0044	0.0000	0.0000	0.0028

Notes: Mean is the average of the estimated parameter values; A.S.E. is the median asymptotic standard error; Median and S.D. are, respectively, the median and standard deviation of the empirical parameter distribution; Size is the empirical size of the *t*-test; O.I. is the empirical size of the chi-square test of the overidentification restrictions; and S.E. is the standard error of the empirical test size.

these discrepancies are not specific to the method of moments and also affect maximum likelihood and indirect inference. A possible strategy to address this issue may be to use bootstrap methods to construct accurate small-sample critical values and confidence intervals (on this, see Hall and Horowitz, 1996).

NOTE

* The financial support of the Social Sciences and Humanities Research Council of Canada is gratefully acknowledged.

REFERENCES

Braun, R.A. (1994), 'Tax disturbances and real economic activity in the postwar United States', *Journal of Monetary Economics*, **33**, 441–62.
Brock, W. and L. Mirman (1972), 'Optimal economic growth and uncertainty: the discounted case', *Journal of Economic Theory*, **4**, 479–513.
Burnside, C., M. Eichenbaum and S. Rebelo (1993), 'Labor hoarding and the business cycle', *Journal of Political Economy*, **101**, 245–73.
Canova, F. and L. Sala (2009), 'Back to square one: identification issues in DSGE models', *Journal of Monetary Economics*, **56**, 431–49.
Cochrane, J.H. (2001), *Asset Pricing*, Princeton, NJ: Princeton University Press.
Christiano, L. and M. Eichenbaum (1992), 'Current real-business cycle theories and aggregate labor-market fluctuations', *American Economic Review*, **82**, 430–50.
Christiano, L., M. Trabant and K. Walentin (2011), 'DSGE models for monetary policy analysis', in B. Friedman and M. Woodford (eds), *Handbook of Monetary Economics*, Amsterdam: North-Holland.
Duffie, D. and K.J. Singleton (1993), 'Simulated moments estimation of Markov models of asset prices', *Econometrica*, **61**, 929–52.
Gorodnichenko, Y. and S. Ng (2010), 'Estimation of DSGE models when the data are persistent', *Journal of Monetary Economics*, **57**, 325–40.
Hall, A.R. (2005), *Generalized Method of Moments*, Oxford: Oxford University Press.
Hall, P. and J.L. Horowitz (1996), 'Bootstrap critical values for test based on generalized method of moments estimators', *Econometrica*, **64**, 891–916.
Hansen, G.D. (1985), 'Indivisible labor and the business cycle', *Journal of Monetary Economics*, **16**, 309–27.
Hansen, L.P. (1982), 'Large sample properties of generalized method of moments estimators', *Econometrica*, **50**, 1929–54.
Hansen, L.P. and K.J. Singleton (1982), 'Generalized instrumental variables estimation of nonlinear rational expectations models', *Econometrica*, **50**, 1269–86.
Iskrev, N. (2010), 'Local identification in DSGE models', *Journal of Monetary Economics*, **57**, 189–202.
Komunjer, I. and S. Ng (2011), 'Dynamic identification of DSGE models', *Econometrica*, **79**(6), 1995–2032.
Lee, B-S. and B.F. Ingram (1991), 'Simulation estimation of time-series models', *Journal of Econometrics*, **47**, 195–205.
Malinvaud, E. (1970), *Statistical Methods of Econometrics*, Amsterdam: North-Holland.
Newey, W.K. (1985), 'Generalized method of moments specification testing', *Journal of Econometrics*, **29**, 229–56.
Racine, J. and J.G. MacKinnon (2004), 'Simulation-based test that can use any number of simulations', Queen's University, mimeo.
Ruge-Murcia, F.J. (2007), 'Methods to estimate dynamic stochastic general equilibrium models', *Journal of Economic Dynamics and Control*, **31**, 1599–2636.
Ruge-Murcia, F.J. (2010), 'Estimating nonlinear DSGE models by the simulated method of moments', CIREQ Working Paper No. 19-2010.
Solow, R.M. (1956), 'A contribution to the theory of economic growth', *Quarterly Journal of Economics*, **70**, 65–94.
Taylor, J. and H. Uhlig (1990), 'Solving nonlinear stochastic growth models: a comparison of alternative solution methods', *Journal of Business and Economic Statistics*, **8**, 1–17.

APPENDIX: MOMENTS OF THE BROCK–MIRMAN MODEL

The unconditional moments of the Brock–Mirman model are derived from

$$\ln(c_t) = \ln(1 - \alpha\beta) + \alpha\ln(k_t) + \ln(z_t), \tag{20A.1}$$

$$\ln(k_{t+1}) = \ln(\alpha\beta) + \alpha\ln(k_t) + \ln(z_t), \tag{20A.2}$$

$$\ln(z_t) = \rho\ln(z_{t-1}) + e_t, \tag{20A.3}$$

where (20A.1) and (20A.2) are the decision rules and (20A.3) is the process of the productivity shock. Recall that $\ln(z) = 0$ and, thus, $E(\ln(z_t)) = 0$ and

$$E((\ln(z_t))^2) = \sigma^2/(1 - \rho^2). \tag{20A.4}$$

Taking unconditional expectations in both sides of (20A.2) delivers

$$E(\ln(k_{t+1})) = \ln(\alpha\beta) + \alpha E(\ln(k_t)).$$

Then

$$E(\ln(k_{t+1})) = \ln(\alpha\beta)/(1 - \alpha). \tag{20A.5}$$

Taking unconditional expectations in both sides of (20A.1) and using (20A.5) deliver

$$E(\ln(c_t)) = \ln(1 - \alpha\beta) + \alpha\ln(\alpha\beta)/(1 - \alpha). \tag{20A.6}$$

For next derivations, it will be useful to compute

$$\begin{aligned} E(\ln(z_t)\ln(k_t)) &= E((\rho\ln(z_{t-1}) + e_t)(\ln(\alpha\beta) + \alpha\ln(k_{t-1}) + \ln(z_{t-1}))), \\ &= \rho E((\ln(z_{t-1}))^2) + \alpha\rho E(\ln(z_{t-1})\ln(k_{t-1})) \end{aligned}$$

where I have used the fact that e_t is an innovation with mean zero to obtain the second equality. Then

$$E(\ln(z_t)\ln(k_t)) = \rho\sigma^2/(1 - \alpha\rho)(1 - \rho^2). \tag{20A.7}$$

Consider now

$$\begin{aligned} E((\ln(k_{t+1}))^2) &= E((\ln(\alpha\beta) + \alpha\ln(k_t) + \ln(z_t))^2), \\ &= (\ln(\alpha\beta))^2 + \alpha^2 E((\ln(k_t))^2) + E((\ln(z_t))^2) + 2\alpha\ln(\alpha\beta)E(\ln(k_t)) \\ &\quad + 2\alpha E(\ln(z_t)\ln(k_t)). \end{aligned}$$

Substituting (20A.4), (20A.5) and (20A.7), and simplifying deliver

$$E((\ln(k_{t+1}))^2) = \sigma^2(1 + \alpha\rho)/\lambda + (\ln(\alpha\beta)/(1 - \alpha))^2. \quad (20A.8)$$

where $\lambda = (1 - \rho^2)(1 - \alpha^2)(1 - \alpha\rho)$. Similarly,

$$\begin{aligned} E((\ln(c_t))^2) &= E((\ln(1 - \alpha\beta) + \alpha\ln(k_t) + \ln(z_t))^2), \\ &= (\ln(1 - \alpha\beta))^2 + \alpha^2 E((\ln(k_t))^2) + E((\ln(z_t))^2) + 2\alpha\ln(1 - \alpha\beta)E(\ln(k_t)) \\ &\quad + 2\alpha E(\ln(z_t)\ln(k_t)), \end{aligned}$$

Substituting (20A.4), (20A.5), (20A.7) and (20A.8), and simplifying deliver

$$E((\ln(c_t))^2) = \sigma^2(1 + \alpha\rho)/\lambda + (\ln(1 - \alpha\beta) + \alpha\ln(\alpha\beta)/(1 - \alpha))^2. \quad (20A.9)$$

Consider now

$$\begin{aligned} E(\ln(k_{t+1})\ln(k_t)) &= E((\ln(\alpha\beta) + \alpha\ln(k_t) + \ln(z_t))\ln(k_t)) \\ &= \ln(\alpha\beta)E(k_t) + \alpha E((\ln(k_t))^2) + E(\ln(z_t)\ln(k_t)). \end{aligned}$$

Substituting (20A.5), (20A.7) and (20A.8), and simplifying deliver

$$E(\ln(k_{t+1})\ln(k_t)) = \sigma^2(\alpha + \rho)/\lambda + (\ln(\alpha\beta)/(1 - \alpha))^2. \quad (20A.10)$$

Finally, consider

$$\begin{aligned} E(\ln(c_t)\ln(c_{t-1})) &= E((\ln(1 - \alpha\beta) + \alpha\ln(k_t) + \ln(z_t))(\ln(1 - \alpha\beta) \\ &\quad + \alpha\ln(k_{t-1}) + \ln(z_{t-1}))) \\ &= E((\ln(1 - \alpha\beta) + \alpha\ln(k_t) + \rho\ln(z_{t-1}) + e_t)(\ln(1 - \alpha\beta) + \alpha\ln(k_{t-1}) + \ln(z_{t-1}))) \\ &= \ln(1 - \alpha\beta)(\ln(1 - \alpha\beta) + \alpha\ln(\alpha\beta)) + \alpha((1 + \alpha)\ln(1 - \alpha\beta) \\ &\quad + \alpha\ln(\alpha\beta))E(\ln(k_{t-1})) + (\alpha + \rho)E((\ln(z_t))^2) + \alpha(2\alpha + \rho)E(\ln(z_{t-1})\ln(k_{t-1})) \\ &\quad + \alpha^3 E((\ln(k_{t-1}))^2) \end{aligned}$$

Substituting (20A.4), (20A.5), (20A.7) and (20A.8), and simplifying deliver

$$E(\ln(c_t)\ln(c_{t-1})) = \sigma^2(\alpha + \rho)/\lambda + (\ln(1 - \alpha\beta) + \alpha\ln(\alpha\beta)/(1 - \alpha))^2. \quad (20A.11)$$

21 Bayesian estimation of DSGE models*

Pablo A. Guerrón-Quintana and James M. Nason

1 INTRODUCTION

Macroeconomists have made substantial investments in Bayesian time series during the last 30 years. One reason is that Bayesian methods afford researchers the chance to estimate and evaluate a wide variety of macro models that frequentist econometrics often find challenging. Bayesian vector autoregressions (BVARs) represent an early return on this research project manifested, for example, by Doan et al. (1984). They show that BVARs are useful forecasting tools.[1] More recent work focuses on developing Bayesian methods capable of estimating time-varying parameter (TVP) VARs, associated with Cogley and Sargent (2005) and Primiceri (2005), and Markov-switching (MS) VARs initiated by Sims and Zha (2006).[2] The complexity of TVP- and MS-VARs underlines the efforts macroeconomists have put into developing useful Bayesian time series tools.[3]

Bayesian times series methods are also attractive for macroeconomists studying dynamic stochastic general equilibrium (DSGE) models. Although DSGE models can be estimated using classical optimization methods, macroeconomists often prefer to use Bayesian tools for these tasks. One reason is that advances in Bayesian theory are providing an expanding array of tools that researchers can employ to estimate and evaluate DSGE models. The popularity of the Bayesian approach is also explained by the increasing computational power available to estimate and evaluate medium- to large-scale DSGE models using Markov chain Monte Carlo (MCMC) simulators. These DSGE models can pose identification problems for frequentist estimators that no amount of data or computing power can overcome.

Macroeconomists are also drawn to the estimation and evaluation framework Bayesians have created because DSGE models are often seen as abstractions of actual economies. A frequentist econometrician might say that DSGE models are misspecified versions of the true model. This is not consistent with the beliefs often held about DSGE models. These beliefs are animated by the well known mantra that 'all models are false'. Since Bayesians eschew the existence of a true model, employing Bayesian methods to study DSGE models dovetails with the views held by many macroeconomists.

This chapter presents an overview of Bayesian time series methods that have been developed to estimate and evaluate linearized DSGE models.[4] We aim to bring the reader to the point where his or her priors and DSGE model can, subsequent to linearization, meet the data to be estimated and evaluated using Bayesian methods. The reader may wonder why this chapter puts aside non-linear estimation of DSGE models. Since these methods represent the frontier, which is being pushed out at an extraordinary rate, a review of Bayesian non-linear estimation of DSGE models waits for more consensus about the merits of the different approaches.[5]

We describe procedures for estimating a medium-scale New Keynesian (NK) DSGE model in this chapter. The NKDSGE model is a descendant of those analyzed by Smets and Wouters (2003) and Christiano et al. (2005). As those authors do, we estimate a linearized approximation of the NKDSGE. The linearization is grounded in the stochastically detrended optimality and equilibrium conditions because the growth rate of the technology shock is stationary. These optimality and equilibrium conditions yield a solution that is cast in state space form, which is the starting point for the Kalman filter. Since the Kalman filter generates predictions and updates of the state vector of the linearized NKDSGE model, we have a platform for computing its likelihood. This likelihood is used by Bayesian MCMC simulators to produce posterior distributions of NKDSGE model parameters given actual data and prior beliefs about these parameters. Posterior distributions represent confidence in an NKDSGE model conditional on the evidence provided by its likelihood. Marginal likelihoods are used to evaluate which member of a suite of NKDSGE models is most favored by the data.

A brief history of DSGE model estimation is presented in the next section. Our purpose is to give a framework for understanding the interaction between the need to connect macro theory to current data and the development of tools to achieve that task. Section 3 outlines the DSGE model we study. The NKDSGE model is prepared for estimation in section 4. This is followed by a discussion of Bayesian methods to estimate the linear approximate solution of the NKDSGE model described in section 5. Results appear in section 6. Section 7 concludes.

2 A BRIEF HISTORY OF DSGE MODEL ESTIMATION

Efforts to estimate and evaluate DSGE models using Bayesian methods began in earnest in the late 1990s. Previously, macroeconomists used classical optimization methods to estimate DSGE models. This section reviews these frequentist approaches to estimate DSGE models, covers the transition from frequentist to Bayesian methods, and ends by mentioning several issues at the frontier of Bayesian estimation of DSGE models.

Non-Bayesians have used maximum likelihood (ML), generalized method of moments (GMM), and indirect inference (II) to estimate DSGE models. These estimators rely on classical optimization either of a log likelihood function or of a GMM criterion.[6]

Early examples of frequentist ML estimation of DSGE models are Altuğ (1989) and Bencivenga (1992). They apply classical optimization routines to the log likelihood of the restricted finite-order vector autoregressive-moving average (VARMA) implied by the linear approximate solutions of their real business cycle (RBC) models. The restrictions arise because the VARMA lag polynomials are non-linear functions of the DSGE model parameters.

A restricted VARMA engages an ML estimator that differs from the approach of Sargent (1989). He maps the linear solution of permanent income (PI) models with a serially correlated endowment shock into likelihoods that are built on Kalman filter innovations of the observed data and the associated covariance matrix. Sargent assumes that the data are ridden with measurement errors, which evolve as independent first-order autoregressions, AR(1)s.[7] This aids in identification because serially correlated measurement errors add restrictions to the VARMA implied by the PI model solution. An extension of Sargent's approach is Ireland (2001). He replaces the independent AR(1) measurement errors with an unrestricted VAR(1); see Curdia and

Reis (2011) for a Bayesian version of this method. Besides measurement error, this VAR(1) inherits the sample data dynamics left unexplained by the RBC model that Ireland studies.

The tools of classical optimization are also useful for GMM estimation of DSGE models. Christiano and Eichenbaum (1992) construct GMM estimates of a subset of the parameters of their RBC model using its steady state conditions and the relevant shock processes as moments. Since the moment conditions are outnumbered by RBC model parameters, only a subset of these parameters are identified by GMM.

Identification also matters for ML estimation of DSGE models. For example, Altuğ, Bencivenga, and Ireland only identify a subset of RBC model parameters after pre-setting or calibrating several other parameters. Analysis by Hall (1996) suggests a reason for this practice. He shows that whether ML or GMM is being used, these estimators are relying on the same sample and theoretical information about first moments to identify DSGE model parameters. Although ML is a full information estimator, which engages all the moment conditions expressed by the DSGE model, GMM and ML rely on the same first moment information for identification. This suggests that problems identifying DSGE models are similar whether ML or GMM is the estimator of choice; see Fernández-Villaverde et al. (2009) for more discussion of these issues.

The frequentist assumption of a true model binds the identification problem to the issue of DSGE model misspecification. The question is whether any parameters of a DSGE model can be identified when it is misspecified. For example, frequentist ML loses its appeal when models are known to be misspecified.[8] Thus, it seems that no amount of data or computing power will solve problems related to the identification and misspecification of DSGE models.

A frequentist response to these problems is II. The first application of II to DSGE models is Smith (1993). He and Gourieroux et al. (1993) note that II yields an estimator and specification tests whose asymptotic properties are standard even though the true likelihood of the DSGE model is not known.[9] The II estimator minimizes a GMM-like criterion in the distance between a vector of theoretical and sample moments. These moments are readily observed in the actual data and predicted by the DSGE model. Estimating DSGE model parameters is 'indirect' because the objective of the GMM-like criterion is to match moments not related directly to the structure of the DSGE model.[10] Theoretical moments are produced by simulating synthetic data from the solution of the DSGE model. A classical optimizer moves the theoretical moments closer to the sample moments by updating the DSGE model parameters holding the structural shock innovations fixed.[11]

Dridi et al. (2007) extend the II estimator by acknowledging that the DSGE model is false. They argue that the purpose of dividing the vector of DSGE model parameters, Θ, into the parameters of interest, Θ_1, and the remaining nuisance or pseudo-parameters, Θ_2, is to separate the part of a DSGE model having economic content from the misspecified part. Thus, Θ_1 represents the part of a DSGE model that is economically relevant for the moments it aims to match. However, Θ_2 cannot be ignored because it is integral to the DSGE model. Fixing Θ_2 or calibrating it with sample information contributes to identifying Θ_1, but without polluting it with the misspecification of the DSGE model encapsulated by Θ_2. This insight is the basis for

Dridi, Guay, and Renault (DGR) to construct an asymptotic distribution of Θ_1 that accounts for misspecification of the DSGE model. The sampling theory is useful for tests of the degree of misspecification of the DSGE model and to gauge its ability to match the data.

Whether identification of DSGE models is a problem for Bayesians is not clear. For many Bayesians all that is needed for identification is a well posed prior.[12] Poirier (1998) points out that this position has potential costs in that prior and posterior distributions can be equivalent if the data are uninformative. This problem differs from identification problems frequentists face. Identification of a model is a problem that arises in population for a frequentist estimator, while for a Bayesian the source of the equivalence is data interacting with the prior. Nonetheless, Poirier provides analysis suggesting that Θ be split into those parameters for which the data are informative, Θ_1, given the priors from those, Θ_2, for which this is not possible.

Bayesians avoid having to assume there exists a true or correctly specified DSGE model because of the likelihood principle (LP). The LP is a foundation of Bayesian statistics and says that all evidence about a DSGE model is contained in its likelihood conditional on the data; see Berger and Wolpert (1998). Since the data's probabilistic assessment of a DSGE model is summarized by its likelihood, the likelihoods of a suite of DSGE models possess the evidence needed to judge which 'best' fit the data. Thus, Bayesian likelihood-based evaluation is consistent with the view that there is no true DSGE model because, for example, this class of models is afflicted with incurable misspecification.

There exist several Bayesian approaches to estimating DSGE models. Most of these methods are fully invested in the LP, which implies likelihood-based estimation. The goal of Bayesian estimation is construction of the posterior distribution, $\mathcal{P}(\Theta|\mathcal{Y}_T)$, of DSGE model parameters conditional on sample data $\mathcal{Y}_T$ of length T. Bayesian estimation exploits the fact that the posterior distribution equals the DSGE model likelihood, $\mathcal{L}(\mathcal{Y}_T|\Theta)$, multiplied by the econometrician's priors on the DSGE model parameters, $\mathcal{P}(\Theta)$, up to a factor of proportionality

$$\mathcal{P}(\Theta|\mathcal{Y}_T) \propto \mathcal{L}(\mathcal{Y}_T|\Theta)\mathcal{P}(\Theta). \tag{21.1}$$

Bayesian estimation of DSGE models is confronted by posterior distributions too complicated to evaluate analytically. The complication arises because the mapping from a DSGE model to its $\mathcal{L}(\mathcal{Y}_T|\Theta)$ is non-linear in Θ, which suggests using simulation to approximate $\mathcal{P}(\Theta|\mathcal{Y}_T)$.

Among the earliest examples of Bayesian likelihood-based estimation of a DSGE model is DeJong et al. (2000a, 2000b). They engage importance sampling to compute posterior distributions of functions of Θ, $\mathcal{G}(\Theta)$.[13] Importance sampling relies on a finite number N of $\mathcal{IID}$ random draws from an arbitrary density $\mathcal{D}(\Theta)$ to approximate $\mathcal{G}(\Theta)$. The approximation is computed with weights that smooth $\mathcal{G}(\Theta)$. The weights, $\mathcal{W}(\Theta_i)$, $i = 1, \ldots, N$, smooth the approximation by giving less (greater) mass to posterior draws of $\mathcal{G}(\Theta_i)$ that occur frequently (infrequently).[14] One drawback of importance sampling is that it is often unreliable when Θ has large dimension. Another is that there is little guidance about updating $\mathcal{P}(\Theta|\mathcal{Y}_t)$, and therefore $\mathcal{G}(\Theta)$, from one draw of $\mathcal{D}(\Theta)$ to the next, given $\mathcal{P}(\Theta)$.

Otrok (2001) reports estimates of a DSGE model grounded on the Metropolis–Hastings (MH) algorithm. This is, perhaps, the first instance of MH-MCMC simulation applied to DSGE model estimation. The MH algorithm proposes to update Θ using a multivariate random walk, but first an initial draw of Θ from $\mathcal{P}(\Theta)$ is needed. The initial Θ is updated by adding to it draws from a distribution of 'shock innovations'. The decision to keep the initial Θ or to move to the updated Θ depends on whether the latter increases $\mathcal{L}(\mathcal{Y}_t|\Theta)$. This process is repeated by sampling from the multivariate random walk to update Θ.

The MH-MCMC simulator is often preferred to importance sampling methods to estimate DSGE models. One reason is that the MH algorithm places less structure on the MCMC simulator. Thus, a wide class of time series models can be estimated by MH-MCMC simulation. Also MH-MCMC simulators generate serial correlation in the posterior distribution, which induces good asymptotic properties, especially compared to importance samplers. These properties reduce the computational burden of updating the prior. Another useful feature of MH-MCMC simulation is that its flexibility lessens the demands imposed by high dimensional Θ. We postpone further discussion of the MH-MCMC simulator to section 5.3.

Bayesian estimation of NKDSGE models leans heavily on MH-MCMC simulation. Smets and Wouters (2003, 2007), Del Negro and Schorfheide (2004), and Del Negro et al. (2007) estimate NKDSGE models similar to the one we estimate below. Open economy NKDSGE models are estimated using MH-MCMC simulators by, among others, Adolfson et al. (2007), Lubik and Schorfheide (2007), Kano (2009), Justiniano and Preston (2010), Rabanal and Tuesta (2010), and Guerrón-Quintana (2013). Evidence of the wide applicability of the MH-MCMC algorithm is its applications to NKDSGE models with labor market search by Sala et al. (2008), with fiscal and monetary policy interactions by Leeper et al. (2010), and that compare sticky price monetary transmission to monetary search frictions by Aruoba and Schorfheide (2011).

Formal Bayesian evaluation of estimated DSGE models relies on Bayes factors or posterior odds ratios. The Bayes factor is

$$\mathcal{B}_{j,s|Y_T} = \frac{\mathcal{L}(Y_T|\Theta_j, \mathcal{M}_j)}{\mathcal{L}(Y_T|\Theta_s, \mathcal{M}_s)}, \tag{21.2}$$

which measures the odds the data prefer DSGE model j, $\mathcal{M}_j$ (with parameter vector Θ_j), over $\mathcal{M}_s$.[15] Multiply $\mathcal{B}_{j,s|\mathcal{Y}_T}$ by the prior odds to find the posterior odds ratio, which as the name suggests is $\mathcal{R}_{j,s|\mathcal{Y}_T} = \mathcal{B}_{j,s|Y_T}\mathcal{P}(\Theta_j)/\mathcal{P}(\Theta_s)$. Put another way, the log of the Bayes factor is the log of the posterior odds of $\mathcal{M}_j$ compared to $\mathcal{M}_s$ net of the log of the prior odds of these DSGE models. Geweke (1999, 2005) and Fernández-Villaverde and Rubio-Ramírez (2004) discuss the foundations of Bayesian evaluation of DSGE models, while Rabanal and Rubio-Ramírez (2005) calculate Bayes factors to gauge the fit of several NKDSGE models.

There are other Bayesian approaches to DSGE model evaluation. Schorfheide (2000) estimates DSGE models using the MH-MCMC simulator as well as a richly parameterized structural BVAR, which serves as a 'reference' model. The fit of the DSGE and reference models to the data is judged within a Bayesian decision problem using a few selected moments under symmetric and asymmetric loss functions. The moments are structural IRFs that have economic meaning within the context of the DSGE models. Problems of DSGE model misspecification are sidestepped in this non-LP-based Bayesian evaluation process because, according to Schorfheide, the moments on which the DSGE models are evaluated are identified by the structural BVAR. He also argues that this approach yields valid DSGE model evaluation when no DSGE model fits the model well, which is not true of the Bayes factor; also see Geweke (2010). This argument is similar to arguments DGR make for parsimony (that is, do not rely on all the moments inherent in the likelihood), when selecting moments to bind the DSGE model to the data for II estimation.[16] DGR are guided to choose moments most economically meaningful for the DSGE model, which is a frequentist analogue to Schorfheide's Bayesian approach.

Another interesting approach to these issues is Guerrón-Quintana (2010). He confronts a NKDSGE model with different sets of observed aggregate variables to ask which data set is most informative for estimating DSGE model parameters. Fixing the NKDSGE models and changing the observed data rules out using the posterior odds ratio to conduct model evaluation. Instead, Guerrón-Quintana engages impulse response functions and out-of-sample forecast exercises to choose among the competing data sets. These evaluation tools reveal that the posterior of a DSGE model is affected by the composition and size of the information sets used in Bayesian MH-MCMC estimation, which is a signal of misspecification.

Identification of DSGE models has become a research frontier for Bayesian econometrics. We briefly mention several here. One approach is Müller (2010). He constructs statistics that unwind the relative contributions of the prior and the likelihood to the posterior. These statistics measure the 'identification strength' of DSGE model parameters with respect to a specific prior. Koop et al. (2011) describe two methods that depend on computing conditional and marginal posterior distributions for checking identification of DSGE models. Another useful approach is found in Guerrón-Quintana et al. (2013). When DSGE models are weakly identified (that is, Bayesian posterior distribution cannot be viewed as frequentist confidence sets), they advocate inverting the Bayes factor to construct confidence intervals with good small sample properties. We return to these issues at the end of this chapter.

3 A CANONICAL NEW KEYNESIAN DSGE MODEL

This section builds a canonical NKDSGE model inspired by the recent literature. The specification of this NKDSGE model is similar to those estimated by Del Negro et al. (2007), Smets and Wouters (2007) and Del Negro and Schorfheide (2008), who in turn build on Smets and Wouters (2003) and Christiano et al. (2005).[17] The main features of the NKDSGE model are: (*a*) the economy grows along a stochastic path; (*b*) prices and wages are assumed to be sticky *à la* Calvo; (*c*) preferences display internal habit formation in consumption; (*d*) investment is costly; and (*e*) there are five exogenous shocks. There are shocks to the monopoly power of the final good firm, the disutility of work, government spending and a shock to the growth rate of labor-neutral total factor productivity (TFP). All of these shocks are stationary AR(1)s. The fifth is a monetary policy shock embedded in a Taylor rule.

3.1 Firms

There is a continuum of monopolistically competitive firms indexed by $j \in [0,1]$. A firm produces an intermediate good using capital services, $k_{j,t}$, and labor services, $L_{j,t}$, which are rented in perfectly competitive markets. The production function of firm j is given by

$$Y_{j,t} = k_{j,t}^{\alpha}(Z_t L_{j,t})^{1-\alpha} - \kappa Z_t, \ \alpha \in (0,1), \ \kappa > 0, \tag{21.3}$$

where Z_t is labor-neutral TFP common to all firms. The term κZ_t is removed from the output of firm j to guarantee that steady state profits are zero as well as to generate the period-by-period fixed cost needed to support monopolistic competition among intermediate goods firms. We assume that the growth rate of the TFP shock, $z_t = \ln(Z_t/Z_{t-1})$, is an AR(1) process

$$z_t = (1-\rho_z)\gamma + \rho_z z_{t-1} + \sigma_z \varepsilon_{z,t}.$$

This AR(1) is stationary around the deterministic TFP growth rate γ (> 0) because $|\rho_z| < 1$ and the innovation of z_t is time invariant and homoskedastic, $\varepsilon_{z,t} \sim \mathcal{NID}(0,1)$ with $\sigma_z > 0$.[18]

Firm j chooses its price $P_{j,t}$ to maximize the present value of profits subject to the restriction that changes in their prices are time dependent. This form of price stickiness is called Calvo pricing; see Yun (1996). At each date t, a fraction of the unit mass of firms are able to update their price to its optimal level. The remaining firms update their prices by a fraction of the economy-wide lagged inflation rate, π_{t-1}. Inflation is defined as the growth rate of the aggregate price level, $\pi_t = P_t/P_{t-1} - 1$. We posit that firms are able to revise their prices at the exogenous probability $1 - \zeta_p$ every date t, while a firm not re-optimizing its price updates according to the rule: $P_{j,t} = (\pi^*)^{1-\iota_p}(\pi_{t-1})^{\iota_p}P_{j,t-1}$, where π^* is steady state inflation and $\iota_p \in [0,1]$. This has firms indexing (the log) of their prices to inflation to a weighted average of steady state inflation and lagged inflation, according to the weight ι_p, in periods when re-optimization is not allowed.

There is a competitive firm that produces the final good using intermediate goods aggregated using the technology

$$Y_t = \left[\int_0^1 Y_{j,t}^{1/(1+\lambda_{f,t})} dj\right]^{1+\lambda_{f,t}},$$

where $\lambda_{f,t}$ is the time-varying degree of monopoly power (that is, the stochastic price elasticity is $[1+\lambda_{f,t}]/\lambda_{f,t}$). This monopoly power evolves according to the AR(1) process

$$\ln\lambda_{f,t} = (1-\rho_{\lambda_f})\ln\lambda_f + \rho_{\lambda_f}\ln\lambda_{f,t-1} + \sigma_{\lambda_f}\varepsilon_{\lambda,t},$$

where $|\rho_{\lambda_f}| < 1$, λ_f, $\sigma_{\lambda_f} > 0$, and $\varepsilon_{\lambda,t} \sim \mathcal{NID}(0,1)$.

3.2 Households

The economy is populated by a continuum of households indexed by address $i \in [0, 1]$. Household i derives utility over 'net' consumption and the disutility of work.[19] This relationship is summarized by the period utility function

$$\mathcal{U}(C_{i,t}, C_{i,t-1}, L_{i,t}; \phi_t) = \ln(C_{i,t} - hC_{i,t-1}) - \phi_t \frac{L_{i,t}^{1+\nu_l}}{1+\nu_l}, \tag{21.4}$$

where $C_{i,t}$ and $L_{i,t}$ are consumption and labor supply of household i, ν_l is the inverse of the Frisch labor supply elasticity, and ϕ_t is an exogenous and stochastic preference shifter. Period utility receives the flow of $C_{i,t}$ net of a fraction h of $C_{i,t-1}$, which is the habit in consumption displayed by preferences. Consumption habit is internal to households and governed by the preference parameter $h \in (0, 1)$. The preference shifter follows the AR(1) process

$$\ln\phi_t = (1 - \rho_\phi)\ln\phi + \rho_\phi \ln\phi_{t-1} + \sigma_\phi \varepsilon_{\phi,t},$$

with $|\rho_\phi| < 1$, $\sigma_\phi > 0$, and $\varepsilon_{\phi,t} \sim \mathcal{NID}(0, 1)$.

Households are infinitely-lived. For household i, this means that it maximizes the expected present discounted value of period utility

$$\mathbb{E}_0^i \sum_{t=0}^{\infty} \beta^t \mathcal{U}(C_{i,t}, C_{i,t-1}, L_{i,t}; \phi_t), \quad \beta \in (0, 1), \tag{21.5}$$

subject to the budget constraint

$$P_t C_{i,t} + P_t[I_{i,t} + a(u_{i,t})\overline{K}_{i,t}] + B_{i,t+1} = R_t^K u_{i,t} \overline{K}_{i,t} + W_{i,t} L_{i,t} + R_{t-1} B_{i,t} + A_{i,t} + \Pi_t + T_{i,t}, \tag{21.6}$$

and the law of motion of capital

$$\overline{K}_{i,t+1} = (1 - \delta)\overline{K}_{i,t} + I_{i,t}\left[1 - \Gamma\left(\frac{I_{i,t}}{I_{i,t-1}}\right)\right], \quad \delta \in (0, 1), \tag{21.7}$$

over uncertain streams of consumption, labor supply, capital intensity, $u_{i,t}$, investment, $I_{i,t}$, capital, $\overline{K}_{i,t+1}$, and 1-period government bonds, $B_{i,t+1}$. Here $\mathbb{E}_t^i$ is the expectation operator conditional on the information set available to household i at time t; $a(\cdot)$ is the cost (in units of the consumption good) household i generates when working $\overline{K}_{i,t+1}$ at intensity $u_{i,t}$; R_t^K is the nominal rental rate of capital; $W_{i,t}$ is the nominal wage household i charges for hiring out $L_{i,t}$; R_{t-1} is the gross nominal interest rate paid on $B_{i,t}$; $A_{i,t}$ captures net payments from complete markets; Π_t corresponds to profits from intermediate goods producers; $T_{i,t}$ corresponds to lump-sum transfers from the government to household i; and $\Gamma(\cdot)$ is a function reflecting costs associated with adjusting the flow $I_{i,t}$ into $\overline{K}_{i,t+1}$. The function $\Gamma(\cdot)$ is assumed to be increasing and convex satisfying $\Gamma(\gamma^*) = \Gamma'(\gamma^*) = 0$ and $\Gamma''(\gamma^*) > 0$, where $\gamma^* \equiv \exp(\gamma)$. Also note that $\overline{K}_t \equiv \int \overline{K}_{i,t} di$ is the aggregate stock of capital. Given $u_{i,t}$ is a choice variable for household i, the nominal return on capital is $R^K_t u_{i,t}\overline{K}_{i,t}$ gross of the real cost $a(u_{i,t})$. The cost function $a(\cdot)$ satisfies the restrictions $a(1) = 0$, $a'(1) > 0$, and $a''(1) > 0$.

3.3 Staggered Nominal Wage Setting

Erceg et al. (2000) introduce Calvo staggered nominal wage setting into an NKDSGE model. We adopt their approach. Assume that household i is a monopolistic supplier of a differentiated labor service, $L_{i,t}$. Households sell these labor services to a firm that aggregates labor and sells it to final firms. This firm aggregates household labor services using the technology

$$L_t = \left[\int_0^1 L_{i,t}^{1/(1+\lambda_W)} dj\right]^{1+\lambda_W}, \quad 0 < \lambda_W < \infty$$

where the nominal wage elasticity is $(1 + \lambda_W)/\lambda_W$.

The role of this firm is to sell aggregate labor services, L_t, to intermediate goods firms in a perfectly competitive market at the aggregate nominal wage, W_t. The relationship between L_t, $L_{i,t}$, $W_{i,t}$, and W_t is given by

$$L_{i,t} = \left[\frac{W_{i,t}}{W_t}\right]^{-(1+\lambda_W)/\lambda_W} L_t.$$

We assume, as Erceg et al. (2000) did to induce wage sluggishness, that household i is allowed to reset its nominal wage in a similar manner to the approach that intermediate goods firms are forced to use to update the prices of their output. Calvo staggered nominal wage setting permits households to re-optimize their labor market decisions at the fixed exogenous probability $1 - \zeta_W$ during each date t. Households not allowed to reset their nominal wages optimally employ the rule $W_{i,t} = (\pi^*\gamma^*)^{1-\iota_W}(\pi_{t-1}\exp(z_{t-1}))^{\iota_W} W_{i,t-1}$ to update, where $\iota_W \in [0,1]$. This rule indexes (the log) of those nominal wages not being set optimally to a weighted average of steady state inflation grossed up by the deterministic growth rate and lagged inflation grossed up by lagged TFP growth, where ι_W determines the weights.

3.4 The Government

As often in the new Keynesian literature, we assume a cashless economy; see Woodford (2003). The monetary authority sets the short-term interest rate according to the Taylor rule used in Del Negro et al. (2007) and Del Negro and Schorfheide (2008)

$$\frac{R_t}{R^*} = \left(\frac{R_{t-1}}{R^*}\right)^{\rho_R}\left[\left(\frac{\pi_t}{\pi^*}\right)^{\psi_1}\left(\frac{Y_t}{Y_t^\tau}\right)^{\psi_2}\right]^{1-\rho_R} \exp(\sigma_R \varepsilon_{R,t}), \tag{21.8}$$

where R^* (> 0) corresponds to the steady state gross nominal interest rate, steady state inflation is π^*, Y_t^τ denotes the target level of output, $\varepsilon_{R,t}$ is a random shock to the systematic component of monetary policy, which is distributed $\mathcal{NID}(0,1)$, and σ_R (> 0) is the size of the monetary shock. The Taylor rule has the central bank systematically smoothing its policy rate by ρ_R as well as responding to deviations of π_t from its steady state π^*, and of Y_t from its target Y_t^τ.

Finally, we assume that government spending is a time-varying fraction of output, $G_t = (1 - 1/g_t)\,Y_t$. The fraction is driven by the shock g_t, which follows the AR(1) process

$$\ln g_t = (1 - \rho_g)\ln g^* + \rho_g \ln g_{t-1} + \sigma_g \varepsilon_{g,t},$$

where $|\rho_g| < 1$, g^*, $\sigma_g > 0$, and $\varepsilon_{g,t} \sim \mathcal{NID}(0,1)$. Although taxes and 1-period bonds are notionally used to finance G_t, the government inhabits a Ricardian world such that along the equilibrium path 1-period bonds are in zero net supply, $B_t = 0$, at all dates t. This forces aggregate lump sum taxes, T_t, always to equal G_t (that is, the primary surplus, $T_t - G_t$, is zero).

4 PREPARING THE NKDSGE MODEL FOR ESTIMATION

The scale of the NKDSGE model suggests that it does not admit a closed-form solution. Hence, we rely on linearization to obtain an approximate solution. The procedure consists of computing a first-order approximation of the NKDSGE model around its non-stochastic steady state.[20]

4.1 Stochastic Detrending

The productivity shock Z_t is non-stationary (that is, has a unit root). Since its growth rate, z_t, is stationary, the NKDSGE model grows along a stochastic path. We induce stationarity in the NKDSGE model by dividing the levels of trending real variables Y_t, C_t, I_t, and $\bar{K}_t$ by Z_t. This is the detrending step, where for example $y_t = Y_t/Z_t$. The nominal wage W_t also needs to be detrended after dividing it by the price level to obtain the detrended real wage, $w_t = W_t/(P_tZ_t)$. To transform the nominal rental rate of capital into the real rate, divide by P_t, $r_t^k = R_t^k/P_t$.

4.2 Linearization

We engage a first-order Taylor or linear approximation to solve the NKDSGE model. The linear approximation is applied to the levels of the variables found in the non-linear optimality and equilibrium conditions of the NKDSGE model.[21] The first step is to detrend the optimality and equilibrium conditions. Consider the production function (21.3), which after detrending becomes

$$y_{j,t} = k_{j,t}^{\alpha} L_{j,t}^{1-\alpha} - \kappa.$$

We avoid excessive notation by representing the original and detrended levels of capital in firm j with k_j. Denote $\tilde{y}_{j,t}$ as the deviation of output from its steady state, $\tilde{y}_{j,t} = y_{j,t} - y_j$. Taking a linear approximation of the previous expression gives

$$\tilde{y}_{j,t} = \alpha \tilde{k}_{j,t} + (1-\alpha)\tilde{L}_{j,t}.$$

The approach is easily extended to the remaining equilibrium and optimality conditions. Del Negro and Schorfheide (2008) present the complete set of linearized optimality and equilibrium conditions of the NKDSGE model.

4.3 Solution

Once the model has been detrended and linearized, the collection of its equilibrium conditions can be cast as an expectational stochastic difference equation

$$\mathbb{E}_t\{\mathcal{F}(N_{t+1}, N_t, X_{t+1}, X_t)\} = 0, \tag{21.9}$$

where X_t and N_t are vectors of predetermined (states) and non-predetermined (controls) variables, respectively. These vectors include

$$X_t \equiv [\tilde{y}_{t-1}\ \tilde{c}_{t-1}\ \tilde{i}_{t-1}\ \tilde{k}_t\ \tilde{w}_{t-1}\ \tilde{R}_{t-1}\ \tilde{\pi}_{t-1}\ \tilde{z}_t\ \tilde{g}_t\ \tilde{\phi}_t\ \tilde{\lambda}_{f,t}]'$$

and

$$N_t \equiv [\tilde{y}_t\ \tilde{c}_t\ \tilde{i}_t\ \tilde{l}_t\ \tilde{r}_t^k\ \tilde{u}_t\ \tilde{w}_t\ \tilde{\pi}_t, \tilde{R}_t]'$$

whose elements are deviations from their steady state values. Hence, finding the solution of the model is tantamount to solving the system of linear stochastic difference equations (21.9). We rely on a suite of programs developed by Stephanie Schmitt-Grohe and Martin Uribe to solve for the linear approximate equilibrium decision rules of the state variables of the NKDSGE model.[22] The solution of the NKDSGE model takes the form

$$\begin{aligned} X_t &= \Pi X_{t-1} + \Phi \xi_t \\ N_t &= \Psi X_t, \end{aligned} \tag{21.10}$$

where the first system of equations is the linear approximate equilibrium decision rules of the state variables, the second set maps from the state variables to the control variables, Π, Φ, and Ψ are matrices that are non-linear functions of the structural parameters of the NKDSGE model, and ξ_t is the vector of structural innovations, $[\varepsilon_{z,t}\ \varepsilon_{\lambda,t}\ \varepsilon_{\phi,t}\ \varepsilon_{R,t}\ \varepsilon_{g,t}]'$.

5 BAYESIAN ESTIMATION OF THE NKDSGE MODEL

This section presents the tools needed to generate Bayesian estimates of the linear approximate NKDSGE model of the previous section. Bayesian estimation employs the Kalman filter to construct the likelihood of the NKDSGE model. Next, priors for the NKDSGE model are reported because the likelihood multiplied by the prior is proportional to the posterior according to expression (21.1). We end this section by reviewing several details of the MH-MCMC simulator.

5.1 The Kalman Filter and the Likelihood

A key step in Bayesian MH-MCMC estimation of a linearized NKDSGE model is evaluation of its likelihood. A convenient tool to evaluate the likelihood of linear models is the Kalman filter. The Kalman filter generates projections or forecasts of the state of the linear approximate solution (21.10) of the NKDSGE model given an information set of observed macro time series. Forecasts of these observables are also produced by the Kalman filter. The Kalman filter is useful for evaluating the likelihood of a linearized NKDSGE model because the forecasts are optimal within the class of all linear models. When shock innovations and the initial state of the NKDSGE model are assumed to be Gaussian (that is, normally distributed), the Kalman filter renders forecasts that are optimal against all data-generating processes of the states and observables. Another implication is that at date t the observables are normally distributed with mean and variance that are functions of forecasts of the state of the linearized NKDSGE model and lagged observables. Thus, the Kalman filter provides the building blocks of the likelihood of a linear approximate NKDSGE model.

We describe the link between the solution of the linearized NKDSGE model with the Kalman filter.[23] Define the expanded vector of states as $\mathbb{S}_t = [N_t' \; X_t']'$. Using this definition, the state space representation of the NKDSGE model consists of the system of state equations

$$\mathbb{S}_t = \mathbb{F}S_{t-1} + \mathbb{Q}\xi_t, \;\; \xi_t \sim \mathcal{NID}(\mathbf{0}, \mathbf{I}_m), \tag{21.11.1}$$

and the system of observation equations

$$\mathbb{Y}_t = \mathbb{M} + \mathbb{H}\mathbb{S}_t + \xi_{u,t}, \;\; \xi_{u,t} \sim \mathcal{NID}(\mathbf{0}, \Sigma_u). \tag{21.11.2}$$

Here, $\mathbb{Y}_t$ corresponds to the vector of observables at time t; $\mathbb{F}$ and $\mathbb{Q}$ are functions of the matrices Π, $\mathbf{\Phi}$, and $\mathbf{\Psi}$; the matrix $\mathbb{H}$, which contains zeros and ones, relates the model's definitions with the data; $\mathbb{M}$ is a vector required to match the means of the observed data; and $\xi_{u,t}$ is a vector of measurement errors. Assume the vector of observables and the vector of states have dimensions m and n, respectively. Also, define $\mathbb{S}_{t|t-1}$ as the conditional forecast or expectation of $\mathbb{S}_t$ given $\{\mathbb{S}_1, \ldots, \mathbb{S}_{t-1}\}$, or $\mathbb{S}_{t|t-1} \equiv \mathbf{E}[\mathbb{S}_t | \mathbb{S}_1, \ldots, \mathbb{S}_{t-1}]$. Its mean square error or covariance matrix is $P_{t|t-1} \equiv \boldsymbol{E}[(\mathbb{S}_t - \mathbb{S}_{t-1})(\mathbb{S}_t - \mathbb{S}_{t-1})']$

The likelihood of the linearized NKDSGE model is built up by generating forecasts from the state space system (21.11.1) and (21.11.2) period-by-period

$$\mathcal{L}(\mathcal{Y}_T | \Theta) = \prod_{t=1}^{T} \mathcal{L}(\mathbb{Y}_t | \mathcal{Y}_{t-1}, \Theta), \tag{21.12}$$

where $\mathcal{L}(\mathbb{Y}_t | \mathcal{Y}_{t-1}, \Theta)$ is the likelihood conditional on the information available up to date $t-1$ and to be clear $\mathcal{Y}_{t-1} \equiv \{\mathbb{Y}_0, \ldots, \mathbb{Y}_{t-1}\}$. The Kalman filter computes this likelihood using the following steps:

1. Set $\mathbb{S}_{1|0} = 0$ and $P_{1|0} = \mathbb{F}P_{0|0}\,\mathbb{F} + \mathcal{Q}', \mathcal{Q}' = \mathbb{Q}\mathbb{Q}'$.[24]
2. Compute $\mathbb{Y}_{1|0} = \mathbb{H}'\mathbb{S}_{1|0} = 0$, $\Omega_{1|0} = E([\mathbb{Y}_1 - \mathbb{Y}_{1|0}][\mathbb{Y}_1 - \mathbb{Y}_{1|0}]') = \mathbb{H}'P_{1|0}\mathbb{H} + \Sigma_u$.

3. The predictions made in Steps 1 and 2 produce the date 1 likelihood:

$$\mathcal{L}(\mathbb{Y}_1|\Theta) = (2\pi)^{-m/2}|\Omega_{1|0}^{-1}|^{1/2}\exp\left[-\frac{1}{2}(\mathbb{Y}_1'\Omega_{1|0}^{-1}\mathbb{Y}_1)\right].$$

4. Next, update the date 1 forecasts:

$$\mathbb{S}_{1|1} = \mathbb{S}_{1|0} + P_{1|0}\mathbb{H}\Omega_{1|0}^{-1}(\mathbb{Y}_1 - \mathbb{Y}_{1|0}),$$

$$P_{1|1} = P_{1|0} - P_{1|0}\mathbb{H}\Omega_{1|0}^{-1}\mathbb{H}'P_{1|0}.$$

5. Repeat steps 2, 3, and 4 to generate Kalman filter predictions of $\mathbb{S}_t$ and $\mathbb{Y}_t$:

$$\mathbb{S}_{t|t-1} = \mathbb{F}\mathbb{S}_{t-1}P_{t|t-1},$$

$$P_{t|t-1} = \mathbb{F}P_{t-1|t-1}\mathbb{F}' + \mathbb{Q}',$$

$$\mathbb{Y}_{t|t-1} = \mathbb{H}'\mathbb{S}_{t|t-1},$$

$$\Omega_{t|t-1} = \mathbf{E}[(\mathbb{Y}_t - \mathbb{Y}_{t|t-1})(\mathbb{Y}_t - \mathbb{Y}_{t|t-1})'] = \mathbb{H}'P_{t|t-1}\mathbb{H} + \Sigma_u,$$

the likelihood,

$$\mathcal{L}(\mathbb{Y}_t|\mathcal{Y}_{t-1},\Theta) = (2\pi)^{-m/2}|\Omega_{t|t-1}^{-1}|^{1/2}\exp\left[-\frac{1}{2}(\mathbb{Y}_t - \mathbb{Y}_{t|t-1})'\Omega_{t|t-1}^{-1}(\mathbb{Y}_t - \mathbb{Y}_{t|t-1})\right]$$

and the updates of the state vector and its mean square error matrix

$$\mathbb{S}_{t|t} = \mathbb{S}_{t|t-1} + P_{t|t-1}\mathbb{H}\Omega_{t|t-1}^{-1}(\mathbb{Y}_t - \mathbb{Y}_{t|t-1}),$$

$$P_{t|t} = P_{t|t-1} - P_{t|t-1}\mathbb{H}\Omega_{t|t-1}^{-1}\mathbb{H}'P_{t|t-1}$$

for $t = 2, \ldots, T$.

The likelihoods, $\mathcal{L}(\mathbb{Y}_1|\Theta)$, $\mathcal{L}(\mathbb{Y}_2|\mathcal{Y}_1,\Theta)$, $\mathcal{L}(\mathbb{Y}_3|\mathcal{Y}_2,\Theta)$, ..., $\mathcal{L}(\mathbb{Y}_{T-1}|\mathcal{Y}_{T-2},\Theta)$, and $\mathcal{L}(\mathbb{Y}_T|\mathcal{Y}_{T-1},\Theta)$, computed at steps 2 and 5 are used to build up the likelihood function (21.12) of the linearized NKDSGE model.

5.2 Priors

Our priors are borrowed from Del Negro and Schorfheide (2008). They construct priors by separating the NKDSGE model parameters into three sets. Their first set consists of those parameters that define the steady state of the NKDSGE model; see Table 2 of Del Negro and Schorfheide (2008, p. 1201). The steady state, which as Hall (1996) shows, ties the steady state of the NKDSGE model to the unconditional first moments of $\mathcal{Y}_T$, has no effect on the mechanism that endogenously propagates exogenous shocks. This mechanism relies on preferences, technologies and market structure. The parameters of these primitives of the NKDSGE model are included in the second set of priors. Along with technology, preference and market structure parameters, Del Negro and Schorfheide add parameters of the Taylor rule (21.8) to this set; see the agnostic sticky price and wage priors of Tables 1 and 2 of Del Negro and Schorfheide (2008, pp. 1200–201). The third set of parameters consist of AR(1) coefficients and standard deviations of the exogenous shocks; see Table 3 of Del Negro and Schorfheide (2008, p. 1201).

We divide the parameter vector Θ into two parts to start. The 25×1 column vector

$$\Theta_1 = [\zeta_p\,\pi^*\,\iota_p\,h\,\nu_l\,a''\,\Gamma''\,\lambda_W\,\zeta_W\,\iota_W\,R^*\,\rho_R\,\psi_1\,\psi_2\,\gamma\,\lambda_f\,\rho_z\,\rho_\phi\,\rho_{\lambda_f}\,\rho_g\,\sigma_z\,\sigma_\phi\,\sigma_{\lambda_f}\,\sigma_g\,\sigma_R]',$$

contains the parameters of economic interest, which are to be estimated, in the order in which they appear in section 3. Under the Del Negro and Schorfheide (2008) prior rubric, the elements of Θ_1 are grouped into the steady state parameter vector

$$\Theta_{1,ss} = [\pi^*\,\gamma\,\lambda_f\,\lambda_W\,R^*]',$$

the parameters tied to endogenous propagation in the NKDSGE model

$$\Theta_{1,prop} = [\zeta_p\,\iota_p\,h\,\nu_l\,a''\,\Gamma''\,\zeta_W\,\iota_W\,\rho_R\,\psi_1\,\psi_2]',$$

and

$$\Theta_{1,exog} = [\rho_z\,\rho_\phi\,\rho_{\lambda_f}\,\rho_g\,\sigma_z\,\sigma_\phi\,\sigma_{\lambda_f}\,\sigma_g\,\sigma_R]'.$$

contains the slope coefficients and standard deviations of the exogenous AR(1) shocks that are the source of fluctuations in the NKDSGE model.

Table 21.1 lists priors for $\Theta_{1,ss}$, $\Theta_{1,prop}$ and $\Theta_{1,exog}$. We draw priors for Θ_1 from normal, beta, gamma and inverse gamma distributions; see Del Negro and Schorfheide (2008) for details. The priors are summarized by the distribution from which we draw, the parameters of the distribution, and implied 95 per cent probability intervals.

Our choices reflect, in part, a desire to elicit priors on Θ_1 that are easy to understand. For example, π^* is endowed with a normally distributed prior. Its mean is 4.3 per cent, which is less than twice its standard deviation, giving a 95 per cent probability interval running from nearly -1 per cent to more than 9 per cent. Thus, the prior reveals the extent of the uncertainty that surrounds steady state inflation.

The beta distribution is useful because it restricts priors on NKDSGE model parameters to the open unit interval. This motivates drawing the sticky price and wage parameter, ζ_p, ι_p, ζ_W, and ι_W, the consumption habit parameters, h, and the AR1 parameters, ρ_R, ρ_z, ρ_ϕ, ρ_{λ_f}, and ρ_g, from the beta distribution. The means and standard deviations of the priors display our uncertainty about these NKDSGE model parameters. For example, the prior on h indicates less uncertainty about it than is placed on the priors for ζ_p, ι_p, ζ_W, and ι_W (that is, the ratio of the mean to the standard deviation of the priors of these parameters is less than 3, while the same ratio for the prior of h is 14). This gives larger intervals on which to draw the sticky price and wage parameters than on h. Also, the prior 95 per cent probability interval of h is in the range that Kano and Nason (2012) show to be relevant for consumption habit to generate business cycle fluctuations in similar NKDSGE models.

Table 21.1 Priors of NKDSGE model parameter

Steady State Parameters: $\Theta_{1,ss}$				
	Priors			Probability intervals, 95%
	Distribution	A_1	A_2	
π^*	Normal	4.30	2.50	[−0.600, 9.200]
γ	Gamma	1.65	1.00	[0.304, 3.651]
λ_f	Gamma	0.15	0.10	[0.022, 0.343]
λ_W	Gamma	0.15	0.10	[0.022, 0.343]
R^*	Gamma	1.50	1.00	[0.216, 3.430]
Endogenous Propagation Parameters: $\Theta_{1,prop}$				
	Priors			Probability intervals, 95%
	Distribution	A_1	A_2	
ζ_p	Beta	0.60	0.20	[0.284, 0.842]
ι_p	Beta	0.50	0.28	[0.132, 0.825]
h	Beta	0.70	0.05	[0.615, 0.767]
ν_l	Gamma	2.00	0.75	[0.520, 3.372]
a''	Gamma	0.20	0.10	[0.024, 0.388]
Γ''	Gamma	4.00	1.50	[1.623, 6.743]
ζ_W	Beta	0.60	0.20	[0.284, 0.842]
ι_W	Beta	0.50	0.28	[0.132, 0.825]
ρ_R	Beta	0.50	0.20	[0.229, 0.733]
ψ_1	Gamma	2.00	0.25	[1.540, 2.428]
ψ_2	Gamma	0.20	0.10	[0.024, 0.388]
Exogenous Propagation Parameters: $\Theta_{1,exog}$				
	Priors			Probability intervals, 95%
	Distribution	A_1	A_2	
ρ_z	Beta	0.40	0.25	[0.122, 0.674]
ρ_ϕ	Beta	0.75	0.15	[0.458, 0.950]
ρ_{λ_f}	Beta	0.75	0.15	[0.458, 0.950]
ρ_g	Beta	0.75	0.15	[0.458, 0.950]
σ_z	Inv-Gamma	0.30	4.00	[0.000, 7.601]
σ_ϕ	Inv-Gamma	3.00	4.00	[2.475, 28.899]
σ_{λ_f}	Inv-Gamma	0.20	4.00	[0.000, 6.044]
σ_g	Inv-Gamma	0.50	4.00	[0.002, 10.048]
σ_R	Inv-Gamma	0.20	4.00	[0.000, 6.044]

Notes: Columns headed A_1 and A_2 contain the means and standard deviations of the beta, gamma and normal distributions. For the inverse-gamma distribution, A_1 and A_2 denote scale and shape coefficients.

The AR(1) coefficients also rely on the beta distribution for priors. The prior on ρ_R suggests a 95 per cent probability interval of draws that range from 0.22 to 0.73. At the upper end of this range, the Taylor rule is smoothing the policy rate R_t. This interval has the same length but is shifted to the left for ρ_z, which endows the technology growth prior with less persistence. The taste, monopoly power, and government spending shocks exhibit more persistence with AR(1) coefficients priors lying between 0.5 and 0.95.

The gamma distribution is applied to NKDSGE model parameters that only require priors that rule out non-negative draws or impose a lower bound. The former restriction describes the use of the gamma distribution for priors on the goods and labor market monopoly power parameters, λ_f and λ_W, the capital utilization parameter, a'', and the Taylor rule parameter on output, ψ_2. A lower bound is placed on the prior of the deterministic growth of technology, γ, the mean policy rate R^*, the labor supply parameter, ν_l, the investment cost parameter, Γ'', and the Taylor rule parameter on inflation, ψ_1. The prior on ψ_1 is set to obey the Taylor principle that R_t rises by more than the increase in π_t net of π^*. This contrasts with the prior on ψ_2 that suggests a smaller response of R_t to the output gap, $Y_t - Y_t^{\tau}$, but this response is non-zero.

The priors on the standard deviations of the exogenous shocks are drawn from inverse-gamma distributions. This distribution has support on an open interval that excludes zero and is unbounded. This allows σ_z, σ_{λ_f}, σ_g, and σ_R to have priors with 95 per cent probability intervals with lower bounds near zero and large upper bounds. These priors show the uncertainty held about these elements of the exogenous shock processes of the NKDSGE model. The same is true for the prior on σ_ϕ, but its scale parameter has a 95 per cent probability interval that exhibits more uncertainty as it is shifted to the right, especially for the upper bound.

The remaining parameters are necessary to solve the linearized NKDSGE model but are problematic for estimation. The fixed or calibrated parameters are collected into

$$\Theta_2 = [\alpha\ \delta\ g^*\ \mathcal{L}_A\ \kappa]'.$$

The calibration of Θ_2 results in

$$[\alpha\ \delta\ g^*\ \mathcal{L}_A\ \kappa]' = [0.33\ 0.025\ 0.22\ 1.0\ 0.0]'.$$

Although these values are standard choices in the DSGE literature, some clarification is in order. As in Del Negro and Schorfheide (2008), our parametrization imposes the constraint that firms make zero profits in the steady state. We also assume that households work one unit of time in steady state. This assumption implies that the parameter ϕ, the mean of the taste shock ϕ_t, is endogenously determined by the optimality conditions in the model. This restriction on steady state hours worked in the NKDSGE model differs from the sample mean of hours worked. We deal with this mismatch by augmenting the measurement equation in the state space representation with a constant or 'add-factor' that forces the theoretical mean of hours worked to match the sample mean; see Del Negro and Schorfheide (2008, p. 1197). This amounts to adding $\mathcal{L}_A$ to the log likelihood of the linearized NKDSGE model

$$\ln \mathcal{L}(\mathcal{Y}_T|\Theta_1; \Theta_2) + \ln \mathcal{L}_A.$$

Also, rather than imposing priors on the great ratios, C^*/Y^*, $I^*/\bar{K}^*$, $\bar{K}^*/Y^*$, and G^*/Y^*, we fix the capital share, α, the depreciation rate, δ, and the share of government expenditure, g^*. This follows well established practices that pre-date Bayesian estimation of NKDSGE models.

5.3 Useful Information about the MH-MCMC Simulator

The posterior distribution of the NKDSGE model parameters in Θ_1 is characterized using the MH-MCMC algorithm. The MH-MCMC algorithm is started up with an initial Θ_1. This parameter vector is passed to the Kalman filter routines described in section 5.1 to obtain an estimate of $\mathcal{L}(\mathcal{Y}_T|\Theta_1;\Theta_2)$. Next, the initial Θ_1 is updated according to the MH random walk law of motion. Inputting the proposed update of Θ_1 into the Kalman filter produces a second estimate of the likelihood of the linear approximate NKDSGE model. The MH decision rule determines whether the initial or proposed update of Θ_1 and the associated likelihood is carried forward to the next step of the MH algorithm. Given this choice, the next step of the MH algorithm is to obtain a new proposed update of Θ_1 using the random walk law of motion and to generate an estimate of the likelihood at these estimates. This likelihood is compared to the likelihood carried over from the previous MH step using the MH decision rule to select the likelihood and Θ_1 for the next MH step. This process is repeated $\mathcal{H}$ times to generate the posterior of the linear approximate NKDSGE model, $\mathcal{P}(\Theta_1|\mathcal{Y}_T;\Theta_2)$.

We summarize this description of the MH-MCMC algorithm with

1. Label the vector of NKDSGE model parameters chosen to initialize the MH algorithm $\hat{\Theta}_{1,0}$.
2. Pass $\hat{\Theta}_{1,0}$ to the Kalman filter routines described in section 5.2 to generate an initial estimate of the likelihood of the linear approximate NKDSGE model, $\mathcal{L}(Y_T|\hat{\Theta}_{1,0};\Theta_2)$.
3. A proposed update of $\hat{\Theta}_{1,0}$ is $\Theta_{1,1}$ which is generated using the MH random walk law of motion, $\Theta_{1,1} = \hat{\Theta}_{1,0} + \varpi\vartheta\varepsilon_1$, $\varepsilon_1 \sim \mathcal{NID}(\mathbf{0}_d, \mathbf{I}_d)$, where ϖ is a scalar that controls the size of the 'jump' of the proposed MH random walk update, ϑ is the Cholesky decomposition of the covariance matrix of Θ_1, and d (= 25) is the dimension of Θ_1. Obtain $\mathcal{L}(\mathcal{Y}_T|\Theta_{1,1};\Theta_2)$ by running the Kalman filter using $\Theta_{1,1}$ as input.
4. The MH algorithm employs a two-stage procedure to decide whether to keep the initial $\hat{\Theta}_{1,0}$ or move to the updated proposal $\Theta_{1,1}$. First, calculate

$$\omega_1 = \min\left\{\frac{\mathcal{L}(\mathcal{Y}_T|\Theta_{1,1};\Theta_2)\mathcal{P}(\Theta_{1,1})}{\mathcal{L}(\mathcal{Y}_T|\hat{\Theta}_{1,0};\Theta_2)\mathcal{P}(\hat{\Theta}_{1,0})}, 1\right\},$$

   where, for example, $\mathcal{P}(\Theta_{1,1})$ is the prior at $\Theta_{1,1}$. The second stage begins by drawing a uniform random variable $\varphi_1 \sim U(0,1)$ to set $\hat{\Theta}_{1,1} = \Theta_{1,1}$ and the counter $\wp = 1$ if $\varphi_1 \leq \omega_1$, otherwise $\hat{\Theta}_{1,1} = \hat{\Theta}_{1,0}$ and $\wp = 0$.
5. Repeat steps 3 and 4 for $\ell = 2, 3, \ldots, \mathcal{H}$ using the MH random walk law of motion

$$\Theta_{1,\ell} = \hat{\Theta}_{1,\ell-1} + \varpi\vartheta\varepsilon_\ell, \quad \varepsilon_\ell \sim \mathcal{NID}(\mathbf{0}_{d\times 1}, \mathbf{I}_d), \tag{21.13}$$

   and drawing the uniform random variable $\varphi_\ell \sim U(0,1)$ to test against

$$\omega_\ell = \min\left\{\frac{\mathcal{L}(\mathcal{Y}_T|\Theta_{1,\ell};\Theta_2)\mathcal{P}(\Theta_{1,\ell})}{\mathcal{L}(\mathcal{Y}_T|\hat{\Theta}_{1,\ell-1};\Theta_2)\mathcal{P}(\hat{\Theta}_{1,\ell-1})}, 1\right\},$$

for equating $\hat{\Theta}_{1,\ell}$ to either $\Theta_{1,\ell}$ or $\hat{\Theta}_{1,\ell-1}$. The latter implies that the counter is updated according to $\wp = \wp + 0$, while the former has $\wp = \wp + 1$.

Steps 1–5 of the MH-MCMC algorithm produce the posterior, $\mathcal{P}(\hat{\Theta}_1|\mathcal{Y}_T;\Theta_2)$, of the linear approximate NKDSGE model by drawing from $\{\hat{\Theta}_{1,\ell}\}_{\ell=1}^{\mathcal{H}}$. Note that in Steps 4 and 5 the decision to accept the updated proposal, $\varphi_\ell \leq \omega_\ell$, is akin to moving to a higher point on the likelihood surface.

There are several more issues that have to be resolved to run the MH-MCMC algorithm to create $\mathcal{P}(\hat{\Theta}_1|\mathcal{Y}_T;\Theta_2)$. Among these are obtaining an $\hat{\Theta}_{1,0}$ to initialize the MH-MCMC, computing ϑ, determining $\mathcal{H}$, fixing ϖ to achieve the optimal acceptance rate for the proposal $\Theta_{1,\ell}$ of $\wp/\mathcal{H}$, and checking that the MH-MCMC simulator has converged.[25]

Step 1 of the MH-MCMC algorithm leaves open the procedure for setting $\hat{\Theta}_{1,0}$. We employ classical optimization methods and an MH-MCMC 'burn-in' stage to obtain $\hat{\Theta}_{1,0}$. First, a classical optimizer is applied repeatedly to the likelihood of the linear approximate NKDSGE model with initial conditions found by sampling 100 times from $\mathcal{P}(\Theta_1)$.[26] These estimates yield the mode of the posterior distribution of Θ_1 that we identify as initial conditions for a 'burn-in' stage of the MH-MCMC algorithm. The point of this burn-in of the MH-MCMC algorithm is to remove dependence of $\mathcal{P}(\hat{\Theta}_1|\mathcal{Y}_T;\Theta_2)$ on the initial condition $\hat{\Theta}_{1,0}$. Drawing $\hat{\Theta}_{1,0}$ from a distribution that resembles $\mathcal{P}(\hat{\Theta}_1|\mathcal{Y}_T;\Theta_2)$ eliminates this dependence. Next, 10000 MH steps are run with $\varpi = 1$ and $\vartheta = \mathbf{I}_d$ to complete the burn-in stage. The final MH step of the burn-in gives $\hat{\Theta}_{1,0}$ to initialize the $\mathcal{H}$ steps of the final stage of the MH-MCMC algorithm. The 10000 estimates of Θ_1 generated during the MH burn-in steps are used to construct an empirical estimate of the covariance matrix $\vartheta\vartheta'$. The Cholesky decomposition of this covariance matrix is the source of ϑ needed for the MH law of motion (21.13).

The scale of the 'jump' from $\Theta_{1,\ell}$ to $\hat{\Theta}_{1,\ell-1}$ determines the speed at which the proposals $\Theta_{1,\ell}$ converge to $\mathcal{P}(\hat{\Theta}_1|\mathcal{Y}_T;\Theta_2)$ within the MH-MCMC simulator. The speed of convergence is sensitive to ϖ as well as to $\mathcal{H}$. The number of steps of the final stage of the MH-MCMC simulator has to be sufficient to allow for convergence. We obtain $\mathcal{H} = 300000$ draws from the posterior $\mathcal{P}(\hat{\Theta}_1|\mathcal{Y}_T;\Theta_2)$, but note that for larger and richer NKDSGE models the total number of draws is often many times larger. Nonetheless, the choice of the scalar ϖ is key for controlling the speed of convergence of the MH-MCMC. Although Gelman et al. (2004) recommend that greatest efficiency of the MH law of motion (21.13) is found with $\varpi = 2.4/\sqrt{d}$, we set ϖ to drive the acceptance rate $\wp/\mathcal{H} \in [0.23, 0.30]$.[27]

It is standard practice to test to check the convergence of the MH-MCMC simulator, besides requiring $\wp/\mathcal{H}$ to 0.23. Information about convergence of the MH-MCMC simulator is provided by the $\hat{R}$ statistic of Gelman et al. (2004, pp. 294–7). This statistic compares the variances of the elements within the sequence of $\{\hat{\Theta}_{1,\ell}\}_{\ell=1}^{\mathcal{M}}$ to the variance across several sequences produced by the MH-MCMC simulator given different initial conditions. These different initial conditions are produced using the same methods already described, with one exception. The initial condition for the burn-in stage of the MH-MCMC algorithm is typically set at the next largest mode of the posterior distribution obtained by applying the classical optimizer to the likelihood of the linear approximate NKSDSGE model. This process is often repeated three to five times. Gelman et al. (2004) suggest that $\hat{R} < 1.1$ for each element of $\hat{\Theta}_1$. If not, across the posteriors of the MH-MCMC chains there is excessive variation relative to the variance within the sequences. When $\hat{R}$ is large, Gelman et al. propose increasing $\mathcal{H}$ until convergence is achieved as witnessed by $\hat{R} < 1.1$.[28]

6 RESULTS

This section describes the data and reports the results of estimating the linear approximate NKDSGE model using the Bayesian procedures of the previous section.

6.1 Data

We follow Del Negro and Schorfheide (2008) in estimating the NKDSGE model given five aggregate US variables. The observables are per capita output growth, per capita hours worked, labor share, inflation, and the nominal interest rate on the 1982Q1–2009 Q4 sample. Thus, Bayesian estimates of the NKDSGE model parameters are conditional on the information set

$$\mathbb{Y}_t = \left[400\Delta \ln Y_t \; 100 \ln L_t \; 100 \ln \frac{W_t L_t}{P_t Y_t} \; 400\pi_t, \; 400 \ln R_t \right]',$$

where Δ is the first difference operator. Per capita output growth, labor share, inflation, and the nominal interest rate are multiplied to obtain data that are annualized, which is consistent with the measurement of per capita hours worked, and in percentages. Real GDP is divided by population (16 years and older) to create per capita output. Hours worked is a series constructed by Del Negro and Schorfheide (2008) that we extend for several more quarters. They interpolate annual observations on aggregate hours worked in the US into the quarterly frequency using the growth rate of an index of hours of all persons in the non-farm business sector. Labor share equals the ratio of total compensation of employees to nominal GDP. Inflation is equated to the (chained) GDP deflator. The effective federal funds rate defines the nominal interest rate.[29]

6.2 Posterior Estimates

Table 21.2 contains summary statistics of the posterior distributions of two NKDSGE models. We include posterior medians, modes and 95 per cent probability intervals of the NKDSGE model parameters in Table 21.2. Estimates of the NKDSGE model labeled $\mathcal{M}_1$ are grounded in the priors that appear in Table 21.1 and discussed in section 5.2. We also estimate an NKDSGE model that fixes ι_p at zero, which defines the weights on π^* and π_{t-1} in the indexation rule used by firms unable to update their prices at any date t.

Table 21.2 Summary of posterior distributions of the NKDSGE models (sample: 1982Q1–2009Q4)

ln Marginal Likelihoods						
	$\mathcal{M}_1 = -39.49$			$\mathcal{M}_2(\iota_p = 0) = -38.69$		
Steady State Parameters: $\Theta_{1,ss}$						
	Posterior		Probability intervals, 95%	Posterior		Probability intervals, 95%
	medians	modes		medians	modes	
π^*	2.822	2.831	[2.133, 3.635]	2.804	2.551	[2.116, 3.559]
γ	1.771	1.766	[1.206, 2.356]	1.773	2.109	[1.191, 2.409]
λ_f	0.178	0.178	[0.160, 0.216]	0.177	0.176	[0.160, 0.211]
λ_W	0.215	0.159	[0.086, 0.458]	0.225	0.274	[0.090, 0.473]
R^*	2.629	2.705	[2.014, 3.242]	2.622	1.915	[2.001, 3.229]
Endogenous Propagation Parameters: $\Theta_{1,prop}$						
	Posterior		Probability intervals, 95%	Posterior		Probability intervals, 95%
	medians	modes		medians	modes	
ζ_p	0.656	0.653	[0.578, 0.734]	0.673	0.725	[0.600, 0.743]
ι_p	0.059	0.007	[0.006, 0.215]	NA	NA	NA
h	0.814	0.825	[0.729, 0.872]	0.816	0.830	[0.736, 0.873]
ν_l	1.157	1.003	[0.717, 1.773]	1.156	1.074	[0.720, 1.787]
a''	0.241	0.198	[0.112, 0.459]	0.238	0.249	[0.109, 0.462]
Γ''	10.05	10.14	[6.948, 13.88]	10.13	13.90	[7.029, 14.18]
ζ_W	0.153	0.113	[0.072, 0.270]	0.154	0.180	[0.076, 0.270]
ι_W	0.461	0.514	[0.228, 0.818]	0.467	0.427	[0.224, 0.803]
ρ_R	0.787	0.780	[0.742, 0.823]	0.784	0.780	[0.739, 0.822]
ψ_1	2.513	2.514	[2.161, 2.902]	2.503	2.356	[2.138, 2.897]
ψ_2	0.055	0.052	[0.025, 0.093]	0.053	0.078	[0.024, 0.093]
Exogenous Propagation Parameters: $\Theta_{1,exog}$						
	Posterior		Probability intervals, 95%	Posterior		Probability intervals, 95%
	medians	modes		medians	modes	
ρ_z	0.256	0.226	[0.080, 0.454]	0.257	0.228	[0.077, 0.469]
ρ_ϕ	0.936	0.934	[0.875, 0.976]	0.936	0.963	[0.878, 0.977]
ρ_{λ_f}	0.915	0.921	[0.797, 0.974]	0.912	0.909	[0.804, 0.971]
ρ_g	0.944	0.944	[0.906, 0.975]	0.944	0.937	[0.906, 0.975]
σ_z	0.739	0.722	[0.659, 0.839]	0.741	0.732	[0.660, 0.846]
σ_ϕ	2.259	1.945	[1.741, 3.224]	2.239	2.133	[1.732, 3.154]
σ_{λ_f}	6.639	6.174	[4.987, 9.624]	6.798	8.474	[5.114, 9.822]
σ_g	0.772	0.757	[0.678, 0.889]	0.772	0.759	[0.679, 0.885]
σ_R	0.195	0.193	[0.170, 0.225]	0.196	0.203	[0.172, 0.226]

This NKDSGE model is labeled $\mathcal{M}_2$. The motivation for estimating $\mathcal{M}_2$ is that Table 6 of Del Negro and Schorfheide (2008, p. 1206) has 90 per cent probability intervals for ι_p with a lower bound of zero for all but one of their priors.

We obtain similar estimates for $\Theta_{1,prop}$ across $\mathcal{M}_1$ and $\mathcal{M}_2$ as listed in the middle panel of Table 21.2, except for ι_p. The posterior distributions of these models indicate substantial consumption habit, $h \in (0.73, 0.87)$, a large Frisch labor supply elasticity, $\nu_l^{-1} \in (0.56, 1.39)$, costly capital utilization, $a'' \in (0.11, 0.46)$, investment costs of adjustments, $\Gamma'' \in (6.9, 14.2)$, sticky prices, $\zeta_p \in (0.58, 0.74)$, nominal wage indexation, $\iota_W \in (0.22, 0.82)$, and interest rate smoothing by a monetary authority, $\rho_R \in (0.74, 0.82)$, that satisfies the Taylor principle, $\psi_1 \in (2.14, 2.90)$. These estimates show which elements of the NKDSGE models interact endogenously to replicate fluctuations found $\mathcal{Y}_T$. These estimates are also in the range often found in the existing literature; for example, see Del Negro and Schorfheide (2008).

Sticky nominal wages, price indexation, and the monetary authority's response to deviations of output from its target appear to matter less for generating endogenous propagation in the NKDSGE models. The 95 per cent probability interval of ι_p has a lower bound of 0.006 in the posterior distribution of $\mathcal{M}_1$. For $\mathcal{M}_1$ and $\mathcal{M}_2$, the estimates of ζ_W and ψ_2 are also relatively small. Thus, sticky prices and nominal wage indexation, not sticky nominal wages and price indexation, matter for endogenous propagation in $\mathcal{M}_1$ and $\mathcal{M}_2$ given $\mathcal{Y}_T$ and our priors.

Estimates of $\Theta_{1,exog}$ show that exogenous propagation matters for creating fluctuations in the posterior distributions of $\mathcal{M}_1$ and $\mathcal{M}_2$. The bottom panel of Table 21.2 shows that the taste shock ϕ_t, the goods market monopoly power shock λ_f, and the government spending shock g_t are persistent. In $\mathcal{M}_1$ and $\mathcal{M}_2$, the half-life of a structural innovation to these shocks is about seven quarters for λ_f and 11 quarters for ϕ_t and g_t at the medians and modes of ρ_{λ_f}, ρ_ϕ, and ρ_g, respectively.[30] The NKDSGE $\mathcal{M}_1$ and $\mathcal{M}_2$ yield estimates of ρ_z that signal much less persistence. Estimates of $\rho_z \in (0.23, 0.47)$ surround estimates of the unconditional first-order autocorrelation coefficient of US output growth; see Cogley and Nason (1995). Further, $\mathcal{M}_1$ and $\mathcal{M}_2$ produce posterior distributions in which the lower end of the 95 per cent probability intervals of ρ_z suggests little or no persistence in z_t.

Exogenous shock volatility contributes to $\mathcal{M}_1$ and $\mathcal{M}_2$ replicating variation in $\mathcal{Y}_T$. The scale parameters σ_ϕ and σ_{λ_f} matter most for this aspect of the fit of the NKDSGE models. Estimates of these elements of $\Theta_{1,exog}$ are 2.5 to more than 9 times larger than estimates of σ_z and σ_g. When σ_R is included in this comparison, it reveals that exogenous variation in monetary policy matters less for $\mathcal{M}_1$ and $\mathcal{M}_2$ to explain variation in $\mathcal{Y}_T$. Thus, $\mathcal{M}_1$ and $\mathcal{M}_2$ attribute the sources of business cycle fluctuations more to taste and goods market monopoly power shocks than to TFP growth, government spending, or monetary policy shocks.

The top panel of Table 21.2 displays estimates of $\Theta_{1,ss}$ that are nearly identical across $\mathcal{M}_1$ and $\mathcal{M}_2$. These estimates indicate that the posterior distributions of these NKDSGE models place a 95 per cent probability that steady state inflation in the US was as low as 2.1 per cent and just a little more than 3.5 per cent.[31] There is greater precision in the posterior estimates of γ. Deterministic TFP growth is estimated to range from 2.85 to 3 per cent per annum with a 95 per cent probability interval according to $\mathcal{M}_1$ and $\mathcal{M}_2$. In contrast, the 95 per cent probability intervals of R^* are shifted slightly to the left of the ones shown for π^*. These estimates suggest the NKDSGE models $\mathcal{M}_1$ and $\mathcal{M}_2$ predict steady state real interest rates near zero.

Del Negro and Schorfheide (2008) report estimates of price and wage stickiness that often differ from those of $\mathcal{M}_1$ and $\mathcal{M}_2$. For example, the middle panel of Table 21.2 shows that the median degree of price stickiness yields a frequency (that is, $1/[1 - \zeta_p]$) at which the firms of $\mathcal{M}_1$ and $\mathcal{M}_2$ change prices about once every two to three quarters. Del Negro and Schorfheide obtain estimates of ζ_p that imply an almost identical frequency of price changes for only three of the six priors they use. Notably, when they adopt priors with greater price stickiness, posterior estimates have firms changing prices as infrequently as once every 10 quarters on average.

Nominal wages exhibit less rigidity in the posterior distributions of $\mathcal{M}_1$ and $\mathcal{M}_2$. The 95 per cent probability intervals of ζ_W range from 0.07 to 0.27. This indicates that the households of $\mathcal{M}_1$ and $\mathcal{M}_2$ change their nominal wages no more than every other quarter. However, at the posterior median and modes of ι_W, those households unable to optimally adjust their nominal wages depend in about equal parts on π^*, γ^*, π_{t-1}, and z_{t-1} when updating to $W_{i,t-1}$. In comparison, the posterior of $\mathcal{M}_1$ shows that firms unable to reset their prices optimally rely almost entirely on π_{t-1} and not π^* when updating because the 95 per cent probability interval of $\iota_p \in (0.0, 0.2)$. The lower end of this interval is near the restriction imposed on ι_p by $\mathcal{M}_2$.

The marginal likelihoods of $\mathcal{M}_1$ and $\mathcal{M}_2$ give evidence about which NKDSGE model is preferred by $\mathcal{Y}_T$. The Bayes factor (21.2) is employed to gauge the relative merits of $\mathcal{M}_1$ and $\mathcal{M}_2$. We adopt methods described in Geweke (1999, 2005) to integrate or marginalize $\hat{\Theta}_1$ out of $\mathcal{L}(\mathcal{Y}_T|\hat{\Theta}_1; \mathcal{M}_j, \Theta_2)$, $j = 1, 2$; also see Chib and Jeliazkov (2001).[32] The top of Table 21.2 lists the log marginal likelihoods of $\mathcal{M}_1$ and $\mathcal{M}_2$. The Bayes factor of the marginal likelihoods of $\mathcal{M}_1$ and $\mathcal{M}_2$ is 2.23. According to Jeffreys (1998), a Bayes factor of this size shows that $\mathcal{Y}_T$'s preference for $\mathcal{M}_2$ over $\mathcal{M}_1$ is 'barely worth mentioning'.[33] Thus, the marginal likelihoods of $\mathcal{M}_1$ and $\mathcal{M}_2$ provide evidence that, although $\mathcal{Y}_T$ support $\iota_p = 0$, the evidence in favor of this restriction is not sufficient for an econometrician with the priors displayed in Table 21.1 to ignore $\mathcal{M}_1$, say, for conducting policy analysis.

7 CONCLUSION

This chapter surveys Bayesian methods for estimating NKDSGE models with the goal of raising the use of these empirical tools. We give an outline of an NKDSGE model to develop intuition about the mechanisms it has to transmit exogenous shocks into endogenous business cycle fluctuations. Studying the sources and causes of these propagation mechanisms requires us to review the operations needed to detrend its optimality and equilibrium conditions, a technique to construct a linear approximation of the model, a strategy to solve for its linear approximate decision rules, and the mapping from this solution into a state space model that can produce Kalman filter projections and the likelihood of the linear approximate NKDSGE model. The projections and likelihood are useful inputs into the MH-MCMC simulator. Since the source of Bayesian estimates of the NKDSGE model is the MH-MCMC simulator, we present an algorithm that implements it. This algorithm relies on our priors of the NKDSGE model parameters and setting initial conditions for the simulator. We employ the simulator to generate posterior distributions of two NKDSGE models. These posterior distributions yield summary statistics of the Bayesian estimates of the NKDSGE model parameters that are compared to results in the extant literature. These posterior distributions are needed as well to address the question of which NKDSGE models are most favored by the data. We also provide a short history of DSGE model estimation as well as pointing to issues that are at the frontier of this research.

We describe Bayesian methods in this chapter that are valuable because DSGE models are useful tools for understanding the sources and causes of business cycles and for conducting policy evaluation. This chapter supplies empirical exercises in which NKDSGE models are estimated and evaluated using data and priors that are standard in the published literature. Thus, it is no surprise that our estimates of the NKDSGE models resemble estimates found in the published literature. Although comforting, the similarity in estimates raises questions about whether the data are truly informative about the NKDSGE models or if posterior distributions of the NKDSGE models are dominated by our priors. Also, little is known about the impact of misspecification on the relationship between data, priors and posterior distributions of NKDSGE models. We hope this chapter acts as a foundation supporting future research on these issues.

NOTES

* The views herein are those of the authors and do not necessarily represent the views of the Federal Reserve Bank of Philadelphia or the Federal Reserve System.

1. L. Kilian gives a progress report on BVARs in this *Handbook* (Chapter 22).
2. This volume has surveys of MS models by J. Gonzalo and J-Y. Pitarakis (Chapter 8) and TVP models by O. Boldea and A. Hall (Chapter 9).
3. L. Bauwens and D. Korobilis provide a chapter on Bayesian methods for macroeconomists in this *Handbook* (Chapter 16).
4. Fernández-Villaverde et al. (2009) and Schorfheide (2011) review Bayesian estimation of DSGE models, while Canova (2007) and DeJong and Dave (2007) give textbook treatments of the subject.
5. An and Schorfheide (2007), Fernández-Villaverde and Rubio-Ramírez (2007), Fernández-Villaverde et al. (2010), Aruoba et al. (2011), and Liu et al. (2011) propose different non-linear estimators of DSGE models.
6. This *Handbook* has a chapter on GMM DSGE model estimation by F. Ruge-Murcia (Chapter 20).
7. Assuming sample data suffers from classical measurement error helps Altuğ identify the Kydland and Prescott (1982) RBC model. Bencivenga achieves the same objective with AR(1) taste shocks in an RBC model.
8. White (1982) develops quasi-ML for misspecified models, but its consistency needs a strong set of assumptions.
9. Gregory and Smith (1990, 1991) anticipate the II approach to DSGE model estimation and evaluation.
10. Also, II can estimate DSGE model parameters by minimizing the distance between the likelihoods of an auxiliary model generated using actual and simulated samples. Simulated quasi-ML yields an asymptotically less efficient estimator because the likelihood of the auxiliary model differs from that of the DSGE model; see Smith (1993).
11. Christiano et al. (2005) estimate an NKDSGE model by matching its predicted impulse responses to those of an SVAR. This approach to moment matching is in the class of II estimators. See Canova and Sala (2009) for a discussion of the identification problem facing this estimator and Hall et al. (2012) for an optimal impulse response matching estimator of DSGE models.
12. This is a proper prior that is independent of the data and has a density that integrates to 1.
13. The objective is to approximate $\mathbf{E}\{\mathcal{G}(\Theta)\} = \int \mathcal{G}(\Theta)\mathcal{P}(\Theta|\mathcal{Y}_t)d\Theta \,/ \int \mathcal{P}(\Theta|\mathcal{Y}_t)d\Theta$.
14. Given N draws from $\mathcal{D}(\Theta)$, $\mathbf{E}\{\mathcal{G}(\Theta)$ is approximated as $\overline{\mathcal{G}}_N = \sum_{i=1}^{N}\mathcal{W}(\Theta_i)\mathcal{G}(\Theta_i)/\sum_{i=1}^{N}\mathcal{W}(\Theta_i)$, where the weights, $\mathcal{W}(\Theta_i)$, equal $\mathcal{P}(\Theta_i|\mathcal{Y}_t)/\mathcal{D}(\Theta_i)$.

15. In general, Bayes factor involves the ratio of marginal likelihoods of $\mathcal{M}_j$ and $\mathcal{M}_s$. The marginal likelihood integrates out Θ_j from $\mathcal{L}(\mathcal{Y}_T|\Theta_j, \mathcal{M}_j)$; see Geweke (2005).
16. Kim (2002), Chernozhukov and Hong (2003) and Sims (2007) give Bayesian treatments of GMM and other limited information estimators.
17. See the chapter in this *Handbook* by Cantore et al. for a plethora of DSGE model specifications (Chapter 18).
18. A strictly positive deterministic growth term γ is also needed to have a well defined steady state around which we can linearize and solve the NKDSGE model.
19. Agents in the economy are given access to complete insurance markets. This assumption is needed to eliminate wealth differentials arising from wage heterogeneity.
20. A first-order approximation is sufficient for many macroeconomic applications. Otherwise, see Fernández-Villaverde et al. (2010, 2011) for tools to solve and estimate DSGE models with higher-order approximations.
21. First-order approximations can also linearize many variables in logs rather than in levels.
22. These programs are available at http://www.columbia.edu/mu2166/2nd_order.htm. Other examples of widely used software to solve DSGE models are found in the Dynare and Iris software packages. This *Handbook* includes reviews of Dynare and Iris by J. Madeira (Chapter 25).
23. For more information on linear filtering see Anderson and Moore (2005), and for details on the Kalman filter and likelihood-based estimation see Harvey (1989) and a chapter by T. Proietti and A. Luati in this *Handbook* (Chapter 15).
24. Let $\Sigma_{\mathbb{S}}$ be the unconditional covariance matrix of $\mathbb{S}$. The state equations (21.11.1) imply $\Sigma_{\mathbb{S}} = \mathbb{F}\Sigma_{\mathbb{S}}\mathbb{F}' + \mathcal{Q}'$. Its solution is vec $(\Sigma_{\mathbb{S}}) = [\mathbf{I}_n - \mathbb{F} \otimes \mathbb{F}]^{-1}$ vec $(\mathcal{Q}')$, where vec $(\mathbb{ABC}) = (\mathbb{C}' \otimes \mathbb{A})$ vec $(\mathbb{B})$, which in turn sets $P_{0|0}$ = vec $(\Sigma_{\mathbb{S}})$.
25. Gelman et al. (2004, pp. 305–307) discuss rules for the MH-MCMC simulator that improve the efficiency of the law of motion (21.13) to give acceptance rates that are optimal.
26. Chris Sims is responsible for the optimizer software that we use. The optimizer is csminwel and available at http://sims.princeton.edu/yftp/optimize/.
27. This involves an iterative process of running the MH-MCMC simulator to calibrate ϖ to reach the desired acceptance rate.
28. Geweke (2005) advocates a convergence test examining the serial correlation within the sequence of each element of $\hat{\Theta}_{1,\ell}$, $\ell = 1, \ldots, \mathcal{H}$.
29. The data are available at http://research.stlouisfed.org/fred2/. This website, which is maintained by the Federal Reserve Bank of St Louis, contains data produced by the Bureau of Economic Analysis (BEA), the Bureau of Labor Statistics (BLS), and the Board of Governors of the Federal Reserve System (BofG). The BEA compiles real GDP, annual aggregate hours worked, total compensation of employees, nominal GDP, and the chained GDP deflator. The BLS provides the population series and the index of hours of all persons in the non-farm business sector. The effective federal funds rate is collected by the BofG.
30. The half-life estimates are computed as $\ln 0.5/\ln\rho_s$, $s = \phi, \lambda_f$, and g.
31. The posterior probability interval differs from a frequentist confidence band. The latter holds the relevant parameter fixed and depends only on data, while the former is conditional on the model, priors and data.
32. Geweke advises computing the marginal likelihood with a harmonic mean estimator along with several refinements that he proposes. Useful instructions for computing marginal likelihoods along these lines are provided by Fernández-Villaverde and Rubio-Ramírez (2004, pp. 169–170).
33. The Bayes factor needs to exceed odds of 3 to 1 before there is 'substantial' evidence against $\mathcal{M}_2$.

REFERENCES

Adolfson, M., S. Laséen, J. Lindé and M. Villani (2007), 'Bayesian estimation of an open economy DSGE model with incomplete pass-through', *Journal of International Economics*, **72**(2), 481–511.

Altuğ, S. (1989), 'Time-to-build and aggregate fluctuations: some new evidence', *International Economic Review*, **30**(4), 889–920.

An, S. and F. Schorfheide (2007), 'Bayesian analysis of DSGE models', *Econometric Reviews*, **26**(2–4), 113–72.

Anderson, B. and J. Moore (2005), *Optimal Filtering*, New York: Dover Publications.

Aruoba, B. and F. Schorfheide (2011), 'Sticky prices versus monetary frictions: an estimation of policy trade-offs', *American Economic Journal: Macroeconomics*, **3**(1), 60–90.

Aruoba, B., L. Bocola and F. Schorfheide (2011), 'A new class of nonlinear time series models for the evaluation of DSGE models', manuscript, Department of Economics, University of Pennslyvania.

Bencivenga, V.R. (1992), 'An econometric study of hours and output variation with preference shocks', *International Economic Review*, **33**(2), 449–71.
Berger, J.O. and R.L. Wolpert (1988), *The Likelihood Principle*, 2nd edn, Hayward, CA: Institute of Mathematical Statistics.
Canova, F. (2007), *Methods for Applied Macroeconomic Research*, Princeton, NJ: Princeton University Press.
Canova, F. and L. Sala (2009), 'Back to square one: identification issues in DSGE models', *Journal of Monetary Economics*, **56**(4), 431–49.
Chernozhukov, V. and H. Hong (2003), 'An MCMC approach to classical estimation', *Journal of Econometrics*, **115**(2), 293–346.
Chib, S. and I. Jeliazkov (2001), 'Marginal likelihood from the Metropolis–Hastings output', *Journal of the American Statistical Association*, **96**, 270–81.
Christiano, L. and M. Eichenbaum (1992), 'Current real-business-cycle theories and aggregate labor-market fluctuations', *American Economic Review*, **82**(3), 430–50.
Christiano, L., M. Eichenbaum and C. Evans (2005), 'Nominal rigidities and the dynamic effects of a shock to monetary policy', *Journal of Political Economy*, **113**(1), 1–45.
Cogley, T. and J.M. Nason (1995), 'Output dynamics in real-business-cycle models', *American Economic Review*, **85**(3), 492–511.
Cogley, T. and T.J. Sargent (2005), 'Drifts and volatilities: monetary policies and outcomes in the post WWII US', *Review of Economic Dynamics*, **8**(2), 262–302.
Curdia, V. and R. Reis (2011), 'Correlated disturbances and US business cycles', manuscript, Department of Economics, Columbia University.
DeJong, D.N. and C. Dave (2007), *Structural Macroeconometrics*, Princeton, NJ: Princeton University Press.
DeJong, D.N., B.F. Ingram and C.H. Whiteman (2000a), 'A Bayesian approach to dynamic macroeconomics', *Journal of Econometrics*, **98**(2), 203–23.
DeJong, D.N., B.F. Ingram and C.H. Whiteman (2000b), 'Keynesian impulses versus Solow residuals: identifying sources of business cycle fluctuations', *Journal of Applied Econometrics*, **15**(3), 311–29.
Del Negro, M. and F. Schorfheide (2004), 'Priors from general equilibrium models for VARs', *International Economic Review*, **45**(2), 643–73.
Del Negro, M. and F. Schorfheide (2008), 'Forming priors for DSGE models (and how it affects the assessment of nominal rigidities)', *Journal of Monetary Economics*, **55**(7), 1191–208.
Del Negro, M., F. Schorfheide, F. Smets and R. Wouters (2007), 'On the fit and forecasting performance of New Keynesian models', *Journal of Business and Economic Statistics*, **25**(2), 123–62.
Doan, T., R. Litterman and C.A. Sims (1984). 'Forecasting and conditional projections using a realistic prior distribution', *Econometric Reviews*, **3**(1), 1–100.
Dridi, R., A. Guay and E. Renault (2007), 'Indirect inference and calibration of dynamic stochastic general equilibrium models', *Journal of Econometrics*, **136**(2), 397–430.
Erceg, C., D. Henderson and A. Levin (2000), 'Optimal monetary policy with staggered wage and price contracts', *Journal of Monetary Economics*, **46**(2), 281–313.
Fernández-Villaverde, J. and J.F. Rubio-Ramírez (2004), 'Comparing dynamic equilibrium models to data: a Bayesian approach', *Journal of Econometrics*, **123**(1), 153–87.
Fernández-Villaverde, J. and J.F. Rubio-Ramírez (2007), 'Estimating macroeconomic models: a likelihood approach', *Review of Economic Studies*, **74**(4), 1059–87.
Fernández-Villaverde, J., P.A. Guerrón-Quintana and J.F. Rubio-Ramírez (2009), 'The new macroeconometrics: a Bayesian approach', in A. O'Hagan and M. West (eds), *The Oxford Handbook of Applied Bayesian Analysis*, Oxford: Oxford University Press.
Fernández-Villaverde, J., P.A. Guerrón-Quintana and J.F. Rubio-Ramírez (2010), 'Fortune or virture: time-variant volatilities versus parameter drifting', Federal Reserve Bank of Philadelphia Working Paper No. 10–14.
Fernández-Villaverde, J., P.A. Guerrón-Quintana, K. Kuester and J.F. Rubio-Ramírez (2011), 'Fiscal volatility shocks and economic activity', Federal Reserve Bank of Philadelphia Working Paper No. 11–32.
Gelman, A., J.B. Carlin, H.S. Stern and D.B. Rubin (2004), *Bayesian Data Analysis*, 2nd edn, Boca Raton, FL: Chapman and Hall/CRC.
Geweke, J. (1999), 'Simulation methods for model criticism and robustness analysis', in J.O. Berger, J.M. Bernado, A.P. Dawid and A.F.M. Smith (eds), *Bayesian Statistics, Vol. 6*, Oxford: Oxford University Press, pp. 275–99.
Geweke, J. (2005), *Contemporary Bayesian Econometrics and Statistics*, Hoboken, NJ: John Wiley & Sons.
Geweke, J. (2010), *Complete and Incomplete Econometric Models*, Princeton, NJ: Princeton University Press.
Gourieroux, C., A. Monfort and E. Renault (1993), 'Indirect inference', *Journal of Applied Econometrics*, **18**(S1), S85–S118.

Gregory, A.W. and G.W. Smith (1990), 'Calibration as estimation', *Econometric Reviews*, **9**(1), 57–89.
Gregory, A.W. and G.W. Smith (1991), 'Calibration as testing: inference in simulated macroeconomic models', *Journal of Business and Economic Statistics*, **9**(3), 297–303.
Guerrón-Quintana, P.A. (2010), 'What you match does matter: the effects of data on DSGE estimation', *Journal of Applied Econometrics*, **25**(5), 774–804.
Guerrón-Quintana, P.A. (2013), 'Common factors in small open economies: inference and consequences', *Journal of International Economics*, forthcoming.
Guerrón-Quintana, P.A., A. Inoue and L. Kilian (2013), 'Frequentist inference in weakly identified DSGE models', *Quantitative Economics*, forthcoming.
Hall, A.R., A. Inoue, J.M. Nason and B. Rossi (2012), 'Information criteria for impulse response function matching estimation of DSGE models', *Journal of Econometrics*, **170**(2), 499–518.
Hall, G.J. (1996), 'Overtime, effort, and the propagation of business cycle shocks', *Journal of Monetary Economics*, **38**(1), 139–60.
Harvey, A.C. (1989), *Forecasting, Structural Time Series Models, and the Kalman Filter*, Cambridge: Cambridge University Press.
Ireland, P.N. (2001), 'Technology shocks and the business cycle: an empirical investigation', *Journal of Economic Dynamics and Control*, **25**(5), 703–19.
Jeffreys, H. (1998), *The Theory of Probability*, 3rd edn, Oxford: Oxford University Press.
Justiniano, A. and B. Preston (2010), 'Monetary policy and uncertainty in an empirical small open-economy model', *Journal of Applied Econometrics*, **25**(1), 93–128.
Kano, T. (2009), 'Habit formation and the present-value model of the current account: yet another suspect', *Journal of International Economics*, **78**(1), 72–85.
Kano, T. and J.M. Nason (2012), 'Business cycle implications of internal consumption habit for New Keynesian models', Federal Reserve Bank of Philadelphia working paper 12–30.
Kim, J-Y. (2002), 'Limited information likelihood and Bayesian analysis', *Journal of Econometrics*, **107**(1–2), 175–93.
Koop, G., M.H. Pesaran and R.P. Smith (2011), 'On identification of Bayesian DSGE models', manuscript, Department of Economics, Birkbeck College, London.
Kydland, F.E. and E.C. Prescott (1982), 'Time to build and aggregate fluctuations', *Econometrica*, **50**(6), 1345–70.
Leeper, E.M., M. Plante and N. Traum (2010), 'Dynamics of fiscal financing in the United States', *Journal of Econometrics*, **156**(2), 304–21.
Liu, Z., D.F. Waggoner and T. Zha (2011), 'Sources of macroeconomic fluctuations: a regime-switching DSGE approach', *Quantitative Economics*, **2**(2), 251–301.
Lubik, T.A. and F. Schorfheide (2007), 'Do central banks respond to exchange rate movements? A structural investigation', *Journal of Monetary Economics*, **54**(4), 1069–87.
Müller, U.K. (2010), 'Measuring prior sensitivity and prior informativeness in large Bayesian models', manuscript, Department of Economics, Princeton University.
Otrok, C. (2001), 'On measuring the welfare cost of business cycles', *Journal of Monetary Economics*, **47**(1), 61–92.
Poirier, D.J. (1998), 'Revising beliefs in nonidentified models', *Econometric Theory*, **14**(4), 483–509.
Primiceri, G. (2005), 'Time varying structural vector autoregressions and monetary policy', *Review of Economic Studies*, **72**(3), 821–52.
Rabanal, P. and J.F. Rubio-Ramírez (2005), 'Comparing New Keynesian models of the business cycle: a Bayesian approach', *Journal of Monetary Economics*, **52**(6), 1151–66.
Rabanal, P. and V. Tuesta (2010), 'Euro-dollar real exchange rate dynamics in an estimated two-country model: an assessment', *Journal of Economic Dynamics and Control*, **34**(4), 780–97.
Sala, L., U. Söderström and A. Trigari (2008), 'Monetary policy under uncertainty in an estimated model with labor market frictions', *Journal of Monetary Economics*, **55**(5), 983–1006.
Sargent, T.J. (1989), 'Two model of measurements and the investment accelerator', *Journal of Political Economy*, **97**(2), 251–87.
Schorfheide, F. (2000), 'Loss function-based evaluation of DSGE models', *Journal of Applied Econometrics*, **15**(6), 645–70.
Schorfheide, F. (2011), 'Estimation and evaluation of DSGE models: progress and challenges', Working Paper No. 11–07, Federal Reserve Bank of Philadelphia.
Sims, C.A. (2007), 'Thinking about instrumental variables', manuscript, Department of Economics, Princeton University.
Sims, C.A. and T. Zha (2006), 'Were there regime switches in US monetary policy?', *American Economic Review*, **96**(1), 54–81.
Smets, F. and R. Wouters (2003), 'An estimated stochastic dynamic general equilibrium model of the euro area', *Journal of the European Economic Association*, **1**(5), 1123–75.

Smets, F. and R. Wouters (2007), 'Shocks and frictions in US business cycles: a Bayesian DSGE approach', *American Economic Review*, **97**(3), 586–606.
Smith, A.A. (1993), 'Estimating nonlinear time-series models using simulated vector autoregressions', *Journal of Applied Econometrics*, **18**(S1), S63–S84.
White, H. (1982), 'Maximum likelihood estimation of mis-specified models', *Econometrica,* **50**(1), 1–25.
Woodford, M. (2003), *Interest and Prices: Foundations of a Theory of Monetary Policy*, Princeton, NJ: Princeton University Press.
Yun, T. (1996), 'Nominal price rigidity, money supply endogeneity, and business cycles', *Journal of Monetary Economics*, **37**(2), 345–70.

PART V

APPLICATIONS II: VECTOR AUTOREGRESSIVE MODELS

22 Structural vector autoregressions*

Lutz Kilian

1 INTRODUCTION

Notwithstanding the increased use of estimated dynamic stochastic general equilibrium (DSGE) models over the last decade, structural vector autoregressive (VAR) models continue to be the workhorse of empirical macroeconomics and finance. Structural VAR models have four main applications. First, they are used to study the expected response of the model variables to a given one-time structural shock. Second, they allow the construction of forecast error variance decompositions that quantify the average contribution of a given structural shock to the variability of the data. Third, they can be used to provide historical decompositions that measure the cumulative contribution of each structural shock to the evolution of each variable over time. Historical decompositions are essential, for example, in understanding the genesis of recessions or of surges in energy prices (see, for example, Edelstein and Kilian, 2009; Kilian and Murphy, 2013). Finally, structural VAR models allow the construction of forecast scenarios conditional on hypothetical sequences of future structural shocks (see, for example, Waggoner and Zha, 1999; Baumeister and Kilian, 2012).

VAR models were first proposed by Sims (1980a) as an alternative to traditional large-scale dynamic simultaneous equation models. Sims' research program stressed the need to dispense with ad hoc dynamic exclusion restrictions in regression models and to discard empirically implausible exogeneity assumptions. He also stressed the need to model all endogenous variables jointly rather than one equation at a time. All of these points have stood the test of time. There is a large body of literature on the specification and estimation of reduced-form VAR models (see, for example, Watson, 1994, Lütkepohl, 2005 and Chapter 6 in this volume). The success of such VAR models as descriptive tools and to some extent as forecasting tools is well established. The ability of structural representations of VAR models to differentiate between correlation and causation, in contrast, has remained contentious.

Structural interpretations of VAR models require additional identifying assumptions that must be motivated based on institutional knowledge, economic theory, or other extraneous constraints on the model responses. Only after decomposing forecast errors into structural shocks that are mutually uncorrelated and have an economic interpretation can we assess the causal effects of these shocks on the model variables. Many early VAR studies overlooked this requirement and relied on ad hoc assumptions for identification that made no economic sense. Such atheoretical VAR models attracted strong criticism (see, for example, Cooley and LeRoy, 1985), spurring the development of more explicitly structural VAR models starting in 1986. In response to ongoing questions about the validity of commonly used identifying assumptions, the structural VAR model literature has continuously evolved since the 1980s. Even today new ideas and insights are being generated. This survey traces the evolution of this literature. It focuses on alternative approaches to the identification of structural shocks within the framework of a reduced-form VAR model, highlighting the conditions under which each approach is valid and discussing potential limitations of commonly employed methods.

Section 2 focuses on identification by short-run restrictions. Section 3 reviews identification by long-run restrictions. Identification by sign restrictions is discussed in section 4. Section 5 summarizes alternative approaches such as identification by heteroskedasticity or identification based on high-frequency financial markets data and discusses identification in the presence of forward-looking behavior. Section 6 discusses the relationship between DSGE models and structural VAR models. The conclusions are in section 7.

2 IDENTIFICATION BY SHORT-RUN RESTRICTIONS

Consider a K-dimensional time series y_t, $t = 1,\ldots,T$. We postulate that y_t can be approximated by a vector autoregression of finite order p. Our objective is to learn about the parameters of the structural vector autoregressive model

$$B_0 y_t = B_1 y_{t-1} + \ldots + B_p y_{t-p} + u_t,$$

where u_t denotes a mean zero serially uncorrelated error term, also referred to as a structural innovation or structural shock. The error term is assumed to be unconditionally homoskedastic, unless noted otherwise. All deterministic regressors have been suppressed for notational convenience. Equivalently the model can be written more compactly as

$$B(L) y_t = u_t,$$

where $B(L) \equiv B_0 - B_1 L - B_2 L^2 - \ldots - B_p L^p$ is the autoregressive lag order polynomial. The variance–covariance matrix of the structural error term is typically normalized such that:

$$E(u_t u_t') \equiv \Sigma_u = I_K.$$

This means, first, that there are as many structural shocks as variables in the model. Second, structural shocks by definition are mutually uncorrelated, which implies that Σ_u is diagonal. Third, we normalize the variance of all structural shocks to unity. The latter normalization does not involve a loss of generality, as long as the diagonal elements of B_0 remain unrestricted. We defer a discussion of alternative normalizations until the end of this section.[1]

In order to allow estimation of the structural model we first need to derive its reduced-form representation. This involves expressing y_t as a function of lagged y_t only. To derive the reduced-form representation, we pre-multiply both sides of the structural VAR representation by B_0^{-1}:

$$B_0^{-1}B_0y_t = B_0^{-1}B_1y_{t-1} + \ldots + B_0^{-1}B_py_{t-p} + B_0^{-1}u_t$$

Hence, the same model can be represented as:

$$y_t = A_1y_{t-1} + \ldots + A_py_{t-p} + \varepsilon_t$$

where $A_i = B_0^{-1}B_i$, $i = 1,\ldots,p$, and $\varepsilon_t = B_0^{-1}u_t$. Equivalently the model can be written more compactly as:

$$A(L)y_t = \varepsilon_t,$$

where $A(L) \equiv I - A_1L - A_2L^2 - \ldots - A_pL^p$ denotes the autoregressive lag order polynomial. Standard estimation methods allow us to obtain consistent estimates of the reduced-form parameters A_i, $i = 1,\ldots,p$, the reduced-form errors ε_t, and their covariance matrix $E(\varepsilon_t\varepsilon_t') \equiv \Sigma_\varepsilon$ (see Lütkepohl, 2005).

It is clear by inspection that the reduced-form innovations ε_t are in general a weighted average of the structural shocks u_t. As a result, studying the response of the vector y_t to reduced-form shocks ε_t will not tell us anything about the response of y_t to the structural shocks u_t. It is the latter responses that are of interest if we want to learn about the structure of the economy. These structural responses depend on B_i, $i = 0,\ldots,p$. The central question is how to recover the elements of B_0^{-1} from consistent estimates of the reduced-form parameters, because knowledge of B_0^{-1} would enable us to reconstruct u_t from $u_t = B_0\varepsilon_t$ and B_i, $i = 1,\ldots,p$, from $B_i = B_0A_i$.

By construction, $\varepsilon_t = B_0^{-1}u_t$. Hence, the variance of ε_t is:

$$E(\varepsilon_t\varepsilon_t') = B_0^{-1}E(u_tu_t')B_0^{-1\prime}$$

$$\Sigma_\varepsilon = B_0^{-1}\Sigma_uB_0^{-1\prime}$$

$$\Sigma_\varepsilon = B_0^{-1}B_0^{-1\prime}$$

where we made use of $\Sigma_u = I_K$ in the last line. We can think of $\Sigma_\varepsilon = B_0^{-1}B_0^{-1\prime}$ as a system of non-linear equations in the unknown parameters of B_0^{-1}. Note that Σ_ε can be estimated consistently and hence is treated as known. This system of non-linear equations can be solved for the unknown parameters in B_0^{-1} using numerical methods, provided the number of unknown parameters in B_0^{-1} does not exceed the number of equations. This involves imposing additional restrictions on selected elements of B_0^{-1} (or equivalently on B_0). Such restrictions may take the form of exclusion restrictions, proportionality restrictions, or other equality restrictions. The most common approach is to impose zero restrictions on selected elements of B_0^{-1}.

To verify that all of the elements of the unknown matrix B_0^{-1} are uniquely identified, observe that Σ_ε has $K(K + 1)/2$ free parameters. This follows from the fact that any covariance matrix is symmetric about the diagonal. Hence, $K(K + 1)/2$ by construction is the maximum number of parameters in B_0^{-1} that one can uniquely identify. This order condition for identification is easily checked in practice, but is a necessary condition for identification only. Even if the order condition is satisfied, the rank condition may fail, depending on the numerical values of the elements of B_0^{-1}. Rubio-Ramirez et al. (2010) discuss a general approach to evaluating the rank condition for global identification in structural VAR models.

The earlier discussion alluded to the existence of alternative normalization assumption in structural VAR analysis. There are three equivalent representations of structural VAR models that differ only in how the model is normalized. All three representations have been used in applied work. In the discussion so far we made the standard normalizing assumption that $\Sigma_u = I_K$, while leaving the diagonal elements of B_0 unrestricted. Identification was achieved by imposing identifying restrictions on B_0^{-1} in $\varepsilon_t = B_0^{-1}u_t$. By construction a unit innovation in the structural shocks in this representation is an innovation of size one standard deviation, so structural impulse responses based on B_0^{-1} are responses to one-standard deviation shocks.

Equivalently, one could have left the diagonal elements of Σ_u unconstrained and set the diagonal elements of B_0 to unity in $u_t = B_0\varepsilon_t$ (see, for example, Keating, 1992). A useful result in this context is that B_0, being lower triangular, implies that B_0^{-1} is lower triangular as well. However, the variance of the structural errors will no longer be unity if the model is estimated in this second representation, so the implied estimate of B_0^{-1} must be rescaled by one residual standard deviation to ensure that the implied structural impulse responses represent responses to one-standard deviation shocks.

Finally, these two approaches may be combined by changing notation and writing the model equivalently as

$$B_0\varepsilon_t = \Upsilon u_t$$

with $\Sigma_u = I_K$ such that $\Sigma_\varepsilon = B_0^{-1}\Upsilon\Upsilon' B_0^{-1\prime}$. The two representations above emerge as special cases of this representation with the alternative normalizations of $B_0 = I_K$ or $\Upsilon = I_K$. The advantage of the third representation is that it allows one to relax the assumption that either $\Upsilon = I_K$ or $B_0 = I_K$, which sometimes facilitates the exposition of the identifying assumptions. For example, Blanchard and Perotti (2002) use this representation with the diagonal elements of Υ normalized to unity, but neither Υ nor B_0 being diagonal.

2.1 Recursively Identified Models

One popular way of disentangling the structural innovations u_t from the reduced-form innovations ε_t is to 'orthogonalize' the reduced-form errors. Orthogonalization here means making the errors uncorrelated. Mechanically, this can be accomplished as follows. Define the lower-triangular $K \times K$ matrix P with positive main diagonal such that $PP' = \Sigma_\varepsilon$. Taking such a *Cholesky decomposition* of the variance–covariance matrix is the matrix analogue of computing the square root of a scalar variance.[2]

It follows immediately from the condition $\Sigma_\varepsilon = B_0^{-1}B_0^{-1\prime}$ that $B_0^{-1} = P$ is *one* possible solution to the problem of how to recover u_t. Since P is lower triangular, it has $K(K + 1)/2$ free parameters, so all parameters of P are exactly identified. As a result, the order condition for identification is satisfied. Given the lower triangular structure of P, there is no need to use numerical solution methods in this case, but if we did impose the recursive exclusion restrictions on B_0^{-1} and solved numerically for the remaining parameters, the results would be identical to the results from the Cholesky decomposition. The advantage of the numerical approach discussed earlier is that it allows for alternative non-recursive identification schemes and for restrictions other than exclusion restrictions.

It is important to keep in mind that the 'orthogonalization' of the reduced-form residuals by applying a Cholesky decomposition is appropriate only if the recursive structure embodied in P can be justified on economic grounds.

- The distinguishing feature of 'orthogonalization' by Cholesky decomposition is that the resulting structural model is recursive (conditional on lagged variables). This means that we impose a particular causal chain rather than learning about causal relationships from the data. In essence, we solve the problem of which structural shock causes the variation in ε_t by imposing a particular solution. This mechanical solution does not make economic sense, however, without a plausible economic interpretation for the recursive ordering.
- The neutral and scientific-sounding term 'orthogonalization' hides the fact that we are making strong identifying assumptions about the error term of the VAR model. In the early 1980s, many users of VARs did not understand this point and thought the data alone would speak for themselves. Such 'atheoretical' VAR models were soon severely criticized (see, for example, Cooley and LeRoy, 1985). This critique spurred the development of structural VAR models that impose non-recursive identifying restrictions (for example, Sims, 1986; Bernanke, 1986; Blanchard and Watson, 1986). It also prompted more careful attention to the economic underpinnings of recursive models. It was shown that in special cases the recursive model can be given a structural or semistructural interpretation.
- P is not unique. There is a different solution for P for each ordering of the K variables in the VAR model. It is sometimes argued that one should conduct sensitivity analysis based on alternative orderings of the K variables. This proposal makes no sense for three reasons:
  1. On the one hand, we claim to be sure that the ordering is recursive, yet on the other hand we have no clue in what order the variables are recursive. This approach is not credible.
  2. For a small VAR model with $K = 4$, for example, there are $4 \cdot 3 \cdot 2 \cdot 1 = 24$ permutations of the ordering. Nobody seriously tries out this many model specifications, nor would there be much hope that the results would be the same in each case, unless the reduced-form errors are uncorrelated, which can be checked by inspecting the off-diagonal elements of Σ_ε.
  3. Even if there were no difference across these 24 specifications, this would only prove that the results are robust among all recursive orderings, but there is no reason for the model to be recursive in the first place. This point is best illustrated by example. Let p_t denote the price and q_t the quantity of a good. Price and quantity are driven by structural demand shocks u_t^d and supply shocks u_t^s. All dynamics are suppressed for expository purposes such that $y_t = \varepsilon_t$:

$$\underbrace{\begin{pmatrix} p_t \\ q_t \end{pmatrix}}_{\varepsilon_t} = \underbrace{\begin{bmatrix} 1 & -0.5 \\ 0.5 & 1 \end{bmatrix}}_{B_0^{-1}} \underbrace{\begin{pmatrix} u_t^d \\ u_t^s \end{pmatrix}}_{u_t}.$$

In this example, by construction Σ_ε is diagonal and the observable data are uncorrelated such that all recursive orderings are identical. This outcome obviously does not imply that any of the recursive orderings are valid. In fact, B_0^{-1} differs from

$$P = chol(\Sigma_\varepsilon) = chol\left(\begin{bmatrix} 1.25 & 0 \\ 0 & 1.25 \end{bmatrix}\right) = \begin{bmatrix} 1.118 & 0 \\ 0 & 1.118 \end{bmatrix}$$

by construction. This point holds more generally. Let $\varepsilon_t = B_0^{-1}u_t$ denote the true structural relationship and $\varepsilon_t = Pu_t^{chol}$ be the Cholesky relationship. Then

$$u_t^{chol} = P^{-1}\varepsilon_t = P^{-1}(B_0^{-1}u_t) \neq u_t,$$

so the Cholesky decomposition will fail to identify the true structural shocks.

2.2 Sources of Identifying Restrictions

The preceding subsection stressed that, unless we can come up with a convincing rationale for a particular recursive ordering, the resulting VAR impulse responses, forecast error variance decompositions, and historical decompositions are economically meaningless. This raises the question of where the economic rationale of identifying restrictions on B_0^{-1} or B_0 comes from. There are a number of potential sources. One is economic theory:

- In some cases, we may wish to impose the structure provided by a specific economic model, although in that case the empirical results will only be as credible as the underlying model. A case in point is Blanchard's (1989) structural VAR analysis of the traditional Keynesian model involving an aggregate demand equation, Okun's law, a price-setting equation, the Phillips curve and a monetary policy rule.
- Another strategy is to specify an encompassing model that includes as special cases various alternative structural models implied by different economic models, allowing tests for overidentifying restrictions. The advantage of this approach is that it avoids conditioning on one specific model that may be incorrect. Of course, this type of structural VAR model no longer admits a Cholesky representation and must be estimated by numerical methods using the Generalized Method of Moments (GMM). This strategy has been used, for example, by Bernanke and Mihov (1998) who model the market for bank reserves as part of a study of US monetary policy. Within a semistructural VAR framework they jointly analyze a vector of policy indicators rather than a single indicator (such as the federal funds rate). Their approach allows for changes in the operating procedures of the Federal Reserve over time.

Often there is no fully developed theoretical model available, in which case identification may be achieved by using extraneous information or by using selective insights from economic theory:

- Information delays: information may not be available instantaneously because data are released only infrequently, allowing us to rule out instantaneous feedback. This approach has been exploited in Inoue et al. (2009), for example.
- Physical constraints: for example, a firm may decide to invest, but it takes time for that decision to be made and for the new equipment to be installed, so measured physical investment responds with a delay.
- Institutional knowledge: for example, we may have information about the inability of suppliers to respond to demand shocks in the short run due to adjustment costs, which amounts to imposing a vertical slope on the supply curve (see, for example, Kilian, 2009). Similarly, Davis and Kilian (2011) exploit the fact that gasoline taxes (excluding *ad valorem* taxes) do not respond instantaneously to the state of the economy because lawmakers move at a slow pace. This feature of the data allows them to treat gasoline taxes as predetermined with respect to domestic macroeconomic aggregates. Moreover, given that consumers are effectively unable to store gasoline, anticipation of gasoline tax changes can be ignored in this setting.
- Assumptions about market structure: another common identifying assumption in empirical work is that there is no feedback from a small open economy to the rest of the world. This identifying assumption has been used, for example, to motivate treating US interest rates as contemporaneously exogenous with respect to the macroeconomic aggregates of small open economies such as Canada (see, for example, Cushman and Zha, 1997). This argument is not without limitations, however. Even if a small open economy is a price taker in world markets, both small and large economies may be driven by a common factor invalidating this exclusion restriction.
- Another possible source of identifying information is homogeneity restrictions on demand functions. For example, Galí (1992) imposes short-run homogeneity in the demand for money when assuming that the demand for real balances is not affected by contemporaneous changes in prices (given the nominal rate and output). This assumption amounts to assuming away costs of adjusting nominal money holdings. Similar homogeneity restrictions have also been used in Bernanke (1986).
- Extraneous parameter estimates: when impact responses (or their ratio) can be viewed as elasticities, it may be possible to impose values for those elasticities based on extraneous information from other studies. This approach has been used by Blanchard and Perotti (2002), for example. Similarly, Blanchard and Watson (1986) impose non-zero values for some structural parameters in B_0 based on extraneous information. If the parameter value cannot be pinned down with any degree of reliability, yet another possibility is to explore a grid of possible structural parameters values, as in Abraham and Haltiwanger (1995). A similar approach has also been used in Kilian (2010) and Davis and Kilian (2011) in an effort to assess the robustness of their baseline results. In a different context, Todd (1990) interprets Sims' (1980b) recursive VAR model of monetary policy in terms of alternative assumptions about the slopes of money demand and money supply curves.
- High-frequency data: in rare cases, it may be possible to test exclusion restrictions

more directly. For example, Kilian and Vega (2011) use daily data on US macroeconomic news to formally test the identifying assumption of no feedback within the month from US macroeconomic aggregates to the price of oil. Their work lends credence to exclusion restrictions in monthly VAR models ruling out instantaneous feedback from domestic macroeconomic aggregates to the price of oil.

It is fair to say that coming up with a set of credible short-run identifying restrictions is difficult. Whether a particular exclusion restriction is convincing, often depends on the data frequency, and in many cases there are not enough credible exclusion restrictions to achieve identification. This fact has stimulated interest in the alternative identification methods discussed in sections 3, 4 and 5.

2.3 Examples of Recursively Identified Models

2.3.1 Example 1: a simple macroeconomic model

Let $y_t = (p_t, gdp_t, m_t, i_t)$ where p_t is the log price level, gdp_t is log real GDP, m_t the log of a monetary aggregate such as M1, and i_t the federal funds rate. The data are quarterly and the proposed identification is recursive such that:

$$\begin{pmatrix} \varepsilon_t^p \\ \varepsilon_t^{gdp} \\ \varepsilon_t^m \\ \varepsilon_t^i \end{pmatrix} = \begin{bmatrix} a & 0 & 0 & 0 \\ b & c & 0 & 0 \\ d & e & f & 0 \\ g & h & i & j \end{bmatrix} \begin{pmatrix} u_t^1 \\ u_t^2 \\ u_t^3 \\ u_t^4 \end{pmatrix}.$$

Note that each line can be viewed as an equation. This may be seen by multiplying through each term on the right-hand side. Each reduced-form shock is a weighted average of selected structural shocks. The letters $a, b, \ldots, j$ represent the weights attached to the structural shocks. For example, the first equation is $\varepsilon_t^p = au_t^1 + 0 + 0 + 0$, the second reads $\varepsilon_t^{gdp} = bu_t^1 + cu_t^2 + 0 + 0$, and so on.

One way of rationalizing this identification would be to interpret the first two equations as an aggregate supply and aggregate demand model with a horizontal AS curve and downward-sloping AD curve. u_t^1 moves the price level and real output, so it must involve a shift of the AS curve. u_t^2 moves real output only, so it must represent a shift of the AD curve. The third equation could be interpreted as a money demand equation derived from the quantity equation: $MV = PY$, where V stands for velocity and Y for real income. Hence, u_t^3 can be interpreted as a velocity shock or money demand shock, if we take real GDP to represent real income. The last equation could represent a monetary policy reaction function. The Federal Reserve systematically responds to ε_t^p, ε_t^{gdp}, and ε_t^m (as well as lags of all variables). Any change in the interest rate not accounted for by this response, would be an exogenous monetary policy (or money supply) shock. Such policy shocks could arise from changes in the composition of the Federal Open Market Committee, for example, or may reflect reactions to idiosyncratic events such as 9/11 or the housing crisis that are not captured by standard policy rules.

It is easy to spot the limitations of this model. For example, why does money demand not respond to the interest rate within a quarter? How plausible is the horizontal supply curve? These are the types of questions that one must ask when assessing the plausibility of a structural VAR model. This example also illustrates that theory typically is not sufficient for identification, even if we are willing to condition on a particular theoretical model. For example, if the AS curve were vertical, but the AD curve horizontal by assumption, the first two equations of the structural model above would have to be modified. More generally, no recursive structure would be able to accommodate a theoretical model in which the AS and AD curves are neither horizontal nor vertical, but upward and downward sloping. This point highlights the difficulty of specifying fully structural models of the macroeconomy in recursive form and explains why such models have been largely abandoned.

2.3.2 Example 2: a model of the global market for crude oil

The second example is a structural VAR model of the global market for crude oil based on Kilian (2009). Let $y_t = (\Delta prod_t, rea_t, rpoil_t)$ where $\Delta prod_t$ denotes the percentage change in world crude oil production, rea_t is a suitably detrended measure of the log of global real economic activity, and $rpoil_t$ is the log of the real price of oil. The data are monthly.

$$\begin{pmatrix} \varepsilon_t^{\Delta prod} \\ \varepsilon_t^{rea} \\ \varepsilon_t^{rpoil} \end{pmatrix} = \begin{bmatrix} a & 0 & 0 \\ b & c & 0 \\ d & e & f \end{bmatrix} \begin{pmatrix} u_t^{flow\ supply} \\ u_t^{flow\ demand} \\ u_t^{other\ oil\ demand} \end{pmatrix}.$$

This model of the global market for crude oil embodies a vertical oil supply curve and a downward-sloping oil demand curve (conditional on lags of all variables). There are two demand shocks that are separately identified by the delay restriction that *other oil-demand shocks* raise the real price of oil, but without slowing down global real economic activity within the same month.

One might question whether one could have imposed an overidentifying restriction of the form $b = 0$. In other words, one would expect that higher oil prices triggered by unanticipated oil supply disruptions would not slow down global real activity within the month any more or less than *other oil demand shocks*. It turns out that the estimate of b is essentially zero, even without imposing that restriction, making this point moot. One also could question whether the short-run supply curve is truly vertical. Defending this assumption requires institutional knowledge of oil markets or extraneous econometric evidence. For example, Kellogg (2011) provides independent microeconomic evidence from Texan oil wells that oil producers are unresponsive to demand shocks in the short run even in competitive environments.

2.3.3 Example 3: models of the transmission of energy price shocks

The preceding two examples are recursively identified VAR models that are fully identified in that each structural shock is identified. Often we do not have enough restrictions to fully identify a VAR model. This has prompted the development of semistructural or partially identified VAR models. The idea of semistructural models is that in some cases we may be satisfied if we can identify a subset of the structural shocks. Often we are interested in one structural shock only. An example are models of the transmission of energy price shocks in which the price of energy is predetermined with respect to all domestic macroeconomic aggregates, consistent with the empirical evidence provided in Kilian and Vega (2011). For example, Edelstein and Kilian (2009) utilized a recursively identified monthly bivariate model similar to the model:

$$\begin{pmatrix} \varepsilon_t^{\Delta p} \\ \varepsilon_t^{\Delta c} \end{pmatrix} = \begin{bmatrix} a & 0 \\ b & c \end{bmatrix} \begin{pmatrix} u_t^1 \\ u_t^2 \end{pmatrix},$$

where Δp denotes the percentage change in US energy prices and Δc denotes the percentage growth in real US consumption. The model is semistructural in that only the innovation in the price of energy, u_t^1, is explicitly identified. The u_t^2 term, in contrast, is a conglomerate of other structural shocks that are not individually identified.

2.3.4 Example 4: semistructural models of monetary policy

Another situation in which we may be interested in identifying one structural shock only are VAR studies of monetary policy shocks. The simplest example is a quarterly model for $y_t = (\Delta gdp_t, \pi_t, i_t)$ where Δgdp_t denotes US real GDP growth, π_t the inflation rate, and i_t the federal funds rate. We use the Cholesky decomposition to compute

$$\begin{pmatrix} \varepsilon_t^{\Delta gdp} \\ \varepsilon_t^{\pi} \\ \varepsilon_t^{i} \end{pmatrix} = \begin{bmatrix} a & 0 & 0 \\ b & c & 0 \\ d & e & f \end{bmatrix} \begin{pmatrix} u_t^1 \\ u_t^2 \\ u_t^3 \end{pmatrix}.$$

The last equation of the model is interpreted as a linear monetary policy reaction function. The interest rate is the policy instrument. In setting ε_t^i, the Federal Reserve responds endogenously to contemporaneous movements in Δgdp and π. The residual left after accounting for all endogenous variation in the interest rate, u_t^3, is interpreted as an exogenous monetary policy shock. This policy shock reflects deviations from the expected (or average) policy response that may arise, for example, from changes in the composition of the Federal Open Market Committee or from discretionary policy decisions in response to extraordinary events. The policy shock, u_t^3, is the only structural shock of interest in this model. No attempt is made to identify the structural shocks u_t^1 and u_t^2.[3]

Models of this type have been commonly used in empirical work. The policy variable in semistructural VAR models need not be the short-term interest rate. A similar approach to identification may be followed with alternative policy indicators such as non-borrowed reserves (see, for example, Strongin, 1995). Regardless of the details of the specification, this identification scheme requires that the shock of interest be ordered at (or near) the bottom of the recursive ordering. Semistructural VAR models of monetary policy have five important weaknesses.

First, the model does not allow for feedback within a given quarter from u_t^3 to Δgdp_t and π_t. This seems implausible at least at quarterly frequency. Because Δgdp_t is not available at higher frequency, there is little we can do about this problem.[4] It might seem that the same identification scheme would be more credible if we replaced Δgdp_t by the growth rate of industrial production and estimated the model at monthly frequency. This is not the case. One problem is that industrial output accounts for only a fraction of total output. Moreover, real GDP is a measure of value added, whereas industrial output is a gross output measure. Finally, it is well known that the Federal Reserve is concerned with broader measures of real activity, making a policy reaction function based on industrial production growth economically less plausible and hence less interesting. In this regard, a better measure of monthly US real activity would be the Chicago Fed's monthly principal components index of US real activity (CFNAI). Yet another approach in the literature has been to interpolate quarterly real GDP data based on the fluctuations in monthly industrial production data and other monthly indicators. Such ad hoc methods not only suffer from the same deficiencies as the use of industrial production data, but they are likely to distort the structural impulse responses to be estimated.

Second, the Federal Reserve may respond systematically to more variables than just Δgdp_t and π_t. Examples are housing prices, stock prices, or industrial commodity prices. To the extent that we have omitted these variables from the model, we will obtain inconsistent estimates of d and e, and incorrect measures of the monetary policy shock u_t^3. In essence, the problem is that the policy shocks must be exogenous to allow us to learn about the effects of monetary policy shocks. Thus, it is common to enrich the set of variables ordered above the interest rate relative to this simple benchmark model and estimate much larger VAR systems (see, for example, Bernanke and Blinder, 1992; Sims, 1992; Christiano et al., 1999).

Adding more variables, however, invites overfitting and undermines the credibility of the VAR estimates. Standard VAR models cannot handle more than half a dozen variables, given typical sample sizes. One potential remedy of this problem is to work with factor augmented VAR (FAVAR) models, as in Bernanke and Boivin (2003), Bernanke et al. (2005), Stock and Watson (2005) or Forni et al. (2009). Alternatively, one can work with large-scale Bayesian VAR models in which the cross-sectional dimension K is allowed to be larger than the time dimension T, as in Banbura et al. (2010). These large-scale models are designed to incorporate a much richer information structure than conventional semistructural VAR models of monetary policy. FAVAR models and large-scale BVAR models have three distinct advantages over conventional small to medium sized VAR models. First, they allow for the fact that central bankers form expectations about domestic real activity and inflation based on hundreds of economic and financial time series rather than a handful of time series. Second, they allow for the fact that economic concepts such as domestic economic activity and inflation may not be well represented by a single observable time series. Third, they allow the user to construct the responses of many variables not included in conventional VAR models. There is evidence that allowing for richer information sets in specifying VAR models improves the plausibility of the estimated responses. It may mitigate the price puzzle, for example.[5]

Third, the identification of the VAR model hinges on the monetary policy reaction function being stable over time. To the extent that policymakers have at times changed the weights attached to their inflation and output objectives or the policy instrument, it becomes essential to split the sample in estimating the VAR model. The resulting shorter sample in turn makes it more difficult to include many variables in the model due to the lack of degrees of freedom. It also complicates statistical inference.

Fourth, the VAR model is linear. It does not allow for a lower bound on the interest rate, for example, making this model unsuitable for studying the quantitative easing of the Federal Reserve Board in recent years.

Fifth, most VAR models of monetary policy ignore the real-time nature of the policy decision problem. Not all data relevant to policymakers are available without delay and when data become available, they tend to be preliminary and subject to further revisions. To the extent that monetary policy shocks are defined as the residual of the policy reaction function, a misspecification of the policymaker's information set will cause biases in the estimated policy shocks. Bernanke and Boivin (2003) is an example of a study that explores the role of real-time data limitations in semistructural VAR models. Their conclusion is that – at least for their sample period – the distinction between real-time data and *ex-post* revised data is of limited importance.

Finally, it is useful to reiterate that the thought experiment contemplated in structural VAR models is an unanticipated monetary policy shock within an existing monetary policy rule. This exercise is distinct from that of changing the monetary policy rule (as happened in 1979 under Paul Volcker or in 2008 following the quantitative easing of the Federal Reserve Board). The latter question is of independent interest, but much harder to answer. The role of systematic monetary policy has been stressed in Leeper et al. (1996) and Bernanke et al. (1997), for example. Econometric evaluations of the role of systematic monetary policy, however, remain controversial and easily run afoul of the Lucas critique (see, for example, Kilian and Lewis (2011) and the references therein).

2.3.5 Example 5: the permanent income model of consumption

Cochrane (1994) proposes another application of the recursive model. His interest is not in identifying demand or supply shocks, but in decomposing permanent and transitory shocks within the framework of the permanent income model of consumption. The standard permanent income model implies that log real consumption (c_t) and log real income (gnp_t) are cointegrated such that the consumption–income ratio is stationary. Cochrane imposes this cointegration restriction on the reduced-form VAR model for (c_t, gnp_t). The permanent income model also predicts that if income changes unexpectedly without a corresponding change in consumption, then consumers will regard the shock to income as having purely transitory effects on income. Cochrane identifies such a shock by ordering innovations to consumption first in the Cholesky decomposition of the reduced-form error–covariance matrix. This decomposition allows him to separate permanent from transitory shocks and to quantify their importance for the variability of consumption and income:

$$\begin{pmatrix} \varepsilon_t^c \\ \varepsilon_t^{gnp} \end{pmatrix} = \begin{bmatrix} a & 0 \\ b & c \end{bmatrix} \begin{pmatrix} u_t^{permanent} \\ u_t^{transitory} \end{pmatrix}.$$

Note that by construction consumption only depends on the permanent shock, whereas income in addition depends on the transitory shock.[6] Cochrane verifies that the response of income to the transitory shock is indeed rapidly mean-reverting, whereas the response of income to a shock that moves both consumption and income on impact has long-lasting effects on income, as expected from a permanent shock. Moreover, much of the consumption response to a permanent shock is immediate, whereas the response of consumption to a transitory shock is close to zero at all horizons.[7] Unlike in our earlier examples, this methodology is silent about the economic interpretation of permanent and transitory shocks. There is no way to determine from the data whether these shocks refer to supply shocks or demand shocks, for example, or to preference shocks, policy shocks, or technology shocks. In general, the transitory and permanent shocks will be a mixture of these deeper economic shocks.

2.4 Examples of Non-recursively Identified Models

Not all structural VAR models have a recursive structure. Increasing skepticism toward atheoretical recursively identified models in the mid-1980s stimulated a series of studies proposing explicitly structural models identified by non-recursive short-run restrictions (see, for example, Bernanke, 1986; Sims, 1986; Blanchard and Watson, 1986). As in the recursive model, the identifying restrictions on B_0 or B_0^{-1} generate moment conditions that can be used to estimate the unknown coefficients in B_0. Efficient estimation of B_0 in these models can be cast in a GMM framework in which, in addition to the predetermined variables in the reduced form, the estimated structural errors are used as instruments in the equations with which the structural errors are assumed uncorrelated. In general, solving the moment conditions for the unknown structural parameters will require iteration, but in some cases the GMM estimator can be constructed using traditional instrumental-variable techniques (see, for example, Watson, 1994; Pagan and Robertson, 1998). An alternative commonly used approach is to model the error distribution as Gaussian and to estimate the structural model by full information maximum likelihood methods. This approach involves the maximization.of the concentrated likelihood with respect to the structural model parameters subject to the identifying restrictions (see, for example, Lütkepohl, 2005).

2.4.1 Example 6: fiscal policy shocks

Blanchard and Perotti (2002) introduce a model of US fiscal policy that deviates from the usual recursive structure. They propose a quarterly model of the US economy for $y_t = (tax_t, gov_t, gdp_t)$, where tax_t refers to real taxes, gov_t to real government spending, and gdp_t to real GDP. All variables are in logs. Ignoring lags, the model can be written as

$$\begin{pmatrix} \varepsilon_t^{tax} \\ \varepsilon_t^{gov} \\ \varepsilon_t^{gdp} \end{pmatrix} = \begin{pmatrix} a\varepsilon_t^{gdp} + bu_t^{gov} + u_t^{tax} \\ c\varepsilon_t^{gdp} + du_t^{tax} + u_t^{gov} \\ e\varepsilon_t^{tax} + f\varepsilon_t^{gov} + u_t^{gdp} \end{pmatrix}$$

Blanchard and Perotti first provide institutional arguments for the delay restriction $c = 0$ which rules out automatic feedback from economic activity to government spending within the quarter. They then show that the within-quarter response of taxes to economic activity, a, can be derived on the basis of extraneous tax elasticity estimates and can be shown to equal $a = 2.08$. The parameters e and f are left unrestricted. The potential endogeneity between taxes and spending is dealt with by imposing either $d = 0$ or $b = 0$. In the latter case, for example, we obtain

$$\begin{pmatrix} \varepsilon_t^{tax} \\ \varepsilon_t^{gov} \\ \varepsilon_t^{gdp} \end{pmatrix} = \begin{pmatrix} 2.08\varepsilon_t^{gdp} + u_t^{tax} \\ du_t^{tax} + u_t^{gov} \\ e\varepsilon_t^{tax} + f\varepsilon_t^{gov} + u_t^{gdp} \end{pmatrix}$$

This system can easily be solved numerically imposing the two exclusion restrictions and the equality restriction on b when constructing the second moments. Note that Blanchard and Perotti effectively treat the first two innovations as mutually exogenous without imposing the overidentifying restriction on d. An obvious concern is that the model does not allow for the anticipation of fiscal shocks. Blanchard and Perotti discuss how this concern may be addressed by changing the timing assumptions and adding further identifying restrictions, if we are willing to postulate a specific form of foresight. Another concern is that the model does not condition on the debt structure (see, for example, Chung and Leeper, 2007). Allowing the debt structure to matter would result in a non-linear dynamic model not contained within the class of VAR models.

2.4.2 Example 7: an alternative simple macroeconomic model

Keating (1992) discusses a variation of the simple macroeconomic model we discussed earlier that does not impose a recursive structure and involves a different economic interpretation:

$$\begin{pmatrix} \varepsilon_t^p \\ \varepsilon_t^{gdp} \\ \varepsilon_t^i \\ \varepsilon_t^m \end{pmatrix} = \begin{pmatrix} u_t^{AS} \\ a\varepsilon_t^p + b\varepsilon_t^i + c\varepsilon_t^m + u_t^{IS} \\ d\varepsilon_t^m + u_t^{MS} \\ e(\varepsilon_t^{gdp} + \varepsilon_t^p) + f\varepsilon_t^i + u_t^{MD} \end{pmatrix}$$

The first equation again represents a horizontal AS curve, but the second equation now can be interpreted as an IS curve, allowing real output to respond to all other model variables. The third equation represents a simple money supply function, according to which the central bank adjusts the rate of interest in relation to the money stock, and the fourth equation is a money demand function in which short-run money holdings rise in proportion to nominal income, yielding the final restriction required for exact identification. Unlike in the earlier example, money holdings are allowed to depend on the interest rate as well. Clearly, this model specification embodies a very different view of what monetary policymakers do than more recently developed structural VAR models motivated by the literature on Taylor rules (see Taylor, 1993).

2.4.3 Limitations of non-recursively identified models

Non-recursively identified VAR models more closely resemble traditional simultaneous equation models. This means that they also are susceptible to the usual weaknesses of such models including the difficulty of finding strong instruments in identifying causal effects. A case in point is the literature on the liquidity effect. The liquidity effect refers to the short-run negative response of interest rates to an unanticipated monetary expansion. Although the presence of such an effect has been suspected for a long time, it has only been in the 1990s that structural VAR studies emerged concluding that there is a liquidity effect. Whereas the evidence of a liquidity effect is at best mixed in recursively identified models of monetary policy, empirical VAR studies based on non-recursive simultaneous equation systems have reliably produced a strong liquidity effect. This evidence might seem to suggest that more explicitly structural models are inherently superior to earlier semistructural models of monetary policy, but Pagan and Robertson (1998) show that the instruments underlying the three most important non-recursive studies of the liquidity effect appear weak in the econometric sense, calling into question any inferences made about the magnitude of the liquidity effect.

3 IDENTIFICATION BY LONG-RUN RESTRICTIONS

One alternative idea has been to impose restrictions on the long-run response of variables to shocks. In the presence of unit roots in some variables but not in others, this may allow us to identify at least some shocks. The promise of this alternative approach to identification is that it will allow us to dispense with the controversy about what the right short-run restrictions are and to focus on long-run properties of models that most economists can more easily agree on. For example, it has been observed that most economists agree that demand shocks such as monetary policy shocks are neutral in the long run, whereas productivity shocks are not. This idea was first introduced in the context of a bivariate model in Blanchard and Quah (1989).

Consider the structural VAR representation $B(L)y_t = u_t$ and the corresponding structural vector moving average (VMA) representation $y_t = B(L)^{-1}u_t = \Theta(L)u_t$. Also consider the reduced-form VAR model $A(L)y_t = \varepsilon_t$ and the corresponding reduced-form VMA representation $y_t = A(L)^{-1}\varepsilon_t = \Phi(L)\varepsilon_t$. By definition

$$\varepsilon_t = B_0^{-1}u_t$$

$$\Sigma_\varepsilon = B_0^{-1}B_0^{-1\prime}$$

where we imposed $\Sigma_u = I_K$. Recall that

$$A(L) = B_0^{-1}B(L)$$

$$B_0^{-1} = A(L)B(L)^{-1}$$

so for $L = 1$

$$B_0^{-1} = A(1)B(1)^{-1}$$

and hence

$$\begin{aligned}\Sigma_\varepsilon &= B_0^{-1}B_0^{-1\prime}\\ &= [A(1)B(1)^{-1}]\underbrace{[A(1)B(1)^{-1}]'}_{[B(1)^{-1}]'A(1)'}\end{aligned}$$

Premultiply both sides by $A(1)^{-1}$ and post-multiply both sides by $(A(1)^{-1})' = [A(1)']^{-1}$:

$$A(1)^{-1}\Sigma_\varepsilon(A(1)^{-1})' = A(1)^{-1}A(1)B(1)^{-1}[B(1)^{-1}]'A(1)'[A(1)']^{-1}$$

$$A(1)^{-1}\Sigma_\varepsilon(A(1)^{-1})' = [B(1)^{-1}][B(1)^{-1}]'$$

$$\Phi(1)\Sigma_\varepsilon\Phi(1)' = \Theta(1)\Theta(1)'$$

$$vec(\Phi(1)\Sigma_\varepsilon\Phi(1)') = vec(\Theta(1)\Theta(1)')$$

The key observation is that the expression on the left-hand side (LHS) can be estimated from the data. Both $\hat{\Sigma}_\varepsilon$ and the cumulative sum $\hat{\Phi}(1) = \hat{A}(1)^{-1}$ are observable based on the reduced-form model, given that $A(1) \equiv I - A_1 - \ldots - A_p$, so if we put enough restrictions on $\Theta(1)$, we can uniquely pin down the remaining elements of $\Theta(1)$ using numerical methods. Because the LHS represents a variance–covariance matrix, as in the case of short-run identification, we need $K(K-1)/2$ restrictions on $\Theta(1)$ to satisfy the order condition for exact identification. If the exclusion restrictions on $\Theta(1)$ are recursive, it suffices to apply a lower triangular Cholesky decomposition to $\hat{\Phi}(1)\hat{\Sigma}_\varepsilon\hat{\Phi}(1)'$.

What does it mean to impose restrictions on $\Theta(1)$? Observe that $\Theta(1) = B(1)^{-1}$ represents the sum of the structural impulse response coefficients. Its elements measure the long-run cumulative effects of each structural shock j on each variable i, so, for an I(1) variable entering the VAR model in log differences,

$$\Theta_{ij}(1) = 0$$

means that the log-level of this variable i is not affected in the long run by structural innovation j. Imposing zero restrictions on selected elements of $\Theta(1)$ allows us to differentiate between structural shocks that affect the log-level of an I(1) variable in the long run and shocks that do not. Clearly, it does not make sense to put any such restrictions on VAR variables that are I(0) because, for I(0) variables expressed in log-levels, $\Theta_{ij}(1) \neq 0 \; \forall j$ by construction.

Given a sufficient number of exclusion restrictions on the elements of $\Theta(1)$ allows us to solve for the remaining elements of $\Theta(1)$, which provides an estimate of

$$B_0^{-1} = A(1)\Theta(1),$$

where $A(1)$ can be consistently estimated. Once we have estimated B_0^{-1}, we can proceed as in the case of short-run identifying restrictions. Although we do not consider this case, note that it would be straightforward to combine short-run and long-run identifying restrictions in estimating B_0^{-1}, when using numerical solution methods. A good example is Galí (1992).

3.1 Examples of Models Identified by Long-run Restrictions

3.1.1 Example 8: a model of aggregate demand and aggregate supply

The first example is the original analysis in Blanchard and Quah (1989). Let ur_t denote the unemployment rate and gdp_t log real GDP. Consider

$$y_t = \begin{pmatrix} \Delta gdp_t \\ ur_t \end{pmatrix}$$

where by assumption $y_t \sim I(0)$, but $gdp_t \sim I(1)$. In principle, any other stationary variable such as the capacity utilization rate would have done just as well as the second element of y_t. After postulating a diagonal Σ_u matrix, we obtain:

$$B(1)y_t = u_t$$

$$\begin{bmatrix} 1 & 0 \\ -b_1 & 1 \end{bmatrix} \begin{pmatrix} \Delta gdp_t \\ ur_t \end{pmatrix} = \begin{pmatrix} u_t^{AS} \\ u_t^{AD} \end{pmatrix}$$

$$\begin{pmatrix} \Delta gdp_t \\ ur_t \end{pmatrix} = \begin{bmatrix} 1 & 0 \\ -a_1 & 1 \end{bmatrix}^{-1} \begin{pmatrix} u_t^{AS} \\ u_t^{AD} \end{pmatrix}$$

$$y_t = \Theta(1) u_t$$

The t-subscripts may be dropped because all relationships are long-run relationships. Equivalently, we could have imposed $\Sigma_u = I_2$. In that case

$$\Theta(1) = \begin{bmatrix} \theta_{11}(1) & 0 \\ \theta_{21}(1) & \theta_{22}(1) \end{bmatrix} = chol(\Phi(1)\Sigma_\varepsilon \Phi(1)')$$

which can also be solved using the Cholesky decomposition instead of numerical methods. Either way the identifying assumption is that aggregate demand shocks do not have long-run level effects on real GDP, whereas aggregate supply shocks do. Most applications of long-run restrictions involve a close variation on the theme of Blanchard and Quah (1989), in which the aggregate supply shock is interpreted as a permanent aggregate productivity shock. The analysis in Galí (1999) is a good example. Even if more variables are included in VAR models based on long-run restrictions, the focus typically is on identifying the responses to aggregate productivity shocks only as opposed to other structural shocks.[8]

3.1.2 Example 9: a Keynesian model

The second example is from Keating (1992). The data vector includes real output (gdp), the real interest rate (r), real money balances ($m - p$) and the monetary aggregate (m). There are four structural shocks: an aggregate supply shock, an IS shock, a money demand shock and a money supply (or monetary policy) shock:

$$gdp = u^{AS}$$
$$r = a_1 gdp + u^{IS}$$
$$m - p = a_2 gdp + a_3 r + u^{MD}$$
$$m = a_4 gdp + a_5 r + a_6(m - p) + u^{MS}$$

which implies

$$C(1) = \begin{bmatrix} 1 & 0 & 0 & 0 \\ -a_1 & 1 & 0 & 0 \\ -a_2 & -a_3 & 1 & 0 \\ -a_4 & -a_5 & -a_6 & 1 \end{bmatrix}^{-1}$$

Although this example is somewhat old-fashioned, it is included as a counterpart to the earlier macroeconomic VAR examples based on short-run restrictions. The first identifying assumption is that in the long run only AS shocks affect real output. Second, monetary shocks do not affect capital accumulation and hence do not affect the IS curve. Third, money supply shocks do not affect real balances in the long run.

3.1.3 Example 10: a model of the neoclassical synthesis

The third example is Shapiro and Watson's (1988) model of the US economy that exploits insights from neoclassical economics about long-run behavior, while allowing for Keynesian explanations of short-run behavior. Unlike the preceding example, Shapiro and Watson do not take a stand on the economic model underlying the short-run behavior. Let h_t denote the log of hours worked, o_t the price of oil, gdp_t the log of real GDP, π_t inflation and i_t the nominal interest rate. Shapiro and Watson decompose fluctuations in $y_t = (\Delta h_t, \Delta o_t, \Delta gdp_t, \Delta\pi_t, i_t - \pi_t)$ in terms of labor supply shocks, technology shocks and two aggregate demand shocks. The first identifying assumption is that aggregate demand shocks have no long-run effects on real GDP or hours worked. The second identifying assumption is that the long-run labor supply is exogenous, which allows Shapiro and Watson to separate the effects of shocks to technology and to labor supply. The third identifying assumption is that exogenous oil price shocks have a permanent effect on the level of all variables but hours worked. The two aggregate demand shocks may be interpreted as goods market (IS) and money market (LM) shocks. No effort is made to identify the two aggregate demand shocks separately. The matrix of long-run multipliers is

$$C(1) = \begin{bmatrix} a & 0 & 0 & 0 & 0 \\ 0 & b & 0 & 0 & 0 \\ c & d & e & 0 & 0 \\ f & g & h & i & j \\ k & l & m & n & o \end{bmatrix}$$

Note that the structure of $C(1)$ is not recursive.

3.2 Limitations of Long-run Restrictions

One important limitation of long-run identification schemes is that they require us to take a stand on the presence of exact unit roots in the autoregressive lag order polynomial $A(L)$. This means that this alternative approach is more limited in scope than VAR models based on short-run restrictions. In addition, there also are serious concerns about the reliability of long-run restrictions:

- One weakness of VAR models identified by long-run restrictions is that they require an accurate estimate of the impulse responses at the infinite horizon. This, however, is akin to pinning down the dominant autoregressive root of the process. We know that it is not possible to estimate accurately the long-run behavior of an economic time series from a short time span of data. For that reason one would expect such structural VAR models to be unreliable in finite samples. Exactly this point was made by Faust and Leeper (1997).
- Second, numerical estimates of the responses in VAR models identified by long-run restrictions are identified only up to their sign. This fact matters. For example,

researchers have been frequently interested in the sign of the response of real output to a productivity shock. Without further identifying assumptions, models based on long-run restrictions cannot resolve this question (also see Taylor, 2004).

- A third concern is that the I(0) variable used to aid in the identification often itself is quite persistent. The unemployment rate used in Blanchard and Quah's (1989) model is a good example. In this regard, Gospodinov (2010) proves that the impulse responses of interest are not consistently estimable under the long-run identification scheme when the process for this variable is parameterized as local to unity. Likewise, standard confidence intervals are invalid. Gospodinov studies the statistical properties of the impulse response estimator in the context of the technology shock example where labor productivity (or real output) is assumed to have an exact unit root, and hours worked (or the unemployment rate) are modeled as a near-integrated process. He expresses this estimation problem as an instrumental variable problem and demonstrates that it is equivalent to a weak-instrument problem. His analysis suggests that many applications of this methodology based on models with highly persistent I(0) variables have been invalid.
- Fourth, it has been observed that the conclusion from Blanchard–Quah type VAR models are sensitive to whether the second variable (for example, unemployment rate or hours worked) is entered in levels or differences. In related work, Gospodinov et al. (2011) clarify the empirical source of the extensive debate on the effect of technology shocks on unemployment/hours worked. They find that the contrasting conclusions from specifying the second VAR variable in levels as opposed to differences can be explained by a small, but important, low frequency co-movement between hours worked and labor productivity or output growth, which is allowed for in the level specification but is implicitly set to zero in the differenced specification. Their theoretical analysis shows that, even when the root of hours is very close to 1 and the low frequency co-movement is quite small, assuming away or explicitly removing the low frequency component can have important implications for the long-run identifying restrictions, giving rise to biases large enough to account for the empirical difference between the two specifications. Which specification is right is ultimately an economic question and continues to be debated. For a closely related analysis see also Canova et al. (2010).

4 IDENTIFICATION BY SIGN RESTRICTIONS

Skepticism toward traditional identifying assumptions based on short-run or long-run exclusion restrictions in recent years has made increasingly popular an alternative class of structural VAR models in which structural shocks are identified by restricting the sign of the responses of selected model variables to structural shocks. This approach was pioneered by Faust (1998), Canova and De Nicolo (2002) and Uhlig (2005) in the context of VAR models of monetary policy. For example, Uhlig (2005) postulated that an unexpected monetary policy contraction is associated with an increase in the federal funds rate, the absence of price increases and the absence of increases in non-borrowed reserves for some time following the monetary policy shock. Uhlig showed that sign-identified models may produce substantially different results from conventional structural VAR models. Sign-identified VAR models have become increasingly popular in other areas as well and are now part of the mainstream of empirical macroeconomics. They have been used to study fiscal shocks (for example, Canova and Pappa, 2007; Mountford and Uhlig, 2009; Pappa, 2009), technology shocks (for example, Dedola and Neri, 2007), and various other shocks in open economies (for example, Canova and De Nicolo, 2002; Scholl and Uhlig, 2008), in oil markets (for example, Baumeister and Peersman, 2012; Kilian and Murphy, 2012, 2013), and in labor markets (for example, Fujita, 2011).

Identification in sign-identified models requires that each identified shock is associated with a unique sign pattern. Sign restrictions may be static, in which case we simply restrict the sign of the coefficients in B_0^{-1}. Unlike traditional exclusion restrictions, such sign restrictions can often be motivated directly from economic theory. In addition, one may restrict the sign of responses at longer horizons, although the theoretical rationale of such restrictions is usually weaker. There is a misperception among many users that these models are more general and hence more credible than VAR models based on exclusion restrictions. This is not the case. Note that sign-identified models by construction are more restrictive than standard VAR models in some dimensions and less restrictive in others. They do not nest models based on exclusion restrictions.

For a given set of sign restrictions, we proceed as follows. Consider the reduced-form VAR model $A(L)y_t = \varepsilon_t$, where y_t is the K-dimensional vector of variables, $A(L)$ is a finite-order autoregressive lag polynomial, and ε_t is the vector of white noise reduced-form innovations with variance–covariance matrix Σ_ε. Let u_t denote the corresponding structural VAR model innovations. The construction of structural impulse response functions requires an estimate of the $K \times K$ matrix B_0^{-1} in $\varepsilon_t = B_0^{-1}u_t$.

Let P denote the lower triangular Cholesky decomposition that satisfies $\Sigma_\varepsilon = PP'$. Then $B_0^{-1} = PD$ also satisfies $\Sigma_\varepsilon = B_0^{-1}B_0^{-1\prime}$ for any orthogonal $K \times K$ matrix D. Unlike P, PD will in general be non-recursive. One can examine a wide range of possible solutions B_0^{-1} by repeatedly drawing at random from the set $\mathbf{D}$ of orthogonal matrices D. Following Rubio-Ramirez et al. (2010) one constructs the set of admissible models by drawing from the set $\mathbf{D}$ and discarding candidate solutions for B_0^{-1} that do not satisfy a set of a priori sign restrictions on the implied impulse responses functions.

The procedure consists of the following steps:

1. Draw a $K \times K$ matrix L of $NID(0, 1)$ random variables. Derive the QR decomposition of L such that $L = Q \cdot R$ and $QQ' = I_K$.
2. Let $D = Q'$. Compute impulse responses using the orthogonalization $B_0^{-1} = PD$. If all implied impulse response functions satisfy the identifying restrictions, retain D. Otherwise discard D.
3. Repeat the first two steps a large number of times, recording each D that satisfies the restrictions (and the corresponding impulse response functions).

The resulting set $\boldsymbol{B}_0^{-1}$ in conjunction with the reduced-form estimates characterizes the set of admissible structural VAR models.

The fraction of the initial candidate models that satisfy the identifying restriction may be viewed as an indicator of how informative the identifying restrictions are about the structural parameters. Note that a small fraction of admissible models is not an indication of how well the identifying restrictions fit the data. There is no way of evaluating the validity of identifying restrictions based on the reduced form. All candidate models by construction fit the data equally well because they are constructed from the same reduced-form model.

4.1 Interpretation

A fundamental problem in interpreting VAR models identified based on sign restrictions is that there is not a unique point estimate of the structural impulse response functions. Unlike conventional structural VAR models based on short-run restrictions, sign-identified VAR models are only set identified. This problem arises because sign restrictions represent inequality restrictions. The cost of remaining agnostic about the precise values of the structural model parameters is that the data are potentially consistent with a wide range of structural models that are all admissible in that they satisfy the identifying restrictions. Without further assumptions there is no way of knowing which of these models is most likely. A likely outcome in practice is that the structural impulse responses implied by the admissible models will disagree on the substantive economic questions of interest.

- One early approach to this problem, exemplified by Faust (1998), has been to focus on the admissible model that is most favorable to the hypothesis of interest. This allows us to establish the extent to which this hypothesis could potentially explain the data. It may also help us to rule out a hypothesized explanation, if none of the admissible models supports this hypothesis. The problem is that this approach is not informative about whether any one of the admissible models is a more likely explanation of the data than some other model. There are examples in which the admissible structural models are sufficiently similar to allow unambiguous answers to the question of economic interest (see, for example, Kilian and Murphy, 2012, 2013). Typically, however, the set of admissible models will be equally consistent with competing economic hypotheses.
- The standard procedure for characterizing the set of admissible models outlined above conditions on a given estimate of the reduced-form VAR model and does not account for estimation uncertainty. A method of constructing classical confidence intervals for sign-identified VAR impulse responses has recently been developed by Moon et al. (2009). Unlike in structural VAR models based on exclusion restrictions, the asymptotic distribution of the structural impulse responses is non-standard and the construction of these non-standard confidence intervals is computationally costly. Moreover, these intervals are not informative about the shape of the impulse response functions in that a given confidence set is consistent with a wide range of different shapes. This fact makes it difficult to interpret the results from an economic point of view.
- The most common approach in the literature has been to rely on Bayesian methods of inference. Under the assumption of a conventional Gaussian-inverse Wishart prior on the reduced-form parameters and a prior on the rotation matrices conditional on a given reduced-form model estimate, one can construct the posterior distribution of the impulse responses by simulating posterior draws from the

reduced-form posterior and applying the identification procedure to each reduced-form posterior draw. In simulating this posterior distribution, care must be taken that the posterior is approximated using a sufficiently large number of reduced-form draws as well as a sufficiently large number of rotations for each posterior draw from the reduced form.

Given the posterior distribution of the structural impulse responses we can make probability statements about the structural impulse responses. The standard approach in the literature for many years has been to report the vector of pointwise posterior medians of the structural impulse responses as a measure of the central tendency of the impulse response functions. This approach suffers from two distinct shortcomings. First, the vector of pointwise posterior median responses (often referred to as the *median response function*) will not correspond to the response function of any of the admissible models, unless the pointwise posterior medians of all impulse response coefficients in the VAR system correspond to the same structural model, which is highly unlikely a priori. Thus, the median response function lacks a structural economic interpretation (see, for example, Fry and Pagan, 2011). Second, median response functions are not a valid statistical summary of the set of admissible impulse response functions. It is well known that the vector of medians is not the median of a vector. In fact, the median of a vector-valued random variable does not exist, rendering the vector of pointwise medians inappropriate as a statistical measure of the central tendency of the impulse response functions. This means that even if there were an admissible structural model with the same impulse response function as the median response function, there would be no compelling reason to focus on this model in interpreting the evidence. In fact, it has been shown that posterior median response functions may be quite misleading about the most likely response dynamics in sign-identified models (see, for example, Kilian and Murphy, 2012; Inoue and Kilian, 2013).

- A solution to this problem has recently been proposed in Inoue and Kilian (2013) who show how to characterize the most likely admissible model(s) within the set of structural VAR models that satisfy the sign restrictions. The most likely structural model can be computed from the posterior mode of the joint distribution of admissible models both in the fully identified and in the partially identified case. The resulting set of structural response functions is well defined from an economic and a statistical point of view. Inoue and Kilian also propose a highest-posterior density credible set that characterizes the joint uncertainty about the set of admissible models. Unlike conventional posterior error bands or confidence bands for sign-identified VAR models, the implied credible sets for the structural response functions characterize the full uncertainty about the structural response functions.
- The reason that classical estimation methods are inherently uninformative about which of the admissible structural models is most likely is that the likelihood is flat with respect to the choice of rotation matrix. An obvious question is how Bayesian methods are able to overcome this problem. The answer is that they rely on a prior distribution over the set $\mathbf{D}$. This prior is not based on economic information, however, and there is no way for the data to overrule this prior even asymptotically because the likelihood does not depend on D. It can be shown that the posterior

distribution of the VAR impulse responses depends on the prior for D as well as the prior for the reduced-form parameters and the likelihood. An open question that is the subject of ongoing research is to what extent the posterior distribution of the impulse responses of sign-identified VAR models depends on the ad hoc prior for the rotation matrices, as opposed to other aspects of the prior or the data.

4.2 Extensions

Since the introduction of VAR models based on sign restrictions several researchers have made proposals to facilitate the interpretation of a set of admissible structural impulse response functions. Broadly speaking, there are two approaches. One approach involves the use of a penalty function to narrow down the set of admissible models to a singleton (see, for example, Uhlig, 2005). For example, Francis et al. (2010) identify a technology shock as that shock which satisfies sign restrictions and maximizes the forecast-error variance share in labor productivity at a finite horizon. Faust (1998) appeals to an analogous argument regarding the effects of monetary policy shocks on real output. Penalty functions help in assessing worst case (or best case) scenarios, based on the set of admissible models, but the results are best thought of as providing evidence that some outcome is possible rather than that it is true or that it is the most likely outcome.

An alternative approach has been to narrow down the set of admissible responses by imposing additional restrictions. The idea is to reduce the set of admissible models to a small number of admissible models that are easier to interpret and, ideally, have similar impulse responses. For example, Canova and De Nicolo (2002) and Canova and Paustian (2011) propose to reduce the number of admissible solutions by imposing additional structure in the form of sign restrictions on dynamic cross-correlations. They motivate these restrictions based on properties of DSGE models and show that these restrictions are needed to recover the DSGE model responses from data generated by DSGE models. In related work, Kilian and Murphy (2011, 2012) propose additional identifying restrictions based on bounds on impact price elasticities in the context of a structural oil market VAR model. This can be considered a special case of imposing a prior distribution on the values of these price elasticities.

Imposing such additional restrictions has been shown to improve the ability of sign-identified VARs to discriminate between alternative data generating processes. The use of all available information in identifying structural shocks from sign-identified models is not merely an option – it is essential. There is a perception among some applied users that remaining agnostic about all but a small number of sign restrictions can only increase the chances of inferring the true structural responses from sign-identified VAR models. This perception is erroneous. In constructing the posterior distribution of the structural responses one implicitly assumes that all admissible models are equally likely a priori. If we know this assumption to be violated and fail to impose further restrictions, we end up averaging models with incorrect probability weights invalidating the implied posterior distribution of the impulse responses. For example, Kilian and Murphy (2012) demonstrate that oil market VAR models identified by sign restrictions only may imply large responses of the real price of oil to oil supply shocks, yet these responses can be ruled out merely by imposing a bound on the short-run price elasticity of oil supply, consistent with long-established views in the literature and extraneous empirical evidence that this elasticity is close to zero. They further show that the failure to impose this additional identifying information would have misled researchers by assigning more importance to oil supply shocks than is warranted by the data.

4.3 Examples of Sign-identified VAR Models

4.3.1 Example 11: an alternative model of monetary policy shocks

Uhlig (2005) proposes replacing a conventional semistructural model of monetary policy by a model based only on sign restrictions. His set of model variables consists of monthly US data for the log of interpolated real US GDP, the log of the interpolated GDP deflator, the log of a commodity price index, total reserves, non-borrowed reserves and the federal funds rate. Uhlig postulates that an unexpected monetary policy contraction is associated with an increase in the federal funds rate, the absence of price increases and the absence of increases in non-borrowed reserves for some time following the policy shock.

$$\begin{pmatrix} \varepsilon_t^{\Delta gdp} \\ \varepsilon_t^{defl} \\ \varepsilon_t^{pcom} \\ \varepsilon_t^{tr} \\ \varepsilon_t^{nbr} \\ \varepsilon_t^{ff} \end{pmatrix} = \begin{bmatrix} \times & \times & \times & \times & \times & \times \\ \times & \times & \times & \times & \times & - \\ \times & \times & \times & \times & \times & - \\ \times & \times & \times & \times & \times & \times \\ \times & \times & \times & \times & \times & - \\ \times & \times & \times & \times & \times & + \end{bmatrix} \begin{pmatrix} u_t^1 \\ u_t^2 \\ u_t^3 \\ u_t^4 \\ u_t^5 \\ u_t^6 \end{pmatrix}.$$

where + and − denotes the postulated sign of the impact response and × denotes no restriction. The model is partially identified in that only the response to an unanticipated monetary tightening is identified. It is also set-identified in that sign restrictions are consistent with a range of admissible models. The same sign restrictions are imposed for half a year following the monetary policy shock. As shown by Uhlig (2005), this model is uninformative even about the direction of the real GDP response to a monetary policy shock. If the identifying restrictions are strengthened by the restriction that the response of real GDP is negative in month 6 following a monetary policy tightening, however, inference can be sharpened considerably (see Inoue and Kilian, 2013). This additional restriction allows us to remain agnostic about the short- and long-run responses of real GDP, while expressing the common conviction that a monetary tightening is associated with a decline in real activity in the foreseeable future.

4.3.2 Example 12: an alternative model of the global market for crude oil

We have already considered a fully identified monthly model of the global market for crude oil based on exclusion restrictions on B_0^{-1}. Inoue and Kilian (2013) provide an alternative fully identified model based on sign restrictions:

$$\begin{pmatrix} \varepsilon_t^{\Delta prod} \\ \varepsilon_t^{rea} \\ \varepsilon_t^{rpoil} \end{pmatrix} = \begin{bmatrix} - & + & + \\ - & + & - \\ + & + & + \end{bmatrix} \begin{pmatrix} u_t^{flow\ supply} \\ u_t^{flow\ demand} \\ u_t^{other\ oil\ demand} \end{pmatrix}.$$

Here the required signs of each element of B_0^{-1} have been indicated by + and −. Flow supply shocks are normalized to correspond to supply disruptions. An unanticipated flow supply disruption causes oil production to fall, the real price of oil to increase, and global real activity to fall on impact. An unanticipated increase in the flow demand for oil driven by the global business cycle causes global oil production, global real activity and the real price of oil to increase on impact. Other positive oil demand shocks (such as shocks to oil inventory demand driven by forward-looking behavior) cause oil production and the real price of oil to increase on impact and global real activity to fall. In addition, the impact price elasticity of oil supply is bounded above by 0.025, as suggested by Kilian and Murphy (2012). This bound is consistent with widely held views among oil economists that the short-run price elasticity of oil supply is close to zero. The elasticity in question can be expressed as the ratio of two impact responses, making it straightforward to discard draws that violate that restriction. Finally, following Baumeister and Peersman (2012) the real price of oil is restricted to be positive for the first year in response to unanticipated oil supply disruptions and in response to positive oil demand shocks.

5 ALTERNATIVE STRUCTURAL VAR APPROACHES

VAR models identified by sign restrictions are the most popular alternative to VAR models identified by short-run or long-run exclusion restrictions, but not the only alternative. Discomfort with semistructural models of monetary policy in particular has stimulated the development of two more methodologies. It has been noted, in particular, that the sequences of policy shocks identified by such models do not always correspond to common perceptions of when policy shocks occurred. For example, Rudebusch (1998) compares estimates of monetary policy shocks from semistructural VAR models to financial market measures of policy shocks and finds little correspondence. He views this as evidence against the identifying assumptions employed in semistructural VAR models of monetary policy (also see Cochrane and Piazzesi, 2002).

5.1 Financial Market Shocks

This critique stimulated a new identification method by Faust et al. (2004) who identify monetary policy shocks in monthly VAR models based on high-frequency futures market data. Using the prices of daily federal funds futures contracts, they measure the impact of the surprise component of Federal Reserve policy decisions on the expected future trajectory of interest rates. It is shown how this information can be used to identify the effects of a monetary policy shock in a standard VAR. This alternative approach to identification is quite different from the conventional identifying restrictions in monetary policy VAR models in that it dispenses with the exclusion restrictions used in semistructural models of monetary policy.

Faust et al.'s procedure involves two key steps: first, they use the futures market to measure the response of expected future interest rates to an unexpected change in the Federal Reserve's target rate. Specifically, they treat the change in the futures rate on the day on which a change in the Fed's target federal funds rate is announced as a measure of the change in market expectations. This interpretation requires that risk premia remain unchanged. Faust et al. further postulate that this change in expectations is due to the policy shock only. In other words, no other news moves the market on that day and the policy announcement itself does not reveal information about other structural shocks. In the second step, they impose that the impulse responses of the funds rate to the monetary policy shock in the VAR model must match the response measured from the futures data.

While these two steps are conceptually straightforward, carefully implementing them in practice requires dealing with several complications. Measuring the response of the funds rate to policy shocks in the futures data requires taking account of several peculiar aspects of the futures market and testing the validity of the underlying assumptions. Moreover, the information from the futures market only set-identifies the structural VAR model. The most striking implication of set identification is that one must give up on point estimation of the structural responses and focus on confidence intervals instead, similar to classical inference in sign-identified VAR models.

In their empirical analysis, Faust et al. find that the usual recursive identification of monetary policy shocks is rejected, as is any identification that insists on a monetary policy shock having no effect on prices contemporaneously. This confirms our earlier concerns with semistructural monetary policy VAR models. Their identification also eliminates the price puzzle – the finding in the benchmark recursive identification that the impulse response of prices first rises slightly but significantly, before falling. Faust et al. nevertheless find that only a small fraction of the variance of output can be attributed to monetary policy shocks, as has been shown by the sign-identification methodology in Faust (1998).

D'Amico and Farka's (2011) analysis of stock market and interest rate data takes this approach a step further. Rather than just estimating the response of stock returns to monetary policy shocks identified from high-frequency data, they propose a VAR methodology for estimating simultaneously the response of stock returns to policy decisions and the Federal Reserve's contemporaneous reaction to the stock market. Their methodology has broad applicability when modeling asset prices. D'Amico and Farka's approach involves two steps. In the first step, the response of the stock market to policy shocks is estimated outside the VAR model by measuring changes in intraday S&P500 futures prices immediately before and after policy announcements. The monthly policy shock is obtained by summing the intraday shocks over the course of a given month. In the second step, D'Amico and Farka impose that external estimate when estimating the response of the federal funds rate to stock returns in a monthly VAR model.

5.2 Identification by Heteroskedasticity

Rigobon (2003) develops yet another method for solving the VAR identification problem based on the heteroskedasticity of the structural shocks. Heteroskedasticity may arise, for example, as a result of financial crises. In the baseline model, Rigobon considers heteroskedasticity that can be described as a two-regime process and shows that the structural parameters of the system are just identified. He also discusses identification under more general conditions such as when there are more than two regimes, when common unobservable shocks exist, and situations in which the nature of the heteroskedasticity is misspecified.

For expository purposes recall the two-equation model of demand and supply based on price and quantity data. All lags have been suppressed for notational convenience:

$$\begin{pmatrix} \varepsilon_t^p \\ \varepsilon_t^q \end{pmatrix} = \begin{bmatrix} 1 & \beta \\ \alpha & 1 \end{bmatrix} \begin{pmatrix} u_t^1 \\ u_t^2 \end{pmatrix}.$$

Under the standard assumption of unconditional homoskedasticity, it can be shown that the reduced-form error covariance matrix is:

$$\Sigma_\varepsilon = \frac{1}{(1 - \alpha\beta)^2} \begin{bmatrix} \beta^2\sigma_2^2 + \sigma_1^2 & \beta\sigma_2^2 + \alpha\sigma_1^2 \\ \cdot & \sigma_2^2 + \alpha^2\sigma_1^2 \end{bmatrix},$$

where σ_1^2 and σ_2^2 denote the variance of the first and the second structural shock. There are three moments in four unknowns (α, β, σ_1^2, σ_2^2), so without further assumptions such as $\alpha = 0$ or $\beta = 0$ it is not possible to identify the structural shocks from the data in this baseline model. This is the basic identification problem discussed throughout this survey.

Now suppose that there are two regimes in the variances of the structural shocks. Further suppose that the difference between regimes is that in one regime the unconditional variance of the supply shock increases relative to the unconditional variance of the demand shocks, while the parameters α and β remain unchanged across regimes. This variance shift suffices to approximate the slope of the demand curve.

As a result of the regime shift, we obtain two expressions of the variance–covariance matrix, one for each regime $r \in \{1,2\}$:

$$\Sigma_{\varepsilon,r} = \frac{1}{(1 - \alpha\beta)^2} \begin{bmatrix} \beta^2\sigma_{2,r}^2 + \sigma_{1,r}^2 & \beta\sigma_{2,r}^2 + \alpha\sigma_{1,r}^2 \\ \cdot & \sigma_{2,r}^2 + \alpha^2\sigma_{1,r}^2 \end{bmatrix}.$$

This means that there are now six moments in six unknowns, allowing us to solve for all six structural parameters (α, β, $\sigma_{1,1}^2$, $\sigma_{2,1}^2$, $\sigma_{1,2}^2$, $\sigma_{2,2}^2$) without restricting α or β. Rigobon (2003) applies this methodology to the problem of characterizing the contemporaneous relationship between the returns on Argentinean, Brazilian and Mexican sovereign bonds – a case in which standard identification methodologies do not apply. Rigobon's approach is of particular interest for modeling asset prices because instantaneous feedback must be assumed when trading is near-continuous. It is not without serious limitations, however. Not only is there uncertainty about the existence, number, and timing of the variance regimes, but in practice we are not likely to know whether a high volatility regime is caused by a relative increase in the volatility of demand shocks or of supply shocks, without assuming the answer to the identification question. This means that we do not know whether we are identifying the supply curve or the demand curve, which is the central question of interest. This problem is particularly apparent in modeling the global market for crude oil. Researchers have proposed competing views of what increased oil price volatility in the 1970s and Rigobon's methodology would not be able to tell us, which view is supported by the data. This concern is less of an issue if the shock of interest can be associated with one variable only, as would be the case when modeling monetary policy shocks within a policy reaction function.

The latter case is discussed in Lanne and Lütkepohl (2008). Lanne and Lütkepohl propose a test of over-identifying restrictions within the structural VAR framework of Bernanke and Mihov (1998). Their test exploits evidence of structural change in the variance–covariance matrix of the reduced-form shocks. As in Rigobon's work, the maintained assumption is that the autoregressive parameters are time invariant. Volatility in the shocks is significantly higher during the Volcker period than the post-Volcker period. This volatility change may be used to test alternative models of the money market. Based on monthly US data for 1965 to 1996, Lanne and Lütkepohl conclude that a model in which monetary policy shocks are associated with shocks to non-borrowed reserves is rejected by the data, whereas a model in which the Federal Reserve accommodates demand shocks to total reserves is not rejected.

In closely related work, Lanne et al. (2010) address the issue of how to detect structural changes in the volatility of the VAR errors in the data. They consider the important special case of volatility shifts that follow a Markov regime switching model (see Sims and Zha, 2006). Identification is achieved by assuming that the shocks are orthogonal across states and that only the variances of the shocks change across states, while the other model parameters remain unaffected. Modeling the reduced-form errors as a Markov regime switching model provides data-dependent estimates of the dates of volatility shifts, conditional on the assumed number of regimes.

Finally, a related identification methodology for vector autoregressions with non-normal residuals has also been discussed by Lanne and Lütkepohl (2010). It is well known that VAR regression errors are frequently non-normal. These errors may be modeled as a mixture of normal distributions. That assumption is useful, for example, when the reduced-form error distribution has heavy tails and a tendency to generate outliers. In that case, one may think of the outliers as being generated by a distribution different from the distribution of the other observations and identification may be obtained by heteroskedasticity across regimes. Unlike in Rigobon's approach, the unconditional error distribution remains homoskedastic, however, and the regime switches in the model are generated endogeneously.

5.3 Identification in the Presence of Forward-looking Behavior

It is important to stress that standard VAR models of monetary policy are concerned with responses to unanticipated policy shocks. They have nothing to say about the effects of anticipated monetary policy shocks. For further discussion see also Leeper et al. (1996), Bernanke and Mihov (1998) and Christiano et al. (1999). The anticipation of shocks is an even greater concern when modeling fiscal policy shocks or productivity shocks and requires fundamental modifications in the analysis. The mere possibility of forward-looking behavior greatly complicates the identification of structural shocks in VAR models.

The maintained assumption in structural VAR analysis is that the structural data-generating process can be represented as a VAR model. In other words, we start with the structural VAR representation with the objective of recovering the structural VMA representation. Suppose that instead we started with the premise that the data-generating process is of the form of the structural VMA

$$y_t = \Theta(L)u_t.$$

where the number of variables equals the number of structural shocks. Not every structural VMA has an equivalent structural VAR representation. Expressing the structural VMA process as a structural VAR process of the form

$$\Theta(L)^{-1}y_t = B(L)y_t = u_t$$

requires all roots of $\det(\Theta(L))$ to be outside the unit circle. This condition rules out models with unit roots in the moving average polynomial, for example, because in that case the moving average polynomial is not invertible. This situation will arise when the data have been overdifferenced. Such cases can be handled by transforming the data appropriately. A more serious complication is that the moving average roots may be inside the unit circle. In this case, the model is said to be non-fundamental. Such representations imply the same autocovariance structure as the fundamental representation, but the underlying structural shocks cannot be recovered from current and past observations of the variables included in the VAR model even asymptotically. Consequently, when the economic model does not guarantee fundamentalness, standard structural impulse response analysis may be misleading (see Lippi and Reichlin, 1993, 1994).

How concerned we should be with that possibility depends on whether non-fundamental representations can be shown to arise in economic theory. In this regard, Hansen and Sargent (1991) illustrated that non-fundamental representations may arise in rational expectations models when agents respond to expectational variables that are not observable to the econometrician. This result suggests extreme caution in interpreting structural VAR models when the VAR information set is smaller than that of the agents making economic decisions in the real world, as would typically be the case in models with forward-looking behavior. If we think of asset prices containing information about expected movements in real macroeconomic aggregates beyond the information in the lagged macroeconomic aggregates, for example, then a VAR including only real macroeconomic aggregates would be misspecified. In particular, we would not be able to recover the true structural shocks of this economy from the reduced-form VAR representation under any possible identification scheme. If we simply ignored this problem, we would end up identifying seemingly structural shocks without economic meaning. For further discussion see Lippi and Reichlin (1993, 1994), Blanchard and Quah (1993), Forni et al. (2009) and Leeper et al. (2011).

A formal test designed to detect non-fundamentalness of this type in a given structural VAR model was proposed by Giannone and Reichlin (2006). Giannone and Reichlin showed that Granger causality from a set of potentially relevant variables that are omitted from the baseline VAR model to the variables already included in the baseline model implies that the structural shocks in the baseline model are not fundamental. Under weak conditions, adding previously omitted Granger causal variables to the VAR model may eliminate this informational inefficiency. Even a model modified in this fashion, however, need not be properly identified. One problem is that there may be expectational variables that affect agents' behavior which are not observable. Thus, passing the Giannone and Reichlin test is necessary, but not sufficient for ruling out identification problems in the structural model. The other problem is that the inclusion of previously omitted Granger causal variables may undermine conventional identification strategies. For example, it may seem that the problem of non-fundamental VAR representations could be mitigated, if not avoided altogether, by simply augmenting the set of VAR variables with forward-looking variables such as asset prices, survey measures of expectations, or professional forecasts. This strategy, however, may invalidate commonly used approaches to identifying monetary policy shocks. Consider a semi-structural model of monetary policy of the type discussed earlier. If we add stock prices to the list of variables the Federal Reserve responds to in setting interest rates, we are implicitly assuming that stock prices do not respond instantaneously to interest rates, which does not seem plausible. If we order stock prices below the interest rate, on the other hand, we prevent the Federal Reserve from responding to a variable that matters for agents' economic decisions and hence should matter to the Federal Reserve. Thus, the presence of forward-looking variables often requires additional modifications in the identification strategy.

Only recently, VAR models have been adapted to allow for forward-looking behavior of some form. Such extensions are non-trivial. Here we consider three illustrative examples. None of the examples provides a generic solution to the problem of modeling forward-looking behavior, but they illustrate that at least in special cases these problems may be overcome.

5.3.1 Example 13: shocks to expectations about future oil demand and oil supply conditions

The first example is a model of the global spot market for crude oil proposed by Kilian and Murphy (2013). Identification is based on a four-variable model including the change in above-ground global inventories of crude oil in addition to the three variables already included in Kilian and Murphy (2012). The key observation is that any change in expectations about future oil demand and oil supply conditions not already captured by flow demand shocks and flow supply shocks must be reflected in a shift in the demand for oil inventories, conditional on past data. By including these inventories (the change of which is denoted by Δinv) in the model and simultaneously identifying all shocks that move inventories, it becomes possible to identify the effect of shifts in expectations without having to measure expectations explicitly. The model is identified by a combination of sign restrictions on the impact responses, bounds on the impact price elasticities of oil demand and of oil supply, and dynamic sign restrictions on the responses to unexpected flow supply disruptions. The impact sign restrictions are:

$$\begin{pmatrix} \varepsilon_t^{\Delta prod} \\ \varepsilon_t^{rea} \\ \varepsilon_t^{rpoil} \\ \varepsilon_t^{\Delta inv} \end{pmatrix} = \begin{bmatrix} - & + & + & \times \\ - & + & - & \times \\ + & + & + & \times \\ \times & \times & + & \times \end{bmatrix} \begin{pmatrix} u_t^{flow\ supply} \\ u_t^{flow\ demand} \\ u_t^{speculative\ demand} \\ u_t^{other\ oil\ demand} \end{pmatrix}.$$

In other words, on impact, a negative flow supply shock shifts the supply curve to the left along the demand curve, resulting in a decline in the quantity and an increase in the price of oil, which causes real activity to decline. A positive flow demand shock is associated with increased real activity. Quantity and price increase, as the demand curve shifts to the right along the supply curve, while real activity increases by construction. The inventory responses to flow supply and flow demand shocks are ambiguous a priori and hence remain unrestricted. A positive speculative demand shock reflecting expectations of a tightening oil market is associated with an increase in inventories and in the real price of oil by construction. The accumulation of inventories requires oil production to increase and oil consumption (and hence real activity) to decline. Effectively, this model further decomposes the *other oil demand shock* in Inoue and Kilian (2013) into a speculative component driven by shifts in expectations and a residual containing only the remaining idiosyncratic oil demand shocks. In addition, the model imposes that the impact price elasticity of oil supply is bounded above and that the impact price elasticity of oil demand (defined to incorporate the inventory response) is restricted to be negative and smaller in magnitude than the long-run price elasticity of oil demand which can be estimated from cross-sectional data. Both elasticities can be expressed as ratios of structural impulse responses on impact. Finally, the model imposes that the sign restrictions on the responses to a flow supply shock remain in effect for one year.

It may seem that this oil market model is incomplete in that it excludes the price of oil futures contracts, which is commonly viewed as an indicator of market expectations about future oil prices. This is not the case. The spot market and the futures market for oil are two distinct markets linked by an arbitrage condition. Thus, if there is speculation in the oil futures market, by arbitrage there should be speculation in the spot market reflected in increased inventory demand (see Alquist and Kilian, 2010). Not only does economic theory imply that oil futures prices are redundant in this model of the spot market, but one can use the Giannone and Reichlin (2006) test to show that the oil futures spread does not Granger cause the variables in the Kilian and Murphy model, consistent with the view that the structural shocks are fundamental.[9]

5.3.2 Example 14: anticipated technology shocks

A second example of a structural VAR model of forward-looking behavior is Barsky and Sims (2011) who focus on expectations about future aggregate productivity. They postulate that the log of aggregate productivity, A_t, is characterized by a stochastic process driven by two structural shocks. The first shock is the traditional surprise technology shock, which impacts the level of productivity in the same period in which agents observe it. The second shock reflects information about future technology and is defined to be orthogonal to the first shock.[10] The two shocks jointly account for all variation in A_t. The two structural shocks are identified as follows:

$$A_t = [B_{11}(L)B_{12}(L)]\begin{pmatrix} u_{1t} \\ u_{2t} \end{pmatrix}$$

where $B_{12}(0) = 0$ such that only u_{1t} affects current productivity, making u_{2t} the future technology shock. Effectively, Barsky and Sims treat A_t as predetermined with respect to the rest of the economy. This identifying assumption leaves a wide range of possible choices for u_{2t}. In practice, u_{2t} is identified as the shock that best explains future movements in $A_{t+1}, \ldots, A_{t+H}$, not accounted for by its own innovation, where H is some finite horizon. This approach, of course, amounts to constructing the best possible case for the role of shocks to expectations rather than necessarily the most likely case.

The estimated VAR model includes a total factor productivity series as well as selected macroeconomic aggregates. A_t is ordered first. The procedure is implemented by constructing candidate solutions of the form PD, where P denotes the lower triangular Cholesky decomposition of Σ_ε and D a conformable orthogonal matrix, as in the case of sign-identified VAR models. The ability of a shock to explain future movements of the data is measured in terms of the forecast-error variance decomposition. Because the contribution of the second shock to the forecast error variance of A_t depends only on the second column of A_0^{-1}, Barsky and Sims choose the second column, γ, to solve the optimization problem:

$$\gamma^* = \arg\max \sum_{h=0}^{H} \Omega_{12}(h),$$

subject to the first element of γ being zero and $\gamma'\gamma = 1$, where $\Omega_{ij}(h)$ denotes the share of the forecast error variance of variable i attributable to structural shock j at horizon h expressed in terms of the structural parameters of the model (also see Lütkepohl, 2005).

5.3.3 Example 15: anticipated tax shocks

In related work, Leeper et al. (2011) address the problem of anticipated tax shocks in the context of the model of Blanchard and Perotti (2002). Although Blanchard and Perotti as part of a sensitivity analysis relaxed the assumption of no foresight in their baseline model, they only investigated a very limited form of tax foresight involving one quarter of anticipation. Clearly, there is no compelling reason for agents not to be more forward-looking.

Leeper et al. propose a more general approach. Their starting point is the observation that the differential US Federal tax treatment of municipal and treasury bonds embeds news about future taxes. The current spread, s_t, between municipal bonds and treasury bonds may be viewed as an implicit tax rate. This implicit tax rate is a weighted average of discounted expected future tax rates and should respond immediately to news about expected future tax changes. This motivates treating s_t as a variable containing expectations of future tax shocks. Assuming market efficiency, the implicit tax rate reveals the extent to which agents do or do not have foresight. A simple test is whether s_t contains useful predictive information for the variables modeled by Blanchard and Perotti. Leeper et al. demonstrate that s_t Granger causes the variables in Blanchard and Perotti's VAR model, indicating that this model is not fundamental. Their solution is to augment the model of Blanchard and Perotti with data on the spread, s, resulting in the four-variable system:

$$\begin{pmatrix} \varepsilon_t^{tax} \\ \varepsilon_t^{gov} \\ \varepsilon_t^{gdp} \\ \varepsilon_t^{s} \end{pmatrix} = \begin{pmatrix} 2.08\varepsilon_t^{gdp} + u_t^{tax} \\ du_t^{tax} + u_t^{gov} \\ e\varepsilon_t^{tax} + f\varepsilon_t^{gov} + u_t^{gdp} \\ g\varepsilon_t^{tax} + h\varepsilon_t^{gov} + i\varepsilon_t^{gdp} + u_t^{s} \end{pmatrix}$$

They add the identifying assumption that news contained in the interest rate spread, u_t^s, has no direct effect on current output, tax revenue and spending. The resulting structural VAR model can be used to construct responses both to unanticipated and anticipated tax revenue shocks. Leeper et al. show that their model produces markedly different impulse response estimates from Blanchard and Perotti's model and suggests that agents' foresight may extend as far as five years.

6 STRUCTURAL VAR MODELS AND DSGE MODELS

Both structural VAR models and DSGE models were developed in response to the perceived failure of traditional large-scale macroeconometric models in the 1970s. Proponents of DSGE models responded to this evidence by developing fully structural models that facilitated policy analysis, but at the expense of requiring strong assumptions about market structures, functional forms and about the exogeneity and dynamic structure of the underlying forcing variables. Proponents of structural VAR models responded by proposing dynamic simultaneous equation models that required minimal assumptions about the dynamics of the model variables, no assumptions about the exogeneity of any variable, and minimal assumptions about the structure of the economy. They dispensed in particular with the imposition of cross-equation restrictions in an effort to make the structural VAR model robust to alternative ad hoc modeling choices.

An obvious question is under what conditions these modeling approaches are compatible and under what conditions one might be able to learn from one approach about the other. This has been less of a concern for DSGE proponents (who often reject the structural VAR approach on a priori grounds) than for proponents of the structural VAR approach, some of whom have viewed results from structural VAR models as informative for DSGE modeling (see, for example, Galí, 1999). Recent research has shown that comparisons of structural VAR estimates with DSGE models are not straightforward:

- Not every DSGE model will have a structural VAR representation. Fernandez-Villaverde et al. (2007) discuss invertibility conditions that must be met for data from a DSGE model to have a structural VAR representation. Whether this fact is a concern for structural VAR modeling depends on whether we view the excluded DSGE models as practically relevant. Moreover, Sims (2012) shows that there may exist situations in which a model has a non-invertible VAR representation, yet structural VAR models nevertheless perform reliably.
- Conversely, not every structural VAR model will correspond to an existing DSGE model. This does not necessarily mean that the structural VAR model lacks theoretical support. It may also reflect our inability to write down and solve more articulated theoretical models.
- The state-space representation of a DSGE model's log-linearized equilibrium often can be expressed in terms of a vector autoregressive moving average (VARMA) process for the observable DSGE model variables. It rarely will take the form of a finite-order VAR process. Integrating out some of the model variables will further affect the nature of the reduced-form VARMA representation. Under suitable conditions, the resulting VARMA model for the observables can be inverted and expressed as a VAR(∞) model, which in turn can be approximated by a sequence of finite-order VAR(k) processes, where k increases with the sample size at a suitable rate. The use of an autoregressive sieve approximation has important implications for lag order selection and for statistical inference in the implied VAR(k) model (see, for example, Inoue and Kilian, 2002).

An obvious concern in practice is how well a VAR(∞) model may be approximated by a VAR(k) in finite samples. One important area of current research is how to select k. The answer depends in part on which aspect of the DSGE model we are interested in. This is an open area of research. Simulation evidence suggests that in some cases the VAR(k) approximation to the VAR(∞) process may be poor for realistic sample sizes for any feasible choice of k. This problem can be severe when the underlying DSGE model has a VARMA representation with a high moving average root.

- The existence of an approximate reduced-form VAR(k) representation is a necessary, but not a sufficient condition for the existence of a structural VAR(k) representation. One additional condition is that the number of shocks in the DSGE model must match the number of shocks in the VAR model. Recall that we postulated that Σ_u is of full column rank. This means that there must be as many shocks as variables in the VAR model. Many DSGE models have fewer shocks than variables. For example, a textbook real business cycle model has only one technology shock, so, when fitting a VAR to output, investment and consumption data generated from this DSGE model, Σ_u would be of reduced rank if the DSGE model were correct. Clearly, the DSGE model and VAR model specifications are incompatible in that case. Users of DSGE models have responded to this problem by either adding ad hoc noise without structural interpretation (such as measurement error) or by augmenting the number of economic shocks in the DSGE model. Examples include preference shocks, fiscal shocks and monetary shocks. This can be problematic if the additional shocks in the DSGE model have no clear structural interpretation or involve questionable exogeneity assumptions.

  Another additional condition is that the restrictions imposed in identifying the structural shocks in the VAR model must be consistent with the underlying DSGE model structure. This is rarely the case when using short-run exclusion restrictions, so caution must be exercised in comparing results from DSGE and structural VAR models. This point was first illustrated by Keating (1990) in the context of a simple rational expectations model. The use of long-run restrictions as in Galí (1999) circumvents this problem in part, but it requires the user to take a strong stand on the presence of unit roots and near-unit roots, it requires the DSGE model to be consistent with these assumptions, it focuses on one shock at the expense of others, and it suffers from its own limitations as discussed earlier. Simulation evidence on the efficacy of this approach is mixed (see, for example, Gust and Vigfusson, 2009). Perhaps the best hope for matching structural VAR models and DSGE models is the use of sign restrictions. Canova and Paustian (2011) report considerable success in recovering responses generated by DSGE models with the help of sign-identified structural VAR models. They stress the importance of not being too agnostic about the identification, however. It is generally easier to recover the underlying population responses when more variables are restricted, for a given number of identified shocks, or when more structural shocks are identified in the VAR model. Moreover, models based on weak identifying restrictions may become unreliable when the variance of the shock in question is small in population. This conclusion is further reinforced by the discussion in Kilian and Murphy (2012) of the dangers of relying on excessively agnostic sign-identified VAR models.
- The earlier comments about forward-looking behavior continue to apply. As noted by Sims (2012), when the data are generated by a DSGE model in which shocks are anticipated by the agents, there is a missing state variable in the structural VAR

representation of the observables, and structural VAR models will be unable to recover the true structural shocks. There is evidence that this problem need not be fatal, however. Even when the conditions for the invertibility of the state-space representation fail, the degree of misspecification of the structural VAR responses may be small.

This discussion highlights that in general caution must be exercised in comparing structural VAR and DSGE model estimates. Interest in such comparisons has further increased in recent years, as Bayesian estimation methods have facilitated the estimation of the state-space representation of DSGE models, making it possible to dispense with VAR models in estimating structural impulse responses. At the same time, there has been increasing recognition that DSGE models are not only sensitive to ad hoc modeling choices, but often suffer from weak identification of the structural parameters. Unless we are very confident about the adequacy of the DSGE model structure, estimates of DSGE models may be misleading, and calibration of the model parameters will be preferable. Moreover, even if the model structure is adequate, structural parameter estimates may be sensitive to the choice of priors. Thus, both the structural VAR approach and the DSGE model approach have to be used with care and the best we can hope for is that both types of models paint a similar picture.

7 CONCLUSION

In addition to continued innovation in the area of the identification of structural shocks from VAR models, recent years have witnessed a number of generalizations of the underlying reduced-form VAR framework. One of the main concerns in the VAR literature we already alluded to is that policy rules and more generally the structure of the economy may evolve over time. One possibility is that structural changes occur infrequently, resulting in occasional breaks in the data that can be handled by splitting the sample. For example, Boivin and Giannoni (2006) consider the possibility that the Great Moderation was caused by a one-time break in the volatilities of the VAR shocks as opposed to improved monetary policy responses. They suggest that, if only the volatilities of the shocks changed during the Great Moderation, structural response functions estimated on pre-break data – after suitable normalizations to control for the magnitude of the shocks – should be identical to structural impulse responses estimated on post-break data, whereas changes in the shape of the response functions would be an indication of a change in the transmission mechanism. Inoue and Rossi (2011), however, document that time-invariant impulse response shapes are not sufficient for structural stability because structural breaks in the autoregressive slope parameters may have offsetting effects on the impulse response functions. Moreover, if there are changes in the shape of the impulse response functions, it is not possible to infer from these changes which parameters in the structural model changed. In particular, it is difficult to infer whether these changes are associated with better policy rules or with other instabilities in the structural model.

A more pernicious form of structural change is associated with smoothly time-varying model parameters. In some cases, such temporal instability may be modeled within a linear VAR framework. For example, Edelstein and Kilian (2009) showed how time variation in the share of energy expenditures in total consumption may be modeled within a linear VAR framework by redefining energy price shocks in terms of shocks to the purchasing power of consumers. A similar approach was taken by Ramey and Vine (2011) in modeling gasoline price rationing. An alternative approach pioneered by Primiceri (2005), Benati (2008), Canova and Gambetti (2009), and Baumeister and Peersman (2012) has been to allow for explicit smooth time variation in the parameters of the structural VAR model. The development of structural TVP-VAR models is challenging because the identifying restrictions themselves may be time-varying. Structural VAR models have also been extended to allow for more specific non-linearities such as regime-switching, threshold non-linearities, or GARCH in mean (see, for example, Elder and Serletis, 2010). Not all non-linearities lend themselves to structural VAR analysis, however. For example, Kilian and Vigfusson (2011a, 2011b) show that certain models involving asymmetric transmissions of shocks may not be represented as structural VAR models. They propose an alternative non-VAR representation of dynamic asymmetric structural models.

A second development in recent years has been the integration of results from the literature on data-dimension reduction in forecasting from large cross-sections. One example is the development of factor augmented VAR (FAVAR) models as in Bernanke et al. (2005) or Stock and Watson (2005). An alternative approach has been the use of large-scale Bayesian VAR models as in Banbura et al. (2010). Both model frameworks allow the user to generate impulse responses for a much larger set of variables than traditional VAR models. A third development has been the increased popularity of panel VAR models (see, for example, Canova, 2007).

These developments illustrate that there is much life left in the research program started by Sims (1980a, 1980b). As with all methodologies, structural vector autoregressions can be powerful tools in the right hands, yet potentially misleading if used blindly. Credible applications require careful consideration of the underlying economic structure. Although not every problem can be cast in a structural VAR framework, structural VAR models are likely to remain an important tool in empirical macroeconomics. There is no indication that DSGE models, in particular, are ready to take the place of structural vector autoregressions. Both approaches have their distinct advantages and disadvantages, and it remains up to the researcher to decide which class of models is more appropriate for a given question.

NOTES

* I thank Ron Alquist, Christiane Baumeister, Fabio Canova, Carlo Favero, Nikolay Gospodinov, Ana María Herrera, Helmut Lütkepohl, and Barbara Rossi for helpful comments on an earlier draft.

1. It is worth noting that, in general, structural shocks do not correspond to particular model variables. For example, in a VAR system consisting of only price and quantity, we can think of a demand shock and a supply shock each shifting prices and quantities. In fact, if price and quantity variables were mechanically associated with price and quantity shocks, this would be an indication that the proposed model is not truly structural.
2. Standard software provides built-in functions for generating the Cholesky decomposition of Σ_ε.
3. Christiano et al. (1999) prove that alternative orderings of $\varepsilon_t^{\Delta gdp}$ and ε_t^{π} will leave u_t^3 unaffected, provided the model is recursive.

4. The Bureau of Economic Analysis does not release monthly US real GDP data. Unofficial measures of monthly US real GDP constructed similarly to the official quarterly data have recently been provided by Macroeconomic Advisers, LLC. These time series for the time being are not long enough for estimating VAR models of monetary policy, however.
5. The price puzzle refers to the finding of a statistically significant increase in the price level in response to an unanticipated monetary tightening in models of this type. Sims (1992) suggested that this puzzle could be resolved by including global commodity prices as an indicator of future inflation in the model. This idea is reasonable because the Federal Reserve considers global commodity prices as a predictor of inflation. Hanson (2004), however, showed that there is little correlation between the ability of alternative measures of global commodity prices to predict inflation and to resolve the price puzzle. Indeed, subsequent research has shown that the price puzzle more often than not persists even after including global commodity prices in the VAR model, suggesting that the model remains misspecified.
6. The terminology of transitory shocks and permanent shocks is somewhat misleading in that any shock by construction involves a one-time disturbance only. A transitory shock, more precisely, is defined as a shock with purely transitory effects on the observables, whereas a permanent shock refers to a shock with permanent (or long-run) effects on the observables.
7. It can be shown that the results of Cochrane's model would be exactly identical to the results from a model in which the transitory shock has no long-run effect on the level of income and consumption, provided consumption follows a pure random walk. Such long-run restrictions will be discussed in section 3.
8. A generalization of the approach of Blanchard and Quah (1989) was proposed by King et al. (1991). King et al. consider a baseline model for output, consumption and investment. Unlike in Blanchard and Quah (1989), in their 3-variable VAR model all variables are driven by the same productivity shock in the long run. In other words, the model variables are cointegrated. King et al. are interested in using this model to differentiate between the three variables' responses to the common productivity shock. One difficulty in models such as this one lies in finding an economically credible identification of the transitory shocks. Another difficulty lies in how to distinguish between multiple permanent shocks when dealing with larger VAR models.
9. One could have considered an alternative specification in which the oil futures spread replaces the change in crude oil inventories, but one-year oil futures contracts did not exist on a monthly basis prior to 1989, so this alternative specification would involve a much smaller sample size. Another advantage of the specification in Kilian and Murphy (2013) is that it remains equally valid even in the absence of an oil futures market (or when arbitrage for some reason is less than perfect). Nor would a model based on the oil futures spread allow the imposition of bounds on the oil demand elasticity.
10. Barsky and Sims refer to this shock as a *news shock*, following a terminology common in the recent macroeconomic literature. This is somewhat misleading in that news shocks have traditionally been defined as unexpected changes to observed aggregates (see, for example, Kilian and Vega, 2011). Rather the second shock captures expected changes in future productivity.

REFERENCES

Abraham, K.G and J.C. Haltiwanger (1995), 'Real wages and the business cycle', *Journal of Economic Literature*, **33**, 1215–64.

Alquist, R. and L. Kilian (2010), 'What do we learn from the price of crude oil futures?', *Journal of Applied Econometrics*, **25**, 539–73.

Banbura, M., D. Giannone and L. Reichlin (2010), 'Large Bayesian vector autoregressions', *Journal of Applied Econometrics*, **25**, 71–92.

Barsky, R.B. and E.R. Sims (2011), 'News shocks and business cycles', *Journal of Monetary Economics*, **58**, 273–89.

Baumeister, C. and L. Kilian (2012), 'Real-time analysis of oil price risks using forecast scenarios', mimeo, University of Michigan.

Baumeister, C. and G. Peersman (2012), 'The role of time-varying price elasticities in accounting for volatility changes in the crude oil market', *Journal of Applied Econometrics*, DOI: 10.1002/jae.2283.

Benati, L. (2008), 'The "Great Moderation" in the United Kingdom', *Journal of Money, Credit and Banking*, **40**, 121–47.

Bernanke, B.S. (1986), 'Alternative explanations of the money–income correlation', *Carnegie-Rochester Conference Series on Public Policy*, **25**, 49–99.

Bernanke, B.S. and A. Blinder (1992), 'The federal funds rate and the channels of monetary transmission', *American Economic Review*, **82**, 901–21.
Bernanke, B.S. and J. Boivin (2003), 'Monetary policy in a data-rich environment', *Journal of Monetary Economics*, **50**, 525–46.
Bernanke, B.S. and I. Mihov (1998), 'Measuring monetary policy', *Quarterly Journal of Economics*, **113**, 869–902.
Bernanke, B.S., J. Boivin and P. Eliasz (2005), 'Measuring monetary policy: a Factor Augmented Vector Autoregressive (FAVAR) approach', *Quarterly Journal of Economics*, **120**, 387–422.
Bernanke, B.S., M. Gertler and M. Watson (1997), 'Systematic monetary policy and the effects of oil price shocks', *Brookings Papers on Economic Activity*, **1**, 91–142.
Blanchard, O.J. (1989), 'A traditional interpretation of macroeconomic fluctuations', *American Economic Review*, **79**, 1146–64.
Blanchard, O.J. and R. Perotti (2002), 'An empirical investigation of the dynamic effects of shocks to government spending and taxes on output', *Quarterly Journal of Economics*, **117**, 1329–68.
Blanchard, O.J. and D. Quah (1989), 'The dynamic effects of aggregate demand and supply disturbances', *American Economic Review*, **79**, 654–73.
Blanchard, O.J. and D. Quah (1993), 'The dynamic effects of aggregate demand and supply disturbances: reply', *American Economic Review*, **83**, 653–8.
Blanchard, O.J. and M.W. Watson (1986), 'Are business cycles all alike?', in R.J. Gordon (ed.), *The American Business Cycle*, Chicago, IL: NBER and Chicago Press, pp. 123–79.
Boivin, J. and M. Giannoni (2006), 'Has monetary policy become more effective?', *Review of Economics and Statistics*, **88**, 445–62.
Canova, F. (2007), *Methods for Applied Macroeconomic Research*, Princeton, NJ: Princeton University Press.
Canova, F. and G. De Nicolo (2002), 'Monetary disturbances matter for business fluctuations in the G-7', *Journal of Monetary Economics*, **49**, 1131–59.
Canova, F. and L. Gambetti (2009), 'Structural changes in the US economy: is there a role for monetary policy?', *Journal of Economic Dynamics and Control*, **33**, 477–90.
Canova, F. and E. Pappa (2007), 'Price dispersions in monetary unions: the role of fiscal shocks', *Economic Journal*, **117**, 713–37.
Canova, F. and M. Paustian (2011), 'Measurement with some theory: using sign restrictions to evaluate business cycle models', *Journal of Monetary Economics*, **58**, 345–61.
Canova, F., D. López-Salido and C. Michelacci (2010), 'The effects of technology shocks on hours and output: a robustness analysis', *Journal of Applied Econometrics*, **25**, 755–73.
Christiano, L., M. Eichenbaum and C. Evans (1999), 'Monetary policy shocks: what have we learned and to what end?', in J.B Taylor and M. Woodford (eds), *Handbook of Macroeconomics*, vol. 1, Amsterdam: Elsevier/North Holland, pp. 65–148.
Chung, H. and E. Leeper (2007), 'What has financed government debt?', NBER Working Paper No. 13425.
Cochrane, J.H. (1994), 'Permanent and transitory components of GNP and stock prices', *Quarterly Journal of Economics*, **109**, 241–65.
Cochrane, J.H. and M. Piazzesi (2002), 'The Fed and interest rates: a high-frequency identification', *American Economic Review*, **92**, 90–95.
Cooley, T.F. and S. LeRoy (1985), 'Atheoretical macroeconometrics: a critique', *Journal of Monetary Economics*, **16**, 283–308.
Cushman, D.O. and T. Zha (1997), 'Identifying monetary policy in a small open economy under flexible exchange rates', *Journal of Monetary Economics*, **39**, 433–48.
D'Amico, S. and M. Farka (2011), 'The Fed and the stock market: an identification based on intraday futures data', *Journal of Business and Economic Statistics*, **29**, 126–37.
Davis, L.W. and L. Kilian (2011), 'Estimating the effect of a gasoline tax on carbon emissions', *Journal of Applied Econometrics*, **26**, 1187–1214.
Dedola, L. and S. Neri (2007), 'What does a technology shock do? A VAR analysis with model-based sign restrictions', *Journal of Monetary Economics*, **54**, 512–49.
Edelstein, P. and L. Kilian (2009), 'How sensitive are consumer expenditures to retail energy prices?', *Journal of Monetary Economics*, **56**, 766–79.
Elder, J. and A. Serletis (2010), 'Oil price uncertainty', *Journal of Money, Credit and Banking*, **42**, 1138–59.
Faust, J. (1998), 'The robustness of identified VAR conclusions about money', *Carnegie-Rochester Conference Series on Public Policy*, **49**, 207–44.
Faust, J. and E. Leeper (1997), 'When do long-run identifying restrictions give reliable results?', *Journal of Business Economics and Statistics*, **15**, 345–53.
Faust, J., E. Swanson and J.H. Wright (2004), 'Identifying VARs based on high frequency futures data', *Journal of Monetary Economics*, **51**, 1107–31.

Fernández-Villaverde, J., J.F. Rubio-Ramírez, T.J. Sargent and M.W. Watson (2007), 'ABCs (and Ds) of understanding VARs', *American Economic Review*, **97**, 1021–26.
Forni, M., D. Giannone, M. Lippi and L. Reichlin (2009), 'Opening the black box: structural factor models with large cross-sections', *Econometric Theory*, **25**, 1319–47.
Francis, N., M. Owyang, J.E. Roush and R. DiCecio (2010), 'A flexible finite-horizon alternative to long-run restrictions with an application to technology shocks', mimeo, Federal Reserve Bank of St Louis.
Fry, R. and A. Pagan (2011), 'Sign restrictions in structural vector autoregressions: a critical review', *Journal of Economic Literature*, **49**, 938–60.
Fujita, S. (2011), 'Dynamics of worker flows and vacancies: evidence from the sign restriction approach', *Journal of Applied Econometrics*, **26**, 89–121.
Galí, J. (1992), 'How Well does the IS–LM model fit postwar US data?', *Quarterly Journal of Economics*, **107**, 709–38.
Galí, J. (1999), 'Technology, employment, and the business cycle: do technology shocks explain aggregate fluctuations?', *American Economic Review*, **89**, 249–71.
Giannone, D. and L. Reichlin (2006), 'Does information help recover structural shocks from past observations?', *Journal of the European Economic Association*, **4**, 455–65.
Gospodinov, N. (2010), 'Inference in nearly nonstationary SVAR models with long-run identifying restrictions', *Journal of Business and Economic Statistics*, **28**, 1–12.
Gospodinov, N., A. Maynard and E. Pesavento (2011), 'Sensitivity of impulse responses to small low frequency co-movements: reconciling the evidence on the effects of technology shocks', *Journal of Business and Economic Statistics*, **29**, 455–67.
Gust, C. and R.J. Vigfusson (2009), 'The power of long-run structural VARs', mimeo, Federal Reserve Board.
Hansen, L.P. and T.J. Sargent (1991), 'Two difficulties in interpreting vector autoregressions', in L.P. Hansen and T.J. Sargent (eds), *Rational Expectations Econometrics*, Boulder, CT: Westview Press, pp. 77–119.
Hanson, M.S. (2004), 'The "price puzzle" reconsidered', *Journal of Monetary Economics*, **51**, 1385–413.
Inoue, A. and L. Kilian (2002), 'Bootstrapping smooth functions of slope parameters and innovation variances in VAR(∞) models', *International Economic Review*, **43**, 309–32.
Inoue, A. and L. Kilian (2013), 'Inference on impulse response functions in structural VAR models', *Journal of Econometrics*, forthcoming.
Inoue, A. and B. Rossi (2011), 'Identifying the sources of instabilities in macroeconomic fluctuations', *Review of Economics and Statistics*, **93**, 1186–204.
Inoue, A., L. Kilian and F.B. Kiraz (2009), 'Do actions speak louder than words? Household expectations of inflation based on micro consumption data', *Journal of Money, Credit, and Banking*, **41**, 1331–63.
Keating, J. (1990), 'Identifying VAR models under rational expectations', *Journal of Monetary Economics*, **25**, 453–76.
Keating, J. (1992), 'Structural approaches to vector autoregressions', *Federal Reserve Bank of St Louis Review*, **74**, 37–57.
Kellogg, R. (2011), 'Short-run responses of oil production to spot and future oil prices', mimeo, University of Michigan.
Kilian, L. (2009), 'Not all oil price shocks are alike: disentangling demand and supply shocks in the crude oil market', *American Economic Review*, **99**, 1053–69.
Kilian, L. (2010), 'Explaining fluctuations in gasoline prices: a joint model of the global crude oil market and the US retail gasoline market', *Energy Journal*, **31**, 87–104.
Kilian, L. and L.T. Lewis (2011), 'Does the Fed respond to oil price shocks?', *The Economic Journal*, **121**, 1047–72.
Kilian, L. and D.P. Murphy (2012), 'Why agnostic sign restrictions are not enough: understanding the dynamics of oil market VAR models', *Journal of the European Economic Association*, **10**, 1166–88.
Kilian, L. and D.P. Murphy (2013), 'The role of inventories and speculative trading in the global market for crude oil', *Journal of Applied Econometrics*, forthcoming.
Kilian, L. and C. Vega (2011), 'Do energy prices respond to US macroeconomic news? A test of the hypothesis of predetermined energy prices', *Review of Economics and Statistics*, **93**, 660–71.
Kilian, L. and R.J. Vigfusson (2011a), 'Are the responses of the US economy asymmetric in energy price increases and decreases?', *Quantitative Economics*, **2**, 419–53.
Kilian, L. and R.J. Vigfusson (2011b), 'Nonlinearities in the oil price–output relationship', *Macroeconomic Dynamics*, **15**(S3), 337–63.
King, R.G., C.I. Plosser, J.H. Stock and M.W. Watson (1991), 'Stochastic trends and economic fluctuations', *American Economic Review*, **81**, 819–40.
Lanne, M. and H. Lütkepohl (2008), 'Identifying monetary policy shocks via changes in volatility', *Journal of Money, Credit, and Banking*, **40**, 1131–49.
Lanne, M. and H. Lütkepohl (2010), 'Structural vector autoregressions with nonnormal residuals', *Journal of Business and Economic Statistics*, **28**, 159–68.

Lanne, M., H. Lütkepohl and K. Maciejowska (2010), 'Structural vector autoregressions with Markov switching', *Journal of Economic Dynamics and Control*, **34**, 121–31.
Leeper, E.M., C.A. Sims and T. Zha (1996), 'What does monetary policy do?', *Brookings Papers on Economic Activity*, **2**, 1–63.
Leeper, E.M., T.B. Walker and S.S. Yang (2011), 'Foresight and information flows', mimeo, Indiana University.
Lippi, M. and L. Reichlin (1993), 'The dynamic effects of aggregate demand and supply disturbances: comment', *American Economic Review*, **83**, 644–52.
Lippi, M. and L. Reichlin (1994), 'VAR analysis, nonfundamental representations, Blaschke matrices', *Journal of Econometrics*, **63**, 307–25.
Lütkepohl, H. (2005), *New Introduction to Multiple Time Series Analysis*, New York: Springer.
Moon, H.R., F. Schorfheide, E. Granziera and M. Lee (2009), 'Inference for VARs identified with sign restrictions', mimeo, University of Southern California.
Mountford, A. and H. Uhlig (2009), 'What are the effects of fiscal policy shocks?', *Journal of Applied Econometrics*, **24**, 960–92.
Pagan, A.R. and J.C. Robertson (1998), 'Structural models of the liquidity effect', *Review of Economics and Statistics*, **80**, 202–17.
Pappa, E. (2009), 'The effects of fiscal shocks on employment and real wages', *International Economic Review*, **50**, 217–44.
Primiceri, G.E. (2005), 'Time varying structural vector autoregressions and monetary policy', *Review of Economic Studies*, **72**, 821–52.
Ramey, V.A. and D.J. Vine (2011), 'Oil, automobiles, and the US economy: how much have things really changed?', *NBER Macroeconomics Annual*, **25**, 333–68.
Rigobon, R. (2003), 'Identification through heteroskedasticity', *Review of Economics and Statistics*, **85**, 777–92.
Rubio-Ramirez, J.F., D. Waggoner and T. Zha (2010), 'Structural vector autoregressions: theory of identification and algorithms for inference', *Review of Economic Studies*, **77**, 665–96.
Rudebusch, G. (1998), 'Do measures of monetary policy in a VAR make sense?', *International Economic Review*, **39**, 907–31.
Scholl, A. and H. Uhlig (2008), 'New evidence on the puzzles: results from agnostic identification on monetary policy and exchange rates', *Journal of International Economics*, **76**, 1–13.
Shapiro, M.D. and M.W. Watson (1988), 'Sources of business cycle fluctuations', in S. Fischer (ed.), *NBER Macroeconomics Annual 1988*, Cambridge, MA: MIT Press, pp. 111–48.
Sims, C.A. (1980a), 'Macroeconomics and reality', *Econometrica*, **48**, 1–48.
Sims, C.A. (1980b), 'Comparison of interwar and postwar business cycles: monetarism reconsidered', *American Economic Review*, **70**, 250–57.
Sims, C.A. (1986), 'Are forecasting models usable for policy analysis?', *Minneapolis Federal Reserve Bank Quarterly Review*, **10**, 2–16.
Sims, C.A. (1992), 'Interpreting the macroeconomic time series facts: the effects of monetary policy', *European Economic Review*, **36**, 975–1011.
Sims, C.A. and T. Zha (2006), 'Were there regime switches in US monetary policy?', *American Economic Review*, **96**, 54–81.
Sims, E.R. (2012), 'News, non-invertibility, and structural VARs', *Advances in Econometrics*, **28**, 81–135.
Stock, J.H. and M.W. Watson (2005), 'Implications of dynamic factor models for VAR analysis', mimeo, Harvard University.
Strongin, S. (1995), 'The identification of monetary policy disturbances: explaining the liquidity puzzle', *Journal of Monetary Economics*, **35**, 463–98.
Taylor, J. (1993), 'Discretion versus policy rules in practice', *Carnegie-Rochester Conference Series on Public Policy*, **39**, 195–214.
Taylor, M.P. (2004), 'Estimating structural macroeconomic shocks through long-run recursive restrictions on vector autoregressive models: the problem of identification', *International Journal of Finance and Economics*, **9**, 229–44.
Todd, R.M. (1990), 'Vector autoregression evidence on monetarism: another look at the robustness debate', *Federal Reserve Bank of Minneapolis Quarterly Review*, Spring, pp. 19–37.
Uhlig, H. (2005), 'What are the effects of monetary policy on output? Results from an agnostic identification procedure', *Journal of Monetary Economics*, **52**, 381–419.
Waggoner, D.F. and T. Zha (1999), 'Conditional forecasts in dynamic multivariate models', *Review of Economics and Statistics*, **81**, 639–51.
Watson, M.W. (1994), 'Vector autoregressions and cointegration', in R.F. Engle and D. McFadden (eds), *Handbook of Econometrics*, Vol. 4, Amsterdam: Elsevier Science, pp. 2844–915.

23 Vector autoregressive models for macroeconomic policy analysis

Soyoung Kim

1 INTRODUCTION

Vector autoregressive (VAR) models have been intensively used for macro policy analysis since Sims (1980) suggested VAR models for macroeconomic analysis. VAR models employ minimal restrictions compared with traditional large-scale models, which impose a large number of incredible restrictions. As a result, VAR models have been used to document data-oriented empirical evidence on the effects of macroeconomic policies.

VAR models were commonly used in the early years to analyze the role of macro policies in business cycle fluctuations. For example, how much does monetary shock contribute to output fluctuations? VAR analysis was later performed as an empirical counterpart of the theoretical model. For example, impulse responses from VAR models are compared with those from Dynamic Stochastic General Equilibrium (DSGE) models to examine the success and failure of theories.

Simple recursive VAR models introduced by Sims (1980) were frequently used in the early years because such models were regarded as models with atheoretical (or normalizing) restrictions. However, subsequent studies showed that the results were usually sensitive to the ordering among variables. Thereafter, providing proper justification for the restrictions has been the most important task. In addition, subsequent studies introduced various methods of identifications, for example, SR non-recursive restrictions, LR zero restrictions, sign restrictions, and so on, because providing justifications for recursive restrictions is often difficult. Subsequent studies also introduced more complicated structures of VAR models, such as the large-scale Bayesian VAR, Factor-Augmented VAR (FAVAR), regime-switching VAR, and time-varying VAR, to better address the policy effects.

This chapter summarizes various methods of analyzing macro policy issues using VAR models. It focuses on summarizing the modeling aspects instead of the results themselves. In particular, this chapter discusses the types of identification methods and the types of VAR models that have been used to analyze macro policies since the literature evolved, as alternative identification methods or new types of VAR models have been introduced. Whereas the previous chapter discussed various identification methods themselves, this chapter focuses on the applications to macro policy analysis.

VAR literature on macro policy analysis began to develop from its application to monetary policy analysis. Thus, in this chapter (from section 2 to section 6), monetary policy analysis is extensively reviewed. More recent analysis on other macro policies are also discussed. Section 7 reviews fiscal policy analysis. Section 8 discusses analysis on open economy policies, such as exchange rate policies and capital controls, and section 9 concludes.

Notation in this chapter is as follows. The reduced form VAR model is

$$y_t = c + A(L)y_t + \varepsilon_t, A(L) \equiv A_1L + A_2L^2 + \ldots + A_pL^p$$

$$E(\varepsilon_t) = 0, E(\varepsilon_t\varepsilon_t') \equiv \Sigma_\varepsilon, t = 1,\ldots,T \quad (23.1)$$

where y_t is a $k \times 1$ data vector, c is a $k \times 1$ constant vector, ε_t is a $k \times 1$ error term vector, and A_js and Σ_ε are $k \times k$ matrices. The structural form VAR model is

$$B_0y_t = d + B(L)y_t + u_t, B(L) \equiv B_1L + B_2L^2 + \ldots + B_pL^p$$

$$E(u_t) = 0, E(u_tu_t') \equiv \Sigma_u, t = 1,\ldots,T \quad (23.2)$$

where d is a $k \times 1$ constant vector, u_t is a $k \times 1$ structural shock vector, B_js are $k \times k$ matrices, and Σ_u is a $k \times k$ diagonal matrix. The structural and reduced forms are related as follows.

$$A_i = B_0^{-1}B_i, c = B_0^{-1}d, i = 1,\ldots,p, \varepsilon_t = B_0^{-1}u_t, \Sigma_\varepsilon = B_0^{-1}\Sigma_uB_0^{-1\prime}.$$

2 EARLY LITERATURE ON MONETARY POLICY

Early studies on the effects of monetary policy using VAR models clearly show that the most important task is identifying exogenous shocks to monetary policy. Monetary policy actions are endogenous to the state of the economy. Unless the exogenous parts of monetary policy actions are identified, the true effects of monetary policy actions will be hard to determine. Distinguishing and disentangling the effects of exogenous policy actions on the state of the economy and the changes in the state of the economy to which monetary policy reacts is not an easy task.

Such problems are found in the old debate between the monetarist and the Keynesian. Friedman and Schwartz (1963) show the timing pattern of monetary aggregates and real activities (that is, money leads real activities) to support the monetarist view. However, Tobin (1970) argues that such timing relation can be observed even in a theoretical model in which monetary policy does not affect real activities, but monetary aggregate endogenously responds to the real activities. This debate suggests that identifying 'exogenous' changes in monetary policies and examining the effects of the exogenous changes are important because monetary aggregates are endogenous to the state of the economy.

Since Sims (1980) introduced VAR models for macroeconomic analysis, VAR models have frequently been used to analyze the effects of monetary policy shocks. VAR models are usually regarded as a useful tool to extract 'surprise' or 'exogenous shocks' of a variable and hence VAR methodology is frequently used in monetary policy analysis.

The initial VAR literature, including Sims' (1980) study, used the SR recursive VAR models (with Cholesky decomposition) and identified innovations in broad monetary aggregates such as M1 and M2 as monetary shocks. However, these studies are faced with the liquidity puzzle.[1] That is, an exogenous monetary expansion is supposed to increase the monetary aggregates and decrease the interest rate. However, in the model that uses innovations in broad monetary aggregate as monetary shocks, both the monetary aggregates and the interest rate increase. This puzzle is usually interpreted as an indication that exogenous shocks to monetary policy actions are not properly identified in the model. Changes in broad monetary aggregates usually respond to non-policy shocks, such as money demand shocks, endogenously. Thus, innovations in broad monetary aggregates are not likely to represent exogenous shocks to monetary policy.

To avoid the liquidity puzzle, subsequent studies, such as Bernanke and Blinder (1992) and Sims (1992), used innovations in short-term interest rate as monetary policy shocks. In recent years, the short-term interest rate has been used as the monetary policy instrument, and it is less likely to be endogenous than the broad monetary aggregates. However, as Sims (1992) suggests, the 'price puzzle' emerges in the model with key macro variables such as the short-term interest rate, real income, price level, and monetary aggregates. That is, an exogenous monetary contraction is supposed to increase the interest rate and decrease the price level. However, monetary policy shocks identified as innovations in short-term interest rate increase the price level. Similar to the liquidity puzzle, the price puzzle is commonly regarded as an indication that exogenous shocks to monetary policy are not properly identified in the model. Sims (1992) suggests that the price puzzle emerges because the monetary authority reacts to inflationary expectation but excludes the variables reflecting inflationary expectation in the model, thus not properly identifying the exogenous shocks to the monetary policy. Sims (1992) resolves the price puzzle in the model by additionally including the commodity price index to capture inflation expectation.[2]

As reviewed in this section, the literature on VAR methods evolved by developing ways to identify exogenous monetary policy shocks. The following sections review the more recent methodologies. Note that these early debates clarify the following concepts. Monetary policy actions can be conceptually divided into two parts, namely, systematic and non-systematic. The systematic part is called the monetary policy rule or the monetary reaction function. Regarding the systematic part, we may analyze how changes in monetary policy rule affect the economy. For example, we can analyze whether the inflation rate is stabilized if the central bank increases the interest rate more steeply in reaction to an inflation rate rise. The non-systematic part is relatively vague conceptually. This part includes discretionary parts that do not follow the policy rule and/or errors in monetary policy actions. The debate suggests that analyses should aim to separate these two parts clearly.

3 MONETARY VAR MODELS WITH SR ZERO RESTRICTIONS

Some studies use SR zero restrictions to resolve the various puzzles discussed in the previous section and to identify exogenous monetary policy shocks. These studies can be divided into three categories: (1) using innovations in short-term interest rates as monetary policy shocks; (2) dividing money demand and money supply using non-recursive models; and (3) modeling detailed monetary policy operating procedure.

Short-term Interest Rate Shocks

As discussed in the previous section, Bernanke and Blinder (1992) and Sims (1992) suggest using innovations in short-term interest rates as monetary policy shocks. This identification method is widely used. Christiano et al. (1996, 1999) further suggest a popular recursive model.

Using a recursive VAR model, Christiano et al. (1996, 1999) assume that the output, price and commodity price are contemporaneously exogenous to the federal funds rate but the federal funds rate is contemporaneously exogenous to other variables, such as non-borrowed reserves, total reserves and monetary aggregates. Such a structure assumes that the monetary authority decides the federal funds rate using information on the current and lagged values of output, price and commodity price as well as the lagged values of other variables. Output and price are the variables that the central bank considers most important. The commodity price index is also included in the recursive VAR model to capture the inflation expectation (as in Sims, 1992). The assumption might be justified since the three variables are directly related to the two important objectives of monetary policy but the assumption can be controversial. Nevertheless, this model has become popular partly because no puzzling responses are observed, the method is easy to implement, and the results are relatively stable as a recursive structure is used. Subsequent studies such as Kim (2001) and Christiano et al. (2005) have used similar models.

Separation of Money Demand and Supply

The second method is to separate money demand and money supply. Monetary aggregates and interest rates are likely to be affected not only by monetary policy shocks (or money supply shocks) but also by money demand shocks. Therefore, by separating money demand and money supply, more exogenous components of monetary policy actions (or money supply) can be identified. Gordon and Leeper (1994), Sims and Zha (2006a, 2006b), Kim (1999), Kim and Roubini (2000), and Cushman and Zha (1997) use this method.

The models in this category typically include the following structural equations:

$$\varepsilon_t^M = a_{1p}\varepsilon_t^P + a_{1y}\varepsilon_t^Y - a_{1R}\varepsilon_t^R + u_t^{MD}$$

$$\varepsilon_t^R = a_{2R}\varepsilon_t^M + a_{2z}\varepsilon_t^I + u_t^{MS} \tag{23.3}$$

where εs are reduced form residuals; *u*s are structural shocks; *M*, *R*, *P*, *Y*, and *I* represent the monetary aggregate, short-term interest rate, price level, output, and an informational variable such as the commodity price index, respectively; and u^{MD} and u^{MS} are money demand and money supply (or monetary policy) shocks, respectively.

The first equation is the money demand equation. Based on the traditional money demand equation, real money balance is assumed dependent on the interest rate and real income.[3] The second equation is the monetary policy reaction function (or the monetary policy rule or money supply equation). The monetary authority is assumed to set the interest rate (or monetary aggregate) after observing contemporaneous values of the monetary aggregate (or the interest rate), the variable I, and the lagged values of all the variables in the model. Unlike in Christiano et al.'s method (1996, 1999), contemporaneous values of output and the price level are not included in the monetary reaction function. The output and the price level are aggregate variables, and contemporaneously obtaining the precise information is difficult because collecting information and aggregation take time. This assumption is called the information delay assumption.

The following model by Sims and Zha (2006a) presents a more concrete example:

$$\begin{bmatrix} a_{11} & a_{12} & a_{13} & a_{14} & a_{15} & a_{16} & a_{17} & a_{18} \\ 0 & a_{22} & a_{23} & 0 & -a_{22} & 0 & -a_{22} & 0 \\ a_{31} & a_{32} & a_{33} & 0 & 0 & 0 & 0 & a_{38} \\ a_{41} & 0 & 0 & a_{44} & a_{45} & a_{46} & a_{47} & a_{48} \\ a_{51} & 0 & 0 & 0 & a_{55} & a_{56} & a_{57} & a_{58} \\ a_{61} & 0 & 0 & 0 & 0 & a_{66} & a_{67} & a_{68} \\ a_{71} & 0 & 0 & 0 & 0 & 0 & a_{77} & a_{78} \\ a_{81} & 0 & 0 & 0 & 0 & 0 & 0 & a_{88} \end{bmatrix} \begin{bmatrix} \varepsilon_t^{PIG} \\ \varepsilon_t^{M} \\ \varepsilon_t^{R} \\ \varepsilon_t^{PIM} \\ \varepsilon_t^{P} \\ \varepsilon_t^{W} \\ \varepsilon_t^{Y} \\ \varepsilon_t^{TBK} \end{bmatrix} = \begin{bmatrix} u_{1,t} \\ u_{MD,t} \\ u_{MP,t} \\ u_{4,t} \\ u_{5,t} \\ u_{6,t} \\ u_{7,t} \\ u_{8,t} \end{bmatrix} \tag{23.4}$$

where *PIG*, *PIM*, *W* and *TBK* represent producers' price index of intermediate goods, producers' price index of intermediate materials, real wage, and the number of personal and business bankruptcy filings, respectively.

The second and the third equations are money demand and money supply equations, respectively. In the money demand equation, the elasticity of real money demand with respect to real income is assumed to be 1. The first equation shows a financial market equilibrium in which the price of intermediate goods instantaneously reflects all the information. The rest of the equations represent the real sector equations, in which real sector variables do not respond to financial market and monetary variables contemporaneously.

Modeling Monetary Policy Operating Procedure

An alternative approach tries to identify monetary policy shocks by carefully modeling the monetary policy operating procedure. For example, Strongin (1995) reviews the history of monetary policy procedure and tries to identify monetary policy shocks for each sub-period in which different monetary policy procedures are adopted. The study, along with other similar studies, suggests that shocks to non-borrowed reserves (or shocks to non-borrowed reserves orthogonal to shocks to total reserves) can represent open market operation precisely because non-borrowed reserves change as a result of open market operation.

Christiano et al. (1996, 1999), Eichenbaum (1992) and Eichenbaum and Evans (1995) utilize this idea to use shocks to non-borrowed reserves as monetary policy shocks in the recursive model, where output, price level and commodity prices are contemporaneously exogenous to non-borrowed reserves.

Bernanke and Mihov (1998) build a model based on monetary policy operating procedure to interpret and compare various existing methods to identify monetary policy shocks. The model by Bernanke and Mihov (1998) is summarized as follows:

$$\varepsilon_t^{TR} = -a_{1FF}\varepsilon_t^{FFR} + u_t^{DTR}$$

$$\varepsilon_t^{TR} - u_t^{NBR} = a_{2FF}\varepsilon_t^{FFR} + u_t^{DBR}$$

$$\varepsilon_t^{NBR} = b_{DTR}u_t^{DTR} + b_{DBR}u_t^{DBR} + u_t^{MP} \qquad (23.5)$$

where TR, FFR and NBR represent total reserves, the federal funds rate, and non-borrowed reserves, respectively. The first equation shows the demand for total reserves, which is a negative function of the federal funds rate. The second equation shows the demand for borrowed reserves (total reserves minus non-borrowed reserves), which is a positive function of the difference between the federal funds rate and the discount rate (the innovations in discount rate are assumed zero). The third equation represents monetary policy function. Non-borrowed reserves are set by an open market operation in reaction to the demand for total reserves and borrowed reserves.

This model comprises various methods as special cases. For example, when $b_{DTR} = 1$ and $b_{DBR} = -1$, monetary policy shocks are innovations in the federal funds rate. When $b_{DTR} = 0$ and $b_{DBR} = 0$, monetary policy shocks are innovations in the non-borrowed reserves.

4 MONETARY VAR MODELS WITH OTHER RESTRICTIONS

LR Restrictions

Some studies use LR restrictions. The long-run neutrality of money is usually exploited as the LR restriction. This identification strategy is attractive, as the long-run neutrality of money is the property shared by most theoretical models with money. In this regard, the identification is consistent with many theoretical models. Thus, the empirical evidence based on such an identification method is a fair benchmark with which to compare different theoretical monetary models.

The study of Blanchard and Quah (1989) is an example of this identification method. The following is the structural VMA representation:

$$\begin{bmatrix} dY_t \\ UR \end{bmatrix} = \begin{bmatrix} h_1 \\ h_2 \end{bmatrix} + \begin{bmatrix} \theta_{11}(L) & \theta_{12}(L) \\ \theta_{21}(L) & \theta_{22}(L) \end{bmatrix} \begin{bmatrix} u_{1t} \\ u_{2t} \end{bmatrix}, \qquad (23.6)$$

where $\theta_{12}(1) = 0$, and UR is the unemployment rate. $\theta_{12}(1) = 0$ implies that u_2 does not have long-run effects on Y. Under this assumption, u_2 can be interpreted as nominal shocks that do not affect real output in the long run.

Although the long-run neutrality assumption is appealing, it may be limited in that there can be structural shocks other than monetary policy shocks that do not affect real output in the long run. For example, money demand shocks are also nominal shocks that are not likely to affect real output in the long run. In addition, temporary real shocks are not likely to have long-run effects on real output.

Using a similar methodology, Lastrapes (1992) and Clarida and Galí (1994) identify nominal or monetary shocks in the open economy set-up. Clarida and Galí (1994) determine monetary shocks using various LR restrictions derived from the Mundell–Fleming–Dornbusch model in the open economy set-up as follows:

$$\begin{bmatrix} dY - dY^* \\ dRER \\ dP - dP^* \end{bmatrix} = \begin{bmatrix} h_1 \\ h_2 \\ h_3 \end{bmatrix} + \begin{bmatrix} \theta_{11}(L) & \theta_{12}(L) & \theta_{13}(L) \\ \theta_{21}(L) & \theta_{22}(L) & \theta_{23}(L) \\ \theta_{31}(L) & \theta_{32}(L) & \theta_{33}(L) \end{bmatrix} \begin{bmatrix} u_{AS} \\ u_{AD} \\ u_M \end{bmatrix}, \theta_{12}(1) = \theta_{13}(1) = \theta_{23}(1) = 0 \quad (23.7)$$

where the variables with * are the foreign variables, *RER* is the real exchange rate, and u_{AS}, u_{AD} and u_M are (the difference between home and foreign) aggregate supply, aggregate demand, and monetary shocks, respectively. $\theta_{13}(1) = \theta_{23}(1) = 0$ implies that monetary shocks do not affect real output and real exchange rate in the long run (LR neutrality of money), and $\theta_{12}(1) = 0$ implies that aggregate demand shocks do not affect real output in the long run, which also holds true in traditional macro models.

By employing both LR and SR restrictions, Galí (1992) separately identifies money supply and money demand shocks. Kim and Lee (2008) use LR restrictions derived from the new open economy macro models to identify various structural shocks, including nominal or monetary shocks. Fung (1998) identifies monetary shocks by combining the cointegration relation for money demand equation and the one-to-one long-run relation between money and price.

Sign Restrictions

As reviewed in previous sections, previous studies usually yield various puzzles, such as the price puzzle and the liquidity puzzle, suggesting that monetary policy shocks identified in these studies may not be truly exogenous. The identification method by sign restrictions is an alternative identification strategy. By imposing the proper signs on impulse responses (or conditional correlation structure), such puzzles can be eliminated by construction.

Uhlig (2005) identifies monetary policy shocks by imposing sign restrictions on impulse responses. Uhlig (2005) defines monetary policy shocks as shocks that increase the federal funds rate, the price level, and the commodity price index but decrease nonborrowed reserves. By defining monetary shocks in this way, price and liquidity puzzles cannot appear by construction. In other words, Uhlig (2005) determines monetary policy shocks as shocks that do not generate the price puzzle and the liquidity puzzle. Scholl and Uhlig (2008) apply a similar method to examine the effect of monetary policy shocks in an open economy context.[4]

To identify monetary shocks, Canova and de Nicolo (2002, 2003) impose sign restrictions on the correlation of impulse responses. Canova and de Nicolo (2002) define monetary policy shocks as the shocks that generate positive correlations between inflation rate and real GDP, between inflation rate and real money balance, and between real money balance and real GDP. Canova and de Nicolo (2002) support these correlations by showing that monetary models predict such correlation structures in general.[5]

5 ALTERNATIVE MONETARY VAR MODELS

Some studies extend the basic VAR model (as shown in equations (23.1) and (23.2)). Large-scale Bayesian VAR and FAVAR models are used to include more variables in the model, as the basic VAR model is often faced with the degree of freedom problem. Such models are useful in analyzing monetary policy, as the monetary authority usually takes action using a lot of information from many variables that are difficult to include in the basic VAR model. On the other hand, monetary policy rule, structure of the economy, and/or variance structure may change over time. Time-varying VAR and regime-switching VAR models are used to capture such changes.

Large-scale VARs

By imposing prior information that does not depend on a specific economic theory, large-scale Bayesian VAR models try to mitigate the degree of freedom problem while maintaining the data-based nature of VAR analysis. For example, the Minnesota prior suggested by Litterman (1986) can be imposed by setting the following moments for the prior distribution of the coefficients in the reduced form VAR model (23.1).

$$E[(A_k)_{ij}] = \begin{cases} 1, j = i, k = 1 \\ 0, \textit{otherwise} \end{cases} \tag{23.8}$$

$$VAR[(A_k)_{ij}] = \begin{cases} g(k)^2\lambda^2, j = i \\ f(i,j)^2 g(k)^2 \lambda^2 \dfrac{\sigma_i^2}{\sigma_j^2}, \textit{otherwise} \end{cases} \tag{23.9}$$

where $(A_k)_{ij}$ is the ith low and jth column of A_k. In addition, a diffuse prior is assumed for each element of c in (23.1). The basic idea is that all equations are centered on the random walk with drift. λ controls the overall tightness. As λ decreases, prior variance of all coefficients decreases, and all equations converge to the random walk with drift. $g(k)$ is a decreasing function of k (for example, $1/k^2$), which implies that prior variance decreases (and the coefficient becomes less important) as the lag length increases. $f(i,j)$ shows the relative importance of lags of other variables to its own lags; $f(i,j)$ is between 0 and 1, so own lags are more important. σ_i is the standard error of a univariate autoregression on equation i. Prior variance is scaled by the standard errors to correct for the different magnitudes of the variables in the system. As this type of prior does not depend on a specific economic theory (but rather depends on a simple belief on the data process itself), it can be useful in increasing the precision on the estimates of the VAR model while maintaining the data-based nature of the VAR analysis. Refer to Doan et al. (1984), Litterman (1986) and the following references for more details.

Some studies use large-scale Bayesian VAR models for structural analysis. Leeper et al. (1996) construct 13- and 18-variable structural Bayesian VAR models (with SR non-recursive restrictions) to identify various types of monetary policy shocks and examine their effects. Banbura et al. (2011) develop structural Bayesian VAR models with 131 variables and conclude that such models can be used for structural analysis.

Bernanke et al. (2005) construct FAVAR models that combine factor analysis and structural VARs. They include about 120 variables. The model is briefly described as follows.

Observable variables (y_t) and unobservable factors (F_t) follow the following VAR process:

$$\begin{bmatrix} F_t \\ y_t \end{bmatrix} = \Phi(L)\begin{bmatrix} F_{t-1} \\ y_{t-1} \end{bmatrix} + \varepsilon_t \tag{23.10}$$

where F_t is a $K \times 1$ vector, y_t is an $M \times 1$ vector, $\Phi(L)$ is a matrix polynominal in lag operator L, and ε_t is the residual vector. $E(\varepsilon_t) = 0$ and $E(\varepsilon_t \varepsilon_t') \equiv \Sigma$.

Assume that x_t, F_t and y_t are related by the following factor model:

$$x_t = \Lambda^f F_t + \Lambda^y y_t + e_t \tag{23.11}$$

where x_t is an $N \times 1$ vector, Λ^f is an $N \times K$ matrix, Λ^y is an $N \times M$ matrix, e_t is the error term vectors, and $E(e_t) = 0$. Therefore, information on unobservable factors (F_t) can be extracted from various observable variables.

Bernanke et al. (2005) use the main policy variable such as the federal funds rate as y_t, which is included directly in (23.10). However, other variables (x_t) used to collect information on the state of the economy are not directly included in (23.10) but only in (23.11), which is used to extract the factors to be included in (23.10). This way, the degree of freedom problem in estimating the VAR equation with all variables is reduced. Then, as in the usual VAR, a structural form can be recovered from the reduced form VAR (23.1). Bernanke et al. (2005) use the SR recursive structure to identify monetary policy shocks.

VARs with Changing Parameters

Various studies, such as Cogley and Sargent (2005), Primiceri (2005), Canova and Gambetti (2009), and Sims and Zha (2006b), enable the use of time variations. These studies mostly find that enabling the use of time variations is important.

A (reduced-form) VAR model that enables time variations in parameters and variance–covariance matrices is described as follows:

$$y_t = c_t + A_t(L)y_t + \varepsilon_t$$

$$E(\varepsilon_t \varepsilon_t') \equiv \Sigma_{\varepsilon,t} \tag{23.12}$$

where elements of $A_t(L)$ and/or $\Sigma_{\varepsilon,t}$, or functions of these elements are usually assumed to follow random walks. Canova and Gambetti (2009) impose sign restrictions to recover structural equations/shocks, whereas Primiceri (2005) imposes SR recursive restrictions.

Sims and Zha (2006b) introduce regime-switching components into contemporaneous structural parameters and the variance of structural shocks. The model may be described in a simple way as follows:

$$B_0(s_t)y_t = d + B(L)y_{t-1} + u_t$$

$$E(u_t u_t') \equiv \Sigma_u(s_t)$$

$$\Pr(s_t = i | s_{t-1} = k) = p_{ik}, i, k = 1,\ldots,h \tag{23.13}$$

where s is an unobserved state, and h is the total number of states. The first equation shows that contemporaneous structural parameters can have different values under different regimes. The second equation shows that the variance of structural shocks can have different values under different regimes. The third equation shows the transition probability. The identification is achieved by SR non-recursive restrictions similar to those of Sims and Zha (2006a).

6 OTHER RELATED STUDIES ON MONETARY POLICY

Narrative Approach

To examine the effects of monetary policy, some studies identify the dates of monetary policy actions following the spirit of Friedman and Schwartz (1963). Romer and Romer (1989) review 'Record of Policy Actions' and 'Minutes of FOMC Meetings', which describe the details on the process of actual monetary policy decisions. They collect the episodes in which the monetary authority takes a monetary contraction to reduce inflation rates. Such episodes are arguably exogenous to output changes because they exclude the episodes in which the monetary authority takes action in reaction to output changes. They treat these episodes (dates) as the dummy variable and regress output on the dummies to examine the effects of monetary policy actions.

Romer and Romer's (1989) regression is as follows:

$$Y_t = a_0 + \sum_{i=1}^{11} a_i SD_{it} + \sum_{j=1}^{24} b_j Y_{t-j} + \sum_{k=1}^{36} c_k D_{t-k} \tag{23.14}$$

where SD is the seasonal dummy, and D is the dummy variable that takes 1 only if the abovementioned monetary contraction takes place and 0 otherwise.

Boschen and Mills (1991) extend Romer and Romer's (1989) study by constructing the index by including the case of expansion (in addition to contraction) and refining it by allocating the value of $\{-2,-1,0,1,2\}$, depending on the strength of the policy actions.

On the other hand, Leeper (1997) criticizes Romer and Romer's (1989) methodology by showing that the price puzzle emerges in response to shocks to the dummy variable in the VAR framework. This finding implies that, unfortunately, Romer and Romer's (1989) measure is not fully exogenous.

Romer and Romer (2004) develop alternative measures to avoid the endogeneity problem. First, they control for the Federal Reserve's forecasts of output and inflation prepared for scheduled FOMC meetings to deal with the central bank's forward-looking behavior. Second, they only consider changes in the federal funds rate scheduled around FOMC meetings, as changes at other times may reflect structural shocks other than monetary policy shocks. The price puzzle does not appear with this new measure, suggesting that this measure may be close to an exogenous one.

Systematic Monetary Policy

In most monetary VAR models, the monetary policy reaction function (or monetary policy rule) is identified when monetary policy shocks are identified. Although past VAR studies on monetary policy focus on the effects of exogenous monetary policy shocks, some studies attempt to obtain the implications for the systematic monetary policy.

Some studies attempt to determine the implied monetary policy reaction function from the monetary VAR models. Clarida and Gertler (1997) estimate Taylor-type monetary policy rules based on the estimates of structural VAR models. Kim (2002, 2003) calculates the elasticity of monetary instruments to changes in various variables based on impulse responses.

Other studies try to calculate the effects of changes in monetary policy rule using structural VAR models. Sims and Zha (2006a) and Kim (1996) perform counterfactual experiments to analyze the effects of changes in monetary policy rule by examining how the impulse responds to each structural shock change when the estimated monetary policy rule is changed to alternative hypothetical policy rules. Such counterfactual experiments in the structural VAR framework are subject to the Lucas critique. However, they are still interesting experiments because they can complement the evidence provided by DSGE models, in which all economic agents are rational, and expectations change instantaneously when the policy rule changes.

Recently, interest on the systematic part of monetary policy has been revived in studies that use VAR models with time variations (that is, Sims and Zha, 2006b; Cogley and Sargent, 2005; Primiceri, 2005; Canova and Gambetti, 2009). While these studies analyze time-varying or regime-switching features, they also discuss how the systematic part of monetary policy changes over time and how changes in the systematic part of monetary policy (in addition to changes in volatility of the non-systematic part of monetary policy) contribute to changes in various business cycle features.

7 FISCAL POLICY

In recent years, VAR analysis on the effects of fiscal policy has expanded rapidly. There are two types of fiscal policies: changes in government spending and changes in net tax. Some studies analyze the effects of both types of policy shocks in one framework, and other studies investigate only government spending shocks because identification is easier, and the theoretical effects can be better understood.

Blanchard and Perotti (2002) use an SR non-recursive model to examine the effects of government spending and tax shocks as follows:

$$\varepsilon_t^T = a_{1GDP}\varepsilon_t^{GDP} + a_{1G}u_t^G + u_t^T$$

$$\varepsilon_t^G = a_{2T}u_t^T + u_t^G$$

$$\varepsilon_t^{GDP} = a_{3T}u_t^T + b_{3G}u_t^G + u_t^{GDP} \tag{23.15}$$

where T, G and GDP represent (real) net tax, (real) government spending, and real GDP, respectively. The first and second equations show the policies on tax and government spending. In the second equation, government spending is assumed not to contemporaneously respond to GDP (within a quarter). Blanchard and Perotti (2002) suggest that such an assumption is consistent with the US institutional process. Government spending does not automatically respond to economic activities. In addition, changing government spending in response to economic activities (for example, to perform a macro stabilization policy) takes at least more than a quarter because of its implementation lag. Blanchard and Perotti (2002) estimate a_{1GDP} (showing how net tax responds to GDP within the period) outside the VAR model and use the estimated value of a_1 in the VAR model. They also assume that either a_{1G} or a_{2T} is zero, which does not affect the result much because ε_t^T and ε_t^G (which are not explained by ε_t^{GDP}) are not correlated much.

Among the various identifying assumptions by Blanchard and Perotti (2002), subsequent studies frequently exploit the restriction that government spending is contemporaneously exogenous to other variables. For example, Fatas and Mihov (2001), Galí et al. (2007), Kim and Roubini (2008), Ilzetzki et al. (2009), Beetsma et al. (2008), Corsetti and Müller (2006), Ravn et al. (2007), and Kim (2009), among many others, use the assumption that government spending is contemporaneously exogenous to other variables. This assumption has become popular partly because it can be imposed in a VAR model with a simple identification method similar to a recursive model.

Mountford and Uhlig (2009) provide an interesting approach with sign restrictions, which simultaneously identifies two types of fiscal shocks. They attempt to extract two types of fiscal shocks by excluding two important structural shocks, namely, non-fiscal business cycle shocks and monetary shocks. Monetary shocks are identified as in Uhlig (2005). Non-fiscal business cycle shocks are defined as the shocks that move government revenue and key macro variables in the same direction. Government revenue shocks and government spending shocks are defined as shocks that increase government revenue and government spending, respectively. Enders et al. (2011) impose sign restrictions derived from the DSGE models to identify government spending shocks in an open economy set-up.

Similar to the narrative approach for monetary policy analysis, Ramey and Shapiro (1998) isolate three arguably exogenous events that lead to large military build-up. Then, they use these dates as a dummy variable and regress real GDP on the dummy variable, as Romer and Romer (1989) do for monetary policy analysis. Edelberg et al. (1999) and Burnside et al. (2004) include the dummy variable in a VAR set-up to examine the effects of the dummy on various variables. Ramey (2009) extends and refines the Ramey and Shapiro (1998) study using richer narrative data on news of military build-ups. Barro and Redlick (2009) use a similar approach.

Fiscal policy actions are commonly anticipated. Thus, recent studies have worked on how to take care of anticipated fiscal shocks in the VAR framework. As discussed in the previous chapter, a problem like non-fundamentalness may arise in the presence of anticipated fiscal shocks. Leeper et al. (2011) include the spread between municipal bonds and treasury bonds in Blanchard and Perotti's (2002) study to overcome such a problem. Fisher and Peters (2009) address the issue using prices of military suppliers as an instrument for military spending. Mountford and Uhlig (2009) analyze the effects of anticipated fiscal shocks by assuming that the impulse responses of fiscal variables are zero for the initial periods but positive after the initial periods.

Some recent studies (Ravn et al., 2007; Kim, 2009; Ilzetzki et al., 2009; Beetsma et al., 2008) employ (structural-form) panel VAR models as follows:

$$B_0 y_t^i = c^i + B(L) y_t^i + u_t^i$$

$$E(u_t^i) = 0, E(u_t^i u_t^{i\prime}) \equiv \Sigma_u, i = 1 \ldots I, t = 1 \ldots T \tag{23.16}$$

where I is the number of countries, and c^i indicates the individual fixed effect that controls country-specific effects not captured in the model. Using cross-sectional information based on the panel VAR model, they group countries with distinct characteristics (that is, fixed vs. floating exchange rate regime and industrial vs. developing countries) and analyze how the effects are different for groups of countries with distinct characteristics.

8 OPEN ECONOMY POLICIES

Exchange Rate Policy

Some previous studies investigate the effects of foreign exchange intervention using VAR frameworks. Kim (2003, 2005) identifies shocks to foreign exchange intervention by imposing SR non-recursive restrictions. As monetary policy is interrelated with foreign exchange intervention, Kim (2003, 2005) jointly identifies shocks to foreign exchange intervention and monetary policy shocks as follows:

$$\varepsilon_t^F = a_{1R} \varepsilon_t^R + a_{1E} \varepsilon_t^E + u_t^{FP}$$

$$\varepsilon_t^R = a_{2M} \varepsilon_t^M + a_{2F} \varepsilon_t^F + a_{2E} \varepsilon_t^E + u_t^{MS} \tag{23.17}$$

where F and E show the indicator of foreign exchange intervention (or foreign exchange reserves) and nominal exchange rate, respectively, and FP stands for foreign exchange policy.

The first equation shows the foreign exchange policy. Foreign exchange reserves (or foreign exchange intervention) are set after observing the contemporaneous values of the exchange rate (as the policy is usually performed to stabilize the exchange rate). The second equation represents the monetary policy. Monetary policy may respond to the exchange rate to stabilize the exchange rate and monetary aggregate, as in the non-recursive model that separates money demand and money supply. In addition, contemporaneous interactions between two policies are allowed. Foreign exchange policy may react to the monetary policy to mitigate the effect of the monetary policy on the exchange rate. If not sterilized, foreign exchange policy affects monetary policy.

In these studies, the foreign exchange intervention function, in addition to the monetary reaction function, is also calculated based on impulse responses. On the other hand,

Kim (2007) uses VAR models with sign restrictions to identify the exchange rate regime based on the degree of exchange rate stabilization policy implied from the impulse response function.

Other studies analyze the effects of exchange rate shocks. In a highly managed exchange rate regime, changes in the exchange rate themselves can be regarded as policy actions. Therefore, examining the effects of exchange rate shocks can be considered an analysis of the effects of exchange rate policy actions. Kamin and Rogers (2000), Kim and Ying (2007) and Kim and Kim (2011) examine the effects of exchange rate shocks in the VAR framework to determine the effects of exchange rate policy actions. Kim and Ying (2007) and Kim and Kim (2011) use SR recursive models in which the exchange rate is allowed to be contemporaneously affected by all variables in the model. Such identifying assumptions can be justified as follows. If the exchange rate is determined in the market to some extent, the exchange rate is likely to reflect instantaneously all the information on the state of the economy. If the exchange rate is fully determined by the policy authority, the policy authority is likely to set the exchange rate after observing all possible contemporaneous information on the state of the economy.

Capital Controls

Some previous studies use the VAR framework to analyze the effectiveness of capital controls. They include the index indicating the degree of capital controls in the VAR model and examine the effects of shocks to the capital control index on various variables, such as capital flows (for example, De Gregorio et al., 2000; Cardoso and Goldfajn, 1997; Carvalho and Garcia, 2008; various studies in *Asian Development Review*, 2012).

A more controversial aspect of these studies is whether such an analysis can properly analyze the effectiveness of capital controls. One important objective of capital controls is to reduce the volatility of capital flows in the presence of various push and pull factors. However, in the basic VAR model, the effects of push and pull factors under high versus low degree of capital controls are treated the same. Merely examining the effects of shocks to the capital control index under such an assumption is not fully satisfactory.

Given the limitation of previous studies, Choi and Kim (2012) analyze the effectiveness of capital controls using the threshold VAR model as follows:

$$Y_t = c^{(1)} + A(L)^{(1)} Y_t + (c^{(2)} + A(L)^{(2)} Y_t) I_t(S_t \geq \gamma) + u_t \qquad (23.18)$$

where $I_t(S_t \geq \gamma)$ is an indicator function whose value is 1 if the degree of capital control, S_t, is larger than the threshold value γ, and 0 otherwise. Choi and Kim (2012) convert the reduced form into the structural form to examine how the effects of shocks to various determinants of capital flows are different under high versus low degree of capital controls to infer the effectiveness of capital controls.[6]

9 CONCLUSION

This chapter reviews how VAR models are applied to macroeconomic policy analysis. The literature is developed by introducing alternative identification methods and models. The VAR model was initially proposed with an SR recursive method, but various alternative identification methods, such as SR non-recursive restrictions, LR restrictions, and sign restrictions, were later introduced. The basic VAR models were extended to allow for a large number of variables (as in large-scale Bayesian VAR and FAVAR), time variations (as in time-varying VAR, regime-switching VAR, and threshold VAR), and cross-sectional information (as in panel VAR). The literature originated from the applications to monetary policy analysis, but it was also extended to other macro policy analyses, such as fiscal policy and exchange rate policy. In the future, new identification methods and models will be continuously introduced, which will be applied to various macro policy applications.

NOTES

1. Refer to Reichenstein (1987) and Leeper and Gordon (1992).
2. However, Hanson (2004) suggests that commodity price does not capture inflation expectation. On the other hand, Beaudry and Devereux (1995) develop a theoretical model to match the price puzzle by regarding the price puzzle as the true effects of monetary policy.
3. There are two interpretations: (1) such relations are applied only to contemporaneous interactions in the structural form equation; (2) they are applied to the relationship between the reduced form residuals and structural shocks.
4. Kim (2013) suggests that monetary policy shocks identified by Uhlig's (2005) method produce other puzzling responses. This may imply that the identified shocks may not be truly exogenous monetary policy shocks despite these two puzzles being avoided by construction.
5. Faust (1998) analyzes the effects of monetary policy shocks on output in the structural VAR models, in which the number of identifying restrictions is smaller than the traditionally required number of identifying restrictions by excluding unsure identifying restrictions. The method of Faust (1998) preludes the methodology of sign restrictions. Refer to Chapter 22 in this volume.
6. An alternative method is to exploit cross-sectional information. Structural shock transmission can be compared for countries of high versus low degree of capital controls. Refer to Miniane and Rogers (2007) for monetary policy transmission and Kim (2009) for fiscal policy transmission.

REFERENCES

Asian Development Review (2012), **29**(2), 1–182.

Banbura, M., D. Giannone and L. Reichlin (2011), 'Large Bayesian vector autoregressions', *Journal of Applied Econometrics*, **25**, 71–92.

Barro, R.J. and C.J. Redlick (2009), 'Macroeconomic effects from government purchases and taxes', NBER Working Paper No. 15369.

Beaudry, P. and M.B. Devereux (1995), 'Money and the real exchange rate with sticky prices and increasing returns', *Carnegie-Rochester Conference Series on Public Policy*, **43**, 55–101.

Beetsma, R., M. Giuliodori and F. Klaassen (2008), 'The effects of public spending shocks on trade balances and budget deficits in the European Union', *Journal of European Economic Association*, **6**, 414–23.

Bernanke, B.S. and A. Blinder (1992), 'The federal funds rate and the channels of monetary transmission', *American Economic Review*, **82**, 901–21.

Bernanke, B.S. and I. Mihov (1998), 'Measuring monetary policy', *Quarterly Journal of Economics*, **113**(3), 869–902.

Bernanke, B.S., J. Boivin and P. Eliasz (2005), 'Measuring the effects of monetary policy: a factor-augmented vector autoregressive (FAVAR) approach', *Quarterly Journal of Economics*, **120**(1), 387–422.
Blanchard, O.J. and R. Perotti (2002), 'An empirical investigation of the dynamic effects of shocks to government spending and taxes on output', *Quarterly Journal of Economics*, **117**, 1329–68.
Blanchard, O.J. and D. Quah (1989), 'The dynamic effects of aggregate demand and supply disturbances', *American Economic Review*, **79**, 655–73.
Boschen, J.F. and L.O. Mills (1991), 'The effects of countercyclical monetary policy on money and interest rates: an evaluation of evidence from FOMC documents', Working Paper No. 91-20, Federal Reserve Bank of Philadelphia.
Burnside, C., M. Eichenbaum and J.D. Fisher (2004), 'Fiscal shocks and their consequences', *Journal of Economic Theory*, **115**, 89–117.
Canova, F. and L. Gambetti (2009), 'Structural changes in the US economy: is there a role for monetary policy?', *Journal of Economic Dynamics and Control*, **33**, 477–90.
Canova, F. and G. de Nicolo (2002), 'Monetary disturbances matter for business cycle fluctuations in the G-7', *Journal of Monetary Economics*, **49**(6), 1131–59.
Canova, F. and G. de Nicolo (2003), 'On the sources of business cycles in the G-7', *Journal of International Economics*, **59**(1), 77–100.
Cardoso, E. and I. Goldfajn (1997), 'Capital flows to Brazil: the endogeneity of capital controls', IMF Working Paper No. 97/115, September.
Carvalho, B.S. de M. and M.G.P. Garcia (2008), 'Ineffective controls on capital inflows under sophisticated financial markets: Brazil in the nineties', in S. Edwards and M.G.P. Garcia (eds), *Financial Markets Volatility and Performance in Emerging Markets*, Chicago, IL: University of Chicago Press, pp. 29–96.
Choi, C. and S. Kim (2012), 'Capital flows and capital controls', working paper, Seoul National University.
Christiano, L., M. Eichenbaum and C. Evans (1996), 'The effects of monetary policy shocks: evidence from the flow of funds', *Review of Economics and Statistics*, **78**, 16–34.
Christiano, L.J., M. Eichenbaum and C.L. Evans (1999), 'Monetary policy shocks: what have we learned and to what end?', in J. Taylor and M. Woodford (eds), *Handbook of Macroeconomics*, Vol. 1A, Amsterdam: Elsevier/North-Holland, pp. 65–148.
Christiano, L.J., M. Eichenbaum and C.L. Evans (2005), 'Nominal rigidities and the dynamic effects of a shock to monetary policy', *Journal of Political Economy*, **113**(1), 1–45.
Clarida, R. and M. Galí (1994), 'Sources of real exchange rate fluctuations: how important are nominal shocks', *Carnegie-Rochester Series on Public Policy*, **41**, 1–56.
Clarida, R. and M. Gertler (1997), 'How the Bundesbank conducts monetary policy', in C.D. Romer and D.H. Romer (eds), *Reducing Inflation: Motivation and Strategy*, Chicago, IL: University of Chicago Press, pp. 363–406.
Cogley, T. and T.J. Sargent (2005), 'Drifts and volatilities: monetary policies and outcomes in the post WWII US', *Review of Economic Dynamics*, **8**(2), 262–302.
Corsetti, G. and G. Müller (2006), 'Twin deficits: squaring theory, evidence and common sense', *Economic Policy*, **21**(8), 597–638.
Cushman, D.O. and T. Zha (1997), 'Identifying monetary policy in a small open economy under flexible exchange rates', *Journal of Monetary Economics*, **39**, 433–48.
De Gregorio, J., S. Edwards and R.O. Valdes (2000), 'Controls on capital inflows: do they work?', *Journal of Development Economics*, **63**, 59–83.
Doan, T., R. Litterman and C.A. Sims (1984), 'Forecasting and conditional projection using realistic prior distributions', *Econometric Reviews*, **3**, 1–100.
Edelberg, W., M. Eichenbaum and J.D.M. Fisher (1999), 'Understanding the effects of a shock to government purchases', *Review of Economic Dynamics*, **2**, 166–206.
Eichenbaum, M. (1992), 'Comments on "Interpreting the macroeconomic time series facts: the effects of monetary policy"', *European Economic Review*, **36**.
Eichenbaum, M. and C. Evans (1995), 'Some empirical evidence on the effects of monetary policy shocks on exchange rates', *Quarterly Journal of Economics*, **110**, 975–1010.
Enders, Z., G.J. Müller and A. Scholl (2011), 'How do fiscal and technology shocks affect real exchange rates?: New evidence for the United States', *Journal of International Economics*, **83**(1), 53–69.
Fatas, A. and I. Mihov (2001), 'The effects of fiscal policy on consumption and employment: theory and evidence', CEPR Discusion Paper No. 2760.
Faust, J. (1998), 'The robustness of identified VAR conclusions about money', *Carnegie-Rochester Conference Series in Public Policy*, **49**, 207–44.
Fisher, J.D.M. and R. Peters (2009), 'Using stock returns to identify government spending shocks', Federal Reserve Bank of Chicago Working Paper No. 2009-03.
Friedman, M. and A.J. Schwartz (1963), *A Monetary History of the United States: 1867–1960*, Princeton, NJ: Princeton University Press.

Fung, B. (1998), 'Monetary shocks in the G-7 countries: is there a puzzle?', *Journal of Monetary Economics*, **42**(3), 575–92.

Galí, J. (1992), 'How well does the IS–LM model fit postwar US data?', *Quarterly Journal of Economics*, **107**, 709–38.

Galí, J., D. López-Salido and J. Vallés (2007), 'Understanding the effects of government spending on consumption', *Journal of the European Economic Association*, **5**(1), 227–70.

Gordon, D.B. and E.M. Leeper (1994), 'The dynamic impacts of monetary policy: an exercise in tentative identification', *Journal of Political Economy*, **102**, 228–47.

Hanson, M.S. (2004), 'The "Price Puzzle" reconsidered', *Journal of Monetary Economics*, **51**(7), 1385–413.

Ilzetzki, E., E.G. Mendoza and C.A. Végh (2009), 'How big (small?) are fiscal multipliers?', NBER Working Paper No. 16479.

Kamin, S.B. and J.H. Rogers (2000), 'Output and the real exchange rate in developing countries: an application to Mexico', *Journal of Development Economics*, **61**, 85–109.

Kim, S. (1996), 'Essays in money and finance in open economies', Ph.D. dissertation, Yale University.

Kim, S. (1999), 'Do monetary policy shocks matter in the G-7 countries? Using common identifying assumptions about monetary policy across countries', *Journal of International Economics*, **48**, 387–412.

Kim, S. (2001), 'International transmission of US monetary policy shocks: evidence from VARs', *Journal of Monetary Economics*, **48**(2), 339–72.

Kim, S. (2002), 'Exchange rate stabilization in the ERM: identifying European monetary policy reactions', *Journal of International Money and Finance*, **21**(3), 413–34.

Kim, S. (2003), 'Monetary policy, foreign exchange intervention, and exchange rate in a unifying framework', *Journal of International Economics*, **60**, 355–86.

Kim, S. (2005), 'Monetary policy, foreign exchange policy, and delayed overshooting', *Journal of Money, Credit, and Banking*, **37**, 775–82.

Kim, S. (2007), 'What is learned from a currency crisis, fear of floating or hollow middle? Identifying exchange rate policy in recent crisis countries', Discussion Paper Series 0712, Institute of Economic Research, Korea University.

Kim, S. (2009), 'Country characteristics and effects of government consumption shocks on current account and real exchange rate', working paper.

Kim, S. (2013), 'What are the effects of monetary policy shocks? Sign restrictions and endogeneity of monetary policy actions', working paper.

Kim, S. and Y. Kim (2011), 'The RMB debate: empirical analysis on the effects of exchange rate shocks in China and Japan', working paper.

Kim, S. and J. Lee (2008), 'International macroeconomic fluctuations: a new open economy macroeconomics interpretation', HKIMR Working Paper No. 23/2008.

Kim, S. and N. Roubini (2000), 'Exchange rate anomalies in the industrial countries: a solution with a structural VAR approach', *Journal of Monetary Economics*, **45**, 561–86.

Kim, S. and N. Roubini (2008), 'Twin deficit or twin divergence? Fiscal policy, current account, and the real exchange rate in the US', *Journal of International Economics*, **74**, 362–84.

Kim, Y. and Y.-H. Ying (2007), 'An empirical assessment of currency devaluation in East Asian countries', *Journal of International Money and Finance*, **26**, 265–84.

Lastrapes, W.D. (1992), 'Sources of fluctuations in real and nominal exchange rates', *Review of Economics and Statistics*, **74**, 530–39.

Leeper, E. (1997), 'Narrative and VAR approaches to monetary policy: common identification problems', *Journal of Monetary Economics*, **40**, 641–57.

Leeper, E.M. and D.B. Gordon (1992), 'In search of the liquidity effect', *Journal of Monetary Economics*, **29**(3), 341–69.

Leeper, E.M., C.A. Sims and T. Zha (1996), 'What does monetary policy do?', *Brookings Papers on Economic Activity*, 1996 (2), 1–63.

Leeper, E.M., T.B. Walker and S.S. Yang (2011), 'Foresight and information flows', working paper, Indiana University.

Litterman, R. (1986), 'Forecasting with Bayesian vector autoregressions: five years of experience', *Journal of Business and Economic Statistics*, **4**, 25–38.

Miniane, J. and J.H. Rogers (2007), 'Capital controls and the international transmission of US money shocks', *Journal of Money, Credit, and Banking*, **39**(5), 1003–35.

Mountford, A. and H. Uhlig (2009), 'What are the effects of fiscal policy shocks?', *Journal of Applied Econometrics*, **24**, 960–92.

Primiceri, G. (2005), 'Time varying structural vector autoregressions and monetary policy', *Review of Economic Studies*, **72**, 821–52.

Ramey, V.A. (2009), 'Identifying government spending shocks: it's all in the timing', NBER Working Paper No. 15464.

Ramey, V.A. and Matthew D. Shapiro (1998), 'Costly capital reallocation and the effects of government spending', *Carnegie-Rochester Conference Series on Public Policy*, **48**(1), 145–94.
Ravn, M.O., S. Schmitt-Grohé and M. Uribe (2007), 'Explaining the effects of government spending shocks on consumption and the real exchange rate', NBER Working Paper No. 13328.
Reichenstein, W. (1987), 'The impact of money on short term interest rates', *Economic Inquiry*, **25**(1), 67–82.
Romer, C. and D. Romer (1989), 'Does monetary policy matter? A new test in the spirit of Friedman and Schwartz', in O.J. Blanchard and S. Fischer (eds), *NBER Macroeconomic Annual*, Cambridge, MA: National Bureau of Economic Research, pp. 121–70.
Romer, C. and D. Romer (2004), 'A new measure of monetary shocks: derivation and implications', NBER Working Paper No. 0966.
Scholl, A. and H. Uhlig (2008), 'New evidence on the puzzles: results from agnostic identification on monetary policy and exchange rates', *Journal of International Economics*, **76**, 1–13.
Sims, C.A. (1980), 'Macroeconomics and reality', *Econometrica*, **48**, 1–48.
Sims, C.A. (1992), 'Interpreting the macroeconomic time series facts: the effects of monetary policy', *European Economic Review*, **36**, 975–1000.
Sims, C.A. and T. Zha (2006a), 'Does monetary policy generate recessions?', *Macroeconomic Dynamics*, **10**, 231–72.
Sims, C.A. and T. Zha (2006b), 'Were there regime switches in US monetary policy?', *American Economic Review*, **96**(1).
Strongin, S. (1995), 'The identification of monetary policy disturbances: explaining the liquidity puzzle', *Journal of Monetary Economics*, **35**, 463–97.
Tobin, J. (1970), 'Money and income: post hoc ergo proctor hoc?', *Quarterly Journal of Economics*, **84**(2), 301–17.
Uhlig, H. (2005), 'What are the effects of monetary policy on output? Results from an agnostic identification procedure', *Journal of Monetary Economics*, **52**, 381–419.

PART VI

APPLICATIONS III: CALIBRATION AND SIMULATIONS

24 Calibration and simulation of DSGE models*

Paul Gomme and Damba Lkhagvasuren

cal·i·bra·tion (kăl′ə-brā′shən) *n.* The process of restricting parameters in an economic model so that the model is consistent with long run growth facts and microeconomic observations.

1 INTRODUCTION

Many interesting macroeconomic models are either sufficiently complex that they must be solved computationally, or the questions being asked are inherently quantitative and so they should be solved computationally. The first group includes almost any empirically relevant version of the neoclassical growth model.[1] The second group includes such basic questions as business cycle fluctuations: How well does the neoclassical growth model do in producing variation in macroaggregates (like output, consumption, investment and hours worked) that 'look like' those seen in the data. These are quantitative questions for which qualitative answers are insufficient. Calibration is an effective tool for imposing discipline on the choice of parameter values that arise in such models, taking what would otherwise be a numerical example into the realm of an empirically relevant exercise with parameters tightly pinned down by either long-run growth facts, or microeconomic observations. As such, calibration is a useful part of the macroeconomist's toolkit.

This chapter is concerned with measurement as it pertains to calibration.[2] Kydland and Prescott (1982) provided the foundations for the calibration procedure; key subsequent developments have been made by Prescott (1986), Cooley and Prescott (1995) and Gomme and Rupert (2007). This chapter builds chiefly on Gomme and Rupert. Like this earlier paper, our goal is to provide a sufficiently careful and detailed description of our procedures for others to be easily able to replicate our work. To further facilitate replication, the underlying data and manipulations are available at *http://alcor.concordia.ca/~pgomme.*

In order to make the presentation as 'hands-on' as possible, section 2 presents the model, the neoclassical growth model which forms the foundation of New Classical and New Keynesian models. The heart of the chapter is in section 3, which presents the calibration of the neoclassical growth model. The first order of business is to choose functional forms for preferences and technology. These choices are guided, in part, by long-run growth considerations. A second key issue is how broadly economic activity should be measured. Cooley and Prescott (1995) think of economic activity very broadly, including not only private market activity but also government and household activity. Gomme and Rupert (2007) focus more narrowly on private market activity. However, as argued in section 3.2, for Cooley and Prescott to aggregate economic activity across the private market, government and household, it must almost certainly be true that each of these sectors has the *same* technology. This chapter follows Gomme and Rupert, focusing narrowly on private market activity since it involves fewer imputations.[3] It is important to remember that if the Cooley and Prescott aggregation is correct, then the Gomme and Rupert measurement should give the same answer as Cooley and Prescott: the converse is not true. Much of the remainder of section 3 describes the nitty gritty details of constructing various calibration targets. The chapter describes how to actually construct more calibration targets than are necessary to calibrate the neoclassical growth model. Section 3.12 describes how to actually calibrate the model, which involves making sure that in steady state, the model is consistent with the calibration targets. It is important to remember that calibration is a process for mapping a set of calibration targets into an identical number of model parameters; it is not simply setting parameter values.

The model is solved and simulated in section 4. Rather than the usual real business cycle practice of comparing two tables of second moments – one for the US data, the other for model-generated data – Solow residuals as measured from the US data are fed into the model as the set of technology shocks. The model is, then, evaluated on its ability to generate time series that are similar to those in the data. The model does reasonably well in replicating the time series behavior of output, consumption and average labor productivity; it does rather poorly with respect to hours, investment and capital.

2 THE ECONOMIC ENVIRONMENT

The organizing framework is the neoclassical growth model that lies at the heart of New Classical and New Keynesian models. The presentation is kept relatively brief since this model should be familiar to most macroeconomists. It should be understood that the variables chosen by households differ from those chosen by firms, and that these differ from aggregate or per capita quantities; in the presentation, no distinction is made between these three sets of variables in the interests of conserving on notation.

Also in the interests of a clean presentation of the model, growth is omitted. There are two logical ways for growth to appear: as labor-embodied technological progress, and in the form of investment-specific technological change.[4] As shown in King et al. (1988) and Gomme and Rupert (2007), including growth is important for delivering certain parameter restrictions in both preferences and technologies. These parameter restrictions are discussed below.

2.1 Households

The problem of the representative household is

$$\max E_0 \sum_{t=0}^{\infty} \beta^t U(c_t, \ell_t), \quad 0 < \beta < 1 \tag{24.1}$$

subject to a budget constraint,

$$c_t + x_t = (1 - \tau_n) w_t n_t + (1 - \tau_k) r_t k_t + \tau_t, \tag{24.2}$$

the law of motion for capital,

$$k_t + 1 = (1 - \delta)k_t + x_t, \quad 0 \leq \delta \leq 1, \tag{24.3}$$

and a constraint on time,

$$n_t + \ell_t = 1. \tag{24.4}$$

The household's preferences are defined over contingent time sequences for consumption, c_t, and leisure, ℓ_t. In the budget constraint, (24.2), the real wage is w_t while the rental rate for capital is r_t. Labor income is taxed at the rate τ_n while capital income is taxed at the rate τ_k.[5] Hours of work are denoted n_t while k_t is the household's beginning-of-period holdings of capital. The household receives a lump-sum transfer of τ_t from the government. Finally, x_t is the household's investment and δ is the depreciation rate of capital.

2.2 Firms

Firms face a sequence of static problems. Each period, a firm hires labor and rents capital to maximize its real profits:

$$\max_{k_t, n_t} F(k_t, n_t; z_t) - w_t n_t - r_t k_t \tag{24.5}$$

where F is a constant-returns-to-scale production function, and z_t is a shock to technology.

In the New Keynesian literature, it is common to assume two sectors, one for final goods, the other for intermediate goods. The final goods sector is perfectly competitive and uses only intermediate goods. The intermediate goods sector is characterized by monopolistic competition, and production employs labor and maybe capital. The reason for the two-sector set-up is because most New Keynesian models include sticky price setting which means that at least some firms must be price setters. The complications of the New Keynesian set-up are suppressed in the interests of clarity.

2.3 Government

The only role for government is to levy distorting factor income taxes, lump-sum rebating the proceeds. In particular, there is no government spending and the government issues no debt. Its budget constraint is

$$\tau_t = \tau_n w_t n_t + \tau_k r_t k_t. \tag{24.6}$$

3 CALIBRATION

At this stage, the task is to choose functional forms, then find calibration targets that can be used to assign values to the parameters of the model.

3.1 Functional Forms

To be consistent with balanced growth, the momentary utility function, U, needs to be homogeneous of some degree in consumption, c. For the most part, the real business cycle literature uses

$$U(c,\ell) = \begin{cases} \frac{(c\ell^{\omega})^{1-\gamma}}{1-\gamma} & \text{if } \gamma \in (0,1) \cup (1,\infty), \\ \ln c + \omega \ln \ell & \text{if } \gamma = 1. \end{cases} \tag{24.7}$$

The utility specification is referred to as 'constant relative risk aversion'. Above, U is homogeneous of degree $(1 - \gamma)$ in c; in other words, this utility function satisfies balanced growth restrictions. In the New Keynesian literature, it is more common to see

$$U(c,n) = \ln c - \omega \frac{n^{1+\xi}}{1+\xi} \tag{24.8}$$

where $1/\xi$ is the Frisch labor supply elasticity.

The production function is specified to be Cobb–Douglas:

$$F(k,n;z) = zk^{\alpha}n^{1-\alpha}, \quad 0 \leq \alpha \leq 1. \tag{24.9}$$

In the literature, the Cobb–Douglas functional form is often justified as being consistent with the following facts:

1. capital's share of output exhibits no secular trend;
2. the return to capital similarly has no secular trend;
3. the real wage rate does have a secular trend.

Swan (1964), Phelps (1966) and King et al. (1988) show that *any* constant-returns-to-scale production function is consistent with these facts. What makes the case for Cobb–Douglas more compelling is to incorporate investment-specific technological change; Gomme and Rupert (2007) make explicit arguments made in Kydland (1995) and Greenwood et al. (1997), and the interested reader is directed to these works for details.

Finally, the productivity shock is assumed to follow a first-order autoregressive process:

$$\ln z_t = \rho \ln z_{t-1} + \varepsilon_t, \quad \varepsilon_t \sim N(0,\sigma^2). \tag{24.10}$$

The set of parameters to be calibrated (assigned values) is summarized in Table 24.1. Since there are nine parameters, procedurally calibration involves the use of nine

Table 24.1 Parameters to be calibrated

Preferences:	β, ω, γ or ξ
Technology:	δ, α, ρ, σ
Government:	τ_n, τ_k

calibration targets. These targets are typically taken from two sources: microeconomic evidence, and long-run growth facts. Long-run growth facts have already implicitly been used to restrict the production function to be Cobb–Douglas, as well as to restrict the utility function. There is an embarrassment of riches since there are more potential calibration targets than parameters.[6] The properties of the technology shock, ρ and σ, can be inferred from the properties of the Solow residual; see section 3.10. The tax rates, τ_n and τ_k, can be obtained directly from National Income and Product Accounts (NIPA) as described in section 3.8. The remaining five parameters can be calibrated using some subset of:

1. factor income shares using data from NIPA;
2. depreciation and capital stock data reported by the Bureau of Economic Analysis (BEA);
3. the investment–output ratio;
4. the capital–output ratio;
5. microeconomic evidence concerning risk aversion;
6. microeconomic evidence regarding the labor supply elasticity;
7. the allocation of time from US time use surveys;
8. the real return to capital.

The remainder of this section discusses the measurement of the above calibration targets.

3.2 How Broadly to Measure Economic Activity

An issue that immediately arises is how broadly one should measure economic activity for the purposes of calibration. Perhaps the best known paper on calibration is that of Cooley and Prescott (1995). They construe economic activity very broadly, encompassing both private market activity, government production, and home activity. Cooley and Prescott include capital in all these sectors, plus the stock of inventories and the value of land, in their measure of the capital stock; output likewise includes output produced by this capital stock. In measuring income flows, Cooley and Prescott must impute capital income flows to government capital since National Income and Product Accounts (NIPA) does not include a measure of government capital income. For similar reasons, they must impute income flows to the stock of consumer durables. Oddly, they do not impute labor income flows for the housing sector, although these flows are largely missing from NIPA. Likewise, Cooley and Prescott's measure of time spent working only includes market time; see the discussion in section 3.7.

An alternative approach is that exemplified by Gomme and Rupert (2007) who measure economic activity more narrowly, focusing on private market activity, when it comes to calibration. If Cooley and Prescott are justified in their aggregation, it should not matter whether one takes the broad or narrow approach to measuring economic activity. To see this point, let sectoral outputs be given by

$$Y_M = K_M^\alpha N_M^{1-\alpha} \tag{24.11}$$

$$Y_G = K_G^\alpha N_G^{1-\alpha} \tag{24.12}$$

$$Y_H = K_H^{\alpha} N_H^{1-\alpha}, \tag{24.13}$$

where an M subscript denotes private market activity, G government activity, and H the household sector. For the Cooley and Prescott aggregation to be valid, it must be the case that all three production functions have the same capital share parameter, α; otherwise, they surely would not be able to write the aggregate production function as

$$Y = (K_M + K_G + K_H)^{\alpha}(N_M + N_G + N_H)^{1-\alpha}. \tag{24.14}$$

To find a value for capital's share, α, it should not matter whether one uses (24.11), as Gomme and Rupert do, or (24.14), as Cooley and Prescott do. Since Cooley and Prescott must impute various income flows while Gomme and Rupert do not, it seems more straightforward to follow the narrow approach of Gomme and Rupert.

Further, there are good reasons for thinking that the three sectors are *not* sufficiently similar to aggregate as in (24.14). For example, the home production literature emphasizes that there is an inherent asymmetry between the market and home sectors: the market sector produces goods that are used in the home sector (namely, investment goods including durables), but the home sector does not produce goods that are used by the market sector; see Benhabib et al. (1991) and Greenwood and Hercowitz (1991).

3.3 Capital's Share of Income

In principle, one of the easiest parameters to calibrate is α, capital's share of income. Given that the production function is Cobb–Douglas, and assuming that factor markets are competitive, factors are paid their marginal products. Capital's share of income can, then, be computed as total payments to capital divided by income. In practice, the calculation is far from straightforward, as already suggested by the discussion of the different approaches of Cooley and Prescott (1995) and Gomme and Rupert (2007).

A further issue relates to the treatment of proprietors' income and indirect taxes less subsidies. The problem is that both go into measured GDP, and both have capital and labor income components that cannot easily be separated out. To see how to proceed, write out market income as:

$$Y_M = Y_{KM} + Y_{NM} + Y_{AM} \tag{24.15}$$

where Y_{AM} denotes ambiguous market income, namely proprietors' income plus indirect taxes less subsidies, Y_{KM} is unambiguous capital income, and Y_{NM} is unambiguous labor income. Some portion of ambiguous income needs to be allocated to capital income, the rest to labor income. The practice in the literature is to assume that the fraction of ambiguous income that should be allocated to capital is the same fraction as income is allocated to capital for the rest of the economy. This idea is, perhaps, clearer when stated as an equation,

$$Y_{KM} + \alpha Y_{AM} = \alpha Y_M, \tag{24.16}$$

where α is the (unknown) capital share. The left-hand side is *total* capital income, including a fraction of ambiguous income; the right-hand side is capital income as a share of total income. Equation (24.16) can be rewritten as

$$\alpha = \frac{Y_{KM}}{Y_{KM} + Y_{NM}}. \tag{24.17}$$

As discussed above, one complication is that market income flows are 'contaminated' by housing income flows. Fortunately, National Income and Product Accounts (NIPA) includes data on the housing sector. Capital market income is given by

$$\begin{aligned} Y_{KM} = {} & \text{Rental Income} - \text{Housing Rental Income} \\ & + \text{Net Interest Income} - \text{Housing Net Interest Income} \\ & + \text{Corporate Profits} - \text{Housing Corporate Profits} \\ & + \underbrace{\text{Gross National Product} - \text{Net National Product}}_{\text{Consumption of Fixed Capital}} \\ & - \underbrace{(\text{Government Gross Value Added} - \text{Government Net Domestic Product})}_{\text{Government Consumption of Fixed Capital}} \\ & - \underbrace{(\text{Housing Gross Value Added} - \text{Net Housing Value Added})}_{\text{Housing Consumption of Fixed Capital}}. \end{aligned} \tag{24.18}$$

In (24.18), consumption of fixed capital (with appropriate adjustments to remove flows associated with the government and housing sectors) reflects compensation to capital for depreciation.

Labor market income is:

$$\begin{aligned} Y_{NM} = {} & \text{Compensation of employees} - \text{Housing compensation of employees} \\ & - \text{Government compensation of employees}. \end{aligned} \tag{24.19}$$

Capital's share of income is, then, computed via (24.17).

3.4 The Depreciation Rate

The Bureau of Economic Analysis (BEA) reports total depreciation for various categories of capital goods, as well as capital stocks. The depreciation rate can, then, be obtained by dividing (nominal) depreciation by the (nominal) capital stock. The depreciation rate on market capital uses data on private equipment and software and private non-residential structures.

For those interested in modeling the home sector, the corresponding categories for computing the depreciation rate for home capital are: private residential fixed assets (structures), and the stock of consumer durables.

Depreciation rates are reported below for market and home capital, as well as their chief components.

3.5 Great Ratios

Two of the so-called 'great ratios' are the investment–output and capital–output ratios. Given the discussion of the measurement of capital's share of income, α, it makes sense that output should correspond to private output (that is, excluding government), net of housing. Investment, then, should include investment in private non-residential structures, and in equipment and software. Inventory investment is excluded from total investment because very few macroeconomic models explicitly model inventories. Output corresponds to the sum of private investment and consumption of non-durables and services.

Measuring the capital–output ratio is fraught with not only similar issues to those for investment, but others unique to the measurement of capital. Specifically, what exactly comprises private market capital? It seems clear that the stock of non-residential structures, and equipment and software should be included. It should be noted, however, that the Bureau of Economic Analysis (BEA)'s inclusion of software in 'capital' is a relatively recent decision. One can make a case for inventories on the basis that National Income and Product Accounts (NIPA) includes changes in the stock of inventories as part of investment. A case can also be made for including land. The problem with land is that its value is computed as a residual from the flow of funds accounts by the Board of Governors of the Federal Reserve System, and the value of land for the US as a whole is sometimes found to be *negative*. In any event, the Board of Governors no longer reports the value of land.

Putting aside these issues, a further problem with capital is that its measurement has been subject to somewhat infrequent but large revisions, as reported in Herman (2000). For broadly defined measures of capital, in 1997 the BEA revised their estimates of the capital stock up by as much as 30 per cent. Alternative measures of the US capital stock, like those of Maddison (1995) give estimates that are even larger. In light of these issues regarding the measurement of capital, using the capital–output ratio as a calibration target seems unwise.

3.6 Microeconomic Evidence

Microeconomic evidence can be brought to bear on two calibration targets: the coefficient of relative risk aversion, and the labor supply elasticity. Since Hall (1978), empirical work on consumption has used an intertemporal Euler equation to estimate key parameters of the utility function. Using this approach, Dynan (1993) reports estimates of the elasticity of intertemporal substitution near 0.1, or a coefficient of relative risk aversion of 10. In contrast, Gruber (2006), using Consumer Expenditure Survey data on total non-durable consumption, estimates a value of around 2, which implies a coefficient of relative risk aversion of 0.5. Using aggregate data, Attanasio and Weber (1995) find an elasticity of intertemporal substitution of either 0.34 or 0.48 – a coefficient of relative risk aversion of roughly 3 or 2. These finds are generally in line with evidence surveyed by Mehra and Prescott (1985); they conclude that the coefficient of relative risk aversion is positive, and restrict its value to be no larger than 10, although the bulk of the evidence points to a smaller value. In the literature, it is fairly common to implicitly set $\gamma = 1$ by assuming logarithmic utility.

Micro evidence on the labor supply elasticity typically use data on men. Typically, this labor supply elasticity is found to be small but positive. Altonji (1986) estimates an elasticity no larger than 0.35, MaCurdy (1981) no larger than 0.5. Pencavel (1986) surveys the empirical literature; he finds that estimates of the male labor supply elasticity are less than 1/3. For the logarithmic case, (24.7) implies a (steady state) Frisch labor supply elasticity given by $\frac{1-h}{h}$. For the largest estimated labor supply elasticity, 0.5, the Frisch labor supply elasticity means that steady state hours are 2/3 of the time endowment; smaller labor supply elasticities correspond to larger fractions of the time endowment. As shown in section 3.7, these fractions are not consistent with US time use evidence. When the utility function is given by (24.8), it seems common to assume a Frisch labor supply elasticity of 1, which would imply $\xi = 1$. There is nothing intrinsic to (24.8) to preclude setting the labor supply elasticity parameter equal to that estimated by labor economists, then using the parameter ω to ensure that hours worked are consistent with the time use survey evidence.

3.7 Time Use Surveys

One of the most comprehensive measurements of time use in the US is the periodic time use surveys which were taken in 1965, 1975, 1985, 1995, and most recently the American Time Use Survey (ATUS), 2003–2006. Based on the American Time Use Survey (ATUS), Gomme and Rubert (2007) report that individuals aged 16 and older spend 25.5 per cent of their discretionary time (that is, excluding time for sleeping and other personal care) working in the market. This fraction is considerably smaller than the value of 1/3 typically used in the literature. Gomme and Rubert compute a higher fraction, 31.5 per cent, for individuals aged 16–64. However, since the majority of macroeconomic models are of a representative agent, there seems to be no good reason to exclude retirees from the calculation of the fraction of time spent working.

Curiously, Cooley and Prescott (1995) calibrate to a working time fraction of 1/3. Given their broad notion of economic activity as including the home sector, it would make sense for them to include both time spent working in the market and time spent working at home. For the 16+ population, Gomme and Rupert (2007) find that an average of 24 per cent of discretionary time is spent performing housework; for those aged 16–64, it is 25.1 per cent. Arguably, then, Cooley and Prescott should have calibrated to an average work time of 49.5 per cent (the 16+ population) or 56.6 per cent (the 16–64 population).

3.8 Taxes

The calculation of tax rates follows the methodology of Mendoza et al. (1994) and Carey and Tchilinguirian (2000); see also Gomme et al. (2011). Auray et al. (2011) construct tax rates for the US and a subset of the EU The first step is to compute the tax rate on general household income, denoted τ_h (as distinct from the tax on earnings, τ_n), as the ratio of total household taxes divided by total household income:

$$\tau_h = \frac{\text{Personal Current Taxes}}{\text{Net Interest} + \text{Proprietors' Income} + \text{Rental Income} + \text{Wages and Salaries}} \qquad (24.20)$$

Next, the tax rate on earnings is obtained as

$$\tau_n = \frac{\text{Labor Income Taxes}}{\text{Labor Income}} \qquad (24.21)$$

where

$$\begin{aligned}\text{Labor Income Taxes} &= \tau_h[\text{Wages and Salaries} + (1-\alpha)\text{Proprietors' Income}]\\ &\quad + \text{Contributions for Government Social Security}, \qquad (24.22)\end{aligned}$$

and

$$\begin{aligned}\text{Labor Income} &= [\text{Wages and Salaries} + (1-\alpha)\text{Proprietors' Income}]\\ &\quad + \text{Employer Contributions for Government Social Security} \qquad (24.23)\end{aligned}$$

In the above, α is capital's share of income; section 3.3.

Finally, the capital income tax rate is given by

$$\tau_k = \frac{\text{Capital Income Taxes}}{\text{Capital Income}} \qquad (24.24)$$

where

$$\begin{aligned}\text{Capital Income Taxes} &= \tau_h[\text{Net Interest} + \alpha\,\text{Proprietors' Income} + \text{Rental Income}]\\ &\quad + \text{Corporate Income Taxes} + \text{Real Estate Property Taxes}\\ &\quad + \text{State Local Other Taxes}, \qquad (24.25)\end{aligned}$$

and

$$\begin{aligned}\text{Capital Income} &= \text{Net Operating Surplus} + \text{Consumption of Private Fixed Capital}\\ &\quad + (1-\alpha)\ \text{Proprietors' Income}, \qquad (24.26)\end{aligned}$$

where it is understood that the income flows, including net operating surplus, are measured net of their corresponding housing income flows. 'State and Local Other Taxes' includes items like licensing fees.

3.9 The Return to Capital

As in Gomme et al. (2011), the after-tax return to capital can be computed from National Income and Product Accounts (NIPA) data by dividing after-tax private market capital income by the corresponding capital stock:

$$R_t = \left[\left(\frac{(\text{After-tax Capital Income})/4}{\text{Market Capital Stock}} \right)^4 - 1 \right] \times 100\% \tag{24.27}$$

where

$$\begin{aligned} \text{After-tax Capital Income} = {} & \text{Net Operating Surplus} - (1 - \alpha)\text{Proprietors Income} \\ & - \tau_h [\text{Net Interest} - \alpha \text{ Proprietors Income} - \text{Rental Income}] \\ & - \text{Taxes on Corporate Income} - \text{Business Property Taxes} \\ & - \text{State and Local Other Taxes.} \end{aligned} \tag{24.28}$$

Since income is reported at an annual rate, the division of income by 4 (24.27) in expresses income at a quarterly rate.

3.10 The Solow Residual

Given data on hours of work, the capital stock and output, and armed with an estimate of α, capital's share of income, the Solow residual can be computed from the aggregate production function, (24.9). Denote the Solow residual by Z_t. To obtain the properties of the productivity shock in (24.10), namely the autoregressive parameter, ρ, and the standard deviation of the innovation, σ, run the following regression:

$$\ln Z_t = \beta_0 + \beta_1 \ln Z_{t-1} + \beta_2 t + u_t. \tag{24.29}$$

The time trend, t, is included to remove secular growth. The estimate of β_1 corresponds to ρ while the standard error of the residual corresponds to σ.

The results of estimating (24.29) over the period 1954Q1 to 2010Q4 are:

$$\ln Z_t = \underset{(0.1145)}{0.3252} + \underset{(0.0158)}{0.9555} \ln Z_{t-1} + \underset{(8.0482 \times 10^5)}{3.4144 \times 10^5} t, \tag{24.30}$$

standard errors in parentheses. The standard deviation of the residual is 0.00861.

3.11 Calibration Targets: Summary

Table 24.2 summarizes the implications of the calculations above for the calibration targets. In order to provide a single source of targets, Table 24.2 includes targets relevant for those interested in modeling the home sector, as well as a disaggregation of the depreciation rates into their constituent components (for the market sector, between structures

Table 24.2 Calibration targets

Target	Value
Risk aversion	1 – 2
Frisch labor supply elasticity	1.0
Time:	
Market, 16+	0.255
Market, 16–64	0.315
Home, 16+	0.24
Home, 16–64	0.251
Capital's share of income	0.2852
Depreciation rates:	
Market	0.0718
Structures	0.0289
Equipment & Software	0.1460
Home	0.0612
Housing	0.0159
Durables	0.2070
Investment–output ratio	0.1617
Capital–output ratio	1.6590
Labor tax rate	0.2417
Capital tax rate	0.4002
Return to capital:	
Pre-tax	9.4115
After-tax	4.9869
Technology shock:	
Autoregressive parameter	0.9555
Standard Deviation of the residual	0.00861

Notes: Average time allocation are based on calculations by Gomme and Rubert (2007) from the 2003–06 American Time Use Survey. Capital's share of income, the depreciation rates, the ratios, tax rates and properties of the technology shock are based on the data for the period 1954Q1 to 2010Q4; see the estimates in (24.30). The return to capital is average over 1954Q1 to 2009Q4.

and equipment and software; for the home sector, between structures (housing) and consumer durables).

A few comments are in order. First, the depreciation rate for market structures is substantially lower than that of equipment and software. The overall market depreciation rate is, clearly, a weighted average of the two components where the weights are given by the relative sizes of the two capital stocks. As shown in Gomme and Rupert (2007), while the market structures–output ratio is relatively constant in the post-World War II period, that of equipment and software has moved up by roughly 10 percentage points.

Second, while the after-tax return to business capital is somewhat higher than the 4 per cent real return that the bulk of the macroeconomics literature calibrates to, the pre-tax return is much higher. The conventional justification for using a 4 per cent return is that it represents a rough average of stock market returns, around 7 per cent according to Mehra and Prescott (1985), and the return to a risk-free bond, 0.8 per cent again according to Mehra and Prescott. Recall, though, that the return to business capital computed above includes income flows that correspond to income from the stock market as well as bonds. What is potentially missing is intangible capital. Omitting intangible capital – which presumably earns a return measured in NIPA – biases up the measured return to business capital. However, as reported in Gomme et al. (2011), the average return to the S&P 500 is somewhat *higher* than the return to business capital, despite the fact that the prices of the stocks making up the S&P 500 should be pricing in the value of intangible capital.

Third, the properties of the technology shock are fairly similar to those of Prescott (1986): an autoregressive parameter of 0.95 and a standard deviation of the innovation of 0.00763.

3.12 Calibration in Action

A model period is set to be one quarter. Recall from Table 24.1 that there are 9 parameters to be calibrated. Some of these parameters can be set directly from Table 24.2. These include: δ, the depreciation rate, based on the depreciation rate of market capital; α, capital's share of income; ρ and σ, the properties of the technology shock (see the estimates in (24.30)); and the tax rates on labor income, τ_n, and capital income, τ_k. For the purposes of this demonstration, the New Classical calibration will be followed, and the coefficient of relative risk aversion is set to 2. The remaining parameters are β, the discount factor, and ω, which determines the importance of leisure in preferences. These parameters should be calibrated to 'high quality' targets, and so are chosen so that the model's steady state delivers the observed fraction of time spent working, 25.5 per cent, and an annual real return to capital of 4.9869 per cent. A reasonable alternative to the return to capital would be the investment–output ratio. Given the discussion above concerning conceptual issues in obtaining the capital–output ratio, as well as the large – if infrequent – revisions to broad definitions of capital, either the return to capital or the investment–output ratio should be strictly preferred as calibration targets over the capital–output ratio.

The equations characterizing a solution to this model consist of:

$$U_1(c_t, 1 - n_t)F_2(k_t, n_t; z_t) = U_2(c_t, 1 - n_t) \tag{24.31}$$

$$U_1(c_{t+1}, 1 - n_{t+1}) = \beta E_t\{U_1(c_{t+1}, 1 - n_{t+1})[(1 - \tau_k)F_1(k_{t+1}, n_{t+1}; z_{t+1}) + 1 - \delta]\} \tag{24.32}$$

$$c_t + k_{t+1} = F(k_t, n_t; z_t) + (1 - \delta)k_t \tag{24.33}$$

Imposing the functional forms above, in steady state, these equations read:

$$\frac{1}{c}(1 - \alpha)\left(\frac{k}{n}\right)^{\alpha} = \frac{\omega}{1 - n} \tag{24.34}$$

$$1 = \beta\left[(1 - \tau_k)\alpha\left(\frac{n}{k}\right)^{1-\alpha} + 1 - \delta\right] \tag{24.35}$$

$$c + \delta k = k^{\alpha}n^{1-\alpha} \tag{24.36}$$

These equations can be solved for c, n, k, ω and β, imposing the additional restrictions that

$$n = 0.255 \tag{24.37}$$

$$(1 - \tau_k)\alpha\left(\frac{n}{k}\right)^{1-\alpha} + 1 - \delta = 1.049869^{\frac{1}{4}} \tag{24.38}$$

Doing so results in the following steady state values and parameter values:

$$k = 5.7659,\ \ h = 0.255,\ \ c = 0.5142,\ \ \beta = 0.9879,\ \ \omega = 2.5205. \tag{24.39}$$

In steady state, output is 0.6206. This calibration implies that the steady state consumption–output ratio is 0.8285, and that the annual capital–output ratio is 2.3228.

4 SIMULATION

While first-order perturbation methods are quite popular for solving dynamic general equilibrium models, here the model is solved by a policy function iteration method (also known as a projection method, or finite element method); see Coleman (1990) for details. This algorithm solves the Euler equations and constraints exactly at a set of grid points for the state variables, with linear interpolation between grid points.

In the business cycle literature, standard practice is to produce one table of second moments for the US economy and a second such table for the model economy (reporting the average over many replications for the model economy). Here, instead, the model is simulated once using the measured innovations to the technology shock (Solow residual). Time series for the model are, then, compared to corresponding series from the US data. In order to remove the secular trend from the data, apply the natural logarithm to the data, then apply the Hodrick and Prescott (1997) filter. The simulated data is similarly filtered.

Constructing quarterly time series is, at times, fraught with difficulties. The principal problem is that some time series are only available annually, at least over part of the desired sample period of 1954Q1 to 2010Q4. Details concerning the various necessary manipulations can be gleaned from the Matlab/Octave file that constructs the data for this chapter, or by referring to Gomme and Rupert (2007) and Gomme et al. (2011).

Figure 24.1a shows a remarkably good 'fit' between the model's prediction for the path of output and that actually observed. This fit can also be seen in the scatter plot in Figure 24.2a where each dot represents a combination of actual and simulated output at some particular period of time. In particular, the scatter plot indicates a positive association between actual and simulated, and a fairly tight fit, as indicated by the fact that the points are reasonably tightly clustered along the 45 degree line.

The story is much the same for consumption, as seen in Figure 24.1b, although the model produces considerably less volatility in consumption since the mid-1980s than is in the data. Nonetheless, there is a high correlation between the actual and simulated

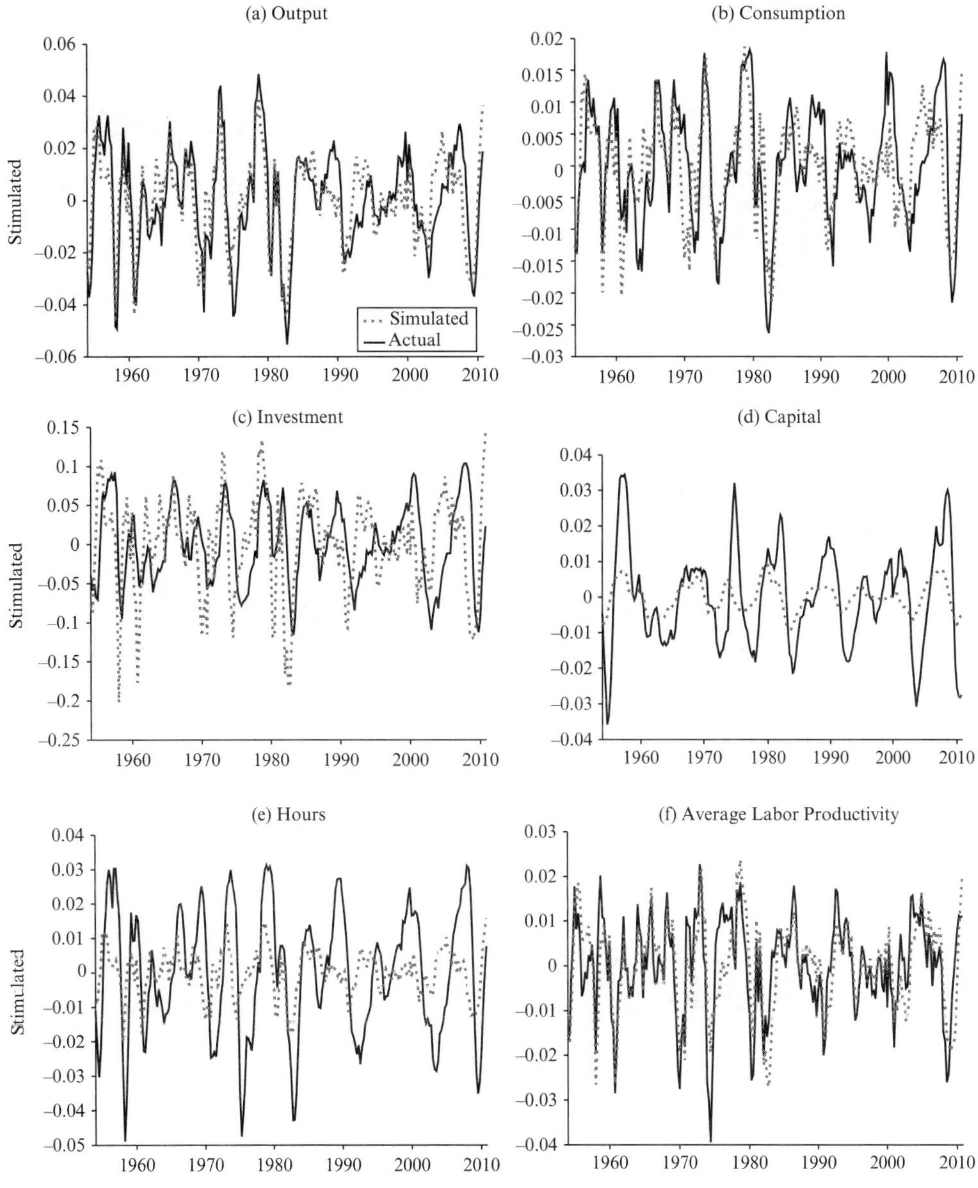

Figure 24.1 Actual and simulated data, time series

consumption series, as seen in Figure 24.2b, although the correlation is not as tight as for output.

The fit between actual and simulated investment is weaker than that seen for output and consumption. Figure 24.1c shows that not only is simulated investment more volatile than actual investment, the correlation between the two series is much

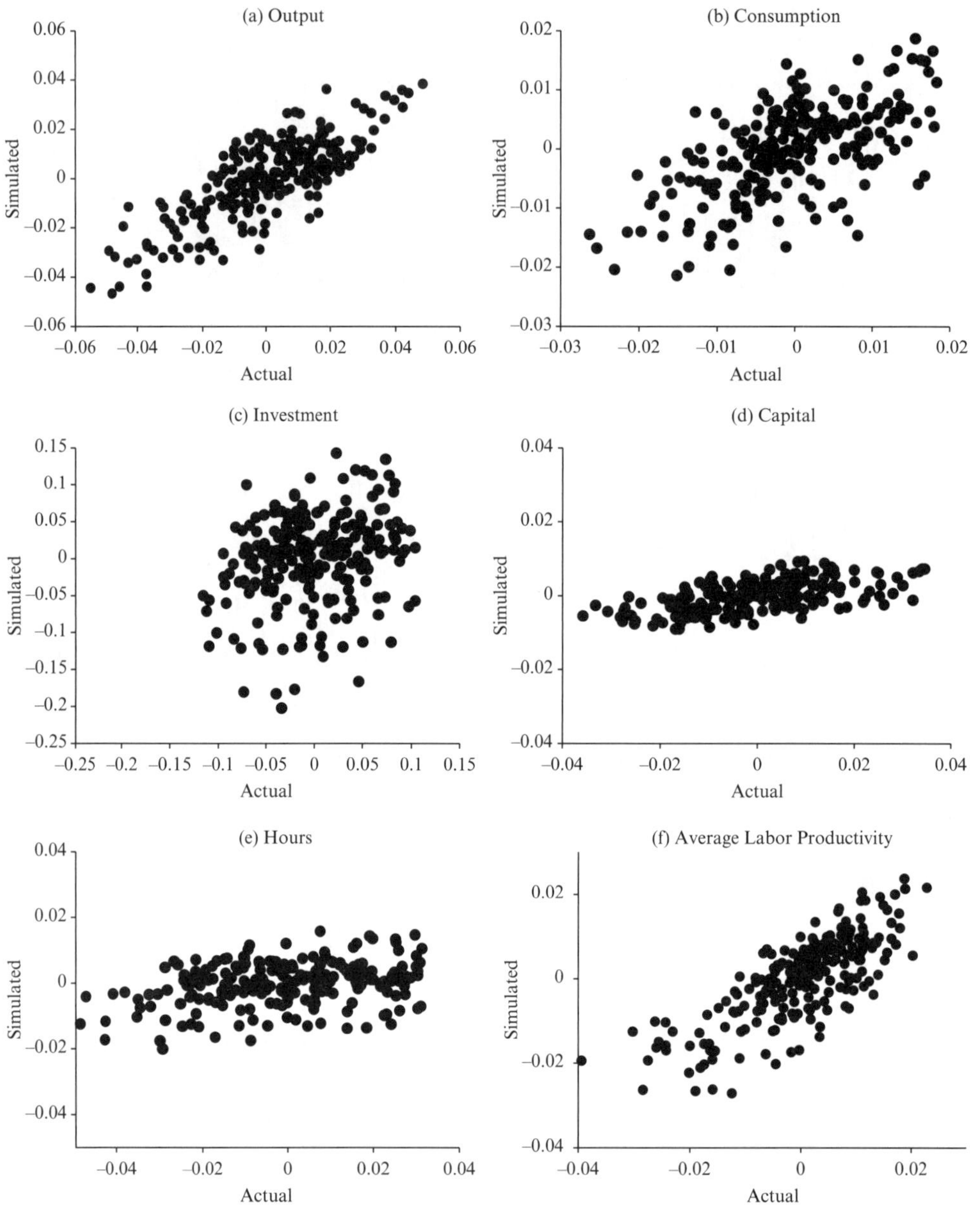

Figure 24.2 Actual and simulated data, scatter plot

weaker. These observations are also borne out in the scatter plot, Figure 24.2c. The behavior of investment feeds into that of capital; see Figure 24.1d. The scatter plot, Figure 24.2d, shows essentially no correlation between the actual and simulated capital stocks.

It is well known from the business cycle literature that models like the one in this chapter deliver too little variability in hours worked. Figure 24.1e confirms this observation. Further, Figure 24.2e shows that there is no correlation between actual and simulated hours.

The model does reasonably well in mimicking the time series pattern of average labor productivity, output divided by hours; see Figure 24.1f. The correlation between actual and simulated productivity is fairly high; see Figure 24.2f. Given that the model does so poorly in predicting the time path of hours worked, its success with respect to productivity is, perhaps, surprising.

5 CONCLUDING REMARKS

This chapter presented, in detail, how to construct calibration targets. To make it easier for others to work with this data, a Matlab/Octave program file is available for download at http://alcor.concordia.ca/~pgomme. This program not only reports calibration targets, it also generates a basic set of data and computes business cycle moments.

The chapter described how to actually calibrate the neoclassical growth model. Since there are more potential calibration targets than parameters, there is some discretion in choosing calibration targets. It was argued that well-measured, high-quality calibration targets should be used whenever possible.

Finally, the model presented simulations of the model, comparing the model's predicted macroeconomic time series with those of the US.

NOTES

* We received helpful comments from Stéphane Auray and David Fuller. The research assistance of Saeed Zaman is gratefully acknowledged. Gomme received financial support from Fonds de Recherche Société et Culture Québec.

1. Except in very special cases, the neoclassical growth model does not allow for closed-form solutions (that is, ones that can be worked out by hand). Perhaps the best known of these is when utility is logarithmic in consumption, separable between consumption and hours worked, the production function is Cobb–Douglas, and depreciation is 100 per cent. These restrictions are very special, and in the case of depreciation, clearly at odds with the data.
2. Measurement is also important in establishing the basic facts to be explained. A basic set of data and business cycle moments are included with the accompanying Matlab/Octave program file, available at *http://alcor.concordia.ca/~pgomme.*
3. As discussed in section 3.2, Cooley and Prescott (1995) must impute government capital income since it is missing from National Income and Product Accounts (NIPA). They should also impute labor income to owner occupied housing (the capital income is already in NIPA), but do not. Given their broad interpretation of economic activity, in calibrating their model, Cooley and Prescott should include time spent on housework, but do not. As discussed in section 3.7, individuals spend a considerable amount of time on housework.
4. Except in the special case of a Cobb–Douglas production function, disembodied technological change is not consistent with balanced growth.
5. The tax on capital is measured net of the capital consumption allowance.
6. The surplus of calibration targets could be handled using formal econometric techniques that take advantage of the 'over identification' of the parameters.

REFERENCES

Altonji, Joeeph G. (1986), 'International substitution in labor supply: evidence from micro data', *Journal of Political Economy*, **94**(3), Part 2: Hoover Institution Labor Conference, S176–S215.

Attanasio, Orazio P. and Gulielmo Weber (1995), 'Is consumption growth consistent with intertemporal optimization? Evidence from the consumer expenditure survey', *Journal of Political Economy*, **103**(6), 1121–57.

Auray, Stéphane, Aurélien Eyquem and Paul Gomme (2011), 'A tale of tax policies in open economies', Working Paper 11-004, Concordia Unversity.

Benhabib, Jess, Richard Rogerson and Randall Wright (1991), 'Homework in macroeconomics: household production and aggregate fluctuations', *The Journal of Political Economy*, **99**(6), 1166–87.

Carey, David and Harry Tchilinguirian (2000), 'Average effective tax rates on capital, labour consumption', OECD Working Paper 258.

Coleman, Wilbur John, II (1990), 'Solving the stochastic growth model by policy-function iteration', *Journal of Business and Economic Statistics*, **8**(1), 27–9.

Cooley, Thomas and Edward C. Prescott (1995), 'Economic growth and business cycles' in Thomas Cooley (ed.), *Frontiers of Business Cycle Research*, Princeton, NJ: Princeton University Press, pp. 1–38.

Dynan, Karen E. (1993), 'How prudent are consumers?', *Journal of Political Economy*, **101**(6), 1104–13.

Gomme, Paul, B. Ravikumar and Peter Rupert (2011), 'The return to capital and the business cycle', *Review of Economic Dynamics*, **14**(2), 262–78.

Gomme, Paul and Peter Rupert (2007), 'Theory, measurement, and calibration of macroeconomic models', *Journal of Monetary Economics*, **54**(2), 460–97.

Greenwood, Jeremy and Zvi Hercowitz (1991), 'The allocation of capital and time over the business cycle', *The Journal of Political Economy*, **99**(6), 1188–214.

Greenwood, Jeremy, Zvi Hercowitz and Per Krusell (1997), 'Macroeconomic implications of capital-embodied technology change', *American Economic Review*, **87**(3), 342–62.

Gruber, Jonathan (2006), 'A tax-based estimate of the elasticity of intertemporal substitution', Working Paper, National Bureau of Economic Research.

Hall, Robert E. (1978), 'Stochastic implications of the life cycle-permanent income hypothesis: theory and evidence', *Journal of Political Economy*, **86**(6), 971–87.

Herman. Shelby W. (2000), 'Fixed assets and consumer goods for 1925–2000', *Survey of Current Business*, **81**(9), 26–38.

Hodrick, Robert J. and Edward C. Prescott (1997), 'Postwar U.S. business cycles: an empirical investigation', *Journal of Money, Credit and Banking*, **29**(1), 1–16.

King, Robert G., Charles I. Plosser and Sergio T. Rebelo (1998), 'Production, growth and business cycles: I. The basic neoclassical model', *Journal of Monetary Economics*, **21**(2/3), 195–232.

Kydland, Finn E. (1995), 'Business cycles and aggregate labor market fluctuations', in Thomas Cooley (ed.), *Frontiers of Business Cycle Research*, Princeton, NJ: Princeton University Press, pp. 126–56.

Kydland, Finn E. and Edward C. Prescott (1982), 'Time to build and aggregate fluctuations', *Econometrica*, **50**(6), 1345–70.

MaCurdy, Thomas E. (1981), 'An empirical model of labor supply in a life-cycle setting', *Journal of Political Economy*, **89**(6), 1059–85.

Maddison, Angus (1995), *Monitoring The World Economy 1820–1992*, Paris and Washington, DC: Organisation for Economic Co-operation and Development.

Mehra, Rajnish and Edward C. Prescott (1985), 'The equity premium: a puzzle', *Journal of Monetary Economics*, **15**(2), 145–61.

Mendoza, Enrique G., Assaf Razin and Linda L. Tesar (1994), 'Effective tax rates in macroeconomics: cross-country estimates of tax rates on factor incomes and consumption', *Journal of Monetary Economics*, **34**(3), 297–323.

Pencavel, John (1986), 'Labor supply of men: a survey', in O. Ashenfelter and R. Layard (eds), *Handbook of Labor Economics, Volume I*, Amsterdam: Elsevier Science Publishers, pp. 3–102.

Phelps, Edmund S (1966), *Golden Rules of Economic Growth: Studies of Efficient and Optimal Investment*, New York: W.W. Norton.

Prescott, Edward C. (1986), 'Theory ahead of business cycle measurement', *Federal Reserve Bank of Minneapolis Quarterly Review*, **10**(4), 9–22.

Swan, Trevor W. (1964), 'Of golden ages production functions', in K. Berrill (ed.), *Economic Development with Special Reference to East Asia: Proceedings of a Conference Held by the International Economic Association*, New York: St. Martin's Press, pp. 3–16.

25 Simulation and estimation of macroeconomic models in Dynare

João Madeira

1 INTRODUCTION

This chapter provides a brief guide to using Dynare. Dynare is free software (available at http://www.dynare.org/) able to simulate and estimate Dynamic Stochastic General Equilibrium (DSGE) models. Dynare is available for Windows, Mac and Linux. Matlab version 7.0 (R14) or above is required to run Dynare. As a free alternative to Matlab it is also possible to run Dynare on GNU Octave version 3.0.0 or above. No additional toolboxes are necessary but having Matlab's 'optimization toolbox' installed allows for additional options when using some commands. Dynare's current development team consists of Stéphane Adjemian, Houtan Bastani, Michel Juillard, Frédéric Karamé, Junior Maih, Ferhat Mihoubi, George Perendia, Marco Ratto and Sébastien Villemot.

1.1 Installation

Start by downloading (or execute the installer directly from the website) the latest version of Dynare for Matlab (Windows) from http://www.dynare.org/. Unzip the compressed file which is now on your computer. The default destination folder is 'c:\dynare\4.x.y' where 'x' and 'y' represent the version number upgrade. This directory contains several sub-directories: 'doc', 'dynare++', 'examples', 'matlab' and 'mex'. The next step is to add the Dynare 'matlab' subdirectory to the MATLAB path. To do this go to Matlab's "File" menu and select the "Set Path" entry, then click on "Add Folder ", and select the 'matlab' sub-directory of your Dynare installation. Finally click on "Save". One must verify that there is no directory coming from another version of Dynare on the Matlab path other than the one that one intends to use.

For Octave installation instructions please consult Dynare's current manual, Adjemian et al. (2011) or the Dynare Wiki.

1.2 Dynare Invocation

The first step is to write a file containing the description of the economic model and the computing tasks required (for example, simulation or estimation of the model). To do this go to Matlab's "File" menu and select the "New" entry, then click on "M-File". Once the *model file* is written (details on how to do this are contained in the remaining sections of this chapter) one must save it with the filename extension '.mod'. Dynare can then be invoked by writing dynare filename.mod in Matlab's "Command Window". Take care to make sure that the folder (you can have it located in any directory on your computer) containing the *model file* is in the Matlab "Current Directory" window. You can do this by clicking in the "Current Directory" window, or typing the path directly in the "Current Directory:" box on the toolbar of Matlab.

When Matlab has concluded the computing tasks required it will show the figures (such as priors/posterior distributions of the model's parameters or impulse response functions) corresponding to the command(s) used in the '.mod' file. You will see several results displayed in the "Command Window"; these could include outputs such as, depending on the command(s) used, parameter estimates or the model's theoretical moments. The results seen in the "Command Window" will be stored in a 'filename.log' Text Document. In the "Workspace" window you can find several other Dynare output results. In particular, the MATLAB workspace will contain the following output variables: 'M_' (structure containing various information about the model), 'options_' (structure contains the values of the various options used by Dynare during the computation) and 'oo_' (structure containing the various results of the computations). The 'M_', 'oo_' and 'options_' structures are saved in a file called 'filename_results.mat'. The figures, '.log' and '_results.mat' files will be automatically saved in the folder containing the '.mod' file used (as can be seen in Matlab's "Current Directory" window).

2 SIMULATION OF DSGE MODELS

This section explains the basics of how to write a *model file* in Dynare and use it to simulate DSGE models. The first subsection will describe a simple DSGE model, consisting of a standard Real Business Cycle (RBC) model similar to that presented by King and Rebelo (1999), Romer (2011) and Campbell (1994) and the second subsection will show how to implement it in Dynare.[1]

2.1 A Basic Real Business Cycle Model

2.1.1 The model

Consider an economy with a continuum of infinitely lived agents and firms on the interval [0,1]. The social planner maximizes the expected value of the representative household utility function:

$$U = E_t \sum_{i=0}^{\infty} \beta^i (\log C_{t+i} + \nu \log L_{t+i}) \tag{25.1}$$

subject to the economy's aggregate budget constraint:

$$Y_t = C_t + I_t + G_t \tag{25.2}$$

and the household's time endowment:

$$L_t + N_t = 1, \tag{25.3}$$

where C_t is consumption, L_t is leisure, Y_t is output, I_t is investment, G_t is government expenses and N_t is hours worked. The parameter $\nu > 0$ measures the utility from leisure and $0 < \beta < 1$ is the household's subjective discount factor.

The aggregate production function is given by:

$$Y_t = A_t K_t^{\alpha}(\gamma^t N_t)^{1-\alpha} \tag{25.4}$$

and the stock of capital (K_t) evolves according to:

$$I_t = K_{t+1} - (1 - \delta)K_t \tag{25.5}$$

where K_t is capital and A_t is Total Factor Productivity (TFP) which follows a stationary process. The parameter α is the capital share of output, γ represents a deterministic labour augmenting technological process and δ is the depreciation rate of capital.

The social planner problem can be solved by first replacing (25.4) and (25.5) in (25.2) and then replacing (25.2) and (25.3) in (25.1). We then take the first order conditions with respect to K_{t+1} and N_t:

$$\frac{1}{C_t} = \beta E_t\left\{\frac{1}{C_{t+1}}[MPK_{t+1} + (1 - \delta)]\right\} \tag{25.6}$$

$$\frac{MPN_t}{C_t} = \frac{v}{1 - N_t}. \tag{25.7}$$

where MPK_t and MPN_t stand respectively for the marginal productivities of capital and labour:

$$MPK_{t+1} = \alpha A_{t+1} K_{t+1}^{\alpha-1}(\gamma^{t+1} N_{t+1})^{1-\alpha} \tag{25.8}$$

$$MPN_t = (1 - \alpha)\gamma^t A_t K_t^{\alpha}(\gamma^t N_t)^{-\alpha}. \tag{25.9}$$

Since the non-stationary technology process γ^t induces a common trend in output, capital, investment, marginal productivity of labour, consumption and government expenditures, it is convenient to express the model in terms of the detrended variables $\tilde{Y}_t = (Y_t/\gamma^t)$, $\tilde{K}_t = (K_t/\gamma^t)$, $\tilde{I}_t = (I_t/\gamma^t)$, $\widetilde{MPN}_t = (MPN_t/\gamma^t)$, $\tilde{C}_t = (C_t/\gamma^t)$ and $\tilde{G}_t = (G_t/\gamma^t)$. The model's equations are then changed in the following way:

$$\tilde{Y}_t = \tilde{C}_t + \tilde{I}_t + \tilde{G}_t \tag{25.10}$$

$$\tilde{Y}_t = A_t \tilde{K}_t^{\alpha} N_t^{1-\alpha} \tag{25.11}$$

$$\tilde{I}_t = \gamma \tilde{K}_{t+1} - (1 - \delta)\tilde{K}_t \tag{25.12}$$

$$\gamma\frac{1}{\tilde{C}_t} = \beta E_t\left\{\frac{1}{\tilde{C}_{t+1}}[MPK_{t+1} + (1 - \delta)]\right\} \tag{25.13}$$

$$\frac{\widetilde{MPN}_t}{\tilde{C}_t} = \frac{v}{1 - N_t} \tag{25.14}$$

$$MPK_{t+1} = \alpha A_{t+1}\widetilde{K}_{t+1}^{\alpha-1}N_{t+1}^{1-\alpha} \tag{25.15}$$

$$\widetilde{MPN}_t = (1-\alpha)A_t\widetilde{K}_t^{\alpha}N_t^{-\alpha}. \tag{25.16}$$

Finally we conclude the description of our model by specifying the stochastic processes for the exogenous variables A_t and $\widetilde{G}_t$. TFP and government spending are both assumed to follow a first-order autoregressive process:

$$\ln(A_t) = (1-\rho_a)\ln(A) + \rho_a\ln(A_{t-1}) + u_t^a \tag{25.17}$$

$$\ln(\widetilde{G}_t) = (1-\rho_g)\ln(\widetilde{G}) + \rho_g\ln(\widetilde{G}_{t-1}) + u_t^g. \tag{25.18}$$

Where u_t^a and u_t^g represent independent shocks with normal distributions of mean zero and respective standard deviations σ_a and σ_g.

2.1.2 Steady state

In a stochastic setting models need to be linearized before being solved. To do this Dynare needs to know the model's steady state. Dynare can solve for the steady state of a model (see the examples in Collard, 2001 and Griffoli, 2007) using numerical methods but it is usually only successful if the initial values entered are close to the true steady state. Since this can prove difficult even for simple models, I normally prefer to enter the steady state solution by hand in Dynare or to write a Matlab program to find the model's steady state. In the case of the Real Business Cycle model described in this section it is simple to find the model's steady state or balanced growth path of the economy (in which output, capital, investment, marginal productivity of labour, consumption and government expenditures all grow at a constant common rate, the exogenous growth rate of the labour augmenting technological process).

Let's start by normalizing $A = 1$. In the steady state all the variables of the detrended model are constant (for example, $\widetilde{Y}_{t+1} = \widetilde{Y}_t = \widetilde{Y}$):

$$\widetilde{Y} = \widetilde{C} + \widetilde{I} + \widetilde{G} \tag{25.19}$$

$$\widetilde{Y} = \widetilde{K}^{\alpha}N^{1-\alpha} \tag{25.20}$$

$$\widetilde{I} = \gamma\widetilde{K} - (1-\delta)\widetilde{K} \tag{25.21}$$

$$\gamma\frac{1}{\widetilde{C}} = \beta\frac{1}{\widetilde{C}}[MPK_t + (1-\delta)] \tag{25.22}$$

$$\frac{\widetilde{MPN}}{\widetilde{C}} = \frac{v}{1-N} \tag{25.23}$$

$$MPK = \alpha\widetilde{K}^{\alpha-1}N^{1-\alpha} \tag{25.24}$$

$$\widetilde{MPN} = (1-\alpha)\widetilde{K}^{\alpha}N^{-\alpha} \tag{25.25}$$

Given values for the parameters $\beta, \alpha, \gamma, \delta$, steady state labour N and $sg = \widetilde{G}/\widetilde{Y}$ it is easy to calculate exact values for the steady state of the remaining variables. One can simplify (25.22) to obtain:

$$MPK = \frac{\gamma}{\beta} - (1 - \delta) \tag{25.26}$$

After this it is easy to calculate steady state capital by solving (25.24) for $\widetilde{K}$:

$$\widetilde{K} = \left(\frac{MPK}{\alpha N^{1-\alpha}} \right)^{\frac{1}{(\alpha - 1)}} \tag{25.27}$$

Then it becomes simple to obtain $\widetilde{Y}$, $\widetilde{I}$ and $\widetilde{MPN}$ from (25.20), (25.21) and (25.25). Steady state government expenditures are given by $\widetilde{G} = sg\widetilde{Y}$. Consumption can now easily be calculated by using (25.19):

$$\widetilde{C} = \widetilde{Y} - \widetilde{I} - \widetilde{G} \tag{25.28}$$

Finally, using (25.23), it is very simple to solve for v:

$$v = \frac{\widetilde{MPN}}{\widetilde{C}} (1 - N) \tag{25.29}$$

2.1.3 Log-linearization of the model

There is no closed form solution to the equations for this model (an exact analytical solution is possible only in the special case of full depreciation of capital and when agents have log utility). An alternative solution method is needed. The strategy is therefore to look for an approximate analytical solution by transforming the model into a system of log-linear difference equations in the unknowns. Log-linearization transforms the domain with a log function, and then approximates with a first order Taylor expansion in the neighbourhood of the steady state balanced growth path. Because in economics the relevant functions in many cases are locally more like exponential functions (such as in growth models) than linear functions, log-linearization provides the best of both worlds – closeness of exponential approximations, and tractability of linear approximations.

Log-linearization is employed as follows. Let X_t be a strictly positive variable, X its steady state and $x_t = log(X_t) - log(X)$ the logarithmic deviation. First notice that, for x near zero, $log(1 + x) \simeq x$, thus:

$$x_t = log(X_t) - log(X) = log(X_t/X) = log(1 + \%change) \simeq \%change.$$

Also notice that you can write $X_t = X(X_t/X) = Xe^{log(X_t/X)} = Xe^{x_t}$. Taking a first order Taylor approximation around the steady state $x = 0$ yields:

$$Xe^{x_t} \simeq Xe^0 + Xe^0(x_t - 0) \simeq X(1 + x_t).$$

By the same logic, you can write:

$$X_t Y_t \simeq X(1 + x_t) Y(1 + y_t) \simeq XY(1 + x_t + y_t + x_t y_t)$$

where $x_t y_t \simeq 0$, since x_t and y_t are both numbers close to zero. Let's now look at an example. Take the production function:

$$\widetilde{Y}_t = A_t \widetilde{K}_t^{\alpha} N_t^{1-\alpha}.$$

Log-linearizing the above expression yields:

$$\widetilde{Y}(1 + \widetilde{y}_t) = A\widetilde{K}^{\alpha} N^{1-\alpha}(1 + a_t + \alpha\widetilde{k}_t + (1 - \alpha)n_t)$$

where lower case letters denote variables in log deviation from the steady state. Simplifying this expression results in:

$$\widetilde{y}_t = a_t + \alpha\widetilde{k}_t + (1 - \alpha)n_t.$$

The Dynare guides by Collard (2001) and Griffoli (2007) focus on examples of models entered in the original non-linear form. My preference, however, is to write the model in log-linear form, expressing variables as percentage deviations from the steady state (the initial values for the model's variables are therefore zero). This also seems to be the favourite choice of many researchers (for example, 46 of the total of 53 models available in the Macro Model Data Base of Wieland et al. 2012, are entered in linear form).

The log-linearized equations of the basic RBC model described in this section are presented below. As in the production function example, I will use lower case letters to denote variables in log deviation from the steady state. Log-linearization of equations (25.10)–(25.18) yields:

$$\widetilde{Y}\widetilde{y}_t = \widetilde{C}\widetilde{c}_t + \widetilde{G}\widetilde{g}_t + \widetilde{I}\widetilde{\imath}_t \tag{25.30}$$

$$\widetilde{y}_t = a_t + \alpha\widetilde{k}_t + (1 - \alpha)n_t \tag{25.31}$$

$$\widetilde{I}\widetilde{\imath}_t = \gamma\widetilde{K}\widetilde{k}_{t+1} - (1 - \delta)\widetilde{K}\widetilde{k}_t \tag{25.32}$$

$$\widetilde{c}_t = E_t\widetilde{c}_{t+1} - \frac{MPK}{MPK + (1 - \delta)} mpk_{t+1} \tag{25.33}$$

$$\widetilde{mpn_t} - \widetilde{c}_t = \frac{N}{1 - N} n_t \tag{25.34}$$

$$mpk_{t+1} = a_{t+1} + (\alpha - 1)\widetilde{k}_{t+1} + (1 - \alpha)n_{t+1} \tag{25.35}$$

$$\widetilde{mpn_t} = a_t + \alpha\widetilde{k}_t - \alpha n_t \tag{25.36}$$

$$a_t = \rho_a a_{t-1} + u_t^a \tag{25.37}$$

$$\widetilde{g}_t = \rho_g \widetilde{g}_{t-1} + u_t^g \tag{25.38}$$

2.2 The Dynare Code

As mentioned previously the estimation and simulation of an economic model in Dynare involves writing a *model file.*[2] This can be done by using an external or internal editor to Matlab (go to Matlab's "File" menu and select the "New" entry, then click on "M-File"). Once the *model file* is written it must be saved with the filename extension '.mod'.

It is useful to think of the structure of the '.mod' file as having four distinct blocks:

1. the preamble which lists variables (endogenous and exogenous) and parameters;
2. the model which outlines the model's equations;
3. the shocks which can be deterministic (temporary or permanent) or stochastic;
4. finally computation which instructs Dynare to undertake certain tasks (such as simulation, estimation or forecasting).

The first non-comment line (write two forward slashes '//' before entering any comments in Dynare, this can be useful to help others, and even oneself, to understand better the code written) in your Dynare code should be: "var" followed by the model's variables' names (all variables apart from the exogenous shocks) and culminating with a semicolon. The Dynare code will not run unless each entry is followed by a semicolon to suppress the output (note that an entry may occupy more than one line). The second line of code should be "varexo" followed by the names of the exogenous shocks. The next command should be "parameters" followed by the names of the model's parameters (which also include the model's steady state values when the model is entered in Dynare in linear form, as is the case here). Below this command one must specify the values of these parameters. Thus, the preamble for the RBC model outlined in this section is:

```
var y c i k n mpk mpn a g;
varexo e_A e_G;
parameters sg beta Nss alpha delta lambdaDT gamma rhoA rhoG
  MPKss Kss Yss Iss MPNss Gss Css v;
sg=0.2; // same as in Romer (2011); in King and Rebelo (1999)
  sg=0
beta=0.984;// Same as in King and Rebelo (1999);
//Romer (2011) uses 1.5% real interest rate (r*),
//since MPKss=r*+delta then r*=(gamma/beta)-1 this implies
  beta=gamma/(1.015)
NSS=0.2;// same as in King and Rebelo (1999); Romer (2011)
  uses 1/3
alpha=1/3;// same as in Romer (2011); alpha=0.333 in King and
  Rebelo (1999)
delta=0.025;// same as in Romer (2011) and as in King and
  Rebelo (1999)
lambdaDT=0.4;// same as in King and Rebelo (1999); Romer
  (2011) uses 0.5
gamma=1+(lambdaDT/100);
```

```
rhoA=0.95;// same as in Romer (2011); King and Rebelo (1999)
  use 0.979
rhoG=0.95;// same as in Romer (2011)
MPKss=(gamma/beta)-(1-delta);
Kss=(MPKss/(alpha*(Nss^(1-alpha))))^(1/(alpha-1));
Yss=(Kss^alpha)*(Nss^(1-alpha));
Iss=gamma*Kss-(1-delta)*Kss;
MPNss=(1-alpha)*(Kss^(alpha))*(Nss^(-alpha));
Gss=sg*Yss;
Css=Yss-Iss-Gss;
v=(MPNss/Css)*(1-Nss);
```

The values for the structural parameters $\beta, \alpha, \gamma, \delta$, steady state labour N, $sg = \widetilde{G}/\widetilde{Y}$, ρ_a and ρ_g are similar to those found in the literature. I have entered comments to compare the values chosen to those used by Romer (2011) and King and Rebelo (1999).

Writing the model block is very straightforward, since Dynare enables the user to do this by entering the model's equations in a manner similar to the way they are written in an academic paper. This block starts with the instruction "model;" and concludes with "end;". Because the model's equations have already been log-linearized in the previous subsection it is necessary to write the term "(linear)" next to the command "model". To write the model block it is important to be aware of a few notational conventions. A variable x with a t subscript is simply written as "x". A variable with a $t + n$ subscript is written as "x(+n)". Similarly, a variable with a $t - n$ subscript is written as "x(−n)". Hence, the model block (consisting of equations 25.30 to 25.38) is as follows:

```
model (linear);
Yss*y=Css*c+Gss*g+Iss*i;
y=a+alpha*k(-1)+(1-alpha)*n;
Iss*i=gamma*Kss*k-(1-delta)*Kss*k(-1);
c=c(+1)-(MPKss/(MPKss+(1-delta)))*mpk;
mpn-c=(Nss/(1-Nss))*n;
mpk=a(+1)+(alpha-1)*k+(1-alpha)*n(+1);
mpn=a+alpha*k(-1)-alpha*n;
//exogenous shocks
a=rhoA*a(-1)+e_A;
g=rhoG*g(-1)+e_G;
end;
```

In Dynare, the default convention is that the timing of a variable reflects when this variable is decided. For example, $\widetilde{k}_t$ is a predetermined variable in the RBC model in the previous section (because it reflects investment decisions made previously, in the case of the model considered here capital is the result of investment decisions implemented at date $t - 1$) and is thus written as "k(−1)".

To specify the shocks block one needs to declare only the non-zero elements of the covariance matrix. Start with the command "shocks;" and conclude with "end;". For the RBC model considered here this block can be written as follows:

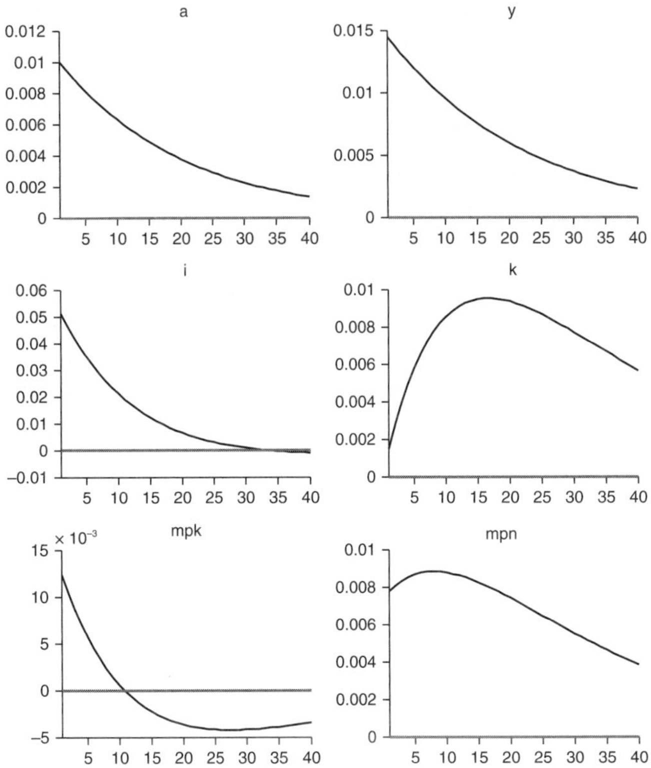

Figure 25.1 RBC model's IRFs to a 1 per cent productivity shock

```
shocks;
var e_A;
stderr 0.01;
var e_G;
stderr 0.01;
end;
```

The model is then solved and simulated using the "stoch_simul;" command:

```
stoch_simul (irf=40,hp_filter=1600) a g y c i k n mpk mpn;
```

This command will compute the model's impulse response functions (IRFs) and various descriptive statistics (moments, variance decomposition, correlation and auto-correlation coefficients). I made use of some options of the "stoch_simul;" command. The option "irf = integer" allows one to choose the number of periods plotted in the IRFs. The default value is 40. The figure Dynare creates for the IRFs to a 1 per cent productivity shock is shown in Figure 25.1.

Notice that Dynare plots the variables being decided at date t. For this reason the initial value of the capital stock is displayed as jumping on impact (the variable plotted is $\widetilde{k}_{t+1}$ and not $\widetilde{k}_t$). If a list of variables is specified after "stoch simul()" then results are displayed only for those variables and in the order in which they are listed (for this reason the order of variables in the impulse response functions is the same as that of the list).

The option "hp_filter = integer" produces theoretical moments (variances, covariances, autocorrelations) after HP filtering the data (the default is to apply no filter to the data), just as in Table 2 of King and Rebelo (1999). This is a very useful option because in order to isolate the business cycle component of economic time series many researchers employ the HP filter. So, one must apply the HP filter to the model's theoretical moments if one wants to compare them to those of HP filtered data from aggregate time series (such as the moments reported in Table 1 of King and Rebelo, 1999). The integer is a number corresponding to the smoothing parameter in the HP filter. For quarterly data (which is typically the frequency of interest for economists studying business cycles) Hodrick and Prescott (1981) recommended a value of 1600.

3 MODEL ESTIMATION

In this section we will look at how to estimate the DSGE model outlined in the previous section using Bayesian techniques as in Smets and Wouters (2003; 2007). To undertake Bayesian estimation it is necessary to have at least as many shocks as there are observable variables. Since the model outlined in the previous section has two exogenous shocks (to productivity and government expenses) the dataset used can contain two time series at most. To estimate the model I used a dataset consisting of seasonally adjusted quarterly US real GDP growth and real investment (so that the time series used are stationary). These same time series were used in Smets and Wouters (2007) but I updated the dataset to include observations for more recent years. Following Galí et al. (2011), I estimated the model for the period 1966Q1 to 2007Q4 due to concerns that the non-linearities induced by the zero lower bound on the federal funds rate could distort the estimates for some of the parameters (whereas Smets and Wouters, 2007, estimated their model with data from 1966Q1 to 2004Q4).

The corresponding measurement equations are:

$$dlGDP_t = \bar{\lambda} + [\widetilde{y}_t - \widetilde{y}_{t-1}], \tag{25.39}$$

$$dlINV_t = \bar{\lambda} + [\widetilde{\iota}_t - \widetilde{\iota}_{t-1}], \tag{25.40}$$

where *dl* stand for log difference and $\bar{\lambda}$ is the common quarterly trend growth rate to real GDP and investment. The parameter $\bar{\lambda}$ is related to the steady state of the model economy as follows: $\gamma = 1 + \frac{\bar{\lambda}}{100}$.

As in the prior section writing the *model file* in Dynare for estimation purposes starts with declaring the model's variables and parameters. This is done exactly as previously described and the preamble block looks very similar (the only difference is that the growth rate of real GDP and investment were added to the endogenous variable list in the first line of the code since the parameter $\bar{\lambda}$ was already previously listed):

```
var y c i k n mpk mpn a g dy dinve;
varexo e_A e_G;
parameters sg beta Nss alpha delta lambdaDT gamma rhoA rhoG
  MPKss Kss Yss Iss MPNss Gss Css v;
sg=0.2; // same as in Romer (2011); in King and Rebelo (1999)
  sg=0
beta=0.984;// Same as in King and Rebelo (1999);
//Romer (2011) uses 1.5% real interest rate (r*),
//since MPKss=r*+delta then r*=(gamma/beta)-1 this implies
  beta=gamma/(1.015)
Nss=0.2;// same as in King and Rebelo (1999); Romer (2011)
  uses 1/3
alpha=1/3;// same as in Romer (2011); alpha=0.333 in King and
  Rebelo (1999)
delta=0.025;// same as in Romer (2011) and as in King and
  Rebelo (1999)
lambdaDT=0.4;// same as in King and Rebelo (1999); Romer
  (2011) uses 0.5
gamma=1+(lambdaDT/100);
rhoA=0.95;// same as in Romer (2011); King and Rebelo (1999)
  use 0.979
rhoG=0.95;// same as in Romer (2011)
MPKss=(gamma/beta)-(1-delta);
Kss=(MPKss/(alpha*(Nss^(1-alpha))))^(1/(alpha-1));
Yss=(Kss^alpha)*(Nss^(1-alpha));
Iss=gamma*Kss-(1-delta)*Kss;
MPNss=(1-alpha)*(Kss^(alpha))*(Nss^(-alpha));
Gss=sg*Yss;
Css=Yss-Iss-Gss;
v=(MPNss/Css)*(1-Nss);
```

Again, the second step is writing the model block (to which the measurement equations must be added) of the Dynare code. Therefore the model block now includes equations 25.30 to 25.40 and looks as follows:

```
model (linear);
Yss*y=Css*c+g+Iss*i;
y=a+alpha*k(-1)+(1-alpha)*n;
Iss*i=gamma*Kss*k-(1-delta)*Kss*k(-1);
c=c(+1)-(MPKss/(MPKss+(1-delta)))*mpk;
mpn-c=(Nss/(1-Nss))*n;
mpk=a(+1)+(alpha-1)*k+(1-alpha)*n(+1);
mpn=a+alpha*k(-1)-alpha*n;
//exogenous shocks
a=rhoA*a(-1)+e_A;
g=rhoG*g(-1)+e_G;
```

```
//measurement equations
dy=lambdaDT+(y-y(-1));
dinve=lambdaDT+(i-i(-1));
end;
```

As in Smets and Wouters (2007) I normalize the exogenous government spending process. I do this by defining a new variable $\tilde{g}_t^* = \tilde{G}\tilde{g}_t$. In this way it is easier to choose a reasonable prior for the standard deviation and it will make it easier to compare the estimate for σ_g obtained for the RBC model described in the prior section with that obtained by Smets and Wouters (2007). As Justiniano et al. (2008) point out, this is 'a practical way to impose correlated priors across coefficients, which is desirable in some cases' and frequently helps 'improve the convergence properties of the MCMC algorithm'.

I now must declare which variables are observable for the estimation procedure. This is done using the command "varobs" followed by the names of the observable variables used in the estimation:

```
varobs dy dinve;
```

The next step is to declare the parameters to be estimated. I choose to estimate values for $\gamma, \alpha, \rho_a, \rho_g, \sigma_a$ and σ_g (the remaining parameters I maintain fixed in the estimation procedure since it would be difficult to identify well all parameters from the data). This is done by writing "estimated_params;" followed by the parameters to be estimated (one in each line) and concluding with "end;":

```
estimated_params;
lambdaDT, 0.4,0.1,0.8, NORMAL_PDF,0.4,0.10;
alpha, 0.33,0.01,1.0, NORMAL_PDF,0.3,0.05;
rhoA, 0.95,.01,.9999, BETA_PDF,0.5,0.2;
rhoG, 0.95,.01,.9999, BETA_PDF,0.5,0.2;
stderr e_A, 0.013,0.01,5, INV_GAMMA_PDF,0.1,2;
stderr e_G, 0.021,0.01,5, INV_GAMMA_PDF,0.1,2;
end;
```

To estimate the RBC model using maximum likelihood (as in Ireland, 2004) one would use the following syntax (fields listed between "[. . .]" are optional) for each estimated parameter: "parameter name, initial value [, lower bound, upper bound];" However, estimating the model with maximum likelihood resulted in an unrealistically high level ($\alpha = 0.6125$) for the capital share. This is a common problem when estimating DSGE models and for this reason the use of Bayesian methods has become very popular among macroeconomic researchers. In Bayesian estimation, each line is written according to the following syntax: "parameter name, [initial value [, lower bound, upper bound]], prior shape, prior mean, prior standard error [, prior third parameter, prior fourth parameter];" I choose prior distributions for the model's parameters to be the same as those in Smets and Wouters (2007). The possible prior shapes are: "beta_pdf", "gamma_pdf", "normal_pdf", "uniform_pdf", "inv_gamma_pdf", "inv_gamma1_pdf" and "inv_gamma2_pdf". Note that "inv_gamma_pdf" is equivalent to "inv_gamma1_ pdf". For the "beta_pdf", "gamma_pdf", "normal_pdf", "inv_gamma_pdf", "inv_gamma1_pdf" and "inv_gamma2_pdf" shapes one must specify values for the prior mean and prior standard error of the distribution. The prior third parameter is used for generalized beta distribution, generalized gamma and for the uniform distribution. The prior fourth parameter is used for the generalized beta distribution and for the uniform distribution. As one uses fields more towards the end of the list, all previous fields must be filled (use empty values if the parameters don't apply). For instance, to specify a uniform distribution between 0 and 1 for α one would enter "alpha, 0.33,0.01,1.0, uniform pdf, , , 0,1;" since the uniform distribution only takes the third and fourth parameters as arguments.

Finally, the model is estimated using the "estimation ();" command:

```
estimation(optim=('MaxIter',200),datafile=
  rbc_model_data,mode_compute=4,
first_obs=71,nobs=172,presample=4,lik_init=2,mode_
  check,prefilter=0,
mh_replic=250000,mh_nblocks=2,mh_jscale=1.08,mh_drop=0.2);
stoch_simul (hp_filter=1600,irf=40) a g y c i k n mpk mpn;
```

This command will display results from posterior optimization, graphs with prior, posterior and mode, marginal log data density, graphs of smoothed shocks, smoothed observation errors, smoothed and historical variables. After estimation with Metropolis iterations Dynare will display the mean and confidence interval from posterior simulation and Metropolis–Hastings convergence graphs.

A result that I consider important to highlight is the marginal log data density. The marginal likelihood of the model gives an indication of the overall likelihood of the model given the data and reflects its prediction performance. It therefore forms a natural benchmark for comparing the overall fit of DSGE models. This can be done by computing the Bayes factor. The Bayes factor (BF) of model 1 against model 2 is the difference of their log marginal likelihoods. Kass and Raftery (1995) suggest that values of 2 logBF above 10 can be considered very strong evidence in favour of model 1. Values between 6 and 10 represent strong evidence, between 2 and 6 positive evidence, while values below 2 are 'not worth more than a bare mention'.

I made use of some options of the "estimation();" command which are explained briefly in the paragraphs below:

The option "optim = (fmincon options)" allows one to set options for fmincon (a function available in Matlab's optimization toolbox).

The option "datafile = filename" specifies the data file (which can be either a '.m' file, a '.mat' file or an '.xls' file) to be used in the estimation process. The data file used 'rbc_model_data.m' contains two vectors of observations: real GDP and real investment growth.[3] This file must be located in the same folder as the '.mod' file.

The option "mode_compute = integer" allows the user to choose the optimizer for the mode computation: 0 the mode isn't computed (mode_file option must be specified); 1 uses fmincon optimization routine (not available under Octave); 2 value no longer used; 3 uses fminunc optimization routine; 4 (default value) uses Chris Sims' csminwel; 5 uses Marco Ratto's newrat; 6 uses a Monte-Carlo based optimization routine (see Dynare

Wiki for more details); 7 uses fminsearch, an optimization routine available under Matlab (if the optimization toolbox is installed) and Octave (if the optim package from Octave-Forge is installed).

The "first obs = integer" option allows one to choose the number of the first observation to be used (default: 1). Even though the observations in my data file start at 1946Q3 with this option, I'm able to choose to use only a subsample of the data (in this case I wish to make use only of data from 1966Q1 onwards to make my results more easy to compare with those of Smets and Wouters, 2007).

The "nobs = integer" option allows the user to specify the number of observations to be used (default: all observations in the datafile). I chose a value of 172 so that Dynare uses data only up to 2007Q4 (while the datafile contains observations up to 2010Q4).

The option "presample = integer" specifies the number of observations to be skipped before evaluating the likelihood (default: 0).

The option "lik_init = integer" specifies the type of initialization of the Kalman filter (default value: 1): 1 is for stationary models while 2 and 3 are for non-stationary models.

The option "mode_check" tells Dynare to plot the posterior density for values around the computed mode for each estimated parameter. This is helpful to diagnose problems with the optimizer.

If the "prefilter = integer" is set to 1 then the estimation procedure demeans the data (default: 0, that is no prefiltering).

The option "mh replic = integer" sets the number of replications for the Metropolis–Hastings algorithm. The default is 20000. I opted to create a sample of 250 000 draws, as in Smets and Wouters (2007).

The option "mh_nblocks = integer" specifies the number of parallel chains for the Metropolis–Hastings algorithm (default: 2).

The "mh_jscale = double precision number" option is used to set the scale of the jumping distribution in the Metropolis–Hastings algorithm (the default is 0.2). The value used should be adjusted to yield an acceptance rate of approximately 23 per cent, the optimal rate proposed by Gelman et al. (1996). For the RBC model estimated in this section a value of 1.08 resulted in an acceptance rate of 23.2 per cent.

The "mh_drop = double precision number" specifies the fraction of initially generated parameter vectors to be dropped before using posterior simulations (default: 0.5). I chose a value of 0.2 as in Smets and Wouters (2007).

The posterior means and confidence intervals obtained are presented below:

```
parameters
            prior   post.    conf.    interval  prior   pstdev
            mean    mean
lambdaDT    0.400   0.4238   0.3921   0.4548    norm    0.1000
alpha       0.300   0.3791   0.3152   0.4409    norm    0.0500
rhoA        0.500   0.9480   0.9257   0.9716    beta    0.2000
rhoG        0.500   0.9500   0.9389   0.9606    beta    0.2000
```

```
standard deviation of shocks
           prior   post.    conf.     interval prior   pstdev
           mean    mean
e_A        0.100   0.4595   0.3805    0.5339   invg    2.0000
e_G        0.100   0.5411   0.4767    0.6009   invg    2.0000
```

The parameter estimates for the RBC model considered are very much in line with the values commonly used in the literature for calibration purposes (as can be seen by comparing them to those used in the previous section) and very similar to the estimates by Smets and Wouters (2007) for equivalent parameters (the respective posterior means found by these authors for $\gamma, \alpha, \rho_a, \rho_g, \sigma_a$ and σ_g were 0.43, 0.19, 0.95, 0.97, 0.45 and 0.53).

If one wishes it is also possible to add the "stoch simul;" command at the end, as shown above. I normally choose to do this so that Dynare uses the estimated results to compute the model's impulse response functions, theoretical moments, variance decomposition, matrix of correlations and coefficients of autocorrelation. For maximum likelihood estimation the parameters and the variance matrix of the shocks are set to the mode. For Bayesian estimation the parameters and the variance matrix of the shocks are set to the posterior mode computation in the case without Metropolis iterations or to the posterior mean after estimation with Metropolis iterations.

4 USEFUL RESOURCES

Dynare can also be used for many other applications which were not explored here, such as deterministic shocks (permanent and temporary), Bayesian VAR, forecasting, optimal policy or sensitivity and identification analysis. Besides the Dynare guides by Collard (2001) and Griffoli (2007), the document by Bhandari et al. (2010) available at the Thomas Sargent webpage (https://files.nyu.edu/ts43/public/research/AP_tom16.pdf) is also a valuable resource where users of Dynare can find examples of '.mod' files for several of these applications. Other resources that I find to be of great use are the forums in the Dynare webpage. These forums allow users to ask questions and get feedback from Dynare developers and fellow researchers. It is often best to start by searching prior posts as it is likely that one's query has been raised previously and that the forum already has answers for most issues a user may experience.

NOTES

1. The essential difference between the model presented here and that in King and Rebelo (1999) is the introduction of exogenous government spending. The only difference relative to Romer (2011) and Campbell (1994) is that I ignore population growth (since in the following section I make use of per capita data to estimate the model).
2. The complete '.mod' files (and the data) used to simulate and estimate the standard RBC model described here are available at: https://sites.google.com/site/joaoantoniorodriguesmadeira/home/dynare.
3. To obtain time series for real GDP and investment growth per capita I made use of data on the Civilian Population age 16 and over, Real GDP, the GDP price deflator and Fixed Private Investment. This data

was obtained from the St. Louis Fed website (http://research.stlouisfed.org/fred2/). Further details are provided in the 'readme.doc' and 'rbc_model_data.xls'.

REFERENCES

Adjemian, S., H. Bastani, M. Juillard, F. Mihoubi, G. Perendia, M. Ratto and S. Villemot (2011), 'Dynare: reference manual, version 4', Dynare Working Papers, 1, CEPREMAP.

Bhandari, A., F. Barillas, R. Colacito, S. Kitao, C. Matthes, T. Sargent and Y. Shin (2010), 'Practicing Dynare', available at: https://files.nyu.edu/ts43/public/research/AP_tom16.pdf.

Campbell, J. (1994), 'Inspecting the mechanism: an analytical approach to the stochastic growth model', *Journal of Monetary Economics*, **33**(3), 463–506.

Collard, F. (2001), 'Stochastic simulations with Dynare: a practical guide', available at: http://www.aynare org/documentation-and support/tutorial.

Galí, J., F. Smets and R. Wouters (2011), 'Unemployment in an estimated New Keynesian model', in D. Acemoglu and M. Woodford (eds), *NBER Macroeconomics Annual*, 26, Chicago, IL: University of Chicago Press.

Gelman, A., G. Roberts and W. Gilks (1996), 'Efficient Metropolis jumping rules', in J. Bernardo, J. Berger, A. David and A. Smith (eds), *Bayesian Statistics V*, Oxford: Oxford University Press, pp. 599–608.

Griffoli, T. (2007), 'Dynare user guide: an introduction to the solution and estimation of DSGE models', available at: http://www.dynare org/documentation-and-support/user-guide.

Hodrick, R. and E. Prescott (1981), 'Post-war US business cycles: an empirical investigation', Discussion Papers 451, Northwestern University, Center for Mathematical Studies in Economics and Management Science.

Ireland, P. (2004), 'A method for taking models to the data', *Journal of Economic Dynamics and Control*, **28**(6), 1205–26.

Justiniano, A., G. Primiceri and A. Tambalotti (2008), 'Investment shocks and business cycles', Working Paper Series WP-08-12, Federal Reserve Bank of Chicago.

Kass, R. and A. Raftery (1995), 'Bayes factors', *Journal of the American Statistical Association*, **90**, 773–95.

King, R. and S. Rebelo (1999), 'Resuscitating real business cycles', in J. Taylor and M. Woodford (eds), *Handbook of Macroeconomics*, Vol. 1A, Amsterdam: Elsevier Science BV, pp. 927–1007.

Romer, D. (2011), *Advanced Macroeconomics*, 4th edn, New York: McGraw-Hill Higher Education.

Smets, F. and R. Wouters (2003), 'An estimated dynamic stochastic general equilibrium model of the euro area', *Journal of the European Economic Association*, **1**(5), 1123–75.

Smets, F. and R. Wouters (2007), 'Shocks and frictions in US business cycles: a Bayesian DSGE approach', *American Economic Review*, **97**(3), 586–606.

Wieland, V., T. Cwik, G. Müller, S. Schmidt and M. Wolters (2012), 'A new comparative approach to macroeconomic modeling and policy analysis', *Journal of Economic Behavior & Organization*, **83**, 523–4.

Index